THIRD EDITION

Foundations of Financial Markets and Institutions

Frank J. Fabozzi

School of Management, Yale University

Franco Modigliani

Sloan School of Management, Massachusetts Institute of Technology

Frank J. Jones

The Guardian Life Insurance Company of America

Michael G. Ferri

School of Business Administration, George Mason University

Prentice
Hall

Upper Saddle River, New Jersey 07458

Library of Congress Cataloging-in-Publication Data

Foundations of financial markets and institutions / Frank j. Fabozzi ... [et al.].-- 3rd ed.
   p. cm.
   Rev. ed. of: Foundations of financial markets and institutions / Frank j. Fabozzi,
Franco Modigaliani, Michael G. Ferri.
   Includes bibliographical references and index.
   ISBN 0-13-018079-3
      1. Finance. 2. Financial institutions. I. Fabozzi, Frank J. Foundations of financial
markets and institutions.

HG173.F29 2001
332.1--dc21

                                                                    2001036188

AVP/Executive Editor: Mickey Cox
Editor-in-Chief: PJ Boardman
Managing Editor (Editorial): Gladys Soto
Assistant Editor: Beth Romph
Editorial Assistant: Kevin Hancock
Marketing Manager: Joshua P. McClary
Marketing Assistant: Christopher Bath
Managing Editor (Production): Cynthia Regan
Production Editor: Carol Samet
Production Assistant: Dianne Falcone
Permissions Coordinator: Suzanne Grappi
Associate Director, Manufacturing: Vincent Scelta
Manufacturing Buyer: Vincent Scelta
Cover Design: Jayne Conte
Cover Illustration/Photo: Bill Binzen/Corbis Stock Market
Manager, Print Production: Christy Mahon
Formatter: Ashley Scattergood-Tooey
Printer/Binder: Courier/Kendallville

Credits and acknowledgments borrowed from other sources and reproduced, with permission, in this textbook appear on appropriate page within text.

Pearson Education LTD.
Pearson Education Australia PTY, Limited
Pearson Education Singapore, Pte. Ltd
Pearson Education North Asia Ltd
Pearson Education, Canada, Ltd
Pearson Educación de Mexico, S.A. de C.V.
Pearson Education–Japan
Pearson Education Malaysia, Pte. Ltd

1 0 9 8 7 6 5 4 3 2
ISBN 0-13-018079-3

To the memory of my parents, Josephine and Alfonso Fabozzi.

_____*Frank J. Fabozzi*

To all of my students, wherever they are.

_____*Franco Modigliani*

To my mother, Margaret C. Jones, and in memory of my father, Walter W. Jones.

_____*Frank J. Jones*

To my mother, Peggy Maginn Ferri, and to the memory of my father, Ferdinand E. Ferri.

_____*Michael G. Ferri*

Brief Contents

Contents

PREFACE

PURPOSE AND STRUCTURE OF TEXT

In the preface to the first edition published in 1994, we wrote that the prior 30 years had been a time of profound, indeed revolutionary, change in the financial markets and institutions of the world. The hallmarks of that change were innovation, globalization, and deregulation. Since 1994, those forces have actually gathered more strength, and the financial landscape continues to undergo large and visible changes around the globe. The discipline that we know as finance has attracted the talents and energies of people from Chicago to Singapore and from Paris to Bombay.

Our purpose in writing this book is to instruct students about this fascinating revolution. We describe the wide array of financial securities that are now available for investing, funding operations, and controlling various types of financial risk. We help the students to see each kind of security as a response to the needs of borrowers, lenders, and investors, who manage assets and liabilities in a world of constantly changing interest rates, asset prices, regulatory constraints, and international competition and opportunities. Our book devotes a considerable amount of space to explaining how the world's key financial institutions manage their assets and liabilities and how innovative instruments support that management. Also, the text gives students a thorough introduction to financial regulation and to major facets of international finance.

It is a safe bet that change will mark the discipline of finance over the foreseeable future and will produce new kinds of institutions, markets, and securities. Our extensive explanation of the developments that dominate today's financial scene provides students with the sense of institutional structure and the analytical tools that they will need to understand the innovations that will surely occur throughout their careers.

Our coverage of institutions, investors, and instruments is as current and up-to-date as we can produce in the face of frequent and significant change both in the United States and around the world. We have made a major effort to get the latest information and data on the players in the global financial game and the rules by which it is played. We think our focus on the actual practices of financial institutions is particularly beneficial to students who will, as noted above, inevitably have to respond to changes in those institutions and their environment.

We believe that our book differs in several key respects from many texts on financial institutions and markets. What follows is an outline of the key differences.

The first difference, and a special feature of this text, is its lengthy coverage of the securitization of assets and the large mortgage market (both residential and commercial). Securitization is the process by which a security, whose collateral is the cash flow from a pool of individually illiquid and often small assets, is created and sold in the capital markets. Asset securitization has been a major innovation of the past 20 years and represents a radical departure from the traditional system for financing needs by manufacturing companies, finance companies, and governments throughout the world. The mortgage-backed security is the prime example of this process and accounts for the largest part of the market for securitized assets. However, the issuance of securitized pools of credit card debt, auto loans, other consumer liabilities, and receivables from intellectual property is becoming a very important part of international financial markets. The text devotes a considerable amount of time to securitized assets and their markets and offers chapters on mortgage loan securitization as well as the securitization of other assets.

The second difference is our commitment to giving the students a substantial amount of information and analysis regarding international or global topics in finance. Our discussions range across a wide field, encompassing markets for bonds and stocks as well as mutual funds in Tokyo, London, Frankfurt, and Paris, among other places. The text gives some detailed explanations about the operations, structure, and regulation of these major markets and institutions. Just a glance at the table of contents shows that this book covers many international topics, which today's students must know in order to function in the increasingly integrated international financial system where they will soon be working.

The third difference is the book's extensive coverage of the markets for derivative securities, such as options, futures, swaps, customized agreements for controlling interest rate risk, and so on. These derivative securities and their markets grow ever more important in global finance. Though the popular press often criticizes and misrepresents these instruments, derivatives enable financial practitioners to control risk and the cost of funding. Because of these instruments, financial markets in the United States and throughout the world are more efficient and can contribute more to economic development and growth.

Our discussion of options naturally contains an explanation of the theoretical principles of pricing. We often show that option pricing theory also applies to complex securities that have embedded options. For example, many kinds of bonds contain optionlike provisions: Issuers may exercise some, and holders may exercise others. Students need to understand options and pricing theory if they are to grasp the valuation of many of today's important assets. Although the text does not delve deeply into trading strategies, it does contain a great deal of information on these contracts and is suitable as a supplementary text for a course dealing with derivatives.

PLANNING AND MANAGING A COURSE

We do not believe that an instructor has the time in a single semester to treat all the topics covered by this book. The following table contains our suggestions for the chapters that should be included in a one-semester course on financial markets and institutions. The table also identifies those chapters that render the text a useful supplement for a course in investments or one in derivative securities.

Chapter number and title	One-semester course on markets and institutions	Supplement for course on derivatives	investments
1. Introduction	x		
2. Financial Intermediaries and Financial Innovation	x		
3. The Role of the Government in Financial Markets	x		
4. Depository Institutions: Activities and Characteristics	x		
5. Central Banks and the Creation of Money	x		
6. Monetary Policy	x		
7. Insurance Companies	x		
8. Investment Companies and Exchange-Traded Funds	x		
9. Pension Funds	x		
10. Properties and Pricing of Financial Assets	(a)	(a)	x

11. The Level and Structure of Interest Rates	x	x	x
12. The Term Structure of Interest Rates	x	x	x
13. Risk/Return and Asset Pricing Models	(a)	(a)	x
14. Primary Markets and the Underwriting of Securities	x		x
15. Secondary Markets	x		x
16. Treasury and Agency Securities Markets	x		x
17. Municipal Securities Markets	x		x
18. Common Stock Markets in the United States	x		x
19. International Stock Markets	x		x
20. Markets for Corporate Senior Instruments: I	x		x
21. Markets for Corporate Senior Instruments: II	x		x
22. The Market for Bank Obligations	x		x
23. The Mortgage Market	x		x
24. Mortgage-Backed Securities Markets	x		x
25. Asset-Backed Securities Markets	x		x
26. Financial Futures Markets	x	x	x
27. Options Markets	x	x	x
28. Pricing of Futures and Options Contracts	x	x	x
29. The Applications of Futures and Options Contracts		x	x
30. Other Derivative Markets: Swaps, Caps, Floor, and Credit Derivatives		x	x
31. The Market for Foreign Exchange Rate Risk Control Instruments		x	x

Note: (a) This chapter should be covered if students have not learned this material in an earlier course.

CHANGES FROM THE SECOND EDITION

We have changed the text in several ways. First, we have updated all discussions of financial institutions in the United States and around the world, and we have revised the tables and charts, using the most current information and numbers we could find. Second, we have substantially revised the following chapters: 7 (Insurance Companies), 8 (Investment Companies and Exchange Traded Funds), 9 (Pension Funds), 18 (Common Stock Markets), 19 (Stock Markets Around the Worlds), and 25 (Asset-Backed Securities Markets).

To help us in updating the book, we recruited another coauthor, Dr. Frank J. Jones, chief investment officer of The Guardian Life Insurance Company of America. His experiences in asset management, as well as his many experiences in the development of financial products prior to joining, provide significant insights.

RENEWING OUR PLEDGE

As we wrote in the first two editions, we would like those who adopt this text to tell us about their experiences with it. Please let us know where you find the book helpful and where it needs changing. Also, we would like to see outlines and syllabi of courses for which this book has been adopted. We have devoted many, many hours to producing the three editions, and we definitely want to know how beneficial our efforts have been to the people who use the text. If all continues to go well, there will be future editions of this book, and we want them to be as good as they can be. For that, we will need your help. For your help, we will all be grateful.

ACKNOWLEDGMENTS

We wish to acknowledge a number of people who have helped us in numerous respects, but who do not bear the burden of any errors or mistakes that may appear in the text. The following people, listed in alphabetical order, read some part or other of the material that has gone into one of the editions of this text: Anand Bhattacharya (Countrywide Securities), Daniel T. Coggin (consultant), Bruce Collins (Western Connecticut State University), Jack Clark Francis (Baruch College, CUNY), Gary L. Gastineau (Nuveen Investments), K. C. Ma (consultant), Scott Richard (Miller, Anderson, & Sherrerd), and Uzi Yaari (Rutgers University).

Over the last few years, we have benefited from discussions on a host of relevant topics with the following individuals: Robert Arnott (First Quadrant), Paul Asquith (MIT), Douglas Bendt (Mortgage Risk Assessment Corp.), Peter Bernstein (Peter L. Bernstein, Inc.), John H. Carlson (Fidelity Investments), John Crockett (George Mason University), Sylvan Feldstein (Guardian Life Insurance), Henry Gabbay (BlackRock Financial Management), Joseph P. Guagliardo (FNX), Gerald Hanweck (George Mason University), Arthur Hogan (Office of Thrift Supervision), Jane Howe (Freedom Capital Management), David P. Jacob (Nomura Securities), Andrew Kalotay (Andrew Kalotay Associates), Frank Keane (Federal Reserve Bank of New York), Robert Kieschnick (Federal Communications Commission), Martin Liebowitz (TIAA-CREF), Ed Murphy (Merchants Mutual Insurance Co.), Mark Pitts (White Oak Capital Management), Chuck Ramsey (Mortgage Risk Assessment Corp.), Dexter Senft (Lehman Brothers), Richard Wilson (consultant), and Jot Yau (George Mason University).

In our end-of-chapter questions, we use excerpts from *Institutional Investor* and several weekly publications of Institutional Investor, Inc., *Wall Street Letter, Bank Management Letter*, and *Portfolio Letter*. We are grateful to Tom Lamont, editor of the weekly publications, for permission to use this material.

Several people served as reviewers of much or all of the material that is contained in this text, and we thank them here: Eleanor Xu, Saint Louis University; Manijeh Sabi, The Sage Colleges; Helen M. Bowers, Wake Forest University; Inayat U. Mangla, Western Michigan University; and Richard Puntillo, University of San Francisco.

We acknowledge permission from Frank J. Fabozzi to use material in several chapters of this book that originally appeared in publications of Frank J. Fabozzi Associates. This includes but is not limited to the majority of the material in Chapters 18–25.

Frank J. Jones received substantial input and support from several sources. They include Jeff W. Smith of Nasdaq; Joanne M. Hill, Goldman Sachs; Steven Wunsch, President, Arizona Stock Exchange; Wayne Wagner, Chairman, The Plexus Group; Dan Friel, International Securities Exchange; and Robin Menzies, Baillie Gifford & Co. JoAnn Chippi's cooperation facilitated the effort overall. Jackie Elfe provided her expertise, efficiency, patience and good humor in preparing the manuscript. Finally, my assistant, Raman Vardharaj, was invaluable in all phases of my contribution to the book, from proofreading and editing to researching topics and authoring entire sections.

We would like to thank our friends at Prentice Hall who have assisted us in ways too numerous to mention, and we want to acknowledge these folks here: Mickey Cox, Executive Editor; Beth Romph, Assistant Editor; Kevin Hancock, Editorial Assistant; and particularly Carol Samet, Production Editor.

Finally, we must express our gratitude to our families, who tolerated much as this third edition was being written and produced.

Frank J. Fabozzi

Franco Modigliani

Frank J. Jones

Michael G. Ferri

ABOUT THE AUTHORS

Frank J. Fabozzi is an Adjunct Professor of Finance at the School of Management at Yale University and editor of the *Journal of Portfolio Management*. From 1986 to 1992, he was a full-time member of the Finance faculty at the Sloan School of Management at MIT. Dr. Fabozzi has authored and edited several widely acclaimed books in finance. He is on the board of directors of the BlackRock complex of closed-end funds and the Guardian Park Avenue Portfolio family of open-end funds. He earned a doctorate in economics in 1972 from The Graduate Center of the City University of New York and is a Chartered Financial Analyst. In 1994, he was awarded an honorary doctorate of Humane Letters from NOVA Southeastern University.

Franco Modigliani is Institute Professor and Professor of Finance and Economics at MIT. He is an Honorary President of the International Economic Association and a former President of the American Economic Association, the American Finance Association, and the Econometric Society. He is a member of several academies, including the National Academy of Science. Professor Modigliani has authored numerous books and articles in economics and finance. In October 1985, he was awarded the Alfred Nobel Memorial Prize in Economic Sciences. He has served as a consultant to the Federal Reserve System, the U.S. Treasury Department, and a number of European banks, as well as to many businesses, and is on several boards of directors. Professor Modigliani received a Doctor of Jurisprudence in 1939 from the University of Rome and a Doctor of Social Science in 1944 from the New School for Social Research, as well as several honorary degrees.

Frank J. Jones is Executive Vice President & Chief Investment Officer of The Guardian Life Insurance Company and President of The Park Avenue Portfolio, Guardian's family of mutual funds. He is also on the board of directors of Guardian Baille Gifford Limited and the International Securities Exchange. He is on the editorial boards of the *Journal of Portfolio Management* and the *Financial Analysts Journal*. He received a doctorate from Stanford University and an M.S. in nuclear engineering from Cornell University. Dr. Jones has been on the Graduate Faculty of Economics at the University of Notre Dame, an associate professor at the San Jose State University College of Business, a lecturer at the Yale University School of Management, and an Adjunct Professor of Finance at New York University. Dr. Jones has been Director of Global Fixed Income Research and Economics at Merrill Lynch & Co. and Senior Vice President at the New York Stock Exchange.

Michael G. Ferri is a Professor of Finance at George Mason University in Fairfax, Virginia, and holds the GMU Foundation Chair in Finance. He received his doctorate in economics from the University of North Carolina in 1975. His numerous articles on financial markets and investments have appeared in a variety of financial and economic journals. He is on the editorial advisory board of the *Journal of Portfolio Management* and several academic journals. He has been a vice-president of the Financial Management Association International and has served as a consultant to agencies of the U.S. government and to several major financial institutions. In 1997, Dr. Ferri held the Coenen Visiting Professorship in the Darden School of the University of Virginia.

C h a p t e r   1

Introduction

Learning Objectives

After reading this chapter, you will understand

■ what a financial asset is and the principal economic functions of financial assets.

■ the distinction between financial assets and tangible assets.

■ what a financial market is and the principal economic functions it performs.

■ the distinction between debt instruments and equity instruments.

■ the various ways to classify financial markets.

■ the differences between the primary and secondary markets.

■ the participants in financial markets.

■ reasons for the globalization of financial markets.

■ the distinction between an internal market and an external market.

■ the distinction between a domestic market, a foreign market, and the Euromarket.

■ the reasons why entities use foreign markets and Euromarkets.

■ what a derivative instrument is and the two basic types of derivative instruments.

■ the role of derivative instruments.

In a market economy, the allocation of economic resources is the outcome of many private decisions. Prices are the signals operating in a market economy that direct economic resources to their best use. The types of markets in an economy can be divided into (1) the market for products (manufactured goods and services), called the *product market*, and (2) the market for the factors of production (labor and capital), called the *factor market*.

Our purpose in this book is to focus on one part of the factor market, the market for financial assets, or, more simply, the **financial market.** In this chapter we will look at the role of financial markets, the "things" that are traded (i.e., bought and sold) in financial markets, and the reasons for the integration of world financial markets.

FINANCIAL ASSETS

We begin with a few basic definitions. An **asset**, broadly speaking, is any possession that has value in an exchange. Assets can be classified as *tangible* or *intangible*. A **tangible asset** is one whose value depends on particular physical properties—examples are buildings, land, or machinery. Intangible assets, by contrast, represent legal claims to some future benefit. Their value bears no relation to the form, physical or otherwise, in which these claims are recorded.

Financial assets are intangible assets. For financial assets, the typical benefit or value is a claim to future cash. This book deals with the various types of financial assets, the markets where they are traded, and the principles for valuing them. Throughout this book we use the terms **financial asset**, *financial instrument*, and *security* interchangeably.

The entity that has agreed to make future cash payments is called the *issuer* of the financial asset; the owner of the financial asset is referred to as the *investor*. Here are just seven examples of financial assets:

➤ a loan by Citibank (investor) to an individual (issuer/borrower) to purchase a car
➤ a bond issued by the U.S. Department of the Treasury
➤ a bond issued by General Motors Corporation
➤ a bond issued by the City of New York
➤ a bond issued by the government of Japan
➤ a share of common stock issued by IBM
➤ a share of common stock issued by Honda Motor Company, a Japanese company.

In the case of the car loan, the terms of the loan establish that the borrower must make specified payments to the commercial bank over time. The payments include repayment of the amount borrowed plus interest. The cash flow for this asset is made up of the specified payments that the borrower must make.

In the case of a U.S. Treasury bond, the U.S. government (the issuer) agrees to pay the holder or the investor the bond interest payments every six months until the bond matures, then at the maturity date repay the amount borrowed. The same is true for the bonds issued by General Motors Corporation, the City of New York, and the government of Japan. In the case of General Motors Corporation, the issuer is a corporation, not a government entity. In the case of the City of New York, the issuer is a municipal government. The issuer of the Japanese government bond is a central government entity.

The common stock of IBM entitles the investor to receive dividends distributed by the company. The investor in this case also has a claim to a pro rata share of the net asset value of the company in case of liquidation of the company. The same is true of the common stock of Honda Motor Company.

Debt versus Equity Instruments

The claim that the holder of a financial asset has may be either a fixed dollar amount or a varying, or residual, amount. In the former case, the financial asset is referred to as a **debt instrument**. The car loan, the U.S. Treasury bond, the General Motors Corporation bond, the City of New York bond, and the Japanese government bond cited above are examples of debt instruments requiring fixed dollar payments.

An **equity instrument** (also called a **residual claim**) obligates the issuer of the financial asset to pay the holder an amount based on earnings, if any, after holders of debt instruments have been paid. Common stock is an example of an equity instrument. A partnership share in a business is another example.

Some securities fall into both categories. Preferred stock, for example, is an equity instrument that entitles the investor to receive a fixed dollar amount. This payment is contingent, however, and due only after payments to debt instrument holders are made. Another "combination" instrument is a convertible bond, which allows the investor to convert debt into equity under certain circumstances. Both debt and preferred stock that pay fixed dollar amounts are called **fixed-income instruments**.

The Price of a Financial Asset and Risk

A basic economic principle is that the price of any financial asset is equal to the present value of its expected cash flow, even if the cash flow is not known with certainty. By cash flow we mean the stream of cash payments over time. For example, if a U.S. government bond promises to pay $30 every six months for the next 30 years and $1,000 at the end of 30 years, then this is its cash flow. In the case of the car loan by Citibank, if the borrower is obligated to pay $500 every month for three years, then this is the cash flow of the loan. We elaborate on this principle throughout this book as we discuss several theories for the pricing of financial assets.

Directly related to the notion of price is the expected return on a financial asset. Given the expected cash flow of a financial asset and its price, we can determine its expected rate of return. For example, if the price of a financial asset is $100, and its only cash flow is $105 one year from now, its expected return would be 5%.

The type of financial asset, whether debt instrument or equity instrument, and the characteristics of the issuer determine the degree of certainty of the expected cash flow. For example, assuming that the U.S. government never defaults on the debt instruments it issues, the cash flow of U.S. Treasury securities is known with certainty. What is uncertain, however, is the purchasing power of the cash flow received.

In the case of the Citibank car loan, the ability of the borrower to repay presents some uncertainty about the cash flow. But, if the borrower does not default on the loan obligation, the investor (Citibank) knows what the cash flow will be. The same is true for the bonds of General Motors and the City of New York.

In the case of the Japanese government bond, the cash flow is known if the Japanese government does not default. The cash flow, however, may be denominated not in U.S. dollars but in the Japanese currency, the yen. Thus, while the cash flow is known in terms of the number of yen that will be received, from the perspective of a U.S. investor, the number of U.S. dollars is unknown. The number of U.S. dollars will depend on the exchange rate between the Japanese yen and the U.S. dollar at the time the cash flow is received.

The holder of IBM common stock is uncertain as to both the amount and the timing of dividend payments. Dividend payments will be related to company profits. The same is true for the cash flow of the common stock of Honda Motor Company. In addition, because Honda will make dividend payments in Japanese yen, there is uncertainty about the cash flow in terms of U.S. dollars.

Although there are various types of risks that we will discuss in this chapter and those to follow, we can see three of them in our examples. The first is the risk attached to potential purchasing power of the expected cash flow. This is called **purchasing power risk**, or **inflation risk**. The second is the risk that the issuer or borrower will default on the obligation. This is called **credit risk**, or **default risk**. Finally, for financial assets whose cash flow is not denominated in U.S. dollars, there is the risk that the exchange rate will change adversely, resulting in less U.S. dollars. This risk is referred to as **foreign-exchange risk**.

Financial Assets versus Tangible Assets

A tangible asset such as plant or equipment purchased by a business entity shares at least one characteristic with a financial asset: Both are expected to generate future cash flow for their owner. For example, suppose a U.S. airline purchases a fleet of aircraft for $250 million. With its purchase of the aircraft, the airline expects to realize cash flow from passenger travel.

Financial assets and tangible assets are linked. Ownership of tangible assets is financed by the issuance of some type of financial asset—either debt instruments or equity instruments. For example, in the case of the airline, suppose that a debt instrument is issued to raise the $250 million to purchase the fleet of aircraft. The cash flow from the passenger travel will be used to service the payments on the debt instrument. Ultimately, therefore, the cash flow for a financial asset is generated by some tangible asset.

The Role of Financial Assets

Financial assets have two principal economic functions. The first is to transfer funds from those who have surplus funds to invest to those who need funds to invest in tangible assets. The second economic function is to transfer funds in such a way as to redistribute the unavoidable risk associated with the cash flow generated by tangible assets among those seeking and those providing the funds. However, as we will see, the claims held by the final wealth holders are generally different from the liabilities issued by the final demanders of funds because of the activity of financial intermediaries that seek to transform the final liabilities into the financial assets that the public prefers.

We can illustrate these two economic functions with three examples.

1. Joe Grasso has obtained a license to manufacture Rugrat wristwatches. Joe estimates that he will need $1 million to purchase plant and equipment to manufacture the watches. Unfortunately, he has only $200,000 to invest, and that is his life savings, which he does not want to invest, even though he has confidence that there will be a receptive market for the watches.
2. Susan Carlson has recently inherited $730,000. She plans to spend $30,000 on some jewelry, furniture, and a few cruises, and to invest the balance, $700,000.
3. Larry Stein, an up-and-coming attorney with a major New York law firm, has received a bonus check that after taxes has netted him $250,000. He plans to spend $50,000 on a BMW and invest the balance, $200,000.

Suppose that, quite by accident, Joe, Susan, and Larry meet at a social function. Sometime during their conversation, they discuss their financial plans. By the end of the evening, they agree to a deal. Joe agrees to invest $100,000 of his savings in the business and sell a 50% interest to Susan for $700,000. Larry agrees to lend Joe $200,000 for four years at an interest rate of 18% per year. Joe will be responsible for operating the business without the assistance of Susan or Larry. Joe now has his $1 million to manufacture the watches.

Two financial claims came out of this meeting. The first is an equity instrument issued by Joe and purchased by Susan for $700,000. The other is a debt instrument issued by Joe and purchased by Larry for $200,000. Thus, the two financial assets allowed funds to be transferred from Susan and Larry, who had surplus funds to invest, to Joe, who needed funds to invest in tangible assets in order to manufacture the watches. This transfer of funds is the first economic function of financial assets.

The fact that Joe is not willing to invest his life savings of $200,000 means that he wanted to transfer part of that risk. He does so by selling Susan a financial asset that gives her a financial claim equal to one-half the cash flow from the business. He further secures an additional amount of capital from Larry, who is not willing to share in the risk of the business (except for credit risk), in the form of an obligation requiring payment of a fixed cash flow, regardless of the outcome of the venture. This shifting of risk is the second economic function of financial assets.

Key Points That You Should Understand Before Proceeding

1. The difference between tangible assets and financial assets and how they are related.
2. The difference between debt instruments and equity instruments.
3. What is meant by the cash flow of a financial asset.
4. Three types of risk associated with investing in financial assets: purchasing power or inflation risk, default or credit risk, and exchange-rate risk.
5. The two principal economic functions of financial assets.

FINANCIAL MARKETS

A financial market is a market where financial assets are exchanged (i.e., traded). Although the existence of a financial market is not a necessary condition for the creation and exchange of a financial asset, in most economies financial assets are created and subsequently traded in some type of financial market. The market in which a financial asset trades for immediate delivery is called the **spot** or **cash market**.

Role of Financial Markets

We previously explained the two primary economic functions of financial assets. Financial markets provide three additional economic functions.

First, the interactions of buyers and sellers in a financial market determine the price of the traded asset. Or, equivalently, they determine the required return on a financial asset. As the inducement for firms to acquire funds depends on the required return that investors demand, it is this feature of financial markets that signals how the funds in the economy should be allocated among financial assets. This is called the **price discovery process**.

Second, financial markets provide a mechanism for an investor to sell a financial asset. Because of this feature, it is said that a financial market offers *liquidity*, an attractive feature when circumstances either force or motivate an investor to sell. If there were not liquidity, the owner would be forced to hold a debt instrument until it matures and an equity instrument until the company is either voluntarily or involuntarily liquidated. While all financial markets provide some form of liquidity, the degree of liquidity is one of the factors that characterize different markets.

The third economic function of a financial market is that it reduces the cost of transacting. There are two costs associated with transacting: **search costs** and **information costs**.

Search costs represent explicit costs, such as the money spent to advertise one's intention to sell or purchase a financial asset, and implicit costs, such as the value of time spent in locating a counterparty. The presence of some form of organized financial market reduces search costs. Information costs are costs associated with assessing the investment merits of a financial asset, that is, the amount and the likelihood of the cash flow expected to be generated. In an efficient market, prices reflect the aggregate information collected by all market participants.

Classification of Financial Markets

There are many ways to classify financial markets. One way is by the type of financial claim, such as debt markets and equity markets. Another is by the maturity of the claim. For example, there is a financial market for short-term debt instruments, called the **money market**, and one for longer-maturity financial assets, called the **capital market**.

Financial markets can be categorized as those dealing with financial claims that are newly issued, called the *primary market*, and those for exchanging financial claims previously issued, called the **secondary market** or the market for seasoned instruments.

Markets are classified as either *cash* or *derivative instruments* markets. (The latter is described later in this chapter.) A market can be classified by its organizational structure: It may be an *auction market*, an *over-the-counter market*, or an *intermediated market*.

These structures are described in Chapter 15. All these classifications are summarized in Table 1-1.

Market Participants

Participants in the global financial markets that issue and purchase financial claims include households, business entities (corporations and partnerships), national gov-

Table 1-1   Summary of Classification of Financial Markets

CLASSIFICATION BY NATURE OF CLAIM:
Debt market
Equity market
CLASSIFICATION BY MATURITY OF CLAIM:
Money market
Capital market
CLASSIFICATION BY SEASONING OF CLAIM:
Primary market
Secondary market
CLASSIFICATION BY IMMEDIATE DELIVERY OR FUTURE DELIVERY:
Cash or spot market
Derivative market
CLASSIFICATION BY ORGANIZATIONAL STRUCTURE:
Auction market
Over-the-counter market
Intermediated market

ernments, national government agencies, state and local governments, and supranationals (such as the World Bank, the European Investment Bank, and the Asian Development Bank).

Business entities include nonfinancial and financial enterprises. Nonfinancial enterprises manufacture products—for example, cars, steel, and computers—and/or provide nonfinancial services—including transportation, utilities, and computer programming. The roles in financial markets played by financial enterprises and a special type of financial enterprise called a financial intermediary are described in Chapter 2.

Finally, while we have focused on market participants that create and/or exchange financial assets a broader definition of market participants would include regulators of financial markets. We discuss regulation in Chapter 3.

Key Points That You Should Understand Before Proceeding

1. The three economic functions of financial markets are to improve the price discovery process, enhance liquidity, and reduce the cost of transacting.
2. There are various ways that financial markets can be classified.
3. The market participants include households, business entities, national governments, national government agencies, state and local governments, supranationals, and regulators.

GLOBALIZATION OF FINANCIAL MARKETS

Because of the globalization of financial markets throughout the world, entities in any country seeking to raise funds need not be limited to their domestic financial market. Nor are investors in a country limited to the financial assets issued in their domestic market. Globalization means the integration of financial markets throughout the world into an international financial market.

The factors that have led to the integration of financial markets are (1) deregulation or liberalization of markets and the activities of market participants in key financial centers of the world; (2) technological advances for monitoring world markets, executing orders, and analyzing financial opportunities; and (3) increased institutionalization of financial markets.

Global competition has forced governments to deregulate (or liberalize) various aspects of their financial markets so that their financial enterprises can compete effectively around the world. We discuss deregulation in Chapter 3.

Technological advances have increased the integration of and efficiency of the global financial market. Advances in telecommunication systems link market participants throughout the world, with the result that orders can be executed within seconds. Advances in computer technology, coupled with advanced telecommunication systems, allow the transmission of real-time information on security prices and other key information to many participants in many places. Therefore, many investors can monitor global markets and simultaneously assess how this information will impact the risk/return profile of their portfolios. Significantly improved computing power allows the instant manipulation of real-time market information so that arbitrage opportunities can be identified. Once these opportunities are identified, telecommunication systems permit the rapid execution of orders to capture them.

The U.S. financial markets have shifted from domination by retail investors to domination by financial institutions. By *retail investors* we mean individuals. For example, when you or I buy a share of common stock, we are referred to as retail investors. Examples of financial institutions are pension funds, insurance companies, mutual funds, commercial banks, and savings and loan associations. We describe these financial institutions in Part 3 of this book. Throughout this book we will refer to these financial institutions as *institutional investors.*

The shifting of the financial markets from dominance by retail investors to institutional investors is referred to as the *institutionalization* of financial markets. The same thing is occurring in other industrialized countries. Unlike retail investors, institutional investors have been more willing to transfer funds across national borders to improve portfolio diversification and/or exploit perceived mispricing of financial assets in foreign countries. The potential portfolio diversification benefits associated with global investing have been documented in numerous studies, which have heightened the awareness of investors about the virtues of global investing.

Classification of Global Financial Markets

Although there is no uniform system for classifying the global financial markets, an appropriate schematic presentation appears in Figure 1-1. From the perspective of a given country, financial markets can be classified as either **internal** or **external**. The *internal market* is also called the **national market**. It is composed of two parts: the **domestic market** and the **foreign market**. The domestic market is where issuers domiciled in a country issue securities and where those securities are subsequently traded.

The foreign market in any country is where the securities of issuers not domiciled in the country are sold and traded. The rules governing the issuance of foreign securities are those imposed by regulatory authorities where the security is issued. For example, securities issued by non-U.S. corporations in the United States must comply with the regulations set forth in U.S. securities law. A non-Japanese corporation that seeks to offer securities in Japan must comply with Japanese securities law and regulations imposed by the Japanese Ministry of Finance. Nicknames have developed to describe the various foreign markets. For example, the foreign market in the United States is called the *Yankee market.* The foreign market in Japan is nicknamed the

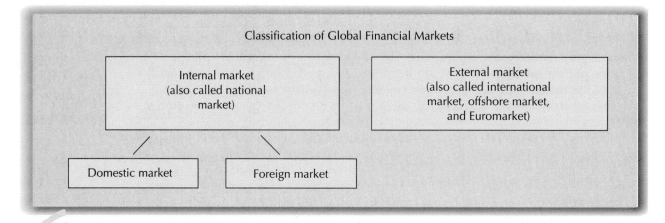

Figure 1-1 Classification of Global Financial Markets

Samurai market, in the United Kingdom the *Bulldog market*, in the Netherlands the *Rembrandt market*, and in Spain the *Matador market*.

The **external market**, also called the **international market**, allows trading of securities with two distinguishing features: (1) at issuance securities are offered simultaneously to investors in a number of countries, and (2) they are issued outside the jurisdiction of any single country. The external market is commonly referred to as the **offshore market**, or, more popularly, the **Euromarket**.[1]

Motivation for Using Foreign Markets and Euromarkets

There are several reasons why a corporation may seek to raise funds outside its domestic market. First, in some countries, large corporations seeking to raise a substantial amount of funds may have no choice but to obtain financing in either the foreign market sector of another country or the Euromarket. This is because the fund-seeking corporation's domestic market is not fully developed and cannot satisfy its demand for funds on globally competitive terms. Governments of developing countries have used these markets in seeking funds for government-owned corporations that they are privatizing.

The second reason is that there may be opportunities for obtaining a lower cost of funding than is available in the domestic market, although with the integration of capital markets throughout the world, such opportunities have diminished. Nevertheless, there are still some imperfections in capital markets throughout the world that may permit a reduced cost of funds. The causes of these imperfections are discussed throughout the book. A final reason for using foreign or Euromarkets is a desire by issuers to diversify their source of funding so as to reduce reliance on domestic investors.

Corporate Financing Week asked the corporate treasurers of several multinational corporations why they used nondomestic markets to raise funds.[2] Their responses reflect one or more of the reasons cited above. For example, the director of corporate finance for General Motors said that the company uses the bond sector of the

---

[1] The classification we use is by no means universally accepted. Some market observers and compilers of statistical data on market activity refer to the external market as consisting of the foreign market and the Euromarket.

[2] Victoria Keefe, "Companies Issue Overseas for Diverse Reasons," *Corporate Financing Week*, November 25, 1991, Special Supplement, pp. 1 and 9.

Eurobond market (discussed in Chapter 21) with the objective of "diversifying funding sources, [and to] attract new investors and achieve comparable, if not cheaper, financing." A managing director of Sears, Roebuck stated that the company "has a long-standing policy of diversifying geographical [funding] sources and instruments to avoid reliance on any specific market, even if the cost is higher." He added that "Sears cultivates a presence in the international market by issuing every three years or so."

In a survey conducted by the Economic Council of Canada of Canadian borrowers who raised funds outside of Canada, 85% cited as a primary reason the lower cost of funding.[3] The other reasons cited by the participants in the survey were: diversification of the investor base (50%); ease of borrowing funds (37%); the presence of a subsidiary, parent, or affiliate in the country of borrowing (43%); the ability to attract new investors (30%); and publicity for the corporation's name (30%).

Key Points That You Should Understand Before Proceeding

1. The three major factors that have integrated financial markets throughout the world.
2. What is meant by the institutionalization of financial markets.
3. What is meant by an internal market (or national market), domestic market, foreign market, and external market (or international market, offshore market, or Euromarket).
4. The motivations for U.S. corporations to raise money outside the United States.

DERIVATIVE MARKETS

So far we have focused on the cash market for financial assets. With some contracts, the contract holder has either the obligation or the choice to buy or sell a financial asset at some future time. The price of any such contract derives its value from the value of the underlying financial asset, financial index, or interest rate. Consequently, these contracts are called **derivative instruments**.

Types of Derivative Instruments

The two basic types of derivative instruments are *futures/forward contracts* and *options contracts*. A futures or forward contract is an agreement whereby two parties agree to transact with respect to some financial asset at a predetermined price at a specified future date. One party agrees to buy the financial asset; the other agrees to sell the financial asset. Both parties are obligated to perform, and neither party charges a fee. The distinction between a futures and forward contract is explained in Chapter 26.

An options contract gives the owner of the contract the right, but not the obligation, to buy (or sell) a financial asset at a specified price from (or to) another party. The buyer of the contract must pay the seller a fee, which is called the option price. When the option grants the owner of the option the right to buy a financial asset from the other party, the option is called a **call option**. If, instead, the option grants the owner of the option the right to sell a financial asset to the other party, the option is called a *put option*. Options are more fully explained in Chapter 27.

Derivative instruments are not limited to financial assets. There are derivative instruments involving commodities and precious metals. Our focus in this book, however, is on derivative instruments where the underlying asset is a financial asset, or some financial benchmark such as a stock index or an interest rate, a credit spread, or

---

[3] A. Nigam, "Canadian Corporations and Governments, Financial Innovation and International Capital Markets," a paper prepared for the Economic Council of Canada, 1989.

foreign exchange. Moreover, there are other types of derivative instruments that are basically "packages" of either forward contracts or option contracts. These include swaps, caps, and floors, all of which are discussed in Chapter 30.

The Role of Derivative Instruments

Derivative contracts provide issuers and investors an inexpensive way of controlling some major risks. While we will describe these risks in later chapters of this book, here are three examples that clearly illustrate the need for derivative contracts:

1.   Suppose that General Motors plans to obtain a bank loan for $100 million two months from now. The key risk here is that two months from now the interest rate will be higher than it is today. If the interest rate is only one percentage point higher, General Motors would have to pay $1 million more in annual interest. Clearly, then, issuers and borrowers want a way to protect against a rise in interest rates.

2.   IBM pension fund owns a portfolio consisting of the common stock of a large number of companies. (We describe the role of pension funds in Chapter 9), but for now the only thing that is important to understand is that the pension fund must make periodic payments to the beneficiaries of the plan.) Suppose the pension fund knows that two months from now it must sell stock in its portfolio to pay beneficiaries $20 million. The risk that IBM pension fund faces is that two months from now when the stocks are sold, the price of most or all stocks may be lower than they are today. If stock prices do decline, the pension fund will have to sell off more shares to realize $20 million. Thus, investors, such as the IBM pension fund, face the risk of declining stock prices and may want to protect against this risk.

3.   Suppose Sears, Roebuck plans to issue a bond in Switzerland and the periodic payments that the company must make to the bondholders are denominated in the Swiss currency, the franc. The amount of U.S. dollars that Sears must pay to receive the amount of Swiss francs it has contracted to pay will depend on the exchange rate at the time the payment must be made. For example, suppose that at the time Sears plans to issue the bonds, the exchange rate is such that 1 U.S. dollar is equal to 1.5 Swiss francs. So, for each 7.5 million Swiss francs that Sears must pay to the bondholders, it must pay U.S. $5 million. If at any time that a payment must be made in Swiss francs, the value of the U.S. dollar declines relative to the Swiss franc, Sears will have to pay more U.S. dollars to satisfy its contractual obligation. For example, if 1 U.S. dollar at the time of a payment changes to 1.25 Swiss francs, Sears would have to pay $6 million to make a payment of 7.5 million Swiss francs. This is U.S. $1 million more than when it issued the bonds. Issuers and borrowers who raise funds in a currency that is not their local currency face this risk.

The derivative instruments that we describe in Part 9 of this book can be used by the two borrowers (General Motors and Sears, Roebuck) and the one investor (IBM pension fund) in these examples to eliminate or to reduce the kinds of risks that they face.

As we will see in later chapters, derivative markets may have at least three advantages over the corresponding cash (spot) market for the same financial asset. First, depending on the derivative instrument, it may cost less to execute a transaction in the derivatives market in order to adjust the risk exposure of an investor's portfolio to new economic information than it would cost to make that adjustment in the cash market. Second, transactions typically can be accomplished faster in the derivatives market. Third, some derivative markets can absorb a greater dollar transaction without an adverse effect on the price of the derivative instrument; that is, the derivative market may be more liquid than the cash market.

The key point here is that derivative instruments play a critical role in global financial markets. A May 1994 report published by the U.S. General Accounting Office (GAO) titled *Financial Derivatives: Actions Needed to Protect the Financial System* recognized the importance of derivatives for market participants. Page 6 of the report states:

> Derivatives serve an important function of the global financial marketplace, providing end-users with opportunities to better manage financial risks associated with their business transactions. The rapid growth and increasing complexity of derivatives reflect both the increased demand from end-users for better ways to manage their financial risks and the innovative capacity of the financial services industry to respond to market demands.

Unfortunately, derivative markets are too often viewed by the general public—and sometimes regulators and legislative bodies—as vehicles for pure speculation (that is, legalized gambling). Without derivative instruments and the markets in which they trade, the financial systems throughout the world would not be as integrated as they are today.

Key Points That You Should Understand Before Proceeding

1. The two basic types of derivative instruments: futures/forward contracts and options.
2. The principal economic role of derivative instruments.
3. The potential advantages of using derivative instruments rather than cash market instruments.

SUMMARY

In this chapter we have explained the role of financial assets and financial markets. A financial asset (or financial instrument or security) entitles the owner to future cash flows to be paid by the issuer as well as to the liquidation value of the asset. The claim can be either an equity or debt claim. The price of any financial asset is equal to the present value of the cash flow expected. Because of uncertainty about the cash flow, in nominal and inflation-adjusted dollars, there is risk in investing in financial assets.

The two principal economic functions of a financial asset are (1) transferring funds from those who have surplus funds to invest to those who need funds to invest in tangible assets, and (2) transferring funds in such a way that redistributes the unavoidable risk associated with the cash flow generated by tangible assets among those seeking and those providing the funds.

Financial markets provide the following three additional functions beyond that of financial assets themselves: (1) They provide a mechanism for determining the price (or, equivalently, the required return) of financial assets, (2) they make assets more liquid, and (3) they reduce the costs of exchanging assets. The costs associated with transacting are search costs and information costs.

There are various ways to classify financial markets: money (or short-term) versus capital markets, debt versus equity markets, primary versus secondary markets, and cash versus derivative markets. Another classification is based on the type of organizational structure: auction versus over-the-counter versus intermediated markets.

The increased integration of financial markets throughout the world can be attributed to three factors: (1) deregulation or liberalization of major financial markets (market deregulation and institutional deregulation); (2) advances in telecommunications and computer technologies; and (3) institutionalization of financial markets. Global financial markets can be classified as the national market of a country, consisting of the domestic market and foreign market, and the external market (overseas or Euromarket).

A derivative instrument is a contract whose value depends on the value of the underlying financial asset. The chief economic function of a derivative instrument is to provide ways to control risk. Derivative markets may offer three advantages over cash markets: (1) lower transactions costs; (2) faster speed at which transactions can be completed; and (3) greater liquidity.

KEY TERMS

- Asset, 1
- Call option, 9
- Capital market, 5
- Debt instrument, 2
- Default risk (also called credit risk), 3
- Derivative instrument, 9
- Domestic market, 7
- Equity instrument (also called residual claim), 2
- External market (also called the international market, the offshore market, or the Euromarket), 8
- Financial asset (or intangible asset), 2
- Financial market, 1

- Fixed-income instrument, 2
- Foreign-exchange risk, 3
- Foreign market, 7
- Information costs, 5
- Internal market (also called national market), 7
- Money market, 5
- Price discovery process, 5
- Purchasing power risk (also called inflation risk), 3
- Search costs, 5
- Secondary market, 5
- Spot market (also called cash market), 5
- Tangible asset, 1

QUESTIONS

1. What is the difference between a financial asset and a tangible asset?
2. What is the difference between the claim of a debtholder of General Motors and an equityholder of General Motors?
3. What is the basic principle in determining the price of a financial asset?
4. Why is it difficult to determine the cash flow of a financial asset?
5. Why are the characteristics of an issuer important in determining the price of a financial asset?
6. What are the two principal roles of financial assets?
7. In September 1990 a study by the U.S. Congress, Office of Technology Assessment, entitled "Electronic Bulls & Bears: U.S. Securities Markets and Information Technology," included this statement:
   Securities markets have five basic functions in a capitalistic economy:
   a. They make it possible for corporations and governmental units to raise capital.
   b. They help to allocate capital toward productive uses.
   c. They provide an opportunity for people to increase their savings by investing in them.
   d. They reveal investors' judgments about the potential earning capacity of corporations, thus giving guidance to corporate managers.
   e. They generate employment and income.
   For each of the functions cited above, explain how financial markets (or securities markets, in the parlance of this Congressional study) perform each function.
8. Explain the difference between each of the following:
   a. Money market and capital market.
   b. Primary market and secondary market.
   c. Domestic market and foreign market.
   d. National market and Euromarket.

9. Indicate whether each of the following instruments trades in the money market or the capital market:
   a. General Motors Acceptance Corporation issues a financial instrument with four months to maturity.
   b. The U.S. Treasury issues a security with 10 years to maturity.
   c. Microsoft Corporation issues common stock.
   d. The State of Alaska issues a financial instrument with eight months to maturity.

10. A U.S. investor who purchases the bonds issued by the government of France made the following comment: "Assuming that the French government does not default, I know what the cash flow of the bond will be." Explain why you agree or disagree with this statement.

11. A U.S. investor who purchases the bonds issued by the U.S. government made the following statement: "By buying this debt instrument I am not exposed to default risk or purchasing power risk." Explain why you agree or disagree with this statement.

12. In January 1992, Atlantic Richfield Corporation, a U.S.-based corporation, issued $250 million of bonds in the United States. From the perspective of the U.S. financial market, indicate whether this issue is classified as being issued in the domestic market, the foreign market, or the offshore market.

13. In January 1992, the Korea Development Bank issued $500 million of bonds in the United States. From the perspective of the U.S. financial market, indicate whether this issue is classified as being issued in the domestic market, the foreign market, or the offshore market.

14. Give three reasons for the trend toward greater integration of financial markets throughout the world.

15. What is meant by the "institutionalization" of capital markets?

16. a. What are the two basic types of derivative instruments?
    b. "Derivative markets are nothing more than legalized gambling casinos and serve no economic function." Comment on this statement.

Financial Intermediaries and Financial Innovation

Learning Objectives

After reading this chapter, you will understand

■ the business of financial institutions.

■ the role of financial intermediaries.

■ the difference between direct and indirect investments.

■ how financial intermediaries transform the maturity of liabilities and give both short-term depositors and longer-term, final borrowers what they want.

■ how financial intermediaries offer investors diversification and so reduce the risks of their investments.

■ the way financial intermediaries reduce the costs of acquiring information and entering into contracts with final borrowers of funds.

■ how financial intermediaries enjoy economies of scale in processing payments from final users of funds.

■ the nature of the management of assets and liabilities by financial intermediaries.

■ how different financial institutions have differing degrees of knowledge and certainty about the amount and timing of the cash outlay of their liabilities.

■ why financial institutions have liquidity concerns.

■ the primary reasons for financial innovation.

■ the nature of asset securitization.

■ the pivotal role of financial intermediaries in securitization.

■ the benefits to issuers, investors, financial markets, and borrowers of securitization.

This chapter serves several purposes. The first is to introduce the financial intermediary. Intermediaries include commercial banks, savings and loan associations, investment companies, insurance companies, and pension funds. The most important contribution of intermediaries is a steady and relatively inexpensive flow of funds from savers to final users or investors. Every modern economy has intermediaries, which perform key financial functions for individuals, households, corporations, small and new businesses, and governments. Germany has large and regional commercial banks, as well as savings banks and credit cooperatives. Japan has nationally branched banks, local banking firms, and trust banks that specialize in savings and investment. Investors in Britain and Italy can choose from among numerous investment companies.

The chapter's second purpose is to convey a sense of the dynamic nature of contemporary finance and financial institutions. We live in a time marked by an unusually rapid pace of financial innovation. This innovation both reflects and responds to two historically significant events in today's world: the arrival of sophisticated telecommunications, Internet, and computer technology, and the globalization of business, especially finance. In a sense, this entire book is a treatise on financial innovation. This chapter provides a brief overview of some of the reasons for and benefits of innovation.

Finally, the chapter calls attention to a special kind of innovation that originates with financial institutions. This innovation is the process by which financial intermediaries pool traditional assets (car loans, mortgages, and so on) and sell securities backed by these loan pools in the capital markets. This process of *securitization* is affecting all kinds of financial institutions and assets today, and it is taking hold in all business centers of the world. Before long, investors will have opportunities to buy bonds based on car loans in India, farm loans in Poland, bad debt loans in Mexico, and truck loans in (just maybe) Russia. Clearly, this is an exciting development and one that needs to be well understood.

FINANCIAL INSTITUTIONS

Business entities include nonfinancial and financial enterprises. Nonfinancial enterprises manufacture products (e.g., cars, steel, computers) and/or provide nonfinancial services (e.g., transportation, utilities, computer programming). Financial enterprises, more popularly referred to as **financial institutions**, provide services related to one or more of the following:

1. Transforming financial assets acquired through the market and constituting them into a different, and more widely preferable, type of asset—which becomes their liability. This is the function performed by **financial intermediaries**, the most important type of financial institution.
2. Exchanging of financial assets on behalf of customers.
3. Exchanging of financial assets for their own accounts.
4. Assisting in the creation of financial assets for their customers, and then selling those financial assets to other market participants.
5. Providing investment advice to other market participants.
6. Managing the portfolios of other market participants.

Financial intermediaries include **depository institutions** (commercial banks, savings and loan associations, savings banks, and credit unions), which acquire the bulk of their funds by offering their liabilities to the public mostly in the form of deposits; insurance companies (life and property and casualty companies); pension funds; and finance companies. Deposit-accepting, or depository institutions, are discussed in Chapter 4. The other financial intermediaries are covered in Chapters 7 through 9.

The second and third services in the list above are the broker and dealer functions, which are discussed in Chapters 14 and 15. The fourth service is referred to as underwriting. As we explain in Chapter 14, typically a financial institution that provides an underwriting service also provides a brokerage and/or dealer service.

Some nonfinancial enterprises have subsidiaries that provide financial services. For example, many large manufacturing firms have subsidiaries that provide financing for the parent company's customer. These financial institutions are called *captive finance companies.* Examples include General Motors Acceptance Corporation (a subsidiary of General Motors) and General Electric Credit Corporation (a subsidiary of General Electric).

Key Points That You Should Understand Before Proceeding

1. The services provided by financial institutions.
2. The special role played by a financial intermediary when it transforms assets acquired from customers or the market into its own liabilities.

ROLE OF FINANCIAL INTERMEDIARIES

As we have seen, financial intermediaries obtain funds by issuing financial claims against themselves to market participants, and then investing those funds. The investments made by financial intermediaries—their assets—can be in loans and/or securities. These investments are referred to as **direct investments**. Market participants who hold the financial claims issued by financial intermediaries are said to have made **indirect investments**.

Two examples will illustrate this. Most readers of this book are familiar with what a **commercial bank** does. Commercial banks accept deposits and may use the proceeds to lend funds to consumers and businesses. The deposits represent the IOU of the commercial bank and a financial asset owned by the depositor. The loan represents an IOU of the borrowing entity and a financial asset of the commercial bank. The commercial bank has made a direct investment in the borrowing entity; the depositor effectively has made an indirect investment in that borrowing entity.

As a second example, consider an **investment company**, a financial intermediary we focus on in Chapter 8, which pools the funds of market participants and uses those funds to buy a portfolio of securities such as stocks and bonds. Investors providing funds to the investment company receive an equity claim that entitles the investor to a pro rata share of the outcome of the portfolio. The equity claim is issued by the investment company. The **portfolio** of financial assets acquired by the investment company represents a direct investment that it has made. By owning an equity claim against the investment company, those who invest in the investment company have made an indirect investment.

We have stressed that financial intermediaries play the basic role of transforming financial assets that are less desirable for a large part of the public into other financial assets—their own liabilities—which are more widely preferred by the public. This transformation involves at least one of four economic functions: (1) providing maturity intermediation; (2) reducing risk via diversification; (3) reducing the costs of contracting and information processing; and (4) providing a payments mechanism. Each function is described below.

Maturity Intermediation

In our example of the commercial bank, two things should be noted. First, the maturity of at least a portion of the deposits accepted is typically short term. For example, certain types of deposit are payable upon demand. Others have a specific maturity date, but most are less than two years. Second, the maturity of the loans made by a commercial bank may be considerably longer than two years. In the absence of a commercial bank, the borrower would have to borrow for a shorter term, or find an entity that is willing to invest for the length of the loan sought, and/or investors who make deposits in the bank would have to commit funds for a longer length of time than they want. The commercial bank by issuing its own financial claims in essence transforms a longer-term asset into a shorter-term one by giving the borrower a loan for the length of time sought and the investor/depositor a financial asset for the desired investment horizon. This function of a financial intermediary is called **maturity intermediation**.

Maturity intermediation has two implications for financial markets. First, it provides investors with more choices concerning maturity for their investments; borrowers have more choices for the length of their debt obligations. Second, because investors are naturally reluctant to commit funds for a long period of time, they will require that long-term borrowers pay a higher interest rate than on short-term borrowing. A financial intermediary is willing to make longer-term loans, and at a lower cost to the borrower than an individual investor would, by counting on successive deposits providing the funds until maturity (although at some risk—see below). Thus, the second implication is that the cost of longer-term borrowing is likely to be reduced.

Reducing Risk via Diversification

Consider the example of the investor who places funds in an investment company. Suppose that the investment company invests the funds received in the stock of a large number of companies. By doing so, the investment company has diversified and reduced its risk. Investors who have a small sum to invest would find it difficult to achieve the same degree of **diversification** because they do not have sufficient funds to buy shares of a large number of companies. Yet by investing in the investment company for the same sum of money, investors can accomplish this diversification, thereby reducing risk.

This economic function of financial intermediaries—transforming more risky assets into less risky ones—is called *diversification*. Although individual investors can do it on their own, they may not be able to do it as cost-effectively as a financial intermediary, depending on the amount of funds they have to invest. Attaining cost-effective diversification in order to reduce risk by purchasing the financial assets of a financial intermediary is an important economic benefit for financial markets.

Reducing the Costs of Contracting and Information Processing

Investors purchasing financial assets should take the time to develop skills necessary to understand how to evaluate an investment. Once those skills are developed, investors should apply them to the analysis of specific financial assets that are candidates for purchase (or subsequent sale). Investors who want to make a loan to a consumer or business will need to write the loan contract (or hire an attorney to do so).

Although there are some people who enjoy devoting leisure time to this task, most prefer to use that time for just that—leisure. Most of us find that leisure time is in short supply, so to sacrifice it, we have to be compensated. The form of compensation could be a higher return that we obtain from an investment.

In addition to the opportunity cost of the time to process the information about the financial asset and its issuer, there is the cost of acquiring that information. All these costs are called *information processing costs*. The costs of writing loan contracts are referred to as **contracting costs**. There is also another dimension to contracting costs, the cost of enforcing the terms of the loan agreement.

With this in mind, consider our two examples of financial intermediaries—the commercial bank and the investment company. People who work for these intermediaries include investment professionals who are trained to analyze financial assets and manage them. In the case of loan agreements, either standardized contracts can be prepared, or legal counsel can be part of the professional staff that writes contracts involving more complex transactions. The investment professionals can monitor compliance with the terms of the loan agreement and take any necessary action to protect the interests of the financial intermediary. The employment of such professionals is cost-effective for financial intermediaries because investing funds is their normal business.

In other words, there are economies of scale in contracting and processing information about financial assets because of the amount of funds managed by financial intermediaries. The lower costs accrue to the benefit of the investor who purchases a financial claim of the financial intermediary and to the issuers of financial assets, who benefit from a lower borrowing cost.

Providing a Payments Mechanism

Although the previous three economic functions may not have been immediately obvious, this last function should be. Most transactions made today are not done with cash. Instead, payments are made using checks, credit cards, debit cards, and electronic transfers of funds. These methods for making payments, called **payment mechanisms**, are provided by certain financial intermediaries.

At one time, noncash payments were restricted to checks written against non-interest-bearing accounts at commercial banks. Similar check writing privileges were provided later by savings and loan associations and savings banks, and by certain types of investment companies. Payment by credit card was also at one time the exclusive domain of commercial banks, but now other depository institutions offer this service. Debit cards are offered by various financial intermediaries. A debit card differs from a credit card in that, in the latter case, a bill is sent to the credit card holder periodically (usually once a month) requesting payment for transactions made in the past. In the case of a **debit card**, funds are immediately withdrawn (that is, debited) from the purchaser's account at the time the transaction takes place.

The ability to make payments without the use of cash is critical for the functioning of a financial market. In short, depository institutions transform assets that cannot be used to make payments into other assets that offer that property.

Key Points That You Should Understand Before Proceeding

1. The difference between a direct investment and an indirect investment.
2. How a financial institution intermediates among investors and borrowers in the area of maturity, reduces risk and offers diversification, reduces the costs of contracting and information processing, and provides payment mechanisms.

OVERVIEW OF ASSET/LIABILITY MANAGEMENT FOR FINANCIAL INSTITUTIONS

In Chapters 4 through 9, we discuss the major financial institutions. To understand the reasons managers of financial institutions invest in particular types of financial assets and the types of investment strategies they employ, it is necessary to have a general understanding of the asset/liability problem faced. In this section, we provide an overview of **asset/liability management**.

The nature of the liabilities dictates the investment strategy a financial institution will pursue. For example, depository institutions seek to generate income by the spread between the return that they earn on assets and the cost of their funds. That is, they buy money and sell money. They buy money by borrowing from depositors or other sources of funds. They sell money when they lend it to businesses or individuals. In essence, they are spread businesses. Their objective is to sell money for more than it costs to buy money. The cost of the funds and the return on the funds sold is expressed in terms of an interest rate per unit of time. Consequently, the objective of a depository institution is to earn a positive *spread* between the assets it invests in (what it has sold the money for) and the costs of its funds (what it has purchased the money for).

Life insurance companies—and, to a certain extent, property and casualty insurance companies—are in the spread business. Pension funds are not in the spread business in that they do not raise funds themselves in the market. They seek to cover the cost of pension obligations at a minimum cost that is borne by the sponsor of the pension plan. Investment companies face no explicit costs for the funds they acquire and must satisfy no specific liability obligations; one exception is a particular type of investment company that agrees to repurchase shares at any time.

Nature of Liabilities

By the **liabilities** of a financial institution we mean the amount and timing of the cash outlays that must be made to satisfy the contractual terms of the obligations issued. The liabilities of any financial institution can be categorized according to four types as shown in Table 2-1. The categorization in the table assumes that the entity that must be paid the obligation will not cancel the financial institution's obligation prior to any actual or projected payout date.

The descriptions of cash outlays as either known or uncertain are undoubtedly broad. When we refer to a cash outlay as being uncertain, we do not mean that it cannot be predicted. There are some liabilities where the "law of large numbers" makes it easier to predict the timing and/or amount of cash outlays. This is the work typically done by actuaries, but of course even actuaries cannot predict natural catastrophes such as floods and earthquakes.

As we describe the various financial institutions in later chapters, keep these risk categories in mind. For now, let's illustrate each one.

Type-I Liabilities.

Both the amount and the timing of the liabilities are known with certainty. A liability requiring a financial institution to pay $50,000 six months from now would be an example. For example, depository institutions know the amount that they are committed to pay (principal plus interest) on the maturity date of a fixed-rate deposit, assuming that the depositor does not withdraw funds prior to the maturity date.

Type-I liabilities, however, are not limited to depository institutions. A major product sold by life insurance companies is a guaranteed investment contract, popularly referred to as a GIC. The obligation of the life insurance company under this contract is that, for a sum of money (called a premium), it will guarantee an interest rate

Table 2-1   Nature of Liabilities of Financial Institutions

LIABILITY TYPE	AMOUNT OF CASH OUTLAY	TIMING OF CASH OUTLAY
Type I	Known	Known
Type II	Known	Uncertain
Type III	Uncertain	Known
Type IV	Uncertain	Uncertain

up to some specified maturity date.[1] For example, suppose a life insurance company for a premium of $10 million issues a five-year GIC agreeing to pay 10% compounded annually. The life insurance company knows that it must pay $16.11 million to the GIC policyholder in five years.[2]

Type-II Liabilities.

The amount of cash outlay is known, but the timing of the cash outlay is uncertain. The most obvious example of a Type-II liability is a life insurance policy. There are many types of life insurance policies that we shall discuss in Chapter 7, but the most basic type is that, for an annual premium, a life insurance company agrees to make a specified dollar payment to policy beneficiaries upon the death of the insured.

Type-III Liabilities.

With this type of liability, the timing of the cash outlay is known, but the amount is uncertain. An example is where a financial institution has issued an obligation in which the interest rate adjusts periodically according to some interest rate benchmark. Depository institutions, for example, issue accounts called **certificates of deposit** (or **CD**), which have a stated maturity. The interest rate paid need not be fixed over the life of the deposit but may fluctuate. If a depository institution issues a three-year floating-rate certificate of deposit that adjusts every three months and the interest rate paid is the three-month Treasury bill rate plus one percentage point, the depository institution knows it has a liability that must be paid off in three years, but the dollar amount of the liability is not known. It will depend on three-month Treasury bill rates over the three years.

Type-IV Liabilities.

There are numerous insurance products and pension obligations that present uncertainty as to both the amount and the timing of the cash outlay. Probably the most obvious examples are automobile and home insurance policies issued by property and casualty insurance companies. When, and if, a payment will have to be made to the policyholder is uncertain. Whenever damage is done to an insured asset, the amount of the payment that must be made is uncertain.

As we explain in Chapter 9, sponsors of pension plans can agree to various types of pension obligations to the beneficiaries of the plan. There are plans where retirement benefits depend on the participant's income for a specified number of years before retirement and the total number of years the participant worked. This will affect the amount of the cash outlay. The timing of the cash outlay depends on when the employee elects to retire, and whether or not the employee remains with the sponsoring plan until retirement. Moreover, both the amount and the timing will depend on how the employee elects to have payments made—over only the employee's life or those of the employee and spouse.

Liquidity Concerns

Because of uncertainty about the timing and/or the amount of the cash outlays, a financial institution must be prepared to have sufficient cash to satisfy its obligations. Also keep in mind that our discussion of liabilities assumes that the entity that holds

---

[1] A GIC doesn't seem like a product that we would associate with a life insurance company because the policyholder doesn't have to die in order for someone to be paid. Yet as we shall see when we discuss life insurance companies in Chapter 7, a major group of insurance company financial products is in the pension benefit area. A GIC is one such product.

[2] This amount is determined as follows: $\$10,000,000 \ (1.10)^5$.

the obligation against the financial institution may have the right to change the nature of the obligation, perhaps incurring some penalty. For example, in the case of a certificate of deposit, the depositor may request the withdrawal of funds prior to the maturity date. Typically, the deposit-accepting institution will grant this request but assess an early withdrawal penalty. In the case of certain types of investment companies, shareholders have the right to redeem their shares at any time.

Some life insurance products have a cash-surrender value. This means that, at specified dates, the policyholder can exchange the policy for a lump-sum payment. Typically, the lump-sum payment will penalize the policyholder for turning in the policy. There are some life insurance products that have a loan value, which means that the policyholder has the right to borrow against the cash value of the policy.

In addition to uncertainty about the timing and amount of the cash outlays, and the potential for the depositor or policyholder to withdraw cash early or borrow against a policy, a financial institution has to be concerned with possible reduction in cash inflows. In the case of a depository institution, this means the inability to obtain deposits. For insurance companies, it means reduced premiums because of the cancellation of policies. For certain types of investment companies, it means not being able to find new buyers for shares.

Regulations and Taxation

Numerous regulations and tax considerations influence the investment policies that financial institutions pursue. When we discuss the various financial institutions in later chapters, we will highlight the key regulations and tax factors.

Key Points That You Should Understand Before Proceeding

1. What is meant by a financial institution being in the spread business.
2. The two dimensions of the liabilities of a financial institution: amount of the cash outlay and the timing of the cash outlay.
3. Why a financial institution must be prepared to have sufficient cash to satisfy liabilities.

FINANCIAL INNOVATION

Categorizations of Financial Innovation

Since the 1960s, there has been a surge in significant financial innovations. Observers of financial markets have categorized these innovations in different ways. Here are just three ways suggested to classify these innovations.

The Economic Council of Canada classifies financial innovations into the following three broad categories:[3]

➤ *market-broadening instruments*, which increase the liquidity of markets and the availability of funds by attracting new investors and offering new opportunities for borrowers

➤ *risk-management instruments*, which reallocate financial risks to those who are less averse to them, or who have offsetting exposure and thus are presumably better able to shoulder them

➤ *arbitraging instruments and processes*, which enable investors and borrowers to take advantage of differences in costs and returns between markets, and which reflect differences in the perception of risks, as well as in information, taxation, and regulations.

---

[3] *Globalization and Canada's Financial Markets* (Ottawa, Canada: Supply and Services Canada, 1989), p. 32.

Another classification system of financial innovations based on more specific functions has been suggested by the Bank for International Settlements: *price-risk-transferring innovations, credit-risk-transferring instruments, liquidity-generating innovations, credit-generating instruments,* and *equity-generating instruments.*[4] Price-risk-transferring innovations are those that provide market participants with more efficient means for dealing with price or exchange-rate risk. Reallocating the risk of default is the function of credit-risk-transferring instruments. Liquidity-generating innovations do three things: (1) They increase the liquidity of the market; (2) they allow borrowers to draw upon new sources of funds; and (3) they allow market participants to circumvent capital constraints imposed by regulations. Instruments to increase the amount of debt funds available to borrowers and to increase the capital base of financial and nonfinancial institutions are the functions of credit-generating and equity-generating innovations, respectively.

Finally, Professor Stephen Ross suggests two classes of financial innovation: (1) new financial products (financial assets and derivative instruments) better suited to the circumstances of the time (for example, to inflation) and to the markets in which they trade, and (2) strategies that primarily use these financial products.[5]

One of the purposes of this book is to explain these financial innovations. For now, let's look at why financial innovation takes place.

Motivation for Financial Innovation

There are two extreme views of financial innovation.[6] There are some who believe that the major impetus for innovation has been the endeavor to circumvent (or **arbitrage**) regulations and find loopholes in tax rules.[7] At the other extreme, some hold that the essence of innovation is the introduction of financial instruments that are more efficient for redistributing risks among market participants.

It would appear that many of the innovations that have passed the test of time and have not disappeared have been innovations that provided more efficient mechanisms for redistributing risk. Other innovations may just represent a more efficient way of doing things. Indeed, if we consider the ultimate causes of financial innovation,[8] the following emerge as the most important:

1. Increased volatility of interest rates, inflation, equity prices, and exchange rates.
2. Advances in computer and telecommunication technologies.
3. Greater sophistication and educational training among professional market participants.
4. Financial intermediary competition.
5. Incentives to get around existing regulation and tax laws.
6. Changing global patterns of financial wealth.

With increased volatility comes the need for certain market participants to protect themselves against unfavorable consequences. This means new or more efficient ways of risk sharing in the financial market are needed. Many of the financial products require the use of computers to create and monitor them. To implement trading

---

[4] Bank for International Settlements, *Recent Innovations in International Banking* (Basle: BIS, April 1986).
[5] Stephen A. Ross, "Institutional Markets, Financial Marketing, and Financial Innovation," *Journal of Finance* (July 1989), p. 541.
[6] Ian Cooper, "Financial Innovations: New Market Instruments," *Oxford Review of Economic Policy* (November 1986).
[7] Merton H. Miller, "Financial Innovation: The Last Twenty Years and the Next," *Journal of Financial and Quantitative Analysis* (December 1986), pp. 459–471.
[8] Cooper, "Financial Innovations," see Table 9. We add inflation to the first category described.

strategies using these financial products also requires computers, as well as telecommunication and Internet networks. Without advances in computer and telecommunication technologies, some innovations would not have been possible. Although financial products and trading strategies created by some market participants may be too complex for other market participants to use, the level of market sophistication, particularly in terms of mathematical understanding, has risen, permitting the acceptance of some complex products and trading strategies.

As you read the chapters on the various sectors of the financial markets that we review in this book, be sure you understand the factors behind any innovations in that market.

Key Points That You Should Understand Before Proceeding

1. The extent of the innovation in many financial markets, securities, and institutions over the last few decades.
2. The causes of innovation, such as the high level of volatility in prices and interest rates, the arrival of technology, the new intensity of competition, and the globalization of markets and institutions.

ASSET SECURITIZATION AS A FINANCIAL INNOVATION

A key financial innovation in the 1980s that dramatically influences the role of financial intermediaries is the phenomenon of **asset securitization**. The process involves the collection or pooling of loans and the sale of securities backed by those loans. This system is radically different from the traditional system for financing the acquisition of assets, which called for one financial intermediary, such as a depository institution or insurance company, to: (1) originate a loan; (2) retain the loan in its portfolio of assets, thereby accepting the credit risk associated with the loan; (3) service the loan—collect payments and provide tax or other information to the borrower; and (4) obtain funds from the public with which to finance its assets (except for the small amount representing the institution's equity).

Asset securitization means that more than one institution may be involved in lending capital. Consider loans for the purchase of automobiles. A lending scenario can look like this: (1) A commercial bank can originate automobile loans; (2) the commercial bank can issue securities backed by these loans; (3) the commercial bank can obtain credit risk insurance for the pool of loans from a private insurance company; (4) the commercial bank can sell the right to service the loans to another company that specializes in the servicing of loans; and (5) the commercial bank can use the services of a securities firm to distribute the securities to individuals and institutional investors.

Besides the original lending bank, an insurance company, another institution that services loans, a securities firm, an individual, and other institutional investors participate. The commercial bank in our example does not have to absorb the credit risk, service the loan, or provide the funding. Although we use automobile loans as an example, this system can be applied to mortgage loans, home equity loans, boat loans, credit card loans, credit sales by finance companies and manufacturing firms, senior bank loans, and lease receivables. By far the largest part of the securitized assets market is the mortgage-backed securities market, where the assets collateralizing the securities are residential mortgage loans. The first public offering of an asset-backed security not backed by mortgage loans was in March 1985 by Sperry Lease Finance Corporation (now Unisys).

Asset securitization has various benefits for issuers, borrowers, and investors as well as far-ranging implications for the U.S. financial system.

Benefits to Issuers[9]

In view of the current and potential growth of securitization globally, it is important to understand the reasons for the proliferation of this innovative technology. From the issuer perspective, securitization offers several advantages, such as the creation of alternative and often cheaper funding sources, conversion of capital-intensive assets to capital-economizing assets, generation of servicing fee income, and, in certain instances, reduced exposure to interest rate volatility.[10]

Diversification and Reduced Cost of Funding.

The securitization of assets enables originators of assets to broaden funding sources and often reduce funding costs. In Chapter 26, we will explain the securitization process in more detail and explain why corporate issuers may find it more cost-effective to raise funds via asset securitization rather than offering a typical corporate bond.

Management of Regulatory Capital.

In later chapters, we will discuss risk-based capital requirements for certain financial institutions. Asset securitization can be used as a tool to manage risk-based capital requirements; this is an issue that directly affects U.S. financial institutions such as banks, thrifts, and insurance companies. However, the concept of using asset securitization as a means of attaining optimal capital adequacy standards is also of direct relevance to European financial institutions, for which increased competition due to deregulation and changing regulatory and environmental trends indicates an increased interest in asset securitization in the context of asset/liability management.

Generation of Servicing Fee Income.

Asset securitization allows the issuer to convert capital-intensive assets to a less-capital-intensive source of servicing fee income, thereby increasing its servicing and origination fees without increasing its capital base. (We will discuss the activity of servicing loans and servicing fees in Chapter 23.) This is done by securitizing and selling the loans while retaining the servicing. The servicing fee that is retained compensates the servicer for providing the normal clerical, computational, and collection functions involved in receiving payments from borrowers and remitting the proceeds to the paying agent for the securitized assets. The issuer of the asset-backed structure is usually also the servicer for the issue. In this respect, financial institutions such as banks, thrifts, and finance companies that are also originators of assets are uniquely positioned to take advantage of the growth of securitization since the infrastructure of these institutions includes the human and technical resources required to service assets.

Management of Interest Rate Volatility.

As we will see in later chapters, financial institutions are exposed to interest rate risk—the risk that a change in interest rates will have an adverse impact on the financial institution. With respect to the management of interest rate volatility, the securitiza-

---

[9] This discussion is adapted from Anand K. Bhattacharya and Frank J. Fabozzi, "The Expanding Frontiers of Asset Securitization," Chapter 1 in Anand K. Bhattacharya and Frank J. Fabozzi (eds.), *Asset-Backed Securities* (New Hope, PA: Frank J. Fabozzi Associates, 1996).

[10] There are also financial reporting advantages in terms of managing corporate earnings, which are not discussed here.

tion of assets fulfills a dual role. The dual role stems from the fact that the institution can securitize assets that expose the institution to higher interest rate risk and retain certain customized parts of the asset securitization transaction to attain an improved asset/liability position. In this respect, the financial institution serves the dual role of issuer and investor.

Benefits to Investors

Securitization converts illiquid loans into securities with greater liquidity and reduced credit risk. Credit risk is reduced because (1) it is backed by a diversified pool of loans, and (2) there is credit enhancement. Credit enhancement is a financial device to reduce the credit risk associated with the loans. This permits investors to broaden their universe of investment opportunities. It also tends to improve returns through the reduction of the cost of intermediation.

Benefits to Borrowers

Because a financial or nonfinancial entity can securitize a loan it originates, or sell it to some entity that will securitize it, the lender now has a more liquid asset that it can sell if capital is needed. This should reduce the spread between lending rates and safe assets such as Treasury securities. We have seen this in the mortgage market and, to some extent, in the automobile loan market. As the market matures, competition among originators should produce lower lending rate spreads in other loan markets.

Implications of Securitization for Financial Markets

Securitization has major implications for financial markets as well as the structure of financial intermediaries. Securitization eventually may replace the traditional system of indirect financing. To understand why, let's briefly review the role of financial intermediaries that we discussed earlier in this chapter.

Financial intermediaries act as conduits in bringing savers and borrowers together. They perform this function in several ways. First, certain financial intermediaries are in a better position than individual investors to assess credit risk. After evaluating credit risk, they may agree to grant a loan and hold the loan as an investment. Furthermore, being in a position to distribute their assets over many different borrowers and industries, they achieve risk reduction through diversification. The returns to investors are further made safe in the case of depository institutions by government-guaranteed liabilities (federal guarantee of deposits will be explained in Chapter 4).

Second, the maturities of loans sought by borrowers may be different from those that investors want. For example, as we shall see in Chapter 4, depository institutions acquire short-term funds and grant loans with longer maturities. This satisfies the objective of investors who may want shorter-term investments and borrowers who want longer-term funds; that is, the institution provides maturity intermediation—although at their risk. Finally, the amount of funds sought by borrowers is typically greater than any one individual investor would be willing to lend. Financial intermediaries make large-dollar loans to borrowers and offer investors investments with smaller dollar denominations. That is, they provide denomination intermediation, transforming very large assets into quite divisible ones. (By **denomination** it is meant the monetary amount of the investment.)

Securitization provides direct financing between borrowers and investors, short-circuiting the traditional intermediaries. Pooling of assets reinforced by private credit enhancement reduces credit risk to more acceptable levels for investors. Furthermore, redirecting cash flows from the pool of loans on a prioritized basis provides varying maturities acceptable to a wide range of investors. Thus, securitization serves a role similar to maturity intermediation while shifting its risk to the lenders. The availability of securities with smaller denominations than the underlying loans accomplishes denomination intermediation. All of this happens without the need for any government guarantees (although such guarantees may enhance the value of securitized instruments).

The success of securitization indicates that it is a more efficient method for linking borrowers and investors than traditional financing through intermediaries. The true innovations in this market are not really the securities themselves but (1) reduction of risk through pooling of assets and private credit enhancement, and (2) repackaging of the cash flows from assets in a way that relieves the intermediary of reliance on its own assets to finance the credit—that is, that permits **off-balance sheet financing**.

The process of asset securitization is not unique to the U.S. financial system. The practice is spreading to other countries, fostered by the capital risk guidelines for commercial banks discussed in Chapter 4.

Social Benefits

There also may be social benefits with asset securitization. Here is an example. In Chapter 10, we will discuss various types of insurance policies. Certain policies provide beneficiaries with a sum of money upon the death of the insured. Some companies in the United States are now offering insured individuals the opportunity to surrender their policy before death. There are non-insurance companies willing to accelerate the death benefit by paying the discounted value of the policy. This is called a "viatical settlement." Viatical settlement companies have come into being that buy insurance policies of individuals with AIDS and non-AIDS-related cancers and other terminal illnesses.

In early 1995, an asset-backed security was issued by Dignity Partners Inc. that was backed by insurance policies purchased from individuals with AIDS and other fatal diseases. The issue size was $35 million.[11] Because of the excellent reception of this issue by investors, subsequent issues backed by viatical settlements were issued at a lower interest cost. This translates into a benefit for those individuals who sell their policies. It is estimated that in a subsequent issuance by Dignity Partners Inc., policyholders were paid an average of $3,000 to $4,000 more because of the greater market acceptance of this security.[12]

Key Points That You Should Understand Before Proceeding

1. The meaning of securitization and the basic structure of the process of securitizing an asset.
2. How asset securitization may benefit issuers in terms of diversification and reduction of funding costs, managing regulatory capital, generating fee income, and managing interest rate volatility.
3. How securitizing an asset helps investors through increasing the opportunities for investment.
4. How securitizing an asset helps borrowers by raising the available capital and reducing its costs.
5. How the increase in securitization affects financial markets.

---

[11] "Ironwood Closes Groundbreaking Dignity Deal," *Private Placement Letter* (March 6, 1995), p. 1.
[12] This statement was made in an acceptance speech by a representative of Dignity Partners Inc. at a ceremony awarding the company for the private asset-backed security deal of 1995.

SUMMARY

Financial institutions provide various types of financial services. Financial intermediaries are a special group of financial institutions that obtain funds by issuing claims to market participants and use these funds to purchase financial assets. Intermediaries transform funds they acquire into assets that are more attractive to the public. By doing so, financial intermediaries do one or more of the following: (1) provide maturity intermediation; (2) provide risk reduction via diversification at lower cost; (3) reduce the cost of contracting and information processing; or (4) provide a payments mechanism.

The nature of their liabilities, as well as regulatory and tax considerations, determines the investment strategy pursued by all financial institutions. The liabilities of all financial institutions will generally fall into one of the four types shown in Table 2-1.

Financial innovation has increased dramatically since the 1960s, particularly in the late 1970s. While financial innovation can be the result of arbitrary regulations and tax rules, innovations that persist after regulations or tax rules have been changed to prevent exploitation are frequently those that have provided a more efficient means for redistributing risk.

Securitization of assets—that is, pooling loans and selling securities backed by the pool of loans—benefits issuers, investors, and borrowers alike. Securitization may be the wave of the future, as it appears to be a more efficient mechanism for bringing borrowers and investors together than traditional financing through financial intermediaries.

KEY TERMS

- Arbitrage, 22
- Asset/liability management, 18
- Asset securitization, 23
- Certificate of deposit (CD), 20
- Commercial bank, 16
- Contracting cost, 17
- Debit card, 18
- Denomination, 25
- Depository institutions, 15
- Direct investments, 16

- Diversification, 17
- Financial institution, 15
- Financial intermediary, 15
- Indirect investment, 16
- Investment company, 16
- Liability, 19
- Maturity intermediation, 17
- Off-balance sheet financing, 26
- Payment mechanism, 18
- Portfolio, 16

QUESTIONS

1. Why is the holding of a claim on a financial intermediary by an investor considered an indirect investment in another entity?
2. The Insightful Management Company sells financial advice to investors. This is the only service provided by the company. Is this company a financial intermediary? Explain your answer.
3. Explain how a financial intermediary reduces the cost of contracting and information processing.
4. "All financial intermediaries provide the same economic functions. Therefore, the same investment strategy should be used in the management of all financial intermediaries." Indicate whether or not you agree or disagree with this statement.
5. A bank issues an obligation to depositors in which it agrees to pay 8% guaranteed for one year. With the funds it obtains, the bank can invest in a wide range of financial assets. What is the risk if the bank uses the funds to invest in common stock?

6. Look at Table 2-1 again. Match the types of liabilities to these four assets that an individual might have:
    a. car insurance policy;
    b. variable-rate certificate of deposit;
    c. fixed-rate certificate of deposit; and
    d. a life insurance policy that allows the holder's beneficiary to receive $100,000 when the holder dies; however, if the death is accidental, the beneficiary will receive $150,000.

7. Each year, millions of American investors pour billions of dollars into investment companies which use those dollars to buy the common stock of other companies. What do the investment companies offer investors who prefer to invest in the investment companies rather than buying the common stock of these other companies directly?

8. Why does increased volatility in financial markets with respect to the price of financial assets, interest rates, and exchange rates foster financial innovation?

9. In a 1989 study entitled "Globalization and Canada's Financial Markets," a research report prepared for the Economic Council of Canada, the following was reported:

    An important feature of the increasing significance of some aspects of financial activity is the greater use of financial markets and instruments that intermediate funds directly—a process called "market intermediation," which involves the issuance of, and trading in, securities such as bonds or stocks—as opposed to "financial intermediation," in which the financial institution raises funds by issuing a claim on itself and provides funds in the form of loans.

    a. Why is asset securitization an example of "market intermediation"?
    b. Identify a benefit that the capital markets get from securitization. Hint: Until recently, most investors could not cheaply or easily take advantage of good returns from making car loans.

10. In classifying financial innovations, the Bank for International Settlements refers to "liquidity-generating instruments." Two characteristics of liquidity-generating instruments are that they increase the liquidity of the market and they allow borrowers to draw upon new sources of funds. Explain why asset securitization results in liquidity-generating instruments.

11. In what way can asset securitization reduce the cost of funds for an issuer?

The Role of the Government in Financial Markets

Learning Objectives

After reading this chapter, you will understand

- the typical justification for governmental regulation of markets.
- the different ways that governments regulate markets, including disclosure regulation, financial activity regulation, financial institution regulation, regulation of foreign firm participation, and regulation of the monetary system.
- the debate about the usefulness of disclosure regulation.
- the role of self-regulatory organizations.
- the various ways that these forms of regulation are implemented in the United States, Japan, Germany, and the United Kingdom.
- the major regulatory agencies in the United States, Japan, Germany, and the United Kingdom.
- the extent of regulatory reform in the 1980s.
- the causes of reform, including financial crisis, financial innovation, and globalization.

The financial markets play a prominent role in many economies, and governments around the world have long deemed it necessary to regulate certain aspects of these markets. In their regulatory capacities, governments have greatly influenced the development and evolution of financial markets and institutions. It is important to realize that governments, markets, and institutions tend to behave interactively and to affect one another's actions in certain ways. Thus, it is not surprising to find that a market's reactions to regulations often prompt a new response by the government, which can cause the institutions participating in a market to change their behavior further, and so on. A sense of how the government can affect a market and its participants is important to an understanding of the numerous markets and securities to be described in the chapters to come. For that reason, we talk about the regulatory function at this early stage.

Because of differences in culture and history, different countries regulate financial markets and financial institutions in varying ways, emphasizing some forms of regulation more than others. In this chapter, we will discuss regulation in the United States and show how regulation in three important financial systems (Japan, Germany, and the United Kingdom) compares with the U.S. approach to regulation. Our purpose is not to provide a detailed account of regulatory structures and rules in any country. Rather, we present a broad view of the goals and types of regulation that governments currently place on their financial systems.

PURPOSES AND FORMS OF REGULATION

Justification for Regulation

The standard explanation or justification for governmental regulation of a market is that the market, left to itself, will not produce its particular goods or services in an efficient manner and at the lowest possible cost. Of course, efficiency and low-cost production are hallmarks of a perfectly **competitive market**. Thus, a market unable to produce efficiently must be one that is not competitive at the time, and that will not gain that status by itself in the foreseeable future. Of course, it is also possible that governments may regulate markets that are viewed as competitive currently but unable to sustain competition, and thus low-cost production, over the long run. A version of this justification for regulation is that the government controls a feature of the economy that the market mechanisms of competition and pricing could not manage without help. A shorthand expression economists use to describe the reasons for regulation is **market failure**. A market is said to fail if it cannot, by itself, maintain all the requirements for a competitive situation.

Governments in most developed economies have created elaborate systems of regulation for financial markets, in part because the markets themselves are complex and in part because financial markets are so important to the general economies in which they operate. The numerous rules and regulations are designed to serve several purposes, which fall into the following categories:

1. To prevent issuers of securities from defrauding investors by concealing relevant information.
2. To promote competition and fairness in the trading of financial securities.
3. To promote the stability of financial institutions.
4. To restrict the activities of foreign concerns in domestic markets and institutions.
5. To control the level of economic activity.

Corresponding to each of these categories is an important form of regulation. We discuss each form in turn and later explore how these forms of regulations affect the four major financial systems of the world.

An Introduction to Forms of Regulation

Disclosure regulation is the form of regulation that requires issuers of securities to make public a large amount of financial information to actual and potential investors. The standard justification for disclosure rules is that the managers of the issuing firm have more information about the financial health and future of the firm than investors who own or are considering the purchase of the firm's securities. The cause of market failure here, if indeed it occurs, is commonly described as **asymmetric information**, which means investors and managers have uneven access to or uneven possession of information. This is referred to as the **agency problem**, in the sense that the firm's managers, who act as agents for investors, may act in their own interests to the disadvantage of the investors. The advocates of disclosure rules say that, in the absence of the rules, the investors' comparatively limited knowledge about the firm would allow the agents to engage in such practices.

It is interesting to note that several prominent economists deny the need and justification for disclosure rules. Led by George Benston, they argue that the securities market would, without governmental assistance, get all the information necessary for a fair pricing of new as well as existing securities. In this view, the rules supposedly extracting key data from agent-managers are redundant.[1] One way to look at this argument is to ask what investors would do if a firm trying to sell new shares did not provide all the data investors would want. In that case, investors either would refuse to buy that firm's securities, giving them a zero value, or would discount or underprice the securities. Thus, a firm concealing important information would pay a penalty in the form of reduced proceeds from sale of the new securities. The prospect of this penalty is potentially as much incentive to disclose as the rules of a governmental agency.

Financial activity regulation consists of rules about traders of securities and trading on financial markets. A prime example of this form of regulation is the set of rules against trading by insiders who are corporate officers and others in positions to know more about a firm's prospects than the general investing public. **Insider trading** is another problem posed by asymmetric information, which is of course inconsistent with a competitive market. A second example of this type of regulation would be rules regarding the structure and operations of exchanges where securities are traded. The argument supporting these rules rests on the possibility that members of exchanges may be able, under certain circumstances, to collude and defraud the general investing public.

Regulation of financial institutions is that form of governmental monitoring that restricts these institutions' activities in the vital areas of lending, borrowing, and funding. The justification for this form of government regulation is that these financial firms have a special role to play in a modern economy. Financial institutions help households and firms to save; they also facilitate the complex payments among many elements of the economy; and in the case of commercial banks they serve as conduits for the government's monetary policy. Thus, it is often argued that the failure of these financial institutions would disturb the economy in a severe way.

Regulation of foreign participants is that form of governmental activity that limits the roles foreign firms can have in domestic markets and their ownership or control of financial institutions.

Authorities use *banking and monetary regulation* to try to control changes in a country's money supply, which is thought to control the level of economic activity. Later chapters will provide a detailed review of this type of governmental regulation. We mention it here briefly in order to provide a comprehensive picture of the government's role in modern financial systems.

Key Points That You Should Understand Before Proceeding

1. The standard explanation for governmental regulation of markets for goods and services.
2. What disclosure is, and the meaning of disclosure regulation.
3. What the term *asymmetric information* means.
4. The reasons why a government might regulate financial activity by certain persons and the behavior of certain financial institutions.

REGULATION IN THE UNITED STATES

The regulatory structure in the United States is largely the result of financial crises that have occurred at various times. Most regulations are the products of the stock market crash of 1929 and the Great Depression in the 1930s. Some of the regulations

---

[1] George J. Benston, "Required Disclosure and the Stock Market: An Evaluation of the Securities Exchange Act of 1934," *American Economic Review* (March 1973), pp. 132–155.

may make little economic sense in the current financial market, but they can be traced back to some abuse that legislators encountered, or thought they encountered, at one time. Furthermore, with the exception of financial institution regulation, the three other forms of regulation are most often a function of the federal government, with state governments playing a secondary role. For that reason, our discussion of regulation in the United States concentrates on the federal government and its agencies. When we discuss certain financial institutions in the United States, we briefly examine the role of state governments.

The United States is firmly committed to regulating the issuance of new securities by means of disclosure. These regulations are contained in two important federal legislations: The **Securities Act of 1933** (or the Securities Act) and the **Securities Exchange Act of 1934** (or the Exchange Act). The acts have been amended periodically. The Securities Act deals primarily with the distribution of *new* securities and has two objectives. First, it requires that investors be given adequate and accurate disclosure concerning the securities distributed to the public.[2] Second, it prohibits fraudulent acts and practices, misrepresentations, and deceit in the sale of securities. While the Exchange Act covers many regulatory issues, one provision deals with the periodic disclosure provisions designed to provide current material information about publicly traded securities. Thus, while the Securities Act deals with the disclosure requirements for securities when they are first issued, the Exchange Act deals with the periodic disclosure requirements for seasoned securities. The **Securities and Exchange Commission (SEC)** is empowered with the responsibility for administering the two acts. The SEC was created by the Exchange Act.

None of the disclosure requirements as set forth in the two acts or the activities of the SEC constitute a guarantee, a certification, or an approval of the securities being issued. Moreover, the government's rules do not represent an attempt to prevent the issuance of risky securities. Rather, the government's (and the SEC's) sole motivation in this regard is to supply diligent and intelligent investors with the information needed for a fair evaluation of the securities. This approach to regulation relies heavily upon the **efficient market hypothesis**, which broadly posits that publicly available, relevant information about the issuers will lead to a correct pricing of freely traded securities in properly functioning markets.[3] (Chapter 15 will discuss efficient markets in more detail.)

U.S. governmental agencies employ a variety of tools in regulating the public trading in securities markets. The SEC has the duty of carefully monitoring the trades that corporate officers, directors, or major stockholders (insiders) make in the securities of their firms. The provisions are set forth in the Exchange Act. To keep the public abreast of these situations, the SEC publishes insiders' trades in its monthly *Official Summary of Securities Transactions and Holdings.*

The **organized exchanges**, such as the New York Stock Exchange and the American Stock Exchange, also play a role in regulation by setting conditions for listing traded stocks and bonds and by monitoring the relationships of brokers with the public. In this regard, the **National Association of Securities Dealers (the NASD)** is an important contributor to the regulation of trading. The NASD is a **self-regulatory organization (or SRO)**, which has SEC authority to require its more than 5,500 member firms to meet certain standards of conduct in issuing securities and selling them to

---

[2] Nancy H. Wojtas, "Regulation of the Securities Markets: Securities and Exchange Commission," Chapter 7 in Frank J. Fabozzi and Frank G. Zarb (eds.), *Handbook of Financial Markets* (Homewood, IL: Dow Jones-Irwin, 1986), pp. 116–118.

[3] Charles J. Johnson, Jr., *Corporate Finance and the Securities Laws* (Englewood Cliffs, NJ: Prentice Hall Law & Business, 1991), p. 43.

the public. Another of the NASD's responsibilities has recently become quite well known to the investing public. The NASD polices the over-the-counter or NASDAQ stock market. The market is very large because shares from nearly 4,500 different companies can be traded on any day, and the volume of daily trading is about 2.1 billion shares. Nasdaq has changed its structure in significant ways recently to address regulatory issues and also competitive challenges from the NYSE. Recently competition between Nasdaq and the NYSE with respect to the cost of transactions has been intense. (See Chapter 18 for more on the Nasdaq's recent changes.)

Two agencies share responsibility for the federal regulation of trading in options and futures, which are derivative securities described in detail in Chapters 26 through 31. The **Commodity Futures Trading Commission (CFTC)** licenses futures exchanges and monitors trading in them, and it authorizes firms to operate the exchanges and provide services to the public. The CFTC also approves individual futures contracts, which must serve the "economic purpose" of being useful for hedging. Approval is not endorsement of a contract, and investors trade these securities at their own risk. The second agency is the SEC, which has responsibility for oversight of options markets, if the asset underlying the option is an equity or set of equities. For example, the SEC regulates the **Philadelphia Stock Exchange (PHLX)**, which lists numerous options on individual stocks. Also, the SEC monitors trading on the Chicago Board of Options Exchange (CBOE), where the Standard & Poor 500 stock index option is traded. Though that option settles in cash, its value reflects the prices of equity shares.

In their work with options and futures, these government agencies receive assistance from several self-regulatory organizations. The most important SRO for futures markets is the **National Futures Association (NFA)**, which has since the early 1980s assisted the CFTC in monitoring trading, preventing fraud, and taking disciplinary action when appropriate. For options, the chief SRO since 1939 has been the NASD. The NASD performs many tasks, including licensing brokers and making sure that they disclose all the risks of options to investors who may want to participate in this market.

In its efforts to promote the stability of financial institutions, the U.S. government has created a truly extensive and complex array of regulations. Although pressure to change the system has been building, and significant change may occur soon, most of these regulations restrict what financial institutions do in the markets and how those institutions manage their liabilities and assets. A major example of these restrictions has been governmental opposition to the creation of national banks with branches in all states and regions. In fact, the United States currently has a large and cumbersome set of state and federal regulations that restrict the thousands of comparatively small banks to specific geographical units. Historically, the Glass-Steagall Act has considerably limited the freedom of commercial banks in the securities markets. However, during 1999 this act was replaced by the Financial Modernization Act of 1999 (the Gramm-Leach-Bliley Act) which significantly increased the flexibility of commercial banks, investment banks and securities firms, and insurance companies to diversify into each others' businesses. (See Chapter 7 for more on the Gramm-Leach-Bliley Act.)

The **Federal Reserve System** (or **Fed**), an independent agency responsible for the nation's money and banking system, places numerous restrictions on depository institutions. For example, the Fed sets minimum requirements for the amount of equity (or shareholder contributions) that banks must have relative to their assets. The current rules are based on a 1988 agreement (called the Basle Agreement) among the major industrialized countries. In the past, the Fed established a maximum level of interest rates commercial banks could pay, but happily the federal government has discontinued such unproductive rule-making. Another governmental agency, the **Office of Thrift Supervision (OTS)**, monitors the type and amount of loans that savings and loan associations make. (As late as the 1970s, a patchwork of regulatory bodies—the **Federal Home Loan Bank Board (FHLBB)** and the Federal Savings and Loan Insurance Corporation, for example—controlled much S&L activity, but many of their elements are now folded into the structure of the OTS.) More discussion of the regulation of asset and liability management in banks and S&Ls appears in Chapter 4. Other financial institutions, such as insurance companies and pension funds, also must work within complex regulatory systems that are described in Chapters 7 and 9, respectively.

Laws and rules about activities of foreign-owned entities in the U.S. financial system generally fall into the two broad categories of banking and securities markets. U.S. regulations permit foreign-owned banks to function generally under the same complicated rules that apply to U.S. domestic banks. Under the provisions of the **International Bank Act of 1978 (IBA)**, foreign banks must select a home state in the United States and comply with the same geographical restrictions and other forms of regulation that domestic banks had been facing for many decades. Nonetheless, foreign banks have continued to open offices in the United States, and hundreds of branches of these banks operate in cities across the country. Another recent development regarding foreign banks has been a series of U.S. agreements with other industrialized countries, through the **Bank for International Settlements (BIS)**, on various proposals regarding the activities of internationally active banking firms. The countries are Japan, Germany, United Kingdom, Canada, and other Western European states. These agreements, which emerged from the Basle Committee on Banking Regulations and Supervisory Practices from 1988 on, specify numerous things, especially the ways to measure the risk in a bank's balance sheet and to identify which country is responsible for supervising a bank with large operations in several countries at the same time.

Like many countries, the United States regulates participation by foreign firms in its domestic financial securities markets. As have most of these countries, however, the United States has been extensively reviewing and changing its policies regarding foreign firms' activities in the financial markets. Some of the changes in the last decade have been particularly worthy of note. In 1984, the federal government abolished the withholding tax on interest payments to nonresident holders of bonds issued by U.S. firms and governmental units. In 1986, the SEC decided to allow certain foreign firms that meet their home-country regulations to be active in U.S. markets without having to prove compliance with U.S. rules. In 1987, U.S. markets obtained permission to trade futures based on foreign government bonds, and the SEC decided to allow foreign firms to trade futures based on these bonds. In that same year, the SEC began to permit institutional investors to purchase unregistered shares of foreign firms.

Through the Federal Reserve System, the government controls the money supply and tries to exert influence on the level of economic activity. As will be described in detail in a later chapter, commercial banks and other depository institutions participate in that process by following rules that the Fed makes.

Key Points That You Should Understand Before Proceeding

1. The main federal acts that set forth the requirements for disclosures: the Securities Act and the Exchange Act.
2. The role of a self-regulatory organization in a market.
3. The scope and implementation of the regulation of financial institutions.
4. The ways in which the United States regulates foreign firms and investors.

REGULATION IN JAPAN

The Japanese **Ministry of Finance (MOF)** is responsible for the regulation of securities markets in Japan. Statutes and laws give the MOF vast direct power for this purpose. Furthermore, the MOF has substantial indirect power, including its duty to provide "administrative guidance" to financial institutions of all kinds and its authority to audit all securities houses that are members of the Tokyo Stock Exchange.

The Japanese system employs disclosure as a form of regulation, somewhat as the U.S. government does. Through its Securities Bureau, which is empowered by the Securities and Exchange Law and is one of seven bureaus, the MOF seeks to keep securities markets fair and competitive. To this end, the Securities Bureau tries to ensure that investors receive a steady flow of information about issuers.[4]

The Japanese approach differs from the U.S. approach in several notable respects. First, the MOF has a long-standing policy of directing funding in the bond markets to only a small group of large and efficient firms in an industry.[5] Second, the system does discourage certain issuers at certain times from issuing debt securities. The regulating body is the Bond Flotation Committee, a group consisting of more than 40 institutions (including large banks and securities firms). Three of the committee's functions are (1) to establish eligibility standards for companies wishing to issue bonds; (2) to monitor the terms and amounts of new issues; and (3) to control the flow of new issues in order to avoid flooding the market. Lately, many Japanese have come to see that this complex system imposes too many burdens and costs on the securities markets. The evidence was that financial business has begun to flee to Singapore, Hong Kong, and London. A Ministry of Finance Commission stated that the flight was happening because of the overregulation of Tokyo's currency and equity markets.[6]

Financial activity regulation is widely practiced in Japan. By law, the MOF's Securities Bureau supervises and licenses securities companies, and only such firms can deal in the full array of securities. Through its Securities Bureau and the **Bank of Japan (BOJ)**, the MOF punishes insider trading and supervises the activities of dealers in the financial markets. In 1992, the government made an additional step toward more careful monitoring of the stock market when it created the **Japan Securities and Exchange Surveillance Commission**. As part of the MOF, the commission will try to prevent the kind of insider trading and favored treatment for big investors that came to light in the 1991 stock market scandal.

As in the United States, the Japanese government imposes numerous restrictions on the activities of its financial institutions. Unlike the United States, Japan allows a few large national banks to do business in every part of the country. Until recently, Japanese rules prohibited commercial banks from full participation in the investment banking or underwriting of securities. Now, banks and other financial firms may, with permission from the Minister of Finance, participate in each other's line of business by forming or acquiring a subsidiary firm in the other's field. Though some restrictions still hold, this change in the regulation of Japanese banks is a significant development for both banking and the securities industry.[7] However, Japanese banks can invest substantial sums in the common stock of publicly traded firms, while current U.S. law prohibits U.S. banks from doing the same. Interestingly, the Japanese government, for

---

[4] Noboru Honjo and Lisa J. Turbessi, "Participants in the Japanese Bond Market," Chapter 3 in Frank J. Fabozzi (ed.), *The Japanese Bond Markets* (Chicago: Probus Publishing Company, 1990), p.56.

[5] Edward William Karp and Akira Koike, "The Japanese Corporate Bond Market," Chapter 11 in ibid., p. 366.

[6] "Hollowing Out Japan's Financial Markets," *Economist* (August 13, 1994), pp. 67–69.

[7] Yasushi Murofushi, "Japan," *International Financial Law Review* (July 1994), Banking Yearbook 1994, pp. 90–95.

many years, fixed the maximum levels of interest rates on bank deposits. In 1987, it abandoned or modified most of the regulations of that type.

In 1995, Japanese bank regulators had to deal with many problems. Between March and August, they were forced to liquidate several fairly large financial institutions, including the first commercial bank to fail since World War II. The disastrous Kobe earthquake affected the ability of many firms and households to repay their loans to banks, further weakening their financial position. Then, in September, the large and prestigious Daiwa Bank had to announce that a securities trader in its U.S. office had lost over $1 billion in investments that may or may not have been properly overseen by his supervisors and high officials in the bank. Following these disclosures, the U.S. government ordered Daiwa to close down its U.S. operations, which extended to 11 states, and accused bank officials of criminal violations of U.S. law. As of this writing, many observers of international banking expect that Japanese banks will encounter additional and even more serious problems in the next few years, as the country tries to recover from its real estate market crash and its stock market plunge, which have badly eroded the health of major financial institutions within Japan.

In recent years, Japan has moderated or discontinued many restrictions against participation in financial securities markets by foreign firms and financial institutions.[8] Some foreign banks are now permitted to participate in trust banking, which focuses on investment management and savings. Securities subsidiaries of foreign financial institutions have opened branches, and through the branches, these institutions have become active in some aspects of underwriting. Foreign firms now own seats on the Tokyo Stock Exchange (TSE), and shares of stock of foreign companies are listed there. The areas of underwriting and asset management remain generally closed to foreign firms, much to the annoyance of U.S. firms, which are expert in both activities. The Ministry of Finance has allowed some progress recently in the field of pension funds management, which has long been completely controlled by a few large Japanese institutions. Though quite modest, this liberalization has led U.S. financial services companies to have some hope that they might eventually be free to compete for the management of Japan's $2.6 trillion in pension plan funds.[9] While numerous official and unwritten rules may remain, it is clear that Japan has achieved meaningful gains in the internationalization and freedom of its financial markets. The Japanese version of the "Big Bang" which was initiated during 1996 with goals to be "fair, free and global," significantly accelerated the changes in Japan's securities markets. (See Chapter 19 for a discussion of these changes.)

The MOF, with the assistance of the Bank of Japan, which functions much as the Fed does in the United States, controls the money supply and seeks to influence short-term interest rates. The way the BOJ implements its policy is described in Chapters 5 and 6.

Key Points That You Should Understand Before Proceeding

1. The extensive role of the Japanese Ministry of Finance.
2. How Japanese regulation differs from U.S. regulation.
3. The scope of Japanese regulation of financial institutions, especially commercial banks.
4. Some ways in which Japan has begun to relax its regulation of foreign participants in its markets.
5. The role of the Bank of Japan.

---

[8] Much of this material is drawn from Issen Sato and E. M. Karnosky, "Historical Development of the Japanese Bond Market," Chapter 2 in Frank J. Fabozzi (ed.), ibid.
[9] Web site, Bank of Japan, Flow of Funds tables.

REGULATION IN GERMANY

The German system uses disclosure regulation to some extent in connection with the issuance of equities. Issuing companies must make public salient facts about the firm in the form of a prospectus. Officials in charge of listing on the exchange where the stock is to be traded must evaluate and approve the prospectus. Furthermore, the firm must make annual and semiannual reports to investors on its operations and finances.[10] Some officials in the U.S. government used to insist that, given the vagueness of German accounting rules, the requirements to disclose are actually weak and effectively permit German firms to deceive investors.[11] Whatever the merit of that charge might once have been, the situation may well be changing dramatically. German accounting rules have undergone serious change, and the desire of German firms for international capital has prompted them to comply with reporting standards that have gained international respect.[12]

The bond market has an interesting structure. A privately owned firm (other than a bank) that wishes to issue a bond must obtain approval of its financial standing and of the bond's collateral. The agency that must give approval is the central bank, or **Bundesbank** (or **Deutsche Bundesbank**), which is a largely autonomous unit of the federal government. This cumbersome regulation has led many German firms to rely on banks for debt capital or to issue bonds in the unregulated Eurobond market, with the result that the bond market in Germany is not strong or active.[13]

There are eight German stock exchanges, and the state government where an exchange is located is an important regulator of the exchange. In a manner reminiscent of the American SROs, the government gets assistance from the exchange's board of governors, which is elected by representatives of firms (especially banks) belonging to the exchange. The board authorizes memberships and the securities to be traded and enforces the rules of the exchange.[14] Until 1994, Germany had no law against insider trading, although industry associations tried to prevent it through contractual agreements with their members, the monitoring of their members' trading, and disciplinary action, when necessary. Now there is such legislation on the books in the form of the Financial Market Promotion Act. This law makes insider trading a serious crime, and it defines *insiders* to include owners, managers, regulators, and others. Furthermore, the law imposes requirements of disclosure of holdings (and changes in holdings) for all those who own more than 5% of the stock in a company.[15]

In the late 1980s, the government authorized the creation of a futures and options market, which is called the **Deutsche Terminbörse**, and enhanced the legal status of those derivative contracts. This market has been successful, and it now offers options and futures contracts on a wide range of securities. Regulations for this derivatives market are quite complex and revolve around the types of companies that are parties to the transactions.

German regulation of financial institutions is significantly less stringent than U.S. law and practice. Most German banks are "universal banks," which take part in all types of financial activity, including commercial banking operations and such lines of securi-

---

[10] O. W. Breycha, "German Equity Markets," in Jess Lederman and Keith K. H. Parks (editors), *The Global Equity Markets* (Chicago: Probus Publishing Company, 1991), p. 132.

[11] Gregg A. Jarrell, "SEC Crimps Big Board's Future," *The Wall Street Journal*, June 19, 1992, p. A15.

[12] "Germany," *Euromoney's 1995 Guide to Developments in the World's Equity and Bond Markets*, Supplement to the September 1995 issue of *Euromoney*, pp. 10–15.

[13] Credit Suisse First Boston, *The Deutsche Mark Bond Markets* (Chicago: Probus Publishing Company, 1991), pp. 158–159.

[14] O. W. Breycha, "German Equity Markets," p. 120.

[15] Andreas J. Roquette, "Germany Makes Insider Trading a Criminal Offense," *International Financial Law Review* (July 1994), p. 16.

ties business as underwriting, trading, and investing in shares. For this reason, banks are the largest investors in Germany, and the German secondary markets for bonds and stocks tend to be **interbank markets** (that is, trading between banks). It is interesting to note that the force of internationalized production is changing the banks' relationship with firms. The shift of production facilities to other parts of Europe is forcing the companies to raise new equity, and that process requires more openness with investors and less coziness with the banks. As a result, the banks are getting pressure to reduce their currently large holdings of equity shares in major German firms.[16]

Nevertheless, the German government, through the powerful Bundesbank, has a regulatory role with respect to the safety of many of the banks' activities. For that reason, the government endorsed and has begun to implement the Basle Agreement, which requires domestic banks to meet certain standards of capital adequacy. In 1995, Germany's Federal Banking Supervisory Office issued a directive designed to establish minimum standards for care and oversight of the banks' trading in equity shares. The regulators cast a wide net, and their directive referred to issues of pay for traders, daily monitoring, and the separation of trading departments from other functions in the banks.

Germany's regulation of financial activities by foreign firms and investors was quite strict and complex until fairly recently. In the 1980s, foreign firms were given greater freedom to sell their securities in Germany, and more than one-third of the shares listed on the main stock market (in Frankfurt) are foreign stocks. The German government bond market became, because of governmental decisions in 1985, one of the most liberal. The Bundesbank granted permission to domestic subsidiaries of foreign firms to participate fully in some important types of investment banking. In 1988, foreign investors gained permission to buy an important type of federal government bond, called a **"Bundes bond" or "Bund"** in international financial circles.

With respect to monetary policy, the European Central Bank (ECB) replaced the central banks of the 11 participating countries of the European Economic and Monetary Union (EMU) on January 4, 1999. Since this time, the ECB, not the venerable German central bank, the Bundesbank, has controlled the money supply, the availability of credit, and short-term interest rates for the EMU members, and has also influenced the uniform currency of the EMU, the euro. (See Chapter 5 and 6 for more information on the ECB and its functions.)

Key Points That You Should Understand Before Proceeding

1. The question about Germany's use of disclosure regulation.
2. The scope of German regulation of commercial banks and the meaning of the term *universal banks.*
3. The reasons for the small size of the German bond market.
4. Some ways in which Germany has begun to relax its regulation of foreign participants in its markets.
5. The role of the Bundesbank.

REGULATION IN THE UNITED KINGDOM

In the **"Big Bang"** of the mid-1980s, which was a sweeping liberalization and restructuring of the securities industry, the British government made a firm commitment to disclosure as a major element in its regulation of securities markets. An important

---

[16] "Equity? Was Ist Das?" *Euromoney* (July 1994), pp. 82–85.
[17] A discussion of the Financial Companies Act may be found in Harriet Creamer, "Issuing Securities in the United Kingdom," *International Financial Law Review* (Special Supplement July 1990), pp. 54–61.

part of that restructuring was the Financial Services Act of 1986.[17] This law imposes a "general duty of disclosure" and applies to any foreign or domestic firm that issues new debt or equity securities, whether or not the securities are to be listed on the London International Stock Exchange. (Listed securities tend to be actively traded issues of well-known firms, while unlisted securities are generally those of new and smaller companies.) The firm must provide investors with an extensive amount of information, including the firm's financial history as well as the method by which the new security is to be marketed to the public. The law mandates penalties for the officers of any firm that either misleads investors or does not take reasonable care to assure the accuracy of its claims. As long as the firm has outstanding issues, it is responsible for disclosing relevant information to the public.

The Financial Services Act assigns responsibility for regulating financial activity to the **Department of Trade and Industry (DTI)**. The DTI delegates much of the task to the **Securities and Investment Board (SIB)**, which is similar in many ways to the U.S. Securities and Exchange Commission. The SIB is the primary agency that authorizes institutions to conduct investment business and monitors their dealings with the public and the adequacy of their funding. In this effort, the SIB gets active support from The Securities Association, which is a powerful self-regulatory organization (or SRO) allied with the Stock Exchange. The Personal Investment Authority, a self-regulatory organization empowered by the SIB, began work in 1994. It is the chief arbitration agent between investors and investment firms and has broad regulatory powers over investment firms. These various governmental and professional bodies also have responsibility for preventing or punishing insider trading, which was not well defined in a legal sense, and occurred rather frequently until the Company Securities Act of 1985. In 1993, new legislation expanded the definition of insider trading and extended the law against it to all securities listed on any European stock exchange.

The **Bank of England** regulates most banking institutions in a way that is similar to the actions of the Federal Reserve Bank in the United States. In addition to managing the money supply, the Bank of England supervises and sets rules for the capital adequacy of banks, as set forth in the Basle Agreement. Until the "Big Bang" of 1986, banks were not permitted to engage in many activities involving the sale of securities. Since then, however, banks have been allowed to own subsidiaries that are members of the stock exchange, which offer investors many financial services linked to investing.

The United Kingdom has been a leader in the process of opening domestic securities markets to participation by foreign firms. Non-British firms may be part of, and even lead, the groups of underwriting firms that sell to the public new issues of debt and equity denominated in pound sterling (the British currency). The shares of numerous foreign companies are listed on London's International Stock Exchange, and subsidiaries of foreign corporations (and banks) may hold memberships on the exchange. The same process of liberalization has affected the United Kingdom's banking laws: Foreign banks operate in large numbers within Great Britain.

The Bank of England has primary responsibility for managing the United Kingdom's money supply. Chapters 5 and 6 provide details on the bank's activities.

Key Points That You Should Understand Before Proceeding

1. The scope of the deregulation that is called the "Big Bang."
2. The responsibility of the Department of Trade and Industry.
3. The responsibility of the Bank of England.
4. The regulation of activities by foreign and domestic commercial banks in the securities markets.

REGULATORY REFORM

Regulatory reform is the result of several forces and developments. First, as we noted earlier, financial crisis often prompts significant shifts in the focus and extent of regulation. Several recent examples from the United States illustrate the point.

At one time, the maximum interest rate that depository institutions were permitted to pay on certain deposit accounts was set by government regulation. When interest rates in the open market rose above the ceiling imposed by the government, funds inevitably flowed out of depository institutions and were used to purchase securities, that is, to make direct investments. When this process of "disintermediation" threatened the economic well-being of many U.S. banks and S&Ls, the Fed and other regulatory bodies were forced to remove the interest rate ceilings.[18] The U.S. savings and loan crisis is another example. Because many S&Ls encountered difficulties, federal legislation passed in 1989 changed the regulatory structure of these deposit-accepting institutions. Finally, the stock market crash of October 1987 produced some shifts in the rules governing the U.S. markets for stock and derivative stock market instruments (stock index futures and stock index options).

A second motivation for regulatory reform in the recent past has been financial innovation, or the development of new financial products. A wide array of new classes of financial assets appeared in the last two decades and forced the introduction of new regulations on trading these products. Specific products that spurred new regulation in the 1980s include the derivative instruments (options and futures) based on stock market indexes. An example of this process was noted above: The German government extensively revised its laws on futures and options and even authorized the establishment of a German exchange for them. The U.S. government has also found it necessary to devise new rules for the use of these innovative products by regulated financial institutions. An example is the complicated experience that S&Ls had with below-investment grade or junk bonds. When these high-yield and risky debt securities emerged as popular and successful investments, S&Ls got permission to invest in them. Congress later (mistakenly) blamed the junk bonds for the problems of many S&Ls and withdrew this permission in 1989.

Globalization of the world's financial markets is the third reason for recent, notable reforms in the regulatory structure of many countries. Naturally, any government's regulations are enforceable only within its borders. If a regulation is too costly, has little economic merit, or simply impedes an otherwise worthwhile financial transaction, market participants can evade it by transacting outside the country. As financial activities move to other nations, many interested parties lose money, and see reason to call for reexamination and reform of the questionable regulation. The German response to the widespread use of futures and options is an example of this phenomenon. Another example is Britain's deregulation of its stock market (or the "Big Bang"), which was, in part, a response to competition from foreign exchanges and trading opportunities.[19]

Another impact of globalization is that it reveals the costs of unwise regulations that prevent financial institutions from competing effectively for business in the world marketplace. Here a good example is regulation of the Japanese financial market. While at one time Japanese banks had sufficient funds to provide funding for non-

---

[18] This change also hurt the depository institutions by increasing their cost of funds. It is interesting to note that a similar event occurred there. In 1987, the Japanese government abandoned or modified a long-standing and complicated policy of fixing maximum levels of interest rates on bank deposits.

[19] Robert A. Schwartz, *Reshaping the Equity Markets* (New York: Harper Business, 1991), p. 69.

Japanese multinational companies domiciled in Japan, regulations kept the banks from lending to foreign firms and from capitalizing on clear financial opportunities. The banks protested to the government, which eventually lifted the regulations and permitted them to compete with non-Japanese banks.

An important result of reform has been structural change in the financial institutions being regulated. As noted above, the U.S. regulatory system has separated the activities performed by different financial institutions. (Similar separation was characteristic of the United Kingdom and Japan.) Today, however, in a change that has a global sweep, regulatory reform gradually has permitted financial institutions to offer a wider range of financial services and to become "financial supermarkets." A major focus of current and prospective regulatory reform, in several major industrial countries, is the outdated and unnecessary distinction between commercial banking and investment banking. We discuss this separation of functions, imposed on the U.S. economy in the 1930s, in Chapter 4.

Key Points That You Should Understand Before Proceeding

1. The meaning of *disintermediation*.
2. How financial innovation and globalization have given impetus to deregulation and regulatory reform.

SUMMARY

Regulation of the financial system and its various component sectors occurs in almost all countries. A useful way to organize the many instances of regulation is to see it as having four general forms: (1) enforcing the disclosure of relevant information; (2) regulating the level of financial activity through control of the money supply as well as trading in financial markets; (3) restricting the activities of financial institutions and their management of assets and liabilities; and (4) constraining the freedom of foreign investors and securities firms in domestic markets.

We have reviewed the regulatory situation in the United States, Japan, Germany, and the United Kingdom. All these countries currently make extensive use of disclosure regulation as well as the regulation of financial activity and trading in markets. In each case, the government gets some assistance from self-regulatory organizations (or SROs) in the financial community and markets.

Germany restricts the activities of financial institutions less than any other country, but other countries are beginning to allow their banks more latitude in the financial securities markets. All four of these countries, however, have endorsed the Basle Agreement on capital adequacy in banks and are pursuing policies based on that agreement. Finally, although every one of these countries has certain rules about activities by foreign-owned banks and firms in domestic capital markets, the clear and strong trend toward liberalization is steadily reducing the number and scope of those rules.

A significant characteristic of the 1980s has been the extensive and still ongoing process of regulatory reform, which has occurred in almost all sectors of the financial system in every country discussed here. This process of reform has been a response to financial crisis, which has revealed flaws in old regulatory arrangements. Reform has also been a consequence of the widespread financial innovation of the last two decades. This innovation has prompted regulators to end old practices and to experiment with new rules. Finally, the irresistible tide of globalization of the financial markets has swept away much of the regulatory apparatus of the major industrial countries. Globalization has brought competition as well as cross-border freedom from onerous and costly regulations. Regulators have abandoned many rules simply because they could not be enforced any more, or because their high cost drove financial activities to other countries.

KEY TERMS

- Agency problems, 30
- Asymmetric information, 30
- Bank for International Settlements (BIS), 34
- Bank of England, 39
- Bank of Japan (BOJ), 35
- Big Bang, 38
- Bundes bond (or Bund), 38
- Bundesbank or Deutsche Bundesbank, 37
- Commodity Futures Trading Commission (CFTC), 33
- Competitive market, 30
- Department of Trade and Industry (DTI), 39
- Deutsche Terminbörse, 37
- Disclosure regulation, 30
- Efficient market hypothesis, 32
- Federal Home Loan Bank Board (FHLBB), 34
- Federal Reserve System (Fed), 33
- Insider trading, 31
- Interbank market, 38
- International Bank Act of 1978 (IBA), 34
- Japan Securities and Exchange Surveillance Commission, 35
- Market failure, 30
- Ministry of Finance (MOF), 35
- National Association of Securities Dealers (NASD), 32
- National Futures Association (NFA), 33
- Office of Thrift Supervision (OTS), 34
- Organized exchanges, 32
- Philadelphia Stock Exchange (PHLX), 33
- Securities Act of 1933, 32
- Securities and Exchange Commission, 32
- Securities and Investment Board (SIB), 39
- Securities Exchange Act of 1934, 32
- Self-regulatory organization (SRO), 32

QUESTIONS

1. a. What is the economic rationale for the widespread use of disclosure regulation?
   b. Do you agree with the view that such regulation is redundant because investors can get the information they need through their power to underprice the securities of firms that do not provide all necessary data?
2. "The Securities and Exchange Commission ensures that securities issued in the United States are not risky and therefore are acceptable investments for the general public." Explain why you agree or disagree with this statement.
3. Why do countries regulate their money supply?
4. What are some key indicators of whether or not a country is liberalizing its rules on financial activities by foreign-owned banks and companies?
5. Identify two key elements in the United Kingdom's "Big Bang" of the mid-1980s.
6. a. Explain how Germany's regulation of banks' roles in the financial securities industry has differed from regulation in other countries.
   b. Why is likely that differences will disappear in the near future?
7. Name some key regulations of trading in common stock that the Securities and Exchange Commission enforces.

Depository Institutions: Activities and Characteristics

Learning Objectives

After reading this chapter, you will understand

■ the role of depository institutions.

■ how a depository institution generates income.

■ differences among commercial banks, savings and loan associations, savings banks, and credit unions.

■ the asset/liability problem all depository institutions face.

■ who regulates commercial banks and thrifts and the types of regulations imposed.

■ the funding sources available to commercial banks and thrifts.

■ the capital requirements imposed on commercial banks and savings and loan associations.

Depository institutions include commercial banks (or simply banks), **savings and loan associations (S&Ls)**, savings banks, and credit unions. All are financial intermediaries that accept deposits. These deposits represent the liabilities (debt) of the deposit-accepting institution. With the funds raised through deposits and other funding sources, depository institutions both make direct loans to various entities and invest in securities. Their income is derived from two sources: (1) the income generated from the loans they make and the securities they purchase and (2) fee income.

It is common to refer to S&Ls, savings banks, and credit unions as *thrifts*, which are specialized types of depository institutions. At one time, thrifts were not permitted to accept deposits transferable by check (negotiable), or, as they are more popularly known, checking accounts. Instead, they obtained funds primarily by tapping the savings of households. Since the early 1980s, however, thrifts have been allowed to offer negotiable deposits entirely equivalent to checking accounts, although they bear a different name (**NOW accounts**, share drafts). By law, the investments that thrifts are permitted to make have been much more limited than those permitted to banks. Recent legislation, however, has expanded the range of investments allowed by thrifts so that they can compete more effectively with banks.

Depository institutions are highly regulated because of the important role that they play in the country's financial system. Demand deposit accounts are the principal means that individuals and business entities use for making payments, and government monetary policy is implemented through the banking system. Because of their important role, depository institutions are afforded special privileges such as access to federal deposit insurance and access to a government entity that provides funds for liquidity or emergency needs. For example, the deposits of most depository institutions are currently insured up to $100,000 per account. We'll give examples of how depository institutions have access to emergency funds later in this chapter.

In this chapter we will look at depository institutions—the nature of their liabilities, where they invest their funds, and how they are regulated. Before we examine the specific institutions, we begin with an overview of the asset/liability problem that a depository institution must manage.

ASSET/LIABILITY PROBLEM OF DEPOSITORY INSTITUTIONS

The asset/liability problem that depository institutions face is quite simple to explain—although not necessarily easy to solve. A depository institution seeks to earn a positive spread between the assets it invests in (loans and securities) and the cost of its funds (deposits and other sources). The spread is referred to as **spread income** or **margin**. The spread income should allow the institution to meet operating expenses and earn a fair profit on its capital.

In generating spread income a depository institution faces several risks. These include **credit risk**, **regulatory risk**, and **interest rate risk**. Credit risk, also called **default risk**, refers to the risk that a borrower will default on a loan obligation to the depository institution or that the issuer of a security that the depository institution holds will default on its obligation. Regulatory risk is the risk that regulators will change the rules so as to adversely impact the earnings of the institution.

Interest Rate Risk

Interest rate risk can be explained best by an illustration. Suppose that a depository institution raises $100 million via deposits that have a maturity of one year and by agreeing to pay an interest rate of 7%. Ignoring for the time being the fact that the depository institution cannot invest the entire $100 million because of reserve requirements, which we discuss later in this chapter, suppose that $100 million is invested in a U.S. government security that matures in 15 years paying an interest rate of 9%. Because the funds are invested in a U.S. government security, there is no credit risk in this case.

It would seem at first that the depository institution has locked in a spread of 2% (9% minus 7%). This spread can be counted on only for the first year, though, because the spread in future years will depend on the interest rate this depository institution will have to pay depositors in order to raise $100 million after the one-year time deposit matures. If interest rates decline, the spread will increase because the depository institution has locked in the 9% rate. If interest rates rise, however, the spread income will decline. In fact, if this depository institution must pay more than 9% to depositors for the next 14 years, the spread will be negative. That is, it will cost the depository institution more to finance the government securities than it will earn on the funds invested in those securities.

In our example, the depository institution has borrowed short (borrowed for one year) and lent long (invested for 15 years). This policy will benefit from a decline in interest rates but be disadvantaged if interest rates rise. Suppose the institution could have borrowed funds for 15 years at 7% and invested in a U.S. government security maturing in one year earning 9%—borrowed long (15 years) and lent short (one year). A rise in interest rates will benefit the depository institution because it can then reinvest the proceeds from the maturing one-year government security in a new one-year government security offering a higher interest rate. In this case a decline in interest rates will reduce the spread. If interest rates fall below 7%, there will be a negative spread.

All depository institutions face this interest rate risk. Managers of a depository institution who have particular expectations about the future direction of interest rates will seek to benefit from these expectations. Those who expect interest rates to rise may pursue a policy to borrow funds for a long time horizon (that is, to borrow long) and lend funds for a short time horizon (to lend short). If interest rates are expected to drop, managers may elect to borrow short and lend long.

The problem of pursuing a strategy of positioning a depository institution based on expectations is that considerable adverse financial consequences will result if those expectations are not realized. The evidence on interest rate forecasting suggests that it is a risky business. We doubt if there are managers of depository institutions who have the ability to forecast interest rate moves so consistently that the institution can benefit should the forecast be realized. The goal of management is to lock in a spread as best as possible, not to wager on interest rate movements.

Inherent in any balance sheet of a depository institution is interest rate risk exposure. Managers must be willing to accept some exposure, but they can take various measures to address the interest rate sensitivity of the institution's liabilities and its assets. Regulators impose restrictions on the degree of interest rate risk a depository institution may be exposed to, as explained later in this chapter. A depository institution will have an asset/liability committee that is responsible for monitoring the interest rate risk exposure. There are several asset/liability strategies for controlling interest rate risk. While a discussion of these strategies is beyond the scope of this chapter, we can point out here that development of several financial instruments (such as floating-rate notes, adjustable-rate mortgages, and interest rate swaps) reflects the asset/liability problem that depository institutions seek to solve.

Liquidity Concerns

Besides facing credit risk and interest rate risk, a depository institution must be prepared to satisfy withdrawals of funds by depositors and to provide loans to customers. There are several ways that a depository institution can accommodate withdrawal and loan demand: (1) attract additional deposits; (2) use existing securities as collateral for borrowing from a federal agency or other financial institution such as an investment bank; (3) raise short-term funds in the money market; or (4) sell securities that it owns.

The first alternative is self-explanatory. The second has to do with the privilege we mentioned earlier. Banks are allowed to borrow at the discount window of the Federal Reserve Banks. The third alternative primarily includes using marketable securities owned as collateral to raise funds in the repurchase agreement market, which we cover in later chapters.

The fourth alternative, selling securities that it owns, requires that the depository institution invest a portion of its funds in securities that are both liquid and have little price risk. By price risk we refer to the prospect that the selling price of the security will be less than its purchase price, resulting in a loss. For example, as we explain in Chapter 10, while a 30-year U.S. government security is a highly liquid security, its price would change dramatically as interest rates rise. A price decline of, say, 25% would not be uncommon in a volatile interest rate environment. A 30-year government bond is therefore highly liquid, but exposes the depository institution to substantial price risk.

In general, as we explain in Chapters 11 and 22, short-term securities entail little price risk. It is therefore short-term, or money market, debt obligations that a depository institution will hold as an investment to satisfy withdrawals and customer loan demand. It does this chiefly by lending federal funds, an investment vehicle that we will discuss later in this chapter. The term to maturity of the securities it holds affects the amount that depository institutions can borrow from some federal agencies because only short-term securities are acceptable collateral.

Securities held for the purpose of satisfying net withdrawals and customer loan demands are sometimes referred to as **secondary reserves**.[1] A disadvantage of holding secondary reserves is that securities with short maturities offer a lower yield than securities with a longer maturity in most interest rate environments. The percentage of a depository institution's assets held as secondary reserves will depend both on the institution's ability to raise funds from the other sources and on its management's risk preference for liquidity (safety) versus yield.

Depository institutions hold liquid assets not only for operational purposes, but also because of the regulatory requirements that we discuss below.

Key Points That You Should Understand Before Proceeding

1. That a depository institution needs to earn a positive spread between the return on its assets and the cost of its funds, which it gets through deposits and other sources.
2. The source and impact of a depository institution's credit risk, interest rate risk, and regulatory risk.
3. The reasons for a depository institution's liquidity concerns and its ways of responding to these concerns.

COMMERCIAL BANKS

As of September 2000, there were 8,375 commercial banks in the United States. A commercial bank can be **chartered** either by the state (state-chartered banks) or by the federal government (national banks). Of the 8,375 commercial banks, 6,133 were state chartered.[2] All national banks must be members of the Federal Reserve System and must be insured by the **Bank Insurance Fund (BIF)**, which is administered by the **Federal Deposit Insurance Corporation (FDIC)**. While federal depository insurance has existed since the 1930s and the insurance program is administered by the FDIC, BIF was created by the **Financial Institutions Reform, Recovery, and Enforcement Act of 1989 (FIRREA)**. Coverage is currently $100,000 per account.

State-chartered banks may elect to join the Federal Reserve System. Their deposits must be insured by the BIF. A minority of state-chartered banks elect to be members of the Federal Reserve System. As of September 2000, of the 6,133 state-chartered banks, only 1,003 elected membership. In spite of the large number of banks that elect not to be members of the Federal Reserve System, banks that are members hold more than 75% of all deposits in the United States. Moreover, with the passage of

---

[1] Roland I. Robinson, *The Management of Bank Funds* (New York: McGraw-Hill, 1962), p. 15. The term *secondary reserves* is used because primary reserves are the reserves required by the Federal Reserve Board, which we will discuss later. If you looked at the balance sheet of a depository institution, you will not see the term *secondary reserves* on it. A depository institution invests in short-term or money market instruments for reasons other than liquidity and does not report the purpose for which it acquires securities.

[2] These data were obtained from the FDIC Web site http://www.fdic.gov/bank/statistical/0009/all-stru.html.

Table 4-1   Distribution of FDIC-Insured Commercial Banks by Size as of September 2000

Asset size	No. of banks	Percent of banks	Assets (in billions)	Percent of assets
Less than $25 million	1,110	13.25	18,323	0.30
$25 to $50 million	1,718	20.51	64,314	1.06
$50 to $100 million	2,094	25.00	150,519	2.48
$100 to $300 million	2,325	27.76	390,751	6.44
$300 to $500 million	432	5.16	165,585	2.73
$500 million to $1 billion	313	3.74	214,204	3.53
$1 to $3 billion	206	2.46	345,082	5.69
$3 to $10 billion	95	1.13	523,002	8.62
$10 billion or more	82	0.98	4,192,305	69.13
Total	8,375	100.00	$6,064,085	100.00

SOURCE: Data obtained to construct this table were obtained from the FDIC Web site:
http://www.fdic.gov/bank/statistical/0009/allstru.html.

the **Depository Institutions Deregulation and Monetary Control Act of 1980 (DIDMCA)**, the reserve requirements that we will discuss for banks that are members of the Federal Reserve System apply also to state-chartered banks.

The size of banks in the United States varies greatly as can be seen from Table 4-1, which shows the distribution for FDIC-insured banks as of September 2000. Shown in the same table are total assets for each asset size. As can be seen, while less than 5% of the banks have total assets in excess of $1 billion, these banks hold more than 85% of the total assets.

The 10 largest U.S. commercial banks, based on total assets as of September 2000, are listed in Table 4-2. The name of the bank holding company for each bank is also listed in Table 4-2. A **bank holding company** is a corporation that owns stock in one or more banks.

Table 4-2   The 10 Largest U.S. Commercial Banks Ranked by Total Assets as of September 2000

Rank	Bank name	Bank location	Holding company name	Assets (in millions)
1	Bank of America	Charlotte, NC	Bank of Amer Corp.	$607,085
2	Citibank	New York, NY	Citigroup	368,998
3	Chase Manhattan	New York, NY	Chase Manhattan Corp.	346,200
4	First Union	Charlotte, NC	First Union Corp.	227,847
5	Morgan Guaranty	New York, NY	J.P. Morgan & Co.	178,264
6	Fleet Na Bank	Providence, RI	FleetBoston Fncl. Corp.	161,710
7	Wells Fargo Bank	San Francisco, CA	Wells Fargo & Co.	103,684
8	Bank One	Chicago, IL	Bank One Corp.	98,120
9	Suntrust Bank	Atlanta, GA	Suntrust Bank	97,352
10	HSBC Bank USA	Buffalo, NY	HSBC North America	84,025

SOURCE: Data for this table were obtained from "Insured U.S.-Chartered Commercial Banks That Have Consolidated Assets of $100 Million or More Ranked by Consolidated Assets as of September 30, 2000." Available: http://www.federalreserve.gov/releases/lbr/lrg_bnk_lst.txt.

Bank Services

Commercial banks provide numerous services in our financial system. The services can be broadly classified as follows: (1) individual banking; (2) institutional banking; and (3) global banking. Of course, different banks are more active in certain of these activities than others. For example, money center banks (defined later) are more active in global banking.

Individual banking encompasses consumer lending, residential mortgage lending, consumer installment loans, credit card financing, automobile and boat financing, brokerage services, student loans, and individual-oriented financial investment services such as personal trust and investment services. Interest income and fee income are generated from mortgage lending and credit card financing. **Mortgage lending** is more popularly referred to as **mortgage banking**. We'll discuss this activity and how fee income is generated in Chapter 23. Fee income is generated from brokerage services and financial investment services.

Loans to nonfinancial corporations, financial corporations, (such as life insurance companies), and government entities (state and local governments in the United States and foreign governments) fall into the category of *institutional banking*. Also included in this category are commercial real estate financing, leasing activities,[3] and factoring.[4] In the case of leasing, a bank may be involved in leasing equipment either as lessors,[5] as lenders to lessors, or as purchasers of leases. Loans and leasing generate interest income, and other services that banks offer institutional customers generate fee income. These services include management of the assets of private and public pension funds, fiduciary and custodial services, and cash management services such as account maintenance, check clearing, and electronic transfers.

It is in the area of *global banking* that banks began to compete head-to-head with investment banking (or securities) firms. Global banking covers a broad range of activities involving corporate financing and capital market and foreign-exchange products and services. Most global banking activities generate fee income rather than interest income.

Corporate financing involves two components. First is the procuring of funds for a bank's customers. This can go beyond traditional bank loans to involve the underwriting of securities. As we shall explain later, legislation in the form of the Glass-Steagall Act at one time limited bank activities in this area. In assisting customers in obtaining funds, banks also provide bankers acceptances, letters of credit, and other types of guarantees for their customers. That is, if a customer has borrowed funds backed by a letter of credit or other guarantee, its lenders can look to the customer's bank to fulfill the obligation. We'll give further examples in Chapter 22. The second area of corporate financing involves advice on such matters as strategies for obtaining funds, corporate restructuring, divestitures, and acquisitions.

Capital market and foreign-exchange products and services involve transactions where the bank may act as a dealer or broker in a service. Some banks, for example, are dealers in U.S. government or other securities. Customers who wish to transact in these securities can do so through the government desk of the bank. Similarly, some banks maintain a foreign-exchange operation, where foreign currency is bought and sold. Bank customers in need of foreign exchange can use the services of the bank.

---

[3] Leasing programs offered by some banks include vendor leasing, direct leasing, and leveraged leasing. For a discussion of these programs and the restrictions imposed on banks with respect to leasing activities, see Peter K. Nevitt, Frank J. Fabozzi, and Edmond J. Seifried, *Equipment Leasing for Commercial Bankers* (Philadelphia, PA: Robert Morris Associates, 1987).

[4] The factoring business involves a bank's purchase of accounts receivable.

[5] This means that the bank buys the equipment and leases it to another party. The bank is the lessor, and the party that uses the leased equipment is the lessee.

In their role as dealers, banks can generate income in three ways: (1) the bid–ask spread; (2) capital gains on the securities or foreign currency they have transacted in; and (3) in the case of securities, the spread between interest income by holding the security and the cost of funding the purchase of that security.

The financial products that banks have developed to manage risk also yield fee income. These products include interest rate swaps, interest rate agreements, currency swaps, forward contracts, and interest rate options. We discuss interest rate swaps and interest rate agreements in Chapter 29, currency swaps in Chapter 30, forward contracts in Chapter 25, and interest rate options in Chapter 29. Banks can generate either commission income (that is, brokerage fees) or spread income from selling such products.

Bank Funding

In describing the nature of the banking business, we have focused so far on how banks generate income. Now let's take a look at how a bank raises funds. There are three sources of funds for banks: (1) deposits; (2) nondeposit borrowing; and (3) common stock and retained earnings. Banks are highly leveraged financial institutions, which means that most of their funds come from borrowing—the first two sources we refer to. Included in nondeposit borrowing are borrowing from the Federal Reserve through the discount window facility, borrowing reserves in the federal funds market, and borrowing by the issuance of instruments in the money and bond markets.

Deposits

There are several types of deposit accounts. **Demand deposits** (checking accounts) pay no interest and can be withdrawn upon demand. Savings deposits pay interest, typically below market interest rates, do not have a specific maturity, and usually can be withdrawn upon demand.

Time deposits, also called **certificates of deposit**, have a fixed maturity date and pay either a fixed or floating interest rate. Some certificates of deposit that we shall describe in Chapter 22 can be sold in the open market prior to their maturity if the depositor needs funds. Other certificates of deposit cannot be sold. If a depositor elects to withdraw the funds from the bank prior to the maturity date, a withdrawal penalty is imposed. A money market demand account is one that pays interest based on short-term interest rates. The market for short-term debt obligations is called the money market, which is how these deposits get their name. They are designed to compete with **money market mutual funds**, which we will describe in Chapter 8.

Reserve Requirements and Borrowing in the Federal Funds Market.

A bank cannot invest $1 for every $1 it obtains in deposit. All banks must maintain a specified percentage of their deposits in a non-interest-bearing account at one of the 12 Federal Reserve Banks. These specified percentages are called **reserve ratios**, and the dollar amounts based on them that are required to be kept on deposit at a Federal Reserve Bank are called **required reserves**. The reserve ratios, which Chapter 5 also examines, are established by the Federal Reserve Board (the Fed). The reserve ratio differs by type of deposit. The Fed defines two types of deposits: transactions and nontransactions deposits. Demand deposits and what the Fed calls "other checkable deposits" (primarily NOW accounts) are classified as transactions deposits. Savings and time deposits are nontransactions deposits. Reserve ratios are higher for transactions deposits than for nontransactions deposits.

To arrive at its required reserves, a bank does not simply determine its transactions and nontransactions deposits at the close of each business day and then multiply each by the applicable reserve ratio. The determination of a bank's required reserves is more complex. Here we'll give a rough idea of how it is done. First, to compute required reserves, the Federal Reserve has established a two-week period called the

deposit computation period. Required reserves are the average amount of each type of deposit held at the close of each business day in the computation period, multiplied by the reserve requirement for each type.

Reserve requirements in each period are to be satisfied by *actual reserves*, which are defined as the average amount of reserves held at the close of business at the Federal Reserve Bank during each day of a two-week reserve maintenance period, beginning on Thursday and ending on Wednesday two weeks later. For transactions deposits, the deposit computation period leads the reserve period by two days. For nontransactions deposits, the deposit computation period is the two-week period four weeks prior to the reserve maintenance period.

If actual reserves exceed required reserves, the difference is referred to as **excess reserves**. Because reserves are placed in non-interest-bearing accounts, there is an opportunity cost associated with excess reserves. At the same time, there are penalties imposed on banks that do not satisfy the reserve requirements. Thus, banks have an incentive to manage their reserves so as to satisfy reserve requirements as precisely as possible.

Banks temporarily short of their required reserves can borrow reserves from banks that have excess reserves. The market where banks can borrow or lend reserves is called the **federal funds market**. The interest rate charged to borrow funds in this market is called the *federal funds rate*.

Borrowing at the Fed Discount Window.

The Federal Reserve Bank is the banker's bank—or, to put it another way, the bank of last resort. Banks temporarily short of funds can borrow from the Fed at its **discount window.** (See Chapter 5 for more discussion of the Fed's use of the discount window.) Collateral is necessary to borrow, but not just any collateral will do. The Fed establishes (and periodically changes) the type of collateral that is eligible. Currently it includes (1) Treasury securities, federal agency securities, and municipal securities, all with a maturity of less than six months, and (2) commercial and industrial loans with 90 days or less to maturity.

The interest rate that the Fed charges to borrow funds at the discount window is called the **discount rate**. The Fed changes this rate periodically in order to implement monetary policy.[6] Bank borrowing at the Fed to meet required reserves is quite limited in amount, despite the fact that the discount rate generally is set below the cost of other sources of short-term funding available to a bank. This is because the Fed views borrowing at the discount window as a privilege to be used to meet short-term liquidity needs, and not a device to increase earnings.

Continual borrowing for long periods and in large amounts is thereby viewed as a sign of a bank's financial weakness or as exploitation of the interest differential for profit. If a bank appears to be going to the Fed to borrow frequently, relative to its previous borrowing pattern, the Fed makes an "informational" call to ask for an explanation for the borrowing. If there is no subsequent improvement in the bank's borrowing pattern, the Fed then makes an "administrative counseling" call in which it tells the bank that it must stop its borrowing practice.

Other Nondeposit Borrowing.

Bank borrowing in the federal funds market and at the discount window of the Fed is short term. Other nondeposit borrowing can be short term in the form of issuing obligations in the money market, or intermediate to long term in the form of issuing securities in the bond market. An example of the former is the repurchase agreement (or "repo") market. An example of intermediate- or long-term borrowing is floating-rate notes and bonds.

---

[6] Although altering the discount rate is a tool to implement monetary policy, along with open market operations and the changing of reserve ratios, today it is not viewed as a primary tool.

Banks that raise most of their funds from the domestic and international money markets, relying less on depositors for funds, are called **money center banks**. A **regional bank** by contrast is one that relies primarily on deposits for funding, and makes less use of the money markets to obtain funds. Larger regional banks have been merging with other regional banks to form so-called superregional banks.

Regulation

Because of the special role that commercial banks play in the financial system, banks are regulated and supervised by several federal and state government entities. At the federal level, supervision is undertaken by the Federal Reserve Board, the Office of the **Comptroller of the Currency**, and the Federal Deposit Insurance Corporation. While much of the legislation defining these activities dates back to the late 1930s, the nature of financial markets and commercial banking has changed in the past 20 years.

Here we will review some of the major regulations concerning the activities of commercial banks. The regulations historically cover four areas:

1. Ceilings imposed on the interest rate that can be paid on deposit accounts.
2. Geographical restrictions on branch banking.
3. Permissible activities for commercial banks.
4. Capital requirements for commercial banks.

Regulation of Interest Rates.

Although regulation of the interest rates that banks can pay has been all but eliminated for accounts other than demand deposits, we discuss the subject because of its historical relevance. Federal regulations prohibit the payment of interest on demand (checking) accounts. **Regulation Q** at one time imposed a ceiling on the maximum interest rate that could be paid by banks on deposits other than demand accounts.

Until the 1960s, market interest rates stayed below the ceiling (except those on checking deposits), so Regulation Q had virtually no impact on the ability of banks to compete with other financial institutions to obtain funds. As market interest rates rose above the ceiling, and ceilings were extended to all depository institutions after 1966, these institutions found it difficult to compete with other financial institutions—such as the money market funds that we will discuss in Chapter 8—to attract funds. As a result, there was **disintermediation**—funds flowed out of commercial banks and thrift institutions and into the other financial institutions.

To circumvent the ceilings on time deposits and recapture the lost funds, banks developed the negotiable certificate of deposit, which in effect had a higher ceiling, and eventually no ceiling at all. They also opened branches outside the United States, where no ceilings were imposed on the interest rate they could offer. As all depository institutions found it difficult to compete in the 1970s, federal legislation in the form of the Depository Institutions Deregulation and Monetary Control Act of 1980 gave banks relief. With a few exceptions, the 1980 act phased out the ceilings on interest rates on time deposits and certificates of deposit. The **Garn-St. Germain Act of 1982** permitted banks to offer money market accounts, accounts that were similar to those offered by money market funds.

Geographical Restrictions.

The **McFadden Act of 1927** allowed each state the right to set its own rules on intrastate branch banking. This legislation was intended to prevent large banks from expanding geographically and thereby forcing out or taking over smaller banking entities, possibly threatening competition. There are some states where banks cannot establish branches statewide—so-called unit-banking states. There are also limit branch banking states, which permit some statewide branches, and other states that have virtually no restrictions on statewide branching.

In 1994 Congress passed the **Riegle-Neal Interstate Banking and Branching Efficiency Act** permitting adequately capitalized and managed *bank holding companies* to acquire banks in any state subject to certain limitations and approval by the Federal Reserve. Starting in June 1997, this legislation allowed interstate mergers between adequately capitalized and managed banks, subject to concentration limits and state laws.

Permissible Activities for Commercial Banks.

The sweeping legislation in bank regulation in recent years has produced changes in the permissible activities for banks and bank holding companies. The key legislation is the **Gramm-Leach Bliley Act of 1999**. To appreciate the major impact of this legislation, we must first review the regulations on permissible bank activities prior to the passage of this legislation.

The activities of banks and bank holding companies are regulated by the Federal Reserve Board. The Fed was charged with the responsibility of regulating the activities of bank holding companies by the Bank Holding Company Act of 1956, subsequently amended in 1966 and 1970. This act states that the permissible activities of bank holding companies are limited to those that are viewed by the Fed as "closely related to banking."

Early legislation governing bank activities developed against the following background:

1. Certain commercial bank lending was believed to have reinforced the stock market crash of 1929.
2. The stock market crash itself led to the breakdown of the banking system.
3. Transactions between commercial banks and their securities affiliates led to abuses. For example, it was discovered that banks were underwriting securities and then selling those securities to customers whose investment accounts they managed or advised. (We'll discuss the underwriting of securities in Chapter 14.)

Against this background, Congress passed the **Banking Act of 1933**, which, among other provisions, created the Federal Deposit Insurance Corporation. Four sections of the 1933 act barred commercial banks from certain investment banking activities—Sections 16, 20, 21, and 32. These four sections are popularly referred to as the *Glass-Steagall Act.*

For banks that are members of the Federal Reserve System, Section 16 provided that the business of dealing in securities and stock by a national bank shall be limited to purchasing and selling such securities and stock without recourse, solely upon the order, and for the account of customers, and in no case for its own account, and the national bank shall not underwrite any issue of securities or stock.

Banks could neither (1) underwrite securities and stock, nor (2) act as dealers in the secondary market for securities and stock, although Section 16 does provide two exceptions. Banks were permitted to underwrite and deal in U.S. government obligations and "general obligations of any state or any political subdivisions thereof." (The latter securities are municipal bonds, which we shall discuss in Chapter 17. The exemption applies to one type of municipal security, general obligation bonds, not another type, revenue bonds.) Section 16 also restricted the activities of banks in connection with corporate securities such as corporate bonds and commercial paper and securities such as mortgage-backed and asset-backed securities (which we will discuss in Chapter 24).

Under Section 20 of the Glass-Steagall Act, commercial banks that were members of the Federal Reserve System were prohibited from maintaining a securities firm. Section 20 states that no member bank shall be affiliated with any organization, association, business trust, or other similar organization engaged principally in the issue, flotation, underwriting, public sale, or distribution at wholesale or retail or through syndicate participation of stocks, bonds, debentures, notes, or other securities.

Section 21 prohibited any "person, firm, corporation, association, business trust, or other similar organization" that receives deposits—that is, depository institutions—from engaging in the securities business as defined in Section 16. Section 32 further prevented banks from circumventing the restrictions on securities activities. It does so by prohibiting banks from placing bank employees or board members in positions with securities firms so that they can obtain indirect but effective control.

The Glass-Steagall Act also imposed restrictions on bank activities in the insurance area. Specifically, it imposed restrictions on the underwriting and selling of insurance. As explained in Chapter 7, regulation of insurance activities was left to the states.

Subsequent legislation, court rulings, and regulatory decisions prior to the passage of the Gramm-Leach Bliley Act of 1999 did erode the barriers against commercial banks' engagement in investment banking activities. The barrier was finally destroyed by the Gramm-Leach Bliley Act of 1999. Specifically, this act did the following:

1. It modified parts of the Bank Holding Company Act to permit affiliations between banks and insurance underwriters.
2. It created a new financial holding company which is authorized to engage in underwriting and selling securities.
3. Although the act preserved the right of states to regulate insurance activities, it did prohibit state actions that would adversely affect bank-affiliated firms from selling insurance on an equal basis with other insurance agents.

Consequently, the underwriting activities described in Chapter 14 and the secondary securities market described in Chapter 15 that were primarily the domain of financial entities referred to as *investment banking firms* were now opened to banks. As a result, subsequent to the act there have been several mergers of large bank holding companies and investment banking firms. In Chapter 7 we will discuss the impact of the Gramm-Leach Bliley Act of 1999 on the insurance industry.

Supporters of this legislation argue that it will ensure that financial institutions in the United States will be able to effectively compete in the increasingly global financial marketplace and that the efficiencies that will result from expanding bank activities will lower costs to consumers and businesses. Alan Greenspan, Chairman of the Federal Reserve Board, in testimony on February 11, 1999, in support of the legislation stated:

> U.S. financial institutions are today among the most innovative and efficient providers of financial services in the world. They compete, however, in a marketplace that is undergoing major and fundamental change driven by a revolution in technology, by dramatic innovations in the capital markets, and by the globalization of the financial markets and the financial services industry.
>
> For these reasons, we support, as we have for many years, major revisions, such as those included in H.R. 10, to the Glass-Steagall Act and the Bank Holding Company Act to remove the legislative barriers against the integration of banking, insurance, and securities activities. There is virtual unanimity among all concerned—private and public alike—that these barriers should be removed. The technologically driven proliferation of new financial products that enable risk unbundling have been increasingly combining the characteristics of banking, insurance, and securities products into single financial instruments. These changes, which are occurring all over the world, have also dramatically altered the way financial services providers operate and the way they deliver their products.

Upon passage of this legislation, then U.S. Treasury Secretary Lawrence Summers stated:

> Today Congress voted to update the rules that have governed financial services since the Great Depression, and replace them with a system for the twenty-first century.

Capital Requirements for Commercial Banks.

The capital structure of banks, like that of all corporations, consists of equity and debt (that is, borrowed funds). Commercial banks, just like the other depository institutions that we discuss in this chapter, and investment banks, which we discuss in Chapter 14, are highly leveraged institutions. That is, the ratio of equity capital to total assets is low, typically less than 8% in the case of banks. This gives rise to regulatory concern about potential insolvency resulting from the low level of capital provided by the owners. An additional concern is that the amount of equity capital is even less adequate because of potential liabilities that do not appear on the bank's balance sheet. These so-called off-balance sheet obligations include commitments such as letters of credit and obligations on customized interest rate agreements (such as swaps, caps, and floors).

Prior to 1989, **capital requirements** for a bank were based solely on its total assets. No consideration was given to the types of assets. In January 1989, the Federal Reserve adopted guidelines for capital adequacy based on the credit risk of the assets held by the bank. These guidelines are referred to as **credit risk-based capital requirements**. The guidelines are based on a framework adopted in July 1988 by the **Basle Committee on Banking Regulations and Supervisory Practices**, which consists of the central banks and supervisory authorities of the G-10 countries.[7]

The principal objectives of the guidelines are as follows. First, regulators in the United States and abroad have sought greater consistency in the evaluation of the capital adequacy of major banks throughout the world. Second, regulators have tried to establish capital adequacy standards that take into consideration the risk profile of the bank. Consider, for example, two banks, A and B, with $1 billion in assets. Suppose that both invest $400 million in identical assets, but the remaining $600 million in different assets. Bank A invests $500 million in U.S. government bonds and $100 million in business loans. Bank B invests $100 million in U.S. government bonds and $500 million in business loans. Obviously, the exposure to default losses is greater for Bank B. While the capital adequacy standards take this greater credit risk into account, they do not recognize liquidity factors or the market price sensitivity to which a bank may be exposed.

The risk-based capital guidelines attempt to recognize credit risk by segmenting and weighting requirements. First, capital is defined as consisting of Tier 1 and Tier 2 capital. Minimum requirements are established for each tier. Tier 1 capital is considered **core capital**; it consists basically of common stockholders' equity, certain types of preferred stock, and minority interest in consolidated subsidiaries. Tier 2 capital is called **supplementary capital**; it includes loan-loss reserves, certain types of preferred stock, perpetual debt (debt with no maturity date), hybrid capital instruments and equity contract notes, and subordinated debt.

Second, the guidelines establish a credit risk weight for all assets. The weight depends on the credit risk associated with each asset. There are four credit risk classi-

---

[7] The countries referred to as the "G-10 countries" include Belgium, Canada, France, Germany, Italy, Japan, Netherlands, Sweden, Switzerland, United Kingdom, and United States.

Table 4-3   Credit Risk Weight Capital Requirement for Various Assets

Risk weight	Example of assets included
0%	U.S. Treasury securities
	Mortgage-backed securities issued by the Government National Mortgage Association
20%	Municipal general obligation bonds
	Mortgage-backed securities issued by the Federal Home Loan Mortgage Corporation or the Federal National Mortgage Association
50%	Municipal revenue bonds
	Residential mortgages
100%	Commercial loans and commercial mortgages
	LDC loans
	Corporate bonds

fications for banks: 0%, 20%, 50%, and 100%, arrived at on no particular scientific basis. Table 4-3 lists examples of assets that fall into each credit risk classification.[8]

The way the credit risk weights work is as follows. The book value of the asset is multiplied by the credit risk weight to determine the amount of core and supplementary capital that the bank will need to support that asset. For example, suppose that the book values of the assets of a bank are as follows:

Asset	Book value (in millions)
U.S. Treasury securities	$ 100
Municipal general obligation bonds	100
Residential mortgages	500
Commercial loans	300
Total book value	$1,000

The risk-weighted assets are calculated as follows:

Asset	Book value (in millions)	Risk weight	Product (in millions)
U.S. Treasury securities	$100	0%	$ 0
Municipal general obligation bonds	100	20	20
Residential mortgages	500	50	250
Commercial loans	300	100	300
Risk-weighted assets	–	–	$570

The risk-weighted assets for this bank would be $570 million.

---

[8] There are special rules for determining the amount of capital required for off-balance sheet items. An off-balance sheet item is a position in interest-sensitive contracts and/or foreign-exchange-related products that is not reported on the balance sheet.

The minimum core (Tier 1) capital requirement is 4% of the book value of assets; the minimum *total* capital (core plus supplementary capital) is 8% of the risk-weighted assets. To see how this works, consider the hypothetical bank we just used to illustrate the calculation of risk-weighted assets. For that bank the risk-weighted assets are $570 million. The minimum core capital requirement is $40 million (0.04 × $1 billion); the minimum total capital requirement is $45.6 million (0.08 × $570 million).[9]

One implication of the new capital guidelines is that it will encourage banks to sell off their loans in the open market. By doing so, the bank need not maintain capital for the loans (assets) sold off. Although the secondary market for individual bank loans has been growing, it has not reached the stage where a bank can efficiently sell large amounts of loans. An alternative is for a bank to pool loans and issue securities that are collateralized by the pool of loans. This is the process of asset securitization, which we discussed in Chapter 2.

The risk-based capital requirements previously mentioned deal with credit risk. Bank regulators have addressed ways in which interest rate risk should be incorporated into capital requirements. The Federal Depository Insurance Corporation Improvement Act of 1991 mandates that banking regulators take into consideration **interest rate risk in setting capital requirements**. Subsequently, banking regulators proposed several measures for quantifying interest rate risk exposure. In August 1995 banking regulators amended the capital requirements for banks based on a bank's exposure to interest rate risk. Exposure was measured in terms of the decline in a bank's economic value due to a change in interest rates. About a year later, a joint policy statement was issued by bank regulators setting sound practices for managing interest rate risk. Although the policy statement does not standardize how interest rate risk exposure should be measured nor quantify how an adjustment should be made to a bank's capital requirements given its interest rate exposure, the policy statement does provides guidance that bank regulators will use to evaluate both the adequacy and effectiveness of a bank's interest rate management policy.[10]

Key Points That You Should Understand Before Proceeding

1. Bank deposits are insured by government-sponsored insurance programs, and state-chartered banks may elect to join the Federal Reserve System.
2. Banks raise funds from deposits, from issuing debt and equity securities, and from their own earnings.
3. U.S. banks must keep a fraction of their deposits in assets that qualify as reserves.
4. Banks may borrow funds from the Federal Reserve System.
5. The implications of the Gramm-Leach Bliley Act of 1999 on banking activities.

SAVINGS AND LOAN ASSOCIATIONS

S&Ls represent a fairly old institution. The basic motivation behind creation of S&Ls was the providing of funds for financing the purchase of a home. The collateral for the loans would be the home being financed.

S&Ls are either mutually owned or have corporate stock ownership. "Mutually owned" means there is no stock outstanding, so technically the depositors are the owners. To increase the ability of S&Ls to expand the sources of funding available to bol-

[9] Other minimum standards imposed by the guidelines cover limitations on supplementary capital elements.
[10] Federal Deposit Insurance Corporation, "Differences in Capital and Accounting Standards Among the Federal Banking and Thrift Agencies; Report to Congressional Committees," *Federal Register*, Vol. 65, No. 127, (June 30, 2000), Notices, p. 40665.

ster their capital, legislation facilitated the conversion of mutually owned companies into a corporate stock ownership structure.

Like banks, S&Ls may be chartered under either state or federal statutes. At the federal level, the primary regulator of S&Ls is the Director of the Office of Thrift Supervision (OTS), created in 1989 by FIRREA. Prior to the creation of OTS, the primary regulator was the Federal Home Loan Bank Board (FHLBB). The FHLBB no longer exists. The Federal Home Loan Banks, which, along with the FHLBB comprised the Federal Home Loan Bank System, still exist and make advances (i.e., loans) to member institutions (S&Ls and commercial banks).

Like banks, S&Ls are now subject to reserve requirements on deposits established by the Fed. Prior to the passage of FIRREA, federal deposit insurance for S&Ls was provided by the Federal Savings and Loan Insurance Corporation (FSLIC). The Savings Association Insurance Fund (SAIF) has replaced FSLIC. SAIF is administered by the FDIC.

Assets

Traditionally, the only assets in which S&Ls were allowed to invest have been mortgages, mortgage-backed securities, and U.S. government securities. Mortgage loans include fixed-rate mortgages, adjustable-rate mortgages, and other types of mortgage designs. While most mortgage loans are for the purchase of homes, S&Ls do make construction loans.

As the structures of S&L balance sheets and the consequent maturity mismatch led to widespread disaster and insolvency, the Garn-St. Germain Act of 1982 expanded the types of assets in which S&Ls could invest. The acceptable list of investments now includes consumer loans (loans for home improvement, automobiles, education, mobile homes, and credit cards), nonconsumer loans (commercial, corporate, business, or agricultural loans), and municipal securities.

Although S&Ls had a comparative advantage in originating mortgage loans, they lacked the expertise to make commercial and corporate loans. Rather than make an investment in acquiring those skills, S&Ls took an alternative approach and invested in corporate bonds because these bonds were classified as corporate loans. More specifically, S&Ls became one of the major buyers of non-investment-grade corporate bonds, more popularly referred to as **junk bonds** or high-yield bonds. Under FIRREA, S&Ls are no longer permitted to invest new money in junk bonds.

S&Ls invest in short-term assets for operational (liquidity) and regulatory purposes. All S&Ls with federal deposit insurance must satisfy minimum liquidity requirements. Acceptable assets include cash, short-term government agency and corporate securities, certificates of deposit of commercial banks,[11] other money market instruments, and federal funds. In the case of federal funds, the S&L is lending excess reserves to another depository institution that is short of funds.

Funding

Prior to 1981, the bulk of the liabilities of S&Ls consisted of passbook savings accounts and time deposits. The interest rate that could be offered on these deposits was regulated. S&Ls were given favored treatment over banks with respect to the maximum interest rate they could pay depositors. They were permitted to pay an interest rate 0.5% higher, later reduced to 0.25%. With the deregulation of interest rates discussed earlier in this chapter, banks and S&Ls now compete head-to-head for deposits. Deregulation also expanded the types of accounts that may be offered by S&Ls—negotiable order of withdrawal (NOW)

---

[11] The S&L is an investor when it holds the CD of a bank, but the CD represents the liability of the issuing bank.

accounts and money market deposit accounts (MMDA). NOW accounts are similar to demand deposits. Unlike demand deposits, NOW accounts pay interest.

In the 1980s, S&Ls became more active in raising funds in the money market. For example, they were able to use the repurchase agreement market to raise funds. Some larger S&Ls have issued commercial paper as well as medium-term notes.[12] They can borrow in the federal funds market and they have access to the Fed's discount window. S&Ls can also borrow from the Federal Home Loan Banks. These borrowings, called **advances**, can be short term or long term in maturity, and the interest rate can be fixed or floating.

Regulation

Federal S&Ls are chartered under the provisions of the **Home Owners Loan Act of 1933**. Federally chartered S&Ls are now supervised by the Office of Thrift Supervisor. State-chartered banks are supervised by the respective states. A further act in 1933 established the Federal Savings and Loan Insurance Corporation, which at that time insured the deposits of federally chartered S&Ls up to $5,000 and allowed state-chartered S&Ls that could qualify to obtain the same insurance coverage. We discuss some of the important legislation and the players below.

As in bank regulation, S&Ls historically have been regulated with respect to the maximum interest rates on deposit accounts, geographical operations, permissible activities (types of accounts and types of investments), and capital adequacy requirements. In addition, there have been restrictions on the sources of nondeposit funds and liquidity requirements. We mentioned liquidity requirements earlier.[13]

The maximum interest rate that is permitted on deposit accounts has been phased out by the Depository Institutions Deregulation and Monetary Control Act of 1980 (DIDMCA). While this allowed S&Ls to compete with other financial institutions to raise funds, it also raised their funding costs. For reasons to be described later, while banks also faced higher funding costs, their balance sheets were better constituted than those of S&Ls to cope with the higher costs resulting from interest rate deregulation.

Besides phasing in the deregulation of interest rates on deposit accounts, DIDMCA was significant in several other ways. First, it expanded the Fed's control over the money supply by imposing deposit reserve requirements on S&Ls. In return, S&Ls were permitted to offer negotiable order of withdrawal (NOW) accounts.

Subsequent legislation, the Garn-St. Germain Act, not only granted thrifts the right to offer money market demand accounts so that S&Ls could compete with money market funds, but also broadened the types of assets in which S&Ls could invest. While S&Ls were first given permission by the FHLBB in 1979 to originate and invest in adjustable-rate mortgage loans, restrictions on the interest rate and other terms stymied their use. Two years later, the FHLBB removed some major impediments.

Permission to raise funds in the money market and the bond market was granted by the Federal Home Loan Bank Board in 1975 (when it allowed the issuance of mortgage pass-through securities by S&Ls) and in 1979 (when it allowed the issuance of commercial paper and Eurodollar issues). FHLBB permission to form finance subsidiaries was granted in 1984. Through these subsidiaries, S&Ls were able to broaden their funding sources by the issuance of mortgage-related securities known as collateralized mortgage obligations.

Geographical operations of S&Ls were restricted until 1981, when the FHLBB permitted thrifts to acquire thrifts in other states.

There are two sets of **capital adequacy standards** for S&Ls as for banks. For S&Ls there are also two ratio tests based on "core" capital and "tangible" capital. The risk-

---

[12] The medium-term note market is discussed in Chapter 20.

[13] Liquidity requirements are not imposed on banks because the majority of their assets are of less than five years' maturity.

based capital guidelines are similar to those for banks. Instead of two tiers of capital, however, there are three: Tier 1—tangible capital, Tier 2—core capital, and Tier 3—supplementary capital.

As with commercial banks, in addition to risk-based capital requirements based on credit risk there are risk-based requirements based on interest rate risk. For S&Ls, regulators have taken a different approach to measuring interest rate risk than regulators of commercial banks. In December 1988, the Federal Home Loan Bank Board, the predecessor to the Office of Thrift Supervision (OTS), stated that it intended to take into consideration interest rate risk exposure in establishing capital requirements. In December 1990, the OTS proposed a rule for dealing with interest rate risk exposure in setting capital requirements. In August 1993 the OTS finally adopted a rule that incorporates interest rate risk into risk-based capital requirements. The rule specifies that if a thrift has greater than "normal" interest rate risk exposure (where normal is defined by the rule), then there would be a deduction of the thrift's total capital for purposes of calculating its risk-based capital requirements. Interest rate risk exposure was specified in the rule as a decline in the net portfolio value (the value of the portfolio after deducting liabilities) resulting from a 200 basis point change (up and down) in market interest rates. What is deducted from the thrift's total capital is one-half the difference between the thrift's measured exposure and the "normal" level of exposure, which is defined as 2% of the estimated economic value of the assets.[14]

The S&L Crisis

The story of the growth of the S&L industry since the late 1960s and the ensuing S&L crisis can't be described in one short chapter, but a basic understanding of the downfall of this industry is possible.

Until the early 1980s, S&Ls and all other lenders financed housing through traditional mortgages at interest rates fixed for the life of the loan. The period of the loan was typically long, frequently up to 30 years. Funding for these loans, by regulation, came from deposits having a maturity considerably shorter than the loans. As we explained earlier in this chapter, this is the funding problem of lending long and borrowing short. It is extremely risky—although regulators took a long time to understand it. There is no problem, of course, if interest rates are stable or declining, but if interest rates rise above the interest rate on the mortgage loan, a negative spread will result, which must result eventually in insolvency. Regulators at first endeavored to shield the S&L industry from the need to pay high interest rates without losing deposits by imposing a ceiling on the interest rate that would be paid by S&Ls and by their immediate competitors, the other depository institutions. But the approach did not and could not work.

With the high volatility of interest rates in the 1970s, followed by the historically high level of interest rates in the early 1980s, all depository institutions began to lose funds to competitors exempt from ceilings, such as the newly formed money market funds; this development forced some increase in ceilings. The ceilings in place since the middle of the 1960s did not protect the S&Ls; the institutions began to suffer from diminished profits, and increasingly from operating losses. A large fraction of S&Ls became technically insolvent as rising interest rates eroded asset market values to the point where they fell short of the liabilities.

But regulators, anxious to cover up the debacle of their empire, let them continue to operate, worsening the problem by allowing them to value their mortgage assets at book value. Profitability worsened with deregulation of the maximum interest rate that S&Ls could pay on deposits. While deregulation allowed S&Ls to compete

---

[14] Federal Deposit Insurance Corporation, "Differences in Capital and Accounting Standards Among the Federal Banking and Thrift Agencies; Report to Congressional Committees."

with other financial institutions for funds, it also raised funding costs. Banks were better equipped to cope with rising funding costs because bank portfolios were not dominated by old, fixed-rate mortgages as S&Ls were. A larger portion of bank portfolios consisted of shorter-term assets and other assets whose interest rate reset to market interest rates after short time periods.

The difficulty of borrowing short and lending long was only part of the problem faced by the industry. As the crisis progressed, and the situation of many S&Ls became hopeless, fraudulent management activities were revealed. Many S&Ls facing financial difficulties also pursued strategies that exposed the institution to greater risk, in the hope of recovering if these strategies worked out. What encouraged managers to pursue such high-risk strategies was that depositors had no reason to be concerned with the risks associated with the institution where they kept their funds because the U.S. government, through federal deposit insurance, guaranteed the deposits up to a predetermined amount. Troubled S&Ls could pay existing depositors through attracting new depositors by offering higher interest rates on deposits than financially stronger S&Ls. In turn, to earn a spread on the higher cost of funds, they had to pursue riskier investment policies.

Key Points That You Should Understand Before Proceeding

1. S&Ls may be chartered by state or federal authorities.
2. The majority of assets owned by S&Ls are mortgages and mortgage-backed securities.
3. S&Ls may obtain funding from deposits and issuance of debt and equity securities.
4. The government regulates many aspects of an S&L's activities, including its capital structure.
5. The fundamental causes of the S&L crisis.

SAVINGS BANKS

Savings banks are institutions similar to, although much older than, S&Ls. They can be either mutually owned (in which case they are called mutual savings banks) or stockholder owned. While conversion of mutual to corporate structure was made easier by the Garn-St. Germain Act, most savings banks are of the mutual form. Only 16 states in the eastern portion of the United States charter savings banks. In 1978, Congress permitted the chartering of federal savings banks.

Although the total deposits at savings banks are less than those at S&Ls, savings banks are typically larger institutions. Asset structures of savings banks and S&Ls are similar. The principal assets of savings banks are residential mortgages. Because states have permitted more portfolio diversification than was permitted by federal regulators of S&Ls, savings bank portfolios weathered funding risk far better than S&Ls. Included in savings bank portfolios are corporate bonds, Treasury and government agency securities, municipal securities, common stock, and consumer loans.

The principal source of funds for savings banks is deposits. Typically, the ratio of deposits to total assets is greater for savings banks than for S&Ls. Savings banks offer the same types of deposit accounts as S&Ls. Deposits can be insured by either the Bank Insurance Fund or Savings Association Insurance Fund.

CREDIT UNIONS

Credit unions are the smallest and the newest of the depository institutions. Credit unions can obtain either a state or federal charter. Their unique aspect is the "common bond" requirement for credit union membership. According to the statutes that regulate federal credit unions, membership in a federal credit union "shall be limited to groups having a common bond of occupation or association, or to groups within a well-defined neighborhood, community, or rural district." They are either cooperatives or mutually owned. There is no corporate stock ownership. The dual purpose of credit unions is, therefore, to serve their members' saving and borrowing needs.

As of the end of 1999, there were 10,628 credit unions —6,566 federally chartered and 4,062 state chartered. Although there are more credit unions than commercial banks, their total assets comprise only a small percentage of that of commercial banks.

Technically, because credit unions are owned by their members, member deposits are called shares. The distribution paid to members is, therefore, in the form of dividends, not interest. Since 1970, the shares of all federally chartered credit unions have been insured by the **National Credit Union Share Insurance Fund (NCUSIF)** for up to $100,000, the same as other depository institutions. State-chartered credit unions may elect to have NCUSIF coverage; for those that do not, insurance coverage is provided by a state agency.

Federal regulations apply to federally chartered credit unions and state-chartered credit unions that have elected to become members of NCUSIF. Most states, however, specify that state-chartered institutions must be subject to the same requirements as federally chartered ones. Effectively, therefore, most credit unions are regulated at the federal level. The principal federal regulatory agency is the **National Credit Union Administration (NCUA)**.

Credit unions obtain their funds primarily from the deposits of their members. With deregulation, they can offer a variety of accounts, including share drafts, which are similar to checking accounts but they pay interest. Playing a role similar to the Fed, as the lender of last resort, is the **Central Liquidity Facility (CLF)**, which is administered by NCUA. CLF provides short-term loans to member credit unions with liquidity needs.

Credit union assets consist of small consumer loans, residential mortgage loans, and securities. Regulations 703 and 704 of NCUA set forth the types of investments in which a credit union may invest. They can make investments in **corporate credit unions**.

What is a corporate credit union? One might think that a corporate credit union is a credit union set up by employees of a corporation. It is not. Federal and state-chartered credit unions are referred to as **"natural person" credit unions** because they provide financial services to qualifying members of the general public. In contrast, corporate credit unions provide a variety of investment services, as well as payment systems, only to natural person credit unions. As of 2000, there were 36 corporate credit unions ranging in size from $5 million to $30 billion. All but three corporate credit unions are federally insured. The U.S. Central Credit Union acts as the chief liquidity center for corporate credit unions by investing surplus funds from the other corporate credit unions.

SUMMARY

Depository institutions (commercial banks, savings and loan associations, savings banks, and credit unions) accept various types of deposits. With the funds raised through deposits and other funding sources, they make loans to various entities and invest in securities. The deposits usually are insured by a federal agency. Income is derived from investments (loans and securities) and fee income. Thrifts (savings and loan associations, savings banks, and credit unions) are specialized types of depository institutions. Historically, they have not been authorized to accept demand accounts, but more recently thrifts have been offering some types of deposits equivalent to checking accounts.

A depository institution seeks to earn a positive spread between the assets it invests in and the cost of its funds. In generating spread income, a depository institution faces credit risk and interest rate risk. A depository institution must be prepared to satisfy net withdrawals of funds by depositors and provide loans to customers. A depository institution can accommodate withdrawals or loan demand by attracting additional deposits, using existing securities as collateral for borrowing from a federal agency, raising short-term funds in the money market, or selling securities that it owns.

All national banks must be members of the Federal Reserve System. State-chartered banks may elect to join the Federal Reserve System. The services provided by commercial banks can be broadly classified as individual banking, institutional banking, and global banking.

There are three sources of funds for banks: (1) deposits; (2) nondeposit borrowing; and (3) retained earnings and sale of equity securities. Banks are highly leveraged financial institutions, meaning that most of their funds are obtained from deposits and nondeposit borrowing, which includes borrowing from the Fed through the discount window facility, borrowing reserves in the federal funds market, and borrowing by the issuance of instruments in the money and bond markets.

Banks must maintain reserves at one of the 12 Federal Reserve Banks, according to reserve requirements established by the Fed. Banks temporarily short of their required reserves can borrow reserves in the federal funds market or borrow temporarily from the Fed at its discount window.

There is both federal and state regulation of banks. At the federal level, supervision of banks is the responsibility of the Federal Reserve Board, the Office of the Comptroller of the Currency, and the Federal Deposit Insurance Corporation. Recent legislation has altered the regulatory structure. The major regulations involve capital requirements and the activities of that are permissible for commercial banks. Until the passage of the Gramm-Leach Bliley Act of 1999, the key legislation regulating bank activities was the Glass-Steagall Act, which effectively separated commercial banking and investment banking activities. The Gramm-Leach Bliley Act of 1999 tore down the walls between commercial banks and investment banks, as well as commercial bank activity in the insurance industry.

Like banks, S&Ls may be chartered under either state or federal statutes. At the federal level, the primary regulator of S&Ls is the Director of the Office of Thrift Supervision. The deposits of S&Ls are subject to reserve requirements established by the Fed. Federal deposit insurance for S&Ls is provided by the Savings Association Insurance Fund.

Much as in the case of bank regulation, S&Ls are regulated with respect to geographical operations, permissible activities, and capital adequacy requirements. S&Ls invest principally in mortgages and mortgage-related securities. Deregulation expanded the types of investments that S&Ls are permitted to make, as well as expanding the types of deposit accounts that may be offered and the available funding sources.

The asset structures of savings banks and S&Ls are similar. As some states have permitted greater portfolio diversification than is permitted by federal regulators of S&Ls, this is reflected in savings bank portfolios. The principal source of funds for savings banks is deposits. Deposits can be federally insured by either the BIF or SAIF.

Credit unions are depository institutions that have a "common bond" requirement for membership. They are owned by their members. Although they can be state or federally chartered, most credit unions effectively are regulated at the federal level by the National Credit Union Administration. The assets of credit unions consist primarily of small consumer loans to their members and credit card loans.

KEY TERMS

- **Advances, 58**
- **Bank holding company, 47**
- **Bank Insurance Fund (BIF), 46**
- **Banking Act of 1933, 52**
- **Basle Committee on Banking Regulations and Supervisory Practices, 54**
- **Capital adequacy standards, 58**
- **Capital requirements, 54**
- **Central Liquidity Facility (CLF), 61**
- **Charter, 46**
- **Comptroller of the Currency, 51**
- **Core capital, 54**

- **Corporate credit union, 61**
- **Credit risk (or default risk), 44**
- **Credit risk-based capital requirements, 54**
- **Credit union, 60**
- **Demand deposit, 49**
- **Deposit computation period, 50**
- **Depository Institutions Deregulation and Monetary Control Act of 1980 (DIDMCA), 47**
- **Discount rate, 50**
- **Discount window, 50**
- **Disintermediation, 51**
- **Excess reserves, 50**

- **Federal Deposit Insurance Corporation (FDIC),** 46
- **Federal funds market, 50**
- **Finacial Institutions Reform, Recovery, and Enforcement Act of 1989 (FIRREA), 46**
- **Garn-St. Germain Act, 51**
- **Gramm-Leach Bliley Act of 1999, 52**
- **Home Owners Loan Act of 1933, 58**
- **Interest rate risk, 44**
- **Interest rate risk-based capital requirements, 56**
- **Junk bonds, 57**
- **McFadden Act of 1927, 51**
- **Money center bank, 51**
- **Money market mutual fund, 49**
- **Mortgage, 48**
- **National Credit Union Administration (NCUA), 61**
- **National Credit Union Share Insurance Fund (NCUSIF), 61**
- **Natural person credit union, 61**
- **NOW (Negotiable Order of Withdrawal) Account, 43**
- **Regional bank, 51**
- **Regulation Q, 51**
- **Regulatory risk, 44**
- **Required reserves, 49**
- **Reserve ratio, 49**
- **Riegle-Neal Interstate Banking and Branching Efficiency Act, 52**
- **Savings and loan association (S&L), 43**
- **Savings bank, 60**
- **Secondary reserves, 46**
- **Spread income (or margin), 44**
- **Supplementary capital, 54**
- **Time deposit (or certificates of deposit), 49**

QUESTIONS

1. Explain the ways in which a depository institution can accommodate withdrawal and loan demand.
2. Why do you think a debt instrument whose interest rate is changed periodically based on some market interest rate would be more suitable for a depository institution than a long-term debt instrument with a fixed interest rate?
3. What is meant by:
   a. Individual banking?
   b. Institutional banking?
   c. Global banking?
4. Explain each of the following:
   a. Reserve ratio.
   b. Required reserves.
5. Explain each of the following types of deposit accounts:
   a. Demand deposit.
   b. Certificate of deposit.
   c. Money market demand account.
6. The following is the book value of the assets of a bank:

Asset	Book value (in millions)
U.S. Treasury securities	$ 50
Municipal general obligation bonds	50
Residential mortgages	400
Commercial loans	200
Total book value	$700

   a. Calculate the credit risk-weighted assets using the following information:

Asset	Risk weight
U.S. Treasury securities	0%
Municipal general obligation bonds	20
Residential mortgages	50
Commercial loans	100

b. What is the minimum core capital requirement?

c. What is the minimum total capital requirement?

7. a. What is meant by the duration of an asset?

b. If the duration of an asset is 5, what does this mean?

8. a. Explain how bank regulators have incorporated interest risk into capital requirements.

b. Explain how S&L regulators have incorporated interest rate risk into capital requirements.

9. You and a friend are discussing the savings and loan crisis. She states that "the whole mess started in the early 1980s. When short-term rates skyrocketed, S&Ls got killed—their spread income went from positive to negative. They were borrowing short and lending long."

a. What does she mean by "borrowing short and lending long"?

b. Are higher or lower interest rates beneficial to an institution that borrows short and lends long?

10. Alan Greenspan, the chairman of the Federal Reserve Board, told the U.S. Senate on July 12, 1990:

> *As you know, the Board has long supported repeal of the provisions of the Glass-Steagall Act that separated commercial and investment banking. We still strongly advocate such repeal because we believe that technology and globalization have continued to blur the distinctions among credit markets, and have eroded the franchise value of the classic bank intermediation process. Outdated constraints will only endanger the profitability of banking organizations and their contribution to the American economy.*

a. What do you think Mr. Greenspan means when he says that the value of the bank intermediation process has been eroded by technology and globalization?

b. What do you think are some of the major benefits and risks of repealing key provisions of the Glass-Steagall Act?

11. Consider this headline from the *New York Times* of March 26, 1933: "Bankers will fight Deposit Guarantees . . . Bad Banking would be encouraged."
What do you think this means?

12. How did the Gramm-Leach Bliley Act of 1999 expand the activities permitted by banks?

13. The following quotation is from the October 29, 1990 issue of *Corporate Financing Week*:

> *Chase Manhattan Bank is preparing its first asset-backed debt issue, becoming the last major consumer bank to plan to access the growing market, Street asset-backed officials said . . . . Asset-backed offerings enable banks to remove credit card or other loan receivables from their balance sheets, which helps them comply with capital requirements.*

a. What capital requirements is this article referring to?

b. Explain why asset securitization reduces capital requirements.

14. Comment on this statement: The risk-based guidelines for commercial banks attempt to gauge the interest rate risk associated with a bank's balance sheet.

15. a. What is the primary asset in which savings and loan associations invest?

b. Why were banks in a better position than savings and loan associations to weather rising interest rates?

Chapter 5

Central Banks
and the Creation
of Money

Learning Objectives

After reading this chapter, you will understand

- the structure of the Federal Reserve System and the nature of the Fed's instruments of monetary policy.
- the meaning of required reserves for banks, and the fractional reserve banking system of the United States.
- the implementation and impact of open market operations and of open market repurchase agreements.
- the role of the Fed's discount rate.
- the different kinds of money and the definitions of key monetary aggregates.
- the money multiplier, and how it generates changes in the monetary aggregates from changes in the banking system's reserves.
- how banks and investors participate, with the Fed, in changing the level of the monetary aggregates.
- how global trade and investment influence the Fed's monetary policy.

In most advanced economies, the process by which the supply of money is created is a complex interaction among several economic agents, which perform different functions at different times. The agents are firms and individuals who both save and borrow, depository institutions that accept savings and make loans to firms or individuals or other institutions, and the nation's central bank, which also lends and buys and sells securities. This chapter gives a brief and general description of the complex process of creating the **money supply**. In so doing, the chapter highlights the role played by U.S. depository institutions and by the financial markets that the process both uses and affects. The chapter also describes the monetary and banking systems of several other major economies.

THE CENTRAL BANK AND MONEY CREATION IN THE UNITED STATES

The Central Bank of the United States: The Federal Reserve System

The most important agent in the money supply process is the Federal Reserve System, which is the central bank of the United States and often called just the Federal Reserve or the Fed. Created in 1913, the Fed is the government agency responsible for the management of the U.S. monetary and banking systems. Most large commercial banks in the United States are members of the Federal Reserve System. The Fed is managed by a seven-member **Board of Governors**, who are appointed by the president and approved by the Congress. These governors have 14-year appointments (with one appointment ending every two years), and one governor is the Board's Chairman. The **Chairmanship of the Fed** is a highly visible and influential position in the world economy. The Federal Reserve System consists of 12 districts covering the entire country; each **district** has a Federal Reserve Bank with its own president.

An important feature of the Fed is that, by the terms of the law that created it, neither the legislative nor the executive branch of the federal government should exert control over it. From time to time, critics charge that the Fed guards this autonomy by accommodating either the White House or Congress (or both) far too much. We have noted in Chapter 3 and 4 that the Fed has substantial regulatory power over the nation's depository institutions, especially commercial banks.

It is worth noting here, before we discuss the Fed's tools for monetary management, that financial innovations in the last two decades have made the Fed's task more difficult. The public's increasing acceptance of money market mutual funds has funneled a large amount of money into what are essentially interest-bearing checking accounts. (See Chapter 8 for more information on mutual funds.) Another relevant innovation is the practice of asset securitization, discussed in Chapter 2. Securitization permits commercial banks to change what once were illiquid consumer loans of several varieties into securities. Selling these securities in the financial markets gives the banks a source of funding that is outside the Fed's influence. The many hedging instruments to be analyzed in Part IX of this book have also affected banks' behavior and their relationship with the Fed. In general, that transformation amounts to reduced Fed control of banks and increased difficulty in implementing monetary policy.

Instruments of Monetary Policy: How the Fed Influences the Supply of Money

The Fed has several tools by which it influences, indirectly and to a greater or lesser extent, the amount of money in the economy and the general level of interest rates. These tools are reserve requirements (whose use is somewhat constricted by Congressional mandate), open market operations, open market repurchase agreements, and the discount rate. These instruments represent the key ways that the Fed interacts with commercial banks in the process of creating money. Our discussion of these tools explains the impact of their use on a generally specified money supply. Later, we describe the money supply in more detail.

Reserve Requirements.

Bank reserves play an important role in the U.S. banking and monetary system and are directly linked to the growth in the money supply. Generally, the higher the growth rate in reserves, the higher the rate of change in the money supply. Later in this chapter, we will discuss this linkage in some detail. At this point, we want to focus on the meaning and function of reserve requirements.

The United States has a **fractional reserve banking system**, which means that a bank must hold or "reserve" some portion of the funds that savers deposit in a form approved by the Fed. As a result, a bank may lend to borrowers only a fraction of what it takes in as deposits. The ratio of mandatory reserves to deposits is the **required reserve ratio**. For many years, the Fed had the authority to set this ratio. In the Depository Institutions Deregulation and Monetary Control Act (DIDMCA) of 1980, Congress assumed much of that responsibility, establishing new rules regarding this ratio to be applied to all depository institutions, including commercial banks, thrifts of various types, and credit unions.

In a key provision of the DIDMCA, Congress adopted a basic ratio of 12% for what are termed checkable or transactional accounts, that is, *demand deposits*, or accounts on which checks may be written often. For nontransactional but short-term deposit accounts—known as *time deposits*—the required reserve ratio is 3%. The 1980 law also authorizes the Fed to change the required reserve ratio on checking accounts to any level between 8% and 14%, and to raise it to 18% under certain conditions. In early 1992, the Fed reduced the ratio to 10% for banks with total checkable accounts at or above $46.8 million. For banks with smaller totals in these accounts, the required reserve ratio is 3%

A bank must maintain the required reserves as either currency on hand (that is, cash in the bank) or deposits in the Federal Reserve itself. The more important form is the deposit, which serves as an asset for the bank and as a liability of the Fed. A bank has *excess reserves* if its reserves amount to more than the Fed requires. A bank's **total reserves** equal its required reserves plus any excess reserves. A bank whose actual reserves fall short of required levels can borrow excess reserves from other banks (see the next chapter and Chapter 22 for more on the federal funds market), or it can borrow reserves from the Fed itself, which we discuss later in this chapter.

Open Market Operations.

The Fed's most powerful instrument is its authority to conduct **open market operations**, which means that the Fed may buy and sell, in open debt markets, government securities for its own account. These securities may be U.S. Treasury bonds, Treasury bills, or obligations of federal agencies. (We describe these securities in more detail in Chapter 16.) The Fed prefers to use Treasury bills because, in that large and liquid market, it can make its substantial transactions without seriously disrupting the prices or yields of bills. When it buys or sells, the Fed does so at prices and interest rates that prevail in these debt markets. The parties to the Fed's transactions may be commercial banks or other financial agents who are dealers in government securities.

The unit of the Fed that decides on the general issues of changing the rate of growth in the money supply, by open market sales or purchase of securities, is the **Federal Open Market Committee,** or **FOMC**. The FOMC consists of the Board of Governors, the president of the Federal Reserve Bank of New York, and presidents of some of the other district Fed banks. This committee meets approximately once a month to analyze economic activity and levels of key economic variables. The variables may include short-term interest rates (such as the federal funds rate), the U.S. dollar's rate of exchange with important foreign currencies, commodity prices, and excess reserves, among other things.[1] After this analysis, the committee sets the direction of monetary policy for the near future. The minutes of these meetings are published at a later time.

The implementation of policy, through open market operations, is the responsibility of the **trading desk of the Federal Reserve Bank of New York.** The desk transacts, in large volume, with bigger securities firms or commercial banks that are dealers, or market makers, in Treasury securities. While the desk does not buy and sell for profit, it functions as a rational investor, buying at the lowest prices and selling at the highest prices offered at the time of the transactions.

Fed purchases augment the amount of reserves in the banking system. If the seller is a commercial bank, it alters the composition, but not the total, of its assets by

[1] D. S. Batten, M. P. Blackwell, I-S. Kim, S. E. Nocera, and Y. Ozeki, *The Conduct of Monetary Policy in the Major Industrial Countries*. Occasional Paper No. 70, International Monetary Fund (Washington: July 1990), p.24.

exchanging the securities for reserves at the Fed. If the seller is not a bank, much or all of the check with which the Fed pays will probably be deposited in a bank. The bank receiving the deposit would experience an increase in liabilities (the customer's deposit) and in assets (the growth in its reserve account at the Fed). In either case, the proceeds from selling the securities to the Fed raise the banking system's total reserves. Such an increase in reserves typically leads to an increase in the money supply. Individual banks whose reserves rise will generally make new loans, equal to the new deposit less required reserves, because loans earn interest while reserves do not. New loans represent growth in the money supply.

Conversely, the Fed's sale of Treasury securities reduces the money supply (or its rate of growth) because the funds that security dealers pay for the securities come from either deposits at banks or, if the dealers are banks, from the banks' own accounts. A reduction in deposits reduces reserves and leaves the banks less to lend.

Open Market Repurchase Agreements.

The Fed often employs variants of simple open market purchases and sales, and these are called the **repurchase agreement** (or **repo**) and the *reverse repo*. The Fed conducts these transactions, which are actually more common than the outright purchases or sales,[2] with large dealers in government securities and, occasionally, with central banks of other countries. In a repurchase agreement, the Fed buys a particular amount of securities from a seller that agrees to repurchase the same number of securities for a higher price at some future time, usually a few weeks. The difference between the original price and the repurchase price is the return to the Fed for letting the dealer have the cash for the life of the agreement and, also, the cost to the dealer of borrowing from the Fed. In a reverse repo (also known as a *matched sale* or a *matched sale-purchase transaction*), the Fed sells securities and makes a commitment to buy them back at a higher price later. The difference in the two prices is the cost to the Fed of the funds and the return to the buyer for lending money.

An example will illustrate some of the points in a Fed repurchase agreement. (A detailed analysis of repos appears in Chapters 16 and 22.) Suppose the Fed wants to increase bank reserves for some reason over a short period of time, and it seeks out a financial institution that has $20 million in Treasury securities but no excess reserves. Suppose further that the institution wants to lend $20 million for seven days to a borrower. After some discussions, the Fed agrees to "buy" the securities from the institution at a price that reflects the current reporate, and to "sell" them back in seven days, when the institution's borrower pays off that loan. The current annualized rate is 4.3%. The transaction would look like this: The Fed would buy the securities for approximately $19,983,292 and sell them back, seven days later, to the institution at the principal value of $20 million. The difference of nearly $16,708 is the interest the institution pays for the seven-day financing and the return to the Fed for lending that money. And for those seven days, the financial institution and the entire banking system can enjoy an increase in reserves, if, of course, the bank keeps the roughly $20 million in its account at the Fed.

The Fed uses repos and reverse repos to bring about a temporary change in the level of reserves in the system or to respond to some event that the Fed thinks will have a significant but not long-lived effect. A particularly good example of such an event is a large payment by the U.S. Treasury (as in tax refunds or Social Security benefits) that

---

[2] David M. Jones and Ellen Rachling, "Monetary Policy: How the Fed Sets, Implements, and Measures Policy Chokes," chapter 2 in Frank J. Fabozzi (ed.), *Handbook of Portfolio Management* (New Hope, PA: Frank J. Fabozzi Associates, 1998).

sharply but temporarily raises reserves at the banks. Of course, these temporary changes in the system's reserves alter the banks' ability to make loans and, ultimately, to prompt growth in the money supply for a short period.

Discount Rate.

As mentioned in Chapter 4, the Fed makes loans to banks that are members of the system. A bank borrowing from the Fed is said to use the *discount window*, and these loans are backed by the bank's collateral. The rate of interest on these loans is the *discount rate*, set at a certain level by the Fed's Board of Governors. As the rate rises, banks are understandably less likely to borrow; a falling rate tends to encourage them to borrow. Proceeds from *discount loans* are also reserves and increase the banks' capacity to make loans. Banks generally do not prefer to gain reserves in this way because the loans cost money as well as invite increased monitoring of the borrowing banks' activities. Accordingly, the flow of this borrowing has a very slight impact on the money banks have and can lend and, therefore, on the supply of money.

There is general agreement that the discount rate is the least effective tool at the Fed's disposal and its use in monetary policy has diminished over time. Today, changes in the discount rate function largely as the Fed's public signals about its intention to change the rate at which the money supply is growing.

Different Kinds of Money

Until now, we have spoken in general terms about the money supply. But we can be more precise and identify several different meanings of the word *money* and several different types of money.

First of all, money is that item which serves as a **numeraire**, or unit of account—in other words, the unit that is used to measure wealth. In the United States, the numeraire is the dollar; in Japan it is the Yen, and so on. Second, we call money any instrument that serves as a medium of exchange, that is, anything that is generally accepted in payment for goods, services, and capital transactions. In the United States, the medium of exchange encompasses currency, which is issued by the Treasury or the Fed, and demand deposits, which support payment by means of checks and are held at depository institutions such as commercial banks. The medium of exchange also performs the function of being a store of value, which means that the exchange medium can be used to carry resources over from the present to the future. Obviously, this function is impaired in times of high and unpredictable inflation.[3] Other accounts that resemble demand deposits include the NOW account (or Negotiable Order of Withdrawal account) and share drafts of credit unions.

Other assets that do not function in the role of medium of exchange have many properties in common with the numeraire. These properties include safety, divisibility, and high liquidity, which is the capacity of being transformed into the medium of exchange promptly and at negligible cost. Because of these properties, these assets are good substitutes for money, in particular, as stores of value. The assets of this type include *time deposits* at commercial banks or thrifts. These accounts earn interest over their specified lives, and the investor may not draw on the money in the account for a transaction, without incurring a penalty, until the deposit's maturity date. Other assets that are substitutes for money include balances in money market mutual funds.

---

[3] The *giro payment*, an alternative to the check, is used in many foreign countries. The giro payment is a direct order to the payer's bank to make a payment to a seller of some good or service. The check, of course, is an order to pay that is drawn on an account at the payer's bank and that the payer gives to the seller.

Money and Monetary Aggregates

Monetary policy and the actions of the Federal Reserve System often concentrate on what are called **monetary aggregates**. The purpose of the aggregates is to measure the amount of money available to the economy at any time.

The most basic monetary aggregate is the **monetary base**. Also termed *high-powered money*, the base is defined as currency in circulation (or coins and Federal Reserve notes held by the public) plus the total reserves in the banking system. It is important to note that reserves make up the bulk of the base, which is under the control of the Fed. Thus, this aggregate is the one that the Fed is most able to influence with its various monetary tools.

The instruments that serve the role of **medium of exchange**—currency and demand deposits—are included in a monetary aggregate that is sometimes referred to as the narrow measure of the money supply and is labeled M_1. Thus, M_1 measures the amount of the medium of exchange in the economy.

M_2 is a more inclusive aggregate because it takes into account all the instruments that substitute for money in the capacity of storing value. Therefore, M_2 is defined as M_1 plus all dollars held in time and savings accounts at banks and thrift institutions, plus all dollars invested in retail money market mutual funds, plus some additional accounts such as overnight repurchase agreements. Some analysts also watch developments in two other monetary aggregates, which are labeled M_3 and **L** (for liquid assets). These aggregates equal M_2 plus certain other financial assets, including long-term time deposits, commercial paper, bankers' acceptances, and some Treasury securities.

The ratio of the money supply to the economy's income (as reflected by the gross national product or some similar measure) is known as the **velocity of money** in circulation. Velocity measures the average amount of transactions carried by a dollar. If the economy's velocity were stable, monetary policy could achieve any desired level of income by simply targeting the aggregate M_1. Unfortunately, velocity is not a stable relationship, and in fact, the linkages between the economy's income and the various aggregates vary considerably over time.

Typically, the monetary aggregates move in somewhat similar patterns, rising and falling at roughly the same rates and at roughly the same times. Table 5-1 shows the growth rates for M_1, M_2, and M_3 during the period from 1980 to 1999. However, the differences among the changes in the aggregates are large and frequent enough to suggest that these aggregates are measuring different things. A major question in Fed policy making (which we discuss below) has revolved around choosing the most appropriate definition of the money supply.

The Money Multiplier: The Expansion of the Money Supply

Our discussion of how the supply of money is created focuses on the linkage between the banking system's reserves and the aggregate M_1. The process we describe, the **money multiplier**, can be generalized to the other monetary aggregates, but the complexities involved in those processes are not relevant to our task now.

We begin by restating that the creation of the money supply, and changes in it, is a complex interaction of four parties: the Fed, banks, savers, and borrowers. The Fed provides reserves to banks and also requires banks to hold, as reserves, a portion of the deposits that the public holds at the banks. The banks, playing their key role in the money multiplier, lend the remainder of the deposits (or most of it) to borrowers at an interest rate that exceeds that of demand deposits. For any one bank, the remainder equals deposits less required reserves, which can be expressed as deposits times (1 − required reserve ratio). Clearly, the funds one bank lends to a borrower can become

Table 5-1   Annual Rates of Growth in Monetary Aggregates 1980–1999

YEAR	M_1	M_2	M_3
1980	6.9%	8.5%	10.3%
1981	6.9	9.7	13.0
1982	8.7	8.8	9.1
1983	9.8	11.3	9.7
1984	5.8	8.6	10.9
1985	12.4	8.0	7.3
1986	16.9	9.5	9.1
1987	3.5	3.6	5.4
1988	4.9	5.8	6.6
1989	0.8	5.5	4.0
1990	4.0	3.8	1.6
1991	8.7	3.1	1.3
1992	14.3	1.6	0.3
1993	10.2	1.6	1.4
1994	1.8	0.4	1.7
1995	−2.0	4.2	6.1
1996	−4.0	4.8	7.3
1997	−0.6	5.8	9.0
1998	1.7	8.8	11.0
1999	2.9	5.9	8.2
2000	−3.0	6.4	8.7

Note: Annual changes are from December to December.
SOURCE: *Economic Report of the President 2000.* 2000 data from www.Federalreserve.gov (Research and Data Section).

the borrower's deposits in another bank. The borrower's decision to hold wealth as deposits rather than cash also affects the money multiplier. Then, that second bank must keep a fraction of those new deposits as reserves and can lend out to other borrowers an amount equal to the deposits less required reserves.

We will illustrate this process with an extended example. Suppose the Fed's required reserve ratio is 12%, and deposits at Bank A are $100 million, while those at Bank B are $50 million. Bank A has reserves of $12 million and outstanding loans of $88 million, and Bank B has reserves of $6 million with loans to borrowers of $44 million. For Bank A, the loan amount to $88 million equals either $100 million of deposits less $12 million of reserves, or $100 million times $(1 − 0.12)$. For Bank B, loans of $44 million equal $50 million minus the 12% required reserves of $6 million. Thus, neither Bank A nor Bank B has any *excess reserves* (which equal total less required reserves). The level of reserves in the banking system has led M_1 to reach the level of (let us say) $900 billion, which equals $250 billion in currency and $650 billion in demand deposits. For this example, we assume that the amount of currency in the system will not change.

The Fed can increase the reserves by either lending to the banks or by purchasing government securities from the banks or other investors. (We ignore here the Fed's authority to change the required reserve ratio.) In this example, we suppose that the Fed buys $5 million of U.S. Treasury securities from a dealer who deposits the check, which is drawn on the Fed, with Bank A. Bank A's reserve account with the Fed has increased by $5 million and so have its (demand) deposits, its total reserves, and the overall level of M_1. But required reserves have risen only by $5 million $\times$ 0.12 or

$600,000. This leaves an additional $4.4 million that the bank is free and eager to invest in order to improve its income.

We continue by assuming that a machinery manufacturing firm borrows all of the $4.4 million in a one-year loan, then buys equipment from a company that places all of that money in a checking account (or demand deposit) at another bank, which is Bank B. Bank A must transfer reserves for the amount of the loan to Bank B. The situation regarding Bank A is this: Its level of deposits remains unchanged at $105 million; its loans have increased by $4.4 million to $92.4 million; its reserves have fallen by $4.4 million from $17 million to $12.6 million; so, its ratio of reserves to deposits is again the required 12% and it has reached its capacity for making loans. Since Bank A's deposits are unchanged, M_1 is also unchanged from its new level of $900.005 billion.

After the transaction, Bank B's deposits have risen by $4.4 million, an increase that raises the amount of M_1 by an additional $4.4 million (or $9.4 million altogether, so far) to $900.0094 billion. Bank B has total reserves of $10.4 million and excess reserves equal to 88% of the $4.4 million in new deposits. Thus, Bank B can lend $3.87 million, keeping $528,000 as required reserves. If loans of $3.87 million are made to borrowers who place those loans as deposits with other banks, the process of creating money, in the form of M_1, will continue.

Where will the process end and what amount of new money, in the form of new demand deposits, will arise from the new reserves? In other words, what is the money multiplier? In this example, the Fed's open market purchase of $5 million of U.S. Treasury securities, along with the banks' incentive to make as many loans as they are permitted to do, has created demand deposits of $9.4 million at the first two banks involved. Still more deposits can be created at other banks. This process will continue as long as other banks use the ever smaller increases in demand deposits to make loans, which become additional demand deposits and excess reserves at still other banks, and so on. Although the process has no set limit in terms of time, there is a maximum number of dollars in new demand deposits that will spring from the new reserves.

This process is a form of a multiplier series that can be expressed in an algebraic formula. If we let ΔTDD be the total demand deposits created, ΔR be the reserves injected into system by the Fed's purchase of Treasury securities, and REQ be the required reserve ratio, then the total of new deposits generated by the expansion of the initial injection of reserves would equal:

$$\Delta TDD = \Delta R + (1 - REQ) \times \Delta R + (1 - REQ)^2 \times \Delta R + (1 - REQ)^3 \\ \times \Delta R + (1 - REQ)^4 \times \Delta R + \ldots \tag{1}$$

Because there are many potential elements in this series, which can get cumbersome, it is best to use this simple version of it:

$$\Delta TDD = \Delta R / REQ \tag{2}$$

In the example, REQ equals 12% and ΔR equals $5 million. Hence, new total demand deposits (if banks lend as much as they can and keep no excess reserves) amount to $5 million/0.12, or $41.67 million. The money multiplier is, therefore, 8.33. As a result, total M_1 will reach $900.04167 billion when the process is completed, which equals the original $900 billion plus $41.67 million in new deposits. Equation (2) clearly shows that the eventual amount of the new demand deposits is negatively related to the required reserve ratio: As REQ falls, the change in TDD rises; and as REQ increases, the change in TDD declines. Thus, if everything in the example were the same, but REQ were 10% instead of 12%, the new demand deposits would reach $50 million.

Obviously, the process of reducing the money supply works in the opposite way. That is, if the Fed wants to drain reserves from the system and reduce the banks' lending ability, it sells securities. The reduction in reserves, as the public trades deposits for marketable securities, allows banks to make fewer new loans or to renew fewer old ones.

The Impact of Interest Rates on the Money Supply

A later chapter describes how changes in the money supply affect interest rates. We note here only that interest rates actually influence the change in the money supply. This point emerges from an evaluation of two key assumptions made above.[4] First, banks are assumed to want to make all the loans they can. If, however, banks were to keep some excess reserves, they would make fewer new loans and generate fewer deposits at other banks, which would affect the amount of M_1 that the Fed's purchase of securities would generate.

One of the important factors in a bank's decisions about excess reserves is the level of market interest rates. High rates make excess reserves costly because they represent loans not made and interest not earned. If rates are low, banks may keep some excess reserves. Hence, the level of interest rates positively influences the amount of M_1 that any increase in reserves will create. Moreover, interest rates can also positively (but probably only slightly) affect the amount of reserves in the system: High market rates may prompt banks to borrow at the discount window in order to make loans, and these borrowed funds are part of reserves.

By the second assumption, borrowers retain none of their loans in cash, but rather deposit all cash flows—proceeds from sold securities, loans, and so on—into checking accounts. In contrast, if borrowers took some of their borrowings in cash, banks would receive fewer deposits and would have fewer reserves from which to make new loans. Accordingly, the public's demand for cash as a portion of its liquid wealth has an impact on the amount of M_1 that arises from the Fed's injection of new reserves.

The level of market rates shapes decisions about cash holdings. Many deposit accounts pay interest, so holding cash imposes an opportunity cost. The higher the rate, the greater the cost, and the more money investors will shuttle into deposits. But the rate on deposits is not the only relevant interest rate. The desired amount of deposits, from which transactions can be easily made, also reflects the rates of return from other assets. As those returns rise, investors would hold more in deposit accounts. For these reasons, the level of interest rates positively affects the size of the money multiplier and, hence, the amount of M_1 that any increase in reserves will produce.

An example will illustrate this point about the impact of rates on the money multiplier and the change in the money supply arising from an infusion of reserves by the Fed. The money multiplier from the previous example was 8.33 or (1/REQ), where REQ was 0.12. Let us now assume that the behavior of banks and depositors responds to interest rates. First, we will assume that the rate of return on bank loans is such that banks do not make all the loans they can but rather want to hold 1% of their deposits (TDD) in excess reserves (ER), with the result that the ratio (ER/TDD) equals 0.01.

---

[4] Lucas Papademos and Franco Modigliani, "The Supply of Money and the Control of Nominal Income," chapter 10 in Benjamin M. Friedman and Frank H. Hahn (eds.), *Handbook of Monetary Economics* (Amsterdam: North-Holland, Elsevier, 1990), pp. 428–430.

Second, let us suppose that the interest rate is at the level where the public will hold only 75% in checkable deposits (rather than 100% as before) and 25% in cash or currency. This means that the ratio (C/TDD) is 0.33. With these assumptions, the formula for the multiplier would now be this:

$$\frac{1 \ + \ (C \ / \ TDD)}{REQ \ + \ (ER \ / \ TDD) \ + \ (C \ / \ TDD)}$$

Plugging in the actual values, we have a much lower multiplier, which is this:

$$\frac{1.33}{0.12 + (0.1) + 0.33} = 2.89$$

Remember, this multiplier is lower because households and banks do not deposit or lend, respectively, all that they can, and these drains from the money creation process reduce the multiplier effect of any increase in reserves.

The Money Supply Process in an Open Economy

Our discussion so far describes central bank activity in what economists call a *closed economy*. A closed economy is one in which foreign transactors—of either goods or financial assets—play a negligible role. In the modern era, almost every country has an **open economy**, where foreign firms and investors account for a large and increasing share of economic activity. This is especially true of the world's largest economy, that of the United States. Understanding of the money supply process, therefore, must include the influence of the foreign sector.

Monetarily, the crucial fact of significant foreign participation in the U.S. economy is that foreign central banks, firms, and individuals hold a substantial number of U.S. dollars. They do so for transactional reasons—buying and selling goods and services in the United States—and for investment purposes—treating the dollar as a financial asset. What makes the foreign holdings of dollars important is that the dollar's exchange rate with currencies of most developed countries floats according to demand and supply in the market. (As we explain in Chapter 6, most central banks, including the Fed, try to keep exchange rates within politically acceptable ranges.)

Shifts in the dollar's exchange rates, obviously, affect the prices of domestic and imported goods, the revenues of U.S. companies, and the wealth of all investors in the country. As a result, the Fed accepts the responsibility to maintain some stability in the exchange rates. A major way to discharge this duty is to *intervene in the foreign exchange markets*. (See Chapter 31 for more detail on foreign currency markets.) The Fed intervenes by buying and selling foreign currencies for its own account. (Most central banks of large economies own, or stand ready to own, a large amount of each of the world's major currencies, which are considered **international reserves**.)

If the Fed thinks the dollar's value is too high and a foreign currency's is too low, it can purchase some of the foreign currency with its own supply of dollars. A purchase involves increasing the outstanding number of dollars and thereby the monetary base. If the Fed thinks the dollar has too low a value relative to some other currency, it might sell some of its holdings of that currency for dollars. Thus, selling foreign currency entails a reduction in the monetary base. Intervention in the currency market is often a response to a particular international event. Moreover, the intervention usually involves a transaction with other central banks, which consists of an immediate exchange of currencies and an agreement for a future offsetting exchange. Thus, this kind of action allows the Fed to know the terms on which the currency deal will terminate and the time when it will terminate.

Our discussion of the elements of monetary policy in Chapter 6 should make it clear that the dollar's exchange rates with important foreign currencies function as a major goal of monetary policy. That is, in forging and implementing policy; the Fed considers the effect of a change in the money supply on the relative value of the dollar in the foreign exchange market.

Dramatic evidence of the growing importance of international policy coordination on monetary matters occurred in two meetings of central bankers of the large industrial nations in the mid-1980s. In 1985, central bank chairmen and directors of the **G-5 countries** (the United States, Great Britain, France, Germany, and Japan) met at the Plaza Hotel in New York. They agreed to coordinate policies in order to bring down the value of the U.S. dollar and to stabilize international exchange rates and trade. In 1987, at the Louvre Museum in Paris, central bankers from the G-5 and Canada agreed to work together to keep exchange rates at their current levels. These efforts at international cooperation on monetary and exchange issues are generally seen as successful.[5]

Key Points That You Should Understand Before Proceeding

1. The Federal Reserve System is the central bank of the United States and responsible for the conduct of monetary policy.
2. The instruments of monetary policy, including reserve requirements, open market operations and repurchase agreements, and the discount rate.
3. The different kinds of money, such as the numeraire, the store of value, and the medium of exchange.
4. The various monetary aggregates and what they are supposed to convey to policymakers.
5. The nature of the money multiplier and how it links reserves in the banking system to monetary aggregates.
6. That interest rates affect the rate at which the money supply changes in response to actions by the Fed.
7. That the openness of an economy to participation by foreign firms, central banks, and individuals affects monetary management.

INTERNATIONAL CENTRAL BANKS

We now turn our attention to the monetary and banking systems of three other significant economies in the world: EMU, the United Kingdom, and Japan.

European Central Bank

The European Central Bank (ECB) replaced the central banks of the 11 participating countries in the European Economic and Monetary Union (EMU) on January 4, 1999. Thus, the ECB replaced the venerable German Bundesbank (the "Buba"), the Bank of France, the Bank of Italy, and so on.

---

[5] "What Should Central Banks Do," Frederic S. Mishkin, *Federal Reserve Bank of St. Louis Review,* November/December 2000, 82, 6, pp. 1–13.

The structure of the ECB is highly decentralized with 17 members making up the ECB's governing council. This council is composed of 11 national central bankers and 6 executive board members. The early presidents of the ECB were selected on a revolving basis beginning with Hans Tietmeyer (the influential German Bundesbanker), followed by Wim Duisenberg from Holland. Banque France Governor Jean-Claude Trichet is scheduled to replace Duisenberg in 2002. He is to be followed by Bank of Italy Governor Antonio Fazio.

The early experience of the ECB shows that it is philosophically in sync with the old Bundesbank but is structurally a blend of the Buba and the U.S. Fed.

The major early issue of the ECB has been the weakness of the Euro, as addressed in Chapter 31. Consider the major aspects of the ECB. The first of these issues is "transparency," that is, the opening up of the ECB's policy deliberations to the public, the press, and national politicians. The ECB provides monthly reports and press conferences. In addition, it has attempted to telegraph its views and actions. However, the ECB has rejected requests to publish minutes of its meetings or voting patterns. In general, the ECB has been somewhat more transparent than the secretive Bundesbank but less transparent than the U.S. Fed or the Bank of England.

The ECB's primary indicator for monetary policy has been inflation, specifically the CPI. It also appears that it pays more attention to overall Euroland CPI rather than individual country inflation. The ECB appears to be operating as if 2% is the inflation ceiling, but the unofficial and unstated target lies between 1% and 1.5%. Consistent with the ECB's focus on inflation, the money supply, as measured by M_3, has taken a backseat as the ECB's primary indicator.

The ECB, while itself under pressure to conduct appropriate monetary policy, has also lectured the national governments to conduct structural reforms, specifically deregulation, and tax, pension, and labor market reforms. Some analysts have observed that getting the 17 members of the ECB to agree on monetary policy is an institutional weakness of the ECB.

Undoubtedly the major issue of the ECB during its first two years of existence was the weakness of the Euro, as mentioned previously.

Bank of England

The Bank of England is the central bank of the United Kingdom. Sometimes known as the "Old Lady of Threadneedle Street," it is located in the financial center of the city of London. Although it has many roles, as with most central banks, its two primary roles are setting and executing monetary policy and maintaining the stability of the financial system, both domestic and international.

The role and responsibility of the Bank of England changed considerably during the late 1990s. On May 6, 1997, the chancellor of the Exchanger, Gordon Brown, announced that the Bank of England was to be given operational responsibility for setting interest rates. The Bank of England Act 1998 executed this change. The common interpretation of this change was that the Bank of England was freed from the control of the Exchequer. Previously, the Exchequer could control Bank of England policies.

Another change was also made at this time. Prior to April 1, 1998, the Bank of England undertook the role of managing the government's debt. From this time onward, the Debt Management Office (DMO), an executive agency of the Treasury, undertook this function.

The Bank's monetary policy objective is to deliver price stability, as discussed below, and without prejudice to that objective, to support the government's economic policy, including its objectives of growth and employment. The government's inflation target is confirmed in each budget statement. Inflation is measured by the retail price index (RPI), which includes mortgage interest rates.

The Bank's Monetary Policy Committee (MPC) sets interest rates to meet the government's inflation target. The MPC meets monthly and decisions are made by a vote of the committee on a "one-person, one-vote" basis, with the governor having the casting vote if there is no majority. The Treasury has the right to be represented in a nonvoting capacity. Decisions on interest rates are announced immediately. The minutes of the meeting, including a record of the vote, are normally published on the Wednesday of the second week after the meeting takes place.

With respect to the Bank of England's independence, the 1997/1998 legislation provides that if, in extreme circumstances, the national interest demands it, the government will have the power to give instructions to the Bank on interest rates for a limited period.

The Bank has 12 agencies across the United Kingdom whose primary role is to assess the economy as seen in the part of the country they cover. The agencies are an important link between business and the Bank. A summary of the information gathered by the agencies is published in a quarterly review entitled *Bank of England Agents' Summary of Business Conditions.* In addition, the Bank's annual report describes the full range of their work.

Bank of Japan

Since World War II, Japan's central bank, the Bank of Japan (BOJ), was controlled in its policy making by Japan's Ministry of Finance (MOF), in effect its Treasury. However, during 1998 Japan's Diet passed a Bank of Japan Law, which became effective on April 1, 1998. This revision was built on the two principles of independence and transparency and was a notable step in reforming the Bank's practices and the financial system of Japan.

The new Bank of Japan Law stated that the objective of monetary policy is "to contribute to the sound development of the national economy through the pursuit of price stability." Japan, like other countries, is still trying to define price stability in terms of a price index (Consumer Price Index, Wholesale Price Index, and GDP deflator) and the desired range. BOJ monetary instruments are, as for other countries, the **official discount rate**, open market operations, and reserve requirements.

The new Bank of Japan Law also made several changes to strengthen the functions of the Policy Board, the BOJ's highest decision-making body. First, the composition of the Policy Board was altered significantly. The previous Policy Board consisted of seven members: the governor of the BOJ; four appointed members; and two government members without voting rights, representing the MOF and the Economic Planning Agency (EPAC). The new Policy Board consists of nine members: the governor, two deputy governors of the BOJ, and six deliberative members.

The main features of the changes are as follows. First, there are no government members on the board. Second, the six deliberative members of the new board can be selected without any restriction on the fields they represent, as long as they are experts. Third, in order to ensure interactive linkage between monetary policy decision making and the BOJ's business operations, the number of members from the management of the Bank was increased from one to three. A balance is struck, however, by appointing six deliberative members so that the three BOJ members are not a majority.

The Policy Board meets once a month. By comparison, the U.S. Federal Open Market Committee meets eight times a year, the Monetary Policy Committee meets once a month, and the ECB meets twice a month as indicated in Table 5-20.

A monthly economic report is provided before each of these meetings. This report, known as the Tankan (Short Term Economic Survey of Enterprises in Japan) is based on a regular business survey. To achieve the goal of transparency of monetary policy specified in the new BOJ law, summaries of discussions and transcripts of regular Policy Board meetings are proposed to be disclosed. The timing of the disclosure is still being discussed.

With respect to the independence of the BOJ from the government, the new system is designed to ensure the autonomy of the central bank in the management of monetary policy while also ensuring adequate communication between the BOJ and the government. To achieve these objectives, the new law permits government representatives to attend Policy Board meetings on monetary control matters and to express their views when necessary. It also grants government representatives the right to make policy proposals regarding monetary control matters, including requests to postpone the board's vote on policies.

The BOJ exercised its independence when on August 11, 2000, it raised its official discount rate to 0.25% despite continuing Japanese economic weakness. This increase was commonly interpreted as the BOJ (and particularly the BOJ Governor Hayami) flexing its muscles of independence rather than necessary monetary policy. Prior to this increase, the BOJ had maintained a zero interest rate policy since February 1999. Such a policy was unprecedented both in and out of Japan and was held to counter the possibility of mounting deflationary pressure.

The BOJ and the Japanese government continue to explore the balance between Bank independence and responsiveness, as do other countries.

SUMMARY

The Federal Reserve System is the U.S. central bank. Its tools of monetary policy include required reserves, open market operations and repurchases, and discount loans to banks. The Fed supplies reserves to the banking system, which participates, along with investors, in generating the money supply. The chief means of supplying reserves is open market operations: The Fed's purchase of government securities provides reserves, and the Fed's sale of securities reduces reserves. The money supply is composed of various types of money as well as demand and time deposits, which can be grouped into monetary aggregates. The fundamental aggregate is the monetary base, composed of currency plus total reserves in the banking system. M_1 equals currency plus all checkable deposits. Other aggregates include various time deposits.

The money multiplier is the process by which changes in bank reserves generate larger changes in the money supply. The banks use the added reserves to buy assets or to make loans; the seller or borrower redeposits these proceeds, which then support additional loans, and so on. The value of the multiplier depends on the required reserve ratio, the public's demand for cash, the banks' willingness to make loans, and the level of interest rates.

The growing international integration of economies requires that the Fed, along with other central banks, consider the impact of its monetary operations on foreign currency exchange rates. Thus, monetary policy must be considered from the standpoint of open economies, not the closed ones of years past.

The central banks of mainland Europe, the United Kingdom, and Japan have all made significant changes during the late 1990's. The ECB was formed and the Bank of England and Bank of Japan experienced significant policy changes. With respect to the key characteristics of independence and transparency, they all became more like the U.S. Fed.

A summary of the central bank meeting schedules and key interest rates is provided in Table 5-2.

Table 5-2   Summary of Central Banks

COUNTRY	CENTRAL BANK	FREQUENCY OF MEETINGS	KEY RATE
United States	Federal Reserve (Fed)	Eight times per year[1]	Fed Funds Rate Discount Rate (Less Used)
United Kingdom	Bank of England (BOE)	Monthly[2]	Repo Rate
European Ecomomic and Monetary Union	European Central Bank (ECB)	Approximately every two weeks[3]	Marginal Lending Facility (Ceiling Rate) Main Refinancing Operations Minimum Bid Rate Deposit Facility (Floor Rate)
Japan	Bank of Japan (BOJ)	Periodic – See below[4]	Overnight Call Rate[5] (Benchmark Rate) Official Discount Rate (ODR) (Less Used)

[1] **Fed 2001 Schedule**
January 30– 31
March 20
May 15
June 26– 27
August 21
October 2
November 6
December 11

[2] **BOE 2001 Schedule**
January 10, 11	*July 4, 5*
February 7, 8	*August 1, 2*
March 7, 8	*September 5, 6*
April 4, 5	*October 3, 4*
May 9, 10	*November 7, 8*
June 5, 6	*December 4, 5*

[3] **ECB 2001 H1 Schedule**
January 4	*April 11*
January 18	*April 26*
February 1	*May 10*
February 15	*May 23*
March 1	*June 7*
March 15	*June 21*
March 29	

[4] **BOJ 2001 H1 Schedule**
January 19	*April 25*
February 9	*May 18*
February 28	*June 15*
March 19	*June 28*
April 13	

[5] Effective March, 2001, the BOJ departed from setting the (uncollateralized) overnight call rate when it went to a "Zero Interest Rate Policy" whereby the call rate would remain close to zero. The BOJ subseqently used as a guideline the outstanding amount of current account balances at the BOJ (the monetary base consists of the current account balances at the BOJ plus the cash in circulation—the cash in circulation accounts for 90% of the monetary base but is much more difficult for the BOJ to control). This policy is called quantitative monetary regime. In effect, the BOJ changes a reserve target (essentially the supply of money) instead of interest rates to guide monetary policy.

KEY TERMS

QUESTIONS

1. Identify each participant and its role in the process by which the money supply changes and monetary policy is implemented.
2. Describe the structure of the board of governors of the Federal Reserve System.
3. a. Explain what is meant by the statement "the United States has a fractional reserve banking system."
   b. How are these items related: total reserves, required reserves, and excess reserves?
4. What is the required reserve ratio, and how has the 1980 Depository Institutions Deregulation and Monetary Control Act constrained the Fed's control over the ratio?
5. In what two forms can a bank hold its required reserves?
6. a. What is an open market purchase by the Fed?
   b. Which unit of the Fed decides on open market policy, and what unit implements that policy?
   c. What is the immediate consequence of an open market purchase?
7. Distinguish between an open market sale and a matched sale (which is the same as a matched sale-purchase transaction or a reverse repurchase agreement).
8. What is the discount rate, and to what type of action by a bank does it apply?
9. Define the monetary base and M_2.
10. Describe the basic features of the money multiplier.
11. Suppose the Fed were to inject $100 million of reserves into the banking system by an open market purchase of Treasury bills. If the required reserve ratio were 10%, what is the maximum increase in M_1 that the new reserves would generate? Assume that banks make all the loans their reserves allow, that firms and individuals keep all their liquid assets in depository accounts, and no money is in the form of currency.
12. Assume the situation from question 11, except now assume that banks hold a ratio of 0.5% of excess reserves to deposits and the public keeps 20% of its liquid assets in the form of cash. Under these conditions, what is the money multiplier? Explain why this value of the multiplier is so much lower than the multiplier from question 11.
13. Briefly describe the governing structure of the ECB and its perceived weakness, if any.
14. Does the ECB target M_3 or CPI?
15. a. Identify some key changes in the role and responsibility of the Bank of England in the late 1990s.
   b. What caused these changes?
16. How does the Bank of England obtain the information about business conditions in the United Kingdom that are relevant to its policy making?
17. Discuss the structure of the Bank of Japan's highest decision-making body, the Policy Board.
18. The following quotation regarding Japan is from the June 22, 2000 issue of *The Economist*:

   Lined up against a rate rise are an impressive range of opponents. These include not only the Liberal Democratic Party, but also big business and the finance ministry which wants monetary policy kept loose so that it has more freedom to begin fixing the government's finances.

   Does the government decide monetary policy in Japan?
19. a. Discuss the recent trends in the ECB, the Bank of England, and the Bank of Japan relative to the U.S. Fed.
   b. What are the major differences between these central banks and the Fed?

C h a p t e r   6

Monetary Policy

Learning Objectives

After reading this chapter, you will understand

- the goals of monetary policy, including price level stability, economic growth, stable interest rates, and stable foreign exchange rates.
- that the operating targets of Fed policy are those monetary and financial variables that are affected by its tools in a predictable way.
- that intermediate targets are economic variables that the Fed can affect indirectly through its work with operating targets.
- that the federal funds rate and bank reserves have often been operating targets of monetary policy.
- that the broad monetary aggregates have sometimes served as intermediate targets, as have certain interest rates.
- the goals and targets of monetary policy in the European Community, Japan, and the United Kingdom.

The previous chapter discussed various components of the monetary and banking structure of the United States. In that chapter, we explained how the Fed, in interaction with banks and other units of the economy, creates money and credit. We also explained the tools that the Fed can use to manage the rate of growth in the money supply.

This chapter examines the **goals of monetary policy**; that is, the conditions in the economy that the Fed seeks to bring about. Although the Fed cannot directly cause these conditions to exist, it can follow policies to target variables that it can influence with its tools. As in the last chapter, we also discuss monetary matters in some other major economies of the world.

MONETARY POLICY IN THE UNITED STATES

Goals of Monetary Policy

The Fed, through such tools as open market operations, which change the reserves in the banking system, can prompt the banking system and depositors to implement desired changes in the money supply and in its rates of growth. The Fed manages the money supply in order to achieve certain economic goals. In this section, we identify some of the more commonly cited goals of Fed policy.[1]

---

[1] Ben Bernanke and Frederic Mishkin, "Guideposts and Signals in the Conduct of Monetary Policy: Lessons from Six Industrialized Countries," presented at the Seventh Annual Conference on Macroeconomics, March 1992.

Stability in the price level is a major goal of the Fed. Price stability gained new respect in the last 20 years as first inflation, then deflation, ravaged entire economies or major sectors such as farm land and commercial real estate. The standard way of measuring inflation is the change in a major price index. Table 6-1 shows the yearly percentage change in the Consumer Price Index between 1980 and 1999, and reveals that the high inflation marking the beginning of the 1980s had largely dissipated by the end of that decade. From this experience, policymakers and economists came to appreciate once more that unstable price levels retard economic growth, provoke volatility in interest rates, stimulate consumption, deter savings, and cause capricious redistribution of income and wealth with attendant social disturbances.

Inflation in advanced economies, however, is seldom (if ever) the result of excessive demand due to monetary or fiscal policy. Rather, a more important source of inflation is an economic shock in the supply of a crucial material, such as the oil shocks of the 1970s, which affected almost all countries. Evidence that the inflation at the end of the 1970s was not related to excessive demand for goods and services is that it occurred with high unemployment and gave the world a period of **stagflation**, which is a condition of both inflation and recession.

It is important to note that, when confronted with a supply shock, a central bank such as the Fed has two choices. First, the banking authorities can refuse to accommodate the higher price levels that follow the shock by matching them with an increase in the money supply. The results of nonaccommodation will initially tend to be higher interest rates and a decline in economic activity. For this reason, central banks and political authorities frequently have opted for the second choice, which is a policy of accommodation and increased growth in the supply of money. Unfortunately, this kind of policy permits the inflation to continue unchecked or possibly to accelerate.

High employment (or low unemployment) of the civilian labor force represents a second major goal for the Fed. While politicians often speak of the U.S. government's commitment to promoting "full employment," most people understand that an unemployment rate of zero is not possible. The reason is that **frictional unemployment**—the temporary unemployment of those changing jobs or seeking new or better ones—is both unavoidable and helpful to an economy. It is unavoidable because people do change jobs, and are likely to do so more readily as employment levels rise, and

Table 6-1   Annual Percentage Changes in the Consumer Price Index from 1980–1999

YEAR	RATE	YEAR	RATE
1980	12.5%	1990	6.1%
1981	8.9	1991	3.1
1982	3.8	1992	2.9
1983	3.8	1993	2.7
1984	3.9	1994	2.7
1985	3.8	1995	2.5
1986	1.1	1996	3.3
1987	4.4	1997	1.7
1988	4.4	1998	1.6
1989	4.6	1999	2.7
		2000	3.4

Note: Annual Changes are from December to December.
SOURCE: *Economic Report of the President 2001.*

because some workers leave and enter the labor market constantly. Frictional unemployment is helpful because it allows a constant reallocation of labor and leads to increased efficiency in the workforce.

Given that zero unemployment is not a feasible aim, the appropriate goal of the Fed and other governmental policymakers is actually a high level of employment. A practical problem, however, is that economists and policymakers cannot agree on a suitable definition or specification of high employment. It does not help to specify a high level of employment as one that approaches 100% less the level of frictional unemployment, because there is also little agreement on the true rate of frictional unemployment.

For practical purposes, many observes consider that a civilian unemployment rate between 4% and 6% indicates an economy operating at or near a level of high employment. This figure allows for frictional unemployment and the effects of the rapid expansion in the workforce over the last several decades. That expansion occurred because of the entry into the workforce of many women, younger workers, and immigrants into the United States.

Table 6-2 provides yearly information on the U.S. level of unemployment in the last 20 years and shows that relatively high employment occurred in the second half of the 1980s and the late-1990s.

It is important to realize that high employment is one of the Fed's goals because, in certain circumstances, the Fed's policy can indirectly influence the level of employment. When the economy is operating sluggishly or below capacity, increases in the money supply can bring about economic expansion and employment because those increases can reduce interest rates, stimulate investment, encourage consumption, and lead to the creation of new jobs. A policy of expansion of the money supply is frequently described as an "easy money policy" because the Fed is said to ease the way for banks to acquire reserves and to extend loans. When the economy's output is close to capacity (given its stock of productive assets and population), however, easy money policies can be disadvantageous because they may kindle inflation and raise interest rates. Policymakers must often wrestle with the tough question of whether easing monetary policy will create more economic growth or simply ignite inflation.

Economic growth, the third goal of the Fed, is the increase in an economy's output of goods and services. Clearly, this goal is closely related to the goal of high employ-

Table 6-2   Annual Rates of Civilian Unemployment in the United States from 1980–1999

YEAR	RATE	YEAR	RATE
1980	7.1%	1990	5.6%
1981	7.6	1991	6.8
1982	9.7	1992	7.5
1983	9.6	1993	6.9
1984	7.5	1994	6.1
1985	7.2	1995	5.6
1986	7.0	1996	5.4
1987	6.2	1997	4.9
1988	5.5	1998	4.5
1989	5.3	1999	4.2
		2000	4.0

SOURCE: *Economic Report of the President 2001.*

ment. As would be expected, there is very little agreement about the exact rate of growth that policymakers should try to achieve. Variously described as "sustainable" or "steady" or "reasonable," the economy's appropriate rate of growth has to be substantial enough to generate high employment in the context of an expanding workforce but low enough to ward off inflation.

Table 6-3 reports the annual growth rate in the gross domestic product (or GDP) over the last 10 years. Note that the rate in one year (1991) was slightly negative. Subsequently, growth exceeded a positive 3% in six years, but it never reached the stunning 7.3% level of 1984, although it was very high during 1998-1999. Interestingly, despite fairly sustained growth in the last decade, inflation has remained rather low. (See Table 6-1.)

Once more, economic growth is a Fed goal because its operations may be able to affect the level of growth. As we note in connection with employment, however, policies expanding the money supply and stimulating growth may be beneficial in some circumstances and detrimental in others, according to the economy's performance relative to its capacity.

The goal of stabilizing interest rates is directly related to the goal of growth and to the Fed's responsibility for the health of the nation's financial and banking system. Table 6-4 reports on yearly averages for the rates on Treasury bills (a short-term security) and on Treasury bonds (a long-term asset). The table reveals that interest rate volatility over the early and mid-1980s was especially pronounced. This volatility has been troublesome to financial institutions such as commercial banks and thrift institutions.

Note that the goal is to stabilize rates, not to prevent changes in rates. Obviously, interest rates move up and down with changes in economic conditions. Those movements may provide signals of important economic developments, and it would be making a mistake for the Fed to try to prevent such changes in rates. However, the Fed may help economic conditions by trying to moderate the impact of large moves in rates. Some increases in rates may reflect temporary or reversible developments, and the Fed can appropriately respond to these changes in a way that eliminates or greatly reduces such increases.

Table 6-3 Annual Rates of Growth in U.S. Gross Domestic Product from 1980–1999

YEAR	RATE	YEAR	RATE
1980	0.0%	1990	1.8%
1981	2.5	1991	−0.5
1982	−1.9	1992	3.0
1983	4.2	1993	2.7
1984	7.3	1994	4.0
1985	3.9	1995	2.7
1986	3.4	1996	3.6
1987	3.5	1997	4.4
1988	4.2	1998	4.4
1989	3.5	1999	4.5
		2000	5.0

Note: Rates are percentage changes in real GDP in 1996 dollars.
SOURCE: *Economic Report of the President 2001.*

Table 6-4   Annual Average Rates of Interest on U.S. Treasury Bills and Bonds from 1980–1999

YEAR	BILLS	BONDS	YEAR	BILLS	BONDS
1980	11.51%	11.27%	1990	7.51%	8.61%
1981	14.03	13.45	1991	5.42	8.14
1982	10.69	12.76	1992	3.45	7.67
1983	8.63	11.18	1993	3.02	6.59
1984	9.58	12.41	1994	4.29	7.37
1985	7.48	10.79	1995	5.51	6.88
1986	5.98	7.78	1996	5.02	6.71
1987	5.82	8.59	1997	5.07	6.61
1988	6.69	8.96	1998	4.81	5.58
1989	8.12	8.45	1999	4.66	5.87
			2000	5.66	5.94

Note: Bills: Rates on new issues. Bonds: Yields on actively traded issues adjusted to constant 30-year maturity by the Department of the Treasury.
SOURCE: *Economic Report of the President 2001.*

Stability in foreign currency exchange rates is the final goal that we will discuss. The foreign exchange market has become much more important in recent years, as the economies of the world have become more integrated, and foreign currency exchange rates have begun to affect ever larger segments of the economy. Because exchange rates are clearly dependent in some ways on the monetary policies of the major countries, the Fed has accepted the goal of stabilizing foreign exchange rates.[2]

Table 6-5 indicates how the U.S. dollar's exchange rates with the German mark (now the Euro) and the Japanese yen have altered over the past 20 years. (The table also reveals that the trend in exchange rates from 1986 to 1995 was in the direction of a cheaper dollar, and the U.S. dollar stabilized and strengthend in the last half of the 1990s.) Clearly, exchange rates have been quite unstable in recent years. In fact, the rates have been unstable since the abrupt abandonment, in the early 1970s, of the fixed exchange rate system, known as the Bretton Woods system, which had been in effect since the end of World War II, or since roughly 1945. Of course, some fluctuations in exchange rates arise for economically sound reasons that monetary policy in one country cannot influence or control. A prime example of such a reason is a pronounced difference in the fiscal policies between two countries. In general, an important explanation of unstable rates among most of the world's major currencies has been the failure of the large industrial economies to coordinate their fiscal and monetary policies.

A chief disadvantage of unstable foreign currency exchange rates is that volatility in the prices of currencies inhibits the international trade that offers a host of benefits to all participating countries. Furthermore, both high and low exchange rates for the dollar are considered detrimental to the U.S. economy. High exchange rates (i.e., a "strong" dollar or one with high value in terms of foreign currencies) reduce demand for U.S.-made products abroad and stimulate the import of foreign goods; the result is a trade imbalance. A "weak" dollar contributes to inflation, as U.S. buyers pay more for the many goods they do import. For these reasons, the Fed's goal of stability in the

[2] Ibid., p. 11.

Table 6-5 Annual Average Rates of Exchange of the U.S. Dollar and the Deutsche Mark and the Japanese Yen from 1980–1999

YEAR	DM/$	YEN/$
1980	1.82	226.63
1981	2.26	220.63
1982	2.43	249.06
1983	2.55	237.55
1984	2.85	237.46
1985	2.94	238.47
1986	2.17	168.35
1987	1.80	144.60
1988	1.76	128.17
1989	1.88	138.07
1990	1.61	145.00
1991	1.66	134.59
1992	1.56	126.78
1993	1.65	111.08
1994	1.62	102.18
1995	1.43	93.96
1996	1.50	108.78
1997	1.73	121.06
1998	1.76	130.99
1999*	1.84 (0.94)	113.73
2000*	2.12 (1.08)	107.83

Note: Average rates during year, as calculated by the Federal Reserve.
*The Euro/$ rate is shown in parentheses.
SOURCE: Economic Report of the President 2001.

currency market often amounts to keeping the value of the dollar, in terms of the major foreign currencies, within some range that is considered politically acceptable and helpful to international trading, especially exporting.

During the late 1990s, due to the moderately strong U.S. dollar, strong U.S. economic growth and weak or anemic economic growth in much of the rest of the world, the United States experienced a very large trade deficit.

Trade-offs and Conflicts among Policies

This account of the widely accepted goals of monetary policy reveals a profound problem in the conduct of monetary policy. The goals are numerous, but the Fed's capabilities are limited to the simple menu of (1) trying to raise the rate of growth in the money supply by providing more reserves to banks, and (2) trying to reduce the rate of monetary expansion by reducing the reserves in the banking system. As a result, it is often the case that one of the goals may require a monetary policy that is inconsistent with some other goal. In other words, a monetary policy that furthers progress toward one goal may actually make attaining another either difficult or impossible.

For example, an easy money policy of expanding the money supply (that is, stimulating higher growth rates for one or more monetary aggregates) may appear to promote growth and low interest rates, but it may also raise the prospect of inflation, affect the exchange rate disadvantageously, and increase interest rates. Another example concerns the goal of price stability and the Fed's responsibility for the health of financial institutions. Suppose that, at a time of high inflation, many such institutions have invested according to inflationary expectations and have made many loans to firms dealing in real assets. Suppose, too, that the Fed decides it needs to take steps to curb the current inflation. In such a situation, the tight monetary policy that accomplishes this goal—a policy of reducing the rate of growth in the money supply—actually may imperil the institutions because the policy might well weaken the financial health of the firms that borrowed from the financial institutions.

Economists frequently describe this problem in this way: The Fed's policy necessarily represents trade-offs among its various goals, which have different levels of relative importance at different times, depending on the state of the economy. Another way of saying this is that the Fed, like any monetary policymaker, has numerous goals but focuses, at any time, on the goal that is most in danger of not being achieved.

Goals and Types of Targets

A second problem in the implementation of monetary policy is that the Fed has no direct control over the goals that are the final objectives of its policies. The Fed cannot, with any of its monetary tools (open market operations, discount rates, etc.), directly influence such complex economic variables as the prices of goods and services, the unemployment rate, foreign currency exchange rates, and the growth in gross domestic product. We know the Fed can affect the rate of growth in the money supply only by means of its control of reserves in the banking system. As we discussed in the previous chapter, the Fed cannot fully determine changes in the money supply. The growth in the money supply depends to a substantial extent on the preferences, actions, and expectations of numerous banks, borrowers, and consumers.

The Fed seeks to achieve its goals through a form of chain reaction, which has the following chronology and structure. The Fed first employs one or more of its tools to affect what are called **operating targets**, which are monetary and financial variables whose changes tend to bring about changes in **intermediate targets**. Intermediate targets, which may include interest rates or monetary aggregates, are variables that have a reasonably reliable linkage with the variables, such as output or employment, that constitute the Fed's goals or *ultimate objectives*. Thus, the Fed exerts whatever influence it has on the intermediate targets in an indirect way, by means of its control over the operating targets. Thus, the Fed's power over the variables that make up its goals is quite indirect and dependent upon the linkages among the various targets and goals.

Although economists have argued many years about the identity of appropriate operating and intermediate target variables, there is no dispute about the chief characteristics of a suitable operating or intermediate target.[3] The first characteristic is *linkage*. An operating target must have an expected connection with the intermediate target, which itself must eventually affect the economy in a way that is consistent with the Fed's goals. The second characteristic is *observability*: Both operating targets and intermediate targets must be readily and regularly observable economic variables, so that the Fed can monitor its success in influencing their levels or rates of change. The third and final characteristic is *responsiveness*: To function as an operating target, a variable must respond quickly and in an expected way to the Fed's use of one or more of its tools; and an appropriate intermediate target is one that reacts, in an anticipated way and a meaningfully short time, to changes in the operating target.

---

[3] A formal treatment of the requirements for targets is available in Benjamin M. Friedman, "Targets and Instruments of Monetary Policy," chapter 22 in Benjamin M. Friedman and Frank H. Hahn, *Handbook of Monetary Economics* (Amsterdam: North-Holland, 1990).

Choosing the Operating Target

In some countries, a key foreign currency exchange rate may well function as an operating target. While the Fed has become more conscious of foreign exchange developments in the last 10 years or so, it has not adopted the dollar's exchange rate with any currency or group of currencies as an operating target. Rather, the Fed's monetary policy has directly targeted either short-term interest rates or some measure of bank reserves.

An important point about the operating target is that the Fed must choose either a short-term rate or the level of some reserves and cannot choose to target both kinds of variables.[4] To understand why the Fed must make a choice, we need to review what the Fed's tools allow it to do. Those tools—whether the secondary ones of discount loans and management of reserve requirements, or the primary tool of open market operations—enable the Fed to change only the level of reserves in the banking system. Obviously, a change in reserves also changes short-term rates because they are determined in the interbank market for excess reserves. Under most circumstances, the change in reserves is negatively related to the change in interest rates: As the Fed supplies more reserves and banks gain more ability to make more loans and buy other assets, the short-term rates fall; as the Fed withdraws reserves and reduces the banks' lending capacity, the short-term rates rise.

Because of this inverse relationship, it might seem possible for the Fed to view each of these variables as a target and to set each of them at the same time. But, in fact, that is impossible. The reason is that the Fed cannot know or predict the *public's* **demand for money,** which is the aggregate demand for holding some of its wealth in the form of liquid balances, such as bank deposits. The public's desire to hold money depends on many factors, especially preferences and anticipations about future income and price inflation, among other things, and unexpected changes in those factors may well shift the public's desired holdings in significant ways. Therefore, the Fed cannot be certain how much impact any change in reserves will have on short-term rates. Without knowledge of what the rate will be for a given change in reserves, the Fed cannot simultaneously determine both the rate and the level of reserves.

In choosing its operating target, then, the Fed makes the decision to let the other variable fluctuate in response to changes in the public's demand for money. When an interest rate is the target, the Fed must let the growth in reserves vary as it strives to keep that interest rate at a certain level or to smooth its transition to a new (higher or lower) level. When some aggregate of reserves is the target, the Fed is forced to allow interest rates to change substantially, so that it can try to bring the level of reserves to that dictated by the Fed's policy. Of course, the Fed can change its target from time to time, in order to rein in the variable that has fluctuated while the Fed focused on the other. But, however often the Fed might change targets, it remains a fact that, at any one time, the Fed cannot target both rates and reserves.

Choosing the Intermediate Target

The best known of the intermediate targets is the money supply, measured by one of the more inclusive monetary aggregates that we described in the previous chapter. In the 1970s, many countries began to target the growth rates of one or more aggregates. The policy, at least as publicly stated, was to supply reserves at a pace that would lead to a selected rate of growth in the aggregates. The idea behind this policy was that the

---

[4] William Poole, "Optimal Choice of Monetary Policy Instrument in a Simple Stochastic Macro Model," *Quarterly Journal of Economics* (1970), pp. 197–216.

goals of central bank activity—growth, stable prices, and so on—would be realized if the money supply were to grow at a known and steady rate.

Over time, other intermediate targets have been specified, and they include foreign exchange rates, the level of national output (such as the gross national product), and the level of actual or expected inflation.[5] Furthermore, the array of interest rates—including rates available to consumers and investors—may also function as a target variable. We have said that a prime characteristic of a suitable intermediate target is that it is readily observable. Obviously, some of these candidates above do not fit that rule: Information on the GNP, for example, is available only on a quarterly basis, while measures of actual or expected inflation may be subject to considerable dispute.[6]

Interestingly, in recent years, many central banks have adopted inflation, despite certain problems in measurement, as a key intermediate variable. The reason is that the monetary aggregates have not had the kind of reliable and persistent relationship either with target variables or with goals that policymakers require. In most European countries, policymakers follow price indexes for sensitive commodities and make decisions about short-term rates and bank reserves on the basis of actual and expected inflation. In the United States, it is commonly said that Fed Chairman Alan Greenspan carefully monitors the price of gold, among other commodities. Thus, the purchasing power of the domestic currency and the foreign exchange rate of the currency have become far more typical intermediate targets than monetary aggregates.

A Review of Recent Federal Reserve Policy

Targeting the Fed Funds Rate, 1970 to 1979.

During most of the 1970s, the Fed viewed the federal funds rate either largely or exclusively as its operating target. Recall that *fed funds* refers to the excess reserves that commercial banks and other depository institutions keep in the form of deposits in the Federal Reserve System and lend among themselves for short periods of time, especially overnight. The rate on these interbank loans is the fed funds rate, and it is a good indicator of the banking system's supply of loanable funds. When banks have a lot of funds and lending capacity, the rate is low; the rate is high when the banking system has drawn its collective reserves close to the required level. It should be noted that the fed funds rate meets the first requirement listed above for an operating target: The rate is readily observable and continuously available because the market for fed funds is large and active.

The Fed targets the fed funds rate by its open market operations. As noted above, a requirement of a good operating target is that the Fed can exert substantial control over its level and changes. If the rate were to rise above the level that the Fed thought conducive to economic growth and high employment, the Fed would engage in open market purchases and inject reserves into the banking system. Through the workings of supply and demand, an increase in the reserves of the banking system would normally cause a fall in the fed funds rate, as many banks would have to borrow less to meet their reserve requirements. If the fed funds rate was too low, the Fed would sell securities and bring about a reduction in the growth of the banking system's total supply of reserves. This action would prompt a rise in the fed funds rate. Furthermore, the Fed has also used open market operations in its effort to smooth the transition of the fed funds rate from one level to another, as the rate varies with conditions in the economy.

The rationale for targeting the fed funds rate lies in the belief that changes in the rate can, over some time, affect the level of economic activity. (Recall, that linkage

---

[5] Bernanke and Mishkin, "Guideposts and Signals in the Conduct of Monetary Policy," p. 41.
[6] Friedman, "Targets and Instruments of Monetary Policy," p. 1203.

is also a prime requirement of a suitable operating target.) That is, if consumers, investors, and bankers believe that a given change in the fed funds rate is permanent and reflects a shift in Federal Reserve policy, such a change in rates can reverberate through the monetary and banking system, and cause a consequent change in the level of economic activity. Generally speaking, this version of monetary policy is associated with **Keynesian** economic theory, and it gives the Fed a great deal of discretion in the conduct of monetary policy.

In the Keynesian view, the Fed's decision to reduce the fed funds rate, by increasing the banking system's excess reserves, should have the following consequences. Banks, as the first economic units to be affected, will have more reserves and lower returns from lending in the fed funds market. As a result, the banks will reduce the cost of loans to businesses and consumers and the return (if any) available to investors on short-term deposits. Investors will now be confronted with lower yields on short-term assets, such as Treasury bills and certificates of deposit. Because of these lower yields, investors will reallocate their holdings from short-term to long-term securities, driving their prices up and raising the wealth of investors in financial securities. Declines in the general cost of funding will encourage firms to expand and increase their output. Consumers, seeing lower costs of borrowing, will increase their demand for more expensive purchases.

Overall, according to this view of the economy, a decline in the fed funds rate should lead to a higher level of output and employment in the economy. Obviously, if the Fed chooses to raise the fed funds rate and uses open market sales to reduce the system's excess reserves, the consequent rise in short-term interest rates will restrain the growth in economic activity. In an important sense, then, the array of short-term rates functions as the intermediate target (or one of the intermediate targets) in this view of monetary policy.

A cautionary note is in order here. Economists in the Keynesian tradition believe that declines in targeted rates can cause the sequence of events just described only if the economy is operating at less than full capacity and employment. If the economy is operating at full employment, these actions by the Fed will generally lead only to an increase in prices (that is, inflation) and interest rates.

A Monetarist Experiment, 1979 to 1982

One historic consequence of the policy of supplying reserves according to movements in the fed funds rate was that the Fed did not concern itself with the behavior of the level of reserves, or of the monetary base and other monetary aggregates, which expanded in an erratic way. On frequent occasions in this period of the 1970s, interest rates were on a rising path, in part because of the oil-price shock and the consequent inflation. The Fed responded to the rising rates by increasing reserves, as it tried to keep the rates from getting to what it considered a too high level. The expansion in the monetary aggregates was particularly rapid from 1975 to 1978, and that expansion (along with the oil shocks) led to serious inflation and a decline in the dollar's value. In 1979, for example, the rate of inflation was in double digits (i.e., above 10%), and the dollar's value, in terms of the Deutsche mark, fell almost 30% between 1975 and 1979.

In October 1979, as a response to inflation, then Chairman of the Fed Paul Volcker announced a new policy. The Fed would henceforth begin to target the banking system's **nonborrowed reserves**, which equal total reserves less those reserves created when banks borrow from the Fed through its discount window. The level of nonborrowed reserves meets the requirements for a good operating target to largely the same extent as the fed funds rate. Moreover, the Fed stated that its purpose in targeting nonborrowed reserves was to control the rate of growth in the money supply, as measured by the monetary aggregates.

This change in policy was widely viewed as a victory for the theory of **monetarism**, which favors a steady, predictable growth in reserves and the monetary base. Monetarists claim that policy that is based on known rules of growth in key monetary aggregates sustains stability in the price level, and that such stability fosters long-run economic growth and employment. Furthermore, monetarists had long criticized the **discretionary** policy whereby the Fed would change the rate of growth in reserves or aggregates in order to achieve short-run adjustments in interest rates or levels of economic activity. Monetarists believe that the "long and variable lags" between the start of a policy and its final impact on the economy make such adjustments unwise and potentially dangerous. This dispute on how best to conduct monetary policy is known as the controversy of "discretion versus rules."

The new Fed policy can be viewed as one where the monetary aggregates became intermediate targets, and the banking system's quantity of nonborrowed reserves was the operating target. Through its open market operations, the Fed has considerable control over this operating target. Movements in that target are, in turn, supposed to generate somewhat predictable changes in the levels of the intermediate targets, or monetary aggregates. The money multiplier, which we introduced in the last chapter, is the link between the reserves and the aggregates. Monetarists believe that the money multiplier is basically steady, so that the link between reserves and the monetary aggregates can be identified. Hence, the appropriate policy is to supply reserves (through open market operations) at that steady pace which will lead to a stable and reasonable rate of growth for the monetary aggregates. The changes in interest rates that may result from changes in money demand (which, in the monetarists' view, does not occur often or to a significant extent) should not be allowed to affect the policy on reserves.

Technically speaking, the Fed had claimed throughout most of the 1970s to be targeting certain aggregates, notably M_1 and M_2 and it had routinely published target ranges and expected growth paths for the aggregates. The Fed's devotion to such a policy was suspect, as the data repeatedly showed the aggregates growing at far faster rates than the Fed said it preferred. When faced with these high growth rates, the Fed often simply adjusted its planned growth path upward. Volcker's 1979 announcement seemed to suggest that the Fed would finally be seriously interested in the growth in aggregates. Indeed, the growth rate in the money supply was far smaller in this time than it had generally been in the 1970s. Also, the new policy stated that the Fed would let interest rates (particularly short-term rates) fluctuate far more freely than they had in the past. In fact, in late 1979 and through the early 1980s, rates of most maturities posted their highest levels in more than a hundred years and displayed a volatility that led to major changes in financial institutions and markets.

Back to the Fed Funds Rate, 1983 to 1991

The Fed did not remain committed to an aggregates policy very long.[7] By 1982, the tight monetary policy had banished the worst of the inflation, which seemed to reach a bottom of about 3% to 4%. Policymakers then faced the prospect of deflation and rising unemployment, which rose to around 10% in 1982. At the end of 1982, the Fed again let the monetary aggregates grow at a rather fast pace. Interest rates fell, employment rose, and economic growth resumed.

In 1983, the Fed adopted a new policy. This time, the Fed identified its operating target as the level of **borrowed reserves**, which are funds that the banks borrow from the Fed through its discount window. It is important to realize that the level of borrowed reserves in the banking system is closely and positively linked to the spread between the

---

[7] Franco Modigliani, "The Monetarist Controversy Revisited," *Contemporary Policy Issues* (October 1988), pp. 3–18.

fed funds rate and the discount rate (the cost of borrowing at the discount window, which the Fed adjusts infrequently). When the fed funds rate goes up relative to the discount rate, all else being equal, the level of borrowed reserves rises because banks are more likely to borrow reserves from the Fed rather than from other banks. Thus, targeting borrowed reserves is equivalent to targeting the fed funds rate.

The Fed's policy beginning in 1983 was to keep the growth in borrowed reserves within some specified range. As a result, the Fed supplied reserves through open market purchases when borrowed reserves rose. Thus, the Fed was essentially supplying reserves when the fed funds rate rose. With this policy, the Fed was once more effectively targeting the fed funds rate, while neglecting changes in the monetary aggregates. In 1987, the Fed admitted that fact and ceased to set targets for growth in M_1, substantially widening the acceptable ranges for growth in the larger aggregates, such as M_2 and M_3. From 1983 to the early 1990s, the Fed's chief operating target has been the level of the fed funds rate. In fact, at the end of 1991, the Fed dramatically lowered short-term rates in a publicly announced effort to stimulate the economy.

Two Developments in the Mid-1980

In the mid-1980s, however, two developments of note occurred. The first was the need for the Fed, which it publicly acknowledged, to become concerned with the level and stability of the U.S. dollar's foreign currency exchange rate. Table 6-5 reveals the dramatic strength in the value of the U.S. dollar through the early 1980s, which made American exports very expensive. In 1985, the Fed implemented an expansionary monetary policy (that is, a policy of expanding aggregates), which drove down the dollar's value. In September 1985, the United States (with the Fed's support) entered into the Plaza Agreement, which was a plan for international coordination of monetary policies by the United States, Great Britain, France, (West) Germany, and Japan. (The Louvre Accord in 1987 was another effort toward coordination.) The result of these actions was a fast decline in the value of the U.S. dollar (see Table 6-5), which the Fed tried to stabilize in 1987. In a sense, then, the U.S. dollar's exchange rate began to function as a kind of intermediate target for Fed policy.

The second development was the shocking fall in equity prices around the world in October 1987. The Fed's immediate response to the crisis was to provide all necessary liquidity. The fall in prices also brought to the fore the need for stability in the financial markets, and the Fed began to treat that as one of its key objectives.

The Same Policy, but with a Twist, 1991 to 1995

The Fed successfully reduced rates across the maturity spectrum, from 1992 to the outset of 1994. The fed funds rate fell to 3%, and the yield on 10-year government bonds was also low, touching 5.72% in December 1993. During 1992 and 1993, economic expansion occurred at a fairly steady rate, with a falling civilian unemployment rate, a growing real GDP, and a modest rate of consumer price inflation.[8]

However, the Fed's expectations regarding the economic environment underwent a change in February 1994. For the first time in two years, the Fed pressured the fed funds rate upward, moving it from 3% to 3.25%. The explanation was the Fed's growing concern that robust economic growth might, at some point, in the relatively near future, spark price inflation. The Fed was not paying much attention to the monetary aggregates, but rather Chairman Alan Greenspan and the FOMC were watching

---

[8] "Monetary Policy and Open Market Operations during 1994," *Federal Reserve Bulletin* (June 1995), pp. 570–584.

the prices of sensitive commodities and the level of industrial capacity being utilized. Thus, the Fed was still targeting rates in order to manage economic activity and to bring about both price level stability and continued expansion. Eventually, the Fed was to nudge rates up seven more times until February 1995, when the fed funds rate reached 6% and the discount rate grew to 5.25% (from its early 1992 level of 3%). These actions had the desired effects: Interest rates on debt of short and long terms to maturities rose and the rate of growth in the economy fell to low but generally positive levels. In 1995, the Fed did not change its mind, and target levels of short-term rates in late 1995 were at their end-of-1994 heights.

The Last Half of the 1990s—Exploring the "New Paradigm"

Despite the seven Fed tightenings of 1994 and early 1995, the economy averted a recession and subsequently experienced strong and noninflationary growth. In fact, based on previous experience, economic growth was stronger than had been expected with little inflation. The explanation for this desirable strong growth–low inflation combination was the "new paradigm."

As of 1995, the conventional wisdom was that the maximum sustainable real GDP growth was approximately $2\frac{1}{4}\%$, 1% due to increases in the labor force and $1\frac{1}{4}\%$ due to productivity increases. And (noninflationary) full employment was thought to be 5% to $5\frac{1}{2}\%$. During 1997/1998, with strong economic growth and unemployment decreasing below $4\frac{1}{2}\%$, Alan Greenspan and the Fed were faced with a dilemma: They had to decide whether to tighten monetary policy to slow economic growth, even though there were no inflationary forces, or to let the economy continue to grow at a rate that had been unsustainable by previous standards.

Greenspan and the Fed exhibited a combination of being cautious and experimental in their approach. Although their main policy tool was to change the fed funds rate (and to make public comments by Greenspan and other FOMC members), their approach was eclectic. They did not concentrate solely on the absolute level of the Fed funds rate, monetary aggregates, or commodity prices.

Greenspan decided to be vigilant but passive, and he permitted the economy to grow beyond what the "old paradigm" would have deemed feasible. In fact, the Fed eased the funds rate three times (by a total of 75 basis points) in 1998 due to a concern about a financial crisis. Another factor was a resulting global weakening due to the Russian default and the problem with a major hedge fund (Long-Term Capital Management) financial crisis.

Greenspan emphasized the traditional reasons for low inflation, including globalization (which reduced the pricing power of suppliers); the strong U.S. dollar; the U.S. trade deficit (by importing international goods, price pressures on U.S.-produced products good were relieved); and immigration (which took pressure off domestic wage rates).

But the overriding explanation for this strong, noninflationary growth was a "new paradigm," which posited that productivity had increased due to the new technology and that accelerated capital expenditures were induced by the new technology. This *capital deepening* increased labor productivity and, thus, sustainable economic growth.

While the Fed was extremely tolerant of strong economic growth, it did enact six fed funds increases (from 4.75% to 6.50%) from June 1999 through May 2000. Overall, the Fed policy during this period could be described as nondoctrinaire, eclectic, and exploratory. For various reasons, Greenspan is credited with having orchestrated the longest postwar expansion, which began during April 1991, and continues to this writing.

Key Points That You Should Understand Before Proceeding

1. The Fed has numerous and complex goals related to conditions in the overall economy, which include price stability, high employment, economic growth, and stability in interest rates and the dollar's value in foreign currencies.
2. Policies that might further the attainment of one goal may make another difficult to realize.
3. The Fed is unable to realize its goals directly but must work through operating targets that it can affect and that, in turn, have some predictable influence on intermediate targets and the economy.
4. The Fed's operating targets have included the fed funds rate and various measures of reserves in the banking system; its primary tool has been open market operations.
5. Intermediate targets may include monetary aggregates, interest rates, or foreign currency exchange rates.
6. Keynesians adopt a monetary policy that largely calls for targeting short-term interest rates.
7. Monetarists adopt a monetary policy that largely calls for targeting reserves in order to achieve a steady growth in monetary aggregates.
8. The targets of Fed policy have changed several times in the last 25 years.

SUMMARY

The goals of monetary policy include a stable price level, economic growth, high employment, stable interest rates, and predictable and steady currency exchange rates. Unfortunately, monetary policies involve difficult trade-offs, and policies that help to achieve one goal may make another less attainable.

Furthermore, the Federal Reserve has no direct control or influence on the complex economic variables that constitute the goals. Hence, it must identify intermediate targets that influence these variables and are, in turn, influenced by operating targets that are variables the Fed can control to a substantial extent. The intermediate targets may be interest rates, monetary aggregates, or possibly exchange rates. The level of bank reserves (borrowed or nonborrowed) and the level of the federal funds rate have served as operating targets from time to time since 1970. The Fed can effectively manage either this rate on interbank loans or the level of various measures of reserves by open market operations that control the flow of reserves to the banking system. However, the Fed cannot target both rates and reserves at the same time. Since 1970, the Fed's policy has alternated among targeting rates, targeting reserves, and an eclectic approach.

KEY TERMS

- **Borrowed reserves**, 91
- **Demand for money**, 88
- **Discretionary monetary policy**, 91
- **Frictional unemployment**, 82
- **Goal of monetary policy**, 81
- **Intermediate target**, 87
- **Keynesian**, 90
- **Monetarism**, 91
- **Nonborrowed reserves**, 90
- **Operating target**, 87
- **Stagflation**, 82

QUESTIONS

1. Name three widely accepted goals of monetary policy.
2. What keeps the Fed from being able to achieve its goals in a direct way?
3. Comment on this statement by an official of the Federal Reserve:

   [the Fed] can control nonborrowed reserves through open market operations (but) it cannot control total reserves, because the level of borrowing at the discount window is determined in the short run by the preferences of depository institutions.

   Quoted from Alfred Broaddus, "A Primer on the Fed," chapter 7 in Sumner N. Levine (ed.), *The Financial Analyst's Handbook* (Homewood, IL: Dow Jones-Irwin, 1988), p. 194.
4. Why is it impossible for the Fed to target, at the same time, both the fed funds interest rate and the level of reserves in the banking system?
5. Explain the change in the Fed's targets that occurred with the 1979 Volcker announcement about inflation and the new Fed policy.

C h a p t e r   7

Insurance Companies

Learning Objectives

After reading this chapter, you will understand

- the nature of the business of insurance companies.
- the differences between the nature of the liabilities of life insurance companies and those of property and casualty insurance companies.
- the different types of life insurance policies.
- the different types of property and casualty insurance policies.
- the types of assets in which life insurance companies and property casualty insurance companies invest.
- the forms of insurance companies: stock and mutual.
- the regulation of insurance companies.
- recent changes in the insurance business and the factors contributing to those changes.
- some important financial developments in the international insurance industry.

Insurance companies provide (sell and service) insurance policies, which are legally binding contracts for which the policyholder (or owner) pays insurance **premiums**. According to the insurance contract, insurance companies promise to pay specified sums contingent on the occurrence of future events, such as death or an automobile accident. Thus, insurance companies are *risk bearers*. They accept or underwrite the risk in return for an insurance premium.

The major part of the insurance company underwriting process is deciding which applications for insurance they should accept and which ones they should reject, and if they accept, determining how much they should charge for the insurance. This is called the *underwriting process*. For example, an insurance company may not provide life insurance to someone with terminal cancer or automobile insurance to someone with numerous traffic violations. And in some cases, they may provide different classes of insurance with different premiums. For example, the company may insure but charge a smoker a larger premium for life insurance than a nonsmoker; and insure someone with a mediocre driving record, but charge more for automobile insurance than an individual with a better driving record. The underwriting process is critical to an insurance company.

Because insurance companies collect insurance premiums initially and make payments later *when* (e.g., the insured person's death) or *if* (e.g., an automobile accident) an insured event occurs, insurance companies maintain the initial premiums collected in an investment portfolio, which generates a return. Thus, insurance companies have two sources of income: the initial **underwriting income** (the insurance premium) and the **investment income**, which occurs over time. The investment returns result from the investment of the insurance premiums until the funds are paid out on the policy. The premium is a fairly stable type of revenue. Investment returns may vary considerably with the performance of the financial markets.

The payments on the insurance policies are one major expense of the insurance company. These payments vary among the different types of insurance policies and companies. The payments may be very unstable, depending on the type of insurance. The other major type of expense is the operating expense of the insurance company. This expense tends to be quite stable.

Insurance company's profits, thus, result from the difference between their insurance premiums and investment returns on the one hand, and their operating expense and insurance payments or benefits on the other. The type of risk insured against, which defines the type of premium collected and benefit paid, defines the insurance company. Table 7-1 summarizes the major risks that insurance companies will insure, many of which are elaborated on in this chapter.

Key Points That You Should Understand Before Proceeding

1. Insurance companies bear risk in return for a fee called the premium.
2. Deciding which risks to underwrite and how much to charge for bearing those risks is critical to an insurance company.

TYPES OF INSURANCE

Life Insurance

For life insurance, the risk insured against is death. The **life insurance company** pays the beneficiary of the life insurance policy in the event of the death of the insured. There are several types of life insurance, which will be examined later in this chapter.

Table 7-1   Major Risks Insurance Companies Face

Life Insurance	Health Insurance	Property and Casualty
- Term Insurance	- Medical	- Property
- Whole Life	• Indemmity	• Automobile
• Fixed	• HMO/PPO/etc.	• House
• Variable	- Dental	• Other
- Universal Life	- Other	- Liability
- Second to Die (Survivorship)		- Other

Other Insurance

- Disability
- Long-Term Care

Structured Settlements

Investment-Oriented Products

- Guaranteed Investment Contracts (GICs)
- Annuities
  • Fixed
  • Variable
  • Mutual Funds

Health Insurance

In the case of health insurance, the risk insured is medical treatment of the insured. The **health insurance company** pays the insured (or the provider of the medical service) all or a portion of the cost of medical treatment by doctors, hospitals, or others. This type of insurance has undergone significant changes in the last decade. As a result, there has been a significant restructuring of the health industry, whereby the largest health insurance companies specialize in health insurance rather than sell health insurance in addition to other products, such as life insurance.

Until the last decade, the major type of health insurance available was *indemnity insurance*. According to indemnity insurance, the insurance company agrees to indemnify (reimburse) the insured for covered medical and hospital expenses. That is, the insurance company pays the medical provider (doctor, hospital, etc.) for the medical services provided to the insured. The provider is selected by the insured and can provide whatever service the provider deems appropriate.

Very often there is an annual minimum amount below which the issuer does not pay for the service, but the insured pays (a *deductible*). Typically, there is also a copayment (a "co-pay") required by the insured. For example, the insured pays 20% of the charge for the service and the insurer pays the other 80%.

Due to the lack of constraints and incentives for cost savings, the medical service insured by indemnity insurance became very expensive. In response, various forms of managed health care have been developed. In general, these forms of managed health care put constraints on the choice of the provider (doctor or hospital) by the insured and on the types of service provided by the provider. The various types of managed care, including health maintenance organizations (HMOs), preferred provider organizations (PPOs), and point of service organizations (POSs), are too diverse and complex to be considered here. It is accurate to assert, however, that no widely acceptable method has yet evolved. While indemnity insurance is still provided on an individual and group basis, the various forms of *managed care* have become common.

There have been and continue to be nonprofit providers of health insurance, such as Blue Cross and Blue Shield, and federal government providers of health insurance, such as Medicare and Medicaid.

The two major classes of medical expense benefits are

> *Basic coverage:* traditional hospital, surgical, and regular expense coverage; and
>
> *Major medical:* designed to reduce the financial burden of heavy medical expenses resulting from catastrophic or prolonged illness or injury.

Property and Casualty Insurance

The risk insured by **property and casualty (P&C) insurance companies** is damage to various types of property. Specifically, it is insurance against financial loss caused by damage, destruction, or loss to property as the result of an identifiable event that is sudden, unexpected, or unusual. The major types of such insurance are:

> A house and its contents against risks such as fire, flood, and theft (home owners insurance and its variants); and
>
> Vehicles against collision, theft, and other damage (automobile insurance and its variants).

Liability Insurance

With liability insurance, the risk insured against is litigation, or the risk of lawsuits against the insured due to actions by the insured or others.

Disability Insurance

Disability insurance insures against the inability of employed persons to earn an income in either their own occupation ("own occ" disability insurance) or any occupation ("any occ"). Typically, "own occ" disability insurance is written for professionals in white-collar occupations and "any occ" for blue-collar workers. Another distinction in disability insurance is the sustainability of the policy. Regarding sustainability, there are two types of policies. The first is *guaranteed renewable* (or guaranteed continuable) whereby the issuer has to sustain the policy for the specified period of time and the issuer cannot make any changes in the policy except that it can change the premium rates for the entire class of policy (but not an individual policyholder). The other type is noncancellable and guaranteed renewable (or simply *noncancellable*) whereby the issuer has no right to make any change in any policy during the specified period. Disability insurance is also divided between short-term disability and long-term disability, with six months being the typical dividing time.

Long-Term Care Insurance

As individuals have been living longer, they have become concerned about outliving their assets and being unable to care for themselves as they age. In addition, custodial care for the aged has become very expensive. Thus, there has been an increased demand for insurance to provide custodial care for the aged who are no longer able to care for themselves. This care may be provided in either the insured's own residence or a separate custodial facility.

Structured Settlements

Structured settlements are fixed, guaranteed periodic payments over a long period of time, typically resulting from a settlement on a disability policy or other type of policy. For example, suppose an individual is hit by an automobile and, as a result, is unable to work for the rest of his or her life. The individual may sue the P&C company for future lost earnings and medical care. To settle the suit, the P&C companies may agree to make specified payments over time to the individual. The P&C company may then purchase a policy from a life insurance company to make the agreed-upon payments.

Investment-Oriented Products

Insurance companies have increasingly sold products that have a significant investment component in addition to their insurance component. The first major investment-oriented product developed by life insurance companies was the **guaranteed investment contract (GIC)**. According to a GIC, a life insurance company agrees, in return for a single premium, to pay the principal amount and a predetermined annual **crediting rate** over the life of the investment, all of which are paid at the maturity date of the GIC. For example, a $10 million five year GIC with a predetermined crediting rate of 10% means that at the end of five years the insurance company pays the guaranteed crediting rate and the principal. The return of the principal depends on the ability of the life insurance company to satisfy the obligation, just as in any corporate debt obligation. The risk that the insurer faces is that the rate earned on the portfolio of supporting assets is less than the guaranteed rate.

The maturity of a GIC can vary from 1 year to 20 years. The interest rate guaranteed depends on market conditions and the rating of the life insurance company. The interest rate will be higher than the yield on U.S. Treasury securities of the same maturity. These policies are purchased by pension plan sponsors as a pension investment.

A GIC is nothing more than the debt obligation of the life insurance company issuing the contract. The word *guarantee* does not mean that there is a guarantor other than the life insurance company. Effectively, a GIC is a zero coupon bond issued by a life insurance company and, as such, exposes the investor to the same credit risk. This credit risk has been highlighted by the default of several major issuers of GICs. The two most publicized were Mutual Benefit, a New Jersey–based insurer, and Executive Life, a California based insurer, which were both seized by regulators in 1991.

Annuity

Another insurance company investment product is an annuity. An **annuity** is often described as "a mutual fund in an insurance wrapper." (Mutual funds are discussed in Chapter 8.) What does this mean? To answer this question, assume that an insurance company investment manager has two identical common stock portfolios, one a mutual fund and the other an annuity. On the mutual fund, all income (that is, the dividend) is taxable, and the capital gains (or losses) realized by the fund are also taxable, although at potentially different tax rates. The income and realized gains are taxable whether they are withdrawn by the mutual fund holder or not. There are no guarantees associated with the mutual fund; its performance depends solely on the portfolio performance.

Because of the insurance wrapper, the annuity is treated as an insurance product and as a result receives a preferential tax treatment. Specifically, the income and realized gains are not taxable if not withdrawn from the annuity product. Thus, the "inside buildup" of returns is not taxable on an annuity, as it is also not on other insurance products.

The "insurance wrapper" on the mutual fund which makes it an annuity can be of various forms. The most common "wrapper" is the guarantee by the insurance company that the annuity policyholder will get back no less that the amount invested in the annuity (there may also be a minimum period before withdrawal to get this benefit). Thus, if an investor invests $100 in a common stock–based annuity and at the time of withdrawal (or at the time of death of the annuity holder) the annuity has a value of only $95, the insurance company will pay the annuity holder (or its beneficiary) $100. Many other types of protection or insurance features have also been developed.

Of course, insurance companies impose a charge for this benefit—an insurance premium for the insurance component of the annuity. Thus, while mutual funds have an expense fee imposed on the fund's performance, an annuity has a *mortality and expense fee* imposed. Annuities are therefore more expensive to the investor than mutual funds. In return, annuity policyholders get the insurance wrapper, which provides the tax benefit. Such annuities can be either fixed annuities, similar to GICs, or variable annuities whose performance is based on the return of a common stock or bond portfolio.

Mutual funds and annuities distributed by insurance companies may have their investments managed by the insurance company investment department or by external investment managers, as discussed in the next section.

Key Points That You Should Understand Before Proceeding

1. Life, property/casualty, and health are among the important categories of risks that insurance companies specialize in.
2. Insurance companies also sell investment products such as GIC (which is essentially a zero coupon bond), and annuity ("a mutual fund in an insurance wrapper").

Table 7-2   Top 10 U.S. Life Insurance Companies (Ranked by 6/30/00 Invested Assets)

RANK	COMPANY	TOTAL INVESTED ASSETS
1	Prudential Insurance Company	$126,253,777
2	Metropolitan Life Insurance Company	122,163,983
3	Teachers Insurance & Ann. Association	111,027,359
4	Northwestern Mutual Life Insurance Company	76,137,876
5	New York Life Insurance Company	64,343,805
6	John Hancock Life Insurance Company	44,243,425
7	Massachusetts Mutual Life Insurance Company	44,067,108
8	Principal Life Insurance Company	41,237,705
9	Equitable Life Assurance Society of the U.S.	38,363,311
10	Jackson National Life Insurance Company	34,366,992

INSURANCE COMPANIES VERSUS TYPES OF PRODUCTS

Whereas in concept these various types of insurance could be combined in different ways in actual companies, traditionally they have been packaged in companies in similar ways. Traditionally, life insurance and health insurance have occurred together in a *life and health insurance company* (L&H company). And property and casualty insurance have been combined in a P&C insurance company. Companies that provide insurance in both insurance products are called **multiline insurance companies.** Investment products tend to be sold by life insurance companies, not P&C companies. Tables 7-2 and 7-3 provide the 10 largest life insurance companies and P&C companies, respectively.

There have been some recent changes in the combinations of products by type of company, however. Health insurance has predominately, but not completely, separated from life insurance and become a separate industry. This change has been due mainly to federal regulation of the health insurance industry. Life insurance companies have also increasingly offered investment-oriented products, both annuities, variable and fixed, and mutual funds. Disability insurance is now sold primarily by pure disability companies but is also offered by some life insurance companies. Long-term care insurance is a fairly new line of business and is offered by different types of com-

Table 7-3   Top 10 U.S. P/C Insurance Companies (Ranked by 3/31/00 Invested Assets)

RANK	COMPANY	TOTAL INVESTED ASSETS
1	State Farm Mutual Auto Insurance Company	$77,026,659
2	Allstate Insurance Company	33,763,148
3	National Indemnity Company	31,503,841
4	Continental Casualty Company	20,604,415
5	Liberty Mutual Insurance Company	17,222,213
6	Nationwide Mutual Insurance Company	15,777,970
7	State Farm Fire & Marine Insurance Company	15,549,002
8	St. Paul Fire & Marine Insurance Company	14,304,535
9	General Reinsurance Corporation	13,226,390
10	Travelers Casualty & Surety Company	10,944,209

panies. In terms of specific product offerings, most companies are unique with respect to the combination of products they offer and how they offer them.

Key Points That You Should Understand Before Proceeding

1. Traditionally, L&H insurers have been distinct from P&C insurers. A few multi-line insurers provide both types of insurance.
2. Increasingly, among L&H insurers, life, health, and disability insurance are being provided by separate companies.

FUNDAMENTALS OF THE INSURANCE INDUSTRY

A fundamental aspect of the insurance industry results from the relationship between revenues and costs. A bread manufacturer purchases its ingredients, uses these ingredients to make bread, and then sells the bread, all over a fairly short timeframe. Therefore, the bread manufacturer's profit margin is easily calculated.

An insurance company, on the other hand, collects its premium income initially and invests these receipts in its portfolio. The payments on the insurance policy occur later and, depending on the type of insurance, may occur in a very unpredictable manner. Consequently, the payments are contingent on potential future events. For example, with respect to life insurance, it is certain that everyone will die. However, it is not known when any individual will die. The timing of the payment on any specific life insurance company is, thus, very uncertain. Although the payments on any single life insurance policy is uncertain, statisticians or actuaries can predict the pattern of deaths on a large portfolio of life insurance policies. Thus, while the payment on a single life insurance policy is uncertain, statistically the payment pattern on a portfolio of life insurance policies is much less uncertain. At the other extreme, whereas payments on home insurance against hurricanes are singularly uncertain, the payments on a portfolio of homes are also uncertain. If one house in South Florida is destroyed by a hurricane, for example, it is likely that many others will also be destroyed.

Thus, there are two very important differences between calculating profitability of bread manufacturers and insurance companies. The first is that the timing and magnitude of the payments are much less certain for an insurance company. The second is that there is a long lag between the receipts and payments for an insurance company, which introduces the importance of the investment portfolio.

These differences in the providers of bread and insurance lead to differences in the way consumers of bread and insurance view their providers. Purchasers of bread are not harmed if the bread manufacturer goes bankrupt the day after they buy the bread. However, while the purchaser of bread receives the bread immediately, the purchaser of insurance receives the payment on his or her insurance policy in the future and, thus, must be concerned about the continued viability of the insurance company. Therefore, the credit rating of an insurance company is important to a purchaser of insurance, especially for the types of insurance that may be paid well into the future, such as life insurance.

Key Points That You Should Understand Before Proceeding

1. The timing and magnitude of payouts to policyholders are highly uncertain for an insurance company.
2. Due to the lag between the premium receipts and policy payouts, the return on the investment portfolio is critical to an insurance company's profitablity.

REGULATION OF THE INSURANCE INDUSTRY

According to the McCarran Ferguson Act of 1945, the insurance industry is regulated by the individual states, not the federal government. However, there has been increasing discussion of federal regulation. Insurance companies whose stock is publicly traded are also regulated by the Securities and Exchange Commission (SEC).

Model laws and regulations are developed by the **National Association of Insurance Commissioners (NAIC)**, a voluntary association of state insurance commissioners, for application on insurance companies in all states. Although the adoption of a model law or regulation by the NAIC is not binding on any state, states typically use these as a model when writing their own laws and regulations.

Insurance companies may also be rated by the rating agencies (Moody's Investor Services, Standard & Poor's, A.M. Best Company, Fitch, and others) for both their "claims paying ability" and their debt outstanding, if any. Public insurance companies (discussed below) are also evaluated by equity analysts who work at investment banks and broker or dealers, with respect to the attractiveness of their outstanding common stock.

The relationship between the premium revenues and the eventual contingent contractual insurance policy payments affects an important aspect of evaluating insurance companies. Insurance companies are monitored by their accountants and auditors, their rating agencies, and their government regulators. These monitors of the insurance companies are concerned about the financial stability of the insurance companies due, among other issues, to the lack of synchronicity between premiums and insurance policy payments and also the volatility of the payments. To assure financial stability, these monitors require insurance companies to maintain reserves or **surplus**, which are the excess of assets over liabilities. These reserves or surpluses are defined differently by regulators and accountants and have different names. Because for regulatory purposes, the treatment of both assets and liabilities is established by the state statutes covering the insurance company, surplus, by this measure, is called **statutory surplus** (or **reserves**) or STAT surplus. **Generally accepted accounting principles (GAAP) surplus** (or reserves) are defined by accountants for their purposes. While statutory and GAAP reserves are measured differently, their purposes are similar, although not identical.

Although specifying the definition of the assets is straightforward, defining liabilities is difficult. The complication in determining the value of liabilities arises because the insurance company has committed to make payments at some time in the future, and those payments are recorded as contingent liabilities on its financial statement. The reserves are simply an accounting entry, not an identifiable portfolio.

Statutory surplus is important because regulators view this as the ultimate amount that can be drawn upon to pay policyholders. The growth of this surplus for an insurance company also determines how much future business it can underwrite.

Key Points That You Should Understand Before Proceeding

1. Insurance companies are regulated by the individual states, typically using the laws developed by the NAIC as a model. They may also be rated by debt rating agencies.
2. Insurance companies whose stock is publicly traded are also regulated by the SEC, and perhaps evaluated by equity analysts.
3. The surplus (i.e., the excess of assets over liabilities) of an insurance company is measured differently for statutory and GAAP purposes, and is an important indicator of its financial standing.

STRUCTURE OF INSURANCE COMPANIES

Based on the previous discussion, insurance companies are really a composite of three companies. First, there is the "home office" or actual insurance company. This company designs the insurance contract ("manufactures" the contract) and provides the backing for the financial guarantees on the contract, that is, assures the policyholder that the contract will pay off under the conditions of the contract. This company is called the *manufacturer* and *guarantor* of the insurance policy. Second, there is the investment component that invests the premiums collected in the investment portfolio. This is the *investment company*.

The third element of an insurance company is the *distribution component* or the sales force. There are different types of distribution forces. First, there are the *agents* who are associated with the company. Agents sell only or mainly the company's own manufactured products. These agents typically are not employees of the company (although some companies also use employees as salespeople), but entrepreneurs financially associated with the company. There are also *brokers* who are not associated with any company but sell the insurance products of many companies. Brokers have traditionally operated individually but are increasingly operating in groups called *producer groups.* As deregulation progresses, commercial banks have also become a natural means of distribution for insurance and investment products. Banks are averse to "manufacturing" insurance products because of their inexperience; the risk borne by manufacturing insurance products; and the long payback period of some insurance products. On the other hand, insurance companies are attracted by commercial bank customer contacts. As a result, commercial bank distribution of insurance company products has grown considerably. This relationship is called **bankassurance**. More recently, the Internet has also been used by some insurance companies to distribute insurance products directly to clients. Internet distribution is very new and has considerable potential but is still in its infancy. This mode of distribution has been most successful in the more commodity-like insurance products, such as term life insurance and automobile insurance.

These three components of insurance companies traditionally have been combined in one overall company, but they are increasingly being separated and the three functions are being provided by different companies. First, as previously mentioned, many insurance companies use independent brokers or producer groups to distribute their products rather than their own agents. Many companies no longer have their own agents and sell all their products exclusively through brokers, producer groups, or on the Internet. Second, insurance companies are increasingly outsourcing parts of their investment portfolio or even the entire portfolio to external independent investment managers. Investment managers are also increasingly diversifying, that is, not specializing in managing any one type of assets such as pension fund assets, mutual funds, or insurance company assets, but managing all of them, including insurance company assets. Third, while the home office component of an insurance company seems to be the core of the insurance company, some home offices use external actuarial firms to design their contracts. And, more importantly, they may *reinsure* some or all of the liabilities they incur in providing insurance. According to the reinsurance transaction, the initial insurer transfers the risk of the insurance to another company, the **reinsurer**. There is an industry of reinsurers who accept the risk incurred by the primary insurance company. The financial guarantee on the insurance policy is, thus, provided by the reinsurer rather than the insurance company, which originally provided or "wrote" the policy.

Given this fragmentation of functions in an insurance company, there is increased discussion of a "virtual insurance company," whereby a small group of executives in the home office have external actuarial firms design the contract; reinsure all the insurance policies written; outsource all the investments; and use brokers to distribute their products. Some insurance companies are currently approaching being a virtual insurance company.

Key Points That You Should Understand Before Proceeding

1. The three key components of an insurance company are the design and financial guarantee of the insurance contract; the distribution of the product; and, the investment of the premiums collected.
2. Traditionally, these components have been combined in a single company, but increasingly separate companies are performing these functions.

FORMS OF INSURANCE COMPANIES: STOCK AND MUTUAL

There are two major forms of life insurance companies: stock and mutual. A **stock insurance company** is similar in structure to any corporation or public company. Shares (of ownership) are owned by independent shareholders and are traded publicly. The shareholders care only about the performance of their shares, that is the stock appreciation and the dividends. Their holding period and, thus, their view may be short term. The insurance policies are simply the products or business of the company.

In contrast, **mutual insurance companies** have no stock and no external owners. Their policyholders are also their owners. The owners, that is, the policyholders, care primarily or even solely about the performance on their insurance policies, notably the company's ability to pay on the policy. Since these payments may occur considerably into the future, the policyholders' view may be long term. Thus, while stock insurance companies have two constituencies, their stockholders and their policyholders, mutual insurance companies only have one, since their policyholders and their owners are the same. Traditionally the largest insurers have been mutual, but recently there have been many *demutualizations*, that is, conversions by mutual companies to stock companies.

The debate on which is the better form of insurance company, stock or mutual, is too involved to be considered in any depth here. However, consider selected comments on this issue. First, consider this issue from the perspective of the policyholder or perhaps the rating agency or regulator, not from the point of view of the insurance company. Mutual holding companies have only one constituency, their policyholder or owner. The liabilities of many types of insurance companies are long term, especially the writers of life insurance. Thus, mutual insurance companies can appropriately have a long time horizon in their strategies and policies. They do not have to make short-term decisions to benefit their shareholders, whose interests are usually short term, via an increase in the stock price or dividend in a way that might reduce their long-term profitability or the financial strength of the insurance company. In addition, if the insurance company makes profits it can pass them onto its policyholders via reduced premiums. (Policies that benefit from an increased profitability of the insurance company are called *participating policies*, as discussed below.) These increased profits do not have to accrue to stockholders because there are none.

Finally, mutual insurance companies can adopt a longer time frame in their investments, which will most likely make possible a higher return. Mutual insurance companies, for example, also hold more common stock. However, whereas the long timeframe of mutual insurance companies may be construed as an advantage over stock companies, it can also be construed as a disadvantage. Rating agencies and others assert that, due to their longer horizon and given their long timeframe, mutual insurance companies may be less efficient and have higher expenses than stock companies. Empirically, rating agencies and others assert that mutual insurance companies typically have reduced their expenses after converting to stock companies. Overall, it can be argued that mutual insurance companies have such long planning horizons that they may not operate efficiently, particularly with respect to expenses. Stock companies, on the other hand, have very short planning horizons and may operate to the long-term disadvantage of their policyholders to satisfy their stockholders in the short run.

Consider now the issue of stock versus mutual companies from the perspective of the insurance company. What have been the motivations of mutual insurance companies to go public (issue stock via an initial public offering [IPO]) in recent years? Several reasons are typically given. First, with the financial industry diversifying, consolidating, and growing, insurance companies have concluded that they need to acquire other financial companies (insurance companies, investment companies, and other financial companies) to prosper or even survive. To conduct these acquisitions they have to have capital. Mutual companies cannot, by definition, issue stock and are limited in the amount of public debt they can issue—mutual insurance companies issue public debt via "surplus notes." In addition, internal surplus has been growing slowly for the insurance industry. Thus, many insurance companies have concluded that to expand as quickly as they deem essential, they have to be able to raise equity capital and, thus, go public. Second, some mutual insurance companies and their advisors believe that, at least some times, stock is a better "acquisition currency" than cash (typically for reasons of taxes and financial accounting), even if the mutual insurance company has enough cash for the acquisition. Finally, company stock and stock options have become a more important form of incentive compensation in many industries, and many insurance companies have concluded that to attract, retain, and motivate the desired executives, they need public stock in their companies.

Whereas many mutual insurance companies go public for these reasons, other mutual insurance companies continue to prosper as mutuals. And while stock insurance companies can raise capital to acquire other companies, they also become vulnerable to being acquired by other companies. Mutual companies cannot be involuntarily acquired.

A new form of insurance company, which is a hybrid between a pure mutual and a pure stock company, has been approved by some states and implemented by some insurance companies in these states since their introduction in 1996. This form is called a **mutual holding company (MHC)**. According to the MHC structure, the upstream holding company is a mutual company (that is, there is no stockholder ownership), and also a holding company (that is, a mutual holding company but not an insurance company). Under the MHC structure, the mutual company forms a stock subsidiary and contributes some or all of its operating businesses to the subsidiary. Policyholders retain membership rights in the mutual holding company and contractual rights in the operating subsidiary. Up to 49.9% of the subsidiary's voting interest can be sold to the public to raise primary capital. The mutual holding company continues to hold a majority ownership in the downstream insurance company. The structure of an MHC is shown in Figure 7-1.

The participating life insurance is written by the downstream public life insurance company. Since the MHC board of directors has majority ownership of the life insurance company, it can and legally must operate the company in the best interests of the participating policyholders. Among the advantages of the MHC are

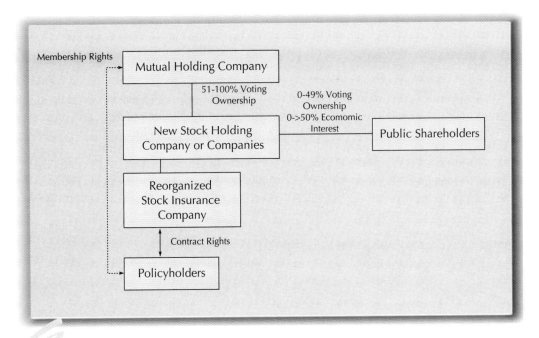

Figure 7-1   Mutual Holding Company—Corporate Structure

Access to external funds, including equity.

Creation of acquisition currency, that is, common stock (which may be superior to cash for acquisitions).

Expansion into new nonparticipating lines of business with these funds.

Retention of majority control of an insurance company.

Management ownership provides incentives to attract and retain top management.

There are also tax advantages to a mutual insurance company becoming an MHC.

MHC laws have been approved by only a few states and even where approved, the laws vary widely by state. The experience with MHCs is not yet sufficient to assess whether this form will be a viable and growing form of life insurance company structure. In fact, the Principal Financial Group, which converted from a mutual to an MHC during 1998 announced in August 2000 a plan to convert to a stock company. Principal cited better access to capital as one of the reasons for this second step.

Key Points That You Should Understand Before Proceeding

1. In terms of ownership, there are two main forms of insurance companies: stock and mutual. A hybrid form, the mutual holding company, has been approved in some states.
2. Traditionally, insurance companies have been mutual, but they are increasingly demutualizing due to the perceived benefits of having a publicly traded stock.

INDIVIDUAL VERSUS GROUP INSURANCE

All the insurance products mentioned in this chapter are sold to individuals. Some insurance products are also sold to groups, typically to the employees of specific companies through their employers, or educational, medical, or other professional associations. Among the major types of products distributed to groups are term life insurance, whole life insurance, medical insurance, disability insurance (short-term and long-term), and investment products such as mutual funds, annuities, and 401 (k) products.

Insurance companies often have different distribution systems for individual and group products. They are typically different because individual product distributors deal with individual and small company owners, and group product distributors deal with human resource departments of corporations and other organizations. In the P&C business, there is also a similar distinction between *personal lines of business* and *commercial lines of business.* Some P&C companies focus mainly or solely on personal lines such as automobile and homeowners insurance; others focus on commercial lines such as business property and liability insurance.

> **Key Point That You Should Understand Before Proceeding**
> 1. Insurance products may be sold either to individuals (e.g. life, automobile) or to groups (e.g. disability, business property).

TYPES OF LIFE INSURANCE

This section elaborates on the types of life insurance products introduced earlier. There are two fundamentally different types of life insurance: **term (life) insurance** and **cash value life insurance**.

Term Insurance

Term insurance is *pure life insurance.* If the insured dies while the policy is intact, the beneficiary of the policy receives the death benefit. If the insured does not die within the period, the policy is invalid and has no value. There is no cash value or investment value for a term insurance policy. In addition, the policyholder cannot borrow against the policy.

With respect to the premium paid, there are two different types of term policies. The first is *level term.* For this type, the premium is constant over the life of the policy. For example, for a 10-year term policy, the premium will be the same for each of the 10 years. Obviously, given the increasing probability of dying with age, the insured overpays early in the life of the policy and underpays late in the policy's life. The second type is *annual renewable term,* whereby the policy provides guaranteed protection over the term of the policy (e.g., 10 years), but at an increasing premium. However, a maximum premium schedule is provided.

Cash Value or Permanent Life Insurance

There is a broad classification of life insurance which is cash-value or permanent or investment-type life insurance. This type is usually called **whole life insurance**. In addition to providing pure life insurance (as does term insurance), whole life insurance builds up a cash value or investment value inside the policy. This cash value can be withdrawn and can also be borrowed against by the owner of the policy. Or, if the owner wishes to let the **policy lapse**, he or she can withdraw the cash value. This cash value develops because of the level premium approach to paying for this type of insurance. The actuarial cost of pure insurance increases with age, but the premium charged on this type of insurance is level. The policyholder is therefore overpaying for insurance early in the life of the policy and underpaying thereafter. The cash value builds up in the policy both for this reason and because the premium is greater than the premium for pure term insurance. Growth in the cash value of the life insurance policy is referred to as the "inside buildup." A major advantage of this and other types of life insurance which have a cash or investment value is that *the inside buildup is not subject to taxation*, as discussed below.

Life insurance and life insurance products are very complex. Only an overview is provided in this chapter.[1] There are two categories with respect to cash value life insurance policies. The first is whether the cash value is *guaranteed* or *variable*. The second is whether the required premium payment is *fixed* or *flexible*. Thus, there are four combinations (see Table 7-4), which we discuss below.

Guaranteed Cash Value Life Insurance.

Traditional cash value life insurance, usually called whole life insurance, has a guaranteed buildup of cash value based on the general account portfolio of the insurance company. The insurance company guarantees a minimum cash value at the end of each year. This guaranteed cash value is based on a minimum dividend paid on the policy. In addition, the policy can be either *participating* or *nonparticipating*. For nonparticipating policies, the minimum dividend and the minimum cash value on the policy are the guaranteed amounts; that is, there is no upside. For the participating policy, the dividend paid on the policy is based on the realized actuarial experience of the company and its investment portfolio. The cash value may be above but not below the guaranteed level for participating policies. Thus, the actual performance of the policy may be substantially affected by the actual policy dividends over the guaranteed amount.

Variable Life Insurance.

Contrary to the guaranteed or fixed cash value policies based on the general account portfolio of the insurance company, variable life insurance policies allow the policyowners to allocate their premium payments to and among separate investment accounts maintained by the insurance company, within limits, and also to be able to shift the policy cash value among the separate accounts. As a result, the amount of the policy cash value and the death benefits depend on the investment results of the separate accounts the policyowners have selected. Thus, there is no guaranteed cash value or death benefit. Both depend on the performance of the selected investment portfolio.

Table 7-4   Classification of Cash Value Insurance

	GUARANTEED DOLLAR CASH VALUE POLICES	VARIABLE LIFE POLICIES
Fixed Premium	Whole life insurance	Variable life insurance
Flexible Premium	Universal life insurance	Variable universal life insurance

---

[1] For an excellent treatment of life insurance, see Ben G. Baldwin, *The New Life Insurance Investment Advisor*, revised edition (Boston, MA: McGraw Hill, 1994). See also *Life Insurance Fact Book*, American Council of Life Insurance, 2000 and *Forum 500 Fact Book*, American Council of Life Insurers, 2000.

The types of separate account investment options offered vary by insurance companies. Typically, the insurance company offers a selection of common stock and bond fund investment opportunities, often managed by the company itself and other investment managers. If the investment options perform well, the cash value buildup in the policy will be significant. However, if the policyholder selects investment options that perform poorly, the variable life insurance policy will perform poorly. There could be little or no cash value buildup, or, in the worst case, the policy could be terminated. This type of life insurance is called **variable life insurance**. Variable life insurance, which typically has common stock investment options, has grown quickly with the stock market rally of the 1990s.

Flexible Premium Policies—Universal Life.

The key element of **universal life** is the flexibility of the premium for the policyowner. This flexible premium concept separates pure insurance protection (term insurance) from the investment (cash value) element of the policy. The policy cash value is set up as the cash value fund (or accumulation fund) to which the investment income is credited and from which the cost of term insurance for the insured (the mortality charge) is debited. The expenses are also debited.

This separation of the cash value from the pure insurance is called the "unbundling" of the traditional life insurance policy. Premium payments for universal life are at the discretion of the policyholder—that is, are flexible—except that there must be a minimum initial premium to begin the coverage. There must also be at least enough cash value in the policy each month to cover the mortality charge and other expenses. If not, the policy will lapse. Both guaranteed cash value and variable life can be written on a flexible premium or fixed premium basis, as summarized in Table 7.4.

Variable Universal Life Insurance.

Variable universal life insurance combines the features of variable life and universal life policies, that is, the choice of separate account investment products and flexible premiums. Since the 1990s, term and variable life insurance have been growing at the expense of whole life insurance during the last decade.

Survivorship (Second to Die) Insurance

Most whole life insurance policies are designed to pay death benefits when one specified insured dies. An added dimension of whole life policies is that two people (usually a married couple) are jointly insured and the policy pays the death benefit not when the first person dies, but when the second person (the "surviving spouse") dies. This is called *survivorship insurance* or *second-to-die insurance*. This survivorship feature can be added to standard cash value whole life, universal life, and variable universal life policies. Thus, each of the four policies listed in Table 7-4 could also be written on a survivorship basis.

In general, the annual premium for a survivorship insurance policy is lower than for a policy on a single person because, by construction, the second of two people to die has a longer life span than the first. Out of the total survivorship sales during the first quarter of 2000, 46% was based on variable universal life, 33% on universal life, and 21% on whole life. Survivorship insurance is typically sold for estate planning purposes.

Key Points That You Should Understand Before Proceeding

1. There are two key types of life insurance: term insurance, which does not have investment value; and, cash value life insurance, which has investment value and can be borrowed against.

2. Cash value insurance products may be 'guaranteed' or 'variable'; with fixed or flexible premiums; and, with or without a survivorship feature.

GENERAL ACCOUNT AND SEPARATE ACCOUNT PRODUCTS

The *general account of an insurance company* refers to the investment portfolio of the overall company. Products "written by the company itself" are said to have a "general account guarantee," that is, they are a liability of the insurance company. When the rating agencies (Moody's, Standard & Poor's, Fitch) provide a credit rating (discussed in Chapter 20), it is on products written by or guaranteed by the general account. Such ratings are on the "claims-paying ability" of the company. Typical products written by and guaranteed by the general account are whole life, universal life, and fixed annuities (including GICs). Insurance companies must support the guaranteed performance of their general account products to the extent of their solvency. These are called **general account products**.

Other types of insurance products receive no guarantee from the insurance company's general account, and their performance is not based on the performance of the insurance company's general account but solely on the performance of an account separate from the general account of the insurance company, often an account selected by the policyholder. These products are called **separate account products**. Variable life insurance and variable annuities are separate account products. The policyholder chooses specific portfolios to support these products. The performance of the insurance product depends almost solely on the performance of the portfolio selected, adjusted for the fees or expenses of the insuring company (which do depend on the insurance company).

> **Key Points That You Should Understand Before Proceeding**
>
> 1. The overall investment portfolio of an insurance company supports its general account products.
> 2. Separate account products depend solely on the performance of an account chosen by the policyholder.

PARTICIPATING POLICIES

The performance of separate account products depends on the performance of the separate account portfolio chosen and is not affected by the performance of the overall insurance company's general account portfolio. In addition, the performance of some general account products is not affected by the performance of the general account portfolio. For example, disability income insurance policies may be written on a general account, and while their payoff depends on the solvency of the general account, the policy performance (for example, its premium) may not participate in the investment performance of the insurance companies' general account investment portfolio.

Other general account insurance products *participate* in the performance of the company's general account performance. For example, whereas a life insurance company provides the guarantee of a minimum dividend on its whole life policies, the policies' actual dividend may increase if the investment portfolio performs well. (This is called the "interest component" of the dividend: The other two components are the expense and mortality components.) Thus, the performance of the insurance policy participates in the overall company's performance. Such a policy is called a *participating policy*, in this case, a participating whole life insurance policy.

Both stock and mutual insurance companies write both general and separate account products. However, most participating general account products are written in mutual companies.

Key Points That You Should Understand Before Proceeding

1. A participating policy pays a higher dividend than the guaranteed minimum if the general account portfolio performs well.
2. General account products may also be non-participating, with fixed payoffs.

INSURANCE COMPANY INVESTMENT STRATEGIES[2]

In general, the characteristics of insurance company investment portfolios should reflect their liabilities, that is, the insurance products they underwrite.

There are many differences among the various types of insurance policies. Among them are the following:

➤ The expected time at which the average payment will be made by the insurance company (technically, the "duration" of the payments);

➤ The statistical or actuarial accuracy of estimates of *when* the event insured against will occur and the *amount* of the payment (that is, the overall risk of the policy); and

➤ Other factors.

In addition, there are tax differences among different types of insurance policies and companies.

The key distinction between life insurance and property and casualty insurance companies lies in the difficulty of projecting whether or not a policyholder will be paid off and how much the payment will be. Although this is no easy task for either a life or a P&C insurance company, it is easier from an actuarial perspective for a life insurance company. The amount and timing of claims on property and casualty insurance companies are more difficult to predict because of the randomness of natural catastrophes and the unpredictability of court awards in liability cases. This uncertainty about the timing and amount of cash outlays to satisfy claims has an impact on the investment strategies of the funds of property and casualty insurance companies compared to life insurance companies.

Without investigating the details for the differences in the portfolios of different types of insurance products, the major differences in the portfolios of life companies and P&C companies are as follows. Life companies on average have less common stock, more private placements, more commercial mortgages, less municipals bonds, and longer maturity bonds. (These securities and financial assets are discussed in later chapters). The difference in municipal bond holdings is due to the tax-exempt characteristic of these securities. The larger holdings of private placements and commercial mortgages indicate the yield orientation of life companies. This yield orientation is also consistent with the low holding of common stock for life insurance companies.

There are also differences in investment strategy between public (or stock) and mutual insurance companies of the same type. The major difference is that stock com-

---

[2] For a more detailed discussion of investment strategies, see Frank J. Jones, "An Overview of Institutional Fixed Income Strategies," *Professional Perspectives on Fixed Income Portfolio Management: Volume 1,* in Frank J. Fabozzi (ed.), (New Hope, PA: Frank J. Fabozzi Associates, 2000), pp. 1–13.

panies tend to have less common stock than mutual companies. The major reason for this difference is that common stock analysts, who make buy-hold-sell recommendations on all public companies for institutional and individual investors, consider mainly regularly recurring operating income in their calculation of income, not volatile returns. Coupon and dividend income tend to be stable, and capital gains tend to be unstable. Thus, these analysts have a bias favoring bonds, which have higher interest income, over stocks, which have higher capital gains and, over the long term, total returns. As a result, mutual insurance companies, which are not rated by common stock analysts, can focus on total return rather than just yield and have more common stock than public companies.

TAXATION OF LIFE INSURANCE

As mentioned previously in this chapter, the inside buildup of cash value life insurance policies is not taxed as either income or capital gains. Neither is the beneficiary of the death benefit of a life insurance policy subject to an income tax. Finally, the death benefit of the policy may or may not be subject to estate tax, depending on how the beneficiary status is structured. Consequently, life insurance products have considerable tax advantages.

Key Points That You Should Understand Before Proceeding

1. Life insurers' portfolios tend to be more yield oriented than those of P&C insurers; mutual insurance company portfolios tend to have more common stock than those of stock insurance companies.
2. Life insurance products have many tax advantages.

CHANGES IN THE INSURANCE INDUSTRY

There have been three major types of changes in the insurance industry in recent years:

> The deregulation of the financial system.
> Internationalization of the insurance industry.
> Demutualization.

We discuss each of these changes below.

The Deregulation of the Financial System

In 1933, Congress passed the Glass-Steagall Act (discussed in Chapter 3). The act separated commercial banking, investment banking, and insurance. That is, a company could be involved in only one of these three types of business. One of the major intentions of this act was to prevent a single organization from having complete control over the sources of corporate funding, specifically lending to and underwriting the securities of a company. An initial celebrated outcome of this Act, which went into effect in 1935, was the breakup of the "House of Morgan," the business of J. P. Morgan. A Morgan son, two Morgan partners, and 25 employees left J. P. Morgan to set up the investment bank, Morgan Stanley. (J. P. Morgan subsequently became Morgan Guaranty Trust Company when it merged with the much larger Guaranty Trust Company in 1959.) Both the bank and the investment bank continue, although in significantly changed forms. J. P. Morgan was acquired by Chase Manhattan in July 2000.

Over time, due to the evolution of the financial system, the implementation of the Glass-Steagall Act became more ambiguous, more difficult to implement, and, in the view of many, counterproductive. With this background, a recent landmark financial event was the revocation of the Glass-Steagall Act. On November 12, 1999, the **Gramm-Leach-Bliley Act (GLB)**, called the Financial Modernization Act of 1999, was signed into law. This act removed the 50-year-old "anti-affiliation restrictions" among commercial banks, investment banks, and insurance companies.

The GLB has facilitated and accelerated affiliations among these three types of institutions. The first mega-institution of this type is the combination of Salomon Brothers, Smith Barney, both investment banks; Travelers, an insurance company; and Citicorp, a commercial bank. This combined firm is now called simply Citigroup and is involved in insurance, commercial banking, investment banking, and security brokerage.

GLB is also asserted to be a reason for the accelerated demutualization of insurance companies. As indicated earlier in this chapter, demutualization permits insurance companies to acquire not only insurance companies but other types of financial institutions. And by demutualizing, insurance companies can acquire capital for acquisitions. The act also certainly accelerates bankassurance.

Even before the passage of the GLB bill, commercial banks were becoming involved in some aspects of commercial banking, but the banks' involvement was accelerated by the passage of the bill. For several years, in addition to selling mutual funds (discussed in Chapter 8), banks have become successful at selling annuities, both variable and fixed, mainly manufactured by other investment managers. In addition, insurance companies have been entering one part of banking, namely trust banking. Many life insurance agents put some of their clients' assets and life insurance policies in trusts. As a result, several life insurance companies have obtained trust licenses.

Few insurers have planned to go into retail commercial banking. However, Metropolitan Life, after having become a public stock insurance company in March 2000, announced in August 2000 that it would acquire Grand Bank, N.A., in New Jersey and go into retail commercial banking, something that could not have been accomplished before the GLB bill was passed.

Internationalization of the Insurance Industry

Globalization has occurred in many industries, including the insurance industry. With respect to the United States, globalization operates in two directions. With respect to the first direction, U.S. insurance companies have both acquired and entered into agreements with international insurance companies and begun operations in other countries. With respect to the second, international insurance companies, mainly European, have become even more active in acquiring U.S. insurance and investment companies.

Some of the recent acquisitions by international insurance companies of U.S. insurance companies and other U.S. financial companies are shown in Table 7-5. Among the reasons for the increased entry by international insurance companies into the U.S. insurance industry and other U.S. financial sectors are (1) the more rapid growth of the U.S. financial businesses relative to the international financial business, (2) the attractive demographics and income of potential U.S. clients, and (3) the less regulated environment of the U.S. insurance industry. Table 7-6 provides the change in rankings of the top ten insurance companies in the United States between 1995 and 1999, including the elevation of the European insurance companies, ING (Dutch), AEGON (Dutch), and Prudential plc (UK).

Table 7-5   Selected International Insurance Company Acquisitions Of U.S.
Insurance Companies

ACQUIRER	ACQUIRED	DATE ANNOUNCED
AXA Group (French)	AXA Financial (Equitable/Alliance/DLJ[*])	August 2000
ING Group (Dutch)	Aetna Financial Services—nonhealth units	July 2000
ING Group (Dutch)	Reliastar Financial Services	May 2000
Allianz (German)	Life USA	May 1999
Fortis (Dutch-Belgian)	American Bankers	March 1999
Royal Bank of Canada	Liberty Life, SC	2000
Aegon (Dutch)	Transamerica Corporation	February 1999
Zurich	Kemper	1996/1998
Fortis	John Alden	1998
ING	United Life & Annuity	1999
Swiss Re	Royal Maccabees Life	1999
ING Group (Dutch)	Equitable of Iowa	1997
AEGON	Providian Life Companies	1996

[*] *AXA sold DLJ to Credit Suisse First Boston during August 2000.*

Table 7-6   U.S. Life Industry Leaders—2001

($ BILLIONS)			
1995 RANK		1999 NET PREMIUMS[a]	RANK[a]
#1	Prudential	MetLife $34.8	#1
2	MetLife	ING 27.3	2
3	Principal	AEGON 23.7	3
4	CIGNA	PRUDENTIAL 20.9	4
5	New York Life	Prudential 17.8	5
6	The Hartford	Principal 15.7	6
7	AEtna	Nationwide® Insurance 14.9	7
8	JohnHancock	AIG 14.2	8
9	Nationwide® Insurance	New York Life 13.6	9
10	AIG	The Hartford 12.5	10

SOURCE: Lehman Brothers, Inc., "The Life Insurance Industry: View from Abroad" *M&A Review*, March 19, 2001.

[a] *Pro forma 2000 and 2001 acquisitions*

Demutualization

Since mid-1995, several insurance companies have changed from mutual companies to stock companies for reasons discussed previously in this chapter. Since insurance companies are regulated by states, such changes have to be preapproved by the state insurance regulatory department. Many industry observers believe that the recent demutualized insurance companies will either acquire other financial companies or will be acquired by other financial companies, or both.

Some states, as indicated above, have approved the mutual holding company status, and so the resident insurance companies had a choice of converting to a mutual holding company or a pure public stock company. Other states, including New York, have not approved the mutual holding company status, and so the only option remaining to a mutual company is to demutualize, that is, become a public stock company.

Key Points That You Should Understand Before Proceeding

1. The Glass-Steagall Act of 1933 prevented any one company from being simultaneously involved in commercial banking, investment banking, and insurance.
2. In response to a changing financial landscape, the Gramm-Leach-Bliley Act of 1999 removed the above restriction and is expected to accelerate mergers among formerly distinct financial institutions.

EVOLUTION OF INSURANCE, INVESTMENT, AND RETIREMENT PRODUCTS

Even prior to the Financial Modernization Act of 1999, there was an increasing overlap of insurance, investment, and pension products and the distribution of those products. The passage of this act has accelerated this convergence. This chapter as well as the next two discuss insurance companies, investment companies, and pension plans with their increasingly overlapping products.

Two decades ago there were three distinct types of products for individuals: insurance, savings/investment, and retirement. The specific products in each distinguishable category were as follows. Insurance products included term life and whole life. Savings/investment products included stocks, bonds, and mutual funds. Retirement products included Social Security (provided by the government), defined benefit and defined contribution plans (provided by employers), and **individual retirement accounts (IRAs)** (provided by investment companies).

During the last two decades, many products have been developed that fit into two or even three of these categories. Into which of these three categories, for example, does an IRA sold to a customer by a life insurance agent fit? Arguably, the correct answer to this question is all three categories. Figure 7-2 provides a summary of some of the products on the insurance/savings/retirement spectrum, which are really *hybrids*. We have discussed the various insurance products in this chapter. Mutual funds and other investment products are discussed in Chapter 8. Retirement products are discussed in Chapter 9. This section discusses products that are hybrid retirement and savings products but which are often manufactured and distributed by insurance companies.

Two products that are a hybrid of retirement and investment products and are often distributed by insurance companies and agents are 401(k)s and IRAs. These products are also often distributed by many insurance companies, and the insurance companies often include some of their own products within these categories. Because these plans are retirement plans, there are tax advantages to both the employee and the employer (if relevant).

Under the 1954 Internal Revenue Service (IRS) rules, *qualified plans* are tax-deferred plans set up by employers for employees. The employees pay taxes only when they withdraw the funds; that is, the contributions are not taxed, they are "before taxes." When employers make contributions to employee plans, the employers also, if they meet several requirements, receive a tax benefit (typically a tax deduction for the payment). Because these plans receive tax benefits and are intended for retirement,

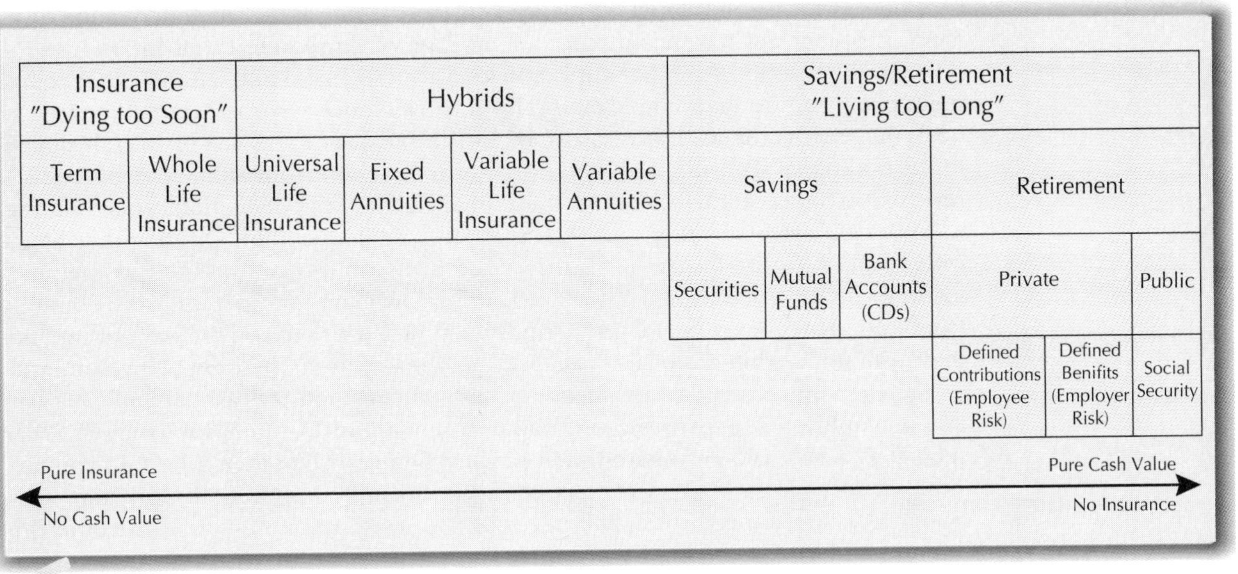

Insurance "Dying too Soon"		Hybrids				Savings/Retirement "Living too Long"				
Term Insurance	Whole Life Insurance	Universal Life Insurance	Fixed Annuities	Variable Life Insurance	Variable Annuities	Savings			Retirement	
						Securities	Mutual Funds	Bank Accounts (CDs)	Private	Public
									Defined Contributions (Employee Risk)	Defined Benifits (Employer Risk)	Social Security

Pure Insurance

No Cash Value

Pure Cash Value

No Insurance

Figure 7-2   Insurance/Savings/Retirement Vehicles
SOURCE: Frank J. Jones, "An Overview of Institutional Fixed Income Strategies," in Volume 1 of *Professional Perspectives on Fixed Income Portfolio Management* (New Hope, PA: Frank J. Fabozzi Associates, 2000).

typically withdrawals prior to age $59\frac{1}{2}$ are subject to a 10% (of principal) penalty tax. In addition, withdrawals must begin by age $70\frac{1}{2}$ to limit the duration of the tax advantage.

401(k) Plans

401(k) plans, which were authorized by the Revenue Act of 1978, are plans provided by an employer whereby an employee may elect to contribute pretax dollars to a qualified tax-deferred retirement plan. The employer offers a range of investment options from which the employee selects a vehicle to invest these funds. The company's own stock, if the company is public, is often one investment option. Most current employer 401(k) plans provide a diversified portfolio of mutual funds to their employees, typically including funds offered by one or more investment companies. 401(k) plans are offered to employers by several distribution systems, primarily insurance companies, investment companies, and others. The employer often matches a certain portion of the employee's contribution. Because of the tax deferral privilege, there are limits on the amount the employee can contribute and also that the employer can match.

IRAs (Individual Retirement Accounts)

While a 401(k) is an *employer-sponsored* retirement program, the most common types of IRAs are *personal* tax-deferred retirement plans; that is, they are set up at the initiative of the employee/investor. IRAs were created by the Employee Retirement Income Security Act (ERISA) of 1974. There are limits on the amount that may be invested in an IRA and the amount of earned income to qualify for an IRA investment.

Some IRAs, however, are employer sponsored. The various types of IRAs, which are both individually sponsored and employer sponsored, are as follows. Individually sponsored IRAs include traditional IRA, Roth IRAs, and rollover IRAs. Employer-sponsored IRAs include Simplified Employee Pension (SEPs) plans, Salary Reduction SEPs (SARSEPs), and Savings Incentive Matching Plan for Employees (SIMPLE).

Traditional and Roth IRAs are vehicles for individuals to set up their own retirement plans outside their employment. Both types permit assets to accumulate free of taxes. In general, the Roth IRA, provided by the Taxpayer Relief Act of 1997, is similar to the traditional IRA, although the taxability of their contributions and withdrawals is reversed. Whereas contributions to traditional IRAs are tax deductible, contributions to Roth IRAs are made after tax (that is, are not tax deductible). On the other hand, with respect to distributions, traditional IRA distributions are taxed as ordinary income (that is, even capital gains are taxed as ordinary income), and distributions from Roth IRAs are tax free. Overall, traditional IRAs are taxed on the way out (at time of distribution), while Roth IRAs are taxed on the way in (at the time of investment).

In general, absent certain special circumstances (such as death, disability, or certain unemployment expenses), withdrawals from either IRA type prior to age $59\frac{1}{2}$ are subject to a 10% IRS early withdrawal penalty. Some of the other rules on voluntary and mandatory distributions are very complex. Contributions to both Roth and traditional IRAs are limited to $2,000 per year, and even the ability to contribute this amount is phased out at higher incomes.

Rollover IRAs, also called "conduit IRAs," are used for rolling over eligible distributions from employer-sponsored retirement plans, such as 401(k)s. Rollover IRAs may be used when an individual is leaving an employer and wants to continue this retirement plan, that is, does not want to be subject to distribution/withdrawal taxes. The employees can roll over assets from an employer-sponsored program into a rollover IRA and subsequently roll it back to another employer-sponsored plan. Traditional and Roth IRAs cannot be rolled into employer-sponsored plans.

SEPs and SIMPLEs are both qualified employer-sponsored IRAs wherein the contributions by the business are tax deductible to the business. The SEP is a type of IRA that allows an employer to make a tax-deductible contribution of from 0 to 15% of earned income per year, per participant, up to $30,000. SEPs are ideal for the self-employed or small business owner. The SARSEP is a modification of the SEP. According to the SIMPLE, which became available during 1997, the employer must match employee contributions up to 3% of compensation or as low as 1%, or must make a nonelective contribution of 2% of compensation to all eligible employees.

As can be seen with respect to both product design and distribution channels, the distinction among insurance, investment, and retirement products has become very blurred.

SUMMARY

In general, insurance companies bear risk from parties who wish to avert risk by transferring it to the insurance companies. The party seeking to transfer the risk pays an insurance premium to the insurance company.

Insurance companies pay the insured when and/or if the insured event occurs. Because insurance companies collect premiums initially and pay the claims later, the initial revenues are invested in a portfolio, and portfolio returns become another important revenue for the insurance company. Consequently, insurance companies are financial intermediaries that function as risk bearers.

The events insured can be death (insured by life insurance companies), health problems (health insurance companies), or housing or automobile damage (property and casualty [P&C] insurance companies). In addition, there are different types of insurance for the different types of risks. Insurance companies have also become active in providing retirement and investment products. These different types of insurance liabilities reflect different types of risks and, therefore, the investment portfolios of these types of insurance companies differ significantly.

Insurance companies can be owned by stockholders (stock or public companies) or by their policyholders (mutual companies). Insurance companies are regulated by states, not the federal government. The regulations can vary significantly from one state to another.

The passage of the Gramm-Leach-Bliley Act (called the Financial Modernization Act of 1999) has eliminated the barriers between insurance companies, commercial banks, and investment banks, and various combinations of these types of companies will continue to evolve.

KEY TERMS

- **401(k)**, 117
- **Annuity**, 100
- **Bankassurance**, 104
- **Cash value life insurance**, 108
- **Crediting rate**, 99
- **GAAP surplus**, 103
- **General account product**, 111
- **Gramm-Leach-Bliley Act (GLB)**, 114
- **Guaranteed investment contract or guaranteed income contract (GIC)**, 99
- **Health insurance company**, 98
- **Investment income**, 96
- **Individual retirement account (IRA)**, 116
- **Life insurance company**, 97
- **Multiline insurance company**, 101
- **Mutual holding company (MHC)**, 106
- **Mutual insurance company**, 105
- **National Association of Insurance Commissioners (NAIC)**, 103
- **Policy lapse**, 108
- **Premium on an insurance policy**, 96
- **Property and casualty insurance company (P&C)**, 98
- **Reinsurer**, 104
- **Separate account product**, 111
- **Statutory surplus (or reserve)**, 103
- **Stock insurance company**, 105
- **Surplus**, 103
- **Term life insurance**, 108
- **Underwriting income**, 96
- **Universal life policy**, 110
- **Variable life insurance**, 110
- **Whole life insurance**, 108

QUESTIONS

1. a. What are the major sources of revenue for an insurance company?
   b. How are its profits determined?
2. Name the major types of insurance and investment-oriented products sold by insurance companies.
3. a. What is a GIC?
   b. Does a GIC carry a "guarantee" like a government obligation?
4. What are some key differences between a mutual fund and an annuity?
5. Why should a purchaser of life insurance be concerned about the credit rating of his or her insurance company?
6. a. Does the SEC regulate all insurance companies?
   b. If not, who regulates them?
7. Does the insurance industry have a self-regulatory group and, if so, what is its role?
8. What is the statutory surplus and why is it an important measure for an insurance company?
9. What is bankassurance?
10. a. What is meant by "demutualization"?
    b. What are the perceived advantages of demutualization?
11. Comment on the following quotation from Frank J. Jones, "An Overview of Institutional Fixed Income Strategies," in Volume 1 of *Professional Perspectives on*

Fixed Income Portfolio Management (New Hope, PA: Frank J. Fabozzi Associates, 2000):

> *An important impediment to the use of the total rate of return objective by stock life insurance companies is the role of equity analysts on Wall Street. . . . These equity analysts emphasize the stability of earnings and thereby prefer stable income to capital gains. Therefore, they consider only income and not capital gains, either realized or unrealized, in operating income—an important measure in their overall rating. While this practice of not considering capital gains may be appropriate for bonds, it certainly is inappropriate for common stock and provides a significant disincentive to life insurance companies for owning common stock in their portfolios. . . . this equity analyst practice does a disservice to policyholders of stock life insurance companies since their insurance companies end up having inferior asset allocations.*

12. Comment on the following statement: "The Mutual Holding Company structure is not vulnerable to a hostile takeover."
13. What is term insurance, whole life insurance, variable life insurance, universal life insurance, and survivorship insurance?
14. Why are all participating policies written in an insurance company's general account?
15. Whose liabilities are harder to predict, life insurers or property and casualty insurers? Explain why.
16. How does the Financial Modernization Act of 1999 affect the insurance industry?

C h a p t e r   8

Investment Companies And Exchange-Traded Funds

Learning Objectives

After reading this chapter, you will understand

- the different types of investment companies: mutual funds, closed-end investment companies, and unit trusts.
- how the share prices of mutual funds and closed-end funds are determined.
- the structure of funds and the costs that they incur.
- how investment companies can differ depending on their investment objectives.
- the economic benefits that investment companies provide, including diversification and reduced costs of investing.
- the meaning of a regulated investment company.
- the structure of investment companies.
- the taxation of mutual funds.
- that the mutual fund industry is highly concentrated, with many of the assets being managed by a relatively few fund families.
- the alternatives to mutual funds being developed.
- the types of investment companies that exist in selected countries around the world.
- what exchange traded funds are.
- the similarities and differences between exchange-traded funds and closed-end funds.

Investment companies are financial intermediaries that sell shares to the public and invest the proceeds in a diversified portfolio of securities. Each share sold represents a proportional interest in the portfolio of securities managed by the investment company on behalf of its shareholders. The type of securities purchased depends on the company's investment objective. Exchange-traded funds are similar to investment companies but have several advantages relative to investment companies.

TYPES OF INVESTMENT COMPANIES

There are three types of investment companies: open-end funds, closed-end funds, and unit trusts.

121

Open-End Funds (Mutual Funds)

Open-end funds, commonly referred to simply as *mutual funds*, are portfolios of securities, mainly stocks, bonds, and money market instruments. There are several important aspects of mutual funds. First, investors in mutual funds own a pro rata share of the overall portfolio. Second, the investment manager of the mutual fund actively manages the portfolio, that is, buys some securities and sells others (this characteristic is unlike unit investment trusts, discussed below). Third, the value or price of each share of the portfolio, called the **net asset value (NAV)**, equals the market value of the portfolio minus the liabilities of the mutual fund divided by the number of shares owned by the mutual fund investors. That is,

$$NAV = \frac{\text{Market value of portfolio} - \text{Liabilities}}{\text{Number of shares outstanding}}$$

For example, suppose that a mutual fund with 10 million shares outstanding has a portfolio with a market value of $215 million and liabilities of $15 million. The NAV is

$$NAV = \frac{\$215,000,000 - \$15,000,000}{10,000,000} = \$20$$

Fourth, the NAV or price of the fund is determined only once each day, at the close of the day. For example, the NAV for a stock mutual fund is determined from the closing stock prices for the day. Business publications provide the NAV each day in their mutual fund tables. The published NAVs are the closing NAVs. Fifth, and very importantly, all new investments into the fund or withdrawals from the fund during a day are priced at the closing NAV (investments after the end of the day or on a non-business day are priced at the next day's closing NAV).

The total number of shares in the fund increases if there are more investments than withdrawals during the day, and vice versa. For example, assume that at the beginning of a day a mutual fund portfolio has a value of $1 million, there are no liabilities, and there are 10,000 shares outstanding. Thus, the NAV of the fund is $100. Assume that during the day $5,000 is deposited into the fund, $1,000 is withdrawn, and the prices of all the securities in the portfolio remain constant. This means that 50 shares were issued for the $5,000 deposited (since each share is $100) and 10 shares redeemed for $1,000 (again, since each share is $100). The net number of new shares issued is then 40. Therefore, at the end of the day there will be 10,040 shares and the total value of the fund will be $1,004,000. The NAV will remain at $100.

If, instead, the prices of the securities in the portfolio change, both the total size of the portfolio and, therefore, the NAV will change. In the previous example, assume that during the day the value of the portfolio doubles to $2 million. Since deposits and withdrawals are priced at the end-of-day NAV, which is now $200 after the doubling of the portfolio's value, the $5,000 deposit will be credited with 25 shares ($5,000/$200) and the $1,000 withdrawn will reduce the number of shares by 5 shares ($1,000/$200). Thus, at the end of the day there will be 10,020 shares (25 − 5 new shares) in the fund with a NAV of $200, and the value of the fund will be $2,004,000. (Note that 10,020 shares × $200 NAV equals $2,004,000, the portfolio value.)

Overall, the NAV of a mutual fund will increase or decrease due to an increase or decrease in the prices of the securities in the portfolio. The number of shares in the fund will increase or decrease due to the net deposits into or withdrawals from the fund. And the total value of the fund will increase or decrease for both reasons.

To summarize, there are three important characteristics of open-end or mutual funds. First, the number of shares of these funds increases or decreases as investors increase their investment or liquidate shares. Second, the fund company facilitates these increases or decreases by selling new shares to or buying existing shares from the investor. Third, these new investments or liquidations occur via the fund company at NAV.

Closed-End Funds

The shares of a **closed-end fund** are very similar to the shares of common stock of a corporation. The new shares of a closed-end fund are initially issued by an underwriter for the fund. And after the new issue, the number of shares remains constant. After the initial issue, there are no sales or purchases of fund shares by the fund company as there are for open-end funds. The shares are traded on a secondary market, either on an exchange or in the over-the-counter market.

Investors can buy shares either at the time of the initial issue (as discussed below), or in the secondary market. Shares are sold only on the secondary market. The price of the shares of a closed-end fund are determined by the supply and demand in the market in which these funds are traded. Thus, investors who transact closed-end fund shares must pay a brokerage commission at the time of purchase and at the time of sale.

The NAV of closed-end funds is calculated in the same way as for open-end funds. However, the price of a share in a closed-end fund is determined by supply and demand, so the price can fall below or rise above the net asset value per share. Shares selling below NAV are said to be "trading at a discount," while shares trading above NAV are "trading at a premium." Newspapers list quotations of the prices of these shares under the heading "Closed-End Funds."

Consequently, there are two important differences between open-end funds and closed-end funds. First, the number of shares of an open-end fund varies because the fund sponsor will sell new shares to investors and buy existing shares from shareholders. Second, by doing so, the share price is always the NAV of the fund. In contrast, closed-end funds have a constant number of shares outstanding because the fund sponsor does not redeem shares and sell new shares to investors (except at the time of a new underwriting). Thus, the price of the fund shares will be determined by supply and demand in the market and may be above or below NAV, as previously discussed.

Although the divergence of the price from NAV is often puzzling, in some cases the reasons for the premium or discount are easily understood. For example, a share's price may be below the NAV because the fund has large built-in tax liabilities, and investors are discounting the share's price for that future tax liability.[1] (We'll discuss this tax liability issue later in this chapter.) A fund's leverage and resulting risk may be another reason for the share's price trading below NAV. A fund's shares may trade at a premium to the NAV because the fund offers relatively cheap access to, and professional management of, stocks in another country about which information is not readily available to small investors. Recently, the Thai and Thai Capital funds have been prominent examples of this situation.[2]

There are, however, "lifeboat provisions" in fund charters that require them to take action to reduce the discount on the share by buying back shares via a tender

---

[1] Harold Bierman, Jr., and Bhaskaran Swaminathan, "Managing a Closed-End Investment Fund," *Journal of Portfolio Management* (Summer 2000), p. 49.

[2] The so-called "Country Funds" were popular in the late 1980s and made up a substantial portion of the closed-end funds issued at that time.

offer for the funds' stock, or doing an outright conversion to an open-end structure. If the fund manager does not believe it is in the best interest of the shareholders to convert or make a tend offer for shares, dissident shareholder groups can buy large blocks of stocks and initiate a proxy fight in order to liquidate the assets or "open-end the fund," in an attempt to increase the value of the fund to its NAV.

Under the **Investment Company Act of 1940**, closed-end funds are capitalized only once. They make an initial initial public offering (IPO), and then their shares are traded on the secondary market, just like any corporate stock, as discussed above. The number of shares is fixed at the IPO; closed-end funds cannot issue more shares. In fact, many closed-end funds become leveraged to raise more funds without issuing more shares.

An important feature of closed-end funds is that the initial investors bear the substantial cost of underwriting the issuance of the funds' shares. The proceeds that the managers of the fund have to invest equals the total paid by initial buyers of the shares minus all costs of issuance. These costs, which average around 7.5% of the total amount paid for the issue, normally include selling fees or commissions paid to the retail brokerage firms that distribute them to the public. The high commissions are strong incentives for retail brokers to recommend these shares to their retail customers, and also for investors to avoid buying these shares on their initial offering.[3]

Historically, closed-end funds have been far less popular than open-end funds in the United States. By year-end 1999, there were approximately 7,700 mutual funds in the United States with assets of $6.5 trillion, while there were 530 closed-end funds with a modest $160 billion in assets. Of the closed-end funds, only 28% were equity funds; the other 72% were bond funds, including municipal and taxable bonds. Bond funds have been, in general, eclipsed by the long rally in stocks during the 1990s.[4]

The relatively new **exchange-traded funds (ETFs)**, which are discussed at the end of this chapter, pose a threat to both mutual funds and closed-end funds. ETFs are essentially hybrid closed-end vehicles, which trade on exchanges but which typically trade very close to NAV.

Since closed-end funds are traded like stocks, the cost to any investor of buying or selling a closed-end fund is the same as that of a stock. The obvious charge is the stockbroker's commission. The bid/offer spread of the market on which the stock is traded is also a cost.

Unit Trusts

A **unit trust** is similar to a closed-end fund in that the number of unit certificates is fixed. Unit trusts typically invest in bonds. They differ in several ways from both mutual funds and closed-end funds that specialize in bonds. First, there is no active trading of the bonds in the portfolio of the unit trust. Once the unit trust is assembled by the sponsor (usually a brokerage firm or bond underwriter) and turned over to a trustee, the trustee holds all the bonds until they are redeemed by the issuer. Typically, the only time the trustee can sell an issue in the portfolio is if there is a dramatic decline in the issuer's credit quality. As a result, the cost of operating the trust will be considerably less than costs incurred by either a mutual fund or a closed-end fund. Second, unit trusts have a fixed termination date, while mutual funds and closed-end funds do not.[5] Third, unlike the mutual fund and closed-end fund investor, the unit trust investor knows that the portfolio consists of a specific portfolio of bonds and has

---

[3] Kathleen Weiss, "The Post-Offering Price Performance of Closed-End Funds," *Financial Management* (Autumn 1989), pp. 57–67.

[4] Richard Karp, "Doomed Dinosaurs?," *Barron's* (February 28, 2000), p. 27.

[5] There are, however, exceptions. Target term closed-end funds have a fixed termination date.

no concern that the trustee will alter the portfolio. While unit trusts are common in Europe, they are not common in the United States.

All unit trusts charge a sales commission. The initial sales charge for a unit trust ranges from 3.5% to 5.5%. In addition to these costs, there is the cost incurred by the sponsor to purchase the bonds for the trust that an investor indirectly pays. That is, when the brokerage firm or bond-underwriting firm assembles the unit trust, the price of each bond to the trust also includes the dealer's spread. There is also often a commission if the units are sold.

In the remainder of this chapter, our primary focus is on open-end (mutual) funds.

Key Points That You Should Understand Before Proceeding

1. The difference between an open-end fund (mutual fund) and a closed-end fund.
2. The meaning of net asset value (NAV) per share.
3. The difference between a closed-end fund and a unit trust.
4. The price of a share of a closed-end fund can trade at a discount or premium to its NAV.

GROWTH OF MUTUAL FUNDS

The number of and assets in mutual funds grew significantly during the 1990s. This section describes that growth and the reasons for this growth.[6]

During the 1990s, there was a significant shift by individual investors from real estate and other tangible assets to financial assets. At the beginning of the decade, nearly 40% of household assets were in real estate and other tangible assets. But by the end of the decade, this share had decreased to 30%. On the other hand, discretionary financial assets increased to 44% of household assets from 34% in 1989. The relative shift toward discretionary financial assets occurred primarily in corporate equities. Nearly one-half of all U.S. households owned stock either directly or indirectly in 1999, up from just under one-third of households at the beginning of 1990.

As households shifted into financial assets, they increased their preference for indirect ownership through mutual funds over direct ownership of stocks and bonds. By the end of 1999, mutual funds accounted for 28% of household discretionary assets, up from 12% at the end of 1989. In addition, 85% of equity-owning households held a portion of their stocks in mutual funds in 1999, up from 50% in 1992.

At the end of the 1990s, households owned approximately 90% of all mutual fund assets. The household base of mutual funds expanded considerably during the 1990s, rising from roughly one-quarter of all U.S. households in 1989 to nearly one-half in 1999. At the end of the decade, 48 million households, representing 83 million individual investors, owned mutual funds. Assets held in mutual funds grew from slightly less than $1 trillion at the beginning of the 1990s to just under $7 trillion by the end of the decade. Mutual funds grew at a 21.4% rate during the 1990s. More than half the growth came from fund performance and 40% from net new investments with the remaining growth from new funds.

The number of mutual funds rose from approximately 2,900 in 1990 to about 8,000 at the end of 1999. Due to the large number of funds, the typical fund has

---

[6] Brian Reid, *The 1990s: A Decade of Expansion and Changes in the U.S. Mutual Fund Industry*, Investment Company Institute, 6, no. 3 (July 2000), pp. 3–6 and 9–10. This report is an excellent summary and analysis of the mutual fund industry in the 1990s.

remained fairly small. Half of the funds in 1990 had less than $50 million in assets. By 1999, median assets had risen to only about $130 million. The average fund size rose from $217 million to about $1 billion in 1999. But only 16% of the funds in 1999 had assets greater than the average fund. That is, there were many small funds and a few very large ones. Table 8-1 shows the assets in various fund categories during 1990 and 1999 and the net flows into these funds during these two years and the decade of the 1990s.

One of the most important factors in the growth of mutual funds was the growth of tax-deferred investing for retirement through defined contribution pension plans, IRAs, and variable annuities held outside of employer-sponsored retirement plans. (We will discuss these types of pension funds in Chapter 9.) By the end of the 1990s, households held 20% of their discretionary financial assets in tax-deferred products, up from 14% at the end of 1989. In addition, tax-deferred accounts became the primary means of owning mutual funds for many households. In 1999, approximately $3 trillion or 48% of household mutual funds assets were held in retirement accounts, up from $234 billion in 1990. Assets from defined contribution plans and IRAs rose from less than one-fifth of all fund assets in 1990 to more than a third in 1999.

At the beginning of the 1990s, most of the retirement assets in mutual funds were held in IRAs. IRAs accounted for approximately 13% of all mutual fund assets in 1990, whereas balances in employer-sponsored plans were a relatively insignificant 6%. During the 1990s, however, employer-sponsored defined contribution plans (either directly from employer-sponsored defined contribution plans or indirectly from rollovers to IRAs) became an important source of new cash flows to mutual funds.

Plan sponsors were attracted to mutual funds for their employees because they provided services such as daily pricing, exchange features, and telephonic access to account information. In addition, many mutual funds had the advantage of widely recognized brand names.

Overall from 1980 until the end of the twentieth century, according to the **Investment Company Institute**, the assets invested in mutual funds have increased significantly, from $134 billion in 1980 to $6,846 billion in 1999. Over the same period, the number of shareholder accounts increased from 12 million to 225 million. The funds industry has responded by providing more funds—564 in 1980 versus 7,791 in 1999. Some observers conclude from these data that there are too many mutual funds and that there will be consolidation in the mutual fund industry.[7]

Table 8-1 Net New Cash Flow and Assets of Mutual Funds, 1990–1999 (in billions)

	1990		1999		1990s Total
	Net Flow	**Assets**	**Net Flow**	**Assets**	**Net Flow**
Equity funds	$13	$ 239	$188	$4,042	$1,207
Bond funds	7	291	−8	808	239
Hybrid funds	1	36	−12	383	128
Money market funds	23	498	104	1,613	717
Total funds	$44	$1,065	$363	$6,846	$2,371

SOURCE: Brian Reid, *The 1990s: A Decade of Expansion and Changes in the U.S. Mutual Fund Industry*, Investment Company Institute, 6, no. 3 (July 2000), p. 2. Reprinted by permission of the Investment Company Institute (www.ici.org).

---

[7] *Mutual Fund Fact Book*, 40th edition (Washington D.C.: Investment Company Institute, 2000), pp. 69–71.

The growth of mutual funds has, however, been slowing recently since a high proportion of potential investors have entered the market and may have significant fund holdings. Some also assert that the advent of the ETFs and other mutual fund alternatives have and will affect the growth of mutual funds, as discussed later in this chapter.

Key Points You Should Understand Before Proceeding

1. During the 1990s, households shifted into financial assets from tangible assets, and into indirect ownership through mutual funds from direct ownership of stocks and bonds.

2. An important reason for the growth of mutual funds in the 1990s was the growth of tax-deferred investing for retirement through defined contribution plans, IRAs and variable annuities.

FUND SALES CHARGES AND ANNUAL OPERATING EXPENSES

There are two types of costs borne by investors in mutual funds. The first is the *shareholder fee*, usually called the *sales charge*. This cost is a "one-time" charge debited to the investor for a specific transaction, such as a purchase, redemption, or exchange. The type of charge is related to the way the fund is sold or distributed. The second cost is the annual fund operating expense, usually called the *expense ratio*, which covers the fund's expenses, the largest of which is for investment management. This charge is imposed annually. This cost occurs on all funds and for all types of distribution. We discuss each cost below.

Sales Charge

Sales charges on mutual funds are related to their method of distribution. The current menu of sales charges and distribution mechanisms has evolved significantly and is now much more diverse than it was a decade ago. To understand the current diversity and the evolution of distribution mechanisms, consider initially the circumstances of a decade ago. At that time, there were two basic methods of distribution, two types of sales charges, and the type of the distribution was directly related to the type of sales charge.

The two types of distribution were sales force (or wholesale) and direct. *Sales-force (wholesale) distribution* occurred via an intermediary, that is, via an agent, a stockbroker, insurance agent, or other entity, who provided investment advice and incentive to the client, actively "made the sale," and provided subsequent service. The distribution approach is active; that is, the fund is typically sold, not bought.

The other approach is *direct* (from the fund company to the investor), whereby there is no intermediary or salesperson to actively approach the client, provide investment advice and service, or make the sale. Rather, the client approaches the mutual fund company, most likely by a "1–800" telephone contact, in response to media advertisements or general information, and opens the account. Little or no investment counsel or service is provided either initially or subsequently. With respect to the mutual fund sale, this is a *passive approach*, although these mutual funds may be quite active in their advertising and other marketing activities. Funds provided by the direct approach are bought, not sold.

There is a *quid pro quo*, however, for the service provided in the sales-force distribution method. The *quid pro quo* is a sales charge borne by the customer and paid to the agent. The sales charge for the agent-distributed fund is called a **load**. The traditional type of load is called a *front-end load*, since the load is deducted initially or "up front." That is, the load is deducted from the amount invested by the client and paid to the agent/distributor. The remainder is the net amount invested in the fund in the client's name. For example, if the load on the mutual fund is 5% and the investor invests $100, the $5 load is paid to the agent and the remaining $95 is the net amount invested in the mutual fund at NAV. Importantly, only $95, not $100, is invested in the fund. The fund is, thus, said to be "purchased above NAV" (i.e., the investor pays $100 for $95 of the fund). The $5 load compensates the sales agent for the investment advice and service provided to the client by the agent. The load to the client, of course, represents income to the agent.

Let's contrast this with directly placed mutual funds. In a directly placed fund, there is no sales agent and, therefore, there is no need for a sales charge. Funds with no sales charges are called **no-load mutual funds**. In this case, if the client provides $100 to the mutual fund, $100 is invested in the fund in the client's name. This approach to buying the fund is called buying the fund "at NAV"; that is, the whole amount provided by the investor is invested in the fund.

A decade ago, many observers speculated that **load funds** would become obsolete and no-load funds would dominate because of the investor's aversion to a sales charge. Increasingly financially sophisticated individuals, the reasoning went, would make their own investment decisions and not need to compensate agents for their advice and service. But, as discussed below, the actual trend has been quite different. Why has there not been a trend away from the more costly agent-distributed funds as many expected? There are two reasons. First, many investors have remained dependent on the investment counsel and service, and, perhaps more importantly, the initiative of the sales agent. Second, sales-force distributed funds have shown considerable ingenuity and flexibility in imposing sales charges, which both compensate the distributors and appear attractive to the clients. Among the recent adaptations of the sales load are **back-end loads** and *level loads*. While the front-end load is imposed at the time of the purchase of the fund, the back-end load is imposed at the time fund shares are sold or redeemed. Level loads are imposed uniformly each year. These two alternative methods both provide ways to compensate the agent. However, unlike with the front-end load, both of these distribution mechanisms permit clients to buy a fund at NAV, that is, not have any of their initial investment debited as a sales charge before it is invested in their account.

The most common type of back-end load currently is the *contingent deferred sales charge* (CDSC). This approach imposes a gradually declining load on withdrawal. For example, a common "3,3,2,2,1,1,0" CDSC approach imposes a 3% load on the amount withdrawn after one year, 3% after the second year, 2% after the third year, and so forth. There is no sales charge for withdrawals after the seventh year.

The third type of load is neither a front-end load at the time of investment nor a (gradually declining) back-end load at the time of withdrawal, but a constant load each year (e.g., a 1% load every year). This approach is called a level load. This type of load appeals to the types of financial planners who charge annual fees (called *fee-based* financial planners) rather than commissions, such as sales charges (called *commission-based* financial planners).

Many mutual fund families often offer their funds with all three types of loads—that is, front-end loads (usually called "A shares"); back-end loads (often called "B shares"); and level loads (often called "C shares")—and permit the distributor and its client to select the type of load they prefer.[8]

---

[8] Edward S. O'Neal, "Mutual Fund Share Classes and Broker Incentives," *Financial Analysts Journal* (September/October 1999), pp. 76–87.

According to the National Association of Securities Dealers (NASD), the maximum allowable sales charge is 8.5%, although most funds impose lower charges. The sales charge for a fund applies to most, even very small, investments (although there is typically a minimum initial investment). For large investments, however, the sales charge may be reduced. For example, a fund with a 4.5% front-end load may reduce this load to 3.0% for investments of more than $1 million. There may be in addition further reductions in the sales charge at greater investments. The amount of investment needed to obtain a reduction in the sales charge is called a *breakpoint*; the breakpoint is $1 million in this example. There are also mechanisms whereby the total amount of the investment necessary to qualify for the breakpoint does not need to be invested up front, but only over time (according to a "letter of intent" signed by the investor).[9]

The sales charge is, in effect, paid by the client to the distributor. How does the fund family, typically called the *sponsor* or manufacturer of the fund, cover its costs and make a profit? That is the topic of the second type of "cost" to the investor, the fund annual operating expense.

Annual Operating Expenses (Expense Ratio)

The *operating expense*, also called the *expense ratio*, is debited annually from the investor's fund balance by the fund sponsor. The three main categories of annual operating expenses are the management fee, distribution fee, and other expenses.

The *management fee*, also called the **investment advisory fee**, is the fee charged by the **investment advisor** for managing a fund's portfolio. If the investment advisor is from a company separate from the fund sponsor, some or all of this investment advisory fee is passed onto the investment advisor by the fund sponsor. In this case, the fund manager is called a *subadvisor*. The management fee varies by the type of fund, specifically by the difficulty of managing the fund. For example, the management fee may increase from money market funds to bond funds, to U.S. growth stock funds, to emerging market stock funds, as illustrated by examples below.

In 1980, the SEC approved the imposition of a fixed annual fee, called the **12b-1 fee**, which is, in general, intended to cover *distribution costs*, including continuing agent compensation and manufacturer marketing and advertising expenses. Such 12b-1 fees are now imposed by many mutual funds. By law, 12b-1 fees cannot exceed 1% of the fund's assets per year. The 12b-1 fee may include a service fee of up to 0.25% of assets per year to compensate sales professionals for providing services or maintaining shareholder accounts. The major rationale for the component of the 12b-1 fee which accrues to the selling agent is to provide an incentive to selling agents to continue to service their accounts after having received a transaction-based fee such as a front-end load. As a result, a 12b-1 fee of this type is consistent with sales-force-sold load funds, not with directly sold, no-load funds. The rationale for the component of the 12b-1 fee, which accrues to the manufacturer of the fund, is to provide incentive and compensate for continuing advertising and marketing costs.

Other expenses include primarily the costs of (1) custody (holding the cash and securities of the fund), (2) the transfer agent (transferring cash and securities among buyers and sellers of securities and the fund distributions, etc.), (3) independent public accountant fees, and (4) directors' fees. The sum of the annual management fee, the annual distribution fee, and other annual expenses is called the *expense ratio*. All the cost information on a fund, including selling charges and annual expenses, are included in the fund prospectus.

---

[9] Daniel C. Inro, Christine X. Jaing, Michael Y. Ho, Wayne Y. Lee, "Mutual Fund Performance: Does Fund Size Matter?" *Financial Analysts Journal* (May/June 1999), pp. 74–87.

Table 8-2   Annual Operating Expenses for Three Mutual Funds

TYPE OF EXPENSE	FIDELITY MAGELLAN	VANGUARD S&P 500 INDEX	AMERICAN INCOME FUND OF AMERICA-A
Management fee	0.57%	0.16%	0.28%
Distribution and/or service (12b-1) fees	0	0	0.24
Other expenses	0.18	0.02	0.07
Total	0.75%	0.18%	0.59%

Table 8-2 shows the expense ratios from the current prospectuses of the three largest mutual funds: the Fidelity Magellan Fund, the Vanguard S&P 500 Index Fund, and the American Income Fund of America Fund. The first two are direct funds and the third is a sales-force fund. The Fidelity Magellan and Vanguard S&P 500 Index funds are directly sold and, thus, have no 12b-1 distribution expenses. The American Income Fund of America, on the other hand, is sales-force sold and has a distribution or 12b-1 fee. With respect to the management fee, index funds are easier to manage and, thus, the Vanguard S&P 500 Index fund has the lowest management fee. The Fidelity Magellan is a very actively managed pure stock fund, which is difficult to manage and has the highest management fee.

In addition to the annual operating expenses, the fund prospectus provides the fees which are imposed only at the time of a transaction. These fees are listed in Table 8-3 for the three largest funds. The Vanguard fund is directly distributed and is a pure no-load fund. The American fund is sales-force distributed and is a front-end load (A share) fund. The Fidelity fund is directly distributed but has a moderate front-end load.

As we explained earlier, many agent-distributed funds are provided in different forms, typically the following: (1) A shares: front-end load; (2) B shares: back-end load (contingent deferred sales charge); and, (3) C shares: level load. These different forms of the same fund are called *share classes*. Table 8-4 provides an example of hypothetical sales charges and annual expenses of funds of different classes for an agent-distributed stock mutual fund. The sales charge accrues to the distributor. The management fee accrues to the mutual fund manager. Other expenses, including custody and transfer fees and the fees of managing the fund company, accrue to the fund sponsor to cover expenses.

Table 8-3   Shareholders Fees for the Three Largest Funds

TYPE OF FEE	FIDELITY MAGELLAN	VANGUARD S&P 500 INDEX	AMERICAN INCOME FUND OF AMERICA-A
Sales charge on purchases	3%	0%	5.75%
Sales charge on reinvested dividend	0	0	0
Redemption fee	0	0	0
Exchange fee	0	0	0

Table 8-4   Hypothetical Sales Charges and Annual Expenses of Funds of Different Classes for an Agent-Distributed Stock Mutual Fund

			Annual Operating Expenses			
SALES CHARGE FRONT BACK LEVEL			MANAGEMENT FEE	DISTRIBUTION (12B-1 FEE)	OTHER EXPENSES	EXPENSE RATIO
A 4.5%	0	0%	0.90%	0.00%	0.15%	1.05%
B 0	*	0	0.90	0.75	0.15	1.80
C 0	0	1	0.90	0.75	0.15	1.80

* *3%, 3%, 2%, 2%, 1%, 0%...*

Multiple Share Classes

During the 1990s, the number of share classes expanded even more quickly than the number of funds, rising from 2,941 in January 1990 to 15,262 in December 1999. Share classes were first offered in 1989 following the SEC's approval of multiple share class. Initially share classes were used primarily by sales-force funds to offer alternatives to the front-end load as a means of compensating brokers. Later, some of these funds used additional share classes as a means of offering the same fund or portfolio through alternative distribution channels in which some fund expenses varied by channel. Offering new share classes was more efficient and less costly than setting up two separate funds.[10] By the end of the decade, the average long-term sales-force fund offered nearly three share classes, as shown in Table 8-5. Direct market funds tended to continue to offer only one share class.

Key Points That You Should Understand Before Proceeding

1. The difference between a load and a no-load mutual fund.
2. The difference between a front-end load, a back-end load, and a level load fund.
3. The difference between a sales charge and an expense ratio.
4. The SEC Rule 12b-1 and the type of fund called a 12b-1 fund.
5. The components of the expense ratio.
6. The nature of a management fee.
7. The meaning of trading at NAV.

Table 8-5   Average Number of Share Classes per Long-Term Fund by Distribution Channel

	1990	1995	1999
Sales force	1.1	1.9	2.7
Direct market	1.0	1.1	1.2

SOURCE: Brian Reid, *The 1990s: A Decade of Expansion and Changes in the U.S. Mutual Fund Industry*, Investment Company Institute, 6, no. 3 (July 2000), p. 15.

---

[10] Reid, *The 1990s: A Decade of Expansion and Changes in the U.S. Mutual Fund Industry*, p. 15.

ECONOMIC MOTIVATION FOR FUNDS

Recall from Chapter 2 that financial intermediaries obtain funds by issuing financial claims against themselves and then investing these funds. An investment company is a financial intermediary in that it pools the funds of individual investors and uses these funds to buy portfolios of securities. Recall the special role in financial markets played by financial intermediaries. Financial intermediaries provide some or all of the following six economic functions: (1) risk reduction via diversification; (2) lower costs of contracting and processing information; (3) professional portfolio management; (4) liquidity; (5) variety; and (6) a payments mechanism. Consider these economic functions as provided by mutual funds.

Consider first the function of risk reduction through diversification. By investing in a fund, an investor can obtain broad-based ownership of a sufficient number of securities to reduce portfolio risk. (We will be more specific about the type of risk that is reduced in Chapter 13.) Although an individual investor may be able to acquire a broad-based portfolio of securities, the degree of diversification will be limited by the amount available to invest. By investing in an investment company, however, the investor can effectively achieve the benefits of diversification at a lower cost even if the amount of money available to invest is not large.

The second economic function is the reduced cost of contracting and processing information because an investor purchases the services of a presumably skilled financial advisor at less cost than if the investor directly and individually negotiated with such an advisor. The advisory fee is lower because of the larger size of assets managed, as well as the reduced costs of searching for an investment manager and obtaining information about the securities. Also, the costs of transacting in the securities are reduced because a fund is better able to negotiate transactions costs; and custodial fees and record-keeping costs are less for a fund than for an individual investor. For these reasons, there are said to be economies of scale in investment management.

Third, and related to the first two advantages, is the advantage of the professional management of the mutual fund. Fourth is the advantage of liquidity. Mutual funds can be bought or liquidated any day at the closing NAV. Fifth is the advantage of the variety of funds available, in general, and even in one particular funds family, as discussed below. Finally, money market funds and some other types of funds provide payment services by allowing investors to write checks drawn on the fund, although this facility may be limited in various ways.

Key Points That You Should Understand Before Proceeding

1. A mutual fund can reduce risk through portfolio diversification.
2. A mutual fund can reduce a variety of costs related to investment and management of portfolios.
3. A mutual fund can provide liquidity.

TYPES OF FUNDS BY INVESTMENT OBJECTIVE

Mutual funds have been provided to satisfy the various **investment objectives** of investors. In general, there are stock funds, bond funds, money market funds, and others. Within each of these categories, there are several subcategories of funds. There are also U.S.-only funds, international funds (no U.S. securities), and global funds (both U.S. and international securities). There are also passive and active funds. Passive (or indexed) funds are designed to replicate an index, such as the S&P 500 Stock Index, the Lehman Aggregate Bond Index, or the Morgan Stanley Capital

International EAFE Index (Europe, Australasia, and the Far East). Active funds, on the other hand, attempt to outperform an index and other funds by actively trading the fund portfolio. There are also many other categories of funds, as discussed below. Each fund's objective is stated in its prospectus, as required by the SEC and the "1940 Act," as discussed below.

Stock funds differ by:

➤ the average market capitalization ("market cap"—large, mid, and small) of the stocks in the portfolio;

➤ style (growth, value, and blend); and

➤ sector—"sector funds" specialize in one particular sector or industry, such as technology, health care, or utilities.

The categories for market cap, while not fixed over time, were as of late 2000 approximately:

➤ small—$0 to $2 billion;

➤ mid—$2 billion to $12 billion; and

➤ large—more than $12 billion.

With respect to style, stocks with high price-to-book and price-to-earnings ratios are considered "growth stocks," and stocks with low price-to-value and price-to-earnings ratios are considered value stocks, although other variables are also considered. There are also blend stocks with respect to style.

Bond funds differ by the creditworthiness of the issuers of the bonds in the portfolio (for example, U.S. government, investment-grade corporate, and high-yield corporate) and by the maturity (or duration) of the bonds (long, intermediate, and short.) There is also a category of bond funds called municipal bond funds whose coupon interest is tax exempt. Municipal funds may also be single state (that is, all the bonds in the portfolio were issued by issuers in the same state) or multistate.

There are also other categories of funds such as asset allocation, hybrid, or balanced funds (all of which hold both stocks and bonds), and convertible bond funds. There is also a category of money market funds (maturities of one year or less) which provide protection against interest rate fluctuations. These funds can have some degree of credit risk (except for the U.S. government money market category). Many of these funds offer check-writing privileges. In addition to taxable money market funds, there are also tax-exempt, municipal money market funds.

Among the other fund offerings are *index funds* and *funds of funds*. Index funds, as discussed above, attempt to passively replicate an index. A fund of funds is a fund that invests in other mutual funds. In 1990, there were only 16 fund of funds with $1.4 billion in assets. By 1999, there were 213 fund of funds with $48 billion in assets.[11] With respect to index funds:

➤ The number of index funds rose from 15 in 1990 to 193 in 1999 with total assets increasing from $3 billion to $383 billion over this period.

➤ The variety of index funds also expanded, domestically and internationally.

➤ Equity funds are the most common type of index funds, accounting for about 88% of these funds and $357 billion in assets.

➤ Funds of funds invest in other funds not in individual securities.

Several organizations provide data on mutual funds. The most popular ones are Morningstar and Lipper. These firms provide data on fund expenses, portfolio man-

---

[11] Reid, *The 1990s: A Decade of Expansion and Changes in the U.S. Mutual Fund Industry*, pp. 14–15.

agers, fund sizes, and fund holdings. But perhaps most importantly, they provide performance (that is, rate of return) data and rankings among funds based on performances and other factors. To compare fund performance on an "apples to apples" basis, these firms divide mutual funds into several categories that are intended to be fairly homogeneous by investment objective. The categories provided by Morningstar and Lipper are similar but not identical and are shown and compared in Table 8-6. Thus, the performance of one Morningstar "large cap blend" fund can be meaning-

Table 8-6   Fund Categories: Morningstar versus Lipper

Morningstar		Lipper		Morningstar		Lipper	
LG	Large Growth	LG	Large Cap Growth	CS	Short Term Bond	SB	Short Term Bond
				GS	Short Government	SU	Short Term US
LV	Large Value	LV	Large Cap Value				
LB	Large Blend	LC	Large Cap Core	GI	Interm. Government	IG	Intmdt US Govt
MG	Mid Cap Growth	MG	Mid Cap Growth	CI	Inter-Term Bond	IB	Intermediate Bond
				MT			Mortgage
MV	Mid Cap Value	MV	Mid Cap Value	CL	Long Term Bond	AB	Long Term Bond
MB	Mid-Cap Blend	MC	Mid Cap Core	GL	Long Government	LU	Long Term US
							Funds
		XG	Multi Cap Growth				
		XC	Multi Cap Core			GT	General US
		XV	Multi Cap Value				Taxable
				CV	Convertibles		
SG	Small Growth	SG	Small Cap Growth	UB	Ultrashort Bond		
				HY	High Yield Bond	HC	High Yield Taxable
SV	Small Value	SV	Small Cap Value	MO	Multisector Bond		
SB	Small Blend	SC	Small Cap Core	IB	International Bond	WB	World Bond
DH	Domestic Hybrid	EI	Equity Income	EB	Emerging Bond		
		BL	Balanced			GM	General Muni
							Debt
FS	Foreign Stock	IL	International Stock (non US)	ML	Muni National Long		
WS	World Stock	GL	Global Stock (incl. US)	MI	Muni National Interm	IM	Intmdt Muni Debt
ES	Europe Stock	EU	European Region				
EM	Diversified Emerging Mkt	EM	Emerging Markets			SM	Short-Term Muni
DP	Diversified Pacific Asia	PR	Pacific Region				
PJ	Pacific Asia ex-Japan					HM	High Yield Muni
JS	Japan Stock					NM	Insured Muni
LS	Latin America Stock	LT	Latin American	SL	Muni Single St. Long	SS	Single State Muni
							Debt
IH	International Hybrid			SI	Muni Single St. Interm.		
		SE	Sector	MS	Muni Single St. Short		
		SQ	Specialty Equity				
ST	Technology	TK	Science & Technology	MY	Muni New York Long		
SU	Utilities	UT	Utility	MC	Muni California Long		
SH	Health	HB	Health & Biotech	MN	Muni New York Interm		
SC	Communication			MF	Muni California Interm		
SF	Financial						
SN	Natural Resources	NR	Natural Resources				
SP	Precious Metals						
SR	Real Estate						

fully compared with another fund in the same category but not with a "small cap value" fund. Morningstar's ranking system, whereby each fund is rated from one star (the worst) to five stars (the best) relative to the other funds in its category, is well-known.

Mutual fund data are also provided by the Investment Company Institute, the national association for mutual funds. Table 8-7 provides data on the assets of the major fund categories as reported by the Investment Company Institute.

Key Points You Should Understand Before Proceeding

1. In order to meet investor needs, mutual funds offered in the market differ by a variety of measures such as asset category (stock vs. bond, etc.); management style (active vs. passive); market segment (small cap vs. large cap in stock funds, investment grade vs. speculative grade in bond funds); and other such measures.

2. Organizations such as Morningstar and Lipper provide key performance data on mutual funds in ways that facilitate meaningful comparisons among them.

THE CONCEPT OF A FAMILY OF FUNDS

A concept that revolutionized the fund industry and benefitted many investors is what the mutual fund industry calls a *family of funds*, a group of funds or a complex of funds. That is, many fund management companies offer investors a choice of numerous funds with different investment objectives in the same fund family. In many cases, investors may move their assets from one fund to another within the family at little or no cost, and with only a phone call. Of course, if these funds are in a taxable account, there may be tax consequences to the sale. Although the same policies regarding loads and other costs may apply to all the members of the family, a management company may have different fee structures for transfers among different funds under its control.

Large fund families usually include money market funds, U.S. bond funds of several types, global stock and bond funds, broadly diversified U.S. stock funds, U.S. stock funds which specialize by market capitalization and style, and stock funds devoted to particular sectors such as health care, technology, or gold companies. Well-known management companies such as Fidelity Investment, Vanguard Group, and American Funds, the three largest fund families, sponsor and manage varied

Table 8-7   Mutual Fund Assets by Major Fund Categories (as of February 2001)

	Assets ($bn)	% of total assets	Number of Funds	Average Assets per Fund ($bn)
Stock funds	3,689.8	53%	4,429	0.8
Hybrid funds	346.5	5%	528	0.7
Taxable bond funds	558.6	8%	1,334	0.4
Municipal bond funds	283.0	4%	862	0.3
Taxable money market funds	1,771.4	26%	704	2.5
Tax-free money market funds	248.1	4%	340	0.7
Total	6,897.4	100%	8,197	0.8

SOURCE: Investment Company Institute

types of funds in a family. Fund families may also use external investment advisors along with their internal advisors in their fund families. The number of family funds has grown from 123 in 1980 to 433 in 1999. Fund data provided in newspapers group the various funds according to their families. For example, all the Fidelity funds are listed under the Fidelity heading, all the Vanguard funds are listed under their name, and so on.

Key Points That You Should Understand Before Proceeding

1. The meaning of the term *family of funds*.
2. The economic benefits that a family of funds can offer to investors.

MUTUAL FUND INDUSTRY CONCENTRATION

Despite the large number of mutual fund families, the industry is quite concentrated, with the top 5 families having 42% of industry assets and the top 10 with 56% at the end of 1999, as shown in Table 8-8. However, even though industry assets grew significantly during the 1990s, asset concentration among the largest mutual fund families underwent only marginal change during the decade. The 5 largest fund companies held 35% of the industry's assets in 1990 and 42% in 1999, as shown in Table 8-8. The result was similar for the largest 10 and 25 families.

The stability in market share during the decade occurred despite the large growth in assets and a high volume of mergers and acquisitions. New entrants, however, contributed to the stability in asset concentration. There were 464 mutual fund complexes at the beginning of the 1900s and 629 by the end of the decade. Among the 464 complexes at the beginning of the 1990s, 313 remained in 1999, with the others having exited through liquidations or mergers.

Finally, a substantial amount of rotation in the rankings of the top 25 largest complexes helped to keep the ratios stable. In 1990, 75% of the industry's assets were in bond and money market funds and 20% in equity funds. In contrast, by the end of the 1990s, domestic equity funds had 50% of assets.

The 10 largest individual mutual funds as of September 2000 are shown in Table 8-9. The 10 largest mutual fund families as of May 2001 are reported in Table 8-10. The largest fund group is managed by Fidelity Investments, which was mentioned above and is mainly a family of actively managed funds. The second largest fund group manager is Vanguard Group, a complex of funds that has enjoyed substantial growth in recent years. Vanguard emphasizes passively managed or index funds. Both of these fund families are primarily directly sold, no-load funds. The largest load family is American Funds. Because the industry manages over $5 trillion, the sizes of these

Table 8-8 Shares of Assets in Long-Term Funds at Largest Mutual Fund Companies

	1990	1994	1999
Top 5 complexes	34%	38%	42%
Top 10 complexes	53	51	56
Top 25 complexes	77	72	76

SOURCE: Brian Reid, *The 1990s: A Decade of Expansion and Changes in the U.S. Mutual Fund Industry*, Investment Company Institute, 6, no. 3 (July 2000), p. 16.

Table 8-9   The Ten Largest Mutual Funds

FUND	ASSETS ($ million)
Fidelity Magellan	86,540
Vanguard Index 500	74,796
Am.A Invest Co of Am	57,445
Am.A WA Mutual Inv	48,216
Am.A Grow Fd of Am	39,385
Fidelity Growth & Inc	34,925
Fidelity Contrafund	33,808
Am.A EuroPacific Gr	32,646
Am.A New Perspective	32,526
PIMCO Instl Tot Ret	31,508

SOURCE: Morningstar® Princilpla®Pro, Release date June 2001.

Table 8-10   The Ten Largest Mutual Fund Families (as of May 2001)

FUND COMPLEX	ASSETS ($ million)
Fidelity	771,273
Vanguard	569,233
American Funds	342,986
Putnam	210,205
Merrill Lynch	192,288
AIM Management	163,808
Franklin Templeton	163,439
Janus	155,713
Federated	147,842
Dreyfus	145,406

SOURCE: Strategic Insight Mutual Fund Research and Consulting, LLC., 2001.

largest fund complexes are noteworthy. Fidelity, for example, manages approximately $650 billion, and Vanguard almost $500 billion.[12]

Key Points That You Should Understand Before Proceeding

1. The extent of concentration in the mutual fund industry.
2. The sizes of the largest mutual funds and mutual fund families.

TAXATION OF MUTUAL FUNDS

Mutual funds must distribute at least 90% of their net investment income earned (bond coupons and stock dividends) exclusive of realized capital gains or losses to shareholders (along with meeting other criteria) to be considered a *regulated investment company* (RIC) and, thus, not be required to pay taxes at the fund level prior to

---

[12] *Mutual Fund Market News* (August 14, 2000), p. 10.

distributions to shareholders. Consequently, funds make these distributions. Taxes are paid on distributions only at the investor level, not the fund level. Even though many mutual fund investors choose to reinvest these distributions, the distributions are taxable to the investor, either as ordinary income or capital gains (long term or short term), whichever is relevant.

Capital gains distributions must occur annually, and typically occur late during the calendar year. The capital gains distributions may be either long-term or short-term capital gains, depending on whether the fund held the security for a year or more. Mutual fund investors have no control over the size of these distributions and, as a result, the timing and amount of the taxes paid on their fund holdings is largely out of their control. In particular, withdrawals by some investors may necessitate sales in the fund, which, in turn, cause realized capital gains and a tax liability to accrue to investors who maintain their holding.

New investors in the fund may assume a tax liability even though they have no gains. That is, all shareholders as of the date of record receive a full year's worth of dividends and capital gains distributions, even if they have owned shares for only one day. This lack of control over capital gains taxes is regarded as a major limitation of mutual funds. In fact, this adverse tax consequence is one of the reasons suggested for a closed-end company's price selling below par value. Also, this adverse tax consequence is one of the reasons for the popularity of exchange-traded funds, to be discussed later.

Of course, the investor must also pay ordinary income taxes on distributions of income. Finally, when the fund investors sell the fund, they will have long-term or short-term capital gains or losses, depending on whether they held the fund for a year or not.

Key Points You Should Understand Before Proceeding

1. Mutual funds must distribute at least 90% of their investment income in order to avoid taxation at the fund level.
2. Fund investors have no control over the size or timing of capital gains distributions, and consequently the associated tax liabilities.

REGULATION OF FUNDS

There are four major laws or acts that relate either indirectly or directly to mutual funds. The first is the Securities Act of 1933 ("the '33 Act"), which provides purchasers of new issues of securities with information regarding the issuer and, thus, helps prevent fraud. Because open-end investment companies issue new shares on a continuous basis, mutual funds must also comply with the '33 Act. The Securities Act of 1934 ("the '34 Act") is concerned with the trading of securities once they have been issued, with the regulation of exchanges, and with the regulation of broker-dealers. Mutual fund portfolio managers must comply with the '34 Act in their transactions.

All investment companies with 100 or more shareholders must register with the SEC according to the Investment Company Act of 1940 ("the '40 Act"). The primary purposes of the '40 Act are to reduce investment company selling abuses and to ensure that investors receive sufficient and accurate information. Investment companies must provide periodic financial reports and disclose their investment policies to investors. The '40 Act prohibits changes in the nature of an investment company's fundamental investment policies without the approval of shareholders. This act also provides some tax advantages for eligible RICs, as indicated below. The purchase and sale of mutual fund shares must meet the requirements of fair dealing that the SEC '40 Act and the NASD, a self-regulatory organization, have established for all securities transactions in the United States.

Finally, the Investment Advisors Act of 1940 specifies the registration requirements and practices of companies and individuals who provide investment advisory services. This Act deals with registered investment advisors (RIAs). Overall, although an investment company must comply with all aspects of the '40 Act, it is also subject to the '33 Act, the '34 Act, and the Investment Advisors Act of 1940.

The SEC also extended the '34 Act in 1988 to provide protections such that advertisements and claims by mutual fund companies would not be inaccurate or misleading to investors. New regulations aimed at potential self-dealing were established in the Insider Trading and Securities Fraud Enforcement Act of 1988, which requires mutual fund investment advisors to institute and enforce procedures that reduce the chances of insider trading.

An important feature of the '40 Act exempts any company that qualifies as a "regulated investment company" from taxation on its gains, either from income or capital appreciation, as previously indicated. To qualify as an RIC, the fund must distribute to its shareholders 90% of its net income excluding capital gains each year. Furthermore, the fund must follow certain rules about the diversification and liquidity of its investments and the degree of short-term trading and short-term capital gains.

Fees charged by mutual funds are also, as noted above, subject to regulation. The foundation of this regulatory power is the government's de facto role as arbiter of costs of transactions regarding securities in general. For example, the SEC and the NASD have established rules as part of the overall guide to fair dealing with customers about the markups dealers can charge financial institutions on the sale of financial assets. The SEC set a limit of 8.5% on a fund's load but allows the fund to pass through certain expenses under the 112b-1 rule. Effective July 1, 1993, the SEC has amended the rule to set a maximum of 8.5% on the total of all fees, inclusive of front-end and back-end loads as well as expenses such as advertising.

Some funds charge a 12b-1 fee, as authorized by the '40 Act. The 12b-1 fee may be divided into two parts. The first component is a *distribution fee*, which can be used for fund marketing and distribution costs. The maximum distribution fee is 0.75% (of net assets per year). The second is a *service fee* (or *trail commission*), which is used to compensate the sales professionals for their ongoing services. The maximum service fee is 0.25%. Thus, the maximum 12b-1 fee is 1%. While no-load funds can have 12b-1 fees, the practice has been that in order to call itself a no-load fund, its 12b-1 fee must be at most 0.25% (all of which would be a distrubution fee). In general, the distribution fee component of the 12b-1 fee is used to develop new customers while the service fee is used for servicing existing customers.

A rule called "prospectus simplification" or "Plain English Disclosure" was enacted on October 1, 1998, to improve the readability of the fund prospectus and other fund documents. According to the SEC, prospectuses and other documents were being written by lawyers for other lawyers and not for the typical mutual fund investor. This initiative mandated that prospectuses and other documents be written from then on in "plain English" for individual investors.

Among the recent SEC priorities that directly affect mutual funds are the following:

1. Reporting after-tax fund returns. This pending requirement would require funds to display the preliquidation and postliquidation impact of taxes on 1-, 5-, and 10-year returns

both in the fund's prospectus and in annual reports. Such reporting could increase the popularity of tax-managed funds (funds with a high tax efficiency).

2. More complete reporting of fees, including fees in dollars-and-cents terms as well as in percentage terms.

3. More accurate and consistent reporting of investment performance.

4. Requiring fund investment practices to be more consistent with the name of a fund to more accurately reflect their investment objectives. The SEC is considering requiring that 80% of a fund's assets be invested in the type of security that its name implies (e.g., health care stocks). The requirement is currently 65%.

5. Disclosing portfolio practices such as "window dressing" (buying or selling stocks at the end of a reporting period to include desired stocks or eliminate undesired stocks from the reports in order to improve the appeared composition of the portfolio), or "portfolio pumping" (buying shares of stocks already held at the end of a reporting period to improve performance during the period).

6. Requiring fund managers to list their security holdings more frequently than the current twice a year.

7. Various rules to increase the effectiveness of independent fund boards.

Key Points That You Should Understand Before Proceeding

1. The '33 Act, the '34 Act, the '40 Act, and the Investment Advisors Act of 1940.
2. The relevance of these acts to a mutual fund.
3. Important aspects of being a regulated investment company.
4. Recent SEC priorities impacting mutual funds.

STRUCTURE OF A FUND

A mutual fund organization is structured as follows:

1. A *board of directors* (also called the *fund trustees*), which represents the *shareholders* who are the owners of the mutual fund.

2. The mutual fund, which is an entity based on the Investment Company Act of 1940.

3. An *investment advisor*, which manages the fund's portfolios and is a registered investment advisor (RIA) according to the Investment Advisor's Act of 1940.

4. A *distributor* or broker-dealer, who is registered under the Securities Act of 1934.

5. Other service providers, both external to the fund (the independent public accountant, custodian, and transfer agent) and internal to the fund (marketing, legal, reporting, etc.).

The structure is illustrated in Figure 8-1.

The role of the **board of directors** is to represent the fund shareholders. The board is composed of both "interested" (or "inside") directors who are affiliated with the investment company (current or previous management) and "independent" (or "outside") directors who have no affiliation with the investment company. The practice is changing such that a majority of the board must be outside directors.

The mutual fund enters into a contract with an investment advisor to manage the fund's portfolios. The *investment advisor* can be an affiliate of a brokerage firm, an insurance company, a bank, an investment management firm, or an unrelated company. The distributor, which may or may not be affiliated with the mutual fund or investment advisor, is a broker-dealer. The role of the custodian is to hold the fund assets, segregating them from other accounts to protect the shareholders' interests. The transfer agent processes orders to buy and redeem fund shares, transfers the secu-

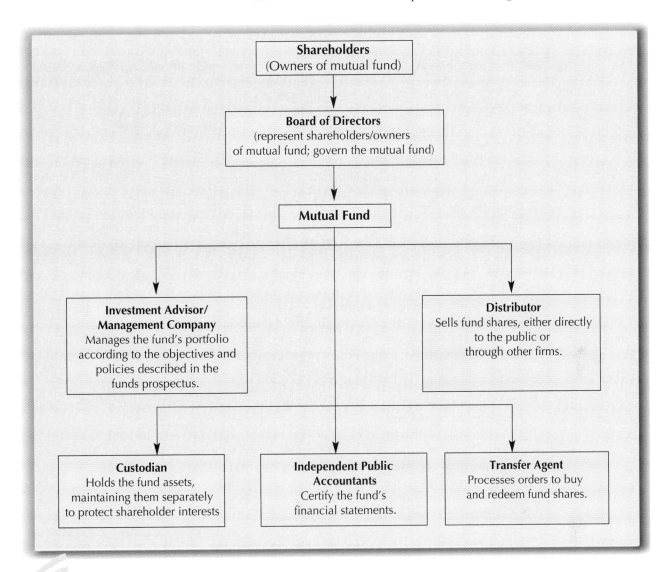

Figure 8-1   The Structure of a Mutual Fund
SOURCE: *Mutual Fund Fact Book*, 40th ed. (Washington D.C.: Investment Company Institute, 2000), p. 34.

rities and cash, collects dividends and coupons, and makes distributions. The independent public accountant audits the fund's financial statements.

Key Points That You Should Understand Before Proceeding
1. The duties of the investment advisor of a fund.
2. The role of the board of directors.

RECENT CHANGES IN THE MUTUAL FUND INDUSTRY

There have been several significant recent changes in the mutual fund industry in addition to those discussed previously in this chapter.

Distribution Channels

As explained earlier in this chapter, at the beginning of the 1990s there were two primary distribution channels, direct sales to investors and sales through brokers. Since then, fund companies and fund distributors developed and expanded sales channels in the 1990s beyond the two traditional channels. By the end of the 1990s, fund companies' use of multiple distribution channels resulted in a blurring of the distinction between direct and sales-force funds that had characterized funds at the beginning of the decade.

Fund companies and distribution companies developed new outlets for selling mutual funds and expanded their traditional sales channels. The changes that occurred are evident in the rising share of sales through third parties and intermediaries. In particular, the estimated share of new direct sales of long-term funds was 18% in 1999, down from 23% in 1990. Over the same period, new sales of long-term funds made through a third party or an intermediary rose from 77% to 82%. However, of this total third-party sales market, the sales-force market also declined, from 63% to 58%. Only the sales through third parties–direct market increased, from 14% to 24%.[13]

Significant market trends account for these changes. In particular, many funds that had previously marketed only directly turned increasingly toward third parties and intermediaries for distribution. For example, in 1990 an estimated 62% of new sales of direct-market funds came through traditional direct sales, whereas by 1999 this share had fallen to 43%. The nontraditional, third-party distribution channels used by direct-market funds were mutual fund supermarkets; mutual fund wrap-account programs; fee-based advisors; variable annuities; employer-sponsored pension plans, and bank trust departments.

Like direct-market funds, funds that were traditionally sold through a sales force moved increasingly to nontraditional sources of sales such as employer-sponsored pension plans, banks, and life insurance companies in the 1990s. Only 41% of new sales of sales-force funds came through nontraditional sources in 1990, whereas 65% came through nontraditional sources in 1999. Below we describe the various nontraditional distribution channels.

Supermarkets.

The introduction of the first mutual fund supermarket in 1992 marked the beginning of a significant change in the distribution of direct market funds. Specifically, during 1992, Charles Schwab & Company introduced its One Source service. With this and other supermarket programs, the organizer of the supermarket offers no-load funds from a number of different mutual fund companies. These supermarkets allow investors to purchase funds from participating companies without investors having to contact each fund company. The organizer of the supermarket also provides the investor with consolidated record keeping and a simple account statement.

These services provide a nontransaction-fee program to provide access to multiple fund families under one roof and to help service the back-office needs of financial advisors. Through this service, investors can access many mutual fund families through one source and buy all the funds with no transaction fee (i.e., no load).

On the one hand, these services make a mutual fund family more accessible to many more investors; on the other hand, they break the direct link between the mutual fund and the investor. According to these services, the mutual fund company does not know the identity of its investors through the supermarkets; only the super-

---

[13] Reid, *The 1990s: A Decade of Expansion and Changes in the U.S. Mutual Fund Industry*, pp. 11–12.

market, which distributes the funds directly to the investor knows their identity. These supermarkets fit the needs of fee-based financial planners very well. For individual investors and planners as well, supermarkets can offer one-stop shopping, including the current "best of the breed." Currently, in addition to Schwab, Fidelity and TD Waterhouse are other major mutual fund supermarkets. Assets in mutual fund supermarkets reached an estimated $500 billion in 1999.

Wrap Programs.

Wrap accounts are managed accounts, typically mutual funds "wrapped" in a service package. The service provided is often asset allocation counsel, that is, advice on the mix of managed funds. Thus, mutual fund wrap programs provide investors with advice and assistance for an asset-based fee rather than the traditional front-end load. Wrap products are currently offered by many fund and nonfund companies. Wrap accounts are not necessarily alternatives to mutual funds but may be different ways to package the funds.

Traditional direct-market funds as well as sales-force funds are marketed through this channel. Mutual funds in wrap programs comprised an estimated $94 billion in late 1999.

Fee-Based Financial Advisors.

Fee-based financial advisors are independent financial planners who charge investors an annual fee, typically as a percentage of assets under management. In return, they provide investment advice to their clients by selecting portfolios of mutual funds and securities. While many planners recommend mutual funds to their clients, others recommend portfolios of planner-selected securities. Mutual fund assets in these accounts reached $150 billion at the end of 1999.

Variable Annuities.

Variable annuities represent another distribution channel. Variable annuities, as discussed in Chapter 7, are described as "mutual funds in an insurance wrapper." Among their insurance features are the tax deferral of investment earnings until they are withdrawn and higher charges (there is a mortality charge for the insurance provided). Variable annuities are sold through insurance agents and other distributors as well as directly through some fund companies. Assets in variable annuities exceeded $800 billion in 1999.

Changes in the Costs of Purchasing Mutual Funds

The purchase cost (or price) of mutual funds declined significantly during the rapid growth of the 1990s. Purchase cost is measured by total shareholder costs, which includes both costs from annual fund expenses and from transaction-based sales loads. The decline in total shareholder costs occurred across all major types of funds. For equity funds, total shareholder costs were 181 basis points per year in 1990 and declined to 135 basis per year in 1998, a decrease of 25%. The corresponding decline for bond funds was from 171 basis points per year in 1990 to 109 basis points. There were also significant decreases in the total costs of bond funds and smaller decreases in money market funds.[14]

In general, load funds responded to the competition of no-load funds by lowering distribution costs. Distribution cost is defined as the sum of the annualized sales

---

[14] For a further discussion of this topic, see Reid, *The 1990s: A Decade of Expansion and Changes in the U.S. Mutual Fund Industry.*

load and 12b-1 fees. The distribution cost is the component of total shareholder cost that reflects the cost of advice and assistance provided by brokers and sales professionals to buyers of mutual funds.

Load funds lowered distribution costs, in part, by reducing front-end sales loads. In addition, load funds introduced alternatives to front-end loads that, depending on the investor's circumstances, could be less costly than front-end loads as a means of compensating sales professionals. One common distribution cost structure combined a 12b-1 fee with a contingent deferred sales load that would be paid by the investor when the shares were redeemed and, depending on the time the fund was held, could be zero.

The reduction in and reallocation of distribution costs during the 1990s was significant. For both equity and bond funds, the lowering of front-end loads along with the growth of alternatives to front-end loads together with more funds adopting 12b-1 fees resulted in 12b-1 fees becoming a much larger portion of distribution costs. A final element in the decline of total shareholder cost was the achievement of economies of scale by many individual costs. Some of the annual fund expenses, mainly those included in "other expenses" and those affected by breakpoints, have declined with the increase in size of some of the larger funds.

Mix and Match

Until recently, fund manufacturers distributed only their own funds; fund distributors distributed only one manufacturer's funds; and typically, employee-defined contribution plans, such as 401(k)s, offered funds from only one distributor. However, the investors' demands for choice and convenience, and also the distributors' need to appear objective, have motivated essentially all institutional users of funds and distribution organizations to offer funds from other fund families in addition to their own (that is, if they also manufacture their own funds). In addition, mutual fund supermarkets distribute funds of many fund families with considerable facility and low costs. Even the biggest fund families, including Fidelity Investments and Vanguard Group, offer funds from other families.

The balance of power between fund manufacturers and distributors currently significantly favors distribution. That is, in general there are more funds available than distributors to sell them. In the mutual fund business, "distribution is king."

Domestic Acquisitions in the U.S. Funds Market

The merger and acquisition (M&A) business in the U.S. asset management business has been active. Just as there has been much M&A activity with fund families being both the acquirer and the acquired, there have also been many "deals" where a U.S. fund family was on one side of the deal and a nonfund U.S. asset manager was on the other. The former type of combination represents the increase in the scale of the mutual fund business, as previously discussed. The latter represents the continued homogenization of asset management in the United States; that is, there has been the consolidation among the following types of asset management:

> Mutual funds/variable annuities
> Institutional
> • Defined benefit
> • Foundation/endowment
> Individual/Separate Account/High Net Worth Individual

The U.S. asset management business continues to grow and consolidate across the various types of asset management.

Internationalization of the U.S. Funds Business

The combination of a U.S. fund company and an international asset manager could occur in either of two directions, that is, with either being the acquirer. But the dominant direction recently has been in the direction of an international asset manager acquiring a U.S. fund company. The reasons U.S. and international asset managers have aggressively acquired U.S. funds include the rapidly growing U.S. mutual fund business; continuing deregulation of the U.S. asset management business; and the general regulatory framework in the United States.

Key Points You Should Understand Before Proceeding

1. During the last decade, indirect sales of mutual funds through intermediaries have grown relative to direct sales.
2. The meaning of the following terms in the context of mutual funds: supermarket, wrap program, variable annuity.
3. The total shareholder costs of owning a mutual fund have decreased in recent years due to a reduction in distribution costs, and due to economies of scale in other fund expenses.

ALTERNATIVES TO MUTUAL FUNDS

Due to the success of mutual funds, investment companies have developed several alternatives to mutual funds. The major alternatives to mutual funds are exchange-traded funds, segregated accounts, and "folios."

Exchange-Traded Funds

Although mutual funds have become very popular with individual investors during the 1980s and 1990s, they are often criticized for two reasons. First, mutual funds shares are priced at, and can be transacted only at, the end-of-the-day (closing) price. Specifically, transactions (i.e., purchases and sales) cannot be made at intraday prices, but only at the end-of-the-day closing prices. The second issue relates to taxes and the investors' control over taxes. As noted earlier in this chapter, withdrawals by some fund shareholders can cause taxable realized capital gains for shareholders who maintain their positions.

During 1993, a new investment vehicle, which has many of the same features of mutual funds but responds to these two limitations, was introduced. This investment vehicle, called *exchange-traded funds* (ETFs), consists of investment companies that are similar to mutual funds but trade like stocks on an exchange. While they are open-ended, ETFs are, in a sense, similar to closed-end funds, which have very small premiums or discounts from their NAV. Since their introduction in 1993, they have only been traded on the American Stock Exchange. Through 2000, these ETFs have been based only on U.S. (e.g., the S&P500) and international (e.g., MSCI EAFE) stock indexes and subindexes, not actively managed portfolios or funds. In addition to broad stock indexes, ETFs are also based on style, sector, and industry-oriented indexes.

In an ETF, it is the investment advisor's responsibility to maintain the portfolio such that it replicates the index and the index's return accurately.[15] Because supply and demand determine the secondary market price of these shares, the exchange price can deviate slightly from the value of the portfolio and, as a result, may provide

---

[15] Among the early investment advisors have been State Street Global Advisors and Barclays Global

some imprecision in pricing. The deviation will be small, however, because arbitrageurs can create or redeem large blocks of shares on any day at NAV, significantly limiting the deviations. Along with being able to transact in ETFs at current prices throughout the day comes the flexibility to place limit orders, stop orders, orders to short sell and buy on margin, none of which can be done with open-end mutual funds. These types of orders are discussed in Chapter 18.

The other major distinction between open-ended mutual funds and ETFs relates to taxation. For both open-ended funds and ETFs, dividend income and capital gains realized when the funds or ETFs are transacted are taxable to the investor. However, in addition, when there are redemptions, open-end mutual funds may have to sell securities (if the cash position is not sufficient to fund the redemptions), thereby causing a capital gain or loss for those who held their shares. ETFs, however, do not have to sell portfolio securities since redemptions are effected by an in-kind exchange of the ETF shares for a basket of the underlying portfolio securities—not a taxable event to the investors. Therefore, investors in ETFs are subject to significant capital gains taxes only when they sell their ETF shares at a price above the original purchase price. However, ETFs do distribute cash dividends and may distribute a limited amount of realized capital gains, and these distributions are taxable. Overall, with respect to taxes, ETFs, like index mutual funds, avoid realized capital gains and the taxation thereof due to their low portfolio turnover. But unlike index mutual funds (or other funds for that matter), they do not cause potentially large capital gains tax liabilities which accrue to those who held their positions in order to meet shareholder redemptions due to the unique way in which they are redeemed.

The pros and cons of mutual funds and ETFs are summarized in Table 8-11. Table 8-12 considers the tax differences in more detail. Overall, the ETFs have the advantages of intraday pricing and tax management, and many, but not all, have lower expenses than their corresponding index mutual funds. However, since open-ended funds are "transacted" through the fund sponsor and ETFs are traded on an exchange, the commissions on each ETF trade may make them unattractive for a strategy that involves several small purchases, as, for instance, would result from strategies such as dollar cost averaging or monthly payroll deductions. However, ETFs may provide a viable alternative to mutual funds for many other purposes.

An indication of the popularity of these ETFs is that their pace of development has accelerated and their use has similarly grown. By mid-2000, the assets in the ETF group increased to $52.6 billion, still small relative to the $7 trillion mutual fund industry, but growing quickly. More specifically, the Qubes (see list that follows) began trading on March 1999 and within 12 months had $9.7 billion in assets; only two U.S. technology funds had a larger market capitalization.

Among the earliest and currently the most popular ETFs are

➤ SPDRS (pronounced *spiders*; Standard and Poor's Depository Receipts) (ticker symbol: SPY)—tracks the S&P500.
➤ DIAMONDS (ticker symbol: DIA)—tracks the Dow Jones Industrial Average.
➤ WEBS (World Equity Benchmarks)—tracks the Morgan Stanley Capital International indexes of various countries. These have been recently renamed *iShares MSCI.*
➤ QQQs (often called *Qubes*; ticker symbol: QQQ)—tracks the Nasdaq 100 index.
➤ i Shares—provided by Barclays Global Investors and tracks 42 different stock indexes.

With respect to continued growth, all the current ETFs are indexed. ETFs based on actively traded portfolios are being planned in the United States and have begun trading in Germany.

Table 8-11   Mutual Funds versus Exchange-Traded Funds

	MUTUAL FUNDS	*ETFs*
Variety	Wide choice.	Choices currently limited to stock indexes, but on many stock indexes.
Taxation	Subject to taxation on dividend and realized capital gains. May have gains/losses when other investors redeem funds. May have gains/losses when stocks in index are changed.	Subject to taxation on dividend and realized capital gain. No gains/losses when other investors redeem funds. May have gains/losses when stocks in index are changed.
Valuation	NAV, based on actual price.	Creations and redemptions at NAV. Secondary market prices may be valued somewhat below NAV, but deviation typically small due to arbitrage.
Pricing	End-of-day.	Continuous.
Expenses	Low for index funds.	Low and, in some cases, even lower than for index mutual funds.
Transaction Cost	None (for no-load funds); sales charge for load funds.	Commission or brokerage.
Management Fee	Depends on fund; even index funds have a range of management fees.	Depends on fund; tends to be very low on many stock index funds.

Table 8-12   Taxes: Mutual Funds versus Exchange-Traded Funds

	MUTUAL FUNDS	ETFs
Holding/Maintaining		
Taxes on Dividend, Income, and Realized Capital Gains	Fully Taxable.	Fully Taxable.
Turnover of Portfolio	Withdrawal by other investors may necessitate portfolio sales and realized capital gains for holder.	Withdrawal by others does not cause portfolio sales and, thus, no realized capital for holder.
Disposition		
Withdrawal of Investment	Capital gains tax on difference between sales and purchase price.	Capital gains tax on difference between sales and purchase price.
Overall	Due to some portfolio turnover, will realize capital gains.	Due to very low portfolio turnover, will not realize significant capital gains.

Segregated (Separately Managed) Accounts

Many high-net-worth individuals object to using mutual funds because of the individual investor's lack of control over taxes, their lack of any input into investment decisions, and the absence of "high-touch" service. The use of separate accounts respond to all these limitations of mutual funds, although they are more expensive. Previously, money managers managed separate accounts for only very large portfolios, typically $1 million and more. Currently, however, many money managers are significantly decreasing the minimum size of their separately managed accounts. As a result, many investors with midsized portfolios are utilizing segregated, individually managed accounts provided by many companies and other investment managers. Typically, asset managers earn higher fees on separately managed accounts but also have higher service costs on these relative to mutual funds.

Folios

A very recent Internet-based product offers a variety of preselected portfolios consistent with any particular investment strategy that investors may desire. For instance, it offers a preselected large cap equity growth portfolio, a small cap equity value portfolio, and so on. These preselected portfolios are called "folios." Investors can also alter the portfolio selections if they choose. After an investor selects and alters one of these portfolios, the portfolio can be transacted through an Internet service at a discount price. Folios are being marketed as an alternative to mutual funds.[16] Among the early products in this field are: Folio[*fn*]; NetFolio; Personal Fund; Smartleaf; and UNX.com.

Key Points That You Should Understand Before Proceeding

1. How ETFs are similar to open-end funds.
2. How ETFs are similar to closed-end funds.
3. The major limitations of open-ended funds.
4. The tax efficiency of ETFs.

COMMERCIAL BANKS AND MUTUAL FUNDS

As we note in several chapters, deregulation has eroded the once solid wall that separated commercial banks from many securities activities. Commercial banks have a dual relationship with mutual funds, both distributing mutual funds from other fund families and also managing their own funds. With respect to distributing funds from other fund families, in 1994, bank sales encompassed 1,000 such nonproprietary funds and raised over $20 billion.[17] At the end of 1995, banks' proprietary funds numbered almost 1,000 and more than 600 of these were either bond or equity funds (money market funds accounted for the remainder). The assets under management in bank-sponsored mutual funds has grown from $158 billion in 1991 to $317 billion in 1995, when sales reached more than $30 billion.

---

[16] Jim McTague, "Basket Weaver," *Barron's* (August 7, 2000); pp. F6–8; and Patrick McGeehan and Danny Hakim, "Online Funds, Built to Order," *New York Times*, August 13, 2000, Money & Business Section, p.1.

[17] Investment Company Institute, *Fundamentals: Mutual Fund Research in Brief* (September/October 1995).

With respect to managing funds, recently the typical bank-managed U.S. stock mutual fund has performed poorly, badly lagging behind the mutual fund industry average in 1999 and the first half of 2000. Many bank funds have continued to be ultra-conservative holdovers from the days of running risk-averse trust accounts.

Even as money has continued to pour into mutual funds industrywide, net sales of bank-managed stock and bond funds have been small. During the first half of 2000, banks' total sales were $1.33 billion, less than half the $2.9 billion in net sales registered in the first half of 1999, according to Financial Research Corporation, a Boston financial services consulting group. The full-year 2000 total sales will be significantly less than the net new investment of $38.9 billion in calendar year 1997.[18] At this time, banks have been more successful in distributing the funds of other advisors than in managing and distributing their own funds.

Key Points That You Should Understand Before Proceeding

1. The extent to which banks have begun to market their own mutual funds.
2. The banks' readiness to sell mutual funds of non-bank financial institutions

---

INTERNATIONAL INVESTMENT COMPANIES

In the remainder of this chapter we discuss investment companies in the United Kingdom and Germany.[19]

United Kingdom

Mutual funds in the United Kingdom generally take one of three forms: (1) unit trusts, (2) open-ended investment companies (commonly known as OEICs), and (3) investment trusts.

Unit Trusts and OEICs.

Unit trusts and OEICs are often referred to as *collective investment schemes*. With a unit trust the investor has a beneficial ownership of the assets held under trust in the form of units. With an OEIC, shares are issued in the company. The unit trust is similar to the open-end fund in the United States, whereas the investment trust is much like the closed-end fund, with shares traded on London's International Stock Exchange. An OEIC takes the best features of the unit trust but is formed within a corporate structure; it is more like the corporate structure found in Europe and the United States.

The essential feature of both unit trusts and OEICs is that investors pool their money into a single fund, thereby benefitting from the economies of scale that can be achieved. A professional fund manager manages the fund whereas an independent trustee company (known as an Authorised Corporate Director in the case of OEICs) holds the assets of the fund on behalf of the investor and monitors the decisions and investments made by the manager. The trustee's duty is to safeguard the assets of the investor. These duties include monitoring the sales and purchases of units or shares by

---

[18] Carrick Mallenkomp and Christopher Oster, "Bank-Run Mutual Funds Perform Poorly," *Wall Street Journal*, August 14, 2000, p. C-1.
[19] The following sections on the United Kingdom and Germany were provided by Robin Menzies of Baillie Gifford & Co., Edinburgh, Scotland.

the management company, distributing payments to unit holders, ensuring that the paperwork is properly done, and overseeing the management company's exercise of its powers.

The principal difference between an OEIC and the unit trust is that an OEIC is founded on the basis of a single pricing mechanism for both buyers and sellers with charges being shown separately. The unit trust, in contrast, normally relies on a dual pricing system with a different price for buyer and seller with charges built in to the quoted price.

Regulation of collective investment schemes is a somewhat complicated matter. At the time of this writing, the British Parliament is in the final throes of agreeing on the details of new legislation that will replace the current regulatory framework. This will result in substantial changes in the way financial services are regulated in the United Kingdom and will, for the first time, consolidate regulation into one statutory authority.

Presently, the Financial Services Act of 1986 imposes the requirement that any fund which is to be advertised to the public must be registered. The authorization procedure now rests in the hands of the Financial Services Authority (FSA), which succeeded the Securities and Investments Board. In turn, the Investment Management Regulatory Organization is responsible for monitoring the activities of the manager. Regulation of unit trusts and OEICs will be consolidated under the auspices of the Financial Services Authority once the final integration of the U.K financial services industry has occurred (expected early in 2001), with the enactment and coming into force of the Financial Services and Markets Bill. This new act will replace in entirety the Financial Services Act 1986 and provide a framework for regulation to reflect the new challenges of the twenty-first century. In the meantime, the Financial Services Authority has laid down a series of conditions for authorization of collective investment schemes with which investment companies must comply. The FSA also has the power to revoke authorization in certain circumstances.

Unit trusts and OEICs have proven to be highly popular. According to the Association of Unit Trust and Investment Funds, in 1998 the U.K. industry expanded with funds under management reaching £183 billion by year-end compared with £113 billion in 1995 and £63 billion in 1992. By the end of November 1999, the figure had reached £238 billion.

U.K. equity funds continue to be the dominant category of investment for the retail buyer, accounting for some 42% of positive net retail sales in 1998. According to the Association of Unit Trust and Investment Funds, this was followed by sales of corporate bond funds. There are now more than 2,000 different funds for the investor to chose from, ranging from one of three main categories: income, capital growth, or specialist funds.

Investment Trusts.

Investment trusts differ from unit trusts and OEICs in that they are companies listed on the London Stock Exchange. They are closed ended, meaning that they have a limited pool of shares in issue at any one time, unlike unit trusts or OEICs where the number of units or shares in issue depends on consumer demand at the time. They have an independent board of directors and shareholders like any other company. An investment trust is dual priced with the difference between buying and selling prices being referred to as the "spread." The spread reflects the difference between the net asset value of the underlying investments and the market price of the investment trust.

Historically, investment trusts have found greater favor with institutional investors, although there has been recent concerted efforts to sell the attractions of unit trusts to retail investors. As of April 2000, the total assets of the investment trust industry amounted to £77 billion, managed by approximately 349 investment trust companies according to the Association of Unit Trust and Investment Funds. An investment trust is registered under the Companies Act and is subject to London Stock Exchange listing rules. In addition, it must obtain Inland Revenue (the equivalent of the U.S. IRS) approval. In this respect it differs quite markedly from unit trusts and OEICs.

Germany

German mutual funds take two general forms: public (or retail) funds and nonpublic funds reserved for institutional buyers. (There are also numerous closed-ended funds that focus on real estate and appeal mostly to institutional investors, which are not discussed here.) The institutional funds are called *Spezialfonds* and account for almost half the money invested in investment companies. The retail funds fall into two broad categories: bond funds (*Rentenfonds*) and equity funds (*Aktienfonds*). Traditionally, German investors have preferred bond funds, but since the early 1990s, equity funds have often received greater annual inflows, reflecting increasing interest in (and good performance of) equities over this period. This shift has accelerated dramatically in recent years.

The growth of *Spezialfonds* can be seen from the volume of assets under management. At the end of October 1999, assets were $428 billion, and more than 7% of this was managed by foreign parent groups.[20] These open-ended investment funds are set up and run by *Kapitalanlagegesellschaften* (management companies).

Adoption of the Euro has created the opportunity for foreign fund managers with specialist knowledge of European investment markets. However, the costs of a foreign operation are expensive, and managers must meet the demanding requirements of the German supervisory authorities (BAKred). Reputation and expertise are essential, but so is the ability to be sensitive to local investment needs.

Although there has been remarkable growth since the 1980s, with German mutual funds now well on the way to being a trillion dollar industry, fund investment per capita is still far below American levels, and even below levels in other large European markets such as France, the United Kingdom, and Italy. The mutual fund industry is quite concentrated because relatively few management companies are responsible for offering all the retail and special funds. Actually totaling around 60, these companies have steadily increased the number of funds available to the varied investing public throughout the 1980s. The German banks, which participate in all segments of the securities industry, are very often partners with these managing firms, and occasionally insurance companies are also partners. Most of the sales to the public are made through banks.

German mutual funds have a distinctive structure. A *Kapitalanlagegesellschaft* has a contractual agreement to manage a pool of assets on behalf of investors who own participations in the asset pool. A custodian bank, called a *Depotbank*, and by law necessarily German, supervises the activities of the management fund. The typical investment company is organized as a limited liability company, which is known as *Gesellschaft mit beschrankter Haftung-GmbH*. The GmbH, as it is often called, has a board that also monitors the management of the assets.

Regulation of the mutual funds follows this pattern. The Investment Company Act (known as KAGG for *Gesetz Uber Kapitalanlagegesellschaften*) requires funds to register and to accept a set of governmental guidelines about the contract between the firm and investors. The Federal Supervisory Agency for Banking (called BAYred for

---

[20] *Financial Times Mandate*, February 14, 2000.

Bundesaufsichtsamt flir fur Kreditwesen) must approve the details of implementation of the contract. KAGG selects a bank to serve as custodian to safeguard the investors' interests regarding types and amounts of investments as well as bookkeeping and accounting matters. Marketing by the funds is monitored by the BAKred because, as previously noted, banks are very often partners in the management firms for the funds.

SUMMARY

Investment companies sell shares to the public and invest the proceeds in a diversified portfolio of securities, with each share representing a proportionate interest in the underlying portfolio of securities. There are three types of investment companies: open-end or mutual funds, closed-end funds, and unit trusts. A wide range of funds with many different investment objectives is available. Securities law requires that a fund clearly set forth its investment objective in its prospectus, and the objective identifies the type or types of assets the fund will purchase and hold.

Mutual funds and closed-end funds provide two crucial economic functions associated with financial intermediaries: risk reduction via diversification and lower costs of contracting and information processing. Money market funds allow shareholders to write checks against their shares, thus providing a payments mechanism, another economic function of financial intermediaries.

Mutual funds are extensively regulated, with most of that regulation occurring at the federal level. The key legislation is the Investment Company Act of 1940. The most important feature regarding regulation is that the funds are exempt from taxation on their gains if the gains are distributed to investors within a relatively short period of time. Even allowing for that special tax-free status, it is necessary to recognize that regulations apply to many features of the funds' administration, including sales fees, asset management, degree of diversification, distributions, and advertising.

In recent years, there has been widespread consumer-investor acceptance of the concept of family (or group or complex) funds. That is, an investment advisory company (such as Fidelity Investments or Vanguard Group) manages dozens of different funds, which span the spectrum of potential investment objectives, from aggressive growth to balanced income to international diversification. The success of these fund families has led to a considerable concentration of the mutual fund industry in a few large fund groups.

The assets in mutual funds have increased significantly since 1980, particularly in stock funds. The shift from stocks to stock funds was caused by the investor need for diversification, convenience, and expert portfolio management. The growth in mutual fund assets may, however, moderate as investor allocations to stock funds have matured and competitors to mutual funds have developed. Among these competitors are variable annuities, exchange traded funds (ETFs), segregated accounts, and Internet-executed folios.

Mutual funds, or their equivalents, have proven popular in countries other than the United States. Many investors make use of unit trusts in Great Britain and *fonds* in Germany. Although regulations and certain institutional features differ from country to country, the basic structure of pooled investments managed by professionals on behalf of investors is common and popular around the globe. Also, the mutual fund industry of many countries tends to be concentrated among a few mutual fund groups, which offer funds covering a wide range of investment objectives. Finally, extensive regulation by governmental authorities is a characteristic of mutual fund activities in many countries.

KEY TERMS

- 12b-1 fee, 129
- Advisory fee, 129
- Back-end load fund, 128
- Board of directors, 140
- Closed-end fund, 123
- Exchange-traded funds (ETFs), 124
- Investment advisor, 129
- Investment Company Act of 1940, 124

- Investment Company Institute, 126
- Investment objective, 132
- Load, 127
- Load funds, 128
- Net asset value per share (NAV), 122
- No-load fund, 128
- Open-end (or mutual) funds, 122
- Unit trust, 124

QUESTIONS

1. An investment company has $1.05 million of assets, $50,000 of liabilities, and 10,000 shares outstanding.
   a. What is its NAV?
   b. Suppose the fund pays off its liabilities while at the same time the value of its assets double. How many shares will a deposit of $5,000 receive?

2. "The NAV of an open-end fund are determined continuously throughout the trading day." Explain why you agree or disagree with this statement.

3. a. What are closed-end funds?
   b. Why do some closed-end funds use leverage to raise more funds rather than issue new shares like mutual funds?

4. Why might the price of a share of a closed-end fund diverge from its NAV?

5. What is the difference between a unit trust and a closed-end fund?

6. a. Describe the following: front-end load, back-end load, level load, 12b-1 fee, management fee.
   b. Is there a limit on the fees that a mutual fund may charge?

7. Why do mutual funds have different classes of shares?

8. a. What is a fund of funds?
   b. What is an index fund?

9. What are the costs incurred by a mutual fund?

10. Why might the investor in a mutual fund be faced with a potential tax liability arising from capital gains even though the investor did not benefit from such a gain?

11. Does an investment company provide any economic function that individual investors cannot provide for themselves on their own? Explain your answer.

12. a. How can a fund qualify as a regulated investment company?
    b. What is the benefit in gaining this status?

13. a. What is an exchange-traded fund?
    b. What are the advantages of an exchange-traded fund relative to open-end and closed-end investment companies?

14. Why have commercial banks been more successful in distributing the funds of other advisors rather than their own funds?

15. The assets under management by mutual funds grew significantly during the 1990s. Did that materially change the degree of asset concentration? Explain your answer.

16. Briefly describe the following in the context of mutual funds:
    a. supermarket
    b. wrap program
    c. folios
    d. segregated accounts
    e. family of funds

17. What is the difference between a unit trust and an investment trust in the United Kingdom?

18. What are *Spezialfonds* in Germany?

19. Briefly discuss the regulation of mutual funds in Germany.

C h a p t e r   9

Pension Funds

Learning Objectives

After reading this chapter, you will understand

- what a pension plan sponsor does.
- the different types of pension plans, including defined contribution plans, defined benefit plans, and a recently developed hybrid plan, the cash balance plan.
- what a 401(k) plan is.
- what an insured plan is.
- the principal provisions of the Employee Retirement Income Security Act (ERISA) of 1974.
- what the Pension Benefit Guaranty Corporation does.
- who the managers of pension funds are.
- the various financial services provided to pension funds.
- the role of mutual funds in contemporary pension plans.
- how pension plans are managed and regulated in Japan, Germany, and the United Kingdom.
- what foundations do.
- the goals of managing money for foundations.

Pension funds, which exist in some form in all developed economies, are major institutional investors and participants in the financial markets. Pension funds have become important for several reasons. First, income and wealth have grown steadily over the post–World War II period, leaving households more money for long-term savings. Second, people are living longer and can expect more financial needs for longer retirement periods. Third, pensions represent compensation to employees that is free of tax liability to the employee until after the workers retire and their income from employment ceases, and employer contributions are tax deductible to the employer.

This chapter discusses **pension plans** and pension fund management. An appendix deals briefly with another interesting financial institution, the foundation. Common in the United States, the foundation is a charitable trust, established in accordance with a network of laws, that supports nonprofit institutions such as universities, hospitals, religious institutions, and museums.

INTRODUCTION TO PENSION PLANS

A pension plan is a fund that is established for the eventual payment of retirement benefits. The entities that establish pension plans, called **plan sponsors**, may be private business entities acting for their employees (called *corporate* or *private plans*); federal, state, and local entities on behalf of their employees (called *public plans*); unions on behalf of their members (called *Taft Hartley plans*); and individuals for themselves (called *individually sponsored plans*). The total assets of U.S. pension funds have grown rapidly since World War II. Total financial assets of private pension plans at the end of 1999 were approximately $5.0 trillion, while those of the pension plans of state and local employees were $3.0 trillion.[1] The two largest corporate-sponsored funds are General Motors and General Electric with over $70 billion in assets in each fund. The two largest government-sponsored funds are California Public Employees Retirement System and New York State Common Retirement Fund with assets of approximately $156 billion and $111 billion, respectively. The 10 largest corporate, public, and union pension funds are shown in Table 9-1.

Pension funds are financed by contributions by the employer. In some plans, employer contributions are matched to some degree by employees. The great success of private pension plans is somewhat surprising because the system involves investing in an asset—the pension contract—that for the most part is very illiquid. It cannot be used, not even as collateral, until retirement. The key factor in explaining pension fund growth is that the employer's contributions and a specified amount of the employee's contributions, as well as the earnings of the fund's assets, are tax exempt. In essence, a pension is a form of employee remuneration for which the employee is *not taxed until funds are withdrawn.* This tax exemption results from meeting many federal requirements. Such plans are called *qualified* pension plans, which means that if the plan meets certain requirements, it qualifies for tax exemptions. Pension funds have also traditionally served to discourage employees from quitting, since the employee, until vested, could lose at least the accumulation resulting from the employer contribution.

Key Points That You Should Understand Before Proceeding

1. The role of the sponsor of a pension plan.
2. The importance of tax exemption to the structure and popularity of pension plans.

TYPES OF PENSION PLANS

There are two basic and widely used types of pension plans: defined benefit plans and defined contribution plans. In addition, a recently developed hybrid type of plan called a cash balance plan, combines features of both these types.

Defined Benefit Plan

In a **defined benefit plan**, the plan sponsor agrees to make specified dollar payments annually to qualifying employees beginning at retirement (and some payments to beneficiaries in case of death before retirement). These payments typically occur monthly. The retirement payments are determined by a formula that usually takes into account the length of service of the employee and the employee's earnings. The pension obligations are effectively a debt obligation of the plan sponsor. The plan sponsor, thereby, assumes the risk of having insufficient funds in the plan to satisfy the regular contractual payments that must be made to retired employees.

---

[1] Federal Reserve Board, *Flow of Funds Summary Statistics—Release Z.7,* June 2000.

Table 9-1   Ten Largest Corporate, Public and Union Pension Plans as of 12/31/99

TEN LARGEST CORPORATE PENSION FUNDS	TOTAL (IN MILLIONS)
1. General Motors	$91,000
2. General Electric	71,456
3. Lucent Technologies	62,267
4. IBM	61,810
5. SBC Communications	60,953
6. Boeing	57,370
7. Ford Motors	55,700
8. Bell Atlantic	54,274
9. Lockheed Martin	34,765
10. AT&T	29,739

TEN LARGEST PUBLIC PENSION FUNDS	TOTAL (IN MILLIONS)
1. State of California Public Employee Retirement	$155,823
2. New York State Common Retirement Fund	111,369
3. California State Teachers Retirement Fund	98,436
4. State Investment Board of Florida	93,152
5. Federal Retirement Thrift Board	85,309
6. New York State Teachers Retirement	81,523
7. Teachers Retirement Fund of Texas	79,377
8. New Jersey Division of Investments	74,927
9. State of Wisconsin Investment Board	57,692
10. Public Employees Retirement System of Ohio	52,760

TEN LARGEST MULTI-EMPLOYER FUNDS	TOTAL (IN MILLIONS)
1. Western States Teamsters	$22,100
2. Central States Teamsters	19,026
3. National Electrical Benefit Fund	9,395
4. United Mineworkers	7,580
5. Operating Engineers	6,268
6. Boilersmakers/Blacksmiths	6,061
7. National Rural Electric	5,753
8. 1199 Healthcare Workers	5,400
9. Bakery and Confectioners Union	5,200
10. IAM National Pension	5,014

SOURCE: *Nelson Information's Directory of Plan Sponsors,* ©2000, used with permission.

A plan sponsor establishing a defined benefit plan can use the payments made into the fund to purchase an annuity policy from a life insurance company. Defined benefit plans that are guaranteed by life insurance products are called **insured benefit plans**. An insured plan is not necessarily safer than a noninsured plan, since it depends on the ability of the life insurance company to make the contractual payments, whereas the uninsured plan depends on the ability of the plan sponsor. Whether a private pension plan is insured or noninsured, a federal agency, the **Pension Benefit Guaranty Corporation (PBGC)**, which was established in 1974 by the ERISA legislation, insures the vested benefits of participants, as discussed below.

Benefits become vested when employees reach a certain age and complete enough years of service so that they meet the minimum requirements for receiving benefits upon retirement. The payment of benefits is not contingent upon a participant's continuation with the employer or union.

Defined Contribution Plan

In a **defined contribution plan**, the plan sponsor is responsible only for making specified contributions into the plan on behalf of qualifying participants, not specified payments to the employee after retirement. The amount contributed is typically either a percentage of the employee's salary and/or a percentage of the employer's profits. The plan sponsor does not guarantee any specific amount at retirement. The payments that will be made to qualifying participants upon retirement depend on the growth of the plan assets. That is, retirement benefit payments are determined by the investment performance of the funds in which the assets are invested and are not guaranteed by the plan sponsor. The plan sponsor gives the participants various options as to the investment vehicles in which they may invest. Defined contribution pension plans come in several legal forms: 401(k) plans, money purchase pension plans, and employee stock ownership plans (ESOPs).

By far the fastest-growing sector of the defined contribution plan is the **401(k) plan**, or its equivalent in the nonprofit sector, the *403(b) plan*, and in the public sector, the *457 plan*. To the firm, this kind of plan offers the lowest costs and the least administrative problems. The employer makes a specified contribution to a specific plan/program, and the employee chooses how it is invested.[2] To the employee, the plan is attractive because it offers some control over how the pension money is managed. In fact, plan sponsors frequently offer participants the opportunity to invest in one or more of a family of mutual funds. Over half of all defined contribution plans (in public institutions such as state governments as well as private firms) use mutual funds, and the percentage of private corporations that use this approach is even higher. By the end of 1999, over $1 trillion had been placed in 401(k) accounts, and the big mutual funds were attracting the bulk of the new money flowing into these accounts.

Employees in the public and corporate sectors have responded favorably, and almost half of all assets in defined contribution pensions are now invested in mutual funds, with the bulk of the money placed in funds emphasizing equities and growth.[3] Recent regulations issued by the U.S. Department of Labor require firms to offer their employees a set of distinctive choices, a development that has further encouraged pension plans to opt for the mutual fund approach because families of mutual funds can readily provide investment vehicles offering different investment objectives.[4]

There are several fundamental differences between defined benefit plans and defined contribution plans. In the defined benefit plan, the plan sponsor: (1) guarantees the retirement benefits; (2) makes the investment choices; and, (3) bears the investment risk if the investments do not earn enough to fund the guaranteed retirement benefits. In contrast, in a defined contribution plan, the employer does not guarantee any retirement benefits. However, the employer does agree to make specified contributions to the employee's account. The employee selects the investment options, and the employee has for retirement only the return on the investment portfolio (plus, of course, the employee and employer contributions). Table 9-2 provides selected data on defined benefit and defined contribution pension plans. About 76% of the assets of the top 1,000 pension plans are defined benefit plans.

---

[2] "Calling It Quits," *Institutional Investor* (February 1991), p. 125.
[3] "Taking a Fancy to Mutual Funds," *Institutional Investor* (May 1992), p. 119.
[4] "The Communication Cloud over 401(k)s," *Institutional Investor* (September 1991), p. 189.

Table 9-2 Selected Data: Defined Benefit and Defined Contribution Pension Plans, 1999 (in billions)

TOP 1,000 ASSETS	$4,958.9	
Defined benefit	3,785.0 (76.3%)	
Defined contribution	1,173.9 (23.7%)	

Largest Employee/Pension Benefit Funds Plans 1999 (in millions)

DEFINED BENEFIT	PUBLIC	CORPORATE
California Public Employees	$155,711	—
New York State Common	111,369	—
California State Teachers	98,400	—
General Motors	—	$69,500

DEFINED CONTRIBUTION	PUBLIC	CORPORATE
Federal Retirement Thrift	$88,309	—
General Electric	—	$26,326
General Motors	—	21,500
Lucent Technologies	—	21,200

SOURCE: *Pensions & Investments*, January 24, 2000. Reprinted by permission of the Investment Company Institute (www.isi.org).

Hybrid Pensions Plans

Defined benefit pension plans are cumbersome for the plan sponsor to administer and are not portable from one job to another by employees in an increasingly mobile workforce. Defined contribution plans put the investment choices and investment risk on the employee. In response to these and other limitations, new forms of **hybrid pension plans**, that is combinations of defined benefit and defined contribution plans, have been developed. Although there are several types of hybrid plans, including pension equity, floor-offset, and others, the most common hybrid form is the cash balance plan.

Cash Balance Pension Plan

The concept of a cash balance pension plan first became widely known when Bank of America adopted a cash balance plan in the mid-1980s as an alternative to the more traditional retirement vehicles. During the late 1990s, the plan received more attention when IBM adopted it.

A cash balance plan is basically a defined benefit that has some of the features of a defined contribution plan. A cash balance plan is a defined benefit plan in that it defines future pension benefits, not employer contributions. Retirement benefits are based on a fixed-amount annual employer contribution and a guaranteed minimum annual investment return. Each participant in a cash balance plan has an account that is credited with a dollar amount that resembles an employer contribution and is generally determined as a percentage of pay. Each participant's account is also credited with interest linked to some fixed or variable index such as the consumer price index (CPI). The plan usually provides benefits in the form of a lump-sum distribution in an annuity. Interest is credited to the employee's account at a rate specified in the plan and is unrelated to the investment earnings of the employer's pension trust. The employee's benefit does not vary based on the interest credit. The promised benefits are fixed, and the investment gains or losses are borne by the employer. However, as in a defined contribution plan, an individual employee can monitor his or her cash balance plan "account" in a regular statement.

Also like a defined contribution plan and important to today's job-changing workforce, many cash balance plans allow the employee to take a lump sum payment of vested benefits when terminating, which can be rolled over into an IRA or to the new employer's plan. That is, cash balance plans are portable from one job to another. Table 9-3 summarizes the features of a cash balance plan that are similar to defined benefit and defined contribution plans.

A cash balance plan is similar to some types of defined contribution plans, particularly money purchase plans and profit sharing plans, according to which the employer contributes at a fixed rate but does not guarantee benefits. Since traditional defined contribution plans are back-ended (i.e., most of the benefit is accrued during the last 10 years of a 20- to 30-year career with a company), younger workers often undervalue the benefit of a pension plan. Cash balance formulas provide for an earlier, more uniform accumulation of retirement pension benefits that can be enjoyed by employees who do not commit their entire careers to one company. Figure 9-1 shows the buildup of retirement benefits over time for defined benefit and defined contribution plans and cash balance plans.[5] As shown, in a traditional plan benefits based on a combination of age and service build up sharply toward the end of the employee's career. In a cash balance plan, benefits build more uniformly each year.

Table 9-3   Features of Cash Balance Plans

DEFINED BENEFIT LIKE FEATURES	DEFINED CONTRIBUTIONS LIKE FEATURES
Plan benefits are fixed based on a formula.	Assets accumulated in an "account" for each employee.
Investment responsibility is borne by the employer.	Vested assets may be taken as a lump sum and rolled into an IRA or another qualified plan when the employee terminates employment.
Employees are automatically included in the plan. Plans are protected by the PBGC.	

Figure 9-1   Plot of Defined Benefit and Cash Balance
SOURCE: Cerulli Associates

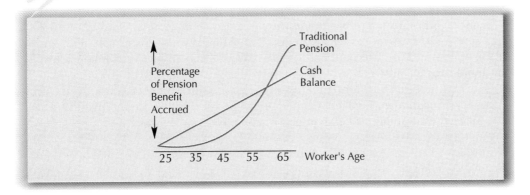

[5] "Cash Balance Plans," *The Cerulli Edge* (June 2000), pp. 14–15.

Many companies have compensated for this by allowing older workers a choice between staying with the old pension plan or converting to the new one. In addition, some companies that convert from defined benefit to cash balance plans autonomously and do not offer their employees the choice of staying in a defined benefit plan have been subject to age discrimination lawsuits. Specifically, from fall 1999 to fall 2000, the U.S. Equal Employment Opportunity Commission received more than 650 complaints of age discrimination from workers and retirees of companies that have converted to cash balance plans from traditional defined benefit plans. The government's position on this issue is not yet well-defined.[6]

A study by Bernstein Research reports that cash balance plans accounted for about $400 billion in assets at the end of 1999, representing approximately 15% of total defined benefit assets, up from about 3% in 1989.

Key Points You Should Understand Before Proceeding

1. In a qualified pension plan, contributions (up to some extent) and earnings thereof are tax-exempt.
2. The difference between a defined benefit pension plan and a defined contribution pension plan.
3. The cash balance pension plan is a new hybrid plan that combines features of the defined benefit plan and the defined contribution plan.

INVESTMENTS

The aggregate asset mix of the 1,000 top defined benefit and defined contribution pension plans at the end of 1999 is summarized in Table 9-4. As indicated, the asset allocations for corporate and public defined benefit plans are very similar, with approximately 75% of their assets in U.S. stocks and bonds. Of the U.S. stock holdings, a significant amount is indexed to a U.S. stock index (most commonly the S&P 500), and the remainder is actively managed. A small amount of U.S. bonds are indexed. Corporate and public defined benefit funds also have approximately 15% of their assets in international equity and fixed income. Private equity and real estate equity together represent approximately 5% of the assets.

The major difference between union plans and the other two types of plans is the small weight in union plans to international investments, only approximately 5% relative to 15% in corporate and public. There are no federal restrictions on investing in non-U.S. investments. The sponsors of a fund, however, are free to restrict the allocation of the fund's assets to domestic investments. It is not uncommon for union-sponsored pension funds, however, to prohibit non-U.S. investments in their portfolios. Most corporate and public funds invest in international assets. From 1993 to 1994, the international equity assets of the top 200 defined benefit plans rose 33%, or by $131 billion, and the international equities rose 21% in defined contribution plans, or by more than $3 billion.[7]

Qualified pension funds are exempt from federal income taxes. Thus, fund assets can accumulate tax free. Consequently, pension funds do not invest in assets that have the advantage of being largely or completely tax exempt.

---

6 "Judge Rejects Claim that Cash Balance Plan Discriminates," *Pensions & Investments* (October 16, 2000), pp. 1 and 50.
7 Marlene Givant Star, "Foreign Equity Stakes Soar," *Pensions & Investments* (January 23, 1995), p. 23.

Table 9-4   Asset Allocation: Defined Benifit and Defined Contribution Pensions
Funds—Top 1,000 at the End of 1999

Defined Benefit Pension Funds

	CORPORATE	PUBLIC	UNION
Domestic equity	49.4%	47.0%	46.1%
Domestic fixed income	25.5	27.9	38.4
International equity	14.9	13.8	4.4
International fixed income	1.5	1.9	0.7
Cash	1.9	1.7	3.1
Private equity	2.9	2.4	0.8
Real estate equity	2.5	3.3	4.2
Mortgage	0.1	1.3	1.2
Other	1.3	0.7	1.1
Total*	100%	100%	100%

Defined Contribution Pension Funds

	CORPORATE	PUBLIC	UNION
Sponsoring Company Stock	31.8%	0%	0%
Other Equity	36.7	57.5	55.8
Fixed Income	5.9	18.3	25.6
Cash	2.5	1.9	9.4
Stable Value	16.4	18.8	4.0
Other	6.7	3.5	5.2
Total*	100%	100%	100%

SOURCE: *Pensions & Investments*, January 24, 2000. Reprinted by permission of the Investment Company Institute
(www.ici.org).

* *Subject to rounding errors.*

Key Points You Should Understand Before Proceeding

1. The largest share of both defined benefit and defined contribution pension fund assets is invested in common stocks, often a U.S. stock index.
2. Qualified pension plans rarely invest in tax-exempt assets.

REGULATION

Because pension plans are so important for U.S. workers, Congress passed comprehensive legislation in 1974 to regulate pension plans. This legislation, the **Employee Retirement Income Security Act of 1974 (ERISA)**, is fairly technical in its details. For our purposes, it is necessary only to understand its major provisions.

First, ERISA established *funding standards* for the minimum contributions that a plan sponsor must make to the pension plan to satisfy the actuarially projected benefit payments. Prior to the enactment of ERISA, many corporate plan sponsors followed a "pay-as-you-go" funding policy. That is, when an employee retired, the corporate plan sponsor paid for the necessary retirement benefits out of current cash flow. Under ERISA, such a practice is no longer allowed, rather the program must be funded. That is, regular contributions to an investment pool along with investment earnings are sufficient to pay the employee retirement benefits.

Second, ERISA established fiduciary standards for pension fund trustees, managers, and advisors. Specifically, all parties responsible for the management of a pension fund are guided by the judgment of what is called a "prudent man" in seeking to determine which investments are proper. Because a trustee is responsible for other people's money, it is necessary to make sure that the trustee takes the role seriously. To fulfill their responsibilities, trustees must act as reasonably prudent people to acquire and use the information that is pertinent to making investment decisions.

Third, ERISA establishes minimum vesting standards. For example, the law specifies that, after five years of employment, a plan participant is entitled to 25% of accrued pension benefits. The percentage of entitlement increases to 100% after 10 years. There are also other vesting requirements.

Finally, ERISA created the Pension Benefit Guaranty Corporation (PBGC) to insure vested pension benefits. The insurance program is funded from annual premiums that must be paid by pension plans.

Responsibility for administering ERISA is delegated to the Department of Labor and the Internal Revenue Service. To ensure that a pension plan is in compliance with ERISA, periodic reporting and disclosure statements must be filed with these government agencies. It is important to recognize that ERISA does not require that a corporation establish a pension plan. If a corporation does establish a defined benefit plan, however, it must comply with the numerous and complex regulations set forth in ERISA.

Key Points That You Should Understand Before Proceeding

1. The scope of ERISA legislation.
2. The meaning of the "prudent man" concept.

MANAGERS OF PENSION FUNDS

A plan sponsor chooses one of the following to manage the defined benefit pension assets under its control: (1) use in-house staff to manage all the pension assets itself; (2) distribute the pension assets to one or more money management firms to manage; or (3) combine alternatives (1) and (2). In the case of a defined contribution pension plan, the plan sponsor typically allows participants to select how to allocate their contributions among funds managed by one or more fund groups.[8]

We have already discussed in Chapter 7 how insurance companies have been involved in the pension business through their issuance of GICs and annuities. Insurance companies also have subsidiaries that manage pension funds. The trust departments of commercial banks, affiliates of investment banks and broker/dealers, and independent money management firms (that is, firms that are not affiliated with an insurance company, bank, investment bank, or broker-dealer) also manage pension funds. Foreign entities are also permitted to participate in the management of pension funds. In fact, several foreign financial institutions have acquired interests in U.S.

---

[8] Keith Ambachtsheer, Ronald Capelle, and Tom Scheibelhut, "Improving Pension Fund Performance," *Financial Analysts Journal* (November/December 1998), pp. 15 ff. Francis Gupta, Eric Stubbs, and Yogi Thambiah, "U.S. Corporate Pension Plans," *The Journal of Portfolio Management* (Summer 2000), pp. 65 ff.

money management firms in order to enter the pension fund money management business.

Table 9-5 lists the largest defined benefit pension managers, and Table 9-6 lists the largest defined contribution managers by type of employer. Managers of pension fund money obtain their income from managing the assets by charging a fee. The annual fee can range from 0.75% of assets under management to as little as 0.01%. Some plan sponsors have entered into management fee contracts based on performance rather than according to a fixed percentage of assets under management.

In addition to money managers, advisors called plan sponsor *consultants* provide other advisory services to pension plan sponsors. Among the functions which consultants provide to plan sponsors are

➤ developing plan investment policy and asset allocation among the major asset classes
➤ providing actuarial advice (liability modeling and forecasting)
➤ designing benchmarks against which the fund's money managers will be measured
➤ measuring and monitoring the performance of the fund's money managers
➤ searching for and recommending money managers to pension plans
➤ providing specialized research

Table 9-5   Largest Institutional Managers of Defined Benefit Pension Funds

FIRM	IN MILLIONS
1. State Street Global	$538,576
2. Barclays Global	490,400
3. Fidelity Investments	396,100
4. TIAA-CREF	285,447
5. Northern Trust	200,864
6. Deutsche Asset	192,748
7. Vanguard Group	176,732
8. PIMCO	163,613
9. J. P. Morgan	143,699
10. Prudential	132,550

SOURCE: Reprinted by permission of the Investment Company Institute (www.ici.org).

Table 9-6   Largest Defined Contribution Managers (Ranked by Internally Managed Assets)—(in Millions) as of 12/31/99

	TOTAL	401(K)	457	403(B)	OTHER
Fidelity Investments	$357,900	$276,000	$12,200	$40,200	$29,500
TIAA-CREF	284,853	0	0	284,853	0
CitiStreet	195,950	173,431	3,066	58	19,395
Barclays Global	101,200	10,900	1,900	0	88,400
Vanguard Group	89,831	77,219	3,640	3,120	5,852

SOURCE: "Mutual Funds Regain Momentum," *Pensions & Investments* (August 7, 2000), p. 21. Reprinted by permission of the Investment Company Institute (www.ici.org).

Key Points That You Should Understand Before Proceeding

1. Who manages pension fund assets.
2. The types of service advisors provide to pension sponsors.

SOCIAL SECURITY

Retirement planning in the United States is described as a three-legged stool, whereby a person's retirement resources are derived from three sources. The three legs of this tool are: (1) a public or government component (specifically Social Security); (2) an employment component (one of the defined benefit, defined contribution, or hybrid plans); and (3) personal savings. Here we discuss the first or public component, that is Social Security. The United States and many other countries have public (government-sponsored) pension plans. The U.S. plan, called *Social Security*, was founded in August 1935. It is essentially a public defined benefit plan supported by a payroll tax. According to the payroll tax, each worker contributes 6.2% of their gross income up to a maximum gross income limit. (The maximum is indexed and was $80,400 in 2000.) The employer matches this employee contribution for a total contribution to Social Security of 12.4% of the employee's gross income up to the limit. Self-employed people must pay the entire 12.4%.

The retirement benefits provided depend on the number of years worked and the income earned. The current maximum Social Security payment is approximately $18,000 per year. This amount is also indexed.

Whereas private pension plans are required to be funded, Social Security is a *pay-as-you-go system*. Unlike a funded plan, where the amount invested for each worker (by the employer and the employee) is calculated to cover the worker's retirement benefits along with accumulated investment earnings, a pay-as-you-go plan is designed so that the amount collected each year covers the retirement benefits paid out during that year. Obviously, the funded method is much more financially sound.

While private pension plans are invested in a wide range of assets, Social Security is invested entirely in Treasury securities. There are currently, however, serious discussions about investing Social Security funds in a wider range of assets. Reforming the Social Security has been and remains an important and controversial issue in the United States. Retired and soon-to-be retired persons are concerned that they will not receive sufficient funds for their retirement. Young people are concerned that they will have to pay significant payroll taxes to support the public retirement system but that when they retire, the system will be unable to pay their earned benefits.

The current problem with the Social Security system is simple. Social Security revenues are based on payroll taxes of employed persons. Social Security outlays result from the payment of retirement benefits and other dependency payments. Currently, Social Security receipts are greater than outlays, and so the Social Security Trust fund assets, which were approximately $1 trillion in 2000, will continue to increase. However, as the average life expectancy increases, the ratio of beneficiaries to workers (the *dependancy ratio*) will increase. Specifically, in 2000 there were approximately 3.4 workers paying into Social Security for every retiree collecting, but by 2030 there will be only 2.

The excess of Social Security receipts over outlays will continue to decrease, eventually becoming zero and then negative. Trust fund assets will continue to increase until the excess of receipts over outlays becomes zero and will then begin to decline. Using current Social Security assumptions, Social Security receipts will exceed outlays until 2015, at which time trust fund assets will be approximately $3 trillion.

After 2015, Social Security outlays will exceed receipts and the assets will decrease. Trust fund assets are projected to be zero during 2037. At this time, receipts will cover only 70% of outlays. Thus, during 2015, the Social Security investment portfolio is projected to start declining and by 2037 it is projected to be gone. Thus, the Social Security problem is a long term but very serious problem.[9]

Due to the potential inadequacy of Social Security to fund future retirement and for other reasons, there have been several proposals to modify the Social Security system. Although the use of the U.S. federal budget surplus to reduce the outstanding federal debt has attracted the most attention, among the other potential changes suggested are

> investing a portion of the Social Security portfolio in non-Treasury assets, including common stock
>
> *Privatizing* a portion of each individual's retirement assets by permitting a participant to invest the assets in personally allocated assets, which would then determine their retirement benefits.

Public policy affecting these public retirement benefits will be an important issue in the future.[10]

Key Points That You Should Understand Before Proceeding

1. What is the key difference between private defined benefit pension plans and Social Security with respect to matching receipts and payments and investment management.
2. Distinguish between a "funded" plan and "a pay-as-you-go" plan.
3. What the proposals are to revise the Social Security system.

OVERVIEW OF RETIREMENT PLANNING

Three decades ago, most individuals felt fairly secure about retirement based on Social Security and a employer defined benefit retirement program. More recently, however, this perceived security has lessened for two reasons. First, given negative publicity and unnerving projections, public confidence in Social Security has lessened. In addition, employers have reduced the number of defined benefit pension plans in favor of defined contribution plans (wherein the employees both have to make their own investment choices and bear the risk of the investment returns).

Thus, Social Security and defined benefit pension plans have become a smaller component of an individual's retirement plans. Defined contribution plans, IRAs, and various types of personal savings have become a larger component. This shift is continuing to have an important effect on the way in which funds are invested in the capital markets, both in the channels of investment and in the specific types of investment.

Key Points You Should Understand Before Proceeding

1. In recent decades, defined contribution plans have grown relative to defined benefit plans.
2. Due to growing concerns about the solvency of Social Security, individuals now bear greater responsibility for their own retirement plans than before.

---

[9] Goldman Sachs & Co., "Global Economics Research Paper No. 56," October 6, 2000.

[10] For a good discussion of issues concerning and remedies for the Social Security System, see Robert Ferguson, "Saving Social Security," *Financial Analysts Journal* (January/February 2000), pp. 6 ff.

PENSION FUNDS AROUND THE WORLD

Many other countries have both public (that is, government) and private (that is, both business and individual) retirement/pension plans. These plans vary considerably by country. In addition, these plans are being changed considerably at present for many reasons, including the changing condition of public finances and the general awareness of the importance of saving for retirement. Perhaps the most important reason for this change, however, is changing demographics. Most developed countries (including the United States, European nations, and Japan) are facing an aging of their populations, whereby very soon there will be a significant increase of the number of retired persons who will be supported by a retirement plan and a corresponding decrease in the number of those employed workers who will fund the older generation's retirement. (In technical terms, there will be an increase in the "dependency ratio.") Table 9-7 provides a list of the world's 100 largest pension funds. Table 9-8 provides the share of the 300 largest pension funds by country, of the countries that hold at least 1% of the total.

Below we provide a brief overview of the pension funds in other major countries, notably Germany and Japan. In general, these systems are in a state of transition.

Table 9-7 World's 300 Largest Pension Funds (U.S. in millions)*

	FUND	COUNTRY	ASSETS		FUND	COUNTRY	ASSETS
1	California Public Employees	U.S.	$155,823	26	North Carolina Retirement	U.S.	52,618
2	Stichting Pensioenfonds ABP	Netherlands	147,820	27	Ohio State Teachers	U.S.	51,399
3	New York State Common	U.S.	111,369	28	Michigan Dept. of Treasury	U.S.	51,127
4	Assoc. of Local Public Service Personnel	Japan	102,605	29	PGGM	Netherlands	50,641
				30	British Telecommunications	U.K.	47,922
5	California State Teachers	U.S.	98,437	31	Pennsylvania School Employees	U.S.	47,279
6	Florida State Board	U.S.	93,152	32	Ontario Teachers	Canada	46,225
7	General Motors	U.S.	91,000	33	CMT Pension Trustee Services	U.K.	45,073
8	Federal Retirement Thrift	U.S.	85,309	34	New York City Teachers	U.S.	44,315
9	New York State Teachers	U.S.	81,523	35	Employees Provident Fund	Malaysia	44,167
10	Texas Teachers	U.S.	79,377	36	University of California	U.S.	41,948
11	National Public Service Personnel	Japan	77,134	37	Washington State Board	U.S.	41,095
				38	Minnesota State Board	U.S.	40,953
12	New Jersey Division of Investment	U.S.	74,927	39	Georgia Teachers	U.S.	38,540
				40	Quebec Public Employees	Canada	35,623
13	General Electric	U.S.	71,456	41	Virginia Retirement	U.S.	35,208
14	Public School Personnel	Japan	67,862	42	Universities Superannuation	U.K.	35,085
15	Allminna Pensionsfonden (Board 1, 2 & 3)	Sweden	65,235	43	Lockheed Martin	U.S.	34,765
				44	Oregon Employees	U.S.	34,546
16	New York City Retirement	U.S.	63,065	45	Japan Pension Fund Association	Japan	33,870
17	Lucent Technologies	U.S.	62,267	46	Electricity Supply Group	U.K.	32,073
18	IBM	U.S.	61,810	47	ATP (Arbejdsmarkedets Tillaegspension)	Denmark	30,886
19	SBC Communications	U.S.	60,953				
20	Wisconsin Investment Board	U.S.	57,692	48	Government Employee Pension Fund	South Africa	30,857
21	Boeing	U.S.	57,370				
22	Ford Motor	U.S.	55,700	49	AT&T	U.S.	29,739
23	Bell Atlantic	U.S.	54,275	50	Maryland State Retirement	U.S.	29,303
24	Central Provident Fund	Singapore	53,061	51	DuPont	U.S.	29,161
25	Ohio Public Employees	U.S.	52,760	52	BellSouth	U.S.	28,277

Table 9-7   World's 300 Largest Pension Funds (U.S. in millions)* (continued)

53	Colorado Employees	U.S.	28,148	76	Connecticut Retirement	U.S.		19,264
54	Los Angeles County Employees	U.S.	27,018	77	Teamsters Central States	U.S.		19,026
55	Massachusetts PRIM	U.S.	26,813	78	National Westminster Bank Staff	U.K.		19,023
56	Private School Teachers & Employees	Japan	26,320	79	Missouri Public Schools	U.S.		18,800
				80	Procter & Gamble	U.S.		18,757
57	Pennsylvania Employees	U.S.	25,979	81	South Carolina Retirement	U.S.		18,737
58	DaimlerChrysler	U.S.	25,414	82	Barclays Bank U.K.	U.K.		18,718
59	Post Office Staff Superannuation Scheme	U.K.	24,869	83	Nippon Telephone & Telegram	Japan		18,621
				84	Northrop Grumman	U.S.		18,292
60	Ontario Municipal Employees	Canada	24,454	85	Shell Contributory Pension Fund	U.K.		18,285
61	Alabama Retirement	U.S.	24,293	86	National Police Personnel	Japan		18,151
62	British Gas Staff Pension Fund	U.K.	24,209	87	Previ (Banco do Brazil)	Brazil		17,772
63	GTE	U.S.	24,163	88	Local Public Service Personnel	Japan		17,742
64	Tennessee Consolidated	U.S.	23,042	89	Allm~nna Pensionsfonden (Board 4)	Sweden		17,263
65	Raytheon	U.S.	23,000					
66	United Nations Joint Staff	U.S.	22,885	90	Philips Pensioenfonds	Netherlands		17,145
67	Railpen Investment	U.K.	22,644	91	Metaalnijverheid	Netherlands		16,914
68	Western Conference Teamsters	U.S.	22,100	92	British Airways	U.K.		16,837
69	Ilinois Teachers	U.S.	21,719	93	SAS Trustee Pooled Funds	Australia		16,826
70	Arizona State Retirement	U.S.	21,622	94	Citigroup	U.S.		16,600
71	British Petroleum	U.K.	20,103	95	Philip Morris	U.S.		15,983
72	Texas Employees	U.S.	19,582	96	Shell Oil	U.S.		15,894
73	Agriculture, Forestry & Fishery Workers	Japan	19,413	97	Mississippi Employees	U.S.		15,542
				98	Queensland State Public Service	Australia		15,136
74	United Technologies	U.S.	19,324	99	Iowa Employees	U.S.		15,113
75	U S WEST	U.S.	19,322	100	Folketrygdfondet	Norway		15,000

SOURCE: Phyllis Feinberg, "World's 300 Largest Pension Funds Grew by 9% during 1999," *Pensions & Investments* (September 18, 2000) pp.14–18. Reprinted by permission of the Investment Company Institute (www.ici.gov).

* *U.S. fund data from the P&I1,000, Jan. 24, 2000; Japan fund data as of March 31, 1999; all other fund data as of Dec. 31, 1999.*

Table 9-8   Percent and Number of 300 Largest Pension Funds by Country

COUNTRY	PERCENT
United States	64.0%
United Kingdom	9.6
Japan	9.1
Netherlands	5.3
Canada	3.6
Sweden	1.5
Switzerland	1.1

SOURCE: Phyllis Feinberg, "World's 300 Largest Pension Funds Grew by 9% during 1999," *Pensions & Investments*, September 18, 2000, pp. 14-18. Reprinted by permission of the Investment Company Institute (www.ici.gov)

However, a discussion of the current or even proposed retirement programs of other countries may be obsolete soon, due to these pending changes.

Germany

First, note the absence of any German pension plan in Tables 9-7 and 9-8. Germany's pension retirement plan has been primarily a public pay-as-you-go pension system. However, demographic changes are causing many to be skeptical of this system.

The German population will age significantly during the first part of the twenty-first century. The German population is projected to decline by approximately 15% between 2000 and 2050, and the ratio of those aged 65 and over to those aged 20 to 65 will increase from 25% to 52%. This aging will strain the current pension system in which pension benefits are financed by current payroll taxes (76%) and transfers from the federal budget (24%)—that is, on a pay-as-you-go basis—not from contributions accumulated by pensioners during their working life. This pay-as-you-go system can be considered as a contract between generations: Workers relinquish part of their income to honor the entitlements of pensioners and, in turn, expect future generations of workers to do likewise.

But the aging of the German population and public skepticism of the current system have prompted proposals for pension reform. Private pension funds and a greater role for company pension plans to support the population during retirement are being proposed. A recent proposal would permit workers to be able to contribute 0.5% of their income to private pension plans or savings/investment funds beginning in 2001, with government subsides added. According to this proposal, pensions would decline from 70% of net income as in 2000 to 64% in 2030. Financial institutions, including banks, would benefit from this program since they would serve as the investment managers.

Many analysts believe that German private and company pension plans will evolve to be similar to those in the United States and United Kingdom.

Japan

Japan has both a public and corporate pension program. In addition, Japan is also experiencing an aging of its population to a greater degree than in the United States and Europe. With respect to Japan's private system, Japanese companies have offered defined benefit plans, which means that low investment returns become liabilities of the corporation. Low investment returns and the aging of the population has left many corporations with substantially underfunded pension fund liabilities on their balance sheets. For these reasons, Japan is planning to introduce a defined contribution plan similar to the 401(k) plan in the United States. The extent of this program, including the tax incentives to be provided, remains under discussion.

SUMMARY

A pension plan is a fund that is established by private employers, governments, or unions for the payment of retirement benefits. Pension plans have grown rapidly, largely because of favorable tax treatment. Qualified pension funds are exempt from federal income taxes, as are employer contributions. The two types of pension funds are defined benefit plans and defined contribution plans. In a defined benefit plan, the sponsor agrees to make specified (or defined) payments to qualifying employees at retirement. In a defined contribution plan, the sponsor is responsible only for making specified (or defined) contributions into the plan on behalf of qualifying employees but does not guarantee any specific amount at retirement.

Recently, some hybrid plans blending features of both basic types of plans have appeared, the most prominent of which is the cash balance plan.

There is federal regulation of pension funds, as embodied in the Employee Retirement Income Security Act of 1974 (ERISA). ERISA sets minimum standards for employer contributions, establishes rules of prudent management, and requires vesting in a specified period of time. Also, ERISA provides for insurance of vested benefits.

Pension funds are managed by the plan sponsor and/or by management firms hired by the sponsor. Management fees may reflect the amount of money being managed or the performance of the managers in achieving suitable rates of return for the funds. In addition, consulting firms provide assistance in the planning, administration, and evaluation of the funds.

Social Security is a U.S. public defined benefit retirement plan based on a payroll tax. Other countries have varying private and public retirement plans, which are currently under review and are being changed.

KEY TERMS

- **401(k) plan,** 157
- **Defined benefit plan,** 155
- **Defined contribution plan,** 157
- **Employee Retirement Income Security Act of 1974 (ERISA),** 161
- **Hybrid pension plan,** 158
- **Insured benefit plan,** 156
- **Pension Benefit Guaranty Corporation (PBGC),** 156
- **Pension plan,** 154
- **Pension plan sponsor,** 154

QUESTIONS

1. What is a plan sponsor?
2. How does a defined benefit plan differ from a defined contribution plan?
3. a. What is a cash balance plan?
   b. Discuss the resemblance of a cash balance plan to a defined benefit and a defined contribution plan.
4. a. What is an insured pension plan?
   b. What is the function of the Pension Benefit Guaranty Corporation?
5. What role do mutual funds play in 401(k) plans?
6. Can and do pension plans invest in foreign securities or tax-exempt securities?
7. a. What is the major legislation regulating pension funds?
   b. Does the legislation require every corporation to establish a pension fund?
8. Discuss ERISA's "prudent man" rule.
9. Who are plan sponsor consultants and what is their role?
10. Consider the following quotation from the October 22, 1998, issue of *The Economist*:

    When Bismarck invented the state pension, with a retirement age of 65, average life expectancy was 45. Now, in the OECD, it is 76 and rising—yet state pensions can still be claimed at 65 or even less.

    Briefly discuss the role played by demographics in the current problem with the Social Security system in the United States.
11. What are the similarities between the problems faced by the Social Security systems in the United States and in Germany?
12. Why are many Japanese corporate pension funds currently underfunded?

Appendix

FOUNDATIONS

Foundations are another group of institutions that have funds to invest in financial markets. These institutions were mainly set up by wealthy individuals and families for the benefit of universities, private schools, hospitals, religious institutions, museums, and others. The initial bequest and the investment income earned is used to gift funds to these beneficiaries. The investment income generated from the funds invested is also used for the operation of the foundation.

Most of the large foundations in the United States are independent of any firm or governmental group. Some foundations are company sponsored or linked to certain communities. Still others are termed *operating foundations* because they award most of their gifts to their own units rather than to organizations outside of the foundations. Table 9A-1 lists the 10 largest foundations, by assets, in the United States as of 1999. All these foundations are independent except for the Getty Trust, which is an operating foundation.[11]

As with pension funds, qualified foundations are exempt from taxation. The board of trustees of the foundation, just like the plan sponsor for a pension fund, specifies the investment objectives and the acceptable investment alternatives. The endowment funds can be managed either in-house or by external money managers. The same organizations that manage money for pension funds also manage funds for foundations. Typically, the managers of a foundation's funds invest in long-term assets and have the primary goal of safeguarding the principal of the fund. For this reason, foundations tend to favor those equities that offer a steady dividend and comparatively little price volatility. Also, foundations often invest in government bonds and corporate bonds of high quality. The second goal, and an important one, is to generate a stream of earnings that allows the foundation to perform its functions of supporting certain operations or institutions.

---

[11] *The Foundation Directory 2000* (New York: The Foundation Center, 2000). http://fdncenter.org.

Table 9-A1   Ten Largest Foundations as of 12/31/99 (in millions)

The Ford Foundation	$11,938
Lilly Endowment	11,538
The David and Lucille Packard Foundation	9,577
J. Paul Getty Trust	8,002
The Robert Wood Johnson Foundation	7,867
W. K. Kellogg Foundation	6,388
Bill & Melinda Gates Foundation	5,369
The Pew Charitable Trusts	4,734
The MacArthur Foundation	4,169
The Rockefeller Foundation	3,838

SOURCE: The Foundation Center.

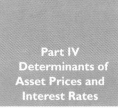

Part IV
Determinants of
Asset Prices and
Interest Rates

C h a p t e r   1 0

Properties and Pricing of Financial Assets

Learning Objectives

After reading this chapter, you will understand

■ the many key properties of financial assets: moneyness; divisibility and denomination; reversibility; cash flow and return; term to maturity; convertibility; currency; liquidity; return predictability or risk; complexity; and tax status.

■ the components of an asset's discount rate or required rate of return.

■ what is meant by a basis point.

■ how the discount rate is structured to encompass the components of an asset's risk.

■ the principles of valuing complex financial assets.

■ the inverse relationship between an asset's price and its discount rate.

■ the principles that reveal how the properties of an asset affect its value, either through the discount rate or through its expected cash flow.

■ what factors affect the price sensitivity of a financial asset to changes in interest rates.

■ what duration means, and how it is related to the price sensitivity of an asset to a change in interest rates.

Financial assets have certain properties that determine or influence their attractiveness to different classes of investors and issuers. This chapter introduces these properties in preparation for a more detailed exposition in later chapters. The chapter also provides the basic principles of the valuation or pricing of financial assets and illustrates how several of the properties of financial assets affect their value. Because the valuation of financial assets requires an understanding of present value, this concept is explained in the appendix.

PROPERTIES OF FINANCIAL ASSETS

The 11 properties of financial assets are (1) **moneyness**, (2) *divisibility and denomination*, (3) *reversibility*, (4) *cash flow*, (5) *term to maturity*, (6) *convertibility*, (7) *currency*, (8) *liquidity*, (9) *return predictability*, (10) *complexity*, and (11) *tax status.*[1]

Moneyness

As we discuss in Chapter 5, some financial assets are used as a medium of exchange or in settlement of transactions. These assets are called *money.* In the United States money con-

---

[1] Some of these properties are taken from James Tobin, "Properties of Assets," undated manuscript, Yale University, New Haven.

sists of currency and all forms of deposits that permit check writing. Other assets, although not money, are very close to money in that they can be transformed into money at little cost, delay, or risk. They are referred to as *near money*. In the case of the United States, these include time and savings deposits and a security issued by the U.S. government called a Treasury bill.[2] Moneyness is clearly a desirable property for investors.

Divisibility and Denomination

Divisibility relates to the minimum size in which a financial asset can be liquidated and exchanged for money. The smaller the size, the more the financial asset is divisible. A financial asset such as a deposit is typically infinitely divisible (down to the penny), but other financial assets have varying degrees of divisibility depending on their denomination, which is the dollar value of the amount that each unit of the asset will pay at maturity. Thus, many bonds come in $1,000 denominations, commercial paper in $25,000 units,[3] and certain types of certificates of deposit in $100,000 and more. In general, divisibility is desirable for investors but not for borrowers.

Reversibility

Reversibility refers to the cost of investing in a financial asset and then getting out of it and back into cash again. Consequently, reversibility is also referred to as **turnaround cost** or *round-trip cost*.

A financial asset such as a deposit at a bank is obviously highly reversible because usually there is no charge for adding to or withdrawing from it. Other transactions costs may be unavoidable, but these are small. For financial assets traded in organized markets or with **market makers** (discussed in Chapter 15), the most relevant component of round-trip cost is the so-called bid–ask spread, to which might be added commissions and the time and cost, if any, of delivering the asset. The spread charged by a market maker varies sharply from one financial asset to another, reflecting primarily the amount of risk the market maker is assuming by "making" a market.

This market-making risk, which is discussed in more detail in Chapter 15, can be related to two main forces. One is the variability of the price as measured, say, by some measure of dispersion of the relative price over time. The greater the variability, the greater the probability of the market maker incurring a loss in excess of a stated bound between the time of buying and reselling the financial asset. The variability of prices differs widely across financial assets. Treasury bills, for example, have a very stable price, for the reason explained at the end of this chapter, while a speculative stock will exhibit much larger short-run variations.

The second determining factor of the bid–ask spread charged by a market maker is what is commonly referred to as the **thickness of the market:** by this is meant essentially the prevailing rate at which buying and selling orders reach the market maker (that is, the frequency of transactions). A **thin market** is one that has few trades on a regular or continuing basis. Clearly, the greater the frequency of order flows, the shorter the time that the security will have to be held in the market maker's inventory, and hence the smaller the probability of an unfavorable price movement while held.

Thickness, too, varies from market to market. A three-month U.S. Treasury bill is easily the thickest market in the world. In contrast, trading in stock of small companies is not thick but thin. Because Treasury bills dominate other instruments both in price stability and thickness, their bid–ask spread tends to be the smallest in the market. A low turnaround cost is clearly a desirable property of a financial asset, and as a result

---

[2] U.S. Treasury bills are discussed in Chapter 16.
[3] Commercial paper is described in Chapter 20.

thickness itself is a valuable property. This explains the potential advantage of larger over smaller markets (economies of scale), along with a market's tendency to standardize the instruments offered to the public.

Cash Flow

The return that an investor will realize by holding a financial asset depends on all the cash distributions that the financial asset will pay its owners; this includes dividends on shares and coupon payments on bonds. The return also considers the repayment of principal for a debt security and the expected sale price of a stock. In computing the expected return, noncash payments, such as stock dividends and options to purchase additional stock, or the distribution of other securities must also be accounted for.

In a world of nonnegligible inflation, it is also important to distinguish between **nominal expected return** and **real expected return**. The expected return that we described above is the nominal expected return. That is, it considers the dollars that are expected to be received, but does not adjust those dollars to take into consideration changes in their purchasing power. The net real expected return is the nominal expected return after adjustment for the loss of purchasing power of the financial asset as a result of anticipated inflation. For example, if the nominal expected return for a one-year investment of $1,000 is 6%, then at the end of one year the investor expects to realize $1,060, consisting of interest of $60 and the repayment of the $1,000 investment. However, if the inflation rate over the same period of time is 4%, then the purchasing power of $1,060 is only $1,019.23 ($1,060 divided by 1.04). Thus, the return in terms of purchasing power, or the real return, is 1.923%. In general, the expected real return can be approximated by subtracting the expected inflation rate from the expected nominal return. In our example, it is approximately 2% (6% – 4%).

Term to Maturity

Term to Maturity is the length of the period until the date at which the instrument is scheduled to make its final payment, or the owner is entitled to demand liquidation. Instruments for which the creditor can ask for repayment at any time, such as checking accounts and many savings accounts, are called *demand instruments*. Maturity is an important characteristic of financial assets such as bonds, and can range from one day to a few decades. In the United Kingdom, there is one well-known type of bond that promises to pay a fixed amount per year indefinitely and not to repay the principal at any time; such an instrument is called a **perpetual**, or a *consul*. Many other instruments, including equities, have no maturity and are thus a form of perpetual.

It should be understood that even a financial asset with a stated maturity may terminate before its stated maturity. This may occur for several reasons, including bankruptcy or reorganization, or because of **call provisions** entitling the debtor to repay in advance, usually at some penalty and only after a number of years from the time of issuance. Sometimes the investor may have the privilege of asking for early repayment. This feature is called a **put option**. Some assets have maturities that may be increased or extended at the discretion of the issuer or the investor. For example, the French government issues a six-year *obligation renouvelable du Trésor*, which allows the investor, after the end of the third year, to switch into a new six-year debt. Similar bonds are issued by the British government. All these features regarding maturity are discussed in later chapters.

Convertibility

As the preceding discussion shows, an important property of some assets is that they are **convertible** into other assets. In some cases, the conversion takes place within one class of assets, as when a bond is converted into another bond. In other situations, the conversion spans classes. For example, a corporate *convertible bond* is a bond that the bondholder can change into equity shares. Preferred stock (discussed in Chapter 21) may be convertible into common stock. It is important to note that the timing, costs, and conditions for conversion are clearly spelled out in the legal descriptions of the convertible security at the time it is issued.

Currency

We have noted throughout our discussion that the global financial system has become increasingly integrated. In light of the freely floating and often volatile exchange rates among the major currencies,[4] this fact gives added importance to the currency in which the financial asset will make cash flow payments. Most financial assets are denominated in one currency, such as U.S. dollars or yen or euros, and investors must choose them with that feature in mind.

Some issuers, responding to investors' wishes to reduce **currency** risk, have issued *dual-currency securities*. For example, some Eurobonds[5] pay interest in one currency but principal or redemption value in a second. U.S. dollars and yen are commonly paired in these cases. Furthermore, some Eurobonds carry a currency option that allows the investor to specify that payments of either interest or principal be made in either one of two major currencies.

Liquidity

This is an important and widely used notion, although there is at present no uniformly accepted definition of liquidity. A useful way to think of liquidity and illiquidity, proposed by Professor James Tobin,[6] is in terms of how much sellers stand to lose if they wish to sell immediately as against engaging in a costly and time-consuming search.

An example of a quite illiquid financial asset is the stock of a small corporation or the bond issued by a small school district. The market for such a security is extremely thin, and one must search for one of a very few suitable buyers. Less suitable buyers, including speculators and market makers, may be located more promptly, but they will have to be enticed to invest in the illiquid financial asset by an appropriate discount in price.

For many other financial assets, liquidity is determined by contractual arrangements. Ordinary deposits, for example, are perfectly liquid because the bank has a contractual obligation to convert them at par on demand. Financial contracts representing a claim on a private pension fund may be regarded on the other hand as totally illiquid because these can be cashed only at retirement.

Liquidity may depend not only on the financial asset but also on the quantity one wishes to sell (or buy). Although a small quantity may be quite liquid, a large lot may run into illiquidity problems. Note that liquidity is again closely related to whether a market is thick or thin. Thinness always has the effect of increasing the turnaround cost, even of a liquid financial asset. But beyond some point, thinness becomes an obstacle to the formation of a market, and it has a direct effect on the illiquidity of the financial asset.

Return Predictability

Return **predictability** is a basic property of financial assets, in that it is a major determinant of their value. Assuming investors are risk averse, the riskiness of an asset can be

---

[4] Exchange rates and the foreign exchange market are the subject of Chapter 30.
[5] Eurobonds are discussed in Chapter 21.
[6] Tobin, "Properties of Assets."

equated with the uncertainty or unpredictability of its return. We will see in Chapter 13 how the unpredictability of future returns can be measured and how it is related to the variability of past returns. But whatever measure of volatility is used,[7] it is obvious that volatility varies greatly across financial assets. There are several reasons for this.

First, as illustrated later in this chapter, the value of a financial asset depends on the cash flow expected and on the interest rate used to discount this cash flow. Hence, volatility will be a consequence of the uncertainty about future interest rates and future cash flow. Now the future cash flow may be contractual, in which case the sole source of its uncertainty is the reliability of the debtor with regard to fulfilling the obligation. The cash flow may be in the nature of a residual equity claim, as is the case for the payments generated by the equity of a corporation. The cash flows from U.S. government securities are the only cash flows generally regarded as altogether riskless. Corporate debt and corporate stock cash flows are generally riskier than cash flows of U.S. government securities. Corporate equities represent a wide range of risk, from public utilities to highly speculative issues.

As for a change in interest rates, it will in principle affect all prices in the opposite direction, but the effect is much larger in the case of the price of a financial asset with a long maturity than one with a short remaining life, as illustrated later in this chapter. Thus, on this account also, short-term U.S. government securities such as Treasury bills tend to be the safest assets, except for cash (if properly insured). For individual stocks the interest effect is generally swamped by cash flow uncertainty, although movements in interest rates have the characteristic of affecting all stocks in the same direction, while change in expected cash flow is largely dependent on a firm's particular financial situation. In general, uncertainty about returns and future prices can be expected to increase as the investment horizon lengthens.

What has been said so far relates to the predictability of nominal returns, although the relevant measure, of course, is real returns—returns corrected for gains or losses of purchasing power attributable to inflation. Of course, if inflation is absent or small, the determinants of real and nominal uncertainty and risk coincide. But in the presence of highly unpredictable inflation (which is usually the case with high inflation), real returns may be drastically harder to predict than nominal returns.

Complexity

Some financial assets are **complex** in the sense that they are actually combinations of two or more simpler assets. To find the true value of such an asset, one must break it down into its component parts and price each separately. The sum of those prices is the value of the complex asset. A good example of a complex asset is the *callable bond,* that is, a bond whose issuer is entitled to repay the debt prior to the maturity date. When investors buy such a bond, they in effect buy a bond and sell to the issuer an option that allows the issuer to redeem the bond at a set price prior to the issue's scheduled maturity. The correct or true price of a callable bond, therefore, is equal to the price of a similar noncallable bond less the value of the issuer's right to retire the bond early.

A complex asset may be viewed as a bundle or package of cash flows and options belonging to either the issuer or the holder, or both. Other examples of a complex asset include a convertible bond, a bond that has payments that can be made in a different currency at the option of the bondholder, and a bond that can be sold back to the issuer at a fixed price (that is, a **putable bond**).

---

[7] Proxy measures for volatility include the standard deviation of expected returns or the range within which the outcome can be expected to fall with some stated probability.

In some cases, the degree of complexity is large: Many convertible bonds are also callable, and some bonds give their issuers the right either to extend the asset's maturity or to redeem it early. Also, some Japanese firms have issued bonds that are convertible into Japanese stock (denominated in yen, of course) but that are sold for, and make coupon and principal payments in, another currency, such as U.S. dollars.

Tax Status

An important feature of any asset is its **tax status**. Governmental regulations for taxing the income from the ownership or sale of financial assets vary widely, if not wildly. Tax rates differ from year to year, from country to country, and even among municipal units within a country (as with state and local taxes in the United States). Moreover, tax rates may differ from financial asset to financial asset, depending on the type of issuer, the length of time the asset is held, the nature of the owner, and so on. For example, in the United States, pension funds are exempt from income taxes (see Chapter 9 for more detail), and coupon payments on municipal bonds are generally free of taxation by the federal government (see Chapter 17).

Key Points That You Should Understand Before Proceeding

1. A financial asset has many properties, and each affects the asset's value in a distinctive and important way.
2. Some properties are intrinsic to the asset, such as its maturity or promised cash flow.
3. Other properties are features of the market for the asset, such as the costs of trading the asset.
4. Still other properties reflect decisions by government about the asset's tax status.
5. A complex asset is one that provides options for the issuer or the investor, or both, and so represents a combination of simpler assets.

PRINCIPLES OF PRICING OF FINANCIAL ASSETS

The fundamental principle of finance is that the true or correct price of an asset equals the **present value** of all cash flows that the owner of the asset expects to receive during its life. In general, the correct price for a financial asset can be expressed as follows:

$$P = \frac{CF_1}{(1+r)^1} + \frac{CF_2}{(1+r)^2} + \frac{CF_3}{(1+r)^3} + \cdots + \frac{CF_N}{(1+r)^N}$$

where

P = the price of the financial asset
CF_t = the cash flow in year t $(t = 1, \ldots, N)$
N = maturity of the financial asset
r = appropriate discount rate

The Appropriate Discount Rate

The appropriate **discount rate**, r, is the return that the market or the consensus of investors requires on the asset. A convenient (but approximate) expression for the appropriate discount rate is this:

$$r = RR + IP + DP + MP + LP + EP$$

where

RR= the **real rate of interest**, which is the reward for not consuming and for lending to other users

IP= the **inflation premium**, which is the compensation for the expected decline in the purchasing power of the money lent to borrowers

DP= the **default risk premium**, which is the reward for taking on the risk of default in the case of a loan or bond or the risk of loss of principal for other assets

MP= the **maturity premium**, which is the compensation for lending money for long periods of time

LP= the **liquidity premium**, which is the reward for investing in an asset that may not be readily converted to cash at a fair market value

EP= the **exchange-rate risk premium**, which is the reward for investing in an asset that is not denominated in the investor's home currency.

Obviously, the price of an asset is inversely related to its discount rate: If the discount rate rises, the price falls; and if the rate declines, the price increases.

Illustration

Let us construct a simple example to illustrate the pricing of a financial asset. We can then use the hypothetical financial asset to illustrate some of the properties explained earlier in this chapter.

Suppose a bond has a maturity of four years and pays annual interest of $50 at the end of each year plus a principal of $1,000 at the conclusion of the fourth year. Since this bond pays $50 per $1,000 of principal, the periodic coupon rate is 5%. This rate is commonly and simply referred to as the **coupon rate**. Thus, using the notation above:

$$N = 4 \quad CF_1 = \$50 \quad CF_2 = \$50 \quad CF_3 = \$50 \quad CF_N = \$1,050$$

Furthermore, assume that the market thinks the real rate is 2.5%, the inflation premium is 3%, the bond's default risk justifies a premium of 2%, the maturity premium is 0.5%, and the liquidity premium is 1%. Since the cash flows are denominated in U.S. dollars, the foreign-exchange rate premium is zero. That is,

$$RR = 2.5\% \quad IP = 3.0\% \quad DP = 2.0\% \quad MP = 0.5\% \quad LP = 1.0\% \quad EP = 0\%$$

Thus, we have this value for the discount rate:

$$r = 2.5\% + 3.0\% + 2.0\% + 0.5\% + 1.0\% + 0\% = 9.0\% \text{ or } 0.09$$

Using the formula for price, the price of this bond is:

$$P = \frac{\$50}{(1.09)^1} + \frac{\$50}{(1.09)^2} + \frac{\$50}{(1.09)^3} + \frac{\$1,050}{(1.09)^4}$$
$$= \$870.41$$

Price and Asset Properties

We can use this hypothetical financial asset to illustrate the effect of some of the properties of financial assets on price or asset value. First, it should be clear that the price of a financial asset changes as the appropriate discount rate, r, changes. More specifically, the price changes in the opposite direction to the change in the appropriate discount rate. An illustration of this principle appears in Table 10-1, which shows the price of our hypothetical financial asset for various discount rates.

Let's look at how reversibility affects an asset's value. Suppose a **broker's commission** of $35 is imposed by brokers to buy or sell the bond. The price of the four-year bond is then:

$$P = -\$35 + \frac{\$50}{(1.09)^1} + \frac{\$50}{(1.09)^2} + \frac{\$50}{(1.09)^3} + \frac{\$1,050 - \$35}{(1.09)^4}$$
$$= \$810.62$$

Notice that the initial commission of $35 is subtracted on an undiscounted basis because that payment is made at the time of purchase.

Suppose also a government entity imposes a transfer tax of $20 on each transaction. Because this rise in the cost of reversing an investment diminishes its reversibility to some extent, the present value of all cash flows associated with owning the bond now looks like this:

$$P = -\$35 - \$20 + \frac{\$50}{(1.09)^1} + \frac{\$50}{(1.09)^2} + \frac{\$50}{(1.09)^3} + \frac{\$1,050 - \$35 - \$20}{(1.09)^4}$$
$$= \$776.45$$

The change in price is significant and demonstrates why financial markets adjust so sharply (and rapidly) when governments impose restrictions on, or raise the cost of, capital market transactions.

To see how default risk affects the price of an asset, assume that, right before you bought the bond, a news story convinced investors that this bond is less risky than they had thought. So, the *default risk premium* falls from 2% to 1%, and the appropriate discount rate thus declines from 9% to 8%. Ignoring commissions and transfer fees, Table 10-1 shows that the price would increase from $870.41 to $900.64.

What about liquidity? Suppose immediately after the purchase of this bond, factors in the market for this bond cause its liquidity to decline. An investor buying this

Table 10-1 Price of a Four-Year Bond for Various Discount Rates

Cash flow:			
CF₁=$50	CF₂=$50	CF₃=$50	CF₄=$1,050
APPROPRIATE DISCOUNT RATE (%)			PRICE ($)
4			1,036.30
5			1,000.00
6			965.35
7			932.26
8			900.64
9			870.41
10			841.51
11			813.85
12			787.39
13			762.04
14			737.77

asset would plan for such a possibility by raising the liquidity premium. Assume that the liquidity premium increases from 1% to 3%. The appropriate discount rate then increases from 9% to 11%. Ignoring the commission and the transfer fee, Table 10-1 shows that the price would be $813.85. The fall in price, from the original $870.41 to $813.85, shows how important liquidity can be.

Now, let's tackle the notion of complexity by assuming that the bond is convertible into a fixed number of shares of common stock of the company that issued the bond. The price of our four-year bond would then be greater than $870.41 by an amount equal to the value that the market assigns to the right to convert the bond into common stock. For example, suppose we observe that the price of our hypothetical bond with the conversion privilege is $1,000.41. This means that the conversion privilege is valued by the market at $130.

The unresolved question is whether or not the $130 is a fair value for this conversion privilege. Valuation techniques to determine the fair value of any type of option such as a conversion privilege are available, and we will discuss these techniques in Chapter 27. For now, it is sufficient to understand why a knowledge of how to value an option is important. Because many financial assets have options embedded in them, failure to assess the options properly may lead to the mispricing of financial assets.

Now, let's turn our attention to currency. Suppose that this bond was issued by a German firm and that all payments are in euros. The cash flow in U.S. dollars that a U.S. investor will receive is uncertain because the dollar-euro exchange rate will fluctuate over the four years. Suppose that the market assigns an exchange premium of 3%. This means that the appropriate discount rate increases from 9% to 12% and the price would be $787.39 (see Table 10-1). To continue with the effect of currency risk, suppose that immediately after the purchase of this bond the market expects that the exchange rate between the U.S. dollar and the euro will become more volatile. The market will adjust for this by increasing the foreign currency risk premium, which, in turn, increases the appropriate discount rate and decreases the price.

It is easy to illustrate the impact of taxes. Suppose that our bond is granted a favorable tax treatment such that the interest and any capital gain from this bond would not be taxed. Suppose that the marginal tax rate on otherwise equivalent taxable bonds is 33.33% and the appropriate discount rate is 9%. This means that the after-tax discount rate would be approximately 6%, as shown below:

$$\text{Pretax discount rate} \times (1 - \text{marginal tax rate})$$
$$0.09 \times (1 - 0.3333) = 6\%$$

Since our hypothetical bond is free of taxes, the appropriate discount rate would be adjusted to compensate for this feature. The discount rate that would be used is 6%, because it is the equivalent of a 9% discount rate and a 33.33% marginal tax rate. From Table 10-1 we see that the price of the bond would be $965.35.

Continuing with the importance of tax features to the price of a financial asset, suppose that immediately after the purchase of this bond, the market comes to expect that the U.S. Congress will raise the marginal tax rate. This expectation would increase the value of the tax-exempt feature by decreasing the discount rate based on the anticipated rise in the marginal tax rate. The opposite would occur if the market came to expect that the U.S. Congress would lower the marginal tax rate.

Although we have used a single discount rate to discount each cash flow, there are theoretical reasons that suggest this is inappropriate. Specifically, in Chapter 12, we will look at the relationship between a bond's maturity and yield. In addition, in Chapter 16 we will see that a financial asset should be viewed as a package of cash flows. Each cash flow should be treated as if it is an individual asset with only one cash flow and that cash flow has its own discount rate that depends upon when it will be received. Consequently, a more general formula for pricing a financial asset would be:

$$P = \frac{CF_1}{(1+r_1)^1} + \frac{CF_2}{(1+r_2)^2} + \frac{CF_3}{(1+r_3)^3} + \cdots + \frac{CF_N}{(1+r_N)^N}$$

where r_t is the discount rate appropriate for period t.

Key Points That You Should Understand Before Proceeding

1. An asset's price is the present value of its expected cash flows, discounted at an appropriate rate.
2. The appropriate discount rate for an asset's cash flows depends upon the properties of the asset.
3. The appropriate discount rate can often be approximated as the sum of rewards for the various risks an asset poses to its buyer.
4. The price of an asset moves in the opposite direction of a change in its discount rate.
5. The price of a complex asset is the sum of the prices of its component parts.

PRICE VOLATILITY OF FINANCIAL ASSETS

As Table 10-1 makes clear, a fundamental principle is that a financial asset's price changes in the opposite direction of the change in the required rate of return. We refer to the required rate of return as the *required* **yield**. This principle follows from the fact that the price of a financial asset is equal to the present value of its cash flow. An increase (decrease) in the yield required by investors decreases (increases) the present value of the cash flow and, therefore, the financial asset's price.

The price sensitivity of a financial asset to a change in the required yield will not be the same for all assets. For example, an increase in the required yield of one percentage point may result in a decline in one asset's price of 20%, but only 3% for another. In this section, we will see how the characteristics of a financial asset and the level of interest rates affect the price responsiveness of a financial asset to a change in the required yield. We also present a measure that can be used to gauge the approximate price sensitivity of a financial asset to changes in the required yield.

It is important to note that the analysis in this section applies fully and directly to bonds and other financial assets that have known expected cash flows and known expected maturities. An analysis of the price sensitivity of other major financial assets, such as preferred stock and common stock (which are perpetuals and have uncertain cash flows), must be postponed to a later chapter.

In our discussion, we will refer to changes in the required yield. It is convenient to measure a change in yield in terms of what market participants refer to as a **basis point** rather than in terms of a percentage change. One basis point is defined as 0.0001, or equivalently, 0.01%. Therefore, 100 basis points is equal to one percentage point, and a yield change from 9% to 10% represents a 100 basis point change in yield. A yield change from 7% to 7.5% is a 50 basis point change, and a yield change from 6% to 8.35% is a 235 basis point change in yield.

The Effect of Maturity

An asset's maturity is a factor that affects its price sensitivity to a change in yield. In fact, a bond's price sensitivity to a change in the discount rate is positively related to the bond's maturity. Consider the case of two bonds that have the same coupon rate, and the same required yield but different maturities. If the required rate were to change, the price sensitivity of the bond with the longer maturity would be greater than that of the bond with the shorter maturity.

An illustration of this link between maturity and price change appears in Table 10-2, which shows the price of a bond that pays $50 annually and $1,000 at maturity—a 5% coupon rate—for various maturities and discount rates. Table 10-3, which is based on Table 10-2, shows the differences across maturities in a bond's dollar price decline and percentage price decline for an increase in the discount rate of 100 basis points. For example, if the discount rate rises from 9% to 10%, the price of a four-year bond falls from $870.41 to $841.51, which represents a price decline of $28.90 and a percentage price decline of 3.32%. In contrast, a similar rise in the discount rate causes the price of a 20-year bond to fall considerably more, from $634.86 to $574.32, which represents a price decline of $60.54 and a percentage price decline of 9.54%.

The Effect of the Coupon Rate

A bond's coupon rate also affects its price sensitivity. More specifically, for two bonds with the same maturity and with the same required yield, the lower the coupon rate, the greater the price responsiveness for a given change in the required yield.

To illustrate this, consider a 5% coupon bond and a 10% coupon bond, each of which has a maturity of 15 years and a principal of $1,000. If the required yield for both bonds is 9%, the price of the 5% coupon bond would be $677.57, and the price of the 10% coupon bond would be $1,080.61. If the required yield increases by 100 basis points, from 9% to 10%, the price of the 5% coupon bond will fall to $619.70, while the price of the 10% coupon bond would fall to $1,000. Thus, the 5% coupon bond's price declines by $57.87 or 8.5% ($57.87/$677.57), while the 10% coupon bond's price declines by $80.61 or by 7.5% ($80.61/$1,080.61). Although the dollar price change is greater for the higher-coupon bond, the percentage price change is less.

In later chapters, we will discuss a special type of bond, one with no coupon rate. This is called a **zero-coupon bond**. The investor who purchases a zero-coupon bond

Table 10-2   Price of a Bond Paying $50 Annually and $1,000 at Maturity For Various Discount Rates and Maturities

DISCOUNT RATE (%)	Number of years to maturity			
	4	10	15	20
4%	$1,036.30	$1,081.11	$1,111.18	$1,135.90
5	1,000.00	1,000.00	1,000.00	1,000.00
6	965.35	926.40	902.88	885.30
7	932.26	859.53	817.84	788.12
8	900.64	798.70	743.22	705.46
9	870.41	743.29	677.57	634.86
10	841.51	692.77	619.70	574.32
11	813.85	646.65	568.55	522.20
12	787.39	604.48	523.24	477.14
13	762.04	565.90	483.01	438.02
14	737.77	530.55	447.20	403.92

Table 10-3   Price Decline if the Discount Rate Increases 100 Basis Points for a Bond Paying $50 Annually and $1,000 at Maturity for Various Discount Rates and Maturities

| | Price Change | | | |
| | Number of years to maturity | | | |
DISCOUNT RATE CHANGES FROM	4	10	15	20
4% to 5%	$−36.30	$−81.11	$−111.18	$−135.91
5 to 6	−34.65	−73.60	−97.20	−114.70
6 to 7	−33.09	−66.87	−85.04	−97.18
7 to 8	−31.62	−60.83	−74.62	−82.66
8 to 9	−30.23	−55.41	−65.65	−70.60
9 to 10	−28.90	−50.52	−57.87	−60.54
10 to 11	−27.66	−46.12	−51.15	−52.12
11 to 12	−26.40	−42.17	−45.13	−45.06
12 to 13	−25.35	−38.58	−40.23	−39.12
13 to 14	−24.27	−35.35	−35.81	−34.12

| | Percentage Price Change | | | |
| | Number of years to maturity | | | |
DISCOUNT RATE CHANGES FROM	4	10	15	20
4% to 5%	−3.50%	−7.50%	−10.01%	−11.96%
5 to 6	−3.47	−7.36	−9.71	−11.47
6 to 7	−3.43	−7.22	−9.42	−10.98
7 to 8	−3.39	−7.08	−9.12	−10.49
8 to 9	−3.36	−6.94	−8.83	−10.01
9 to 10	−3.32	−6.80	−8.54	−9.54
10 to 11	−3.29	−6.66	−8.25	−9.08
11 to 12	−3.25	−6.52	−7.97	−8.63
12 to 13	−3.22	−6.38	−7.69	−8.20
13 to 14	−3.18	−6.25	−7.41	−7.79

receives no periodic interest payment. Instead, the investor purchases the bond at a price below its principal and receives the principal at the maturity date. The difference between the principal and the price at which the zero-coupon bond is purchased represents interest earned by the investor over the bond's life. For example, consider a zero-coupon bond with a principal of $1,000 and a maturity of 15 years. If the required yield is 9%, the price of this bond would be $274.54.[8] The difference between the principal of $1,000 and the price of $274.54 is the interest that the investor realizes at the maturity date.

A zero-coupon bond will have greater price sensitivity than a bond with a coupon rate selling at the same required yield and with the same maturity. For example, consider once again the 15-year zero-coupon bond. If the required yield increases from 9% to 10%, the price of this bond would fall to $239.39, a percentage price decline of 12.8% ($35.15/$274.54). This percentage change is greater than the declines in price for the 15-year maturity 5% coupon and 15-year 10% coupon bonds.

---

[8] The price is the present value of $1,000 15 years from now discounted at 9%.

The Effect of the Level of Yields

Tables 10-2 and 10-3 also bring out another interesting property about asset prices. Notice that, for a given maturity, the dollar price change and the percentage price change is higher for the lower initial discount rates than at the higher initial discount rates. For example, consider the 15-year bond when the discount rate is 5%. The price of the bond falls from $1,000 to $902.88 when the discount rate increases from 5% to 6%, a price decline of $97.20 and a percentage price decline of 9.72%. In contrast, a rise in the discount rate of 100 basis points from 13% to 14% reduces the same bond's price by $35.81 (from $483.01 to $447.20) and by the percentage of 7.41%.

The implication is that the lower the level of yields, the greater the affect a change in interest rates will have on the price of a financial asset.

Measuring Price Sensitivity to Interest Rate Changes: Duration

From our discussion thus far, we see that three factors affect the price sensitivity of an asset to changes in interest rates: the maturity, the coupon rate, and the level of interest rates. In managing the price sensitivity of a portfolio, market participants seek a measure of the sensitivity of assets to interest rate changes that encompasses all three factors.

A useful way to approximate an asset's price sensitivity to interest rate changes is to examine how the price changes if the yield changes by a small number of basis points. To do this, we will use the following notation:

Δy = change in yield (in decimal)
P_0 = initial price of the asset
P_- = asset's price if the yield is decreased by Δy
$P+$ = asset's price if the yield is increased by Δy

Then, for a small decrease in yield, the percentage price change is:

$$\frac{P_- - P_0}{P_0}$$

The percentage price change per basis point change is found by dividing the percentage price change by the number of basis points (Δy times 100). That is,

$$\frac{P_- - P_0}{P_0(\Delta y)100}$$

Similarly, the percentage price change per basis point increase in yield is:

$$\frac{P_0 - P_+}{P_0(\Delta y)100}$$

The percentage price change for an increase and decrease in interest rates will not be the same. Consequently, the average percentage price change per basis point change in yield can be calculated. This is done as follows:

$$\frac{1}{2}\left[\frac{P_- - P_0}{P_0(\Delta y)100} + \frac{P_0 - P_+}{P_0(\Delta y)100}\right]$$

or equivalently,

$$\frac{P_- - P_+}{2P_0(\Delta y)100}$$

The approximate percentage price change for a 100 basis point change in yield is found by multiplying the previous formula by 100:

$$\frac{P_- - P_+}{2 P_0 (\Delta y)}$$

For example, the price of a 5% coupon bond with a principal of $1,000 and a maturity of 15 years is $677.57. If the yield is increased by 50 basis points from 9% to 9.5%, the price would be $647.73. If the yield is decreased by 50 basis points from 9% to 8.5%, the price would be $709.35. Then we have these values:

$$\Delta y = 0.005$$
$$P_0 = \$677.57$$
$$P_- = \$709.35$$
$$P_+ = \$647.73$$

The application of the foregoing formula provides this number:

$$\frac{\$709.35 - \$647.73}{2(\$677.57)(0.005)} = 9.09$$

This measure of price sensitivity is popularly referred to as **duration**—a concept we introduced in Chapter 4 when discussing the interest rate risk of a depository institution. Table 10-4 shows how the duration is determined for a 5% coupon bond with different maturities when the interest rate is initially at 9%.

Table 10-5 shows the duration for three coupon bonds with different maturities, under the assumption of different initial yields. As can be seen from this table, the relative magnitude of duration is consistent with the properties we described earlier. Specifically, (1) for bonds with the same coupon rate and the same yield, the longer the maturity the greater the duration; (2) for bonds with the same maturity and at the same yield, the lower the coupon rate the greater the duration; and (3) the lower the initial yield, the greater the duration for a given bond. Thus, duration picks up the effect of all three factors: maturity, coupon rate, and initial level of yield.

Duration is related to the price sensitivity as follows:

Approximate percentage change in a financial asset's price =
− Duration × (Yield change in decimal form) × 100

Table 10-4 Determination of Duration for a 5% Coupon Bond with a Principal of $1,000 and an Initial Required Yield of 9%

	Number of years to maturity			
	4	10	15	20
Price at 9% (P_0)	870.41	743.29	677.57	634.86
Price at 9.5% (P+)	855.80	717.45	647.73	603.44
Price at 8.5% (P_)	885.35	770.35	709.35	668.78
Duration	3.40	7.12	9.09	10.29

$$\text{Duration} = \frac{P_- - P_+}{2(P_0)(0.005)}$$

Table 10-5   Duration for Various Bonds by Maturity, Coupon Rate, and Yield Level.

COUPON RATE	YIELD	Number of years to maturity			
		4	10	15	20
5%	5%	3.55	7.73	10.39	12.48
5	9	3.40	7.12	9.09	10.29
5	12	3.29	6.67	8.16	8.79
10	5	3.36	6.93	9.15	10.95
10	9	3.21	6.30	7.91	8.97
10	12	3.10	5.85	7.05	7.69
0	5	3.81	9.53	14.30	19.08
0	9	3.67	9.18	13.77	18.38
0	12	3.57	8.93	13.40	17.88

For example, suppose that the required yield on the 5% coupon, 15-year bond increases from 9% to 10% (0.01 in decimal form). Then, since this bond's duration is 9.09:

$$\text{Approximate percentage change in price} = -9.09 \times (0.01) \times 100 = -9.09\%$$

We showed earlier that the actual percentage change in price if the required yield increases from 9% to 10% would be a fall of 8.5%. Thus, duration is a close approximation of the percentage price change. The approximation is better for smaller changes in the required yield. For example, if the required yield changes by 20 basis points (0.002 in decimal form) from 9% to 9.20% rather than 100 basis points, then based on duration the approximate percentage change in price would be −1.82%. The actual price if the required yield increased by 20 basis points is $665.41, a decline of $12.16 from the price of $677.57 at 9%. The actual percentage price change is therefore −1.79% (−$12.16/$677.57). Duration did an excellent job of approximating the percentage price change in this case.

In general, one can interpret duration as follows: *the approximate percentage change in price for a 100 basis point change in interest rates around the prevailing yield.* Duration does a good job of approximating the price change for a small change in yield on the order of 50 basis points in either direction. The larger the yield change, the poorer the approximation that duration provides.

Although we have developed duration in the context of bonds, we want to note that the basic principle applies equally to other financial assets. For example, consider a financial asset whose cash flow is as follows:

Year	Cash flow
1	$ 30
2	75
3	120
4	140
5	200
6	250
7	300

Suppose that the appropriate discount rate is 7%. Then the price of this financial asset would be $794.31. If the yield is decreased by 50 basis points to 6.5%, the price would be $812.82. If the yield is increased by 50 basis points to 7.5%, the price would be $776.36. Thus, for this financial asset we know:

$$\Delta y = 0.005$$
$$P_0 = \$794.31$$
$$P_- = \$812.82$$
$$P_+ = \$776.36$$

The duration is then 4.59, as follows:

$$\frac{\$812.82 - \$776.36}{2(\$794.31)(0.005)} = 4.59$$

Although we have focused on the price sensitivity of individual financial assets to changes in interest rates, we can extend the principle to a portfolio of financial assets. The duration of a portfolio of assets is simply the weighted average of the duration of the individual assets. The weight used for each asset is its market value in the portfolio.

Moreover, the principle can be extended to a liability stream. A liability can be viewed as a financial asset with a negative cash flow. The present value of the cash outlays is equal to the value or price of the liability stream. When interest rates change, the value of the liability stream changes. A duration for a liability stream can be calculated in the same way as the duration of a financial asset.

Importance of Measuring Price Sensitivity to Interest Rate Changes

The importance of being able to measure the sensitivity of an individual asset, a portfolio of assets, and a liability cannot be overemphasized. To control interest rate risk, it is necessary to be able to measure it. An investor with a portfolio of assets wants to be able to measure her exposure to interest rate changes in order to assess whether or not the exposure is acceptable. If it is not, she can alter the exposure. Various instruments that we describe later in this book provide a means for doing so. Financial institutions manage assets against liabilities. The interest rate risk exposure of a financial institution is the difference between the duration of its assets and the duration of its liabilities.

From our discussion, it may seem simple to calculate the duration of an asset. Unfortunately, this is not the case. The reason is that for most assets, the cash flow can change when interest rates change. In our illustrations, we have assumed that when interest rates change, the cash flows are unchanged. However, as we describe the various financial instruments in later chapters, we will see that as interest rates change either the issuer or the investor can alter the cash flow. Consequently, if a change in the cash flow is not considered when interest rates change, the duration calculation can be misleading.

When a duration is calculated under the assumption that the cash flows do not change when interest rates change, the resulting duration is called **modified duration**. In contrast, a duration calculated assuming that the cash flow changes when interest rates change is called **effective duration**. The difference between modified duration and effective duration for some assets can be quite dramatic. For example, with some of the more complex financial instruments discussed later in this book, the modified duration could be 4 while the effective duration could be 25! This means that an investor might believe that the price of the asset will change by approximately 4% for a 100 basis point change in interest rates (modified duration) when, in fact, it would change by approximately 25% for a 100 basis point change in interest rates (effective duration).

Macaulay Duration

The term *duration* was first used in 1938 by Frederick Macaulay as a measure of the weighted average time to maturity of a bond.[9] It can be shown that the measure Macaulay developed is related to the price sensitivity of a bond to interest rate changes. Unfortunately, too many market participants interpret duration as some measure of average life instead of a measure of price sensitivity to interest rate changes. This misinterpretation has been a key factor in several financial blunders. For example, for some complex financial assets, the effective duration is greater than the **Macaulay duration**. Market participants who interpret duration as a measure of the average life of an asset find this difficult to believe.

Consequently, when you hear the term *duration* used, interpret it as a measure of price sensitivity to rate changes, not some measure of the asset's average life. In addition, understand what type of duration measure is being used, effective duration or modified duration. Effective duration is the appropriate measure. Finally, if someone thinks that Macaulay duration means something for managing a portfolio or the asset/liability position of a financial institution, photocopy this page and tell them to review this discussion!

Key Points That You Should Understand Before Proceeding

1. Assets have different degrees of price sensitivity to a change in the discount rate or required yield.
2. Factors that influence an asset's price sensitivity include its maturity, its coupon rate, and the initial level of the required yield.
3. The longer an asset's maturity, the greater its price sensitivity to a change in the discount rate, other things being constant.
4. The larger an asset's coupon rate, the lower its price sensitivity to a change in the discount rate, if all else is the same.
5. The lower the initial discount rate, the greater the price sensitivity of most assets to a change in that rate.
6. Duration is a measure of price sensitivity that incorporates maturity, coupon, and level of yield; it provides an approximation of the percentage price change for small changes in yield.
7. It is important to be able to measure the price sensitivity of an asset or liability to interest rate changes and the appropriate measure is the effective duration.

---

[9] Frederick R. Macaulay, *Some Theoretical Problems Suggested by the Movements of Interest Rates, Bond Yields, and Stock Prices in the United States Since 1865* (New York: National Bureau of Economic Research, 1938).

SUMMARY

In this chapter we have introduced some key properties of financial assets: moneyness, divisibility and denomination, reversibility, cash flow, term to maturity, convertibility, currency, liquidity, return predictability or risk, complexity, and tax status. These properties, which determine much of an asset's appeal and value to different classes of investors, are discussed in greater detail in later chapters. Furthermore, we have illustrated how various properties fit into the theory and practice of pricing assets. We presented a number of illustrations of the way to compute the prices of assets. The illustrations rely on the basic financial principle that price is the present value of expected future cash flows and that the discount rate contains rewards for accepting various features of the asset. Many properties, such as risk of default or term to maturity, influence prices through the required rate of return, which is inversely related to price. Other properties, such as reversibility and tax status, may affect the price of an asset through its expected cash flow.

Because it is so important to contemporary finance and to much of the material in this book, we decided that this first chapter on prices was the right place to introduce the concept of complexity in financial assets. Many assets contain rights, which are, in fact, options for issuers or investors to do something important with the assets. Options are valuable, and they affect the price of the assets that carry them. Later chapters provide extensive and detailed developments of the theme and notion of complexity.

The price of a financial asset will change in the opposite direction of the change in the discount rate or required yield. There are two characteristics of a financial asset that affect its price sensitivity: maturity and coupon rate (in the case of a bond). All other factors constant, the longer the maturity of a financial asset, the greater its price sensitivity to a change in the required yield. All other factors constant, the lower the coupon rate, the greater the price sensitivity to a change in the required yield. The level of interest rates or yields is another factor that affects price sensitivity to interest rate changes: the lower the yield level, the greater the price sensitivity.

Duration is a measure of the approximate price sensitivity of a financial asset to interest rate changes. In general, duration is the approximate percentage price sensitivity of a financial asset to a 100 basis point change in interest rates around some initial level of required yield.

KEY TERMS

- Basis point, 180
- Broker's commission, 178
- Call provision, 173
- Complexity, 175
- Convertibility, 173
- Coupon rate, 177
- Currency, 174
- Default risk premium, 177
- Discount rate, 176
- Divisibility, 172
- Duration, 184
- Effective duration, 186
- Exchange rate premium, 177
- Inflation premium, 177
- Liquidity premium, 177
- Macaulay duration, 187
- Market maker, 172
- Maturity premium, 177
- Modified duration, 186
- Moneyness, 171
- Nominal return, 173
- Perpetual, 173
- Predictability, 174
- Present value, 176
- Put option, 173
- Putable bond, 175
- Real rate of interest, 177
- Real return, 173
- Reversibility, 172
- Tax status, 176
- Term to maturity, 173
- Thickness, 172
- Thin market, 172
- Turnaround cost, 172
- Yield, 180
- Zero-coupon bond, 181

QUESTIONS

1. Your broker is recommending that you purchase U.S. government bonds. Here is the explanation:

   Listen, in these times of uncertainty, with many companies going bankrupt, it makes sense to play it safe and purchase long-term government bonds. They're issued by the U.S. government, so they are risk free.

   How would you respond to the broker?

2. You just inherited 30,000 shares of a company you have never heard of, ABD Corporation. You call your broker to find out if you have finally struck it rich. After several minutes she comes back on the telephone and says: "I don't have a clue about these shares. It's too bad they are not traded in a financial market. That would make life a lot easier for you." What does she mean by this?

3. Suppose you own a bond that pays $75 yearly in coupon interest and that is likely to be called in two years (because the firm has already announced that it will redeem the issue early). The call price will be $1,050. What is the price of your bond now, in the market, if the appropriate discount rate for this asset is 9%?

4. Your broker has advised you to buy shares of Hungry Boy Fast Foods, which has paid a dividend of $1.00 per year for 10 years and will (according to the broker) continue to do so for many years. The broker believes that the stock, which now has a price of $12, will be worth $25 per share in five years. You have good reason to think that the discount rate for this firm's stock is 22% per year, because that rate compensates the buyer for all pertinent risks. Is the stock's present price a good approximation of its true financial value?

5. You have been considering a zero-coupon bond, which pays no interest but will pay a principal of $1,000 at the end of five years. The price of the bond is now $712.99, and its required rate of return is 7.0%. This morning's news contained a surprising development. The government announced that the rate of inflation appears to be 5.5% instead of the 4% that most people had been expecting. (Suppose most people had thought the real rate of interest was 3%.) What would be the price of the bond, once the market began to absorb this new information about inflation?

6. State the difference in basis points between each of the following:
   a. 5.5% and 6.5%
   b. 7% and 9%
   c. 6.4% and 7.8%
   d. 9.1% and 11.9%

7. a. Does a rise of 100 basis points in the discount rate change the price of a 20-year bond as much as it changes the price of a 4-year bond, assuming that both bonds have the same coupon rate and offer the same yield?
   b. Does a rise of 100 basis points in the discount rate change the price of a 4% coupon bond as much as it changes the price of a 10% coupon bond, assuming that both bonds have the same maturity and offer the same yield?
   c. Does a rise of 100 basis points in the discount rate change the price of a 10-year bond to the same extent if the discount rate is 4% as it does if the discount rate is 12%?

8. During the early 1980s, interest rates for many long-term bonds were above 14%. In the early 1990s, rates on similar bonds have been far lower. What do you think this dramatic decline in market interest rates means for the price volatility of bonds in response to a change in interest rates?

9. a. What is the cash flow of a 6% coupon bond that pays interest annually, matures in seven years, and has a principal of $1,000?
   b. Assuming a discount rate of 8%, what is the price of this bond?

      c. Assuming a discount rate of 8.5%, what is the price of this bond?

      d. Assuming a discount rate of 7.5%, what is the price of this bond?

      e. What is the duration of this bond, assuming that the price is the one you calculated in part (b)?

      f. If the yield changes by 100 basis points, from 8% to 7%, by how much would you approximate the percentage price change to be using your estimate of duration in part (e)?

      g. What is the actual percentage price change if the yield changes by 100 basis points?

10. Why is it important to be able to estimate the duration of a bond or bond portfolio?

11. Explain why you agree or disagree with the following statement: "Determining the duration of a financial asset is a simple process."

12. Explain why the effective duration is a more appropriate measure of a complex financial instrument's price sensitivity to interest rate changes than is modified duration.

Appendix

REVIEW OF PRESENT VALUE

In the body of this chapter, we explained that the price or value of any financial asset is equal to the present value of the expected cash flow. The purpose of this appendix is to review how the present value of some amount of money to be received in the future is determined.

We begin by looking at how much some amount of money invested today will grow in the future. The formula to determine the future value of an amount invested today and earning some annual interest rate is:

$$\text{Future value} = \text{Amount invested}\,(1 + \text{Interest rate})^n$$

where n is the number of years that the amount will be invested.

For example, if $142.60 is invested today for five years, and the interest rate that can be earned on that investment is 7%, then the future value is:

$$\text{Future value} = \$142.60(1.07)^5$$
$$= \$200$$

Now we can illustrate how to work the process in reverse; that is, given the future value of an investment, we will illustrate how to determine the amount that must be invested today in order to realize that future value. The amount of money that must be invested today is called the *present value*.

The present value can be determined by solving the future value formula for the amount to be invested:

$$\text{Amount invested} = \frac{\text{Future value}}{(1 + \text{Interest rate})^n}$$

But the amount invested is the present value, so we can rewrite the above formula as

$$\text{Present value} = \frac{\text{Future value}}{(1 + \text{Interest rate})^n}$$

For example, suppose that $200 will be received five years from now and that an investor can earn 7% a year on any amount invested today. The present value is then:

$$\text{Present value} = \frac{\$200}{(1.07)^5}$$
$$= \$142.50$$

If the interest rate that could be earned is 10% rather than 7%, then the present value of $200 is:

$$\text{Present value} = \frac{\$200}{(1.10)^5}$$
$$= \$124.18$$

There are two properties of the present value that should be understood. First, the higher the interest rate that can be earned, the lower the present value. Our examples show this: When the interest rate is 7%, the present value of $200 five years from now is $142.50, but it is $124.18 if the interest rate is 10%. In the present value calculation, the interest rate is called the *discount rate*. The second property is that the farther in the future a cash flow is to be received, the lower is its present value.

Thus far we have calculated the present value of a single cash flow to be received in the future. Most financial assets will generate more than one cash flow in the future. To calculate the present value of any cash flow stream, the present value of each cash flow is calculated and then all the values are summed. In the table below, a cash flow stream is shown in the second column. The present value for each of these cash flows is shown for three discount rates (7%, 10%, and 4%). The present value of $1 shown in the table is equal to:

$$\text{Present value of } \$1 = \frac{\$1}{(1 + \text{Interest rate})^n}$$

The product of the cash flow for any year and the present value of $1 at a given discount rate is the present value of the cash flow for that year. The total present value for the cash flow, for each discount rate, is shown in the last line of the table. As can be seen, the higher the discount rate, the lower the present value.

Year	Cash flow	PV of $1 7%	PV of CF	PV of $1 10%	PV of CF	PV of $1 4%	PV of CF
1	30	0.9346	28.04	0.9091	27.27	0.9615	28.85
2	75	0.8734	65.51	0.8264	61.98	0.9246	69.34
3	120	0.8163	97.96	0.7513	90.16	0.8890	106.68
4	140	0.7629	106.81	0.6830	95.62	0.8548	119.67
5	200	0.7130	142.60	0.6209	124.18	0.8219	164.39
6	250	0.6663	166.59	0.5645	141.12	0.7903	197.58
7	300	0.6227	186.82	0.5132	153.95	0.7599	227.98
Total present value			794.31		694.29		914.48

The Level and Structure of Interest Rates

Learning Objectives

After reading this chapter, you will understand

- Fisher's classical approach to explaining the level of the interest rate.
- the role in Fisher's theory of the saver's time preference and the borrowing firm's productivity of capital.
- the meaning of equilibrium and how changes in the demand and supply function affect the equilibrium level of the interest rate.
- the structure of Fisher's Law, which states that the nominal and observable interest rate is composed of two unobservable variables; the real rate of interest and the premium for expected inflation.
- the loanable funds theory, which is an expansion of Fisher's theory.
- the meaning of liquidity preference in Keynes's theory of the determination of interest rates.
- how an increase in the money supply can affect the level of the interest rate through an impact on liquidity, income, and price expectations.
- the features of a bond issue.
- how the yield to maturity of a bond is calculated.
- why historically the yields on securities issued by the U.S. Department of the Treasury have been used as the benchmark interest rates throughout the world.
- the reason why the yields on U.S. Treasury securities are no longer as popular as benchmark interest rates and what alternative benchmarks are being considered by market participants.
- the different types of bonds.
- what factors affect the yield spread between two bonds.

In this chapter, we deal with two issues. The first is the theory of interest rate determination, and our discussion focuses on the general level of the interest rate in an economy. Second, we explain how interest rates function in the pricing of bonds. That explanation leads to consideration of the many different interest rates that an economy presents a borrower or an investor. We show how the rates are related to one another and to key features of bonds and economic conditions.

THE THEORY OF INTEREST RATES

An interest rate is the price paid by a borrower (or debtor) to a lender (or creditor) for the use of resources during some interval. The amount of the loan is the *principal*, and the price paid is typically expressed as a percentage of the principal per unit of time (generally, a year). In this section, we present the two most influential theories of the determination of the interest rate: **Fisher's theory**, which underlies the loanable funds theory, and Keynes's **liquidity preference theory**.

We focus first on the interest rate that provides the anchor for other rates, namely, the short-term, risk-free, real rate. By the *real rate*, we mean the rate that would prevail in the economy if the average prices for goods and services were expected to remain constant during the loan's life. By the *risk-free rate*, we mean the rate on a loan whose borrower will not default on any obligation. By *short term*, we mean the rate on a loan that has one year to maturity. All other interest rates differ from this rate according to particular aspects of the loan, such as its maturity or risk of default, or because of the presence of inflation.

Fisher's Classical Approach

Irving Fisher analyzed the determination of the level of the interest rate in an economy by inquiring why people save (that is, why they do not consume all their resources) and why others borrow.[1] Here, we outline his theory in the context of a very simplified economy. That economy contains only individuals who consume and save with their current income, firms that borrow unconsumed income in loans and invest, a market where savers make loans of resources to borrowers, and projects in which firms invest. The interest rate on loans embodies no premium for default risk because borrowing firms are assumed to meet all obligations. (The prospect of inflation and its impact on the interest rate will be discussed in short order.)

Decisions on Saving and Borrowing.

Saving is the choice between current and future consumption of goods and services. Individuals save some of their current income in order to be able to consume more in the future. A chief influence on the saving decision is the individual's **marginal rate of time preference**, which is the willingness to trade some consumption now for more future consumption. Individuals differ in their time preferences. Some people may have a rate of time preference that leads them to forgo current consumption for an increase of 10% in their future consumption, while others might save only if their future consumption possibilities rise by 20%.

Another influence on the saving decision is *income*. Generally, higher current income means the person will save more, although people with the same income may have different time preferences. The third variable affecting savings is the *reward for saving*, or the rate of interest on loans that savers make with their unconsumed income. Interest is what borrowers pay for the loans, and it makes greater future consumption possible. As the interest rate rises, each person becomes willing to save more, given that person's rate of time preference.

This description of the savings decision applies to all the people in the economy. The total savings (or the total supply of loans) available at any time is the sum of everybody's savings and a positive function of the interest rate. The relationship between total savings and the interest rate is graphed as the upward sloping supply function, *S*, in Figure 11-1, which relates the amount of savings/investment on the horizontal axis to the interest rate on the vertical axis.[2]

---

[1] Irving Fisher, *The Theory of Interest Rates* (New York: Macmillan, 1930).

[2] For a more extensive analysis of the supply of savings, including the reason why the supply can reach negative levels and the reason why the supply curve can itself turn negative, see Frank J. Fabozzi and Franco Modigliani, *Capital Markets: Institutions and Instruments* (Englewood Cliffs, N.J.: Prentice Hall, 1992), pp. 338ff.

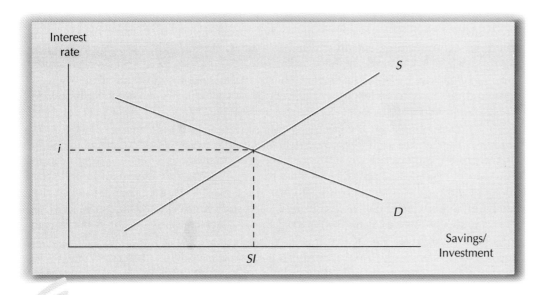

Figure 11-1   Equilibrium in the Market for Savings

There can be no reward for savings if there is no demand for borrowed resources because someone must pay the interest. In our simple economy, firms do all the borrowing, and they borrow from savers in order to invest. Investment means directing resources to assets that will increase the firms' future capacity to produce. An important influence on the borrowing decision is the *gain from investment*, which is the positive difference between the resources used by a process and the total resources it will produce in the future. The gain is not constant, at any one time, across all possible projects and levels of total investment. The reason is that, at any time, only a certain number of projects are available, some offering high gains, others promising moderate gains, and still others yielding low gains. Firms will direct borrowed resources to projects in order of their profitability, starting with the most profitable and proceeding to those with lower gains. The gain from additional projects, as investment increases, is the **marginal productivity of capital**, which is negatively related to the amount of investment. In other words, as the amount of investment grows, additional gains necessarily fall, as more of the less profitable projects are accepted.

The maximum that a firm will invest depends on the *rate of interest*, which is the cost of loans. The firm will invest only as long as the marginal productivity of capital exceeds or equals the rate of interest. In other words, firms will accept only projects whose gain is not less than their cost of financing. Thus, the firm's demand for borrowing is negatively related to the interest rate. If the rate is high, only limited borrowing and investment make sense. At a low rate, more projects offer a profit, and the firm wants to borrow more. This negative relationship exists for each and all firms in the economy. The economy's total demand for borrowed resources (or loans of unconsumed income), as a function of the interest rate, appears as the downward-sloping line labeled *D* in Figure 11-1.

Equilibrium in the Market.
The equilibrium rate of interest is determined by interaction of the supply and demand functions. As a cost of borrowing and a reward for lending, the rate must

reach the point where total supply of savings equals total demand for borrowing and investment. Figure 11-1 shows that this equilibrium rate of interest, labeled i, occurs at the intersection of the demand and supply curves, D and S. The equilibrium level of savings (which is the same as the equilibrium level of borrowing and investment) is given as SI. Clearly, Fisher's theory emphasizes that the long-run level of the interest rate and the amount of investment depend on a society's propensity to save and on technological development.

Let us now consider the effects of a sudden increase in technological capability, which makes production cheaper. With no change in any other relevant variable, lower production costs mean more gain on investments and a higher marginal productivity of capital. The resulting increase in firms' desired investment and borrowing through loans, at any level of the interest rate, is actually an upward shift in the demand function, as shown in Figure 11-2. That shift (from D to D^*) prompts a rise in the equilibrium interest rate, from i to i^*, and an increase in equilibrium borrowing and investment from SI to SI^*.

Now consider circumstances where individuals suddenly grow more willing to save, which amounts to a fall in the marginal rate of time preference. (All other economic considerations stay the same.) As Figure 11-3 depicts this change, the supply of loans function would shift downward (from S to S^*), and savings would be higher at every level of the interest rate. The equilibrium interest rate would also fall, from i to i^*. Total investment would rise, from SI to SI^*, as firms would get more funds and more projects would be profitable, at any interest rate.

The Real Rate and the Nominal Rate.

It is useful here to consider the distinction between the **nominal rate of interest** and the *real rate of interest*. The real rate is the growth in the power to consume over the life of a loan. The nominal rate of interest, by contrast, is the number of monetary units to be paid per unit borrowed, and is, in fact, the observable market rate on a loan. In the

Figure 11-2   The Results of a Shift in the Demand for Savings

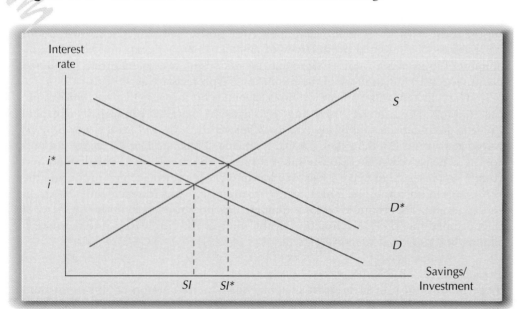

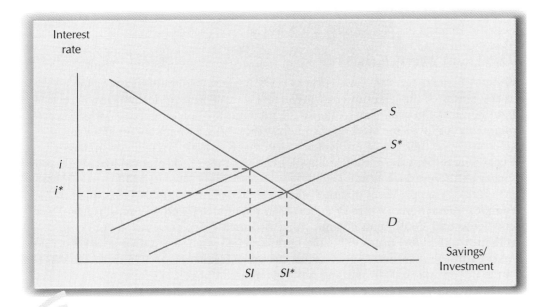

Interest rate

Savings/Investment

Figure 11-3   The Results of a Shift in the Supply of Savings

absence of inflation, the nominal rate equals the real rate. Because we assume in our discussion that the purchasing power of the monetary units in a loan stays the same over the loan's life, the equilibrium interest rate we have discussed is both the nominal and the real rate of interest.

In the presence of inflation, however, the nominal rate is different from, and must exceed, the real rate. The reason is that savers demand a premium above the real rate as compensation for the expected loss in the purchasing power of their interest and principal. The relationship between inflation and interest rates is the well-known **Fisher's Law**, which can be expressed this way:

$$(1 + i) = (1 + r) \times (1 + p), \tag{1}$$

where i is the nominal rate, r is the real rate, and p is the expected percentage change in the price level of goods and services over the loan's life. Equation (1) shows that the nominal rate, i, reflects both the real rate and expected inflation. Also, the compensation demanded by savers applies to both the interest payment and the principal because the left-hand side variable is 100% plus the interest rate, or the full loan plus its interest.

Equation (1) can be simplified to a formula that appeared in Chapter 10 and, in most circumstances, approximates equation (1) closely enough:

$$i = r + p \tag{2}$$

The only quantities from equation (1) not present in equation (2) are the values of 1, which cancel one another out, and the product of r and p, which is usually small enough to be ignored. For example, if the real rate is 3% or 0.03, and the expected inflation rate is 5% or 0.05, their product equals only 0.0015, or 0.15 of 1%. It is important to realize that the expected rate of inflation and the real rate are not observable. With fairly good estimates of expected inflation, p, it is possible to get a reasonable estimate of r from the nominal rate, but the precise value of the real rate must remain elusive.

The Loanable Funds Theory

Fisher's theory is a general one and obviously neglects certain practical matters, such as the power of the government (in concert with depository institutions) to create money and the government's often large demand for borrowed funds, which is frequently immune to the level of the interest rate. Also, Fisher's theory does not consider the possibility that individuals and firms might invest in cash balances. Expanding Fisher's theory to encompass these situations produces the **loanable funds theory of interest rates**.

This theory proposes that the general level of interest rates is determined by the complex interaction of two forces. The first is the total demand for funds by firms, governments, and households (or individuals), which carry out a variety of economic activities with those funds. This demand is negatively related to the interest rate (except for the government's demand, which may frequently not depend on the level of the interest rate). If income and other variables do not change, then an increase in the interest rate will reduce the demand for borrowing on the part of many firms and individuals, as projects become less profitable, and consumption and holding cash grow more costly. The second force affecting the level of the interest rate is the total supply of funds by firms, governments, banks, and individuals. Supply is positively related to the level of interest rates, if all other economic factors remain the same. With rising rates, firms and individuals save and lend more, and banks are more eager to extend more loans. (A rising interest rate probably does not significantly affect the government's supply of savings.)

In an equilibrium situation much like that depicted in Figure 11-1, the intersection of the supply and demand functions sets the interest rate level and the level of loans. In equilibrium, the demand for funds equals the supply of funds. This means that all agents are borrowing what they want, investing to the desired extent, and holding all the money they wish to hold. In other words, equilibrium extends through the money market, the bond market, and the market for investment assets.

As in Fisher's theory, shifts in the demand and supply curves may occur for many reasons: changes in the money supply, government deficits, changed preferences by individuals, new investment opportunities, and so on. These shifts affect the equilibrium level of the interest rate and of investment in predictable ways. Finally, the expectation of inflation can affect the equilibrium rate through the supply of funds curve, as savers demand higher rates (because of inflation) for any level of savings. Note that this analysis has excluded the question of default on loans: the rate discussed is the risk-free rate, either in its real or nominal form.

The Liquidity Preference Theory

The liquidity preference theory, originally developed by John Maynard Keynes,[3] analyzes the equilibrium level of the interest rate through the interaction of the supply of money and the public's aggregate demand for holding money. Keynes assumed that most people hold wealth in only two forms: "money" and "bonds." For Keynes, money is equivalent to currency and demand deposits, which pay little or no interest but are liquid and may be used for immediate transactions. Bonds represent a broad Keynesian category and include long-term, interest-paying financial assets that are not

---

[3] John Maynard Keynes, *The General Theory of Employment, Interest and Money* (New York: Harcourt, Brace & World, 1936).

liquid and that pose some risk because their prices vary inversely with the interest rate level. Bonds may be liabilities of governments or firms. (Default risk is not considered here, and the rate is the risk-free rate, in real or nominal form.)

Demand, Supply, and Equilibrium.

The public (consisting of individuals and firms) holds money for several reasons: ease of transactions, precaution against unexpected events, and speculation about possible rises in the interest rate. Although money pays no interest, the demand for money is a negative function of the interest rate. At a low rate, people hold a lot of money because they do not lose much interest by doing so and because the risk of a rise in rates (and a fall in the value of bonds) may be large. With a high interest rate, people desire to hold bonds rather than money, because the cost of liquidity is substantial in terms of lost interest payments and because a decline in the interest rate would lead to gains in the bonds' values. The negative linkage between the interest rate and the demand for money appears as curve D in Figure 11-4, which relates the interest rate to the amount of money in the economy, given the level of income and expected price inflation.

For Keynes, the supply of money is fully under the control of the central bank (which is the Fed in the United States). Moreover, the money supply is not affected by the level of the interest rate. (Recall the discussion in Chapter 5 about the positive link between the interest rate and the growth in the money supply.) Thus, the supply of money appears, in Figure 11-4, as the vertical line, $\overline{MS}$, and the line above the MS indicates a quantity not varying with the interest rate. Equilibrium in the money market requires, of course, that the total demand for money equals total supply. In Figure 11-4, equilibrium implies an interest rate of i. Furthermore, equilibrium in the money market implies the equilibrium of the bond market.

Shifts in the Rate of Interest.

The equilibrium rate of interest can change if there is a change in any variable affecting the demand or supply curves. On the demand side, Keynes recognized the impor-

Figure 11-4 Equilibrium in Keynes's Market for Money

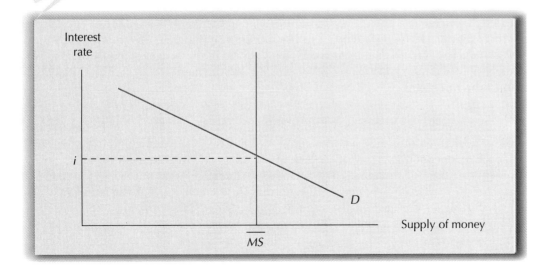

tance of two such variables: the level of income and the level of prices for goods and services. A rise in income (with no other variable changing) raises the value of money's liquidity and shifts the demand curve to the right, increasing the equilibrium interest rate. Because people want to hold amounts of "real money," or monetary units of specific purchasing power, a change in expected inflation would also shift the demand curve to the right and raise the level of interest.

The money supply curve can shift, in Keynes's view, only by actions of the central bank. The central bank's power over interest rates arises because of its ability to buy and sell securities (open market operations), which can alter the amount of money available in the economy. Generally, Keynes thought that an increase in the money supply would, by shifting the supply curve to the right, bring about a decline in the equilibrium interest rate. Similarly, he reasoned that a reduction in the money supply would raise rates. As we note in Chapter 6, however, there is now widespread recognition that the question of linkage between the money supply and the level of the interest rate is rather more complex than that.

Changes in the Money Supply and Interest Rates

In Chapter 6, we provide a general account of how changes in the money supply affect the level of interest rates. Now, we can discuss the matter in more detail, because the Keynesian money demand model that we just developed is a particularly useful framework for analyzing the relationship between the money supply and the level of the interest rate.

A change in the money supply has three different effects upon the level of the interest rate: the **liquidity effect**, the **income effect**, and the **price expectations effect**. These effects do not usually occur in a simultaneous manner but rather tend to be spread out over some time period following the change in the money supply. These effects move rates in different ways and to different extents. One effect may even cancel or overwhelm an earlier effect. The final magnitude and direction of the impact of a change in the money supply depends on the economy's level of output and employment.

Liquidity Effect.

This effect represents the initial reaction of the interest rate to a change in the money supply. With an increase in the money supply, the initial reaction should be a fall in the rate. The reason for the fall is that a rise in the money supply represents a shift in the supply curve. For example, let us suppose that (in the United States) the Fed increases the supply of money by buying bonds, raising excess reserves, and allowing banks to offer more loans. With demand unchanging, the increase in the money supply amounts to a rightward shift of the supply and causes a fall in the equilibrium interest rate, from i to i^*. Figure 11-5 depicts the rise in the money supply (from $\overline{MS}$ to $\overline{MS}^*$) and the decline in the interest rate from i to i^*. (A decrease in the money supply would cause the supply of money function to shift to the left and the liquidity effect of an initial rise in the interest rate.)

Income Effect.

It is well-known that changes in the money supply affect the economy. A decline in the supply would tend to cause a contraction. An increase in the money supply, generally speaking, is economically expansionary: more loans are available and extended, more people are hired or work longer, and consumers and producers purchase more goods and services. Thus, money supply changes can cause income in the system to vary. Let us focus on an increase in the money supply, which raises income. Because the demand for money is a function of income, a rise in income shifts the demand function and increases the amount of money that the public will want to hold at any level of the interest rate. Figure 11-6 depicts the income effect by indicating that the shift of

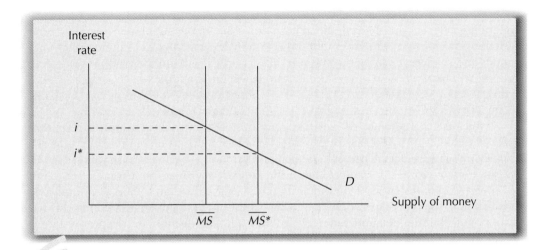

Figure 11-5   The Liquidity Effect of an Increase in the Money Supply

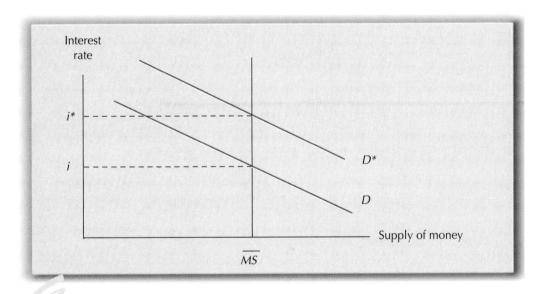

Figure 11-6   The Income Effect of a Change in the Money Supply

the demand function to the right, brought on by the increase in the money supply, causes a rise in the equilibrium interest rate.

No empirical data or economic theory can predict whether the income effect of a money supply increase will override its liquidity effect, or if so, after what interval of time. Under most circumstances, the income effect is likely to reverse some of the liquidity effect. But the relative magnitude of these two effects depends greatly on the state of the economy at the time the money supply changes.

Price Expectations Effect.
Although an increase in the money supply is an economically expansionary policy, the resultant increase in income depends substantially on the amount of slack in the econ-

omy at the time of the Fed's action. Chapter 6 addressed this issue: If the economy is operating at less than full strength, an increase in the money supply can stimulate production, employment, and output; if the economy is producing all or almost all of the goods and services it can (given the size of the population and the amount of capital goods), then an increase in the money supply will largely stimulate expectations of a rising level of prices for goods and services. Thus, the price expectations effect usually occurs only if the money supply grows in a time of high output.

Because the price level (and expectations regarding its changes) affects the money demand function, the price expectations effect is an increase in the interest rate. That increase occurs because the demand for money balances shifts upward. This positive effect moves the interest rate in the same direction as the income effect, and in the opposite direction of the liquidity effect. (Of course, in a time of inflation, a reduction in the rate of growth in the money supply might dampen inflationary expectations and shift the demand curve to the left, leading to declines in the interest rate.)

There is no general guide to the relative size of the price expectations effect: It may be great enough to overwhelm the liquidity effect, or it may cancel only part of it. The magnitude of the income effect depends upon how much of the economy's productive capacity it is utilizing when the money supply rises.

Key Points That You Should Understand Before Proceeding

1. Interest is the price paid for the temporary use of resources, and the amount of a loan is its principal.

2. Fisher's theory of interest analyzes the equilibrium level of the interest rate as the result of the interaction of savers' willingness to save and borrowers' demand for investment funds.

3. In Fisher's terms, the interest rate reflects the interaction of the savers' marginal rate of time preference and borrowers' marginal productivity of capital.

4. Fisher's Law states that the observable nominal rate of interest is composed of two unobservable variables: the real rate of interest and the premium for expected inflation.

5. The loanable funds theory is an extension of Fisher's theory and proposes that the equilibrium rate of interest reflects the demand and supply of funds, which depend on savers' willingness to save, borrowers' expectations regarding the profitability of investing, and the government's action regarding money supply.

6. The liquidity preference theory is Keynes's view that the rate of interest is set in the market for money balances.

7. The demand for money, in this theory, reflects the liquidity of money by comparison with long-term financial instruments and depends on the interest rate, income, and the price level.

8. Changes in the money supply can affect the level of interest rates through the liquidity effect, the income effect, and the price expectations effect; their relative magnitudes depend upon the level of economic activity at the time of the change in the money supply.

THE DETERMINANTS OF THE STRUCTURE OF INTEREST RATES

There is not one interest rate in any economy. Rather, there is a structure of interest rates. The interest rate that a borrower will have to pay will depend on a myriad of factors. Although we describe these various factors, in the process, we provide an overview of the fixed-income instruments that we examine in much more detail in later chapters. We begin with a basic description of a bond.

Features of a Bond

A bond is an instrument in which the issuer (debtor/borrower) promises to repay to the lender/investor the amount borrowed plus interest over some specified period of time. The term to maturity of a bond is the number of years during which the issuer has promised to meet the conditions of the obligation. The **maturity** of a bond refers to the day the debt will cease to exist and the day the issuer will redeem the bond by paying the amount owed. The practice in the bond market, however, is to refer to the *term to maturity* of a bond as simply its *maturity* or *term*. As we explain below, there may be provisions that allow either the issuer or bondholder to alter a bond's term to maturity.

The **principal value** (or simply **principal**) of a bond is the amount that the issuer agrees to repay the bondholder at the maturity date. This amount is also referred to as the **par value, maturity value, redemption value,** or **face value**.

The *coupon rate* is the interest rate that the issuer agrees to pay each year. The annual amount of the interest payment made to owners during the term of the bond is called the *coupon*. The coupon rate when multiplied by the principal of the bond provides the dollar amount of the coupon. For example, a bond with an 8% coupon rate and a principal of $1,000 will pay annual interest of $80. In the United States and Japan, the usual practice is for the issuer to pay the coupon in two equal semiannual installments. In contrast, bonds issued in most European bond markets and the Eurobond market make coupon payments only once per year.

Yield on a Bond

The yield on a bond investment should reflect the coupon interest that will be earned plus either (1) any capital gain that will be realized from holding the bond to maturity, or (2) any capital loss that will be realized from holding the bond to maturity. For example, if a four-year bond with a coupon rate of 5% and a par value of $1,000 is selling for $900.64, the yield should reflect the coupon interest of $50 (5% times $1,000) every year plus the capital gain of $99.36 ($1,000 − $900.64) when the bond is redeemed at maturity. Moreover, the yield should also reflect the time value of money by considering the timing of the various payments associated with the bond.

The **yield to maturity** is a formal, widely accepted measure of the rate of return on a bond. As typically defined, the yield to maturity of a bond takes into account the coupon interest and any capital gain or loss, if the bond were to be held to maturity. The yield to maturity is defined as the interest rate that makes the present value of the cash flow of a bond equal to the bond's market price. In mathematical notation, the yield to maturity, y, is found by solving the following equation for y:

$$P = \frac{C}{(1+y)^1} + \frac{C}{(1+y)^2} + \frac{C}{(1+y)^3} + \cdots + \frac{C+M}{(1+y)^n}$$

where
P = market price of bond
C = coupon interest
M = maturity value
n = time to maturity

The yield to maturity is determined by a trial-and-error process. Even the algorithm in a calculator or computer program, which computes the yield to maturity (or internal rate of return) in an apparently direct way, uses a trial-and-error process. The steps in that process are as follows:

Step 1: Select an interest rate.

Step 2: Compute the present value of each cash flow using the interest rate selected in Step 1.

Step 3: Total the present value of the cash flows found in Step 2.

Step 4: Compare the total present value found in Step 3 with the market price of the bond and, if the total present value of the cash flows found in Step 3 is:

➤ equal to the market price, then the interest rate used in Step 1 is the yield to maturity;

➤ greater than the market price, then the interest rate is not the yield to maturity. Therefore, go back to Step 1 and use a higher interest rate;

➤ less than the market price, then the interest rate is not the yield to maturity. Therefore, go back to Step 1 and use a lower interest rate.

For example, suppose that a four-year bond that pays interest annually has a par value of $1,000, a coupon rate of 5%, and is selling in the market for $900.64. Table 11-1 shows the procedure for calculating the yield to maturity. When a 2% interest rate is tried, the total present value is equal to $1,136.52. As this value is greater than the market price of $900.64, it is not the yield to maturity and, therefore, a higher interest rate must be tried. Suppose a 12% interest rate is tried. Now the total present value of $787.39 is smaller than the market price, so a lower interest rate must be tried. When an 8% interest rate is tried, the total present value is equal to the market price, so the yield to maturity is 8%.

Had the market price of this bond been $813.85 rather than $900.64, the yield to maturity would be 11%. Notice that the lower the market price, the higher the yield to maturity.

There are several interesting points about the relationship among the coupon rate, market price, and yield to maturity that can be seen in Table 11-1:

Table 11-1   Yield to Maturity of an Annual Pay Four-Year Bond with a Coupon Rate of 5% and a Market Price of $900.64

C = $50	M = $1,000	P = $900.64	n = 4
INTEREST RATE TRIED		TOTAL PRESENT VALUE	
2%		$1,136.52	
3		1,106.57	
4		1,036.30	
5		1,000.00	
6		965.35	
7		932.26	
8		900.64	
9		870.41	
10		841.51	
11		813.85	
12		787.39	

1. If the market price is equal to the par value, then the yield to maturity is equal to the coupon rate;
2. If the market price is less than the par value, then the yield to maturity is greater than the coupon rate, and;
3. If the market price is greater than the par value, then the yield to maturity is less than the coupon rate.

In our illustration, we assumed that coupon payments are made once per year. As noted earlier, however, the practice in the U.S. bond market is to pay coupon interest every six months. This does not affect the procedure for calculating the yield to maturity; that is, it is still the interest rate that will make the present value of the cash flow equal to the market price. The cash flow, however, is not annual. Instead, the coupon payment is every six months and is equal to one-half the annual coupon payment. The resulting yield to maturity is then a semiannual yield to maturity. To annualize the semiannual yield, the *convention* adopted in the bond market is to double the semiannual yield. The resulting yield to maturity is said to be calculated on a **bond-equivalent yield basis**.

For example, consider an 18-year bond with a coupon rate of 6% and a par value of $1,000. Suppose that the bond pays interest semiannually and is selling for $700.89. The cash flow for this bond is $30 every six months for 35 six-month periods and $1,030 36 six-month periods from now. That is:

$C = \$30$ $M = \$1,000$ and $n = 36$ (double the number of years to maturity)

Table 11-2 shows the calculation of the yield to maturity for this bond. Notice that the interest rate that makes the total present value equal to the market price of $700.89 is 4.75%. This is the semiannual yield to maturity. Doubling this semiannual yield gives 9.5%, which is the yield to maturity on a bond-equivalent yield basis.

In the discussion to follow, we will refer to the yield to maturity of a bond as simply its yield. The difference between the yield on any two bond issues is called a **yield spread**, or simply **spread**. The spread is typically measured in basis points. For example, if the yield on bond A is 9%, and the yield on bond B is 8.5%, the yield spread is 50 basis points.

Table 11-2   Yield to Maturity of a Semiannual Pay 18-Year Bond with a Coupon Rate of 6% and a Market Price of $700.89

C = $30 M = $1,000 P = $700.89 n = 36	
INTEREST RATE TRIED	TOTAL PRESENT VALUE
3.25%	$947.40
3.50	898.54
3.75	853.14
4.00	810.92
4.25	771.61
4.50	735.01
4.75*	700.89

* *Semiannual yield to maturity. Therefore, the yield to maturity on a bond-equivalent yield basis is 9.5% (2 times 4.75%).*

The Base Interest Rate

Now that we have examined the characteristics of a bond and how to measure the yield on a bond, we will now look at the structure of interest rates. In our discussion, we use the terms *interest rate* and *yield* interchangeably.

The securities issued by the U.S. Department of the Treasury, popularly referred to as **Treasury securities** or simply **Treasuries**, are backed by the full faith and credit of the U.S. government. Consequently, market participants throughout the world view them as having no credit risk. As a result, historically the interest rates on Treasury securities have served as the benchmark interest rates throughout the U.S. economy, as well as in international capital markets.

The fact that the U.S. Treasury is the largest single issuer of debt in the world and the large size of any single issue has contributed to making the Treasury market the most active and, hence, the most liquid market in the world. However, in recent years, the U.S. Department of the Treasury has reduced its issuance of Treasury securities, particularly long-term securities, as well as buying back long-term Treasury securities in the market. This has decreased the supply of these securities and, as a result, there are market participants who feel that the yields on Treasury securities are no longer a suitable benchmark for interest rates throughout the world. As a result, as of this writing, there is a search for other benchmarks that can be used as the benchmark interest rates.[4] Moreover, outside of the United States, other countries have been developing benchmark interest rates. In Europe, the yield on German government bonds have been used as the benchmark.

Despite the potential decline of U.S. Treasury securities as a benchmark, in this book we will continue to use them as the benchmark interest rates. Any other benchmark that may be selected by market participants in the future must recognize the additional risks associated with the benchmark, as will be explained as we proceed.

There are two categories of U.S. Treasury securities: discount and coupon securities. The fundamental difference between the two types is in the form of the stream of payments that the holder receives, which, in turn, is reflected in the prices at which the securities are issued. Coupon securities pay interest every six months, plus principal at maturity. Discount securities pay only a contractually fixed amount at maturity. Treasury securities are typically issued on an auction basis according to regular cycles for securities of specific maturities. Current Treasury practice is to issue all securities with maturities of one year or less as discount securities. These securities are called *Treasury bills.* All securities with maturities of two years or longer are issued as Treasury *coupon securities.*

The most recently auctioned Treasury issues for each maturity are referred to as **on-the-run** or **current coupon issues**. Table 11-3 shows the on-the-run U.S. Treasury yields as of the close of business on September 15, 2000. Issues auctioned prior to the current coupon issues are typically referred to as **off-the-run issues;** they are not as liquid as on-the-run issues, and, therefore, offer a higher yield than the corresponding on-the-run Treasury issue.

The minimum interest rate or **base interest rate** that investors will demand for investing in a non-Treasury security is the yield offered on a comparable maturity for an on-the-run Treasury security. So, for example, if an investor wanted to purchase a 10-year bond on September 15, 2000, the minimum yield the investor would seek is 5.84%, the on-the-run Treasury yield reported in Table 11-3. The base interest rate is also referred to as the **benchmark interest rate**.

---

[4] For a further discussion, see Michael J. Fleming, "The Benchmark U.S. Treasury Market: Recent Performance and Possible Alternatives," *FRBNY Economic Policy Review* (April 2000).

Table 11-3   Yields for On-the-Run Treasuries on September 15, 2000

MATURITY	YIELD
3-month	6.14%
6-month	6.21
1-year	6.11
2-year	6.06
5-year	5.91
10-year	5.84
30-year	5.90

The Risk Premium

Market participants talk of interest rates on non-Treasury securities as "trading at a spread" to a particular on-the-run Treasury security (or a spread to any particular benchmark interest rate selected). For example, if the yield on a 10-year non-Treasury security is 7% and the yield on a 10-year Treasury security is 6%, the spread is 100 basis points. This spread reflects the additional risks the investor faces by acquiring a security that is not issued by the U.S. government and, therefore, can be called a *risk premium*. Thus, we can express the interest rate offered on a non-Treasury security as:

$$\text{Base interest rate + Spread}$$

or equivalently,

$$\text{Base interest rate + Risk premium}$$

We have discussed the factors that affect the base interest rate. One of the factors is the expected rate of inflation. That is, the base interest rate can be expressed as:

$$\text{Base interest rate = Real rate of interest + Expected rate of inflation}$$

How can the real rate of inflation required by market participants be estimated? Since 1997, the U.S. Department of the Treasury has issued securities indexed to the Consumer Price Index. These securities are called *Treasury Inflation Protection Securities* (TIPS), and we discuss these securities in Chapter 16. What is important for us to understand here is that the yield on these securities can be used as an estimate of the real rate of interest. For example, the yield on a 10-year TIPS issue is an estimate of the real interest rate for a 10-year bond. On September 15, 2000, for example, the yield on the on-the-run 10-year TIPS issue was 4.02%. How do we get the expected rate of inflation? This is found by subtracting the real rate of interest (from the TIPS issue) from the base interest rate (i.e., the yield for the on-the-run non-TIPS issue). For example, as can be seen in Table 11-3, the base interest rate (i.e., the yield for the on-the-run 10-year issue) on September 15, 2000 was 5.84%. The yield on the 10-year TIPS issue on the same day was 4.02%. Therefore, the expected rate of inflation was 1.82% (5.84% – 4.02%).

Turning to the spread, the factors that affect it are (1) the type of issuer; (2) the issuer's perceived creditworthiness; (3) the term or maturity of the instrument; (4)

provisions that grant either the issuer or the investor the option to do something; (5) the taxability of the interest received by investors; and (6) the expected liquidity of the issue. Notice that these factors are the ones that we discussed in the previous chapter as affecting the price of a security.

It is important to note that yield spreads must be interpreted relative to the benchmark interest rate used. This is particularly important to keep in mind for the second and last factors that affect the spread when the benchmark interest rate is other than the yield on U.S. Treasury securities.

Types of Issuers.

A key feature of a debt obligation is the nature of the issuer. In addition to the U.S. government, there are agencies of the U.S. government, municipal governments, corporations (domestic and foreign), and foreign governments that issue bonds.

The bond market is classified by the type of issuer, and groups of securities of the various kinds of issuers are referred to as **market sectors.** The spread between the interest rates offered in two sectors of the bond market on obligations with the same maturity is referred to as an **intermarket sector spread.**

Excluding the Treasury market sector, the other market sectors include a wide range of issuers, each with different abilities to satisfy their contractual obligations. For example, within the corporate market sector, issuers are classified as follows: (1) utilities; (2) industrials; (3) finance; and (4) banks. The spread between two issues within a market sector is called an **intramarket sector spread.**

Perceived Creditworthiness of Issuer.

Default risk or *credit risk* refers to the risk that the issuer of a bond may be unable to make timely principal or interest payments. Most market participants rely primarily on commercial rating companies to assess the default risk of an issuer. These companies perform credit analyses and express their conclusions by a system of ratings. The three commercial rating companies in the United States are (1) Moody's Investors Service, (2) Standard & Poor's Corporation, and (3) Fitch.

In all systems the term **high grade** means low credit risk, or conversely, high probability of future payments. The highest-grade bonds are designated by Moody's by the symbol Aaa, and by S&P and Fitch by the symbol AAA. The next highest grade is denoted by the symbol Aa (Moody's) or AA (S&P and Fitch); for the third grade all rating systems use A. The next three grades are Baa or BBB, Ba or BB, and B, respectively. There are also C grades. Moody's uses 1, 2, or 3 to provide a narrower credit quality breakdown within each class, and S&P and Fitch use plus and minus signs for the same purpose.

Bonds rated triple A (AAA or Aaa) are said to be *prime*; double A (AA or Aa) are of *high quality*; single A issues are called *upper medium grade*, and triple B are *medium grade*. Lower-rated bonds are said to have speculative elements or be distinctly speculative.

Bond issues that are assigned a rating in the top four categories are referred to as *investment-grade bonds*. Issues that carry a rating below the top four categories are referred to as *noninvestment-grade bonds*, or more popularly as *high-yield bonds* or *junk bonds*. Thus, the bond market can be divided into two sectors: the investment-grade and noninvestment-grade markets.

The spread between Treasury securities and non-Treasury securities that are identical in all respects except for quality is referred to as a **quality spread** or **credit spread.** For example, for the week of September 15, 2000, the yield on single-A, 10-year industrial bonds was 7.13% and the corresponding yield for the 10-year on-the-run Treasury (see Table 11-3) was 5.84%. Therefore, the quality spread was 129 basis points (7.13% − 5.84%).

Let us return to the interpretation if the yield spread on a non-U.S. Treasury security is used as the benchmark interest rate. Since the U.S. Treasury securities are viewed by market participants as free of credit risk, the yield spread to U.S. Treasury securities is reflecting credit risk, as well as the other risks to be discussed. In the search for a new benchmark interest rate, it is desirable to use a benchmark that has minimal credit risk. There are three possible candidates for the benchmark. The first is the yield on securities offered by government-sponsored enterprises. These entities are discussed in Chapter 16. They are currently viewed as having a triple A rating (AAA or Aaa) and therefore have minimal credit risk. The second alternative is corporate bond issuers that have triple A ratings. As we will see in our discussion of liquidity, corporate bond issuers may not be a viable candidate to replace Treasury securities as the benchmark. The third candidate is one that comes from a market that we discuss in Chapter 30 of this book, the interest rate swap market. A measure that comes out of the swap market is called the *swap spread*, which many market participants, particularly in Europe, have been using as a benchmark.

While these are the alternatives being considered to replace Treasuries as the benchmark, there is a benchmark that is well established as a benchmark for floating-rate securities. As explained in Chapter 21, the coupon interest rate for these securities changes is based on some reference interest rate. The benchmark used for these securities is the London interbank offer rate (LIBOR). What this rate is and why it is used as the benchmark is discussed in Chapter 22.

Term to Maturity

As we explained in the previous chapter, the price of a financial asset will fluctuate over its life as yields in the market change. As we demonstrated, the volatility of a bond's price is dependent on its maturity. More specifically, with all other factors constant the longer the maturity of a bond, the greater the price volatility resulting from a change in market yields. The spread between any two maturity sectors of the market is called a **maturity spread** or **yield curve spread**. Table 11-4 shows various maturity spreads on September 15, 2000.

The relationship between the yields on comparable securities but different maturities is called the **term structure of interest rates**. The term-to-maturity topic is of such importance that we devote the entire next chapter to it.

Inclusion of Options

It is not uncommon for a bond issue to include a provision that gives either the bondholder and/or the issuer an option to take some action against the other party. An option that is included in a bond issue is referred to as an **embedded option**.

Table 11-4   Various Maturity Spreads on September 15, 2000

MATURITIES	MATURITY SPREAD (IN BASIS POINTS)
5-year to 2-year	−15
10-year to 5-year	−8
30-year to 2-year	−16
30-year to 10-year	6

SOURCE: Lehman Brothers, *Relative Value Report*, Fixed Income Research, September 15, 2000, p. T-3 © 2000 Lehman Brothers, Inc. All rights reserved.

The most common type of option in a bond issue is a **call provision**. This provision grants the issuer the right to retire the debt, fully or partially, before the scheduled maturity date. The inclusion of a call feature benefits issuers by allowing them to replace an old bond issue with a lower interest cost issue should interest rates in the market decline. Effectively, a call provision allows the issuer to alter the maturity of a bond. A call provision is detrimental to the bondholder because the bondholder will be uncertain about maturity and might have to reinvest the proceeds received at a lower interest rate if the bond is called and the bondholder wants to keep his or her funds in issues of similar risk of default.

An issue may also include a provision that allows the bondholder to change the maturity of a bond. An issue with a **put provision** grants the bondholder the right to sell the issue back to the issuer at par value on designated dates. Here, the advantage to the investor is that, if interest rates rise after the issue date and result in a price that is less than the par value, the investor can force the issuer to redeem the bond at par value.

A **convertible bond** is an issue giving the bondholder the right to exchange the bond for a specified number of shares of common stock. This feature allows the bondholder to take advantage of favorable movements in the price of the issuer's common stock.

The presence of these embedded options has an effect on the spread of an issue relative to a Treasury security and the spread relative to otherwise comparable issues that do not have an embedded option. In general, market participants will require a larger spread over a comparable Treasury security for an issue with an embedded option that is favorable to the issuer (e.g., a call option) than for an issue without such an option. In contrast, market participants will require a smaller spread over a comparable Treasury security for an issue with an embedded option that is favorable to the investor (for example, put option and conversion option). In fact, for a bond with an option that is favorable to an investor, the interest rate on an issue may be less than that on a comparable Treasury security!

To illustrate the impact of an embedded option on the spread, Table 11-5 shows the yield spread on government-sponsored enterprise securities—issuers that are discussed in Chapter 16—for issues with 5-year and 10-year maturities without a call provision (referred to as "noncallable" in the table) and with a call provision (identified as "noncallable for" a specified number of years) on September 15, 2000. So the issues that are callable (i.e., have an embedded option) are those identified in the table as "noncallable for". The restriction is simply that the issuer cannot call the issue for a specified number of years. The yield spread shown in the last column of the table is

Table 11-5   Yield Spread on Government-Sponsored Enterprise Issues: Noncallable and Callable Issues on 9/15/00

MATURITY	CALL PROVISION	YIELD SPREAD (BP)
5-year	Noncallable	80
5-year	Noncallable for 1 year	144
5-year	Noncallable for 2 years	120
5-year	Noncallable for 3 years	107
10-year	Noncallable	116
10-year	Noncallable for 3 years	167
10-year	Noncallable for 5 years	140

based on the yield spread between the issue and the on-the-run Treasury issue. Notice that for both the 5-year and 10-year issues, the yield spread relative to the on-the-run Treasury is larger for the callable issues than for the noncallable issue.

Also note that for the 5-year and 10-year issues there is more than one callable issue. The callable issues differ with respect to when the issuer may call the bond issue. For example, consider the 5-year issue. There is an issue shown that is "noncallable for 1 year". While we will explain this in more detail in Chapter 21, this simply means that the issuer may call the bond (that is, there is an embedded option) but the issuer cannot call the bond issue for one year. Similarly, there is a 5-year issue identified as "noncallable for 2 years" and as "noncallable for 3 years. What is important to note from the table is that the longer the time before the issuer is permitted to call the bond, the lower the spread for a given maturity.

A major part of the bond market is the mortgage market. There is a wide range of mortgage-backed securities that we discuss in Chapter 24. But these securities expose an investor to a form of call risk called "prepayment risk." Consequently, a yield spread between a mortgage-backed security and a comparable on-the-run Treasury security reflects this call risk. To see this, consider a basic mortgage-backed security called a Ginnie Mae passthrough security. This security is backed by the full faith and credit of the U.S. government. Consequently, the yield spread between a Ginnie Mae passthrough security and a comparable Treasury security is not due to credit risk. Rather, it is primarily due to call risk.

Taxability of Interest

Unless exempted under the federal income tax code, interest income is taxable at the federal level. In addition to federal income taxes, there may be state and local taxes on interest income.

The federal tax code specifically exempts the interest income from qualified municipal bond issues from taxation at the federal level. **Municipal bonds** are securities issued by state and local governments and by their creations, such as "authorities" and special districts. The large majority of outstanding municipal bonds are tax-exempt securities. Because of the tax-exempt feature of municipal bonds, the yield on municipal bonds is less than that on Treasuries with the same maturity. The difference in yield between tax-exempt securities and Treasury securities is typically measured not in basis points but in percentage terms. More specifically, it is measured as the percentage of the yield on a tax-exempt security relative to a comparable Treasury security.

The yield on a taxable bond issue after federal income taxes are paid is equal to:

$$\text{After-tax yield} = \text{Pretax yield} \times (1 - \text{Marginal tax rate})$$

For example, suppose a taxable bond issue offers a yield of 9% and is acquired by an investor facing a marginal tax rate of 39.6%. The after-tax yield would then be:

$$\text{After-tax yield} = 0.09 \times (1 - 0.396) = 0.0544 = 5.44\%$$

Alternatively, we can determine the yield that must be offered on a taxable bond issue to give the same after-tax yield as a tax-exempt issue. This yield is called the **equivalent taxable yield** and is determined as follows:

$$\text{Equivalent taxable yield} = \frac{\text{Tax-exempt yield}}{(1 - \text{Marginal tax rate})}$$

For example, consider an investor facing a 39.6% marginal tax rate who purchases a tax-exempt issue with a yield of 5.44%. The equivalent taxable yield is then:

$$\text{Equivalent taxable yield} = \frac{0.0544}{(1-039.6\%)} = 0.09 = 9\%$$

Notice that the lower the marginal tax rate, the lower the equivalent taxable yield. Thus, in our previous example, if the marginal tax rate is 25% rather than 39.6%, the equivalent taxable yield would be 7.25% rather than 9%, as shown below:

$$\text{Equivalent taxable yield} = \frac{0.0544}{(1-0.25)} = 0.0725 = 7.25\%$$

State and local governments may tax interest income on bond issues that are exempt from federal income taxes. Some municipalities exempt interest income paid on all municipal issues from taxation; others do not. Some states exempt interest income from bonds issued by municipalities within the state but tax the interest income from bonds issued by municipalities outside of the state. The implication is that two municipal securities of the same quality rating and the same maturity may trade at some spread because of different tax policies and, hence, the relative demand for bonds of municipalities in different states. For example, in a high income tax state such as New York, the demand for bonds of municipalities will drive down their yield relative to municipalities in a low income tax state such as Florida.

Municipalities are not permitted to tax the interest income from securities issued by the U.S. Treasury. Thus, part of the spread between Treasury securities and taxable non-Treasury securities of the same maturity reflects the value of the exemption from state and local taxes.

Expected Liquidity of an Issue.

Bonds trade with different degrees of liquidity. The greater the expected liquidity with which an issue will trade, the lower the yield that investors would require. As noted earlier, Treasury securities are the most liquid securities in the world. The lower yield offered on Treasury securities relative to non-Treasury securities reflects, to a significant extent, the difference in liquidity. Even within the Treasury market, some differences in liquidity occur, because on-the-run issues have greater liquidity than off-the-run issues.

An important factor that affects the liquidity of an issue is the size of the issue. One of the reasons that U.S. Treasury securities are highly liquid is the large size of each individual issue. As we will explain in Chapter 16, government-sponsored enterprises in recent years have dramatically increased their issuance size. They have done this in their attempt to have the yield on their securities become the benchmark interest rates in the U.S. economy. As we noted earlier, the triple A **credit rating** of government sponsored enterprises makes the yield on their securities an attractive candidate to replace the yield on Treasury securities as the benchmark interest rates. The large size and therefore liquidity of the securities issued by government-sponsored enterprises increase their attractiveness as an alternative benchmark. We also noted earlier that the yield on corporate bond issues rated triple A may make them a potential alternative benchmark. However, the size of each issue for the various triple A corporate bond issuers is considerably smaller than that of the securities issued by government-sponsored enterprises. For this reason, triple A corporate bond issuers may not be received by market participants as a benchmark alternative.

Key Points That You Should Understand Before Proceeding

1. Historically, the on-the-run Treasury security of a given maturity is the base or benchmark interest rate.
2. With the decline in the issuance of Treasury securities by the U.S. Department of the Treasury, there is now a search for an alternative interest rate benchmark.
3. Non-Treasury securities will trade at a spread (measured in basis points) relative to an on-the-run Treasury security.
4. The factors that affect yield spreads in the bond market are the type of issuer, credit risk, term to maturity, the presence of embedded options, the tax treatment of interest income, and liquidity.
5. The credit risk of an issuer is gauged by ratings assigned by commercial rating companies (Moody's, S&P, and Fitch).
6. Embedded options can either reduce the spread to Treasuries, if the option benefits the bondholder, or increase the spread to Treasuries, if the option benefits the issuer.
7. The interest income from municipal securities is generally exempt from federal income taxation, and as a result municipals offer a lower yield than Treasury securities.

SUMMARY

Two important theories of the determination of the level of the interest rate are Fisher's theory, adapted to the loanable funds model, and Keynes's liquidity preference theory. Fisher considers the reasons for saving to be the marginal rate of time preference, which is the willingness to forgo current consumption for enhanced future consumption, the level of income, and the rate of interest. The demand for borrowing arises because of firms' investment opportunities. The marginal productivity of capital is the gain from additional investment and it is negatively related to the interest rate. The equilibrium rate of interest is determined by the interaction of the demand for and supply of savings. In the presence of inflation, the equilibrium rate is composed of both the real rate of interest and a premium for expected inflation.

Keynes's theory emphasizes the role of liquid balances or money in transaction and states that the interest rate is determined in the money market. Demand for money reflects income and the level of prices for goods and services, and it is negatively related to the level of interest rates. The supply of money, in this theory, is controlled by the central bank, which can, by changing the money supply, affect the rate of interest. In fact, changes in the money supply can have three possibly conflicting effects on the level of the interest rate, depending on the economy's level of output and employment. Those effects are the liquidity effect, the income effect, and the price expectations effect.

The basic features of a bond include the coupon rate, the term to maturity, and the principal or par value. The yield to maturity of a bond is the interest rate that makes the total present value of the bond's cash flow equal to its market price.

In every economy there is not just one interest rate but a structure of interest rates. The difference between the yield on any two bonds is called the yield spread. Historically, the interest rate or yield on U.S. Treasury securities have been the benchmark interest rates throughout the world. Today, because of the substantial reduction in issuance of U.S. Treasury securities, market participants believe that another benchmark will eventually be selected. The candidates suggested have been the yield on securities issued by government-sponsored enterprises, the yield on securities issued by triple A rated corporate bond issues, and the swap spread in the interest rate swap market. Moreover, as bond markets outside the United States develop, some countries are developing their own benchmark interest rates.

As of this writing, the base interest rate in the United States is the yield on a Treasury security. The base interest rate is equal to the real rate of interest plus the expected rate of inflation. The risk premium is the the yield spread between a non-Treasury security and a comparable on-the-run Treasury security. The factors that affect the spread include: (1) the type of issuer (agency, corporation, municipality); (2) the issuer's perceived creditworthiness as measured by the rating system of commercial rating companies; (3) the term or maturity of the instrument; (4) the embedded options in a bond issue (e.g., call, put, or conversion provisions); (5) the taxability of interest income at the federal and municipal levels; and (6) the expected liquidity of the issue.

KEY TERMS

- Base interest rate (also called benchmark interest rate), 206
- Bond-equivalent yield, 205
- Call provision, 209
- Convertible bond, 210
- Credit rating (or quality rating), 212
- Embedded option, 209
- Equivalent taxable yield, 211
- Fisher's Law, 197
- Fisher's theory of interest, 194
- High-grade bond, 208
- Income effect, 200
- Intermarket sector spread, 208
- Intramarket sector spread, 208
- Liquidity effect, 200
- Liquidity preference theory of interest, 194
- Loanable funds theory of interest, 198
- Marginal productivity of capital, 195
- Marginal time preference, 194

- Market sectors, 208
- Maturity, 203
- Maturity spread, 209
- Municipal bonds, 211
- Nominal rate of interest, 196
- Off-the-run Treasury issue, 206
- On-the-run Treasury issue (also called current coupon issue), 206
- Price expectations effect, 200
- Principal value (also called principal, par value, maturity value, redemption value and face value), 203
- Put provision, 210
- Quality spread (or credit spread), 208
- Term structure of interest rates, 209
- Treasury security (also called Treasuries), 206
- Yield curve spread, 209
- Yield spread (or spread), 205
- Yield to maturity, 203

QUESTIONS

1. Explain what these terms mean in Fisher's theory of interest rates;
   a. the *marginal rate of time preference*;
   b. the *marginal productivity of capital*; and
   c. the *equilibrium interest rate*.

2. a. How does the loanable funds theory expand Fisher's theory of interest rate determination?
   b. How does a change in the government's deficit affect the equilibrium rate in the loanable funds theory?

3. a. How do the assets, money and bonds, differ in Keynes's liquidity preference theory?
   b. How does a change in income affect the equilibrium level of the interest rate in Keynes's theory?
   c. How does a change in the money supply affect that rate?

4. a. Explain these terms: the *liquidity effect*; the *income effect*; and the *price expectations effect*.
   b. How is it determined which of these three effects on interest rates an increase in the money supply will have?

5. Consider three bonds, all with a par value of $1,000:

Bond	Coupon rate	Market price
A	8%	$1,100
B	7	900
C	9	1,000

a. What is the yield to maturity of bond C?
b. Is the yield to maturity of bond A greater than or less than 8%?
c. Is the yield to maturity of bond B greater than or less than 9%?
6. Consider the following bond: 19 years to maturity, 11% coupon rate, pays interest semiannually, $1,000 par value. Suppose that the market price of this bond is $1,233.64. Given the information below, determine the yield to maturity for this bond on a bond-equivalent yield basis.

Interest rate tried	Total present value of cash flow
3.00%	$1,562.32
3.25	1,486.96
3.50	1,416.82
3.75	1,351.46
4.00	1,290.52
4.25	1,233.64

7. a. Show the cash flows for the two bonds below, each of which has a par value of $1,000 and pays interest semiannually:

Bond	Coupon rate	Years to maturity	Price
W	7%	5	$884.20
Y	9	4	967.70

b. Calculate the yield to maturity for the two bonds.
8. In the May 29, 1992, *Weekly Market Update*, published by Goldman Sachs & Co., the following information was reported in various exhibits for the Treasury market as of the close of business Thursday, May 28, 1992:

On-the-Run Treasuries

Maturity	Yield
3-month	3.77%
6-month	3.95
1-year	4.25
2-year	5.23
3-year	5.78
5-year	6.67
7-year	7.02
10-year	7.37
20-year	7.65
30-year	7.88

Key Off-the-Run Treasuries

Issue	Yield
Old 10-year	7.42%
Old 30-year	7.90

a. What is the credit risk associated with a Treasury security?
b. Why is the Treasury yield considered the base interest rate?
c. What is meant by *on-the-run Treasuries*?

d. What is meant by *off-the-run Treasuries*?

e. What are the yield spreads between (i) the off-the-run 10-year Treasury issue and the on-the-run 10-year Treasury issue, and (ii) the off-the-run 30-year Treasury issue and the on-the-run 30-year Treasury issue?

f. What does the yield spread between the off-the-run Treasury issue and the on-the-run Treasury issue reflect?

9. In the May 29, 1992, *Weekly Market Update*, published by Goldman Sachs & Co., the following information was reported in various exhibits for certain corporate bonds as of the close of business Thursday, May 28, 1992:

Issuer	Rating	Yield	Spread	Treasury benchmark
General Electric Capital Co.	Triple A	7.87%	50	10
Mobil Corp.	Double A	7.77	40	10
Southern Bell Tel & Teleg	Triple A	8.60	72	30
Bell Tel Co Pa	Double A	8.66	78	30
AMR Corp	Triple B	9.43	155	30

a. What is meant by *rating*?

b. Which of the five bonds has the greatest credit risk?

c. What is meant by *spread*?

d. What is meant by *Treasury benchmark*?

e. Using the information for the Treasury market reported for May 29, 1992, in question 8, explain how each of the spreads reported above was determined.

f. Why does each spread reported above reflect a risk premium?

10. For the corporate bond issues reported in the previous question, answer the following questions:

a. Should a triple A-rated bond issue offer a higher or lower yield than a double A-rated bond issue of the same maturity?

b. What is the spread between the General Electric Capital Company issue and the Mobil Corporation issue?

c. Is the spread reported in (b) consistent with your answer to (a)?

d. The yield spread between these two bond issues reflects more than just credit risk. What other factors would the spread reflect?

e. The Mobil Corporation issue is not callable. However, the General Electric Capital Company issue is callable. How does this information help you in understanding the spread between these two issues?

11. For the corporate bond issues reported in question 9, answer the following questions:

a. What is the yield spread between the Southern Bell Telephone and Telegraph bond issue and the Bell Telephone Company (Pennsylvania) bond issue?

b. The Southern Bell Telephone and Telegraph bond issue is not callable but the Bell Telephone Company (Pennsylvania) bond issue is callable. What does the yield spread in (a) reflect?

c. AMR Corporation is the parent company of American Airlines and is therefore classified in the transportation industry. The bond issue cited is not callable. What is the yield spread between AMR Corporation and Southern Bell Telephone and Telegraph bond issue, and what does this spread reflect?

12. Historically, what has been the reason that the yields on U.S. Treasury securities have been viewed as the benchmark interest rates throughout the world?

13. Two possible candidates to replace the yields U.S. Treasury securities as the benchmark interest rates are the yields on securities issued by government spon-

sored enterprises and the yields on triple A-rated corporate issuers. Which of the two alternatives is likely to be better? Explain why.

14. In the May 29, 1992, *Weekly Market Update*, published by Goldman Sachs & Co., the following information was reported in an exhibit for high-grade, tax-exempt securities as of the close of business Thursday, May 28, 1992:

Maturity	Yield	Yield as a percent of Treasury yield
1-year	3.20%	76.5%
3-year	4.65	80.4
5-year	5.10	76.4
10-year	5.80	78.7
30-year	6.50	82.5

   a. What is meant by a *tax-exempt security*?
   b. What is meant by a *high-grade* issue?
   c. Why is the yield on a tax-exempt security less than the yield on a Treasury security of the same maturity?
   d. What is meant by the *equivalent taxable yield*?
   e. Also reported in the same issue of the Goldman Sachs report is information on "Intra-market Yield Spreads." What is an intra-market yield spread?

15. a. What is meant by an *embedded option* in a bond?
   b. Give three examples of an embedded option that might be included in a bond issue.
   c. Does an embedded option increase or decrease the risk premium relative to the base interest rate?

Chapter 12

The Term Structure of Interest Rates

Learning Objectives

After reading this chapter, you will understand

- what is meant by the term structure of interest rates.
- what the yield curve is.
- the different shapes that the term structure can take.
- what is meant by a spot rate and a spot rate curve.
- how a theoretical spot rate curve can be determined from the Treasury yield curve.
- what is meant by an implicit forward rate and how it can be calculated.
- how long-term rates are related to the current short-term rate and short-term forward rates.
- the different theories about the determinants of the shape of the term structure: pure expectations theory, the liquidity theory, the preferred habitat theory, and the market segmentation theory.
- the risks associated with investing in bonds when interest rates change—price risk and reinvestment risk.

In this chapter, we extend the theories and principles of the last chapter to the relationship between the yield on a bond and its maturity. Since the maturity of a bond is referred to as its *term to maturity* or simply *term*, the relationship between yield and maturity is referred to as the **term structure of interest rates**. We also explain the various theories about the determinants of the term structure of interest rates.

THE YIELD CURVE AND THE TERM STRUCTURE

The graphic that depicts the relationship between the yield on bonds of the same credit quality but different maturities is known as the **yield curve**. Market participants have tended to construct yield curves from observations of prices and yields in the Treasury market. Two reasons account for this tendency. First, Treasury securities are free of default risk, and differences in creditworthiness do not affect yield estimates. Second, as the largest and most active bond market, the Treasury market offers the fewest problems of illiquidity or infrequent trading. Figure 12-1 shows the shape of three hypothetical Treasury yield curves that have been observed from time to time in the United States. However, as noted in the previous chapter, new benchmarks are being considered by market participants because of the dwindling supply of U.S. Treasury securities. Nevertheless, the principles set forth in this chapter apply to any other benchmark selected.

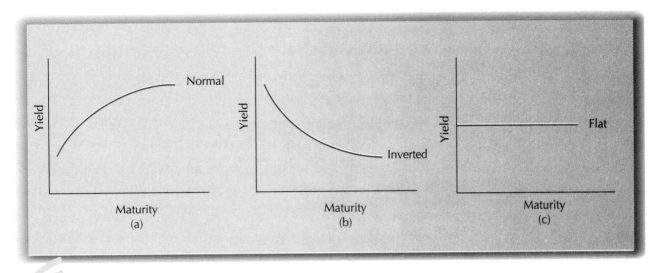

Figure 12-1   Three Hypothetical Yield Curves

From a practical viewpoint, as we explained in the previous chapter, the Treasury yield curve functions mainly as a benchmark for pricing bonds and setting yields in many other sectors of the debt market—bank loans, mortgages, corporate debt, and international bonds. More recently market participants have come to realize that the traditionally constructed Treasury yield curve is an unsatisfactory measure of the relation between required yield and maturity. The key reason is that securities with the same maturity may actually provide different yields. As we will explain below, this phenomenon reflects the role and impact of differences in the bonds' coupon rates. Hence, it is necessary to develop more accurate and reliable estimates of the Treasury yield curve. In what follows, we will show the problems posed by traditional approaches to the Treasury yield curve, and offer an innovative and increasingly popular approach to building a yield curve. The approach consists of identifying yields that apply to zero-coupon bonds and, therefore, eliminates the problem of nonuniqueness in the yield–maturity relationship.

Using the Yield Curve to Price a Bond

As we explained in Chapter 10, the price of any financial asset is the present value of its cash flow. However, in our illustrations and our discussion to this point in the book, we have assumed that one interest rate should be used to discount all the cash flows from a financial asset. In the previous chapter, we indicated that the appropriate interest rate is the yield on a Treasury security with the same maturity as the financial asset, plus an appropriate yield premium or spread.

As noted above, however, there is a problem with using the Treasury yield curve to determine the appropriate yield at which to discount the cash flow of a bond. To illustrate this problem, consider the following two hypothetical five-year Treasury bonds, A and B. The difference between these two Treasury bonds is the coupon rate, which is 12% for A and 3% for B. The cash flow for these two bonds per $100 of par value for the ten six-month periods to maturity would be:

Period	Cash Flow for A	Cash Flow for B
1–9	$ 6.00	$ 1.50
10	106.00	101.50

Because of the different cash flow patterns, it is not appropriate to use the same interest rate to discount all cash flows. Instead, each cash flow should be discounted at a unique interest rate that is appropriate for the time period in which the cash flow will be received. But what should be the interest rate for each period?

The correct way to think about bonds A and B is not as bonds but as packages of cash flows. More specifically, they are packages of zero-coupon instruments. As noted in Chapter 10, a **zero-coupon instrument** is one that is purchased at an amount below its maturity value and that pays no interest periodically. Instead, the interest is earned at the maturity date when the investor receives the maturity or principal value. Thus, the interest earned is the difference between the maturity value and the price paid. For example, bond A can be viewed as 10 zero-coupon instruments: one with a maturity value of $6 maturing six months from now; a second with a maturity value of $6 maturing one year from now; a third with a maturity value of $6 maturing 1.5 years from now, and so on. The final zero-coupon instrument matures 10 six-month periods from now and has a maturity value of $106.

Likewise, bond B can be viewed as ten zero-coupon instruments: one with a maturity value of $1.50 maturing six months from now; one with a maturity value of $1.50 maturing one year from now; one with a maturity value of $1.50 maturing 1.5 years from now, and so on. The final zero-coupon instrument matures 10 six-month periods from now and has a maturity value of $101.50. Obviously, in the case of each coupon bond, the value or price of the bond is equal to the total value of its component zero-coupon instruments.

In general, any bond can be viewed as a package of zero-coupon instruments. That is, each zero-coupon instrument in the package has a maturity equal to its coupon payment date or, in the case of the principal, the maturity date. The value of the bond should equal the value of all the component zero-coupon instruments. As we show in the appendix to Chapter 16, if this does not hold, it is possible for a market participant to generate riskless profits. Because no one can pass up riskless and certain profits, the market must drive these two prices to equality, and our discussion here assumes that equality.

To determine the value of each zero-coupon instrument, it is necessary to know the yield on a zero-coupon Treasury with that same maturity. This yield is called the **spot rate**, and the graphical depiction of the relationship between the spot rate and its maturity is called the **spot rate curve**. Below we will see how to derive this curve from theoretical considerations of the yields of the actually traded Treasury securities. Such a curve is called a *theoretical spot rate curve.*

Constructing the Theoretical Spot Rate Curve

In this section, we explain how the theoretical spot rate curve is constructed from the yield curve that is based on the observed yields of Treasury bills and Treasury coupon securities. The process of creating a theoretical spot rate curve in this way is called **bootstrapping**.[1] To explain this process, we'll use the data for the hypothetical price, annualized yield (yield to maturity) and maturity of the 20 Treasury securities shown

Table 12-1   Maturity and Yield to Maturity for 20 Hypothetical Treasury Securities

MATURITY (YEARS)	COUPON RATE	YIELD TO MATURITY	PRICE
0.50	0.0000	0.0800	$ 96.15
1.00	0.0000	0.0830	92.19
1.50	0.0850	0.0890	99.45
2.00	0.0900	0.0920	99.64
2.50	0.1100	0.0940	103.49
3.00	0.0950	0.0970	99.49
3.50	0.1000	0.1000	100.00
4.00	0.1000	0.1040	98.72
4.50	0.1150	0.1060	103.16
5.00	0.0875	0.1080	92.24
5.50	0.1050	0.1090	98.38
6.00	0.1100	0.1120	99.14
6.50	0.0850	0.1140	86.94
7.00	0.0825	0.1160	84.24
7.50	0.1100	0.1180	96.09
8.00	0.0650	0.1190	72.62
8.50	0.0875	0.1200	82.97
9.00	0.1300	0.1220	104.30
9.50	0.1150	0.1240	95.06
10.00	0.1250	0.1250	100.00

in Table 12-1. (In practice, all the coupon rates are estimated so that the price of each bond is par.)

Throughout the analysis and illustrations to come, it is important to remember that the basic principle underlying bootstrapping is that the value of the Treasury coupon security should be equal to the value of the package of zero-coupon Treasury securities that duplicates the coupon bond's cash flow.

Consider the six-month Treasury bill in Table 12-1. As we explained in the previous chapter, a Treasury bill is a zero-coupon instrument. Therefore, its annualized yield of 8% is equal to the spot rate. Similarly, for the one-year Treasury, the cited yield of 8.3% is the one-year spot rate. Given these two spot rates, we can compute the spot rate for a theoretical 1.5-year zero-coupon Treasury. The price of a theoretical 1.5-year

[1] In practice, the Treasury securities that are used to construct the theoretical spot rate curve are the most recently auctioned Treasury securities of a given maturity. Such issues are referred to as the *on-the-run Treasury issues.* As we will explain in Chapter 16, there are actual zero-coupon Treasury securities with a maturity greater than one year that are outstanding in the market. These securities are not issued by the U.S. Treasury but are created by certain market participants from actual coupon Treasury securities. It would seem logical that the observed yield on zero-coupon Treasury securities can be used to construct an actual spot rate curve, but there are problems with this approach. First, the liquidity of these securities is not as great as that of the coupon Treasury market. Second, there are maturity sectors of the zero-coupon Treasury market that attract specific investors who may be willing to trade off yield in exchange for an attractive feature associated with that particular maturity sector, thereby distorting the term structure relationship.

zero-coupon Treasury should equal the present value of the three cash flows from an actual 1.5-year coupon Treasury, where the yield used for discounting is the spot rate corresponding to the cash flow. Using $100 as par, the cash flow for the 1.5-year Treasury with the 8.5% coupon rate is:

0.5 years	$0.085 \times \$100 \times 0.5$	$= \$ \ \ 4.25$
1.0 years	$0.085 \times \$100 \times 0.5$	$= \$ \ \ 4.25$
1.5 years	$0.085 \times \$100 \times 0.5 + 100$	$= \$104.25$

The present value of the cash flow is then:

$$\frac{4.25}{(1+z_1)^1} + \frac{4.25}{(1+z_2)^2} + \frac{104.25}{(1+z_3)^3}$$

where

z_1 = one-half the annualized six-month theoretical spot rate
z_2 = one-half the one-year theoretical spot rate
z_3 = one-half the 1.5-year theoretical spot rate

Since the six-month spot rate and one-year spot rate are 8.0% and 8.3%, respectively, we know these facts:

$$z_1 = 0.04 \ \text{ and } \ z_2 = 0.0415$$

We can compute the present value of the 1.5-year coupon Treasury security as:

$$\frac{4.25}{(1.0400)^1} + \frac{4.25}{(1.0415)^2} + \frac{104.25}{(1+z_3)^3}$$

Since the price of the 1.5-year coupon Treasury security (from Table 12-1) is $99.45, the following relationship between market price and the present value of the cash flow must hold:

$$99.45 = \frac{4.25}{(1.0400)^1} + \frac{4.25}{(1.0415)^2} + \frac{104.25}{(1+z_3)^3}$$

We can solve for the theoretical 1.5-year spot rate as follows:

$$99.45 = 4.08654 + 3.91805 + \frac{104.25}{(1+z_3)^3}$$

$$91.44541 = \frac{104.25}{(1+z_3)^3}$$

$$(1+z_3)^3 = 1.140024$$

$$z_3 = 0.04465$$

Doubling this yield, we obtain the bond equivalent yield of 0.0893 or 8.93%, which is the theoretical 1.5-year spot rate. That rate is the rate that the market would apply to a 1.5-year zero-coupon Treasury security if, in fact, such a security existed.

Given the theoretical 1.5-year spot rate, we can obtain the theoretical two-year spot rate. The cash flow for the two-year coupon Treasury in Table 12-1 is:

$$
\begin{array}{lll}
0.5 \text{ years} & 0.090 \times \$100 \times 0.5 & = \$ \ \ 4.50 \\
1.0 \text{ years} & 0.090 \times \$100 \times 0.5 & = \$ \ \ 4.50 \\
1.5 \text{ years} & 0.090 \times \$100 \times 0.5 & = \$ \ \ 4.50 \\
2.0 \text{ years} & 0.090 \times \$100 \times 0.5 + 100 & = \$104.50
\end{array}
$$

The present value of the cash flow is then:

$$
\frac{4.50}{(1+z_1)^1} + \frac{4.50}{(1+z_2)^2} + \frac{4.50}{(1+z_3)^3} + \frac{104.50}{(1+z_4)^4}
$$

where z_4 is one-half the two-year theoretical spot rate. Since the six-month spot rate, one-year spot rate, and 1.5-year spot rate are 8.0%, 8.3%, and 8.93%, respectively, then:

$$
z_1 = 0.04, \ z_2 = 0.0415, \ \text{and} \ \ z_3 = 0.04465
$$

Therefore, the present value of the two-year coupon Treasury security is:

$$
\frac{4.50}{(1.0400)^1} + \frac{4.50}{(1.0415)^2} + \frac{4.50}{(1.04465)^3} + \frac{104.50}{(1+z_4)^4}
$$

Since the price of the two-year coupon Treasury security is $99.64, the following relationship must hold:

$$
99.64 = \frac{4.50}{(1.0400)^1} + \frac{4.50}{(1.0415)^2} + \frac{4.50}{(1.04465)^3} + \frac{104.50}{(1+z_4)^4}
$$

We can solve for the theoretical two-year spot rate as follows:

$$
99.64 = 4.32692 + 4.14853 + 3.94730 + \frac{104.25}{(1+z_4)^4}
$$

$$
87.21725 = \frac{104.50}{(1+z_4)^4}
$$

$$
(1+z_4)^4 = 1.198158
$$

$$
z_4 = 0.046235
$$

Doubling this yield, we obtain the theoretical two-year spot rate bond-equivalent yield of 9.247%.

One can follow this approach sequentially to derive the theoretical 2.5-year spot rate from the calculated values of z_1, z_2, z_3, and z_4 (the six-month, one-year, 1.5-year,

Table 12-2   Theoretical Spot Rates

MATURITY (YEARS)	YIELD TO MATURITY	THEORETICAL SPOT RATE
0.50	0.0800	0.08000
1.00	0.0830	0.08300
1.50	0.0890	0.08930
2.00	0.0920	0.09247
2.50	0.0940	0.09468
3.00	0.0970	0.09787
3.50	0.1000	0.10129
4.00	0.1040	0.10592
4.50	0.1060	0.10850
5.00	0.1080	0.11021
5.50	0.1090	0.11175
6.00	0.1120	0.11584
6.50	0.1140	0.11744
7.00	0.1160	0.11991
7.50	0.1180	0.12405
8.00	0.1190	0.12278
8.50	0.1200	0.12546
9.00	0.1220	0.13152
9.50	0.1240	0.13377
10.00	0.1250	0.13623

and two-year rates), and the price and coupon of the bond with a maturity of 2.5 years. Furthermore, one could derive theoretical spot rates for the remaining 15 half-yearly rates. The spot rates thus obtained are shown in Table 12-2. They represent the term structure of interest rates for maturities up to 10 years, at the particular time to which the bond price quotations refer.

Column 2 of Table 12-2 reproduces the calculated yield to maturity for the coupon issue listed in Table 12-1. A comparison of this column with the last column giving the yield to maturity of a zero-coupon bond is instructive, for it confirms that bonds of the same maturity may have different yields to maturity. That is, the yield of bonds of the same credit quality does not depend on their maturity alone. While the two columns do not change much at the beginning, they diverge more after the third year, and by the ninth year the zero-coupon yield is nearly 100 basis points higher than that of the same maturity with a coupon of 13% and selling at a premium.

Using Spot Rates to Value a Bond

Given the spot rates, the theoretical value of a bond can be calculated. This is done by discounting a cash flow for a given period by the corresponding spot rate for that period. This is illustrated in Table 12-3.

The bond in our illustration is a ten-year, 10% coupon Treasury bond. The second column of Table 12-2 shows the cash flow per $100 of par value for a 10% coupon bond. The third column shows the theoretical spot rates. The fourth column is simply one half of the annual spot rate of the previous column. The last column shows the present value of the cash flow in the second column when discounted at the semiannual spot rate. The value of this bond is the total present value, $85.35477.

Table 12-3   Illustration of How to Value a 10-Year, 10% Treasury Bond Using Spot Rates

MATURITY (YEARS)	CASH FLOW	SPOT RATE	SEMIANNUAL SPOT RATE	PRESENT VALUE
0.5	5	0.08000	0.04000	4.8077
1.0	5	0.08300	0.04150	4.6095
1.5	5	0.08930	0.04465	4.3859
2.0	5	0.09247	0.04624	4.1730
2.5	5	0.09468	0.04734	3.9676
3.0	5	0.09787	0.04894	3.7539
3.5	5	0.10129	0.05065	3.5382
4.0	5	0.10592	0.05296	3.3088
4.5	5	0.10850	0.05425	3.1080
5.0	5	0.11021	0.05511	2.9242
5.5	5	0.11175	0.05588	2.7494
6.0	5	0.11584	0.05792	2.5441
6.5	5	0.11744	0.05872	2.3813
7.0	5	0.11991	0.05996	2.2128
7.5	5	0.12405	0.06203	2.0274
8.0	5	0.12278	0.06139	1.9274
8.5	5	0.12546	0.06273	1.7774
9.0	5	0.13152	0.06576	1.5889
9.5	5	0.13377	0.06689	1.4613
10.0	105	0.13623	0.06812	28.1079
Total				85.35477

Key Points That You Should Understand Before Proceeding

1. What the yield curve represents.
2. Why any financial asset can be viewed as a package of zero-coupon instruments.
3. What is meant by spot rates and how the theoretical spot rates can be constructed from a Treasury yield curve.
4. How to value a bond using spot rates.

FORWARD RATES

Thus far we have seen that from the Treasury yield curve we can extrapolate the theoretical spot rates. In addition, we can extrapolate what some market participants refer to as the *market's consensus of future interest rates*. To see the importance of knowing the market's consensus for future interest rates, consider the following two investment alternatives for an investor who has a one-year investment horizon:

Alternative 1: Investor buys a one-year instrument.
Alternative 2: Investor buys a six-month instrument and when it matures in six months the investor buys another six-month instrument.

With Alternative 1, the investor will realize the one-year spot rate and that rate is known with certainty. In contrast, with Alternative 2, the investor will realize the six-month spot rate, but the six-month rate six months from now is unknown. Therefore,

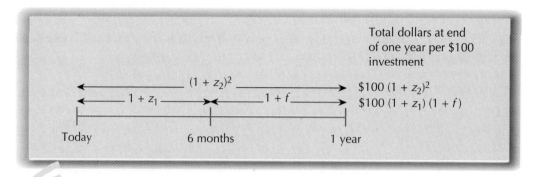

Figure 12-2 Two Alternative One-Year Investments

for Alternative 2, the rate that will be earned over one year is not known with certainty. This is illustrated in Figure 12-2.

Suppose that this investor expected that six months from now the six-month rate will be higher than it is today. The investor might then feel Alternative 2 would be the better investment. However, this is not necessarily true. To understand why and to appreciate the need to understand why it is necessary to know what the market's consensus of future interest rates is, let's continue with our illustration.

The investor will be indifferent to the two alternatives if they produce the same total dollars over the one-year investment horizon. Given the one-year spot rate, there is some rate on a six-month instrument six months from now that will make the investor indifferent between the two alternatives. We will denote that rate by f.

The value of f can be readily determined given the one-year spot rate and the six-month spot rate. If an investor placed $100 in a one-year instrument (Alternative 1), the total dollars that will be generated at the end of one year is:

$$\text{Total dollars at the end of year for Alternative 1} = \$100(1 + z_2)^2$$

where z_2 is the one-year spot rate. (Remember we are working in six-month periods, so the subscript 2 represents two six-month periods, or one year.)

The proceeds from investing at the six-month spot rate will generate the following total dollars at the end of six months:

$$\text{Total dollars at the end of six months for Alternative 2} = \$100(1 + z_1)$$

where z_1 is the six-month spot rate. If this amount is reinvested at the six-month rate six months from now, which we denoted f, then the total dollars at the end of one year would be:

$$\text{Total dollars at the end of year for Alternative 2} = \$100(1 + z_1)(1 + f)$$

The investor will be indifferent between the two alternatives if the total dollars are the same. Setting the two equations for the total dollars at end of one year for the two alternatives equal we get:

$$\$100 = (1 + z_2)^2 = \$100(1 + z_1)(1 + f)$$

Solving the preceding equation for f, we get

$$f = \frac{(1 + z_2)^2}{(1 + z_1)} - 1$$

Doubling f gives the bond-equivalent yield for the six-month rate six months from now that we are interested in.

We can illustrate the calculation of f using the theoretical spot rates shown in Table 12-2. From that table, we know that:

Six-month spot rate = 0.080, therefore z_1 = 0.0400
One-year spot rate = 0.083, therefore z_2 = 0.0415

Substituting into the formula, we have:

$$f = \frac{(1.0415)^2}{(1.0400)} - 1$$
$$= 0.043$$

Therefore, the forward rate on a six-month security, quoted on a bond-equivalent basis, is 8.6% (0.043×2).

Here is how we use this rate of 8.6%. If the six-month rate six months from now is less than 8.6%, then the total dollars at the end of one year would be higher by investing in the one-year instrument (Alternative 1). If the six-month rate six months from now is greater than 8.6%, then the total dollars at the end of one year would be higher by investing in the six-month instrument and reinvesting the proceeds six months from now at the six-month rate at the time (Alternative 2). Of course, if the six-month rate six months from now is 8.6%, the two alternatives give the same total dollars at the end of one year.

Now that we have the rate f in which we are interested and we know how that rate can be used, let's return to the question we posed at the outset. From Table 12-2, the six-month spot rate is 8%. Suppose that the investor expects that six months from now, the six month rate will be 8.2%. That is, the investor expects that the six-month rate will be higher than its current level. Should the investor select Alternative 2 because the six-month rate six months from now is expected to be higher? The answer is no. As we explained in the previous paragraph, if the rate is less than 8.6%, then Alternative 1 is the better alternative. Since this investor expects a rate of 8.2%, then he or she should select Alternative 1 despite the fact that he or she expects the six-month rate to be higher than it is today.

This is a somewhat surprising result for some investors. But the reason for this is that the market prices its expectations of future interest rates into the rates offered on investments with different maturities. This is why knowing the market's consensus of future interest rates is critical. The rate that we determined for f is the market's consensus for the six-month rate six months from now. A future interest rate calculated from either the spot rates or the yield curve is called a **forward rate** or an **implied forward rate**.

Similarly, borrowers need to understand what a forward rate is. For example, suppose a borrower must choose between a one-year loan and a series of two six-month loans. If the forward rate is less than the borrower's expectations of six-month rates six months from now, then the borrower will be better off with a one-year loan. If, instead, the borrower's expectations are that six-month rates six months from now will be less than the forward rate, the borrower will be better off by choosing a series of two six-month loans.

There are two elements to the forward rate. The first is when in the future the rate begins. The second is the length of time for the rate. For example, the two-year forward rate three years from now means a rate three years from now for a length of two years. The notation used for a forward rate, f, will have two subscripts—one before f and one after f as shown below:

$$_t f_m$$

The subscript before f is t and is the length of time that the rate applies. The subscript after f is m and is when the forward rate begins. That is,

the length of time of the forward rate f when the forward rate begins

Remember our time periods are still six-month periods. Given the above notation, here is what the following mean:

Notation	Interpretation for the forward rate
$_1 f_{12}$	six-month (one-period) forward rate beginning six years (12 periods) from now
$_2 f_8$	one-year (two-period) forward rate beginning four years (8 periods) from now
$_6 f_4$	three-year (six-period) forward rate beginning two years (4 periods) from now
$_8 f_{10}$	four-year (eight-period) forward rate beginning five years (10 periods) from now

It can be demonstrated that the formula to compute any forward rate is

$$_t f_m = \left[\frac{(1 + z_{m+t})^{m+t}}{(1 + z_m)^m} \right]^{1/t} - 1$$

Notice that if t is equal to 1, the formula reduces to the one-period (six-month) forward rate.

To illustrate, for the spot rates shown in Table 12-2, suppose that an investor wants to know the two-year forward rate three years from now. In terms of the notation, t is equal to 4 and m is equal to 6. Substituting for t and m into the equation for the forward rate we have

$$_4 f_6 = \left[\frac{(1 + z_{6+4})^{6+4}}{(1 + z_6)^6} \right]^{1/4} - 1$$

This means that the following two spot rates are needed: z_6 (the three-year spot rate) and z_{10} (the five-year spot rate). From Table 12-3 we know

z_6 (the three-year spot rate) = 9.9787% / 2 = 4.894% = 0.04894
z_{10} (the five-year spot rate) = 13.623% / 2 = 6.812% = 0.06812

then

$$_4f_6 = \left[\frac{(1.06812)^{10}}{(1.04894)^6}\right]^{1/4} - 1 = 0.09755 = 9.755\%$$

Therefore, $_4f_6$ is equal to 9.755%, and doubling this rate gives 19.510% the forward rate on a bond-equivalent basis.

We can verify this result. Investing $100 for 10 periods at the semiannual spot rate of 6.812% will produce the following value:

$$\$100\,(1.06812)^{10} = \$193.286.$$

By investing $100 for six periods at 4.894% and reinvesting the proceeds for four periods at the forward rate of 9.755% gives the same value

$$\$100\,(1.04894)^6\,(1.09755)^4 = \$193.286.$$

Relationship between Spot Rates and Short-Term Forward Rates

Suppose an investor purchases a five-year, zero-coupon Treasury security for $58.48 with a maturity value of $100. The investor could instead buy a six-month Treasury bill and reinvest the proceeds every six months for five years. The number of dollars that will be realized will depend on the six-month forward rates. Suppose that the investor can actually reinvest the proceeds maturing every six months at the implied six-month forward rates. Let us see how many dollars would accumulate at the end of five years. The implied six-month forward rates were calculated for the yield curve given in Table 12-2. Letting f_t denote the six-month forward rate beginning t six-month periods from now, then the semiannual implied forward rates using the spot rates shown in Table 12-2 are:

$$
\begin{array}{llll}
f_1 = 0.043000 & f_2 = 0.050980 & f_3 = 0.051005 & f_4 = 0.051770 \\
f_5 = 0.056945 & f_6 = 0.060965 & f_7 = 0.069310 & f_8 = 0.064625 \\
f_9 = 0.062830
\end{array}
$$

By investing the $58.48 at the six-month spot rate of 4% (8% on a bond-equivalent basis) and reinvesting at the foregoing forward rates, the number of dollars accumulated at the end of five years would be:

$$\$58.48(1.04)(1.043)(1.05098)(1.051005)(1.05177)(1.056945)$$
$$(1.060965)(1.069310)(1.064625)(1.06283) = \$100$$

Therefore, we see that if the implied forward rates are realized, the $58.48 investment will produce the same number of dollars as an investment in a five-year, zero-coupon Treasury security at the five-year spot rate. From this illustration, we can see that the five-year spot rate is related to the current six-month spot rate and the implied six-month forward rates.

In general, the relationship between a t-period spot rate, the current six-month spot rate, and the implied six-month forward rates is as follows:

$$z_t = [(1+z_1)(1+f_1)(1+f_2)(1+f_3)...(1+f_{t-1})]^{1/t} - 1$$

To illustrate how to use this equation, look at how the five-year (10-period) spot rate is related to the six-month forward rates. Substituting into the preceding equation the relevant forward rates just given and the one-period spot rate of 4% (one-half the 8% annual spot rate), we obtain

$$\begin{aligned} z_{10} &= [(1.04)(1.043)(1.05098)(1.051005)(1.05177)(1.056945) \\ &\quad (1.060965)(1.069310)(1.064625)(1.06283))]^{1/10} - 1 \\ &= 5.51\% \end{aligned}$$

Doubling 5.51% gives an annual spot rate of 11.02%, which agrees with the spot rate given in Table 12-2.

Forward Rate as a Hedgeable Rate

A natural question about forward rates is how well they do at predicting future interest rates. Studies have demonstrated that forward rates do not do a good job in predicting future interest rates.[2] Then, why the big deal about understanding forward rates? The reason, as we demonstrated in our illustration of how to select between two alternative investments, is that the forward rates indicate how an investor's expectations must differ from the market consensus in order to make the correct decision.

In our illustration, the six-month forward rate may not be realized. That is irrelevant. The fact is that the six-month forward rate indicated to the investor that if expectations about the six-month rate six months from now are less than 8.6%, the investor would be better off with Alternative 1.

For this reason, as well as others explained later, some market participants prefer not to talk about forward rates as being market consensus rates. Instead, they refer to forward rates as being *hedgeable rates*. For example, by buying the one-year security, the investor was able to hedge the six-month rate six months from now.

DETERMINANTS OF THE SHAPE OF THE TERM STRUCTURE

If we plot the term structure—the yield to maturity, or the spot rate, at successive maturities against maturity—what is it likely to look like? Figure 12-1 shows three shapes that have appeared with some frequency over time. Panel A shows an upward-sloping yield curve; that is, yield rises steadily as maturity increases. This shape is commonly referred to as a normal or positive yield curve. Panel B shows a downward-sloping or inverted yield curve, where yields decline as maturity increases. Finally, panel C shows a flat yield curve.

Two major theories have evolved to account for these observed shapes of the yield curve: the *expectations theory* and the *market segmentation theory*.

There are several forms of the expectations theory—the **pure expectations theory**, the *liquidity theory*, and the *preferred habitat theory*. All share a hypothesis about the behavior of short-term forward rates and also assume that the forward rates in current long-term contracts are closely related to the market's expectations about future short-

---

[2] Eugene F. Fama, "Forward Rates as Predictors of Future Spot Rates," *Journal of Financial Economics*, 3, no. 4 (1976), pp. 361–377.

term rates. These three theories differ, however, on whether or not other factors also affect forward rates, and how. The pure expectations theory postulates that no systematic factors other than expected future short-term rates affect forward rates; the liquidity theory and the preferred habitat theory assert that there are other factors. Accordingly, the last two forms of the expectations theory are sometimes referred to as *biased expectations theories*. Figure 12-3 depicts the relationship between these three theories.

The Pure Expectations Theory

According to the pure expectations theory, the forward rates exclusively represent the expected future rates. Thus, the entire term structure at a given time reflects the market's current expectations of the family of future short-term rates. Under this view, a rising term structure, as in Panel A of Figure 12-1, must indicate that the market expects short-term rates to rise throughout the relevant future. Similarly, a flat term structure reflects an expectation that future short-term rates will be mostly constant, while a falling term structure must reflect an expectation that future short rates will decline steadily.

We can illustrate this theory by considering how an expectation of a rising short-term future rate would affect the behavior of various market participants, so as to result in a rising yield curve. Assume an initially flat term structure, and suppose that economic news subsequently leads market participants to expect interest rates to rise.

1. Those market participants interested in a long-term investment would not want to buy long-term bonds because they would expect the yield structure to rise sooner or

Figure 12-3   Term Structure Theories
SOURCE: Frank J. Fabozzi, *Valuation of Fixed Income Securities and Derivatives* (New Hope, PA: Frank J. Fabozzi Associates, 1995), p. 49.

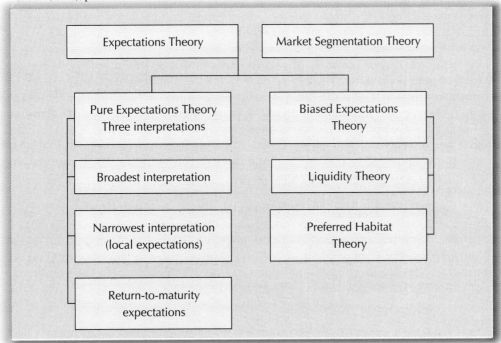

later, resulting in a price decline for the bonds and a capital loss on the long-term bonds purchased. Instead, they would want to invest in short-term debt obligations until the rise in yield had occurred, permitting them to reinvest their funds at the higher yield.

2.   Speculators expecting rising rates would anticipate a decline in the price of long-term bonds and, therefore, would want to sell any long-term bonds they own and possibly to "short sell" some they do not now own.[3] (Should interest rates rise as expected, the price of longer-term bonds will fall. Since the speculator sold these bonds short and can then purchase them at a lower price to cover the short sale, a profit will be earned.) The proceeds received from the selling of long-term debt issues the speculators now hold or the shorting of longer-term bonds will be invested in short-term debt obligations.

3.   Borrowers wishing to acquire long-term funds would be pulled toward borrowing now, in the long end of the market, by the expectation that borrowing at a later time would be more expensive.

All these responses would tend either to lower the net demand for, or to increase the supply of, long-maturity bonds, and two responses would increase demand for short-term debt obligations. Clearing of the market would require a rise in long-term yields in relation to short-term yields; that is, these actions by investors, speculators, and borrowers would tilt the term structure upward until it is consistent with expectations of higher future interest rates. By analogous reasoning, an unexpected event leading to the expectation of lower future rates will result in the yield curve sloping down.

Unfortunately, the pure expectations theory suffers from one shortcoming, which, qualitatively, is quite serious. It neglects the risks inherent in investing in bonds and like instruments. If forward rates were perfect predictors of future interest rates, then the future prices of bonds would be known with certainty. The return over any investment period would be certain and independent of the maturity of the instrument initially acquired and of the time at which the investor needed to liquidate the instrument. However, with uncertainty about future interest rates and hence about future prices of bonds, these instruments become risky investments in the sense that the return over some investment horizon is unknown.

Similarly, from a borrower or issuer's perspective, the cost of borrowing for any required period of financing would be certain and independent of the maturity of the instrument initially sold if the rate at which the borrower must refinance debt in the future is known. But with uncertainty about future interest rates, the cost of borrowing is uncertain if the borrower must refinance at some time over the periods in which the funds are initially needed.

In the following section, we examine more closely the sources and types of risk that the pure expectations theory ignores.

Risks Associated with Bond Investment.
There are two risks that cause uncertainty about the return over some investment horizon. The first is the uncertainty about the price of the bond at the end of the investment horizon. For example, an investor who plans to invest for five years might consider the following three investment alternatives: (1) invest in a five-year bond and hold it for five years; (2) invest in a 12-year bond and sell it at the end of five years; and

---

[3] Short selling means selling a security that is not owned but borrowed. The process for selling stocks short is described in Chapter 15.

(3) invest in a 30-year bond and sell it at the end of five years. The return that will be realized for the second and third alternatives is not known because the price of each long-term bond at the end of five years is not known. In the case of the 12-year bond, the price will depend on the yield on seven-year debt securities five years from now; and the price of the 30-year bond will depend on the yield on 25-year bonds five years from now. Since forward rates implicit in the current term structure for a future 12-year bond and a future 25-year bond are not perfect predictors of the actual future rates, there is uncertainty about the price for both bonds five years from now.

The risk that the price of the bond will be lower than currently expected at the end of the investment horizon is called **price risk**. An important feature of price risk is that it is greater, the longer the maturity of the bond. The reason should be familiar from our discussions in Chapter 10, and it is that the longer the maturity, the greater the price volatility of a bond when yields rise. Thus, investors are exposed to price risk when they invest in a bond that will be sold prior to the bond's maturity date.

The second risk has to do with uncertainty about the rate at which the proceeds from a bond that matures prior to the maturity date can be reinvested until the maturity date. For example, an investor who plans to invest for five years might consider the following three alternative investments: (1) invest in a five-year bond and hold it for five years; (2) invest in a six-month instrument and, when it matures, reinvest the proceeds in six-month instruments over the entire five-year investment horizon; and (3) invest in a two-year bond and, when it matures, reinvest the proceeds in a three-year bond. The risk in the second and third alternatives is that the return over the five-year investment horizon is unknown because rates at which the proceeds can be reinvested until maturity are unknown. This risk is referred to as **reinvestment risk**.

Interpretations of the Pure Expectations Theory.

There are several interpretations of the pure expectations theory that have been put forth by economists. These interpretations are not exact equivalents, nor are they consistent with each other, in large part because they offer different treatments of the two risks associated with realizing a return that we have just explained.[4]

The broadest interpretation of the pure expectations theory suggests that investors expect the return for any investment horizon to be the same, regardless of the maturity strategy selected.[5] For example, consider an investor who has a five-year investment horizon. According to this theory, it makes no difference if a five-year, 12-year, or 30-year bond is purchased and held for five years because the investor expects the return from all three bonds to be the same over five years. A major criticism of this very broad interpretation of the theory is that, because of price risk associated with investing in bonds with a maturity greater than the investment horizon, the expected returns from these three very different bond investments should differ in significant ways.[6]

A second interpretation, referred to as the *local expectations* form of the pure expectations theory, suggests that the return will be the same over a short-term investment horizon starting today. For example, if an investor has a six-month investment horizon, buying a 5-year, 10-year, or 20-year bond will produce the same six-month return. It has been demonstrated that the local expectations formulation, which is nar-

---

[4] These formulations are summarized by John Cox, Jonathan Ingersoll, Jr., and Stephen Ross, "A Re-examination of Traditional Hypotheses About the Term Structure of Interest Rates," *Journal of Finance* (September 1981), pp. 769–799.

[5] F. Lutz, "The Structure of Interest Rates," *Quarterly Journal of Economics* (1940–41), pp. 36–63.

[6] Cox, Ingersoll, and Ross, "A Re-examination of Traditional Hypotheses," pp. 774–775.

row in scope, is the only one of the interpretations of the pure expectations theory that can be sustained in equilibrium.[7]

The third and final interpretation of the pure expectations theory suggests that the return that an investor will realize by rolling over short-term bonds to some investment horizon will be the same as holding a zero-coupon bond with a maturity that is the same as that investment horizon. (A zero-coupon bond has no reinvestment risk, so future interest rates over the investment horizon do not affect the return.) This variant is called the *return-to-maturity expectations* interpretation.

For example, let's once again assume that an investor has a five-year investment horizon. By buying a five-year zero-coupon bond and holding it to maturity, the investor's return is the difference between the maturity value and the price of the bond, all divided by the price of the bond. According to return-to-maturity expectations, the same return will be realized by buying a six-month instrument and rolling it over for five years. At this time, the validity of this interpretation is subject to considerable doubt.

The Liquidity Theory

We have explained that the drawback of the pure expectations theory is that it does not consider the risks associated with investing in bonds. Nonetheless, we have just shown that there is indeed risk in holding a long-term bond for one period, and that risk increases with the bond's maturity because maturity and price volatility are directly related.

Given this uncertainty, and the reasonable consideration that investors typically do not like uncertainty, some economists and financial analysts have suggested a different theory. This theory states that investors will hold longer-term maturities if they are offered a long-term rate higher than the average of expected future rates by a risk premium that is positively related to the term to maturity.[8] Put differently, the forward rates should reflect both interest rate expectations and a "liquidity" premium (really a risk premium), and the premium should be higher for longer maturities.

According to this theory, which is called the **liquidity theory of the term structure**, the implicit forward rates will not be an unbiased estimate of the market's expectations of future interest rates because they embody a liquidity premium. Thus, an upward-sloping yield curve may reflect expectations that future interest rates either (1) will rise, or (2) will be flat or even fall, but with a liquidity premium increasing fast enough with maturity so as to produce an upward-sloping yield curve.

The Preferred Habitat Theory

Another theory, known as the **preferred habitat theory**, also adopts the view that the term structure reflects the expectation of the future path of interest rates as well as a risk premium. However, the habitat theory rejects the assertion that the risk premium must rise uniformly with maturity.[9] Proponents of the habitat theory say that the latter conclusion could be accepted if all investors intend to liquidate their investment at the first possible date, while all borrowers are eager to borrow long, but that this is an assumption that can be rejected for a number of reasons.

In the first place, it is obvious that many investors wish to carry resources forward for appreciable periods of time—to buy a house, for example, or to provide for retirement. Such investors are concerned with the amount available at the appropriate

---

[7] Ibid.

[8] John R. Hicks, *Value and Capital*, 2nd ed. (London: Oxford University Press, 1946), pp. 141–145.

[9] Franco Modigliani and Richard Sutch, "Innovations in Interest Rate Policy," *American Economic Review* (May 1966), pp. 178–197.

time, and not the path by which that goal is reached. Hence, risk aversion dictates that they should prefer an instrument with a maturity matching the period for which they wish to invest over shorter-term investment vehicles. If these investors buy a shorter instrument, they will bear reinvestment risk—the risk of a fall in the interest rates available for reinvesting proceeds of the shorter instrument. Investors can avoid that risk only by locking in the current long rate through a long-term contract. Similarly, if they buy an instrument with maturity longer than the time they wish to invest for, they will bear the risk of a loss in the price of the asset (price risk) when liquidating it before its maturity, because of a rise in interest rates. Entirely analogous considerations apply to borrowers; prudence and safety call for borrowing for a maturity by matching the length of time for which funds are required.

In the second place, a lot of the demand for and supply of securities these days comes from financial intermediaries, which have liabilities with specified maturities, as we explained in Chapters 2, 4, 7, and 9. These institutions seek to match as closely as possible the maturity of their liabilities with the cash flow of a portfolio of assets. In constructing such a portfolio, a financial institution will restrict its investments to certain maturity sectors.

To illustrate this preference for maturity sectors, consider a life insurance company that has issued a five-year guaranteed investment contract.[10] The insurance company will not want to invest in six-month instruments because of the associated reinvestment risk. As another example, assume a thrift has borrowed funds at a fixed rate for one year with the proceeds from the issuance of a one-year certificate of deposit. The thrift is exposed to price (or interest rate) risk if the borrowed funds are invested in a bond with 20 years to maturity. Clearly, then, either of these institutions faces some kind of risk if it invests outside its preferred maturity sector.

The preferred habitat theory asserts that, to the extent that the demand and supply of funds in a given maturity range does not match, some lenders and borrowers will be induced to shift to maturities showing the opposite imbalances. However, they will need to be compensated by an appropriate risk premium whose magnitude will reflect the extent of aversion to either price or reinvestment risk.

Thus, this theory proposes that the shape of the yield curve is determined by both expectations of future interest rates and a risk premium, positive or negative, to induce market participants to shift out of their preferred habitat. Clearly, according to this theory, yield curves sloping up, down, flat, or humped are all possible.

Market Segmentation Theory

The **market segmentation theory** also recognizes that investors have preferred habitats dictated by saving and investment flows. This theory also proposes that the major reason for the shape of the yield curve lies in asset/liability management constraints (either regulatory or self-imposed) and/or creditors (borrowers) restricting their lending (financing) to specific maturity sectors.[11] However, the market segmentation theory differs from the preferred habitat theory in that it assumes that neither investors nor borrowers are willing to shift from one maturity sector to another to take advantage of opportunities arising from differences between expectations and forward rates.

---

[10] See Chapter 7 for a discussion of guaranteed investment contracts.
[11] This theory was suggested in J. M. Culbertson, "The Term Structure of Interest Rates," *Quarterly Journal of Economics* (November 1957), pp. 489–504.

Thus, for the segmentation theory, the shape of the yield curve is determined by supply of and demand for securities within each maturity sector. This formulation seems untenable because it presupposes the prevalence of absolute risk aversion, while the evidence does not support that proposition. Thus, market participants must be expected to shift away from their habitat when there are sufficiently large discrepancies between market and expected rates. This potential shifting ensures that the differences between market and expected rates will not grow too large, and this consideration leads back to the preferred habitat theory.

Key Points That You Should Understand Before Proceeding

1. The different shapes that have been observed for the yield curve.
2. The common hypothesis about the behavior of short-term forward rates shared by the various forms of the expectations theory.
3. The implications of the shape of the yield curve for future interest rates based on the pure expectations theory.
4. The two types of risks associated with investing in bonds and how these two risks affect the pure expectations theory.
5. How the two biased expectations theories differ from the pure expectations theory.

SUMMARY

The relationship between yield and maturity is referred to as the term structure of interest rates. The graphical depiction of the relationship between the yield on bonds of the same credit quality but different maturities is known as the yield curve. Since historically the yield on Treasury securities is the base rate off which a non-government bond's yield often is benchmarked, the most commonly constructed yield curve is the Treasury yield curve.

There is a problem with using the Treasury yield curve to determine the one yield at which to discount all the cash payments of any bond. Each cash flow within a bond's total pattern of cash flows should be discounted at a unique interest rate that is applicable to the time period when the cash flow is to be received. Since any bond can be viewed as a package of zero-coupon instruments, its value should equal the value of all the component zero-coupon instruments. The rate on a zero-coupon bond is called the spot rate. The theoretical spot rate curve for Treasury securities can be estimated from the Treasury yield curve using a methodology known as bootstrapping.

Under certain assumptions, the market's expectation of future interest rates can be extrapo-lated from the theoretical Treasury spot rate curve. The resulting forward rate is called the implicit forward rate. The spot rate is related to the current six-month spot rate and the implicit six-month forward rates. A knowledge of the forward rates implicit in the current long-term rate is relevant in formulating both investment strategies and borrowing policies.

Several theories have been proposed about the determination of the term structure. The pure expectations theory hypothesizes that the one-period forward rates simply represent the market's expectations of future actual rates. Thus, the long-term spot rate would itself be explained fully by the market expectations of future short rates. The term structure might then be rising, falling, or flat, according to whether the market expects rising, falling, or unchanged short-term rates. This formulation fails to recognize the risks associated with investing in bonds—price risk and reinvestment risk—when investors buy bonds whose maturity is different from the time for which they plan to hold the bond.

The fact that there is price risk in investing in long-term bonds, and that it seems to increase with maturity, has given rise to an alternative liquidity theory of the term structure. According to this theory, forward rates are the sum of expected future rates and a risk premium that increases for more and more distant future rates and, hence, rises with the maturity of a bond. This formulation has shortcomings because it presupposes that all lenders want to lend short and all borrowers want to borrow long. If so, long borrowers would have to offer lenders a premium, rising with maturity, to accept the risk of going long. But in reality both lenders and borrowers have quite varied maturity preferences. Each market participant can eliminate risk, not by borrowing or lending short, but by lending (or borrowing) for a period coinciding with their preferred habitat. But, at the same time, agents would presumably be willing to depart from their preferred habitat by the inducement of a risk premium.

Accordingly, the third version of the expectations theory—namely, the preferred habitat theory—suggests, like the liquidity theory, that forward rates are the sum of a component reflecting expected future rates and a risk premium. However, the premium will not rise continuously with maturity but will materialize in any maturity neighborhood where supply exceeds demand. A negative premium or discount would be expected if supply exceeds demand.

One final theory explains the shape of the term structure by the concept of market segmentation. In common with the preferred habitat theory, it recognizes that participants in the bond market have maturity preferences. However, it postulates that these preferences are absolute and cannot be overcome by the expectation of a higher return from a different maturity, no matter how large. Each maturity is therefore a separate market, and the interest rate in every such market is determined by the given demand and supply. Thus, the interest rate at any maturity is totally unrelated to expectations of future rates. This formulation is of doubtful use because it implies highly irrational, implausible, and counterfactual behavior.

KEY TERMS

- **Bootstrapping, 220**
- **Forward rate (also called implied forward rate), 227**
- **Liquidity theory, 234**
- **Market segmentation theory, 235**
- **Preferred habitat theory, 234**
- **Price risk, 233**

- **Pure expectations theory, 230**
- **Reinvestment risk, 233**
- **Spot rate, 220**
- **Spot rate curve, 220**
- **Term structure, 218**
- **Yield curve, 218**
- **Zero-coupon instrument, 220**

QUESTIONS

1. a. What is a yield curve?
   b. Historically, why has the Treasury yield curve been the one that is most closely watched by market participants?
2. What is meant by a spot rate?
3. Explain why it is inappropriate to use one yield to discount all the cash flows of a financial asset.
4. Explain why a financial asset can be viewed as a package of zero-coupon instruments.
5. Why is it important for lenders and borrowers to have a knowledge of forward rates?
6. How are spot rates related to forward rates?
7. You are a financial consultant. At various times you have heard the following comments on interest rates from one of your clients. How would you respond to each comment?
   a. "The yield curve is upward sloping today. This suggests that the market consensus is that interest rates are expected to increase in the future."
   b. "I can't make any sense out of today's term structure. For short-term yields (up to three years), the spot rates increase with maturity; for maturities greater than three years but less than eight years, the spot rates decline with

maturity; and for maturities greater than eight years the spot rates are virtually the same for each maturity. There is simply no theory that explains a term structure with this shape."

c. "When I want to determine the market's consensus of future interest rates, I calculate the implicit forward rates."

8. You observe the Treasury yield curve below (all yields are shown on a bond-equivalent basis):

Year	Yield to maturity	Spot rate
0.5	5.25%	5.25%
1.0	5.50	5.50
1.5	5.75	5.76
2.0	6.00	?
2.5	6.25	?
3.0	6.50	?
3.5	6.75	?
4.0	7.00	?
4.5	7.25	?
5.0	7.50	?
5.5	7.75	7.97
6.0	8.00	8.27
6.5	8.25	8.59
7.0	8.50	8.92
7.5	8.75	9.25
8.0	9.00	9.61
8.5	9.25	9.97
9.0	9.50	10.36
9.5	9.75	10.77
10.0	10.00	11.20

All the securities maturing from 1.5 years on are selling at par. The 0.5-year and 1-year securities are zero-coupon instruments.

a. Calculate the missing spot rates.

b. What should the price of the six-year Treasury security be?

c. What is the implicit six-month forward rate starting in the sixth year?

9. You observe the following Treasury yield curve (all yields are shown on a bond-equivalent basis):

Year	Yield to maturity	Spot rate
0.5	10.00%	10.00%
1.0	9.75	9.75
1.5	9.50	9.48
2.0	9.25	9.22
2.5	9.00	8.95
3.0	8.75	8.68
3.5	8.50	8.41
4.0	8.25	8.14
4.5	8.00	7.86
5.0	7.75	7.58
5.5	7.50	7.30
6.0	7.25	7.02

6.5	7.00	6.74
7.0	6.75	6.46
7.5	6.50	6.18
8.0	6.25	5.90
8.5	6.00	5.62
9.0	5.75	5.35
9.5	5.50	?
10.0	5.25	?

All the securities maturing from 1.5 years on are selling at par. The 0.5-year and 1-year securities are zero-coupon instruments.

  a. Calculate the missing spot rates.

  b. What should the price of the four-year Treasury security be?

10. Using the theoretical spot rates in Table 12-2, calculate the theoretical value of a 7%, six-year Treasury bond.

11. a. Using the theoretical spot rates in Table 12-2, calculate the two-year forward rate four years from now.

    b. Verify the answer by assuming an investment of $100 is invested for six years.

12. Explain the role that forward rates play in making investment decisions.

13. "Forward rates are poor predictors of the actual future rates that are realized. Consequently, they are of little value to an investor." Explain why you agree or disagree with this statement.

14. An investor is considering two alternative investments. The first alternative is to invest in an instrument that matures in two years. The second alternative is to invest in an instrument that matures in one year and at the end of one year, reinvest the proceeds in a one-year instrument. The investor believes that one-year interest rates one year from now will be higher than they are today and, therefore, is leaning in favor of the second alternative. What would you recommend to this investor?

15. What is the common hypothesis about the behavior of short-term forward rates shared by the various forms of the expectations theory?

16. What are the types of risks associated with investing in bonds and how do these two risks affect the pure expectations theory?

17. Give three interpretations of the pure expectations theory.

18. What are the two biased expectations theories about the term structure of interest rates?

19. What are the underlying hypotheses of the two biased expectations theories of interest rates?

Risk/Return and Asset Pricing Models

Learning Objectives

After reading this chapter, you will understand

- the fundamental principles of portfolio theory.
- how to calculate the historical single-period investment return for a security or portfolio of securities.
- how to calculate the expected return and variability of expected return of a portfolio.
- the components of a portfolio's total risk: systematic risk and unsystematic risk.
- what the beta of a stock measures.
- why diversification eliminates unsystematic risk.
- the capital asset pricing model, the relevant measure of risk in this model, and the limitations of the model.
- the development of the multifactor capital asset pricing model.
- the empirical difficulties of testing the capital asset pricing model.
- the fundamental principles underlying the arbitrage pricing theory model.
- the empirical difficulties of testing the arbitrage pricing theory model.

Portfolio theory deals with the selection of optimal portfolios by rational risk-averse investors—that is, by investors who attempt to maximize their expected portfolio returns consistent with individually acceptable levels of portfolio risk. Capital markets theory deals with the implications for security prices of the decisions made by these investors—that is, the relationship that should exist between security returns and risk if investors behave in this optimal fashion. Together, portfolio and capital markets theories provide a framework to specify and measure investment risk and to develop relationships between expected security return and risk (and hence between risk and required return on investment).

The purpose of this chapter is to introduce portfolio and capital markets theories. We begin with the basic concepts of portfolio theory and then build upon these concepts to develop the theoretical relationship between the expected return on a security and risk. Because the risk and return relationship indicates how much expected return a security should generate, given its relevant risks, it also tells us how assets should be priced. Hence, the risk and return relationship is also referred to as an asset pricing model.

The three asset pricing models that we present in this chapter are those that dominate financial thinking today: the capital asset pricing model, the multifactor capital asset pricing model, and the arbitrage pricing theory model. Our focus is on the key elements underlying portfolio theory and asset pricing theory. We do not attempt to provide a rigorous mathematical presentation of these theories.

PORTFOLIO THEORY

In designing a portfolio, investors seek to maximize the expected return from their investment, given some level of risk they are willing to accept.[1] Portfolios that satisfy this requirement are called **efficient (or optimal) portfolios**.[2] To construct an efficient portfolio, it is necessary to understand what is meant by **expected return** and risk. The latter concept, risk, could mean any one of the many types of risk that we have referred to in earlier chapters in this book. We shall be more specific about its meaning as we proceed in the development of portfolio theory. We begin our exploration of portfolio theory with the concept of investment return.

Investment Return

The return on an investor's portfolio during a given interval is equal to the change in value of the portfolio plus any distributions received from the portfolio, expressed as a fraction of the initial portfolio value. It is important that any capital or income distributions made to the investor be included, or the measure of return will be deficient. Another way to look at return is as the amount (expressed as a fraction of the initial portfolio value) that can be withdrawn at the end of the interval while maintaining the principal intact. The return on the investor's portfolio, designated R_p, is given by

$$R_p = \frac{V_1 - V_0 + D_1}{V_0} \tag{1}$$

where V_1 = the portfolio market value at the end of the interval
V_0 = the portfolio market value at the beginning of the interval
D_1 = the cash distributions to the investor during the interval

The calculation assumes that any interest or dividend income received on the portfolio of securities and not distributed to the investor is reinvested in the portfolio (and thus reflected in V_1). Furthermore, the calculation assumes that any distributions occur at the end of the interval, or are held in the form of cash until the end of the interval. If the distributions were reinvested prior to the end of the interval, the calculation would have to be modified to consider the gains or losses on the amount reinvested. The formula also assumes no capital inflows during the interval. Otherwise, the calculation would have to be modified to reflect the increased investment base. Capital inflows at the end of the interval (or held in cash until the

---

[1] Alternatively stated, investors seek to minimize the risk to which they are exposed, given some target expected return.
[2] The theoretical framework for selecting efficient portfolios was developed in Harry M. Markowitz, "Portfolio Selection," *Journal of Finance* (March 1952), pp. 71–91, and *Portfolio Selection: Efficient Diversification of Investments* (New York: John Wiley & Sons, Inc., 1959).

end), however, can be treated as just the reverse of distributions in the return calculation.

Thus, given the beginning and ending portfolio values, plus any contributions from or distributions to the investor (assumed to occur at the end of an interval), equation (1) lets us compute the investor's return. For example, if the XYZ pension fund had a market value of $100,000 at the end of June, a distribution of $5,000 made at the end of July, and an end-of-July market value of $103,000, the return for the month would be 8%:

$$R_p = \frac{103,000 - 100,000 + 5,000}{100,000} = 0.08$$

In principle, this sort of calculation of returns could be carried out for any interval of time, say, for one month or 10 years. Yet there are several problems with this approach. First, it is apparent that a calculation made over a long period of time, say, more than a few months, would not be very reliable because of the underlying assumption that all cash payments and inflows are made and received at the end of the period. Clearly, if two investments have the same return as calculated from the formula above, but one investment makes a cash payment early and the other late, the one with early payment will be understated. Second, we cannot rely on the formula to compare return on a one-month investment with that on a 10-year return portfolio. For purposes of comparison, the return must be expressed per unit of time—say, per year.

In practice, we handle these two problems by first computing the return over a reasonably short unit of time, perhaps a quarter of a year or less. The return over the relevant horizon, consisting of several unit periods, is computed by averaging the return over the unit intervals.[3]

Portfolio Risk

The definition of investment risk leads us into less explored territory. Not everyone agrees on how to define risk, let alone measure it. Nevertheless, there are some attributes of risk that are reasonably well accepted.

An investor holding a portfolio of Treasury bills until the maturity date faces no uncertainty about monetary outcome. The value of the portfolio at maturity of the securities will be identical with the predicted value; the investor bears no monetary risk. In the case of a portfolio composed of common stocks, however, it will be impossible to predict the value of the portfolio at any future date. The best an investor can do is to make a best-guess or most-likely estimate, qualified by statements about the range and likelihood of other values. In this case, the investor does bear risk.

One measure of risk is the extent to which possible future portfolio values are likely to diverge from the expected or predicted value. More specifically, risk for most

---

[3] There are three generally used methods of averaging: (1) the arithmetic average return, (2) the time-weighted rate of return (also referred to as the geometric rate of return), and (3) the dollar-weighted return. The averaging yields a measure of return per unit of time period. The measure can be converted to an annual or other period yield by standard procedures. For an explanation of these three methods of averaging, see Franco Modigliani and Gerald A. Pogue, "Risk, Return, and CAPM: Concepts and Evidence," Chapter 37 in Summer N. Levine (ed.), *The Financial Analysts Handbook* (Homewood, IL: Dow Jones-Irwin, 1988).

investors is related to the chance that future portfolio values will be less than expected. That is, if the investor's portfolio has a current value of $100,000, and an expected value of $110,000 at the end of the next year, what matters is the probability of values less than $110,000.

Before proceeding to the quantification of risk, it is convenient to shift our attention from the terminal value of the portfolio to the portfolio rate of return, R_p, because the increase in portfolio value is related directly to R_p.

Expected Portfolio Return.

A particularly useful way to quantify the uncertainty about the portfolio return is to specify the probability associated with each of the possible future returns. Assume, for example, that an investor has identified five possible outcomes for the portfolio return during the next year. Associated with each return is a subjectively determined probability, or relative chance of occurrence. The five possible outcomes are:

Outcome	Possible return	Subjective probability
1	50%	0.1
2	30	0.2
3	10	0.4
4	−10	0.2
5	−30	0.1

Note that the probabilities sum to 1 so that the actual portfolio return is confined to one of the five possible values. Given this **probability distribution**, we can measure the expected return and risk for the portfolio.

The expected return is simply the weighted average of possible outcomes, where the weights are the relative chances of occurrence. In general, the expected return on the portfolio, denoted $E(R_p)$, is given by

$$E(R_p) = P_1 R_1 + P_2 R_2 + \cdots + R_n P_n \tag{2}$$

or

$$E(R_p) = \sum_{j=1}^{n} P_j R_j$$

where the R_js are the possible returns, the P_js the associated probabilities, and n is the number of possible outcomes.

The expected return of the portfolio in our illustration is:

$$E(R_p) = 0.1(50.0) + 0.2(30.0) + 0.4(10.0) + 0.2(-10.0) + 0.1(-30.0)$$
$$= 10\%$$

Variability of Expected Return

If risk is defined as the chance of achieving returns lower than expected, it would seem logical to measure risk by the dispersion of the possible returns below the expected value. Risk measures based on below-the-mean variability are difficult to work with, however, and moreover are unnecessary as long as the distribution of future return is

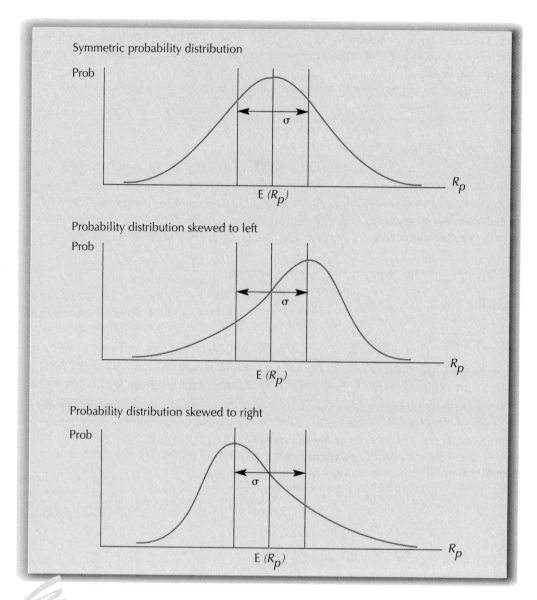

Figure 13-1   Possible Shapes for Probability Distributions

reasonably symmetric about the expected value. Figure 13-1 shows three probability distributions: the first symmetric, the second skewed to the left, and the third skewed to the right. For a **symmetrical distribution**, the dispersion of returns on one side of the expected return is the same as the dispersion on the other side of the expected return.

Empirical studies of realized rates of return on diversified common stock portfolios show that **skewness** is not a significant problem.[4] If future distributions are shaped like historical distributions, it makes little difference whether we measure variability of

---

[4] For example, see Marshall E. Blume, "Portfolio Theory: A Step Toward Its Practical Application," *Journal of Business* (April 1970), pp. 152–173.

returns on one or both sides of the expected return. If the probability distribution is symmetric, measures of the total variability of return will be twice as large as measures of the portfolio's variability below the expected return. Thus, if total variability is used as a risk surrogate, the risk ranking for a group of portfolios will be the same as when variability below the expected return is used. It is for this reason that total variability of returns has been used so widely as a surrogate for risk.

It now remains to choose a specific measure of total variability of returns. The most commonly used measures are the **variance** and **standard deviation** of returns.

The variance of return is a weighted sum of the squared deviations from the expected return. Squaring the deviations ensures that deviations above and below the expected value contribute equally to the measure of variability regardless of sign. The variance for the portfolio, designated σ_p^2, is given by

$$\sigma_p^2 = P_1[R_1 - E(R_p)]^2 + P_2[R_2 - E(R_p)]^2 \\ + \cdots + P_n[R_n - E(R_p)]^2$$

or

$$\sigma_p^2 = \sum_{j=1}^{n} P_j[R_j - E(R_p)]^2 \tag{3}$$

In the previous example, the variance for the portfolio is

$$\sigma_p^2 = 0.1(50.0 - 10.0)^2 + 0.2(30.0 - 10.0)^2 \\ + 0.4(10.0 - 10.0)^2 + 0.2(-10.0 - 10.0)^2 \\ + 0.1(-30.0 - 10.0)^2 \\ = 480\% \text{ squared}$$

The standard deviation (σ_p) is defined as the square root of the variance. It is equal to 22% in our example. The larger the variance or standard deviation, the greater the possible dispersion of future realized values around the expected value, and the larger the investor's uncertainty. As a rule of thumb for symmetric distributions, it is often suggested that roughly two-thirds of the possible returns will lie within one standard deviation on either side of the expected value, and that 95% will be within two standard deviations of the expected value.

A final remark before leaving portfolio risk measures. We have assumed implicitly that investors are *risk averse*; that is, they seek to minimize risk for a given level of return. This assumption appears to be valid for most investors in most situations. The entire theory of portfolio selection and capital asset pricing rests on the assumption that investors on the average are risk averse.

Diversification

Empirically, a comparison of the distribution of historical returns for a large portfolio of randomly selected stocks (say, 50 stocks) with the distribution of historical returns for an individual stock in the portfolio has indicated a curious relationship. It is not uncommon to find that (1) the standard deviation of return for the individual stocks in the portfolio is considerably larger than that of the portfolio, and (2) the average return of an individual stock is less than the portfolio return. Is the market so imperfect that it tends to reward substantially higher risk with lower stock return?

Not so. The answer lies in the fact that not all of an individual stock's risk is relevant. Much of the **total risk** (which equals standard deviation of return) is **diversifiable**. That is, if an investment in an individual stock is combined with other securities, a portion of the variation in its returns could be smoothed or canceled by complementary variation in the other securities. The same portfolio diversification effect accounts for the low standard deviation of return for a large stock portfolio. In fact, the portfolio standard deviation is lower than that of the typical security in the portfolio. Much of the total risk of the component securities has been eliminated by diversification. As long as much of the total risk can be eliminated simply by holding a stock in a portfolio, there is no economic requirement for the anticipated return to be in line with the total risk. Instead, we should expect realized returns to be related to that portion of security risk that cannot be eliminated by portfolio combination—so-called **systematic risk**. (We will have more to say on risk/return relationships later in this chapter.)

Diversification results from combining securities whose returns are less than perfectly correlated in order to reduce portfolio risk. The portfolio return is simply a weighted average of the individual security returns, no matter the number of securities in the portfolio. Therefore, diversification will not systematically affect the portfolio return, but it will reduce the variability (standard deviation) of return. In general, the less the **correlation** among security returns, the greater the impact of diversification on reducing variability. This is true no matter how risky the securities of the portfolio are when considered in isolation.

Theoretically, if we could find sufficient securities with uncorrelated returns, we could eliminate portfolio risk completely. Unfortunately, this situation is not typical in real financial markets, where returns are positively correlated to a considerable degree because they tend to respond to the same set of influences (for example, to business cycles and interest rates). Thus, while portfolio risk can be reduced substantially by diversification, it cannot be eliminated entirely.

This has been demonstrated very clearly by Wayne Wagner and Sheila Lau, who measured the standard deviations of randomly selected portfolios including various numbers of New York Stock Exchange (NYSE) securities.[5] Their study shows that the average return and the standard deviation for portfolios from the average return is unrelated to the number of issues in the portfolio. Yet the standard deviation of return declines as the number of holdings increases. On the average, Wagner and Lau find that approximately 40% of the risk of an individual common stock is eliminated by forming randomly selected portfolios of 20 stocks. They also find (1) additional diversification yields rapidly diminishing reduction in risk, with the improvement only slight when the number of securities held is increased beyond, say, 10, and (2) a rapid decline in total portfolio risk as the portfolios were expanded from 1 to 10 securities.

Another key finding of the Wagner-Lau study was that the return on a diversified portfolio follows the market very closely. The degree of association is measured by the correlation coefficient of each portfolio with an unweighted index of NYSE stocks. Two securities with perfectly correlated patterns will have a correlation coefficient of 1.0. Conversely, if the return patterns are perfectly negatively correlated, the correlation coefficient will equal −1.0. Two securities with uncorrelated (that is, statistically unrelated) returns will have a correlation coefficient of zero. The 20-security portfolio in the Wagner-Lau study had a correlation of 0.89 with the market. The implication is that the risk remaining in the 20-stock portfolio is predominantly a reflection of uncertainty about the performance of the stock market in general.

---

[5] Wayne H. Wagner and Sheila Lau, "The Effect of Diversification on Risk," *Financial Analysts Journal* (November–December 1971), pp. 2–7.

These results of the Wagner-Lau study show that, while some risks can be eliminated through diversification, others cannot. Thus, we are led to distinguish between a security's **unsystematic risk**, which can be washed away by mixing the security with other securities in a diversified portfolio, and its *systematic risk*, which cannot be eliminated by diversification. As the Wagner-Lau study shows, total portfolio risk declines as the number of holdings increases. Increasing diversification gradually tends to eliminate the unsystematic risk, leaving only systematic, that is, market-related risk. The remaining variability results from the fact that the return on nearly every security depends to some degree on the overall performance of the market. This is illustrated in Figure 13-2. Consequently, the return on a well-diversified portfolio is highly correlated with the market, and its variability or uncertainty is basically the uncertainty of the market as a whole. Investors are exposed to market uncertainty no matter how many stocks they hold.

The Risk of Individual Securities

From the empirical evidence we have cited, we can conclude that the systematic risk of an individual security is that portion of its total risk (which, again, is the same as standard deviation of return) that cannot be eliminated by combining it with other securities in a well-diversified portfolio. We now need a way of quantifying the systematic risk of a security and relating the systematic risk of a portfolio to that of its component securities. This can be accomplished by dividing a security's return into two parts: one perfectly correlated with and proportionate to the market return, and a second inde-

Figure 13-2   Systematic and Unsystematic Risk

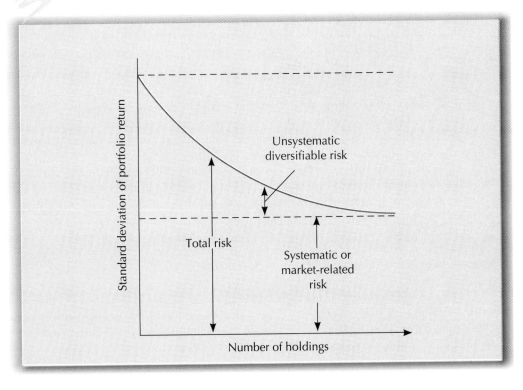

pendent from (uncorrelated with) the market. The first component of return is usually referred to as *systematic*, the second as *unsystematic*. Thus, we have

$$\text{Security return} = \text{Systematic return} + \text{Unsystematic return} \qquad (4)$$

As the systematic return is proportional to the market return, it can be expressed as the symbol **beta** (or β) times the market return, R_m. The proportionality factor of beta is a market sensitivity index, indicating how sensitive the security return is to changes in the market level. (How to estimate beta for a security or portfolio is discussed later.) The unsystematic return, which is independent of market returns, is usually represented by the symbol *epsilon* (ϵ'). Thus, the security return, R, may be expressed

$$R = \beta R_m + \epsilon' \qquad (5)$$

For example, if a security has a β factor of 2.0, then a 10% market return will generate a 20% systematic return for the stock. The security return for the period would be the 20% plus the unsystematic component.

The unsystematic component in equation (5) depends on factors that are unique or specific to the company that issued the security, such as labor difficulties, unexpectedly high or low sales, managerial issues, and so on. Thus, the unsystematic component is not linked to the overall market or economic system. It is important to note that a security's return variability that is due to this unsystematic component is diversifiable precisely because that variability represents events or situations that are specific (or unique) to the firm that issued the security. If a portfolio contains many securities issued by many companies, then events that are specific to any firm and affect that firm's returns can readily be offset by contrary or opposite developments that are unique to other firms and that influence their returns in different ways.

The security returns model given by equation (5) is usually written in such a way that the average value of the residual term, ϵ', is zero. This is accomplished by adding a factor, **alpha** (α), to the model to represent the average value of the unsystematic returns over time. That is, we set $\epsilon' = \alpha + \epsilon$ so that

$$R = \alpha + \beta R_m + \epsilon \qquad (6)$$

where the average ϵ over time should tend to zero. The reason the average value of the term is zero is that the term represents the eventual impact of unexpected events that are particular to the firm. If those events are random and unpredictable, their overall impact should be zero.

The model for security returns given by equation (6) is usually referred to as the **market model**.[6] Graphically, the model can be depicted as a line fitted to a plot of security returns against rates of return on the market index. This kind of line fitting is shown for a hypothetical security in Figure 13-3.

The beta factor can be thought of as the slope of the line. It gives the expected increase in security return for a 1% increase in market return. In Figure 13-3, the security has a beta of 1.0. Thus, a 10% market return will result, on the average, in a 10% security return.

The alpha factor is represented by the intercept of the line on the vertical security return axis. It is equal to the average value over time of the unsystematic returns (ϵ') on the stock. For most stocks, the alpha factor tends to be small and unstable.

---

[6] It is also referred to as the *single-index market model* and the *characteristic line*.

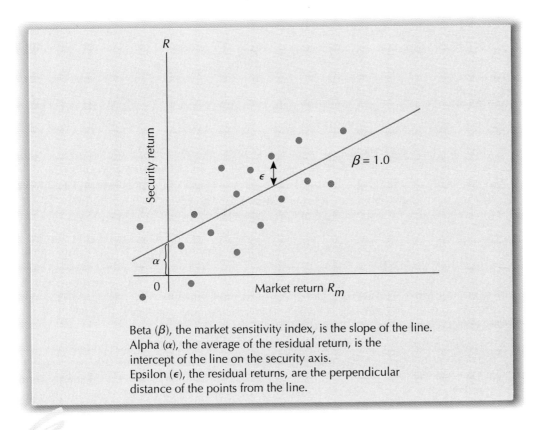

Beta (β), the market sensitivity index, is the slope of the line.
Alpha (α), the average of the residual return, is the
intercept of the line on the security axis.
Epsilon (ϵ), the residual returns, are the perpendicular
distance of the points from the line.

Figure 13-3   The Market Model for Security Returns

Using this definition of security return given by the market model, the specification of systematic and unsystematic risk is simply the standard deviations of the two return components.

The systematic risk of a security is equal to β times the standard deviation of the market return:

$$\text{Systematic risk} = \beta\sigma_m \tag{7}$$

The unsystematic risk equals the standard deviation of the residual return factor ϵ, or

$$\text{Unsystematic risk} = \sigma_\epsilon \tag{8}$$

Given measures of individual-security systematic risk, we can now compute the systematic risk of the portfolio. It is equal to the beta factor for the portfolio, β_p, times the risk of the market index, σ_m:

$$\text{Portfolio systematic risk} = \beta_p\sigma_m \tag{9}$$

The portfolio beta factor in turn can be shown to be simply an average of the individual security betas, weighted by the proportion of each security in the portfolio, or

$$\beta_p = X_1\beta_1 + X_2\beta_2 + \cdots + X_n\beta_n$$

or more concisely as

$$\beta_p = \sum_{i=1}^{n} X_i \beta_i \qquad (10)$$

where X_i = the proportion of portfolio market value represented by security i
          n = the number of securities

Thus, the systematic risk of a portfolio is simply the market value-weighted average of the systematic risk of the individual securities. It follows that the β for a portfolio consisting of all stocks is 1. If a stock's β exceeds 1, it is above the average; if its beta is below 1, it is below the average. If the portfolio is composed of an equal dollar investment in each stock, the β_p is simply an unweighted average of the component security betas.

The unsystematic risk of the portfolio is also a function of the unsystematic security risks, but the form is more complex. The important point is that, with increasing diversification, this risk approaches zero.

To summarize these results, first, roughly 40% to 50% of total security risk can be eliminated by diversification. Second, the remaining systematic risk is equal to the security β times market risk. Third, portfolio systematic risk is a weighted average of security systematic risks.

The implications of these results are substantial. First, we would expect realized rates of return over substantial periods of time to be related to the systematic as opposed to the total risk of securities. As the unsystematic risk is relatively easily eliminated, we should not expect the market to offer investors a risk premium for bearing such risk. Second, because security systematic risk is equal to the security beta times σ_m (which is common to all securities), beta is useful as a *relative* risk measure. The β gives the systematic risk of a security (or portfolio) relative to the risk of the market index. Thus, it is often convenient to speak of systematic risk in relative terms, that is, in terms of beta rather than beta times σ_m.

Estimating Beta

The beta of a security or portfolio can be estimated using statistical analysis. More specifically, we use regression analysis on historical data to estimate the market model given by equation (6). The estimated slope for the market model is the estimate of beta. A series of returns is computed according to equation (1) over some time interval for some broad market index (such as the S&P 500 stock market index) and for the stock (or portfolio). For example, monthly returns can be calculated for the past five years; thus, there would be 60 return observations for both the market index and the stock or portfolio. Or, weekly returns can be calculated for the past year.

There is nothing in portfolio theory that indicates whether weekly, monthly, or even daily returns should be used. Nor does theory indicate any specific number of observations, except that statistical methodology entails that more observations will give a more reliable measure of beta.[7] Our purpose here is not to provide an explanation of the mechanics of calculating beta but to point out the practical problems in obtaining beta. (There are many statistical issues also, but we do not focus on these.)

There will be a difference in the calculated beta depending on: (1) the length of time over which a return is calculated (e.g., daily, weekly, monthly); (2) the number of observations used (e.g., three years of monthly returns or five years of

---

[7] This assumes that the economic determinants that affect the beta of a stock do not change over the measurement period.

monthly returns); (3) the specific time period used (January 1, 1996 to December 31, 2000, for example, or January 1, 1995 to December 31, 1999); and (4) the market index selected (for instance, the S&P 500 stock market index or an index consisting of all stocks traded on exchanges weighted by their relative market value). Moreover, there is the question of the stability of beta over different time intervals—that is, does the beta of a stock or portfolio remain relatively unchanged over time, or does it change?

A very interesting question has to do with the economic determinants of the beta of a stock. The risk characteristics of a company should be reflected in its beta. Several empirical studies have attempted to identify these macroeconomic and microeconomic factors.

Key Points That You Should Understand Before Proceeding

1. Risk aversion means that investors want to minimize risk for any given level of expected return, or want to maximize return, for any given level of risk.
2. Risk is the likelihood that an actual return will deviate from the expected return.
3. Investors hold diversified portfolios rather than individual securities because portfolios eliminate some of the risk of most securities.
4. The relevant risk of any individual security is not total variability in returns but rather systematic variability, which is that portion of total variability that cannot be eliminated by combining it with other securities in a diversified portfolio.
5. The market model is the hypothesis that a security's return may be attributed to two forces, the returns on securities in general or the market, and events related to the firm itself.
6. The index of the sensitivity of a security's returns to movement in the market is the security's beta, which can be estimated with regression techniques from historical data.

THE CAPITAL ASSET PRICING MODEL

We have now developed two measures of risk: one is a measure of total risk (standard deviation), the other a relative index of systematic or nondiversifiable risk (beta). The beta measure would appear to be the more relevant for the pricing of securities. Returns expected by investors logically should be related to systematic as opposed to total risk. Securities with higher systematic risk should have higher expected returns.

The question of interest now is the form of the relationship between risk and return. In this section we describe a relationship called the **capital asset pricing model** (CAPM), which is based on elementary logic and simple economic principles.[8] The basic postulate underlying this finance theory is that assets with the same systematic risk should have the same expected rate of return; that is, the prices of assets in the capital markets should adjust until equivalent risk assets have identical expected returns. This principle is called the "law of one price".

To see the implications of this postulate, consider an investor who holds a risky portfolio that has the same risk as the market portfolio (beta equal to 1.0).[9] What return should she expect? Logically, she should expect the same return as that of the

---

[8] CAPM theory was developed by William F. Sharpe, "Capital Asset Prices: A Theory of Market Equilibrium Under Conditions of Risk," *Journal of Finance* (September 1964), pp. 425–442.

[9] We use the term *portfolio* in a general sense, including the case where the investor holds only one security. Because portfolio return and (systematic) risk are simply weighted averages of security values, risk/return relationships that hold for securities must also be true for portfolios, and vice versa.

market portfolio. Consider another investor who holds a riskless protfolio, or one with a beta equal to zero. In this case, the investor should expect to earn the rate of return on riskless assets, such as Treasury bills. In other words, the investor who takes no risk earns only the riskless rate of return.

Now, consider the case of an investor who holds a mixture of these two portfolios. Assume he invests a proportion X of his money in the risky portfolio and the rest, or $(1-X)$, in the riskless portfolio. What systematic risk does he bear, and what return should he expect? The risk of the composite portfolio is easily computed. Recall that the beta of a portfolio is simply a weighted average of the component security betas, where the weights are the portfolio proportions. Thus, the portfolio beta, β_p, is a weighted average of the beta of the market portfolio and that of the riskless portfolio. The market beta is 1.0, and the beta of the risk-free asset is 0. Thus,

$$\beta_p = (1 - X) \times 0 + X \times 1 \qquad (11)$$
$$= X$$

Thus, β_p is equal to the fraction of the money invested in the risky portfolio. If 100% or less of the investor's funds are invested in the risky portfolio, the portfolio beta will be between 0 and 1. If the investor borrows at the risk-free rate and invests the proceeds in the risky portfolio, so that X is larger than 1 and $(1-X)$ is negative, the portfolio beta will be greater than 1.

The expected return of the composite portfolio is also a weighted average of the expected returns on the two portfolios; that is,

$$E(R_p) = (1 - X) \times R_f + X \times E(R_m) \qquad (12)$$

where $E(R_p)$ and $E(R_m)$ are the expected returns on the portfolio and the market index, and R_f is the risk-free rate. Now, from equation (11) we know that X is equal to β_p. Substituting into equation (12), we have

$$E(R_p) = (1 - \beta_p) \times R_f + \beta_p \times E(R_m) \qquad (13)$$

or

$$E(R_p) = R_f + \beta_p \left[E(R_m) - R_f \right]$$

Equation (13) is the capital asset pricing model. This extremely important theoretical result says that the expected return on a portfolio should exceed the riskless rate of return by an amount that is proportional to the portfolio beta. That is, the relationship between expected return and risk should be linear.

The CAPM is often stated in risk premium form. Risk premiums or excess returns are obtained by subtracting the risk-free rate from the rate of return. The expected portfolio and market risk premiums—designated $E(r_p)$ and $E(r_m)$, respectively—are given by

$$E(r_p) = E(R_p) - R_f,$$

and

$$E(r_m) = E(R_m) - R_f$$

Substituting these risk premiums into equation (13), we obtain

$$E(r_p) = \beta_p E(r_m) \qquad (14)$$

In this form, the CAPM states that the expected risk premium for the investor's portfolio is equal to its beta value times the expected market risk premium. Or, equivalently stated, the expected risk premium should be equal to the *quantity of* risk (as measured by beta) and the *market price of risk* (as measured by the expected market risk premium).

We can illustrate the model by assuming that the short-term (risk-free) interest rate is 6% and the expected return on the market is 10%. The expected risk premium for holding the market portfolio is simply the difference between the 10% and the short-term interest rate of 6%, or 4%. Investors who hold the market portfolio expect to earn 10%, which is 4% greater than they could earn on a short-term market instrument for certain. In order to satisfy equation (13), the expected return on securities or portfolios with different levels of risk must be as follows:

Beta	Expected return
0.0	6%
0.5	8
1.0	10
1.5	12
2.0	14

The predictions of the model are inherently sensible. For safe investments ($\beta = 0$), the model predicts that investors would expect to earn the risk-free rate of interest. For a risky investment, ($\beta > 0$), investors would expect a rate of excess return proportional to the market sensitivity (or β) of the investment. Thus, stocks with lower-than-average market sensitivities would offer expected returns less than the expected market return. Stocks with above-average values of beta would offer expected returns in excess of the market.

Underlying Assumptions

In our development of the CAPM, we have implicitly made a number of assumptions that are required if the model is to be established on a rigorous basis. These assumptions involve investor behavior and conditions in the capital markets. The following assumptions are sufficient to allow a single derivation of the model:

1. The market is made up of risk-averse investors who measure risk in terms of standard deviation of portfolio return. This assumption provides a basis for the use of risk measures such as beta.

2. All investors have a common time horizon for investment decision making (for example, one month, one year, and so on). This assumption allows us to measure investor expectations over some common interval, thus making comparisons meaningful.

3. All investors are assumed to have the same expectations about future security returns and risks. The only reason why they choose different portfolios is differences in systematic risk and in risk preferences. Without this assumption, the analysis would become much more complicated.

4. Capital markets are perfect in the sense that all assets are completely divisible, there are no transactions costs or differential taxes, and borrowing and lending rates are equal to each other and the same for all investors. Without these conditions, there would exist frictional barriers to the equilibrium conditions on which the model is based.

Although these assumptions are sufficient to derive the model, it is not clear that all are necessary in this exact form. It may well be that several of the assumptions can be relaxed substantially without major change in the form of the model. A good deal of research has been conducted toward this end.

Tests of the Capital Asset Pricing Model

The CAPM is indeed a simple and elegant model, but these qualities do not in and of themselves guarantee that it will be useful in explaining observed risk/return patterns. Here we briefly review the empirical literature on attempts to verify the model.

The major difficulty in testing the CAPM is that the model is stated in terms of investors' expectations and not in terms of realized returns. To test the CAPM, it is necessary to convert the theoretical CAPM given by equation (14) into a form that can be tested empirically. We will not go through this exercise here, but will simply provide a general statement of the model that is typically tested.[10] Nor will we delve into the statistical problems associated with testing the CAPM, although we will discuss later an important theoretical issue that raises serious questions about the testability of the CAPM and therefore the empirical findings of researchers.

The empirical analogue of equation (14) asserts that, over the period of time analyzed, (1) there is a linear relationship between the average risk premium return on the market and the average risk premium return on a stock or portfolio, and its slope is β, and (2) the linear relationship should pass through the origin. Moreover, according to the CAPM, beta is a complete relative measure of a stock's risk. Consequently, various alternative risk measures that might be proposed, the most common being the standard deviation of return, should not be significant contributors to the explanation of a stock's return. Recall that the standard deviation measures a stock's total risk and includes both systematic and unsystematic components.

The CAPM theoretically applies to both individual securities and portfolios. Therefore, the empirical tests can be based on either. However, there are statistical problems associated with estimating the magnitude of the risk/return trade-off using individual securities. By grouping securities into portfolios, we can eliminate most of the statistical problems encountered for individual stocks and thereby get a much clearer view of the relationship between return and systematic risk.

The major results of the empirical tests conducted are summarized below:[11]

1. The evidence shows a significant positive relationship between realized returns and systematic risk as measured by beta. The average market risk premium estimated is usually less than that predicted by the CAPM, however.

2. The relationship between risk and return appears to be linear. The studies give no evidence of significant curvature in the risk/return relationship.

3. Tests that attempt to discriminate between the effects of systematic and unsystematic risk do not yield definitive results. Both kinds of risk appear to be positively related to security returns, but there is substantial support for the proposition that the relationship

---

[10] The interested reader can find the procedure for developing the empirical model tested in Franco Modigliani and Gerald A. Pogue, "Introduction to Risk and Return: Concepts and Evidence: Part II," *Financial Analysts Journal* (May–June 1974), pp. 69–86.

[11] Some of the earlier studies are Nancy Jacob, "The Measurement of Systematic Risk for Securities and Portfolios: Some Empirical Results," *Journal of Financial and Quantitative Analysis* (March 1971), pp. 815–834; Merton H. Miller and Myron S. Scholes, "Rates of Returns in Relation to Risk: A Reexamination of Recent Findings," and Fischer Black, Michael C. Jensen, and Myron S. Scholes, "The Capital Asset Pricing Model: Some Empirical Evidence," in Michael C. Jensen (ed.), *Studies in the Theory of Capital Markets* (New York: Praeger Books, 1972); Marshall E. Blume and Irwin Friend, "A New Look at the Capital Asset Pricing Model," *Journal of Finance* (March 1973), pp. 19–33; and Eugene F. Fama and James D. MacBeth, "Risk, Return and Equilibrium: Empirical Tests," Working Paper No. 7237, University of Chicago, Graduate School of Business, August 1972.

between return and unsystematic risk is at least partly spurious—that is, partly a reflection of statistical problems rather than the true nature of capital markets.

Obviously, we cannot claim that the CAPM is absolutely right. On the other hand, the early empirical tests do support the view that beta is a useful relative risk measure and that high-beta stocks tend to be priced so as to yield correspondingly high rates of return.

In 1977, however, Richard Roll wrote a paper criticizing previously published tests of the CAPM.[12] Roll argued that while the CAPM is testable in principle, no correct test of the theory had yet been presented. He also argued that there was practically no possibility that a correct test would ever be accomplished in the future.

The reasoning behind Roll's assertions is based on his observation that there is only one potentially testable hypothesis associated with the CAPM, namely, that the true market portfolio is mean-variance efficient. (This means that the market portfolio must have minimum risk for its level of return.) Furthermore, because the true market portfolio must contain all worldwide assets, the value of most of which cannot be observed (for example, human capital), the hypothesis is in all probability untestable.

Since 1977, there have been a number of studies that purport either to support or reject the CAPM. These tests have attempted to examine implications of the CAPM other than the linearity of the risk/return relation as the basis of their methodology. Unfortunately, none provides a definitive test, and most are subject to substantial criticism, suffering from the same problem of identifying the "true" market portfolio.

Key Points That You Should Understand Before Proceeding

1. The capital asset pricing model (or CAPM) hypothesizes that assets with the same level of systematic risk should experience the same level of returns.

2. The level of returns expected from any asset (which may be an individual security or a portfolio of securities) is a linear function of the risk-free rate, the asset's beta, and the returns expected on the market portfolio of risky assets.

3. Some reservations about the CAPM are inevitable because it makes many assumptions about investors' behavior and the structure of the market where assets are traded.

4. A major criticism of the CAPM is that it is basically untestable because the true or relevant market portfolio is an unobservable or unattainable portfolio diversified across all risky assets in the world.

THE MULTIFACTOR CAPM

The CAPM described above assumes that the only risk that an investor is concerned with is uncertainty about the future price of a security. Investors, however, usually are concerned with other risks that will affect their ability to consume goods and services in the future. Three examples would be the risks associated with future labor income, the future relative prices of consumer goods, and future investment opportunities.

Recognizing these other risks that investors face, Robert Merton has extended the CAPM to describe consumers deriving their optimal lifetime consumption when they face these **"extra-market" sources of risk**.[13] These extra-market sources of risk are

---

[12] Richard Roll, "A Critique of the Asset Pricing Theory: Part I. On the Past and Potential Testability of the Theory," *Journal of Financial Economics* (March 1977), pp. 129–176.

[13] Robert C. Merton, "An Intertemporal Capital Asset Pricing Model," *Econometrica* (September 1973), pp. 867–888.

also referred to as *factors*, so the model derived by Merton is called a *multifactor CAPM* and is given below in risk premium form:

$$E(r_p) = B_{pm} \ E(r_m) + B_{pF1} \ E(r_{F1}) + B_{pF2} \ E(r_{F2}) + \cdots + B_{pFK} \ E(r_{FK}) \tag{15}$$

where
$$K = \text{number of factors or extra-market sources of risk}$$
$$B_{pFk} = \text{the sensitivity of the portfolio to the } k\text{th factor}$$
$$E(r_{Fk}) = \text{the expected return of factor } k \text{ minus the risk-free rate}$$

The total extra-market sources of risk are equal to

$$B_{pF1} \ E(r_{F1}) + B_{pF2} \ E(r_{F2}) + \cdots + B_{pFK} \ E(r_{FK}) \tag{16}$$

Equation (15) says that investors want to be compensated for the risk associated with each source of extra-market risk, in addition to market risk. Note that, if there are no extra-market sources of risk, equation (15) reduces to the CAPM as given by equation (14). In the case of the CAPM, investors hedge the uncertainty associated with future security prices through diversification by holding the market portfolio, which can be thought of as a mutual fund that invests in all securities based on their relative capitalizations. In the multifactor CAPM, besides investing in the market portfolio, investors will also allocate funds to something equivalent to a mutual fund that hedges a particular extra-market risk. While not all investors are concerned with the same sources of extra-market risk, those that are concerned with a specific extra-market risk will basically hedge them in the same way.

As individual securities are nothing more than portfolios consisting of only one security, equation (15) must hold for each security, *i*. That is,

$$E(r_i) = B_{im} \ E(r_m) + B_{iF1} \ E(r_{F1}) + B_{iF2} \ E(r_{F2}) + \cdots + B_{iFK} \ E(r_{FK}) \tag{17}$$

From an empirical perspective, it may be difficult to identify the relevant extra-market risks. Moreover, it is difficult to distinguish the multifactor CAPM empirically from the next risk and return model described.

Key Points That You Should Understand Before Proceeding

1. The multifactor CAPM posits that extra-market factors influence expected returns on securities or portfolios.
2. This approach entails that a security's return has a beta like sensitivity to each factor.

ARBITRAGE PRICING THEORY MODEL

An alternative model to the CAPM and the multifactor CAPM was developed by Stephen Ross in 1976.[14] This model is based purely on arbitrage arguments, and hence is called the **Arbitrage Pricing Theory** (APT) model. It postulates that a secu-

---

[14] Stephen A. Ross, "The Arbitrage Theory of Capital Asset Pricing," *Journal of Economic Theory* (December 1976), pp. 343–362.

rity's expected return is influenced by a variety of factors, as opposed to just the single market index of the CAPM.

The APT model assumes that there are several factors that determine the rate of return on a security, not just one as in the case of the CAPM. To understand this, look back at equation (5), which states that the return on a security is dependent on its market sensitivity index and an unsystematic return. The APT in contrast states that the return on a security is linearly related to H factors. The APT does not specify what these factors are, but it is assumed that the relationship between security returns and the factors is linear.

For now, to illustrate the APT model, let's assume a simple world with a portfolio consisting of three securities in the presence of two factors. The notation is as follows:

$\tilde{R}_i$ = the random rate of return on security i ($i = 1, 2, 3$)
$\mathrm{E}(R_i)$ = the expected return on security i ($i = 1, 2, 3$)
$\tilde{F}_h$ = the hth factor that is common to the returns of all three assets ($h = 1, 2$)
β_{ih} = the sensitivity of the ith security to the hth factor
$\tilde{e}_i$ = the unsystematic return for security i ($i = 1, 2, 3$)

The APT model asserts that the random rate of return on security i is given by the relationship:

$$\tilde{R}_i = \mathrm{E}(R_i) + \beta_{i1}\,\tilde{F}_1 + \beta_{i2}\,\tilde{F}_2 + \tilde{e}_i \tag{18}$$

For equilibrium to exist among these three assets, an arbitrage condition must be satisfied: Using no additional funds (wealth) and without increasing risk, it should not be possible, on average, to create a portfolio to increase return. In essence, this condition states that there is no "money machine" available in the market. Ross has shown that the following risk and return relationship, in risk premium form, will result for each security i:

$$\mathrm{E}(r_i) = \beta_{iF1}\,\mathrm{E}(r_{F1}) + \beta_{iF2}\,\mathrm{E}(r_{F2}) \tag{19}$$

where
r_i = the excess return of security i over the risk-free rate
β_{iFi} = the sensitivity of security i to the jth factor
r_{Fi} = the excess return of the jth systematic factor over the risk-free rate, which can be thought of as the price (or risk premium) for the ith systematic risk

Equation (19) can be generalized to the case where there are H factors as follows:

$$\mathrm{E}(r_i) = \beta_{iF1}\,\mathrm{E}(r_{F1}) + \beta_{iF2}\,\mathrm{E}(r_{F2}) + \cdots + \beta_{iFH}\,\mathrm{E}(r_{FH}) \tag{20}$$

Equation (20) is the APT model. It states that investors want to be compensated for all the factors that systematically affect the return of a security. The compensation is the sum of the product of the quantity of systematic risk accepted for factor i, which is measured by the beta of the security with respect to the factor, and how the financial market prices that factor's risk, which is measured by the difference between the expected return for the factor and the risk-free rate. As in the case of the two other risk and return models described earlier, an investor is not compensated for accepting unsystematic risk.

Contrast equation (20) with the CAPM. If there is only one factor, equation (20) reduces to equation (14), and the one factor would be market risk. The CAPM is, therefore, a special case of the APT model. Now, contrast equation (20) with the multifactor CAPM given by equation (15). They look similar. Both say that investors are compensated for accepting all systematic risk and no unsystematic risk. The multifactor CAPM states that one of these systematic risks is market risk, while the APT model does not.

Supporters of the APT model argue that it has several major advantages over the CAPM or the multifactor CAPM. First, it makes less restrictive assumptions about investor preferences toward risk and return. The CAPM theory assumes investors trade off between risk and return solely on the basis of the expected returns and standard deviations of prospective investments. The APT, on the other hand, simply requires that some rather unobtrusive bounds be placed on potential investor utility functions. Second, no assumptions are made about the distribution of security returns. Finally, as the APT does not rely on identifying the true market index, the theory is potentially testable.

Empirical Evidence

To date, attempts to test the APT model empirically in the stock market have been inconclusive. Indeed, because of an inability to find a set of factors that consistently explains security returns, some question whether or not the APT is testable at all. The APT gives no direction as to the choice of the factors themselves or even how many factors might be required. Thus, the APT replaces the problem of the market portfolio in the CAPM with uncertainty over the choice and measurement of the underlying factors.

One study by Nai-fu Chen, Richard Roll, and Stephen Ross suggests four plausible economic factors:[15]

1. Unanticipated changes in industrial production.
2. Unanticipated changes in the spread between the yield on low-grade and high-grade bonds.
3. Unanticipated changes in interest rates and the shape of the yield curve.
4. Unanticipated changes in inflation.

It is interesting to note that one study expands that list to five factors, some similar to the previous group and some new.[16] The factors whose unexpected changes are said to have systematic impact on stock returns are these:

1. The business cycle, as measured by the Index of Industrial Production.
2. Interest rates, as given by the yields on long-term government bonds.
3. Investor confidence, as proxied by the spread between yields on high-grade and yields on low-grade bonds that are similar with regard to call provisions, maturity, and other features.
4. Short-term inflation, as measured by month-to-month changes in the Consumer Price Index.
5. Inflationary expectations, as represented in the changes in the short-term risk-free interest rate.

As this study points out, some stocks are responsive to some factors, while other stocks are closely linked to different factors. Portfolio building involves identifying the pertinent factors and finding the price/risk reward for them. In its consideration of differ-

---

[15] Nai-fu Chen, Richard Roll, and Stephen A. Ross, "Economic Forces and the Stock Market: Testing the APT and Alternative Asset Pricing Theories," Journal of Business (July 1980), pp. 383–403.

[16] Roll and Ross Asset Management Corporation, *APT: Balancing Risk and Return* (undated), p. 14.

ing sensitivities to various systematic variables, the APT departs significantly from the CAPM.

SUMMARY

This chapter explains the principles of portfolio theory, a theory that deals with the construction of optimal portfolios by rational risk-averse investors, and its implications for the returns on different assets and, hence, security prices. One way to evaluate the risk of a portfolio is by estimating the extent to which future portfolio values are likely to deviate from expected portfolio return. This is measured by the variance of the portfolio's return and is called the total portfolio risk. Total portfolio risk can be broken down into two types of risk: systematic risk and unsystematic risk.

Systematic risk, also called *market risk*, is the risk that affects all securities. The beta of any security or portfolio is the relative systematic risk of the asset and is measured statistically (using historical return data) by the slope of the regression between the asset's and the market's returns. The regression line estimated is called the market model. Unsystematic risk is the risk that is unique to a company, and it can be eliminated by diversifying the portfolio. Thus, systematic risk and unsystematic risk are referred to as nondiversifiable and diversifiable risk, respectively.

The capital asset pricing model is an economic theory that attempts to provide a relationship between risk and return, or, equivalently, it is a model for the pricing of risky securities. The CAPM asserts that the only relevant risk that investors will require compensation for assuming is systematic risk because that risk cannot be eliminated by diversification. Basically, CAPM says that the expected return of a security or a portfolio is equal to the rate on a risk-free security plus a risk premium. The risk premium in the CAPM is proportional to the secu-

rity or the portfolio beta. More specifically, the risk premium is the product of the quantity of risk and the market price of risk, measured by beta, and the difference between the expected market return and risk-free rate, respectively.

The CAPM assumes that investors are concerned with only one risk: the risk having to do with the future price of a security. However, there are other risks, such as the capacity of investors to consume goods and services in the future. The multifactor CAPM assumes investors face such extra-market sources of risk called factors. The expected return in the multifactor CAPM is the market risk, as in the case of the basic CAPM, plus a package of risk premiums. Each risk premium is the product of the beta of the security or portfolio with respect to the particular factor and the difference between the expected return for the factor and the risk-free rate.

The arbitrage pricing theory model is developed purely on arbitrage arguments. It postulates that the expected return on a security or a portfolio is influenced by several factors. Proponents of the APT model cite its use of less restrictive assumptions as a feature that makes it more appealing than the CAPM or the multifactor CAPM. Moreover, testing the APT model does not require identification of the true market portfolio. It does, however, require empirical determination of the factors because they are not specified by the theory. Consequently, the APT model replaces the problem of identifying the market portfolio in the CAPM with the problem of choosing and measuring the underlying factors.

All things considered, the CAPM, the multifactor CAPM, and the APT model all provide interesting conceptual insights into the issues of the pricing of risk and portfolio selection in securities markets. None can be said to dominate the others in terms of theoretical content or the simplicity of empirical testing. Only the future will decide which has the best claim to the ultimate truth. Indeed, on this question, all three pricing theories will probably make valuable contributions to development of the next generation of equilibrium models.

KEY TERMS

- **Alpha, 248**
- **Arbitrage pricing theory (APT) model, 256**
- **Beta, 248**
- **Capital asset pricing model (CAPM), 251**
- **Correlation, 246**
- **Diversifiable risk, 246**
- **Efficient (or optimal) portfolio, 241**
- **Expected return, 241**
- **Extra-market source of risk, 255**

- **Market model, 248**
- **Probability distribution, 243**
- **Skewness, 244**
- **Standard deviation, 245**
- **Symmetric distribution, 244**
- **Systematic risk, 246**
- **Total risk, 246**
- **Unsystematic risk, 247**
- **Variance of a probability distribution, 245**

QUESTIONS

1. A friend has asked you to help him figure out a statement he received from his broker. It seems that, at the start of last year, your friend paid $900 for a bond, and sold it at the end of the year for $890. During the year, he received a single coupon payment of $110. The statement claims that his return (not including commissions and taxes) is 11.11% for the year. Is this claim correct?

2. Suppose the probability distribution for the one-period return of some asset is as follows:

Return	Probability
0.20	0.10
0.15	0.20
0.10	0.30
0.03	0.25
−0.06	0.15

   a. What is this asset's expected one-period return?
   b. What is this asset's variance and standard deviation for the one-period return?

3. "A portfolio's expected return and variance of return are simply the weighted average of the expected return and variance of the individual assets." Do you agree with this statement?

4. In the January 25, 1991, issue of *The Value Line Investment Survey*, you note the following:

Company	Beta (β)
IBM	0.95
Bally Manufacturing	1.40
Cigna Corporation	1.00
British Telecom	0.60

a. How do you interpret these betas?

b. Is it reasonable to assume that the expected return on British Telecom is less than that on IBM shares?

c. "Given that Cigna Corporation has a β of 1.00, one can mimic the performance of the stock market as a whole by buying only these shares." Do you agree with this statement?

5. Assume the following:

$$\text{Expected market return} = 15\%$$
$$\text{Risk-free rate} = 5.7\%$$

If a security's beta is 1.3, what is its expected return according to the CAPM?

6. Professor Harry Markowitz, corecipient of the 1990 Nobel Prize in Economics, wrote the following:

A portfolio with sixty different railway securities, for example, would not be as well diversified as the same size portfolio with some railroad, some public utility, mining, various sorts of manufacturing, etc.

Why is this true?

7. Following is an excerpt from an article, "Risk and Reward," in *The Economist* of October 20, 1990:

Next question: is the CAPM supported by the facts? That is controversial, to put it mildly. It is a tribute to Mr. Sharpe [cowinner of the 1990 Nobel Prize in Economics] that his work, which dates from the early 1960s, is still argued over so heatedly. Attention has lately turned away from beta to more complicated ways of carving up risk. But the significance of CAPM for financial economics would be hard to exaggerate.

a. Summarize Roll's argument on the problems inherent in empirically verifying the CAPM.

b. What are some of the other "more complicated ways of carving up risk"?

8. a. What are the difficulties in practice of applying the arbitrage pricing theory model?

b. Does Roll's criticism also apply to this pricing model?

c. "In the CAPM investors should be compensated for accepting systematic risk: for the APT model, investors are rewarded for accepting both systematic risk and unsystematic risk." Do you agree with this statement?

Primary Markets and the Underwriting of Securities

Learning Objectives

After reading this chapter, you will understand

- the role investment bankers play in the distribution of newly issued securities.
- the risk associated with the underwriting of a security.
- the different types of underwriting arrangements.
- the types of entities that are involved in investment banking.
- how the SEC regulates the distribution of newly issued securities.
- what a registration statement is.
- the impact of the SEC Rule 415 (shelf registration).
- what is a bought deal underwriting for a bond issue, and why it is used.
- what a competitive bidding underwriting is.
- what a rights offering for the sale of common stock is.
- the advantages and disadvantages from an issuer's perspective of a private placement.
- the reason for Rule 144A and its potential impact on the private placement market.

As we explain in Chapter 1, financial markets can be categorized as those dealing with financial claims that are newly issued, called the **primary market,** and those for exchanging financial claims previously issued, called the *secondary market*, or the market for seasoned securities. In this chapter we focus on the primary market for securities; the next chapter covers the secondary market.

The primary market involves the distribution to investors of newly issued securities by central governments, its agencies, municipal governments, and corporations.[1] The participants in the marketplace that work with issuers to distribute newly issued securities are called **investment bankers**. The activity of investment banking is undertaken by basically two types of firms: securities houses and commercial banks. In this

---

[1] This also includes the offering of securities of government-owned companies to private investors. This process is referred to as *privatization*. An example in the United States is the initial public offering of the U.S. government-owned railroad company Conrail in March 1987. Non-U.S. examples include Great Britain's British Telecom, Chile's Pacifica, and France's Paribas.

chapter, we explain the various ways that investment banking firms are involved in the issuance of new securities, the regulation of the primary market, and the private placement market.

THE TRADITIONAL PROCESS FOR ISSUING NEW SECURITIES

The traditional process in the United States for issuing new securities involves investment bankers performing one or more of the following three functions: (1) advising the issuer on the terms and the timing of the offering, (2) buying the securities from the issuer, and (3) distributing the issue to the public.[2] The advisor role may require investment bankers to design a security structure that is more palatable to investors than a particular traditional instrument. For example, the high interest rates in the United States in the late 1970s and early 1980s increased the cost of borrowing for issuers of even the highest-quality rating. To reduce the cost of borrowing for their clients, investment bankers designed securities with characteristics that were more attractive to investors but not onerous to issuers. They also designed security structures for low-quality bond issues, so-called high-yield or junk bond structures. We'll give several examples of these financial innovations in later chapters.

In the sale of new securities, investment bankers need not undertake the second function—buying the securities from the issuer. An investment banker may merely act as an advisor and/or distributor of the new security. The function of buying the securities from the issuer is called **underwriting**. When an investment banking firm buys the securities from the issuer and accepts the risk of selling the securities to investors at a lower price, it is referred to as an *underwriter*. When the investment banking firm agrees to buy the securities from the issuer at a set price, the underwriting arrangement is referred to as a **firm commitment**. In contrast, in a **best efforts** arrangement, the investment banking firm agrees only to use its expertise to sell the securities—it does not buy the entire issue from the issuer.

The fee earned from underwriting a security is the difference between the price paid to the issuer and the price at which the investment bank reoffers the security to the public. This difference is called the **gross spread**, or the **underwriter discount**. There are numerous factors that affect the size of the gross spread. Typical gross spreads for common stock offerings, **initial public offerings (IPOs)**, and bond offerings are shown in Table 14-1. IPOs are typically common stock offerings issued by companies that had not previously issued common stock to the public. Because of the risk associated with pricing and then selling IPOs to investors, the gross spread is higher.

The typical underwritten transaction involves so much risk of capital loss that a single investment banking firm undertaking it alone would be exposed to the danger of losing a significant portion of its capital. To share this risk, an investment banking firm forms a **syndicate** of firms to underwrite the issue. The gross spread is then divided among the lead underwriter(s) and the other firms in the underwriting syndicate. The lead underwriter manages the deal (or "runs the books" for the deal). In many cases, there may be more than one lead underwriter, so that the lead underwriters are said to colead or comanage the deal.

To realize the gross spread, the entire securities issue must be sold to the public at the planned reoffering price. This usually requires a great deal of marketing muscle. Investment banking firms have an investor client base (retail and institutional) to

---

[2] When an investment banking firm commits its own funds on a long-term basis by either taking an equity interest or creditor position in companies, this activity is referred to as merchant banking.

Table 14-1   Gross Spread by Offering Size During 1999: Stocks and Bonds

Initial Public Offerings of Stocks

SIZE OF INDIVIDUAL ISSUE (IN MILLIONS)	TOTAL PRINCIPAL ISSUED IN THE RANGE (IN MILLIONS)	ISSUE MARKET SHARE	# OF ISSUES	TOTAL GROSS SPREAD OVER ALL ISSUES (IN MILLIONS)	GROSS SPREAD AS A % OF PRINCIPAL
$10–30	$ 1256.5	1.8%	64	$ 83.2	6.62%
30–60	8381.2	11.9	186	564.8	6.74
60–150	19897.9	28.2	222	1326.3	6.67
150 +	40999.4	58.1	75	1829.7	4.46
Industry total	$70534.9	100.0%	547	$3804.0	5.39%

Secondary Common Stock Offerings

SIZE OF INDIVIDUAL ISSUE (IN MILLIONS)	TOTAL PRINCIPAL ISSUED IN THE RANGE (IN MILLIONS)	ISSUE MARKET SHARE	# OF ISSUES	TOTAL GROSS SPREAD OVER ALL ISSUES (IN MILLIONS)	GROSS SPREAD AS A % OF PRINCIPAL
$10–30	$ 821.6	0.8%	39	$ 46.4	5.65%
30–60	3729.7	3.7	81	199.0	5.34
60–150	13568.9	13.6	136	662.2	4.88
150 +	81908.1	81.9	183	2605.0	3.18
Industry total	$100028.3	100.0%	439	$3512.6	3.51%

Fixed Income Offerings*

SIZE OF INDIVIDUAL ISSUE (IN MILLIONS)	TOTAL PRINCIPAL ISSUED IN THE RANGE (IN MILLIONS)	ISSUE MARKET SHARE	# OF ISSUES	TOTAL GROSS SPREAD OVER ALL ISSUES (IN MILLIONS)	GROSS SPREAD AS A % OF PRINCIPAL
$ 0–500	$152293.1	73.8%	1221	$ 763.4	0.50%
500–5000	54048.9	26.2	65	286.2	0.53
Industry total	$206342.0	100.0%	1286	$1049.6	0.51%

SOURCE: Thomson Financial Securities Data.

* *Characteristics of included issues: underwritten, public, nonconvertible, U.S. corporate, bullet, issue size under $5 billion.*

which they attempt to sell the securities. To increase the potential investor base, the lead underwriter will put together a **selling group**. This group includes the underwriting syndicate plus other firms that are not in the syndicate. Members of the selling group can buy the security at a concession price—a price less than the reoffering price. The gross spread is thereby divided among the lead underwriter, members of the underwriting syndicate, and members of the selling group.

A successful underwriting of a security requires that the underwriter have a strong sales force. The sales force provides feedback on advance interest in the security, and the traders (also called market makers) provide input in pricing the security as well. (Traders are discussed in Chapter 15.) It would be a mistake to think that once the securities are all sold the investment banking firm's ties with the deal are ended. In the case of bonds, those who bought the securities will look to the investment banking firm to make a market in the issue. This means that the investment banking firm must be willing to take a principal position in secondary market transactions.

> **Key Points That You Should Understand Before Proceeding**
>
> 1. There are three functions performed by investment bankers in the offering of new securities.
> 2. Depending on the type of underwriting agreement, the underwriting function may expose the investment banking firm to the risk of selling the securities to the public at a price less than the price paid to the issuer.
> 3. The gross spread earned by the underwriter depends on numerous factors.
> 4. Because of the risks associated with the underwriting of securities, an underwriting syndicate and a selling group are typically formed.

INVESTMENT BANKERS

Investment banking is performed by two groups: commercial banks, which we discussed in Chapter 4, and securities houses. As discussed in Chapters 4 and 7, prior to 1999, the Glass-Steagall Act separated the activities of commercial banks, investment banks, and insurance companies and thereby restricted the types of securities that commercial banks in the United States could underwrite. This act had been on the books since the Great Depression. No restrictions were placed on the investment activities of commercial banks outside of the United States. The Gramm-Leach-Bliley Financial Services Modernization Act of 1999 (the "GLB Act") supplanted the Glass-Steagall Act and eliminated the restrictions on the activities conducted by companies in each financial sector. Now commercial banks (which have since recently underwritten securities) as well as insurance companies (which have not underwritten securities) can underwrite securities.

Securities houses are firms that not only distribute newly issued securities but also are involved in the secondary market as market makers and brokers. Just as in the United States, the securities laws and banking regulations of each country specify the entities that are permitted to underwrite securities. Japanese securities law, for example, places even greater restrictions on the underwriting activities of commercial banks than the Glass Steagall Act in the United States. In countries such as Germany, there is no separation of commercial banking and investment banking activities. Banks in Germany are referred to as *universal banks* because they are involved in both activities. The underwriting of new securities is primarily done by commercial banks in Germany.

A country will also regulate the activities of foreign firms in its financial market. For example, a country may not permit a foreign commercial bank or securities house to participate in the primary market for a government and/or corporate security. The liberalization of financial markets in recent years has opened up investment banking activities to foreign entities.

Table 14-2 shows a selective list of major national U.S. investment banks, major non-U.S. national investment banks, and regional firms.[3] The list shown in the table

---

[3] At one time a popular classification of U.S. securities firms involved in the underwriting of securities was as follows: bulge-bracket firms, major bracket firms, submajor bracket firms, and regional firms. *Bulge-bracket firms* were viewed as the premier investment banking firms because of their size, reputation, presence in key markets, and customer base. Large investment banking firms that do not have the same status as the bulge-bracket firms but nevertheless provide full-line services were called major bracket firms. *Submajor bracket firms* were frequently New York–based firms that catered to smaller issuing companies. Firms located outside New York and that served regional issuers (corporate and local governments) were classified as *regional firms*.

Table 14-2   Selective List of Investment Banks as of 12/31/00

Major National U.S. Investment Banks	Major Non-U.S. National Investment Banks
Merrill Lynch & Company	UBS Warburg LLC
Goldman Sachs & Company	• Dillion Read
Morgan Stanley Dean Witter	• Paine Webber
Lehman Brothers	Credit Suisse First Boston Corporation
Salomon Smith Barney, Inc. (part of Citigroup)	• Donaldson, Lufkin & Jenrette
Chase H&Q	ABN AMRO, Inc.
• J. P. Morgan & Company	CIBC World Markets
Bear, Stearns & Company, Inc.	• Oppenheimer Securities
Bank of America	Deutsche Bank
	• Banker's Trust
	• Alex Brown
	Barclays Bank

Regional Firms

Jeffries & Company, Inc.
SG Cowen
U.S. Bankcorp Piper Jeffray
Robertson Stephens (subsidiary of Fleet Financial)

has changed rapidly due to mergers and acquisitions. For example, in 2000 the following occurred: Chase Manhattan Bank acquired J. P. Morgan and Co.; Credit Suisse Group, the large Swiss bank, acquired Donaldson, Lufkin & Jenrette; and UBS, another large Swiss bank, acquired PaineWebber.

In Japan, the major securities houses—popularly referred to as the Big Four—are Nomura, Daiwa, Yamaichi, and Nikko. These firms are actively involved in the underwriting of securities issued in the United States and the Euromarket, as well as in Japan.

Key Points That You Should Understand Before Proceeding

1. The two groups that underwrite securities are investment banking firms and commercial banks. The limitations on commercial bank underwriting activities have been significantly reduced by the GLB Act.
2. There are four major firms that dominate investment banking in Japan.

REGULATION OF THE PRIMARY MARKET

Underwriting activities are regulated by the Securities and Exchange Commission (SEC). The Securities Act of 1933 governs the issuance of securities. The act requires that a **registration statement** be filed with the SEC by the issuer of a security. The type of information contained in the registration statement is the nature of the business of the issuer, key provisions or features of the security, the nature of the investment risks associated with the security, and the background of management.[4] Financial statements must be included in the registration statement, and they must be certified by an independent public accountant.[5]

The registration is actually divided into two parts. Part I is the **prospectus**. It is this part that is typically distributed to the public as an offering of the securities. Part II contains supplemental information, which is not distributed to the public as part of the offering but is available from the SEC upon request.

The act provides for penalties in the form of fines and/or imprisonment if the information provided is inaccurate or material information is omitted. Moreover, investors who purchase the security are entitled to sue the issuer to recover damages if they incur a loss as a result of the misleading information. The underwriter may also be sued if it can be demonstrated that the underwriter did not conduct a reasonable investigation of the information reported by the issuer. One of the most important duties of an underwriter is to perform **due diligence.** The following quotation comes from a court decision that explains the obligation of an underwriter to perform due diligence:

> An underwriter by participating in an offering constructively represents that statements made in the registration materials are complete and accurate. The investing public properly relies upon the underwriter to check the accuracy of the statements and the soundness of the offer; when the underwriter does not speak out, the investor reasonably assumes that there are no undisclosed material deficiencies. The representations in the registration statement are those of the underwriter as much as they are those of the issuer.[6]

The filing of a registration statement with the SEC does not mean that the security can be offered to the public. The registration statement must be reviewed and approved by the SEC's Division of Corporate Finance before a public offering can be made. Typically, the staff of this division will find a problem with the registration statement. The staff then sends a "letter of comments" or "deficiency letter" to the issuer explaining the problem it has encountered. The issuer must remedy any problem by filing an amendment to the registration statement. If the staff is satisfied, the SEC will issue an order declaring that the registration statement is "effective," and the underwriter can solicit sales. The approval of the SEC, however, does not mean that the securities have investment merit or are properly priced or that the information is accurate. It merely means that the appropriate information appears to have been disclosed.

The time interval between the initial filing of the registration statement and the time the registration statement becomes effective is referred to as the **waiting period**: (also called the "cooling-off period"). During the waiting period, the SEC does allow the underwriters to distribute a preliminary prospectus. Because the prospectus has not become effective, its cover page states this in red ink and, as a result, the preliminary prospectus is commonly called a **red herring**. During the waiting period, the underwriter cannot sell the security, nor may it accept written offers from investors to buy the security.

In 1982 the SEC approved Rule 415, which permits certain issuers to file a single registration document indicating that they intend to sell a certain amount of a certain

---

[4] SEC Regulation S-K and the Industry Guidelines (SEC Securities Act Release No. 6384, March 3, 1982) specify the information that must be included in the registration statement.

[5] SEC Regulation S-X specifies the financial statements that must be disclosed.

[6] Chris-Craft Industries, Inc. *v.* Piper Aircraft Corp, 1973.

class of securities at one or more times within the next two years.[7] Rule 415 is popularly referred to as the **shelf registration rule** because the securities can be viewed as sitting on a "shelf," and can be taken off that shelf and sold to the public without obtaining additional SEC approval. In essence, the filing of a single registration document allows the issuer to come to market quickly because the sale of the security has been preapproved by the SEC. Prior to establishment of Rule 415, there was a lengthy period required before a security could be sold to the public. As a result, in a fast-moving market, issuers could not come to market quickly with an offering to take advantage of what they perceived to be attractive financing opportunities. For example, if a corporation felt that interest rates were low and wanted to issue a bond, it had to file a registration statement and could not issue the bond until the registration statement became effective. The corporation was then taking the chance that during the waiting period interest rates would rise, making the bond offering more costly.

Key Points That You Should Understand Before Proceeding

1. The SEC regulates underwriting activities.
2. An issuer must file a registration statement, one part of which is the prospectus.
3. The underwriter must exercise due diligence to assure that there are no misstatements or omissions of fact in the registration statement or prospectus.
4. SEC Rule 415 (the shelf registration rule) gives greater flexibility to certain issuers by permitting them to file a single registration document for the offering of certain securities at one or more times within the next two years.

VARIATIONS IN THE UNDERWRITING PROCESS

Not all deals are underwritten using the traditional syndicate process we have described. Variations in the United States, the Euromarkets, and foreign markets include the **bought deal** for the underwriting of bonds, the auction process for both stocks and bonds, and a rights offering for underwriting common stock.

Bought Deal

The bought deal was introduced in the Eurobond market in 1981 when Credit Suisse First Boston purchased from General Motors Acceptance Corporation a $100 million issue without lining up an underwriting syndicate prior to the purchase. Thus, Credit Suisse First Boston did not use the traditional syndication process to diversify the capital risk exposure associated with an underwriting that we described earlier.

The mechanics of a bought deal are as follows. The lead manager or a group of managers offers a potential issuer of debt securities a firm bid to purchase a specified amount of the securities with a certain interest (coupon) rate and maturity. The issuer is given a day or so (maybe even only a few hours) to accept or reject the bid. If the bid is accepted, the underwriting firm has bought the deal. It can, in turn, sell the securities to other investment banking firms for distribution to their clients and/or distribute the securities to its clients. Typically, the underwriting firm that buys the deal will have presold most of the issue to its institutional clients.

---

[7] The issuer qualifies for Rule 415 registration if the securities are investment-grade securities and/or the securities of companies that have historically filed registration statements and whose securities comply with minimum flotation requirements.

The bought deal appears to have found its way into the United States in mid-1985 when Merrill Lynch underwrote a bond issue for which it was the only underwriter. The gross spread on the bond, a $50 million issue of Norwest Financial, was 0.268%. This is far less than the 0.7% gross spread typical of that time. Merrill Lynch offered a portion of the securities to investors and the balance to other investment banking firms.

There are several reasons why some underwriting firms find the bought deal attractive. While Rule 415 gives certain issuers timing flexibility to take advantage of windows of opportunities in the global marketplace, it requires that underwriting firms be prepared to respond on short notice to commit funds to a deal. This fact favors the bought deal because it gives the underwriting firm very little time to line up a syndicate. A consequence of accepting bought deals, however, is that underwriting firms need to expand their capital so that they can commit greater amounts of funds to such deals.

The risk of capital loss in a bought deal may not be as great as it first appears. There are some deals that are so straightforward that a large underwriting firm may have enough institutional investor interest to keep the risks of distributing the issue at the reoffering price quite small. Moreover, in the case of bonds, hedging strategies using the interest rate risk control tools that we discuss in Chapters 25 and 26 can reduce or eliminate the risk of realizing a loss of selling the bonds at a price below the reoffering price.

Auction Process

Another variation for underwriting securities is the auction process. In this method, the issuer announces the terms of the issue, and interested parties submit bids for the entire issue. The auction form is mandated for certain securities of regulated public utilities and many municipal debt obligations. It is more commonly referred to as a **competitive bidding underwriting**. For example, suppose that a public utility wishes to issue $100 million of bonds. Various underwriters will form syndicates and bid on the issue. The syndicate that bids the lowest yield (i.e., the lowest cost to the issuer) wins the entire $100 million bond issue and then reoffers it to the public.

In a variant of the process, the bidders indicate the price they are willing to pay and the amount they are willing to buy. The security is then allocated to bidders from the highest bid price (lowest yield in the case of a bond) to the lower ones (higher yield in the case of a bond) until the entire issue is allocated. For example, suppose that an issuer is offering $500 million of a bond issue, and nine bidders submit the following yield bids:

Bidder	Amount (in millions)	Bid
A	$150	5.1%
B	110	5.2
C	90	5.2
D	100	5.3
E	75	5.4
F	25	5.4
G	80	5.5
H	70	5.6
I	85	5.7

The first four bidders—A, B, C, and D—will be allocated the amount for which they bid because they submitted the lowest-yield bids. In total, they will receive $450 million of the $500 million to be issued. That leaves $50 million to be allocated to the next-lowest bidders. Both E and F submitted the next lowest yield bid, 5.4%. In total, they bid for $100 million. Since the total they bid for exceeds the remaining $50 million, they will receive an amount proportionate to the amount for which they bid. Specifically, E will be allocated three-quarters ($75 million divided by $100 million) of the $50 million or $37.5 million, and F will be allocated one-quarter ($25 million divided by $100 million) of the $50 million or $12.5 million.

The next question concerns the yield that all of the six winning bidders—A, B, C, D, E, and F—will have to pay for the amount of the issue allocated to them. One way in which a competitive bidding can occur is all bidders pay the highest winning yield bid (or, equivalently, the lowest winning price). In our example, all bidders would buy the amount allocated to them at 5.4%. This type of auction is referred to as a *single-price auction* or a **Dutch auction**. Another way is for each bidder to pay whatever each one bid. This type of auction is called a *multiple-price auction*. As we explain in Chapter 16, historically both procedures have been used in the auctioning of U.S. Treasury securities.

Using an auction allows corporate issuers to place newly issued debt obligations directly with institutional investors rather than follow the indirect path of using an underwriting firm. Internet auctions of municipal originations to underwriters began during 1997. As will be explained in Chapter 17, one method of issuing municipal securities (i.e., securities issued by state and local governments and their authorities) is via a competitive bidding process. During November 1997, MuniAuction auctioned over the Internet $70 million City of Pittsburgh municipal bonds despite the opposition of some major Wall Street traditional, competitive bond underwriters. In 1999, the City of Pittsburgh used MuniAuction to offer bonds directly to institutional investors, allowing them to bypass traditional underwriters. By late 2000, MuniAuction reports it conducted more than 250 municipal auctions totaling $13.4 billion. As of late November 2000, 14% of all competitive municipal bond underwritings were conducted over the MuniAuction system. By contrast, with the exception of two corporate bonds sales (Dow Chemical and Deutsche Bank), the corporate bond market had not adopted electronic bidding for new issues.

Investment bankers' response to the practice of direct purchase of publicly registered securities is that, as intermediaries, they add value by searching their institutional client base, which increases the likelihood that the issuer will incur the lowest cost, after adjusting for the underwriting fees. By dealing with just a few institutional investors, investment bankers argue, issuers cannot be sure of obtaining funds at the lowest cost. In addition, investment bankers say that they often play another important role: They make a secondary market in the securities they issue. This market improves the perceived liquidity of the issue and, as a result, reduces the cost to issuers. The question whether or not investment bankers can obtain lower-cost funding (after accounting for underwriting fees) to issuers, by comparison to the cost of funding from a direct offering, is an interesting empirical question.

Preemptive Rights Offering

A corporation can issue new common stock directly to existing shareholders via a **preemptive rights offering**. A preemptive right grants existing shareholders the right to buy some proportion of the new shares issued at a price below market value. The price at which the new shares can be purchased is called the *subscription price*. A rights offering ensures that current shareholders may maintain their proportionate equity interest in the corporation. In the United States, the practice of issuing common stock via a preemptive rights offering is uncommon. In other countries it is much more common; in some countries, it is the only means by which a new offering of common stock may be sold.

For the shares sold via a preemptive rights offering, the underwriting services of an investment banker are not needed. However, the issuing corporation may use the services of an investment banker for the distribution of common stock that is not subscribed to. A **standby underwriting arrangement** will be used in such instances. This arrangement calls for the underwriter to buy the unsubscribed shares. The issuing corporation pays a **standby fee** to the investment banking firm.

To demonstrate how a rights offering works, the effect on the economic wealth of shareholders, and how the terms set forth in a rights offering affects whether or not the issuer will need an underwriter, we will use an illustration. Suppose that the market price of the stock of XYZ Corporation is $20 per share and that there are 30,000 shares outstanding. Thus, the capitalization of this firm is $600,000. Suppose that the management of XYZ Corporation is considering a rights offering in connection with the issuance of 10,000 new shares. Each current shareholder would receive one right for every three shares owned. The terms of the rights offering are as follows: for three rights and $17 (the subscription price) a new share can be acquired. The subscription price must always be less than the market price or the rights will not be exercised. In our illustration, the subscription price is 15% ($3/20) below the market price.[8]

In addition to the number of rights and the subscription price, there are two other elements of a rights offering that are important. First is the choice to transfer the rights. This is done by selling the right in the open market. This is critical since, as we will see, the right has a value and that value can be captured by selling the right. The second element is the time when the right expires (that is, when it can no longer be used to acquire the stock). Typically, the time period before a right expires is short.

The value of a right can be found by calculating the difference between the price of a share before the rights offering and the price of a share after the rights offering.[9] That is,

Value of a right = Price before rights offering – Price after rights offering

Or, equivalently,

Value of a right = Share price rights on – Share price ex rights

Table 14-3 shows the impact of the rights offering on the price of a share. The price after the rights offering will be $19.25. Therefore, the value of a right is $0.75 ($20 – $19.25).

The difference between the price before the rights offering and after the rights offering expressed as a percentage of the original price is called the *dilution effect of the rights issue*. In the present case, the dilution effect is $0.75/$20, or 3.75%. The larger the dilution is, the larger the ratio of old and new shares is, and the larger the discount is.[10]

---

[8] Note that the same results can be achieved by issuing one right per share but requiring three rights plus the subscription price for a new share (except for rounding-off problems and implications for the value of one right discussed below).

[9] Alternatively, the value of a right can be found as follows:

$$\frac{\text{Price after rights offering} - \text{Subscription price}}{\text{Number of rights required to buy a share}}$$

[10] Specifically:

$$\text{Dilution effect} = \frac{\text{Discount \%}}{1 + (\text{Ratio of old to new shares})}$$

In our illustration the discount is 15% and the ratio of old to new shares is 30,000/10,000 or 3, so the dilution effect is 15%/4, or 3.75%.

Table 14-3   Analysis of Rights Offering on the Market Price of XYZ Corporation

I. *Before rights issue*	
1. Capitalization	$600,000
2. Number of shares	30,000
3. Share price (rights on)	$20.00
II. *After issuance of shares via rights offering*	
4. Number of shares	40,000 (= 30,000 + 10,000)
5. Capitalization	$770,000 (= $600,000 + 10,000 × $17)
6. Share price (ex rights)	$19.25 (= $770,000/40,000)
7. Value of one right	$0.75 (= $20.00 − $19.25)
III. *Net gain or loss to initial stockholder*	
8. Loss per share due to dilution	$0.75 (= 3.75% × $20)
9. Gain per share from selling or exercising a right	$0.75
10. Net gain or loss	$ 0

The last section of Table 14-3 shows the net gain or loss to the initial shareholder as a result of the rights offering. The loss per share due to dilution is $0.75, but that is exactly equal to the value of a right which, if the shareholder desires, can be sold in the market. This result is important because it shows that the rights offering as such will not affect the sum of the value of the share without rights (referred to as ex rights) plus the value of the rights the shareholder receives, no matter how much the dilution or the initial discount offered is. This is because a larger dilution is exactly compensated by the increase in the value of the rights.[11]

Key Points That You Should Understand Before Proceeding

1. There are variations in the traditional underwriting process.
2. In a bought deal, a lead manager or a group of managers offers a potential issuer of debt securities a firm bid to purchase a specified amount of a security.
3. An offering of a new security can be made by means of an auction process.
4. A corporation can offer existing shareholders new shares in a preemptive rights offering, and using a standby underwriting arrangement, the corporation can have an investment banking firm agree to distribute any shares not subscribed to.

PRIVATE PLACEMENT OF SECURITIES

In addition to underwriting securities for distribution to the public, securities may be placed with a limited number of institutional investors such as insurance companies, investment companies, and pension funds. **Private placement**, as this process is known, differs from the public offering of securities that we have described so far. Life insurance companies are the major investors in private placements. At the end of 1999, life insurance companies held $353.5 billion of private placements.[12]

---

[11] For a further discussion of why the size of the discount and dilution is relevant for the welfare of the stockholders and the factors that will affect the success of a rights offering, see Frank J. Fabozzi and Franco Modigliani, *Capital Markets: Institutions and Instruments* (Englewood Cliffs, N.J.: Prentice Hall, 1996), pp. 133–136.

[12] *Fact Book 2000*, American Council of Life Insurance, p. 121.

Public and private offerings of securities differ in terms of the regulatory requirements that the issuer must satisfy. The Securities Act of 1933 and the Securities Exchange Act of 1934 require that all securities offered to the general public must be registered with the SEC, unless there is a specific exemption.

The Securities Acts allow three exemptions from federal registration. First, intrastate offerings—that is, securities sold only within a state—are exempt. Second, there is a small-offering exemption (Regulation A). Specifically, if the offering is for $1 million or less, the securities need not be registered. Finally, Section 4(2) of the 1933 act exempts from registration "transactions by an issuer not involving any public offering." At the same time, the 1933 act does not provide specific guidelines to identify what is a private offering or placement.

In 1982, the SEC adopted Regulation D, which sets forth the guidelines that determine if an issue is qualified for exemption from registration. The guidelines require that, in general, the securities cannot be offered through any form of general advertising or general solicitation that would prevail for public offerings. Most importantly, the guidelines restrict the sale of securities to "sophisticated" investors. Such "accredited" investors are defined as those who (1) have the capability to evaluate (or who can afford to employ an advisor to evaluate) the risk and return characteristics of the securities, and (2) have the resources to bear the economic risks.[13]

The exemption of an offering does not mean that the issuer need not disclose information to potential investors. In fact, the issuer must still furnish the same information deemed material by the SEC. The issuer supplies this information in a private placement memorandum, as opposed to a prospectus for a public offering. The distinction between the private placement memorandum and the prospectus is that the former does not include information deemed by the SEC "nonmaterial," if such information is required in a prospectus. Moreover, unlike a prospectus, the private placement memorandum is not subject to SEC review.

Investment banking firms assist in the private placement of securities in several ways. They work with the issuer and potential investors on the design and pricing of the security. Often it has been in the private placement market that investment bankers first design new security structures. Field testing of many of the innovative securities that we describe in this book occurred in the private placement market.

The investment bankers may be involved with lining up the investors as well as designing the issue. Or, if the issuer has already identified the investors, the investment banker may serve only in an advisory capacity. An investment banker can also participate in the transaction on a best efforts underwriting arrangement.

Rule 144A

In the United States, one restriction imposed on buyers of privately placed securities is that they may not be resold for two years after acquisition. Thus, there is no liquidity in the market for that time period. Buyers of privately placed securities must be compensated for the lack of liquidity, which raises the cost to the issuer of the securities.

In April 1990, however, SEC **Rule 144A** became effective. This rule eliminates the two-year holding period by permitting large institutions to trade securities acquired in a private placement among themselves without having to register these securities with the SEC.

---

[13] Under the current law, an accredited investor is one who satisfies either a net worth test (at least $1 million excluding automobiles, home, and home furnishings) or an annual income test (at least $200,000 for a single individual, $300,000 for a couple for the last two years, with expectations of such income to continue for the current year).

Private placements are now classified as Rule 144A offerings or non-Rule 144A offerings. The latter are more commonly referred to as traditional private placements. Rule 144A offerings are underwritten by investment bankers.

Rule 144A encourages non-U.S. corporations to issue securities in the U.S. private placement market for two reasons. First, it will attract new large institutional investors into the market that were unwilling previously to buy private placements because of the requirement to hold the securities for two years. Such an increase in the number of institutional investors may encourage non-U.S. entities to issue securities. Second, foreign entities were unwilling to raise funds in the United States prior to establishment of Rule 144A because they had to register their securities and furnish the necessary disclosure set forth by U.S. securities laws. Private placement requires less disclosure. Rule 144A also improves liquidity, reducing the cost of raising funds.

Key Points That You Should Understand Before Proceeding

1. A private placement is the distribution of shares to a limited number of institutional investors rather than through a public offering.
2. The SEC specifies the conditions that must be satisfied to qualify for a private placement.
3. Investment bankers will typically work with issuers in the design of a security for a private placement and line up the potential investors.
4. SEC Rule 144A improves the liquidity of securities acquired by certain institutional investors in a private placement.

SUMMARY

The primary market involves the distribution to investors of newly issued securities. Investment bankers perform one or more of three functions: (1) advising the issuer on the terms and the timing of the offering, (2) buying the securities from the issuer, and (3) distributing the issue to investors. The second function is referred to as the underwriting function. Investment banking activities are performed by commercial banks and securities houses.

The SEC is responsible for regulating the issuance of new securities, with the major provisions set forth in the Securities Act of 1933. The act requires that the issuer file a registration statement for approval by the SEC. Rule 415, the shelf registration rule, permits certain issuers to file a single registration document indicating that they intend to sell a certain amount of a certain class of securities at one or more times within the next two years.

Variations in the underwriting process include the bought deal for the underwriting of bonds, the auction process for both stocks and bonds, and a rights offering coupled with a standby arrangement for underwriting common stock.

A private placement is different from the public offering of securities in terms of the regulatory requirements that must be satisfied by the issuer. If an issue qualifies as a private placement, it is exempt from the more complex registration requirements imposed on public offerings. Rule 144A has contributed to the growth of the private placement market by improving the liquidity of securities issued in this market.

KEY TERMS

- Best efforts underwriting, 263
- Bought deal, 268
- Competitive bidding underwriting, 269
- Due diligence, 267
- Dutch auction, 270
- Firm commitment underwriting, 263
- Gross spread (or underwriter discount), 263
- Initial public offering (IPO), 263
- Investment bankers, 262
- Preemptive rights offering, 270
- Primary market, 262
- Private placement, 272

- Prospectus, 267
- Red herring, 267
- Registration statement, 266
- Rule 144A, 273
- Selling group, 264
- Shelf registration (or SEC Rule 415), 268
- Standby fee, 271
- Standby underwriting arrangement, 271
- Underwriting, 263
- Underwriting syndicate, 263
- Waiting period, 267

QUESTIONS

1. a. What are the three ways in which an investment banking firm may be involved in the issuance of a new security?
    b. What is meant by the underwriting function?
2. What is the difference between a firm commitment underwriting arrangement and a best efforts arrangement?
3. a. What is meant by a bought deal?
    b. Why do bought deals expose investment banking firms to greater capital risk than traditional underwriting?
4. A corporation is issuing a bond on a competitive bidding basis. The corporation has indicated that it will issue $200 million of an issue. The following yield bids and the corresponding amounts were submitted:

Bidder	Amount (in millions)	Bid
A	$20	7.4%
B	40	7.5
C	10	7.5
D	50	7.5
E	40	7.6
F	20	7.6
G	10	7.7
H	10	7.7
I	20	7.8
J	25	7.9
K	28	7.9
L	20	8.0
M	18	8.1

   a. Who are the winning bidders?
   b. How much of the security will be allocated to each winning bidder?
   c. If this auction is a single-price auction, at what yield will each winning bidder be awarded the security?
   d. If this auction is a multiple-price auction, at what yield will each winning bidder be awarded the security?
5. a. What is a preemptive right?
    b. What is a preemptive rights offering?

    c. Is a preemptive rights offering common in the United States?

6. The market price of the stock of the Bernstein Corporation is $50 per share and there are one million shares outstanding. Suppose that the management of this corporation is considering a rights offering in connection with the issuance of 500,000 new shares. Each current shareholder would receive one right for every two shares owned. The terms of the rights offering are as follows: For two rights and $30 (the subscription price), a new share can be acquired.

    a. What would the share price be after the rights offering?

    b. What is the value of one right?

    c. Demonstrate the effect on the economic well-being of the initial shareholders as a result of the rights offering.

7. What is a registration statement?

8. What is meant by the waiting period?

9. An underwriter is responsible for performing due diligence before offering a security to investors. What does due diligence mean?

10. The following statements come from the December 24, 1990, issue of *Corporate Financing Week*:

As in the public market, growth in the private placement market was slowed this year by a rise in interest rates that pushed many issuers to the sidelines, by the Mideast crisis and by a flight to quality by investors. . . . Foreign private placements saw a marked increase due to Rule 144A.

    a. What are the key distinctions between a private placement and a public offering?

    b. What is Rule 144A?

    c. Why do you think Rule 144A has increased foreign private placements?

Secondary Markets

Learning Objectives

After reading this chapter, you will understand

■ the definition of a secondary market.

■ the need for secondary markets for financial assets.

■ the various trading locations for securities.

■ the difference between a continuous and a call market.

■ the requirements of a perfect market.

■ frictions that cause actual financial markets to differ from a perfect market.

■ why brokers are necessary.

■ the role of a dealer as a market maker and the costs associated with market making.

■ what is meant by the operational efficiency of a market.

■ what is meant by the pricing efficiency of a market.

■ the implications of pricing efficiency.

■ the different forms of pricing efficiency.

■ the implications of pricing efficiency for market participants.

In Chapter 1, we describe the various functions of financial markets. We note in that chapter that financial markets can be divided into primary and secondary markets. It is in the secondary market where already issued financial assets are traded. The key distinction between a primary market (as described in the last chapter) and a secondary market is that, in the secondary market, the issuer of the asset does not receive funds from the buyer. Rather, the existing issue changes hands in the secondary market, and funds flow from the buyer of the asset to the seller.

In this chapter, we explain the various features of secondary markets. These features are common to the trading of any type of financial instrument. We take a closer look at individual markets in later chapters.

FUNCTION OF SECONDARY MARKETS

It is worthwhile to review once again the function of secondary markets. In the secondary market, an issuer of securities—whether it is a corporation or a governmental unit—may obtain regular information about the value of the asset. The periodic trading of the asset reveals to the issuer the consensus price that the asset commands in an open market. Thus, firms can discover what value investors attach to their stocks, and firms or noncorporate issuers can observe the prices of their bonds and the implied interest rates investors expect and demand from them. Such information helps issuers assess how well they are using the funds acquired from earlier primary market activities, and it also indicates how receptive investors would be to new offerings. The other service that a secondary market offers issuers is the opportunity for the original buyer of an asset to reverse the investment by selling it for cash. Unless investors are confident that they can shift from one financial asset to another as they may feel necessary, they would naturally be reluctant to buy any financial asset. Such reluctance would harm potential issuers in one of two ways: Either issuers would be unable to sell new securities at all, or they would have to pay a higher rate of return, as investors would increase the discount rate in compensation for expected illiquidity in the securities.

Investors in financial assets receive several benefits from a secondary market. Such a market obviously offers them liquidity for their assets as well as information about the assets' fair or consensus values. Furthermore, secondary markets bring together many interested parties and thereby reduce the costs of searching for likely buyers and sellers of assets. Moreover, by accommodating many trades, secondary markets keep the cost of transactions low. By keeping the costs of both searching and transacting low, secondary markets encourage investors to purchase financial assets.

Key Points You Should Understand Before Proceeding

1. Secondary markets help the issuer of securities to track their values and required returns.
2. Secondary markets benefit investors by providing liquidity.

TRADING LOCATIONS

One indication of the usefulness of secondary markets is that they exist throughout the world. Here, we give just a few examples of these markets.

In the United States, secondary trading of common stock occurs in a number of trading locations. Many shares are traded on major national **stock exchanges** (the largest of which is the New York Stock Exchange) and regional stock exchanges, which are organized and somewhat regulated markets in specific geographical locations. Additional significant trading in stock takes place on the so-called **over-the-counter** or **OTC market**, which is a geographically dispersed group of traders linked to one another via telecommunication systems. The dominant OTC market for stocks in the United States is Nasdaq. Some bonds are traded on exchanges, but most trading in bonds in the United States and throughout the world occurs in the OTC market. The U.S. secondary markets for common stocks are discussed in Chapter 18.

The London Stock Exchange (LSE) is basically an over-the-counter market whose members are in various places but communicate directly with one another through sophisticated electronic and computer facilities. Assets traded on the LSE include stocks of domestic and international firms as well as a wide array of bonds and options. The dominant German exchange is the Destche Borse AG, which is owned by the Frankfurt Stock Exchange (FSE) and seven other regional stock exchanges. On these exchanges, trading is done by a new electronic trading system (Xetra). There are six Japanese stock exchanges, but the Tokyo Stock Exchange (TSE) is dominant. The trading floor of the TSE was closed during April 1999, and all trading occurs purely through a computer-based system without any designated market maker. The international secondary markets for common stocks are discussed in Chapter 19.

Key Points You Should Understand Before Proceeding

1. What an organized exchange is.
2. A large volume of trading may also occur on a market with no fixed location and with geographically dispersed traders.

MARKET STRUCTURES

Many secondary markets are **continuous**, which means that prices are determined continuously throughout the trading day as buyers and sellers submit orders. For example, given the order flow at 10:00 A.M., the market clearing price of a stock on some organized stock exchange may be $70; at 11:00 A.M. of the same trading day, the market-clearing price of the same stock, but with different order flows, may be $70.75. Thus, in a continuous market, prices may vary with the pattern of orders reaching the market and not because of any change in the basic situation of supply and demand. We will return to this point later.

A contrasting market structure is the **call market**, in which orders are batched or grouped together for simultaneous execution at the same price. That is, at certain times in the trading day (or possibly more than once in a day), a market maker holds an auction for a stock. The auction may be oral or written. In either case, the auction will determine or fix the market clearing price at a particular time of the trading day. (This use of the word **fix** is traditional, and not pejorative or suggestive of illegal activity. For example, the *Financial Times* reports on the activities of the London gold bullion market, which is a call market, and records prices set at the "morning fix" and the "afternoon fix." These fixes take place at the two call auctions which are held daily.) Until the mid-1980s, the Paris *Bourse* was a call market, with auctions for large stocks being oral and auctions for smaller issues being written. It has since become a continuous market, and trading takes place *en continu*.

Currently, some markets are mixed, using elements of the continuous and the call frameworks. For example, the New York Stock Exchange begins trading (at 9:30 A.M.) with a call auction. With opening prices set in that manner, trading proceeds in a continuous way until closing.

Key Points You Should Understand Before Proceeding

1. The basic features of the call method of trading.
2. What a continuous market is.
3. Some markets conduct the day's initial trades with a call method and most other trades in a continuous way.

PERFECT MARKETS

In order to explain the characteristics of secondary markets, we first describe a **perfect market** for a financial asset. Then we can show how common occurrences in real markets keep them from being theoretically perfect.

In general, a perfect market results when the number of buyers and sellers is sufficiently large, and all participants are small enough relative to the market so that no individual market agent can influence the commodity's price. Consequently, all buyers and sellers are price-takers, and the market price is determined where there is equality of supply and demand. This condition is more likely to be satisfied if the commodity traded is fairly homogeneous (for example, corn or wheat). But a market is not perfect only because market agents are price takers. A perfect market is also free of transactions costs and any impediment to the interaction of supply and demand for the commodity. Economists refer to these various costs and impediments as **frictions**. The costs associated with frictions generally result in buyers paying more than in the absence of frictions and/or in sellers receiving less.

In the case of financial markets, frictions would include:

➤ commissions charged by brokers

➤ bid–ask spreads charged by dealers

➤ order handling and clearance charges

➤ taxes (notably on capital gains) and government-imposed transfer fees

➤ costs of acquiring information about the financial asset

➤ trading restrictions, such as exchange-imposed restrictions on the size of a position in the financial asset that a buyer or seller may take

➤ restrictions on market makers

➤ halts to trading that may be imposed by regulators where the financial asset is traded.

An investor who expects that the price of a security will increase can benefit from buying that security. However, suppose that an investor expects that the price of a security will decline and wants to benefit should the price actually decline. What can the investor do? The investor may be able to sell the security without owning it. How can this happen? There are various institutional arrangements that allow an investor to borrow securities so that the borrowed security can be delivered to satisfy the sale. We describe this for the stock market in Chapter 18.

This practice of selling securities that are not owned at the time of sale is referred to as *selling short*. The security is purchased subsequently by the investor and returned to the party that lent it. In this way, the investor covers a short position. A profit will be realized if the purchase price is less than the price at which the issuer sold short the security.

The ability of investors to sell short is an important mechanism in financial markets. In the absence of an effective short-selling mechanism, security prices will tend to be biased toward the view of more optimistic investors, causing a market to depart from the standards of a perfect price-setting situation. In fact, many large and developed securities markets allow short selling, although regulatory bodies tend to monitor this practice more closely than other features of markets. Nonetheless, the prevalence of short selling is clear evidence of its usefulness to the price-setting function of securities markets.

Key Points You Should Understand Before Proceeding

1. A market can be perfect, in a theoretical sense, only if it meets many conditions regarding number of participants, flow of information, freedom from regulation, and freedom from costs that hinder trading.
2. Market imperfections are called frictions.
3. A perfect market must also permit short selling, which is the sale of borrowed securities.

ROLE OF BROKERS AND DEALERS IN REAL MARKETS

Common occurrences in real markets keep them from meeting the theoretical standards of being perfect. Because of these occurrences, **brokers** and dealers are necessary to the smooth functioning of a secondary market.

Brokers

One way in which a real market might not meet all the exacting standards of a theoretically perfect market is that many investors may not be present at all times in the marketplace. Furthermore, a typical investor may not be skilled in the art of the deal or completely informed about every facet of trading in the asset. Clearly, most investors in even smoothly functioning markets need professional assistance. Investors need someone to receive and keep track of their orders for buying or selling, to find other parties wishing to sell or buy, to negotiate for good prices, to serve as a focal point for trading, and to execute the orders. The broker performs all these functions. Obviously, these functions are more important for the complicated trades, such as the small or large trades, than for simple transactions or those of typical size.

A broker is an entity that acts on behalf of an investor who wishes to execute orders. In economic and legal terms, a broker is said to be an *agent* of the investor. It is important to realize that the brokerage activity does not require the broker to buy and sell or hold in inventory the financial asset that is the subject of the trade. (Such activity is termed *taking a position* in the asset, and it is the role of the dealer, another important financial market participant discussed below.) Rather, the broker receives, transmits, and executes investors' orders with other investors. The broker receives an explicit commission for these services, and the commission is a *transactions cost* of the securities markets. If the broker also provides other services, such as research, record keeping, or advising, investors may pay additional charges.

Dealers as Market Makers

A real market might also differ from the perfect market because of the possibly frequent event of a temporary imbalance in the number of buy and sell orders that investors may place for any security at any one time. Such unmatched or unbalanced flow causes two problems. One is that the security's price may change abruptly, even if there has been no shift in either supply or demand for the security. Another problem is that buyers may have to pay higher than market-clearing prices (or sellers accept lower ones) if they want to make their trade immediately.

An example can illustrate these points. Suppose that the consensus price for ABC security is $50, which was determined in several recent trades. Now, suppose that a flow of buy orders from investors who suddenly have cash arrives in the market, but there is no accompanying supply of sell orders. This temporary imbalance could be sufficient to push the price of ABC security to, say, $55. Thus, the price has changed sharply even though there has been no change in any fundamental financial aspect of the issuer. Buyers who want to buy immediately must pay $55 rather than $50, and this difference can be viewed as the price of **immediacy**. By immediacy, we mean that buyers and sellers do not want to wait for the arrival of sufficient orders on the other side of the trade, which would bring the price closer to the level of recent transactions.

The fact of imbalances explains the need for the **dealer** or market maker, who stands ready and willing to buy a financial asset for its own account (to add to an inventory of the financial asset) or sell from its own account (to reduce the inventory of the financial asset). At a given time, dealers are willing to buy a financial asset at a price (the bid price) that is less than what they are willing to sell the same financial asset for (the ask price).

In the 1960s, two economists, George Stigler[1] and Harold Demsetz,[2] analyzed the role of dealers in securities markets. They viewed dealers as the suppliers of immediacy—the ability to trade promptly—to the market. The bid–ask spread can be viewed in turn as the price charged by dealers for supplying immediacy together with short-run price stability (continuity or smoothness) in the presence of short-term order imbalances. There are two other roles that dealers play: providing reliable price infor-

---

[1] George Stigler, "Public Regulation of Securities Markets," *Journal of Business* (April 1964), pp. 117–134.

[2] Harold Demsetz, "The Cost of Transacting," *Quarterly Journal of Economics* (October 1968), pp. 35–36.

mation to market participants, and, in certain market structures, providing the services of an auctioneer in bringing order and fairness to a market.[3]

The price stabilization role follows from our earlier example of what may happen to the price of a particular transaction in the absence of any intervention when there is a temporary imbalance of orders. By taking the opposite side of a trade when there are no other orders, the dealer prevents the price from materially diverging from the price at which a recent trade was consummated.

Investors are concerned not only with immediacy, but also with being able to trade at prices that are reasonable, given prevailing conditions in the market. While dealers do not know with certainty the true price of a security, they do have a privileged position in some market structures with respect not just to the flow of market orders but also to **limit orders**, which are special orders that can be executed only if the market price of the asset changes in a specified way. (See Chapter 18 for more on limit orders.) For example, the dealers of the organized markets, called *specialists* and discussed in Chapter 18, have just such a privileged position from which they get special information about the flow of market orders.

Finally, the dealer acts as an **auctioneer** in some market structures, thereby providing order and fairness in the operations of the market. For example, as we will explain in Chapter 18, the market maker on organized stock exchanges in the United States performs this function by organizing trading to make sure that the exchange rules for the priority of trading are followed. The role of a market maker in a call market structure is that of an auctioneer. The market maker does not take a position in the traded asset, as a dealer does in a continuous market.

What factors determine the price dealers should charge for the services they provide? Or equivalently, what factors determine the *bid–ask spread*? One of the most important is the order processing costs incurred by dealers. The costs of equipment necessary to do business and a dealer's administrative and operations staff are examples. The lower these costs, the narrower the bid–ask spread. With the reduced cost of computing and better-trained personnel, these costs have declined since the 1960s.

Dealers also have to be compensated for bearing risk. A **dealer's position** may involve carrying inventory of a security (a *long position*) or selling a security that is not in inventory (a *short position*). There are three types of risks associated with maintaining a long or short position in a given security. First, there is the uncertainty about the future price of the security. A dealer who has a net long position in the security is concerned that the price will decline in the future; a dealer who is in a net short position is concerned that the price will rise.

The second type of risk has to do with the expected time it will take the dealer to unwind a position and its uncertainty. And this, in turn, depends primarily on the thickness of the market for the security. Finally, while a dealer may have access to better information about order flows than the general public, there are some trades where the dealer takes the risk of trading with someone who has better information.[4] This results in the better-informed trader obtaining a better price at the expense of the dealer. Consequently, a dealer in establishing the bid–ask spread for a trade will assess whether or not the trader might have better information.[5]

---

[3] For a more detailed discussion, see Chapter 1 in Robert A. Schwartz, *Equity Markets: Structure, Trading, and Performance* (New York: Harper & Row Publishers, 1988), pp. 389–397.

[4] Walter Bagehot, "The Only Game in Town," *Financial Analysts Journal* (March–April 1971), pp. 12–14, 22.

[5] Some trades that we will discuss in Chapter 18 can be viewed as *informationless trades*. This means that the dealer knows or believes that a trade is being requested to accomplish an investment objective that is not motivated by the potential future price movement of the security.

> **Key Points You Should Understand Before Proceeding**
>
> 1. The relationship between a broker and an investor.
> 2. How a dealer makes a profit when making a market.
> 3. The benefits that a market derives from the actions of dealers.

MARKET EFFICIENCY

The term *efficient* capital market has been used in several contexts to describe the operating characteristics of a capital market. There is a distinction, however, between an **operationally (or internally) efficient market** and a **pricing (or externally) efficient capital market**.[6]

Operational Efficiency

In an operationally efficient market, investors can obtain transaction services as cheaply as possible, given the costs associated with furnishing those services. For example, in national equity markets throughout the world the degree of operational efficiency varies. At one time, brokerage commissions in the United States were fixed, and the brokerage industry charged high fees and functioned poorly. But that began to change in May 1975, as the American exchanges adopted a system of competitive and negotiated commissions. Non-U.S. markets have been moving toward more competitive brokerage fees. France, for example, adopted a system of negotiated commissions for large trades in 1985. In its "Big Bang" of 1986, the London Stock Exchange abolished fixed commissions. The Japanese version of the Big Bang began during 1996. One of its many goals was the liberalization of commissions.

Commissions are only part of the cost of transacting, as we note above. The other part is the dealer spread. As explained in Chapter 18, minimum bid–offer spreads in the stock market have declined significantly in recent years. The minium spread was one-eighths ("eighths") until 1997, a vestige of the early days of stock trading. The NYSE and other markets began trading in one-sixteenths ("teenies") on June 24, 1997. Effective August 24, 2000, the minimum spread was reduced to one cent ("decimals"), with trades on all stocks in decimals beginning on August 9, 2001. Bid–offer spreads for bonds vary by type of bond. For example, the bid–ask spread on U.S. Treasury securities is much smaller than for other bonds such as mortgage-backed bonds and derivative mortgage-backed instruments, which are key topics in later chapters. Even within the U.S. Treasury securities market, certain issues have a narrower bid–ask spread than other issues.

Pricing Efficiency

Pricing efficiency refers to a market where prices at all times fully reflect all available information that is relevant to the valuation of securities. That is, investors quickly adjust the demand and supply schedules for a security when new information about it becomes available, and those actions quickly impound the information into the price of the security.

---

[6] Richard R. West, "Two Kinds of Market Efficiency," *Financial Analysts Journal* (November–December 1975), pp. 30–34.

A price efficient market has implications for the investment strategy that investors may wish to pursue. Throughout this book, we refer to various active strategies employed by investors. In an **active strategy**, investors seek to capitalize on what they perceive to be the mispricing of a security or securities. In a market that is price efficient, active strategies will not consistently generate a return after taking into consideration transactions costs and the risks associated with a strategy of frequent trading. The other strategy, in a market which seems to be price efficient, is simply to buy and hold a broad cross section of securities in the market. Some investors pursue this strategy through **indexing**, which is a policy that has the goal of matching the performance of some financial index from the market. We look at the pricing efficiency of the stock market in Chapter 18. It is in this market where the greatest amount of empirical evidence exists.

Key Points You Should Understand Before Proceeding

1. What makes a market operationally or internally efficient.
2. The key characteristic of a market that has pricing or external efficiency.

ELECTRONIC TRADING: THE CASE OF BONDS

In later chapters of this book we will discuss the various types of bonds. Traditionally, bond trading has been based on broker-dealer trading desks, which take principal positions to fill customer buy and sell orders. In recent years, however, there has been an evolution away from traditional bond trading toward electronic trading. This evolution toward electronic trading is likely to continue.

There are several related reasons for the transition to the electronic trading of bonds. Because the bond business has been a principal rather than an agency business, the capital of the market makers is critical. Whereas the amount of capital of the broker-dealers has increased during the last several years, the amount of capital of U.S. institutional investors (pension funds, mutual funds, insurance companies, and commercial banks) and international customers has increased much more, and the size of the orders has increased significantly. As a result, making markets in bonds has become more risky for the market makers.

In addition, the increase in the volatility of bond markets has increased the capital required of bond broker-dealers. Finally, the profitability of bond market making has declined since many of the products have become more commodity-like and their bid–offer spreads have decreased.

The combination of the increased risk and the decreased profitability of bond market making has induced the major market markets to deemphasize this business in the allocation of capital. Broker-dealer firms have determined that it is more efficient to employ their capital in other activities such as underwriting, asset management, and other agency-type brokerage businesses than in principal-type market-making businesses. As a result, the liquidity of the traditionally principal-oriented bond markets has declined, and this decline in liquidity has opened the way for other market-making mechanisms.

This retreat by traditional market-making firms opened the door for electronic trading. In fact, as indicated below, the same Wall Street firms that have been the major market makers in bonds have also been the supporters of electronic trading in bonds.

Electronic trading in bonds has helped fill this developing vacuum and provided liquidity to the bond markets. The growth of electronic trading will necessarily continue. Among the overall advantages of electronic trading are (1) providing liquidity to the markets; (2) price discovery (particularly for less liquid markets); (3) utilization of new technologies; and (4) trading and portfolio management efficiencies. As an example of the last advantage, portfolio managers can load their buy/sell orders in a web site, trade from these orders, and then clear these orders.

There are a variety of types of electronic trading systems for bonds. The two major types of electronic trading systems are the *dealer-to-customer systems* and the *exchange systems.*

Dealer-to-customer systems can be a *single-dealer system* or *multiple-dealer system.* Single-dealer systems are based on a customer dealing with a single, identified dealer over the computer. The single-dealer system simply computerizes the traditional customer–dealer market making mechanism. Multi-dealer systems provide some advancement over the single-dealer method. A customer can select from any of several identified dealers whose bids and offers are provided on a computer screen. The customer knows the identity of the dealer and the transaction is cleared through the dealer's procedures.

The exchange system is quite different and has potentially significantly greater value added. According to the exchange system, dealer and customer bids and offers are entered into the system on an anonymous basis, and the clearing of the executed trades is done through a common process. As a result, a common clearinghouse and common membership criteria based on the credit acceptability of the members have to be developed. This mechanism requires a much more onerous structure than the dealer-to-customer systems. Although there is a common clearinghouse for common stocks (Depository Trust Company [DTC]), there is none for bonds. Thus, the development of an open architecture system for bonds will be more difficult than for stocks.

Two different major types of exchange systems are those based on continuous trading and call auctions described previously in this chapter. Continuous trading permits trading at continuously changing market determined prices throughout the day and is appropriate for liquid bonds, such as Treasury and agency securities. Call auctions provide for fixed price auctions (that is, all the transaction or exchanges occur at the same "fixed" price) at specific times during the day and are appropriate for less liquid bonds such as corporate bonds and municipal bonds. Table 15-1 summarizes the major issues in electronic bond trading.

Table 15-1   Summary of Major Issues in Electronic Bond Trading

	DEALER TO CUSTOMER— MULTIPLE DEALER	EXCHANGE SYSTEMS
Characteristics	Customer and dealer know the identity of the counterparty	Counterparties are anonymous
	Clearing through specific dealer's clearing system	Common clearing through same system
	Counterparty credit determined by individual broker-dealer and customer	Counterparty credit determined by common clearing organization
	Large trades done as block trades through individual dealers	Large trades done as block trades through individual dealers
Ideal products	Liquid, tradable type products: Treasuries, agencies, and MBS	Inventory-type products: CMOs, ABS, corporate bonds, municipal bonds, other less liquid products
Examples	Trade Web (Sponsors: CSFB, Goldman Sachs, Lehman Brothers, Salomon Smith Barney, Merrill Lynch, Morgan Stanley Dean Witter)	Bondbook-prospective (Sponsors: Goldman Sachs, Merrill Lynch, Morgan Stanley); Bloomberg-prospective

Currently a large share of Treasuries are traded via the dealer-to-customer Tradeweb system. Two exchange systems are scheduled to begin operations during 2001, namely Bondbook and a system sponsored by Bloomberg.

SUMMARY

A secondary market in financial assets is one where existing or outstanding assets are traded among investors. A secondary market serves several needs of the firm or governmental unit that issues securities in the primary market. The secondary market provides the issuer with regular information about the value of its outstanding stocks or bonds, and it encourages investors to buy securities from issuers because it offers them an ongoing opportunity for liquidating their investments in securities.

Investors also get services from the secondary market: The market supplies them with liquidity and prices for the assets they are holding or want to buy; and the market brings interested investors together, thereby reducing the costs of searching for other parties and of making trades.

Secondary markets for financial securities exist around the world. Such markets may be continuous, where trading and price determination go on throughout the day as orders to buy and sell reach the market. Some markets are call markets: Prices are determined by executions of batched or grouped orders to buy and sell at a specific time (or times) within the trading day. Some secondary markets combine features of call and continuous trading.

Even the most developed and smoothly functioning secondary market falls short of being perfect in the economically theoretical meaning of the term. Actual markets tend to have numerous frictions that affect prices and investors' behavior. Some key frictions are transactions costs, which include commissions, fees, and execution costs.

Because of imperfections in actual markets, investors need the services of two types of market participants: dealers and brokers. Brokers aid investors by collecting and transmitting orders to the market, by bringing willing buyers and sellers together, by negotiating prices, and by executing orders. The fee for these services is the broker's commission.

Dealers perform three functions in markets: (1) They provide the opportunity for investors to trade immediately rather than waiting for the arrival of sufficient orders on the other side of the trade (immediacy), and they do this while maintaining short-run price stability (continuity); (2) they offer price information to market participants; and (3) in certain market structures, dealers serve as auctioneers in bringing order and fairness to a market. Dealers buy for their own account and maintain inventories of assets, and their profits come from selling assets at higher prices than the prices at which they purchased them.

A market is operationally efficient if it offers investors reasonably priced services related to buying and selling. A market is price efficient if at all times prices fully reflect all available information that is relevant to the valuation of securities. In such a market, active strategies pursued will not consistently produce superior returns after adjusting for risk and transactions costs.

Electronic bond trading has improved the liquidity of the bond market as the commitment to bond trading by dealers has not kept pace with the liquidity needs of institutional investors. The two major types of electronic trading systems are the dealer-to-customer systems (single-and multiple-dealer systems) and the *exchange systems*. In exchange systems, dealer and customer bids and offers are entered into the system on an anonymous basis, and the clearing of the executed trades is done through a common process. There are continuous trading and call auction exchange-trading systems.

KEY TERMS

- Active investment strategy, 284
- Auctioneer, 282
- Broker, 280
- Call market, 279
- Continuous market, 279
- Dealer, 281
- Dealer's position, 282
- Fix, 279
- Frictions, 279
- Immediacy, 281
- Indexing, 284
- Limit order, 282
- Operational or internal efficiency, 283
- Over-the-counter (OTC) market, 278
- Perfect market, 279
- Pricing or external efficiency, 283
- Short sale, 280
- Stock exchange, 278

QUESTIONS

1. Consider two transactions. The Norwegian government sells bonds in the United States. The buyer of one of those bonds is an insurance company, which, after holding the bond for a year, sells it to a mutual fund. Which of these transactions occurs in the primary market and which in the secondary market? Does the Norwegian government get any proceeds from the sale between the insurance company and the mutual fund?

2. Some years ago, Japan's four largest brokerage firms (Yamaichi Securities Co., Nomura Securities Co., Daiwa Securities Co., and Nikko Securities Co.) formally asked their government to lift bans that restrict their freedom to invest in stocks. One of those bans prevents a brokerage firm from trading for its own account (that is, buying and selling for itself rather than for clients) during certain times of the trading day. The other ban restricts a brokerage firm participating in more than 30% of the trading of any one stock within a month. Consider these restrictions in terms of the role of dealers in financial markets and the requirements for operational and price efficiency in a market. Do you think that lifting the restrictions would help the Tokyo Stock Exchange to be more efficient with regard to price and operations?

3. The residential real estate market boasts many brokers but very few dealers. What explains this situation?

4. Some years ago, legislators in a state claimed that speculation on land was driving prices to too high a level. They proposed to pass a law that would require the buyer of any piece of land in the state to hold the land for at least three years before he or she could resell it.
   a. Analyze this proposal in terms of perfect markets and possible frictions that have been described in this chapter.
   b. If that proposal had passed, do you think land prices would have risen or fallen?

5. What is meant by the statement that "dealers offer both immediacy and price continuity to investors"?

6. In 1990, a trader on the Paris *Bourse* claimed to one of the authors of this book that "now, we are just like New York; everything is continuous." Do you think that the *Bourse*'s change from a call market to a continuous market, which took place in the 1980s, could have improved either price or operational efficiency in that market enough to warrant this assertion?

7. If a security is highly liquid, explain whether it would be more advantageous to develop a trading system with continuous trading or call auction.

8. Outline the problems associated with fixed brokerage commissions.

9. Indicate whether or not you agree with the following statement: "The minimum bid-offer spread on common stock is in terms of one-eighths."

10. Assume that UND stock normally has a bid–offer spread of three-eights, or $0.375. What do you think would happen to that spread on a day when the stock market begins to fall very sharply? Explain your answer. Also, what would happen to the spread if the company announced that it was buying back 20% of its outstanding shares and would complete that repurchase within three months? Explain your view.

11. Suppose the federal government imposed a tax of $0.10 on each stock-buying transaction. Would stock prices in general rise or fall on such news? Explain your answer.

12. If the Japanese government mandates that all commissions on stock sales be negotiable, would stock prices rise or fall because of this information? Why?

13. What are the reasons for the development of electronic bond trading?

Part VI
Markets for
Government Debt

Treasury and Agency Securities Markets

Learning Objectives

After reading this chapter, you will understand

- the importance of the Treasury market.
- the different types of securities issued by the Treasury.
- the operation of the primary market for Treasury securities.
- the role of government dealers and government brokers.
- the secondary market for Treasury securities.
- how Treasury securities are quoted in the secondary market.
- how government dealers use the repurchase agreement market.
- the zero-coupon Treasury securities market.
- the difference between government-sponsored enterprises and federally related institutions.
- functions of government-sponsored enterprises that issue securities.
- non-U.S. government bond markets.

Treasury securities are issued by the U.S. Department of the Treasury and are backed by the full faith and credit of the U.S. government. Consequently, market participants view them as having no credit risk. As explained in Chapter 11, historically, interest rates on Treasury securities have been the benchmark interest rates throughout the U.S. economy. However, since the late 1990s, the deficit of the U.S. government has been declining. As a result, the U.S. Department of the Treasury has reduced its issuance of long-term securities and has pursued a policy of buying back longer term securities. As a result, while U.S. Treasury securities still play a prominent role in financial markets, there is currently a search for a sector of the bond market to take over the role of Treasury securities as the benchmark. We mentioned in Chapter 11 three candidates. In this chapter, we discuss the Treasury securities market and the market for U.S. agency securities. It is, in fact, the yields on securities of U.S. agencies (more specifically, government-sponsored enterprises) that are seeking to become the new benchmark interest rates. At the end of this chapter, we discuss non-U.S. government bond markets.

TREASURY SECURITIES[1]

Two factors account for the prominent role of U.S. Treasury securities: volume (in terms of dollars outstanding) and liquidity. The Department of the Treasury is the largest single issuer of debt in the world. The large volume of total debt and the large size of any single issue have contributed to making the Treasury market the most active and hence the most liquid market in the world. The spread between bid and ask prices is considerably narrower than in other sectors of the bond market, and most issues can be traded easily. Many issues in the corporate and municipal markets are illiquid by contrast and cannot be traded readily.

Treasury securities are available in book-entry form at the Federal Reserve Bank. This means that the investor receives only a receipt as evidence of ownership instead of an engraved certificate. An advantage of book-entry is ease in transferring owner-ship of the security. Interest income from Treasury securities is subject to federal income taxes but is exempt from state and local income taxes.

Types of Treasury Securities

There are two categories of government securities: **discount** and **coupon securities**. The fundamental difference between the two types lies in the form of the stream of payments that the holder receives, which is reflected in turn in the prices at which the securities are issued. Coupon securities pay interest every six months, plus principal at maturity. Discount securities pay only a contractually fixed amount at maturity, called maturity value or face value. Discount instruments are issued below maturity value, and return to the investor the difference between maturity value and issue price.

Current Treasury practice is to issue all securities with maturities of one year or less as discount securities. These securities are called **Treasury bills**. All securities with maturities of two years or longer are issued as coupon securities. Treasury coupon securities issued with original maturities between 2 and 10 years are called **Treasury notes**; those with original maturities greater than 10 years are called **Treasury bonds**. While there is therefore a distinction between Treasury notes and bonds, in this chap-ter we refer to both as simply Treasury bonds.

Treasury Inflation-Protection Securities.

On January 29, 1997, the U.S. Department of the Treasury issued for the first time Treasury securities that adjust for inflation. These securities are popularly referred to as **Treasury inflation protection securities** (TIPS). (The Treasury refers to these secu-rities as Treasury inflation indexed securities [TIIS].) The Treasury has issued TIPS that are notes and bonds. TIPS work as follows. The coupon rate on an issue is set at a fixed rate. That rate is determined via the auction process described later in this sec-tion. The coupon rate is called the "real rate" since it is the rate that the investor ulti-mately earns above the inflation rate. The inflation index that the government has decided to use for the inflation adjustment is the nonseasonally adjusted U.S. City Average All Items Consumer Price Index for All Urban Consumers (CPI-U).

The adjustment for inflation is as follows. The principal on which the Treasury Department will base both the dollar amount of the coupon payment and the maturity value is adjusted semiannually. This is called the inflation-adjusted principal. For example, suppose that the coupon rate for a TIPS is 3.5% and the annual inflation rate is 3%. Suppose further that an investor purchases on January 1, $100,000 of par

---

[1] Portions of this section are adapted from Chapter 3 in Frank J. Fabozzi, *Bond Portfolio Management* (New Hope, PA: Frank J. Fabozzi Associates, 2001) and in other published writings by Frank J. Fabozzi.

value (principal) of this issue. The semiannual inflation rate is 1.5% (3% divided by 2). The inflation-adjusted principal at the end of the first six-month period is found by multiplying the original par value by the semiannual inflation rate. In our example, the inflation-adjusted principal at the end of the first six-month period is $101,500. It is this inflation-adjusted principal that is the basis for computing the coupon interest for the first six-month period. The coupon payment is then 1.75% (one-half the real rate of 3.5%) multiplied by the inflation-adjusted principal at the coupon payment date ($101,500). The coupon payment is therefore $1,776.25

Let us look at the next six months. The inflation-adjusted principal at the beginning of the period is $101,500. Suppose that the semiannual inflation rate for the second six-month period is 1%. Then the inflation-adjusted principal at the end of the second six-month period is the inflation-adjusted principal at the beginning of the six-month period ($101,500) increased by the semiannual inflation rate (1%). The adjustment to the principal is $1,015 (1% times $101,500). So, the inflation-adjusted principal at the end of the second six-month period (December 31 in our example) is $102,515 ($101,500 + $1,015). The coupon interest that will be paid to the investor at the second coupon payment date is found by multiplying the inflation-adjusted principal on the coupon payment date ($102,515) by one-half the real rate (i.e., one-half of 3.5%). That is, the coupon payment will be $1,794.01.

As can be seen, part of the adjustment for inflation comes in the coupon payment since it is based on the inflation-adjusted principal. However, the U.S. government has decided to tax the adjustment each year. This feature reduces the attractiveness of TIPS as an investment in the accounts of tax-paying entities.

Because of the possibility of disinflation (i.e., price declines), the inflation-adjusted principal at maturity may turn out to be less than the initial par value. However, the Treasury has structured TIPS so that they are redeemed at the greater of the inflation-adjusted principal and the initial par value.

An inflation-adjusted principal must be calculated for a settlement date. The inflation-adjusted principal is defined in terms of an index ratio, which is the ratio of the reference CPI for the settlement date to the reference CPI for the issue date. The reference CPI is calculated with a three-month lag. For example, the reference CPI for May 1 is the CPI-U reported in February. The U.S. Department of the Treasury publishes and makes available on its web site (www.publicdebt.treas.gov) a daily index ratio for an issue.

The Primary Market

The primary market is the market for the issuance of newly issued Treasury securities.

Auction Cycles.

The U.S. Department of the Treasury makes the determination of the procedure for auctioning new Treasury securities, when to auction them, and what maturities to issue. There have been occasional changes in the auction cycles and the maturity of the issues auctioned. Currently, there are weekly three-month and six-month bill auctions. For coupon securities, there are monthly two-year note and five-year note auctions, and quarterly auctions for the 10-year note and 30-year bond (the "refunding" auction).[2]

On the announcement day, the Treasury announces the amount of each issue to be auctioned, the auction date, and maturities to be issued. Occasionally an outstand-

---

[2] At one time the U.S. Department of the Treasury offered three-year, four-year, and seven-year Treasury notes and 15-year and 20-year Treasury bonds.

ing issue is **reopened** (that is, the amount of an outstanding note is increased) at an auction instead of a new issue auctioned. In recent years, the Department of the Treasury has re-opened the ten-year note several times.

Determination of the Results of an Auction.

The auction for Treasury securities is conducted on a competitive bidding basis. Competitive bids must be submitted on a yield basis. Noncompetitive tenders may also be submitted for up to a $1 million face amount. Such tenders are based only on quantity, not yield.

The auction results are determined by first deducting the total noncompetitive tenders and nonpublic purchases (such as purchases by the Federal Reserve itself) from the total securities being auctioned. The remainder is the amount to be awarded to the competitive bidders. For example, in April 1996 there was an auction for the two-year Treasury note. The amount auctioned by the Treasury was $19.946 billion. The noncompetitive bids totaled $1.169 billion. This meant that there was $18.777 billion to be distributed to competitive bidders. For this auction, there were bids for $47.604 billion.

The bids are then arranged from the lowest-yield bid to the highest-yield bid. This is equivalent to arranging the bids from the highest price to the lowest price. Starting from the lowest-yield bid, all competitive bids are accepted until the amount to be distributed to the competitive bidders is completely allocated. The highest yield accepted by the Treasury is referred to as the **stop yield**, and bidders at that yield are awarded a percentage of their total tender offer. For the two-year Treasury auction in April 1996, the stop yield was 5.939%. Bidders higher in yield than the stop yield are not distributed any of the new issue. Such bidders are said to have "missed" or were "shut out."

At what yield is a winning bidder awarded the security? All U.S. Treasury auctions are single-price auctions. In a single-price auction, all bidders are awarded securities at the highest yield of accepted competitive tenders (i.e., the stop yield). This type of auction is called a "Dutch auction." Historically, the Treasury auctioned securities through multiple-price auctions. With multiple-price auctions, the Treasury still accepted the lowest-yielding bids up to the yield required to sell the amount offered (less the amount of noncompetitive bids), but accepted bids were awarded at the particular yields bid, rather than at the stop-out yield. In September 1992, the Treasury started conducting single-price auctions for the two- and five-year notes. In November 1998, the Treasury adopted the single-price method for all auctions.

To illustrate the auction process, suppose that the auction results for a Treasury security were as follows:

Total issue	$9.00 billion
Less noncompetitive bids	0.64
Less Federal Reserve	2.80
Left for competitive bidders	$5.56 billion

Total competitive bids might have been received as shown in Table 16-1.

The Treasury allocates securities to competitive bidders from the low-yield bid to the high-yield bid until $5.56 billion is distributed. Those who bid 7.55% to 7.61% will be awarded the entire amount for which they bid. The total that would be awarded to these bidders is $4.36 billion, leaving $1.2 billion to be awarded, less than the $1.52 billion bid at 7.62%. Each of the bidders at 7.62% would be awarded 79% ($1.2/$1.52) of the amount it bid. For example, if a financial institution bid for $100 million at 7.62%, it would be awarded $79 million. The results of the auction would show 7.55%

Table 16-1   Bids at Hypothetical Treasury Auction

AMOUNT (IN BILLIONS)	BID
$0.20	7.55% (lowest yield/highest price)
0.26	7.56
0.33	7.57
0.57	7.58 (average yield/average price)
0.79	7.59
0.96	7.60
1.25	7.61
1.52	7.62 (stop or highest yield/stop or lowest price)

high, 7.58% average, and 7.62% the stop yield, with 79% awarded at the stop. All winning bidders are awarded securities at the stop yield of 7.62%. Bidders higher in yield than 7.62% were shut out.

The difference between the average yield of all the bids accepted by the Treasury and the stop yield is called the **tail**. Market participants use the tail as a measure of the success of the auction. The larger the tail, the less successful the auction. This is because the average price at which accepted bidders realized securities was considerably lower than the highest price paid. The hypothetical Treasury auction in our illustration above had a tail of 0.04—the stop yield of 7.62% less the average yield of 7.58%.

Primary Dealers.

Any firm can deal in government securities, but in implementing its open market operations, the Federal Reserve will deal directly only with dealers that it designates as **primary dealers** or *recognized dealers*. Basically, the Federal Reserve wants to be sure that firms requesting status as primary dealers have adequate capital relative to positions assumed in Treasury securities and do a reasonable amount of volume in Treasury securities. Table 16-2 lists the primary government dealers as of January 12, 2001.

When a firm requests status as a primary dealer, the Federal Reserve requests first that the applying firm informally report its positions and trading volume. If these are acceptable to the Federal Reserve, it gives the firm status as a *reporting dealer*. This means that the firm will be put on the Federal Reserve's regular reporting list. After the firm serves for some time as a reporting dealer, the Federal Reserve will make it a primary dealer if it is convinced that the firm will continue to meet the criteria established.

Submission of Bids.

Until 1991, primary dealers and large commercial banks that were not primary dealers would submit bids for their own account and for their customers. Others who wished to participate in the auction process could only submit competitive bids for their own account, not their customers. Consequently, a broker-dealer in government securities that was not a primary dealer could not submit a competitive bid on behalf of its customers. Moreover, unlike primary dealers, nonprimary dealers had to make large cash deposits or provide guarantees to ensure that they could fulfill their obligation to purchase the securities for which they bid.

Table 16-2   List of the Primary Government Securities Dealers Reporting to the
Securities Reports Division of the Federal Reserve Bank of New York

ABN AMRO Incorporated
BNP Paribas Securities Corp.
Banc of America Securities LLC
Banc One Capital Markets, Inc.
Barclays Capital Inc.
Bear, Stearns & Co., Inc.
CIBC World Markets Corp.
Credit Suisse First Boston Corporation
Daiwa Securities America Inc.
Deutsche Banc Alex. Brown Inc.
Dresdner Kleinwort Benson North America LLC.
Fuji Securities Inc.
Goldman, Sachs & Co.
Greenwich Capital Markets, Inc.
HSBC Securities (USA) Inc.
J. P. Morgan Securities, Inc./Chase Securities Inc.*
Lehman Brothers Inc.
Merrill Lynch Government Securities Inc.
Morgan Stanley & Co. Incorporated
Nesbitt Burns Securities Inc.
Nomura Securities International, Inc.
SG Cowen Securities Corporation
Salomon Smith Barney Inc.
UBS Warburg LLC.
Zions First National Bank

SOURCE: Securities Reports Division, Federal Reserve Bank of New York, January 12, 2001
For an updated list of primary dealers go to: http://www.ny.frb.org/pihome/news/opnmktops/

This change results from the merger of J. P. Morgan & Co. Incorporated and Chase Manhattan Corporation at the holding company level (effective December 31, 2000). The two primary dealers, which are now affiliates, are expected to merge at the end of the first quarter or early in the second quarter of 2001.

Well-publicized violations of the auction process by Salomon Brothers in the summer of 1991 forced Treasury officials to more closely scrutinize the activities of primary dealers and also reconsider the procedure by which Treasury securities are auctioned.[3] Specifically, the Treasury announced that it would allow qualified broker-dealers to bid for their customers at Treasury auctions. If a qualified broker-dealer establishes a payment link with the Federal Reserve system, no deposit or guaranty is required. Moreover, the auction is no longer handled by the submission of hand-delivered sealed bids to the Federal Reserve. The new auction process is a computerized auction system, which can be electronically accessed by qualified broker-dealers.

---

[3] Salomon Brothers admitted that it repeatedly violated a restriction that limited the amount that any one firm could purchase at the Treasury auction. The firm also admitted that it submitted unauthorized bids for some of its customers.

The Secondary Market

The secondary market for Treasury securities is an over-the-counter market where a group of U.S. government securities dealers offer continuous bid and ask prices on outstanding Treasuries.[4] There is virtual 24-hour trading of Treasury securities. The three primary trading locations are New York, London, and Tokyo. The normal settlement period for Treasury securities is the business day after the transaction day ("next day" settlement).

The most recently auctioned issue of a given maturity is referred to as the *on-the-run issue* or the *current issue*. For example, in May 1999, the on-the-run 30-year Treasury issue was the 5.25s of 2/15/2029. Securities that are replaced by the on-the-run issue are called *off-the-run issues*. For example, prior to the issuance of the 5.25s of 2/15/2029, the on-the-run 30-year Treasury issue was the 5.25s of 11/15/2028 and in May 1999 became an off-the run issue. At a given point in time, there may be more than one off-the-run issue with approximately the same remaining maturity as the on-the-run issue. Issues that have been replaced by several on-the-run issues are said to be "well off-the-run issues." For example, in May 1999, the 30-year 6.5% coupon issued in November 1996 and due in May 2026 was a well off-the-run issue.

When-Issued Market.

Treasury securities are traded prior to the time they are issued by the Treasury. This component of the Treasury secondary market is called the **when-issued market, or wi market**. When-issued trading for both bills and coupon securities extends from the day the auction is announced until the issue day.

Government Brokers.

Government dealers trade with the investing public and with other dealer firms. When they trade with each other, it is through intermediaries known as *interdealer brokers or* **government brokers**. Dealers leave firm bids and offers with interdealer brokers who display the highest bid and lowest offer in a computer network tied to each trading desk and displayed on a monitor. Dealers use interdealer brokers because of the speed and efficiency with which trades can be accomplished. Interdealer brokers keep the names of the dealers involved in trades confidential. The quotes provided on the government dealer screens represent prices in the "inside" or "interdealer" market.

Bid and Offer Quotes on Treasury Bills.

The convention for quoting bids and offers is different for Treasury bills and Treasury coupon securities. Bids and offers on Treasury bills are quoted in a special way. Unlike bonds that pay coupon interest, Treasury bill values are quoted on a bank discount basis, not on a price basis. The **yield on a bank discount basis** is computed as follows:

$$Y = \frac{D}{F} \times \frac{360}{t}$$

where Y = annualized yield on a bank discount basis
 (expressed as a decimal)

D = dollar discount, which is equal to the difference between the face value and the price

F = face value

t = number of days remaining to maturity

As an example, a Treasury bill with 100 days to maturity, a face value of $100,000, and selling for $97,569 would be quoted at 8.75% on a bank discount basis:

$$D = \$100,000 - \$97,569$$
$$= \$2,431$$

Therefore:

$$Y = \frac{\$2,431}{\$100,000} \times \frac{360}{100}$$
$$= 8.75\%$$

Given the yield on a bank discount basis, the price of a Treasury bill is found by first solving the formula for Y, for the dollar discount as follows:

$$D = Y \times F \times t/360$$

The price is then:

$$\text{Price} = F - D$$

For the 100-day Treasury bill with a face value of $100,000, if the yield on a bank discount basis is quoted as 8.75%, D is equal to:

$$D = 0.0875 \times \$100,000 \times 100/360$$
$$= \$2,431$$

Therefore:

$$\text{Price} = \$100,000 - \$2,431$$
$$= \$97,569$$

The quoted yield on a bank discount basis is not a meaningful measure of the return from holding a Treasury bill for two reasons. First, the measure is based on a face value investment rather than on the actual dollar amount invested. Second, the yield is annualized according to a 360-day rather than 365-day year, making it difficult to compare Treasury bill yields with Treasury notes and bonds, which pay interest on a 365-day basis. Despite its shortcomings as a measure of return, this is the method dealers have adopted to quote Treasury bills.

Bid and Offer Quotes on Treasury Coupon Securities.

Treasury coupon securities are quoted differently from Treasury bills. They trade on a dollar price basis in price units of $\frac{1}{32}$ here of 1% of par (par is taken to be $100). For example, a quote of 92-14 refers to a price of 92 and $^{14}\!/_{32}$. If a Treasury coupon security has a $100,000 par value, then a change in price of 1% equates to $1,000, and $\frac{1}{32}$ equates to $31.25. A plus sign following the number of 32nds means that a 64th is added to the price. For example, 92-14+ refers to a price of 92 and $^{29}\!/_{64}$, or 92.453125% of par value.

On quote sheets and screens, the price quote is followed by some *yield to maturity* measure, a calculation we explain in Chapter 11.

Regulation of the Secondary Market.

In the stock market congressional and SEC actions have resulted in movement toward a consolidated tape for reporting trades on exchanges and the over-the-counter market, with a composite quotation system for the collection and display of bid and ask quotations. In the Treasury market, however, despite the fact that trading activity is concentrated in the over-the-counter market, and that daily trading volume exceeds $100 billion, reporting of trades does not exist. Nor is there a display of bid and ask quotations that provides reliable price quotes at which the general public can transact. Such quotations do exist, as we explained earlier, in the interdealer market on government broker screens. While nonprimary dealers can subscribe to the government broker screens, the information that they can obtain on these screens is limited. In particular, the government dealers that permit access to their screens provide information on only the best bid and offer quotation but not the size of the transaction.

Moreover, the rules for the sale of U.S. government securities have been exempt from most SEC provisions and rules.[5] Thus, government broker-dealers are not required to disclose the bid–ask spread on the Treasury securities that they buy from or sell to customers. There are guidelines established by the National Association of Security Dealers for reasonable bid–ask spreads, but lack of disclosure to customers makes it difficult for customers to monitor the pricing practice of a broker-dealer.

Dealer Use of the Repurchase Agreement Market.

Suppose a government securities dealer has purchased $10 million of a particular Treasury security. Where does the dealer obtain the funds to finance that position? Of course, the dealer can use its own funds or borrow from a bank. Typically, however, the dealer uses the *repo* market to obtain financing. In the repo market the dealer can use the $10 million of Treasury security purchased as collateral for a loan. The term of the loan and the interest rate that the dealer agrees to pay (called the *repo rate*) are specified. When the term of the loan is one day, it is called an **overnight repo**; a loan for more than one day is called a **term repo**.

The transaction is referred to as a repurchase agreement because it calls for the sale of the security and its repurchase at a future date. Both the sale price and the purchase price are specified in the agreement. The difference between the purchase (repurchase) price and the sale price is the dollar interest cost of the loan.

Now, let's return to the dealer who needs to finance $10 million of a Treasury security. Suppose that the dealer plans to hold the bonds overnight. Suppose also that a customer of the dealer has excess funds of $10 million. (The customer might be a municipality with tax receipts that it has just collected, and no immediate need to disburse the funds.) The dealer would agree to deliver ("sell") $10 million of the Treasury security to the customer for an amount determined by the repo rate and buy ("repurchase") the same Treasury security from the customer for $10 million the next day. Suppose that the overnight repo rate is 6.5%. Then, the dealer would agree to deliver the Treasury securities for $9,998,194 and repurchase the same securities for $10 million the next day. The $1,806 difference between the "sale" price of $9,998,194

---

[5] Broker-dealers who sell government securities are always subject to the general fraud provisions of the Securities Act of 1933.

and the repurchase price of $10 million is the dollar interest on the financing. From the customer's perspective, the agreement is called a *reverse repo*.

The advantage to the dealer of using the repo market for borrowing on a short-term basis is that the rate is less than the cost of bank financing. From the customer's perspective, the repo market offers an attractive yield on a short-term secured transaction that is highly liquid.

Although the example illustrates financing a dealer's long position in the repo market, dealers can also use the market to cover a short position. For example, suppose a government dealer sold $10 million of Treasury securities two weeks ago and must now cover the position—that is, deliver the securities. The dealer can do a reverse repo (agree to buy the securities and sell them back). Of course, the dealer eventually would have to buy the Treasury security in the market in order to cover its short position.

There is a good deal of Wall Street jargon describing repo transactions. To understand it, remember that one party is lending money and accepting the security as collateral for the loan;[6] the other party is borrowing money and giving collateral to borrow money. When someone lends securities in order to receive cash (that is, to borrow money), that party is said to be *reversing out* securities. A party that lends money with the security as collateral is said to be *reversing in* securities. The expressions *to repo securities* and *to do repo* are also used. The former means that someone is going to finance securities using the security as collateral; the latter means that the party is going to invest in a repo. Finally, the expressions *selling collateral* and *buying collateral* are used to describe a party financing a security with a repo on the one hand, and lending on the basis of collateral, on the other.

It is important to note that both parties to the transaction are exposed to credit risk. The failure of a few small government securities dealer firms involved in repo transactions in the 1980s has made market participants more cautious about the creditworthiness of the counterparty to a repo. Repos are now more carefully structured to reduce credit risk exposure.[7]

There is no one repo rate; rates vary from transaction to transaction depending on factors such as the term of the repo and the availability of collateral. The more difficult it is to obtain the collateral, the lower the repo rate. To understand why this is so, remember that the borrower (or equivalently the seller of the collateral) has a security that is a **hot** or **special issue**. The party that needs the collateral will be willing to lend funds at a lower repo rate in order to obtain the collateral.

Although the factors given above determine the repo rate on a particular transaction, the federal funds rate determines the general level of repo rates. The repo rate will be slightly below the federal funds rate because a repo involves collateralized borrowing, while a federal funds transaction is unsecured borrowing.

Because it is used by dealer firms (investment banking firms and money center banks acting as dealers) to finance positions and cover short positions, the repo market has evolved into one of the largest sectors of the money market. Financial and non-financial firms participate in the market as both sellers and buyers, depending on the circumstances they face. Thrifts and commercial banks are typically net sellers of collateral (that is, net borrowers of funds); money market funds, bank trust departments, municipalities, and corporations are typically net buyers of collateral (that is, providers of funds).

---

[6] The collateral in a repo is not limited to government securities. Money market instruments, federal agency securities, and mortgage-backed securities are also used.

[7] For a description of the procedures used to reduce credit risk, see Frank J. Fabozzi (ed.), *Securities Lending and Repurchase Agreements* (New Hope, PA: Frank J. Fabozzi Associates, 1997).

Although a dealer firm uses the repo market as the primary means for financing its inventory and covering short positions, it will also use the repo market to run a matched book where it takes on repos and reverse repos with the same maturity. The firm will do so to capture the spread at which it enters into the repo and reverse repo agreements. For example, suppose that a dealer firm enters into a term repo of 10 days with a money market fund and a reverse repo rate with a thrift for 10 days in which the collateral is identical. This means that the dealer firm is borrowing funds from the money market fund and lending money to the thrift. If the rate on the repo is 7.5% and the rate on the reverse repo is 7.55%, the dealer firm is borrowing at 7.5% and lending at 7.55%, locking in a spread of 0.05% (five basis points).

A Note on Terminology in the Repo Market.

As noted in Chapter 5, the Federal Reserve conducts open market operations by the outright purchase or sale of government securities or, more often, by repurchase agreements. In these agreements, the Fed either purchases or sells collateral. By buying collateral (that is, lending funds), the Fed injects money into the financial markets, thereby exerting downward pressure on short-term interest rates. When the Fed buys collateral for its own account, this is called a *system repo*. The Fed also buys collateral on behalf of foreign central banks in repo transactions that are referred to as *customer repos*. It is primarily through system repos that the Fed attempts to influence short-term rates. By selling securities for its own account, the Fed drains money from the financial markets, thereby exerting upward pressure on short-term interest rates. This transaction is called a *matched sale*.

Note the language that is used to describe the transactions of the Fed in the repo market. When the Fed lends funds based on collateral, we call it a system or customer repo, not a reverse repo. Borrowing funds using collateral is called a matched sale, not a repo. The jargon is confusing, which is why we used the terms of *buying collateral* and *selling collateral* to describe what parties in the repo market are doing.

Stripped Treasury Securities

The Treasury does not issue zero-coupon notes or bonds. In August 1982, however, both Merrill Lynch and Salomon Brothers created synthetic zero-coupon Treasury receipts. Merrill Lynch marketed its Treasury receipts as Treasury Income Growth Receipts (TIGRs); Salomon Brothers marketed its as Certificates of Accrual on Treasury Securities (CATS). The procedure was to purchase Treasury bonds and deposit them in a bank custody account. The firms then issued (that is, sold) receipts representing an ownership interest in each coupon payment on the underlying Treasury bond in the account and a receipt for ownership of the underlying Treasury bond's maturity value. This process of separating each coupon payment, as well as the principal (called the *corpus*), and selling securities against them is referred to as *coupon stripping*. Although the receipts created from the coupon-stripping process are not issued by the U.S. Treasury, the underlying bond deposited in the bank custody account is a debt obligation of the U.S. Treasury, so the cash flow from the underlying security is certain.

To illustrate the process, suppose $100 million of a Treasury bond with a 10-year maturity and a coupon rate of 10% is purchased to create zero-coupon Treasury securities. The cash flow from this Treasury bond is 20 semiannual payments of $5 million each ($100 million times 0.10 divided by two) and the repayment of principal (corpus) of $100 million 10 years from now. This Treasury bond is deposited in a bank custody account. Receipts are then issued, each with a different single payment claim on the bank custody account. As there are 41 different payments to be made by the Treasury, a receipt representing a single payment claim on each payment is issued,

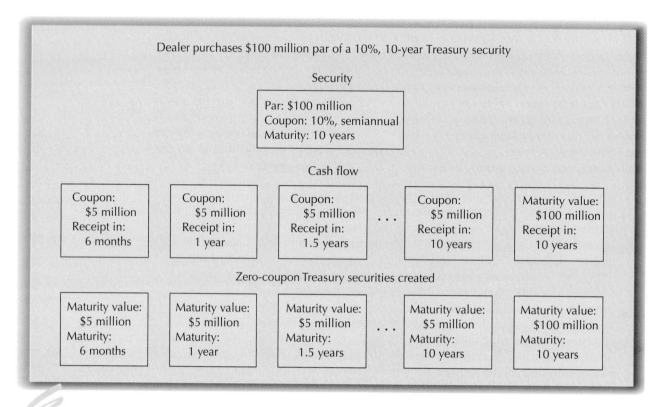

Dealer purchases $100 million par of a 10%, 10-year Treasury security

Security

Par: $100 million
Coupon: 10%, semiannual
Maturity: 10 years

Cash flow

| Coupon: $5 million Receipt in: 6 months | Coupon: $5 million Receipt in: 1 year | Coupon: $5 million Receipt in: 1.5 years | . . . | Coupon: $5 million Receipt in: 10 years | Maturity value: $100 million Receipt in: 10 years |

Zero-coupon Treasury securities created

| Maturity value: $5 million Maturity: 6 months | Maturity value: $5 million Maturity: 1 year | Maturity value: $5 million Maturity: 1.5 years | . . . | Maturity value: $5 million Maturity: 10 years | Maturity value: $100 million Maturity: 10 years |

Figure 16-1 Coupon Stripping: Creating Zero-Coupon Treasury Securities

which is effectively a zero-coupon bond. The amount of the maturity value for a receipt on a particular payment, whether coupon or corpus, depends on the amount of the payment to be made by the Treasury on the underlying Treasury bond. In our example, 20 coupon receipts each have a maturity value of $5 million, and one receipt, the corpus, has a maturity value of $100 million. The maturity dates for the receipts coincide with the corresponding payment dates by the Treasury. This is illustrated in Figure 16-1.

Other investment banking firms followed suit by creating their own receipts.[8] They all are referred to as **trademark zero-coupon Treasury securities** because they are associated with particular firms.[9] Receipts of one firm were rarely traded by competing dealers, so the secondary market was not liquid for any one trademark. Moreover, the investor was exposed to the risk—as small as it may be—that the custodian bank may go bankrupt.

To broaden the market and improve liquidity of these receipts, a group of primary dealers in the government market agreed to issue generic receipts that would not be directly associated with any of the participating dealers. These generic receipts are referred to as **Treasury receipts (TRs)**. Rather than representing a share of the

---

[8] Lehman Brothers offered "Lehman Investment Opportunities Notes" (LIONs); E. F. Hutton offered "Treasury Bond Receipts" (TBRs); and Dean Witter Reynolds offered "Easy Growth Treasury Receipts" (ETRs). There were also GATORs, COUGARs, and—you'll like this one—DOGS (Dibs on Government Securities).

[9] They are also called "animal products" for obvious reasons.

trust as the trademarks do, TRs represent ownership of a Treasury security. A common problem with both trademark and generic receipts was that settlement required physical delivery, which is often cumbersome and inefficient.

In February 1985, the Treasury announced its Separate Trading of Registered Interest and Principal of Securities (**STRIPS**) program to facilitate the stripping of designated Treasury securities. Specifically, all new Treasury bonds and all new Treasury notes with maturities of ten years and longer are eligible. The zero-coupon Treasury securities created under the STRIPS program are direct obligations of the U.S. government. Moreover, the securities clear through the Federal Reserve's book-entry system.[10] Creation of the STRIPS program ended the origination of trademarks and generic receipts.

Today, **stripped Treasury securities** are simply referred to as *Treasury strips*. On dealer quote sheets and vendor screens they are identified by whether the cash flow is created from the coupon (denoted "ci"), principal from a Treasury bond (denoted "bp"), or principal from a Treasury note (denoted "np"). Strips created from coupon payments are called *coupon strips* and those created from the principal are called *principal strips*. The reason why a distinction is made between coupon strips and the principal strips has to do with the tax treatment by non-U.S. entities, as discussed below.

A disadvantage of a taxable entity investing in Treasury strips is that accrued interest is taxed each year even though interest is not paid. Thus, these instruments are negative cash flow instruments until the maturity date. They have negative cash flow since tax payments on interest earned but not received in cash must be made. One reason for distinguishing between strips created from the principal and coupon is that some foreign buyers have a preference for the strips created from the principal (i.e., the principal strips). This preference is due to the tax treatment of the interest in their home country. Some country's tax laws treat the interest as a capital gain if the principal strip is purchased. The capital gain receives a preferential tax treatment (i.e., lower tax rate) compared to ordinary income.

Coupon Stripping and the Theoretical Value of Treasury Securities

Financial theory tells us that the theoretical value of a Treasury security should be equal to the present value of the cash flow where each cash flow is discounted at the appropriate theoretical spot rate. We review this theory in Chapter 12. What we do not do in that chapter, however, is demonstrate what economic force will assure that the actual market price of a Treasury security will not depart significantly from its theoretical value. We were not able to do that in Chapter 12 because we had not yet introduced stripped Treasury securities. Given our discussion of these instruments, we can now demonstrate the economic force that will move the actual price of a Treasury security toward its theoretical value.

To demonstrate this, we will use the Treasury yield curve as represented by the 20 hypothetical Treasury securities given in Table 12-1 in Chapter 12. The longest-maturity bond given in that table is the 10-year, 12.5% coupon issue selling at par and, therefore, with a yield to maturity of 12.5%. Suppose that a government dealer buys a 14%, 10-year Treasury security. Since this is a 10-year security, using the yield for 10-year instruments 12.5% given in Table 12-1 would suggest that this issue should sell to

---

[10] In 1987, the Treasury permitted the conversion of stripped coupons into book-entry form under its Coupons Under Book-Entry Safekeeping (CUBES) program.

offer a yield of 12.5%. Table 16-3 shows the price of a 14%, 10-year Treasury issue if it is selling in the market to yield 12.5%. The present value of the cash flows when discounted at 12.5% is $108.4305 per $100 of par value.

Suppose that this issue is selling at that price. A government dealer can purchase that issue and strip it. The stripped Treasury securities should offer approximately the theoretical spot rate. Table 12-2 shows the theoretical spot rates. Table 16-4 shows the theoretical value of the 14% coupon issue if the cash flows are discounted at the theoretical spot rates. The theoretical value is $108.7889 per $100 par value. Thus, if a dealer purchased this issue for $108.4305, stripped it, and subsequently resold the zero-coupon instruments created at about the theoretical spot rates, the dealer would generate $108.7889 per $100 par value. This would result in an arbitrage profit of $0.3584 per $100 of par value. The only way to eliminate this arbitrage profit is for this security to sell for approximately $108.7889—its theoretical value as determined by the theoretical spot rates.

In this instance, coupon stripping shows that the sum of the parts is greater than the whole. Consider instead of a 10-year, 14% coupon Treasury one in which the coupon rate is 10%. In Chapter 12, we show that the theoretical value for that issue based on the spot rates would be $85.35477. If the cash flows are instead discounted at the 12.5% yield for 10-year Treasury securities, it can be shown that the price would be $85.9491. Thus, if the market price was $85.9491 when the theoretical value based on spot rates indicated a value of $85.35477, a dealer would not want to strip this issue. The proceeds received by selling the zero-coupon instruments created would be less than the cost of purchasing the issue.

Table 16-3   Price of a 10-Year, 14% Coupon Treasury Based on the 10-Year Yield of 12.5%

MATURITY	CASH FLOW PER $100 PAR	REQUIRED YIELD OF 0.125	SEMIANNUAL YIELD	PRESENT VALUE
0.5	$ 7	0.125	0.0625	$ 6.5882
1.0	7	0.125	0.0625	6.2007
1.5	7	0.125	0.0625	5.8359
2.0	7	0.125	0.0625	5.4927
2.5	7	0.125	0.0625	5.1696
3.0	7	0.125	0.0625	4.8655
3.5	7	0.125	0.0625	4.5793
4.0	7	0.125	0.0625	4.3099
4.5	7	0.125	0.0625	4.0564
5.0	7	0.125	0.0625	3.8178
5.5	7	0.125	0.0625	3.5932
6.0	7	0.125	0.0625	3.3818
6.5	7	0.125	0.0625	3.1829
7.0	7	0.125	0.0625	2.9957
7.5	7	0.125	0.0625	2.8194
8.0	7	0.125	0.0625	2.6536
8.5	7	0.125	0.0625	2.4975
9.0	7	0.125	0.0625	2.3506
9.5	7	0.125	0.0625	2.2123
10.0	107	0.125	0.0625	31.8277
Total				$108.4305

Table 16-4   Theoretical Value of a 10-Year, 14% Coupon Treasury Based on the Theoretical Spot Rate

MATURITY	CASH FLOW PER $100 PAR	SPOT RATE	SEMIANNUAL SPOT RATE	PRESENT VALUE
0.5	$ 7	0.08000	0.04000	$ 6.7308
1.0	7	0.08300	0.04150	6.4533
1.5	7	0.08930	0.04465	6.1402
2.0	7	0.09247	0.04624	5.8423
2.5	7	0.09468	0.04734	5.5547
3.0	7	0.09787	0.04894	5.2554
3.5	7	0.10129	0.05065	4.9534
4.0	7	0.10592	0.05296	4.6324
4.5	7	0.10850	0.05425	4.3512
5.0	7	0.11021	0.05511	4.0939
5.5	7	0.11175	0.05588	3.8491
6.0	7	0.11584	0.05792	3.5618
6.5	7	0.11744	0.05872	3.3338
7.0	7	0.11991	0.05996	3.0979
7.5	7	0.12405	0.06203	2.8384
8.0	7	0.12278	0.06139	2.6983
8.5	7	0.12546	0.06273	2.4883
9.0	7	0.13152	0.06576	2.2245
9.5	7	0.13377	0.06689	2.0458
10.0	107	0.13623	0.06812	28.6433
Total				$108.7889

In such cases, a dealer can purchase in the market a package of zero-coupon stripped Treasury securities such that the cash flow of the package of securities replicates the cash flow of the mispriced coupon Treasury security. By doing so, the dealer will realize a yield higher than the yield on the coupon Treasury security. By buying 20 zero-coupon bonds with maturity values identical to the cash flow for the 10%, 10-year Treasury, the dealer is effectively purchasing a 10-year Treasury coupon security at a cost of $85.35477 instead of $85.9491. This procedure to generate an arbitrage profit is referred to as **reconstitution**.

It is the process of coupon stripping and reconstituting that forces the price of a Treasury security to trade near its theoretical value based on spot rates.

Key Points That You Should Understand Before Proceeding

1. U.S. Treasury securities play a prominent role in global financial markets because they do not have credit risk.
2. Treasury securities are issued on an auction basis with regular cycles for securities of specific maturities.
3. In the secondary market, the most actively traded Treasury securities are the on-the-run issues, and government brokers are used as intermediaries for trading among primary dealers.
4. Securities dealers use the repo market to finance their position in Treasury securities.
5. Stripped Treasury securities are zero-coupon instruments that, while not issued by the U.S. government, are backed by Treasury securities from which they are created.
6. Why a Treasury security's price must reflect its theoretical value based on theoretical spot rates.

FEDERAL AGENCY SECURITIES[11]

Federal agency securities can be classified by the type of issuer, those issued by federally related institutions and those issued by government sponsored enterprises.

Federally related institutions (also referred to as *government-owned agencies*) are arms of the federal government and generally do not issue securities directly in the marketplace. The major issuers have been the Tennessee Valley Authority (TVA) and the Government National Mortgage Association (Ginnie Mae). All federally related institutions are exempt from SEC registration. With the exception of securities of the TVA and the Private Export Funding Corporation, the securities are backed by the full faith and credit of the United States government.

Government-sponsored enterprises (**GSEs**) are privately owned, publicly chartered entities. They were created by Congress to reduce the cost of capital for certain borrowing sectors of the economy deemed to be important enough to warrant assistance. The entities in these privileged sectors include farmers, homeowners, and students. Government-sponsored enterprises issue securities directly in the marketplace.

Today there are five GSEs that issue securities: Federal Farm Credit System, Federal Home Loan Bank System, Federal National Mortgage Association (Fannie Mae), Federal Home Loan Bank Corporation (Freddie Mac), and Student Loan Marketing Association (Sallie Mae). The Federal Farm Credit Bank System is responsible for the credit market in the agricultural sector of the economy. The Federal Home Loan Bank, Freddie Mac, and Fannie Mae are responsible for providing credit to the housing sectors. Sallie Mae provides funds to support higher education. With the exception of the securities issued by the Farm Credit Financial Assistance Corporation, GSE securities are not backed by the full faith and credit of the U.S. government, as is the case with Treasury and federally related securities. Consequently, investors purchasing GSEs are exposed to credit risk.

The securities issued by GSEs are one of two types: debentures and mortgage-backed/asset-backed securities. *Debentures* do not have any specific collateral backing the bond. The ability to repay bondholders depends on the ability of the issuing GSE to generate sufficient cash flows to satisfy the obligation. The other type of security issued is a security backed by specific pools of either mortgage loans or other type of loan. These securities are called mortgage-backed securities or asset-backed securities. We will discuss these securities in Chapters 24 and 25.

Below we describe the debentures issued by three GSEs: Fannie Mae and Freddie Mac, and the Federal Home Loan Banks.[12] These two GSEs are frequent issuers of debentures and therefore have developed regular programs for securities that they issue. Both are hoping that their securities will appeal to investors as a substitute for Treasury securities and thereby take the place of U.S. Treasury securities as the benchmark interest rates in the United States.

Fannie Mae issues short-term debentures, Benchmark Bills, discount notes, medium-term notes, Benchmark Notes, Benchmark Bonds, Callable Benchmark Notes, and global bonds. We will discuss medium-term notes in Chapter 21. Short-term debentures have maturities of one year or less and pay interest semiannually.

---

[11] Portions of this section are adapted from Chapter 3 in Frank J. Fabozzi, *Bond Portfolio Management* (New Hope, PA: Frank J. Fabozzi Associates, 2001).

[12] For a further discussion of federal agency securities, see Frank J. Fabozzi and Michael Fleming, "U.S. Treasury and Agency Securities," Chapter 8 in Frank J. Fabozzi (ed.), *The Handbook of Fixed Income Securities: 6th ed.* (New York: McGraw Hill, 2001).

They may be noncallable or have a callable feature. A call feature allows the issuer to pay off an issue prior to the stated maturity date. (We will discuss this feature in Chapter 21.) Benchmark Bills and discount notes are issued at a discount from their maturity value and have maturities of 360 days or less. Benchmark Notes are large issues ($2 to $5 billion in initial size) of 5-year to 10-year maturity and are non-callable. Fannie Mae expects either to issue a new Benchmark Note monthly or to reopen a current issue according to a published issuance calendar. Benchmark Bonds are large ($2 to $4 billion initial size), 30-year maturity issues that are issued or reopened twice a year. Both Benchmark Notes and Bonds are eligible for stripping; that is, the issue can be stripped in the same way that Treasury securities are stripped.

Freddie Mac issues Reference Bills, discount notes, medium-term notes, Reference Notes, Callable Reference Bonds, Reference Notes, and global bonds. Reference Bills and discount notes are issued with maturities of one year or less. Reference Notes and Callable Reference Notes have maturities of 2 to 10 years and are the equivalent to Fannie Mae's Benchmark Notes and Callable Benchmark Notes. Freddie Mac will issue and/or reopen Reference Bills, Reference Notes, and 30-year Reference Bonds according to a published issuance calendar. Initial Reference Note sizes will be $3 to $6 billion, with $2 billion minimum reopenings and initial Reference Bond sizes of $2 billion with $1 billion minimum reopenings. Freddie Mac Reference Notes and Reference Bonds are eligible for stripping.

The Federal Home Loan Banks (FHLB) issues discount notes and medium term notes. The FHLB established its benchmark securities program, which is called the Tap Issue Program, in the summer of 1999. The program reopens coupon securities of four common maturities up to twice a day for three months. The securities are sold via a competitive auction.

Key Points That You Should Understand Before Proceeding

1. Federal agencies securities fall into two categories: federally related institutions securities and government-sponsored enterprises securities.
2. Federally related institutions are generally backed by the full faith and credit of the U.S. government.
3. Government-sponsored enterprises are privately owned, publicly chartered entities that, unlike federally related institutions, do issue securities directly in the marketplace.
4. In general, the securities issued by government-sponsored enterprises are not backed by the full faith and credit of the U.S. government.

A LOOK AT NON-U.S. GOVERNMENT BOND MARKETS

The U.S. bond market is the largest government bond market in the world, although that may change in the future as the U.S. deficit declines. Major government bond markets outside the United States include those of Japan, Germany, France, United Kingdom, Italy, Spain, Belgium, Holland, Sweden, and Denmark. The yields on German government bonds are viewed as benchmark interest rates in Europe.

Types of Securities Issued

Most central governments issue fixed-rate coupon bonds just as issued by the U.S. Department of the Treasury. Non-U.S. central governments also offer bonds with other characteristics. For example, the British government, whose bonds are referred to as gilts, offer bonds called convertibles. These gilts have short maturities that give the holder the option to convert into a specified amount of a longer-maturity gilt (or more than one gilt) for a number of years. The British government also offers index-linked gilts. These gilts have coupons and final redemption amounts linked to the General Index of Retail Price (RPI), an index which is released each month by the Central Statistical Office. Index-linked gilts have low coupons, 2% to 2½, which, in effect, reflect the real rate of return. Maturities of index-linked gilts vary from short term to 2024.

Other central governments have offered bonds linked to inflation. For example, in 1991, the Canadian government issued its first issue of real return bonds ($700 million, due in 2021). The issue was priced to yield a real return equal to 4.25%. The Australian government has small amounts of index-linked Treasury bonds that have either interest payments or capital linked to the Australian Consumer Price Index. Interest-indexed securities pay a fixed coupon every six months plus an arrears adjustment that amounts to the increase in the CPI. Capital-indexed securities also pay a fixed coupon (usually 4%) with the increase in the CPI added to the capital value of the bond and paid on maturity.

Methods of Distribution

There are four methods of distribution that have been used by central governments in issuing government bonds: regular auction calendar/Dutch-style system, the regular auction calendar/minimum-price offering, ad hoc auction system, and the tap system.

In the *regular auction calendar/Dutch-style system*, winning bidders are allocated securities at the yield (price) they bid. At one time, this distribution method was used by the U.S. Department of the Treasury.

In the *regular auction calendar/minimum-price offering system*, there is a regular calendar of offerings. The winners and the amount they will receive are determined in the same manner as in the regular auction calendar/Dutch-style system. However, the price (yield) at which winning bidders are awarded the securities is different. Rather than awarding winning bidders at the yield (price) they bid, all winning bidders are awarded securities at the highest yield accepted by the government (i.e., the stop yield). As noted earlier, U.S. Treasury securities are issued using this auction system, which we referred to as the single-price auction. The regular auction calendar/minimum-price offering method is used in Germany and France.

In the *ad hoc auction system*, governments announce auctions when prevailing market conditions appear favorable. It is only at the time of the auction that the amount to be auctioned and the maturity of the security to be offered are announced. This is one of the methods used by the Bank of England in distributing British government bonds. There are two advantages of an ad hoc auction system rather than a regular auction calendar from the issuing government's perspective. First, a regular auction calendar introduces greater market volatility than an ad hoc auction, since yields tend to rise as the announced auction date approaches and then fall afterward. Second, there is reduced flexibility in raising funds with a regular auction calendar. After the election of the Conservative Party in England in 1992, there was a significant drop in the yields on British government bonds. The Bank of England used that window to obtain almost a third of the government's funding needs for fiscal year 1992 1993 in just the first two months of its fiscal year.

In a *tap system*, additional bonds of a previously outstanding bond issue are auctioned. The government announces periodically that it is adding this new supply. The tap system has been used in the United Kingdom and the Netherlands, as well as in the United States for the 10-year note.

SUMMARY

The U.S. Treasury market is closely watched by all participants in the financial markets because interest rates on Treasury securities are the benchmark interest rates throughout the world. The Treasury issues three types of securities: bills, notes, and bonds. Treasury bills have a maturity of one year or less, are sold at a discount from par, and do not make periodic interest payments. Treasury notes and bonds are coupon securities. In 1997, the Treasury began issuing inflation protection securities.

Treasury securities are issued on a competitive bid auction basis, according to a regular auction cycle. The auction process relies on the participation of the primary government securities dealers, with which the Federal Reserve deals directly. The auction process has been revised to allow greater participation by eligible nonprimary dealers.

The secondary market for Treasury securities is an over-the-counter market, where dealers trade with the general investing public and with other dealers. In the secondary market, Treasury bills are quoted on a bank discount basis; Treasury coupon securities are quoted on a price basis. Government brokers are used by primary dealers to trade among themselves. Pressure has been placed on primary dealers to provide greater access to prices of Treasury securities.

Treasury dealers finance their position in the repo market. They also use the repo market to cover short positions.

Although the Treasury does not issue zero-coupon Treasury securities, government dealers have created these instruments synthetically by a process called coupon stripping. Zero-coupon Treasury securities include trademarks, Treasury receipts, and STRIPS. Creation of the first two types of zero-coupon Treasury securities has ceased; STRIPS now dominate the market. The ability to strip Treasury coupon securities and reconstitute stripped Treasury securities forces the market price of a Treasury security to sell at a price close to its theoretical value based on theoretical spot rates.

Government-sponsored enterprise securities and federally related institution securities comprise the federal agency securities market. The former are privately owned, publicly chartered entities created to reduce the cost of borrowing for certain sectors of the economy. Federally related institutions are arms of the federal government whose debt is guaranteed by the U.S. government. While government-sponsored enterprises issue their own securities.

The U.S. government bond market is the largest in the world, followed by the Japanese, Italian, and German government bond markets. Some central governments offer bonds indexed to the country's inflation. There are four methods of distribution that have been used by the central governments in issuing bonds: regular auction calendar/Dutch-style system, the regular auction calendar/minimum-price offering, ad hoc auction system, and the tap system.

KEY TERMS

- Federally related institutions, 304
- Government brokers, 295
- Government-sponsored enterprises (GSEs), 304
- Hot issue (also called special issue), 298
- Overnight repo, 297
- Primary dealers, 293
- Reconstitution, 303
- Reopened issue, 292
- Stop yield, 292
- Stripped Treasury security, 301
- STRIPS, 301
- Tail, 293

- Term repo, 297
- Trademark zero-coupon Treasury securities, 300
- Treasury bills, 290
- Treasury bonds, 290
- Treasury coupon securities, 290
- Treasury discount securities, 290
- Treasury inflation protection security (TIPS), 290
- Treasury notes, 290
- Treasury receipt (TR), 300
- When-issued (or wi) market, 295
- Yield on a bank discount basis, 295

QUESTIONS

1. Why do government dealers use government brokers?
2. Suppose that the price of a Treasury bill with 90 days to maturity and a $1 million face value is $980,000. What is the yield on a bank discount basis?
3. The bid and ask yields for a Treasury bill were quoted by a dealer as 5.91% and 5.89%, respectively. Shouldn't the bid yield be less than the ask yield because the bid yield indicates how much the dealer is willing to pay, and the ask yield is what the dealer is willing to sell the Treasury bill for?
4. Suppose a portfolio manager purchases $1 million of par value of a Treasury inflation protection security. The real rate (determined at the auction) is 3.2%.
   a. Assume that at the end of the first six months the CPI-U is 3.6% (annual rate). Compute (i) the inflation adjustment to principal at the end of the first six months, (ii) the inflation-adjusted principal at the end of the first six months, and (iii) the coupon payment made to the investor at the end of the first six months.
   b. Assume that at the end of the second six months the CPI-U is 4.0% (annual rate). Compute (i) the inflation adjustment to principal at the end of the second six months, (ii) the inflation-adjusted principal at the end of the second six months, and (iii) the coupon payment made to the investor at the end of the second six months.
5. a. What is the measure of the rate of inflation selected by the U.S. Treasury for determining the inflation adjustment for Treasury inflation protection securities?
   b. Suppose that there is deflation over the life of a Treasury inflation protection security resulting in an inflation-adjusted principal at the maturity date that is less than the initial par value. How much will the U.S. Treasury pay at the maturity date to redeem the principal?
   c. Why is it necessary for the U.S. Treasury to report a daily index ratio for each TIPS issue?
6. Calculate the dollar price for the following Treasury coupon securities:

	Price quoted	Par
a.	95–4	$ 100,000
b.	87–16	1,000,000
c.	102–10	10,000,000
d.	116–30	10,000
e.	102–4+	100,000

7. a. Does the U.S. Department of the Treasury use a single-price or multiple-price auction in the issuance of Treasury coupon securities?
   b. How is the yield of winning bidders determined in a Treasury auction?
8. The following is from the March 1991 monthly report published by Blackstone Financial Management:

The Treasury also brought $34.5 billion in new securities to the market in February as part of the normal quarterly refunding. . . . The auctions went slightly better than expected given the significant size and the uncertainties surrounding the duration of the war. The 3-year was issued at a 6.98% average yield, the 10-year at a 7.85% average yield, and the 30-year at a 7.98% average yield. All bids were accepted at the average yield or better (that is, with no tail), indicating ample demand for the securities.

a. What is meant by the average yield and the tail?

b. Why does the absence of a tail indicate ample demand for the Treasuries auctioned?

9. a. What is the difference between a STRIP, a trademark Treasury zero-coupon security, and a Treasury receipt?

b. What is the most common type of Treasury zero-coupon security?

10. a. How can a repurchase agreement be used by a dealer firm to finance a long position in a Treasury security?

b. One party in a repo transaction is said to "buy collateral," the other party to "sell collateral." Why?

c. When there is a shortage of a specific security for a repo transaction, will the repo rate increase or decrease?

11. Which rate should be higher: the overnight repo rate, or the overnight federal funds rate? Why?

12. What is the difference between a government-sponsored enterprise and a federally related institution?

13. Are government-sponsored enterprise securities backed by the full faith and credit of the U.S. government?

14. What is the difference between an agency debenture and an agency mortgage-backed security?

15. a. What are Reference Notes and Benchmark Notes?

b. What government-sponsored enterprises are seeking to have the rates that they offer viewed as the benchmark interest rates in the U.S. financial market?

16. What economic mechanism forces the actual market price of a Treasury security toward its theoretical value based on theoretical spot rates?

17. a. Based on a yield to maturity of 12.5% for 10-year Treasury securities, demonstrate that the price of a 13% coupon, 10-year Treasury would be $102.8102 per $100 par value if all cash flows are discounted at 12.5%.

b. Based on the theoretical spot rates in Table 16-4, show that the theoretical value would be $102.9304 per $100 par value.

c. Explain why the market price for this Treasury security would trade close to its theoretical value.

18. a. The interest rates on what European country's government bond market are viewed as the benchmark rates in Europe?

b. What is a gilt?

19. What are the different methods for the issuance of government securities throughout the world?

Municipal Securities Markets

Learning Objectives

After reading this chapter, you will understand

■ who buys municipal securities and why the securities are attractive investments to these buyers.

■ the types of municipal securities and why they are issued.

■ the risks unique to investment in municipal securities.

■ the primary and secondary markets for municipal securities.

■ the yield relationship between municipal securities and taxable bonds.

■ the yield relationships among municipal securities within the municipal market.

■ the degree of regulation of the municipal securities market.

In this chapter, we discuss municipal securities and the market in which they trade. Municipal securities are issued by state and local governments and by entities that they establish. All states issue municipal securities. Local governments include cities and counties. Political subdivisions of municipalities that issue securities include school districts and special districts for fire prevention, water, sewer, and other purposes. Public agencies or instrumentalities include authorities and commissions.

The attractiveness of municipal securities is due to their tax treatment at the federal income tax level. Most municipal securities are tax exempt. This means that interest on municipal bonds is exempt from federal income taxation. The exemption applies to interest income, not capital gains. The exemption may or may not extend to the state and local levels. Each state has its own rule as to how interest on municipal securities is taxed.[1] While most municipal bonds outstanding are tax exempt, there are issues that are taxable at the federal level.

Municipal securities are issued for various purposes. Short-term notes typically are sold in anticipation of the receipt of funds from taxes or proceeds from the sale of a bond issue, for example. The proceeds from the sale of short-term notes permit the issuing municipality to cover seasonal and temporary imbalances between outlays for expenditures and tax inflows. Municipalities issue long-term bonds as the principal means for financing both (1) long-term capital projects such as the construction of schools, bridges, roads, and airports, and (2) long-term budget deficits that arise from current operations.

---

[1] The tax treatment at the state level will be one of the following: (1) exemption of interest from all municipal securities, (2) taxation of interest from all municipal securities, (3) exemption of interest from municipal securities where the issuer is in the state but taxation of interest where the issuer is out of the state.

As the single most important advantage of municipal securities to investors is the exemption of interest income from federal taxation, the investor groups that have purchased these securities are those that benefit the most from this exemption. The three categories of investors dominating the municipal securities market are households (retail investors), commercial banks, and property and casualty insurance companies. Individual investors may purchase municipal securities directly or through investment companies.

TYPES AND FEATURES OF MUNICIPAL SECURITIES[2]

There are basically two types of municipal security structures: **tax-backed debt** and **revenue bonds**. There are also securities that share characteristics of tax-backed debt and revenue bonds.

Tax-Backed Debt

Tax-backed debt obligations are instruments issued by states, counties, special districts, cities, towns, and school districts that are secured by some form of tax revenue. Tax-backed debt includes general obligation debt, appropriation-backed obligations, and debt obligations supported by public credit enhancement programs.

General Obligation Debt.

The broadest type of tax-backed debt is **general obligation debt.** There are two types of general obligation pledges: unlimited and limited. An unlimited tax general obligation debt is the stronger form of general obligation pledge because it is secured by the issuer's unlimited taxing power. The tax revenue sources include corporate and individual income taxes, sales taxes, and property taxes. Unlimited tax general obligation debt is said to be secured by the full faith and credit of the issuer. A limited tax general obligation debt is a limited tax pledge because for such debt there is a statutory limit on tax rates that the issuer may levy to service the debt.

Certain general obligation bonds are secured not only by the issuer's general taxing powers to create revenues accumulated in a general fund but also by certain identified fees, grants, and special charges, which provide additional revenues from outside the general fund. Such bonds are known as double-barreled in security because of the dual nature of the revenue sources. For example, the debt obligations issued by special purpose service systems may be secured by a pledge of property taxes, a pledge of special fees/operating revenue from the service provided, or a pledge of both property taxes and special fees/operating revenues. In the last case, they are double-barreled.

Appropriation-Backed Obligations.

Agencies or authorities of several states have issued bonds that carry a potential state liability for making up shortfalls in the issuing entity's obligation. The appropriation of funds from the state's general tax revenue must be approved by the state legislature. However, the state's pledge is not binding. Debt obligations with this nonbinding pledge of tax revenue are called **moral obligation bonds.** Because a moral obligation bond requires legislative approval to appropriate the funds, it is classified as an **appropriation-backed obligation.** The purpose of the moral obligation pledge is to enhance the creditworthiness of the issuing entity. However, the investor must rely on the best

---

[2] For a further discussion of these securities, see Chapter 5 in Frank J. Fabozzi, *Fixed Income Securities* (New Hope, PA: Frank J. Fabozzi Associates, 1998).

efforts of the state to approve the appropriation. Another type of appropriation-backed obligation is lease-backed debt.

Debt Obligations Supported by Public Credit Enhancement Programs. While a moral obligation is a form of credit enhancement provided by a state, it is not a legally enforceable or legally binding obligation of the state. There are entities that have issued debt that carries some form of public credit enhancement that is legally enforceable. This occurs when there is a guarantee by the state or a federal agency or when there is an obligation to automatically withhold and deploy state aid to pay any defaulted debt service by the issuing entity. Typically, the latter form of public credit enhancement is used for debt obligations of a state's school systems.

Some examples of state credit enhancement programs include Virginia's bond guarantee program that authorizes the governor to withhold state aid payments to a municipality and divert those funds to pay principal and interest to a municipality's general obligation holders in the event of a default. South Carolina's constitution requires mandatory withholding of state aid by the state treasurer if a school district is not capable of meeting its general obligation debt. Texas created the Permanent School Fund to guarantee the timely payment of principal and interest of the debt obligations of qualified school districts. The fund's income is obtained from land and mineral rights owned by the state of Texas.

Revenue Bonds

The second basic type of security structure is found in a revenue bond. Such bonds are issued for either project or enterprise financings where the bond issuers pledge to the bondholders the revenues generated by the operating projects financed. A feasibility study is performed before the endeavor is undertaken to determine whether or not it will be self-supporting.

Following are examples of revenue bonds: airport revenue bonds, college and university revenue bonds, hospital revenue bonds, single-family mortgage revenue bonds, multifamily revenue bonds, public power revenue bonds, resource recovery revenue bonds, seaport revenue bonds, sports complex and convention center revenue bonds, student loan revenue bonds, toll road and gas tax revenue bonds, and water revenue bonds.

Hybrid and Special Bond Structures

Some municipal securities have special security structures that share characteristics of tax-backed debt and revenue bonds. These include **insured bonds**, prefunded bonds, and structured/asset-based bonds.

Insured Bonds.

Insured bonds, in addition to being secured by the issuer's revenue, are also backed by insurance policies written by commercial insurance companies. Insurance on a municipal bond is an agreement by an insurance company to pay the bondholder any bond principal and/or coupon interest that is due on a stated maturity date but that has not been paid by the bond issuer. Once issued, this municipal bond insurance usually extends for the term of the bond issue, and it cannot be canceled by the insurance company.

Prefunded Bonds.

Although originally issued as either revenue or general obligation bonds, municipals are sometimes prefunded and called **prefunded municipal bonds**. (They are also called **refunded bonds**.) A prefunding usually occurs when the original bonds are escrowed or collateralized by direct obligations guaranteed by the U.S. government.[3] By this it is meant that a portfolio of securities guaranteed by the U.S. government is placed in a trust. The portfolio of securities is assembled such that the cash flows from the securities match the obligations that the issuer must pay. For example, suppose that a municipality has a 7% $100 million issue with 12 years remaining to maturity. The municipality's obligation is to make payments of $3.5 million every six months for the next 12 years and $100 million 12 years from now. If the issuer wants to prefund this issue, a portfolio of U.S. government obligations can be purchased that has a cash flow of $3.5 million every six months for the next 12 years and $100 million 12 years from now.

Once this portfolio of securities whose cash flows match those of the municipality's obligation is in place, the prefunded bonds are no longer secured as either general obligation or revenue bonds. The bonds are now supported by cash flows from the portfolio of securities held in an escrow fund. Such bonds, if escrowed with securities guaranteed by the U.S. government, have little, if any, credit risk. They are the safest municipal bonds available.

The escrow fund for a prefunded municipal bond can be structured so that the bonds to be refunded are to be called at the first possible call date or a subsequent call date established in the original bond indenture. Although prefunded bonds are usually retired at their first or subsequent call date, some are structured to match the debt obligation to the maturity date. Such bonds are known as *escrowed-to-maturity bonds.*

Asset-Backed Bonds.

In recent years, states and local governments began issuing bonds where the debt service is to be paid from so-called "dedicated" revenues such as sales taxes, tobacco settlement payments, fees, and penalty payments. These structures mimic the asset-backed bonds that are discussed in Chapter 25. **Asset-backed bonds** are also referred to as **dedicated revenue bonds** and **structured bonds**.

Municipal Notes

Municipal securities issued for periods up to three years are considered to be short term in nature. These include **tax anticipation notes** (TANs), **revenue anticipation notes** (RANs), **grant anticipation notes** (GANs), and **bond anticipation notes** (BANs).

TANs, RANs, GANs, and BANs are temporary borrowings by states, local governments, and special jurisdictions. Usually, notes are issued for a period of 12 months, although it is not uncommon for notes to be issued for periods as short as three months and for as long as three years. TANs and RANs (also known as TRANs) are issued in anticipation of the collection of taxes or other expected revenues. The purpose of these borrowings is to even out irregular flows into the treasuries of the issuing entity. BANs are issued in anticipation of the sale of long-term bonds.

Redemption Features

Municipal bonds are issued with one of two debt retirement structures or a combination of both. Either a bond has a **serial maturity structure** or a **term maturity structure**. A serial maturity structure requires a portion of the debt obligation to be retired each

---

[3] Because the interest rate that a municipality must pay on borrowed funds is less than the interest rate paid by the U.S. government, in the absence of any restrictions in the tax code, a municipal issuer can realize a tax arbitrage. This can be done by issuing a bond and immediately investing the proceeds in a U.S. government security. Tax rules may prevent such arbitrage in some cases. Should a municipal issuer violate the tax arbitrage rules, the issue will be ruled to be taxable. If subsequent to the issuance of a bond, however, interest rates decline so that the issuer will find it advantageous to call the bond, the establishment of the escrow fund will not violate the tax arbitrage rules.

year. A term maturity structure provides for the debt obligation to be repaid at the end of the bond's planned life. Usually, term bonds have maturities ranging from 20 to 40 years. Such bonds often have sinking fund provisions that call for partial and systematic retirement of the debt on a set schedule that begins five or ten years before the time of maturity. Another provision that permits the early redemption of a term bond is the call privilege, which allows the issuer, under certain and well-specified circumstances, to pay off the debt prior to the scheduled maturity. Sinking fund and call provisions are noted features of corporate debt and will be discussed further in Chapter 21.

Key Points That You Should Understand Before Proceeding

1. There are two types of municipal securities: tax-backed debt and revenue bonds.
2. A general obligation bond is secured by the issuer's unlimited taxing power.
3. A revenue bond is issued for either project or enterprise financings where the bond issuer pledges the revenues generated by the project that is financed to the bondholders.
4. Municipal notes are issued for periods up to three years and represent temporary borrowings by states, local governments, and special jurisdictions.
5. The debt retirement structure for a municipal bond can be either a serial maturity structure or a term maturity structure.

MUNICIPAL BOND RATINGS

Although municipal bonds have long been considered second in safety only to U.S. Treasury securities, today there are new concerns about the credit risks of many municipal bonds.[4]

The first concern came out of the New York City billion-dollar financial crisis in 1975. On February 25, 1975, the state of New York's Urban Development Corporation defaulted on a $100 million note issue that was the obligation of New York City. Many market participants had been convinced that the state of New York would not allow the issue to default. Although New York City was able later to obtain a $140 million revolving credit from banks to cure the default, lenders became concerned that the city would face difficulties in repaying its accumulated debt, which stood at $14 billion on March 31, 1975.[5] This financial crisis sent a loud and clear warning to market participants: Despite supposedly ironclad protection for the bondholder, when issuers such as large cities have severe financial difficulties, the financial stakes of public employee unions, vendors, and community groups may be dominant forces in balancing budgets. This reality was reinforced by the federal bankruptcy law taking effect in October 1979, which makes it easier for the issuer of a municipal security to go into bankruptcy.

The second reason for concern about the credit risk of municipal securities is the proliferation in this market of innovative financing techniques to secure new bond issues. In addition to the established general obligation bonds and revenue bonds, there are now more innovative, and legally untested, security mechanisms that do not require voters' approval of new debt. What distinguishes these newer bonds from the more traditional general obligation and revenue bonds is that there is no history of

---

[4] For a history of defaults of municipal bonds, see Chapter 2 in Sylvan G. Feldstein and Frank J. Fabozzi, *The Dow Jones-Irwin Guide to Municipal Bonds* (Homewood, IL: Dow Jones-Irwin, 1987).

[5] Securities and Exchange Commission Staff Report on *Transactions in Securities of the City of New York* (Washington, D.C.: U.S. Government Printing Office, 1977), p. 2. The reasons for the New York City financial crisis are documented in Donna E. Shalala and Carol Bellamy, "A State Saves a City: The New York Case," *Duke Law Journal* (January 1976), pp. 1119–1126.

court decisions or other case law that firmly establishes the rights of the bondholders and the obligations of the issuers. It is not possible to determine in advance the probable legal outcome if the newer financing mechanisms were to be challenged in court. The importance of this uncertainty is illustrated most dramatically by the bonds of the Washington Public Power Supply System (WPPSS) where bondholder rights to certain revenues were not upheld by the highest court in the state of Washington.

More recently, municipal bond investors have been increasingly concerned with those who manage the investment funds of municipalities. This concern was the result of the collapse of the Orange County (California) Investment Pool, which lost $1.7 billion as a result of a poorly conceived investment strategy by Robert L. Citron, the county treasurer. Citron followed a strategy which resulted in a leveraged position in securities that benefited if interest rates declined. Basically, he used the repurchase agreement described in Chapter 16. Instead of using the repurchase agreement as a short-term investment vehicle, he used it to create leverage via a reverse repurchase agreement. The loss resulting from this strategy, as well as investments in instructured notes (described in Chapter 20), resulted in the bankruptcy of Orange County. To date, this is the largest municipal failure in U.S. history.[6]

Many institutional investors in the municipal bond market rely on their own in-house municipal credit analysts for determining the creditworthiness of a municipal issue; other investors rely on the three nationally recognized rating companies. The assigned rating system is the same as that used for corporate bonds that we discussed in Chapter 21.

To evaluate general obligation bonds, the commercial rating companies assess information in four basic categories. The first category includes information on the issuer's debt structure and overall debt burden. The second category relates to the issuer's ability and political discipline to maintain sound budgetary policy. The focus of attention here usually is on the issuer's general operating funds and whether it has maintained at least balanced budgets over three to five years. The third category involves determining the specific local taxes and intergovernmental revenues available to the issuer, as well as obtaining historical information both on tax collection rates, which are important when looking at property tax levies, and on the dependence of local budgets on specific revenue sources. The fourth and last category of information necessary to the credit analysis is an assessment of the issuer's overall socioeconomic environment. The determinations that have to be made here include trends of local employment distribution and composition, population growth, real estate property valuation, and personal income, among other economic factors.

While there are numerous security structures for revenue bonds, the underlying principle in rating is whether or not the project being financed will generate sufficient cash flow to satisfy the obligations due bondholders.

Key Points That You Should Understand Before Proceeding

1. The investor in a municipal security is exposed to credit risk.
2. Commercial rating companies evaluate the credit risk associated with municipal securities and express the results of their analysis in the form of rating categories.
3. The factors used to determine a rating for a general obligation bond are different from those used for a revenue bond.

---

[6] For an excellent account of the Orange County bankruptcy, see Philipe Jorion, *Big Bets Gone Bad* (New York: Academic Press, 1995).

TAX RISKS ASSOCIATED WITH INVESTING IN MUNICIPAL SECURITIES

There are two types of tax risk to which tax-exempt municipal securities buyers are exposed. The first is the risk that the federal income tax rate will be reduced. The higher the marginal tax rate, the more valuable the tax-exemption feature. As the marginal tax rate declines, the price of a tax-exempt municipal security will decline. Proposals to reduce the marginal tax rate result in less demand for municipal securities and, as a result, a decline in their price. This occurred most recently in 1995 when there were proposals of a flat tax in which the tax rate would be less than the prevailing rate.

The second type of tax risk is that a municipal bond issued as a tax-exempt issue may be eventually declared by the Internal Revenue Service to be taxable. This could happen because many municipal revenue bonds have elaborate security structures that could be subject to future adverse Congressional action and IRS interpretation. A loss of the tax-exemption feature will cause the municipal bond to decline in value in order to provide a yield comparable to similar taxable bonds. An example of this risk is the following situation: In June 1980, the Battery Park City Authority sold $97.315 million in notes, which at the time of issuance seemed to be exempt from federal income taxation. In November 1980, however, the IRS held that interest on these notes was not exempt. The legal question was not settled until September 1981, when the authority and the IRS signed a formal agreement resolving the matter so as to make the interest on the notes tax-exempt.

> **Key Points That You Should Understand Before Proceeding**
>
> 1. A tax risk associated with investing in municipal bonds is that the highest marginal tax rate will be reduced, resulting in a decline in the value of municipal bonds.
> 2. Another tax risk associated with investing in municipal bonds is that a tax-exempt issue may be eventually declared by the Internal Revenue Service to be taxable.

THE PRIMARY MARKET

A substantial number of municipal obligations are brought to market each week. A state or local government can market its new issue by offering bonds publicly to the investing community or by placing them privately with a small group of investors. When a public offering is selected, the issue usually is underwritten by investment bankers and/or municipal bond departments of commercial banks. Public offerings may be marketed by either competitive bidding or direct negotiations with underwriters. In a competitive process, the bidder submitting the highest bid price for the security gets the right to market the debt to investors.[7]

Most states mandate that general obligation issues be marketed through competitive bidding, but generally this is not necessary for revenue bonds. Usually, state and local governments require a competitive sale to be announced in a recognized financial publication, such as *The Bond Buyer*, which is a trade publication for the municipal bond industry. *The Bond Buyer* also provides information on upcoming competitive sales and most negotiated sales, as well as the results of previous weeks. However the debt is marketed, the municipal unit prepares an *official statement* describ-

---

[7] See Chapter 14 for more information about underwriting.

ing its financial situation and the terms of the issue. These terms include the call and sinking fund provisions mentioned above.

THE SECONDARY MARKET

Municipal bonds are traded in the over-the-counter market supported by municipal bond dealers across the country. Markets for the debts of smaller issuers (referred to as *local credits*) are maintained by regional brokerage firms, local banks, and by some of the larger Wall Street firms. Markets for the bonds of larger issuers (referred to as *general names*) are supported by the larger brokerage firms and banks, many of whom have investment banking relationships with these issuers. There are brokers who serve as intermediaries in the sale of large blocks of municipal bonds among dealers and large institutional investors. In Chapter 15, we described electronic bond trading. Beginning in 2000, bonds in the secondary market as well as some new issue competitive and negotiated issues began to be auctioned and sold over the Internet by large and small broker-dealers to institutional and individual investors.

In the municipal bond market, an odd lot of bonds is $25,000 or less in par value for retail investors. For institutions, anything below $100,000 in par value is considered an odd lot. Dealer spreads depend on several factors. For the retail investor, the spread can range from as low as one-quarter of one point ($12.50 per $5,000 par value) on large blocks of actively traded bonds to four points ($200 per $5,000 of par value) for odd-lot sales of an inactive issue. For institutional investors, the dealer spread rarely exceeds one-half of one point ($25 per $5,000 of par value).

The convention for both corporate and Treasury bonds is to quote prices as a percentage of par value with 100 equal to par. Municipal bonds, however, generally are traded and quoted in terms of yield (yield to maturity or yield to call). The price of the bond in this case is called a *basis price*. The exception is certain long-maturity revenue bonds. A bond traded and quoted in dollar prices (actually, as a percentage of par value) is called a *dollar bond*.

YIELDS ON MUNICIPAL BONDS

Because of the tax-exempt feature of municipal bonds, the yield on municipal bonds is less than that on Treasuries with the same maturity. Table 17-1 shows this relationship on August 16, 1999, for AAA rated general obligation bonds. The difference in yield between tax-exempt securities and Treasury securities is typically measured not in basis points but in percentage terms. More specifically, it is measured as the percentage of the yield on a municipal security relative to a comparable Treasury security. This is reported in Table 17-1.

The yield ratio has changed over time. The higher the tax rate, the more attractive the tax-exempt feature and the lower the yield ratio. The yield ratio for 10-year AAA general obligation bonds and 10-year Treasury securities varied in the 1990s from a low of 0.72 on September 30, 1994, to a high of 0.94 on September 30, 1998.

In the municipal bond market, several benchmark curves exist. In general, a benchmark yield curve is constructed for AAA-quality-rated state general obligation.

In the Treasury and corporate bond markets, it is not unusual to find at different times shapes for the yield curve described in Chapter 11. In general, the municipal yield curve is positively sloped. There was a brief period where the municipal yield curve became inverted. In fact, during the period when the Treasury yield curve was inverted, the municipal yield curve maintained its upward-sloping shape. Prior to 1986 the municipal yield curve was consistently steeper than the Treasury yield curve as

Table 17-1   Yield Ratio for AAA General Obligation Municipal Bonds to U.S.
Treasuries of the Same Maturity on August 16, 1999

MATURITY	YIELD ON AAA GENERAL OBLIGATION	YIELD ON U.S. TREASURY	YIELD RATIO
3 months	3.29%	4.93%	0.67
6 months	3.43	5.21	0.66
1 year	3.56	5.55	0.64
2 years	4.03	5.78	0.70
3 years	4.23	5.84	0.72
4 years	4.37	6.00	0.73
5 years	4.46	5.87	0.76
7 years	4.66	6.20	0.75
10 years	4.95	5.99	0.83
15 years	5.33	6.39	0.83
20 years	5.50	6.47	0.85
30 years	5.55	6.26	0.89

SOURCE: Bloomberg Financial Markets.

measured by the spread between the 30-year and 1-year issues. Between 1986 and 1990, the steepness was comparable. In 1991, the municipal yield curve became steeper than the Treasury yield curve.

REGULATION OF THE MUNICIPAL SECURITIES MARKET[8]

Congress has specifically exempted municipal securities from both the registration requirements of the Securities Act of 1933 and the periodic reporting requirements of the Securities Exchange Act of 1934. Antifraud provisions apply nevertheless to offerings of, or dealings in, municipal securities.

The reasons for the exemption afforded municipal securities appear to relate to (1) a desire for harmonious and cooperative relations among the various levels of government in the United States; (2) the absence of recurrent abuses in transactions involving municipal securities; (3) the greater level of sophistication of investors in this segment of the securities markets (the market was long dominated by institutional investors); and (4) the fact that there had been few defaults by municipal issuers. Consequently, between the enactment of federal securities acts in the early 1930s and the early 1970s, the municipal securities market was relatively free from federal regulation.

In the early 1970s, however, circumstances changed. As incomes rose, individual investors began to participate in the municipal securities market to a much greater extent, and public concern over selling practices was expressed with greater frequency. Moreover, the financial problems of some municipal issuers, notably New York

---

[8] Parts of this section are drawn from Thomas F. Mitchell, "Disclosure and the Municipal Bond Industry," Chapter 40, and Nancy H. Wojtas, "The SEC and Investor Safeguards," Chapter 42 in Frank J. Fabozzi, Sylvan G. Feldstein, Irving M. Pollack, and Frank Zarb (eds.), *The Municipal Bond Handbook: Volume I* (Homewood, IL: Dow Jones-Irwin, 1983).

City, made market participants aware that municipal issuers have the potential to experience severe financial difficulties approaching bankruptcy levels.

Congress passed the Securities Act Amendment of 1975 to broaden federal regulation in the market for municipal debt. This legislation brought brokers and dealers in the municipal securities market, including banks that underwrite and trade municipal securities, under the regulatory umbrella of the Securities Exchange Act of 1934. The legislation mandated also that the SEC establish a 15-member Municipal Securities Rulemaking Board (MSRB) as an independent, self-regulatory agency whose primary responsibility is to develop rules governing the activities of banks, brokers, and dealers in municipal securities. Rules adopted by the MSRB must be approved by the SEC. The MSRB has no enforcement or inspection authority. That authority is vested with the SEC, the National Association of Securities Dealers, and certain regulatory banking agencies such as the Federal Reserve Bank.

The Securities Act Amendment of 1975 does not require municipal issuers to comply with the registration requirement of the 1933 act or the periodic reporting requirement of the 1934 act, despite several legislative proposals to mandate such financial disclosure. Even in the absence of federal legislation dealing with the regulation of financial disclosure, however, underwriters began insisting upon greater disclosure as it became apparent that the SEC was exercising stricter application of the antifraud provisions. Moreover, underwriters recognized the need for improved disclosure to sell municipal securities to an investing public that had become much more concerned about the credit risk of municipal issuers.

On June 28, 1989, the SEC formally approved the first bond disclosure rule, effective January 1, 1990. While the disclosure rule has several exemptions, in general it applies to new issue municipal securities offerings of $1 million or more.

SUMMARY

Municipal securities are issued by state and local governments and their authorities, with the interest on most issues being exempt from federal income taxes. The primary investors in these securities are households (which includes mutual funds), commercial banks, and property and casualty insurance companies.

There are both tax-exempt and taxable municipal securities, where "tax-exempt" means that interest on a municipal security is exempt from federal income taxation; most municipal securities that have been issued are tax-exempt.

There are basically two types of municipal security structures: tax-backed debt and revenue bonds. Tax-backed debt obligations are instruments issued by states, counties, special districts, cities, towns, and school districts that are secured by some form of tax revenue. Tax-backed debt includes general obligation debt (the broadest type of tax-backed debt), appropriation-backed obligations, and debt obligations supported by public credit enhancement programs. A general obligation bond is said to be double-barreled when it is secured not only by the issuer's general taxing powers to create

revenues accumulated in a general fund but also by certain identified fees, grants, and special charges, which provide additional revenues from outside the general fund. Revenue bonds are issued for enterprise financings that are secured by the revenues generated by the completed projects themselves, or for general public-purpose financings in which the issuers pledge to the bondholders the tax and revenue resources that were previously part of the general fund.

Insured bonds, in addition to being secured by the issuer's revenue, are backed by insurance policies written by commercial insurance companies. Prefunded bonds are no longer secured as either general obligation or revenue bonds but are supported by a portfolio of securities held in an escrow fund. If escrowed with securities guaranteed by the U.S. government, refunded bonds are the safest municipal bonds available. A prefunded municipal bond is one in which the escrow fund is structured so that the bonds are to be called at the first possible call date or a subsequent call date established in the original bond indenture. There are municipal securities structured as asset-backed securities that are backed by "dedicated" revenues such as sales taxes, tobacco settlement payments, fees, and penalty payments.

Municipal notes are issued for shorter periods (one to three years) than municipal bonds. Municipal bonds may be retired with a serial maturity structure, a term maturity structure, or a combination of both. Investing in municipal securities exposes investors to credit risk and tax risk.

KEY TERMS

- Anticipation note, 313
- Appropriation-backed bond, 311
- Asset-backed bond (or structured bond or dedicated revenue bond), 313
- General obligation debt, 311
- Insured bonds, 312
- Moral obligation bond, 311
- Prefunded bonds (or refunded bonds), 312
- Revenue bonds, 311
- Serial maturity structure, 313
- Tax-backed debt, 311
- Term maturity structure, 313

QUESTIONS

1. Explain why you agree or disagree with the following statement: "All municipal bonds are exempt from federal income taxes."
2. a. Who are the three major investors in municipal securities?
   b. What aspect of their situation and what feature of these bonds attract these investors to this market?
3. If it is expected that Congress will change the tax law so as to increase marginal tax rates, what do you think will happen to the price of municipal bonds?
4. What is the major difference between a tax-backed debt and a revenue bond?
5. What is the difference between a limited and unlimited general obligation bond?
6. a. Why are more municipal bonds insured today than in 1970?
   b. In your view, would the typical AAA-rated municipal bond be insured?
7. "A moral obligation bond is a form of a limited general obligation bond." Explain why you agree or disagree with this statement.
8. a. What is a prerefunded bond?
   b. Identify two reasons why an issuing municipality would want to prerefund an outstanding bond.
9. Why does a properly structured prerefunded municipal bond have no credit risk?
10. In recent years, municipalities have begun to issue asset-backed securities. What are the revenues of these securities backed by?
11. For years, observers and analysts of the debt market believed that municipal securities were free of any risk of default. Why do most people now believe that municipal debt can carry a substantial amount of credit or default risk?
12. Because many people know that interest payments on municipal debt generally are exempt from taxation by the federal government, they would undoubtedly be surprised by the term tax risk of investing in municipal bonds. Can you explain this term, and state why an astute investor should always be aware of this risk when buying municipal bonds?
13. How does the shape of the Treasury yield curve compare to that of the municipal yield curve?
14. Why isn't the Treasury yield curve used as a benchmark in measuring yield spreads between different sectors of the municipal bond market?

C h a p t e r   1 8

Common Stock Markets in the United States

Learning Objectives

After reading this chapter, you will understand

■ the reasons why the stock market has undergone significant structural changes.

■ where stocks are traded.

■ key federal government laws and actions affecting common stock markets.

■ trading mechanisms such as the types of orders, short selling, and margin transactions.

■ the key structural difference between a stock exchange and an over-the-counter market.

■ trading arrangements to accommodate institutional traders such as block trades and program trades.

■ what the upstairs market is and its role in institutional trading.

■ price limits and collars imposed by exchanges.

■ the role played by stock market indicators and how those indicators are constructed.

■ various stock market indicators of interest to market participants.

■ evidence on the pricing efficiency of the stock market.

■ the implications of pricing efficiency for a common stock strategy.

O ur focus in this chapter is on the secondary market for common stock in the United States. It is in the stock market that investors express their opinions about the economic prospect of a company through the trades they make. The aggregate of these trades gives the market consensus opinion about the price of the stock. This market has undergone significant changes since the 1960s, reflecting primarily the three interacting factors we described in Chapter 1, which have led to globalization of markets: (1) the institutionalization of the stock market as a result of a shift away from traditional small investors to large institutional investors; (2) changes in government regulation of the market; and (3) innovation, largely due to advances in computer technology.

The institutionalization of this market has had important implications for the design of trading systems because the demands made by institutional investors are different from those made by traditional small investors. We describe in this chapter the arrangements that have evolved to accommodate institutional investors in the secondary market for common stocks. We also review evidence on how efficiently common stocks are priced and the implications of efficiency for investment strategies.

321

CHARACTERISTICS OF COMMON STOCK

Equity securities represent an ownership interest in a corporation. Holders of equity securities are entitled to the earnings of the corporation when those earnings are distributed in the form of dividends; they are also entitled to a pro rata share of the remaining equity in case of liquidation. There are two types of equity securities: preferred stock and common stock. The key distinction between the two forms of equity securities is the degree to which their holders may participate in any distribution of earnings and capital and the priority given to each class in the distribution of earnings. Typically, preferred stockholders are entitled to a fixed dividend, which they receive before common stockholders can receive any dividends. We refer, therefore, to **preferred stock** as a senior corporate security, in the sense that preferred stock interests are senior to the interests of common stockholders. We postpone an explanation of preferred stock to Chapter 21 where we discuss the market for senior corporate securities.

> **Key Points That You Should Understand Before Proceeding**
> 1. The rights of an owner of a common share of stock.
> 2. The rights of an owner of a share of preferred stock.

WHERE STOCK TRADING OCCURS

In the United States, secondary market trading in common stocks has occurred in two different ways. The first is on organized **exchanges**, which are specific geographical locations called *trading floors*, where buyers and sellers physically meet. The trading mechanism on exchanges is the *auction system*, which results from the presence of many competing buyers and sellers assembled in one place.

The second type is via **over-the-counter (OTC) trading**, which results from geographically dispersed traders or market-makers linked to one another via telecommunication systems. That is, there is no trading floor. This trading mechanism is a *negotiated system* whereby individual buyers negotiate with individual sellers.

Exchange markets are called *central auction specialist systems* and OTC markets are called *multiple market-maker systems*. Recently, however, a new method of trading common stocks via independently owned and operated **electronic communications networks (ECNs)** has developed and is growing quickly.

In the United States, there are two national stock exchanges: (1) the New York Stock Exchange (NYSE), commonly called the **Big Board**, and (2) the American Stock Exchange (AMEX or ASE), also called the Curb. National stock exchanges trade stocks of not only U.S. corporations but also non-U.S. corporations. In addition to the national exchanges, there are regional stock exchanges in Boston, Chicago (called the Midwest Exchange), Cincinnati, San Francisco (called the Pacific Coast Exchange) and Philadelphia. Regional exchanges primarily trade stocks from corporations based within their region.

The major OTC market in the United States is **Nasdaq (the National Association of Securities Dealers Automated Quotation System)**, which is owned and operated by the NASD (the National Association of Securities Dealers). The NASD is a securities industry self-regulatory organization (SRO) that operates subject to the oversight of the SEC. Nasdaq is a national market. During 1998, Nasdaq and AMEX merged to form the Nasdaq–AMEX Market Group, Inc.

The NYSE is the largest exchange in the United States, with approximately 3,000 companies' shares listed. The AMEX is the second largest national stock exchange in the United States, with more than 750 issues listed for trading. Nasdaq has a greater number of listed stocks but with much less *market capitalization* than the NYSE.

In Chapter 15, we discussed the Securities Act of 1934. According to that act, there are two categories of traded stocks. The first is exchange traded stocks, which are also called listed stocks. The second is OTC stocks, which are also non-exchange traded stocks and are, thereby, by inference, nonlisted. However, as we will describe later in this chapter, certain Nasdaq stocks have listing requirements (the Nasdaq National Market and the Nasdaq Small Capitalization Market). Thus, a more useful and practical categorization of these categories is as follows:

1. Exchange listed stocks (national and regional exchanges)
2. Nasdaq listed OTC stocks
3. Non-Nasdaq OTC stocks.

We will focus on each of these markets later in this section.

The four major types of markets on which stocks are traded are referred to as follows:

First Market—Trading on exchanges of stocks listed on an exchange

Second Market—Trading in the OTC market of stocks not listed on an exchange

Third Market—Trading in the OTC market of stocks listed on an exchange

Fourth Market—Private transactions between institutional investors who deal directly with each other without utilizing the services of a broker-dealer intermediary.

These types of markets are discussed below.

EXCHANGES

Stock exchanges are formal organizations, approved and regulated by the Securities and Exchange Commission (SEC). They are made up of members who use the exchange facilities and systems to exchange or trade listed stocks. These exchanges are physical locations where members assemble to trade. Stocks that are traded on an exchange are said to be **listed stocks**. That is, these stocks are individually approved for trading on the exchange by the exchange. To be listed, a company must apply and satisfy requirements established by the exchange for minimum capitalization, shareholder equity, average closing share price, and other criteria. Even after being listed, exchanges may delist a company's stock if it no longer meets the exchange requirements.[1]

To have the right to trade securities or make markets on an exchange floor, firms or individuals must become a *member* of the exchange, which is accomplished by buying a **seat on the exchange**. The number of seats is fixed by the exchange and the cost of a seat is determined by supply and demand of those who want to sell or buy seats. In early 2001, there were 1,366 seats on the NYSE, and the cost of a seat was $2 million.

---

[1] Stocks may also be delisted because they have merged with another company or by the choice of the company. For example, a corporation may choose to list its stock on another exchange or on Nasdaq. Since 1976, the listing of a common stock on more than one exchange—for example on a national and a regional exchange—has been permitted.

Two kinds of stocks are listed on the five regional stock exchanges: (1) stocks of companies that either could not qualify for listing on one of the major national exchanges or could qualify for listing but chose not to list; and (2) stocks that are also listed on one of the major national exchanges. The latter are called *dually listed stocks.* The motivation of a company for dual listing is that a local brokerage firm that purchases a membership on a regional exchange can trade their listed stocks without having to purchase a considerably more expensive membership on the national stock exchange where the stock is also listed. Alternatively, a local brokerage firm could use the services of a member of a major national stock exchange to execute an order, but in this case it would have to give up part of its commission.

The regional stock exchanges compete with the NYSE for the execution of smaller trades. Major national brokerage firms have in recent years routed such orders to regional exchanges because of the lower cost they charge for executing orders or better prices, as we will discuss later.

The NYSE

Trading in stocks listed on the NYSE is conducted as a centralized continuous auction market at a designated location on the trading floor, called a **post**, with brokers representing their customers' buy and sell orders. A single **specialist** is the market-maker for each stock. A member firm may be designated as a specialist for the common stock of more than one company; that is, several stocks can trade at the same post. But only one specialist is designated for the common stock of each listed company.

A specialist for each stock stands at a trading position around one of the 17 NYSE posts. Each post is essentially an auction site where orders, bids and offers, arrive. Most orders arrive from floor brokers and via an electronic delivery system called the *SuperDot.* SuperDot is an electronic order routing and reporting system which links member firms electronically worldwide directly to the specialist's post on the trading floor of the NYSE. The majority of NYSE orders are processed electronically through SuperDot.

In addition to the single specialist market-maker on an exchange, other firms that are members of an exchange can trade for themselves or on behalf of their customers. NYSE member firms, which are broker-dealer organizations that serve the investing public, are represented on the trading floor by brokers who serve as fiduciaries in the execution of customer orders.

The largest membership category on the NYSE is that of the commission broker. A *commission broker* is an employee of one of the nearly 500 securities houses (stockbrokers or wirehouses) devoted to handling business on the exchange. Commission brokers execute orders for their firm on behalf of their customers at agreed commission rates. These houses may deal for their own account as well as on behalf of their clients.[2]

Other transactors on the exchange floor include the following categories. *Independent floor brokers* work on the exchange floor and execute orders for other exchange members who have more orders than they can handle alone or who require assistance in carrying out large orders. Floor brokers take a share in the commission received by the firm they are assisting. *Registered traders* are individual members who buy and sell for their own account. Alternatively, they may be trustees who maintain membership for the convenience of dealing and to save fees.

---

[2] Banks, however, are not allowed to act as principals and may only deal on their customers' behalf.

The last type of exchange participant is the specialist.

NYSE Specialist.

As explained earlier, *specialists* are dealers or market-makers assigned by the NYSE to conduct the auction process and maintain an orderly market in one or more designated stocks. Specialists may act as both a broker (agent) and a dealer (principal). In their role as a broker or agent, specialists represent customer orders in their assigned stocks, which arrive at their post electronically or are entrusted to them by a floor broker to be executed if and when a stock reaches a price specified by a customer (limit or stop order). As a dealer or principal, specialists buy and sell shares in their assigned stocks for their own account as necessary to maintain an orderly market. Specialists must always give precedence to public orders over trading for their own account.

In general, public orders for stocks traded on the NYSE, if they are not sent to the specialist's post via SuperDot, are sent from the member firm's office to its representative on the exchange floor, who attempts to execute the order in the trading crowd. Later in this chapter we discuss the various types of orders that an investor can ask a broker to execute. There are certain types of orders where the order will not be executed immediately on the trading floors. These are limit orders and stop orders. If the order is at a limit order or a stop order and the member firm's floor broker cannot transact the order immediately, the floor broker can wait in the trading crowd or give the order to the specialist in the stock, who will enter the order in that specialist's **limit order book** (or simply, *book*) for later execution based on the relationship between the market price and the price specified in the limit or stop order. The book is the list on which specialists keep the limit and stop orders that are given to them, arranged with size, from near the current market price to further away from it. Whereas the book used to be an actual physical paper book, it is now electronic. Only the specialists can see the orders in the book for their stock. This exclusivity with respect to the limit order book is obviously an advantage to the specialists, which to some degree offsets their obligation to make fair and orderly markets. At the time of this writing, however, the NYSE was planning to make the specialists' book available to investors electronically.

A significant advantage of the NYSE market is its diversity of participants. At the exchange, public orders meet each other often with minimal dealer intervention, contributing to an efficient mechanism for achieving fair securities prices. The liquidity provided in the NYSE market stems from the active involvement of the following principal groups: the individual investor; the institutional investor; the member firm acting as both agent and dealer; the member-firm broker on the trading floor acting as agent, representing the firm's customer orders; the independent broker on the trading floor acting as agent and handling customer orders on behalf of other member firms; and the specialist, with assigned responsibility in individual securities on the trading floor. Together these groups provide depth and diversity to the market.

NYSE-assigned specialists have four major roles:

1. As dealers, they trade for their own accounts when there is a temporary absence of public buyers or sellers, and only after the public orders in their possession have been satisfied at a specified price.

2. As agents, they execute market orders entrusted to them by brokers, as well as orders awaiting a specific market price.

3. As catalysts, they help to bring buyers and sellers together.

4. As auctioneers, they quote current bid–ask prices that reflect total supply and demand for each of the stocks assigned to them.

In carrying out their duties, specialists may, as indicated, act as either an agent or a principal. When acting as an *agent*, the specialists simply fill customer market orders or limit or stop orders (either new orders or orders from their book) by opposite orders (buy or sell). When acting as a *principal*, the specialists are charged with the responsibility of maintaining a *fair and orderly market*. Specialists are prohibited from engaging in transactions in securities in which they are registered unless such transactions are necessary to maintain a fair and orderly market. Specialists profit only from those trades in which they are involved; that is, they realize no revenue for trades in which they are an agent.

The term *fair and orderly market* means a market in which there is price continuity and reasonable depth. Thus, specialists are required to maintain a reasonable spread between bids and offers and small changes in price between transactions. Specialists are expected to bid and offer for their own account if necessary to promote such a fair and orderly market. They cannot put their own interests ahead of public orders and are obliged to trade on their own accounts against the market trend to help maintain liquidity and continuity as the price of a stock goes up or down. They may purchase stock for their investment account only if such purchases are necessary to create a fair and orderly market.

Specialists are responsible for balancing buy and sell orders at the opening of the trading day in order to arrange an equitable opening price for the stock. Specialists are expected to participate in the opening of the market only to the extent necessary to balance supply and demand for the security to effect a reasonable opening price. While trading throughout the day is via a continuous auction-based system, the opening is conducted via a single-priced call auction system. The specialists conduct the call and determine the single price.

If there is an *imbalance* between buy and sell orders either at the opening of or during the trading day and the specialists cannot maintain a fair and orderly market, then they may, under restricted conditions, close the market in that stock (that is, discontinue trading) until they are able to determine a price at which there is a balance of buy and sell orders. Such closes of trading can occur either during the trading day or at the opening, which is more common, and can last for minutes or days. Closings of a day or more may occur when, for example, there is an acquisition of one firm by another or when there is an extreme announcement by the corporation (for this reason, many announcements are made after the close of trading).

NYSE trading officials oversee the activities of the specialists and trading-floor brokers. Approval from these officials must be sought for a delay in trading at the opening or to halt trading during the trading day when unusual trading situations or price disparities develop.

Because of their critical public role and the necessity of capital in performing their function as a market-maker, capital requirements are imposed by the exchanges for specialists. Specialists must be able to assume a position of at least 150 round lots in each common stock in which they are registered.

As of February 1, 2001, there were 18 specialist firms on the NYSE. Traditionally, NYSE specialist firms were small, private family-owned businesses. However, recently NYSE specialist firms have consolidated, been acquired by public companies, or have gone public themselves. The increased capital requirements for specialists has been one factor that has led to a consolidation of the specialist firms. These specialists will continue to face increasing competition such as electronic communication networks.

Nevertheless, the specialist business is very profitable—its return on capital exceeds that of most brokerage firms.[3]

Commissions.

Before 1975, stock exchanges were allowed to set minimum commissions on transactions. The fixed commission structure did not allow the commission rate to decline as the number of shares in the order increased, thereby ignoring the economies of scale in executing transactions. For example, brokers incur lower total costs in executing an order of 10,000 shares of one stock for one investor than in executing 100 orders for the same stock from 100 investors. Consequently, fixed commissions did not reflect economies of scale.

Pressure from institutional investors, who transacted large trades, led the SEC to eliminate fixed commission rates in May 1975. Since 1975, commissions have been fully negotiable between investors and their brokers. May 1, 1975, called Black Thursday, began a period of severe price competition among brokers, with many firms failing, and a consolidation of firms taking place in the brokerage industry. This liberalization of commissions was the U.S. version of the "Big Bang," which was later followed in the U.K. during 1986 and Japan during 1996, which we will discuss in Chapter 19.

Since the introduction of negotiated commissions, the opportunity has arisen for the development of **discount brokers.** These brokers charge commissions at rates much less than those charged by other brokers, but offer little or no advice or any other service apart from the execution of the transaction. Discount brokers have been particularly effective in inducing retail investors to participate in the market for individual stock.

THE OTC MARKET

The OTC market is called the market for unlisted stocks. As explained previously, technically while there are listing requirements for exchanges, there are also listing requirements for the Nasdaq National and Small Capitalization OTC markets. Nevertheless, exchange traded stocks are called listed, and stocks traded on the OTC markets are called unlisted.

There are three parts to the OTC market: two under the aegis of NASD (the Nasdaq markets) and a third market for truly unlisted stocks, the non-Nasdaq OTC markets.

Nasdaq Stock Market

Established in 1971, the Nasdaq stock market was developed as a wholly owned subsidiary of the NASD. The NASD is a national securities association, an SRO subject to oversight by the SEC. NASD, a private organization, represents and regulates the dealers in the OTC market. Nasdaq is the flagship market of the NASD.

Nasdaq is essentially a telecommunication network that links thousands of geographically dispersed, market-making participants. Nasdaq is an electronic quotation system that provides price quotations to market participants on Nasdaq listed stocks.

---

[3] See Jeff D. Opdyke, "Goldman Boosts Clout in Trading," *Wall Street Journal* (January 30, 2001), pp. C1, C18; Charles Gasparino, "Bear Stearns to Acquire Specialist," *Wall Street Journal* (February 15, 2001), pp. C1, C16; Patrick McGeehan, "A Bear Stearns Partnership Expands Its Stock Trading Role," *New York Times* (February 16, 2001), p. C1.

Table 18-1   Nasdaq and Its National Market and Small Cap Market

Components of Nasdaq			
	NASDAQ (NMS)	NATIONAL MARKET (NNM)	SMALL CAP MARKET
Share Volume (in billions)*	442.8	424.0	18.8
Dollar Volume (in billions)	$20,395.3	$20,273.7	$121.7
Market Value (in billions)	$3,597.1	$3,579.4	$17.7
Companies	4,734	3,827	907
Issues	5,053	4,010	1,043

SOURCE: www.marketdata.nasdaq.com

Volume data is for the year 2000. The other data is as of December 31, 2000.

Although there is no central trading floor, Nasdaq has become an electronic "virtual trading floor." As shown in Table 18-1, there are more than 4,700 common stocks included in the Nasdaq system with a total market value of over $3.5 trillion. Some 535 dealers, known as market-makers, representing some of the world's largest securities firms, provide competing bids to buy and offers to sell Nasdaq stocks to investors.

Nasdaq Market Tiers.

The Nasdaq stock market has two broad tiers of securities: (1) the *Nasdaq National Market (NNM)* and the *Small Capitalization Market.* Newspapers contain separate sections for these two tiers of stocks (sections labeled the "Nasdaq National Market" and the "Nasdaq Small Capitalization Market"). The Nasdaq NMS is the dominant OTC market in the United States.

As of December 2000, there were approximately 3,800 stocks on the Nasdaq NNM system and 900 on the Small Cap Market. Some features of the two tiers of Nasdaq are shown in Table 18-1. Note that the Small Cap Market is smaller in every way.

Securities are actually listed on both tiers of Nasdaq; that is, they must meet fairly stringent listing requirements for size, issuer profitability, trading volume, governance, public disclosure, and other factors. Securities traded on these Nasdaq tiers must meet specified minimum standards for both initial listing and continued listing. The financial criteria for listing in the Small Cap Market are not as stringent as in the NNM system, although the corporate governance standards for the two are the same. Small Cap companies often grow and move up to the NNM market. The NNM issues are more widely known, have more trading volume, and have more market-makers.

Many stocks that qualify for listing on the NYSE remain on Nasdaq, including Microsoft and Intel, as of the end of 2000. Occasionally companies switch from Nasdaq to the NYSE. However, only one has switched from the NYSE to Nasdaq since 1970 (Aeroflex, Inc.).

Some firms are market-makers only and others brokers only. Thus, brokers would have to conduct their OTC business through market-makers. However, many firms, including the national wirehouses, have become vertically integrated. Increasingly, large wirehouses have acquired major Nasdaq trading firms which were independent. A major reason for these acquisitions is that Nasdaq trading is becoming increasingly retail and the large investment banks wanted to maintain and increase their retail business.

The structure of Nasdaq is quite different from that of the NYSE. Nasdaq has been completely owned by the NASD, a nonprofit organization. NASD has approximately 5,500 member firms, and there are no meaningful ownership rights. However, Nasdaq is a for-profit organization. Thus, Nasdaq would not upstream all its profits to NASD. Nasdaq and NASD sold 62.6% of their ownership in Nasdaq via two private equity offerings during 2000 and early 2001 to broker dealers and companies whose shares trade on Nasdaq. Nasdaq is planning an initial public offering to become a public company during 2001 or 2002, and NASD plans to sell all of its ownership rights to Nasdaq which would liquify its previous private issues.

Clearly, changes in the structure of U.S. trading markets have been accelerating. Such changes have also been accelerating internationally, as we will discuss in the next chapter.

Other OTC Markets

Whereas the Nasdaq stock markets are the major parts of the U.S. OTC markets, the vast majority of the OTC issues (about 8,000) do not trade on either of the two Nasdaq systems. There are two types of markets for these stocks. The securities traded on these markets are not listed; that is, they have no listing requirements. Thus, these two OTC markets are not "issuer services" but are "subscriber services." That is, subscribers can make bids and offers for any stock not listed on exchanges or Nasdaq.

The first of these two non-Nasdaq OTC markets is the **OTC Bulletin Board (OTCBB)**, sometimes called simply the Bulletin Board. OTCBB is owned and operated by Nasdaq and regulated by NASD. The OTCBB displays real-time quotes, last-sale prices and volume information for approximately 5,500 securities. It includes stocks not traded on NYSE, Amex, or Nasdaq.

The second non-Nasdaq OTC market is the **Pink Sheets**, which is owned and operated by the National Quotation Bureau. Prior to the creation of Nasdaq in 1971, dealer quotations were disseminated by paper copy only. These copies were printed on pink paper, for which reason these OTC securities were called Pink Sheet stocks. The Pink Sheets are still published weekly. In addition, an electronic version of the Pink Sheets is updated daily and disseminated over market data vendor terminals. Pink Sheet securities are often pejoratively called *penny stocks*.

THE THIRD MARKET

A stock may be both listed on an exchange and also traded in the OTC market, called the **third market**. Dealers in this market could not be members of the NYSE until the NYSE Rule 390 was repealed during 1999. Consequently, these non-NYSE member dealers were not restricted by the fixed minimum commissions set prior to 1975. The third market grew as institutional investors used it in the early 1960s to avoid these fixed minimum commissions. Even after 1975, however, only a handful of dealers actively participated in the third market, primarily because of NYSE Rule 390. After the repeal of Rule 390 during 1999, however, third-market activity for NYSE-listed stocks has the potential to grow significantly.

Like Nasdaq, the third market is a network of broker-dealers that aggregates quotation information and provides interparticipant order routing tools but leaves order execution to market participants. Dealers that make markets in the third market operate under the regulatory jurisdiction of the NASD. While the third market is not owned by the NASD, market-makers in the third market use some of the facilities provided by Nasdaq. When the NASD created Nasdaq in 1971, it included substantially similar functionality for third-market listed trading, including the **CQS (Consolidated Quotations Service)** for third-market quotes, and CTS for third-market trades.

ALTERNATIVE TRADING SYSTEMS—THE FOURTH MARKET

It is not necessary for two parties to a transaction to use an intermediary. That is, the services of a broker or a dealer are not required to execute a trade. The direct trading of stocks between two customers without the use of a broker is called the *fourth market*. This market grew for the same reasons as the third market—the excessively high minimum commissions established by the exchanges.

A number of proprietary **alternative trading systems (ATSs)**, which comprise the fourth market, are operated by the NASD members or member affiliates. These fourth-market ATSs are for-profit "broker's brokers" that match investor orders and report trading activity to the marketplace via Nasdaq or the third market. In a sense, ATSs are similar to exchanges because they are designed to allow two participants to meet directly on the system and are maintained by a third party who also serves a limited regulatory function by imposing requirements on each subscriber.

Broadly, there are two types of ATSs: electronic communications networks and crossing networks.

Electronic Communications Networks

Electronic communications networks (ECNs) are privately owned broker-dealers that operate as market participants within the Nasdaq system. They display quotes that reflect actual orders and provide institutions and Nasdaq market-makers with an anonymous way to enter orders. Essentially, an ECN is a limit order book that is widely disseminated and open for continuous trading to subscribers who may enter and access orders displayed on the ECN. ECNs offer transparency, anonymity, automated service, and reduced prices, and are therefore effective for handling small orders. ECNs are used to disseminate firm commitments to trade (firm bids or offers) to participants, or subscribers, which have typically either purchased or leased hardware for the operation of the ECN or have built a custom connection to the ECN. ECNs may also be linked into the Nasdaq marketplace via a quotation representing the ECN's best buy and sell quote. In general, ECNs use the Internet to link buyers and sellers, bypassing brokers and trading floors.

Since ECNs are part of the Nasdaq execution, their volume is counted as part of the Nasdaq volume. ECNs account for over 30% of Nasdaq trading in exchange trading. However, even after the repeal of NYSE Rule 390, ECNs amount to less than 5% of executed volume on the NYSE.

Instinet, the first ECN, began operating in 1969, and continues to be a very large ECN in terms of activity. Since 1969, nine additional ECNs have been created. Two of the ECNs have applied to the SEC to become exchanges.

Crossing Networks

Crossing networks are systems developed to allow institutional investors to **cross trades**—that is, match buyers and sellers directly—typically via computer. These networks are batch processes that aggregate orders for execution at prespecified times.

Crossing networks provide anonymity and reduced cost, and are specifically designed to minimize a trading cost that we will describe later (market impact cost). They vary considerably in their approach to market structure, including the type of order information that can be entered by the subscriber and the amount of pre-trade transparency that is available to participants.

At present, there are three major crossing networks.

OTHER TYPES OF COMMON STOCK TRADING

There are other types of common stock trading vehicles and security types as well. Some of these are discussed in the sections that follow.

Rule 144A Securities

Rule 144A is designed to facilitate secondary market trading in "nonfungible" unregistered securities among qualified institutional buyers (QIBs) by providing a "safe harbor" from the registration requirements of the Securities Act of 1933. QIBs are institutions that have $100 million invested in securities of issuers that are not affiliated with the qualified buyer. Basically, Rule 144A permits the issue of nonregistered securities and their purchase by qualified institutions.

American Depository Receipts

American depository receipts (ADRs) are negotiable certificates in registered form, which are issued in the United States by a U.S. bank and which certify that a specific number of foreign shares have been deposited with an overseas branch of the bank (or another financial institution), that, in turn, acts as a custodian of the shares in the country of origin. ADRs provide an opportunity for investors who want to invest in the shares of a foreign corporation to buy, hold, and sell their interests in these foreign securities without having to take physical possession of the securities. ADRs are discussed in more detail in the next chapter.

Key Points That You Should Understand Before Proceeding

1. The differences between organized exchanges and the OTC market.
2. The role and duties of a specialist on an organized exchange.
3. The role of market-makers on the OTC markets.
4. The meaning and structure of the Nasdaq National Market and the Small Cap Market.
5. The role of the third market.
6. The roles of ATS, ECNs, and crossing networks.

THE ROLE AND REGULATION OF DEALERS IN EXCHANGE AND OTC MARKETS

In Chapter 15 we explained the role of dealers in secondary markets. There is an important structural difference between exchanges and the OTC market with respect to the activities of dealers. The main difference is whether there is a single market-maker (as on the exchanges) or multiple market-makers (as on the OTC). On exchanges, there is only one market-maker or dealer per stock, and the dealer is called the specialist.

Since there is only one specialist for a given stock, there is no competition from other market-makers on the exchange. Does this mean that the specialist has a monopolistic position? Not necessarily. Specialists face competition from several sources. Brokers in the crowd might have public market or limit orders that compete with specialists. In the case of multiple-listed stocks, there is also competition from specialists on other exchanges where the stock is listed. Since Rule 390 was repealed in late 1999, there could also be competition from dealers in the OTC market. Finally, as we will discuss later in this chapter, when a block trade is involved, specialists compete with the upstairs market.

In the OTC market, there can be many dealers for a stock. The number of dealers depends on the volume of trading in a stock. For example, at the time of this writing, there were nearly 82 dealers on Nasdaq for Microsoft. If a stock is not actively traded, there may be only one or two dealers. As trading activity increases in a stock, there are no barriers preventing more entities from becoming dealers in that stock, other than satisfaction of capital requirements. Competition from more dealers, or the threat of new dealers, forces bid–ask spreads to more competitive levels. Moreover, the capital-providing capacity of more than one dealer could be thought to be more beneficial to markets than that of a single specialist performing the role of a market-maker.

Those who think the OTC market is superior to an organized exchange often cite the greater competition from numerous dealers and the greater amount of capital they bring to the trading in a security. The exchanges, however, insist that the commitment of the dealers to provide a market for shares in the OTC market is not the same obligation as that of the specialist on the exchange. On the NYSE, as we described previously, specialists are obligated to maintain fair and orderly markets. Failure to fulfill this obligation results in a loss of specialist status. A dealer in the OTC market is under no such obligation to continue its market-making activity during volatile and uncertain market conditions.

Overall, NYSE specialists have an obligation to make fair and orderly markets. And NNM market-makers have an affirmative obligation to continuously post firm two-sided quotes good for 1,000 shares (for most stocks). However, both types of market-makers have escape valves for extenuating circumstances. If the NYSE specialists are unable to maintain a balanced market, then, with the approval of the Exchange authorities, they can close the market until they are able to restore the balance. Similarly, Nasdaq market-makers are relieved of their obligation to make markets if companies make news announcements or in cases of unusual trading when an issuer's executives cannot be reached. Nasdaq market-makers are considering requesting the SEC to give Nasdaq authorities greater latitude in halting and canceling aberrant trades in stocks.

On the NYSE, 8 out of 10 trades happen directly between a buyer and a seller; that is, there is no intermediate market-maker who collects a spread. Thus, each side simply pays only his or her own broker for the service. The exchange levies a fee only on orders larger than 2,100 shares. On the other hand, most Nasdaq trades take place through a market-maker who benefits from the bid–offer spread.

Consider this age-old securities debate: Are investors better off in a central market distilling highly accurate prices from a huge pool of liquidity, as at the NYSE, at the risk of sanctioning a lethargic monopoly? Or are they better off in a sea of competing market-makers, as Nasdaq offers? An SEC study of the costs of trading in these two markets sheds some light on this issue. On January 8, 2001, the SEC released a study indicating that for many types of orders, investors get worse prices when they trade on the Nasdaq than on the NYSE. The study was based on the cost of trading comparable stocks on the NYSE and Nasdaq during the week of June 5, 2000.

The SEC study found that for orders of 100 to 499 shares, the spread was between $0.057 and $0.109 per share wider for Nasdaq stocks for all but the very largest stocks. Offsetting this negative finding for Nasdaq, the study found that on small orders of 100 to 499 shares, orders are executed by 10 to 19 seconds faster on Nasdaq; on 500 to 1,999 share orders there is little difference; and, on 2,000 to 4,999 share orders, the NYSE is faster by 29 to 47 seconds. The study also found that limit orders are filled more often on the NYSE than on Nasdaq.[4]

The study identified, however, structural differences between the NYSE and Nasdaq that could explain the cost differences. As discussed previously in this chapter, the NYSE is a central agency–auction market where more than 80% of the volume in its stocks is executed on the floor. This maximizes the chances that a buyer will transact directly with a seller. In contrast, Nasdaq is decentralized or "fragmented," with no market-maker or ECN responsible for a majority of the volume. Thus, dealers fill a much greater portion of the orders on Nasdaq (where they are called market-makers) than on the NYSE (the specialist). As a result, the investor of a Nasdaq stock is less likely to do better than the quoted bid or ask (that is, receive "price improvement") because the market-maker captures the spread as profit. On the NYSE, however, buyers and sellers are typically matched at the bid, the ask, or in between. That means either the buyer, the seller, or both do better than the quoted spread.

Overall, dealers attempt to profit at the price at which they trade with customers, and their greater involvement on Nasdaq may lead to higher customer transaction costs. Thus, the disparity in trading costs can be due simply to differences between a "dealer" stock market such as Nasdaq and an "auction market" such as the NYSE.

Nasdaq proponents also point out that Nasdaq stocks are smaller (on average) and technology related, and such stocks are more volatile. It is argued that this accounts for the difference in trading costs. Investigations on this topic continue.

TRADING MECHANICS

Here we describe the key features involved in trading stocks. Later in the chapter, we discuss trading arrangements (block trades and program trades) that developed specifically for coping with the trading needs of institutional investors.

Types of Orders and Trading Priority Rules

When an investor wants to buy or sell a share of common stock, the price and conditions under which the order is to be executed must be communicated to a broker. The simplest type of order is the **market order**, an order to be executed at the best price available in the market. If the stock is listed and traded on an organized exchange, the best price is assured by the exchange rule that when more than one order on the same side of the buy/sell transaction reaches the market at the same time, the order with

---

[4] Grey Ip and Michael Schroeder, "SEC Price Study Deals Blow to Nasdaq," *Wall Street Journal* (January 9, 2001), pp. C1, C4; Gretchen Morgenson, "A Friendlier Nasdaq: Work in Progress," *New York Times* (January 9, 2001), Business section, pp. 1, 12.

the best price is given priority. Thus, buyers bidding a higher price are given priority over those bidding a lower price; sellers offering a lower price are given priority over those offering a higher price.

Another **priority rule** of exchange trading is needed to handle receipt of more than one order at the same price. Most often, the priority in executing such orders is based on the time of arrival of the order—first orders in are the first orders executed—although there may be a rule that gives higher priority to certain types of market participants over other types of market participants who are seeking to transact at the same price. For example, on exchanges, orders can be classified as either **public orders** or orders of those member firms dealing on behalf of their own account (both nonspecialists and specialists). Exchange rules require that public orders be given priority over orders of member firms dealing for their own account.

The danger of a market order is that an adverse move may take place between the time the investor places the order and the time the order is executed. To avoid this danger, the investor can place a *limit order* that designates a price threshold for the execution of the trade. A *buy limit order* indicates that the stock may be purchased only at the designated price or lower. A *sell limit order* indicates that the stock may be sold at the designated price or higher. The key disadvantage of a limit order is that there is no guarantee that it will be executed at all; the designated price may simply not be obtainable. A limit order that is not executable at the time it reaches the market is recorded in a limit order book that we mentioned earlier in this chapter.

The limit order is a *conditional order*: It is executed only if the limit price or a better price can be obtained. Another type of conditional order is the **stop order**, which specifies that the order is not to be executed until the market moves to a designated price, at which time it becomes a market order. A *buy stop order* specifies that the order is not to be executed until the market rises to a designated price, that is, until it trades at or above, or is bid at or above, the designated price. A *sell stop order* specifies that the order is not to be executed until the market price falls below a designated price, that is, until it trades at or below, or is offered at or below, the designated price. A stop order is useful when an investor cannot watch the market constantly. Profits can be preserved or losses minimized on a stock position by allowing market movements to trigger a trade. In a sell (buy) stop order, the designated price is lower (higher) than the current market price of the stock. In a sell (buy) limit order, the designated price is higher (lower) than the current market price of the stock. The relationships between the two types of conditional orders, and the market movements which trigger them, appear in Table 18-2.

Two dangers are associated with stop orders. Stock prices sometimes exhibit abrupt price changes, so the direction of a change in a stock price may be quite temporary, resulting in the premature trading of a stock. Also, once the designated price is reached, the stop order becomes a market order and is subject to the uncertainty of the execution price noted earlier for market orders.

A *stop-limit order*, a hybrid of a stop order and a limit order, is a stop order that designates a price limit. In contrast to the stop order, which becomes a market order if the stop is reached, the stop-limit order becomes a limit order if the stop is reached. The stop-limit order can be used to cushion the market impact of a stop order. The investor can limit the possible execution price after the activation of the stop. As with a limit order, the limit price may never be reached after the order is activated, which therefore defeats one purpose of the stop order—to protect a profit or limit a loss.

An investor can also enter a **market if touched order**. This order becomes a market order if a designated price is reached. A market if touched order to buy becomes a

Table 18-2 Conditional Orders and the Direction of Triggering Security Price Movements

PRICE OF SECURITY	LIMIT ORDER	MARKET IF TOUCHED ORDER	STOP LIMIT ORDER	STOP ORDER
Higher price	Price specified for a *sell limit order*	Price specified for a *sell market if touched order*	Price specified for a limit *buy stop order*	Price specified for a *buy stop order*
Current price	—	—	—	—
Lower price	Price specified for a *buy limit order*	Price specified for a *buy market if touched order*	Price specified for a *sell stop limit order*	Price specified for a *sell stop order*
Comment	Can be filled only at price or better; that is, does not become a market order when price is reached	Becomes market order when price is reached	Does not become a market order when price is reached; can be executed only at price or better.	Becomes market order when price is reached

market order if the market falls to a given price, whereas a stop order to buy becomes a market order if the market rises to a given price. Similarly, a market if touched order to sell becomes a market order if the market rises to a specified price, while the stop order to sell becomes a market order if the market falls to a given price. We can think of the stop order as an order designed to get out of an existing position at an acceptable price (without specifying the exact price), and the market if touched order as an order designed to get into a position at an acceptable price (also without specifying the exact price).

Orders can be placed to buy or sell at the open or the close of trading for the day. An opening order indicates a trade to be executed only in the opening range for the day, and a closing order indicates a trade is to be executed only within the closing range for the day.

An investor may enter orders that contain order cancellation provisions. A **fill or kill order** must be executed as soon as it reaches the trading floor or it is immediately canceled. Orders may designate the time period for which the order is effective: a day, week, or month, or perhaps by a given time within the day. An **open order**, or good till canceled order, is good until the investor specifically terminates the order.

Orders are also classified by size. One **round lot** is typically 100 shares of a stock. An **odd lot** is defined as less than a round lot. For example, an order of 75 shares of Digital Equipment Corporation (DEC) is an odd lot order. An order of 350 shares of DEC includes an odd lot portion of 50 shares. A block trade is defined on the NYSE as an order of 10,000 shares of a given stock or a total market value of $200,000 or more.

Both the major national stock exchanges and the regional stock exchanges have systems for routing orders of a specified size (that are submitted by brokers) through a computer directly to the specialists' posts where the orders can be executed. On the NYSE, this system is the SuperDOT (Super Designated Order Turnaround) system. The AMEX's Post Execution Reporting system allows orders up to 2,000 shares to be routed directly to specialists. The regional stock exchanges have computerized systems for routing small orders to specialists. The Small Order Execution system of the NASDAQ routes and executes orders up to 1,000 shares of a given stock.

Short Selling

As we explained in Chapter 15, short selling involves the sale of a security not owned by the investor at the time of sale. The investors can arrange to have their broker borrow the stock from someone else, and the borrowed stock is delivered to implement the sale. To cover their short position, the investors must subsequently purchase the stock and return it to the party that lent the stock.

Let us look at an example of how this is done in the stock market. Suppose Ms. Stokes believes that Wilson Steel common stock is overpriced at $20 per share and wants to be in a position to benefit if her assessment is correct. Ms. Stokes calls her broker, Mr. Yats, indicating that she wants to sell 100 shares of Wilson Steel. Mr. Yats will do two things: (1) sell 100 shares of Wilson Steel on behalf of Ms. Stokes, and (2) arrange to borrow 100 shares of that stock to deliver to the buyer. Suppose that Mr. Yats is able to sell the stock for $20 per share and borrows the stock from Mr. Jordan. The shares borrowed from Mr. Jordan will be delivered to the buyer of the 100 shares. The proceeds from the sale (ignoring commissions) will be $2,000. However, the proceeds do not go to Ms. Stokes because she has not given her broker the 100 shares. Thus, Ms. Stokes is said to be "short 100 shares."

Now, let's suppose one week later the price of Wilson Steel stock declines to $15 per share. Ms. Stokes may instruct her broker to buy 100 shares of Wilson Steel. The cost of buying the shares (once again ignoring commissions) is $1,500. The shares purchased are then delivered to Mr. Jordan, who lent 100 shares to Ms. Stokes. At this point, Ms. Stokes has sold 100 shares and bought 100 shares. So, she no longer has any obligation to her broker or to Mr. Jordan; she has covered her short position. She is entitled to the funds in her account that were generated by the selling and buying activity. She sold the stock for $2,000 and bought it for $1,500. Thus, she realizes a profit before commissions of $500. From this amount, commissions are subtracted.

Two more costs will reduce the profit further. First, a fee will be charged by the lender of the stock. Second, if there are any dividends paid by Wilson Steel while the stock is borrowed, Ms. Stokes must compensate Mr. Jordan for the dividends to which he would have been entitled.

If instead of falling, the price of Wilson Steel stock rises, Ms. Stokes will realize a loss when she is forced to cover her short position. For example, if the price rises to $27, Ms. Stokes will lose $700, to which must be added commissions and the cost of borrowing the stock (and possibly dividends).

Exchanges impose restrictions as to when a short sale may be executed; these so-called **tick-test rules** are intended to prevent investors from destabilizing the price of a stock when the market price is falling. A short sale can be made only when either (1) the sale price of the particular stock is higher than the last trade price (referred to as an *uptick trade*), or (2) if there is no change in the last trade price of the particular stock (referred to as a *zero uptick*), the previous trade price must be higher than the trade price that preceded it. For example, if Ms. Stokes wanted to short Wilson Steel at a price of $20, and the two previous trade prices were $20 $\frac{1}{8}$, and then $20, she could not do so at this time because of the uptick trade rule. If the previous trade prices were $19 $\frac{7}{8}$, $19 $\frac{7}{8}$, and then $20, she could short the stock at $20 because of the uptick trade rule. Suppose that the sequence of the last three trades is $19 $\frac{7}{8}$, $20, and $20. Ms. Stokes could short the stock at $20 because of the zero uptick rule.

Margin Transactions

Investors can borrow cash to buy securities and use the securities themselves as collateral. For example, suppose Mr. Boxer has $10,000 to invest and is considering buying Wilson Steel, which is currently selling for $20 per share. With his $10,000, Mr. Boxer can buy 500 shares. Suppose his broker can arrange for him to borrow an additional $10,000 so that Mr. Boxer can buy an additional 500 shares. Thus, with a $20,000 investment, he can purchase a total of 1,000 shares. The 1,000 shares will be used as collateral for the $10,000 borrowed, and Mr. Boxer will have to pay interest on the amount borrowed.

A transaction in which an investor borrows to buy shares using the shares themselves as collateral is called **buying on margin**. By borrowing funds, an investor creates financial leverage. Note that Mr. Boxer, for a $10,000 investment, realizes the consequences associated with a price change of 1,000 shares rather than 500 shares. He will benefit if the price rises but be worse off if the price falls (compared to borrowing no funds).

To illustrate, we now look at what happens if the price subsequently changes. If the price of Wilson Steel rises to $29 per share, ignoring commissions and the cost of borrowing, Mr. Boxer will realize a profit of $9 per share on 1,000 shares, or $9,000. Had Mr. Boxer not borrowed $10,000 to buy the additional 500 shares, his profit would be only $4,500. Suppose, instead, the price of Wilson Steel stock decreases to $13 per share. Then, by borrowing to buy 500 additional shares, he lost $7 per share on 1,000 shares instead of $7 per share on just 500 shares.

The funds borrowed to buy the additional stock will be provided by the broker, and the broker gets the money from a bank. The interest rate that banks charge brokers for funds of this purpose is named the **call money rate** (also labeled the broker loan rate). The broker charges the borrowing investor the call money rate plus a service charge.

Setting Initial Margin Requirements

The broker is not free to lend as much as it wishes to the investor to buy securities. The Securities Exchange Act of 1934 prohibits brokers from lending more than a specified percentage of the market value of the securities. The **initial margin requirement** is the proportion of the total market value of the securities that the investor must pay as an equity share, and the remainder is borrowed from the broker. The 1934 act gives the board of governors of the Federal Reserve (the Fed) the responsibility to set initial margin requirements, which it does under Regulations T and U. The Fed changes margin requirements as an instrument of economic policy. The initial margin requirement has been below 40%; it is 50% as of this writing. Initial margin requirements vary for stocks and bonds.

Maintenance Margin

The Fed also establishes a **maintenance margin requirement**. This is the minimum proportion of (1) the equity in the investor's margin account to (2) the total market value. If the investor's margin account falls below the minimum maintenance margin (which would happen if the share's price fell), the investor is required to put up additional cash. The investor receives a margin call from the broker specifying the additional cash to be put into the investor's margin account. If the investor fails to put up the additional cash, the broker has the authority to sell the securities for the investor's account.

Let us illustrate maintainance. Assume an investor buys 100 shares of stock at $60 per share for $6,000 of stock on 50% margin and the maintenance margin is 25%. By purchasing $6,000 of stock on 50% margin, the investor must put up $3,000 of cash (or other equity) and, thus, borrows $3,000 (referred to as the *debit balance*). The investor, however, must maintain 25% of margin. To what level must the stock price decline to hit the maintenance margin level? The price is $40. At this price, the stock position has a value of $4,000 ($40 × 100 shares). With a loan of $3,000, the equity in the account is $1,000 ($4,000 − $3,000), or 25% of the account value ($1,000/$4,000 = 25%). If the price of the stock decreases below $40, the investor must deposit more equity to bring the equity level up to 25%. In general, the account level has to decrease to 4/3 times the amount borrowed (the debit balance) to hit the minimum maintenance margin level.

There are also margin practices for short selling. Consider a similar margin example for a short position. An investor shorts (borrows and sells) 100 shares of stock at $60 for total stock value of $6,000. With an initial margin of 50%, the investor must deposit $3,000 (in addition to leaving the $6,000 from the sale in the account). This leaves the investor with a *credit balance* of $9,000 (which does not change with the stock price since it is in cash). However, the investor owes 100 shares of the stock at the current market price. To what level must the stock price increase to hit the maintenance margin level, assumed to be 30% (which is the equity in the account as a percentage of the market value of the stock)? The answer is $69.23, for a total stock value of $6,923. If the stock is worth $6,923, there is $2,077 of equity in the account ($9,000 − $6,923), which represents 30% of the market value of the stock ($2,077/$6,923 = 30%). The value of the stock that triggered the maintenance level is calculated by multiplying the credit balance by 10/13 (10/13 × $9,000 = $6,923).

TRANSACTION COSTS

An important aspect of an investment strategy is controlling the transaction costs necessary to implement the strategy. Trading costs can be decomposed into two major components: *explicit costs* and *implicit costs*. Explicit costs are the direct costs of trading, such as broker commissions, fees, and taxes. Implicit costs represent such indirect costs as the price impact of the trade and the opportunity costs of failing to execute in a timely manner or at all. Whereas explicit costs are associated with identifiable accounting charges, no such reporting of implicit costs occurs.

Explicit Costs

The main explicit cost is the commission paid to the broker for execution. Commission costs are fully negotiable and vary systematically by broker type and market mechanism. The commission may depend on both the price per share and the number of shares in the transaction.[5] In addition to commissions, there may be other explicit costs. These explicit costs include custodial fees (the fees charged by an institution that holds securities in safekeeping for an investor) and transfer fees (the fees associated from transferring an asset from one owner to another).

Implicit Costs

Implicit trading costs include impact costs, timing costs, and opportunity costs.

Impact Costs.

The **impact cost** of a transaction is the change in market price due to supply/demand imbalances caused by the presence of the trade. Bid–ask spread estimates, although

---

[5] For more on this point, see Bruce M. Collins and Frank J. Fabozzi, "A Methodology for Measuring Transactions Costs," *Financial Analysts Journal* (March/April 1991), pp. 27–36.

informative, fail to capture the fact that large trades—those that exceed the number of shares the market-maker is willing to trade at the quoted bid and ask prices—may move prices in the direction of the trade. That is, large trades can increase the price for buy orders and decrease the price for sell orders. The resulting market impact or price impact of the transaction can be thought of as the deviation of the transaction price from the "unperturbed price" that would have prevailed had the trade not occurred. As discussed previously, crossing networks are designed to minimize impact costs.

Timing Costs.

The **timing cost** is measured as the price change between the time the parties to the implementation process assume responsibility for the trade and the time they complete the responsibility. Timing costs occur when orders are on the trading desk of a buy side firm (e.g., an investment mangement firm) but have not been released to the broker because the trader fears that the trade may swamp the market.

Opportunity Costs.

The opportunity cost is the "cost" of securities not traded. This cost results from missed or only partially completed trades. These costs are the natural consequence of the release delays. For example, if the price moves too much before the trade can be completed, the manager will not make the trade. In practice, this cost is measured on shares not traded based on the difference between the market price at the time of decision and the closing price 30 days later.

Whereas commissions and impact costs are actual and visible out-of-pocket costs, opportunity costs and timing costs are the costs of foregone opportunities and are invisible. Opportunity costs can arise for two reasons. First, some orders are executed with a delay, during which the price moves against the investor. Second, some orders incur an opportunity cost because they are only partially filled or are not executed at all.

TRADING ARRANGEMENTS FOR RETAIL AND INSTITUTIONAL INVESTORS

Trades are executed by both individuals, called *retail investors*, and institutions. There are several differences in the way they trade. The first is size: institutions typically transact much larger orders than individuals. The second is commissions: consistent with their larger size, institutions typically pay lower commissions than individuals.

The third difference is the method of order execution. Although both an individual and an institution can trade through a broker-dealer, the ways in which their orders are entered and executed may be considerably different, even if the trades are through the same broker-dealer. An individual trading through a broker-dealer typically goes through a stockbroker (although stockbrokers now have a variety of different names, such as financial consultant [FC]). These orders go to a retail exchange execution desk and from there to the NYSE (usually through SuperDot) or to the OTC execution desk, where the order is transacted through another market-maker on Nasdaq or it is internalized.

Institutional investors typically give their order directly to the institutional broker-dealer execution desk, for both exchange and OTC orders. Exchange orders may be sent to the broker-dealer's floor broker, and OTC orders may be transacted with another broker-dealer or internalized at a competitive bid or offer. Competing bids or offers are typically obtained in all cases.

Because of these differences in the execution of stock trades by individuals and institutions, the trends in common stock holdings is of consequence. During the last 50 years, common stock holdings in the United States have become increasingly institutionalized. The major institutional holders are pension funds (private [usually corporate], state and local government, and labor union), investment companies (mutual funds and closed end funds), life insurance companies, bank trusts, endowments, and foundations.

Historically, there has been a decline in the direct household ownership of common stocks. This decline does not necessarily lead to the conclusion that households have decreased their common stock holdings. Rather, it means that households are holding more of their common stock through intermediaries such as mutual funds rather than directly in the form of common stock. Thus, households have "intermediated" their stock holdings. Although households hold more total common stock than before, they hold less common stock directly, and, thus, increasingly the stock executions are done by institutions, such as mutual funds, rather than by individuals.

Retail Stock Trading

One of the reasons, as explained in Chapter 8, that individuals own stocks through mutual funds rather than directly is transaction costs; that is, institutions can transact stocks more cheaply than individuals. Although this advantage to institutions remains, transaction costs for individuals have declined significantly during the last decade.

Since May Day 1975, stock trading commissions have declined both for institutions and individuals. However, prior to 1990 (approximately), individuals traded stocks mainly through so-called full-service brokers, where their commissions reflected not only the stock trade execution but also the counsel of a stockbroker and perhaps research. The largest full-service broker-dealers are also known as wire-houses. These firms typically do institutional trading and investment banking as well as retail business. The commissions for these full-service brokers have declined since 1975.

A discount broker industry has also developed in which the stockbroker provides advice and no research. Individuals enter their orders via a telephone. More recently, individuals are able to enter their orders via their computer: These are called online or Web-based brokerage firms. Consistent with the lower provision of service by discount brokers and online brokers, stock trading commissions decreased significantly. Thus, individuals could trade and own stocks more efficiently.

To remain competitive to a wide range of clients in this environment, the traditional full-service brokerage firms responded by offering their customers alternative means of transacting common stock. For example, many full-service brokerage firms offer the traditional services of a stockbroker and research at a high commission, and, in addition, offer direct order entry only at a lower commission. On the other hand, some discount brokers have begun to offer more service at a higher commission.

Institutional Trading

With the increase in trading by institutional investors, trading arrangements more suitable to these investors had to be developed. Their needs included trading in large size and trading groups of stocks, both at a low commission and with low market impact. This has resulted in the evolution of special arrangements for the execution of certain types of orders commonly sought by institutional investors: (1) orders requiring the execution of a trade of a large number of shares of a given stock, and (2) orders requiring the execution of trades in a large number of different stocks at as near the same time as possible. The former types of trades are called **block trades**; the latter are called **program trades**. An example of a block trade is a mutual fund that seeks to buy 15,000 shares of IBM stock. An example of a program trade is a pension fund that wants to buy shares of 200 names (companies) at the end of a trading day ("at the close").

The institutional arrangement that has evolved to accommodate these two types of institutional trades is the development of a network of trading desks of the major securities firms and other institutional investors that communicate with each other by means of electronic display systems and telephones. This network is referred to as the **upstairs market**. Participants in the upstairs market play a key role by (1) providing liquidity to the market so that such institutional trades can be executed, and by (2) arbitrage activities that help to integrate the fragmented stock market.

Block Trades

On the NYSE, block trades are defined as either trades of at least 10,000 shares of a given stock or trades of shares with a market value of at least $200,000, whichever is less. In 1961, there were about nine block trades per day, which accounted for about 3% of the trading volume of NYSE. By contrast, in 1999 there were 16,600 block trades per day, accounting for 50.2% of the reported trading volume. On the Nasdaq National Market (NNM), block trades were 24.6% of the total NNM trading volume during 1999.

Since the execution of large numbers of block orders places strains on the specialist system in the NYSE, special procedures have been developed to handle them. Typically, an institutional customer contacts its salesperson at a brokerage firm, indicating that it wishes to place a block order. The salesperson then gives the order to the brokerage firm's block execution department. Notice that the salesperson does not submit the order to be executed to the exchange where the stock might be traded or, in the case of an unlisted stock, try to execute the order on the Nasdaq system. The sales traders in the block execution department then contact other institutions to attempt to find one or more institutions that would be willing to take the other side of the order. That is, they use the upstairs market in their search to fill the block trade order. If this can be accomplished, the execution of the order is completed.

If the sales traders cannot find enough institutions to take the entire block (for example, if the block trade order is for 40,000 shares of IBM, but only 25,000 can be "crossed" with other institutions), then the balance of the block trade order is given to the firm's market-maker. There are two choices. First, the brokerage firm can take a position in the stock and buy the shares for its own account. Second, the unfilled order can be executed by using the services of competing market-makers. In the former case, the brokerage firm is committing its own capital.

A block trade is defined by its size, not the method of execution. Although negotiation in the informal "upstairs" market provides better execution than the "downstairs" market (i.e., the NYSE floor) for large trades, these differences are economically small. The study found that traders who can credibly signal that their trades are liquidity motivated use upstairs markets. Thus, upstairs markets allow trades that may not otherwise occur. The study concluded that "downstairs" on the NYSE floor market is a significant source of liquidity.[6]

---

[6] Minder Cheng and Ananth Madhavan. "In Search of Liquidity: Block Trades in the Upstairs and Downstairs Markets," *The Review of Financial Studies*, Volume 10, Number 1, 1997, p.175–203.

Program Trades.

Program trades involve the buying and/or selling of a large number of names simultaneously. Such trades are also called **basket trades** because effectively a "basket" of stocks is being traded. The NYSE defines a program trade as any trade involving the purchase or sale of a basket of at least 15 stocks with a total value of $1 million or more.

The two major applications of program trades are asset allocation and index arbitrage. With respect to asset allocation trades, some examples of why an institutional investor may want to use a program trade are deployment of new cash into the stock market; implementation of a decision to move funds invested in the bond market to the stock market (or vice versa); and rebalancing the composition of a stock portfolio because of a change in investment strategy. A mutual fund money manager can, for example, move funds quickly into or out of the stock market for an entire portfolio of stocks through a single program trade. All these strategies are related to asset allocation.

The growth of mutual fund sales and massive equity investments by pension funds and insurance companies during the 1990s have all given an impetus to such methods to trade baskets or bundles of stocks efficiently. Other reasons for which an institutional investor may have a need to execute a program trade should be apparent later when we discuss an investment strategy called *indexing.*

Program trading is also used for a strategy called *index arbitrage.* In Chapter 26, we discuss futures contracts traded on stock indexes, called *stock index futures.* In Chapter 28, we will see that the price of a stock index futures contract is derived from the underlying cash product, namely the stocks included in the stock index. Specifically, there is a mathematical relationship between the price of the stock index futures contracts and the value of the stocks included in the index taking into account transaction costs and the cost of borrowing funds. This relationship establishes bounds for the price of the stock index futures contract. When the price of the stock index futures contract deviates from these bounds, there is an opportunity for a riskless profit by trading the two. For example, suppose that the price of the S&P 500 futures contract (which we will discuss in Chapter 26) is higher than the upper bound established by the cash market price of the basket of 500 stocks and transaction costs and borrowing costs. Then, it would be profitable to sell the index in the futures market and buy the basket in the cash market. To the NYSE specialists, this would show up as a large simultaneous purchase of all stocks in the S&P 500 index. Index fund managers sometimes use program trades to choose between taking a position in the stock market by buying or selling stock or by buying or selling stock index futures contracts.

Several commission arrangements are available to an institution for a program trade, and each arrangement has numerous variants. Considerations in selecting one (in addition to commission costs) are the risks of failing to realize the best execution price and that the brokerage firms be solicited about executing the program trade will use their knowledge of the program trade to benefit from the anticipated price movement that might result—in other words, that they will **frontrun** the transaction, for example, buying a stock for their own account before filling the customer buy order.

From a dealer's perspective, program trades can be conducted in two ways, namely, on an agency basis and on a principal basis. An intermediate type of program trade, the agency incentive arrangement, is also an alternative. A program trade executed on an *agency basis* involves the selection by the investor of a brokerage firm solely on the basis of commission bids (cents per share) submitted by various brokerage firms. The brokerage firm selected uses its best efforts as an agent of the institution to obtain the best price. Such trades have low explicit commissions. To the investor, the disadvantage of the agency program trade is that, while commissions may be the lowest, the execution price may not be the best because of impact costs and the potential frontrunning by the brokerage firms that were solicited to submit a commission bid. The investor knows in advance the commission paid but does not know the price at which its trades will be executed. Another disadvantage is that there is increased risk of adverse selection of the counterparty in the execution process.

Related to the agency basis is an *agency incentive arrangement*, in which a benchmark portfolio value is established for the group of stocks in the program trade. The price for each "name" (i.e., specific stock) in the program trade is determined as either the price at the end of the previous day or the average price of the previous day. If the brokerage firm can execute the trade on the next trading day such that a better-than-benchmark portfolio value results—a higher value in the case of a program trade involving selling, or a lower value in the case of a program trade involving buying— then the brokerage firm receives the specified commission plus some predetermined additional compensation. In this case, the investor does not know in advance the commission or the execution price precisely but has a reasonable expectation that the price will be better than a threshold level.

What if the brokerage firm does not achieve the benchmark portfolio value? It is in such a case that the variants come into play. One arrangement may call for the brokerage firm to receive just a previously agreed-upon commission. Other arrangements may involve sharing the risk of not realizing the benchmark portfolio value with the brokerage firm. That is, if the brokerage firm falls short of the benchmark portfolio value, it must absorb a portion of the shortfall. In these risk-sharing arrangements, the brokerage firm is risking its own capital. The greater the risk-sharing that the brokerage firm must accept, the higher the commission it will charge.

The brokerage firm can also choose to execute the trade on a *principal basis*. In this case, the dealer would commit its own capital to buy or sell the portfolio and complete the investor's transaction immediately. Since the dealer incurs market risk, it would also charge higher commissions. The key factors in pricing principal trades are liquidity characteristics, absolute dollar value, nature of trade, customer profile, and market volatility. In this case, the investor knows the trade execution price in advance but pays a higher commission.

To minimize frontrunning, institutions often use other types of program trade arrangements. They call for brokerage firms to receive aggregate statistical information about key portfolio parameters rather than specific names and quantities of stocks. Several brokerage firms then bid on a cents-per-share basis on the entire portfolio (also called blind baskets), guaranteeing execution at either closing price (termed market-at-close) or a particular intra-day price to the customer. Note that this is a principal trade. Since mutual fund net asset values (see Chapter 8) are calculated using closing prices, a mutual fund that follows an indexing strategy (i.e., an index fund), for instance, would want guaranteed market-at-close execution to minimize its risk of not performing as well as the stock index. When the winning bidder has been selected, it receives the details of the portfolio. Although the commission in this type of transaction is higher, this procedure increases the risk to the brokerage firm of successfully executing the program trade.

However, the brokerage firm can use stock index futures (described in Chapter 26) to protect itself from marketwide movements if the characteristics of the portfolio in the program trade are similar to the index underlying the stock index futures contract.

Brokerage firms can also execute the trade in the upstairs market or send orders electronically to exchange floors or Nasdaq system through the automated order-routing systems such as the SuperDot system on the NYSE.

To a specialist on an exchange, the counterparties in program trades are uninformed traders; that is, the specialist knows that the trade is being made for indexwide or portfoliowide reasons and not stock-specific reasons. Such trades are called *informationless trades*.

Key Points That You Should Understand Before Proceeding

1. The reasons retail stock trading has become more attractive.
2. Because of the dominance of institutional investors, trading arrangements have been developed to accommodate their trading needs. Block trading and program trading are two such arrangements.
3. Block trades are large orders in a single stock and are often executed through the upstairs market.
4. Program trades are simultaneous transactions in a large number of stocks and are made for reasons such as asset allocation and index arbitrage.
5. There are several commission arrangements for program trading.
6. The meaning of the term *frontrunning* and how institutional investors can avoid this problem.

PRICE LIMITS AND COLLARS

Trading limits (or price limits) specify a minimum price limit, below which the market price index level may not decline due to an institutionally mandated termination of trading, at least at prices below the specified price(the price limit), for a specified period of time. For example, if the Dow Jones Industrial Average (DJIA) was trading at 11,000 and its price limit was 500 points below that, then no trades could occur below 10,500. This pause in trading is intended to "give the market a breather" to at least calm emotions. Previously, trading limits had been used in the futures markets but not in the stock market.

These price limits have been modified several times For example, on April 15, 1998, the NYSE, implemented Rule 80b to increase and widen thresholds at which trading can be halted for single-day declines in the DJIA. The point levels are set quarterly at 10%, 20%, and 30% of the DJIA by using the DJIA average closing value of the previous month and are adjusted on January 1, April 1, July 1, and October 1.

STOCK MARKET INDICATORS

Stock market indicators have come to perform a variety of functions, from serving as benchmarks for evaluating the performance of professional money managers to answering the question "How did the market do today?" Thus, **stock market indicators** (**indexes** or averages) have become a part of everyday life. Even though many of the stock market indicators are used interchangeably, it is important to realize that each indicator applies to, and measures, a different facet of the stock market.

The most commonly quoted stock market indicator is the Dow Jones Industrial Average (DJIA). Other stock market indicators cited in the financial press are the Standard & Poor's 500 Composite (S&P 500), the New York Stock Exchange Composite Index (NYSE Composite), the Nasdaq Composite Index, and the Value Line Composite Average (VLCA). Other stock market indicators include the Wilshire stock indexes and the Russell stock indexes, which are followed primarily by institutional money managers.

In general, market indexes rise and fall in fairly similar patterns. Table 18-3 shows the correlation coefficients, which measure the degree of similarity in changes in value, for eight prominent market indexes. Although the coefficients are high, the indexes do not move in exactly the same ways at all times. The differences in movement reflect the different ways in which the indexes are constructed. Three factors enter into that construction: the universe of stocks represented by the sample underlying the index, the relative weights assigned to the stocks included in the index, and the method of averaging across all the stocks.

Some indexes represent only stocks listed on an exchange. Examples are DJIA and the NYSE Composite, which represent only stocks listed on the Big Board. By contrast, the Nasdaq includes only stocks traded over the counter. A favorite of professionals is the S&P 500 because it contains both NYSE-listed and OTC-traded shares. Each index relies on a sample of stocks from its universe, and that sample may be small or quite large. The DJIA uses only 30 of the largest corporations, while the NYSE Composite includes every one of the NYSE listed shares. The Nasdaq also includes all shares in its universe, while the S&P 500 has a sample that contains only 500 of the more than 8,000 shares in the universe it represents.

The stocks included in a stock market index must be combined in certain proportions, and each stock must be given a weight. The three main approaches to weighting are these: (1) weighting by the **market capitalization** of the stock's company, which is the value of the number of shares times price per share; (2) weighting by the price of the stock; and (3) equal weighting for each stock, regardless of its price or its firm's market value. With the exception of the Dow Jones averages (such as the DJIA) and the VLCA, all of the most widely used indexes are market-value weighted. The DJIA is a price-weighted average, and the VLCA is an equally weighted index.

Stock market indicators can be classified into three groups: (1) those produced by stock exchanges based on all stocks traded on the exchanges; (2) those produced by organizations that subjectively select the stocks to be included in indexes; and (3) those where stock selection is based on an objective measure, such as the market capitalization of the company. The first group includes the New York Stock Exchange Composite Index, which reflects the market value of all stocks traded on the exchange. Although it is not an exchange, the Nasdaq Composite Index falls into this category because the index represents all stocks tracked by the Nasdaq system.

Table 18-3   Correlation Coefficients for Selected U.S. Stock Indexes, Based on Monthly Returns (January 1987 to March 2000)

	DOW JONES 30	NASDAQ COMPOSITE	NYSE COMPOSITE	RUSSELL 1000	RUSSELL 2000	S&P 500	VALUE LINE COMPOSITE	WILSHIRE 5000
Dow Jones 30	1.00							
Nasdaq Composite	0.74	1.00						
NYSE Composite	0.95	0.80	1.00					
Russell 1000	0.93	0.85	0.98	1.00				
Russell 2000	0.70	0.88	0.76	0.79	1.00			
S&P 500	0.95	0.83	0.98	0.99	0.75	1.00		
Value Line Composite	0.87	0.84	0.92	0.91	0.90	0.89	1.00	
Wilshire 5000	0.92	0.89	0.97	0.99	0.85	0.98	0.93	1.00

SOURCE: Investment Technologies, Inc.

The three most popular stock market indicators in the second group are the Dow Jones Industrial Average, the Standard & Poor's 500, and the Value Line Composite Average. The DJIA is constructed from 30 of the largest blue-chip industrial companies. The companies included in the average are those selected by Dow Jones & Company, publisher of the *Wall Street Journal*. The S&P 500 represents stocks chosen from the two major national stock exchanges and the over-the-counter market. The stocks in the index at any given time are determined by a committee of Standard & Poor's Corporation, which may occasionally add or delete individual stocks or the stocks of entire industry groups. The aim of the committee is to capture present overall stock market conditions as reflected in a very broad range of economic indicators. The VLCA, produced by Value Line, Inc., covers a broad range of widely held and actively traded NYSE, AMEX, and OTC issues selected by Value Line.

In the third group, we have the Wilshire indexes produced by Wilshire Associates (Santa Monica, California) and Russell indexes produced by the Frank Russell Company (Tacoma, Washington), a consultant to pension funds and other institutional investors. The criterion for inclusion in each of these indexes is solely a firm's market capitalization. The most comprehensive index is the Wilshire 5000, which currently includes more than 6,700 stocks, up from 5,000 at its inception. The Wilshire 4500 includes all stocks in the Wilshire 5000 except for those in the S&P 500. Thus, the shares in the Wilshire 4500 have smaller capitalization than those in the Wilshire 5000. The Russell 3000 encompasses the 3,000 largest companies in terms of their market capitalization. The Russell 1000 is limited to the largest 1,000 of those, and the Russell 2000 has the remaining smaller firms.

Two methods of averaging may be used. The first and most common is the arithmetic average. An arithmetic mean is just a simple average of the stocks, calculated by summing them (after weighting, if appropriate) and dividing by the sum of the weights. The second method is the geometric mean, which involves multiplication of the components, after which the product is raised to the power of 1 divided by the number of components.

Key Points That You Should Understand Before Proceeding

1. What a market index is and what it is supposed to convey.
2. The key differences among the important stock market indexes in terms of the universe each index represents, the sample of stocks on which it is based, the method of weighting, the method of averaging, and the entity responsible for producing and publishing the index.

PRICING EFFICIENCY OF THE STOCK MARKET

As explained in Chapter 15, a price efficient market is one in which security prices at all times fully reflect all available information that is relevant to their valuation. When a market is price efficient, investment strategies pursued to outperform a broad-based stock market index will not consistently produce superior returns after adjusting for risk and transaction costs.

Numerous studies have examined the pricing efficiency of the stock market. While it is not our intent in this chapter to provide a comprehensive review of these studies, we can summarize their basic findings and their implications for investment strategies.

Forms of Efficiency

The three different **forms of pricing efficiency** are (1) weak form, (2) semistrong form, and (3) strong form. The distinctions among these forms lie in the relevant information that is believed to be taken into consideration in the price of the security at all times. *Weak-form efficiency* means that the price of the security reflects the past price and trading history of the security. *Semistrong-form efficiency* means that the price of the security fully reflects all public information (which, of course, includes but is not limited to, historical price and trading patterns). *Strong-form efficiency* exists in a market where the price of a security reflects all information, whether it is publicly available or known only to insiders such as the firm's managers or directors.

The preponderance of empirical evidence supports the claim that the common stock market is efficient in the weak form. The evidence emerges from statistical tests that explore whether or not historical price movements can be used to project future prices in such a way as to produce returns above what one would expect from market movements and the risk class of the security. Such returns are known as **positive abnormal returns**. The implications are that investors who follow a strategy of selecting stocks solely on the basis of price patterns or trading volume—such investors are referred to as **technical analysts** or **chartists**—should not expect to do better than the market. In fact, they may fare worse because of higher transactions costs associated with frequent buying and selling of stocks.

Evidence on whether or not the stock market is price efficient in the semistrong form is mixed. Some studies support the proposition of efficiency when they suggest that investors who select stocks on the basis of **fundamental security analysis**—which consists of analyzing financial statements, the quality of management, and the economic environment of a company—will not outperform the market. This result is certainly reasonable: There are so many analysts using the same approach, with the same publicly available data, that the price of the stock remains in line with all the relevant factors that determine value. On the other hand, a sizable number of other studies have produced evidence indicating that there have been instances and patterns of pricing inefficiency in the stock market over long periods of time. Economists and financial analysts often label these examples of inefficient pricing as **anomalies in the market**, that is, phenomena that cannot be easily explained.

Empirical tests of strong form pricing efficiency fall into two groups: (1) studies of the performance of professional money managers, and (2) studies of the activities of insiders (individuals who are either company directors, major officers, or major stockholders). Studying the performance of professional money managers to test the strong form of pricing efficiency has been based on the belief that professional managers have access to better information than the general public. Whether or not this is true is moot because the empirical evidence suggests professional managers have not been able to outperform the market consistently. In contrast, evidence based on the activities of insiders has generally revealed that this group often achieves higher returns than the stock market. Of course, insiders could not get those high abnormal returns if the stock prices fully reflected all relevant information about the values of the firms. Thus, the empirical evidence on insider trading argues against the notion that the market is efficient in the strong-form sense.

Implications for Investing in Common Stock

Common stock investment strategies can be classified into two general categories: active strategies and passive strategies. *Active strategies* are those that attempt to outperform the market by one or more of the following: timing the selection of transactions, such as in the case of technical analysis, identifying undervalued or overvalued stocks using fundamental security analysis, or selecting stocks according to one of the market anomalies. Obviously, the decision to pursue an active strategy must be based on the belief that there is some type of gain from such costly efforts, but gains are possible only if pricing inefficiencies exist. The particular strategy chosen depends on why the investor believes this is the case.

Investors who believe that the market prices stocks efficiently should accept the implication that any attempts to outperform the market cannot be systematically successful, except by luck. This implication does not mean that investors should shun the stock market, but rather that they should pursue a *passive strategy*, which is one that does not attempt to outperform the market. Is there an optimal investment strategy for someone who holds this belief in the pricing efficiency of the stock market? Indeed there is. Its theoretical basis is the modern portfolio theory and capital market theory that we discussed in Chapter 13. According to modern portfolio theory, the market portfolio offers the highest level of return per unit of risk in a market that is price efficient. A portfolio of financial assets with characteristics similar to those of a portfolio consisting of the entire market—the market portfolio—will capture the pricing efficiency of the market.

How can such a passive strategy be implemented? More specifically, what is meant by a *market portfolio*, and how should that portfolio be constructed? In theory, the market portfolio consists of all financial assets, not just common stock. The reason is that investors compare all investment opportunities, not just stock, when committing their capital. Thus, our principles of investing must be based on capital market theory, not just stock market theory. When the theory is applied to the stock market, the market portfolio has been defined as consisting of a large universe of common stocks. But how much of each common stock should be purchased when constructing the market portfolio? Theory states that the chosen portfolio should be an appropriate fraction of the market portfolio; hence, the weighting of each stock in the market portfolio should be based on its relative market capitalization. Thus, if the aggregate market capitalization of all stocks included in the market portfolio is $T and the market capitalization of one of these stocks is $A, then the fraction of this stock that should be held in the market portfolio is $A/$T.

The passive strategy that we have just described is called *indexing*. As pension fund sponsors have increasingly come in the 1990s to believe that money managers are unable to outperform the stock market, the amount of funds managed using an indexing strategy has grown substantially. Index funds, however, still account for a relatively small fraction of institutional stock investments.

Key Points That You Should Understand Before Proceeding

1. The relevant information that is believed to be discounted in the price of a stock at all times for the three forms of pricing efficiency (weak form, semistrong form, and strong form).

2. The implications of the weak form of pricing efficiency for chartists or technical analysts.

3. The implications of the semistrong form of pricing efficiency for fundamental security analysts.

4. The general conclusion about pricing efficiency that empirical research into U.S. markets tends to support.

5. Why the price efficiency of a market influences the decision as to whether an investor will pursue an active strategy or passive strategy.

SUMMARY

Common stock represents an ownership interest in a corporation. In the United States, secondary trading of common stock occurs in one or more of the following trading locations: two major national stock exchanges (the NYSE and AMEX), five regional stock exchanges, and the OTC market (Nasdaq system). More recent alternative trading systems, which includes electronic communication networks and cross-trading networks, permit a new type of stock trading.

The secondary market for common stock has undergone significant changes since the 1970s. The major participants are now institutional investors rather than retail investors, although the availability of discount brokers with their low commissions have induced some retail investors to become more active traders. Advances in computer technology have ushered in developments for linking the various market locations and systems for institution-to-institution direct trading.

Different types of orders may be submitted to the stock markets. The most common type is a market order, which means that the order must be filled immediately at the best price. Other types of orders, such as stop and limit orders, are filled only if the market price reaches a price specified in the order.

An important structural difference between exchanges and the OTC market is that on exchanges there is only one market-maker, or dealer, per stock—the specialist—whereas there is no restriction on the number of dealers per stock in the OTC market. There are mandated obligations by both types of market-makers, although these obligations are quite different.

The brokerage commission is the most obvious type of trading cost and object of competition among broker-dealers for both institutional and retail investors. However, other types of trading costs, such as impact costs and opportunity costs, may be larger than commissions.

To accommodate the trading needs of institutional investors who tend to place orders of larger sizes and with a large number of names, special arrangements have evolved. Block trades are trades of 10,000 shares or more of a given stock or trades with a market value of $200,000 or more. Program trades, or basket trades, involve the buying and/or selling of a large number of names simultaneously. The institutional arrangement that has evolved to accommodate these needs is the upstairs market, which is a network of trading desks of the major securities firms and institutional investors that communicate with each other by means of electronic display systems and telephones.

Stock market indicators can be classified into three groups: (1) those produced by stock exchanges and that include all stocks to be traded on the exchange (such as the Nasdaq Composite Index and the NYSE Composite Index); (2) those in which a committee subjectively selects the stocks to be included in the index (such as the S&P 500 Index); and (3) those in which the stocks selected are based solely on stocks' market capitalizations (such as the Russell 3000, 1000, and 2000 indexes).

There are three forms of pricing efficiency according to what is hypothesized to be the relevant information that is believed to be embodied in the price of a stock at all times: (1) weak form, (2) semistrong form, and (3) strong form. Most of the empirical evidence appears to suggest that markets are efficient in the weak form. The evidence on the semistrong form is mixed, as pockets of inefficiency have been observed. Empirical tests of strong-form pricing efficiency have also produced conflicting results.

Active investment strategies, consisting of efforts to time purchases and select stocks, are pursued by investors who believe that securities are mispriced enough that it is possible to capitalize on strategies that are designed to exploit the perceived inefficiency. The optimal strategy to pursue when the stock market is perceived to be price efficient is indexing because it allows the investor to capture the efficiency of the market.

KEY TERMS

- **Abnormal returns, 347**
- **Alternative trading systems (ATS), 330**
- **Anomalies in the market, 347**
- **Big Board, 322**
- **Block trades, 341**
- **Call money rate, 337**
- **Capitalization (or market capitalization), 345**
- **Chartist, 347**
- **Consolidated Quotation System (CQS), 330**
- **Cross trading systems, 330**

- **Discount brokers, 327**
- **Electronic communications networks (ECNs), 322**
- **Exchange, 322**
- **Fill or kill order, 335**
- **First market, 323**
- **Forms of pricing efficiency, 347**
- **Fourth market, 323**
- **Frontrun, 342**
- **Fundamental security analysis, 347**
- **Impact cost, 338**
- **Initial margin requirement, 337**
- **Limit order book, 325**
- **Listed stock, 323**
- **Maintenance margin requirement, 337**
- **Margin buying, 337**
- **Market if touched order, 334**
- **Market index (or indicator), 344**
- **Market order, 333**
- **National Association of Securities Dealers Automated Quotation System (Nasdaq), 322**
- **Odd lot, 335**
- **Open order, 335**
- **OTC Bulletin Board (OTCBB), 329**
- **Over-the-counter (OTC) trading, 322**
- **Pink sheets, 329**
- **Post on an exchange, 324**
- **Preferred stock, 322**
- **Program (or basket) trade, 341**
- **Public order, 334**
- **Round lot, 335**
- **Rule 144A, 331**
- **Seat on an exchange, 323**
- **Second market, 323**
- **Specialist, 324**
- **Stop order, 334**
- **Third market, 323**
- **Tick-test rules, 336**
- **Timing cost, 339**
- **Trading priority rules, 334**
- **Upstairs market, 341**

QUESTIONS

1. "Stocks traded on the Nasdaq are nonlisted stocks." Explain why you agree or disagree with this statement.
2. When the NYSE refers to a "fair and orderly market," what does that mean?
3. What is meant by the "Pink Sheets" and the "Bulletin Board"?
4. Give three examples of ECNs.
5. This quotation is from an interview with William Donaldson, Chairman of the New York Stock Exchange, that appeared in the *New York Times* of January 30, 1990:

   Sure it's possible to beat the market. . . . By investing for the long term with an individual selection of stocks, it's quite possible to beat the market. . . .

   My concern is that by simply buying an index, investors are not channeling their capital into the best investments, and that has long-term negative implications for the cost of capital in this country. The risk of indexing and treating all companies the same is to give in to a very mediocre goal.

   What can you infer about Donaldson's views on pricing efficiency from his comment?
6. This quotation is from the same interview with William Donaldson:

   There's a need to understand the advantages of an auction market versus a dealer market. The auction market allows a buyer and a seller to get together and agree on a price and the dealer is not involved at all. That's opposed to a dealer market where the house is on both sides of the trade and the dealer makes the spread rather than having the spread shared by the buyer and the seller. One of the things we're coming to the forefront on now is the whole idea of what makes a good market. I think the best market is where you have the maximum number of people coming together in a single location and bidding against each other. . . . That is far superior to what we are getting now, which is a fractionalization of the market. Traders on machines, trades in the closet, trades in many areas where buyers and sellers don't have the opportunity to meet

Discuss Donaldson's opinion. In your answer, be sure to address the pros and cons of the different trading locations and practices addressed in the chapter.

7. What do crossing networks seek to do?
8. What is Rule 144A?
9. Following is a quotation from "The Taxonomy of Trading Strategies" by Wayne H. Wagner that appears in *Trading Strategies and Execution Costs*, published by The Institute of Chartered Financial Analysts in 1988. (The publication is the product of a conference held in New York City on December 3, 1987.)

    The NYSE is not the only operating market; there are ancillary markets that provide trading facilities beyond what is available on the Exchange floor. This suggests that some needs are not well served by the process as it occurs on the Exchange. Examples of how the NYSE is augmented by other trading facilities include the supporting specialists (particularly on the regional exchange); the upstairs brokers. . . the third market, the fourth market, and crossing networks; and the informal floor accommodations. All of these structures are intended to accommodate trading. Without these facilities, the NYSE as it exists today probably could not exist. . . .

    Explain what is meant by:
    a. the upstairs brokers.
    b. the third market.
    c. the fourth market.
10. What factors led to the development of the third market?
11. The following quote is taken from Wayne H. Wagner, "The Taxonomy of Trading Strategies," in Katrina F. Sherrerd (ed.), *Trading Strategies and Execution Costs* (Charlottesville, VA: The Institute of Chartered Financial Analysts, 1988).

    When a trader decides how to bring an order to the market, he or she must deal with some very important issues; to me, the most important is: What kind of trade is this? It could be either an active or a passive trade. The type of trade will dictate whether speed of execution is more or less important than cost of execution. In other words, do I want immediate trading (a market order); or am I willing to forgo the immediate trade for the possibility of trading less expensively if I am willing to "give" on the timing of the trade (a limit order)?

    a. What is meant by a market order?
    b. Why would a market order be placed when an investor wants immediate trading?
    c. What is meant by a limit order?
    d. What are the risks associated with a limit order?
12. Suppose that Mr. Mancuso has purchased a stock for $45 and that he sets a maximum loss that he will accept on this stock of $6. What type of order can Mr. Mancuso place?
13. What is a program trade?
14. What are the various types of commission arrangements for executing a program trade and the advantages and disadvantages of each?

15. What types of restriction on stock price movements are imposed by the New York Stock Exchange?
16. Explain these terms:
    a. public order
    b. stop loss order
    c. block trade
17. a. Explain the mechanics and some key rules of a short sale.
    b. What restrictions are imposed on short selling activities?
18. What role does the broker loan rate play in a margin purchase?
19. a. What is meant by maintenance margin when stocks are purchased on margin?
    b. What is meant by debit balance?
    c. What is meant by credit balance?
20. What were the findings of the SEC cost study?
21. The following statements are taken from Greta E. Marshall's article "Execution Costs: The Plan Sponsor's View," which appears in *Trading Strategies and Execution Costs*, published by The Institute of Chartered Financial Analysts in 1988. (The publication is the product of a conference held in New York City on December 3, 1987):
    a. "There are three components of trading costs. First there are direct costs which may be measured—commissions. Second, there are indirect—or market impact—costs. Finally, there are the undefined costs of not trading."
    What are market impact costs, and what do you think the "undefined costs of not trading" represent?
    b. "Market impact, unlike broker commissions, is difficult to identify and measure." Why is market impact cost difficult to measure?
22. What is the difference between a market-value-weighted index and an equally weighted index?
23. What are the main features of the S & P 500 common stock index?
24. "The stocks selected for the S & P 500 are the largest 500 companies in the United States." Indicate whether you agree or disagree with this statement.
25. There are participants and analysts in the stock market that are called chartists or technical analysts. What does the theory that the market is weak-form efficient say about these investors' chances of beating the market?
26. The November 1985 prospectus of the Merrill Lynch Phoenix Fund, Inc., a mutual fund, stated the following investment objective:

    Based upon the belief that the pricing mechanism of the securities markets lacks perfect efficiency so that prices of securities of troubled issuers are often depressed to a greater extent than warranted by the condition of the issuer and that, while investment in such securities involves a high degree of risk, such investments offer the opportunity for significant capital gains.

    What does this strategy assume about the pricing efficiency of the stock market?
27. Why should an investor who believes that the market is efficient pursue an indexing strategy?

C h a p t e r   1 9

International Stock Markets

Learning Objectives

After reading this chapter, you will understand

- the basic characteristics of the major international stock exchanges.
- the trading costs of international stock markets.
- the motivation for investors to invest outside of their domestic stock market.
- the reasons why issuers raise equity funds outside of their domestic stock market.
- the correlation of the price movements of world equity markets and the implications for international investing.
- recent European stock market reorganizations and stock market activities.
- that some stock markets enjoy extensive freedom for self-management, whereas others experience substantial control by governments, and still others are dominated by commercial banks.
- that most exchanges allow prices of actively traded stocks to be set continuously during the day as buy and sell orders reach the market.
- that some exchanges determine opening prices or prices of inactively traded shares through a call auction procedure, which batches orders for simultaneous execution.
- that computerization has caused most markets to become competitive dealer markets.
- the major stock market indexes.
- what Global Depositary receipts and American Depositary receipts are and why they make international equity investing easier.

Both individual and institutional investors invest in stocks of companies within their country and outside of their country. The purpose of investing in stocks of companies outside their country is to enhance returns and to reduce risk through diversification. We'll see how this is accomplished in this chapter. Increasingly, investors have been able to invest in international stocks more conveniently through financial instruments called American Deposit Receipts and Global Deposit Receipts that are listed on markets in their own countries.

On the issuance side also, corporations have issued equities outside their home market to finance subsidiaries in other countries or to reduce the cost of raising equity capital. In fact, new equity issues may be offered in more than one country simultaneously. The term *Euroequity* applies to a stock issue that is offered simultaneously in several countries by an international syndicate. In addition, U.S. corporations engage in equity offerings which, in addition to the primary U.S. component, include a portion of the issuance reserved for sale in the Euromarkets. This portion of a newly issued stock is referred to as a **Euroequity tranche**. Similarly, European firms offer equity securities with a U.S. *tranche*. The innovation of the Euroequity markets was not a matter of new equity securities or structures. Rather, the innovation consisted of an efficient international system for selling and distributing equity offerings to various markets in different countries at the same time.

Thus, on both the investing and issuing sides, the international markets are critical to the world's equity markets. Investors and issuers cannot follow the U.S. equity markets without also following the international equity markets. This chapter discusses various aspects of the international stock markets.

OVERVIEW OF MAJOR INTERNATIONAL STOCK MARKETS AND INDEXES

Tables 19-1 and 19-2 provide the size, in U.S. dollars, of two major world stock indexes and the countries included. Both indexes are products of Morgan Stanley Capital International (MSCI) and are the most widely used indexes of their type. Table 19-1 provides the Europe, Australasia, and the Far East Index (**EAFE Index**). EAFE includes the world's developed countries, excluding the United States and Canada, as the name indicates. Note that Japan has the largest market capitalization (25.4% of EAFE) and the United Kingdom second (21.4%). At the bottom of Table 19-1 is the MSCI *World Index*, which includes EAFE as well as the United States and Canada. The United States comprises 52.8% of the MSCI World Index.

Table 19-2 provides the composition of the MSCI Emerging Market Index (EM), which covers developing countries in Asia, Latin America, Europe, and the Middle East. Note that Taiwan (15.3% of the index), Brazil (10.9%), and Mexico (9.9%) have the highest market capitalizations in the EM Index.

Selected international stock indexes are discussed in more detail later in this chapter.

Multiple Listings on National Markets

Stocks of corporations can be listed for trading on stock exchanges in other countries as well as an exchange in their own country. Stocks of some very large corporations are listed on stock exchanges in several countries. As an example, the number of stocks of firms from other countries that were listed on the German national exchange (Deutsche Borse) as of year-end 1999 was 7,682. German domestic companies only numbered 933. As another example, in the United Kingdom there were 1,945 domestic companies listed on the London Stock Exchange as of year end 1999 and 499 foreign companies.[1] **Multiple listing** of stocks is clearly an increasingly common phenomenon.

The readiness of an exchange to list and trade the shares of a foreign company varies by country and exchange according to their international orientation. Foreign firms that seek listing for their shares on U.S. exchanges may face some costs in terms of disclosure standards in some countries. In other countries, however, regulations on the listing and trading of the stock of a foreign company are not stringent.

There are several reasons why firms want to list their shares on the exchanges of several countries. Firms seek to diversify their sources of capital across national boundaries and to tap all the various funds available globally for investment in new issues. In addition, firms may believe that an internationally varied ownership diminishes the prospect of takeover by other domestic concerns. Finally, firms may expect a foreign listing to boost their name awareness and, as a result, the sales of their products.[2]

---

[1] This information was obtained from *The Salomon Smith Barney Guide to World Equity Markets, 2000* (Euromoney Books, 2000).

[2] Bruno Solnik, *International Investments*, 2nd ed. (Reading, MA: Addison Wesley, 1991), pp. 112–113.

Table 19-1   Capitalization of Stock Markets Included in the Morgan Stanley
Capital International Indexes: Europe and Far East (EAFE) Index*

MARKET	ESTIMATED MARKET CAP OF THE COUNTRY** (IN BILLIONS)	MARKET CAP INCLUDED IN THE EAFE INDEX*** (IN BILLIONS)	PERCENT OF TOTAL EAFE INDEX
Europe			
United Kingdom	$2,639.0	$1,888.8	21.0%
France	1,426.6	1,048.6	11.7
Germany	1,348.0	818.7	9.1
Switzerland	759.4	631.1	7.0
Netherlands	812.8	507.6	5.7
Italy	781.8	440.4	4.9
Spain	371.5	285.6	3.2
Sweden	353.9	257.3	2.9
Finland	243.6	210.7	2.3
Denmark	124.9	90.8	1.0
Belgium	179.8	81.8	0.9
Ireland	76.1	57.2	0.6
Portugal	69.3	50.6	0.6
Norway	58.8	40.1	0.4
Austria	26.6	21.2	0.2
Asia and Far East			
Japan	3,410.1	2,005.0	22.3%
Australia	387.9	249.8	2.8
Hong Kong	334.3	197.6	2.2
Singapore	155.2	87.9	1.0
New Zealand	20.4	10.7	0.1
Total	$13,580.0	$8,981.5	100.0%

World Index			
MARKET	ESTIMATED MARKET CAP (IN BILLIONS)	MARKET CAP INCLUDED IN THE WORLD INDEX (IN BILLIONS)	PERCENT OF TOTAL WORLD INDEX
United States	$15,834.4	$9,987.6	51.4%
EAFE	13,580.0	8,981.5	46.2
Canada	789.0	471.7	2.4
Total	$30,203.4	$19,440.8	100.0%

* *As of January 31, 2001.*

** *Actual total market cap of a country is larger than what is included in the index.*

*** *Europe, Australasia, and the Far East Index (EAFE).*

SOURCE: Morgan Stanley Capital International, Blue Book (January 2001).

Research tends to support these views of multiple listing. Firms whose shares are listed on exchanges in different countries tend to be quite large and to have a relatively substantial amount of foreign sales revenue.[3]

---

[3] Shahrokh M. Saudagran, "An Emprical Study of Selected Factors Influencing the Decision to List on Foreign Stock Exchanges," *Journal of International Business Studies* (Spring 1988), pp. 101–127.

Table 19-2   Capitalization of Stock Markets Included in the Morgan Stanley Capital International Index: Emerging Market Index.*

MARKET	ESTIMATED MARKET CAP OF THE COUNTRY** (IN BILLIONS)	MARKET CAP INCLUDED IN THE EM INDEX*** (IN BILLIONS)	PERCENT OF TOTAL EM INDEX
Asia			
Taiwan	$320.0	$191.7	14.2%
China Free	194.1	148.3	11.0
Korea	189.5	134.1	9.9
India	161.1	93.3	6.9
Malaysia	122.5	70.3	5.2
Thailand	35.1	19.4	1.4
Philippines	59.4	14.3	1.1
Indonesia	32.9	10.8	0.8
Pakistan	6.3	4.1	0.3
Sri Lanka	1.0	0.3	0.0
Latin America			
Brazil	$249.9	$141.6	10.5%
Mexico	157.5	111.0	8.2
Chile	65.5	36.2	2.7
Argentina	32.3	18.8	1.4
Venezuela	10.1	5.7	0.4
Peru	9.4	4.3	0.3
Colombia	7.9	3.1	0.2
Europe & Middle East			
South Africa	$221.3	$104.1	7.7%
Israel	58.5	58.4	4.3
Greece	103.3	57.0	4.2
Turkey	76.9	40.5	3.0
Russia	49.7	39.8	2.9
Poland	30.6	21.2	1.6
Hungary	12.7	10.3	0.8
Czech Republic	11.7	9.1	0.7
Jordan	5.1	2.9	0.2
Total	$2,224.3	$1,350.6	100.0%

*As of January 31, 2001.

**Actual total market cap of a country is larger than what is included in the index.

***Emerging Markets (EM) Index.

SOURCE: Morgan Stanley Capital International, Red Book (January 2001).

An important question is whether or not a share traded in different markets has different prices in those markets. The answer is "no" because investors can buy or sell the shares in any of the markets, and they would arbitrage any meaningful differences in prices. To "arbitrage" is to exploit the presence of different prices for the same item in different markets. That is, if the price of a stock were significantly lower in country X than in country Y, investors would buy as many shares as they could in country X and sell shares in country Y. Investors would do this until the pressure they were putting on prices in both markets would drive the prices together. A decreasing gap in prices means that the arbitrage profits would decline. Investors would stop arbitraging when profits due to the price differences equaled the costs of the transactions. Therefore, when the various costs of the transactions, including commissions and taxes and costs of exchanging currencies, are fully acknowledged, the price of any share tends to be the same across the different markets where it is traded.

Trading Costs in International Stock Markets

Trading costs vary considerably internationally and, as discussed in the previous chapter, affect investment returns. Salomon Smith Barney has constructed an equity index called the *Broad Market Index (BMI)*, composed of 23 countries, and has estimated the one-way costs of trading market benchmark portfolios in these countries.[4]

The BMI is divided into two components, the Primary Market Index (PMI), which contains the shares of the largest 80% of the BMI by total market value, and the Extended Market Index (EMI), which contains the shares of the remaining smaller companies. In effect, the PMI is the large cap index and the EMI the small cap index, in each country. That is, each country has some stocks in the PMI and some in the EMI. For example, as shown in Tables 19-3a and 19-3b, Finland has one stock in the

Table 19-3a   Primary Market Indexes

COUNTRY	WEIGHT	NUMBER OF ISSUES	AVERAGE BID–ASK COST	VOLATILITY COST	TOTAL COST
Canada	2.47%	72	16	13	29
United States	53.11	346	13	12	25
Australia	1.32	41	13	6	19
Hong Kong	1.80	26	29	18	47
Japan	11.14	210	14	13	27
New Zealand	0.06	14	55	9	64
Singapore	0.47	19	33	12	45
France	4.58	33	10	8	18
Germany	3.76	29	9	9	18
Italy	2.58	38	16	8	24
Netherlands	2.32	16	8	4	12
Spain	1.34	10	6	27	33
Denmark	0.39	15	62	17	79
Norway	0.22	28	25	19	44
Sweden	1.13	25	32	12	44
Switzerland	2.50	10	8	7	15
United Kingdom	8.49	66	20	8	28
Austria	0.13	21	24	8	32
Belgium	0.62	18	19	15	34
Finland	0.73	1	10	21	31
Greece	0.33	61	23	23	46
Ireland	0.27	9	81	15	96
Portugal	0.24	11	18	10	28
Total	100.00%	1,119	14	11	25

[4] Keith Miller et al., "Global Equity Impact Cost Model and Market Liquidity Monitor, Monthly Update," Salomon Smith Barney (February 15, 2001), pp. 3–4.

Table 19-3b Extended Market Indexes

COUNTRY	WEIGHT	NUMBER OF ISSUES	AVERAGE BID–ASK COST	VOLATILITY COST	TOTAL COST
Canada	2.28%	272	51	12	63
United States	53.22	2,967	27	13	40
Australia	1.04	135	41	7	48
Hong Kong	1.16	120	43	26	69
Japan	10.51	1,049	32	16	48
New Zealand	0.04	11	50	9	59
Singapore	0.39	59	52	17	69
France	5.16	206	28	15	43
Germany	4.65	262	20	149	169
Italy	2.34	143	23	11	34
Netherlands	1.89	107	23	9	32
Spain	1.40	74	18	14	32
Denmark	0.39	44	79	9	88
Norway	0.16	38	65	14	79
Sweden	1.34	128	56	13	69
Switzerland	3.20	140	44	9	53
United Kingdom	8.62	544	70	7	77
Austria	0.07	21	34	5	39
Belgium	0.36	43	55	16	71
Finland	1.14	77	47	17	64
Greece	0.19	79	46	25	71
Ireland	0.25	31	104	19	123
Portugal	0.17	13	17	38	55
Total	100.00%	6,563	33	19	52

PMI and 77 in the EMI. These indexes are market capitalization weighted (with the market capitalization based on free float, as discussed below).

Tables 19-3a and 19-3b provide the trading costs for the PMI and the EMI, respectively, at the end of 2000. Among the PMI, the least expensive markets were Australia, France, Germany, the Netherlands, and Switzerland. The United States had average trading costs. Among the EMI, the least expensive markets were Italy, the Netherlands, and Spain.

Global Diversification: Correlation of World Equity Markets

Numerous studies have documented the potential portfolio diversification benefits of global investing. Specifically, the inclusion of securities from other countries can increase a portfolio's expected return without increasing its risk or its variability in returns (as discussed in Chapter 13 in more detail). Similarly, including securities from other countries in a portfolio may reduce the portfolio's risk with no decrease in its expected return. The basis of these benefits from diversification is that international capital markets are less than perfectly correlated; that is, their returns do not increase and decrease in unison. Correlation is a statistical measurement of the similarity in the movement of two variables, such as rates of return on groups of stocks from two different countries. Stock markets that are not highly correlated move in ways different from one another.

This dissimilarity in changes in market returns is not surprising. Different countries tend to have different experiences in such important areas as taxation, monetary management, banking policies, political goals and stability, population growth, and so on. And because for many stocks the largest influences on stock prices are domestic or local events and policies, the prices of groups of stocks from different areas tend to move up or down at somewhat different times and to somewhat different degrees. This pattern of dissimilar security price changes allows investors to diversify away a certain amount of risk in individual countries and creates the benefits of international or global investing.

Tables 19-4 and 19-5 provide evidence regarding the degree of dissimilarity in the movement of stock prices on selected national stock exchanges. Table 19-4 presents the correlation coefficients for the monthly returns for the stock market indexes of eight developed countries. Table 19-5 does the same for the stock market indexes of 16 emerging market countries. The correlations are based on the general level of share prices on the exchanges in those countries for the period 1970 to 2000. (Specific stock price indexes for the markets of the world are discussed below in this chapter.)

To interpret the table, it is necessary to keep in mind a few properties of the correlation coefficient. The correlation coefficient has a maximum value of 1.00, which occurs if two variables always move in the same way; and a minimum value of −1.00, which occurs if two variables always move in the exact opposite way. Thus, any variable has a correlation of 1.00 with itself, which simply means that it moves in exactly the same way that it does. For example, Australia's index moves just as Australia's index does, and so the correlation of Australia's index with itself is 1.00, as indicated in Table 19-4. A positive correlation that is less than 1.00 but greater than 0 means that the two variables move generally in the same direction. For example, in Table 19-4 it can be seen that Germany's stock market has a correlation coefficient of 0.61 with France's market, which implies that these two markets do not move identically to each other but move in the same way much of the time. Finally, the correlation of Germany's market with France's is the same as the correlation of France's market with Germany's. So Table 19-4 reports that coefficient only once in the row for France. As a result, the table of coefficients is diagonal and only half-filled.

Table 19-4 reveals some interesting points. First, these international stock markets behave quite differently from one another; that is the correlations of their returns tend to be substantially less than unity. Although the highest coefficient is 0.71 between the U.S. and Canada, many values are below 0.50. Thus, investors can diversify their holdings by spreading their portfolio across these various markets.

Table 19-4   Correlation Coefficients of Selected Developed Market Stock Indexes

COUNTRY	UNITED STATES	FRANCE	UNITED KINGDOM	JAPAN	GERMANY	SWITZERLAND	CANADA	AUSTRALIA
United States	1.00	0.44	0.51	0.29	0.38	0.49	0.71	0.47
France		1.00	0.54	0.39	0.61	0.60	0.44	0.37
United Kingdom			1.00	0.36	0.43	0.56	0.50	0.47
Japan				1.00	0.36	0.41	0.30	0.30
Germany					1.00	0.67	0.34	0.30
Switzerland						1.00	0.44	0.39
Canada							1.00	0.59
Australia								1.00

Note: *Correlations are based on monthly returns for the period January 1970 to December 2000.*
SOURCE: Correlations were calculated from gross monthly index level data available on www.msci.com.

Table 19-5   Correlation Coefficients of Selected Emerging Market Stock Indexes

COUNTRY	CHILE	CHINA	COLOMBIA	INDIA	INDONESIA	ISRAEL	KOREA	MALAYSIA	MEXICO	PAKISTAN	PHILIPPINES	POLAND	S.AFRICA	TURKEY
Chile	1.00													
China	0.41	1.00												
Colombia	0.34	0.04	1.00											
India	0.40	0.18	0.09	1.00										
Indonesia	0.50	0.36	0.25	0.21	1.00									
Israel	0.32	0.14	0.06	0.30	0.20	1.00								
Korea	0.26	0.15	0.12	0.12	0.36	0.04	1.00							
Malaysia	0.42	0.46	0.23	0.24	0.56	0.17	0.26	1.00						
Mexico	0.45	0.38	0.10	0.28	0.30	0.43	0.18	0.26	1.00					
Pakistan	0.32	0.17	0.39	0.39	0.18	0.20	0.06	0.24	0.24	1.00				
Philippines	0.50	0.51	0.14	0.13	0.59	0.12	0.30	0.60	0.35	0.15	1.00			
Poland	0.24	0.20	0.09	0.24	0.26	0.20	0.21	0.30	0.34	0.12	0.26	1.00		
South Africa	0.48	0.45	0.01	0.13	0.34	0.26	0.36	0.39	0.44	0.18	0.60	0.28	1.00	
Turkey	0.24	0.09	0.21	0.13	0.18	0.31	0.02	0.19	0.28	0.25	0.11	0.16	0.22	1.00

Note: All the above are MSCI US$ indexes. "China" is the Chine Free index. "Malaysia" is the Malaysia Emerging Market index. Correlations are based on monthly returns for the period January 1993 to December 2000.

SOURCE: Investment Technologies, Inc.

The second notable point is that geography and political alliances do influence the correlations. Thus, stock prices in Germany and Japan move less similarly (correlation equals 0.36) than do the prices in Germany and France (correlation of 0.61) or the prices in the United States and Canada (correlation of 0.71). Consequently, investors seeking diversification must choose carefully from among the various markets.

Finally, it is interesting that all the correlations are positive and well above zero. This implies the absence of complete dissimilarity in the movement of stock prices. The positive values mean that the world's stock prices are, like their economies, somewhat integrated. Thus, the benefit of international diversification has limits. In other words, the markets of the world are members of a somewhat loosely connected system of economies, and allocating funds among the various economies provides some, but not complete, reduction of variability in returns on securities.

There are two factors, however, that have tended to increase the correlation among the various countries' stock markets during the 1990s; that is, these factors have tended to reduce the advantages of diversification among the world's equity markets. One of these factors is behavioral and the other is due to the structure of the economies and their stock markets. The first relates to the behavior of investors during times of financial crisis, the times when investors would find diversification potentially the most beneficial. At such times, the reasoning goes, investors become very risk averse and flee to safety and liquidity. So if a crisis starts in one country for a legitimate fundamental reason, investors will sell stocks (and perhaps bonds) in not just that country or region alone, but in many or all other countries as well. This "flight to quality" will result in unusually high temporary demand for low risk, high liquidity assets (most likely U.S. Treasuries), and a simultaneous decrease in the demand for and price of all risky assets. Such a crisis mentality increases the correlation among all or most risky assets and does so at a time when diversification is needed most.

The second factor that may increase international correlation relates to the structure of national economies and their stock markets. A country's economy can be postulated to be made up of two sectors, a global sector and a country sector. The *global sector* provides goods and services that are provided in the global economy through international trade. Thus, the companies in a country's global sector respond more to global forces than to national forces according to this reasoning. Microchip manufacturing, automobile manufacturing, and telecommunications are examples of global sectors. A microchip manufacturer in one country is affected by economic forces much more like a microchip manufacturer in other countries than like nonglobal companies in the same country.

In contrast, the *country sector* produces goods and services mainly for the local economy. Companies in this sector are affected by economic forces more like the other local economy companies in the same country than like the global companies in that country. Railroads, retailing, and construction are examples of country sectors.

The conclusion is that companies in global sectors tend to follow the global market for their goods and services rather than their local economy and consequently are not highly diversifying. For example, the stocks of telecommunications companies all over the world declined significantly during 2000. Companies in the country sector, in contrast, follow the indigenous economy and their stocks, and therefore would be diversifying in a global portfolio.

An example of this concept is that a U.S. stock investor would not buy the Finland stock index to pursue international stock diversification since Nokia, which manufactures telecommunications equipment, represents approximately 67% of the Finland stock index.

The evidence indicates that the share of global sectors has been increasing relative to country sectors in most developed countries during the last several years. As a result, globally diversified portfolios currently provide less market diversification than they did previously.[5]

Overall, however, diversification continues to provide a benefit to an investment portfolio, although the diversification exercise may need to be done more carefully by considering both the country effects and the sector effects.

Key Points That You Should Understand Before Proceeding

1. The motivation for investors for investing internationally.
2. The reasons why corporations raise equity funds outside of their domestic equity market.
3. Why there cannot be any meaningful differences in prices of the same stock throughout the world.
4. Why large international firms have their stocks listed on several national exchanges.
5. What the level of correlation between national market indexes says about the benefits from diversifying investments across those countries.
6. The implications and reasons for the increase in correlation between national market indexes.

MAJOR INTERNATIONAL STOCK EXCHANGES

In this section we will review the main characteristics of selected major international stock markets. Included in these discussions are their recent stock market reforms. Recent financial reforms of the stock markets of the world have made them more efficient and open to domestic and international investors. The U.S. stock market engaged in a major financial reform in 1975 when it eliminated fixed commissions, as discussed in Chapter 18. Since then, stock market reforms have continued throughout much of the world.

United Kingdom

The London Stock Exchange (LSE) plays a vital role in maintaining London's position as one of the world's leading financial centers. One of the three major exchanges globally, it is also the world's leading international equity market, with more international companies listed and more international equities traded than on any other exchange.

In 1973, all seven exchanges in the British Isles amalgamated to form the Stock Exchange of Great Britain and Ireland, with trading floors in London, Birmingham, Manchester, Liverpool, Glasgow, and Dublin. Regional trading floors in the United Kingdom ceased operations in the late 1980s, however, and all trading, even in regional stocks, was routed through the central market in London. In December 1995, the Dublin Stock Exchange separated from the UK exchange, which then became formally known as the London Stock Exchange.

The current LSE market includes not only the ordinary shares of local and foreign companies and fixed-interest securities issued by private borrowers, but also the primary and secondary markets in British government (gilt-edged) securities. At the end of 2000, there were 2,428 domestic listed companies with a market capitalization of £1,812 billion.

---

[5] See Stefano Cavaglia, Christopher Brightman, and Michael Akid, "The Increasing Importance of Industry Factors," *Financial Analysts Journal* (September/October, 2000), pp. 41–54, and Sean P. Baca, Brian L. Garbe, and Richard Weiss, "The Rise of Sector Effects in Major Equity Markets," *Financial Analysts Journal*, (September/October 2000), pp. 34–40.

Operations.

During 1986, the **Big Bang** significantly changed the way the LSE operated. One outcome was that during 1987 the LSE's trading floor system was closed and replaced by "screen" trading, that is, a dealer over-the-counter market.

In October 1997, the introduction of the new order book transformed the way that the FTSE 100 shares, the major U.K. stock index (international stock indexes are discussed later in this chapter) are traded. Under the new system (called the Stock Exchange Trading Service, or SETS), when bid and offer prices match, orders are automatically executed against one another on the screen.

Shares outside the FTSE 100 are traded using the quote-driven trading structure introduced during the Big Bang of 1986. This system is based on the competing market-maker system. Throughout the trading day, registered market makers are obliged to display to the market their bid and offer prices and the corresponding maximum sizes. These quotes are displayed on the exchange's **Stock Exchange Automated Quotations (SEAQ)** bulletin board.

In 1999, the LSE announced a program of twice-yearly upgrades to its trading systems. This program would deliver improvements to functionality and bring the market in line with the European Market Model that the LSE had agreed upon with seven other European exchanges.

On March 15, 2000, the exchange shareholders approved allowing the exchange to become a public company with transferable shares, thus allowing the exchange to operate on a fully commercial basis. This change had not been implemented at the time of this writing.

Reforms.

Financial reform occurred in England in 1986. This reform was called the Big Bang after the astronomical theory that the universe originated from a gigantic explosion. The reforms centered on the LSE and were a response to:

1. The decline of the status of the British securities market (the LSE's volume was only a small fraction of that of New York and Tokyo).

2. The delayed response of the British securities markets to internationalization; foreign, mainly U.S., traders were supplanting British firms in their own markets.

3. Technological developments and the expansion of transactions occurring outside the exchange.

As a result, the following reforms were adopted in October 1986. First, the liberalization of commissions, specifically minimum commissions, were abolished. Second, the rule prohibiting non–stock exchange members from investing in stock exchange members was abolished. Prior to the Big Bang, only members of the LSE were permitted to make investments in stock exchange members' companies. As a result of this reform, external capital (the capital of non–stock exchange members) was permitted to expand the capital base of LSE member companies.

Perhaps the biggest change related to market participants. Historically there had long been a rigid division between stock exchange member firms that are brokers (agents) and those that are "jobbers" (the British word for dealers, who are principals in a transaction). According to the Independent Certification System (ICS), the former acted solely as agents on behalf of investors but did not make markets, and the latter made markets, quoting two-way prices, but had no direct contact with the public. This policy made it very difficult for U.K. traders to compete with foreign traders. The introduction of "dual capacity" in 1986 permitted member firms to become broker-dealers; that is, they were permitted to become both brokers and jobbers. Trading is now based on a system of committed market-makers who are also free to conduct agency business. Equally, broker-dealers executing client orders can take positions but are obliged to state clearly in any given transaction whether they are acting as a principal or as an agent. Some brokers have elected to conduct agency business only.

As a result of these Big Bang changes, LSE stock commissions declined, the financial sector in the U.K. grew, London grew as a center of European investment banking, and U.K. brokers and jobbers were increasingly acquired by English merchant banks and U.S. financial companies.

Germany

The Frankfurt Stock Exchange (FSE) was one of the first German exchanges to reopen after World War II, but it did not regain its importance until after the subsequent stabilization of the currency and the recovery of the German economy.

Since 1991, the FSE has been operated by **Frankfurt Wertpapierbörsen AG (FWB)**, a stock corporation controlled by both domestic and foreign market participants. The exchange is denoted by FWB, as defined above, but is commonly referred to as the FSE. In late 1992, the FWB was renamed the Deutsche Borse (DB) AG. DB is owned by international and German banks, official ledger brokers (Kursmakler and Freimakler), and the other regional German stock exchanges.

There are eight technically independent stock exchanges in Frankfurt, Düsseldorf, Munich, Hamburg, Berlin, Stuttgart, Hanover, and Bermen. However, they actually cooperate closely. Recently the stock exchanges of Frankfurt, Düsseldorf, and Munich extended their cooperation in order to establish uniform pricing mechanisms for the DAX 100 securities (the DAX is an index that we will described later in this chapter). Although these several regional exchanges exist, equity trading is highly concentrated in Frankfurt, where floor trading and electronic trading coexist for cash transactions. Each exchange operates three market segments: the official market, the regulated market, and the Neuer Market for smaller growth companies.

In January 1990, the DB formed the DTB (Deutsche TerminBorse, the German Financial Futures and Options Exchange), a fully computerized exchange for trading equity options and futures. In 1998, the DTB and the derivatives exchange Sofex (Switzerland) merged to form the world's derivatives exchange, **Eurex**.

There were 1,088 domestic companies listed on the German stock exchanges at the end of 2000. The market capitalization of shares traded on the DB amounted to 1,352.9 billion Euros.

Owners or prospective buyers of securities can bring orders to the FSE only through a bank represented on the FSE since, according to the Banking Act, "the purchase and sale of securities for the accounts of others" is a banking transaction.

In November 1997, the exchange introduced a new electronic trading system, **Exchange Electronic Trading (Xetra)**. Xetra is a modern, cost-efficient, order-driven trading system with automatic matching, which brings together wholesale and retail trading in a central order book. Limit and market orders can be entered with various validity constraints, trading limits, and conditions for execution, and can be kept in the order book for up to one year. The order book, which is basically transparent, is designed to give all market participants the opportunity to react quickly to changes in the market while preserving their anonymity. In the event of sharp price swings, the system reacts with volatility interruptions to support price continuity. In 1999, more than 15 million trades worth 1,169 billion Euros were executed by Xetra. The system was again upgraded in April 2000.

Germany still has minimum fees for brokered exchange transactions. Germany has not experienced a Big Bang as have other countries.

Japan

The Japanese stock market has a history of more than 120 years, beginning with the establishment of the Tokyo Stock Exchange (TSE) in 1878. During the 1980s, the Japanese securities market changed substantially, with rapid deregulation and globalization. More recently, during November 1999, the TSE launched a new market, Mothers, for stocks of emerging companies with high-growth potential, in order to contribute to the fostering of new companies and to provide investors with a wider range of investment products. This market adds to the shares listed on the TSE first and second sections (discussed later) and thereby offers investors a wider range of investment products.

Since March 2000, when the Hiroshima and Niigata exchanges were merged with the TSE, there have been six stock exchanges in Japan. They are located in Tokyo, Osaka, Nagoya, Kyoto, Fukuoka, and Sapporo.

Shares listed on the TSE are generally classified into either the **first section** or the *second section*, depending principally upon size, turnover, and share ownership. During April 2001, there were 2,079 domestic companies listed on the Tokyo Stock Exchange, of which 1,471 were listed on the first section. Total market capitalization was 350.6 trillion yen during April 2001. Related data by market are provided in Table 19-6.

Operations.

The TSE market is a continuous auction market where buy and sell orders directly interact with one another. The trading of shares is carried out under the "zaraba method," which is similar to an open outcry system. Prices are first established at the beginning of the trading session based on orders placed by regular members before the start of trading. The central book is kept by "Saitori members," who function solely as intermediaries between the regular members. They are not allowed to trade any listed stock for their own account, nor to accept orders from the investing public. After the opening price is established, Saitori members match orders in accordance with price priority and time precedence.

All securities, whether money market or capital market issues, must be traded through an authorized securities dealer who is a member of the Japan Securities Dealer's Association. The three main dealers are Nomura, Nikko, and Daiwa. Collectively, these three firms handle the major portion of all transactions in shares by domestic securities companies. Transactions of all shares take place under the **Computer-Assisted Order-Routing and Execution System (CORES)**. (The TSE closed its trading floor in April 1999.)

Table 19-6   Number of Listed Companies and Market Value of Tokyo Stock Exchange (as of April 2001)

	NUMBER OF LISTED COMPANIES	MARKET CAP (BILLION YEN)
First Section	1471	342,851
Second Section	575	6,959
Mothers*	33	816
Total	2,079	350,626

Market of the high growth and emerging stocks.

SOURCE: The website of Tokyo Stock Exchange.

Reforms.

Until the late 1970s, Japan's financial markets were highly regulated. During November 1996, the Japanese prime minister proposed the Japanese version of the Big Bang to engage in significant financial market reform with the goal of revitalizing the Japanese financial market and making Tokyo competitive with New York and London with a completion date of 2001. The Japanese Big Bang was known locally as "Kinyu biggo ban," literally "financial big bang."

In general, the goals of the Big Bang were for the Japanese financial markets to be "fair, free, and global." More specifically, the four general goals of the Big Bang reforms were to develop:

1. A free market that employs market principles.
2. A fair and transparent market.
3. A market that is global.
4. A market that is less susceptible to domestic political pressures.

More pragmatically, the Big Bang intended to lower the barriers separating banks, securities companies, and insurance companies, and to ease the regulation of the products financial companies offered and the fees they could charge.

The Japanese Big Bang was partially a response to two factors. The first was the increasing internationalization of the financial markets and Japan's inability to compete. The second was the bursting of Japanese asset bubble in stocks and real estate during 1990 to 1995.

The first step in the Big Bang was the deregulation of the foreign exchange markets on April 6, 1998. This change enabled Japanese investors to invest more easily in other countries.

These Big Bang developments continue to evolve.[6]

China

China is the most populous country in the world and while its stock market is currently rudimentary, given the recent actual growth and the potential growth of the Chinese economy, China's stock market will inevitably be an important world stock market.

Prior to February 2001, the Chinese stock market was divided into two types: A shares, which were restricted to Chinese investors, and B-shares, which were reserved for foreign (non-Chinese) investors.

The A share market was denominated in Chinese yuan (which are nonconvertible) and was much larger than the B-share market. While very large, the A-share market was primarily limited to state-owned companies; private companies have very limited access to the larger A-share market.

The B-share market was started in 1991 to give private companies and entrepreneurs access to foreign capital (although there are government listing requirements) and to give foreigners with hard currency the opportunity to invest in Chinese companies. Shanghai B-shares are quoted in U.S. dollars and Shenzen B shares are quoted in Hong Kong dollars, although these two currencies are linked. The B-share market, however, never developed and grew as the Chinese government intended. It had only 114 listed shares as of the beginning of 2001. In fact, B-share trading was not dominated by foreigners but by Chinese using various ploys. Another indication of the lack

---

[6] One evolving result of the Big Bang is the breakdown of the "convoy" system, whereby banks were not allowed to fail. Previously, a single weak bank was supported by a convoy of healthy banks, which shared the burden of the weak bank, thus allowing the weak bank to postpone the provisions for and sale of bad loans.

of success of the B-share market was that the prices of the few companies listed on both the A- and B-share markets were considerably higher on the A-share market.

In addition, Chinese disclosure and accounting standards, which foreign investors have deemed inadequate, led to offerings of Chinese shares in Hong Kong (called H shares). Finally, "red chips"—that is, Hong Kong companies with strong Chinese ties—were traded in Hong Kong.

As a result of these failings in the B-share market and China's increasing participation in the global markets of all types, in February 2001 the Chinese government legalized Chinese ownership of B shares and Chinese investors were allowed to transfer foreign currencies into a trading account under new rules by the China Securities Regulatory Commissions (CSRC) to fund these purchases. In addition, all Chinese companies, private and state-owned, were permitted to sell either A or B shares. Thus, Chinese investors were given more access to the Class B market and companies more access to the Class A market. In fact, these changes could cause an amalgamation of the Class A, B, and H markets.[7]

The initial trading in B shares after the implementation of these policies on Febuary 28, 2001, was very volatile. At the time of this writing, however, the success of these new regulations could not be evaluated.[8]

Key Points That You Should Understand Before Proceeding

1. The structure of trading on the major exchanges in the United Kingdom, Germany, Japan, and China.
2. The major financial reforms in the United Kingdom and Japan.

RECENT EUROPEAN STOCK MARKET REORGANIZATIONS

In the 1990s, stock exchanges throughout the world became more efficient and transparent not only to better serve their domestic investors, but also to remain competitive in an increasingly globalized stock market. Recent changes in the stock markets of the United States are discussed in Chapter 18, and of the United Kingdom, Germany, Japan, and China earlier in this chapter. But, in addition to these global forces, Europe has had competition from within as a result of the formation of the European Monetary Union (EMU) and the adoption of the single currency, the Euro, on January 1, 1999, as discussed in Chapter 31. And since the United Kingdom did not become a member of the EMU, there were also competitive dynamics between the United Kingdom and Continental Europe. Thus, it is perhaps not surprising that the amount of actual and attempted exchange organizational activity in Europe exceeded that of other parts of the world.

Here we summarize some of the European exchange activity during the late 1990s and the early 2000s, even though not all came to fruition and even though the European exchange structure was not yet in equilibrium at the time of this writing and would inevitably continue to change.[9]

---

[7] Leslie P. Norton, "China Moves Toward Reducing Stock-Trading Complexity," *Barron's* (February 26, 2001), p. MW 17; and Craig S. Smith, "Chinese Investors May Get Access to Wider Market," *New York Times*, February 21, 2001, p. C1.

[8] Craig S. Smith, "Hot Trading in B Shares Chills Rapidly for Chinese," *New York Times* (March 8, 2001), p. W1.

[9] Justin Schack, "Europe's New Cost Consciousness," *Institutional Investor*, (November 2000), pp. 95–105.

London Stock Exchange

Much of the European exchange activity centered on the LSE. The LSE was once regarded as very technology savvy. In 1985, it launched the first electronic market for trading pan-European stocks, the SEAQ International (Stock Exchange Automated Quotation). In 1997, LSE developed an order-driven system known as SETS (Stock Exchange Electronic Trading Service) for the largest 100 stocks, which was later expanded to about 200 stocks. Investors wanting to trade other stocks, however, still had to go through a market-maker. But subsequently, the LSE was unable to stay ahead of its rivals in technology.[10]

As a result of this issue and others, the LSE met with Frankfurt's Deutsche Boerse (DB) in the spring of 1998 to discuss a combination. During April 2000, it was announced that the LSE would merge with the Deutsche Borse to create iX (for "international exchange"), a market for all European shares. But the talks bogged down over whose technology to use (SETS versus Xetra). In addition, both sides felt short-changed by a proposed 50%/50% merger. The proposed merger, which was announced in May 2000, was called off in September 2000.

Another effort regarding the LSE which overlapped the DB discussions involved OM Gruppen, a Swedish technology company. During 1998, OM Gruppen acquired the Stockholm Stock Exchange, the first takeover of a national bourse. This takeover was quickly followed by an electronic link between the Stockholm and Copenhagen exchanges.

In August 2000, OM Gruppen made an informal friendly bid to acquire the LSE, which was quickly rejected by the LSE. One of the obstacles was the Swedish concern's majority ownership of Jiway, a retail order executing system as discussed below, which would present a direct conflict with the corresponding LSE systems. Another was OM's ownership and governance structure, which included a minority stake held by the Swedish government. OM Gruppen followed with a formal hostile bid (for 1 billion U.K. pounds), which was also rejected. This effort by OM ended. The LSE believed that it could continue and deliver a pan-European market alone.

In July 1999, the LSE determined that it would convert from mutual to public ownership to enable it to combine with other exchanges. As of this writing, there was no movement on this issue.

Deutsche Borse

In the wake of iX's demise, the FSE of the Deutsche Borse appeared similarly isolated, particularly considering that it had twice come close to joining Paris as part of Euronext, discussed below, before attempting the deal with LSE. The FSE transformed itself from just one of Germany's eight stock exchanges to Europe's second-largest stock exchange. In addition, the FSE turned itself into a systems provider as much as an exchange. In fact, the FSE invested so much in its Xetra trading system, launched in 1997, that it may have to make it a European standard to recoup its investment.

In addition, the FSE has sponsored two other exchanges. First, the DB owns 50% of Eurex, the world's largest derivative exchange. Second, DB's Neuer Mart, formed in 1998, trades high technology companies, as discussed below. A trading alliance between Eurex and the Chicago Board of Trade (CBOT) has also been discussed but was encountering difficulties at the time of this writing.

On Febuary 5, 2001, the DB completed an IPO, selling 3.2 million shares, or 27% of its equity, for 1.1 billion euros ($1 billion). Through this IPO, the DB raised plenti-

---

[10] "How It Became a Foggy Day on the London Exchange," *Wall Street Journal* (November 2, 2000), pp. C1, C15.

ful acquisition currency to potentially use in the consolidation of the European stock exchanges.

Euronext

In September 2000, the Paris, Brussels, and Amsterdam exchanges merged to form **Euronext**, with ownership shares of 60%, 32%, and 8%, respectively. The goal of Euronext was to form a pan-European stock market. Euronext planned to put all three markets onto a common trading system during 2000, though the markets remained legally separate and have slightly different trading rules. Euronext also had discussions with the LSE concerning an alliance. As of April 2001, Euronext ranked first in Europe in trading volume, and second by market capitalization of the companies on its boards. LSE was the largest by market capitalization.

In addition to forming this merger with the Dutch and Belgian exchanges, the Paris stock exchange sold its trading technology to several foreign markets. The Deutsche Borse and the Paris **Bourse** are believed to be Europe's two best stock markets in terms of technology and market model.

Other European Stock Market Activities

In 2000, Nasdaq, the U.S. OTC market, explored an alliance with the LSE, and was also in discussions with the DB, Euronext, and other European exchanges to form a pan-European trading platform, with Nasdaq providing the U.S. link. Nasdaq has also explored an alliance with the Japanese market.[11]

Nasdaq in March 2001 announced a plan to acquire a 58% stake in Easdaq, a new exchange discussed below. Easdaq is a pioneering European exchange set up five years earlier as a pan-European electronic marketplace for small but fast-growing young companies. After the takeover by Nasdaq, it was announced that Easdaq would adopt an entirely new trading system in June 2001. Renamed Nasdaq Europe, the new exchange is soon expected to trade blue chips as well as technology stocks, and form a pan-European market linked to Nasdaq's trading systems in the U.S. and Japan.[12]

Nasdaq also announced in March 2001 a partnership with the London International Financial Futures and Options Exchange, or Liffe, to jointly introduce single stock futures in the United States during the later part of 2001. U.S. investors have been barred from trading in stock futures due to fears of market manipulation. However, regulations permitting such investments are expected to be fully enacted by December 2001. The Nasdaq–Liffe partnership hopes to benefit from the resulting growth in the equity derivatives market in the U.S. Single stock futures (known at the Liffe as Universal Stock Futures) on some Nasdaq-listed stocks such as Cisco and Microsoft already trade on Liffe. The partnership is expected to use Liffe's Connect Electronic Trading System and trade during the U.S. business day. This venture will be U.S.-regulated.[13]

The New York Stock Exchange has also explored alliances with several world markets, including Euronext.

In addition to the Deutsche Borse, four other major exchanges in the world, in Stockholm, Hong Kong, Singapore, and Australia, are run by publicly traded entities. Euronext, Europe's second-largest bourse, and itself the result of a merger during

---

[11] Greg Ip, "Nasdaq Looks to Europe: Are Preparations Prelude to a Bid for London Exchange?" *Wall Street Journal* (November 2000) pp. C1, C17.
[12] Edmund L. Andrews, "Nasdaq is Set to Control Counterpart in Europe," *New York Times* (March 28, 2001), p. W1.
[13] Silvia Ascarelli, "Nasdaq, Liffe Plan Stock-Futures Venture," *New York Times* (March 27, 2001).

2000 among the French, Dutch and Belgian markets, also plans to go public during 2001. As indicated in Chapter 18, Nasdaq plans to go public during 2001, and the NYSE is considering becoming a public company.

Clearly there are economic and financial forces toward the centralization of European stock trading.[14] However, European bourses are viewed as national treasures. They are owned by local brokerages, national banks, and sometimes governments, which often complicates strategic decision making. Merging them into one seamless unit will require either considerable diplomacy (which, in some cases, has already failed) or contentious discussions.

Similar to the United States, the development of new electronic markets are getting a boost from the traditional bourses' lack of progress in merging to form a pan-European exchange. Electronic systems such as Tradepoint and E-Crossnet are already pan-European. These systems have strong backers. Tradepoint is majority-owned by an Instinet-led consortium of U.S. firms. E-Crossnet, which would completely eliminate the need for brokerages entirely, is backed by Merrill Lynch & Company and Barclays Global Investors. And Morgan Stanley and OM Gruppen co-own Jiway, a proposed pan-European system for executing retail orders.

NEW EUROPEAN EXCHANGES

As we discussed in Chapter 18, in the United States, due to the more stringent listing requirements on the NYSE and other exchanges, newer and smaller companies tend to be traded on the Nasdaq OTC markets. During the late 1990s, Europe's traditional exchanges also began to develop such markets. Their goal was to replicate Nasdaq in their country, and specifically to give European start-up companies access to equity capital and to stem the flow of entrepreneurial talent to the United States.[15]

The largest of these markets is the **Neuer Markt** in Frankfurt, started by the Deutsche Borse in March 1997. The Neuer Markt traded 338 companies with a combined market capitalization of $114 billion at the end of 2000.

The Nouveau Marche, started in March 1996 by the Paris bourse, has 158 companies with a combined market value of more than $20 billion. The first of such markets was the Alternative Investments Market (AIM), started by the London Stock Exchange in June 1995, with more than 500 stocks listed, but with a market capitalization of only $22 billion.

Finally, Easdaq, an electronic trading network modeled after Nasdaq and based in Brussels, started in November 1996 as a pan-European exchange and has only 62 stocks listed with a market capitalization of $23 billion. Easdaq's major shareholder was Knight Trading Group, Inc., the U.S. market-marker, before a 58% share was bought by Nasdaq during March 2001, as discussed earlier.

NEW JAPANESE EXCHANGES

Japan has three markets for emerging companies. The combined trading volume of these three markets, however, remains small. The newest and fastest changing of these markets is Nasdaq Japan. This market, which was launched during June 2000 as a section of the Osaka Securities Exchange, is as a market for start-up companies.

---

[14] Peter Bennett, "An Architecture for a Single European Stock Exchange," *The Bridge Handbook of World Stock, Derivative and Commodity Exchanges 2000*, Mondo Visione, 2000, pp. XXXV–XXXVI.

[15] Edmund Andrews, "Think Nasdaq. Now Double the Pain," *New York Times* (January 28, 2001), Money & Business, Section 3, pp. 1, 12, 13.

Initially all issues on this market traded via an auction market, under which buy/sell orders are directly matched. However, under a hybrid system planned to be introduced at the end of 2001, issues will be classified into two categories based on trading volume, market capitalization, and other factors. Small issues will be traded through the market-making system (similar to that used by Nasdaq), and large issues will be traded via either the market-making system or the auction system (similar to that used by the NYSE).

All currently listed issues are classified as small issues. The market-making system enables investors to trade stocks even with small numbers of shares outstanding. On the other hand, stocks with large numbers of shares outstanding can be traded by the auction method used by the NYSE.

The OTC market adopted a market-making system at the end of 1998. The number of issues subject to trading via market-making represents 30% of the issues listed, and there are 28 market-makers. This OTC market also plans to improve its market-making system during 2001.

OWNERSHIP AND CONTROL OF NATIONAL STOCK EXCHANGES

A convenient and informative way of outlining key comparisons among some of the larger and more established national stock markets is to analyze traditional patterns of ownership and control of the exchanges.[16] One group of markets has enjoyed great freedom. In Chapter 3, we pointed out that although stock exchanges in the United States are regulated by the SEC, they are privately owned and competitive entities. The exchanges decide upon the number of memberships, the rules for acquiring membership, and the criteria for listed securities. The exchanges and related self-regulatory organizations (SROs) supervise the activities of members, and commissions are fully negotiable. Furthermore, the various exchanges are actually in competition with one another, and market participants are free to conduct private trades without funneling them through an exchange. For these reasons, it can be said that the U.S. equity markets are in fact private markets, which basically regulate themselves but comply with some governmental regulations.

Market structures that have similar ownership and management traditions exist in Japan, the United Kingdom, Canada, Hong Kong, and Australia. These exchanges are privately owned and self-regulating, with the government largely playing the role of monitor. Competition among exchanges occurs in some of these countries. Japan, for example, has eight major exchanges, but more than 98% of the trades occur on the Tokyo Stock Exchange, the Osaka Exchange, and the Nagoya Exchange. Canada has large exchanges in both Montreal and Toronto. In contrast, the United Kingdom has one dominant exchange, the London Stock Exchange in London, and it represents a consolidation of regional exchanges that occurred almost 40 years ago. The Stock Exchange of Hong Kong similarly represents a unification of four previously separate, small exchanges.[17] In many countries where exchanges are privately owned, deregulation has resulted in either fully or partially negotiable commissions.

The rules for membership and listing securities represent another important feature of the exchanges. In Great Britain, Canada, Hong Kong, and Australia, the

---

[16] Categorizing markets by ownership and management is a concept suggested by Solnik, *International Investments*, p. 106.

[17] Kie Ann Wong, "The Hong Kong Stock Market," in Richard Yan-Ki Ho et al. (eds.), *The Hong Kong Financial System* (Hong Kong: Oxford University Press, 1991), pp. 222–223.

exchanges determine which securities will be listed and the criteria that firms must meet for membership. Japan handles this matter somewhat differently: the Ministry of Finance (MOF) must approve all listed securities;[18] and while the exchange has set a limit on the number of members, only financial firms licensed by the MOF can become members.

A second group of national markets includes those where the stock exchange has traditionally been a public or quasi-public institution. In these countries, the government has exercised considerable control over the exchange's operations and activities. For example, the government has selected brokers (mostly individuals, but occasionally limited partnerships) and given them a monopoly over the bulk of stock transactions. Often, too, the government has fixed commission rates or has given its approval to fixed rates. Typically, the government has required that all transactions go through the exchange and that a broker get a fee, even if a buyer and a seller conclude a private deal without the assistance of a broker.

Most countries whose stock markets were owned and operated in this fashion are European and include France, Belgium, Spain, and Italy. However, the 1980s—a time of extensive liberalization, innovation, and computerization in the international securities industries—brought about several significant changes in these markets. In recent years, the governments mandated that individual brokers be replaced by corporations with limited liability, public shareholders, and authority to conduct both brokerage and dealer functions. Shares in these firms can be owned by foreign firms as well as by banks in the home country. In France and Belgium, a brokerage firm is a **Société de Bourse;** in Italy, it is a **Societá di Intermediazione Mobilaire**; and in Spain, brokerage firms are **Sociedades de Valores.**

Despite this change, government agencies exercise extensive supervisory authority over the exchanges. For example, membership on an exchange may still require government approval or licensing and government agencies set minimum capital requirements as insurance against insolvency.[19] In several of these countries, negotiable fees are replacing fixed commissions at varying speeds. In another significant change, computerized trading systems, frequently modeled on the Toronto Stock Exchange's **Computer Assisted Trading System (CATS)**, are now integral features of these markets. In some countries (such as France), off-exchange trading among dealers is permitted for large blocks of stock, while in Spain and Italy all trading must be handled by a licensed securities firm on the exchange.

The last group of national markets includes those countries in which the majority of exchange trading is done through banks. This type of structure appears in Switzerland and Austria. The domination by the banks reflects regulatory or government policy.

TRADING PROCEDURES AND COMPUTERIZATION

In Chapter 15, we explained the difference between continuous and call markets. In the former, prices are determined continuously throughout the trading day as buyers and sellers submit orders. In a call market, orders are batched for simultaneous execution at the same price and at a particular time (or times) during the day. We also note that some markets (such as the New York Stock Exchange in the United States)

---

[18] Stuart Allen and Selina O'Connor (eds.), *The Guide to World Equity Markets 1992* (London: Euromoney Publications PLC, 1992), p. 288.

[19] Stuart Allen and Selina O'Connor (eds.), *The Guide to World Equity Markets 1992*, (London: Euromoney Publications PLC, 1992), p. 266.

that are largely continuous in nature will set opening prices with a call auction procedure based on bids submitted over night, when the market is closed.

Equity markets in Canada, Japan, Hong Kong, and most of Europe employ the method of continuous trading. The Tokyo Stock Exchange is an example of an exchange that has continuous trading but that opens trading with a call market auction. The auction method is the **Itayosa** method. Essentially, it involves the grouping of orders to buy and sell the stock and identifying the representative price as a central price that will bring about a trade or batch of trades. After the opening, the market uses the **Zaraba** auction method, which arranges individual trades that match the lowest sale price to the highest buy price. The markets of Germany and Austria still use call-based trading for the stocks of smaller companies.

The widespread adoption of computerized and electronic technology has brought many changes to the world's equity markets. Continuous markets that adopted the new technology saw a substantial rise in their volumes of trading. Furthermore, the technology has increased the amount of information that dealers and brokers can get, which has contributed to the efficiency of the trading on the exchanges.[20] Some outstanding successes of computer technology in stock exchanges include the following: Toronto Stock Exchange's CATS, which means Computer Assisted Trading System; the London Stock Market's Stock Exchange Automatic Quotation System (SEAQ); the Frankfurt Sock Exchange's Xetra (Exchange Electronic Trading); and the Tokyo Stock Exchange's CORES, which means Computerized Order Routing and Execution System and which handles all but the largest stocks (the First Section) because they are traded on the trading floor.

One of the most interesting consequences of computerized trading is the conversion of traditional call markets to continuous markets.[21] France is a good example of this change. Once a rather large call market, the Paris Bourse adopted the Toronto Stock Exchange's CATS in the mid-1980s. The French renamed the system CAC, for **Cotation Assistée en Continu.** CAC or CATS is a fully automated electronic trading system that enables traders to work from computer screens without being physically present on a trading floor (except for unusual or possibly very large orders). Spain, Belgium, Italy, and Sweden are other examples of markets where the implementation of computerized trading (often, some version of CATS) has spurred the advance of continuous market structures (except possibly for the initial trades of the day).[22]

DEALERS IN MAJOR MARKETS[23]

A continuous stock market can actually take two forms, according to how the dealer's function is carried out. One form has been adopted by the organized U.S. stock exchanges, such as the New York and American exchanges. The exchange designates a specialist for specific shares who is the sole market-maker or dealer for those shares. The second form is the competitive dealer system like the one found in the U.S. over-the-counter or Nasdaq market. Here, several dealers may be market-makers for any stock, and the dealers do not have a special authorization from the exchange to play this role.

Outside the United States, the specialist system appears only in the Montreal Exchange. The Amsterdam Stock Exchange gives certain firms the specialist's status and

---

[20] Roger D. Huang and Hans R. Stoll, *Major World Equity Markets: Current Structure and Prospects for Change* (New York: New York University Salomon Center Monograph in Finance and Economics, 1991), p. 44.

[21] For a discussion of how this is being done and the advantages of this approach, see Chapter 10 of Robert A. Schwartz, *Reshaping the Equity Markets: A Guide for the 1990s* (New York: HarperBusiness, 1991).

[22] "European Equity Markets," a supplement to the January 1992 issue of *Euromoney*, p. 48.

[23] Schwartz, *Reshaping the Equity Markets*, contains more information on large markets around the world.

duties; a firm of this type is called a **hoekman**. The hoekman is responsible for acting as market-maker only for trades of small to moderate size, and large trades are managed by the transacting parties themselves. Market-makers on the Toronto Stock Exchange are similar to specialists. Limited in number and selected by the exchange, these registered traders trade for their own accounts and try to create orderly price changes in stocks that the exchange has assigned to them. Also, these traders are obligated to post bid and ask prices all through the day and to keep their bid–ask spreads rather small.

Aside from these exceptions, all continuous markets in the world employ some version of the competitive dealer mechanism. The London Stock Exchange is a good example of a full-scale commitment to this approach. On the LSE, any well-capitalized firm that abides by certain regulations can enter the competition as a dealer on any security. Market-makers publish firm bid–ask quotes for their stocks in standardized lots. There are more than 10 dealers for the majority of the large and actively traded shares.

The Tokyo Stock Exchange employs a variant of the competitive dealer system. A broker, called a **saitori**, functions as an intermediary between the dealers and the brokers who are members of the exchange. The *saitoris* cannot buy or sell for their own accounts but rather arrange transactions among dealers. *Saitoris* also conduct the auctions during the trading day and match buy and sell orders submitted by the brokers on behalf of their own accounts or those of their clients.

The final point we want to consider here has to do with the execution of block trades, which are trades of large numbers of shares and typically represent investment activities of large institutional investors. The size of block trades calls for special procedures, such as the upstairs market in the U.S. system, which uses negotiation among institutions in order to bypass the specialist of the organized exchanges as well as the dealers of the OTC market. (See Chapter 18 for more on block trades.)

Dealers in London tend to take larger positions—they commit more of their capital than American dealers do.[24] Also, the London SEAQ system does not quote the full size of an offered block trade, thus protecting block traders from a disclosure of their needs to potential parties on the other side of the trades. For these reasons, while block trading in London also uses negotiation among institutions, the trades go through the computerized trading system in the normal manner. Because the CATS system of Toronto and Paris provides more information about bids than London's SEAQ does, as noted previously, it discloses more about block trades than those initiating the trades generally want to disclose. Thus, block traders do not find Paris and Toronto well-suited to block trades, and large institutional trades have flowed toward New York and London. In response, the Paris Bourse is experimenting with more off-exchange trading of large orders.

Key Points That You Should Understand Before Proceeding

1. How and why exchanges can differ in significant respects among different countries.
2. The role of dealers in national stock exchanges.

STOCK MARKET INDEXES

There are many indexes of stock prices that chart and measure the performance of foreign stock markets. In every country where stock trading takes place, there is at least one index that measures general share price movements. If a country has more

---

[24] Huang and Stoll, *Major World Equity Markets*, p. 49.

than one stock exchange, each exchange usually has its own index. Also, news organizations and financial advisory services create indexes. In the United States, examples of the exchange indexes are the NYSE Composite Index and the AMEX Composite Index, while examples of the indexes constructed by nonexchange firms include Standard & Poor's 500 Common Stock Index and the Dow Jones Industrial Average.

In Japan, there are two major indexes. The Tokyo Stock Exchange produces the **Tokyo Stock Price Index (TOPIX)**. This is a composite index, which is based on all the shares in the Tokyo market's First Section, a designation reserved for the established and large companies whose shares are the most actively traded and widely held. (The TOPIX is computed based on the included firms' market value, not just their prices.) A financial information firm, Nihon Keizai Shimbun, Inc., calculates and publishes the **Nikkei 225 Stock Average**. This average (computed in the same way as the Dow Jones 30) is based on 225 of the largest companies in the First Section.

The United Kingdom's London Stock Exchange is covered by several widely followed indexes. The **Financial Times Industrial Ordinary Index** is based on the prices of shares of 30 leading companies and is known as the **FT 30**. A broader index is the **Financial Times–Stock Exchange 100**, which is a market-value index and is commonly referred to as the **FTSE 100** (and pronounced "Footsie 100"). This index is based on the shares of the largest 100 U.K. firms, whose market value makes up a majority of the market value of all U.K. equities.[25] Indexes for different sectors, and a composite index across sectors, are produced by the *Financial Times* and the Institute for Actuaries. These FT-A indexes are very broadly based, with the composite including more than 700 shares.

The primary German stock index is the **DAX**, which stands for the *Deutscher Aktienindex*, produced by the Frankfurt Stock Exchange. (The German name for this exchange is the *Frankfurter Wertpapier börse*. Some financial services regularly refer to the exchange by its initials, FWB.) The DAX is based on the 30 most actively traded shares listed on the Frankfurt exchange. The **FAZ Index** is another popular German index. Compiled by the Frankfurter *Allgemeine Zeitung*, which is a daily newspaper, the FAZ Index is computed from the share prices of the 100 largest companies listed on the Frankfurt exchange.

In France, a national association of stockbrokers and the Paris Bourse produce an index based on the shares of 40 large and prominent firms traded on the exchange. The index is known as the **CAC 40 Index**, after the name of the Bourse's electronic trading system. Given the increasing economic integration of Europe, the CAC 40, like the FTSE 100 and possibly the DAX, may well be reliable indicators of the overall performance of European stocks and markets.

Other widely followed national stock indexes include the **Hang Seng Index** produced by the Stock Exchange of Hong Kong, the **TSE 300 Composite** of the Toronto Stock Exchange, and the **Swiss Performance Index (SPI)**, which applies to almost 400 firms and is published by the stock exchanges in that country.

To meet the increased interest in global equity investing, financial institutions have crafted several respected international equity indexes. The international equity index followed most by U.S. pension funds is the *Morgan Stanley Capital International Europe, Australasia, and the Far East Index (EAFE Index)*. This index, started by Capital International in 1968 and acquired by Morgan Stanley in 1986, covers more than 2,000 companies in 21 countries. Relatively new international equity indexes include the **Financial Times World Index** (a joint product of the Institute of Actuaries in the United Kingdom, Goldman Sachs & Co., and Wood MacKenzie & Co.), the *Salomon Smith Barney–Russell Global Equity Index* (a joint product of Salomon Smith Barney and

---

[25] Euromoney, *The Guide to World Equity Markets 1995* (London: Euromoney Publications PLC, 1995), p. 348.

Frank Russell, Inc.), and the **Global Index** (a joint product of First Boston Corporation and London-based *Euromoney* magazine).

Free Float

In 2000, an issue regarding the weights used in an international (or global) stock index elevated. The widely used MSCI indexes are market capitalization weighted. The market capitalizations used to weight each country index are the total amounts of stock outstanding in each country, no matter who owns the stock. However, in many countries other corporations own (and typically hold) the shares of other corporations—called "cross holdings"—and some governments also hold shares of stocks in their country. These holdings are not available for trading on the public stock markets. Only the remainder of the stocks, called the **free float**, is available for trading. It is estimated that 20% of the MSCI EAFE Index is not available for purchase on the public stock markets. And the free float varies considerably by country. For example, Singapore, Japan, and Continental Europe have low degrees of free float, and the United States, United Kingdom, and Iceland have high degrees of free float.[26]

In concept, only the free float is available for investors and, thus, the free float market capitalization, not the total market capitalization, should be used as weights in the construction of an international stock index.

And this issue leads to a difference among various international stock indexes. Among the major indexes, the MSCI EAFE has used the total market capitalization as weights, whereas the Salomon Smith Barney BMI (and PMI and EMI) indexes that we described earlier in this chapter are free float weighted. However, during December 2000, MSCI announced that it would convert to float weighting, and by June 2002, all of the major index sponsors will produce free float weighted international stock indexes.

GLOBAL DEPOSITARY RECEIPTS

When a corporation's equities are traded in a foreign market, whether they were issued in the foreign market or not, they are typically in the form of a **Global Depositary Receipt (GDR)**. GDRs are issued by banks as evidence of ownership of the underlying stock of a foreign corporation that the bank holds in trust. Each GDR may represent ownership of one or more shares of common stock of a corporation. The advantage of the GDR structure to the corporation is that the corporation does not have to comply with all of the regulatory issuing requirements of the foreign country where the stock is to be traded. GDRs are typically, but as discussed below not always, sponsored by the issuing corporation. That is, the issuing corporation will work with a bank to offer its common stock in a foreign country via the sale of GDRs.

As an example, consider the U.S. version of the GDR, the **American Depositary Receipt (ADR)**. The combination of GDRs and ADRs for a given company is called simply a *DR (Depository Receipt)*. The initial success of the ADR structure in the United States resulted in the rise of GDRs throughout the world. ADRs are denominated in U.S. dollars and pay dividends in U.S. dollars. Although ADRs are priced in U.S. dollars and their dividends are paid in U.S. dollars, the basis for these payments is the local currency of the underlying stock. Thus, a change in the exchange rate between the local currency of the underlying corporation and the U.S. dollar will affect the ADRs' U.S. dollar price and dividend.

---

[26] Phyllis Feinberg, "Consultants Recommend Clients Switch to Salomon Indexes," *Pensions & Investments* (April 2, 2001), pp. 6, 34.

ADRs can be created in one of two ways. First, one or more banks or brokerage firms can assemble a large block of the shares of a foreign corporation and issue ADRs without the participation of the foreign corporation. These are *nonsponsored* ADRs. More typically, however, ADRs are *sponsored* by the foreign corporation that seeks to have its stock traded in the United States. In these instances, there is only one depositary bank that issues the ADRs. Periodic financial reports are provided by the issuing corporation in English to the holders of an ADR. The Bank of New York is the leading U.S. depository bank for ADRs.

By construction, ADRs are not a direct holding in the company but a derivative created by a financial institution that holds the underlying securities. The holder of an ADR typically does not have voting or preemptive rights. The decision to treat ADR holders differently than direct stockholders, however, is at the discretion of the company. That is, such a distinction may sometimes not be applied.[27]

ADRs can either be traded on one of the two major organized stock exchanges (the New York Stock Exchange and the American Stock Exchange) or traded on the over-the-counter market. The nonsponsored ADR is typically traded on the over-the-counter market. Since ADRs can be continuously created to meet investor demand, they provide the same trading liquidity as the home market securities they represent.

There are several advantages to a U.S. investor to buy an ADR of an international company rather than hold the international stock directly. First, the investor can trade the stock on a U.S. market (exchange or OTC) during U.S. hours and according to U.S. trading practices. Second, the investor makes and receives payments in U.S. dollars rather than foreign currency, although as indicated above, the investor is subject to foreign exchange risk. Finally, the U.S. investor can use a U.S., rather than a global, custodian, which can be easier and save costs and, in some cases, avoid some country-specific taxes.

As U.S. investors, both institutional and individual, have become more open to international investing, the popularity of U.S. ADRs has increased significantly. The share volume of listed Depository Receipt Programs (DRPs), a total of ADRs and GDRs, increased by 71% (from 16.8 billion shares to 28.7 billion shares) from 1999 to 2000 and the U.S. dollar volume by 78% (from $667 billion to $1,185 billion). The number of sponsored DR programs grew from 352 representing 24 countries in 1990 to over 1,800 from 78 countries in 2001.[28]

There are such a sufficient number of ADRs listed in the United States that Merrill Lynch has constructed ADR indexes for various regions, countries, and sectors. In addition, the Bank of New York has created a group of ADR indexes, a Composite Index, three regional subindexes (Europe, Asia, and Latin America), three market subindexes (Developed, Emerging, and Euroland), and 20 country indexes. These indexes are capitalization weighted and are calculated continuously throughout the trading day.

Key Points That You Should Understand Before Proceeding

1. The major stock market indexes throughout the world.
2. The significance of free float market capitalization.
3. What a Global Depositary Receipt (GDR) and what an American Depositary Receipt are.
4. How the GDR is a response to often stringent governmental regulation about the issuance of foreign shares.

---

[27] Craig Karmin, "ADR Holders Find They Have Unequal Rights," *Wall Street Journal* (March 1, 2001), pp. C1, C15.

[28] The Bank of New York Web site: www.adrbny.com.

SUMMARY

The markets for goods and services have become increasingly internationalized through the export and import of good and services, the migration of labor, and the location of production and distribution operations in other countries. Similarly, the markets for common stocks have become increasingly internationalized. Institutional and individual investors invest in stocks of other countries to enhance returns and reduce risk through diversification. The increased availability of GDRs and ADRs makes it easier for investors to trade international stocks in their own time and in their own currency and through their normal settlement and clearance institutions.

Issuers of common stock issue their shares internationally to reduce financing costs, broaden their ownership, and improve their brand internationally. Listing their shares in other countries via GDRs and ADRs helps accomplish these objectives.

International stocks are usually segmented into stocks of developed and emerging countries. Among the developed countries, the United States, Japan, and the United Kingdom have the largest market capitalizations. Among the emerging countries, Taiwan, China, and Brazil have the largest market capitalizations.

The prices of stocks on markets around the world do not move together in an exact way because the economic systems in which those markets are located have dissimilar environments in terms of taxation, industrial growth, political stability, monetary policy, and other factors. Low levels of comovement of stock prices offer investors a benefit from diversifying their holdings across the markets of countries. That is, investors who allocate some of their portfolio to shares from other countries can reduce the portfolio's expected return with no increase in risk. This benefit of international diversification has led many investors to allocate some of their wealth to foreign markets and shares of foreign firms.

Methods of trading vary considerably throughout the world. Electronically assisted market-maker trading has become prevalent throughout the world. The NYSE and the other U.S. exchanges are among the few markets to have a trading floor and trade via the auction method with specialists. Thus, the market-maker system has become more common and the specialist system less common. Exchanges in Europe and throughout the world are

setting up exchanges to imitate Nasdaq, thus permitting the trading of the shares of newer and smaller companies.

Another trend in trading organizations is that they are becoming or are considering becoming public companies wherein their stock in the exchange is owned and traded by the public. The corporate form of organization provides more flexibility and capital for mergers and acquisitions and to make capital expenditures for technology. The Deutsche Borse went public during 2001, Euronext is expected to do so soon, and exchanges in Stockholm, Hong Kong, Singapore, and Australia previously became publicly traded entities.

Finally, the importance of technology has become increasingly important to stock trading organizations. The purposes of technology include: a reduction of costs; an increase in the speed and efficiency of order routing, trade execution, and price reporting; and an improvement in the efficiency of the settlement and clearance process to assure fair and transparent order execution. Many stock markets are significant "technology companies," and their success as a trading market depends on the quality of their technology and systems. Some exchanges even cover their technology costs by selling their technology to other exchanges.

A stock market may be a continuous market or a call market. Many markets use call auction procedures to set an opening price and then allow prices to be determined on a continuous basis. Many former call markets have, with the advent of computerization, become continuous markets. Computerization has had great success across the world, from Tokyo to Toronto to London, and many markets have adopted computerized trading systems.

It is possible to group the stock market structures throughout the world into three categories. The first includes private markets that are basically self-regulated. Markets in the United States, England, Hong Kong, Canada, Japan, and Australia fit this description. Second, some markets are public institutions, for which the government plays a traditionally active role in licensing brokers and directing operations of some key exchange activities. Exchanges in France, Spain, Italy, and Belgium fall into this category. The third category includes stock markets where the majority of trading is done through banks. Switzerland and Austria are members of this group.

Every market in the world has an index, which is a measure of the general movement in the prices of shares on the market. Some indexes are produced by exchanges and some by financial news services or other nonexchange organizations. The large markets have well-known and widely followed indexes: the TOPIX and the Nikkei 225 in Japan; the FTSE 100 in the United Kingdom; the DAX and FAZ indexes in Germany; and the CAC 40 in France. Popular international equity price indexes are based on several markets; good examples are the Morgan Stanley EAFE Index, which covers Europe, Australasia, and the Far East, and the Morgan Stanley Emerging Market Index. The Salomon Smith Barney Basic Market Index and Emerging Market Index are also in use.

A more convenient method for trading shares in foreign corporations is the Global Depositary Receipt. The U.S. version is the American Depositary Receipt.

KEY TERMS

- American Depositary Receipt (ADR), 376
- Big Bang, 363
- Bourse, 369
- CAC 40 Index, 375
- Computer Assisted Trading System (CATS), 372
- Computer-Assisted Order-Routing and Execution System (CORES), 365
- Cotation Assistée en Continu (CAC), 373
- DAX, 375
- EAFE Index, 354
- Eurex, 364
- Euronext, 369
- Euroequity tranche, 353
- Exchange Electronic Trading (Xetra), 364
- FAZ Index, 375
- Financial Times Industrial Ordinary Index (or FT 30), 375
- Financial Times–Stock Exchange 100 (FTSE 100), 375
- Financial Times World Index, 375
- First section, 365
- Frankfurt Wertpapierbörse AG (FWB), 364
- Free float, 376
- Global Depositary Receipt (GDR), 376
- Global Index, 376
- Hang Seng Index, 375
- Hoekman, 374
- Itayosa and Zaraba, 373
- Multiple listing, 354
- Neuer Markt, 370
- Nikkei 225 Stock Average, 375
- Saitori, 374
- Sociedades de Valores, 372
- Societá di Intermediazione Mobiliare, 372
- Société de Bourse, 372
- Stock Exchange Automatic Quotation System (SEAQ), 363
- Swiss Performance Index (SPI), 375
- Tokyo Stock Price Index (TOPIX), 375
- TSE 300 Composite, 375

QUESTIONS

1. a. What is a Euroequity issue and a Euroequity tranche?
   b. What is the most important innovation that Euroequities have achieved?
2. Some stocks are listed on several exchanges around the world. Give three reasons why a firm might want its stock to be listed on an exchange in the firm's home country as well as on exchanges in other countries.
3. Suppose the stock of company UNA is selling for $10 per share in New York and for $10.75 per share (after adjustment for the dollar-to-pound exchange rate) on the London Stock Exchange.
   a. Would you buy 1,000 shares in New York and sell them in London if the total cost of both transactions and all related fees were $375?
   b. What is the lowest dollar price on the LSE that would make this arbitrage unprofitable? (Again, assume costs of $375 per 1,000 shares.)
4. Provide a general explanation for why stocks of Dutch companies in Holland might sustain a significant decline over the same time period that brings about a

sharp increase in the value of shares of a typical Australian company, which are traded in Australia.

5. a. What is the correlation coefficient and how does a low value (say, +0.30) of correlation between stocks in two countries offer investors an interesting investment opportunity?
    b. Why, if the correlation coefficient were +0.95, would the same kind of opportunity not exist?
    c. Claudia Barelli and Roberto Moro-Visconti, in their working paper titled, "The Link Between Volatility and Correlation in International Stock Markets," report that share price volatility, especially sharp falls as in times of market "crashes," actually encourages investors to increase the international diversification of their holdings because they want to protect themselves against severe market declines. Comment on whether or not you find this analysis intuitively appealing.

6. What two factors have tended to increase the correlation among the various countries' stock markets during the 1990s?

7. A country's economy can be postulated to be made up of two sectors, a global sector and a country sector. What are these two sectors?

8. Explain how rules of structure and ownership help to group the world's stock markets into three broad categories.

9. a. Identify the types of trades for which many markets use the call auction method.
    b. Why do markets tend to favor continuous methods for the pricing of actively traded stocks?
    c. Name and distinguish the two methods of auction used by the Tokyo Stock Exchange?

10. Identify the meaning of these acronyms: CORES, SEAQ, CATS, and CAC.

11. a. What does the term *First Section* mean on the Tokyo Stock Exchange?
    b. What are the key differences between the two major Japanese stock market indexes, the TOPIX and the Nikkei 225?
    c. What is "Mothers"?

12. a. Which markets in the world use some form of the specialist system that is favored by the organized U.S. exchanges?
    b. What system do most markets use instead of the specialist arrangement?

13. a. What is the Broad Market Index (BMI)?
    b. What is the difference between the Primary Market Index (PMI) and the Extended Market Index (EMI)?

14. Often a news report will survey the day's trading with a statement like this: "The Footsie 100 rose 1.5% today, while the DAX dropped 0.25% and the CAC 40 finished unchanged." What are the formal names of the indexes referred to, and to which country do they apply?

15. a. What is a GDR?
    b. How does a GDR facilitate issuance of a domestic firm's securities in a foreign country?

16. What is meant by a sponsored and unsponsored GDR?

17. a. What is meant by free float market capitalization?
    b. How does free float market capitalization lead to a difference among various international stock market indexes?

Markets for Corporate Senior Instruments: I

Learning Objectives

After reading this chapter, you will understand

- the various financing alternatives available to corporations.
- The different forms of credit risk: default risk, credit spread risk, and downgrade risk.
- the importance of credit ratings.
- what commercial paper is.
- the types of commercial paper: directly placed paper and dealer paper.
- the differences between the U.S. commercial paper market and the Eurocommercial paper market.
- what a medium-term note is.
- what a syndicated loan is.
- the two different ways a syndicated loan can be sold: assignment and participation.
- the basic terms of a loan agreement.
- what a lease financing transaction is.
- the difference between a single-investor lease and a leveraged lease.

Corporate senior instruments are financial obligations of a corporation that have priority over its common stock in the case of bankruptcy. They include debt obligations and preferred stock.

The market for corporate debt obligations can be classified into five sectors: (1) commercial paper market; (2) medium-term note market; (3) bank loan market; and (4) bond market. In this chapter, we look at the first four sectors, while in the next chapter we cover the corporate bond market, as well as another market for long-term funding, the preferred stock market. Unlike our discussion of common stock, in which we focused first on the U.S. equity market and then the non-U.S. equity market, here we discuss both the U.S. markets and Euromarkets in which corporations can borrow funds.

Securities such as commercial paper, Euronotes, medium-term notes, and bonds represent alternatives to bank loans for companies needing to raise funds. The issuance of securities in the international market has increased substantially since the 1980s, in stark contrast to the bank borrowing trend. This phenomenon of borrower preference for issuing securities over borrowing directly from banks is referred to as the *securitization* of capital markets. The term *securitization* is actually used in two ways. It is in the broader sense that we use it here. In the more narrow sense, the term *securitization*, more specifically, *asset securitization*, is used to describe the process of pooling loans and issuing securities backed by these loans. We described asset securitization in Chapter 2.

CREDIT RISK

Unlike investing in a U.S. Treasury security, an investor who lends funds to a corporation by purchasing its debt obligation is exposed to *credit risk*. But what is credit risk? Traditionally credit risk is defined as the risk that the borrower will fail to satisfy the terms of the obligation with respect to the timely payment of interest and repayment of the amount borrowed. This form of credit risk is called *default risk*.

In addition to default risk, there are other risks associated with the investment in debt securities that are also components of credit risk. Even in the absence of default, the investor is concerned that the market value of a debt instrument will decline in value and/or the relative price performance of that instrument will be worse than that of other debt obligations which the investor is compared against. As explained in Chapter 11, the yield on a corporate debt instrument is made up of two components: (1) the yield on a similar maturity Treasury issue and (2) a premium to compensate for the risks associated with the debt instrument that do not exist in a Treasury issue, referred to as a *spread*. The part of the risk premium or spread attributable to credit risk is called the *credit spread*.

The price performance of a non-Treasury debt obligation and its return over some investment horizon will depend on how the credit spread changes. If the credit spread increases—investors say that the spread has "widened"—the market price of the debt obligation will decline. The risk that an issuer's debt obligation will decline due to an increase in the credit spread is called *credit spread risk*.

We explained credit risk first in our discussion of municipal securities. Professional money managers analyze an issuer's financial information and the specifications of the debt instrument itself in order to estimate the ability of the issuer to live up to its future contractual obligations. This activity is known as *credit analysis*. Some large institutional investors have their own credit analysis department but most individual and institutional investors do not conduct such analytical studies. Instead, they rely primarily on commercial rating companies that perform credit analysis and express their conclusions by a system of ratings. As we explained in Chapter 11, there are three commercial rating companies: Standard & Poor's Corporation, Moody's Investors Service, Inc., and Fitch.

Once a rating is assigned to a corporate debt instrument, it can be changed based on subsequent economic and financial developments. An improvement in the credit quality of an issue or issuer is rewarded with a better credit rating, referred to as an *upgrade*; a deterioration in the credit quality of an issue or issuer is penalized by the assignment of an inferior credit rating, referred to as a *downgrade*. An unanticipated downgrading of an issue or issuer increases the credit spread sought by the market, resulting in a decline in the price of the issue or the issuer's debt obligation. This risk is referred to as *downgrade risk*.

The credit-rating companies play a key role in the functioning of debt markets. Investors take great comfort in knowing that the rating companies monitor the creditworthiness of issuers and keep the investing public informed of their findings. One would expect that other countries would have organizations that provide a similar function. This has not been the case. Only in recent years have credit-rating companies appeared in other countries. For example, in Japan it was not until 1977 that a formal corporate bond-rating system was introduced. The original system for rating corporate bonds that was introduced in Japan in 1959 was based solely on the size of the issue.[1]

---

[1] Edward W. Karp and Akira Koike, "The Japanese Corporate Bond Market," Chapter 11 in Frank J. Fabozzi (ed.), *The Japanese Bond Markets* (Chicago: Probus Publishing, 1990), p. 377.

Key Points That You Should Understand Before Proceeding

1. Corporate debt obligations expose an investor to credit risk.
2. Credit risk consists of default risk, credit spread risk, and downgrade risk.
3. Credit risk is typically measured by the credit or quality ratings assigned by nationally recognized commercial rating companies.
4. Commercial rating companies play a key role in the functioning of debt markets in the United States, and their role in other countries is increasing.

COMMERCIAL PAPER

Commercial paper is a short-term unsecured promissory note issued in the open market that represents the obligation of the issuing corporation. The issuance of commercial paper is an alternative to bank borrowing for large corporations (nonfinancial and financial) with strong credit ratings.

While the original purpose of commercial paper was to provide short-term funds for seasonal and working capital needs, companies have used this instrument for other purposes in recent years. It has been used quite often for *bridge financing*. For example, suppose that a corporation needs long-term funds to build a plant or acquire equipment. Rather than raising long-term funds immediately, the corporation may elect to postpone the offering until more favorable capital market conditions prevail. The funds raised by issuing commercial paper are used until longer-term securities are sold. Interestingly, commercial paper has sometimes been used as bridge financing to finance corporate takeovers.[2]

In the United States, the maturity of commercial paper is typically less than 270 days, with the most common maturity range 30 to 50 days or less.[3] There are reasons for this pattern of maturities. First, as explained in Chapter 3, the Securities Act of 1933 requires that securities be registered with the SEC. Special provisions in the 1933 act exempt commercial paper from registration so long as the maturity does not exceed 270 days. Hence, to avoid the costs associated with registering issues with the SEC, firms rarely issue commercial paper with maturities exceeding 270 days. Another consideration in determining the maturity is whether or not the commercial paper would be eligible collateral for a bank borrowing from the Federal Reserve Bank's discount window. In order to be eligible, the maturity of the paper may not exceed 90 days. Since eligible paper trades at a lower cost than paper that is not eligible, firms prefer to issue paper whose maturity does not exceed 90 days.

To pay off holders of maturing paper, issuers generally use the proceeds obtained by selling new commercial paper. This process is often described as rolling over short-term paper. The risk that the investor in commercial paper faces is that the issuer will be unable to sell new paper at maturity. As a safeguard against this rollover risk, commercial paper is typically backed by unused bank credit lines. The commitment fee the bank charges for providing a credit line increases the effective cost of issuing commercial paper.

Investors in commercial paper are institutional investors. Money market mutual funds purchase roughly one-third of all the commercial paper issued. Pension funds, commercial bank trust departments, state and local governments, and nonfinancial

---

[2] Commercial paper also has been used as part of an interest rate swap transaction. We discuss these transactions in Chapter 29.
[3] *Money Market Instruments* (New York: Merrill Lynch Money Markets Inc., 1989), p. 16.

corporations seeking short-term investments purchase the balance. The minimum round-lot transaction is $100,000, though some issuers will sell commercial paper in denominations of $25,000.

There is very little secondary trading of commercial paper. Typically, an investor in commercial paper is an entity that plans to hold it until maturity. This is understandable because an investor can purchase commercial paper in a direct transaction with the issuer, which will sell paper with the specific maturity the investor desires.

Issuers of Commercial Paper

Corporate issuers of commercial paper can be divided into financial companies and nonfinancial companies. The majority of commercial paper outstanding was issued by financial companies. As of June 1997, financial firms issued 78% of all commercial paper outstanding.[4]

There are three types of financial companies: **captive finance companies**, *bank-related finance companies*, and *independent finance companies*. Captive finance companies are subsidiaries of equipment manufacturing companies. Their primary purpose is to secure financing for the customers of the parent company. For example, the three major U.S. automobile manufactures have captive finance companies: General Motors Acceptance Corporation (GMAC), Ford Credit, and Chrysler Financial. GMAC is by the far the largest issuer of commercial paper in the United States. Furthermore, a bank holding company may have a subsidiary that is a finance company, which provides loans to enable individuals and businesses to acquire a wide range of products. Independent finance companies are those that are not subsidiaries of equipment manufacturing firms or bank holding companies.

Although the issuers of commercial paper typically have high credit ratings, smaller and less well-known companies with lower credit ratings have been able to issue paper in recent years. They have been able to do so by means of credit support from a firm with a high credit rating (such paper is called *credit-supported commercial paper*) or by collateralizing the issue with high-quality assets (such paper is called *asset-backed commercial paper*). An example of credit-supported commercial paper is one supported by a *letter of credit*. The terms of a letter of credit specify that the bank issuing the letter guarantees that the bank will pay off the paper when it comes due, if the issuer fails to do so. The bank will charge a fee for the letter of credit. From the issuer's perspective the fee enables it to enter the commercial paper market and thereby obtain funding at a lower cost than that of bank borrowing. Commercial paper issued with this credit enhancement is referred to as **LOC paper**. The credit enhancement may also take the form of a surety bond from an insurance company.[5]

Both domestic and foreign corporations issue commercial paper in the United States. Commercial paper issued by foreign entities is called **Yankee commercial paper**.

The three rating companies assign ratings to commercial paper. These ratings are shown in Table 20-1.

Directly Placed versus Dealer-Placed Paper

Commercial paper is classified as either **direct paper** or **dealer-placed paper**. Directly placed paper is sold by the issuing firm directly to investors without the help of an agent or an intermediary. A large majority of the issuers of direct paper are financial

---

[4] See Susan Stojanovic and Mark D. Vaughan "Who's Minding the Shop?" *The Regional Economist*, St. Louis Federal Reserve (April 1998), pp. 1–8.

[5] A surety bond is a policy written by an insurance company to protect another party against loss or violation of a contract.

Table 20-1   Commercial Paper Ratings*

	COMMERCIAL RATING COMPANY		
CATEGORY	FITCH	MOODY'S	S&P
Investment grade	F-1+		A-1+
	F-1	P-1	A-1
	F-2	P-2	A-2
	F-3	P-3	A-3
Noninvestment grade	F-S	NP (Not Prime)	B
			C
In default	D		D

SOURCE: Mitchell A. Post. "The Evolution of the U.S. Commercial Paper Market Since 1980," *Federal Reserve Bulletin* (December 1992), p. 882.

* *The definition of ratings varies by rating agency*

companies. These entities require continuous funds in order to provide loans to customers. As a result, they find it cost-effective to establish a sales force to sell their commercial paper directly to investors.

Dealer-placed commercial paper requires the services of an agent to sell an issuer's paper. The agent distributes the paper on a best efforts underwriting basis. (For more on best efforts underwriting, see Chapter 14.) Historically, the dealer paper market was dominated by securities houses because commercial banks were prohibited from underwriting commercial paper by the Glass-Steagall Act. In June 1987, however, the Fed granted subsidiaries of bank holding companies permission to underwrite commercial paper. While securities houses still dominate the dealer market, commercial banks are making inroads. This seems natural because, for the most part, the funds being raised in the commercial paper market represent those previously raised through short-term bank loans. Banks are seeking to generate underwriting fees associated with commercial paper underwriting in order to recoup part of the interest income lost from borrowers that have come to favor commercial paper issuance rather than short-term bank borrowing.

Non-U.S. Commercial Paper Markets

Other countries have developed their own commercial paper markets. For example, in November 1987, the Japanese Ministry of Finance (MOF) approved the issuance of commercial paper by Japanese corporations in its domestic market. A few months later, the MOF approved the issuance of yen-denominated commercial paper in Japan by non-Japanese entities. Such paper is referred to as **Samurai commercial paper.**

Eurocommercial paper is issued and placed outside the jurisdiction of the currency of denomination. There are several differences between U.S. commercial paper and Eurocommercial paper with respect to the characteristics of the paper and the structure of the market. First, commercial paper issued in the United States usually has a maturity of less than 270 days, with the most common maturity range 30 to 50 days or less. The maturity of Eurocommercial paper can be considerably longer. Second, while an issuer in the United States must have unused bank credit lines, it is possible to issue commercial paper without such backing in the Eurocommercial paper market. Third, while in the United States commercial paper can be directly placed or dealer placed, Eurocommercial paper is almost always dealer placed. The fourth distinction is that numerous dealers participate in the Eurocommercial paper market, while only a few dealers dominate the market in the United States. Finally, because of the longer maturity of Eurocommercial paper, that paper is traded more often in the secondary market than U.S. commercial paper. Investors in commercial paper in the United States typically buy and hold to maturity, and the secondary market is thin and illiquid.

Key Points That You Should Understand Before Proceeding

1. Commercial paper is a short-term unsecured promissory note that is issued in the open market and that represents the obligation of the issuing corporation. It is an alternative to bank borrowing for large corporations.
2. By using credit support, smaller and less well-known companies with lower credit ratings have been able to issue paper.
3. Commercial paper is rated by private rating companies.
4. Commercial paper can be directly placed by the issuer or issued by using the services of an agent or intermediary.
5. Other countries have developed their own commercial paper markets, and there is a Eurocommercial paper market.

MEDIUM-TERM NOTES

A **medium-term note (MTN)** is a corporate debt instrument, with the unique characteristic that notes are offered continuously to investors by an agent of the issuer. Investors can select from several maturity ranges: 9 months to 1 year, more than 1 year to 18 months, more than 18 months to 2 years, and so on up to 30 years. Medium-term notes are registered with the Securities and Exchange Commission under Rule 415 (the shelf registration rule), which gives a corporation the maximum flexibility for issuing securities on a continuous basis.[6]

The term "medium-term note" to describe this corporate debt instrument is misleading. Traditionally, the term "note" or "medium term" was used to refer to debt issues with a maturity greater than 1 year but less than 15 years. Certainly, this is not a characteristic of MTNs, since they have been sold with maturities from 9 months to 30 years, and even longer. For example, in July 1993, Walt Disney Corporation issued a security with a 100-year maturity off its medium-term note shelf registration.

General Motors Acceptance Corporation first used medium-term notes in 1972 to fund automobile loans with maturities of five years and less. The purpose of the MTN was to fill the funding gap between commercial paper and long-term bonds. It is for this reason that they are referred to as "medium term." The medium-term notes were issued directly to investors without the use of an agent. Only a few corporations issued MTNs in the 1970s. About $800 million of MTNs were outstanding by 1981.

The modern-day medium-term note was pioneered by Merrill Lynch in 1981. The first medium-term note issuer was Ford Motor Credit Company. By 1983, GMAC and Chrysler Financial used Merrill Lynch as an agent to issue medium-term notes. Merrill Lynch and other investment banking firms committed funds to make a secondary market for MTNs, thereby improving liquidity. In 1982, Rule 415 was adopted, making it easier for issuers to sell registered securities on a continuous basis.

---

[6] The shelf registration rule is explained in Chapter 14.

Euro medium-term notes are those issued in the Euromarket. The market began in 1987. Euro medium-term notes are issued by sovereign issuers (i.e., governments and governmental agencies), nonfinancial corporations, and financial institutions. The last two entities are now the major issuers, accounting for about two-thirds of issuance volume in 1991.[7] Euro medium-term notes have been issued in a variety of currencies. Borrowers from 19 countries have issued Euro medium-term notes. Most Euro medium-term notes were issued via the private placement market.

Size of Market and Issuers[8]

The public offering of MTNs by U.S. corporations between 1983 through 1998 increased from $5.5 billion in 1983 to $150 billion in 1998. In 1983, there were only 12 issuers of MTNs. By 1998, 94 U.S. corporations issued MTNs and the MTNs of more than 451 corporations was outstanding.

The growth of the domestic medium-term note market and its importance as a funding source can be seen by comparing it to the amount of intermediate and long-term corporate debt issued. The ratio of outstanding MTNs to the amount of outstanding public corporate debt (MTNs plus public corporate bonds) was 9% in 1989 and 41% in 1999. For financial firms and nonfinancial firms the share in 1999 was 57% and 12%, respectively.

Borrowers have flexibility in designing MTNs to satisfy their own needs. They can issue fixed- or floating-rate debt. The coupon payments can be denominated in U.S. dollars or in a foreign currency. In the next chapter we describe corporate bonds and the various security structures. These structures have been used by MTN issuers.

When the treasurer of a corporation is contemplating an offering of either MTNs or corporate bonds, there are two factors that affect the decision. The most obvious is the cost of the funds raised after consideration of registration and distribution costs. This cost is referred to as the *all-in-cost of funds.* The second is the flexibility afforded to the issuer in structuring the offering. The tremendous growth in the MTN market is evidence of the relative advantage of MTNs with respect to cost and flexibility for some offerings. However, the fact that there are corporations that raise funds by issuing both bonds and MTNs is evidence that there is no absolute advantage in all instances and market environments.

As with commercial paper, MTNs are rated by the nationally recognized rating companies. In 1998, about 99% of all MTNs issued received an investment-grade rating at the time of issuance. Most outstanding MTNs were rated investment grade.

The Primary Market

Medium-term notes differ from corporate bonds in the manner in which they are distributed to investors when they are initially sold. Although some investment-grade corporate bond issues are sold on a best efforts basis, typically they are underwritten by investment bankers. MTNs have been traditionally distributed on a best efforts basis by either an investment banking firm or other broker-dealers acting as agents. Another difference between corporate bonds and MTNs when they are offered is that MTNs are usually sold in relatively small amounts on a continuous or an intermittent basis, while corporate bonds are sold in large, discrete offerings.

---

[7] *Eurobonds and Euro Medium-Term Notes: 1991 Review* (New York: Salomon Brothers Inc, 1992), pp. 11–12.

[8] Data about medium-term note issuance by corporations are provided on the Federal Reserve Bank's web site: www.federalreserve/releases/medterm.

Table 20-2   An Offering Rate Schedule for a Medium-Term Note Program

Medium-term notes			Treasury securities	
MATURITY RANGE	YIELD (PERCENT)	YIELD SPREAD OF MTN OVER TREASURY SECURITIES (BASIS POINTS)	MATURITY	YIELD (PERCENT)
9 months to 12 months	(a)	(a)	9 months	3.35
12 months to 18 months	(a)	(a)	12 months	3.50
18 months to 2 years	(a)	(a)	18 months	3.80
2 years to 5 years	4.35	35	2 years	4.00
3 years to 4 years	5.05	55	3 years	4.50
4 years to 5 years	5.60	60	4 years	5.00
5 years to 6 years	6.05	60	5 years	5.45
6 years to 7 years	6.10	40	6 years	5.70
7 years to 8 years	6.30	40	7 years	5.90
8 years to 9 years	6.45	40	8 years	6.05
9 years to 10 years	6.60	40	10 years	6.20
10 years	6.70	40	10 years	6.30

SOURCE: Leland E. Crabbe, "The Anatomy of the Medium-Term Note Market," *Federal Reserve Bulletin* (August 1993), p. 753.

[a] *No rate posted.*

A corporation that wants an MTN program will file a shelf registration with the SEC for the offering of securities. While the SEC registration for MTN offerings is between $100 and $1 billion, once the total is sold, the issuer can file another shelf registration.[9] The registration will include a list of the investment banking firms, usually two to four, that the corporation has arranged to act as agents to distribute the MTNs. The large New York–based investment banking firms dominate the distribution market for MTNs.

The issuer then posts rates over a range of maturities: for example, 9 months to 1 year, 1 year to 18 months, 18 months to 2 years, and annually thereafter. Table 20-2 provides an example of an offering rate schedule for a medium-term note program. Usually, an issuer will post rates as a spread over a Treasury security of comparable maturity. For example, in the two- to three-year maturity range, the offering rate is 35 basis points over the two-year Treasury. Since the two-year Treasury is shown in the table at 4%, the offering rate is 4.35%. Rates will not be posted for maturity ranges that the issuer does not desire to sell. For example, in Table 20-2 the issuer does not wish to sell MTNs with a maturity of less than two years.

The agents will then make the offering rate schedule available to their investor base interested in MTNs. An investor who is interested in the offering will contact the agent. In turn, the agent contacts the issuer to confirm the terms of the transaction. Since the maturity range in the offering rate schedule does not specify a specific maturity date, the investor can choose the final maturity subject to approval by the issuer. The minimum size that an investor can purchase of an MTN offering typically ranges from $1 million to $25 million.

---

[9] Leland E. Crabbe, "Medium-Term Notes," Chapter 12 in Frank J. Fabozzi (ed.), *The Handbook of Fixed Income Securities*, 6th ed. (New York: McGraw Hill, 2001).

The rate offering schedule can be changed at any time by the issuer either in response to changing market conditions or because the issuer has raised the desired amount of funds at a given maturity. In the latter case, the issuer can either not post a rate for that maturity range or lower the rate.

Structured MTNs

It is common today for issuers of MTNs to couple their offerings with transactions in the derivative markets (options, futures/forwards, swaps, caps, and floors) so as to create debt obligations with more interesting risk/return features than are available in the corporate bond market. Specifically, an issue can be floating rate over all or part of the life of the security and the coupon reset formula can be based on a benchmark interest rate, equity index or individual stock price, a foreign exchange rate, or a commodity index. There are even MTNs with coupon reset formulas that vary inversely with a benchmark interest rate. That is, if the benchmark interest rate increases (decreases), the coupon rate decreases (increases). Debt instruments with this coupon characteristic are called *inverse floating-rate securities.*

MTNs created when the issuer simultaneously transacts in the derivative markets are called **structured notes**. It is estimated today that new-issue volume of structured notes is 20% to 30% of new-issuance volume. The most common derivative instrument used in creating structured notes is a swap—a derivative instrument that we discuss in Chapter 30.

Key Points That You Should Understand Before Proceeding

1. A unique characteristic of medium-term notes is that they are continuously offered to investors over a period of time by an agent of the issuer.
2. Medium-term notes are rated by the nationally recognized rating companies.
3. Investors can select issues from several maturity bands.
4. Unlike corporate bonds, medium-term notes are typically issued on a best efforts basis rather than underwritten by an investment banker.
5. A structured note is a medium-term note in which the issuer couples its offering with a position in a derivative instrument in order to create instruments with more interesting risk/return characteristics.

BANK LOANS

As an alternative to the issuance of securities, a corporation can raise funds by borrowing from a bank.[10] There are five sourcing alternatives for a corporation: (1) a domestic bank in the corporation's home country; (2) a subsidiary of a foreign bank that is established in the corporation's home country; (3) a foreign bank domiciled in a country where the corporation does business; (4) a subsidiary of a domestic bank that has been established in a country where the corporation does business; or (5) an offshore or Eurobank. Loans made by offshore banks are referred to as **Eurocurrency loans**.[11]

Syndicated Bank Loans

A **syndicated bank loan** is one in which a group (or syndicate) of banks provides funds to the borrower. The need for a group of banks arises because the amount sought by a

---

[10] Bank debt is widely used as the senior financing for a leveraged buyout, acquisition, or recapitalization. These are collectively referred to as *highly leveraged transactions* or HLTs.

[11] A loan can be denominated in a variety of currencies. Loans denominated in U.S. dollars are called *Eurodollar loans*. Similarly there are *Euroyen loans* and *Eurodeutschemark* loans.

borrower may be too large for any one bank to be exposed to the credit risk of that borrower. Therefore, the syndicated bank loan market is used by borrowers who seek to raise a large amount of funds in the loan market rather than through the issuance of securities.

These bank loans are called **senior bank loans** because they have a priority position over subordinated lenders (bondholders) with respect to repayment of interest and principal. The interest rate on a syndicated bank loan is a rate that **floats**, which means that the loan rate is based on some reference rate. The loan rate is periodically reset at the reference rate plus a spread. The reference rate is typically the London Interbank Offered Rate (LIBOR), although it could be the prime rate (that is, the rate that a bank charges its most creditworthy customers) or the rate on certificates of deposits. The term of the loan is fixed. A syndicated loan is typically structured so that it is amortized according to a predetermined schedule, and repayment of principal begins after a specified number of years (typically not longer than five or six years). Structures in which no repayment of the principal is made until the maturity date can be arranged. Such loan structures are referred to as **bullet loans**.

A syndicated loan is arranged by either a bank or a securities house. The arranger then lines up the syndicate. Each bank in the syndicate provides the funds for which it has committed. The banks in the syndicate have the right to sell their parts of the loan subsequently to other banks.

Syndicated loans are distributed by two methods: assignment or participation. Each method has its relative advantages and disadvantages, with the method of assignment the more desirable of the two.

The holder of a loan who is interested in selling a portion can do so by passing the interest in the loan by the *method of assignment*. In this procedure, the seller transfers all rights completely to the holder of the assignment, now called the *assignee*. The assignee is said to have *privity of contract* with the borrower. Because of the clear path between the borrower and assignee, assignment is the more desirable choice of transfer and ownership.

A *participation* involves a holder of a loan "participating out" a portion of the holding in that particular loan. The holder of the participation does not become a party to the loan agreement, and has a relationship not with the borrower but with the seller of the participation. Unlike an assignment, a participation does not confer privity of contract on the holder of the participation, although the holder of the participation has the right to vote on certain legal matters concerning amendments to the loan agreement. These matters include changes regarding maturity, interest rate, and issues concerning the loan collateral. Because syndicated loans can be sold in this manner, they have become marketable.

In response to the large amount of bank loans issued in the 1980s and their strong credit protection, some commercial banks and securities houses have shown a willingness to commit capital and resources to facilitate trading as broker-dealers. Also, these senior bank loans have been securitized through the same innovations discussed in Chapter 2 for the securitization of mortgage loans.[12] Further development of the senior bank loan market will no doubt eventually erode the once important distinction between a security and a loan: A security has long been seen as a marketable financial asset, while a loan has not been marketable. Interestingly, the trading of these loans is not limited to **performing loans**, which are loans whose borrowers are

---

[12] For a discussion of the trading and securitization of senior bank loans, see John H. Carlson and Frank J. Fabozzi (eds.), *The Trading and Securitization of Senior Bank Loans* (Chicago: Probus Publishing, 1992).

fulfilling contractual commitments. There is also a market in the trading of nonperforming loans—loans in which the borrowers have defaulted.

Lease Financing

The market for lease financing is a segment of the larger market for equipment financing. Any type of equipment that can be purchased with borrowed funds can also be leased. Our interest here is in the leasing of equipment that can be classified as a big-ticket item (that is, equipment costing more than $5 million). Included in this group are commercial aircraft, large ships, large quantities of production equipment, and energy facilities. A special type of leasing arrangement, known as a **leveraged lease**, is used in financing such equipment.

Leasing works as follows. The potential equipment user, called the **lessee**. first selects the equipment and the dealer or manufacturer from whom the equipment will be purchased. The lessee negotiates such aspects of the transaction as the purchase price, specifications, warranties, and delivery date. When the lessee accepts the terms of the deal, another party, such as a bank or finance company, buys the equipment from the dealer or manufacturer and leases it to the lessee. This party is called the **lessor**. The lease is so arranged that the lessor realizes the tax benefits associated with the ownership of the leased equipment.

Basically, leasing is a vehicle by which tax benefits can be transferred from the user of the equipment (the lessee), who may not have the capacity to take advantage of the tax benefits associated with equipment ownership (such as depreciation and any tax credits), to another entity who can utilize them (the lessor). In exchange for these tax benefits, a lessor provides lower-cost financing to the lessee than the lessee could get by purchasing the equipment with borrowed funds. Such leases are referred to as **tax-oriented leases**.

There are two possible ways for the lessor to finance the purchase of the equipment. One way is to provide all the financing from its own funds and therefore be at risk for 100% of the funds used to purchase the equipment. Such leasing arrangements are referred to as **single-investor or direct leases**. Essentially, such leases are two-party agreements (the lessee and the lessor). The second way is for the lessor to use only a portion of its own funds to purchase the equipment, and to borrow the balance from a bank or group of banks. This type of leasing arrangement is called a *leveraged lease*. There are three parties to a leveraged lease agreement: the lessee, the lessor, and the lender. The leveraged lease arrangement allows the lessor to realize all the tax benefits from owning the equipment and the tax benefits from borrowing funds—deductible interest payments—while putting up only a portion of its own funds to purchase the equipment. Because of this, leveraged leasing is commonly used in financing big-ticket items.

In a leveraged lease transaction, it is necessary for a party to arrange for the equity and the debt portions of the funding involved. The same party can arrange both. The equity portion is typically provided by one or more institutional investors. The debt portion is arranged with a bank. Since leveraged lease transactions are for large-ticket items, the bank debt is typically arranged as a syndicated bank loan.

The financing of aircraft is normally accomplished through leveraged lease financing. For example, between May and October 1991, Japanese banks arranged $1 billion in leveraged lease financing for airlines throughout the world.[13] One large Japanese bank, Mitsubishi Trust, arranged for a total of almost $250 million of equity

---

[13] *International Financial Review*, Issue 902 (November 2, 1991), p. 12.

and debt financing for British Airways to acquire four aircraft. Mitsubishi Trust also arranged for the equity financing in purchases by Quantas.[14]

Key Points That You Should Understand Before Proceeding

1. Bank loans are an alternative to the issuance of securities
2. A syndicated bank loan is one in which a group of banks provides funds to the borrower, with the reference rate on the loan typically the London Interbank Offered Rate.
3. Senior loans can be distributed by either assignment or participation.
4. Any type of equipment that can be purchased with borrowed funds can also be leased.
5. A tax-oriented lease effectively allows the lessee to obtain a financing at less cost than by bank borrowing.

SUMMARY

Corporate senior instruments include debt obligations and preferred stock. Holders of these obligations have priority over holders of a corporation's common stock in the case of bankruptcy. In this chapter we discuss four sectors of this market: the commercial paper market, the medium-term note market, and the bank loan market.

Investors typically do not perform their own analysis of the issuer's credit-worthiness. Instead, they rely on a system of credit rating developed by commercial ratings companies. The four companies in the United States that rate corporate debt in terms of the likelihood of default are (1) Moody's Investors Service, (2) Standard & Poor's Corporation, and (3) Fitch.

Commercial paper is a short-term unsecured promissory note issued in the open market that represents the obligation of the issuing entity. Generally, commercial paper maturity is less than 90 days. Financial and nonfinancial corporations issue commercial paper, with the majority issued by the former. Directly placed paper is sold by the issuing firm directly to investors without using an agent as an intermediary; for dealer-placed commercial paper, the issuer uses the services of an agent to sell its paper. Commercial paper markets have been developed in other countries. Eurocommercial paper is paper issued and placed outside the jurisdiction of the currency of denomination.

Medium-term notes are corporate debt obligations offered on a continuous basis. The maturities range from 9 months to 30 years and have provided a financing alternative with maturities between those of commercial paper and long-term bonds.

Bank loans represent an alternative to the issuance of securities. A syndicated bank loan is one in which a group of banks provides funds to the borrower. Senior bank loans have become marketable; they are now more actively traded and have been securitized.

Leasing is a form of bank borrowing. Basically leasing is a vehicle by which tax benefits can be transferred from the user of the equipment (the lessee), who may not have the capacity to utilize the tax benefits associated with equipment ownership, to another entity who can utilize them. A single-investor lease is a two-party agreement involving the lessee and the lessor. In a leveraged lease, the lessor uses only a portion of its own funds to purchase the equipment and borrows the balance from a bank or group of banks.

KEY TERMS

- Bullet loan, 390
- Captive finance companies, 384
- Commercial paper, 383
- Dealer-placed paper, 384
- Directly placed paper, 384
- Eurocommercial paper, 385
- Eurocurrency loans, 389
- Euro medium-term notes, 387
- Floating rate, 390
- Lessee, 391
- Lessor, 391
- Leveraged lease, 391

---

[14] Ibid., p. 11.

QUESTIONS

1. What are the different forms of credit risk?
2. What role do rating companies play in financial markets?
3. What is meant by a credit or quality spread?
4. a. Why is commercial paper an alternative to short-term bank borrowing for a corporation?
   b. What is the difference between directly placed paper and dealer-placed paper?
5. What does the yield spread between commercial paper and Treasury bills of the same maturity reflect?
6. a. What is Eurocommercial paper?
   b. How does it differ from U.S. commercial paper?
7. a. What is a medium-term note?
   b. What determines the yield that will be offered on a medium-term note?
   c. What is a Euro medium-term note?
8. What is a structured note?
9. a. What is a syndicated bank loan?
   b. What is the reference rate typically used for a syndicated bank loan?
   c. What is the difference between an amortized bank loan and a bullet bank loan?
10. Explain the two ways in which a bank can sell its position in a syndicated loan.
11. a. For a lease financing transaction, who is the lessee and the lessor?
    b. Who is entitled to the tax benefits, and what are those tax benefits?
    c. If a manufacturing corporation has no taxable income, is it likely to buy equipment or lease equipment? Why?
12. What is the difference between a single-investor lease and a leveraged lease?

Corporate Senior Instruments: II

Learning Objectives

After reading this chapter, you will understand

- the key provisions of a corporate bond issue.
- the risks associated with investing in corporate bonds.
- what a callable bond is.
- bonds with special features and why they are issued.
- the high-yield or junk bond sector of the corporate bond market.
- the purpose for which junk bond issuers use bond proceeds.
- the different type of bond structures used in the junk bond market.
- the Eurobond market and the different types of bond structures issued.
- the difference between preferred stock, corporate debt, and common stock.
- the difference between the various types of preferred stock: fixed-rate, adjustable-rate, and auction and remarketed preferred stock.
- the basic provisions in the Bankruptcy Reform Act of 1978.
- the difference between a liquidation and a reorganization.
- the principle of absolute priority in a bankruptcy.

In this chapter, we continue coverage of corporate senior instruments, focusing on corporate bonds and preferred stock. Preferred stock is classified as a senior instrument in that holders of these securities have priority over common stockholders in the case of bankruptcy. We conclude this chapter with a discussion of corporate bankruptcy.

CORPORATE BONDS

Corporate bonds are classified by the type of issuer. The four general classifications used by bond information services are: (1) utilities; (2) transportations; (3) industrials; and (4) banks and finance companies. Finer breakdowns are often made to create more homogeneous groupings. For example, utilities are subdivided into electric power companies, gas distribution companies, water companies, and communication companies. Transportations are further divided into airlines, railroads, and trucking companies. Industrials are the catchall class, and the most heterogeneous of the groupings with respect to investment characteristics. Industrials include all kinds of manufacturing, merchandising, and service companies. In recent years, industrials have raised the largest amount in the corporate bond market, followed by financial institutions and then utilities.[1] The largest investor group is life insurance companies, followed by pension funds, public and private. Historically, these institutional investors hold more than half of outstanding corporate bonds. The balance is held by households, foreign investors, depository institutions, non-life insurance companies, and mutual funds and securities brokers and dealers.

Basic Features of a Corporate Bond Issue

The essential features of a corporate bond are relatively simple. The corporate issuer promises to pay a specified percentage of par value (known as the coupon payments) on designated dates, and to repay par or principal value of the bond at maturity. Failure to pay either principal or interest when due constitutes legal default, and court proceedings can be instituted to enforce the contract. Bondholders, as creditors, have a prior legal claim over common and preferred stockholders as to both income and assets of the corporation for the principal and interest due them.

The promises of corporate bond issuers and the rights of investors who buy them are set forth in great detail in contracts called **bond indentures**. If bondholders were handed the complete indenture, they would have trouble understanding its language, and even greater difficulty in determining at a particular time whether or not the corporate issuer were keeping all its promises. These problems are solved for the most part by bringing in a corporate trustee as a third party to the contract. The indenture is made out to the corporate trustee as a representative of the interests of bondholders; that is, the trustee acts in a fiduciary capacity for investors who own the bond issue. A corporate trustee is a bond or trust company with a corporate trust department and officers who are experts in performing the functions of a trustee.

A bond's indenture clearly outlines three important aspects: its maturity, its security, and its provisions for retirement.

Maturity of Bonds.

Most corporate bonds are *term bonds*; that is, they run for a term of years, then become due and payable. Term bonds are often referred to as **bullet-maturity**, or, simply, **bullet bonds**. Any amount of the liability that has not been paid off prior to maturity must be paid off at that time. The bond's term may be long or short. Generally, obligations due less than ten years from the date of issue are called *notes*.[2]

Most corporate borrowings take the form of *bonds* due in 20 to 30 years. Term bonds may be retired by payment at final maturity or retired prior to maturity if provided for in the indenture. Some corporate bond issues are so arranged that specified principal amounts become due on specified dates prior to maturity. Such issues are called **serial bonds**. Equipment trust certificates (discussed later) are structured as serial bonds.

Security for Bonds.

Either real property (using a mortgage) or personal property may be pledged to offer security beyond that of the general credit standing of the issuer. A **mortgage bond**

---

[1] *Moody's Bond Survey*, selected, year-end issues.

[2] From our discussion of the various debt instruments in the previous chapter, it can be seen that the word *notes* is used to describe a variety of instruments—medium-term notes and Euronotes. The use of the term *notes* here is as a market convention distinguishing notes and bonds on the basis of the number of years to maturity at the time the security is issued.

grants the bondholders a lien against the pledged assets. A *lien* is a legal right to sell mortgaged property to satisfy unpaid obligations to bondholders. In practice, foreclosure and sale of mortgaged property are unusual. If a default occurs, there is usually a financial reorganization of the issuer when provision is made for settlement of the debt to bondholders. The mortgage lien is important, though, because it gives the mortgage bondholders a very strong bargaining position relative to other creditors in determining the terms of a reorganization.

Some companies do not own fixed assets or other real property, and so have nothing on which they can give a mortgage lien to secure bondholders. Instead, these firms own securities of other companies and, thus, are *holding companies*. The firms whose shares are owned are *subsidiaries*. To satisfy the desire of bondholders for security, the holding companies pledge stocks, notes, bonds, or whatever other kind of financial instruments they own. These assets are termed *collateral* (or personal property), and bonds secured by such assets are called **collateral trust bonds**.

Many years ago the railway companies developed a way of financing the purchase of cars and locomotives, called *rolling stock*, that enabled them to borrow at just about the lowest rates in the corporate bond market. Railway rolling stock has for a long time been regarded by investors as excellent security for debt. The equipment is sufficiently standardized that it can be used by one railway as well as another. And of course it can readily be moved from the tracks of one railroad to those of another. Therefore, there is generally a good market for lease or sale of cars and locomotives. The railroads have taken advantage of these characteristics of rolling stock by developing a legal arrangement for giving investors a legal claim on it that is different from, and generally superior to, a mortgage lien.

The legal arrangement in this situation is one that vests legal title to railway equipment in a trustee. When a railway company orders some cars and locomotives from a manufacturer, the manufacturer transfers legal title to the equipment to a trustee. The trustee, in turn, leases the equipment to the railroad, and at the same time sells **equipment trust certificates** to obtain the funds to pay the manufacturer. The trustee collects lease payments from the railroad and uses these receipts to pay interest and principal on the certificates. The principal is therefore paid off on specified dates, a provision that makes a certificate different from a term bond.

The general idea of the equipment trust arrangement has also been used by companies engaged in providing other kinds of transportation. For example, trucking companies finance the purchase of huge fleets of trucks in the same manner; airlines use this kind of financing to purchase transport planes; and international oil companies use this financing method to buy huge tankers.

A **debenture bond** is not secured by a specific pledge of property, but that does not mean that this type of bond has no claim on property of issuers or on their earnings. Debenture bondholders have the claim of general creditors on all assets of the issuer not pledged specifically to secure other debt. Also, holders of debentures even have a claim on pledged assets to the extent that these assets have value greater than necessary to satisfy secured creditors. A **subordinated debenture bond** is an issue that ranks after secured debt, after debenture bonds, and often after some general creditors in its claim on assets and earnings.

The type of corporate security issued determines the cost to the issuer. For a given corporation, mortgage bonds will cost less than debenture bonds; debenture bonds will cost less than subordinated debenture bonds.

A **guaranteed bond** is an obligation guaranteed by another entity. The safety of a guaranteed bond depends upon the financial capability of the guarantor to satisfy the terms of the guarantee, as well as the financial capability of the issuer. The terms of the guarantee may call for the guarantor to guarantee the payment of interest and/or repayment of the principal.

It is important to recognize that a superior legal status will not prevent bond-holders from suffering financial loss when the issuer's ability to generate cash flow adequate to pay its obligations is seriously eroded.

Provisions for Paying Off Bonds.

Most corporate issues have a call provision allowing the issuer an option to buy back all or part of the issue prior to maturity. Some issues carry a sinking fund provision, which specifies that the issuer must retire a predetermined amount of the issue periodically.[3]

An important question in negotiating the terms of a new bond issue is whether or not the issuer shall have the right to redeem the *entire amount* of bonds outstanding on a date before maturity. Issuers generally want this right because they recognize that at some time in the future the general level of interest rates may fall sufficiently below the issue's coupon rate, so that redeeming the issue and replacing it with another issue carrying a lower coupon rate would be attractive. For reasons discussed later in this chapter, this right represents a disadvantage to the bondholder.

The usual practice is a provision that denies the issuer the right to redeem bonds during the first 5 to 10 years following the date of issue with proceeds received from the sale of lower-cost debt obligations that have an equal or superior rank to the debt to be redeemed. This type of redemption is called **refunding**. While most long-term issues have these refunding restrictions, they may be immediately callable, in whole or in part, if the source of funds is something other than money raised with debt of a lower interest. Under such a provision, acceptable sources include cash flow from operations, proceeds from a common stock sale, or funds from the sale of property.

Investors often confuse refunding protection with call protection. Call protection is much more comprehensive because it prohibits the early redemption of the bonds *for any reason*. Refunding restrictions, by contrast, provide protection only against the one type of redemption mentioned above.

As a rule, corporate bonds are callable at a premium above par. Generally, the amount of the premium declines as the bond approaches maturity and often reaches zero after a number of years following issuance. The initial amount of the premium may be as much as one year's coupon interest, or as little as the coupon interest for one-half of a year.

If the issuer has the choice to retire all or part of an issue prior to maturity, the buyer of the bond takes the chance that the issue will be called away at a disadvantageous time. This risk is referred to as **call risk**, or **timing risk**. There are two disadvantages of call provisions from the investor's perspective. First, as explained in Chapter 10, a decline in interest rates in the economy will increase the price of a debt instrument, although in the case of a callable bond, the price increase is somewhat limited. If and when interest rates decline far enough below the coupon rate to make call an immediate or prospective danger, the market value of the callable bond will not rise as much as that of noncallable issues that are similar in all other respects. Second, when a bond issue is called as a result of a decline in interest rates, the investor must reinvest

---

[3] For a more detailed explanation of corporate call provisions, see Richard S. Wilson and Frank J. Fabozzi, *Corporate Bonds: Structures & Analysis* (New Hope, PA: Frank J. Fabozzi Associates, 1996).

the proceeds received at a lower interest rate (unless the investor chooses debt of greater risk).

Corporate bond indentures may require the issuer to retire a specified portion of an issue each year. This **sinking fund provision** for the repayment of the debt may be designed to liquidate all of a bond issue by the maturity date, or it may call for the liquidation of only a part of the total by the end of the term. If only a part of the outstanding bond is paid before retirement, the remainder is called a *balloon maturity*. The purpose of the sinking fund provision is to reduce credit risk. Generally, the issuer may satisfy the sinking fund requirement by either (1) making a cash payment of the face amount of the bonds to be retired to the corporate trustee, who then calls the bonds for redemption using a lottery, or (2) delivering to the trustee bonds with a total face value equal to the amount that must be retired from bonds purchased in the open market.

Bonds with Special Features

Prior to the 1970s, securities issued in the U.S. bond market had a simple structure. They had a fixed coupon rate and a fixed maturity date. The only option available to the issuer was the right to call all or part of the issue prior to the stated maturity date. The historically high interest rates that prevailed in the United States in the late 1970s and early 1980s, and the volatile interest rates since the 1970s, prompted introduction of new structures or the increased use of existing structures with special features that made issues more attractive to both borrowers and investors. Various bond structures are reviewed below.

Convertible and Exchangeable Bonds.

The conversion provision in a corporate bond issue grants the bondholder the right to convert the bond to a predetermined number of shares of common stock of the issuer. A **convertible bond** is therefore a corporate bond with a call option to buy the common stock of the issuer. An **exchangeable bond** grants the bondholder the right to exchange the bonds for the common stock of a firm *other* than the issuer of the bond. For example, Ford Motor Credit exchangeable bonds are exchangeable for the common stock of its parent company, Ford Motor Company.

Issues of Debt with Warrants.

Warrants may be attached as part of a bond issue. A **warrant** grants the holder the right to purchase a designated security at a specified price from the issuer of the bond. A warrant is simply a call option. It may permit the holder to purchase the common stock of the issuer of the debt or the common stock of a firm other than the issuer's. Or, the warrant may grant the holder the right to purchase a debt obligation of the issuer. Generally, warrants can be detached from the bond and sold separately. Typically, in exercising the warrant, an investor may choose either to pay cash or to offer the debt, to be valued at par, that was part of the offering. A major difference between warrants and either convertible or exchangeable bonds is that an investor exercising the option provided by the latter must turn the bond in to the issuer.

Putable Bonds.

A **putable bond** grants the bondholder the right to sell the issue back to the issuer at par value on designated dates. The advantage to the bondholder is that if interest rates rise after the issue date, thereby reducing the market value of the bond, the bondholder can sell the bond back to the issuer for par.

Zero-Coupon Bonds.

Zero-coupon bonds are, just as the name implies, bonds without coupon payments or a stated interest rate. We discussed zero-coupon bonds in Chapter 16, where we covered stripped Treasury securities. In the Treasury market, the U.S. government does not issue zero-coupon bonds. Dealers strip issues and create these bonds from the cash flow of a coupon Treasury bond. Corporations, however, can and do issue zero-coupon bonds. The first such public offering was in the spring of 1981. The attractiveness of a zero-coupon bond from the investor's perspective is that the investor who holds the bond to the maturity date will realize a predetermined return on the bond, unlike a coupon bond where the actual return realized, if the bond is held to maturity, depends on the rate at which coupon payments can be reinvested.

Floating-Rate Securities.

The coupon interest on **floating-rate securities** is reset periodically to follow changes in the level of some predetermined benchmark rate. For example, the coupon rate may be reset every six months to a rate equal to a spread of 100 basis points over the six-month Treasury bill rate.

Floating-rate securities are attractive to some institutional investors because they allow them to buy an asset with an income stream that closely matches the floating nature of the income of some of their liabilities. Certain floating-rate instruments are viewed by some investors as a passive substitute for short-term investments, particularly that part of a short-term portfolio that is more or less consistently maintained at certain minimum levels. Thus, floating-rate securities save on the costs of constantly rolling over short-term securities as they reach maturity.

Why do corporations issue floating-rate securities? Closer matching of their income flows from variable-rate assets with floating-rate liabilities is of major importance, especially with lenders such as banks, thrifts, and finance companies. Issuers can fix or lock in a spread between the cost of borrowed funds and the rate at which those funds are lent out. Another reason might be to avoid uncertainties associated with what could be an unreceptive market at some future date. The issuer can tap a new source for intermediate- to long-term funds at short-term rates, thereby making fewer trips to the marketplace and avoiding related issuance costs.

Also, in the presence of inflation, a floating-rate security (rolled over, if needed) may have a lower interest cost than a fixed-rate, long-term security. The reason is that, with inflation, the long rate may incorporate a substantial premium against the uncertainty of future inflation and interest rates. Finally, as we note in our Chapter 29 discussion of the innovative world of swaps, an issuer may find that it can issue a floating-rate security and convert its payments into a fixed-rate stream through an interest rate swap agreement. An issuer will elect this approach if the cost of issuing a floating-rate security and then using an interest rate swap will result in a lower cost than simply issuing a fixed-rate security.

There may be other features in a floating-rate issue. For example, many floating-rate issues include a put option. Some issues are exchangeable either automatically at a certain date (often five years after issuance) or at the option of the issuer into fixed-rate securities. A few issues are convertible into the common stock of the issuer. Some floating-rate issues have a ceiling or maximum interest rate for the coupon rate; some have a floor or minimum interest rate for the coupon rate.

Corporate Bond Credit Ratings

As we stated in the previous chapter, market participants typically do not do their own credit analysis of a debt obligation. Instead, they rely primarily on nationally recog-

Table 21-1   Summary of Corporate Bond Rating Systems and Symbols

MOODY'S	S&P	FITCH	BRIEF DEFINITION
Investment grade—High creditworthiness			
Aaa	AAA	AAA	Gilt edge, prime, maximum safety
Aa1	AA+	AA+	
Aa2	AA	AA	Very high grade, high quality
Aa3	AA–	AA–	
A1	A+	A+	
A2	A	A	Upper medium grade
A3	A–	A–	
Baa1	BBB+	BBB+	
Baa2	BBB	BBB	Lower medium grade
Baa3	BBB–	BBB–	
Distinctly speculative—Low creditworthiness			
Ba1	BB+	BB+	
Ba2	BB	BB	Low grade, speculative
Ba3	BB–	BB–	
B1	B+	B+	
B2	B	B	Highly speculative
B3	B–	B–	
Predominantly speculative—Substantial risk in default			
	CCC+		
Caa	CCC	CCC	Substantial risk, in poor standing
	CCC–		
Ca	CC	CC	May be in default, extremely speculative
C	C	C	Even more speculative than those above
	C1		C1 = Income bonds—no interest is being paid
		DDD	Default
		DD	
	D	D	

SOURCE: Richard S. Wilson and Frank J. Fabozzi, *Corporate Bonds: Structures & Analysis* (New Hope, PA: Frank J. Fabozzi Associates, 1996).

nized rating companies that perform credit analysis and issue their conclusions in the form of ratings. The three nationally recognized rating companies are (1) Moody's Investors Service, (2) Standard & Poor's Corporation, and (3) Fitch. The rating systems use similar symbols, as shown in Table 21-1.

In all systems the term *high grade* means low credit risk, or conversely, high probability of future payments. The highest-grade bonds are designated by Moody's by the symbol Aaa, and by the other three rating systems by the symbol AAA. The next highest grade is denoted by the symbol Aa (Moody's) or AA (the other three rating systems); for the third grade all rating systems use A. The next three grades are Baa or BBB, Ba or BB, and B, respectively. There are also C grades. Moody's uses 1, 2, or 3 to provide a narrower credit quality breakdown within each class, and the other three rating companies use plus and minus signs for the same purpose.

Bonds rated triple A (AAA or Aaa) are said to be *prime*; double A (AA or Aa) are of high quality; single A issues are called *upper medium grade*, and triple B are *medium grade*. Lower-rated bonds are said to have speculative elements or be distinctly speculative.

Bond issues that are assigned a rating in the top four categories are referred to as **investment-grade bonds**. Issues that carry a rating below the top four categories are referred to as *noninvestment-grade bonds*, or more popularly as **high-yield bonds** or **junk bonds**. Thus, the corporate bond market can be divided into two sectors: the investment-grade and noninvestment-grade markets.

Ratings of bonds change over time. Issuers are upgraded when their likelihood of default as assessed by the rating company improves and downgraded when their likelihood of default as assessed by the rating company deteriorates. The rating companies publish the issues that they are reviewing for possible rating change. These lists are called *credit watch lists*.

Each rating agency periodically publishes a table showing the upgrade and downgrade history of the issues that it rated. Such a table is called a *rating transition matrix*. The table shows the percentage of issues of each rating at the beginning of a time period that were downgraded, upgraded, or unchanged by the end of some time period. This information helps investors assess the prospects that an issue will be downgraded or upgraded over some time period.

Occasionally, the ability of an issuer to make interest and principal payments is seriously and unexpectedly changed by (1) a natural or industrial accident or some regulatory change, or (2) a takeover or corporate restructuring. These risks are referred to generically as *event risk*. Two examples of the first type of event risk are (a) a change in the accounting treatment of loan losses for commercial banks, and (b) the cancellation of nuclear plants by public utilities.

An example of the second type of event risk is the takeover in 1988 of RJR Nabisco for $25 billion through a financing technique known as a **leveraged buyout (LBO)**. The new company took on a substantial amount of debt to finance the acquisition of the firm.[4] In the case of RJR Nabisco, the debt and equity after the leveraged buyout were $29.9 and $1.2 billion, respectively. Because of the need to service a larger amount of debt, the company's quality rating was reduced. RJR Nabisco's quality rating as assigned by Moody's dropped from A1 to B3. As a result, investors demanded a higher credit spread because of this new capital structure with a greater proportion of debt. The yield spread to a benchmark Treasury rate increased from about 100 basis points to 350 basis points.

High-Yield Sector

As we have noted, high-yield bonds are issues with a credit rating below triple B. Bond issues in this sector of the market may have been rated investment grade at the time of issuance and have been downgraded subsequently to noninvestment grade, or they may have been rated noninvestment grade at the time of issuance, called *original-issue, high-yield bonds*.

Bonds that have been downgraded fall into two groups: (1) issues that have been downgraded because the issuer voluntarily significantly increased their debt as a result of a leveraged buyout or a recapitalization and (2) issues that have been downgraded

---

[4] For a discussion of event risk associated with takeovers, see N. R. Vijayarghavan and Randy Snook, "Takeover Event Risk and Corporate Bond Portfolio Management," in Frank J. Fabozzi (ed.), *Advances and Innovations in Bond and Mortgage Markets* (Chicago: Probus Publishing, 1989).

for other reasons. The latter issues are commonly referred to as **fallen angels**. As of year-end 1992, 14% of the high-yield market was made up of issues downgraded because of leveraged buyouts and recapitalizations, 16% were fallen angels, and 70% were original-issue high-yield bonds.[5]

The modern high-yield market began in the late 1970s.[6] The high-yield market grew from approximately $24 billion at year-end 1977 to approximately $199 billion by year-end 1992, reaching $215 billion in 1990.[7] Due to the market's dramatic successes (such as the $1.5 billion leveraged buyout of Metromedia by John Kluge in 1984 and Kolberg Kravis Roberts & Company's 1986 LBO of Beatrice, a company with many well-known brand names), the media began to report stories helping to bring to a peak investors' appetites. The market's early growth was dominated by a single investment bank, Drexel Burnham Lambert, and it was not until the mid-1980s that this firm began to experience serious competition from other investment banks, namely, Merrill Lynch, Morgan Stanley, and First Boston.[8] As of year-end 1992, the high-yield sector represented about 23% of the total corporate bond market.

As of year-end 1992, the largest holders of high-yield bonds were mutual funds and independent money managers who owned 43% of outstanding issues, followed by insurance companies (25%) and pension funds (15%).[9]

The Role of High-Yield Bonds in Corporate Finance.

The introduction of original-issue, high-yield bonds has been a very important financial innovation with wide impact throughout the financial system. There was a common view that high default risk bonds would not be attractive to the investing public, at least at interest rates that would be acceptable to the borrower. The view rested on the skewed nature of the outcomes offered by the instrument: The maximum return that an investor may obtain is capped by the coupon and face value, but the loss could be as large as the principal invested. It was the merit of Drexel Burnham Lambert, and particularly of Michael Milken of that firm, to disprove that view as evidenced by the explosive growth of that market.

Before development of the high-yield market, U.S. corporations that could not issue securities in the public debt market would borrow from commercial banks or finance companies on a short-term to intermediate-term basis or would be shut off from credit. With the advent of the high-yield bond structure, financing shifted from commercial banks to the public market. One study estimated that about two-thirds of the $90 to $100 billion of the high-yield bonds issued represent simply a replacement of commercial bank borrowing. The same study concluded that high-yield bonds are "no more a threat to the stability of the financial system than that bank debt itself was."[10]

In essence, the high-yield bond market shifts the risk from commercial banks to the investing public in general. There are several advantages to such a shift. First,

---

[5] Joseph C. Bencivenga, "The High-Yield Corporate Bond Market," Chapter 15 in Frank J. Fabozzi (ed.), *The Handbook of Fixed Income Securities* (Burr Ridge, Il: Irwin Professional Publishing, 1995), Exhibit 15-8.
[6] The evolution of the high-yield market since the early 1900s is described in J. Thomas Madden and Joseph Balestrino, "Evolution of the High-Yield Market;" Chapter 2 in Frank J. Fabozzi (ed.), *The New High-Yield Debt Market* (New York: Harper & Row, 1991).
[7] Bencivenga, "The High-Yield Corporate Bond Market," p. 307.
[8] Drexel Burnham Lambert underwrote more than 45% of new high-yield issues.
[9] Bencivenga, "The High-Yield Corporate Bond Market," Exhibit 15-9, p. 314.
[10] November 1986 speech by John Paulus, chief economist at Morgan Stanley, at a conference sponsored by Citizens for a Sound Economy.

when commercial banks lend to high credit risk borrowers, that risk is accepted indirectly by all U.S. citizens, who may not wish to accept the risk. The reason is that commercial bank liabilities are backed by the Federal Deposit Insurance Company. If high credit risk corporations default on their loans, causing an FDIC bailout, all taxpayers eventually may have to pay. The liabilities of other investors (excluding thrifts that have invested in high-yield bonds) are not backed by the U.S. government (and, therefore, not by U.S. citizens). The risks of this investing are accepted by the specific investor group willing to accept them.

The second advantage is that commercial bank loans are typically short-term, floating-rate loans, which make debt financing less attractive to corporations. High-yield bond issues give corporations the opportunity to issue long-term, fixed-rate debt. Third, commercial banks set interest rates based on their credit analysis. When high-yield bonds are traded in a public market, the investing public establishes the interest rate. Finally, the high-yield market opens the possibility of funding for some firms that previously had no means to it.

Corporate bond issuers use the proceeds from a bond sale for a number of purposes. These include working capital, expansion of facilities, refinancing of outstanding debt, and financing takeovers (mergers and acquisitions). In the case of noninvestment-grade bonds, it is the use of the proceeds to finance takeovers (particularly hostile takeovers) that has aroused some public concern over the excessive use of debt by U.S. corporations.[11] According to one source, while just over half the proceeds raised in 1987 were used for either a leveraged buyout, to repay LBO debt, or for recapitalization, only 6% were used for that purpose in 1992.[12] Instead, about 80% of the proceeds raised in 1992 were applied toward debt retirement.

High-Yield Bond Structures.

In the early years of the high-yield market, all the issues had a conventional structure; that is, the issues paid a fixed coupon rate and were term bonds. Today, however, there are more complex bond structures in the junk bond area, particularly for bonds issued for LBO financing and recapitalizations producing higher debt.

In an LBO or a recapitalization, the heavy interest payment burden that the corporation assumes placed severe cash flow constraints on the firm. To reduce this burden, firms involved in LBOs and recapitalizations have issued bonds with deferred coupon structures that permit the issuer to avoid using cash to make interest payments for a period of three to seven years. There are three types of deferred coupon structures: (1) deferred-interest bonds, (2) step-up bonds, and (3) payment-in-kind bonds.

Deferred-interest bonds are the most common type of **deferred coupon structure**. These bonds sell at a deep discount and do not pay interest for an initial period, typically from three to seven years. (Because no interest is paid for the initial period, these bonds are sometimes referred to as zero-coupon bonds.) **Step-up bonds** do pay coupon interest, but the coupon rate is low for an initial period and then increases ("steps up") to a higher coupon rate. Finally, **payment-in-kind (PIK) bonds** give the issuer an option to pay cash at a coupon payment date or give the bondholder a similar bond (i.e., a bond with the same coupon rate and a par value equal to the amount of the coupon payment that would have been paid). The period during which the issuer can make this choice varies from 5 to 10 years.

---

[11] A hostile takeover is one in which the targeted firm's management resists the merger or acquisition.

[12] Indepth Data Inc.

Secondary Market

There are really two secondary corporate bond markets: the exchange market and the over-the-counter (OTC) market. Almost all trading volume takes place in the OTC market, which is the market used by institutional investors and professional money managers.

Here is how corporate bond trading by institutional investors works today in the over-the-counter market. An institutional investor may want to buy a specific corporate bond with certain characteristics, or an institutional investor may have a specific corporate bond in its portfolio. The portfolio manager would then contact brokers at several different brokerage firms to inquire about prices (to buy or to sell, whatever the case may be). The broker will obtain prices from its trading desk, and these prices will depend on the inventory of that corporate bond that the trading desk has. Thus, the institutional investor must do a search for the corporate bonds that he or she is interested in buying or selling.

The over-the-counter market relies on a commitment of capital from bond dealers trading desks to make a market in corporate bonds by carrying inventory of corporate bonds. In general, capital allocation by dealer desks has been declining. For example, consider the high-yield corporate bond sector. In 1988, there was $200 billion outstanding and dealer capital as a percentage of that was 1%. Ten years later, the high-yield corporate bond sector was $572 billion, and dealer capital was at 0.6%. This suggests that while the size of the high-yield corporate bond market tripled, capital to service that sector by the dealer community has nearly halved.

The concern in the corporate bond market is on the transparency of prices and trades. The Nasdaq's **Fixed Income Pricing System (FIPS)** is an electronic trading system for disseminating price quote and reporting trades for high-yield corporate bonds. FIPS began operations in April 1994. However, FIPS is not really a reporting system per se. It is reporting to the Securities and Exchange Commission and Nasdaq, but those prices don't go anywhere. The self-regulatory organizations have abrogated the control of the bond market to the dealer community, and the dealers do not want those prices out and that is the reason why they are not out. This is why high-yield bond prices are not transparent to the investment community.

In recent years several electronic trading systems have been developed via the Internet. There are online bond trading web sites sponsored by Wall Street firms, as well as independent bond trading web sites. Electronic trading could carve a niche for itself by enabling investors to transact more efficiently. The major advantage to a broker-dealer is that the dealer can show its bond inventory to its customers and representatives efficiently. Instead of a customer calling a trading desk to find prices for a bond that meets certain criteria, the customer can do the query himself or herself. Thus, the broker-dealer can do more trades without having to add people to trading desks. Customers get better pricing as they can see more inventory and can choose the best prices. It is much more efficient to check a computer monitor for different quotes on a particular bond than to call several broker dealers.

The liquidity of corporate bonds varies from issue to issue. The bonds of large firms, usually sold to the public in large amounts, can have a high degree of liquidity. However, the issues of smaller, less well-known firms may be quite illiquid.

Eurobond Market

The **Eurobond** sector of the global bond market includes bonds with several distinguishing features: (1) they are underwritten by an international syndicate; (2) at issuance they are offered simultaneously to investors in a number of countries; (3)

they are issued outside the jurisdiction of any single country; and (4) they are in unregistered form. Although Eurobonds are typically listed on a national stock exchange (the most common are the Luxembourg, London, or Zurich exchanges), the bulk of all trading is in the over-the-counter market. Firms list these bonds purely to circumvent restrictions imposed on some institutional investors that are prohibited from purchasing securities not listed on an exchange. Some of the stronger issuers privately place their debt with international institutional investors.

Borrowers in the Eurobond market include nonfinancial corporations, banks, sovereign governments, entities whose debt is guaranteed by a sovereign government, provinces, municipalities, cities, and supranational entities such as the World Bank. The major issuer group is nonfinancial corporations, followed by banks. Traditionally, the main currency used in Eurobond offerings has been the U.S. dollar, although the share of Eurobond offerings denominated in U.S. dollars has been declining.

The Eurobond market has been characterized by new and innovative bond structures to accommodate particular needs of issuers and investors throughout the world. Some issues, of course, are the "plain vanilla," fixed-rate coupon bonds, referred to as **Euro straights**. Because they are issued on an unsecured basis, they are usually the debt of high-quality entities.

Coupon payments on Eurobonds are made annually, rather than semiannually. There are also zero-coupon bond issues, deferred-coupon issues, and step-up issues. Some of the innovative issues in this market are **dual-currency issues**: They pay coupon interest in one currency but the principal in a different currency. For example, the coupon interest payments can be made in Swiss francs, while the principal may be paid in U.S. dollars.

Some Eurobonds are convertible or exchangeable, and bonds with attached warrants represent a large part of the market. Most warrants on Eurobonds are detachable from the bond with which they originally came to market. That is, the bondholder may detach the warrant from the bond and sell it separately.

The warrants on Eurobonds are varied: some are equity warrants, others are debt warrants, and still others may be currency warrants. An equity warrant permits the warrant owner to buy the common stock of the issuer at a specified price. A debt warrant entitles the warrant owner to buy additional bonds from the issuer at the same price and yield as the host bond. The debt warrant owner will benefit if interest rates decline because the warrant allows the owner to purchase a bond with a higher coupon than the same issuer would offer. A currency warrant permits the warrant owner to exchange one currency for another at a set price (that is, a fixed exchange rate). This feature protects the bondholder against a depreciation of the foreign currency in which the bond's cash flows are denominated. Finally, we also note that some warrants are gold warrants and allow the warrant holder to purchase gold from the bond issuer at a prespecified price.

Eurobonds make use of a wide variety of floating-rate structures. Almost all the floating-rate notes are denominated in U.S. dollars, and non-U.S. banks are the major issuers of these bonds. The coupon rate on a floating-rate note is some stated margin over the London Interbank Offered Rate (LIBOR), the bid on LIBOR (referred to as LIBID), or the arithmetic average of LIBOR and LIBID (referred to as LIMEAN). Many floating-rate issues have either a minimum rate (or floor) that the coupon rate cannot fall below or a maximum rate (or cap) that the coupon rate cannot exceed. An issue that has both a floor and a cap is said to be *collared*. Some floating-rate issues grant the borrower the right to convert the floating coupon rate into a fixed coupon rate at some time. Some issues, referred to as *drop-lock bonds*, automatically convert the floating coupon rate into a fixed coupon rate under certain circumstances.

Key Points that You Should Understand Before Proceeding

1. The bond indenture sets forth the obligations of the issuer and the rights of the bondholders.
2. Either real property or personal property may be pledged to offer security beyond that of the general credit standing of the issuer.
3. Bonds typically carry provisions that allow for the principal to be repaid prior to the stated maturity date, with the most common provision being the right of the issuer to call the issue. This is an advantage to the issuer and a disadvantage to the bondholder.
4. There is a wide variety of bond structures with special features that make issues more attractive to both borrowers and investors.
5. In addition to credit risk, corporate bond investors are exposed to event risk.
6. High-yield bonds are issues whose quality rating is designated as noninvestment grade, and there are several unique bond structures in this sector of the market.
7. The Eurobond market has been characterized by new and innovative bond structures to accommodate particular needs of issuers and investors throughout the world.

PREFERRED STOCK

Preferred stock is a class of stock, not a debt instrument, but it shares characteristics of both common stock and debt. Like the holder of common stock, the preferred stockholder is entitled to dividends. Unlike those on common stock, however, preferred dividends are a specified percentage of par or face value.[13] The percentage is called the dividend rate; it need not be fixed, but may float over the life of the issue.

Failure to make preferred stock dividend payments cannot force the issuer into bankruptcy. Should the issuer not make the preferred stock dividend payment, usually paid quarterly, one of two things can happen, depending on the terms of the issue. First, the dividend payment can accrue until it is fully paid. Preferred stock with this feature is called **cumulative preferred stock**. If a dividend payment is missed and the securityholder must forgo the payment, the preferred stock is said to be **noncumulative preferred stock**. Second, the failure to make dividend payments may result in the imposition or certain restructions on management. For example, if dividend payments are in arrears, preferred stockholders might be granted voting rights.

Preferred stock differs from debt in a major way: The current tax code for corporations treats payments made to preferred stockholders as a distribution of earnings and not as tax-deductible expenses, which is how the tax code views interest payments. While this difference in tax status raises the after-tax cost of funds for a corporation issuing preferred stock rather than borrowing, another factor in the tax code reduces the cost differential. A provision in the tax code exempts 70% of qualified dividends from federal income taxation, if the recipient is a qualified corporation.

For example, if Corporation A owns the preferred stock of Corporation B, then only $30 of each $100 that A receives in dividends from B will be taxed at A's marginal tax rate. The purpose of this provision is to mitigate the effect of the double taxation of corporate earnings. There are two implications of this tax treatment of preferred

---

[13] Almost all preferred stock limits the securityholder to the specified amount. Historically, there have been issues entitling the preferred stockholder to participate in earnings distribution beyond the specified amount (based on some formula). Preferred stock with this feature is referred to as participating preferred stock.

stock dividends. First, the major buyers of preferred stock are corporations seeking tax-advantaged investments. Second, the cost of preferred stock issuance is lower than it would be in the absence of the tax provision, because the tax benefits are passed through to the issuer by the willingness of buyers to accept a lower dividend rate.

Preferred stock, particularly cumulative preferred stock, has some important similarities with debt: (1) The issuer promises fixed cash payments to preferred stock-holders, and (2) preferred stockholders have priority over common stockholders with respect to dividend payments and the distribution of assets in the case of bankruptcy. (The position of noncumulative preferred stock is considerably weaker.) It is because of this second feature that preferred stock is called a senior corporate instrument—it is senior to common stock. Note, however, that preferred stock is classified as equity on corporate balance sheets.

Almost all preferred stock has a sinking fund provision, and some preferred stock is convertible into common stock. Preferred stock may be issued without a maturity date. This is called **perpetual preferred stock**.

The preferred stock is a relatively small part of the financial system. Historically, utilities have been the major issuers of preferred stock, accounting for more than half of each year's issuance. Since 1985, major issuers have become financially oriented companies—finance companies, banks, thrifts, and insurance companies.

The same four commercial companies that assign ratings to corporate bond issues also rate preferred stock issues.

There are three types of preferred stock: (1) fixed-rate preferred stock, (2) adjustable-rate preferred stock, and (3) auction and remarketed preferred stock. Before 1982, all publicly issued preferred stock was fixed-rate preferred stock. In May 1982, the first adjustable-rate preferred stock issue was sold in the public market.[14]

Adjustable-Rate Preferred Stock

The dividend rate on an **adjustable-rate preferred stock (ARPS)** is fixed quarterly and based on a predetermined spread from the highest of three points on the Treasury yield curve.[15] The predetermined spread is called the *dividend reset spread*. The motivation for linking the dividend rate to the highest of the three points on the Treasury yield curve is to provide the investor with protection against unfavorable shifts in the yield curve.

Most ARPS is perpetual, with a floor and ceiling imposed on the dividend rate of most issues. Because most ARPS is not putable, it can trade below par if, after issuance, the spread demanded by the market to reflect the issuer's credit risk is greater than the dividend reset spread.

The major issuers of ARPS have been bank holding companies. There are two reasons bank holding companies have become major issuers of ARPS. First, floating-rate obligations provide a better liability match, given the floating-rate nature of bank assets. Second, bank holding companies are seeking to strengthen their capital positions, and regulators permit bank holding companies to count perpetual preferred

---

[14] Private placement of ARPS occurred as early as 1978—illustrating how an innovation is first developed in this market. For historical background on the development of the ARPS market, see Richard S. Wilson, "Adjustable Rate Preferred Stocks," Chapter 3 in Frank J. Fabozzi (ed.), *Floating Rate Instruments: Characteristics, Valuation and Portfolio Strategies* (Chicago: Probus Publishing, 1986).

[15] The Treasury yield curve is described in Chapter 12. The three points on the yield curve (called the benchmark rate) to which the dividend reset spread is either added or subtracted are the highest of: (1) the three-month Treasury bill rate; (2) the two-year constant maturity rate; or (3) a 10-year or 30-year constant maturity rate. The Treasury constant maturity rate is reported in the Federal Reserve Report H.15(519). It is based on the closing market bid yields on actively traded Treasury securities.

stock as part of their primary capital. Issuing ARPS provides not only a better asset/liability match, but also permits bank holding companies to improve primary capital without having to issue common stock.

Auction and Remarketed Preferred Stock

The popularity of ARPS declined when instruments began to trade below their par value—because the dividend reset rate is determined at the time of issuance, not by market forces. In 1984, a new type of preferred stock, **auction preferred stock (APS)**, was designed to overcome this problem, particularly for corporate treasurers who sought tax-advantaged short-term instruments to invest excess funds.[16] The dividend rate on APS is set periodically, as with ARPS, but it is established through an auction process.[17] Participants in the auction consist of current holders and potential buyers. The dividend rate that participants are willing to accept reflects current market conditions.

In the case of **remarketed preferred stock (RP)**, the dividend rate is determined periodically by a remarketing agent who resets the dividend rate so that any preferred stock can be tendered at par and be resold (remarketed) at the original offering price. An investor has the choice of dividend resets every seven days or every 49 days.

Since 1985, APS and RP have become the dominant type of preferred stock issued.

Key Points that You Should Understand Before Proceeding

1. Preferred stock is a class of stock in which the dividend rate is typically a fixed percentage of par or face value.
2. Payments made to preferred stockholders are treated as a distribution of earnings and therefore are not tax deductible to the issuing corporation.
3. Because the tax code exempts 70% of qualified dividends from federal income taxation if the recipient is a qualified corporation, the major buyers of preferred stock are corporations seeking tax-advantaged investments; these investors are willing to accept a lower dividend rate.
4. Preferred stock has some important similarities with debt.
5. There are various types of preferred stock: fixed-rate, adjustable-rate, auction, and remarketed preferred stock.

BANKRUPTCY AND CREDITOR RIGHTS

In this chapter and the previous one, we refer to *senior* corporate securities. By senior, we mean that the holder of the security has priority over the equity owners in the case of bankruptcy of a corporation. And, as we explain in this chapter, there are creditors who have priority over other creditors. In this section, we provide an overview of the bankruptcy process and then look at what actually happens to creditors in bankruptcies.

The law governing bankruptcy in the United States is the **Bankruptcy Reform Act of 1978**.[18] One purpose of the act is to set forth the rules for a corporation to be

---

[16] Each investment bank developed its own trademark name for APS. The instrument developed by Shearson Lehman/American Express was called Money Market Preferred (MMP). Salomon Brothers called it Dutch Auction Rate Transferable Securities (DARTS).

[17] The auction process is described in Richard S. Wilson, "Money Market Preferred Stock," Chapter 4 in Frank J. Fabozzi (ed.), *Floating Rate Instruments*, pp. 85–88.

[18] For a discussion of the Bankruptcy Reform Act of 1978 and a nontechnical description of its principal features, see Jane Tripp Howe, "Investing in Chapter 11 and Other Distressed Companies," Chapter 20 in Frank J. Fabozzi (ed.), *The Handbook of Fixed Income Securities*.

liquidated or reorganized. *Liquidation* means that all the assets of the corporation will be distributed to holders of claims on the corporation, and no corporate entity will survive. In a *reorganization*, a new corporate entity will result. Some holders of claims on the bankrupt corporation will receive cash in exchange for their claims; others may receive new securities in the corporation that results from the reorganization; and still others may receive a combination of both cash and new securities in the resulting corporation.

Another purpose of the bankruptcy act is to give a corporation time to decide whether to reorganize or to liquidate, and then provide the necessary time to formulate a plan to accomplish either a reorganization or liquidation. This is achieved because a bankruptcy filing allows the corporation protection from creditors who seek to collect their claims.[19] A company that files for protection under the bankruptcy act generally becomes a **debtor-in-possession**, and continues to operate its business under the supervision of the court.

The bankruptcy act has 15 chapters, each covering a particular type of bankruptcy. Of particular interest to us are two of the chapters, **Chapter 7** and **Chapter 11**. Chapter 7 deals with the liquidation of a company; Chapter 11 covers reorganization.

When a company is liquidated, creditors receive distributions based on the **absolute priority rule** to the extent assets are available. The absolute priority rule is the principle that senior creditors are paid in full before junior creditors are paid anything. For secured creditors and unsecured creditors, the absolute priority rule guarantees their seniority to equity holders.

In liquidations, the absolute priority rule generally holds, but in reorganizations under Chapter 11, it is often violated. Studies of actual reorganizations under Chapter 11 have found that the violation of absolute priority is the rule rather than the exception.[20]

There are several reasons that have been suggested as to why, in a reorganization, the distribution made to claimholders will diverge from that required by the absolute priority principle.[21] One reason commonly cited has to do with the negotiation process that takes place among the various classes of claimholders in a reorganization. In a reorganization, a committee representing the various claimholders is appointed with the purpose of formulating a plan of reorganization. To be accepted, a plan of reorganization must be approved by at least two-thirds of the amount and a majority of the number of claims voting, and at least two-thirds of the outstanding shares of each class of interests. Consequently, a long-lasting bargaining process is expected. The longer the negotiation process among the parties, the more likely the company is to be operated in a manner that is not in the best interest of the creditors and, as a result, the smaller the amount to be distributed to all parties. Since all impaired classes including equityholders generally must approve the plan of reorganization, creditors often convince equityholders to accept the plan by offering to distribute some value to them.

Consequently, while investors in the debt of a corporation may feel that they have priority over the equity owners and priority over other classes of debtors, the

---

[19] The petition for bankruptcy can be filed either by the company itself, in which case it is called a *voluntary bankruptcy*, or be filed by its creditors, in which case it is called an *involuntary bankruptcy*.
[20] See: Julian R. Franks and Walter N. Torous, "An Empirical Investigation of U.S. Firms in Reorganization," *Journal of Finance*, (July 1989), pp. 747–769; Lawrence A. Weiss, "Bankruptcy Resolution: Direct Costs and Violation of Priority of Claims," *Journal of Financial Economics* (1990), pp. 285–314; and Frank J. Fabozzi, Jane Tripp Howe, Takashi Makabe, and Toshihide Sudo, "Recent Evidence on the Distribution Patterns in Chapter 11 Reorganizations," *Journal of Fixed Income* (Spring 1993), pp. 6–23.
[21] For a discussion of these reasons, see Fabozzi, et. al., "Recent Evidence on the Distribution Patterns in Chapter 11 Reorganizations," op. cit.

actual outcome of a bankruptcy may be far different from what the terms of the debt agreement state.

> ### Key Points that You Should Understand Before Proceeding
>
> 1. The Bankruptcy Reform Act of 1978 is the law governing bankruptcy in the United States.
> 2. Chapter 7 of the act deals with the liquidation of a company, and Chapter 11 deals with the reorganization of a company.
> 3. When a company is liquidated, creditors receive distributions based on the absolute priority rule to the extent assets are available.
> 4. In liquidations, the absolute priority rule generally holds, but in reorganizations under Chapter 11, it is often violated.

SUMMARY

Corporate bonds are debt obligating a corporation to pay periodic interest with full repayment at maturity. The promises of the corporate bond issuer and the rights of the investors are set forth in the bond indenture. Provisions to be specified include call and sinking fund provisions.

Security for bonds may be real or personal property. Debenture bonds are not secured by a specific pledge of property. Subordinated debenture bonds are issues that rank after secured debt, after debenture bonds, and often after some general creditors in their claim on assets and earnings.

Special corporate bond features include convertible and exchangeable bonds, units of debt with warrants, putable bonds, zero-coupon bonds, and floating-rate securities. Junk bonds or high-yield bonds are issues with quality ratings below triple B. Recent years have seen the introduction of several complex bond structures in the junk bond area, particularly bonds issued for LBO financing and recapitalizations producing higher levels of debt to equity. These include deferred-coupon bonds (deferred-interest bonds, step-up bonds, and payment-in-kind bonds) and extendable reset bonds.

Many innovative bond structures have been introduced in the Eurobond market such as dual-currency issues and various types of convertible bonds and bonds with warrants. A warrant permits its owner to enter into another financial transaction with the issuer if the owner will benefit as a result of exercising. The floating-rate sector of the Eurobond market is dominated by U.S. dollar-denominated issues.

Preferred stock as a class of stock has characteristics of both common stock and debt. Because a special provision in the tax code allows taxation of only a portion of dividends when they are received by a corporation, the major buyers of preferred stock are corporations. There are three types of preferred stock besides the traditional fixed-rate preferred stock: adjustable-rate preferred stock, auction preferred stock, and remarketed preferred stock.

The Bankruptcy Reform Act of 1978 governs the bankruptcy process in the United States. Chapter 7 of the bankruptcy act deals with the liquidation of a company. Chapter 11 deals with the reorganization of a company. Creditors receive distributions based on the absolute priority rule to the extent assets are available. This means that senior creditors are paid in full before junior creditors are paid anything. Generally, this rule holds in the case of liquidations. In contrast, the absolute priority rule is typically violated in a reorganization.

KEY TERMS

- **Absolute priority rule, 409**
- **Adjustable-rate preferred stock (ARPS), 407**
- **Auction preferred stock (APS), 408**
- **Bankruptcy Reform Act of 1978, 408**
- **Bond indenture, 395**
- **Bullet bond (or bullet-maturity bond), 395**
- **Call risk (or timing risk), 397**
- **Chapter 7, 409**
- **Chapter 11, 409**

- **Collateral trust bond, 396**
- **Convertible bond, 398**
- **Cumulative preferred stock, 406**
- **Debenture bond, 396**
- **Debtor-in-possession, 409**
- **Deferred coupon structure, 403**
- **Deferred-interest bond, 403**
- **Dual-currency issue, 405**
- **Equipment trust certificate, 396**

QUESTIONS

1. a. What are the disadvantages of investing in a callable bond?
   b. What is the advantage to the issuer of issuing a callable bond?
   c. What is the difference between a noncallable bond and a nonrefundable bond?
2. a. What is a sinking fund requirement in a bond issue?
   b. "A sinking fund provision in a bond issue benefits the investor." Do you agree with this statement?
3. What is a:
   a. Serial bond?
   b. Mortgage bond?
   c. Equipment trust certificate?
   d. Collateral bond?
4. What is the difference between a convertible bond and an exchangeable bond?
5. Do you agree or disagree with this statement: "Zero-coupon corporate bonds are created in the same way as in the Treasury market—by stripping coupon bonds"?
6. a. What is event risk?
   b. Give two examples of event risk.
7. What is meant by a rating transition matrix?
8. What is the difference between a fallen angel and an original-issue, high-yield bond?
9. Indicate why you agree or disagree with the following statement: "Today, the proceeds from most original-issue, high-yield bonds are used for leveraged buyouts and recapitalizations."
10. a. What is a Eurobond?
    b. How often is the coupon payment on a Eurobond made?
    c. Name the two currencies most often used to denominate Eurobonds.
11. What is a dual-currency bond?
12. a. Explain what an institutional investor will do to purchase or sell a corporate bond.
    b. What has happened to the commitment of capital of dealer firms to the high-yield corporate bond market in recent years?
13. a. Why are corporate treasurers the main buyers of preferred stock?
    b. What was the reason for the popularity of auction and remarketed preferred stock?
14. a. What is the difference between a liquidation and a reorganization?
    b. What is the difference between a Chapter 7 and Chapter 11 bankruptcy filing?
    c. What is meant by a debtor-in-possession?
15. a. What is meant by the principle of absolute priority?
    b. Comment on this statement: "An investor who purchases the mortgage bonds of a corporation knows that, should the corporation become bankrupt, mortgage bondholders will be paid in full before the common stockholders receive any proceeds."

The Markets for Bank Obligations

Learning Objectives

After reading this chapter, you will understand

- a categorization of banks that is useful for understanding the supply of bank obligations.
- what a negotiable certificate of deposit or CD is, and the different types of certificates of deposit.
- what a Euro CD is and how it differs from a Yankee CD.
- what determines a CD's yield or rate of interest.
- what federal funds are, and how banks use them to meet Federal Reserve requirements.
- what the effective fed funds rate is.
- the size of the fed funds market and the role brokers play in it.
- what a bankers acceptance or BA is, and how it is created.
- what the BA's credit risk is, and what an eligible BA is.

Commercial banks are special types of corporations. We describe their activities and how they raise funds to finance these activities in Chapter 4. Banks will raise equity in the same manner that we described in Chapter 14. Larger banks will also raise funds using the various debt markets described in the previous two chapters. In this chapter, we describe three other debt obligations: large-denomination certificates of deposit, federal funds, and **bankers acceptances**. All these instruments trade in what is collectively known as the *money market*, the market for short-term debt instruments. Typically, money market instruments have a maturity of one year or less. While our discussion focuses on commercial banks, other depository institutions may also issue the same types of obligations.

TYPES OF BANKS OPERATING IN THE UNITED STATES

Banks in the United States can be classified into four groups. First are the **money center banks**—banks that raise most of their funds from the domestic and international money markets and rely less on depositors for funds. The second group is **regional banks**, which rely primarily on deposits for funding and make less use of the money markets to obtain funds. **Japanese banks** are the third group of banks. Japanese banks are classified as one of the following: city banks, local banks, long-term credit banks, trust banks, and mutual banks.[1] City banks are the most powerful depository institutions in Japan, with 13 city banks holding approximately 20% of all deposits in Japan.

---

[1] For a discussion of these different institutions, see Chapters 4 and 5.

The fourth group of banks are **Yankee banks**. These are foreign banks with U.S. branches. Included in this group are non-Japanese branches of foreign banks, such as Credit Lyonnais and Deutsche Bank.

LARGE-DENOMINATION NEGOTIABLE CDS

A **certificate of deposit (CD)** is a financial asset issued by a bank or thrift that indicates a specified sum of money has been deposited at the issuing depository institution. CDs are issued by banks and thrifts to raise funds for financing their business activities. A CD bears a maturity date and a specified interest rate, and can be issued in any denomination. CDs issued by banks are insured by the Federal Deposit Insurance Corporation but only for amounts up to $100,000. There is no limit on the maximum maturity, but by Federal Reserve regulations CDs cannot have a maturity of less than seven days.

A CD may be *nonnegotiable* or **negotiable**. In the former case, the initial depositor must wait until the maturity date of the CD to obtain the funds. If the depositor chooses to withdraw funds prior to the maturity date, an early withdrawal penalty is imposed. In contrast, a negotiable CD allows the initial depositor (or any subsequent owner of the CD) to sell the CD in the open market prior to the maturity date.

Negotiable CDs were introduced in the early sixties. At that time the interest rate banks could pay on various types of deposits was subject to ceilings administered by the Federal Reserve (except for demand deposits defined as deposits of less than one month that by law could pay no interest). For complex historical reasons, these ceiling rates started very low, rose with maturity, and remained below market rates up to some fairly long maturity. Before introduction of the negotiable CD, those with money to invest for, say, one month had no incentive to deposit it with a bank, for they would get a below-market rate unless they were prepared to tie up their capital for a much longer period of time. When negotiable CDs came along, they could buy a three-month or longer negotiable CD yielding a market interest rate, and recoup all or more than the investment (depending on market conditions) by selling it in the market.

This innovation was critical in helping banks to increase the amount of funds raised in the money market, a position that had languished in the earlier postwar period. It also motivated competition among banks, ushering in a new era. There are now two types of negotiable CDs. The first is the large-denomination CD, usually issued in denominations of $1 million or more. These are the negotiable CDs whose history we describe above.

In 1982, Merrill Lynch entered the retail CD business by opening up a primary and secondary market in small-denomination (less than $100,000) CDs. While it made the CDs of its numerous banking and savings institution clients available to retail customers, Merrill Lynch also began to give these customers the negotiability enjoyed by institutional investors by standing ready to buy back the CDs prior to maturity. Today, several retail-oriented brokerage firms offer CDs that are salable in a secondary market. These are the second type of negotiable CD. Our focus in this chapter, though, is on the large-denomination negotiable CD, and we refer to them simply as CDs throughout the chapter.

The largest group of CD investors is investment companies, and money market funds make up the bulk of them. Far behind are banks and bank trust departments, followed by municipal entities and corporations. One indication of the size of the market available to these investors is the Federal Reserve Board's data series for "Time Deposits in amounts of $100,000 or more." In the mid-1980s, the value of these deposits was near $400 billion. Although recently down to a level of $170 billion, these deposits/securities still represent a meaningful part of the money market and the obligations of the banking system of the United States.

CD Issuers

CDs can be classified into four types, according to the issuing institution. First are CDs issued by domestic banks. Second are CDs that are denominated in U.S. dollars but are issued outside the United States. These CDs are called **Eurodollar CDs.** A third type of CD is the **Yankee CD**, which is a CD denominated in U.S. dollars and issued by a foreign bank with a branch in the United States. Finally, **thrift CDs** are those issued by savings and loan associations and savings banks.

Money center banks and large regional banks are the primary issuers of domestic CDs. Most CDs are issued with a maturity of less than one year. Those issued with a maturity greater than one year are called **term CDs**.

Unlike Treasury bills, commercial paper, and bankers acceptances, yields on domestic CDs are quoted on an interest-bearing basis. CDs with a maturity of one year or less pay interest at maturity. For purposes of calculating interest, a year is treated as having 360 days. Term CDs issued in the United States normally pay interest semiannually, again with a year taken as 360 days.

A **floating-rate CD (FRCD)** is one whose interest rate changes periodically in accordance with a predetermined formula that indicates the spread (or margin) above some index at which the rate will reset periodically. There are FRCDs that reset the coupon daily, weekly, monthly, quarterly, or semiannually. Typically FRCDs have maturities from 18 months to 5 years.

Eurodollar CDs are U.S. dollar–denominated CDs issued primarily in London by U.S., European, Canadian, and Japanese banks. The yields on Eurodollar CDs play an important role in the world financial markets because they are viewed globally as the cost of bank borrowing since they are effectively the rates at which major international banks offer to pay each other to borrow money by issuing a Eurodollar (CD) with given maturities. The interest rate paid is called the **London interbank offered rate (LIBOR)**.

Yields on CDs

The yields posted on CDs vary depending on three factors: (1) the credit rating of the issuing bank; (2) the maturity of the CD; and (3) the supply and demand for CDs. With respect to the third factor, banks and thrifts issue CDs as part of their liability management strategy, so the supply of CDs will be driven by the demand for bank loans and the cost of alternative sources of capital to fund these loans. Moreover, bank loan demand will depend on the cost of alternative funding sources such as commercial paper. When loan demand is weak, CD rates decline. When demand is strong, the rates rise. The effect of maturity depends on the shape of the yield curve, a topic we covered in Chapter 12.

Credit risk has become more of an issue. At one time domestic CDs issued by money center banks traded on a *no-name basis*. Recent financial crises in the banking industry, however, have caused investors to take a closer look at issuing banks. **Prime CDs** (those issued by high-rated domestic banks) trade at a lower yield than **nonprime CDs** (those issued by lower-rated domestic banks). Because of the unfamiliarity investors have with foreign banks, generally Yankee CDs trade at a higher yield than domestic CDs.

As just noted, the rate or yield offered on Eurodollar CDs is LIBOR. This yield is higher than the yield on domestic CDs. There are three reasons for this. First, there are reserve requirements imposed by the Federal Reserve on CDs issued by U.S. banks in the United States that do not apply to issuers of Eurodollar CDs. The reserve requirement effectively raises the cost of funds to the issuing bank because it cannot invest all the proceeds it receives from the issuance of a CD, and the amount that must be kept as reserves will not earn a return for the bank. Because it will earn less on funds raised by selling domestic CDs, the domestic issuing bank will pay less on its domestic CD than a Eurodollar CD. Second, the bank issuing the CD must pay an insurance premium to the FDIC, which again raises the cost of funds. Finally, Eurodollar CDs are dollar obligations that are payable by an entity operating under a foreign jurisdiction, exposing the holders to a risk (referred to as sovereign risk) that their claim may not be enforced by the foreign jurisdiction. As a result, a portion of the spread between the yield offered on Eurodollar CDs and domestic CDs reflects what can be termed a sovereign risk premium. This premium varies with the degree of confidence in the international banking system.

The maturities for the Eurodollar CD range from overnight to five years. So, references to "three-month LIBOR" indicate the interest rate that major international banks are offering to pay to other such banks on a CD that matures in three months. During the 1990s, LIBOR has increasingly become the reference rate of choice for borrowing arrangements—loans and floating-rate securities. When we discuss derivatives instruments used to control interest rate risk, we will see that the reference rate for many of them (particularly interest rate swaps) is LIBOR.

CD yields are higher than yields on Treasury securities of the same maturity. The spread is due mainly to the credit risk that a CD investor is exposed to and the fact that CDs offer less liquidity. The spread due to credit risk will vary with both economic conditions and confidence in the banking system, increasing when there is a "flight to quality" (which means investors shift their funds in significant amounts to debt of high quality or little risk), or when there is a crisis in the banking system.

At one time, there were more than 30 dealers who made markets in CDs. The presence of that many dealers provided good liquidity to the market. Today, fewer dealers are interested in making markets in CDs, and the market can be characterized as an illiquid one.

Key Points That You Should Understand Before Proceeding

1. A negotiable CD allows the initial depositor (or any subsequent owner of the CD) to sell the CD in the open market prior to the maturity date.
2. CDs can be classified into four types, based on the issuing entity: domestic CD, Eurodollar CD, Yankee CD, and thrift CD.
3. The yield offered on a CD depends on the credit rating of the issuing bank, the maturity of the CD, and the supply and demand for CDs.
4. CD yields are higher than yields on Treasury securities of the same maturity.
5. The important role played by the Eurodollar CD and the rate paid, LIBOR.

FEDERAL FUNDS

The rate determined in the federal funds market is the major factor that influences the rates paid on all the other money market instruments described in this chapter. As we explained in Chapter 4, depository institutions (commercial banks and thrifts) are required to maintain reserves. The reserves are deposits at their district Federal Reserve Bank, which are called *federal funds*. The level of the reserves that a bank must maintain is based on its average daily deposits over the previous 14 days. Of all depository institutions, commercial banks are by far the largest holders of federal funds.

No interest is earned on federal funds. Consequently, a depository institution that maintains federal funds in excess of the amount required incurs an opportunity cost—the loss of interest income that could be earned on the excess reserves. At the same time, there are depository institutions whose federal funds are less than the amount required. Typically, smaller banks have excess reserves, while money center banks find themselves short of reserves and must make up the shortfall. Banks maintain federal funds desks whose managers are responsible for the bank's federal funds position.

Most transactions involving fed funds last for only one night; that is, a bank with insufficient reserves that borrows excess reserves from another financial institution will typically do so for the period of one full day. Because these loans last for such a short time, fed funds are often referred to as *overnight money*.

One way that banks with less than the required reserves can bring reserves to the required level is to enter into a repurchase agreement (or *repo*, as described in Chapter 16) with a nonbank customer. The repo, which consists of the sale of a security and an agreement by the bank to repurchase it later, will provide funds for a short period of time, after which the bank buys back the security, as previously agreed. An alternative to the repo is for the bank to borrow federal funds from a bank that has excess reserves. The market in which federal funds are bought (borrowed) by banks that need these funds and sold (lent) by banks that have excess federal funds is called the federal funds market. The equilibrium interest rate, which is determined by the supply and demand for federal funds, is the federal funds rate.

Federal Funds Rate

The federal funds rate and the repo rate are tied together because both are a means for a bank to borrow. The federal funds rate is higher because the lending of federal funds is done on an unsecured basis; this differs from the repo, where the lender has a security as collateral. The spread between the two rates varies depending on market conditions; typically the spread is around 25 basis points.

The rate most often cited for the fed funds market is known as the **effective fed funds rate**. The *Federal Reserve Bulletin* defines "the daily effective rate" as "a weighted average of rates on trades through N.Y. brokers." This weighting process, which takes the size of transactions into account, can be illustrated in an example. Suppose only two transactions took place on September 1, one for $50 million at 3.375% and another for $150 million at 3.625%. The simple arithmetic average of this day's rates would be $(3.375\% + 3.625\%)/2$, or 3.5%. By contrast, the transactions-weighted average for that day is $(50/200)(3.375\%) + (150/200)(3.625\%)$, or 3.5625%. The weighted average exceeds the arithmetic average because the larger transaction occurred at the higher interest rate.

As we explained in Chapter 6, the fed funds rate is frequently a significant operating target of the Federal Reserve Board's monetary policy. Through its open market operations that lower or raise the level of excess reserves in the banking system, the Fed will often change the fed funds rate as part of its effort to change the rate of activity in the country's economy. For this reason, the fed funds rate often shows a high level of volatility over short periods of time. Although this rate does generally tend to move in the direction of other money market rates, the fed funds rate often is the first of these rates to change, and frequently it changes more substantially than the other money market rates.

Market for Federal Funds

Although the term of most federal funds transactions is overnight, there are longer-term transactions that range from one week to six months. Trading typically takes place directly between the buyer and seller—usually between a large bank and one of its correspondent banks. Some federal funds transactions require the use of a broker. The broker stays in constant touch with likely buyers and sellers of funds and arranges deals between them for a commission. Brokers provide another service to this market in (normally) unsecured loans because they often can give lenders credit analyses of borrowers if the lenders have not done business with them previously.[2]

Key Points That You Should Understand Before Proceeding

1. The rate determined in the federal funds market is the major factor that influences the rate paid on all other private money market instruments.
2. Commercial banks are by far the largest holders of federal funds, with most transactions involving fed funds lasting for only one night.
3. Borrowing in the federal funds market is an alternative to borrowing in the repo market.
4. The federal funds rate is higher than the repo rate because the lending of federal funds is done on an unsecured basis.
5. The effective fed funds rate is the rate most often cited for the fed funds market.

BANKERS ACCEPTANCES

Simply put, a bankers acceptance is a vehicle created to facilitate commercial trade transactions. The instrument is called a bankers acceptance because a bank accepts the ultimate responsibility to repay a loan to its holder. The use of bankers acceptances to finance a commercial transaction is referred to as **acceptance financing**.

The transactions in which bankers acceptances are created include (1) the importing of goods into the United States; (2) the exporting of goods from the United States to foreign entities; (3) the storing and shipping of goods between two foreign countries where neither the importer nor the exporter is a U.S. firm;[3] and (4) the storing and shipping of goods between two entities in the United States.

Bankers acceptances are sold on a discounted basis just as Treasury bills and commercial paper. (See Chapter 16 for a discussion of discount securities.) The major investors in bankers acceptances are money market mutual funds and municipal entities.

Illustration of the Creation of a Bankers Acceptance

The best way to explain the creation of a bankers acceptance is by an illustration.

Several entities are involved in our transaction:

➤ Car Imports Corporation of America (Car Imports), a firm in New Jersey that sells automobiles
➤ Germany Fast Autos Inc. (GFA), a manufacturer of automobiles in Germany
➤ First Hoboken Bank (Hoboken Bank), a commercial bank in Hoboken, New Jersey
➤ West Berlin National Bank (Berlin Bank), a bank in Germany
➤ High-Caliber Money Market Fund, a mutual fund in the United States that invests in money market instruments.

Car Imports and GFA are considering a commercial transaction. Car Imports wants to import 15 cars manufactured by GFA. GFA is concerned with the ability of Car Imports to make payment on the 15 cars when they are received.

Acceptance financing is suggested as a means for facilitating the transaction. Car Imports offers $300,000 for the 15 cars. The terms of the sale stipulate payment to be made to GFA 60 days after it ships the 15 cars to Car Imports. GFA determines whether it is willing to accept the $300,000. In considering the offering price, GFA must calcu-

---

[2] Marvin Goodfriend, "Federal Funds," in *Instruments of the Money Market*, Federal Reserve Bank of Richmond, 1993.
[3] Bankers acceptances created from these transactions are called third-country acceptances.

late the present value of the $300,000, because it will not be receiving payment until 60 days after-shipment. Suppose that GFA agrees to these terms.

Car Imports arranges with its bank, Hoboken Bank, to issue a letter of credit. The letter of credit indicates that Hoboken Bank will make good on the payment of $300,000 that Car Imports must make to GFA 60 days after shipment. The letter of credit, or time draft, will be sent by Hoboken Bank to GFA's bank, Berlin Bank. Upon receipt of the letter of credit, Berlin Bank will notify GFA, which will then ship the 15 cars. After the cars are shipped, GFA presents the shipping documents to Berlin Bank and receives the present value of $300,000. GFA is now out of the picture.

Berlin Bank presents the time draft and the shipping documents to Hoboken Bank. The latter will then stamp "accepted" on the time draft. By doing so, Hoboken Bank has created a bankers acceptance. This means that Hoboken Bank agrees to pay the holder of the bankers acceptance $300,000 at the maturity date. Car Imports will receive the shipping documents so that it can procure the 15 cars once it signs a note or some other type of financing arrangement with Hoboken Bank.

At this point, the holder of the bankers acceptance is the Berlin Bank. It has two choices. It can continue to hold the bankers acceptance as an investment in its loan portfolio, or it can request that Hoboken Bank make a payment of the present value of $300,000. Let's assume that Berlin Bank requests payment of the present value of $300,000.

Now the holder of the bankers acceptance is Hoboken Bank. It has two choices: retain the bankers acceptance as an investment as part of its loan portfolio, or sell it to an investor. Suppose that Hoboken Bank chooses the latter, and that High-Caliber Money Market Fund is seeking a high-quality investment with the same maturity as that of the bankers acceptance. Hoboken Bank sells the bankers acceptance to the money market fund at the present value of $300,000. Rather than sell the instrument directly to an investor, Hoboken Bank could sell it to a dealer, who would then resell it to an investor such as a money market fund. In either case, at the maturity date, the money market fund presents the bankers acceptance to Hoboken Bank, receiving $300,000, which the bank in turn recovers from Car Imports.

Accepting Banks

All four groups of banks that we describe earlier in this chapter create bankers acceptances (that is, are **accepting banks**). They have their own sales forces to sell bankers acceptances rather than using the services of a dealer. The larger regional banks maintain their own sales forces to sell the bankers acceptances they create but will use dealers to distribute those they cannot sell.

Eligible Bankers Acceptance.

An accepting bank that has decided to retain a bankers acceptance in its portfolio may be able to use it as collateral for a loan at the discount window of the Federal Reserve. The reason we say "may" is that, to be used as collateral, bankers acceptances must meet certain eligibility requirements established by the Federal Reserve. One requirement for eligibility is maturity, which with a few exceptions cannot exceed six months. While the other requirements for eligibility are too detailed to review here, the basic principle is simple.[4] The bankers acceptance should be financing a self-liquidating commercial transaction.

---

[4] The eligibility requirements are described in Jean M. Hahr and William C. Melton, "Bankers' Acceptances," *Quarterly Review*, Federal Reserve Bank of New York, Summer 1981.

Eligibility is also important because the Federal Reserve imposes a reserve requirement on funds raised via bankers acceptances that are ineligible. Bankers acceptances sold by an accepting bank are potential liabilities of the bank, but no reserve requirements are imposed for eligible bankers acceptances. Consequently, most bankers acceptances satisfy the various eligibility criteria. Finally, the Federal Reserve also imposes a limit on the amount of eligible bankers acceptances that may be issued by a bank.[5]

Rates Banks Charge on Acceptances.

To calculate the rate to be charged the customer for issuing a bankers acceptance, the bank determines the rate for which it can sell its bankers acceptance in the open market. To this rate it adds a commission.

Dealers

We mentioned that banks may sell their bankers acceptances directly to investors, or may sell all or part to dealers. When the bankers acceptance market was growing in the early 1980s, there were over 25 dealers. By 1989, the decline in the amount of bankers acceptances issued drove many one-time major dealers such as Salomon Brothers out of the business. Today, the major dealer is Merrill Lynch. Lehman Brothers is another dealer in bankers acceptances. The other key dealers are commercial banks such as Bankers Trust and Morgan Guaranty.

Credit Risk

Investing in bankers acceptances exposes the investor to credit risk. This is the risk that neither the borrower nor the accepting bank will be able to pay the principal due at the maturity date. The market interest rates that acceptances offer investors reflect this risk because BAs have higher yields than risk-free Treasury bills. As detailed in Chapter 10, a yield may also include a premium for relative illiquidity. The BA yield has such a premium because its secondary market is far less developed than that of the T-bill. Hence, the spread between BA rates and T-bill rates represents a combined reward to investors for bearing the higher risk and relative illiquidity of the acceptance. That spread is not constant over time. The change in the spread reveals shifting investor valuation of the risk and illiquidity differences between the assets.

Key Points That You Should Understand Before Proceeding

1. A bankers acceptance is a vehicle created to facilitate commercial trade transactions wherein a bank accepts the ultimate responsibility to repay a loan to its holder.
2. Banks creating banker acceptances are money center banks, regional banks, Japanese banks, and Yankee banks.
3. Eligible bankers acceptances held in a bank's portfolio may be used as collateral for a loan at the discount window of the Federal Reserve.
4. A bank may sell its bankers acceptances directly to investors, or may sell all or part to dealers.
5. The investor in a bankers acceptance is exposed to credit risk.

---

[5] It may not exceed 150% of a bank's capital and surplus.

SUMMARY

Commercial banks raise funds in the same equity and debt markets that we describe in earlier chapters of the book. In addition, they can issue special debt obligations: large-denomination CDs, federal funds, and bankers acceptances.

Certificates of deposit are issued by banks and thrifts to raise funds for financing their business activities. Unlike other bank deposits, these are negotiable in the secondary market. CDs can be classified into four types: domestic CDs, Eurodollar CDs, Yankee CDs, and thrift CDs. Unlike Treasury bills, commercial paper, and bankers acceptances, yields on domestic CDs are quoted on an interest-bearing basis. A floating-rate CD is one whose coupon interest rate changes periodically in accordance with a predetermined formula. The rate paid on Eurodollar CDs has become an important rate because it is viewed as the global cost of borrowing. The rate or yield paid on Eurodollar CDs is the London interbank offered rate (LIBOR).

The federal funds market is the market where depository institutions borrow (buy) and sell (lend) excess reserves held in the form of deposits in a Federal Reserve bank. The federal funds rate, which is the rate at which all money market interest rates are anchored, is determined in this market. The federal funds rate is higher than the repo rate because borrowing done in the federal funds market is unsecured borrowing. The fed funds rate is often a target of the Fed's monetary policy, so it can exhibit a considerable amount of volatility or change in level over time.

A bankers acceptance is a vehicle created to facilitate commercial trade transactions, particularly international transactions. The name, bankers acceptance, arises because a bank accepts the responsibility to repay a loan to the holder of the vehicle created in a commercial transaction in case the debtor fails to perform. Bankers acceptances are sold on a discounted basis as are Treasury bills and commercial paper.

KEY TERM

- Acceptance financing, 417
- Accepting bank, 418
- Bankers acceptance (BA), 412
- Certificate of deposit (CD), 413
- Effective fed funds rate, 416
- Eurodollar certificate of deposit, 414
- Floating-rate certificate of deposit (FRCD), 414
- Japanese banks, 412
- London interbank offered rate (LIBOR), 414
- Money center bank, 412
- Negotiable certificate of deposit, 413
- Nonprime CD, 414
- Prime CD, 414
- Regional bank, 412
- Term certificate of deposit, 414
- Thrift certificate of deposit, 414
- Yankee bank, 413
- Yankee certificate of deposit, 414

QUESTIONS

1. Explain the difference between a domestic U.S. bank and a Yankee bank.
2. Explain what a negotiable certificate of deposit is.
3. What are the four types of negotiable CDs?
4. a. What is the chief reason that the yield on a six-month CD exceeds that on a six-month Treasury bill?
   b. Explain why a Eurodollar CD should offer a higher yield than a domestic CD issued by the same bank for the same time to maturity.
5. a. What is the London interbank offered rate?
   b. Why has this rate become so important in financial markets?
6. Explain how federal funds are related to the reserve requirements that the Federal Reserve places on commercial banks.
7. How does a repurchase agreement that a bank might enter into with a securities dealer regarding a U.S. Treasury bill substitute for the borrowing of federal funds from another bank?

8. Why are fed funds called overnight money?
9. Explain whether or not the rate on an overnight repurchase agreement can be higher than the rate on overnight federal funds.
10. What is the chief reason that the fed funds rate is an unusually volatile short-term interest rate?
11. What are the four transactions whose financing can lead to the creation of bankers acceptances?
12. Why is a bank that creates a BA called an accepting bank?
13. Why is the eligibility of a bankers acceptance important?
14. How does a bank determine the rate it will charge its customer for issuing a bankers acceptance?

C h a p t e r   2 3

The Mortgage Market

Learning Objectives

After reading this chapter, you will understand

- what a mortgage is.
- the difference between a residential mortgage loan and a commercial mortgage loan.
- who the major originators of residential mortgages are.
- the mortgage origination process.
- the borrower and property characteristics considered by a lender in evaluating the credit risk of an applicant for a mortgage loan.
- the risks associated with the origination process for residential mortgage loans.
- what the servicing of a residential mortgage loan involves.
- the fixed-rate, level-payment, fully amortized mortgage instrument (or traditional mortgage), and its cash flow characteristics.
- what a prepayment is.
- what a prepayment penalty mortgage is.
- deficiencies of the traditional mortgage: mismatch and tilt problems.
- alternative mortgage instruments, their cash flow characteristics, and how they correct for the deficiencies of the traditional mortgage instrument.
- risks associated with investing in mortgages.
- the significance of prepayment risk.
- the features of a commercial mortgage loan and provisions for protecting the lender against prepayment risk.
- the measures used to assess the credit risk of a commercial mortgage loan.

The **mortgage market** is a collection of markets, which includes a primary (or origination) market and a secondary market where mortgages trade. We look in this chapter at the market participants (mortgage originators and investors) and the risks they face. We also review the various types of mortgage instruments. We discuss the development of the current secondary mortgage market in the next chapter, when we explain the securitization of mortgage loans. We postpone the discussion because development of the secondary market is tied to development of the market for instruments backed by mortgage loans (that is, mortgage-backed securities).

WHAT IS A MORTGAGE?

By definition, a **mortgage** is a pledge of property to secure payment of a debt. Typically, property refers to real estate, which is often in the form of a house; the debt is the loan given to the buyer of the house by a lender. Thus, a mortgage might be a pledge of a house to secure payment of a loan. If a homeowner (the **mortgagor**) fails to pay the lender (the **mortgagee**), the lender has the right to foreclose the loan and seize the property in order to ensure that it is repaid.

When the loan is based solely on the credit of the borrower and on the collateral for the mortgage, the mortgage is said to be a **conventional mortgage**. The lender also may take out mortgage insurance to provide a guarantee for the fulfillment of the borrower's obligations. There are three forms of mortgage insurance guaranteed by the U.S. government if the borrower can qualify: Federal Housing Administration (FHA), Veterans Administration (VA), and Rural Housing Service (RHS) insurance. There are also private mortgage insurers such as Mortgage Guaranty Insurance Company (owned by Northwestern Mutual) and PMI Mortgage Insurance Company (owned by Sears, Roebuck). The cost of mortgage insurance is paid to the guarantor by the mortgage originator but passed along to the borrower in the form of higher mortgage payments.

The types of real estate properties that can be mortgaged are divided into two broad categories: single-family (one-to four-family) residential and commercial properties. The former category includes houses, condominiums, cooperatives, and apartments. Commercial properties are income-producing properties: multifamily properties (i.e., apartment buildings), office buildings, industrial properties (including warehouses), shopping centers, hotels, and health care facilities (e.g., senior housing care facilities).

Our primary focus in this chapter is on mortgage loans for residential property. At the end of this chapter we will discuss commercial mortgage loans.

MORTGAGE ORIGINATION

The original lender is called the **mortgage originator**. The principal originators of residential mortgage loans are thrifts, commercial banks, and mortgage bankers. Other private mortgage originators are life insurance companies and, to a much lesser extent, pension funds.

Mortgage originators may generate income from mortgage activity in one or more ways. First, they typically charge an **origination fee.** This fee is expressed in terms of points, where each point represents 1% of the borrowed funds. For example, an origination fee of two points on a $100,000 mortgage loan is $2,000. Originators also may charge application fees and certain processing fees. The second source of revenue is the profit that might be generated from selling a mortgage at a higher price than it originally cost. This profit is called *secondary market profit.* If mortgage rates rise, an originator will realize a loss when the mortgages are sold in the secondary market.

Although technically the sources of revenue attributable to the origination function are origination fees and secondary marketing profits, there are two other potential sources. First, mortgage originators may service the mortgages they originate, for which they obtain a **servicing fee.** Servicing of the mortgage involves collecting monthly payments from mortgagors and forwarding proceeds to owners of the loan, sending payment notices to mortgagors, reminding mortgagors when payments are overdue, maintaining records of mortgage balances, furnishing tax information to mortgagors, administering an escrow account for real estate taxes and insurance purposes, and, if necessary, initiating foreclosure proceedings. The servicing fee is a fixed percentage of the outstanding mortgage balance, typically 50 basis points to 100 basis points per year. The mortgage originator may sell the servicing of the mortgage to another party who would then receive the servicing fee. Second, the mortgage originator may hold the mortgage in its investment portfolio.

Historically, regulatory and tax considerations have encouraged thrifts to invest in mortgages, and, until quite recently, they tried to keep mortgages in their portfolios. Lately, however, both because they have become more conscious of the problem of mismatching maturities (their liabilities being short term and mortgage loans being long term), and because the tax benefits have been reduced by the 1986 tax act, banks and thrifts have tended to sell a good portion of what they originate and to become increasingly dependent on the fees generated from originating and servicing mortgages.

Mortgage banking refers to the activity of originating mortgages. As explained above, banks and thrifts undertake mortgage banking. However, there are companies not associated with a bank or thrift that are involved in mortgage banking. These mortgage bankers, unlike banks and thrifts, typically do not invest in the mortgages that they originate. Instead, they derive their income from the origination fees. Commercial banks derive their income from all three sources, but there are no regulatory benefits to them from investing in mortgages or mortgage-backed securities.

The Mortgage Origination Process

Someone who wants to borrow funds to purchase a home will apply for a loan from a mortgage originator. The potential homeowner completes an application form, which provides financial information about the applicant, and pays an application fee; then the mortgage originator performs a credit evaluation of the applicant. The two primary factors in determining whether or not the funds will be lent are the (1) **payment-to-income** (PTI) ratio, and (2) the **loan-to-value** (LTV) ratio. The first is the ratio of monthly payments to monthly income, which measures the ability of the applicant to make monthly payments (both mortgage and real estate tax payments). The lower this ratio, the greater the likelihood that the applicant will be able to meet the required payments.

The difference between the purchase price of the property and the amount borrowed is the borrower's down payment. The LTV is the ratio of the amount of the loan to the market (or appraised) value of the property. The lower this ratio, the greater the protection for the lender if the applicant defaults on the payments and the lender must repossess and sell the property. For example, if an applicant wants to borrow $150,000 on property with an appraised value of $200,000, the LTV is 75%. Suppose the applicant subsequently defaults on the mortgage. The lender can then repossess the property and sell it to recover the amount owed. But the amount that will be received by the lender depends on the market value of the property. In our example, even if conditions in the housing market are weak, the lender will still be able to recover the proceeds lent, if the value of the property declines by $50,000. Suppose, instead, that the applicant wanted to borrow $180,000 for the same property. The LTV would then be 90%. If the lender had to sell the property because the applicant defaults, there is less protection for the lender.

If the lender decides to lend the funds, it sends a **commitment letter** to the applicant. This letter commits the lender to provide funds to the applicant. The length of time of the commitment varies between 30 and 60 days. At the time of the commitment letter, the lender will require that the applicant pay a commitment fee. It is important to understand that the commitment letter obligates the lender—not the applicant—to perform. The commitment fee that the applicant pays is lost if the applicant decides not to purchase the property or uses an alternative source of funds to purchase the property. Thus, the commitment letter states that, for a fee, the applicant has the right but not the obligation to require the lender to provide funds at a certain interest rate and on certain terms.

At the time the application is submitted, the mortgage originator will give the applicant a choice among various types of mortgages. Basically, the choice is between a *fixed-rate mortgage* or an **adjustable-rate mortgage**. In the case of a fixed-rate mortgage, the lender typically gives the applicant a choice as to when the interest rate on the mortgage will be determined. The three choices may be: (1) at the time the loan application is submitted; (2) at the time a commitment letter is issued to the borrower; or (3) at the closing date (the date that the property is purchased).

These choices granted the applicant—the right to decide whether or not to close on the property and the right to select when to set the interest rate—expose the mortgage originator to certain risks, against which the originator will protect itself.

Mortgage originators can either (1) hold the mortgage in their portfolio; (2) sell the mortgage to an investor that wishes to hold the mortgage in its portfolio or that will place the mortgage in a pool of mortgages to be used as collateral for the issuance of a security; or (3) use the mortgage themselves as collateral for the issuance of a security. When a mortgage is used as collateral for the issuance of a security, the mortgage is said to be *securitized*. We discussed the process of securitizing loans in Chapter 4. In the next chapter, we will discuss the securitization of mortgage loans.

When a mortgage originator intends to sell the mortgage, it will obtain a commitment from the potential investor (buyer). Two federally sponsored agencies and several private companies buy mortgages. As these agencies and private companies pool these mortgages and sell them to investors, they are called **conduits**.

Two agencies, the Federal Home Loan Mortgage Corporation and the Federal National Mortgage Association, purchase only **conforming mortgages**—that is, a mortgage loan that meets the agency underwriting standards to be included in a pool of mortgages underlying a security that they guarantee. Three underwriting standards established by these agencies in order to qualify as a conforming mortgage are (1) a maximum PTI; (2) a maximum LTV; and (3) a maximum loan amount. If an applicant does not satisfy the underwriting standards, the mortgage is called a **nonconforming mortgage**.[1] The mortgages acquired by the agency may be held as a portfolio investment or securitized.

Examples of private conduits are Residential Funding Corporation, GE Capital Mortgage Services, Countrywide, and Prudential Home Mortgage. Both conforming and nonconforming mortgages are purchased.

Nonconforming mortgages do not necessarily have greater credit risk. For example, an individual with an annual income of $500,000 may apply for a mortgage loan of $200,000 on real estate that she wants to purchase for $1 million. This would be a nonconforming mortgage because the amount of the mortgage exceeds the limit currently established for a conforming mortgage, yet the individual's income can easily accommodate the monthly mortgage payments. Moreover, the lender's risk exposure is minimal, as it has lent $200,000 backed by collateral of $1 million.

The mortgage rate that the originator will set on the loan will depend on the mortgage rate required by the investor who plans to purchase the mortgage. At any

---

[1] Loans that exceed the maximum loan amount and therefore do not qualify as conforming mortgages are called jumbo loans.

time, there are different mortgage rates for delivery at different future times (30 days, 60 days, or 90 days).

The Risks Associated with Mortgage Origination

The loan applications being processed and the commitments made by a mortgage originator together are called its **pipeline**. *Pipeline risk* refers to the risks associated with originating mortgages. This risk has two components: *price risk* and **fallout risk**.

Price risk refers to the adverse effects on the value of the pipeline if mortgage rates rise. If mortgage rates rise, and the mortgage originator has made commitments at a lower mortgage rate, it will either have to sell the mortgages when they close at a value below the funds lent to homeowners, or retain the mortgages as a portfolio investment earning a below-market mortgage rate. The mortgage originator faces the same risk for mortgage applications in the pipeline where the applicant has elected to fix the rate at the time the application is submitted.

Fallout risk is the risk that applicants or those who were issued commitment letters will not close (complete the transaction by purchasing the property with funds borrowed from the mortgage originator). The chief reason that potential borrowers may cancel their commitment or withdraw their mortgage application is that mortgage rates have declined sufficiently so that it is economic to seek an alternative source of funds. Fallout risk is the result of the mortgage originator giving the potential borrower the right but not the obligation to close (that is, the right to cancel the agreement). There are reasons other than a decline in mortgage rates that may cause a potential borrower to fall out of the pipeline. There may be an unfavorable property inspection report, or the purchase could have been predicated on a change in employment that does not occur.

Mortgage originators have several alternatives to protect themselves against pipeline risk. To protect against price risk, the originator could get a commitment from the agency or the private conduit to whom the mortgage originator plans to sell the mortgage.[2] This sort of commitment is effectively a forward contract, a contract that we will describe in Chapter 25. The mortgage originator agrees to deliver a mortgage at a future date, and another party (either one of the agencies or a private conduit) agrees to buy the mortgage at that time at a predetermined price (or mortgage rate).

Consider what happens, however, if mortgage rates decline, and potential borrowers elect to cancel the agreement. The mortgage originator has agreed to deliver a mortgage with a specified mortgage rate. If the potential borrower does not close, and the mortgage originator has made a commitment to deliver the mortgage to an agency or private conduit, the mortgage originator cannot back out of the transaction. As a result, the mortgage originator will realize a loss—it must deliver a mortgage at a higher mortgage rate in a lower mortgage rate environment. This is fallout risk.

Mortgage originators can protect themselves against fallout risk by entering into an agreement with an agency or private conduit for optional rather than mandatory delivery of the mortgage. In such an agreement, the mortgage originator is effectively buying an option that gives it the right, but not the obligation, to deliver a mortgage. The agency or private conduit has sold that option to the mortgage originator and, therefore, charges a fee for allowing optional delivery.

---

[2] This commitment that the mortgage originator obtains to protect itself should not be confused with the commitment that the mortgage originator gives to the potential borrower.

> **Key Points That You Should Understand Before Proceeding**
>
> 1. The mortgage originator is the original lender of mortgage funds, and the activity of originating mortgages is called mortgage banking.
> 2. The principal originators of residential mortgage loans are thrifts, commercial banks, and mortgage bankers.
> 3. Mortgage originators may generate income from origination fees, secondary market profit, servicing fees, and investment income from holding the mortgages.
> 4. The two primary factors in determining whether funds will be lent to a mortgage loan applicant are the payment-to-income ratio and the loan-to-value ratio.
> 5. Two federally sponsored agencies and several private companies buy mortgages for purposes of pooling them and selling them to investors.
> 6. Pipeline risk is the risk associated with mortgage origination; it is made up of price risk and fallout risk.

TYPES OF MORTGAGE DESIGNS

Between the mid-1930s and the early 1970s, only one type of mortgage loan was available in the United States: the fixed-rate, level-payment, fully amortized mortgage. The deficiencies of this mortgage design, commonly referred to as the *traditional mortgage*, led to the introduction of new mortgage designs.

Fixed-Rate, Level-Payment, Fully Amortized Mortgages

The basic idea behind the design of the traditional mortgage is that the borrower pays interest and repays principal in equal installments over an agreed-upon period of time, called the maturity or term of the mortgage. Thus, at the end of the term, the loan has been fully amortized—there is no mortgage balance remaining. The interest rate is generally above the risk-free rate because of servicing costs, default risk that is present despite the collateral, and some further risks discussed below. The frequency of payment is typically monthly, and the prevailing term of the mortgage is 15 to 30 years.

Cash Flow Characteristics of the Traditional Mortgage.
Each monthly mortgage payment for a level-payment, fixed-rate mortgage is due on the first of each month and consists of:

1. Interest of $1/12$th of the fixed annual interest rate times the amount of the outstanding mortgage balance at the beginning of the previous month, and
2. A repayment of a portion of the outstanding mortgage balance (principal).

The difference between the monthly mortgage payment and the portion of the payment that represents interest equals the amount that is applied to reduce the outstanding mortgage balance. The monthly mortgage payment is designed so that after the last scheduled monthly payment of the loan is made, the amount of the outstanding mortgage balance is zero (that is, the mortgage is fully repaid).

As an illustration of a level-payment, fixed-rate mortgage, consider a 30-year (360-month), $100,000 mortgage with a 9.5% mortgage rate. The monthly mortgage payment would be $840.85. Table 23-1 shows for selected months how each monthly mortgage payment is divided between interest and repayment of principal. At the beginning of Month 1, the mortgage balance is $100,000, the amount of the original loan. The mortgage payment for Month 1 includes interest on the $100,000 borrowed for the month. As the interest rate is 9.5%, the monthly interest rate is 0.0079167

Table 23-1   Amortization Schedule for a Level-Payment, Fixed-Rate Mortgage

		Mortgage loan: $100,000			
		Mortgage rate: 9.5%			
		Monthly payment: $840.85			
		Term of loan: 30 years (360 months)			
MONTH	BEGINNING MORTGAGE BALANCE	MONTHLY MORTGAGE PAYMENT	INTEREST FOR MONTH	PRINCIPAL REPAYMENT	ENDING MORTGAGE BALANCE
1	$100,000.00	$840.85	$791.67	$49.19	$99,950.81
2	99,950.81	840.85	791.28	49.58	99,901.24
3	99,901.24	840.85	790.88	49.97	99,851.27
4	99,851.27	840.85	790.49	50.37	99,800.90
5	99,800.90	840.85	790.09	50.76	99,750.14
6	99,750.14	840.85	789.69	51.17	99,698.97
7	99,698.97	840.85	789.28	51.57	99,647.40
8	99,647.40	840.85	788.88	51.98	99,596.42
9	99,595.42	840.85	788.45	52.39	99,543.03
10	99,543.03	840.85	788.05	52.81	99,490.23
...	...	...	...	...	...
...	...	...	...	...	...
...	...	...	...	...	...
98	99,862.54	840.85	735.16	105.69	92,756.85
99	92,756.85	840.85	734.33	106.53	92,650.32
100	92,640.32	840.85	733.48	107.37	92,542.95
101	92,542.95	840.85	732.63	108.22	92,434.72
102	92,434.72	840.85	731.77	109.08	92,325.64
103	92,325.64	840.85	730.91	109.94	92,215.70
104	92,215.70	840.85	730.04	110.81	92,104.89
105	92,104.89	840.85	729.16	111.69	91,993.20
106	91,993.20	840.85	728.28	112.57	91,880.62
...	...	...	...	...	...
...	...	...	...	...	...
...	...	...	...	...	...
209	74,177.40	840.85	587.24	253.62	73,923.78
210	73,923.78	840.85	585.23	255.62	73,668.16
211	73,668.16	840.85	583.21	257.65	73,410.51
212	73,410.51	840.85	581.17	259.69	73,150.82
...	...	...	...	...	...
...	...	...	...	...	...
...	...	...	...	...	...
354	5,703.93	840.85	45.16	795.70	4,908.23
355	4,908.23	840.85	38.86	802.00	4,106.24
356	4,106.24	840.85	35.21	808.35	3,297.89
357	3,297.89	840.85	26.11	814.75	2,483.14
358	2,483.14	840.85	19.66	821.20	1,661.95
359	1,661.95	840.85	13.16	827.70	834.25
360	834.25	840.85	6.60	834.26	0.00

(0.095 divided by 12). Interest for Month 1 is therefore $791.67 ($100,000 times 0.0079167). The $49.18 difference between the monthly mortgage payment of $840.85 and the interest of $791.67 is the portion of the monthly mortgage payment that represents repayment of principal. This $49.18 in Month 1 reduces the mortgage balance.

The mortgage balance at the end of Month 1 (beginning of Month 2) is then $99,950.81 ($100,000 minus $49.19).[3] The interest for the second monthly mortgage payment is $791.28, which equals the monthly interest rate (0.0079167) times the mortgage balance at the beginning of Month 2 ($99,950.81). The difference between the $840.85 monthly mortgage payment and the $791.28 interest is $49.57, representing the amount of the mortgage balance paid off with that monthly mortgage payment. Notice that the last monthly mortgage payment is sufficient to pay off the remaining mortgage balance. When a loan repayment schedule is structured in this way, so that the payments made by the borrower will completely pay off the interest and principal, the loan is said to be self-amortizing. Table 23-1 is referred to as an amortization schedule.

As Table 23-1 clearly shows, the portion of the monthly mortgage payment applied to interest declines each month, and the portion applied to reducing the mortgage balance increases. The reason for this is that, as the mortgage balance is reduced with each monthly mortgage payment, the interest on the mortgage balance declines. Because the monthly mortgage payment is fixed, a larger part of the monthly payment is applied to reduce the principal in each subsequent month.

Prepayments.

In our illustration of the cash flow from a level-payment, fixed-rate mortgage it is assumed that the homeowner does not pay off any portion of the mortgage balance prior to the scheduled due date. But homeowners do pay off all or part of their mortgage balances prior to the maturity date. Payments made in excess of the scheduled principal repayments are called **prepayments**.

Prepayments occur for one of several reasons. First, homeowners prepay the entire mortgage when they sell their house for any number of reasons that require moving. Second, the borrower has the right to pay off all or part of the mortgage balance at any time. Effectively, those who invest in mortgages grant the borrower an option to prepay the mortgage, and the debtor will have an incentive to do so as the interest rate in the mortgage market falls below the mortgage rate that the borrower is paying. Third, if homeowners cannot meet their mortgage obligations, the property is repossessed and sold, with the proceeds from the sale used to pay the lender in the case of a conventional mortgage. For an insured mortgage, the insurer will pay off the mortgage balance. Finally, if property is destroyed by fire, or another insured catastrophe occurs, the insurance proceeds are used to pay off the mortgage.

When the borrower prepays, the typical mortgage design permits the borrower to do so at par. That is, there is typically no penalty for prepaying. So, if the borrower's outstanding mortgage balance is $92,756 and the borrower sells her home and pays off the $92,756 balance—that is, prepays—the only amount paid is the outstanding mortgage balance.

While the majority of mortgages outstanding do not penalize the borrower from prepaying any part or all of the outstanding mortgage balance, in recent years mortgage originators have begun originating **prepayment penalty mortgages (PPMs)**. We will discuss this type of mortgage later.

---

[3] Because Table 23-1 is computer generated, rounding results in slightly different values in the table.

Deficiencies of the Traditional Mortgage.

There are problems with the traditional mortgage design. In the presence of high and variable inflation, this mortgage design suffers from two basic and serious shortcomings: the **mismatch problem** and the **tilt problem**.

Savings and loan associations have faced the mismatch problem during most of the post–World War II period because mortgages—a very long-term asset—have been financed largely by depository institutions that obtain their funds through deposits that are primarily, if not entirely, of a short-term nature. These institutions have engaged inevitably in a highly speculative activity: borrowing short and lending very long. That is, there is a mismatch of the maturity of the assets (mortgages) and the liabilities raised to fund those assets. Speculation of this sort will prove a losing proposition if interest rates rise, as is bound to happen in the presence of significant inflation. The institution may be earning the contractual rate, but to attract the deposits needed to finance the loan, it will have to pay the current higher market rate. Considering that the intermediation margin or spread is modest—some 100 to 200 basis points—it will not take much inflation or rise in interest rates before an institution runs into a loss.

Another way to describe the mismatch problem is in terms of the balance sheet rather than the income statement. The difference between lending and borrowing rates will cause the lending institution to become technically insolvent, in the sense that the market value of its assets will be insufficient to cover its liabilities. The reason for this is that the institution's liabilities are related to the face value of its mortgage assets, but the market value of these assets will be below the face value of the mortgage loan. For these reasons, both losses and technical insolvencies have occurred on a large scale since the late 1960s, especially in the 1970s and early 1980s.

One obvious way to resolve this problem is for the institution that primarily finances fixed-rate mortgages to lengthen its liabilities through term deposits or analogous instruments. Actually, this has been done in recent years, but only to a modest extent. In fact, it is doubtful that this approach could go very far in meeting the problem, for what has made S&Ls so popular is unquestionably the highly liquid, riskless nature of their deposits. If they were allowed to finance mortgages only by long-term deposits, we might expect a substantial decline in the volume of funds available to them for mortgage financing. A second alternative is to design a different sort of mortgage.

The tilt problem refers to what happens to the real burden of mortgage payments over the life of the mortgage as a result of inflation. If the general price level rises, the real value of the mortgage payments will decline over time. If a homeowner's real income rises over time, this coupled with a decline in the real value of the mortgage payments will mean that the burden of the mortgage payments will decline over time. Thus, the mortgage obligation represents a greater burden in real terms for the homeowner in the initial years. In other words, the real burden is "tilted" to the initial years. This discourages people purchasing a home in their early earning years. The tilt problem is behind the development of other types of mortgage instruments.

Adjustable-Rate Mortgages

One way to resolve the mismatch problem is to redesign the traditional mortgage so as to produce an asset whose return would match the short-term market rates, thus better matching the cost of the liabilities. One instrument that satisfies these requirements, and that has won considerable popularity, is the so-called *adjustable-rate mortgage*.

Characteristics of the Adjustable-Rate Mortgage.

The adjustable-rate mortgage (ARM) calls for resetting the interest rate periodically, in accordance with some appropriately chosen index reflecting short-term market rates. This mortgage represents an approach applied to many other instruments, such as bank loans, especially in the Eurodollar market. By using a short-term rate as the index, S&Ls are able to improve the matching of their returns to their cost of funds. An instrument earning the market rate could be expected to remain close to par whether interest rates rise or fall, thus avoiding the problems of technical insolvency that have plagued the S&Ls relying on the traditional mortgage. Note also that, with high and variable rates of inflation, an adjustable-rate, in principle, reduces risk for the borrower—reduced inflation generally is accompanied by a fall in interest rates, which will benefit borrowers with an adjustable-rate contract.

The adjustable-rate contracts currently popular in the United States call for resetting the interest rate either every month, six months, year, two years, or three years. The interest rate at the reset date is equal to a benchmark index plus a spread. The spread is between 100 and 200 basis points.

The two most popular indexes are the one-year Treasury rate and the 11th District Cost of Funds Index (called COFI). The latter index is a calculation based on the monthly weighted average interest cost for liabilities of thrifts in the 11th Federal Home Loan Bank Board District.[4] This district includes the states of California, Arizona, and Nevada.

ARMs have been popular with lenders because they shift interest rate risk from the lender to the borrower. To be sure, the risk resulting from falling rates tends to be shifted from the borrower to the lender, but then this risk is born by the lenders anyway, at least in part, because of the borrower's prepayment option. Thrifts accordingly prefer to hold ARMs in their portfolios rather than fixed-rate mortgages such as the traditional mortgage, because ARMs provide a better matching with their liabilities. As liabilities are closely tied to the calculated cost of funds index, thrifts prefer ARMs benchmarked to the 11th District Cost of Funds.

The basic ARM is one that resets periodically and has no other terms that affect the monthly mortgage payment.[5] Typically, the mortgage rate is affected by other terms. These include: (1) **periodic caps** and (2) **lifetime rate caps** and floors. Periodic caps limit the amount that the interest rate may increase or decrease at the reset date. The periodic rate cap is expressed in percentage points. Most ARMs have an upper limit on the mortgage rate that can be charged over the life of the loan. This lifetime loan cap is expressed in terms of the initial rate; the most common lifetime cap is 5% to 6%. For example, if the initial mortgage rate is 7% and the lifetime cap is 5%, the maximum interest rate that the lender can charge over the life of the loan is 12%. Many ARMs also have a lower limit (floor) on the interest rate that can be charged over the life of the loan.

Balloon/Reset Mortgages.

Another type of adjustable-rate mortgages is the **balloon/reset mortgage**. The primary difference between a balloon/reset mortgage design and the basic ARM is that the mortgage rate is reset less frequently.

Although new to the U.S. mortgage market, the balloon/reset mortgage has long been used in Canada, where it is referred to as a *rollover mortgage*. In this mortgage design, the borrower is given long-term financing by the lender but at specified future dates the contract rate is renegotiated. Thus, the lender is providing long-term funds for what is effectively a short-term borrowing, how short depending on the frequency of the renegotiation period. Effectively, it is a short-term balloon loan in which the lender agrees to provide financing for the remainder of the term of the mortgage. The balloon payment is the original amount borrowed less the amount amortized.

---

[4] The cost of funds is calculated by first computing the monthly interest expenses for all thrifts included in the 11th District. The interest expenses are summed and then divided by the average of the beginning and ending monthly balance.

[5] There are ARMs that can be converted into fixed-rate mortgages called *convertible ARMs*.

The Federal Home Loan Bank Board attempted to introduce this mortgage design in January 1980, when it proposed a prototype rollover mortgage design. The prototype called for the contract rate to be renegotiated every three to five years (with the specific time period determined at the time the mortgage is originated), with a maximum contract rate change of 50 basis points for each year in the renegotiation period (for example, 150 basis points if renegotiated every three years and 250 basis points if every five years), and the lender guaranteeing to provide new financing. There were several proposals as to how the new contract rate should be determined.

Although the rollover mortgage was hailed as an important step in alleviating the mismatch problem that thrifts face, it did not catch on until 1990. Now called *balloon/reset mortgages*, or simply *balloon mortgages*, these mortgages are the focal points of purchase programs of two government-sponsored entities, Fannie Mae and Freddie Mac. Freddie Mac's 30-year balloon/resets, for example, can have either a renegotiation period of five years ("30-due-in-5" FRMs) or seven years ("30-due-in-7" FRMs). If certain conditions are met, Freddie Mac guarantees the extension of the loan. The contract rate set by Freddie Mac is based on its 30-year, single-family, fixed-rate 60-day delivery mortgage rate. If the borrower elects to extend the mortgage, a $250 processing fee is charged.

Assessment of Adjustable-Rate Mortgages.

On the whole, the adjustable-rate mortgage and its variants have the merit of providing a manageable solution to the problem of the mismatch of maturities. To borrowers, these mortgages reduce the risk associated with uncertain inflation. Unfortunately, the merits of the ARM have been significantly impaired by arbitrary and misguided regulatory rules, particularly interest rate caps. These caps, meant to protect the borrower, might make sense if rates were set unilaterally by the lender, but they do not make sense when they are tied to an objective market rate, or to the cost of funds to the lending institution. Furthermore, we know that an increase in nominal rates tends to occur when there is an appreciable rise in inflation, in which case the borrower, in general, can afford to pay the higher interest rate while it lasts.

The main effect of caps is to increase the risk of inflation to intermediary lenders who have no way of putting a cap on the rate they have to pay. Nor is a lower cap adequate compensation, because borrowers have the right to repay. Of course, some of the expected loss will tend to be recouped by a higher spread, and thus finally unloaded on some borrowers; even so, it would be best to leave the matter of caps to private bargaining.

Unfortunately, regulators have still not grasped these simple principles. Nor have they understood that in many cases the consumer generally pays for "consumer protection" in the form of higher rates or other less favorable terms. Finally, the adjustable-rate mortgage is not a satisfactory answer to inflation-swollen interest rates because it does not address the tilt problem. And the tilt problem remains in effect because, in these mortgages, the payments are still based on a nominal rather than a real interest rate.

Mortgage Designs to Deal with Inflation

The traditional mortgage was designed so that the borrower would repay the debt in constant nominal installments. This form of repayment would seem highly desirable from the debtor's point of view, so long as inflation is zero or small, because a level nominal repayment rate in that case implies a level real rate of repayment. But when there is significant inflation, the traditional mortgage turns into a malfunctioning, very undesirable vehicle for home financing. The reason is not, as frequently supposed, that inflation increases interest rates. To be sure, with a 10% rate of inflation we would expect nominal interest rates to rise by roughly 10 percentage points—say, from 5% to 15%. But this rise does not, per se, make the lender any better off or the borrower any worse off, as the increase is offset by inflation losses and gains, leaving the real rate largely unchanged. The higher interest rate is, by and large, compensated for by the erosion of the principal in terms of purchasing power. (In nominal terms, the higher rate is offset by the rise in the value of the property.)

Rather, the reason for the unsatisfactory performance of the traditional mortgage lies in the tilt effect: With 10% steady inflation, if the nominal payment is level, then the real payment will decrease at 10% per year. By the twentieth year, it will be down to some 15% of the initial installment payment. If the creditor is to receive the same real amount as in the absence of inflation, the gradual erosion of the repayments in terms of purchasing power will have to be made up by sufficiently high initial real (and hence nominal) payments. Indeed, with the interest rate rising from 5% to 15%, the first payment on a long-term mortgage will rise roughly threefold.

The nature of the distortion or tilt in the real payment path is illustrated in Figure 23-1 for different rates of inflation. Notice that, for an 8% rate of inflation, the path starts at more than twice the no-inflation level, to terminate at well below half. The high initial payment caused by inflation has the effect of foreclosing home ownership to large segments of the population, or forcing buyers to scale down their demands. Indeed, not many people would be able to pay a multiple of what they were paying in the preinflation period for the same home. This is especially true in the case of young people who have little asset accumulation.

The first thing to note about this problem is that it is not addressed by the adjustable-rate mortgage. That mortgage uses throughout a nominal interest rate

Figure 23-1   Nature of Tilt Problem: Real Value of Monthly Payments
SOURCE: D. Tucker, "The Variable-Rate Graduated Payment Mortgage," *Real Estate Review* (Spring 1975), p. 72.

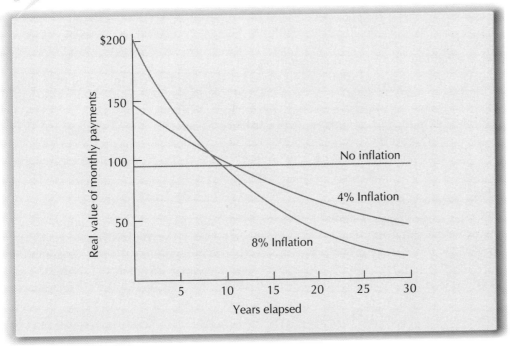

comparable to the fixed-rate mortgage. In particular, the critical early payment will be roughly as high as with a traditional mortgage. Actually, one can show that the adjustable rate is, in some ways, even worse for borrowers than the traditional mortgage. It starts with a rate as high as the traditional mortgage independently of inflation, and will make a substantial jump every time the interest rate is adjusted and the payment shifts from one nominal level to another—even though the rate of payment is level as long as the interest rate does not change.

Can the tilt problem be remedied? It is clear that in principle a solution must involve reducing the interest rate used in the early payments and recouping later. Three mortgage designs (with many variants) have been offered to solve the tilt problem: the **graduated-payment mortgage**, the **price-level-adjusted mortgage**, and the **dual-rate mortgage**.

Graduated-Payment Mortgage.

A graduated-payment mortgage (GPM) is one whose nominal monthly payment grows at a constant rate during a portion of the life of the contract, thereafter leveling off. The mortgage rate is fixed for the life of the loan, despite the fact that the monthly mortgage payment gradually increases. The terms of a GPM plan include (1) the mortgage rate; (2) the term of the mortgage; (3) the number of years over which the monthly mortgage payment will increase (and when the level payments will begin); and (4) the annual percent increase in the mortgage payments. The most popular 30-year GPM plan that qualifies for FHA insurance calls for monthly payments that increase by 7.5% for five years, then at the beginning of the sixth year remain constant for the remaining 25 years. The monthly mortgage payments under this GPM program for a $100,000, 30-year, 10% mortgage would be: (1) $667.04 per month in the first year; (2) $717.06 per month in the second year; (3) $770.84 in the third year; (4) $828.66 in the fourth year; (5) $890.80 in the fifth year; and (6) $957.62 for the remaining term of the mortgage, beginning with the sixth year.

Because this mortgage design involves a fixed rate over the life of the loan, while the rate of inflation may be highly variable over the same period, the GPM is not likely to succeed in assuring the debtor anything approaching a level real repayment stream. Thus, it does not solve the tilt problem. It should be apparent that it cannot solve the mismatching problem. These shortcomings have probably contributed to the decreasing popularity of GPMs in recent years. In fact, the only two basic mortgage designs that can provide a more or less foolproof solution to both problems are the price-level-adjusted mortgage and the dual-rate mortgage.

There is another problem with the GPM that is unrelated to its ability to deal with inflation. In the earlier years of a GPM, the mortgage payments will be less than the interest on the mortgage balance. What happens is that any shortfall in the interest is added to the outstanding mortgage balance. So instead of the mortgage balance declining in the earlier years of a GPM—that is, the mortgage balance amortizing—the mortgage balance increases. This is called *negative amortization* and increases the credit risk to the lender.

Price-Level-Adjusted Mortgage.

This mortgage design is similar to the traditional mortgage except that monthly payments are designed to be level in purchasing power terms rather than in nominal terms, and that the fixed rate is the "real" rather than the nominal rate.[6] To compute the monthly payment under a *price-level-adjusted mortgage* (PLAM), the terms of the contract must be specified, namely: (1) the real interest rate; (2) the term of the loan;

[6] The real rate, it will be recalled from Chapter 11, is the interest rate that one could expect to prevail if there were no inflation in the economy.

and (3) the index to be used to measure the price level, usually the Consumer Price Index (CPI). On the basis of an ordinary mortgage table, the annual payment and the unpaid balance at the end of each year, corresponding to the stipulated real interest and maturity, can then be computed. These figures represent payments and balances in real terms. To compute the payments actually due in each year, we simply multiply the real payment by an inflation-correction factor equal to the ratio of the stipulated index in the last year to the value of the index in the initial year. Similarly, to compute the actual debt, we multiply the real debt by the inflation-correction factor.[7]

The PLAM is not a new concept; it has been used for decades in many countries with high inflation, where the housing industries could not possibly have survived with the traditional mortgage. These include Finland right after World War II, many South American countries, and Israel. Somewhat surprisingly, it has not been used to any significant extent in the United States. This is largely explained because no innovation in home financing has been possible without some sanction of government regulators, and regulators have been unimaginative, and rather disinclined toward real indexation of any type. Critical in this respect has been HUD's lack of approval for FHA insurance. Quite recently, however, HUD seems poised to change this attitude and to issue regulations to standardize these mortgages. PLAM may soon be making its debut in the United States.

Dual-Rate Mortgage.

Also referred to as the **inflation-proof mortgage**, the dual-rate mortgage (DRM) is similar in spirit and objective to the PLAM: Payments start low—at current mortgage rates of around 10%, payments would start around 30% to 40% below those required by the traditional mortgage or by the ARM. They then rise smoothly at the rate of inflation, if any, achieving, like the PLAM, annual payments approximately level in terms of purchasing power. Finally, by construction, the debt is fully amortized by the end of the contract.

The DRM differs from the PLAM in that the amount owed by the borrower is computed on the basis of a floating short-term rate. This has several important consequences. First, just as in the case of other instruments where a fluctuating rate is indexed to short-term market rates, the market value of the instrument is not subject to interest rate risk but should instead remain close to par, except of course for credit risk. Second, there is little danger of prepayment risk, that is, of the borrower taking the option to repay when rates fall, for the DRM rate would automatically fall. And finally, this mortgage can be financed through the existing institution of short-term nominal deposits.

A DRM requires specification of three parameters. The first is the payment rate. This is a real rate of interest fixed for the life of the loan, much as with a PLAM. The purpose of this rate is not to establish how much the debtor will pay, but rather how the amount will be paid—to make possible a desirable and affordable distribution of payments over the life of the instrument. The second parameter is the effective or debiting rate, a short-term rate that, as in the ARM, determines how much the borrower effectively pays (or is debited for) and how much the creditor earns. This debiting rate changes periodically, say, once a year, on the basis of an agreed-upon reference short-term rate (for example, the one-year Treasury bill). And the third parameter is the life of the mortgage, just as for any other fully amortized mortgage contract.

So far, the DRM has had rather limited application in the United States, largely because it has not yet received FHA approval for insurance. The DRM has had some

---

[7] For a discussion of the PLAM, see Susan E. Woodward and David A. Crowe, "A Power-Packed Mortgage," *Secondary Mortgage Markets* (Fall 1988), pp. 2–7.

application abroad and should have a future also in the United States after the PLAM has been introduced. There are a number of variants of the DRM that improve the working of the instrument in some directions, at the cost of reduced effectiveness in other directions.[8]

Other Mortgage Designs[9]

There are other mortgage designs that are available to meet the unique needs of some borrowers. Lenders have also started to make loans to borrowers with blemished credit, reduced documentation with nonstandard specifications, and even loans that require less down payment than previously, or do not need any down payment at all. Addressing the distinctive needs of various mortgagors in the changing mortgage market, lenders have come to offer such specialized programs as high-LTV, Alt-A, and sub-prime loans, which are discussed below.

Prepayment Penalty Mortgages.

As explained previously in this chapter, the majority of mortgages outstanding do not penalize the borrower from prepaying any part or all of the outstanding mortgage balance. However, in recent years mortgage originators have begun originating *prepayment penalty mortgages* (PPMs).

The laws and regulations governing the imposition of prepayment penalties are established at the federal and state levels.[10] Usually, the applicable laws for fixed-rate mortgages are specified at the state level. There are states that do not permit prepayment penalties on fixed-rate mortgages with a first lien. There are states that do permit prepayment penalties but restrict the type of penalty. For some mortgage designs, such as adjustable-rate and balloon mortgages, there are federal laws that override state laws.

The basic structure of a PPM is as follows. There is specified time period where prepayments are not permitted. This time period is called the *lockout period*. Typically, this period is either three years or five years. Depending on the structure, a certain amount of prepayments can be made during the lockout period without the imposition of a prepayment penalty. The common prepayment penalty structure is one that allows partial prepayments up to 20% of the original loan amount in any consecutive 12-month period without a prepayment penalty. When a prepayment penalty is imposed, it is typically as follows:[11]

> ➤ If there is a three-year lockout period, the prepayment penalty is the lesser of 2% of any prepayment amount within three years that is greater than 20% of the original mortgage, or six months of interest on the portion of the prepayment amount that exceeds 20% of the original principal balance.

> ➤ If there is a five-year lockout period, the prepayment penalty is six months' interest on any prepayment amount in the first five years that is greater than 20% of the original principal balance.

---

[8] For a further discussion, of the DRM, its variants, and the difference between the PLAM and DRI, see Chapter 7 of Frank J. Fabozzi and Franco Modigliani, *Mortgage and Mortgage-Backed Securities Markets* (Boston: Harvard Business School Press, 1992).

[9] Portions of the discussion in this section draw from Anand K. Bhattacharya, Frank J. Fabozzi, and S. Esther Chang, "Overview of the Mortgage Market," Chapter 1 in Frank J. Fabozzi (ed.), *The Handbook of Mortgage-Backed Securities*, 5th ed. (New York: McGraw Hill, 2001).

[10] For a discussion of these laws and regulations, see Anand K. Bhattacharya and Paul C. Wang, "Prepayment Penalty MBS,", *The Handbook of Mortgage-Backed Securities*, 5th ed. The information in this section draws from that chapter.

[11] The prepayment penalty structures are explained in Bhattacharya and Wang, "Prepayment Penalty MBS," op. cit.

For example, suppose that a borrower with a PPM with a mortgage rate of 8.5%, original principal balance of $150,000, and a lockout period of five years refinances within the first five years and prepays the entire balance. The prepayment penalty will be six months of interest on the amount prepaid in excess of the 20% of the original principal balance. Since 20% of the original principal balance of $150,000 is $120,000 and interest for one year at 8.5% is $10,200 (8.5% times $120,000), the prepayment penalty is six-months' interest, $5,100.

The motivation for the PPM is that it reduces prepayment risk (discussed later in this chapter) for the lender during the lockout period. It does so by effectively making it more costly for the borrower to prepay. In exchange for this reduction in prepayment risk, the lender will offer a mortgage rate that is less than that of an otherwise comparable mortgage loan without a prepayment penalty.

Growing-Equity Mortgage.

A variation of the GPM that does not have negative amortization is the **growing-equity mortgage (GEM)**, which has a fixed-rate mortgage whose monthly mortgage payments increase over time. Rather, the higher monthly mortgage payments serve to pay down the principal faster and shorten the term of the mortgage. For example, a 30-year, $100,000 GEM loan with a contract rate of 9.5% might call for an initial monthly payment of $840.85. However, the GEM payment would gradually increase, and the GEM might be fully paid in only 15 years.

Thus, a GEM effectively shortens the life of a mortgage. The advantage of this mortgage design for the borrower is that because it has a shorter life than a level-payment mortgage, in an upward-sloping yield curve environment a lender will be willing to provide a lower mortgage rate than for a level-payment mortgage. As the borrower's income grows over time, the borrower can afford to make the higher payments that lead to the shorter life for the mortgage.

Reverse Mortgages.

Reverse mortgages are designed for senior homeowners who want to convert their home equity into cash. Fannie Mae, for instance, offers two types of reverse mortgages for senior borrowers. The Home Keeper Mortgage is an adjustable-rate conventional reverse mortgage for borrowers who are of at least 62 years of age, that either own the home outright, or have a very low amount of unpaid principal balance. The maximum amount that can be borrowed is based upon the homeowner's age, the property's value, and the interest rate. The borrower will not have to repay the loan until they no longer occupy the home as their principal residence, and cannot be forced to sell or vacate the home to pay off the loan as long as the property is maintained. The other type of reverse mortgage, Home Keeper for Home Purchase, enables senior borrowers to buy a new home with a combination of personal funds and calculated amount of reverse mortgage that is based upon the borrower's age, number of borrowers, the adjusted property value, and the equity share option chosen.

High-LTV Loans.

Traditionally for a conventional, conforming loan, borrowers typically were required to make a down payment of 20% when qualifying for a mortgage. However, today a mortgagor with good credit has the option of making a lesser down or no down payment, resulting in loans with higher LTVs. Hence, these mortgage loans are called **high-LTV loans**. For borrowers interested in conventional, nonconforming loans, there are programs available with 103% LTV that require no down payment because 100% of the home's price, as well as an additional 3% for closing costs, can be financed into the mortgage.

Alt-A Loans.

Alt-A loans are made to borrowers whose qualifying mortgage characteristics do not meet the conforming underwriting criteria established by the government-sponsored enterprises that we will discuss in the next chapter. For instance, the borrower may be self-employed and may not be able to provide all the necessary documentation for income verification. In such respects, Alt-A loans allow reduced or alternate forms of documentation to qualify for the loan. An Alt-A loan borrower, however, should not be confused with borrowers with blemished credits. The typical Alt-A borrower will have an excellent credit rating—referred to as an "A" rating, and hence the loan is referred to an Alt-A loan—which is especially important to the originator since the credit quality of the borrower must compensate for the lack of other necessary documentation. What is appealing to borrowers about the Alt-A program is the flexibility that the program offers in terms of documentation, and borrowers will pay a premium for the privilege. Typically, rates on Alt-A loans range between 75 to 125 basis points above the rate on otherwise comparable standard mortgage rates.

Subprime Loans.

Borrowers who apply for **subprime loans** vary from those who have or had credit problems due to difficulties in repayment of debt brought on by an adverse event, such as job loss or medical emergencies, to those that continue to mismanage their debt and finances. The distinguishing feature of a subprime mortgage is that the potential universe of subprime mortgagors can be divided into various risk grades, ranging from A through D. The risk gradation is a function of past credit history and the magnitude of credit blemishes existing in the history. Additionally, some of the higher grades in this loan category have also been labeled as "fallen angels" to indicate the fact that the creditworthiness of such borrowers was hampered by a life event, such as job loss or illness. Since such borrowers tend to have lower credit scores and pose greater credit risk, subprime mortgages command a pricing premium over standard mortgages.

Key Points That You Should Understand Before Proceeding

1. The fixed-rate, level-payment fully amortized mortgage (or traditional mortgage) is the most common type of mortgage design in the United States.

2. A prepayment is a payment made by the borrower in excess of the amount due. While for most mortgages there is no penalty for prepaying, in recent years prepayment penalty mortgages have been introduced into the mortgage market to make it more costly for a borrower to prepay.

3. In the presence of high and variable inflation, the traditional mortgage design suffers from two basic and serious shortcomings: the mismatch problem and the tilt problem.

4. An adjustable-rate mortgage is a mortgage design whose rate resets periodically in accordance with some appropriately chosen index reflecting short-term market rates and overcomes the mismatch problem but not the tilt problem.

5. To overcome the tilt problem, several mortgage designs that take inflation into account have been developed or proposed.

6. To address the distinctive needs of various mortgagors in the changing mortgage market, lenders have come to offer loans to borrowers with blemished credit, reduced documentation with nonstandard specifications, and even loans that require less down payment than previously, or do not need any down payment at all.

COMMERCIAL MORTGAGE-BACKED SECURITIES

Commercial mortgage loans are loans for income-producing properties. These properties include multifamily properties (i.e., apartment buildings), office buildings, industrial properties (including warehouses), shopping centers, hotels, and health care facilities (e.g., senior housing care facilities).

Unlike residential mortgage loans where the lender relies on the ability of the borrower to repay and has recourse to the borrower if the payment terms are not satisfied, commercial mortgage loans are *nonrecourse loans*. This means that the lender can only look to the income-producing property backing the loan for interest and principal repayment. If there is a default, the lender looks to the proceeds from the sale of the property for repayment and has no recourse to the borrower for any unpaid balance. Basically, this means that the lender must evaluate each property using measures that have been found useful in assessing credit risk.

Measures Used in Evaluating the Credit Risk of Commercial Mortgage Loans

Regardless of the property type, the two measures that have been found to be key indicators of the potential credit performance is the debt-to-service coverage ratio and the loan-to-value ratio. The **debt-to-service coverage (DSC)** ratio is the ratio of the property's net operating income (NOI) divided by the debt service. The NOI is defined as the rental income reduced by cash operating expenses (adjusted for a replacement reserve). A ratio greater than 1 means that the cash flow from the property is sufficient to cover debt servicing. The higher the ratio, the more likely that the borrower will able to meet debt servicing from the property's cash flow.

Prepayment Protection for Lenders

We discussed earlier that there is prepayment risk with mortgage loans and that for residential mortgages prepayments are typically penalty-free (the typical residential mortgage loan) or there may be a penalty. For a commercial mortgage loan, prepayment (or call) protection is provided. It can take one of the following forms: (1) prepayment lockout, (2) defeasance, (3) prepayment penalty points, or (4) yield maintenance charges.

A *prepayment lockout* is a contractual agreement that prohibits any prepayments during a specified period of time, called the lockout period. The lockout period at issuance can be from two to five years. After the lockout period, call protection comes in the form of either prepayment penalty points or yield maintenance charges. Prepayment lockout and defeasance are the strongest forms of prepayment protection.

With *defeasance*, rather than prepaying a loan, the borrower provides sufficient funds for the servicer to invest in a portfolio of Treasury securities that replicates the cash flows that would exist in the absence of prepayments. Unlike the other call protection provisions discussed next, there is no distribution made to the bondholders when the defeasance takes place. Moreover, the substitution of the cash flow of a Treasury portfolio for that of the borrower improves the credit quality of the loan.

Prepayment penalty points are predetermined penalties that must be paid by the borrower if the borrower wishes to refinance. For example, 5-4-3-2-1 is a common prepayment penalty point structure. That is, if the borrower wishes to prepay during the first year, he or she must pay a 5% penalty for a total of $105 rather than $100 (which is the norm in the residential market). Likewise, during the second year, a 4% penalty would apply, and so on. Today, prepayment penalty points are not common in newly originated commercial mortgage loans. Instead, the next form of call protection discussed, yield maintenance charges, is more commonly used

Yield maintenance charge, in its simplest terms, is designed to make the lender indifferent as to the timing of prepayments. The yield maintenance charge, also called the *make whole charge*, makes it uneconomical for the borrower to refinance solely to get a lower mortgage rate. The simplest and most restrictive form of yield maintenance charge ("Treasury flat yield maintenance") penalizes the borrower based on the difference between the mortgage coupon and the prevailing Treasury rate.

INVESTMENT RISKS

The principal investors in mortgage loans include thrifts and commercial banks. Pension funds and life insurance companies also invest in these loans, but their ownership is small compared to that of the banks and thrifts.

Investors face four main risks by investing in mortgage loans: (1) *credit risk;* (2) *liquidity risk;* (3) *price risk;* and (4) *prepayment risk.*

Credit Risk

Credit risk is the risk that the homeowner/borrower will default. For FHA-, VA-, and FmHA-insured mortgages, this risk is minimal. For privately insured mortgages, the risk can be gauged by the credit rating of the private insurance company that has insured the mortgage. For conventional mortgages, the credit risk depends on the borrower. The LTV provides a useful measure of the risk of loss of principal in case of default. When LTV is high, default is more likely because the borrower has little equity in the property.

Liquidity Risk

Although there is a secondary market for mortgage loans, which we discuss in the next chapter, the fact is that bid–ask spreads are large compared to other debt instruments. That is, mortgage loans tend to be rather illiquid because they are large and indivisible.

Price Risk

As explained in Chapter 10, the price of a fixed-income instrument will move in an opposite direction from market interest rates. Thus, a rise in interest rates will decrease the price of a mortgage loan.

Prepayments and Cash Flow Uncertainty

Payments made in excess of the scheduled principal repayments are called *prepayments.* Prepayments occur for one of several reasons. First, homeowners prepay the entire mortgage when they sell their house for any number of reasons that require moving. Second, the borrower has the right to pay off all or part of the mortgage balance at any time. Effectively, those who invest in mortgages grant the borrower an option to prepay the mortgage, and the debtor will have an incentive to do so as the interest rate in the mortgage market falls below the mortgage rate that the borrower is paying. Third, if homeowners cannot meet their mortgage obligations, the property is repossessed and sold, with the proceeds from the sale used to pay the lender in the case of a conventional mortgage. For an insured mortgage, the insurer will pay off the mortgage balance. Finally, if property is destroyed by fire, or another insured catastrophe occurs, the insurance proceeds are used to pay off the mortgage.

The effect of the prepayment right is that the cash flow from a mortgage is not known with certainty. This is true not only for level-payment, fixed-rate mortgages but also for all the mortgages we discussed in this chapter.

Key Points That You Should Understand Before Proceeding

1. There are four main risks associated with investing in mortgages: credit risk, liquidity risk, price risk, and prepayment risk.
2. Credit risk can be reduced if the mortgage is insured by a government agency or a private insurance company.
3. Mortgages are not liquid assets—they tend to have a large bid–ask spread.
4. Because of prepayments, the investor is uncertain about the cash flows that will be realized from investing in a mortgage.

SUMMARY

The types of real estate properties that can be mortgaged are single-family residential and commercial properties. Single-family residential properties include one- to four-family dwellings. Commercial properties are income-producing properties.

The major originators of residential mortgage loans are thrifts, banks, and mortgage bankers. The risks associated with originating mortgages (pipeline risk) include price risk and fallout risk.

The traditional type of mortgage, characterized by a fixed-rate, level (nominal) payment, and full amortization, performed well in the first years of the postwar period, becoming the dominant vehicle for house financing. But this design showed drawbacks in the presence of high and variable inflation. First, traditional mortgages were financed mainly by depository institutions with very short-term funds, even though a mortgage is a very long-term instrument; this mismatch of maturities proved catastrophic when short-term rates rose sharply, leading to widespread insolvency of S&Ls, the major lenders. Second, in the presence of inflation-driven high interest rates, mortgage repayment in real terms is no longer level, but instead starts high and ends low, shutting off many would-be borrowers.

Two remedies in use in the United States are the adjustable-rate mortgage (ARM) and the graduated-payment mortgage (GPM). The first addresses the mismatch problem, and the second (imperfectly) the tilt problem; neither addresses both. Two other solutions, the price-level-adjusted mortgage (PLAM) and the dual-rate mortgage (DRM), fairly effectively address both problems, but neither of these instruments has yet been adopted on a large scale in the United States.

There are several types of mortgage designs offered to borrowers with features that make them more appealing to specific borrower groups with special needs or objectives. These include growing-equity mortgages, reverse mortgages, and loans to borrowers with blemished credit (subprime mortgages), reduced documentation with nonstandard specifications (Alt-A mortgages), and loans that require less down payment than a standard mortgage loan or no downpayment at all (high-LTV mortgages).

Although prepayments—mortgage payments that exceed the amount that is due—can typically be made by the borrower without a penalty, in recent years prepayment penalty mortgages have been offered.

There is uncertainty associated with investing in any of these mortgages; because of prepayments, the cash flow is not known with certainty. This uncertainty is called prepayment risk. Investors in mortgages also face marketability risk and price risk, and may be exposed to credit risk.

Commercial mortgage loans are for income-producing properties that include multifamily properties (i.e., apartment buildings), office buildings, industrial properties (including warehouses), shopping centers, hotels, and health care facilities (e.g., senior housing care facilities). Commercial mortgage loans are nonrecourse loans, meaning that that the lender can only look to the income-producing property backing the loan for interest and principal repayment. The two measures that have been found to be key indicators of the potential credit performance of commercial property are the debt-to-service coverage ratio and the loan-to-value ratio. There are various provisions in a commercial mortgage loan to protect the lender against prepayments.

KEY TERMS

- Adjustable-rate mortgage, 425
- Alt-A loan, 438
- Balloon/reset mortgage, 431
- Commitment letter, 424
- Conduits, 425
- Conforming mortgage, 425
- Conventional mortgage, 423
- Debt-to-service coverage ratio (DSC), 439
- Dual-rate mortgage (DRM) (also called inflation-proof mortgage), 434, 435
- Fallout risk, 426
- Graduated-payment mortgage (GPM), 434
- Growing-equity mortgage (GEM), 437
- High-LTV Loans, 437
- Lifetime cap, 431
- Loan-to-value (LTV) ratio, 424
- Mismatch problem, 430
- Mortgage banking, 424

- Mortgage loan (or simply mortgage), 423
- Mortgage market, 422
- Mortgage originator, 423
- Mortgage servicing, 423
- Mortgagee, 423
- Mortgagor, 423
- Nonconforming mortgage, 425
- Origination fee, 423
- Payment-to-income (PTI) ratio, 424
- Periodic cap, 431
- Pipeline risk, 426
- Prepayment, 429
- Prepayment penalty mortgage (PPM), 429
- Price-level-adjusted mortgage (PLAM), 434
- Reverse mortgage, 437
- Subprime loan, 438
- Tilt problem, 430

QUESTIONS

1. What are the sources of revenue arising from mortgage origination?
2. What are the risks associated with the mortgage origination process?
3. What are the two primary factors in determining whether or not funds will be lent to an applicant for a residential mortgage loan?
4. What can mortgage originators do with a loan after originating it?
5. Explain why in a fixed-rate, level-payment mortgage the amount of the mortgage payment applied to interest declines over time, while the amount applied to the repayment of principal increases.
6. Consider the following fixed-rate, level-payment mortgage

    maturity = 360 months
    amount borrowed = $100,000
    annual mortgage rate = 10%
    monthly mortgage payment = $877.57

    a. Construct an amortization schedule for the first 10 months.
    b. What will the mortgage balance be at the end of the 360th month?
7. Why is the interest rate on a mortgage loan not necessarily the same as the interest rate that the investor receives?
8. a. Why is the cash flow of a residential mortgage loan unknown?
    b. In what sense has the investor in a residential mortgage loan granted the borrower (homeowner) a call option?
9. If the borrower prepays a residential mortgage loan, what is the prepayment penalty?
10. a. What features of an adjustable-rate mortgage will affect its cash flow?
    b. What are the two categories of benchmark indexes used in adjustable-rate mortgages?
11. What is the motivation for the design of price-level-adjusted mortgages and dual-rate mortgages?

12. With respect to a default by the borrower, how does a residential mortgage loan differ from a commercial mortgage loan?

13. What types of provisions are usually included in a commercial loan to protect the lender against prepayment risk?

14. Why is the debt to service coverage ratio used to assess the credit risk of a commercial mortgage loan?

Mortgage-Backed Securities Market

Learning Objectives

After reading this chapter, you will understand

- the development of the current mortgage market, and the role of public and private conduits.
- the agency pass-through market.
- the nonagency pass-through market.
- the investment characteristics of mortgage pass-through securities.
- the importance of prepayments.
- why a collateralized mortgage obligation is created.
- how different types of collateralized mortgage obligation bond classes are created.
- the investment characteristics of stripped mortgage-backed securities.
- the features of a commercial mortgage-backed security and the types of deals.

Our major focus in this chapter is on the market for securities created from residential mortgage loans. The basic mortgage-backed security is the mortgage pass-through security. From this security, derivative mortgage-backed securities are created: collateralized mortgage obligations and stripped mortgage-backed securities. We begin by describing how the process of securitizing mortgages resulted in the strong secondary mortgage market that exists today. At the end of the chapter, we will discuss mortgage-backed securities backed by commercial mortgage loans.

DEVELOPMENT OF THE SECONDARY MORTGAGE MARKET

The driving force in the development of a strong secondary market for residential mortgage loans was a financial innovation that involves the packaging (or "pooling") of mortgages and the issuance of securities collateralized by these mortgages. As we explained in Chapter 2, this system, called *asset securitization*, is radically different from the traditional system for financing the acquisition of assets, which calls for one financial intermediary, such as a commercial bank, thrift, or insurance company, to: (1) originate a loan; (2) retain the loan in its portfolio of assets, thereby accepting the credit risk associated with the loan; (3) service the loan (that is, collect payments and provide tax or other information to the borrower); and (4) obtain funds from the public with which to finance its assets (except for the small amount representing the institution's equity).

With asset securitization more than one institution may be involved in lending capital. In the case of mortgage activities, a lending scenario can look like this: (1) A thrift or commercial bank can originate a mortgage loan; (2) the thrift or commercial bank can sell its mortgages to an investment banking firm that creates a security backed by the pool of mortgages; (3) the investment banker can obtain credit risk insurance for the pool of mortgages from a private insurance company; (4) the investment banker can sell the right to service the loans to another thrift or a company specializing in serving mortgages; and (5) the investment banking firm can sell the securities to individuals and institutional investors. Besides the original bank or thrift, participants include an investment bank, an insurance company, another thrift, an individual, and other institutional investors. The bank or thrift in this case does not have to absorb the credit risk, service the mortgage, or provide the funding.

Foundations of the Mortgage Market

The foundations for the secondary mortgage market can be traced back to the Great Depression and the legislation that followed. Congress's response to the Depression and its effects on financial markets was to establish several public purpose agencies. The Federal Reserve provided increased liquidity for commercial banks through the Federal Reserve discount window. Liquidity for thrifts was provided by the creation of the Federal Home Loan Banks (FHLBs), which were granted the right to borrow from the Treasury.

Another creation of Congress, the Federal Housing Administration (FHA), addressed the problems presented by the mortgages used at that time. It is this government agency that developed and promoted the fixed-rate, level-payment, fully amortized mortgage. The FHA also reduced credit risk for investors by offering insurance against mortgage defaults. Not all mortgages could be insured, however—the mortgage applicant had to satisfy FHA underwriting standards, which made the FHA the first to standardize mortgage terms. While we may take this for granted today, standardization is the basis for the development of a secondary mortgage market. In 1944, the Veterans Administration began insuring qualified mortgages.

But who was going to invest in these mortgages? Thrifts could do so, especially with the inducement provided by several tax and regulatory advantages. But the investment would be illiquid in the absence of a market where mortgages are traded. Congress thought of that, too. It created another government-sponsored agency, the Federal National Mortgage Association (FNMA). This agency, popularly known as Fannie Mae, was charged with the responsibility to create a liquid secondary market for FHA- and VA-insured mortgages, which it tried to accomplish by buying mortgages. Fannie Mae needed a funding source in case it faced a liquidity squeeze. Congress provided this by giving Fannie Mae a credit line with the Treasury.

Despite the creation of Fannie Mae, the secondary mortgage market did not develop to any significant extent. During periods of tight money, Fannie Mae could do little to mitigate the housing crisis. In 1968, Congress divided Fannie Mae into two organizations: (1) the current Fannie Mae, and (2) the Government National Mortgage Association (popularly known as Ginnie Mae). Ginnie Mae's function is to use the "full faith and credit of the U.S. government" to support the FHA and VA mortgage market. Two years later, in 1970, Congress authorized Fannie Mae to purchase conventional mortgage loans (that is, those not insured by the FHA or VA) and created the Federal Home Loan Mortgage Corporation (popularly known as Freddie Mac) to provide support for FHA/VA insured mortgages and conventional mortgages.

Securitization of Mortgages

Ginnie Mae accomplished its objective by guaranteeing securities issued by private entities who pooled mortgages together and then used these mortgages as collateral for the security sold. Freddie Mac and Fannie Mae purchased mortgages, pooled these mortgages, and issued securities using the pool of mortgages as collateral. The securities created are called **mortgage pass-through securities**. They are purchased by many types of investors (domestic and foreign) who had previously shunned investment in the mortgage market.

In the 1980s, private issuers of mortgage pass-through securities who did not use the backing of the three agencies but instead some form of private credit enhancement began issuing pass-through securities backed by conventional family mortgages and commercial real estate mortgages.

> ### Key Points That You Should Understand Before Proceeding
>
> 1. The securitization of a mortgage loan to create mortgage pass-through securities was the key factor in the development of a strong secondary mortgage market.
> 2. Securitization of mortgage loans is one form of asset securitization.
> 3. Three government agencies were created to promote the secondary mortgage market: Ginnie Mae, Fannie Mae, and Freddie Mac.

MORTGAGE PASS-THROUGH SECURITIES

As we noted in the previous chapter, investing in mortgages exposes the investor to default risk, price risk, liquidity risk, and prepayment risk. A more efficient investment technique is to invest in a *mortgage pass-through security*. This is a security created when one or more holders of mortgages form a collection (pool) of mortgages and sell shares or participation certificates in the pool. A pool may consist of several thousand mortgages or only a few. The first mortgage pass-through security was created in 1968. Risk-averse investors prefer investing in a pool to investing in a single mortgage, partly because a mortgage pass-through security is considerably more liquid than an individual mortgage.

When a mortgage is included in a pool of mortgages that is used as collateral for a mortgage pass-through security, the mortgage is said to be **securitized**. More than one-third of mortgages for one- to four-family houses have been securitized. Only 25% of conventional mortgages have been securitized, but 85% of FHA/VA insured mortgages have been. Less than 10% of multifamily unit mortgages have found their way into a mortgage pool backing a mortgage pass-through security.

Cash Flow Characteristics

The cash flow of a mortgage pass-through security depends on the cash flow of the underlying mortgages. As we explained in the previous chapter, the cash flow consists of monthly mortgage payments representing interest, the scheduled repayment of principal, and any prepayments.

Payments are made to securityholders each month. The amounts and the timing of the cash flow from the pool of mortgages and the cash flow passed through to investors, however, are not identical. The monthly cash flow for a pass-through security is less than the monthly cash flow of the underlying mortgages by an amount equal to servicing and other fees. The other fees are those charged by the issuer or guarantor of the pass-through security for guaranteeing the issue (discussed later).[1]

The timing of the cash flow is also different. The monthly mortgage payment is due from each mortgagor on the first day of each month, but there is a delay in pass-

---

[1] Actually, the servicer pays the guarantee fee to the issuer or guarantor.

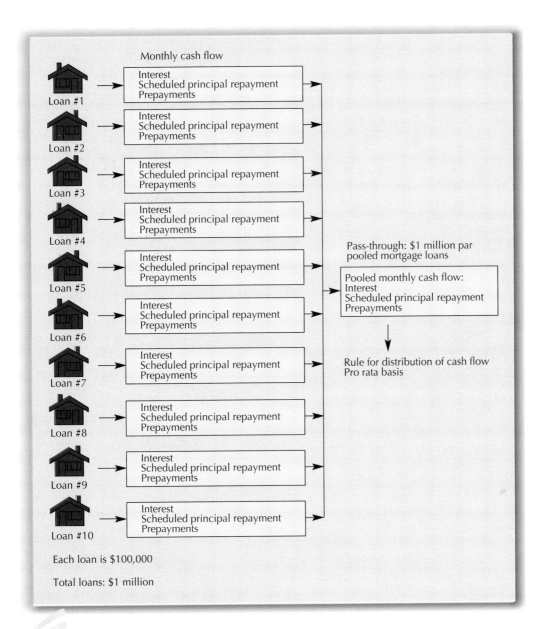

Figure 24-1   Illustration of Creation of a Mortgage Pass-Through Security

ing through the corresponding monthly cash flow to the securityholders. The length of the delay varies by the type of pass-through security.

Figure 24-1 illustrates the process of creating a mortgage pass-through security.

Issuers of Mortgage Pass-Through Securities

The three major types of pass-through securities are guaranteed by the agencies created by Congress to increase the supply of capital to the residential mortgage market and to provide support for an active secondary market: Government National

Mortgage Association (Ginnie Mae), Federal Home Loan Mortgage Corporation (Freddie Mac), and Federal National Mortgage Association (Fannie Mae).

Although Fannie Mae and Freddie Mac are commonly referred to as *agencies* of the U.S. government, in fact both are corporate instrumentalities of the government. Their stock trades on the New York Stock Exchange; therefore, they are effectively quasi-private corporations. They do not receive a government subsidy or appropriation, and are taxed like any other corporation. Fannie Mae and Freddie Mac are more appropriately referred to as *government-sponsored enterprises (GSEs)*. Their guarantee does not carry the full faith and credit of the U.S. government. Ginnie Mae, by contrast, is a federally related institution because it is part of the Department of Housing and Urban Development. Its guarantee, therefore, carries the full faith and credit of the U.S. government.

The securities associated with these three entities are known as **agency pass-through securities**. About 98% of all pass-through securities are agency pass-through securities. The balance of mortgage pass-through securities are privately issued. These securities are called **nonagency mortgage pass-through securities**. While the major portion of pass-throughs issues have residential mortgages as their collateral, pass-throughs collateralized by mortgages on commercial property also have been issued.

Government National Mortgage Association

Ginnie Mae's mortgage-backed securities represent the largest proportion of mortgage pass-through securities outstanding. They are guaranteed by the full faith and credit of the U.S. government with respect to timely payment of both interest and principal. That is, the interest and principal will be paid when due even if mortgagors fail to make their monthly mortgage payment.

Although Ginnie Mae provides the guarantee, it is not the issuer. Pass-through securities are issued by lenders it approves, such as thrifts, commercial banks, and mortgage bankers. These lenders receive approval only if the underlying mortgages satisfy the underwriting standards established by Ginnie Mae. When it guarantees securities issued by approved lenders, Ginnie Mae permits these lenders to convert illiquid individual mortgages into liquid securities backed by the U.S. government. In the process, Ginnie Mae accomplishes its goal to supply funds to the residential mortgage market and provide an active secondary market. For the guarantee, Ginnie Mae receives a fee, called the *guaranteeing fee*.

The security guaranteed by Ginnie Mae is called a *mortgage-backed security* (MBS). These securities are sold in minimum denominations of $25,000 and in increments of $5,000 thereafter. The first MBS was issued in 1968. Only mortgages insured or guaranteed by either the Federal Housing Administration, the Veterans Administration, or the Farmers Home Administration can be included in a mortgage pool guaranteed by Ginnie Mae.

Federal Home Loan Mortgage Corporation

The second largest category of agency pass-through securities contains those issued by the Federal Home Loan Mortgage Corporation (FHLMC). The security issued by Freddie Mac is called a **participation certificate (PC)**. The first PCs were issued in 1971.

Most of the pools of mortgages underlying Freddie Mac participation certificates consist of conventional mortgages, although participation certificates with underlying pools consisting of FHA-insured and VA-guaranteed mortgages have been issued. While there are participation certificates that guarantee the timely payment of both interest and principal, most Freddie Mac participation certificates guarantee only the timely payment of interest. The scheduled principal is passed through as it is collected, with Freddie Mac guaranteeing only that the scheduled payment will be made no later than one year after it is due. A Freddie Mac guarantee is not a guarantee by the U.S. government. Most market participants, though, view Freddie Mac participation certificates as similar in credit-worthiness to Ginnie Mae pass-throughs, which are fully guaranteed by the U.S. government.

Freddie Mac has two programs from which it creates PCs: the Cash Program and the Guarantor/Swap Program. The underlying loans for both programs are conventional mortgages (i.e., mortgages not backed by a government agency). Conventional Regular PCs are issued under the Cash Program. In this program, the mortgages that back the PC include individual conventional one- to four-family mortgage loans that Freddie Mac purchases from mortgage originators, pools, and sells. Under the Conventional Guarantor/Swap Program, Freddie Mac allows originators to swap pooled mortgages for PCs in those same pools. For example, a thrift may have $50 million of mortgages. It can swap these mortgages for a Freddie Mac PC whose underlying mortgage pool is the $50 million mortgage pool the thrift swapped for the PC.

Both programs provide capital to the residential mortgage market and foster a secondary mortgage market. The Guarantor/Swap Program was designed specifically to provide liquidity to the troubled thrift industry. It allows thrifts to swap mortgages trading below par (because mortgage rates are lower than the current mortgage rate) without recognizing an accounting loss for financial reporting purposes. The PC that the thrift gets in exchange for the mortgage pool can then be either (1) held as an investment; (2) used as collateral for either short-term or long-term borrowing; or (3) sold. The Guarantor/Swap program has been a huge success and is one of the reasons for the significant growth of the amount of PCs issued.

In the fall of 1990, Freddie Mac introduced its Gold PC, which it issues in both its Cash Program and Guarantor/Swap Program. The Gold PC is the only type of pass-through it will issue in the future. Gold PCs are guaranteed with respect to timely payment of both interest and principal.

Federal National Mortgage Association

Although it was created by Congress in 1938, the Federal National Mortgage Association (FNMA), in its current form, is the newest player in the agency pass-through securities market. Fannie Mae was charged by Congress with promoting a secondary market for conventional and FHA/VA single- and multifamily mortgages. To meet that obligation, since 1972 it has purchased these mortgages and held them as investments. It was not until 1981 that Fannie Mae pooled these mortgages and issued its first mortgage pass-through securities, called *mortgage-backed securities* (MBS). These pass-throughs are guaranteed with respect to the timely payment of both interest and principal. Like Freddie Mac participation certificates, Fannie Mae mortgage-backed securities are not obligations of the U.S. government. Fannie Mae also has a swap program similar to that of Freddie Mac. It provides liquidity to mortgage originators such as thrifts.

Nonagency Pass-Through Securities

The mortgages that the agencies could purchase or guarantee in securitized form are restricted to those that meet their underwriting standards related to the maximum size of the loan and the maximum ratio of the amount of the loan to the market value of the mortgaged property. Such mortgages are called *conforming mortgages*. A mortgage that fails to satisfy the underwriting standard is called a *nonconforming mortgage*. Mortgage loans that are greater than the maximum permissible loan size are referred to as **jumbo loans**. While Congress has periodically increased the maximum amount of the loan that may be included in pass-throughs guaranteed by the three agencies, the loan size is still often below the typical average cost of a home in certain geographical areas.

The agencies cannot affect the liquidity of nonconforming mortgages such as jumbo mortgages. This sector of the mortgage market has had to be securitized by the private sector, without government guarantee.

Privately issued—that is, *nonagency*—pass-throughs were first issued in 1977 by the Bank of America, but faced many impediments to widespread acceptance. The government wanted to see the private sector market develop, not only to improve its liquidity, but also because it was concerned about the huge potential liability of the U.S. government, should the agencies have to make good on their guarantee in the event of massive homeowner defaults. One of the objectives of the Presidential Commission on Housing, established in mid-1981, was to recommend a number of private-sector alternatives.

The commission's report in April 1982 recommended the privatization of Fannie Mae and Freddie Mac and the development of private-sector alternatives to the two government-sponsored enterprises. The commission identified three major problems to be solved before an efficient private-sector market could be developed. First, private pass-throughs were being crowded out by agency issues. Second, private issuers faced federal and state laws or regulations that either limited the demand for private label products, or resulted in security structures that were not cost-efficient for issuers. Moreover, these restrictions had no economic justification. For example, federal or state regulators would not permit such securities to be treated as qualified investments for the institutions they regulated. Tax rules regarding how a transaction must be structured in order to qualify as a nontaxable conduit resulted in needlessly expensive security structures. Finally, private issues lacked standardization, and this deficiency limited liquidity.

The development of the nonagency pass-through market has been the result of government intervention to foster the growth of this sector, as well as initiatives undertaken by the private sector to structure pass-throughs to enhance their credit quality.

Government Intervention.

Several legislative acts and regulatory changes helped foster the development of the nonagency mortgage-backed securities market. The **Secondary Mortgage Market Enhancement Act of 1984 (SMMEA)** included provisions to improve the marketability of mortgage-related securities earning a double-A quality rating or better from one of the nationally recognized commercial rating companies. More specifically, SMMEA made such securities legal investments for federally chartered banks and thrifts. These investments are referred to as *SMMEA-qualified securities.*

This legislation also made SMMEA-qualified securities permissible investments for state-regulated financial institutions (depository institutions and insurance companies), which are permitted to invest in Treasury securities or federal agency securities. This action opened the door to enormous pools of investment capital. The SMMEA grants individual states the right to override this particular provision of the act by October 1991. As many states have exercised their prerogative and overridden this provision of the act, they have reduced funds from the entities they regulate that could invest in the private-sector market. The Department of Labor, which has the responsibility of regulating pension funds, has since made nonagency pass-throughs acceptable assets for pension plans.

The peculiarities of creating pass-throughs made it difficult for issuers to comply with SEC registration regulations. The SEC, for example, requires that a prospectus provide pertinent information about the underlying pool of mortgages. In the creation of mortgage-backed securities, however, issuers sell the securities while they are assembling the underlying pool of mortgage loans. Thus, the final pool would be unknown at the time of registration and could not be indicated in the prospectus. SEC regulations prevented the registration of these *blind pools* and refused to allow such underwriting on a shelf registration basis (Rule 415). Issuers also had to contend with the periodic reporting requirements after a mortgage-backed security was issued. None of these actions was required for agency mortgage-backed securities, because such securities are exempt from SEC registration. All these factors—the increased cost associated with the inability to time issuances through shelf registration, the lost flexibility to assemble pools prior to the offering, and the ongoing reporting requirements—made private issuance unattractive and impeded development of the private label pass-through market.

Recognizing this, the SEC significantly modified the requirements for private pass-through issuers in 1983 by permitting the registration of securities backed by blind pools, so long as the issuer commits to obtain a specified quality rating and provides sufficient information about the potential pool in the prospectus. When the final pool is assembled, that information must be sent to investors. Private mortgage-backed security issuers can now also qualify for shelf registration, and the periodic reporting requirements are less stringent than for corporate issuers.

The Tax Reform Act of 1986 also made the structuring of private mortgage-related securities less costly from a tax perspective. The 1986 act expanded the types of structures that could be issued, and exempted from separate taxation the legal entity that distributes the cash flow if certain conditions are satisfied. Finally, brokers and dealers could use agency pass-throughs as collateral for margin transactions. Prior to 1983, private pass-throughs were not marginable. In January 1983, the Federal Reserve Board amended Regulation T to allow the same margin requirements as for over-the-counter nonconvertible bonds.

The Issuers.

Nonagency pass-throughs have been issued by conduits of (1) commercial banks, (2) investment banking firms, and (3) entities not associated with either commercial banks or investment banking firms. The following are some of the issuers of nonagency pass-through securities: Countrywide, Residential Funding Corporation, Citicorp/Citibank Housing, Chase Mortgage Finance, Prudential Home, Saxon Mortgage, and GE Capital Mortgage.

In addition, the Resolution Trust Corporation (RTC) was an important issuer in this market. The RTC used the mortgages it acquired by taking over S&Ls to create mortgage pass-through securities. While the RTC was a government entity, an investor in the securities issued by this entity is not protected against credit risk by the U.S. government.

Credit Enhancement.

Unlike agency pass-through securities, nonagency mortgage pass-through securities are rated. Often they are supported by credit enhancements so that they can obtain a high rating. The senior tranches of most nonagency mortgage pass-through securities have a rating of at least double A. The development of private credit enhancement is the key to the success of this market and, indeed, the key to the development of all asset securitization. Credit enhancement may take the form of either (1) corporate guarantees; (2) pool insurance from a mortgage insurance company; (3) a bank letter of credit; or (4) senior/subordinated interests.

In the case of a corporate guarantee, the issuer of a conventional pass-through uses its own credit rating to back the security. Under the second approach to credit enhancement, a mortgage pool policy is obtained to cover defaults up to a specified amount. The rating of the mortgage insurance company that writes the policy must be equal to or higher than the rating that the issuer seeks for the pass-through security. For example, if an issuer seeks a double-A rating for the pass-through, it cannot obtain a pool insurance policy from a single-A rated mortgage insurance company. The cost of a letter of credit is relatively high because of the limited number of financial institutions willing to issue such guarantees, and therefore this form of credit enhancement is not common.

The fourth approach to credit enhancement is the senior/subordinated structure, also known as the A/B pass-through. In this structure, a mortgage pool is partitioned into senior certificates and subordinated certificates. The senior certificate holder has priority on the cash flow from the underlying collateral. It is the senior certificates that are rated and sold to investors as conventional pass-throughs. The subordinated certificates absorb the default risk. The amount of subordinated certificates relative to senior certificates that a mortgage pool is divided into will determine its credit rating. The greater the portion of subordinated certificates relative to senior certificates, the higher the credit rating that can be obtained.[2]

We discuss these credit enhancements in more detail in the next chapter where we cover asset-backed securities.

Prepayment Risks Associated with Pass-Through Securities

An investor who owns pass-through securities does not know what the cash flow will be because cash flow depends on prepayments. The risk associated with prepayments is called **prepayment risk**.

To understand prepayment risk, suppose an investor buys a 10% coupon Ginnie Mae at a time when mortgage rates are 10%. Let's consider what will happen to prepayments if mortgage rates decline to, say, 6%. There will be two adverse consequences. First, as we explained in Chapter 11, the price of an option-free bond such as a Treasury bond will rise. In the case of a pass-through security, the rise in price will not be as large as that of an option-free bond, because a fall in interest rates will increase the probability that the market rate will fall below the rate the borrower is paying. This fall in rates gives the borrower an incentive to prepay the loan and refinance the debt at a lower rate. To the extent that this happens, the securityholder will be repaid not at a price incorporating the premium but at par value. The holder risks capital loss, which reflects the fact that the anticipated reimbursements at par will not yield the initial cash flow.

The adverse consequences when mortgage rates decline are the same as those faced by holders of callable corporate and municipal bonds. As in the case of those instruments, the upside price potential of a pass-through security is truncated because of prepayments. This should not be surprising because a mortgage loan effectively grants the borrower the right to call the loan at par value. The adverse consequence when mortgage rates decline is referred to as **contraction risk**.

Now let's look at what happens if mortgage rates rise to 15%. The price of the pass-through, like the price of any bond, will decline. But again it will decline more because the higher rates will tend to slow down the rate of prepayment, in effect increasing the amount invested at the coupon rate, which is lower than the market rate. Prepayments will slow down because homeowners will not refinance or partially prepay their mortgages when mortgage rates are higher than the contractual rate of 10%. Of course, this is just the time when investors want prepayments to speed up so that they can reinvest the prepayments at the higher market interest rate. This adverse consequence of rising mortgage rates is called **extension risk**.

---

[2] For a more detailed description of this structure, see Chapter 8 of Frank J. Fabozzi and Chuck Ramsey, *Collateralized Mortgage Obligations: Structures and Analysis*, 3rd ed. (New Hope, PA: Frank J. Fabozzi Associates, 1998).

Therefore, prepayment risk encompasses contraction risk and extension risk. Prepayment risk makes pass-throughs unattractive for certain financial institutions to hold from an asset/liability perspective. Let's look at why particular institutional investors may find pass-throughs unattractive:

1. Thrifts and commercial banks, as we explained in Chapter 4, want to lock in a spread over their cost of funds. Their funds are raised on a short-term basis. If they invest in fixed-rate pass-through securities, they will be mismatched because a pass-through is a longer-term security. In particular, depository institutions are exposed to extension risk when they invest in pass-through securities.

2. To satisfy certain obligations of insurance companies, pass-through securities may be unattractive. More specifically, consider a life insurance company that has issued a four-year GIC. The uncertainty about the cash flow from a pass-through security, and the like-lihood that slow prepayments will result in the instrument being long-term, make it an unappealing investment vehicle for such accounts. In such instances, a pass-through security exposes the insurance company to extension risk.

3. Consider a pension fund that wants to fund a 15-year liability. Buying a pass-through security exposes the pension fund to the risk that prepayments will speed up and that the maturity of the investment will shorten to considerably less than 15 years. Prepayments will speed up when interest rates decline, thereby forcing reinvestment of the prepaid amounts at a lower interest rate. In this case, the pension fund is open to contraction risk.

We can see that some institutional investors are concerned with extension risk and others with contraction risk when they purchase a pass-through security. Is it possible to alter the cash flow of a pass-through so as to reduce the contraction risk and extension risk for institutional investors? This is explained later in this chapter when we cover collateralized mortgage obligations.

Prepayment Conventions

The only way to project a cash flow is to make some assumption about the prepayment rate over the life of the underlying mortgage pool. The prepayment rate assumed is called the *prepayment speed* or, simply, *speed*.

Conditional Prepayment Rate.

The **conditional prepayment rate (CPR)** assumes that some fraction of the remaining principal in the pool is prepaid each year for the remaining term of the mortgage. The prepayment rate assumed for a pool is based on the characteristics of the pool (including its historical prepayment experience) and the current and expected future economic environment. It is referred to as a *conditional* rate because it is conditional on the remaining mortgage balance.

The CPR is an annual prepayment rate. To estimate monthly prepayments, the CPR must be converted into a monthly prepayment rate, commonly referred to as the *single-monthly mortality rate* (SMM). The following formula can be used to determine the SMM for a given CPR:

$$SMM = 1 - (1 - CPR)^{1/12} \qquad (1)$$

Suppose that the CPR used to estimate prepayments is 6%. The corresponding SMM is:

$$SMM = 1 - (1 - 0.06)^{1/12}$$
$$= 1 - (0.94)^{0.08333} = 0.005143$$

An SMM of $w\%$ means that approximately $w\%$ of the remaining mortgage balance at the beginning of the month, less the scheduled principal payment, will prepay that month. That is,

$$\text{Prepayment for month } t = \text{SMM} \times (\text{Beginning mortgage balance for month } t \\ - \text{Scheduled pricipal payment for month } t) \qquad (2)$$

For example, suppose that an investor owns a pass-through in which the remaining mortgage balance at the beginning of some month is $290 million. Assuming that the SMM is 0.5143% and the scheduled principal payment is $3 million, the estimated prepayment for the month is:

$$0.005143 \times (\$290,000,000 - \$3,000,000) = \$1,476,041$$

PSA Benchmark.

The **Public Securities Association (PSA) prepayment benchmark** is expressed as a monthly series of annual prepayment rates. The PSA benchmark assumes that prepayment rates are low for newly originated mortgages and then will speed up as the mortgages become seasoned.

The PSA benchmark assumes the following CPRs for 30-year mortgages:

1. a CPR of 0.2% for the first month, increased by 0.2% per year per month for the next 30 months when it reaches 6% per year, and
2. a 6% CPR for the remaining years.

This benchmark, referred to as *100% PSA* or simply *100 PSA*, is graphically depicted in Figure 24-2. Mathematically, 100 PSA can be expressed as follows:

$$\text{If } t \le 30, \text{ then CPR} = 6\%\,(t/30)$$
$$\text{If } t > 30, \text{ then CPR} = 6\%$$

where t is the number of months since the mortgage originated.

Slower or faster speeds are then referred to as some percentage of PSA. For example, 50 PSA means one-half the CPR of the PSA benchmark prepayment rate; 150 PSA means one-and-a-half times the CPR of the PSA benchmark prepayment rate; 300 PSA means three times the CPR of the benchmark prepayment rate. A prepayment rate of 0 PSA means that no prepayments are assumed.

The CPR is converted to an SMM using equation (1). For example, the SMMs for month 5, month 20, and months 31 through 360 assuming 100 PSA are calculated as follows:

For month 5:

$$\text{CPR} = 6\%\,(5/30) = 1\% = 0.01$$
$$\text{SMM} = 1 - (1 - 0.01)^{1/12}$$
$$= 1 - (0.99)^{0.083333} = 0.000837$$

For month 20:

$$\text{CPR} = 6\%\,(20/30) = 4\% = 0.04$$
$$\text{SMM} = 1 - (1 - 0.04)^{1/12}$$
$$= 1 - (0.96)^{0.083333} = 0.003396$$

For months 31 to 360:

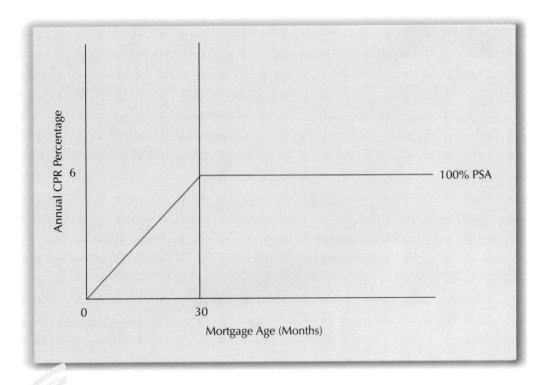

Figure 24-2   Graphical Depiction of 100 PSA

$$CPR = 6\%$$
$$SMM = 1 - (1 - 0.06)^{1/12}$$
$$= 1 - (0.94)^{0.083333} = 0.005143$$

The SMMs for month 5, month 20, and months 31 through 360 assuming 165 PSA are computed as follows:
For month 5:

$$CPR = 6\%(5/30) = 1\% = 0.01$$
$$165\ PSA = 1.65(0.01) = 0.0165$$
$$SMM = 1 - (1 - 0.0165)^{1/12}$$
$$= 1 - (0.9835)^{0.083333} = 0.001386$$

For month 20:

$$CPR = 6\%(20/30) = 4\% = 0.04$$
$$165\ PSA = 1.65(0.04) = 0.066$$
$$SMM = 1 - (1 - 0.066)^{1/12}$$
$$= 1 - (0.934)^{0.083333} = 0.005674$$

For months 31 to 360:

$$CP = 6\%$$
$$165\ PSA = 1.65(0.06) = 0.099$$
$$SMM = 1 - (1 - 0.099)^{1/12}$$
$$= 1 - (0.901)^{0.083333} = 0.007828$$

Notice that the SMM assuming 165 PSA is not just 1.65 times the SMM assuming 100 PSA. It is the CPR that is a multiple of the CPR assuming 100 PSA.

Illustration of Monthly Cash Flow Construction

We now show how to construct a monthly cash flow for a hypothetical pass-through given a PSA assumption. For the purpose of this illustration, the underlying mortgages for this hypothetical pass-through are assumed to be fixed-rate, level-payment mortgages and the pass-through rate is assumed to be 7.5%. Furthermore, it is assumed that the weighted average maturity (WAM) of the pool of mortgages is 357 months.[3]

Table 24-1 shows the cash flow for selected months assuming 100 PSA. The cash flow is broken down into three components: (1) interest (based on the pass-through rate), (2) the regularly scheduled principal repayment, and (3) prepayments based on 100 PSA.

Let's walk through Table 24-1 column by column.

Column 1: This is the month.
Column 2: This column gives the outstanding mortgage balance at the beginning of the month. It is equal to the outstanding balance at the beginning of the previous month reduced by the total principal payment in the previous month.
Column 3: This column shows the SMM for 100 PSA. Two things should be noted in this column. First, for month 1, the SMM is for a pass-through that has been seasoned three months. That is, the CPR is 0.8%. This is because the WAM is 357. Second, from month 27 on, the SMM is 0.00514, which corresponds to a CPR of 6%.
Column 4: The total monthly mortgage payment is shown in this column. Notice that the total monthly mortgage payment declines over time as prepayments reduce the mortgage balance outstanding. There is a formula to determine what the monthly mortgage balance will be for each month given prepayments.[4]
Column 5: The monthly interest paid to the pass-through investor is found in this column. This value is determined by multiplying the outstanding mortgage balance at the beginning of the month by the pass-through rate of 7.5% and dividing by 12.
Column 6: This column gives the regularly scheduled principal repayment. This is the difference between the total monthly mortgage payment (the amount shown in column 4) and the gross coupon interest for the month. The gross coupon interest is 8.125% multiplied by the outstanding mortgage balance at the beginning of the month, then divided by 12.
Column 7: The prepayment for the month is reported in this column. The prepayment is found by using equation (2). So, for example, in month 100, the beginning mortgage balance is $231,249,776, the scheduled principal payment is $332,298, and the SMM at 100 PSA is 0.00514301 (only 0.00514 is shown in the table to save space), so the prepayment is:

$$0.00514301 \times (\$231,249,776 - \$332,928) = \$1,187,608$$

Column 8: The total principal payment, which is the sum of columns 6 and 7, is shown in this column.
Column 9: The projected monthly cash flow for this pass-through is shown in this last column. The monthly cash flow is the sum of the interest paid to the pass-through investor (column 5) and the total principal payments for the month (column 8).

---

[3] It is necessary to calculate a WAM for a pool of mortgages because not all the mortgages have the same number of months remaining to maturity.
[4] The formula is presented in Chapter 20 of Frank J. Fabozzi, *Fixed Income Mathematics: Analytical and Statistical Techniques* (Chicago: Probus Publishing, 1993).

Table 24-1 Monthly Cash Flow for a $400 Million, 7.5% Pass-through Rate with a WAC of 8.125% and a WAM of 357 Months Assuming 100 PSA

(1)	(2)	(3)	(4)	(5)	(6)	(7)	(8)	(9)
MONTH	OUTSTANDING BALANCE	SMM	MORTGAGE PAYMENT	NET INTEREST	SCHEDULED PRINCIPAL	PREPAY-MENT	TOTAL PRINCIPAL	TOTAL CASH FLOW
1	$400,000,000	0.00067	$2,975,868	$2,500,000	$267,535	$ 267,470	$ 535,005	$3,035,005
2	399,464,995	0.00084	2,973,877	2,496,656	269,166	334,198	603,364	3,100,020
3	398,861,631	0.00101	2,971,387	2,492,885	270,762	400,800	671,562	3,164,447
4	398,190,069	0.00117	2,968,399	2,488,688	272,321	467,243	739,564	3,228,252
5	397,450,505	0.00134	2,964,914	2,484,066	273,843	533,493	807,335	3,291,401
6	396,643,170	0.00151	2,960,931	2,479,020	275,327	599,514	874,841	3,353,860
7	395,768,329	0.00168	2,956,453	2,473,552	276,772	665,273	942,045	3,415,597
8	394,826,284	0.00185	2,951,480	2,467,664	278,177	730,736	1,008,913	3,476,577
9	393,817,371	0.00202	2,946,013	2,461,359	279,542	795,869	1,075,410	3,536,769
10	392,741,961	0.00219	2,940,056	2,454,637	280,865	860,637	1,141,502	3,596,140
11	391,600,459	0.00236	2,933,608	2,447,503	282,147	925,008	1,207,155	3,654,658
12	390,393,304	0.00254	2,926,674	2,439,958	283,386	988,948	1,272,333	3,712,291
13	389,120,971	0.00271	2,919,254	2,432,006	284,581	1,052,423	1,337,004	3,769,010
14	387,783,966	0.00288	2,911,353	2,423,650	285,733	1,115,402	1,401,134	3,824,784
15	386,382,832	0.00305	2,902,973	2,414,893	286,839	1,177,851	1,464,690	3,879,583
16	384,918,142	0.00322	2,894,117	2,405,738	287,900	1,239,739	1,527,639	3,933,378
17	383,390,502	0.00340	2,884,789	2,396,191	288,915	1,301,033	1,589,949	3,986,139
18	381,800,553	0.00357	2,874,992	2,386,253	289,884	1,361,703	1,651,587	4,037,840
19	380,148,966	0.00374	2,864,730	2,375,931	290,805	1,421,717	1,712,522	4,088,453
20	378,436,444	0.00392	2,854,008	2,365,228	291,678	1,481,046	1,772,724	4,137,952
21	376,663,720	0.00409	2,842,830	2,354,148	292,503	1,539,658	1,832,161	4,186,309
22	374,831,559	0.00427	2,831,201	2,342,697	293,279	1,597,525	1,890,804	4,233,501
23	372,940,755	0.00444	2,819,125	2,330,880	294,005	1,654,618	1,948,623	4,279,503
24	370,992,132	0.00462	2,806,607	2,318,701	294,681	1,710,908	2,005,589	4,324,290
25	368,986,543	0.00479	2,793,654	2,306,166	295,307	1,766,368	2,061,675	4,367,841
26	366,924,868	0.00497	2,780,270	2,293,280	295,883	1,820,970	2,116,852	4,410,133
27	364,808,016	0.00514	2,766,461	2,280,050	296,406	1,874,688	2,171,094	4,451,144
28	362,636,921	0.00514	2,752,233	2,266,481	296,879	1,863,519	2,160,398	4,426,879
29	360,476,523	0.00514	2,738,078	2,252,978	297,351	1,852,406	2,149,758	4,402,736
30	358,326,766	0.00514	2,723,996	2,239,542	297,825	1,841,347	2,139,173	4,378,715
100	231,249,776	0.00514	1,898,682	1,445,311	332,928	1,187,608	1,520,537	2,965,848
101	229,729,239	0.00514	1,888,917	1,435,808	333,459	1,179,785	1,513,244	2,949,052
102	228,215,995	0.00514	1,879,202	1,426,350	333,990	1,172,000	1,505,990	2,932,340
103	226,710,004	0.00514	1,869,538	1,416,938	334,522	1,164,252	1,498,774	2,915,712
104	225,211,230	0.00514	1,859,923	1,407,570	335,055	1,156,541	1,491,596	2,899,166
105	223,719,634	0.00514	1,850,357	1,398,248	335,589	1,148,867	1,484,456	2,882,703
200	109,791,339	0.00514	1,133,751	686,196	390,372	562,651	953,023	1,639,219
201	108,838,316	0.00514	1,127,920	680,239	390,994	557,746	948,740	1,628,980
202	107,889,576	0.00514	1,122,119	674,310	391,617	552,863	944,480	1,618,790
203	106,945,096	0.00514	1,116,348	668,407	392,241	548,003	940,243	1,608,650
204	106,004,852	0.00514	1,110,607	662,530	392,866	543,164	936,029	1,598,560
205	105,068,823	0.00514	1,104,895	656,680	393,491	538,347	931,838	1,588,518
300	32,383,611	0.00514	676,991	202,398	457,727	164,195	621,923	824,320
301	31,761,689	0.00514	673,510	198,511	458,457	160,993	619,449	817,960
302	31,142,239	0.00514	670,046	194,639	459,187	157,803	616,990	811,629
303	30,525,249	0.00514	666,600	190,783	459,918	154,626	614,545	805,328
304	29,910,704	0.00514	663,171	186,942	460,651	151,462	612,113	799,055
305	29,298,591	0.00514	659,761	183,116	461,385	148,310	609,695	792,811

(continued)

Table 24-1   (*Continued*)

(1)	(2)	(3)	(4)	(5)	(6)	(7)	(8)	(9)
MONTH	OUTSTANDING BALANCE	SMM	MORTGAGE PAYMENT	NET INTEREST	SCHEDULED PRINCIPAL	PREPAY-MENT	TOTAL PRINCIPAL	TOTAL CASH FLOW
350	4,060,411	0.00514	523,138	25,378	495,645	18,334	513,979	539,356
351	3,546,432	0.00514	520,447	22,165	496,435	15,686	512,121	534,286
352	3,034,311	0.00514	517,770	18,964	497,226	13,048	510,274	529,238
353	2,524,037	0.00514	515,107	15,775	498,018	10,420	508,437	524,213
354	2,015,600	0.00514	512,458	12,597	498,811	7,801	506,612	519,209
355	1,508,988	0.00514	509,823	9,431	499,606	5,191	504,797	514,228
356	1,004,191	0.00514	507,201	6,276	500,401	2,591	502,992	509,269
357	501,199	0.00514	504,592	3,132	501,199	0	501,199	504,331

Table 24-2 shows selected monthly cash flows for the same pass-through assuming 165 PSA.

Average Life

The stated maturity of a mortgage pass-through security is an inappropriate measure of the security's life because of prepayments. Instead, market participants commonly use the security's average life. The **average life** of a mortgage-backed security is the average time to receipt of principal payments (scheduled principal payments and projected prepayments), weighted by the amount of principal expected. Mathematically, the average life is expressed as follows:

$$\text{Average life} = \sum_{t=1}^{T} \frac{t \times \text{Principal received at time } t}{12\,(\text{Total principal})}$$

where T is the number of months.

Table 24-2   Monthly Cash Flow for a $400 Million, 7.5% Pass-through Rate with a WAC of 8.125% and a WAM of 357 Months Assuming 165 PSA

(1)	(2)	(3)	(4)	(5)	(6)	(7)	(8)	(9)
MONTH	OUTSTANDING BALANCE	SMM	MORTGAGE PAYMENT	NET INTEREST	SCHEDULED PRINCIPAL	PREPAY-MENT	TOTAL PRINCIPAL	TOTAL CASH FLOW
1	$400,000,000	0.00111	$2,975,868	$2,500,000	$267,535	$ 442,389	$ 709,923	$3,209,923
2	399,290,077	0.00139	2,972,575	2,495,563	269,048	552,847	821,896	3,317,459
3	398,468,181	0.00167	2,968,456	2,490,426	270,495	663,065	933,560	3,423,986
4	397,534,621	0.00195	2,963,513	2,484,591	271,873	772,949	1,044,822	3,529,413
5	396,489,799	0.00223	2,957,747	2,478,061	273,181	882,405	1,155,586	3,633,647
6	395,334,213	0.00251	2,951,160	2,470,839	274,418	991,341	1,265,759	3,736,598
7	394,068,454	0.00279	2,943,755	2,462,928	275,583	1,099,664	1,375,246	3,838,174
8	392,693,208	0.00308	2,935,534	2,454,333	276,674	1,207,280	1,483,954	3,938,287

(continued)

Table 24-2   (*Continued*)

(1)	(2)	(3)	(4)	(5)	(6)	(7)	(8)	(9)
MONTH	OUTSTANDING BALANCE	SMM	MORTGAGE PAYMENT	NET INTEREST	SCHEDULED PRINCIPAL	PREPAY-MENT	TOTAL PRINCIPAL	TOTAL CASH FLOW
9	391,209,254	0.00336	2,926,503	2,445,058	277,690	1,314,099	1,591,789	4,036,847
10	389,617,464	0.00365	2,916,666	2,435,109	278,631	1,420,029	1,698,659	4,133,769
11	387,918,805	0.00393	2,906,028	2,424,493	279,494	1,524,979	1,804,473	4,228,965
12	386,114,332	0.00422	2,894,595	2,413,215	280,280	1,628,859	1,909,139	4,322,353
13	384,205,194	0.00451	2,882,375	2,401,282	280,986	1,731,581	2,012,567	4,413,850
14	382,192,626	0.00480	2,869,375	2,388,704	281,613	1,833,058	2,114,670	4,503,374
15	380,077,956	0.00509	2,855,603	2,375,487	282,159	1,933,203	2,215,361	4,590,848
16	377,862,595	0.00538	2,841,068	2,361,641	282,623	2,031,931	2,314,554	4,676,195
17	375,548,041	0.00567	2,825,779	2,347,175	283,006	2,129,159	2,412,164	4,759,339
18	373,135,877	0.00597	2,809,746	2,332,099	283,305	2,224,805	2,508,110	4,840,210
19	370,627,766	0.00626	2,792,980	2,316,424	283,521	2,318,790	2,602,312	4,918,735
20	368,025,455	0.00656	2,775,493	2,300,159	283,654	2,411,036	2,694,690	4,994,849
21	365,330,765	0.00685	2,757,296	2,283,317	283,702	2,501,466	2,785,169	5,068,486
22	362,545,596	0.00715	2,738,402	2,265,910	283,666	2,590,008	2,873,674	5,139,584
23	359,671,922	0.00745	2,718,823	2,247,950	283,545	2,676,588	2,960,133	5,208,083
24	356,711,789	0.00775	2,698,575	2,229,449	283,338	2,761,139	3,044,477	5,273,926
25	353,667,312	0.00805	2,677,670	2,210,421	283,047	2,843,593	3,126,640	5,337,061
26	350,540,672	0.00835	2,656,123	2,190,879	282,671	2,923,885	3,206,556	5,397,435
27	347,334,116	0.00865	2,633,950	2,170,838	282,209	3,001,955	3,284,164	5,455,002
28	344,049,952	0.00865	2,611,167	2,150,312	281,662	2,973,553	3,255,215	5,405,527
29	340,794,737	0.00865	2,588,581	2,129,967	281,116	2,945,400	3,226,516	5,356,483
30	337,568,221	0.00865	2,566,190	2,109,801	280,572	2,917,496	3,198,067	5,307,869
100	170,142,350	0.00865	1,396,958	1,063,390	244,953	1,469,591	1,714,544	2,777,933
101	168,427,806	0.00865	1,384,875	1,052,674	244,478	1,454,765	1,699,243	2,751,916
102	166,728,563	0.00865	1,372,896	1,042,054	244,004	1,440,071	1,684,075	2,726,128
103	165,044,489	0.00865	1,361,020	1,031,528	243,531	1,425,508	1,669,039	2,700,567
104	163,375,450	0.00865	1,349,248	1,021,097	243,060	1,411,075	1,654,134	2,675,231
105	161,721,315	0.00865	1,337,577	1,010,758	242,589	1,396,771	1,639,359	2,650,118
200	56,746,664	0.00865	585,990	354,667	201,767	489,106	690,874	1,045,540
201	56,055,790	0.00865	580,921	350,349	201,377	483,134	684,510	1,034,859
202	55,371,280	0.00865	575,896	346,070	200,986	477,216	678,202	1,024,273
203	54,693,077	0.00865	570,915	341,832	200,597	471,353	671,950	1,013,782
204	54,021,127	0.00865	565,976	337,632	200,208	465,544	665,752	1,003,384
205	53,355,375	0.00865	561,081	333,471	199,820	459,789	659,609	993,080
300	11,758,141	0.00865	245,808	73,488	166,196	100,269	266,465	339,953
301	11,491,677	0.00865	243,682	71,823	165,874	97,967	263,841	335,664
302	11,227,836	0.00865	241,574	70,174	165,552	95,687	261,240	331,414
303	10,966,596	0.00865	239,485	68,541	165,232	93,430	258,662	327,203
304	10,707,934	0.00865	237,413	66,925	164,912	91,196	256,107	323,032
305	10,451,827	0.00865	235,360	65,324	164,592	88,983	253,575	318,899
350	1,235,674	0.00865	159,202	7,723	150,836	9,384	160,220	167,943
351	1,075,454	0.00865	157,825	6,722	150,544	8,000	158,544	165,266
352	916,910	0.00865	156,460	5,731	150,252	6,631	156,883	162,614
353	760,027	0.00865	155,107	4,750	149,961	5,277	155,238	159,988
354	604,789	0.00865	153,765	3,780	149,670	3,937	153,607	157,387
355	451,182	0.00865	152,435	2,820	149,380	2,611	151,991	154,811
356	299,191	0.00865	151,117	1,870	149,091	1,298	150,398	152,259
357	148,802	0.00865	149,809	930	148,802	0	148,802	149,732

The average life of a pass-through depends on the PSA prepayment assumption. To see this, the average life follows for different prepayment speeds for the pass-through we used to illustrate the cash flow for 100 PSA and 165 PSA in Table 24-1 and Table 24-2:

PSA speed	50	100	165	200	300	400	500	600	700
Average life	15.11	11.66	8.76	7.68	5.63	4.44	3.68	3.16	2.78

Key Points That You Should Understand Before Proceeding

1. A mortgage pass-through security is created when one or more holders of mortgages form a collection (pool) of mortgages and sell shares or participation certificates in the pool.

2. The cash flow of a mortgage pass-through security depends on the cash flow of the underlying mortgages, which consists of monthly mortgage payments representing interest, the scheduled repayment of principal, and any prepayments.

3. The three major types of pass-through securities are guaranteed by either Ginnie Mae (a federally related entity), Fannie Mae (a government-sponsored enterprise), or Freddie Mac (a government-sponsored enterprise), and are referred to as agency pass-through securities.

4. There are private issuers of mortgage pass-through securities that are not explicitly or implicitly guaranteed by the U.S. government; these securities are called nonagency pass-through securities.

5. Of the mortgage pass-through securities guaranteed by one of the three agencies, only those guaranteed by Ginnie Mae carry the full faith and credit of the U.S. government; nonagency pass-through securities are rated by a commercial rating company, and often they are supported by credit enhancements so that they can obtain a high rating.

6. An investor in a mortgage pass-through security is exposed to prepayment risk, which can be decomposed into two types of risk, contraction risk and extension risk.

7. The cash flow of a mortgage pass-through is projected based on an assumed PSA assumption.

COLLATERALIZED MORTGAGE OBLIGATIONS

Some institutional investors are concerned with extension risk and others with contraction risk when they invest in a pass-through. This problem can be mitigated by redirecting the cash flows of mortgage pass-through securities to different bond classes, called **tranches**, so as to create securities that have different exposure to prepayment risk and, therefore, different risk/return patterns than the pass-through securities from which the tranches were created.

When the cash flows of pools of mortgage pass-through securities are redistributed to different bond classes, the resulting securities are called **collateralized mortgage obligations (CMO)**. The creation of a CMO cannot eliminate prepayment risk; it can only distribute the various forms of this risk among different classes of bondholders. The CMO's major financial innovation is that the securities created more closely satisfy the asset/liability needs of institutional investors and thus broaden the appeal of mortgage-backed products to traditional bond investors.

Rather than list the different types of tranches that can be created in a CMO structure, we will show how the tranches can be created. This will provide an excellent illustration of financial engineering. Although there are many different types of CMOs that have been created, we will only look at three of the key innovations in the CMO market: sequential-pay tranches, accrual tranches, and planned amortization class bonds. Two other important tranches that are not illustrated here are the *floating-rate tranche* and *inverse floating-rate tranche.*

Sequential-Pay CMOs

The first CMO was created in 1983 and was structured so that each class of bond would be retired sequentially. Such structures are referred to as **sequential-pay CMOs**. To illustrate a sequential-pay CMO, we discuss CMO-1, a hypothetical deal made up to illustrate the basic features of the structure. The collateral for this hypothetical CMO is a hypothetical pass-through with a total par value of $400 million and the following characteristics: (1) The pass-through coupon rate is 7.5%, (2) the weighted average coupon (WAC) is 8.125%, and (3) the **weighted average maturity (WAM)** is 357 months. This is the same pass-through that we used earlier in this chapter to describe the cash flow of a pass-through based on some PSA assumption.

From this $400 million of collateral, four bond classes or tranches are created. Their characteristics are summarized in Table 24-3. The total par value of the four tranches is equal to the par value of the collateral (i.e., the pass-through security). In this simple structure, the coupon rate is the same for each tranche and also the same as the coupon rate on the collateral. There is no reason why this must be so, and, in fact, typically the coupon rate varies by tranche.

Now remember that a CMO is created by redistributing the cash flow—interest and principal—to the different tranches based on a set of payment rules. The payment rules at the bottom of Table 24-3 describe how the cash flow from the pass-through (i.e., collateral) is to be distributed to the four tranches. There are separate rules for the payment of the coupon interest and the payment of principal, the principal being the total of the regularly scheduled principal payment and any prepayments.

In CMO-1, each tranche receives periodic coupon interest payments based on the amount of the outstanding balance at the beginning of the month. The disbursement of the principal, however, is made in a special way. A tranche is not entitled to receive principal until the entire principal of the tranche has been paid off. More specifically, tranche A receives all the principal payments until the entire principal amount owed to that bond class, $194,500,000, is paid off; then tranche B begins to receive principal and continues to do so until it is paid the entire $36,000,000.

Table 24-3   CMO-1: A Hypothetical Four-Tranche, Sequential-Pay Structure

TRANCHE	PAR AMOUNT	COUPON RATE
A	$194,500,000	7.5%
B	36,000,000	7.5
C	96,500,000	7.5
D	73,000,000	7.5
Total	$400,000,000	

Payment rules:

1. *For payment of periodic coupon interest:* Disburse periodic coupon interest to each tranche on the basis of the amount of principal outstanding at the beginning of the period.
2. *For disbursement of principal payments:* Disburse principal payments to tranche A until it is completely paid off. After tranche A is completely paid off, disburse principal payments to tranche B until it is completely paid off. After tranche B is completely paid off, disburse principal payments to tranche C until it is completely paid off. After tranche C is completely paid off, disburse principal payments to tranche D until it is completely paid off.

Tranche C then receives principal, and when it is paid off, tranche D starts receiving principal payments.

Although the priority rules for the disbursement of the principal payments are known, the precise amount of the principal in each period is not. This will depend on the cash flow and, therefore, on the principal payments of the collateral, which will depend on the actual prepayment rate of the collateral. An assumed PSA speed allows the cash flow to be projected. Table 24-2 shows the cash flow (interest, regularly scheduled principal repayment, and prepayments) assuming 165 PSA. Assuming that the collateral does prepay at 165 PSA, the cash flow available to all four tranches CMO-1 will be precisely the cash flow shown in Table 24-2.

To demonstrate how the priority rules for CMO-1 work, Table 24-4 shows the cash flow for selected months assuming the collateral prepays at 165 PSA. For each tranche,

Table 24-4 Monthly Cash Flow for Selected Months for CMO- 1 Assuming 165 PSA

	Tranche A			Tranche B		
MONTH	BALANCE	PRINCIPAL	INTEREST	BALANCE	PRINCIPAL	INTEREST
1	$194,500,000	$ 709,923	$1,215,625	$36,000,000	$ 0	$225,000
2	193,790,077	821,896	1,211,188	36,000,000	0	255,000
3	192,968,181	933,560	1,206,051	36,000,000	0	225,000
4	192,034,621	1,044,822	1,200,216	36,000,000	0	225,000
5	190,989,799	1,155,586	1,193,686	36,000,000	0	225,000
6	189,834,213	1,265,759	1,186,464	36,000,000	0	225,000
7	188,568,454	1,375,246	1,178,553	36,000,000	0	225,000
8	187,193,208	1,483,954	1,169,958	36,000,000	0	225,000
9	185,709,254	1,591,789	1,160,683	36,000,000	0	225,000
10	184,117,464	1,698,659	1,150,734	36,000,000	0	225,000
11	182,418,805	1,804,473	1,140,118	36,000,000	0	225,000
12	180,614,332	1,909,139	1,128,840	36,000,000	0	225,000
75	12,893,479	2,143,974	80,584	36,000,000	0	225,000
76	10,749,504	2,124,935	67,184	36,000,000	0	225,000
77	8,624,569	2,106,062	53,904	36,000,000	0	225,000
78	6,518,507	2,087,353	40,741	36,000,000	0	225,000
79	4,431,154	2,068,807	27,695	36,000,000	0	225,000
80	2,362,347	2,050,422	14,765	36,000,000	0	225,000
81	311,926	311,926	1,950	36,000,000	1,720,271	225,000
82	0	0	0	34,279,729	2,014,130	214,248
83	0	0	0	32,265,599	1,996,221	201,660
84	0	0	0	30,269,378	1,978,468	189,184
85	0	0	0	28,290,911	1,960,869	176,818
95	0	0	0	9,449,331	1,793,089	59,058
96	0	0	0	7,656,242	1,777,104	47,852
97	0	0	0	5,879,138	1,761,258	36,745
98	0	0	0	4,117,880	1,745,550	25,737
99	0	0	0	2,372,329	1,729,979	14,827
100	0	0	0	642,350	642,350	4,015
101	0	0	0	0	0	0
102	0	0	0	0	0	0
103	0	0	0	0	0	0
104	0	0	0	0	0	0
105	0	0	0	0	0	0

(continued)

Table 24-4 Continued

	Tranche C			Tranche D		
MONTH	BALANCE	PRINCIPAL	INTEREST	BALANCE	PRINCIPAL	INTEREST
1	96,500,000	0	603,125	73,000,000	0	456,250
2	96,500,000	0	603,125	73,000,000	0	456,250
3	96,500,000	0	603,125	73,000,000	0	456,250
4	96,500,000	0	603,125	73,000,000	0	456,250
5	96,500,000	0	603,125	73,000,000	0	456,250
6	96,500,000	0	603,125	73,000,000	0	456,250
7	96,500,000	0	603,125	73,000,000	0	456,250
8	96,500,000	0	603,125	73,000,000	0	456,250
9	96,500,000	0	603,125	73,000,000	0	456,250
10	96,500,000	0	603,125	73,000,000	0	456,250
11	96,500,000	0	603,125	73,000,000	0	456,250
12	96,500,000	0	603,125	73,000,000	0	456,250
95	96,500,000	0	603,125	73,000,000	0	456,250
96	96,500,000	0	603,125	73,000,000	0	456,250
97	96,500,000	0	603,125	73,000,000	0	456,250
98	96,500,000	0	603,125	73,000,000	0	456,250
99	96,500,000	0	603,125	73,000,000	0	456,250
100	96,500,000	1,072,194	603,125	73,000,000	0	456,250
101	95,427,806	1,699,243	596,424	73,000,000	0	456,250
102	93,728,563	1,684,075	585,804	73,000,000	0	456,250
103	92,044,489	1,669,039	575,278	73,000,000	0	456,250
104	90,375,450	1,654,134	564,847	73,000,000	0	456,250
105	88,721,315	1,639,359	554,508	73,000,000	0	456,250
175	3,260,287	869,602	20,377	73,000,000	0	456,250
176	2,390,685	861,673	14,942	73,000,000	0	456,250
177	1,529,013	853,813	9,556	73,000,000	0	456,250
178	675,199	675,199	4,220	73,000,000	170,824	456,250
179	0	0	0	72,829,176	838,300	455,182
180	0	0	0	71,990,876	830,646	449,943
181	0	0	0	71,160,230	823,058	444,751
182	0	0	0	70,337,173	815,536	439,607
183	0	0	0	69,521,637	808,081	434,510
184	0	0	0	68,713,556	800,690	429,460
185	0	0	0	67,912,866	793,365	424,455
350	0	0	0	1,235,674	160,220	7,723
351	0	0	0	1,075,454	158,544	6,722
352	0	0	0	916,910	156,883	5,731
353	0	0	0	760,027	155,238	4,750
354	0	0	0	604,789	153,607	3,780
355	0	0	0	451,182	151,991	2,820
356	0	0	0	299,191	150,389	1,870
357	0	0	0	148,802	148,802	930

the table shows: (1) the balance at the end of the month, (2) the principal paid down (regularly scheduled principal repayment plus prepayments), and (3) interest. In month 1, the cash flow for the collateral consists of principal payment of $709,923 and interest of $2.5 million (0.075 times $400 million divided by 12). The interest payment is distributed to the four tranches based on the amount of the par value outstanding. So, for example, tranche A receives $1,215,625 (0.075 times $194,500,000 divided by

12) of the $2.5 million. The principal, however, is all distributed to tranche A. Therefore, the cash flow for tranche A in month 1 is $1,925,548. The principal balance at the end of month 1 for tranche A is $193,790,076 (the original principal balance of $194,500,000 less the principal payment of $709,923). No principal payment is distributed to the three other tranches because there is still a principal balance outstanding for tranche A. This will be true for months 2 through 80.

After month 81, the principal balance will be zero for tranche A. For the collateral, the cash flow in month 81 is $3,318,521, consisting of a principal payment of $2,032,196 and interest of $1,286,325. At the beginning of month 81 (end of month 80), the principal balance for tranche A is $311,926. Therefore, $311,926 of the $2,032,196 of the principal payment from the collateral will be disbursed to tranche A. After this payment is made, no additional principal payments are made to this tranche as the principal balance is zero. The remaining principal payment from the collateral $1,720,271, is disbursed to tranche B. According to the assumed prepayment speed of 165 PSA, tranche B then begins receiving principal payments in month 81.

Table 24-4 shows that tranche B is fully paid off by month 100, when tranche C now begins to receive principal payments. Tranche C is not fully paid off until month 178, at which time tranche D begins receiving the remaining principal payments. The maturity (i.e., the time until the principal is fully paid off) for these four tranches assuming 165 PSA would be 81 months for tranche A, 100 months for tranche B, 178 months for tranche C, and 357 months for tranche D.

Let's look at what has been accomplished by creating the CMO. First, as shown earlier in this chapter, the average life for the pass-through is 8.76 years, assuming a prepayment speed of 165 PSA. Table 24-5 reports the average life of the collateral and the four tranches assuming different prepayment speeds. Notice that the four tranches have average lives that are both shorter and longer than the collateral, thereby attracting investors who have a preference for an average life different from that of the collateral.

There is still a major problem: There is considerable variability of the average life for the tranches. We'll see how this can be tackled later on. However, there is some protection provided for each tranche against prepayment risk. This is because prioritizing the distribution of principal (i.e., establishing the payment rules for principal) effectively protects the shorter-term tranche A in this structure against extension risk. This

Table 24-5   Average Life for the Collateral and the Four Tranches of CMO-1

PREPAYMENT SPEED (PSA)	Average life for				
	COLLATERAL	TRANCHE A	TRANCHE B	TRANCHE C	TRANCHE D
50	15.11	7.48	15.98	21.02	27.24
100	11.66	4.90	10.86	15.78	24.58
165	8.76	3.48	7.49	11.19	20.27
200	7.68	3.05	6.42	9.60	18.11
300	5.63	2.32	4.64	6.81	13.36
400	4.44	1.94	3.70	5.31	10.34
500	3.68	1.69	3.12	4.38	8.35
600	3.16	1.51	2.74	3.75	6.96
700	2.78	1.38	2.47	3.30	5.95

protection must come from somewhere, so it comes from the three other tranches. Similarly, tranches C and D provide protection against extension risk for tranches A and B. At the same time, tranches C and D benefit because they are provided protection against contraction risk, the protection coming from tranches A and B.

Accrual Bonds

In CMO-1, the payment rules for interest provide for all tranches to be paid interest each month. In many sequential-pay CMO structures, at least one tranche does not receive current interest. Instead, the interest for that tranche would accrue and be added to the principal balance. Such a bond class is commonly referred to as an **accrual tranche**, or a *Z bond* (because the bond is similar to a zero-coupon bond). The interest that would have been paid to the accrual bond class is then used to speed up paying down the principal balance of earlier bond classes.

To see this, consider CMO-2, a hypothetical CMO structure with the same collateral as CMO-1 and with four tranches, each with a coupon rate of 7.5%. The structure is shown in Table 24-6. The difference is in the last tranche, Z, which is an accrual bond.

Let's look at month 1 and compare it to month 1 in Table 24-4 based on 165 PSA. The principal payment from the collateral is $709,923. In CMO-1, this is the principal paydown for tranche A. In CMO-2, the interest for tranche Z, $456,250, is not paid to that tranche but instead is used to pay down the principal of tranche A. So, the principal payment to tranche A is $1,166,173, the collateral's principal payment of $709,923 plus the interest of $456,250 that was diverted from tranche Z.

The inclusion of the accrual tranche results in a shortening of the expected final maturity for tranches A, B, and C. The final payout for tranche A is 64 months rather than 81 months, for tranche B it is 77 months rather than 100 months, and for tranche C it is 112 rather than 178 months.

The average lives for tranches A, B, and C are shorter in CMO-2 compared to CMO-1 because of the inclusion of the accrual bond. For example, at 165 PSA, the average lives are as follows:

Table 24-6   CMO-2: A Hypothetical Four-Tranche Sequential-Pay Structure with an Accrual Bond Class

TRANCHE	PAR AMOUNT	COUPON RATE
A	$194,500,000	7.5%
B	36,000,000	7.5
C	96,500,000	7.5
Z (Accrual)	73,000,000	7.5
Total	$400,000,000	

Payment rules:

1. *For payment of periodic coupon interest:* Disburse periodic coupon interest to tranches A, B, and C on the basis of the amount of principal outstanding at the beginning of the period. For tranche Z, accrue the interest based on the principal plus accrued interest in the previous period. The interest for tranche Z is to be paid to the earlier tranches as a principal paydown.

2. *For disbursement of principal payments:* Disburse principal payments to tranche A until it is completely paid off. After tranche A is completely paid off, disburse principal payments to tranche B until it is completely paid off. After tranche B is completely paid off, disburse principal payments to tranche C until it is completely paid off. After tranche C is completely paid off, disburse principal payments to tranche Z until the original principal balance plus accrued interest is completely paid off.

Structure	Tranche A	Tranche B	Tranche C
CMO-2	2.90	5.86	7.87
CMO-1	3.48	7.49	11.19

The reason for the shortening of the nonaccrual tranches is that the interest that would be paid to the accrual bond is being allocated to the other tranches. Tranche Z in CMO-2 will have a longer average life than tranche D in CMO-1.

Thus, shorter-term tranches and a longer-term tranche are created by including an accrual bond. The accrual bond appeals to investors who are concerned with reinvestment risk. Since there are no coupon payments to reinvest, reinvestment risk is eliminated until all the other tranches are paid off.

Planned Amortization Class Tranches

Many investors were still concerned about investing in an instrument that they continued to perceive as posing significant prepayment risk because of the substantial average like variability despite the innovations designed to reduce prepayment risk. Traditional corporate bond buyers sought a structure with both the characteristics of a corporate bond (either a bullet maturity or a sinking fund type of schedule for principal repayment) and high credit quality. While CMOs satisfied the second condition, they did not satisfy the first.

In 1987, CMO issuers began issuing bonds with the characteristic that if prepayments are within a specified range, the cash flow pattern is known. The greater predictability of the cash flow for these classes of bonds, referred to as **planned amortization class (PAC)** bonds, occurs because there is a principal repayment schedule that must be satisfied. PAC bondholders have priority over all other classes in the CMO issue in receiving principal payments from the underlying collateral. The greater certainty of the cash flow for the PAC bonds comes at the expense of the non-PAC classes, called the **support** or *companion* bonds. It is these bonds that absorb the prepayment risk. Because PAC bonds have protection against both extension risk and contraction risk, they are said to provide *two-sided prepayment protection*.

To illustrate how to create a PAC bond, we will use as collateral the $400 million pass-through with a coupon rate of 7.5%, a WAC of 8.125%, and a WAM of 357 months. The second column of Table 24-7 shows the principal payment (regularly scheduled principal repayment plus prepayments) for selected months assuming a prepayment speed of 90 PSA, and the next column shows the principal payments for selected months assuming that the pass-through prepays at 300 PSA.

The last column of Table 24-7 gives the *minimum* principal payment if the collateral speed is 90 PSA or 300 PSA for months 1 to 349. (After month 346, the outstanding principal balance will be paid off if the prepayment speed is between 90 PSA and 300 PSA.) For example, in the first month, the principal payment would be $508,169.52 if the collateral prepays at 90 PSA and $1,075,931.20 if the collateral prepays at 300 PSA. Thus, the minimum principal payment is $508,169.52, as reported in the last column of Table 24-7. In month 103, the minimum principal payment is also the amount if the prepayment speed is 90 PSA, $1,446,761, compared to $1,458,618.04 for 300 PSA. In month 104, however, a prepayment speed of 300 PSA would produce a principal payment of $1,433,539.23, which is less than the principal payment of $1,440,825.55 assuming 90 PSA. So, $1,433,539.23 is reported in the last column of Table 24-7. In fact, from month 104 on, the minimum principal payment is the one that would result assuming a prepayment speed of 300 PSA.

In fact, if the collateral prepays at *any* speed between 90 PSA and 300 PSA, the minimum principal payment would be the amount reported in the last column of

Table 24-7   Monthly Principal Payment for $400 Million, 7.5% Coupon Pass-
through with an 8.125% WAC and a 357 WAM Assuming Prepayment
Rates of 90 PSA and 300 PSA

MONTH	AT 90% PSA	AT 300% PSA	MINIMUM PRINCIPAL PAYMENT—THE PAC SCHEDULE
1	$ 508,169.52	$1,075,931.20	$ 508,169.52
2	569,843.43	1,279,412.11	569,843.43
3	631,377.11	1,482,194.45	631,377.11
4	692,741.89	1,683,966.17	692,741.89
5	753,909.12	1,884,414.62	753,909.12
6	814,850.22	2,083,227.31	814,850.22
7	875,536.68	2,280,092.68	875,536.68
8	935,940.10	2,474,700.92	935,940.10
9	996,032.19	2,666,744.77	996,032.19
10	1,055,784.82	2,855,920.32	1,055,784.82
11	1,115,170.01	3,041,927.81	1,115,170.01
12	1,174,160.00	3,224,472.44	1,174,160.00
13	1,232,727.22	3,403,265.17	1,232,727.22
14	1,290,844.32	3,578,023.49	1,290,844.32
15	1,348,484.24	3,748,472.23	1,348,484.24
16	1,405,620.17	3,914,344.26	1,405,620.17
17	1,462,225.60	4,075,381.29	1,462,225.60
18	1,518,274.36	4,231,334.57	1,518,274.36
101	1,458,719.34	1,510,072.17	1,458,719.34
102	1,452,725.55	1,484,126.59	1,452,725.55
103	1,446,761.00	1,458,618.04	1,446,761.00
104	1,440,825.55	1,433,539.23	1,433,539.23
105	1,434,919.07	1,408,883.01	1,408,883.01
211	949,482.58	213,309.00	213,309.00
212	946,033.34	209,409.09	209,409.09
213	942,601.99	205,577.05	205,577.05
346	618,684.59	13,269.17	13,269.17
347	617,071.58	12,944.51	12,944.51
348	615,468.65	12,626.21	12,626.21
349	613,875.77	12,314.16	3,432.32
350	612,292.88	12,008.25	0
351	610,719.96	11,708.38	0
352	609,156.96	11,414.42	0
353	607,603.84	11,126.28	0
354	606,060.57	10,843.85	0
355	604,527.09	10,567.02	0
356	603,003.38	10,295.70	0
357	601,489.39	10,029.78	0

Table 24-7. For example, if we had included principal payment figures assuming a prepayment speed of 200 PSA, the minimum principal payment would not change: From month 11 through month 103, the minimum principal payment is that generated from 90 PSA, but from month 104 on, the minimum principal payment is that generated from 300 PSA.

This characteristic of the collateral allows for the creation of a PAC bond, assuming that the collateral prepays over its life at a constant speed between 90 PSA and 300

PSA. A schedule of principal repayments that the PAC bondholders are entitled to receive before any other bond class in the CMO is specified. The monthly schedule of principal repayments is as specified in the last column of Table 24-7, which shows the minimum principal payment. Although there is no assurance that the collateral will prepay between these two speeds, a PAC bond can be structured to assume that it will.

Table 24-8 shows a CMO structure, CMO-3, created from the $400 million, 7.5% coupon pass-through with a WAC of 8.125% and a WAM of 357 months.

There are just two bond classes in this structure: a 7.5% coupon PAC bond created assuming 90 to 300 PSA with a par value of $243.8 million, and a support bond with a par value of $156.2 million.

Table 24-9 reports the average life for the PAC bond and the support bond in CMO-3 assuming various *actual* prepayment speeds. Notice that between 90 PSA and 300 PSA, the average life for the PAC bond is stable at 7.26 years. However, at slower or

Table 24-8   CMO-3 CMO Structure with One PAC Bond and One Support Bond

TRANCHE	PAR AMOUNT	COUPON RATE
P (PAC)	$243,800,000	7.5%
S (Support)	156,200,000	7.5%
Total	$400,000,000	

Payment rules:

1. *For payment of periodic coupon interest:* Disburse periodic coupon interest to each tranche on the basis of the amount of principal outstanding at the beginning of the period.
2. *For disbursement of principal payments:* Disburse principal payments to tranche P based on its schedule of principal repayments. Tranche P has priority with respect to current and future principal payments to satisfy the schedule. Any excess principal payments in a month over the amount necessary to satisfy the schedule for tranche P are paid to tranche S. When tranche S is completely paid off, all principal payments are to be made to tranche P regardless of the schedule.

Table 24-9   Average Life for PAC Bond and Support Bond in CMO-3 Assuming Various Prepayment Speeds

PREPAYMENT RATE (PSA)	PAC BOND (P)	SUPPORT BOND (S)
0	15.97	27.26
50	9.44	24.00
90	7.26	18.56
100	7.26	18.56
150	7.26	12.57
165	7.26	11.16
200	7.26	8.38
250	7.26	5.37
300	7.26	3.13
350	6.56	2.51
400	5.92	2.17
450	5.38	1.94
500	4.93	1.77
700	3.70	1.37

faster PSA speeds, the schedule is broken, and the average life changes, lengthening when the prepayment speed is less than 90 PSA and shortening when it is greater than 300 PSA. Even so, there is much greater variability for the average life of the support bond. The average life for the support bond is substantial.

Key Points That You Should Understand Before Proceeding

1. A CMO is a security backed by a pool of mortgage pass-through securities or mortgages and is referred to as a derivative security.

2. In a CMO structure there are several bond classes called tranches.

3. With the exception of support bonds, a CMO reduces the uncertainty concerning the maturity of a tranche, thereby providing a risk/return pattern not available with typical mortgage pass-through securities.

4. Tranche types that have been included in a CMO structure are sequential-pay bonds, accrual bonds (or Z-bonds), planned amortization class bonds, and support bonds.

5. A PAC bond is a class of bonds designed to reduce prepayment risk by specifying a schedule for the amortization of the principal owed to the bondholder; the reduction in the prepayment risk comes at the expense of the support bonds.

STRIPPED MORTGAGE-BACKED SECURITIES

Stripped mortgage-backed securities, introduced by Fannie Mae in 1986, are another example of derivative mortgage securities. A mortgage pass-through security divides the cash flow from the underlying pool of mortgages on a pro rata basis to the securityholders. A stripped mortgage-backed security is created by altering that distribution of principal and interest from a pro rata distribution to an unequal distribution. The result is that some of the securities created will have a price/yield relationship that is different from the price/yield relationship of the underlying mortgage pool. Stripped mortgage-backed securities, if properly used, provide a means by which investors can hedge prepayment risk.

The first generation of stripped mortgage-backed securities were partially stripped. We can see this by looking at the stripped mortgage-backed securities issued by Fannie Mae in mid-1986. The Class B stripped mortgage-backed securities were backed by FNMA pass-through securities with a 9% coupon. The mortgage payments from the underlying mortgage pool are distributed to Class B-1 and Class B-2 so that both classes receive an equal amount of the principal, but Class B-1 receives one-third of the interest payments while Class B-2 receives two-thirds.

In a subsequent issue, Fannie Mae distributed the cash flow from the underlying mortgage pool in a far different way. Using FNMA 11% coupon pools, Fannie Mae created Class A-1 and Class A-2. Class A-1 was given 4.95% of the 11% coupon interest, while Class A-2 received the other 6.05%. Class A-1 was given almost all of the principal payments, 99%, while Class A-2 was allotted only 1% of the principal payments.

In early 1987, stripped mortgage-backed securities began to be issued allocating all the interest to one class (called the **interest-only** or **IO class**) and all the principal to the other class (called the **principal-only** or **PO class**). The IO class receives no principal payments.

The PO security is purchased at a substantial discount from par value. The yield an investor realizes depends on the speed at which prepayments are made. The faster the prepayments, the higher the investor's yield. For example, suppose there is a mortgage pool consisting of only 30-year mortgages, with $400 million in principal, and that investors can purchase POs backed by this mortgage pool for $175 million. The dollar return on this investment will be $225 million. How quickly that dollar return is recovered by PO investors determines the yield that will be realized. In the extreme case, if all homeowners in the underlying mortgage pool decide to prepay their mortgage loans immediately, PO investors will realize the $225 million immediately. At the other extreme, if all homeowners decide to remain in their homes for 30 years and make no prepayments, the $225 million will be spread out over 30 years, which would result in a lower yield for PO investors.

A PO is a security whose price would rise when interest rates decline and fall when interest rates rise. This is typical of all the bonds we have discussed thus far in this book. A characteristic of a PO is that its price is very sensitive to changes in interest rates.

An IO has no par value. In contrast to the PO investor, the IO investor wants prepayments to be slow. The reason is that the IO investor receives interest only on the amount of the principal outstanding. When prepayments are made, less dollar interest will be received as the outstanding principal declines. In fact, if prepayments are too fast, the *IO investor may not recover the amount paid for the IO*. The unique aspect of an IO is that its price changes in the *same* direction as the change in interest rates. Moreover, as in the case of the PO, its price is highly responsive to a change in interest rates.

Because of these price volatility characteristics of stripped mortgage-backed securities, institutional investors have used them to control the risk of a portfolio of mortgage-backed securities so as to create a risk/return pattern that better fits their needs.

Key Points That You Should Understand Before Proceeding

1. A stripped mortgage-backed security is created by distributing the principal and interest from a pool of underlying mortgages on an unequal basis to two classes of securityholders.
2. A stripped mortgage-backed security is another example of a derivative mortgage security.
3. Stripped mortgage-backed securities can be used to hedge a portfolio exposed to prepayment risk.
4. There are two types of stripped mortgage-backed securities: partially stripped, and interest-only/principal-only securities.

YIELDS ON MORTGAGE-BACKED SECURITIES

Although many of the securities issued in the mortgage-backed securities market carry the explicit or implicit guarantee of the U.S. government, this does not mean that they will offer the same yield as U.S. Treasury securities or other government agency securities. The primary reason for a difference in yields lies in the uncertainty of the cash flow of a mortgage-backed security and the exposure to prepayment risk. This risk arises because the investor has granted the homeowner/borrower the right to prepay a loan at any time without penalty. Of course, investors require a higher potential yield as compensation for prepayment risk. This situation is not any different from that of an investor who buys a callable corporate bond and seeks compensation for the call risk associated with such a bond. In a CMO structure, classes that are exposed to less prepayment risk are willing to accept a lower yield than other classes such as the support bond classes that are exposed to greater prepayment risk.

The problem of calculating a yield for a mortgage-backed security is a complex one. As explained in Chapter 11, calculating the yield requires a determination of the cash flow. In the case of a mortgage-backed security, the cash flow is not known because of prepayments. This means that, to calculate the potential yield, projections of prepayments must be made for a mortgage-backed security. The PSA convention described earlier is used. What is important, however, is recognition that the yield on any mortgage-backed security is based on some assumption about prepayments. For a nonagency mortgage-backed security a projection must be made regarding defaults and recoveries of the mortgages in the underlying pool.

COMMERCIAL MORTGAGE-BACKED SECURITIES

As explained in the previous chapter, the mortgage market is comprised of the residential mortgage market and the commercial mortgage market. Thus far in this chapter, our focus has been on the securitization of residential mortgage loans. We conclude this chapter with a brief look at securities back by commercial mortgage loans.

With the exception of some securities backed by a pool of multifamily houses issued by the government-sponsored enterprises, **commercial mortgage-backed securities** have been issued by private entities that do not have any implicit or explicit government guarantee. As with nonagency mortgage-backed securities backed by a pool of residential loans, commercial mortgage-backed securities must be credit enhanced.

In the previous chapter, we described how, unlike residential mortgage loans, commercial mortgage loans are nonresource loans. We explained how the debt-to-service coverage ratio and the loan-to-value ratio are used to gauge the credit risk of an individual commercial mortgage loan. When assessing the credit quality of a commercial mortgage-backed security, investors look not only at these two measures for the individual loans in the pool but also at the concentration of loans by property type and by geographical location

In the previous chapter we reviewed the types of prepayment protection afforded the lender in a commercial mortgage loan. That is, there is loan-level protection against prepayment risk. For a commercial mortgage-backed security, there is additional prepayment protection that can be provided for some tranches of a deal. This type of call protection available at the deal level is referred to as *structural protection* and is provided by creating tranches similar to those in a collateralized mortgage obligation. That is, a sequential pay structure for the tranches in a deal allow for the redistribution of prepayment risk.

Today there are different types of CMBS deals. A **multiproperty single borrower deal** is one where the pool of commercial mortgage loans consists of multiple properties for which there is only one borrower. For example, the pool can include apartment buildings and strip malls owned by by one borrower. A **conduit-originated deal** has as its collateral multiproperties with multiple borrowers. Conduits are commercial-lending entities that are established for the sole purpose of generating collateral to securitize, and this is the fastest growing segment of the CMBS market. A special type of conduit deal is a *fusion conduit deal.* In such deals there is a large loan (greater than $50 million) included with smaller loans. **Liquidating trusts** (also called *nonperforming trusts*) are deals backed by nonperforming mortgage loans (i.e., loans where the borrowers are in default).

SUMMARY

In this chapter we have discussed the market for mortgage-backed securities and the important role that securitization played in the development of the secondary mortgage market. The basic mortgage-backed security is the mortgage pass-through security. The types of mortgage pass-through securities are agency and nonagency pass-through securities.

The latter require private credit enhancements in order to receive a high credit rating.

To address the prepayment risk associated with investing in mortgage pass-through securities—contraction risk and extension risk—collateralized mortgage obligations (CMOs) were created. Another derivative mortgage-backed security, the stripped mortgage-backed security, was created for better controlling the risk of a portfolio of mortgage-backed securities.

The market for agency pass-through securities is now the second most liquid long-term fixed-income market in the United States, the first being the U.S. Treasury securities market. The greater liquidity, coupled with new mortgage designs and security structures, has resulted in increased participation by a greater number of nondepository financial institutions. This development, in turn, has assured a supply of funds to the mortgage market so that mortgage rates are in line with rates in other sectors of the long-term debt market. Rates in the mortgage market, therefore, more nearly reflect supply and demand in the capital markets rather than the fortunes or misfortunes of the thrifts that historically have been the primary suppliers of funds to the mortgage market.

Securities backed by a pool of commercial mortgage loans are called commercial mortgage-backed securities. Typically, these securities are issued by private entities that do not have any implicit or explicit government guarantee and therefore require credit enhancement. The tranches in a CMBS deal can be structured to provide additional prepayment protection above and beyond that provided at the loan level. CMBS deals are classified as multiproperty single borrower deals, conduit-originated deals, and liquidating trusts.

KEY TERM

- Accrual tranche, 465
- Agency pass-through security, 448
- Average life, 458
- Collateralized mortgage obligation (CMO), 460
- Commercial mortgage-backed securities, 471
- Conditional prepayment rate (CPR), 453
- Conduit-originated deal, 471
- Contraction risk, 452
- Extension risk, 452
- Interest-only (IO) class, 469
- Jumbo loan, 449
- Liquidating trust, 471
- Mortgage pass-through security, 446
- Multiproperty single borrower deal, 471

- Nonagency pass-through security, 448
- Participation certificate (PC), 448
- Planned amortization class (PAC) tranche, 466
- Prepayment risk, 452
- Principal-only (PO) class, 469
- PSA prepayment benchmark, 454
- Secondary Mortgage Market Enhancement Act of 1984 (SMMEA), 450
- Securitized mortgage, 446
- Sequential-pay CMO, 461
- Stripped mortgage-backed securities, 469
- Support bond, 466
- Tranche, 460
- Weighted average maturity (WAM), 461

QUESTIONS

1. What is a mortgage pass-through security?
2. Describe the cash flow of a mortgage pass-through security.
3. How has securitization enhanced the liquidity of mortgages?
4. a. What are the different types of agency pass-through securities?
   b. Which type of agency pass-through carries the full faith and credit of the U.S. government?
5. a. Who are the issuers of nonagency pass-through securities?
   b. Why must a nonagency CMO be credit enhanced?
6. What is meant by prepayment risk, contraction risk, and extension risk?
7. Why would a pass-through be an unattractive investment for a savings and loan association?
8. What is meant by the average life of a pass-through?
9. Why is an assumed prepayment speed necessary to project the cash flow of a pass-through?
10. A cash flow for a pass-through typically is based on some prepayment benchmark. Describe the benchmark.

11. What does a conditional prepayment rate of 8% mean?
12. What does 150 PSA mean?
13. How does a collateralized mortgage obligation alter the cash flow from mortgages so as to shift the prepayment risk across various classes of bondholders?
14. "By creating a CMO, an issuer eliminates the prepayment risk associated with the underlying mortgages." Do you agree with this statement? Explain.
15. Explain the effect of including an accrual tranche in a CMO structure on the average lives of the sequential-pay structures.
16. What types of investors would be attracted to an accrual bond?
17. What was the motivation for the creation of PAC bonds?
18. Describe how the schedule for a PAC tranche is created.
19. a. In a commercial mortgage-backed securities deal, explain why the investor in a security is provided prepayment protection at the loan level and may be afforded prepayment protection at the deal level.
    b. Why would an investor in a commercial mortgage-backed security be concerned with the concentration of loans by property type and by geographical location?
20. What is the difference between a multiproperty single-borrower commercial mortgage-backed securities deal and a conduit-originated commercial mortgage-backed securities deal?

Asset-Backed Securities Markets [1]

Learning Objectives

After reading this chapter, you will understand

- what an asset-backed security is.
- the role of a special purpose vehicle in an asset-backed securities transaction.
- the motivation for an entity needing funds to issue an asset-backed security rather than a straight debt issue.
- the difference between amortizing assets and nonamortizing assets and why the former may have prepayments.
- the difference between an external and internal credit enhancement.
- the different types of external and internal credit enhancements.
- the difference between a pass-through structure and a pay-through structure.
- the cash flow for securities backed by closed-end home equity loans, open-end home equity loans, manufactured housing loans, student loans, SBA loans, and credit card receivables.
- the types of bonds used as collateral for a collateralized bond obligation.
- the basic structure of a collateralized bond obligation and the types of tranches.
- the difference between a true securitization and a hybrid securitization.

While the securitization of residential mortgage loans is by far the largest type of asset that has been securitized, securities backed by other assets (consumer and business loans and receivables) have been securitized. The largest sectors of the asset-backed securities market in the United States are securities backed by credit card receivables, auto loans, home equity loans, manufactured housing loans, student loans, Small Business Administration loans, and bond obligations. Since home equity loans and manufactured housing loans are backed by real estate property, the securities backed by them are referred to as *real estate-backed asset-backed securities.* Other asset-backed securities include securities backed by home improvement loans, health care receivables, agricultural equipment loans, equipment leases, commercial mortgage loans, music royalty receivables, movie royalty receivables, and municipal parking ticket receivables. The list is continually expanding. Moreover, asset-backed securities are not limited to the U.S. market. Many countries have developed asset-backed securities backed by a wide range of loans and receivables.

---

[1] This chapter is adapted from material written by Frank J. Fabozzi and published in several books by Frank J. Fabozzi Associates on the topic.

In this chapter, we will discuss the basic features of asset-backed securities. These products are used by both corporations, federal agencies, and municipalities to raise funds. The issuer must structure the transaction so as to deal with both credit risk and prepayment risk. We begin with the motivation for a corporation to use an asset-backed security rather than a straight corporate bond offering. The same rationale applies to other entities such as federal agencies and municipalities in deciding whether to issue a traditional bond or an asset-backed security.

MOTIVATION FOR ISSUING AN ASSET-BACKED SECURITY

For a corporation, an asset-backed security is an alternative means for raising funds than issuing a straight corporate bond. Why doesn't a corporation simply issue a corporate bond or medium-term note rather than an asset-backed security? To understand why, consider a triple BBB-rated corporation that manufactures construction equipment. We will refer to this corporation as XYZ Corp. Some of its sales are for cash, and others are on an installment sales basis. The installment sales are assets on the balance sheet of XYZ Corp. shown as "installment sales receivables."

Suppose XYZ Corp. wants to raise $75 million. If it issues a corporate bond, for example, XYZ Corp.'s funding cost would be whatever the benchmark Treasury yield is, plus a yield spread for BBB issuers. Suppose, instead, that XYZ Corp. has installment sales receivables that are more than $75 million. XYZ Corp. can use the installment sales receivables as collateral for a bond issue. What will its funding cost be? It will probably be the same as if it issued a corporate bond. The reason is if XYZ Corp. defaults on any of its obligations, the creditors will go after all of its assets, including the installment sales receivables.

However, suppose that XYZ Corp. can create another corporation or legal entity and sell the installment sales receivables to that entity. We'll refer to this entity as SPV Corp. If the transaction is done properly, SPV Corp. owns the installment sales receivables, not XYZ Corp. This means that if XYZ Corp. is forced into bankruptcy, its creditors cannot go after the installment sales receivables because they are owned by SPV Corp. What are the implications?

Suppose that SPV Corp. sells securities backed by the installment sales receivables. Now creditors will evaluate the credit risk associated with collecting the receivables independent of the credit rating of XYZ Corp. What credit rating will be assigned to the securities issued by SPV Corp.? Whatever SPV Corp. wants the rating to be! It may seem strange that the issuer (SPV Corp.) can get any rating it wants, but that is the case. The reason is that SPV Corp. will show the characteristics of the collateral for the security (i.e., the installment sales receivables) to a rating agency. In turn, the rating agency will evaluate the credit quality of the collateral and inform the issuer what must be done to obtain a specific rating.

More specifically, the issuer will be asked to "credit enhance" the securities. There are various forms of credit enhancement that we will review later. Basically, the rating agencies will look at the potential losses from the pool of installment sales receivables and make a determination of how much credit enhancement is needed for it to issue a specific rating. The higher the credit rating sought by the issuer, the greater the credit enhancement. Thus, XYZ Corp., which is BBB rated, can obtain funding using its installment sales receivables as collateral to obtain a better credit rating for the securities issued. In fact, with enough credit enhancement it can issue an AAA-rated security.

The key to a corporation issuing a security with a higher credit rating than the corporation's own credit rating is the SPV Corp. Actually, this legal entity that a corporation sells the assets to is called a **special purpose vehicle** or **special purpose corporation**. It plays a critical role in the ability to create a security—an asset-backed security—that separates the assets used as collateral from the corporation that is seeking financing.

Why doesn't a corporation always seek the highest credit rating (AAA) for its securities backed by collateral? The answer is that credit enhancement does not come without a cost. As will be described later, the company would require credit enhancement mechanisms, which increase the costs associated with a securitized borrowing via an asset-backed security. So the corporation must monitor the trade-off when it is seeking a higher rating between the additional cost of credit enhancing the security versus the reduction in funding cost by issuing a security with a higher credit rating.

Additionally, if bankruptcy occurs, there is the risk that a bankruptcy judge could decide that the assets of the special purpose vehicle are assets that the creditors of the corporation seeking financing (XYZ Corp. in our example) may go after. This is an important but unresolved legal issue in the United States. Legal experts have argued that this is unlikely. A legal opinion addressing this issue is given in the prospectus of an asset-backed security. This is the reason that special purpose vehicles in the United States are referred to as "bankruptcy remote" entities.

Key Points That You Should Understand Before Proceeding

1. The motivation for any entity to issue an asset-backed security rather than a standard corporate bond is the opportunity to reduce funding cost by separating the credit rating of the issuer from the credit quality of the pool of loans or receivables.
2. The separation of the pool of assets from the issuer is accomplished by means of a special purpose vehicle or special purpose corporation.

FEATURES OF AN ASSET-BACKED SECURITY

Before we discuss the major types of asset-backed securities, let's first look at the general features of the underlying collateral and the structure.

Amortizing versus Nonamortizing Assets

The collateral for an asset-backed security can be classified as either amortizing or nonamortizing assets. **Amortizing assets** are loans in which the borrower's periodic payment consists of scheduled principal and interest payments over the life of the loan. The schedule for the repayment of the principal is called an *amortization schedule*. The standard residential mortgage loan falls into this category. Auto loans and certain types of home equity loans (specifically, closed-end home equity loans discussed later in this chapter) are amortizing assets. Any excess payment over the scheduled principal payment is called a *prepayment*. Prepayments can be made to pay off the entire balance or a partial prepayment, called a curtailment.

In contrast to amortizing assets, nonamortizing assets do not have a schedule for the periodic payments that the individual borrower must make. Instead, a nonamortizing asset is one in which the borrower must make a minimum periodic payment. If that payment is less than the interest on the outstanding loan balance, the shortfall is added to the outstanding loan balance. If the periodic payment is greater than the interest on the outstanding loan balance, then the difference is applied to the reduction of the outstanding loan balance. There is no schedule of principal payments (i.e., no amortization schedule) for a nonamortizing asset. Consequently, the concept of a prepayment does not apply. Credit card receivables and certain types of home equity loans described later in this chapter are examples of nonamortizing assets.

For an amortizing asset, projection of the cash flows requires projecting prepayments. One factor that may affect prepayments is the prevailing level of interest rates relative to the interest rate on the loan. In projecting prepayments it is critical to determine the extent to which borrowers take advantage of a decline in interest rates below the loan rate in order to refinance the loan.

As with nonagency mortgage-backed securities described in the previous chapter, modeling defaults for the collateral is critical in estimating the cash flows of an asset-backed security. Proceeds that are recovered in the event of a default of a loan prior to the scheduled principal repayment date of an amortizing asset represents a prepayment and are referred to as an *involuntary prepayment.* Projecting prepayments for amortizing assets requires an assumption of the default rate and the recovery rate. For a nonamortizing asset, while the concept of a prepayment does not exist, a projection of defaults is still necessary to project how much will be recovered and when.

The analysis of prepayments can be performed on a pool level or a loan level. In pool-level analysis, it is assumed that all loans comprising the collateral are identical. For an amortizing asset, the amortization schedule is based on the *gross weighted average coupon* (GWAC) and weighted average maturity (WAM) for that single loan. Pool-level analysis is appropriate where the underlying loans are homogeneous. Loan-level analysis involves amortizing each loan (or group of homogeneous loans).

The maturity of an asset-backed security is not a meaningful parameter. Instead, the average life of the security is calculated. This measure was introduced in the previous chapter when we discussed agency pass-through securities.

Fixed Rate versus Floating Rate

There are fixed-rate and floating-rate asset-backed securities. Floating-rate asset-backed securities are typically created where the underlying pool of loans or receivables pay a floating rate. The most common are securities backed by credit card receivables, home equity line of credit receivables, closed-end home equity loans with an adjustable rate, student loans, Small Business Administration loans, and trade receivables. As demonstrated in the previous chapter, fixed-rate loans also can be used to create a structure that has one or more floating-rate tranches. For example, there are closed-end home equity loans with a fixed rate that can be pooled to create a structure with floating-rate tranches.

Credit Enhancements

All asset-backed securities are **credit enhanced**. That means that support is provided for one or more of the bondholders in the structure. Credit enhancement levels are determined relative to a specific rating desired by the issuer for a security by each rating agency. Specifically, an investor in an AAA-rated security expects to have "minimal," that is to say, virtually no chance of losing any principal due to defaults. For example, a rating agency may require credit enhancement equal to four times expected losses to obtain an AAA rating or three times expected losses to obtain an AA rating. The amount of credit enhancement necessary depends on rating agency requirements.

There are two general types of credit enhancement structures: external and internal. We describe each type below.

External credit enhancements.

External credit enhancements come in the form of **third-party guarantees** that provide for protection against losses up to a specified level, for example, 10%. This third-party protection is referred to as *first loss protection* since it provides protection against losses before the internal credit enhancements, discussed later, are drawn upon to provide protection. The most common forms of external credit enhancements are

➤ a corporate guarantee
➤ a letter of credit from a bank
➤ bond insurance.

Typically, external credit enhancement is not used as the primary protection but to supplement other forms of credit enhancement discussed below. For example, suppose that a $300 million asset-backed securities deal is issued, and the sponsor (i.e., effectively the seller of the securities) agrees to guarantee $10 million. Then, if losses exceed $10 million, the sponsor is not responsible for the excess over $10 million. Bond insurance provides the same function as in municipal bond structures. However, in the case of asset-backed securities, the insurance covers only up to a specified amount of the loss.

An asset-backed security with external credit support is subject to the credit risk of the third-party guarantor. Should the third-party guarantor be downgraded, the issue itself could be subject to downgrade even if the structure is performing as expected. This is based on the "weak link" test followed by rating agencies. According to this test, when evaluating a proposed structure, credit quality of the issue is only as good as the weakest link in credit enhancement regardless of the quality of underlying loans.

Internal credit enhancements.

Internal credit enhancements come in more complicated forms than external credit enhancements. The most common forms of internal credit enhancement are **reserve funds**, overcollateralization, and senior/subordinated structures.

Reserve funds come in two forms: cash reserve funds and excess servicing spread accounts. *Cash reserve funds* are straight deposits of cash generated from issuance proceeds. In this case, part of the underwriting profits from the deal are deposited into a fund which typically invests in money market instruments. Cash reserve funds are typically used in conjunction with external credit enhancements.

Excess servicing spread accounts involve the allocation of excess spread or cash into a separate reserve account after paying out the net coupon, servicing fee, and all other expenses on a monthly basis. For example, suppose that:

1. Gross weighted average coupon (gross WAC) is 8.00%—this is the interest rate paid by the borrowers.
2. Servicing and other fees are 0.25%.
3. Net weighted average coupon (net WAC) is 7.25%—this is the rate that is paid to all the tranches in the structure.

So, for this hypothetical deal, 8.00% is available to make payments to the tranches, to cover servicing fees and to cover other fees. Of that amount, 0.25% is paid for servicing and other fees, and 7.25% is paid to the tranches. This means that only 7.50% must be paid out, leaving 0.50% (8.00% – 7.50%). This 0.50% or 50 basis points is called the excess servicing spread. This amount is placed in a reserve account—the excess servicing spread account—and it will gradually increase and can be used to pay for possible future losses.

Overcollateralization works as follows. The total par value of the tranches is the liability of the structure. So, if a structure has two tranches with a par value of $200 million, then that is the amount of the liability. The amount of the collateral backing the structure must be at least equal to the amount of the liability. If the amount of the collateral exceeds the amount of the liability of the structure, the deal is said to be over-collateralized. The amount of overcollateralization represents a form of internal credit enhancement because it can be used to absorb losses. For example, if the liability of the structure is $200 million and the collateral's value is $214 million, then the structure is overcollateralized by $14 million. Thus, the first $14 million of losses will not result in a loss to any of the tranches.

The last form of credit enhancement is the **senior-subordinated structure**. In this structure, there is a senior tranche and at least one junior or subordinated tranche. For example, suppose a deal has $300 million as collateral (i.e., a pool of loans or receivables). The structure may look as follows:

senior tranche	$280 million
subordinated tranche	$ 20 million

This means that the first $20 million of losses are absorbed by the subordinated tranche.

There is no reason why there must be only one subordinated tranche. The structure can have more than one subordinated tranche. For example, the structure could be as follows:

senior tranche	$280 million
subordinated tranche 1	$ 15 million
subordinated tranche 2	$ 5 million

In this structure, the subordinate tranches 1 and 2 are called the *nonsenior tranches.* The senior tranche still has protection up to $20 million as in the previous structure with only one subordinated tranche. In the second structure, the first $5 million of losses is absorbed by the subordinated tranche 2. Hence, this tranche is referred to as the first loss tranche. Subordinated tranche 1 has protection of up to $5 million in losses, the protection provided by the first loss tranche.

The basic concern in the senior-subordinate structure is that while the subordinated tranches provide a certain level of credit protection for the senior tranche at the closing of the deal, the level of protection changes over time due to prepayments. The objective after the deal closes is to distribute any prepayments such that the credit protection for the senior tranche does not deteriorate over time.

In real estate–related asset-backed securities, as well as nonagency mortgage-backed securities, there is a well-developed mechanism used to address this concern called the *shifting interest mechanism.* Here is how it works. The percentage of the mortgage balance of the subordinate tranche to that of the mortgage balance for the entire deal is called the *level of subordination* or the *subordinate interest.* The higher the percentage, the greater the level of protection for the senior tranches. The subordinate interest changes after the deal is closed due to prepayments. That is, the subordinate interest shifts (hence the term *shifting interest*). The purpose of a shifting interest mechanism is to allocate prepayments so that the subordinate interest is maintained at an acceptable level to protect the senior tranche. In effect, by paying down the senior tranche more quickly, the amount of subordination is maintained at the desired level.

Pass-Through versus Pay-Through Structures

In the previous chapter, we saw how a mortgage pass-through security is created. A pool of mortgage loans is used as collateral, and certificates (securities) are issued with each certificate entitled to a pro rata share of the cash flow from the pool of mortgage loans. So, if a $100 million mortgage pool is the collateral for a pass-through security and 10,000 certificates are issued, then the holder of one certificate is entitled to 1/10,000 of the cash flow from the collateral.

The same type of structure, a **pass-through structure**, can be used for an asset-backed security deal. That is, each certificate holder is entitled to a pro rata share of the cash flow from the underlying pool of loans or receivables. For example, consider the following asset-backed security structure:

senior tranche	$280 million	10,000 certificates issued
subordinated tranche	$ 20 million	1,000 certificates issued

Each certificate holder of the senior tranche is entitled to receive 1/10,000 of the cash flow to be paid to the senior tranche from the collateral. Each certificate holder of the subordinated tranche is entitled to receive 1/1,000 of the cash flow to be paid to the subordinated tranche from the collateral.

In the previous chapter, we saw how a pass-through security can be used to create a collateralized mortgage obligation (CMO). That is, pass-through securities are pooled and used as collateral for a CMO. Another name for a CMO structure is a pay-through structure. In the case of an asset-backed security, the loans are either pooled and issued as a pass-through security or as a pay-through security. That is, unlike in the agency mortgage-backed securities market, a pass-through is not created first, and then the pass-through is used to create a pay-through security.

In a pay-through structure, the senior tranches can be simple sequential-pays, just as we described for CMOs in the previous chapter. Or, there could be a PAC structure with, say, senior tranche 1 being a short average life PAC, senior tranche 2 being a long average life tranche, and the other two senior tranches being support tranches.

It is important to emphasize that the senior-subordinated structure is a mechanism for redistributing credit risk from the senior tranche to the subordinated tranches and is referred to as *credit tranching*. When the senior tranche is carved up into tranches with different exposures to prepayment risk in a pay-through structure, prepayment risk can be transferred among the senior tranches as in a nonagency CMO. This is referred to as prepayment tranching or *time tranching*.

Key Points That You Should Understand Before Proceeding

1. The collateral for an asset-backed security can be either amortizing assets or nonamortizing assets.

2. For amortizing assets, projection of the cash flow requires projecting prepayments; for nonamortizing assets, prepayments by an individual borrower do not apply since there is no schedule of principal repayments.

3. Asset-backed securities must be credit enhanced; that is, there must be support from somewhere to absorb a certain amount of losses.

4. Credit enhancement levels are determined relative to a specific rating desired for a security, and there are two general types of credit enhancement structures: external and internal.

5. External credit enhancements come in the form of third-party guarantees that provide for first loss protection against losses up to a specified level: (a) a corporate guarantee, (b) a letter of credit, and (c) bond insurance.

6. Reserve funds, overcollateralization, and senior/subordinated structures are the most common forms of internal credit enhancements.

7. A structure can be a pass-through or pay-through structure, the latter occuring when the senior tranche is carved up to create several senior tranches with different exposures to prepayment risk.

MAJOR ASSET CLASSES SECURITIES

As noted at the outset of this chapter, the collateral that has been used for creating asset-backed securities is continually expanding. Below we provide a summary of some of the major sectors of the ABS market.

Home Equity Loans

A *home equity loan* (HEL) is a loan backed by residential property. At one time, the loan was typically a second lien on property that was already pledged to secure a first lien. In some cases, the lien was a third lien. In recent years, the character of a home equity loan has changed. Today, a home equity loan is often a first lien on property where the borrower has either an impaired credit history and/or the payment-to-income ratio is too high for the loan to qualify as a conforming loan for securitization by Ginnie Mae, Fannie Mae, or Freddie Mac. Typically, the borrower uses a home equity loan to consolidate consumer debt using the current home as collateral rather than to obtain funds to purchase a new home.

Home equity loans can be either **closed end** or *open end*. Most home equity loan-backed deals have been backed by closed-end HELs. A closed-end HEL is structured the same way as a fully amortizing residential mortgage loan. That is, it has a fixed maturity and the payments are structured to fully amortize the loan by the maturity date.

There are both fixed-rate and variable-rate closed-end HELs. Typically, variable-rate loans have a reference rate of six-month LIBOR and have periodic caps and lifetime caps. (A periodic cap limits the change in the mortgage rate from the previous time the mortgage rate was reset; a lifetime cap sets a maximum that the mortgage rate can ever be for the loan.) The cash flow of a pool of closed-end HELs is comprised of interest, regularly scheduled principal repayments, and prepayments, just as with mortgage-backed securities. Thus, it is necessary to have a prepayment model and a default model to forecast cash flows. The prepayment speed is measured in terms of a conditional prepayment rate (CPR).

Borrower characteristics and the seasoning process must be kept in mind when trying to assess prepayments for a particular deal. In the prospectus of an offering, a base case prepayment assumption is made: the initial speed and the amount of time until the collateral is expected to be seasoned. Thus, the prepayment benchmark is issuer specific. The benchmark speed in the prospectus is called the *prospectus prepayment curve* (PPC). As with the PSA benchmark described in the previous chapter, slower or faster prepayments speeds are a multiple of the PPC.

Typically, **home equity loan-backed securities** are securitized by both closed-end fixed-rate and adjustable-rate (or variable-rate) HELs. The securities backed by the latter are called *HEL floaters*. The reference rate of the underlying loans typically is six-month LIBOR. The cash flow of these loans is affected by periodic and lifetime caps on the loan rate.

Institutional investors that seek securities that better match their floating-rate funding costs are attracted to securities that offer a floating-rate coupon. To increase the attractiveness of home equity loan-backed securities to such investors, the securities typically have been created in which the reference rate is one-month LIBOR. Because of (1) the mismatch between the reference rate on the underlying loans and that of the HEL floater and (2) the periodic and life caps of the underlying loans, there is a cap on the coupon rate for the HEL floater. Unlike a typical floater, which has a cap that is fixed throughout the security's life, the effective periodic and lifetime cap of a HEL floater is variable. The effective cap, referred to as the *available funds cap*, will depend on the amount of funds generated by the net coupon on the principal, less any fees.

Let's look at one issue, Advanta Mortgage Loan Trust 1995-2 issued in June 1995. At the offering, this issue had approximately $122 million closed-end HELs. There were 1,192 HELs consisting of 727 fixed-rate loans and 465 variable-rate loans. There were five classes (A-1, A-2, A-3, A-4, and A-5) and a residual. The five classes are summarized below:

Class	Par amount	Pass-through coupon rate
A-1	$ 9,229,000	7.30%
A-2	30,330,000	6.60
A-3	16,455,000	6.85
A-4	9,081,000	Floating rate
A-5	56,917,000	Floating rate

The collateral is divided into group I and group II. The 727 fixed-rate loans are included in group I and support Classes A-1, A-2, and A-3 certificates. The 465 variable-rate loans are in group II and support Classes A-4 and A-5 certificates.

Manufactured Housing–Backed Securities

Manufactured housing-backed securities are backed by loans for manufactured homes. In contrast to site-built homes, manufactured homes are built at a factory and then transported to a manufactured home community or private land. The loan can be either a mortgage loan (for both the land and the mobile home) or a consumer retail installment loan.

Manufactured housing–backed securities are issued by Ginnie Mae and private entities. The former securities are guaranteed by the full faith and credit of the U.S. government. The manufactured home loans that are collateral for the securities issued and guaranteed by Ginnie Mae are loans guaranteed by the Federal Housing Administration (FHA) or Veterans Administration (VA). Loans not backed by the FHA or VA are called conventional loans. Manufactured housing–backed securities that are backed by such loans are called conventional manufactured housing–backed securities. These securities are issued by private entities.

The typical loan for a manufactured home is 15 years to 20 years. The loan repayment is structured to fully amortize the amount borrowed. Therefore, as with residential mortgage loans and HELs, the cash flow consists of net interest, regularly scheduled principal, and prepayments. However, prepayments are more stable for manufactured housing–backed securities because they are not sensitive to refinancing. There are several reasons for this. First, the loan balances are typically small so that there is no significant dollar savings from refinancing. Second, the rate of depreciation of mobile homes may be such that in the earlier years, depreciation is greater than the amount of the loan paid off. This makes it difficult to refinance the loan. Finally, borrowers are typically of lower credit quality and therefore find it difficult to obtain funds to refinance.

As with residential mortgage loans and HELs, prepayments on manufactured housing–backed securities are measured in terms of CPR.

The payment structure is the same as with nonagency mortgage-backed securities and home equity loan-backed securities. For example, consider the Green Tree Manufactured Housing Contract Trust 1995-3 issue. There are four classes in this $502.1 million issue: A-1, M-1, B-1, and B-2. Class A-1 is the senior class, Classes M-1, B-1, and B-2 are the subordinated or junior classes. The priority of payments is as follows: first payments are made to Class A-1, then to Class M-1, then to Class B-1, and then finally Class B-2. The losses, however, are realized in reverse order; that is, B-2, B-1, M-1, and finally A-1.

Auto Loan-Backed Securities

Auto loan-backed securities are issued by

➤ the financial subsidiaries of auto manufacturers (domestic and foreign)
➤ commercial banks
➤ independent finance companies and small financial institutions specializing in auto loans.

Auto loans can range in maturity from three years to six years.

The cash flow for auto loan-backed securities consists of regularly scheduled monthly loan payments (interest and scheduled principal repayments) and any prepayments. For securities backed by auto loans, prepayments result from (1) sales and trade-ins requiring full payoff of the loan, (2) repossession and subsequent resale of the automobile, (3) loss or destruction of the vehicle, (4) payoff of the loan with cash to save on the interest cost, and (5) refinancing of the loan at a lower interest cost. Although refinancings may be a major reason for prepayments of mortgage loans, they are of minor importance for automobile loans. Moreover, the interest rates for the automobile loans underlying some deals are substantially below market rates since they are offered by manufacturers as part of a sales promotion.

Prepayments for auto loan-backed securities are measured in terms of the **absolute prepayment speed (ABS)**. The ABS is the monthly prepayment expressed as a percentage of the original collateral amount. As explained in the previous chapter, the SMM (monthly CPR) expresses prepayments based on the prior month's balance.

There are auto loan-backed deals that are pass-through structures and paythrough structures. In a typical pass-through structure there is a senior tranche and a subordinate tranche. There is also an interest-only class. Whereas more deals are structured as pass-throughs, this structure is typically used for smaller deals. Larger deals usually have a pay - through structure.

Student Loan-Backed Securities

Student loans are made to cover college cost (undergraduate, graduate, and professional programs such as medical and law school) and tuition for a wide range of vocational and trade schools. Securities backed by student loans, popularly referred to as *SLABS* (student loan asset-backed securities), have similar structural features as the other asset-backed securities we discussed above.

The student loans that have been most commonly securitized are those that are made under the Federal Family Education Loan Program (FFELP). Under this program, the government makes loans to students via private lenders. The decision by private lenders to extend a loan to a student is not based on the applicant's ability to repay the loan. If a default of a loan occurs and the loan has been properly serviced, then the government will guarantee up to 98% of the principal plus accrued interest.

Loans that are not part of a government guarantee program are called *alternative loans*. These loans are basically consumer loans, and the lender's decision to extend an alternative loan will be based on the ability of the applicant to repay the loan. Alternative loans have been securitized.

Congress created Fannie Mae and Freddie Mac to provide liquidity in the mortgage market by allowing these government-sponsored enterprises to buy mortgage loans in the secondary market. Congress created the Student Loan Marketing Association (nicknamed "Sallie Mae") as a government-sponsored enterprise to purchase student loans in the secondary market and to securitize pools of student loans. Since its first issuance in 1995, Sallie Mae is now the major issuer of SLABS, and its issues are viewed as the benchmark issues. Other entities that issue SLABS are either traditional corporate entities (e.g., the Money Store and PNC Bank) or nonprofit organizations (Michigan Higher Education Loan Authority and the California Educational Facilities Authority). The SLABS of the latter typically are issued as tax-exempt securities and therefore trade in the municipal market. In recent years, several not-for-profit entities have changed their charter and applied for "for profit" treatment.

Let's first look at the cash flow for the student loans themselves. There are different types of student loans under the FFELP, including subsidized and unsubsidized Stafford loans, Parental Loans for Undergraduate Students (PLUS), and Supplemental Loans to Students (SLS). These loans involve three periods with respect to the borrower's payments: deferment period, grace period, and loan repayment period. Typically, student loans work as follows. While a student is in school, no payments are made by the student on the loan. This is the deferment period. Upon leaving school, the student is extended a grace period of usually six months when no payments on the loan must be made. After this period, payments are made on the loan by the borrower.

Prior to July 1, 1998, the reference rate for student loans originated under FFELP was the three-month Treasury bill rate plus a margin of either 250 basis points (during the deferment and grace periods) or 310 basis points (during the repayment period). Since July 1, 1998, the Higher Education Act changed the reference rate to the 10-year Treasury note. Specifically, the interest rate is the 10-year Treasury note rate plus 100 basis points. The spread over the reference rate varies with the cycle period for the loan.

Typically, non-Sallie Mae issues have been LIBOR-based floaters. For Sallie Mae issues, there is an indirect government guarantee. Sallie Mae has typically issued SLABS indexed to the three-month Treasury bill rate. However, late in the second quarter of 1999, Sallie Mae issued bonds in which the buyer of the two-year average life tranche had the choice of receiving either LIBOR plus 8 basis points or the three-month Treasury bill rate plus 87 basis points. There are available funds caps in SLABS because of the different reference rates for the loans and the securities.

Prepayments typically occur due to defaults or loan consolidation. Even if there is no loss of principal faced by the investor when defaults occur, the investor is still exposed to contraction risk. This is the risk that the investor must reinvest the proceeds at a lower spread and in the case of a bond purchased at a premium, the premium will be lost. Studies have shown student loan prepayments are insensitive to the level of interest rates. Consolidations of a loan occurs when the student who has loans over several years combines them into a single loan. The proceeds from the consolidation are distributed to the original lender and, in turn, distributed to the bondholders.

SBA Loan-Backed Securities

The Small Business Administration (SBA) is an agency of the U.S. government empowered to guarantee loans made by approved SBA lenders to qualified borrowers. The loans are backed by the full faith and credit of the government. Most SBA loans are variable-rate loans where the reference rate is the prime rate. The rate on the loan is reset monthly on the first of the month or quarterly on the first of January, April, July, and October. SBA regulations specify the maximum coupon allowable in the secondary market. Newly originated loans have maturities between 5 and 25 years.

The Small Business Secondary Market Improvement Act passed in 1984 permitted the pooling of SBA loans. When pooled, the underlying loans must have similar terms and features. The maturities typically used for pooling loans are 7, 10, 15, 20, and 25 years. Loans without caps are not pooled with loans that have caps.

Most variable-rate SBA loans make monthly payments consisting of interest and principal repayment. The amount of the monthly payment for an individual loan is determined as follows. Given the coupon formula of the prime rate plus the loan's quoted margin, the interest rate is determined for each loan. Given the interest rate, a level payment amortization schedule is determined. It is this level payment that is paid monthly until the coupon rate is reset.

The monthly cash flow that the investor in an SBA-backed security receives consists of

> ➤ the coupon interest based on the coupon rate set for the period
> ➤ the scheduled principal repayment (i.e., scheduled amortization)
> ➤ prepayments.

Prepayments for SBA-backed securities are measured in terms of CPR. Voluntary prepayments can be made by the borrower without any penalty. There are several factors contributing to the prepayment speed of a pool of SBA loans. A factor affecting prepayments is the maturity date of the loan. It has been found that the fastest speeds on SBA loans and pools occur for shorter maturities. The purpose of the loan also affects prepayments. There are loans for working capital purposes and loans to finance real estate construction or acquisition. It has been observed that SBA pools with maturities of 10 years or less made for working capital purposes tend to prepay at the fastest speed. In contrast, loans backed by real estate that are long maturities tend to prepay at a slow speed. All other factors constant, pools that have capped loans tend to prepay more slowly than pools of uncapped loans.

Credit Card Receivable-Backed Securities

Credit card receivable-backed securities are backed by credit card receivables. Credit cards are issued by:

> ➤ banks (e.g., Visa and MasterCard)
> ➤ retailers (e.g., JC Penney and Sears)
> ➤ travel and entertainment companies (e.g., American Express).

Credit card deals are structured as a *master trust*. With a master trust the issuer can sell several series from the same trust. For example, consider the following two deals: Sears Credit Account Master Trust II, Series 1995-4, and Standard Credit Card Master Trust I, Series 1995-A.

Sears offers several open-end revolving credit plans. From these various plans, Sears generates a portfolio of receivables. As of July 1995, the master trust comprised $4 billion of principal receivables. These receivables were randomly selected from the entire portfolio of receivables of Sears Roebuck and Company. About 38% of the accounts had credit limits of $1,999 and about 61% were seasoned at least five years. All series issued from this Master Trust II share in the cash flow from the pool of receivables that were randomly selected. Information about the specific accounts in the pool selected for Master Trust II was not disclosed; however, because of the random selection process, an investor might expect that the composition did not differ significantly from the entire portfolio of receivables. Each time a new series of securities is issued, more receivables are randomly selected to be added to the trust. The Sears Credit Account Master Trust II, Series 1995-4 was the sixth of a series issued by Group One of Sears Credit Account Master Trust II. There were two classes of certificates that were offered to the public: Class A Master Trust Certificates and Class B Master Trust Certificates. The principal for the former was $500 million and for the latter $22.5 million.

The Standard Credit Card Master Trust I is a Citibank master trust. The master trust as of May 22, 1995, was comprised of 20,092,662 accounts with principal receivables of approximately $24.3 billion and approximately $290.8 million of finance charge receivables. The average credit limit was $3,282 and the average principal balance of the accounts was $1,210. About 69% of the accounts were seasoned more than two years. The SCCMTI Series 1995A is the twenty-second in a series issued by Group One of Standard Credit Card Master Trust I and is a Euro issue. There was only one certificate offered to the public—$300 million of Floating Rate Class A Credit Card Participation Certificates.

The 10 largest Master Trusts as of March 1999 were: (1) MBNA Master Trust II, (2) Citibank, (3) First USA, (4) Discover, (5) Chase, (6) First Chicago, (7) AT&T Universal, (8) Sears Master Trust II, (9) Capital One, and (10) Fleet/Advanta.

Cash Flow

For a pool of credit card receivables, the cash flow consists of finance charges collected, fees, and principal. Finance charges collected represent the periodic interest the credit card borrower is charged based on the unpaid balance after the grace period. Fees include late payment fees and any annual membership fees.

Interest to securityholders is paid periodically (e.g., monthly, quarterly, or semiannually). The interest rate may be fixed or floating; roughly half of the securities are floaters. The floating rate is uncapped.

A credit card receivable-backed security is a nonamortizing security. For a specified period of time, referred to as the **lockout period** or **revolving period**, the principal payments made by credit card borrowers comprising the pool are retained by the trustee and reinvested in additional receivables to maintain the size of the pool. The lockout period can vary from 18 months to 10 years. So, during the lockout period, the cash flow that is paid out to securityholders is based on finance charges collected and fees.

After the lockout period, the principal is no longer reinvested but paid to investors. This period is referred to as the **principal-amortization period**.

Performance of the Portfolio of Receivables

Several concepts must be understood in order to assess the performance of the portfolio of receivables and the ability of the issuer to meet its interest obligation and repay principal as scheduled.

We begin with the concept of the *gross portfolio yield*. This yield includes finance charges collected and fees. Charge-offs represent the accounts charged off as uncollectible. Net portfolio yield is equal to gross portfolio yield minus charge-offs. The net portfolio yield is important because it is from this yield that the bondholders will be paid. So, for example, if the average yield (WAC) that must be paid to the various tranches in the structure is 5% and the net portfolio yield for the month is only 4.5%, there is the risk that the bondholder obligations will not be satisfied.

Delinquencies are the percentages of receivables that are past due for a specified number of months, usually 30, 60, and 90 days. They are considered an indicator of potential future charge-offs.

The *monthly payment rate* (MPR) expresses the monthly payment (which includes finance charges, fees, and any principal repayment) of a credit card receivable portfolio as a percentage of credit card debt outstanding in the previous month. For example, suppose a $500 million credit card receivable portfolio in January realized $50 million of payments in February. The MPR would then be 10% ($50 million divided by $500 million).

There are two reasons why the MPR is important. First, if the MPR reaches an extremely low level, there is a chance that there will be extension risk with respect to the principal payments on the bonds. Second, if the MPR is very low, then there is a chance that there will not be sufficient cash flows to pay off principal. This is one of the events that could trigger early amortization of the principal (described below).

At issuance, portfolio yield, charge-offs, delinquency, and MPR information are provided in the prospectus. Information about portfolio performance is then available from various sources.

Early Amortization Triggers.

There are provisions in credit card receivable-backed securities that require early amortization of the principal if certain events occur. Such provisions, which are referred to as either **early amortization** or *rapid amortization*, are included to safeguard the credit quality of the issue. The only way that the principal cash flows can be altered is by the triggering of the early amortization provision.

Typically, early amortization allows for the rapid return of principal in the event that the three-month average excess spread earned on the receivables falls to zero or less. When early amortization occurs, the credit card tranches are retired sequentially (i.e., first the AAA bond then the AA-rated bond, etc.). This is accomplished by paying the principal payments made by the credit card borrowers to the investors instead of using them to purchase more receivables. The length of time until the return of principal is largely a function of the monthly payment rate. For example, suppose that an AAA tranche is 82% of the overall deal. If the monthly payment rate is 11%, then the AAA tranche would return principal over a 7.5-month period (82%/11%). An 18% monthly payment rate would return principal over a 4.5-month period (82%/18%).

Collateralized Bond Obligations

A **collateralized bond obligation (CBO)** is an asset-backed security backed by a diversified pool of one or more of the following types of debt obligations:

➤ noninvestment grade (i.e., high yield) corporate bonds
➤ emerging market bonds
➤ bank loans to corporate entities.

When an asset-backed security has only bank loans, it is referred to as a *collateralized loan obligation* (CLO).

There is an asset manager responsible for managing the portfolio of debt obligations. There are restrictions imposed by the rating agencies as to what the asset manager may do and certain tests that must be satisfied for the tranches in the CBO to maintain their credit rating at the time of issuance. We'll discuss some of these requirements below.

CBO Structure.

The typical structure of a CBO is as follows. There is (1) a senior tranche, (2) different layers of subordinate or junior debt tranches, and (3) an equity tranche. The senior tranche is between 70% and 80% of the deal and receives a floating-rate payment in order to attract floating-rate investors. The junior tranches, in contrast, receive a fixed-coupon rate. So, the collateral from the diversified pool of debt obligations is going to pay the tranche holders, the majority of whom (i.e., the senior tranche investors) are being paid a floating rate. Do the debt obligations pay a fixed or floating rate? Whereas the bank loans are typically floating rate, the other debt obligations in which the asset manager may invest typically pay a fixed rate. Now that presents a problem—paying the majority of the tranche investors a floating rate when the majority of the debt obligations pay a fixed rate.

To deal with this problem, the asset manager uses derivative instruments to be able to convert fixed-rate payments into floating-rate payments. In particular, interest rate swaps are used. We will discuss interest rate swaps in Chapter 30. Because of the mismatch between the nature of the cash flows of the debt obligations in which the asset manager invests and the floating-rate liability for the senior tranche, the asset manager must use an interest rate swap. A rating agency will require the use of swaps to eliminate this mismatch.

The junior tranches receive a fixed rate. The rate is a spread over a comparable maturity Treasury security. The amount of the spread varies with market conditions and the credit rating of a junior tranche. For example, the fixed rate for a junior tranche might be the Treasury rate plus 185 basis points.

The equity tranche receives any remaining interest that is received from the collateral but not paid to the senior and junior tranches. To understand how the equity tranche generates cash flows, consider again the basic CBO structure in terms of collateral and debt tranches, and look at what is being received from the collateral and what is being paid to the senior and junior tranches. Depending on market conditions at the time the CBO is issued, the fixed-rate debt obligations in which the asset manager invests will offer a spread to Treasury securities that is quite large to reflect the low credit quality of the bonds purchased. Let's assume the following:

Assumption 1: The CBO is a $100 million structure. That is, the assets purchased will be $100 million.

Assumption 2: The collateral consists of bonds that all mature in 10 years, and the coupon rate for every bond is the 10-Treasury rate plus 400 basis points.

Assumption 3: The senior tranche comprises 80% of the structure ($80 million) and pays interest based on the following coupon formula (remember the senior tranche is a floating-rate tranche): LIBOR plus 70 basis points.

Assumption 4: There is only one junior tranche ($10 million) with a coupon rate that is fixed. The coupon rate is the Treasury rate plus 200 basis points.

Assumption 5: The asset manager enters into an agreement with another party in which it agrees to pay a fixed rate each year equal to the 10-year Treasury rate plus 100 basis points and receive LIBOR. The notional amount of the agreement is $80 million.

The last assumption may be difficult to appreciate at this point since we have not discussed interest rate swaps. For now, we'll be able to lay out the principle without setting forth what an interest swap is. Keep in mind that the goal is to show how the equity tranche can expect to generate a return.

Note that given that the senior tranche is $80 million and the junior tranche is $10 million, the equity tranche must be $10 million ($100 million minus $90 million).

Let's assume that the 10-year Treasury rate at the time the CBO is issued is 7%. Now we can walk through the cash flows for each year. Look first at the collateral. The collateral will pay interest each year (assuming no defaults) equal to the 10-year Treasury rate of 7% plus 400 basis points (Assumption 2). So the interest will be:

$$\text{Interest from collateral: } 11\% \times \$100,000,000 = \$11,000,000$$

Now let's determine the interest that must be paid to the senior and junior tranches. For the senior tranche, the interest payment (Assumption 3) will be:

$$\text{Interest to senior tranche: } \$80,000,000 \times (\text{LIBOR} + 70 \text{ b.p.})$$

The coupon rate for the junior tranche is 7% plus 200 basis points (Assumption 4). So, the coupon rate is 9% and the interest is:

$$\text{Interest to junior tranche: } 9\% \times \$10,000,000 = \$900,000$$

Finally, let's look at the interest rate swap. In this agreement, the asset manager agrees to pay some third party (we'll call this party the "swap counterparty") each year 7%

(the 10-year Treasury rate) plus 100 basis points, or 8%. But 8% of what? In an interest rate swap, payments are based on a notional amount. In our illustration (Assumption 5), the notional amount is $80 million. The reason the asset manager selected the $80 million was because this is the amount of principal for the senior tranche. So, the asset manager pays to the swap counterparty:

$$\text{Interest to swap counterparty: } 8\% \times \$80,000,000 = \$6,400,000$$

The interest payment received from the swap counterparty (Assumption 5) is LIBOR based on a notional amount of $80 million. That is,

$$\text{Interest from swap counterparty: } \$80,000,000 \times \text{LIBOR}$$

Now we can put this all together. Let's look at the interest coming into the CBO:

Interest from collateral:	$11,000,000
Interest from swap counterparty:	$80,000,000 × LIBOR
Total interest received:	$11,000,000 + $80,000,000 × LIBOR

The interest to be paid out to the senior and junior tranches and to the swap counterparty include:

Interest to senior tranche:	$80,000,000 × (LIBOR 70 b.p.)
Interest to junior tranche:	$900,000
Interest to swap counterparty:	$6,400,000
Total interest paid:	$7,300,000 + $80,000,000 × (LIBOR + 70 b.p.)

Netting the interest payments coming in and going out we have:

Total interest received:	$11,000,000 + $80,000,000 × LIBOR
Total interest paid:	$7,300,000 + $80,000,000 × (LIBOR + 70 b.p.)
Net interest:	$3,700,000 − $80,000,000 × (70 b.p.)

Since 70 b.p. × $80 million = $560,000, the net interest remaining is $3,140,000 (= $3,700,000 − $560,000). From this amount, any fees (including the asset management fee) must be paid. The balance is then the amount available to pay the equity tranche.

Obviously, some simplifying assumptions have been made. For example, it is assumed that there are no defaults. It is assumed that all of the issues are non-callable, and therefore the coupon rate would not decline because issues are called. Moreover, as explained below, after some period the asset manager must begin repaying principal to the senior and junior tranches. Consequently, the interest swap must be structured to take this into account since the entire amount of the senior tranche is not outstanding for the life of the collateral. Despite the simplifying assumptions, the illustration does demonstrate the basic economics of the CBO, the need for the use of an interest rate swap, and how the equity tranche will realize a return.

Activities of the Asset Manager.

The CBO structure described above is the type that is predominately issued today. The CBO is structured to generate cash flow for the senior and junior tranches without the active trading of bonds. Older CBO deals were typically structured so that the cash flow for the structure was based on the active trading of bonds. The cash flow needed to pay principal and interest to the senior and junior tranches had to be generated from capital gains as well as coupon interest. With the difficulties encountered in the high-yield bond sector in the late 1980s and early 1990s, CBOs structured in this way lost their appeal and their issuance declined.

Because the cash flows from the structure are designed to accomplish the objective for each tranche, restrictions are imposed on the asset managers. The asset manager is not free to buy and sell bonds. The conditions for disposing of issues held are specified and are usually driven by credit risk management. Also, in assembling the portfolio, the asset manager must meet certain requirements set forth by the rating agency or agencies that rate the deal. These requirements have to do with constructing a diversified portfolio and minimum ratings for the issues acquired. The asset manager must monitor the collateral to ensure that certain tests or covenants are being met.

CREDIT CONSIDERATION FOR A CORPORATE BOND VERSUS AN ASSET-BACKED SECURITY

We conclude this chapter with a look at how the rating of an asset-backed security transaction differs from that of a corporate bond issue. To understand the difference, it important to appreciate how the cash flow that must be generated differs for an asset-backed security transaction and a corporate bond issue.

In a corporate bond issue, management through its operations must undertake the necessary activities that will produce revenues and collect revenues. Management will incur costs in creating products and services. These costs include management compensation, employees salaries, the costs of raw materials, and financial costs. Consequently, in evaluating the credit risk of a corporate bond issue, a rating agency will examine these factors.

In contrast, in an asset-backed security transaction, there are assets (loans or receivables) that are to be collected and distributed to bondholders. There are no operating or business risks such as the competitive environment or existence of control systems that are needed to assess the cash flow. What is important is the quality of the collateral in generating the cash flow needed to make interest and principal payments. It is the greater predictability of the cash flow in an asset-backed security transaction due to the absence of operational risks that distinguishes it from a corporate bond issue.

In a "true" asset-backed security transaction, the role of the servicer is to simply collect the cash flow. There is no active management with respect to the collateral as is the case of the management necessary to operate a corporation to generate cash flow to pay bondholders. Standard & Poor's defines a "true" asset-backed security transaction (which this rating agency refers to as a "true securitization") as follows:

> In a true securitization, repayment is not dependent on the ability of the servicer to replenish the pool with new collateral or to perform more than routine administrative functions.[2]

There are asset-backed security transactions where the role of the servicer is more than administrative. Where the role of the servicer is more than administrative, Standard & Poor's, for example, refers to such transactions as "hybrid transactions". This is because such transactions have elements of an asset-backed security transaction and a corporation performing a service. According to Standard & Poor's:

> In a hybrid transaction, the role of the servicer is akin to that of a business manager. The hybrid servicer performs not only administrative duties, as in

---

[2] Standard & Poor's, "Rating Hybrid Securitizations," *Structured Finance* (October 1999), p. 2.

a true securitization, but also . . . [other] services that are needed to generate cash flow for debt service.[3]

Moreover, Standard & Poor's notes that:

> Unlike a true securitization, where the servicer is a fungible entity replaceable with few, if any, consequences to the transaction, bondholders depend on the expertise of the hybrid servicer for repayment. . . . Not coincidentally, these are the same attributes that form the basis of a corporate rating of the hybrid servicer. They also explain the rating linkage between the securitization and its hybrid servicer.[4]

Standard & Poor's provides an illustration of the distinction between a true asset-backed securitization transaction and one requiring a more active role for the servicer.[5] Consider a railcar company that has several hundred leases and the leases are with a pool of diversified highly rated companies. Suppose that each lease is for 10 years, and it is the responsibility of the customers—not the railcar company—to perform the necessary maintenance on the leased railcars. If there is an asset-backed security transaction backed by these leases and the term of the transaction is 10 years, then the role of the servicer is minimal. Since the leases are for 10 years and the securities issued are for 10 years, the servicer is just collecting the lease payments and distributing them to the holders of the securities. In such a transaction, it possible for this issue to obtain a high investment-grade rating as a true asset-backed security transaction.

Suppose we change the assumptions as follows. The securities issued are for 25 years, not 10 years. Also, assume that the railcar company, not the customers, are responsible for the servicing. Now the role of the servicer changes. The servicer will be responsible for finding new companies to release the railcars to when the original leases terminate in 10 years. This is necessary because the securities issued have a maturity of 25 years but the original leases only cover payments to securityholders for the first 10 years. It is the releasing of the railcars that is required for the last 15 years. The servicer under this new set of assumptions is also responsible for the maintenance of the railcars leased. Thus, the servicer must be capable of maintaining the railcars or have ongoing arrangements with one or more companies that have the ability to perform such maintenance.

How do rating agencies evaluate hybrid transactions? These transactions will be rated both in terms of a standard methodology for rating an asset-backed security transaction and using a "quasi-corporate approach" (in the words of Standard & Poor's) which involves an analysis of the servicer. The relative weight of the evaluations in assigning a rating to an asset-backed security transaction will depend on the involvement of the servicer. The more important the role of the servicer, the more weight will be assigned to the quasi-corporate approach analysis.

SUMMARY

Asset-backed securities are securities backed by a pool of loans or receivables. Throughout the world, the types of loans and receivables being used as collateral for an asset-backed security continues to grow. The motivation for issuers to issue an asset-backed security rather than a traditional debt obligation is that there is the opportunity to reduce funding cost by separating the credit rating of the issuer

---

[3] Ibid., p. 3.

[4] Standard & Poor's, "Rating Hybrid Securitizations," *Structured Finance* (October 1999), p. 2.

[5] Ibid., p. 3.

from the credit quality of the pool of loans or receivables. The separation of the pool of assets from the issuer is accomplished by means of a special purpose vehicle or special purpose corporation.

In obtaining a credit rating for an asset-backed security, the rating agencies require that the issue be credit enhanced; the higher the credit rating sought, the greater the credit enhancement needed. There are two general types of credit enhancement structures: external and internal. External credit enhancements come in the form of third-party guarantees that provide for first loss protection against losses up to a specified level. The most common forms of external credit enhancements are (1) a corporate guarantee, (2) a letter of credit, and (3) bond insurance. The most common forms of internal credit enhancements are reserve funds, overcollateralization and senior/subordinate structures. The creation of a senior-subordinated structure is a means of credit tranching; that is, reallocating credit risk from one tranche to another. When the senior tranche is carved up to create several senior tranches with different exposures to prepayment risk, the structure is referred to as a pay-through security.

Fundamentally, because of the absence of operational risk an asset-backed security transaction generally has greater certainty about the cash flow than a corporate bond issue. A true asset-backed security transaction involves minimal involvement by the servicer beyond administrative functions. In a hybrid asset-backed security transaction, the service has more than an administrative function; the greater the importance of the servicer, the more the transaction should be evaluated as a quasi-corporate entity.

The collateral for an asset-backed security can be either amortizing assets (e.g., auto loans and closed-end home equity loans) or nonamortizing assets (e.g., credit card receivables). For amortizing assets, projection of the cash flow requires projecting prepayments. For nonamortizing assets, prepayments by an individual borrower do not apply since there is no schedule of principal repayments. One factor that may affect prepayments is the prevailing level of interest rates relative to the interest rate on the loan. Since a default is a prepayment (an involuntary prepayment), prepayment modeling for an asset-backed security backed by amortizing assets requires a model for projecting the amount that will be recovered and when it will be recovered.

The collateral for a home equity loan is typically a first lien on residential property, and the loan fails to satisfy the underwriting standards for inclusion in a loan pool of Ginnie Mae, Fannie Mae, or Freddie Mac. Typically, a home equity loan is used by a borrower to consolidate consumer debt using the current home as collateral rather than to obtain funds to purchase a new home. Home equity loans can be either closed end (i.e., structured the same way as a fully amortizing residential mortgage loan) or open end (i.e., homeowner given a credit line). The monthly cash flow for a home equity loan–backed security backed by closed-end HELs consists of (1) net interest, (2) regularly scheduled principal payments, and (3) prepayments.

Manufactured housing–backed securities are backed by loans on manufactured homes (i.e., homes built at a factory and then transported to a site). Manufactured housing–backed securities are issued by Ginnie Mae and private entities, the former being guaranteed by the full faith and credit of the U.S. government. A manufactured housing loan's cash flow consists of net interest, regularly scheduled principal, and prepayments. Prepayments are more stable for manufactured housing–backed securities because they are not sensitive to refinancing.

Auto loan-backed securities are issued by the financial subsidiaries of auto manufacturers, commercial banks, independent finance companies, and small financial institutions specializing in auto loans. The cash flow for auto loan-backed securities consists of regularly scheduled monthly loan payments (interest and scheduled principal repayments), and any prepayments. Prepayments on auto loans are not sensitive to interest rates. Prepayments on auto loan-backed securities are measured in terms of the absolute prepayment speed, which measures monthly prepayments relative to the original collateral amount.

SLABS are asset-backed securities backed by student loans. The student loans most commonly securitized are those that are made under the Federal Family Education Loan Program (FFELP), whereby the government makes loans to students via private lenders and the government guarantees up to 98% of the principal plus accrued interest. Alternative loans are student loans that are not part of a government guarantee program and are basically consumer loans. In contrast to government-guaranteed loans, the lender's decision to extend an alternative loan is based on the ability of the applicant to repay the loan. Student loans involve three periods with respect to the borrower's payments: deferment period, grace period, and loan repayment period. Prepayments typically occur due to defaults or a loan consolidation (i.e, a loan to consolidate loans over several years into a single loan). Issuers of SLABs include the Student Loan Marketing Association (Sallie Mae, a government-sponsored enterprise), traditional corporate entities, and nonprofit organizations.

Small Business Administration (SBA) loans are backed by the full faith and credit of the U.S. government. Most SBA loans are variable-rate loans where the reference rate is the prime rate with monthly payments consisting of interest and principal repayment. Prepayments for SBA-backed securities are measured in terms of CPR. Voluntary prepayments can be made by the SBA borrower without any penalty.

Credit card receivable-backed securities are backed by credit card receivables for credit cards issued by banks, retailers, and travel and entertainment companies. Credit card deals are structured as a master trust. For a pool of credit card receivables, the cash flow consists of finance charges collected, fees, and principal. The principal repayment of a credit card receivable-backed security is not amortized; instead, during the lockout period, the principal payments made by credit card borrowers are retained by the trustee and reinvested in additional receivables and after the lockout period (the principal-amortization period), the principal received by the trustee is no longer reinvested but paid to investors. There are provisions in credit card receivable-backed securities that require early amortization of the principal if certain events occur.

A collateralized bond obligation (CBO) is an asset-backed security backed by a diversified pool of one or more of the following types of debt obligations: noninvestment grade corporate bonds, emerging market bonds, and/or bank loans to corporate entities. There is an asset manager in a CBO responsible for assembling and managing the debt obligations in which the asset manager may invest, subject to restrictions on the bond manager's activities. The typical structure of a CBO consists of a senior tranche (the majority of the structure) that receives a floating rate, different layers of subordinate or junior debt tranches that receive a fixed coupon rate, and an equity tranche. Because of the mismatch between a CBO's collateral (which primarily pays a fixed rate) and the floating-rate payment made to the senior tranche, the asset manager must employ derivatives such as an interest rate swap to better match the interest payments received and paid out.

KEY TERMS

- **Absolute prepayment speed (ABS)**, 483
- **Amortizing assets**, 476
- **Auto loan-backed security**, 483
- **Closed-end home equity loan**, 481
- **Collateralized bond obligation (CBO)**, 487
- **Credit card receivable-backed security**, 485
- **Credit enhancement**, 477
- **Early amortization**, 487
- **Home equity loan-backed security**, 481
- **Lockout period**, 486

- **Manufactured housing–backed security**, 482
- **Overcollateralization**, 478
- **Pass-through structure**, 480
- **Principal-amortization period**, 486
- **Reserve funds**, 478
- **Revolving period**, 486
- **Senior/subordinated structure**, 479
- **Special purpose vehicle or special purpose corporation**, 475
- **Third-party guarantee**, 477

QUESTIONS

1. A financial corporation with a BBB rating has a consumer loan portfolio. An investment banker has suggested that this corporation consider issuing an asset-backed security where the collateral for the security is the consumer loan portfolio. What would be the advantage of issuing an asset-backed security rather than a straight offering of corporate bonds?

2. What is the role played by a special purpose vehicle in an asset-backed security structure?

3. a. What are the various forms of external credit enhancement for an asset-backed security?

b. What is the disadvantage of using an external credit enhancement in an asset-backed security structure?

4. Suppose that the collateral for an asset-backed securities structure has a gross weighted average coupon of 8.6%. The servicing fee is 50 basis points. The tranches issued have a weighted average coupon rate of 7.1%. What is the excess servicing spread?

5. Suppose that the structure for an asset-backed security transaction is as follows:

senior tranche	$220 million
subordinated tranche 1	$50 million
subordinated tranche 2	$30 million

and that the value of the collateral for the structure is $320 million. Subordinated tranche 2 is the first loss tranche.

a. How much is the overcollateralization in this structure?

b. What is the amount of the loss for each tranche if losses due to defaults over the life of the structure total $15 million?

c. What is the amount of the loss for each tranche if losses due to defaults over the life of the structure total $35 million?

d. What is the amount of the loss for each tranche if losses due to defaults over the life of the structure total $85 million?

e. What is the amount of the loss for each tranche if losses due to defaults over the life of the structure total $110 million?

6. What is the difference between a pass-through structure and a pay-through structure?

7. An asset-backed security has been credit enhanced with a letter of credit from a bank with a single A credit rating. If this is the only form of credit enhancement, explain why this issue is unlikely to receive a triple A credit rating.

8. Why would it be critical for insurance companies that offer bond insurance for asset-backed security transactions to maintain a triple A credit rating?

9. What is the difference between a cash reserve fund and an excess servicing spread account?

10. a. Explain why a senior-subordinated structure is a form of internal credit enhancement.

b. Explain the need for a shifting interest mechanism in a senior-subordinated structure when the underlying assets are subject to prepayments.

11. Indicate whether you agree or disagree with the following statement: "Typically, closed-end home equity loans are loans to borrowers of the highest credit quality."

12. a. What are the components of the cash flow for a home equity loan-backed security and manufactured housing-backed security?

b. What are the reasons why prepayments due to refinancing are not significant for manufactured housing loans?

13. a. What are the components of the cash flow for an auto loan-backed security?

b. How important are prepayments due to refinancing for auto loans?

14. For a student loan-backed security, what is the difference between the deferment period and the grace period?

15. a. What are the components of the cash flow for a Small Business Administration-backed security?

b. What reference rate is used for setting the coupon interest, and how often is the coupon rate reset?

16. What is the cash flow for a credit card receivable-backed security during the lockout or revolving period?

17. How is the principal received from credit card borrowers handled during the lockout or revolving period for a credit card receivable-backed security?

18. a. What is meant by the monthly payment rate for a credit card deal?
    b. What is the significance of the monthly payment rate?
    c. How is the net portfolio yield determined for a credit card deal?
19. a. What is the typical collateral for a collateralized bond obligation?
    b. Explain why you agree or disagree with the following statement: "The asset manager for a CBO is free to actively manage the portfolio without any constraints."
    c. Explain why you agree or disagree with the following statement: "By using an interest rate swap, the asset manager for a CBO increases the risk associated with meeting the obligations that must be paid to the senior tranche."
    d. What is the equity tranche in a CBO entitled to receive?
20. Consider the following CBO transaction:
    1. The CBO is a $200 million structure. That is, the assets purchased will be $200 million.
    2. The collateral consists of bonds that all mature in eight years and the coupon rate for every bond is the eight-year Treasury rate plus 600 basis points.
    3. The senior tranche comprises 75% of the structure ($150 million) and pays interest based on the following coupon formula: LIBOR plus 90 basis points.
    4. There is only one junior tranche ($30 million) with a coupon rate that is fixed. The coupon rate is the eight-year Treasury rate plus 300 basis points.
    5. The asset manager enters into an agreement with a counterparty in which it agrees to pay the counterparty a fixed rate each year equal to the eight-year Treasury rate plus 120 basis points and receive LIBOR. The notional amount of the agreement is $150 million.
    a. How much is the equity tranche in this CBO?
    b. Assume that the eight-year Treasury rate at the time the CBO is issued is 6%. Assuming no defaults, what is the cash flow for each year and how is it distributed?
    c. Ignoring the asset management fee, what is the amount available each year for the equity tranche?
21. a. Some asset-backed security transactions may be characterized as "true securitizations," while others may be more properly classified as "hybrid transactions." What is the distinguishing feature of a "true securitization" and a "hybrid transaction"?
    b. How is the credit quality of a "hybrid transaction" evaluated?
22. Explain whether you would consider a collateralized bond obligation a true securitization or a hybrid securitization?

C h a p t e r   2 6

Financial Futures
Markets

Learning Objectives

After reading this chapter, you will understand

■ what a futures contract is.

■ the basic economic function of a futures contract.

■ the differences between futures and forward contracts.

■ the role of the clearinghouse.

■ the mark-to-market and margin requirements of a futures contract.

■ the role of futures markets in the economy.

■ features of U.S. stock index futures contracts.

■ features of interest rate futures contracts.

■ findings of the GAO study on financial derivatives.

■ what a forward rate agreement is.

In this chapter, we describe the financial futures market and the various contracts traded in it. The basic economic function of futures markets is to provide an opportunity for market participants to hedge against the risk of adverse price movements.

Futures contracts are products created by exchanges. To create a particular futures contract, an exchange must obtain approval from the Commodity Futures Trading Commission (CFTC), a government regulatory agency. In its application to the CFTC, the exchange must demonstrate that there is an economic purpose for the contract. While numerous futures contracts obtain approval for trading, only those contracts that spark investor interest and serve investor needs ultimately succeed.

Prior to 1972, only futures contracts involving traditional agricultural commodities (such as grain and livestock), imported foodstuffs (such as coffee, cocoa, and sugar), or industrial commodities were traded. Collectively, such futures contracts are known as *commodity futures*. Futures contracts based on a financial instrument or a financial index are known as *financial futures*. Financial futures can be classified as (1) stock index futures; (2) interest rate futures; and (3) currency futures.

As the value of a futures contract is derived from the value of the underlying instrument, futures contracts are commonly called *derivative instruments*. Options, discussed in the next chapter, are another example of derivative instruments. The pricing of derivative contracts and their uses by market participants are the topics of Chapters 28 and 29, respectively.

In the United States, the development of the markets for futures and options on stock indexes and debt obligations was a response to the need for an efficient risk-transference mechanism as stock price and interest rate volatility in the United States increased. Other countries have shared the U.S. experience with volatility and, as a result, developed derivative markets.

FUTURES CONTRACTS

A **futures contract** is a firm legal agreement between a buyer and a seller, in which:

1. The buyer agrees to take delivery of something at a specified price at the end of a designated period of time.
2. The seller agrees to make delivery of something at a specified price at the end of a designated period of time.

Of course, no one buys or sells anything when entering into a futures contract. Rather, the parties to the contract agree to buy or sell a specific amount of a specific item at a specified future date. When we speak of the "buyer" or the "seller" of a contract, we are simply adopting the jargon of the futures market, which refers to parties of the contract in terms of the future obligation they are committing themselves to.

Let's look closely at the key elements of this contract. The price at which the parties agree to transact in the future is called the **futures price**. The designated date at which the parties must transact is called the **settlement date** or **delivery date**. The "something" that the parties agree to exchange is called the **underlying**.

To illustrate, suppose there is a futures contract traded on an exchange where the underlying to be bought or sold is Asset XYZ, and the settlement is three months from now. Assume further that Bob buys this futures contract, and Sally sells this futures contract, and the price at which they agree to transact in the future is $100. Then $100 is the futures price. At the settlement date, Sally will deliver Asset XYZ to Bob. Bob will give Sally $100, the futures price.

When an investor takes a position in the market by buying a futures contract (or agreeing to buy at the future date), the investor is said to be in a **long position** or to be **long futures**. If, instead, the investor's opening position is the sale of a futures contract (which means the contractual obligation to sell something in the future), the investor is said to be in a **short position** or to be **short futures**.

The buyer of a futures contract will realize a profit if the futures price increases; the seller of a futures contract will realize a profit if the futures price decreases. For example, suppose that one month after Bob and Sally take their positions in the futures contract, the futures price of Asset XYZ increases to $120. Bob, the buyer of the futures contract, could then sell the futures contract and realize a profit of $20. Effectively, he has agreed to buy, at the settlement date, Asset XYZ for $100 and to sell Asset XYZ for $120. Sally, the seller of the futures contract, will realize a loss of $20.

If the futures price falls to $40 and Sally buys the contract, she realizes a profit of $60 because she agreed to sell Asset XYZ for $100 and now can buy it for $40. Bob would realize a loss of $60. Thus, if the futures price decreases, the buyer of the futures contract realizes a loss while the seller of a futures contract realizes a profit.

Liquidating a Position

Most financial futures contracts have settlement dates in the months of March, June, September, or December. This means that at a predetermined time in the contract settlement month the contract stops trading, and a price is determined by the exchange for settlement of the contract. The contract with the closest settlement date is called the **nearby futures contract**. The next futures contract is the one that settles just after the nearby contract. The contract farthest away in time from settlement is called the **most distant (or deferred) futures contract.**

A party to a futures contract has two choices on liquidation of the position. First, the position can be liquidated prior to the settlement date. For this purpose, the party must take an offsetting position in the same contract. For the buyer of a futures contract, this means selling the same number of identical futures contracts; for the seller of a futures contract, this means buying the same number of identical futures contracts.

The alternative is to wait until the settlement date. At that time the party purchasing a futures contract accepts delivery of the underlying; the party that sells a futures contract liquidates the position by delivering the underlying at the agreed-upon price. For some futures contracts that we shall describe later in this chapter, settlement is made in cash only. Such contracts are referred to as **cash settlement contracts.**

A useful statistic measuring the liquidity of a contract is the number of contracts that have been entered into but not yet liquidated. This figure is called the contract's **open interest**. An open interest figure is reported by an exchange for all the futures contracts traded on the exchange.

The Role of the Clearinghouse

Associated with every futures exchange is a **clearinghouse**, which performs several functions. One of these functions is to guarantee that the two parties to the transaction will perform. To see the importance of this function, consider potential problems in the futures transaction described earlier from the perspective of the two parties—Bob the buyer and Sally the seller. Each must be concerned with the other's ability to fulfill the obligation at the settlement date. Suppose that at the settlement date the price of Asset XYZ in the cash market is $70. Sally can buy Asset XYZ for $70 and deliver it to Bob, who in turn must pay her $100. If Bob does not have the capacity to pay $100 or refuses to pay, however, Sally has lost the opportunity to realize a profit of $30. Suppose, instead, that the price of Asset XYZ in the cash market is $150 at the settlement date. In this case, Bob is ready and willing to accept delivery of Asset XYZ and pay the agreed-upon price of $100. If Sally cannot deliver or refuses to deliver Asset XYZ, Bob has lost the opportunity to realize a profit of $50.

The clearinghouse exists to meet this problem. When someone takes a position in the futures market, the clearinghouse takes the opposite position and agrees to satisfy the terms set forth in the contract. Because of the clearinghouse, the two parties need not worry about the financial strength and integrity of the party taking the opposite side of the contract. After initial execution of an order, the relationship between the two parties ends. The clearinghouse interposes itself as the buyer for every sale and the seller for every purchase. Thus, the two parties are then free to liquidate their positions without involving the other party in the original contract, and without worry that the other party may default.

Besides its guarantee function, the clearinghouse makes it simple for parties to a futures contract to unwind their positions prior to the settlement date. Suppose that Bob wants to get out of his futures position. He will not have to seek out Sally and work out an agreement with her to terminate the original agreement. Instead, Bob can unwind his position by selling an identical futures contract. As far as the clearinghouse is concerned, its records will show that Bob has bought and sold an identical futures contract. At the settlement date, Sally will not deliver Asset XYZ to Bob but will be instructed by the clearinghouse to deliver to someone who bought and still has an open futures position. In the same way, if Sally wants to unwind her position prior to the settlement date, she can buy an identical futures contract.

Margin Requirements

When a position is first taken in a futures contract, the investor must deposit a minimum dollar amount per contract as specified by the exchange. This amount, called **initial margin**, is required as a deposit for the contract. Individual brokerage firms are free to set margin requirements above the minimum established by the exchange. The initial margin may be in the form of an interest-bearing security such as a Treasury bill. As the price of the futures contract fluctuates each trading day, the value of the investor's **equity** in the position changes. The equity in a futures account is the sum of all margins posted and all daily gains less all daily losses to the account. We develop this important concept throughout this section.

At the end of each trading day, the exchange determines the **settlement price** for the futures contract. The settlement price is different from the closing price, which many people know from the stock market and which is the price of the security in the final trade of the day (whenever that trade occurred during the day). The settlement price by contrast is that value that the exchange considers to be representative of trading at the end of the day. The representative price may in fact be the price in the day's last trade. But, if there is a flurry of trading at the end of the day, the exchange looks at all trades in the last few minutes and identifies a median or average price among those trades. The exchange uses the settlement price to mark to market the investor's position, so that any gain or loss from the position is quickly reflected in the investor's equity account.

Maintenance margin is the minimum level (specified by the exchange) to which an investor's equity position may fall as a result of an unfavorable price movement before the investor is required to deposit additional margin. The additional margin deposited is called **variation margin**, and it is an amount necessary to bring the equity in the account back to its initial margin level. Unlike initial margin, the variation margin must be in cash rather than interest-bearing instruments. Any excess margin in the account may be withdrawn by the investor. If a party to a futures contract who is required to deposit variation margin fails to do so within 24 hours, the exchange closes the futures position out.

Although there are initial and maintenance margin requirements for buying securities on margin, the concept of margin differs for securities and futures. When securities are acquired on margin, the difference between the price of the security and the initial margin is borrowed from the broker. The security purchased serves as collateral for the loan, and the investor pays interest. For futures contracts, the initial margin, in effect, serves as good faith money, an indication that the investor will satisfy the obligation of the contract. Normally, no money is borrowed by the investor who takes a futures position.

To illustrate the mark-to-market procedure, let's assume the following margin requirements for Asset XYZ:

Initial margin	$7 per contract
Maintenance margin	$4 per contract

Let's assume that Bob buys 500 contracts at a futures price of $100, and Sally sells the same number of contracts at the same futures price. The initial margin for both Bob and Sally is $3,500, which is determined by multiplying the initial margin of $7 by the number of contracts, which is 500. Bob and Sally must put up $3,500 in cash or Treasury bills or other acceptable collateral. At this time, $3,500 is also called the equity in the account. The maintenance margin for the two positions is $2,000 (the maintenance margin per contract of $4 multiplied by 500 contracts). The equity in the account may not fall below $2,000. If it does, the party whose equity falls below the maintenance margin must put up additional margin, which is the variation margin. There are two things to note here. First, the variation margin must be cash. Second, the amount of variation margin required is the amount to bring the equity up to the initial margin, not to the maintenance margin.

To illustrate the mark-to-market procedure, we assume the following settlement prices at the end of several trading days after the transaction was entered into. Those prices are:

Trading day	Settlement price
1	$ 99
2	97
3	98
4	95

First, consider Bob's position. At the end of trading day 1, Bob realizes a loss of $1 per contract or $500 for the 500 contracts he bought. Bob's initial equity of $3,500 is reduced by $500 to $3,000. No action is taken by the clearinghouse because Bob's equity is still above the maintenance margin of $2,000. At the end of the second day, Bob realizes a further loss as the price of the futures contract has declined another $2 to $97, resulting in an additional reduction in his equity position by $1,000. Bob's equity is then $2,000: the equity at the end of trading day 1 of $3,000 minus the loss on trading day 2 of $1,000. Despite the loss, no action is taken by the clearinghouse, because the equity still meets the $2,000 maintenance requirement. At the end of trading day 3, Bob realizes a profit from the previous trading day of $1 per contract or $500. Bob's equity increases to $2,500. The drop in price from $98 to $95 at the end of trading day 4 results in a loss for the 500 contracts of $1,500 and consequent reduction of Bob's equity to $1,000. As Bob's equity is now below the $2,000 maintenance margin, Bob is required to put up additional margin of $2,500 (variation margin) to bring the equity up to the initial margin of $3,500. If Bob cannot put up the variation margin his position will be liquidated.

Now, let's look at Sally's position. Sally as the seller of the futures contract benefits if the price of the futures contract declines. As a result, her equity increases at the end of the first two trading days. In fact, at the end of trading day 1, she realizes a profit of $500, which increases her equity to $4,000. She is entitled to take out the $500 profit and use these funds elsewhere. Suppose she does, and her equity therefore remains at $3,500 at the end of trading day 1. At the end of trading day 2, she realizes an additional profit of $1,000 that she also withdraws. At the end of trading day 3, she realizes a loss of $500 with the increase of the price from $97 to $98. This results in a reduction of her equity to $3,000. Finally, on trading day 4, she realizes a profit of $1,000, making her equity $4,000. She can withdraw $500.

Leveraging Aspect of Futures

A party taking a position in a futures contract need not put up the entire amount of the investment. Instead, the exchange and/or clearinghouse requires only the initial margin to be put up. To see the crucial consequences of this fact, suppose Bob has $100 and wants to invest in Asset XYZ because he belives its price will appreciate. If Asset XYZ is selling for $100, he can buy one unit of the asset. His payoff will then be based on the price action of one unit of Asset XYZ.

Suppose further that the exchange where the futures contract for Asset XYZ is traded requires an initial margin of only 5%, which in this case would be $5. This means Bob can purchase 20 contracts with his $100 investment. (We ignore the fact that Bob may need funds for variation margin.) His payoff will then depend on the price action of 20 units of Asset XYZ. Thus, he can leverage the use of his funds. (The degree of leverage equals 1/margin rate. In this case, the degree of leverage equals 1/0.05 or 20.) While the degree of leverage available in the futures market varies from contract to contract, as the initial margin requirement varies, the leverage attainable is considerably greater than in the cash market.

At first, the leverage available in the futures market may suggest that the market benefits mainly those who want to speculate on price movements. As we shall see in Chapter 29, however, futures markets can also be used to reduce price risk. Without the leverage possible in futures transactions, the cost of reducing price risk using futures would be too high for many market participants.

Market Structure

All futures exchanges in the United States trade more than one futures contract. On the exchange floor, each futures contract is traded at a designated location in a polygonal or circular platform called a *pit*. The price of a futures contract is determined by open outcry of bids and offers in an auction market. Because of the large number of traders attempting to communicate to other traders the price and quantity at which they wish to transact, pit traders are often forced to communicate using a system of hand signals. There is no designated market maker in the futures market as there is on an exchange where common stock is traded.

Trading on the floor of the exchange is restricted to members of the exchange. A membership is called a *seat on the exchange*. Its price is determined by supply and demand. Nonexchange members can lease a seat, which conveys to them the right to trade on an exchange. Floor traders include two types: **locals** and **floor brokers** (also called **pit brokers**). Locals buy and sell futures contracts for their own account, thereby risking their own capital. They are professional risk takers whose presence in the futures market adds liquidity to the market and brings bid and offer prices closer together. Consequently, collectively they play the same effective role as the market maker. Most locals do not maintain an open position overnight. The number of locals and the amount of capital that they can commit to the market far exceeds that of the floor brokers.

Floor brokers, just like locals, buy and sell for their own account. They execute customer orders as well. These orders come through an authorized futures broker, called a **futures commissions merchant**, or in the form of orders requested by other floor traders. For trades that they execute on behalf of others, floor brokers receive a commission. While floor brokers can both execute orders for customers and trade for their own account, most of their trades involve the former. When floor brokers do trade for their own account, such trades must not conflict with the interests of customers for whom they are executing trades.

The system of trading whereby participants meet at a trading pit during the trading hours of the exchange and price is determined by open outcry is still the dominant form of price determination in the futures market. However, the futures exchanges have introduced various forms of electronic trading to accommodate 24-hour trading and order routing. For example, the Chicago Mercantile Exchange's electronic trading system (GLOBEX2) provides access around the clock and the Chicago Board of Trade's alliance with Eurex (the all-electronic German/Swiss derivatives exchange) will create a single global electronic trading system by the end of 2001.

Daily Price Limits

The exchange has the right to impose a limit on the daily price movement of a futures contract from the previous day's closing price. A **daily price limit** sets the minimum and maximum price at which the futures contract may trade that day.[1] When a daily price limit is reached, trading does not stop but rather continues at a price that does not violate the minimum or maximum price.

The rationale offered for the imposition of daily price limits is that they provide stability to the market at times when new information may cause the futures price to exhibit extreme fluctuations. Those who support daily price limits argue that giving market participants time to digest or reassess such information if trading ceases when price limits would be violated gives them greater confidence in the market. Not all economists agree with this rationale. The question of the role of daily price limits and whether they are necessary remains the subject of extensive debate.

Key Points That You Should Understand Before Proceeding

1. A futures contract is a firm legal agreement between a buyer and a seller in which the buyer agrees to take delivery of something at the futures price at the settlement date and the seller agrees to make delivery.
2. A party to a futures contract can liquidate a position prior to the settlement date by taking an offsetting position in the same contract.
3. Associated with every futures exchange is a clearinghouse, which provides a guarantee function.
4. Parties to a futures contract must satisfy margin requirements (initial, maintenance, and variation), and futures contracts are marked to market at the end of each trading day.
5. Futures contracts are leveraged instruments that can be used to control risk.

FUTURES VERSUS FORWARD CONTRACTS

A **forward contract**, just like a futures contract, is an agreement for the future delivery of something at a specified price at the end of a designated period of time. Futures contracts are standardized agreements as to the delivery date (or month) and quality of the deliverable, and are traded on organized exchanges. A forward contract is usually nonstandardized because the terms of each contract are negotiated individually between buyer and seller. Also, there is no clearinghouse for trading forward contracts, and secondary markets are often nonexistent or extremely thin. Unlike a futures contract, which is an exchange-traded product, a forward contract is an over-the-counter instrument.

Although both futures and forward contracts set forth terms of delivery, futures contracts are not intended to be settled by delivery. In fact, generally fewer than 2% of outstanding contracts are settled by delivery. Forward contracts, in contrast, are intended for delivery.

Futures contracts are marked to market at the end of each trading day. Consequently, futures contracts are subject to interim cash flows as additional margin may be required in the case of adverse price movements, or as an investor who has experienced favorable price movements withdraws any cash that exceeds the account's margin requirement. A forward contract may or may not be marked to market, depending on the wishes of the two parties. For a forward contract that is not marked

---

[1] For a discussion of price limits on equity index futures contracts on the Chicago Mercantile Exchange go to: *http://www.cme.com/market/riskman/pricelmt.html* and *http://www.cme.com/market/riskman/pricelmtfaq.html.*

to market, there are no interim cash flow effects because no additional margin is required.

Finally, the parties in a forward contract are exposed to credit risk because either party may default on the obligation. Credit risk is minimal in the case of futures contracts because the clearinghouse associated with the exchange guarantees the other side of any transaction.

Other than these differences, which reflect the institutional arrangements in the two markets, most of what we say about futures contracts applies equally to forward contracts.

THE ROLE OF FUTURES IN FINANCIAL MARKETS

Without financial futures, investors would have only one trading location to alter portfolio positions when they get new information that is expected to influence the value of assets—the cash market. If they hear economic news that is expected to impact the value of an asset adversely, investors want to reduce their price risk exposure to that asset. The opposite would be true if the new information is expected to impact the value of an asset favorably: an investor would increase price risk exposure to that asset. There are, of course, transactions costs associated with altering exposure to an asset— explicit costs (commissions), and execution costs (bid–ask spreads and market impact costs), which we discussed in Chapter 18.

The futures market is an alternative market that investors can use to alter their risk exposure to an asset when new information is acquired. But which market—cash or futures—should the investor employ to alter a position quickly on the receipt of new information? The answer is simple: the one that most efficiently achieves the objective. The factors to consider are liquidity, transactions costs, taxes, and leverage advantages of the futures contract.

The market that investors consider more efficient for their investment objective should be the one where prices will first be established that reflect the new economic information. That is, this will be the market where price discovery takes place. Price information is then transmitted to the other market. For many of the financial assets that we have discussed, it is in the futures market that it is easier and less costly to alter a portfolio position. Therefore, it is the futures market that will be the market of choice and will serve as the price discovery market. It is in the futures market that investors send a collective message about how any new information is expected to impact the cash market.

How is this message sent to the cash market? To understand how, it is necessary to understand that there is a relationship between the futures price and the cash price. More specifically, in Chapter 28 we will demonstrate that the futures price and the cash market price are tied together by the cost of carry. If the futures price deviates from the cash market price by more than the cost of carry, arbitrageurs (in attempting to obtain arbitrage profits) would pursue a strategy to bring them back into line. Arbitrage is the mechanism that assures that the cash market price will reflect the information that has been collected in the futures market.

Some investors and the popular press consider that the introduction of a futures market for a financial asset will increase the price volatility of that financial asset in the cash market. That is, some market observers believe that, as a result of speculative trading of futures contracts, the cash market instrument does not reflect its fundamental economic value. The implication here is that the price of the financial asset would better reflect its true economic value in the absence of a futures market for that financial asset.

Whether or not the introduction of futures markets destabilizes prices of financial assets is an empirical question. Whether or not the introduction of futures contracts increases cash market price volatility, we might ask whether greater volatility has negative effects on financial markets. At first glance, it might seem that volatility has adverse effects from the points of view of allocative efficiency and participation in financial markets.

Actually, it has been pointed out that this inference may not be justified if, say, the introduction of futures markets lets prices respond more promptly to changes in factors that affect the economic value of a financial asset, and if these factors themselves are subject to large shocks.[2] Thus, the greater volatility resulting from an innovation may simply more faithfully reflect the actual variability of factors that affect the economic value of financial assets. In this case, "more" volatility of a financial asset's price need not be bad but, rather, may be a manifestation of a well-functioning market. Of course, to say that more volatility need not be bad does not mean that it is good.

For example, we describe below one type of futures contract in which the underlying is a stock market index. Critics of these futures contracts assert that their introduction has created greater volatility for stock market prices. While the empirical evidence has not supported this view, the key point is that increased volatility of stock market prices may be due to the greater quantity and frequency of information released by the government about important economic indicators that affect the value of the common stock of all companies. That information itself is subject to a great deal of variability. Thus, if there is any observed increase in the volatility of stock prices, that volatility may be due to the substantial variability of economic information, not to the presence of a futures contract on a stock market index.

Clearly, price volatility greater than what can be justified by relevant new information is undesirable. By definition, it makes prices inefficient. This is referred to as "excess volatility."[3]

Key Points That You Should Understand Before Proceeding

1. The key role of futures contracts is that, in a well-functioning futures market, these contracts provide a more efficient means for investors to alter their risk exposure to an asset.

2. A futures market will be the price discovery market when market participants prefer to use this market rather than the cash market to change their risk exposure to an asset.

3. The futures market and the cash market for an asset are tied together by an arbitrage process.

4. The argument that futures markets destabilize the prices of the underlying financial assets is an empirical question, but greater price volatility by itself is not an undesirable attribute of a financial market.

U.S. FINANCIAL FUTURES MARKETS

In this section we review the more important financial futures markets in the United States.

---

[2] Eugene F. Fama, "Perspectives on October 1987, or What Did We Learn from the Crash?" in Robert J. Barro, et al. (eds.), *Black Monday and the Future of Financial Markets* (Homewood, IL: Dow Jones-Irwin, 1989), p. 72.

[3] Franklin R. Edwards, "Futures Trading and Cash Market Volatility: Stock Index and Interest Rate Futures," *The Journal of Futures Markets*, Vol. 8, No. 4 (1988), p. 423.

Stock Index Futures Markets

In 1982, three futures contracts on broadly based common stock indexes made their debut: the Standard & Poor's 500 futures contract traded on the international Monetary Market of the Chicago Mercantile Exchange, the New York Stock Exchange Composite futures contract traded on the New York Futures Exchange, and the Value Line Average traded on the Kansas City Board of Trade. Since then, broad-based and specialized stock index futures contracts have been introduced. Table 26-1 lists the stock index futures contracts traded in the United States. The most actively traded contract is the S&P 500 futures contract. There are not yet contracts on individual stocks.

Stock index futures contracts are regulated by the Commodity Futures Trading Commission, although in recent years there have been proposals to shift regulatory authority to the SEC.

The dollar value of a stock index futures contract is the product of the futures price and the contract's multiple; that is,

Dollar value of a stock index futures contract = Futures price × Muliple

The **multiples for the key contracts** are indicated in the last column of Table 26-1. For example, if the futures price for the S&P 500 is 1300, since the multiple is $250, the dollar value of a stock index futures contract is:

$$310 \times \$250 = \$325,000$$

If an investor buys (takes a long position in) an S&P 500 futures contract at 1300 and sells it at 1315, the investor realizes a profit of 15 times $250, or $3750. If the futures contract is sold instead for 1280, the investor will realize a loss of 20 times $250, or $5000.

Stock index futures contracts are cash settlement contracts. This means that, at the settlement date, cash will be exchanged to settle the contract. For example, if an

Table 26-1   List of Stock Index Futures Contracts Traded on Exchanges in the United States

INDEX FUTURES CONTRACT	INDEX DESCRIPTION	EXCHANGE	CONTRACT SIZE/MULTIPLE
Standard & Poor's 500	500 stocks, cap weighted	CME	Index × $250
Standard & Poor's Midcap	400 stocks, cap weighted	CME	Index × $500
Russell 2000 Index	2000 stocks, cap weighted	CME	Index × $500
Nikkei 225 Index	225 stocks, price weighted	CME	Index × $5
Major Market Index	20 stocks, price weighted	CME	Index × $500
S&P 500/BARRA Growth Index	100+ stocks, cap weighted	CME	Index × $250
Standard & Poor's BARRA Value	300+ stocks, cap weighted	CME	Index × $250
NASDAQ 100 Index	100 stocks, cap weighted	CME	Index × $100
IPC Stock Index	35 stocks, cap weighted	CME	Futures × $25
NYSE Composite Index	2600+ stocks, cap weighted	NYFE	Index × $500

Symbols Directory
CME = Chicago Mercantile Exchange
NYFE = New York Futures Exchange

SOURCE: Exhibit 12 in Bruce M. Collins and Frank J. Fabozzi, *Derivatives and Equity Portfolio Management* (New Hope, PA: Frank J. Fabozzi Associates, 1999), p. 33.

investor buys an S&P 500 futures contract at 1300 and the settlement index is 1350, settlement would be as follows. The investor has agreed to buy the S&P 500 for 1300 times $250, or $325,000. The S&P 500 value at the settlement date is 1350 times $250, or $337,500. The seller of this futures contract must pay the investor $12,500 ($337,500 − $325,000). Had the index at the settlement date been 1280 instead of 1350, the value of the S&P 500 would be $320,000 (1280 × $250). The investor must pay the seller of the contract $5,000 ($325,000 − $320,000).

Interest Rate Futures Markets

In October 1975, the Chicago Board of Trade (CBT) pioneered trading in a futures contract based on a fixed-income instrument—Government National Mortgage Association certificates. Three months later, the International Monetary Market (IMM) of the Chicago Mercantile Exchange (CME) began trading futures contracts based on 13-week Treasury bills. Other exchanges soon followed with their own interest rate futures contracts. The more actively traded interest rate futures contracts are described below.

Treasury Bill Futures.

The Treasury bill futures contract, which is traded on the IMM, is based on a 13-week (three-month) Treasury bill with a face value of $1 million. More specifically, the seller of a Treasury bill futures contract agrees to deliver to the buyer at the settlement date a Treasury bill with 13 weeks remaining to maturity and a face value of $1 million. The Treasury bill that would be delivered by the terms of this contract can be newly issued or seasoned. The futures price is the price at which the Treasury bill will be sold by the short and purchased by the buyer. For example, a nine-month Treasury bill futures contract requires that, nine months from now, the short deliver to the long $1 million face value of a Treasury bill with 13 weeks remaining to maturity. The Treasury bill could be a newly issued 13-week Treasury bill or a Treasury bill that was issued one year prior to the settlement date and that therefore, at the settlement, has only 13 weeks remaining to maturity.

As we explained in Chapter 16, Treasury bills are quoted in the cash market in terms of the annualized yield on a bank discount basis. The Treasury bill futures contract is not quoted directly in terms of yield but instead on an index basis that is related to the yield on a bank discount basis as follows:

$$\text{Index price} = 100 - (\text{Yield on a bank discount basis} \times 100)$$

For example, if the yield on a bank discount basis is 8%, then

$$\text{Index price} = 100 - (0.08 \times 100) = 92$$

Eurodollar CD Futures

As we explained in Chapter 22, Eurodollar certificates of deposit (CDs) are denominated in dollars but represent the liabilities of banks outside the United States. The rate paid on Eurodollar CDs is the London Interbank Offered Rate (LIBOR). The three-month Eurodollar CD is the underlying for the Eurodollar CD futures contract. As with the Treasury bill futures contract, this contract is for $1 million of face value and is traded on an index price basis. The contract is traded on both the International Monetary Market of the Chicago Mercantile Exchange and the London International Financial Futures Exchange.

The unique feature of the Eurodollar CD futures contract is that the settlement procedure requires the parties to settle in cash for the value of a Eurodollar CD based on LIBOR at the settlement date. Of the two futures contracts based on short-term instruments, Eurodollar CD futures are more commonly employed by institutional investors than Treasury bill futures.

Treasury Bond Futures

The underlying for a Treasury bond futures contract is $100,000 par value of a hypothetical 20-year, 6% coupon bond. While prices and yields of the Treasury bond futures contract are quoted in terms of this hypothetical Treasury bond (see Chapter 16 for details on price quotations of Treasury bonds), the seller of the futures contract has the choice of several actual Treasury bonds that are acceptable to deliver. The Chicago Board of Trade (where the contract is traded) allows the seller to deliver any Treasury bond that has at least 15 years to maturity from the date of delivery if it is not callable; in the case of callable bonds, the issue must not be callable for at least 15 years from the first day of the delivery month. Settling a contract calls for an acceptable bond to be delivered. That is, the contract is not a cash settlement contract.

The delivery process for the Treasury bond futures contract makes the contract interesting. At the settlement date, the seller of a futures contract (the short) is required to deliver to the buyer (the long) $100,000 par value of a 6%, 20-year Treasury bond. Since no such bond exists, the seller must choose from the list of acceptable, deliverable bonds that the exchange has specified. But this choice raises a problem. Suppose the seller is entitled to deliver $100,000 of a 4%, 20-year Treasury bond to settle the futures contract. The value of this bond, of course, is less than the value of a 6%, 20-year bond. If the seller delivers the 4%, 20-year, this would be unfair to the buyer of the futures contract who contracted to receive $100,000 of a 6%, 20-year Treasury bond. Alternatively, suppose the seller delivers $100,000 of a 10%, 20-year Treasury bond. The value of a 10%, 20-year Treasury bond is greater than that of a 6%, 20-year bond, so this would be a disadvantage to the seller.

How can this problem be resolved? To make delivery equitable to both parties, and to tie cash prices to futures prices, the CBT has introduced **conversion factors** for determining the invoice price of each acceptable deliverable Treasury issue against the Treasury bond futures contract. The conversion factor is determined by the CBT before a contract with a specific settlement date begins trading. The conversion factor is based on the price that a deliverable bond would sell for, at the beginning of the delivery month, if it were to yield 6%. The conversion factor is constant throughout the trading period of the futures contract. The short must notify the long, one day before the delivery date, of the actual bond that will be delivered.

The invoice price paid by the buyer of the Treasury bonds which the seller delivers is determined using the formula:

Invoice price = Contract size × Future contract settlement price × Conversion factor

Suppose the Treasury bond futures contract settles at 96 (0.96 in decimal form) and that the short elects to deliver a Treasury bond issue with a conversion factor of 1.15. As the contract size is $100,000, the invoice price is:

$$\$100,000 \times 0.96 \times 1.15 = \$110,400$$

The invoice price in the formula is just for the principal. The buyer of the futures contract must also pay the seller accrued interest on the bond delivered.

In selecting the issue to be delivered, the short will select from all the deliverable issues the bond that is cheapest to deliver. This issue is referred to as the **cheapest-to-deliver issue** and is found by determining the issue that will produce the largest rate of return in a cash-and-carry trade. That is, for each deliverable issue the rate of return is calculated by assuming the issue is purchased and held to the futures delivery date. The rate of return calculated is called the *implied repo rate*. The cheapest-to-deliver issue is the one that offers the largest implied repo rate from among all the deliverable issues. This issue may change over the life of the contract. The cheapest-to-deliver issue plays a key role in the pricing of this futures contract.

In addition to the option of which acceptable Treasury issue to deliver—sometimes referred to as the **quality** or **swap option**—the short position has two more options granted under CBT delivery guidelines. First, the short position is permitted to decide when in the delivery month actually to make the delivery. This is called the **timing option**. The second option is the right of the short position to give notice of intent to deliver up to 8:00 P.M. Chicago time after the closing of the exchange (3:15 P.M. Chicago time) on the date when the futures settlement price has been fixed. This option is referred to as the **wild card option**. The quality option, the timing option, and the wild card option (in sum referred to as the *delivery options*) mean that the long position can never be sure which Treasury bond will be delivered or when it will be delivered.

Treasury Note Futures.

There are three Treasury note futures contracts: 10-year, 5-year, and 2-year. All three contracts are modeled after the Treasury bond futures contract and are traded on the CBT. The underlying instrument for the 10-year Treasury note futures contract is $100,000 par value of a hypothetical 6%, 10-year Treasury note. There are several acceptable Treasury issues that may be delivered by the short. An issue is acceptable if the maturity is not less than 6.5 years and not greater than 10 years from the first day of the delivery month. The delivery options granted to the short position and the minimum price fluctuation are the same as for the Treasury bond futures contract.

For the five-year Treasury note futures contract, the underlying is $100,000 par value of a 6% notional coupon U.S. Treasury note that satisfies the following conditions: (1) an original maturity of not more than five years and three months, (2) a remaining maturity no greater then five years and three months, and (3) a remaining maturity not less than four years and two months. The minimum price fluctuation for this contract is $1/64$ of 1%. The dollar value of a 64th for a $100,000 par value is $15.625 and is therefore the minimum price fluctuation.

The underlying for the two-year Treasury note futures contract is $200,000 par value of a 6% notional coupon U.S. Treasury note with a remaining maturity of not more than two years and not less than one year and nine months. Moreover, the *original maturity* of the note delivered to satisfy the two-year futures cannot be more than five years and three months. The minimum price fluctuation for this contract is $1/128$ of 1%. The dollar value of a 128th for a $200,000 par value is $15.625 and is therefore the minimum price fluctuation.

The two-year and five-year note futures are less liquid than the 10-year note futures.

Agency Futures Contract.

As will be explained in Chapter 29, managers can use Treasury futures for controlling interest rate risk. However, interest rate risk has two dimensions: the risk of changes in the level of Treasury yields and the risk of changes in the spread in the yield between non-Treasury securities and otherwise comparable Treasury securities. The latter risk, spread risk, has increased significantly since the summer of 1998. At the same time, there had been a considerable reduction in the issuance of long-term Treasury securities and a buy back by the U.S. Department of Treasury of its bonds. As explained in Chapter 10, agencies, specifically, Fannie Mae and Freddie Mac, have stepped in to issue debenture securities that they hope will become the benchmark interest rates in the financial market.

As a result of the anticipated important role of agency securities for becoming the benchmark yields and the greater spread risk, the CBT and the Chicago Mercantile Exchange (CME) began trading in 2000 futures contracts in which the underlying is a Fannie Mae or Freddie Mac agency security.

The underlying for the CBT 10-year agency note futures is one Fannie Mae Benchmark Note or Freddie Mac Reference Note having a face value of $100,000 at maturity with a notional coupon of 6%. As with the Treasury futures contract, there is more than one issue that is deliverable. For an issue to be deliverable it must be (1) a noncallable Fannie Mae Benchmark Note or Freddie Mac Reference Note maturing at least 6.5 years but not more than 10.25 years (original maturity) from the first day of the delivery month, (2) have an original issuance of $3 billion or greater, and (3) pay semiannual fixed coupons. The tick size is one-half of $1/32$ of one point ($15.625) rounded up to the nearest full cent. The contract delivery months are March, June, September, and December. As with the Treasury futures contract there is a conversion factor for each eligible issue.

The 10-year Agency Note futures contract of the CME is similar to that of the CBT but has a notional coupon of 6.5% instead of 6%. For an issue to be deliverable, the CME requires that the original maturity is 10 years, which does not mature for a period of at least 6.5 years from the date of delivery.

The CBT and the CME also have a five-year Agency Note futures contract. Again, the CBT's underlying is a 6% notional coupon and the CME's is a 6.5% notional coupon. As a result, of the many issues that are deliverable, there is a cheapest-to-deliver issue. This issue is found in exactly the same way as with the Treasury futures contract.

Bond Buyer's Municipal Bond Index Futures

The underlying product for this contract traded on the CBT is a basket, or index, of 40 municipal bonds. The Bond Buyer, publisher of *The Bond Buyer* (a trade publication of the municipal bond industry), serves as the index manager for the contract and prices each bond in the index according to prices received from five municipal bond brokers. It is necessary to obtain several independent prices from brokers because municipal bonds trade in the over-the-counter market.

Once the prices for a given issue are received from the five pricing brokers, the lowest and the highest prices are dropped. The remaining three prices then are averaged, with the resulting value referred to as the *appraisal value*. As delivery on all 40 bonds in the index is not practicable, the contract is a cash settlement contract, with settlement price based on the value of the index on the delivery date.

FINANCIAL FUTURES MARKETS IN OTHER COUNTRIES

Other countries have developed financial futures exchanges that have introduced a wide range of contracts. Many of these contracts are modeled after those developed in the U.S. futures markets. Many of the stock index futures contracts, for example, are cash settlement contracts, which is the settlement procedure used in the United States. In the case of futures on government bonds, the short (the seller of the futures contract) has the right to deliver one of several acceptable government issues. Table 26-2 lists stock index futures contracts traded on non-U.S. exchanges.

Key Points That You Should Understand Before Proceeding

1. Stock index futures contracts are cash settlement contracts whose underlying is a common stock index.
2. The dollar value of a stock index futures contract is the product of the futures price and the contract's multiple.
3. An interest rate futures contract is one whose underlying asset is a fixed-income instrument or an interest rate.
4. The more actively traded interest rate futures contracts are the Treasury bill futures contract, the Eurodollar CD futures contract (a cash settlement contract), the Treasury bond and note futures contracts, and the Bond Buyer's Municipal Bond Index futures contract (a cash settlement contract).
5. The Treasury bond and note futures contracts are unique in that the short is granted options as to which issue to deliver and during the delivery month when to deliver.
6. Non-U.S. exchanges have introduced a wide range of contracts, and many of these contracts are modeled after those developed in the U.S. futures markets.

THE GAO STUDY ON FINANCIAL DERIVATIVES

We've just explored our first derivative instrument, and we'll have more to say about other derivatives in the remaining chapters of this book. As we will see, some of these products are exchange traded, such as the futures contracts we discussed in this chapter. Other products are created by commercial banks and investment banking firms, as we explain in Chapters 30 and 31. These customized derivative products are called *over-the-counter* or *OTC derivatives*. Forward contracts are an example of an OTC derivative product. Swaps are another example of an OTC derivative. There are also OTC options.

There is public concern that commercial banks are creating OTC derivative products that put them in a position that could result in severe financial problems. Because it is the larger commercial banks that are creating OTC derivatives, this could have a rippling effect on the U.S. financial system. Specifically, there is concern that banks creating OTC derivative products do not have the proper risk-management systems in place to effectively monitor their risk exposure. For example, a July 1993 report by a highly influential bank group—the Group of Thirty—recommended how to improve bank risk-management systems. However, the recommendations did not appear to be uniformly adopted since they did not carry the force of law. Moreover, end-users of derivatives—financial institutions and businesses—may not have the requisite skills and risk-management systems to use derivatives or might be using them for speculative purposes rather than controlling financial risk.

In May 1994, the General Accounting Office (GAO) prepared a report on *Financial Derivatives: Actions Needed to Protect the Financial System*. The study recognized the importance of derivatives for market participants. Page 6 of the report states:

> Derivatives serve an important function of the global financial marketplace, providing end-users with opportunities to better manage financial risks associated with their business transactions. The rapid growth and increasing complexity of derivatives reflect both the increased demand from end-users for better ways to manage their financial risks and the inno-

Table 26-2   Selected Non-U.S. Stock Index Futures Contracts

INDEX FUTURES CONTRACT	INDEX DESCRIPTION	EXCHANGE	CONTRACT SIZE/MULTIPLE
JSE Actuaries Top 40 All Shares Index (South Africa)	40, cap weighted	SFFEX	Index × R10
Australian All Ordinaries	300+ stocks, cap weighted	SFE	Index × $25
Hang Seng Index (Hong Kong)	600+ stocks, cap weighted	HKFE	Index × $50
Nikkei 225 Average (Japan)	225 stocks, price weighted	OSE	Index × ¥1,000
Nikkei 300 Average (Japan)	300 stocks, cap weighted	OSE	Index × ¥10,000
SIMEX MSCI Singapore Stock Index	35 stocks, cap weighted	SIMEX	Index × S$200
Nikkei 225 Average (Japan)	225 stocks, price weighted	SIMEX	Index × ¥500
Nikkei 300 Average (Japan)	300 stocks, cap weighted	SIMEX	Index × ¥10,000
Kuala Lumpur Composite Index (Malaysia)	50 stocks, cap weighted	KLOFFE	Index × RM100
NZSE 10 Index (New Zealand)	10 stocks, cap weighted	NZFOE	Index × NZ$25
FTSE 100 Index (U.K.)	100 stocks, cap weighted	LIFFE	Index ×£10
FTSE 250 Index (U.K.)	250 stocks, cap weighted	LIFFE	Index ×£10
Eurotop 100 (European Stocks)	100 stocks, cap weighted	LIFFE	Index × ECU20
Dow Jones STOXX 50*	50 stocks, cap weighted	EUREX	Index × ECU10
Dow Jones EURO STOXX 50*	50 stocks, cap weighted	MATIF	Index × ECU10
DAX 30 Index (Germany)	30 stocks, cap weighted	DTB	Index × DM100
CAC 40 Index (France)	40 stocks, cap weighted	MATIF	Index × FF200
IBEX 35 Stock Index (Spain)	35 stocks, cap weighted	RV	Index × ESP1,000
Milan Stock Exchange MIB 30 (Italy)	30 stocks, cap weighted	IDEM	Index × ITL 10,000
TSE 35 Index (Canada)	35 stocks, cap weighted	TFE	Index × C$500
Bovespa Index (Brazil)	51 stocks, cap weighted	BM&F	Index × BRL3

Symbols Directory
SEFEX = Sydney Futures Exchange
SFE = IPC is the principal stock index of the Bolsa Mexicana de Valores
OSE = Osaka Stock Exchange
SIMEX = Singapore International Monetary Exchange
LIFFE = London International Financial Futures and Options Exchange
KLOFFE = Kuala Lumpur Options and Futures Exchange
TSE = Toronto Stock Exchange
TFE = Toronto Futures Exchange
HKFE = Hong Kong Futures Exchange
DTB = Deutsche Terminborse
NZFOE = New Zealand Futures and Options Exchange
MATIF = Marche a Terme International de France
RV = Meff Renta Variable
IDEM = Italian Derivatives Market; Italian Stock Exchange
BM&F = Bolsa de Mercadorias & Futuros
EUREX = The Swiss-German Futures and Options Exchange

* Dow Jones STOXX 50 and Dow Jones EURO STOXX 50 futures contracts trade on both the EUREX and the MATIF. Options on the futures trade on the DTB.

SOURCE: Exhibit 12 in Bruce M. Collins and Frank J. Fabozzi, *Derivatives and Equity Portfolio Management* (New Hope, PA: Frank J. Fabozzi Associates, 1999), p. 33.

vative capacity of the financial services industry to respond to market demands.

Despite the importance of derivatives, the study goes on to state:

> However, Congress, federal regulators, and some members of the industry are concerned about these products and the risk they may pose to the financial system, individual firms, investors, and U.S. taxpayers. These concerns have been heightened by recent reports of substantial losses by some derivative end-users.

The GAO study was undertaken because of these concerns. The cover letter to the GAO report stated that the objectives of the report were to determine:

> (1) what the extent and nature of derivatives use was, (2) what risks derivatives might pose to individual firms and to the financial system, (3) whether gaps and inconsistencies existed in U.S. regulation of derivatives, (4) whether existing accounting rules resulted in financial reports that provided market participants and investors with adequate information about firms' use of derivatives, and (5) what the implications of the international use of derivatives were for U.S. regulations.

Here are some of the principal conclusions of the study. First, boards of directors and senior management have primary responsibility for managing derivative risks and, therefore, should have the necessary internal controls in place to carry out this responsibility. Moreover, regulations should provide a legal framework that would require OTC derivative product dealers to comply with a common set of basic standards to effectively manage risk.

Second, financial reporting requirements for derivative instruments are inadequate and the Financial Accounting Standards Board should implement comprehensive accounting rules for derivative products. Third, improving regulations for derivatives in the United States without coordinating with foreign regulators will reduce the effectiveness of the regulations. Finally, policymakers and regulators should not stifle the use of derivatives. Rather, a proper balance should be struck between allowing the financial services to be innovative in creating products useful to end-users and protecting the safety and soundness of the financial system.

FORWARD RATE AGREEMENTS

A **forward rate agreement** (FRA) is the over-the-counter equivalent of the exchange-traded futures contracts on short-term rates. Typically, the short-term rate is LIBOR.

The elements of an FRA are the contract rate, reference rate, settlement rate, notional amount, and settlement date. The parties to an FRA agree to buy and sell funds on the settlement date. The FRA's *contract rate* is the rate specified in the FRA at which the buyer of the FRA agrees to pay for funds and the seller of the FRA agrees to receive for investing funds. The reference rate is the interest rate used. For example, the *reference rate* could be three-month LIBOR or six-month LIBOR. The benchmark from which the interest payments are to be calculated is specified in the FRA and is called the *notional amount* (or notional principal amount). This amount is not exchanged between the two parties. The *settlement rate* is the value of the reference rate at the FRA's settlement date. The source for determining the settlement rate is specified in the FRA.

The buyer of the FRA is agreeing to pay the contract rate, or equivalently, to buy funds at the settlement date at the contract rate; the seller of the FRA is agreeing to receive the contract rate, or equivalently to sell funds at the settlement date at the contract rate. So, for example, if the FRA has a contract rate of 5% for three-month LIBOR (the reference rate) and the notional amount is for $10 million, the buyer is agreeing to pay 5% to buy or borrow $10 million at the settlement date and the seller is agreeing to receive 5% to sell or lend $10 million at the settlement date.

If at the settlement date the settlement rate is greater than the contract rate, the FRA buyer benefits because the buyer can borrow funds at a below-market rate. If the settlement rate is less than the contract rate, this benefits the seller who can lend funds at an above-market rate. If the settlement rate is the same as the contract rate, neither party benefits. This is summarized as follows:

> FRA buyer benefits if settlement rate > Contract rate
>
> FRA seller benefits if contract rate > Settlement rate
>
> Neither party benefits if settlement rate = Contract rate

As with the Eurodollar CD futures contract, FRAs are cash settlement contracts. At the settlement date, the party that benefits based on the contract rate and settlement rate must be compensated by the other. Assuming the settlement rate is not equal to the contract rate, then:

> Buyer receives compensation if settlement rate > Contract rate
>
> Seller receives compensation if contract rate > Settlement rate

To determine the amount one party must compensate the other, the following is first calculated assuming a 360-day count convention:

If settlement rate > contract rate:

$$\text{Interest differential} = (\text{Settlement rate} - \text{Contract rate}) \\ \times (\text{Days in contract period}/360) \times \text{Notional amount}$$

If contract rate > settlement rate:

$$\text{Interest differential} = (\text{Contract rate} - \text{Settlement rate}) \\ \times (\text{Days in contract period}/360) \times \text{Notional amount}$$

The amount that must be exchanged at the settlement date is not the interest differential. Instead, the present value of the interest differential is exchanged. The discount rate used to calculate the present value of the interest differential is the settlement rate. Thus, the compensation is determined as follows:

$$\text{Compensation} = \frac{\text{Interest differential}}{[1 + \text{Settlement rate} \times (\text{Days to contract period} / 360)]}$$

To illustrate, assume the following terms for an FRA: Reference rate is three-month LIBOR, the contract rate is 5%, the notional amount is for $10 million, and the number of days to settlement is 91 days. Suppose the settlement rate is 5.5%. This means that the buyer benefits, since the buyer can borrow at 5% (the contract rate) when the market rate (the settlement rate) is 5.5%. The interest differential is:

$$\text{Interest differential} = (0.055 - 0.05) \times (91/360) \times \$10,000,000 = \$12,638.89$$

Table 26-3　Effect of Rate Changes on Parties to an FRA and an Interest Rate Futures Contract

	Interest rates				
	Decrease			Increase	
PARTY	FRA	FUTURES		FRA	FUTURES
Buyer	Loses	Gains		Gains	Loses
Seller	Gains	Loses		Loses	Gains

The compensation or payment that the seller must make to the buyer is:

$$\text{Compensation} = \frac{\$12,638.89}{[1 + 0.055 \times 91 / 360]}$$

$$\frac{\$12,638.89}{1.0139027} = \$12,465.58$$

It is important to note the difference of who benefits when interest rates move in an FRA and an interest rate futures contract. The buyer of an FRA benefits if the reference rate increases and the seller benefits if the reference rate decreases. In a futures contract, the buyer benefits from a falling rate while the seller benefits from a rising rate. This is summarized in Table 26-3. This is because the underlying for each of the two contracts is different. In the case of an FRA, the underlying is a rate. The buyer gains if the rate increases and loses if the rate decreases. In contrast, in a futures contract the underlying is a fixed-income instrument. The buyer gains if the fixed-income instrument increases in value. This occurs when rates decline. The buyer loses when the fixed-income instrument decreases in value. This occurs when interest rates increase. The opposite occurs for the seller of a futures contract.

SUMMARY

The traditional purpose of futures markets is to provide an important opportunity to hedge against the risk of adverse future price movements. Futures contracts are creations of exchanges, which require initial margin from parties. Each day positions are marked to market. Additional (variation) margin is required if the equity in the position falls below the maintenance margin. The clearinghouse guarantees that the parties to futures contracts will satisfy their obligations.

A buyer (seller) of a futures contract realizes a profit if the futures price increases (decreases). The buyer (seller) of a futures contract realizes a loss if the futures price decreases (increases). Because only initial margin is required when an investor takes a futures position, futures markets provide investors with substantial leverage for the money invested.

A forward contract differs in several important ways from a futures contract. In contrast to a futures contract, the parties to a forward contract are exposed to the risk that the other party to the contract will fail to perform. The positions of the parties are not marked to market, so there are no interim cash flows associated with a forward contract. Finally, unwinding a position in a forward contract may be difficult.

Investors can use the futures market or the cash market to react to economic news that is expected to change the value of an asset. Well-functioning futures markets are typically the market of choice for altering asset positions, and therefore represent the price discovery market, because of the lower transactions costs involved and the greater speed with which orders can be executed. The actions of arbitrageurs assure that price discovery in the futures markets will be transmitted to the cash market.

Critics of futures markets believe that these contracts are the source of greater price volatility in the cash market for the underlying asset. Although this is an empirical question not fully discussed here, even if price volatility in the cash market were greater because of the introduction of futures markets, this does not necessarily mean that greater volatility is bad for the economy.

The financial futures contracts traded in the United States include stock index futures contracts (with the most actively traded contract the S&P 500 futures contract), short-term interest rate futures contracts (Treasury bill and Eurodollar CD futures contracts), and Treasury bond and note futures contracts. Other countries have developed their financial futures markets with many of the contract features similar to those in the United States.

The General Accounting Office study addresses the concerns of Congress and regulators regarding derivative products. There is concern that major banks and end-users do not have adequate risk-management systems in place. Inadequate accounting disclosure and the lack of coordination with foreign regulators were other concerns highlighted by the study.

A forward rate agreement is the over-the-counter equivalent of the exchange-traded futures contracts on short-term rates and is a cash settlement contract. Typically, the short-term reference rate is LIBOR. The elements of an FRA are the contract rate, reference rate, settlement rate, notional amount, and settlement date. The buyer of the FRA agrees to pay the contract rate and the seller of the FRA agrees to receive the contract rate. The amount that must be exchanged at the settlement date is the present value of the interest differential. In contrast to a position in an interest rate futures contract, the buyer of an FRA benefits if the reference rate increases and the seller benefits if the reference rate decreases.

KEY TERMS

- Cash settlement futures contract, 498
- Cheapest-to-deliver issue, 508
- Clearinghouse, 498
- Conversion factor for a Treasury bond or note futures contracts, 507
- Daily price limit, 501
- Equity in a futures account, 499
- Floor brokers (also called pit brokers), 501
- Forward contract, 502
- Forward rate agreement (FRA), 512
- Futures commissions merchant, 501
- Futures contract, 497
- Futures price, 497
- Initial margin, 499
- Locals, 501
- Long futures position, 497
- Maintenance margin, 499
- Most distant (or deferred) futures contract, 497
- Multiple of an index futures contract, 505
- Nearby futures contract, 497
- Open interest, 498
- Quality option (also called swap option), 508
- Settlement date (or delivery date), 497
- Settlement price, 499
- Short futures position, 497
- Timing option, 508
- Underlying, 497
- Variation margin, 499
- Wild card option, 508

QUESTIONS

1. The chief financial officer of the corporation you work for recently told you that he had a strong preference to use forward contracts rather than futures contracts to hedge: "You can get contracts tailor-made to suit your needs." Comment on the CFO's statement. What other factors influence the decision to use futures or forward contracts?
2. Explain the functions of a clearinghouse associated with a futures exchange.
3. On April 1, 1992, you bought a stock index futures contract for 200 and were required to put up initial margin of $10,000. The value of the contract is 200 times the $500 multiple, or $100,000. On the next three days, the contract's settlement price was at these levels: day 1, 205; day 2, 197; day 3, 190.

     a. Calculate the value of your margin account on each day.

     b. If the maintenance margin for the contract is $7,000, how much variation margin did the exchange require you to put up at the end of the third day?

     c. If you had failed to put up that much, what would the exchange have done?

4. How do margin requirements in the futures market differ from margin requirements in the cash market?

5. "The futures market is where price discovery takes place." Do you agree with this statement? If so, why? If not, why not?

6. a. What is meant by a cash settlement futures contract?

   b. What two contracts in the United States are cash settlement futures contracts?

7. Two years ago Osaka became the first Japanese exchange to come out with a financial future—a stock-index future known as the Osaka 50. It was only a modest success, mainly because it had to be delivered in shares rather than cash.

This claim comes from the September 1989 issue of *Institutional Investor*. Why is cash settlement preferred for stock index futures?

8. a. What is meant by open interest?

   b. Why is open interest important to an investor?

9. a. In the Treasury bond futures contract, there are choices or options granted to one of the parties to the contract. Which party has these choices, the buyer or seller?

   b. What are the options that are granted to the party?

10. a. What was the motivation for the introduction of the agency note futures contracts?

   b. 'The agency note futures contract is a cash settlement contract." Explain why you agree or disagree with this statement.

11. On September 1, you sold 100 S&P 500 futures contracts at 1000 with multiples of $250, expiration date in three months, and an initial margin of 10%. After that date, the index fell steadily and you were not required to post any additional margin, but you also did not withdraw any of the cash profits you were earning. On November 1, the futures price of the contract was 900, and you reversed your position by buying 100 contracts.

   a. How much money did you make (ignoring taxes and commissions)?

   b. What was the rate of return on your invested funds?

   c. In those two months the S&P 500 futures price fell 10%. Explain why your rate of return is so much higher than this level.

12. What is meant by an OTC derivative product?

13. What is the major concern with banks creating OTC derivative products?

14. Hieber Manufacturing Corporation purchased the following forward rate agreement from the First Commercial Bank Corporation: (1) reference rate is three-month LIBOR, (2) contract rate is 6%, (3) notional amount is for $20 million, and (4) the number of days to settlement is 91 days.

   a. Suppose the settlement rate is 6.5%. Which party must compensate the other at the settlement date?

   b. If the settlement rate is 6.5%, how much will the compensation be?

15. Explain whether you agree or disagree with the following statement: "Both the buyers of an interest rate futures contract and forward rate agreement benefit if interest rates decline."

Options Markets

Learning Objectives

After reading this chapter, you will understand

- what an option contract is, and the basic features of an option.
- the difference between a call option and a put option.
- why an option is a derivative instrument.
- the difference between an American option and a European option.
- the difference between an exchange-traded option and options traded in the over-the-counter market.
- the difference between a futures contract and an option contract.
- the risk/return characteristics of call and put options, to both the seller and the buyer of the options.
- the hedging role of options in financial markets.
- the extensive role that organized exchanges play in standardizing and guaranteeing option contracts traded on exchanges.
- how stock options can change the risk/return profile of a portfolio.
- the basic features of stock index options.
- the basic features of interest rate options.
- what an exotic option is.
- some key aspects of non-U.S. options markets.
- the basic features of options on futures or futures options.

In the previous chapter, we introduced our first derivative instrument, a futures contract. In this chapter we introduce a second derivative contract, an options contract, and we discuss the differences between the two. In Chapter 28 we show how to determine the price of an **option**, and in Chapter 29 we explain how market participants can use these contracts.

OPTIONS CONTRACTS

There are two parties to an option contract: the *buyer* and the **writer** (also called the *seller*). In an option contract, the writer of the option grants the buyer of the option the right, but not the obligation, to purchase from or sell to the writer something at a specified price within a specified period of time (or at a specified date). The writer grants this right to the buyer in exchange for a certain sum of money, which is called the **option price** or **option premium**. The price at which the underlying (that is, the asset or commodity) may be bought or sold is called the **exercise price** or **strike price**. The date after which an option is void is called the **expiration date** or **maturity date**. Our focus in this chapter is on options where the underlying is a financial instrument or financial index.

When an option grants the buyer the right to purchase the underlying from the writer (seller), it is referred to as a **call option**, or simply, a **call**. When the option buyer has the right to sell the underlying to the writer, the option is called a **put option**, or simply, a **put**.

The timing of the possible exercise of an option is an important characteristic of the contract. There are options that may be exercised at any time up to and including the expiration date. Such options are referred to as **American options**. Other options may be exercised only at the expiration date; these are called **European options**.

Let's use an illustration to demonstrate the fundamental option contract. Suppose that Jack buys a call option for $3 (the option price) with the following terms:

1. The underlying asset is one unit of Asset XYZ.
2. The exercise price is $100.
3. The expiration date is three months from now, and the option can be exercised any time up to and including the expiration date (that is, it is an American option).

At any time up to and including the expiration date, Jack can decide to buy from the writer (seller) of this option one unit of Asset XYZ, for which he will pay a price of $100. If it is not beneficial for Jack to exercise the option, he will not, and we'll explain shortly how he decides whether or not it will be beneficial. Whether Jack exercises the option or not, the $3 he paid for the option will be kept by the option writer. If Jack buys a put option rather than a call option, then he would be able to sell Asset XYZ to the option writer for a price of $100.

The maximum amount that an option buyer can lose is the option price. The maximum profit that the option writer (seller) can realize is the option price. The option buyer has substantial upside return potential, while the option writer has substantial downside risk. We will investigate the risk/reward relationship for option positions later in this chapter.

There are no margin requirements for the buyer of an option once the option price has been paid in full. Because the option price is the maximum amount that the investor can lose, no matter how adverse the price movement of the underlying asset, no margin is needed. Because the writer (seller) of an option has agreed to accept all of the risk (and none of the reward) of the position in the underlying asset, the writer is generally required to put up the option price received as margin. In addition, as price changes occur that adversely affect the writer's position, the writer is required to deposit additional margin (with some exceptions) as the position is marked to market.

Options, like other financial instruments, may be traded either on an organized exchange or in the over-the-counter (OTC) market. An exchange that wants to create an options contract must obtain approval from either the Commodity Futures Trading Commission or the Securities and Exchange Commission.[1] **Exchange-traded options** have three advantages. The first is standardization of the exercise price, the quantity of the underlying, and the expiration date of the contract. Second, as in the case of futures contracts, the direct link between buyer and seller is severed after the order is executed because of the interchangeability of exchange-traded options. The clearing-

---

[1] By an agreement between the CFTC and the SEC and pursuant to an act of Congress, options on futures (discussed later in this chapter) are regulated by the former.

house associated with the exchange where the option trades performs the same function in the options market it does in the futures market. Finally, the transactions costs are lower for exchange-traded options than for OTC options.

The higher cost of an OTC option reflect the cost of customizing the option for the common situation where an institutional investor needs to have a tailor-made option because the standardized exchange-traded option does not satisfy its investment objectives. Investment banking firms and commercial banks act as principals as well as brokers in the OTC options market. Most institutional investors are not concerned that an OTC option is less liquid than an exchange-traded option because they use OTC options as part of an asset/liability strategy in which they intend to hold them to expiration.

Key Points That You Should Understand Before Proceeding

1. An option is a contract in which the writer of the option grants the buyer the right, but not the obligation, to purchase from or sell to the writer something at the exercise (or strike) price within a specified period of time (until the expiration date).
2. The price paid by the option buyer is called the option price or option premium.
3. A call option grants the option buyer the right to buy something from the option writer, and a put option grants the option buyer the right to sell something to the option writer.
4. The maximum amount that an option buyer can lose is the option price, while the maximum profit that the option writer can realize is the option price; the option buyer has substantial upside return potential, while the option writer has substantial downside risk.
5. Options may be traded either on an organized exchange or in the over-the-counter market.

DIFFERENCES BETWEEN OPTIONS AND FUTURES CONTRACTS

One distinction between futures and options contracts, is that one party to an option contract is not obligated to transact at a later date. Specifically, the option buyer has the right but not the obligation to exercise the option. The option writer (seller), though, does have the obligation to perform, if the buyer of the option insists on exercising it. In the case of a futures contract, both buyer and seller are obligated to perform. Of course, a futures buyer does not pay the seller to accept the obligation, while an option buyer pays the seller an option price.

Consequently, the risk/reward characteristics of the two contracts are also different. In the case of a futures contract, the buyer of the contract realizes a dollar-for-dollar gain when the price of the futures contract increases, and suffers a dollar-for-dollar loss when the price of the futures contract drops. The opposite occurs for the seller of a futures contract. Options do not provide this symmetric risk/reward relationship. The most that the buyer of an option can lose is the option price. While the buyer of an option retains all the potential benefits the gain is always reduced by the amount of the option price. The maximum profit that the writer (seller) may realize is the option price; this is offset against substantial downside risk. This difference between options and futures is extremely important because, as we shall see in subsequent chapters, investors can use futures to protect against symmetric risk and options to protect against asymmetric risk.

We will return to the difference between options and futures later in this chapter when we discuss the application of these derivative contracts for hedging purposes.

Key Points That You Should Understand Before Proceeding

1. Unlike a futures contract, only one party to an option contract is obligated to transact at a later date: the option writer.
2. Futures have a symmetric risk/reward relationship, while options do not because the buyer of an option retains all the potential benefits, but the gain is always reduced by the amount of the option price.

RISK AND RETURN CHARACTERISTICS OF OPTIONS

Here we illustrate the risk and return characteristics of the four basic option positions: buying a call option (which market participants refer to as being **long a call option**), selling a call option (**short a call option**), buying a put option (**long a put option**), and selling a put option (**short a put option**). The illustrations assume that each option position is held to the expiration date and not exercised early. Also, to simplify the illustrations, we ignore transactions costs.

Buying Call Options

Assume that there is a call option on Asset XYZ that expires in one month and has a strike price of $100. The option price is $3. Suppose that the current price of Asset XYZ is $100. What is the profit or loss for the investor who purchases this call option and holds it to the expiration date?

The profit and loss from the strategy will depend on the price of Asset XYZ at the expiration date. A number of outcomes are possible.

1. If Asset XYZ's price at the expiration date is less than $100, the investor will not exercise the option. It would be foolish to pay the option writer $100 when Asset XYZ can be purchased in the market at a lower price. In this case, the option buyer loses the entire, original option price of $3. Notice, however, that this is the maximum loss that the option buyer will realize regardless of how low Asset XYZ's price declines.
2. If Asset XYZ's price is equal to $100 at the expiration date, again, there is no economic value in exercising the option. As in the case where the price is less than $100, the buyer of the call option will lose the entire option price, $3.
3. If Asset XYZ's price is more than $100 but less than $103 at the expiration date, the option buyer will exercise the option. By exercising, the option buyer can purchase Asset XYZ for $100 (the strike price) and sell it in the market for the higher price. Suppose, for example, that Asset XYZ's price is $102 at the expiration date. The buyer of the call option will realize a $2 gain by exercising the option. Of course, the cost of purchasing the call option was $3, so $1 is lost on this position. By failing to exercise the option, the investor loses $3 instead of only $1.
4. If Asset XYZ's price is equal to $103 at the expiration date, the investor will exercise the option. In this case, the investor breaks even, realizing a gain of $3 that offsets the cost of the option, $3.
5. If Asset XYZ's price is more than $103 at the expiration date, the investor will exercise the option and realize a profit. For example, if the price is $113, exercising the option will generate a profit on Asset XYZ of $13. Reducing this gain by the cost of the option ($3), the investor will realize a net profit of $10 from this position.

Table 27-1   Profit/Loss Profile for a Long Call Position

Assumptions: Option price = $3 Strike price = $100 Time to expiration = 1 month			
PRICE OF ASSET XYZ AT EXPIRATION DATE	NET PROFIT/LOSS*	PRICE OF ASSET XYZ AT EXPIRATION DATE	NET PROFIT/LOSS*
$150	$47	100	−3
140	37	99	−3
130	27	98	−3
120	17	97	−3
115	12	96	−3
114	11	95	−3
113	10	94	−3
112	9	93	−3
111	8	92	−3
110	7	91	−3
109	6	90	−3
108	5	89	−3
107	4	88	−3
106	3	87	−3
105	2	86	−3
104	1	85	−3
103	0	80	−3
102	−1	70	−3
101	−2	60	−3

* Price at expiration − $100 − $3.
Maximum loss = −$3.

Table 27-1 shows the profit and loss for the buyer of the hypothetical call option in tabular form, whereas Figure 27-1 graphically portrays the result. While the break-even point and the size of the loss depend on the option price and the strike price, the profile shown in Figure 27-1 will hold for all buyers of call options. The shape indicates

Figure 27-1   Profit/Loss Profile for a Long Call Position

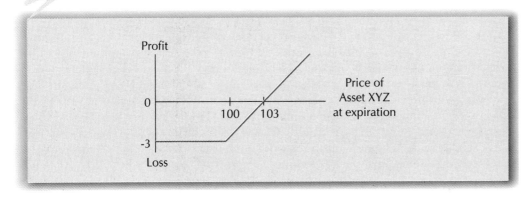

that the maximum loss is the option price and that there is substantial upside potential.

It is worthwhile to compare the profit and loss profile of the call option buyer to that of someone taking a long position in one unit of Asset XYZ. The payoff from the position depends on Asset XYZ's price at the expiration date. Consider again the five price outcomes given above (and again ignore transactions costs):

1. If Asset XYZ's price at the expiration date is less than $100, the investor in the call option loses the entire option price of $3. In contrast, a long position in Asset XYZ will have one of three possible losses:
   a. If Asset XYZ's price is less than $100 but greater than $97, the loss on the long position in Asset XYZ will be less than $3.
   b. If Asset XYZ's price is $97, the loss on the long position in Asset XYZ will be $3.
   c. If Asset XYZ's price is less than $97, the loss on the long position in Asset XYZ will be greater than $3. For example, if the price at the expiration date is $80, the long position in Asset XYZ will result in a loss of $20.

2. If Asset XYZ's price is equal to $100, the buyer of the call option will realize a loss of $3 (option price). Similarly, there will be no gain or loss on the long position in Asset XYZ.

3. If Asset XYZ's price is more than $100 but less than $103, the option buyer will realize a loss of less than $3, while the long position in Asset XYZ will realize a profit.

4. If the price of Asset XYZ at the expiration date is equal to $103, there will be no loss or gain from buying the call option. The long position in Asset XYZ, however, will produce a gain of $3.

5. If Asset XYZ's price at the expiration date is greater than $103, both the call option buyer and the long position in Asset XYZ will post a profit. However, the profit for the buyer of the call option will be $3 less than that for the long position. For example, if Asset XYZ's price is $113, the profit from the call position is $10, while the profit from the long position in Asset XYZ is $13.

Table 27-2 compares the long call strategy and the long position in Asset XYZ. This comparison clearly demonstrates the way in which an option can change the risk/return profile for investors. An investor who takes a long position in Asset XYZ realizes a profit of $1 for every $1 increases in Asset XYZ's price. As Asset XYZ's price falls, however, the investor loses dollar-for-dollar. If the price drops by more than $3, the long position in Asset XYZ results in a loss of more than $3. The long call strategy, in contrast, limits the loss to only the option price of $3 but retains the upside potential, which will be $3 less than for the long position in Asset XYZ.

Which alternative is better, buying the call option or buying the asset? The answer depends on what the investor is attempting to achieve. This will become clearer in Chapter 29 where we explain various strategies using either option positions or cash market positions.

This hypothetical example demonstrates another important feature of options: their speculative appeal. Suppose an investor has strong expectations that Asset XYZ's price will rise in one month. At an option price of $3, the speculator can purchase 33.33 call options for each $100 invested. If Asset XYZ's price rises, the investor realizes the price appreciation associated with 33.33 units of Asset XYZ, while with the same $100, the investor could have bought only one unit of Asset XYZ selling at $100, realizing the appreciation associated with only one unit if Asset XYZ's price increases. For example, suppose that in one month the price of Asset XYZ rises to $120. The long call position will result in a profit of $566.50 [($20 × 33.33) − $100)] or a return of 566.5% on the $100 investment in the call option. By comparison, a $100 investment in the long position in Asset XYZ results in a profit of $20, for only a 20% return on $100.

Table 27-2   Comparison of Long Call Position and Long Asset Position

Assumptions:
Initial price of Asset XYZ = $100
Option price = $3
Strike price = $100
Time to expiration = 1 month

PRICE OF ASSET XYZ AT EXPIRATION DATE	Net profit/loss for		PRICE OF ASSET XYZ AT EXPIRATION DATE	Net profit/loss for	
	LONG CALL	LONG ASSET XYZ		LONG CALL	LONG ASSET XYZ
$150	$47	$50	100	−3	0
140	37	40	99	−3	−1
130	27	30	98	−3	−2
120	17	20	97	−3	−3
115	12	15	96	−3	−4
114	11	14	95	−3	−5
113	10	13	94	−3	−6
112	9	12	93	−3	−7
111	8	11	90	−3	−8
110	7	10	91	−3	−9
109	6	9	90	−3	−10
108	5	8	89	−3	−11
107	4	7	88	−3	−12
106	3	6	87	−3	−13
105	2	5	86	−3	−14
104	1	4	85	−3	−15
103	0	3	80	−3	−20
102	−1	2	70	−3	−30
101	−2	1	60	−3	−40

It is this greater leverage that attracts investors to options when they wish to speculate on price movements. There are some drawbacks of leverage, however. Suppose that Asset XYZ's price is unchanged at $100 at the expiration date. The long call position (33.33 options) results, in this case, in a loss of the entire investment of $100, while the long position in Asset XYZ produces neither a gain nor a loss.

Writing (Selling) Call Options

To illustrate the option seller's (writer's) position, we use the same call option as in the example of buying a call option. The profit and loss profile of the short call position (that is, the position of the call option writer) is the mirror image of the profit and loss profile of the long call position (the position of the call option buyer). Consequently, the profit of the short call position for any given price of Asset XYZ at the expiration date is the same as the loss of the long call position. Furthermore, the maximum profit that the short call position can produce is the option price. The maximum loss is not limited because it is the highest price reached by Asset XYZ on or before the expiration date, less the option price; this price can be indefinitely high. These relationships can be seen in Figure 27-2, which shows the profit/loss profile for a short call position.

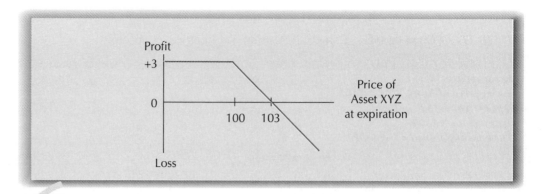

Figure 27-2 Profit/Loss Profile for a Short Call Position

Buying Put Options

To illustrate the position of the buyer of a put option, we assume a hypothetical put option on one unit of Asset XYZ with one month to maturity and a strike price of $100. Assume the put option is selling for $2 and that the current price of Asset XYZ is $100. The profit or loss for this position at the expiration date depends on the market price of Asset XYZ. The possible outcomes are:

1. If Asset XYZ's price is greater than $100, the buyer of the put option will not exercise it because exercising would mean selling Asset XYZ to the writer for a price that is less than the market price. In this case, a loss of $2 (the original price of the option) will result from buying the put option. Once again, the option price represents the maximum loss to which the buyer of the put option is exposed.

2. If Asset XYZ's price at expiration is equal to $100, the put will not be exercised, leaving the put buyer with a loss equal to the option price of $2.

3. If Asset XYZ's price is less than $100 but greater than $98, the option buyer will experience a net loss on the position; exercising the put option, however, limits the loss to less than the option price of $2. For example, suppose that the price is $99 at the expiration date. By exercising the option, the option buyer will realize a loss of only $1. This is because the buyer of the put option can sell Asset XYZ, purchased in the market for $99, to the writer for $100, realizing a gain of $1. Deducting the $2 cost of the option results in a net loss of $1 to the position.

4. If Asset XYZ's price is $98 at the expiration date, the put buyer will break even. The investor will realize a gain of $2 by selling Asset XYZ to the writer of the option for $100, and this gain exactly offsets the cost of the option ($2).

5. If Asset XYZ's price is below $98 at the expiration date, the long put position (the put buyer) will realize a profit. For example, suppose the price falls at expiration to $80. The long put position will produce a profit of $18: a gain of $20 for exercising the put option less the $2 option price.

The profit and loss profile for the long put position is shown in tabular form in the second column of Table 27-3 and in graphical form in Figure 27-3. As with all long option positions, the loss is limited to the option price. The profit potential, however, is substantial: the theoretical maximum profit is generated if Asset XYZ's price falls to zero. Contrast this profit potential with that of the buyer of a call option. The theoretical maximum profit for a call buyer cannot be determined beforehand, because it depends on the highest price that can be reached by Asset XYZ before or at the option expiration date, a price that is indeterminate.

Table 27-3   Profit/Loss Profile for a Long Put Position in Comparison to a Short
Asset Position

Assumptions:
Initial price of Asset XYZ = $100
Option price = $2
Strike price = $100
Time to expiration = 1 month

PRICE OF ASSET XYZ AT EXPIRATION DATE	Net profit/loss for		PRICE OF ASSET XYZ AT EXPIRATION DATE	Net profit/loss for	
	LONG PUT*	SHORT ASSET XYZ**		LONG PUT*	SHORT ASSET XYZ**
$150	−$2	−$50	91	7	9
140	−2	−40	90	8	10
130	−2	−30	89	9	11
120	−2	−20	88	10	12
115	−2	−15	87	11	13
110	−2	−10	86	12	14
105	−2	−5	85	13	15
100	−2	0	84	14	16
99	−1	1	83	15	17
98	0	2	82	16	18
97	1	3	81	17	19
96	2	4	80	18	20
95	3	5	75	23	25
94	4	6	70	28	30
93	5	7	65	33	35
92	6	8	60	38	40

* *$100 – Price at expiration – $2.*
Maximum loss = – $2.
** *$100 – Price of Asset XYZ.*

Figure 27-3   Profit/Loss Profile for a Long Put Position

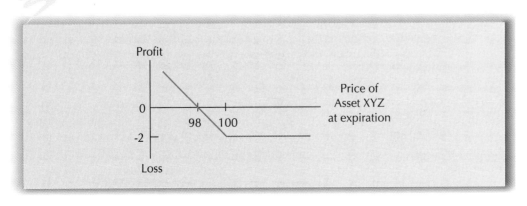

To see how an option alters the risk/return profile for an investor, we again compare it to a position in Asset XYZ. The long put position is compared to taking a short position in Asset XYZ because this is the position that would realize a profit if the price of the asset falls.[2] Suppose an investor sells Asset XYZ short for $100. The short position in Asset XYZ would produce the following profit or loss compared with the long put position (without considering transactions costs):

1. If Asset XYZ's price rises above $100, the long put option results in a loss of $2, but the short position in Asset XYZ realizes one of the following:
   a. If the price of Asset XYZ is less than $102, there will be a loss of less than $2, which is the loss to the long put position.
   b. If the price of Asset XYZ is equal to $102, the loss will be $2, the same as the maximum loss of the long put position.
   c. If the price of Asset XYZ is greater than $102, the loss will be greater than $2. For example, if the price is $125, the short position will realize a loss of $25, because the short seller must now pay $125 for Asset XYZ that he sold short at $100.

2. If Asset XYZ's price at expiration is equal to $100, the long put position will realize a $2 loss, while there will be no profit or loss on the short position in Asset XYZ.

3. If Asset XYZ's price is less than $100 but greater than $98, the long put position will experience a loss of less than $2, but the short position will realize a profit. For example, a price of $99 at the expiration date will result in a loss of $1 for the long put position but a profit of $1 for the short position.

4. If Asset XYZ's price is $98 at the expiration date, the long put position will break even, but the short position in Asset XYZ will generate a $2 profit.

5. If Asset XYZ's price is below $98, both positions will generate a profit; however, the profit for the long put position will always be $2 less than the profit for the short position.

Table 27-3 presents a detailed account of this comparison of the profit and loss profiles for the long put position and short position in Asset XYZ. While the investor who takes a short position in Asset XYZ faces all the downside risk as well as the upside potential, the long put position limits the downside risk to the option price while still maintaining upside potential (reduced only by an amount equal to the option price).

Writing (Selling) Put Options

The profit and loss profile for a short put option is the mirror image of the long put option. The maximum profit from this position is the option price. The theoretical maximum loss can be substantial should the price of the underlying asset fall; at the outside, if the price were to fall all the way to zero, the loss would be as large as the strike price less the option price. Figure 27-4 graphically depicts this profit and loss profile.

To summarize these illustrations of the four option positions, we can say the following: Buying calls or selling puts allows the investor to gain if the price of the underlying asset rises; and selling calls and buying puts allows the investor to gain if the price of the underlying asset falls.

Considering the Time Value of Money

Our illustrations of the four option positions do not take into account the time value of money. Specifically, the buyer of an option must pay the seller the option price at the time the option is purchased. Thus, the buyer must finance the purchase price of the option or, assuming the purchase price does not have to be borrowed, the buyer

---

[2] See Chapter 18 for more detail on selling short in a securities market.

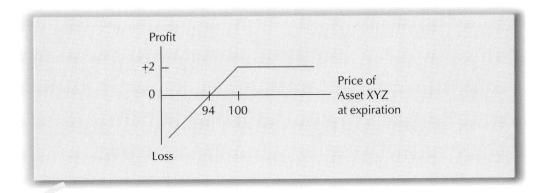

Figure 27-4   Profit/Loss Profile for a Short Put Position

loses the income that can be earned by investing the amount of the option price until the option is sold or exercised. In contrast, assuming that the seller does not have to use the option price amount as margin for the short position or can use an interest-earning asset as security, the seller has the opportunity to earn income from the proceeds of the option sale.

The time value of money changes the profit/loss profile of the option positions we have discussed. The breakeven price for the buyer and the seller of an option will not be the same as in our illustrations. The breakeven price for the underlying asset at the expiration date is higher for the buyer of the option; for the seller, it is lower.

Our comparisons of the option position with long and short positions in the underlying asset also ignore the time value of money. We have not considered the fact that the underlying asset may generate interim cash flows (dividends in the case of common stock, interest in the case of bonds). The buyer of a call option is not entitled to any interim cash flows generated by the underlying asset. The buyer of the underlying asset, however, would receive any interim cash flows and would have the opportunity to reinvest them. A complete comparison of the long call option position and the long position in the underlying asset must take into account the additional dollars from reinvesting any interim cash flows. Moreover, any effect on the price of the underlying asset as a result of the distribution of cash must be considered. This occurs, for example, when the underlying asset is common stock and, as a result of a dividend payment, the stock declines in price.

Key Points That You Should Understand Before Proceeding

1. There are four basic option positions: buying a call option, selling a call option, buying a put option, and selling a put option.
2. An option can be used to alter the risk/reward relationship from that of a position in the underlying.
3. The buyer of a call option benefits if the price of the underlying rises; the writer (seller) of a call option benefits if the price of the underlying is unchanged or falls.
4. The buyer of a put option benefits if the price of the underlying falls; the writer (seller) of a put option benefits if the price of the underlying is unchanged or rises.
5. In determining the payoff from an option, the time value of money as a result of having to finance the option price must be considered.

ECONOMIC ROLE OF THE OPTION MARKETS

Futures contracts allow investors to hedge the risks associated with adverse price movements. Hedging with futures lets a market participant lock in a price, and thereby eliminates price risk. In the process, however, the investor gives up the opportunity to benefit from a favorable price movement. In other words, hedging with futures involves trading off the benefits of a favorable price movement for protection against an adverse price movement.

Hedging with options has a variety of potential benefits, which we discuss in Chapter 29. For now, we provide an overview of how options can be used for hedging, and how the outcomes of hedging with options differ from those of hedging with futures. A good way to show the hedging uses of options is to return to the initial illustration in this chapter where the underlying for the option is Asset XYZ.

First let's consider an investor who owns Asset XYZ, currently selling for $100, which she expects to sell one month from now. The investor's concern is that, one month from now, Asset XYZ's price may decline below $100. One alternative available to this investor is to sell Asset XYZ now. Suppose, however, the investor does not want to sell this asset now because either some restrictions prevent this or she thinks that the price may rise during the month. Suppose also that an insurance company offers to sell the investor an insurance policy providing that, if at the end of one month Asset XYZ's price is less than $100, the insurance company will make up the difference between $100 and the market price. For example, if one month from now Asset XYZ's price is $80, the insurance company will pay the investor $20.

The insurance company naturally charges the investor a premium to write this policy. Let's suppose that the premium is $2. Holding aside the cost of the insurance policy, the payoff that this investor then faces is as follows. The minimum price for Asset XYZ that the investor can receive is $100 because, if the price is less, the insurance company will make up the difference. If Asset XYZ's price is greater than $100, however, the investor will receive the higher price. The premium of $2 that is required to purchase this insurance policy effectively assures the investor of a minimum price of $98 ($100 minus $2), while if the price is above $100 the investor realizes the benefits of a higher price (reduced always by the $2 for the insurance policy). In buying this policy, the investor has purchased protection against an adverse price movement, while maintaining the opportunity to benefit from a favorable price movement.

Insurance companies do not offer such policies, but we have described an option strategy that provides the same protection. Consider the put option on Asset XYZ with one month to expiration, a strike price of $100, and an option price of $2 that we discussed earlier in this chapter. The payoff to a long position in this put is identical to the insurance policy. The option price resembles the hypothetical insurance premium; this is the reason why the option price is referred to as the option premium. Thus, a put option can be used to hedge against a decline in the price of the underlying instrument.

The long put's payoff is quite different from that of a futures contract. Suppose that a futures contract with Asset XYZ as the underlying instrument has a futures price equal to $100 and a settlement date one month from now. By selling this futures contract, the investor would be agreeing to sell Asset XYZ for $100 one month from now. If Asset XYZ's price falls below $100, the investor is protected because she will receive $100 upon delivery of the asset to satisfy the futures contract. If Asset XYZ's price rises above $100, however, the investor will not realize the price appreciation because she must deliver the asset for an agreed-upon amount of $100. By selling the futures contract, the investor has locked in a price of $100, and fails to realize a gain if the price rises while avoiding a loss if the price declines.

Call options, too, are useful for hedging. A call option can be used to protect against a rise in the price of the underlying instrument while maintaining the opportunity to benefit from a decline in the price of the underlying instrument. Suppose, for example, that an investor expects to receive $100 one month from now, and plans to use that money to purchase Asset XYZ, which is selling currently for $100. The risk that the investor faces is that Asset XYZ's price will rise above $100 one month from now. Let us further suppose there is a call option such as we described earlier in the chapter. The option costs $3 and has a strike price of $100 and a month to expiration. By purchasing that call option, the investor has hedged the risk of a rise in the price of Asset XYZ.

The hedge outcome is as follows. If the price rises above $100 one month from now, the investor would exercise the call option and realize the difference between the market price of Asset XYZ and $100. Thus, if we hold aside the cost of the option for the moment, we can see that the investor is insuring that the maximum price she will have to pay for Asset XYZ is $100. Should the asset's price fall below $100, the call option expires worthless, but the investor benefits by being able to purchase Asset XYZ at a price less than $100. Once the $3 cost of the option is considered, the payoff is as follows. Regardless of the eventual price of the asset, the maximum price that the investor will have to pay for Asset XYZ is $103 (the strike price plus the option price). If the price of the asset declines below $100, the investor will benefit by the amount of the price decline less $3.

Compare this situation to a futures contract where Asset XYZ is the underlying instrument, the settlement is in one month, and the futures price is $100. Suppose that the investor buys this futures contract. If one month from now the price of Asset XYZ rises above $100, the investor has contracted to buy the asset for $100, thereby eliminating the risk of a price rise; if the price falls below $100, however, the investor cannot benefit because she has contracted to pay $100 for the asset.

It should be clear now how hedging with options differs from hedging with futures. This difference cannot be overemphasized—options and futures are not interchangeable instruments.

Although our focus has been on hedging price risk, options also allow investors an efficient way to expand the range of return characteristics available. That is, investors can use options to "mold" a return distribution for a portfolio to fit particular investment objectives.[3]

Key Points That You Should Understand Before Proceeding

1. Hedging with futures involves trading off the benefits of a favorable price movement for protection against an adverse price movement.
2. Hedging with options allows the option buyer to limit risk but maintain the potential to benefit from a favorable price movement.
3. Options allow the investor to mold a risk/return relationship.

U.S. OPTIONS MARKETS

There are a variety of options traded in the United States. Here, we provide a survey of the major ones.

---

[3] See Stephen A. Ross, "Options and Efficiency," *Quarterly Journal of Economics* (February 1976), pp. 75–89; and Fred Arditti and Kose John, "Spanning the State Space with Options," *Journal of Financial and Quantitative Analysis* (March 1980), pp. 1–9.

Stock Options

Options on individual shares of common stock have been traded for many years. Trading of standardized call options on common stock began on the Chicago Board Options Exchange (CBOE) in April 1973. Since then, the Securities and Exchange Commission (SEC) has granted permission to other exchanges to trade options: the American Stock Exchange in 1974, the Philadelphia Exchange in 1975, the Pacific and the Midwest Stock Exchanges in 1976, the New York Stock Exchange in 1982, and the International Securities Exchange (ISE) in 2000. SEC permission to trade put options on common stocks on organized exchanges was not granted until March 1977.

The SEC approved the creation of a national clearing system for options, the **Options Clearing Corporation (OCC)**, jointly established by the CBOE and the American Stock Exchange. Since its establishment in 1974, the OCC has issued, guaranteed, registered, cleared, and settled all transactions involving listed options on all exchanges.

Exchange-traded stock options have a standardized quantity: One contract applies to 100 shares of the designated common stock. While most underlying stocks are those of listed companies, stock options on a number of over-the-counter stocks are also available. However, all the companies are large and their shares are actively traded.

The Options Clearing Corporation has established standard strike price guidelines for listed options. For stocks with a price above $100, option strike prices are set at $10 intervals; for stocks with a price below $100 and above $30, strike prices are set at $5 intervals; and for stocks priced between $10 and $30 the interval is $2.50. While the strike price of exchange-traded options is not changed because of cash dividends paid to common stockholders, the strike price is adjusted for stock splits, stock dividends, reorganization, and other recapitalizations affecting the value of the underlying stock.

All exchange-traded stock options in the United States may be exercised any time before the expiration date; that is, they are American options. They expire at 11:59 P.M. Eastern Standard Time on the Saturday following the third Friday of the expiration month. Exchange rules require that investors wishing to exercise an expiring option must instruct a broker about the exercise no later than 5:30 P.M. Eastern time on the business day immediately preceding the expiration date. Notices to exercise a nonexpiring option on a date other than the expiration date must be made between 10:00 A.M. and 8:00 P.M. Eastern Standard Time. When a nonexpiring option is exercised, the OCC assigns the obligation the next day to someone who has an outstanding short position in an option of the same exercise price, expiration date, and underlying stock. This assignment is on a random basis.

Options are designated by the name of the underlying common stock, the expiration month, the strike price, and the type of option (put or call). Thus, an IBM call option with a strike price of 103 and expiring in April is referred to as the "Exxon April 103 call."

The expiration dates are standardized. Each stock is assigned an option cycle, the three option cycles being January, February, and March. The expiration months for each option cycle are as follows:

Option cycle	Expiration months
January	January, April, July, October
February	February, May, August, November
March	March, June, September, December

In addition, the practice is to trade options with an expiration date of the current calendar month, the next calendar month, and the next two expiration months in the cycle. For example, suppose a stock is assigned the January option cycle. In February, options with the following expiration months would be traded: February (the current calendar month), March (the next calendar month), April (first next expiration month in January option cycle), and July (second next option cycle month in January option cycle). In May the following expiration months would be traded for a stock assigned to the January option cycle: May (the current calendar month), April (the next calendar month), July (first next expiration month in January option cycle), and October (second next option cycle month in January option cycle).

Stock Index Options

In March 1983, a revolution in stock options and investments in general occurred. At that time, trading in an option whose underlying instrument was a stock index, the S&P 100 (originally called the CBOE 100), began on the Chicago Board Options Exchange. Shortly afterward, the American Stock Exchange initiated trading in an option based on what the exchange called the Major Market Index (MMI).[4] These index options have proven useful and popular with many kinds of investors. As in the case of options on individual stocks, stock index options are regulated by the Securities and Exchange Commission.

Table 27-4 presents a list of stock index option contracts trading on exchanges in the United States. The most liquid index options are those on the S&P 100 index (OEX) and the S&P 500 index. Both trade on the CBOE. Index options can be listed as American or European. The S&P 500 index option contract is European, while the OEX is American. Both index option contracts have specific standardized features and contract terms. Moreover, both have short expiration cycles. Table 27-4 also shows selected industry options, sector options, and style options.

The level of trading volume for each contract differs. A useful statistic measuring the liquidity of a contract is the number of contracts that have been entered into but not yet liquidated. This figure is called the contract's *open interest*. An open interest figure is reported for all listed contracts.

If a stock option is exercised, a stock must be delivered. It would be complicated, to say the least, to settle a stock index option by delivering all the stocks that make up the index. Instead, stock index options are *cash settlement contracts*. This means that, if the option is exercised, the exchange-assigned option writer pays cash to the option buyer. There is no delivery of any stock.

The dollar value of the stock index underlying an index option is equal to the current cash index value multiplied by the contract's multiple. That is,

$$\text{Dollar value of the underlying index} = \text{Cash index value} \times \text{Contract multiple}$$

Each stock index option has a contract multiple. The contract multiple for the S&P 100 is $100. So, for example, if the cash index value for the S&P 100 is 720, then the dollar value of the S&P 100 contract is $720 \times \$100 = \$72,000$.

For a stock option, the price at which the buyer of the option can buy or sell the stock is the strike price. For an index option, the strike index is the index value at which the buyer of the option can buy or sell the underlying stock index. The strike index is converted into a dollar value by multiplying the strike index by the multiple

---

[4] The index includes 20 stocks and was constructed to be similar to the Dow Jones Industrial Average.

Table 27-4   U.S. Listed Equity Index Option Contracts

CONTRACT	INDEX DESCRIPTION	EXCHANGE	EXERCISE PROVISIONS
Large Cap Contracts			
Major Market Index	20 stocks, price weighted	AMEX	European, FLEX
Dow Jones Industrial Average	30 stocks, price weighted	CBOE	European, FLEX
NASDAQ 100	100 stocks, cap weighted	CBOE	European, FLEX
Standard & Poor's 100	100 stocks, cap weighted	CBOE	American, FLEX
Standard & Poor's 500	500 stocks, cap weighted	CBOE	European, FLEX
NYSE Composite Index	2,600+ stocks, cap weighted	CBOE	European, FLEX
Institutional Index	75 stocks, cap weighted	AMEX	European, FLEX
Small Cap Contracts			
Russell 2000 Index	2,000 stocks, cap weighted	CBOE	European
Standard & Poor's Small Cap 600	600 stocks, cap weighted	CBOE	European
PSE Wilshire Small Cap 250	250 stocks, cap weighted	PSE	European
Style or Nonindustry Sector Options			
Standard & Poor's BARRA Growth	100+ stocks, cap weighted	CBOE	European
Standard & Poor's BARRA Value	300+ stocks, cap weighted	CBOE	European
AMEX MS Consumer Index	30 stocks, equal weighted	AMEX	European
AMEX MS Cyclical Index	30 stocks, equal weighted	AMEX	European
AMEX MS Gold Bugs Index	13 stocks, equal weighted	AMEX	European
AMEX MS Commodity Related	21 stocks, equal weighted	AMEX	European
CBOE Lipper Analytical Salomon Brothers Growth Fund	30 stocks, equal weighted	CBOE	European
CBOE Lipper Analytical Salomon Brothers Growth & Income Fund	30 stocks, equal weighted	CBOE	European
CBOE Morgan Stanley Multinational Company Index	40+ stocks, cap weighted	CBOE	European
Dow Jones Transportation Average	20 stocks, price weighted	CBOE	European
Dow Jones Utility Average	15 stocks, price weighted	CBOE	European
PSE Morgan Stanley Emerging Growth Index	50 stocks, cap weighted	PSE	European
Sector Options			
Chicago Board Options Exchange	10 CBOE Sector Indexes	CBOE	European
	6 Goldman Sachs Technology Indexes		
	6 S&P Industry Sectors		
American Stock Exchange	15+ AMEX Sector Indexes	AMEX	European
	5+ MS Sector Indexes		
Philadelphia Stock Exchange	12 PHLX Sector Indexes	PHLX	European

Symbols Directory

AMEX = *American Stock Exchange*

CBOE = *Chicago Board Options Exchange*

PHLX = *Philadelphia Stock Exchange*

SOURCE: Exhibit 4 in Bruce M. Collins and Frank J. Fabozzi, *Derivatives and Equity Portfolio Management* (New Hope, PA: Frank J. Fabozzi Associates, 1999), pp. 20–21.

for the contract. For example, if the strike index is 700 for an S&P 100 index option, the dollar value is $70,000 (700 × $100). If an investor purchases a call option on the S&P 100 with a strike index of 700, and exercises the option when the index value is 720, then the investor has the right to purchase the index for $70,000 when the dollar value of the index is $72,000. The buyer of the call option would then receive $2,000 from the option writer.

As can be seen in Table 27-4, exercise provisions for stock index options come in both the American and European variety. The S&P 100 index options are American options. The S&P 500, the Major Market, and the Institutional index options are European options (which means that they cannot be exercised until expiration). (Later we'll explain what "FLEX" means in Table 27-4.) Institutional investors find European options attractive because they need not fear that a short position they take in an option in order to accomplish an investment objective will be exercised early. Index options expire on the Saturday following the third Friday of the contract month.

There are also options on stock index futures. These options are not as widely used as options on stock indexes. Options on futures contracts are the contracts of choice in the interest rate options market, so we will postpone our discussion of options on futures until later in this chapter.

Long-Term Equity Anticipation Securities

For an individual stock and a stock index, only the next two expiration months are traded on an exchange. Consequently, the longest time before expiration of a standard exchange-traded option is six months. **Long-Term Equity Anticipation Securities (LEAPS)** are option contracts designed to offer option contracts with longer maturities. These contracts are available on individual stocks and some indexes. Stock option LEAPS are comparable to standard stock options except the maturities can range up to 39 months from the origination date. Index options LEAPS differ in size compared with standard index options having a multiplier of 10 rather than 100.

Interest Rate Options

Interest rate options can be written on cash instruments or futures. At one time, there were several exchange-traded option contracts whose underlying instrument was a debt instrument. These contracts are referred to as **options on physicals**. For reasons explained later, options on futures that are based on debt instruments have been far more popular than options on physicals.

In recent years, market participants have made increasingly greater use of over-the-counter options on Treasury, agency debentures, and mortgage-backed securities.[5] Certain institutional investors who want to purchase an option on a specific Treasury security or a Ginnie Mae pass-through can do so on an over-the-counter basis. There are government and mortgage-backed securities dealers who make a market in options on specific securities. Typically, the maturity of the option coincides with the time period over which the buyer of the option wants to hedge, so the buyer is not concerned with the option's liquidity.

Besides options on fixed-income securities, investors can obtain OTC options on a yield spread (such as the spread between mortgage pass-through securities and Treasuries or between double-A corporates and Treasuries).

---

[5] For a more detailed discussion of over-the-counter options, see Chapter 2 of Mark Pitts and Frank J. Fabozzi, *Interest Rate Futures and Options* (Chicago: Probus Publishing, 1989).

FLEX Options[6]

A **FLEX option** is an option contract with some terms that have been customized. It is traded on an options exchange and cleared and guaranteed by the associated clearinghouse for the exchange. The need for customization of certain terms is a result of the wide range of portfolio strategy needs of institutional investors that cannot be satisfied by standard exchange-traded options.

A FLEX option can be created for individual stocks, stock indexes, and Treasury securities. The value of FLEX options is the ability to customize the terms of the contract along four dimensions: underlying, strike price, expiration date, and settlement style (i.e., American versus European). Moreover, the exchange provides a secondary market to offset or alter positions and an independent daily marking of prices.

The development of the FLEX option is a response to the growing over-the-counter market. The exchanges seek to make the FLEX option attractive by providing price discovery through a competitive auction market, an active secondary market, daily price valuations, and the virtual elimination of counterparty risk. The FLEX option represents a link between listed options and OTC products.

Exotic Options

OTC options can be customized in any manner sought by an institutional investor. Basically, if a dealer can reasonably hedge the risk associated with the opposite side of the option sought, it will create the option desired by a customer. OTC options are not limited to European or American types. An option can be created in which the option can be exercised at several specified dates as well as the expiration date of the option. Such options are referred to as **limited exercise options**, **Bermuda options**, and **Atlantic options**.

The more complex options created are called **exotic options**. Here are just two types of such exotic options: alternative options and outperformance options. An **alternative option**, also called an **either-or option**, has a payoff which is the best independent payoff of two distinct assets. For example, suppose that Donna buys an alternative call option with the following terms:

1. The underlying asset is one unit of Asset M or one unit of Asset N.
2. The strike price for Asset M is $80.
3. The strike price for Asset N is $110.
4. The expiration date is three months from now.
5. The option can only be exercised three months from now (that is, it is a European option).

At the expiration date, Donna can decide to buy from the writer of this option *either* one unit of Asset M at $80 or Asset N at $110. Donna will buy the asset with the larger payoff. So, for example, if Asset M and Asset N at the expiration date are $84 and $140, respectively, then the payoff would be $4 if Donna elects to exercise to buy Asset M but $30 if she elects to exercise to buy Asset N. Thus, she will exercise to buy Asset N. If the price for either asset at the expiration date is below their strike price, Donna will let the option expire worthless.

An **outperformance option** is an option whose payoff is based on the relative payoff of two assets at the expiration date. For example, consider the following outperformance call option purchased by Karl:

---

[6] For a more detailed description of FLEX options, see James J. Angel, Gary L. Gastineau, and Clifford J. Weber, *Equity FLEX Options* (New Hope, PA: Frank J. Fabozzi Associates, 1999).

1. Portfolio A consists of the stock of 50 public utility companies with a market value of $1 million.
2. Portfolio B consists of the stock of 50 financial services companies with a market value of $1 million.
3. The expiration date is six months from now and is a European option.
4. The strike is equal to:

Market value of Portfolio B – Market value of Portfolio A

At the expiration date, if the market value of Portfolio A is greater than the market value of Portfolio B, then there is no value to this option and it will expire worthless. The option will be exercised if the market value of Portfolio B exceeds the market value of Portfolio A at the expiration date.

> **Key Points That You Should Understand Before Proceeding**
>
> 1. There are options traded on individual shares of common stock and options traded on common stock indexes.
> 2. The dollar value of a stock index option contract is equal to the index value multiplied by the contract's multiple.
> 3. There are interest rate options in which the underlying is a debt instrument (called an option on a physical) and a futures contract (called a futures option).
> 4. Exchange-traded options on futures that are based on debt instruments have been far more popular than exchange-traded options on physicals.
> 5. There has been increased use by institutional investors of over-the-counter options on Treasury and mortgage-backed securities.
> 6. Complex OTC options are called exotic options.

OPTIONS MARKETS OUTSIDE THE UNITED STATES

Options markets have developed in many countries. In the United Kingdom, the London Traded Options Market is part of the International Stock Exchange and hosts trading in options on stocks and on indexes. In Canada, numerous options are traded on both the Toronto Stock Exchange and the Montreal Exchange. The European Options Exchange is in Amsterdam and it sponsors trading in a wide variety of European equity options and index options.

Table 27-5 shows selected international stock index options. Among the latest arrivals of international options are options traded on the Dow Jones STOXX 50 and the Dow Jones EURO 50 stock indexes. The indexes comprise 50 industrial, commercial, and financial European blue-chip companies.

FUTURES OPTIONS

An option on a futures contract, commonly referred to as a **futures option**, gives the buyer the right to buy from or sell to the writer a designated futures contract at a designated price at any time during the life of the option. If the futures option is a call option, the buyer has the right to purchase one designated futures contract at the exercise price. That is, the buyer has the right to acquire a long futures position in the designated futures contract. If the buyer exercises the call option, the writer (seller) acquires a corresponding short position in the futures contract.

A put option on a futures contract grants the buyer the right to sell one designated futures contract to the writer at the exercise price. That is, the option buyer has

Table 27-5   International Listed Stock Index Option Contracts

CONTRACT	INDEX DESCRIPTION	EXCHANGE	EXERCISE PROVISIONS
Dow Jones STOXX 50	50 stocks, cap weighted	DTB	European
Dow Jones EURO STOXX 50	50 stocks, cap weighted	DTB	European
Eurotop 100	225 stocks, price weighted	AMSE	European
Nikkei 225 Average (Japan)	100 stocks, price weighted	OSE	American
TOPIX (Japan)	1,300+ stocks, cap weighted	TSE	American
FTSE 100 Index (United Kingdom)	100 stocks, cap weighted	LIFFE	American, FLEX
DAX 30 Index (Germany)	30 stocks, cap weighted	DTB	American
CAC 40 Index (France)	40 stocks, cap weighted	MONEP	American
Hang Seng Index (Hong Kong)	600+ stocks, cap weighted	HKFE	European
Australian All Ordinaries	300+ stocks, cap weighted	ASE	American

Symbols Directory

OSE *Osaka Stock Exchange*
TSE *Tokyo Stock Exchange*
LIFFE *London International Financial Futures and Options Exchange*
DTB *Deutsche Terminborse*
MONEP *Marche des Options Negociables de*
HKFE *Hong Kong Futures Exchange*
ASE *Australian Stock Exchange*
AMSE *Amsterdam Stock Exchange*

SOURCE: Exhibit 4 in Bruce M. Collins and Frank J. Fabozzi, *Derivatives and Equity Portfolio Management* (New Hope, PA: Frank J. Fabozzi Associates, 1999), pp. 20–21.

the right to acquire a short position in the designated futures contract. If the put option is exercised, the writer acquires a corresponding long position in the designated futures contract.

There are futures options on all the interest rate futures contracts reviewed in the previous chapter.

Mechanics of Trading Futures Options

As the parties to the futures option will realize a position in a futures contract when the option is exercised, the question is: What will the futures price be? That is, at what price will the long be required to pay for the instrument underlying the futures contract, and at what price will the short be required to sell the instrument underlying the futures contract?

Upon exercise, the futures price for the futures contract will be set equal to the exercise price. The position of the two parties is then immediately marked to market based on the then-current futures price. Thus, the futures position of the two parties will be at the prevailing futures price. At the same time, the option writer or seller must pay the option buyer the economic benefit from exercising. In the case of a call futures option, the option writer must pay the difference between the current futures price and the exercise price to the buyer of the option. In the case of a put futures option, the option writer must pay the option buyer the difference between the exercise price and the current futures price.

For example, suppose an investor buys a call option on some futures contract in which the exercise price is 85. Assume also that the futures price is 95, and that the buyer exercises the call option. Upon exercise, the call buyer is given a long position in the futures contract at 85, and the call writer is assigned the corresponding short position in the futures contract at 85. The futures position of the buyer and the writer is immediately marked to market by the exchange. Since the prevailing futures price is 95, and the exercise price is 85, the long futures position (the position of the call buyer) realizes a gain of 10 while the short futures position (the position of the call writer) realizes a loss of 10. The call writer pays the exchange 10 and the call buyer receives 10 from the exchange. The call buyer, who now has a long futures position at 95, can either liquidate the futures position at 95 or maintain a long futures position. If the former course of action is taken, the call buyer sells a futures contract at the prevailing futures price of 95. There is no gain or loss from liquidating the position. Overall, the call buyer realizes a gain of 10. If the call buyer elects to hold the long futures position, then he or she will face the same risk and reward of holding such a position. But the call buyer still has realized a gain of 10 from the exercise of the call option.

Suppose, instead, that the futures option is a put rather than a call, and the current futures price is 60 rather than 95. If the buyer of this put option exercises it, the buyer would have a short position in the futures contract at 85; the option writer would have a long position in the futures contract at 85. The exchange then marks the position to market at the then-current futures price of 60, resulting in a gain to the put buyer of 25 and a loss to the put writer of the same amount. The put buyer, now having a short futures position at 60, can either maintain that position or liquidate it by buying a futures contract at the prevailing futures price of 60. In either case the put buyer realizes a gain of 25 from exercising the put option.

The exchange imposes no margin requirements for the buyer of a futures option once the option price has been paid in full. Because the maximum amount the buyer can lose is the option price, regardless of how adverse the price movement of the underlying instrument, there is no need for margin.

Because the writer (seller) of an option has agreed to accept all of the risk (and none of the reward) of the position in the underlying instrument, the writer (seller) is required to deposit not only the margin required on the interest rate futures contract position if that is the underlying instrument, but, with certain exceptions, also the option price that is received for writing the option. In addition, if prices for the underlying futures contract adversely affect the writer's position, the writer would be required to deposit variation margin as it is marked to market.

Reasons for the Popularity of Futures Options

There are three reasons why futures options on fixed-income securities have largely supplanted options on physicals as the options vehicle used by institutional investors.[7] First, unlike options on fixed-income securities, futures options on Treasury coupon futures do not require payments for accrued interest to be made. Consequently, when a futures option is exercised, the call buyer and the put writer need not compensate the other party for accrued interest.

Second, futures options are believed to be "cleaner" instruments because of the reduced likelihood of delivery squeezes. Market participants who must deliver an instrument are concerned that the instrument to be delivered will be in short supply at the time of delivery, resulting in a higher price to acquire it. As the deliverable supply of futures contracts is more than adequate for futures options currently traded, there is no concern about a delivery squeeze.

---

[7] Laurie Goodman, "Introduction to Debt Options," Chapter 1 in Frank J. Fabozzi (ed.), *Winning the Interest Rate Game: A Guide to Debt Options* (Chicago: Probus Publishing, 1985), pp. 13–14.

Finally, in order to price any option, it is imperative to know at all times the price of the underlying instrument. As we mentioned in our discussions of the various bond markets, current bond prices are not easily available. In contrast, futures prices are readily available.

Key Points That You Should Understand Before Proceeding

1. A futures option gives the buyer the right to buy from or sell to the writer a designated futures contract at a designated price at any time during the life of the option.
2. If the buyer of the futures option exercises, the futures price for the futures contract will be set equal to the exercise price, but the position of the two parties is then immediately marked to market based on the then-current futures price.
3. There are several reasons why futures options on fixed-income securities have been used more by institutional investors than options on physicals.

SUMMARY

An option is a contract between two parties, the buyer and the seller (or writer). The buyer pays a price or premium to the seller for the right (but not the obligation) to buy or sell a certain amount of a specified item at a set price for a specified period of time. The right to buy is a call option, and the right to sell is a put option. The set price is the exercise or strike price. The period ends on the maturity or expiration date. If the right cannot be exercised until that date, the option is called a European option. If the option can be exercised at any time before the maturity date, the option is an American option. The item to which the option applies is the underlying asset, and its value determines the value of the option. Hence, options are called derivative instruments.

Options traded on exchanges are standardized and guaranteed by the exchange and its clearinghouse, and trading in these options is monitored by the Securities and Exchange Commission. Customized options are traded in the unregulated OTC market.

Options differ from futures in several key ways. First, both parties to a futures contract accept an obligation to transact, but only the writer of an option has an obligation, and that occurs if the buyer wishes to exercise the option. Second, the option buyer has a limited, known maximum loss. Third, the risk/return profile of an option position is asymmetric, while that of a futures position is symmetric.

The risk/return profile of the option buyer is the mirror image of the risk/return profile of the option writer, whether the option is a put or a call, American or European. The purchase of a call option is like taking a long position in the underlying asset but with a fixed, maximum loss. The purchase of a put option resembles the short sale of the underlying asset but with a known maximum loss.

The essence of hedging with options is that it minimizes loss while reducing gains only by the price of the option. Thus, hedging with options is very much like taking out an insurance policy. Hedging with options differs from hedging with futures because the latter establishes a known, future price and does not allow the hedger to participate in gains that price changes might generate for the investor.

Options may be written on individual stocks or on bundles and groups of stocks. Those written on groups are called index options, the most popular being the S&P 100. Several stock index options are traded on major exchanges around the world. The exercise of stock options involves an exchange of cash for shares. By contrast, stock index options are cash settlement contracts, where the buyer receives the cash value of the difference between the exercise price (called the strike index) and the actual level of the stock market index. Options based on important government debt securities are also traded on major exchanges.

LEAPS and FLEX options essentially modify an existing feature of either a stock option, an index option, or both. LEAPS are designed to offer options with longer maturities. FLEX options allow users to specify the terms of the option contract.

An option on a futures contract gives the buyer the right to acquire a position in a futures contract—a long position in the case of a call option and a short position in the case of a put option.

These options, referred to as futures options, are the option of choice in the fixed-income market.

OTC options can be customized in any manner sought by an institutional investor. Exotic options are the more complex options created in the OTC market. Two examples of exotic options are alternative options and outperformance options.

KEY TERMS

- Alternative option (also called an either-or option), 534
- American option, 518
- Bermuda option (also called an Atlantic option or a limited exercise option), 534
- Call option (call), 518
- European option, 518
- Exchange-traded option, 518
- Exercise (or strike) price, 518
- Exotic option, 534
- Expiration (or maturity) date, 518
- FLEX option, 534

- Futures option, 535
- Long option position, 520
- Long-Term Equity Anticipation Securities (LEAPs^{TM}), 533
- Option, 517
- Option on a physical, 533
- Option price (or option premium), 517
- Options Clearing Corporation (OCC), 530
- Outperformance option, 534
- Put option, 518
- Short option position, 520
- Writer of option, 517

QUESTIONS

1. Identify and explain the key features of an option contract.
2. What is the difference between a put option and a call option?
3. What is the difference between an American option and a European option?
4. Why does an option writer need to post margin?
5. Identify two important ways in which an exchange-traded option differs from a typical over-the-counter option.
6. a. What are the main ways in which an option differs from a futures contract?
   b. Why are options and futures labeled *derivative securities*?
7. Explain how this statement can be true: "A long call position offers potentially unlimited gains, if the underlying asset's price rises, but a fixed, maximum loss if the underlying asset's price drops to zero."
8. Suppose a call option on a stock has an exercise price of $70 and a cost of $2, and suppose you buy the call. Identify the profit to your investment, at the call's expiration, for each of these values of the underlying stock: $25, $70, $100, $400.
9. Consider again the situation in question 8. Suppose you had sold the call option. What would your profit be, at expiration, for each of the stock prices?
10. Explain why you agree or disagree with this statement: "Buying a put is just like short selling the underlying asset. You gain the same thing from either position, if the underlying asset's price falls. If the price goes up, you have the same loss."
11. Why do stock index options involve cash settlement rather than delivery of the underlying stocks?
12. Suppose you bought an index call option for 5.50 that has a strike price of 200 and that, at expiration, you exercised it. Suppose, too, that at the time you exercised the call option, the index has a value of 240.
    a. If the index option has a multiple of $100, how much money does the writer of this option pay you?
    b. What profit did you realize from buying this call option?
13. How do LEAPS differ from standard stock options and standard index options?
14. a. What are the terms that can be customized in a FLEX option?

b. Why was the FLEX option introduced by exchanges?

15. Suppose that you buy an alternative call option with the following terms:
    - The underlying asset is one unit of Asset G or one unit of Asset H.
    - The strike price for Asset G is $100.
    - The strike price for Asset H is $115.
    - The expiration date is four months from now.
    - The option can only be exercised at the expiration date.

    a. What is the payoff from this option if at the expiration date the price of Asset G is $125 and price of Asset H is $135?
    b. What is the payoff from this option if at the expiration date the price of Asset G is $90 and price of Asset H is $125?
    c. What is the payoff from this option if at the expiration date the price of Asset G is $90 and price of Asset H is $105?

16. Suppose that you buy an outperformance call option with the following terms:
    - Portfolio X consists of bonds with a market value of $5 million.
    - Portfolio Y consists of stocks with a market value of $5 million.
    - The expiration date is nine months from now and is a European option.
    - The strike price is equal to:

    Market value of Portfolio X – Market value of Portfolio Y

    What is the payoff of this option if at the expiration date the market value of Portfolio X is $10 million and the market value of Portfolio Y is $12 million?

17. Suppose you have a long position in a call option on a futures contract, and the strike price is 80. The futures contract price is now 87, and you want to exercise your option. Identify the gains from exercise, specifying any cash inflow and the futures position you get (and the price of the futures contract).

C h a p t e r 2 8

Pricing of Futures and Options Contracts

Learning Objectives

After reading this chapter, you will understand

- the theory of pricing a futures contract.
- how arbitrage between the futures market and the cash or spot market links the prices of those markets.
- the meaning of the terms *cost of carry* and *net financing cost*.
- the convergence of the futures and cash prices for a particular asset at the settlement date of the futures contract.
- why the actual futures price may differ from the theoretical futures price.
- how the market price of an option can be broken down into an intrinsic value and a time premium.
- why arbitrage ensures that the prices of calls and puts on the same underlying asset with the same exercise price and expiration date have a certain relationship to each other.
- the factors that affect the price of an option: the underlying asset's current price and expected price volatility, the contract's expiration date and exercise price, the short-term rate of interest, and any cash flows from the underlying asset.
- the principles of the binomial option pricing model and how the model is derived.

In the previous two chapters, we described the various types of futures and options contracts. In this chapter, we explain how to determine the theoretical price of these contracts using arbitrage arguments. A close examination of the underlying assumptions necessary to derive the theoretical price indicates how it must be modified to price the specific contracts described in the previous two chapters.

PRICING OF FUTURES CONTRACTS

To understand what determines the futures price, consider once again the futures contract in Chapter 26 where the underlying instrument is Asset XYZ. We make several assumptions:

1. Asset XYZ is selling for $100 in the cash market.
2. Asset XYZ pays the holder (with certainty) $12 per year in four quarterly payments of $3, and the next quarterly payment is exactly three months from now.
3. The futures contract requires delivery three months from now.
4. The current three-month interest rate at which funds can be lent or borrowed is 8% per year.

541

What should the price of this futures contract be? That is, what should the futures price be? Suppose the price of the futures contract is $107. Consider this strategy:

> Sell the futures contract at $107
> Purchase Asset XYZ in the cash market for $100
> Borrow $100 for three months at 8% per year

The borrowed funds are used to purchase Asset XYZ, resulting in no initial cash outlay for this strategy. At the end of three months, $3 will be received from holding Asset XYZ. Three months from now, Asset XYZ must be delivered to settle the futures contract, and the loan must be repaid. This strategy produces an outcome as follows:

1. From settlement of the futures contract:

Proceeds from sale of Asset XYZ to settle the futures contract	= $107
Payment received from investing in Asset XYZ for three months	= 3
Total proceeds	= $110

2. From the loan:

Repayment of principal of loan	= $100
Interest on loan (2% for three months)	= 2
Total outlay	= $102

3. Profit: $ 8

Notice that this strategy guarantees a profit of $8. Moreover, this profit is generated with no investment outlay; the funds needed to buy Asset XYZ were borrowed. The profit is realized regardless of what the futures price at the settlement date is. In financial terms, the profit arises from a riskless arbitrage between the price of Asset XYZ in the cash or spot market and the price of Asset XYZ in the futures market. Obviously, in a well-functioning market, arbitrageurs who could get this riskless gain for a zero investment would sell the futures and buy Asset XYZ, forcing the futures price down and bidding up Asset XYZ's price so as to eliminate this profit.

This strategy that resulted in the capturing of the arbitrage profit is referred to as a **cash and carry trade**. The reason for this name is that it involves borrowing cash to purchase a security and "carrying" that security to the futures settlement date.

Suppose instead that the futures price is $92 and not $107. Let's consider this strategy:

> Buy the futures contract at $92
> Sell (short) Asset XYZ for $100
> Invest (lend) $100 for three months at 8% per year[1]

Once again, there is no initial cash outlay for the strategy: The cost of the long position in the futures contract is zero, and there is no cost to selling the asset short and lending the money. Three months from now, Asset XYZ must be purchased to settle the long position in the futures contract. Asset XYZ accepted for delivery will then be used to cover the short position—to cover the short sale of Asset XYZ in the cash market. Shorting Asset XYZ requires the short seller to pay the lender of Asset XYZ the proceeds that the lender would have earned for the quarter. Therefore, the strategy

---

[1] Consider the first strategy (cash and carry trade), which had these elements:
Technically, a short seller may not be entitled to the full use of the proceeds resulting from the sale. We will discuss this later in this section.

requires a payment of $3 to the lender of Asset XYZ. The outcome in three months would be as follows:

1. From settlement of the futures contract:

Price paid for purchase of Asset XYZ to settle futures contract	= $ 92
Proceeds to lender of Asset XYZ to borrow the asset	= 3
Total outlay	= $ 95

2. From the loan:

Principal from maturing of investment	= $100
Interest earned on loan ($2 for three months)	= 2
Total proceeds	= $102

3. Profit: $ 7

The $7 profit from this strategy is also a riskless arbitrage profit. This strategy requires no initial cash outlay, but will generate a profit whatever the price of Asset XYZ is at the settlement date. Clearly, this opportunity would lead arbitrageurs to buy futures and short Asset XYZ, and the effect of these two actions would be to raise the futures price and lower the cash price until the profit again disappeared.

This strategy that resulted in the capturing of the arbitrage profit is referred to as a **reverse cash and carry trade**. That is, with this strategy a security is sold short and the proceeds received from the short sale are invested.

At what futures price would the arbitraging stop? Another way to ask this question is this: Is there a futures price that would prevent the opportunity for the riskless arbitrage profit? Yes, there is. There will be no arbitrage profit if the futures price is $99. Let's look at what happens if the two previous strategies (cash and carry trade and reverse cash and carry trade) are followed, now assuming a futures price of $99.

Consider the first strategy (cash and carry), which had these elements:

Sell the futures contract at $99
Purchase Asset XYZ in the cash market for $100
Borrow $100 for three months at 8% per year

In three months the outcome will be as follows:

1. From settlement of the futures contract:

Proceeds from sale of Asset XYZ to settle the futures contract	= $ 99
Payment received from investing in Asset XYZ for 3 months	= 3
Total proceeds	= $102

2. From the loan:

Repayment of principal of loan	= $100
Interest on loan (2% for three months)	= 2
Total outlay	= $102

3. Profit: $ 0

If the futures price is $99, the arbitrage profit has disappeared.

Next, consider the strategy consisting of these actions:

Buy the futures contract at $99
Sell (short) Asset XYZ for $100
Invest (lend) $100 for three months at 8% per year

The outcome in three months would be as follows:

1. From settlement of the futures contract:

Price paid for purchase of Asset XYZ to settle futures contract	= $ 99
Proceeds to lender of Asset XYZ to borrow the asset	= 3
Total outlay	= $102

2. From the loan:

Principal from maturing of investment	= $100
Interest earned on loan ($2 for three months)	= 2
Total proceeds	= $102

3. Profit: $ 0

Thus, if the futures price were $99, neither strategy would result in an arbitrage profit. Hence, a futures price of $99 is the equilibrium price because any higher or lower futures price will permit riskless arbitrage profits.

Theoretical Futures Price Based on Arbitrage Model

According to the arbitrage arguments we have just presented, we see that the equilibrium or theoretical futures price can be determined on the basis of the following information:

1. The price of the asset in the cash market.
2. The cash yield earned on the asset until the settlement date. In our example, the cash yield on Asset XYZ is $3 on a $100 investment or 3% quarterly (12% annual cash yield).
3. The **financing cost**, which is the interest rate for borrowing and lending until the settlement date. In our example, the financing cost is 2% for the three months.

To develop a theory of futures pricing, we will use the following notation:

$$F = \text{Futures price (\$)}$$
$$P = \text{Cash market price (\$)}$$
$$r = \text{Financing cost (\%)}$$
$$y = \text{Cash yield (\%)}$$

Now, consider the cash and carry trade:

Sell (or take a short position in) the futures contract at F
Purchase Asset XYZ for P
Borrow P at a rate of r until the settlement date

The outcome at the settlement date would be:

1. From settlement of the futures contract:

Proceeds from sale of Asset XYZ to settle the futures contract	= F
Payment received from investing in Asset XYZ	= yP
Total proceeds	= $F + yP$

2. From the loan:

Repayment of principal of loan	= P
Interest on loan	= rP
Total outlay	= $P + rp$

The profit will equal:

$$\text{Profit} = \text{Total proceeds} - \text{Total outlay}$$
$$\text{Profit} = F + yP - (P + rP)$$

The equilibrium futures price is the price that ensures that the profit from this arbitrage strategy is zero. Thus, equilibrium requires that:

$$0 = F + yP - (P + rP)$$

Solving for the theoretical futures price gives this equation:

$$F = P + P(r - y)$$

In other words, the equilibrium futures price is simply a function of the cash price, the financing cost, and the cash yield on the asset.

Alternatively, let us consider the reverse cash and carry trade illustrated in our example above, which looks like this:

Buy the futures contract at F

Sell (short) Asset XYZ for P

Invest (lend) P at a rate of r until the settlement date

The outcome at the settlement date would be:

1. From settlement of the futures contract:

Price paid for purchase of asset to settle futures contract	$=$	F
Payment to lender of asset in order to borrow the asset	$=$	yP
Total outlay		$= F + yP$

2. From the loan:

Principal from maturing of investment	$=$	P
Interest earned on loan	$=$	rP
Total proceeds		$= P + rP$

The profit will equal:

$$\text{Profit} = \text{Total proceeds} - \text{Total outlay}$$
$$\text{Profit} = P + rP - (F + yP)$$

Setting the profit equal to zero, so that there will be no arbitrage profit, and solving for the futures price, we obtain the same equation for the futures price as derived earlier:

$$F = P + P(r - y)$$

It is instructive to apply this equation to our previous example to determine the theoretical futures price. In that example, the key variables have these values:

$$r = 0.02$$
$$y = 0.03$$
$$P = \$100$$

Then the theoretical futures price is:

$$F = \$100 - \$100 \ (0.03 - 0.02)$$
$$= \$100 - \$1 = \$99$$

This agrees with the equilibrium futures price we proposed earlier.

The theoretical futures price may be at a premium to the cash market price (higher than the cash market price) or at a discount from the cash market price (lower than the cash market price), depending on the value of $P(r - y)$. The term, $r - y$, which reflects the difference between the cost of financing and the asset's cash yield, is called the **net financing cost**. The net financing cost is more commonly called the **cost of carry**, or simply, **carry**. **Positive carry** means that the yield earned is greater than the financing cost; **negative carry** means that the financing cost exceeds the yield earned. We can summarize the effect of carry on the difference between the futures price and the cash market price in this way:

Carry	**Futures price**
Positive $(y > r)$	will sell at a discount to cash price $(F < P)$
Negative $(y < r)$	will sell at a premium to cash price $(F > P)$
Zero $(r = y)$	will be equal to the cash price $(F = P)$

Price Convergence at the Delivery Date

At the delivery date, which is when the futures contract settles, the futures price must equal the cash market price because a futures contract with no time left until delivery is equivalent to a cash market transaction. Thus, as the delivery date approaches, the futures price will converge to the cash market price. This fact is evident from the equation for the theoretical futures price. As the delivery date approaches, the financing cost approaches zero, and the yield that can be earned by holding the investment approaches zero. Hence, the cost of carry approaches zero, and the futures price will approach the cash market price.

A Closer Look at the Theoretical Futures Price

To derive the theoretical futures price using the arbitrage argument, we made several assumptions. When the assumptions are violated, the actual futures price will diverge from the theoretical futures price. That is, the difference between the two prices will differ from the value of carry. Next we examine those assumptions and identify practical reasons why the actual prices of all financial futures contracts tend to deviate from their theoretical prices.

Interim Cash Flows.

Our theoretical analysis assumes that no interim cash flows arise because of changes in futures prices and the variation margin of the organized exchanges on which futures are traded. In addition, our approach assumes implicitly that any dividends or coupon interest payments are paid at the delivery date rather than at some time between initiation of the cash position and expiration of the futures contract. However, we know that interim cash flows of either type can and do occur in practice.

In the case of stock index futures, incorporating interim dividend payments into the pricing model is necessary because a cash position in a set of 100 or 500 stocks (the number of stocks underlying an index) generates cash flows in the form of dividends from the stocks. The dividend rate and the pattern of dividend payments are not known with certainty. They must be projected from the historical dividend payments of the companies in the index. Once the dividend payments are projected, they can be incorporated into the pricing model. The only problem is that the value of the dividend payments at the settlement date will depend on the interest rate at which the dividend payments can be reinvested from the time they are projected to be received until the settlement date. The lower the dividend, and the closer the dividend payments to the settlement date of the futures contract, the less important the reinvestment income is in determining the futures price.

It is important to note that, in the absence of initial and variation margins, the theoretical price for the contract is technically the theoretical price for a forward contract, not the theoretical price for a futures contract. This is because, unlike a futures contract, a forward contract is not marked to market at the end of each trading day, and therefore does not require variation margin and does not generate cash inflows from gains or outflows from losses.

Differences between Lending and Borrowing Rates.

In deriving the theoretical futures price, we assumed that the investor's borrowing rate and lending rate are equal. Typically, however, the borrowing rate is higher than the lending rate. The impact of this inequality is important and easy to identify. We will begin by adopting these symbols for the two rates:

$$r_B = \text{Borrowing rate}$$
$$r_L = \text{Lending rate}$$

Now, consider the cash and carry trade:

> Sell the futures contract at F
> Purchase the asset for P
> Borrow P until the settlement date at r_B

Clearly, the futures price that would produce no arbitrage profit is:

$$F = P + P(r_B - y)$$

Recall that the reverse cash and carry trade is:

> Buy the futures contract at F
> Sell (short) the asset for P
> Invest (lend) P at r_L until the settlement date

The futures price that would prevent a riskless profit is:

$$F = P + P(r_L - y)$$

These two equations together provide boundaries between which the futures price will be in equilibrium. The first equation establishes the upper boundary, and the second equation the lower boundary. For example, assume that the borrowing rate is 8% per year, or 2% for three months, while the lending rate is 6% per year, or 1.5% for three months. According to the first equation, the upper boundary is:

$$F \text{ (upper boundary)} = \$100 + \$100 \ (0.02 - 0.03) = \$99$$

The lower boundary according to the second equation is:

$$F \text{ (lower boundary)} = \$100 + \$100 \ (0.015 - 0.03) = \$98.50$$

Thus, equilibrium is achieved if the futures price takes on any value between the two boundaries. In other words, equilibrium requires that $\$98.50 \leq F \leq \$99$.

Transaction Costs.

In deriving the theoretical futures price, we ignored transaction costs of the elements in the arbitrage strategies. In actuality, the costs of entering into and closing the cash position as well as round-trip transaction costs for the futures contract do affect the futures price. It is easy to show, as we do above for borrowing and lending rates, that transaction costs widen the boundaries for the equilibrium futures price. The details need not concern us here.

Short Selling.

In the strategy involving short selling of Asset XYZ when the futures price is below its theoretical value, we explicitly assumed in the reverse cash and carry trade that the proceeds from the short sale are received and reinvested. In practice, for individual investors, the proceeds are not received, and, in fact, the individual investor is required to put up margin (securities margin and not futures margin) to short sell. For institutional investors, the asset may be borrowed, but there is a cost to borrowing. This cost of borrowing can be incorporated into the model by reducing the yield on the asset.

For strategies applied to stock index futures, a short sale of the stocks in the index means that all stocks in the index must be sold simultaneously. The stock exchange rule for the short selling of stock, which we explained in Chapter 18, may prevent an investor from implementing the arbitrage strategy. The short selling rule for stocks specifies that a short sale can be made only at a price that is higher than the previous trade (referred to as an uptick), or at a price that is equal to the previous trade (referred to as a zero tick) but higher than the last trade at a different price. If the arbitrage requires selling the stocks in the index simultaneously, and the last transaction for some of the stocks is not an uptick, the stocks cannot be shorted simultaneously. Thus, an institutional rule may in effect keep arbitrageurs from bringing the actual futures price in line with the theoretical futures price.

Known Deliverable Asset and Settlement Date.

Our example illustrating arbitrage strategies assumes that (1) only one asset is deliverable, and (2) the settlement date occurs at a known, fixed point in the future. Neither assumption is consistent with the delivery rules for some futures contracts. The case of U.S. Treasury bond and note futures contracts illustrates the point: An investor in a long position cannot know either the specific Treasury bond to be delivered or the specific date within the contract month when it might be delivered. This substantial uncertainty is a result of the delivery options that the short position in a futures contract has. As a reflection of the short positions' options and advantages, the actual futures price will be less than the theoretical futures price for the Treasury bond and note futures contracts.

The Deliverable Is a Basket of Securities.

Some futures contracts involve a single asset, but other contracts apply to a basket of assets or an index. Stock index futures and the municipal bond index futures contracts are examples. The problem in arbitraging these two futures contracts is that it is too expensive to buy or sell every security included in the index. Instead, a portfolio containing a smaller number of assets may be constructed to track the index (which means having price movements that are very similar to changes in the index). Nonetheless, arbitrage based on this tracking portfolio is no longer risk-free because of the risk that the portfolio will not track the index exactly. Clearly, then, the actual price of futures based on baskets of assets may diverge from the theoretical price because of transactions costs as well as uncertainty about the outcome of the arbitrage.

Different Tax Treatment of Cash and Futures Transactions.

The basic arbitrage model presented in this chapter ignores not only taxes but also different tax treatment of cash market transactions and futures transactions. Obviously, these factors can keep the actual futures price from being equal to the theoretical price.

Key Points That You Should Understand Before Proceeding

1. The equilibrium or theoretical futures price can be determined through arbitrage arguments.
2. The strategy that can be used to capture the arbitrage profit for an overpriced futures contract is the cash and carry trade; the strategy that can be used to capture the arbitrage profit for an underpriced futures contract is the reverse cash and carry trade.
3. The theoretical futures price depends on the price of the underlying asset in the cash market, the cost of financing a position in the underlying asset, and the cash yield on the underlying asset.
4. At the delivery date, the price of a futures contract converges to the cash market price.
5. The actual futures price will diverge from the theoretical futures price because of interim cash flows, differences between lending and borrowing rates, transaction costs, restrictions on short selling, and uncertainty about the deliverable asset and the date it will be delivered.

PRICING OF OPTIONS

The theoretical price of an option is also derived from arbitrage arguments. However, the pricing of options is not as simple as the pricing of futures contracts.

Basic Components of the Option Price

The option price is the sum of the option's **intrinsic value** and a premium over intrinsic value that is often referred to as the *time value* or *time premium*. While the former term is more common, we will use the term **time premium** to avoid confusion between the time value of money and the time value of the option.

Intrinsic Value.

The intrinsic value of an option, at any time, is its economic value if it is exercised immediately. If no positive economic value would result from exercising immediately, the intrinsic value is zero.

Computationally, the intrinsic value of a call option is the difference between the current price of the underlying asset and the strike price. If that difference is positive, then the intrinsic value equals that difference; if the difference is zero or negative, then the intrinsic value is set equal to zero. For example, if the strike price for a call option is $100 and the current asset price is $105, the intrinsic value is $5. That is, an option buyer exercising the option and simultaneously selling the underlying asset would realize $105 from the sale of the asset, which would be covered by acquiring the asset from the option writer for $100, thereby netting a $5 gain.

When an option has intrinsic value, it is said to be **in the money**. When the strike price of a call option exceeds the current asset price, the call option is said to be **out of the money**, it has no intrinsic value. An option for which the strike price is equal to the current asset price is said to be **at the money**. Both at-the-money and out-of-the-money options have intrinsic values of zero because it is not profitable to exercise them. Our call option with a strike price of $100 would be: (1) in the money when the current asset price is more than $100; (2) out of the money when the current asset price is less than $100; and (3) at the money when the current asset price is equal to $100.

For a put option, the intrinsic value is equal to the amount by which the current asset price is below the strike price. For example, if the strike price of a put option is $100, and the current asset price is $92, the intrinsic value is $8. That is, the buyer of the put option who simultaneously buys the underlying asset and exercises the put option will net $8 by exercising. The asset will be sold to the writer for $100 and purchased in the market for $92. For our put option with a strike price of $100, the option would be: (1) in the money when the current asset price is less than $100; (2) out of the money when the current asset price exceeds $100; (3) at the money when the current asset price is equal to $100.

Time Premium.

The time premium of an option is the amount by which the option's market price exceeds its intrinsic value. The option buyer hopes that, at some time prior to expiration, changes in the market price of the underlying asset will increase the value of the rights conveyed by the option. For this prospect, the option buyer is willing to pay a premium above the intrinsic value. For example, if the price of a call option with a strike price of $100 is $9 when the current asset price is $105, the time premium of this option is $4 ($9 minus its intrinsic value of $5). Had the current asset price been $90 instead of $105, then the time premium of this option would be the entire $9 because the option has no intrinsic value. Clearly, other things being equal, the time premium of an option will increase with the amount of time remaining to expiration.

An option buyer has two ways to realize the value of a position taken in the option. The first way is to exercise the option. The second way is to sell the call option for its market price. In the first example above, selling the call for $9 is preferable to exercising, because the exercise will realize a gain of only $5 but the sale will realize a gain of $9. As this example shows, exercise causes the immediate loss of any time premium. It is important to note that there are circumstances under which an option may be exercised prior to the expiration date. These circumstances depend on whether the total proceeds at the expiration date would be greater by holding the option or exercising and reinvesting any received cash proceeds until the expiration date.

Put–Call Parity Relationship

There is an important relationship between the price of a call option and the price of a put option on the same underlying instrument, with the same strike price and the same expiration date. An example can illustrate this relationship, which is commonly referred to as the **put–call parity relationship**.

Our example comes from the previous chapter and assumes that a put option and a call option are available on the same underlying asset (Asset XYZ), and that both options have one month to expiration and a strike price of $100. The example assumes the price of the underlying asset to be $100. The call and put prices are assumed to be $3 and $2, respectively.

To see if the two prices have the right relationship, consider what happens if an investor pursues this strategy:

>Buy Asset XYZ at a price of $100
>Sell a call option at a price of $3
>Buy a put option at a price of $2

This strategy generates these positions:

>Long Asset XYZ
>Short the call option
>Long the put option

Table 28-1 shows the profit and loss profile at the expiration date for this strategy. Notice that, no matter what Asset XYZ's price is at the expiration date, the strategy will produce a profit of $1. The net cost of creating this position is the cost of purchasing Asset XYZ ($100) plus the cost of buying the put ($2) less the cost from selling the call ($3), which is $101. Suppose that the net cost of creating the position for one month is less than $1. Then, by borrowing $101 to create the position so that no investment outlay is made by the investor, this strategy will produce a net profit of $1 (as shown in the last column of Table 28-1) less the cost of borrowing $101, which is assumed to be less than

Table 28-1   Profit/Loss Profile for a Strategy Involving a Long Position in Asset XYZ, Short Call Option Position, and Long Put Option Position

Assumptions:
Price of Asset XYZ = $100
Call option price = $3
Put option price = $2
Strike price = $100
Time to expiration = 1 month

PRICE OF ASSET XYZ AT EXPIRATION DATE	PROFIT FROM ASSET XYZ*	PRICE RECEIVED FOR CALL	PRICE PAID FOR PUT	OVERALL PROFIT
$150	0	3	−2	1
140	0	3	−2	1
130	0	3	−2	1
120	0	3	−2	1
115	0	3	−2	1
110	0	3	−2	1
105	0	3	−2	1
100	0	3	−2	1
95	0	3	−2	1
90	0	3	−2	1
85	0	3	−2	1
80	0	3	−2	1
75	0	3	−2	1
70	0	3	−2	1
65	0	3	−2	1
60	0	3	−2	1

* There is no profit because at a price above $100 Asset XYZ will be called from the investor at a price of $100, and at a price below $100, Asset XYZ will be put by the investor at a price of $100.

$1. This situation cannot exist in an efficient market. As market participants implement the strategy to capture the $1 profit, their actions will have one or more of the following consequences, which will tend to eliminate the $1 profit: (1) the price of Asset XYZ will increase; (2) the call option price will drop; and/or (3) the put option price will rise.

Our example clearly implies that, if Asset XYZ's price does not change, the call price and the put price must tend toward equality. But our example ignores the time value of money (financing and opportunity costs, cash payments, and reinvestment income). Also, our example does not consider the possibility of early exercise of the options. Thus, we have been considering a put–call parity relationship for only European options.

It can be shown that the put–call parity relationship for options where the underlying asset makes cash distributions and where the time value of money is recognized is:

$$\text{Put option price} - \text{Call option price} = \text{Present value of strike price} + \text{Present value of cash distribution} - \text{Price of underlying asset}$$

Once more, we note that this relationship is actually the put–call parity relationship for European options. However, the values of puts and calls that are American options do conform approximately to this relationship. If this relationship does not hold, arbitrage opportunities exist. That is, investors will be able to construct portfolios consisting of long and short positions in the asset and related options that will provide an extra return with (practical) certainty.

Factors that Influence the Option Price

Six factors influence the price of an option:

1. Current price of the underlying asset.
2. Strike price.
3. Time to expiration of the option.
4. Expected price volatility of the underlying asset over the life of the option.
5. Short-term, risk-free interest rate over the life of the option.
6. Anticipated cash payments on the underlying asset over the life of the option.

The impact of each of these factors may depend on whether (1) the option is a call or a put, and (2) the option is an American option or a European option. A summary of the effect of each factor on put and call option prices is presented in Table 28-2. Here we briefly explain why the factors have the particular effects.

Table 28-2   Summary of Factors that Affect the Price of an Option

FACTOR	Effect of an increase of factor on	
	CALL PRICE	PUT PRICE
Current price of underlying asset	Increase	Decrease
Strike price	Decrease	Increase
Time to expiration of option	Increase	Increase
Expected price volatility	Increase	Increase
Short-term interest rate	Increase	Decrease
Anticipated cash payments	Decrease	Increase

Current Price of the Underlying Asset.

The option price will change as the price of the underlying asset changes. For a call option, as the price of the underlying asset increases (all other factors constant), the option price increases. The opposite holds for a put option: As the price of the underlying asset increases, the price of a put option decreases.

Strike Price.

The strike price is fixed for the life of the option. All other factors equal, the lower the strike price, the higher the price for a call option. For put options, the higher the exercise price, the higher the option price.

Time to Expiration of the Option.

An option is a *wasting asset*. That is, after the expiration date the option has no value. All other factors equal, the longer the time to expiration of the option, the higher the option price. This is because, as the time to expiration decreases, less time remains for the underlying asset's price to rise (for a call buyer) or fall (for a put buyer), and therefore the probability of a favorable price movement decreases. Consequently, for American options, as the time remaining until expiration decreases, the option price approaches its intrinsic value.

Expected Price Volatility of the Underlying Asset over the Life of the Option.

All other factors equal, the greater the expected volatility (as measured by the standard deviation or variance) of the price of the underlying asset, the more an investor would be willing to pay for the option, and the more an option writer would demand for it. This occurs because the greater the volatility, the greater the probability that the price of the underlying asset will move in favor of the option buyer at some time before expiration.

Notice that it is the standard deviation or variance, not the systematic risk as measured by beta, as described in Chapter 13, that is relevant in the pricing of options.

Short-Term, Risk-Free Interest Rate over the Life of the Option.

Buying the underlying asset ties up one's money. Buying an option on the same quantity of the underlying asset makes the difference between the asset price and the option price available for investment at an interest rate at least as high as the risk-free rate. Consequently, all other factors constant, the higher the short-term, risk-free interest rate, the greater the cost of buying the underlying asset and carrying it to the expiration date of the call option. Hence, the higher the short-term, risk-free interest rate, the more attractive the call option will be relative to the direct purchase of the underlying asset. As a result, the higher the short-term, risk-free interest rate, the greater the price of a call option.

Anticipated Cash Payments on the Underlying Asset over the Life of the Option.

Cash payments on the underlying asset tend to decrease the price of a call option because the cash payments make it more attractive to hold the underlying asset than to hold the option. For put options, cash payments on the underlying asset tend to increase the price.

Option Pricing Models

We have shown that the theoretical price of a futures contract can be determined on the basis of arbitrage arguments. An option pricing model uses a set of assumptions and arbitrage arguments to derive a theoretical price for an option. As we shall see below, deriving a theoretical option price is much more complicated than deriving a theoretical futures price because the option price depends on the expected price volatility of the underlying asset over the life of the option.

Several models have been developed to determine the theoretical value of an option. The most popular one was developed by Fischer Black and Myron Scholes in 1973 for valuing European call options.[2] Several modifications to their model have followed. We use another pricing model called the *binomial option pricing model* to see how arbitrage arguments can be used to determine a fair value for a call option.[3]

Basically, the idea behind the arbitrage argument is that if the payoff from owning a call option can be replicated by (1) purchasing the asset underlying the call option, and (2) borrowing funds, the price of the option is then (at most) the cost of creating the replicating strategy.

Deriving the Binomial Option Pricing Model

To derive a one-period binomial option pricing model for a call option, we begin by constructing a portfolio consisting of: (1) a long position in a certain amount of the asset, and (2) a short call position in the underlying asset. The amount of the underlying asset purchased is such that the position will be hedged against any change in the price of the asset at the expiration date of the option. That is, the portfolio consisting of the long position in the asset and the short position in the call option is riskless and will produce a return that equals the risk-free interest rate. A portfolio constructed in this way is called a *hedged portfolio*.

We can show how this process works with an extended illustration. Let us assume first that there is an asset that has a current market price of $80, and that only two possible future states can occur one year from now. Each state is associated with one of only two possible values for the asset, and they can be summarized in this way:

State	Price
1	$100
2	70

We assume further that there is a call option on this asset with a strike price of $80 (the same as the current market price), and that it expires in one year. Let us suppose an investor forms a hedged portfolio by acquiring two-thirds of a unit of the asset and selling one call option. The two-thirds of a unit of the asset is the so-called *hedge ratio* (how we derive the hedge ratio is explained later). Let us consider the outcomes for this hedged portfolio corresponding to the two possible outcomes for the asset.

If the price of the asset one year from now is $100, the buyer of the call option will exercise it. This means that the investor will have to deliver one unit of the asset in exchange for the strike price, $80. As the investor has only two-thirds of a unit of the asset, she has to buy one-third at a cost of $33 ⅓ (the market price of $100 times ⅓). Consequently, the outcome will equal the strike price of $80 received, minus the $33

[2] Fischer Black and Myron Scholes, "The Pricing of Corporate Liabilities," *Journal of Political Economy* (May–June 1973), pp. 637–659.

[3] John C. Cox, Stephen A. Ross, and Mark Rubinstein, "Option Pricing: A Simplified Approach," *Journal of Financial Economics* (September 1979), pp. 229–263; Richard J. Rendleman and Brit J. Bartter, "Two-State Option Pricing," *Journal of Finance* (December 1979), pp. 1093–1110; and William F. Sharpe, *Investments* (Englewood Cliffs, N.J.: Prentice Hall, 1981), Chapter 16.

⅓ cost to acquire the one-third unit of the asset to deliver, plus whatever price the investor initially sold the call option for. That is, the outcome will be:

$$80 - 33 \tfrac{1}{3} + \text{Call option price} = 46 \tfrac{2}{3} + \text{Call option price}.$$

If, instead, the price of the asset one year from now is $70, the buyer of the call option will not exercise it. Consequently, the investor will own two-thirds of a unit of the asset. At the price of $70, the value of two-thirds of a unit is $46 ⅔. The outcome in this case is then the value of the asset plus whatever price the investor received when she initially sold the call option. That is, the outcome will be:

$$46 \tfrac{2}{3} + \text{Call option price}.$$

It is apparent that, given the possible asset prices, the portfolio consisting of a short position in the call option and two-thirds of a unit of the asset will generate an outcome that hedges changes in the price of the asset; hence, the hedged portfolio is riskless. Furthermore, this riskless hedge will hold regardless of the price of the call, which affects only the magnitude of the outcome.

Deriving the Hedge Ratio.
To show how to calculate the hedge ratio, we use the notation:

S = current asset price
u = 1 plus the percentage change in the asset's price if the price goes up in the next period
d = 1 plus the percentage change in the asset's price if the price goes down in the next period
r = a risk-free one-period interest rate (the risk-free rate until the expiration date)
C = current price of a call option
C_u = intrinsic value of the call option if the asset price goes up
C_d = intrinsic value of the call option if the asset price goes down
E = strike price of the call option
H = hedge ratio, that is, the amount of the asset purchased per call sold

In our illustration, u and d are:

$$u = 1.250 \ (\$100/\$80)$$
$$d = 0.875 \ (\$70/\$80)$$

Furthermore, State 1 in our illustration means that the asset's price goes up, and State 2 means that the asset's price goes down.

The investment made in the hedged portfolio is equal to the cost of buying H amount of the asset minus the price received from selling the call option. Therefore, because

$$\text{Amount invested in the asset} = HS,$$

then

$$\text{Cost of the hedged portfolio} = HS - C.$$

The payoff of the hedged portfolio at the end of one period is equal to the value of the *HS* amount of the asset purchased minus the call option price. The payoffs of the hedged portfolio for the two possible states are defined in this way:

$$\text{State 1, if the asset's price goes up: } uHS - C_u$$
$$\text{State 2, if the asset's price goes down: } dHS - C_d$$

In our illustration, we have these payoffs:

$$\text{If the asset's price goes up: } 1.250\ H\ \$80 - C_u \text{ or } \$100\ H - C_u$$
$$\text{If the asset's price falls: } 0.875\ H\ \$80 - C_d \text{ or } \$70\ H - C_d$$

If the hedge is riskless, the payoffs must be the same. Thus,

$$uHS - C_u = dHS - C_d \tag{1}$$

Solving equation (1) for the hedge ratio, *H*, we have

$$H = \frac{C_u - C_d}{(u - d)S} \tag{2}$$

To determine the value of the hedge ratio, *H*, we must know C_u and C_d. These two values are equal to the difference between the price of the asset and the strike price in the two possible states. Of course, the minimum value of the call option, in any state, is zero. Mathematically, the differences can be expressed as follows:

$$\text{If the asset's price goes up: } C_u = \text{Max}\,[0, (uS - E)]$$
$$\text{If the asset's price goes down: } C_d = \text{Max}\,[0, (dS - E)]$$

As the strike price in our illustration is $80, the value of *uS* is $100, and the value of *dS* is $70. Then,

$$\text{If the asset's price goes up: } C_u = \text{Max}\,[0, (\$100 - \$80)] = \$20$$
$$\text{If the asset's price goes down: } C_d = \text{Max}\,[0, (\$70 - \$80)] = \$0$$

To continue with our illustration, we substitute the values of *u*, *d*, *S*, C_u, and C_d into equation (2) to obtain the hedge ratio's value:

$$H = \frac{\$20 - \$0}{(1.25 - 0.875)\$80} = \frac{2}{3}$$

This value for *H* agrees with the amount of the asset purchased when we introduced this illustration.

Now we can derive a formula for the call option price. Figure 28-1 diagrams the situation. The top left half of the figure shows the current price of the asset for the current period and at the expiration date. The lower left-hand portion of the figure does the same thing using the notation above. The upper right-hand side of the figure gives the current price of the call option and the value of the call option at the expiration date; the lower right-hand side does the same thing using our notation. Figure 28-2 uses the values in our illustration to construct the outcomes for the asset and the call option.

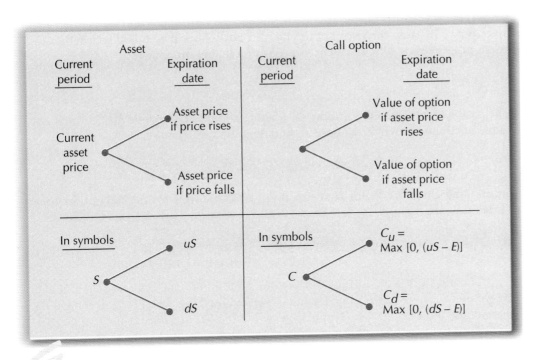

Figure 28-1   One-Period Option Pricing Model

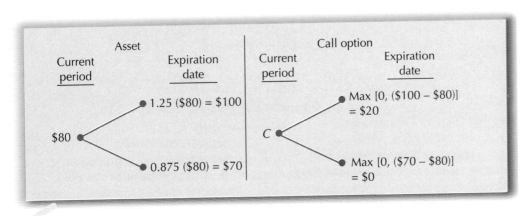

Figure 28-2   One-Period Option Pricing Model Illustration

Deriving the Price of a Call Option.

To derive the price of a call option, we can rely on the basic principle that the hedged portfolio, being riskless, must have a return equal to the risk-free rate of interest. Given that the amount invested in the hedged portfolio is $HS - C$, the amount that should be generated one period from now is:

$$(1 + r)(HS - C) \tag{3}$$

We also know what the payoff will be for the hedged portfolio if the asset's price goes up or down. Because the payoff of the hedged portfolio will be the same whether the asset's price rises or falls, we can use the payoff if it goes up, which is

$$uHS - C_u$$

The payoff of the hedged portfolio given above should be the same as the initial cost of the portfolio given by equation (3). Equating the two, we have:

$$(1 + r)(HS - C) = uHS - C_u \tag{4}$$

Substituting equation (2) for H in equation (4), and solving for the call option price, C, we find

$$C = \left(\frac{1 + r - d}{u - d}\right)\left(\frac{C_u}{1 + r}\right) + \left(\frac{u - 1 - r}{u - d}\right)\left(\frac{C_d}{1 + r}\right) \tag{5}$$

Equation (5) is the formula for the one-period binomial option pricing model. We would have derived the same formula if we had used the payoff for a decline in the price of the underlying asset. This derivation is left as an exercise for the reader.

Applying equation (5) to our illustration where

$$u = 1.250$$
$$d = 0.875$$
$$r = 0.10$$
$$C_u = \$20$$
$$C_d = \$0$$

we get

$$C = \left(\frac{1 + 0.10 - 0.875}{1.25 - 0.875}\right)\left(\frac{\$20}{1 + 0.10}\right) + \left(\frac{1.25 - 1 - 0.10}{1.25 - 0.875}\right)\left(\frac{\$0}{1 + 0.10}\right)$$
$$= \$10.90$$

The approach we present for pricing options may seem oversimplified, given that we assume only two possible future states for the price of the underlying asset. In fact, we can extend the procedure by making the period shorter and shorter, and in that way calculate a fair value for an option. It is important to note that extended and comprehensive versions of the binomial pricing model are in wide use throughout the world of finance. Moreover, the other popular option pricing model, the Black-Scholes model mentioned earlier, is in reality the mathematical equivalent of the binomial approach as the periods become very short. Thus, the approach we have described in detail here provides the conceptual framework for much of the analysis of option prices that today's financial market participants regularly perform.

Fixed-Income Option Pricing Models

Because of the assumptions required for the binomial model described above, such models may have limited applicability to the pricing of options on fixed-income securities. More specifically, the binomial model assumes that (1) the price of the security can take on any positive value with some probability—no matter how small; (2) the short-term interest rate is constant over the life of the option; and (3) the volatility of the price of the security is constant over the life of the option.

These assumptions are unreasonable for an option on a fixed-income security. First, the price of a fixed-income security cannot exceed the undiscounted value of the cash flow. Any possibility that the price can go higher than this value implies that interest rates can be negative. Second, the price of an interest rate option will change as interest rates change. A change in the short-term interest rate changes the rates along the yield curve. Therefore, to assume that the short-term rate will be constant is inappropriate for interest rate options. The third assumption, that the variance of prices is constant over the life of the option, is inappropriate because as a bond moves closer to maturity its price volatility declines.

Fortunately, it is possible to avoid the problem of negative interest rates. We can develop a binomial option pricing model that is based on the distribution of interest rates rather than prices. Once a binomial interest rate tree is constructed, it can be converted into a binomial price tree by using its interest rates to determine the prices of the bond at the end of the period. We can apply to these prices the same procedure described earlier to calculate the option price by working backward from the value of the call option at the expiration date.

Although the binomial option pricing model based on yields is superior to models based on prices, it still has a theoretical drawback. All theoretically valid option pricing models must satisfy the put–call parity relationship. The problem with the binomial model based on yields is that it does not satisfy this relationship. It violates the relationship because it fails to take into consideration the yield curve, thereby allowing arbitrage opportunities.

The most elaborate models that take the yield curve into consideration, and as a result eliminate arbitrage opportunities, are called *yield curve option pricing models* or *arbitrage-free option pricing models*. These models can incorporate different volatility assumptions along the yield curve. They are theoretically superior to the other models we have described.[4]

Key Points That You Should Understand Before Proceeding

1. The price of an option can be separated into two parts, its intrinsic value and its time premium.
2. The put–call parity relationship is the relationship between the price of a call option and the price of a put option on the same underlying instrument, with the same strike price and the same expiration date.
3. There are six factors that influence the price of an option: the current price of the underlying asset, the strike price, the time to expiration of the option, the expected price volatility of the underlying asset over the life of the option, the short-term, risk-free interest rate over the life of the option, and the anticipated cash payments on the underlying asset over the life of the option.
4. The theoretical price of an option can be determined on the basis of arbitrage arguments, but is much more complicated to determine than the theoretical price of a futures contract because the option price depends on the expected price volatility of the underlying asset over the life of the option.
5. Several models have been developed to determine the theoretical value of an option.
6. The value of an option is equal to the cost of creating a replicating hedge portfolio.

---

[4] For a discussion of yield curve or arbitrage-free option pricing models see: Mark Pitts and Frank J. Fabozzi, *Interest Rate Futures and Options* (Chicago: Probus Publishing, 1989), Chapter 9; and Lawrence J. Dyer and David P. Jacob, "Guide to Fixed Income Option Pricing Models," in Frank J. Fabozzi (ed.), *The Handbook of Fixed Income Options* (Chicago: Probus Publishing, 1989).

SUMMARY

Using simple arbitrage arguments, the theoretical or equilibrium futures price can be determined. Specifically, to capture the arbitrage profit for an overpriced futures contract a cash and carry trade can be implemented and to capture the arbitrage profit for an underpriced futures contract a reverse cash and carry trade. The ability of market participants to implement these two trades (or arbitrage strategies) result in the theoretical futures price being equal to the cash market price plus the cost of carry. The cost of carry is the net financing cost, that is, the difference between the financing rate and the cash yield on the underlying asset. The theoretical futures price will be less than the cash market price if the cost of carry is positive, equal to the cash market price if the cost of carry is zero, and more than the cash market price if the cost of carry is negative.

Developing the theoretical futures price with arbitrage arguments requires certain assumptions. When these assumptions are violated for a specific futures contract, the theoretical futures price must be modified. Because of the difference between borrowing and lending rates and because of transaction costs, there is not one theoretical futures price but, rather, a boundary around the theoretical futures price. So long as the actual futures price remains within this boundary, arbitrage profits cannot be realized.

The price of an option consists of two components: the intrinsic value and the time premium. The intrinsic value is the economic value of the option if it is exercised immediately. If there is no positive economic value resulting from exercising immediately, the intrinsic value is zero. The time premium is the amount by which the option price exceeds the intrinsic value. Six factors influence the option price: (1) the current price of the underlying asset; (2) the strike price of the option; (3) the time remaining to the expiration of the option; (4) the expected price volatility of the underlying asset; (5) the short-term, risk-free interest rate over the life of the option; and (6) the anticipated cash payments on the underlying asset.

The relationship among the call option price, the put option price, and the price of the underlying asset is known as the put–call parity relationship. The theoretical option price can be calculated with the binomial option pricing model, which also employs arbitrage arguments. Application of the binomial model to the pricing of options on fixed-income securities poses problems because of the model's underlying assumptions.

GLOSSARY

- **At-the-money option, 550**
- **Cash and carry trade, 542**
- **Cost of carry (or simply carry), 546**
- **Financing cost, 544**
- **In-the-money option, 550**
- **Intrinsic value, 549**
- **Negative carry, 546**

- **Net financing cost, 546**
- **Out-of-the-money option, 550**
- **Positive carry, 546**
- **Put–call parity relationship, 550**
- **Reverse cash and carry trade, 543**
- **Time premium, 549**

QUESTIONS

1. Models for pricing futures and options are said to be based on arbitrage arguments.
   a. What does arbitrage mean?
   b. What is the investor's incentive to engage in arbitrage?
2. Suppose there is a financial Asset ABC, which is the underlying asset for a futures contract with settlement six months from now. You know the following about this financial asset and the futures contract:
   1. In the cash market, ABC is selling for $80.
   2. ABC pays $8 per year in two semiannual payments of $4, and the next semiannual payment is due exactly six months from now.

3. The current six-month interest rate at which funds can be loaned or borrowed is 6%.
   a. What is the theoretical (or equilibrium) futures price?
   b. What action would you take if the futures price is $83?
   c. What action would you take if the futures price is $76?
   d. Suppose that ABC pays interest quarterly instead of semiannually. If you know that you can reinvest any funds you receive three months from now at 1% for three months, what would the theoretical futures price for six-month settlement be?
   e. Suppose that the borrowing rate and lending rate are not equal. Instead, suppose that the current six-month borrowing rate is 8% and the six-month lending rate is 6%. What are the boundaries for the theoretical futures price?

3. a. Explain why restrictions on short selling of stocks would cause the actual price of a stock index futures contract to diverge from its theoretical price.
   b. Explain why creating a portfolio of stocks in which the number of stocks is less than the number of stocks in the index underlying a stock index futures contract would result in an arbitrage that is not riskless.

4. Why do the delivery options in a Treasury bond futures contract cause the actual futures price to diverge from its theoretical price?

5. "Of course the futures are more expensive than the cash price—there's positive carry." Do you agree with this statement?

6. Consider the following call option with three months to expiration:

   Strike price = $72
   Current price of underlying assets = $87
   Market price of option = $6

   a. What is the intrinsic value for this call option?
   b. What is the time premium for this call option?

7. Suppose the option in the previous question is a put option rather than a call option.
   a. What is the intrinsic value for this put option?
   b. What is the time premium for this put option?

8. You obtain the following price quotes for call options on Asset ABC. It is now December, with the near contract maturing in one month's time. Asset ABC's price is currently trading at $50.

Strike	January	March	June
$40	$11	$12	$11.50
50	6	7	8.50
60	7	8	9.00

   Glancing at the figures, you note that two of these quotes seem to violate some of the rules you learned regarding options pricing.
   a. What are these discrepancies?
   b. How could you take advantage of the discrepancies? What is the minimum profit you would realize by arbitraging based on these discrepancies?

9. Indicate whether you agree or disagree with the following statements:
   a. "To determine the theoretical value of an option, we will need some measure of the price volatility of the underlying asset. Because financial theorists tell us that the appropriate measure of risk is beta (that is, systematic risk), then we should use this value."
   b. "If the expected price volatility of an option increases, the theoretical value of an option decreases."

    c. "It does not make sense that the price of a call option should rise in value if the price of the underlying asset falls."

10. Consider two options with the same expiration date and for the same underlying asset. The two options differ only in the strike price. Option 1's strike price is greater than that of Option 2.
    a. If the two options are call options, which option will have a higher price?
    b. If the two options are put options, which option will have a higher price?

11. Consider two options with the same strike price and for the same underlying asset. The two options differ only with respect to the time to expiration. Option A expires in three months and Option B expires in six months.
    a. If the two options are call options, which option will have the higher intrinsic value (assuming the options are in the money)?
    b. If the two options are call options, which option will have a higher time premium?
    c. Would your answers to (a) and (b) be different if the option is a put rather than a call?

12. In an option pricing model, what statistical measure is used as a measure of the price volatility of the underlying asset?

13. For an asset that does not make cash distributions over the life of an option, it does not pay to exercise a call option prior to the expiration date. Why?

14. Consider two strategies:

Strategy 1: Purchase one unit of Asset M currently selling for $103. A distribution of $10 is expected one year from now.

Strategy 2: (a) Purchase a call option on Asset M with an expiration date one year from now and a strike price of $100; and (b) place sufficient funds in a 10% interest-bearing bank account to exercise the option at expiration ($100) and to pay the cash distribution that would be paid by Asset M ($10).
    a. What is the investment required under Strategy 2?
    b. Give the payoffs of Strategy 1 and Strategy 2, assuming that the price of Asset M one year from now is:
        (i) $120
        (ii) $103
        (iii) $100
        (iv) $ 80
    c. For the four prices of Asset M one year from now, demonstrate that the following relationship holds:

Call option price ≥ Max [0, (Price of underlying asset − Present value of strike price − Present value of cash distribution)]

15. What is meant by a hedge ratio in developing an option pricing model?

16. a. Calculate the option value for a two-period European call option with the following terms:

    Current price of underlying asset = $100
    Strike price = $10
    One-period, risk-free rate = 5%

The stock price can either go up or down by 10% at the end of one period.
    b. Recalculate the value for the option when the stock price can move either up or down by 50% at the end of one period. Compare your answer with the calculated value in part (a).

17. What is the problem encountered in applying the binomial pricing model to the pricing of options on fixed-income securities?

The Applications of Futures and Options Contracts

Learning Objectives

After reading this chapter, you will understand

■ how participants use stock index futures to control a stock portfolio's risk and other portfolio applications.

■ how investors in fixed-income securities employ interest rate futures to control the interest rate risk of a portfolio and other portfolio applications.

■ how and under what circumstances futures can be used to enhance portfolio returns.

■ how futures can be used to alter the allocation of a portfolio between equities and bonds.

■ the differences in hedging with futures and options.

■ how stock options and stock index options allow investors to protect the values of their stock portfolios.

■ how interest rate options enable fixed-income investors to hedge against adverse changes in interest rates.

■ what is meant by the basis and that the basis can change over time.

■ that hedging with futures eliminates price risk but exposes the hedged position to basis risk.

■ what is meant by cross hedging and the risks associated with cross hedging.

■ the difference between the long or buy hedge and the short or sell hedge, both in direct hedging and cross hedging.

In the previous three chapters, we focused on the general properties of financial futures and options contracts, the specific contracts available, and how they are priced. While we have alluded to various applications of these contracts, particularly their use in hedging, we did not cite specific applications. In this chapter, we provide an overview of how market participants can and do employ derivative instruments. The appendix to this chapter explains the general principles of hedging with futures contracts.

APPLICATIONS OF FUTURES CONTRACTS

We begin with the various ways in which market participants can use stock index futures and interest rate futures.

Stock Index Futures

Institutional investors can use stock index futures for seven distinct investment strategies. We describe these strategies below.

Speculating on the Movement of the Stock Market.

Prior to the development of stock index futures, an investor who wanted to speculate on the future course of aggregate stock prices had to buy or short individual stocks. Now, a stock index can be bought or sold in the futures market. However, making speculation easier for investors is not the main function of stock index futures contracts. The other strategies discussed below show how institutional investors can use stock index futures effectively to meet investment objectives.

Controlling the Risk of a Stock Portfolio.

An institution that wishes to alter its exposure to the market can do so by revising the portfolio's beta. This can be done by rebalancing the portfolio with stocks that will produce the target beta, but there are transactions costs associated with rebalancing a portfolio. Because of the leverage embedded in futures, institutions can use stock index futures to achieve a target beta at a considerably lower transaction cost. Buying stock index futures will increase a portfolio's beta, and selling futures will reduce it.

Hedging against Adverse Stock Price Movements.

Hedging is a special case of controlling a stock portfolio's exposure to adverse price changes. In a hedge, the objective is to alter a current or anticipated stock portfolio position so that its beta is zero. A portfolio with a beta of zero should generate a risk-free interest rate. Such a return from a zero-beta portfolio is consistent with the capital asset pricing model discussed in Chapter 13, and also consistent with our discussion of the pricing of futures contracts in the previous chapter.

Remember that using stock index futures for hedging locks in a price, and that the hedger cannot then benefit from a favorable movement in the portfolio's value. (As we explain later, using stock index options has downside protection but retains the upside potential reduced by the cost of the option.)

Two examples of how investment banking firms can use stock index futures to hedge their activities became known shortly after stock index futures began trading. In June 1982, International Harvester traded its stock portfolio to Goldman Sachs in exchange for a bond portfolio.[1] As recipient of the stock portfolio, Goldman Sachs was exposed to market risk. To protect itself against a decline in the value of the stock portfolio, Goldman Sachs placed a hedge on a "significant" portion of the stock portfolio, using all three stock index futures trading at the time to implement the hedge.

The second example involves Salomon Brothers, which used stock index futures to protect itself against a decline in stock prices in a transaction involving $400 million of stock. In that transaction, the New York City Pension Fund switched $400 million of funds that were being managed by Alliance Capital to Bankers Trust so that the latter could manage the funds with an indexing approach. Salomon Brothers guaranteed prices at which the Pension Fund and Bankers Trust could purchase or sell the stocks in the portfolio being transferred. To do this, Salomon Brothers used options on individual stocks to protect against price changes in certain stocks, but also used stock index futures to protect itself against broad market movements that would decrease the value of the stocks in the portfolio.

---

[1] Kimberly Blanton, "Index Futures Contracts Hedge Big Block Trades," *Pension & Investments Age* (July 19, 1982), pp. 1, 38.

Constructing Indexed Portfolios.

As we explain in Chapter 18, an increasing number of institutional equity funds are indexed to some broad-based stock market index. Creating a portfolio that replicates a targeted stock index requires outlays for management fees and transactions costs. The higher these costs, the greater the divergence between the performance of the indexed portfolio and the target index. To control costs, many fund managers creating an indexed portfolio will not purchase all the stocks that comprise the index, but will purchase a group that "tracks the targeted index" or moves in much the same way as the index. As a result, the indexed portfolio produces **tracking error risk**, which is the chance that its movements will not precisely follow those of the index. To avoid the problems of using the cash market to construct an indexed portfolio, the manager can use stock index futures.

However, it is important to note that index fund managers can use stock index futures to create an index fund only if stock index futures contracts are fairly priced or cheap. If the futures price is less than the theoretical futures price (that is, the futures contracts are cheap), the index fund manager can enhance the indexed portfolio's return by buying the futures and buying the Treasury bills. That is, the return on the futures/Treasury bill portfolio will be greater than that on the underlying index when the position is held to the settlement date. In this case, the stock index futures contracts offer still another advantage to the manager.

Index Arbitrage.

Opportunities to enhance returns as a result of the mispricing of the futures contract are not restricted to index fund management. Money managers and arbitrageurs monitor the cash and futures market to see when the differences between the theoretical futures price and actual futures price are sufficiently large to generate an arbitrage profit. These investors respond to those opportunities by selling the futures index if it is expensive and buying stocks, or buying the futures index if it is cheap and selling the stocks. **Index arbitrage** plays an important role in linking futures prices and cash prices. Program trading is used to execute the buy and sell orders.[2]

Creating Portfolio Insurance.

As explained in the previous chapter, a put option can protect the value of an asset. At the expiration date of the put option, the minimum value for the asset will be the strike price minus the cost of the put option. Put options on stock indexes can do the same for a diversified portfolio of stocks.

Alternatively, an institutional investor can create a put option synthetically by using either (1) stock index futures, or (2) stocks and a riskless asset. Of course, the portfolio manager must change the allocation of the portfolio's funds to stock index futures or between stocks and a riskless asset, as market conditions change.[3] A strategy that seeks to insure the value of a portfolio through the use of a synthetic put option strategy is called **dynamic hedging**.

Given that put options on stock indexes are available to portfolio managers, why should they bother with dynamic hedging? There are four reasons. First, the size of the market for options on stock indexes is not as large as that for stock index futures and therefore may not easily accommodate a large portfolio insurance program with-

---

[2] Program trading is discussed in Chapter 18.
[3] For a more detailed explanation of this strategy, see Mark Rubinstein and Hayne Leland, "Replicating Options with Positions in Stock and Cash," *Financial Analysts Journal* (July–August 1981), pp. 63–72.

out moving the price of the option substantially. Second, exchanges impose limits on the number of contracts in which an investor can have a position. Institutions wishing to protect large equity portfolios may find that position limits effectively prevent them from using exchange-traded index options to protect their portfolio. Third, existing exchange-traded index options contracts are of shorter maturity than the period over which some investors seek protection. Finally, the cost of a put option may be higher than the transactions costs associated with dynamic hedging.

In one way, however, hedging with put options does offer an advantage. While the cost of a put option is known (and is determined by expected price volatility), the cost of creating portfolio insurance by using stock index futures or stocks will be determined by actual price volatility in the market. The greater the market's price volatility, the more rebalancing of the portfolio is necessary, and the higher the cost of creating portfolio insurance.

Asset Allocation.

The decision on how to divide funds across the major asset classes (for example, equities, bonds, foreign securities, real estate) is referred to as the **asset allocation decision**. Futures and options can be used to implement an asset allocation decision more effectively than transacting in the cash markets.

For example, suppose that a pension fund sponsor with assets of $1 billion has allocated $300 million to the bond market and $700 million to the stock market. Suppose further that the sponsor has decided to alter that bond/stock mix to $600 million in bonds and $400 million in stock. Liquidation of $300 million in stock will involve significant transactions costs—both commissions and execution (market impact) costs.[4] Moreover, the external money managers who are managing the stock portfolios will face disruption as funds are withdrawn by the sponsor. Rather than liquidating the stock portfolio immediately, the sponsor can sell an appropriate number of stock index futures contracts. This effectively decreases the exposure of the pension fund to the stock market. To increase the fund's exposure to the bond market, the sponsor can buy interest rate futures contracts.

Interest Rate Futures

Market participants can employ interest rate futures in various ways, which we will now discuss.

Speculating on the Movement of Interest Rates.

The price of a futures contract moves in the opposite direction from interest rates: when rates rise (fall), the futures price will fall (rise). An investor who wants to speculate that interest rates will rise (fall) can sell (buy) interest rate futures. Before interest rate futures were available, investors who wanted to speculate on interest rates did so with the long-term Treasury bond: shorting it if they expected interest rates to rise, and buying it if they expected interest rates to fall.

There are three advantages of using interest rate futures instead of the cash market (trading long-term Treasuries themselves). First, the transactions costs of using futures are lower than those in the corresponding cash market. Second, margin requirements are lower for futures than for Treasury securities; using futures thus per-

---

[4] These costs are described in Chapter 18.

mits greater leverage. Finally, it is easier to take a short position in the futures market than to sell short in the Treasuries market. We repeat here what we said when we discussed the use of stock index futures to speculate on stock price movements: Making speculation easier for investors is not the function of interest rate futures contracts.

Controlling the Interest Rate Risk of a Portfolio.

Stock index futures can be used to change the market risk of a diversified stock portfolio; that is, to alter the beta of a portfolio. Likewise, interest rate futures can be used to alter the interest rate sensitivity of a portfolio. As we explained in Chapter 10, duration is a measure of the interest rate sensitivity.

Investment managers with strong expectations about the direction of the future course of interest rates will adjust the durations of their portfolios so as to capitalize on their expectations. Specifically, a manager expecting rates to increase will reduce the interest rate sensitivity of a portfolio. A manager expecting rates to decrease will raise the interest rate sensitivity of the portfolio. While investment managers can alter the interest rate sensitivity of their portfolios with cash market instruments, a quick and inexpensive means for doing so (on either a temporary or permanent basis) is to use futures contracts.

Hedging against Adverse Interest Rate Movements.

Interest rate futures can be used to hedge against adverse interest rate movements by locking in either a price or an interest rate. Some examples of hedging with interest rate futures will illustrate the basic concepts.

1. Suppose that a pension fund manager knows that bonds must be liquidated in 40 days to make a $5 million payment to the beneficiaries of the pension fund. If interest rates rise in 40 days, more bonds will have to be liquidated to realize proceeds of $5 million. The pension fund manager can hedge by selling in the futures market to lock in a selling price.

2. A pension fund manager expecting substantial cash contributions that must be invested, but concerned that interest rates may fall, can hedge against declining returns by buying interest rate futures. Also, a money manager who knows that bonds are maturing in the near future and who expects that interest rates will be lower at the time of reinvestment can buy interest rate futures. In both cases, interest rate futures are used to hedge against a fall in interest rates that would cause cash flows to be reinvested at a lower interest rate.

3. A corporation planning to sell long-term bonds two months from now can protect itself against a rise in interest rates by selling or taking a short position in interest rate futures now.

4. A thrift or commercial bank can hedge its cost of funds by locking in a rate using the Eurodollar CD futures contract.

5. A corporation that plans to sell commercial paper one month from now can use Treasury bill futures or Eurodollar CD futures to lock in a commercial paper rate.

6. Investment banking firms can use interest rate futures to protect both the value of positions held by their trading desks and positions assumed by the underwriting of new bond issues. An example of the latter is a 1979 Salomon Brothers underwriting of $1 billion of IBM bonds. To protect itself against a rise in interest rates, which would reduce the value of the IBM bonds, Salomon Brothers sold (shorted) Treasury futures. In October 1979, interest rates rose upon an announcement by the Federal Reserve Board that it was allowing interest rates more flexibility to move. While the value of the IBM bonds held by Salomon Brothers declined in value, so did the Treasury bond futures contracts. Because Salomon Brothers had sold these futures, it realized a gain and thus reduced the loss on the IBM bonds it underwrote.

Enhancing Returns When Futures Are Mispriced.

In our discussion of stock index futures earlier, we explained that institutional investors look for the mispricing of stock index futures to create arbitrage profits and thereby to enhance portfolio returns. We referred to this strategy as index arbitrage because it involves a stock index. If interest rate futures are mispriced (even after considering the pricing problems we discussed in the previous chapter), institutional investors can enhance returns in the same way that they do in equities.

Asset Allocation.

As noted earlier, interest rate futures and stock index futures are quick, cheap, and effective ways to change the composition of a portfolio between bonds and stocks.

Key Points That You Should Understand Before Proceeding

1. Investors can use stock index futures to speculate on stock prices, control a portfolio's price risk exposure, hedge against adverse stock price movements, construct indexed portfolios, engage in index arbitrage, and create a synthetic put option.
2. Market participants can employ interest rate futures to speculate on interest rate movements, control a portfolio's risk exposure to interest rate changes, hedge against adverse interest rate movements, and enhance returns when futures are mispriced.
3. Because futures are highly leveraged and transactions costs are less than in the cash market, market participants can alter their risk exposure to a market (stock or bond) more efficiently in the futures market.
4. Buying a futures contract increases a market participant's exposure to a market; selling a futures contract decreases a market participant's exposure to a market.
5. A money manager can use both stock index futures and interest rate futures to more efficiently allocate funds between the stock market and the bond market.

APPLICATIONS OF OPTIONS CONTRACTS

Stock Options and Stock Index Options

Stock options can be used to take advantage of the anticipated price movement of individual stocks. Alternatively, they can help protect current or anticipated positions in individual stocks. For example, an investor can protect against a decline in the price of a stock in her portfolio by buying a put option on that stock. The put guarantees a minimum price equal to the strike price minus the cost of buying the option. This strategy is called a **protective put buying strategy**. Also, if an investor anticipates buying a stock in the future but fears that the stock price will rise over that time, she can buy a call option on the stock. This strategy guarantees that the maximum price that will be paid in the future is the strike price plus the option price.

Now consider an institutional investor that holds a portfolio consisting of a large number of stock issues. Using stock options to protect against an adverse price movement in the portfolio's value, the institutional investor would have to buy a put on every stock in the portfolio, which would be quite costly. By taking an appropriate position in a suitable stock index option, an institutional investor can create a protective put for the entire, diversified portfolio. For example, suppose that an institutional investor, who holds a diversified portfolio of common stock that is highly correlated with the S&P 100, is concerned that the stock market will decline in value over the next three months. Suppose, too, that a three-month put option on the S&P 100 is available. Because the put option buyer gains when the price of the underlying stock index declines, purchasing a put option will offset any adverse movements in the portfolio's value due to a decline in the stock market. This protective put buying strategy obviously offers a cheap, effective, and flexible alternative to either buying puts on the various stocks or liquidating the entire portfolio and converting holdings into cash.

When stock options or stock index options are used to protect an existing or anticipated position, the investor need not exercise the option if the prices of the held stocks move in the direction that the investor wants. This freedom not to exercise makes options more suited than futures to the task of protecting a cash position. An institutional investor can obtain downside protection using options at a cost equal to the option price, but preserve upside potential (reduced by the option price).

Interest Rate Options

An institutional investor can use interest rate options or options on interest rate futures to speculate on fixed-income security price movements based on expectations of interest rate changes. Because a call option increases in price if interest rates decline, an investor can buy call options if he or she expects interest rates to move in that direction. Alternatively, because the writer of a put option will benefit if the price increases, an investor who expects interest rates to fall can write put options. Purchasing put options and/or selling call options would be appropriate for an investor who expects interest rates to rise. Remember that, unlike interest rate futures, interest rate options limit downside risk while permitting upside potential that is reduced only by the amount of the option price.

As noted, institutional investors can use interest rate options to hedge against adverse interest rate movements but still let the investor benefit from a favorable interest rate movement. It is important to recognize that hedging in this way can basically set a floor or ceiling on an institution's targeted interest rate. We will use the illustrations given earlier for interest rate futures to explain how this works using options.

1.   Suppose that a pension fund manager knows that bonds must be liquidated in 40 days to make a $5 million payment to the beneficiaries of the pension fund. If interest rates rise in 40 days, more bonds will have to be liquidated to realize $5 million. The hedger will buy put options (that is, follow a protective put buying strategy). Should interest rates rise, the value of the bonds to be sold will decline, but the put options purchased will rise in value. If the transaction is properly structured, the gain on the put options will offset the loss on the bonds. The cost of the safety bought by this strategy will then be the option price paid. If, instead, interest rates decline, the value of the bonds will rise. The pension fund manager will not exercise the put option. A gain equal to the rise in the bond value minus the put option price will be realized.

2.   Suppose a pension fund manager knows there will be substantial cash contributions flowing into the fund and is concerned that interest rates may fall. Or suppose that a money manager knows that bonds are maturing in the near future and expects interest rates to fall. In both cases, proceeds will be reinvested at a lower interest rate. Call options can be purchased in this situation. Should interest rates fall, the call options will increase in value, offsetting the loss in interest income that will result when the proceeds must be invested at a lower interest rate. The cost of this hedge strategy is the call option price. Should interest rates rise instead, the proceeds can be invested at a higher rate. The benefit of the higher rate will be reduced by the cost of the call option, which expires worthless.

3.   A corporation plans to issue long-term bonds two months from now. To protect itself against a rise in interest rates, the corporation can buy put options. If interest rates rise, the interest cost of the bonds issued two months from now will be higher,

but the put option will have increased in value. Buying an appropriate number of put options yields a gain on the put options sufficient to offset the higher interest cost of the bond issue. Again, the cost of this strategy is the price of the put options. Should interest rates decline instead, the corporation will benefit from a lower interest cost when the bonds are issued, a benefit reduced by the cost of the put options.

4.   A thrift or commercial bank wants to make sure that the cost of its funds will not exceed a certain level. This can be done by buying put options on Eurodollar CD futures.

5.   A corporation plans to sell commercial paper one month from now. Buying put options on Treasury bill futures or Eurodollar CD futures lets the corporation set a ceiling on its commercial paper interest cost.

Key Points That You Should Understand Before Proceeding

1. Market participants can obtain downside protection using options at a cost equal to the option price, but preserve upside potential (reduced by the option price).
2. A protective put buying strategy can be used to reduce the risk exposure of a stock portfolio to a decline in stock prices, guaranteeing a minimum price equal to the strike price minus the cost of buying the put option.
3. The purchase of a call option can be used to guarantee that the maximum price that will be paid in the future is the strike price plus the option price.
4. By taking an appropriate position in a suitable stock index option, an institutional investor can create a protective put for a diversified portfolio.
5. Interest rate options or options on interest rate futures can be used by investors and issuers to hedge against adverse interest rate movements but still benefit from a favorable interest rate movement.

SUMMARY

Market participants, both investors and borrowers, can use derivative contracts in a variety of ways. The contracts can be used to speculate on stock prices or interest rates, to alter the risk exposure of a stock or bond portfolio, to hedge the risk associated with a stock position or bond position, to hedge the issuance of future debt, or to change the allocation of funds between stocks and bonds. When contracts are mispriced, a market participant can capitalize on this opportunity by enhancing returns, in the case of an investor, or reduce the cost of issuing an obligation, in the case of an issuer of securities.

KEY TERMS

- **Asset allocation decision, 566**
- **Basis, 573**
- **Basis risk, 573**
- **Cross hedging, 573**
- **Cross-hedging risk, 573**
- **Index arbitrage, 565**
- **Long hedge (also called a buy hedge), 573, 574**
- **Perfect hedge (or textbook hedge), 573**
- **Portfolio strategy (also called dynamic hedging), 565**
- **Protective put buying strategy, 568**
- **Short hedge (also called a sell hedge), 573**
- **Tracking error risk, 565**

QUESTIONS

1. a. If a stock portfolio's indicator of volatility is its beta, explain how stock index futures can be used to change the portfolio's volatility.
    b. Suppose an institutional investor wants to increase the beta of a portfolio of stocks. Should the institutional investor buy or sell S&P 500 futures contracts?

2. a. What is the difference between an index arbitrage strategy and an indexing strategy?
    b. Why would a portfolio manager find it advantageous to use stock index futures in an indexing strategy?

3. Suppose a corporation plans to issue bonds three months from now and wants to protect against a rise in interest rates. Should the corporation buy or sell interest rate futures contracts?

4. a. What is meant by a synthetic put option?
    b. What is meant by dynamic hedging?

5. Assume you own an asset and there are both futures contracts and options contracts on that asset. Provide a clear account of the difference between hedging against a price decline with futures and hedging with options. Direct your analysis to the potential gains from options and the nature of losses from a futures position.

6. a. What is the basis of a futures contract?
    b. Explain why hedging with futures contracts substitutes basis risk for price risk.

7. Under what conditions would a perfect hedge occur?

8. a. Why is a short futures hedge called a sell hedge?
    b. Why is a long futures hedge called a buy hedge?

9. In the August 18, 1989, issue of the *Wall Street Journal* there appeared an article entitled "Program Trading Spreads from Just Wall Street Firms." Following are two quotations from that article:

    Brokerage firms in the business, which tiptoed back into program trading after the post-crash furor died down, argue that such strategies as stock-index arbitrage—rapid trading between stock index futures and stocks to capture fleeting price differences–link two related markets and thus benefit both.

    The second quotation in the article is from a senior vice president at Twenty-First Securities Corp:

    Program trading is a product that is here, links markets, and it is not going to disappear. It is a function of the computerization of Wall Street.

    Do you agree with these statements?

10. This quotation is from the June 8, 1987, issue of *Business Week.*

    The idea sounds almost un-American. Instead of using your smarts to pick stocks that will reach the sky, you put money in a fund that merely tracks a broad market index. But that is precisely what institutional investors are doing. . . . Indexing is a new force in the stock market. . . . But the impact of index-funds reaches far beyond stock prices.

    Discuss how indexing may have contributed to the growth of the stock index derivatives markets.

11. This quotation appeared in the December 1988 issue of *Euromoney.*

The proliferation of futures and options markets has created new opportunities for international investors. It is now possible to change investment exposure from one country to another through the use of derivative instruments, augmented by a limited number of individual securities. Asset allocation in most major markets is now feasible using futures and options.

Discuss this quotation and the reasons for using derivative rather than cash instruments to facilitate asset allocation decisions.

12. What are the risks associated with cross hedging?

13. Donald Singleton is an investment banker for a regional firm. One of his clients, Dolby Manufacturing, Inc., is a private company that will be making an initial public offering of 20 million shares of common stock. Mr. Singleton's firm will buy the issue at $10 per share. He has suggested to the managing director of the firm, John Wilson, that the firm should hedge the position using stock index futures contracts. What should Mr. Wilson's response be?

14. a. Explain why you agree or disagree with the following statement by Gary Gastineau ("A Short History of Program Trading," *Financial Analysts Journal,* September–October 1991):

Stock index futures and options were introduced in the early 1980s. Their introduction was partly a response to institutional portfolio managers' preference for trading portfolios rather than individual stocks and partly a way of reducing transaction costs in the implementation of asset-allocation and market-timing decisions.

b. In the same article, Gary Gastineau made the following statement:

Long positions in stock index futures combined with short-term fixed income securities are an almost perfect substitute for a stock index portfolio. Conversely, selling futures contracts against a portfolio of stocks is a low-cost way to reduce market exposure.

Explain the conditions that must hold for this statement to be true.

Appendix

GENERAL PRINCIPLES OF HEDGING WITH FUTURES

In this appendix, we explain the general principles of hedging with futures contracts. This explanation introduces numerous key concepts that underlie the applications and examples presented in this chapter.

The major function of futures markets is to transfer price risk from hedgers to speculators. That is, risk is transferred from those willing to pay to avoid risk to those wanting to assume the risk in the hope of gain. Hedging in this case is the employment of a futures transaction as a temporary substitute for a transaction in the cash market. The hedge position locks in a value for the cash position. As long as cash and futures prices move together, any loss realized on one position (whether cash or futures) will be offset by a profit on the other position. When the profit and loss are equal, the hedge is called a **perfect** or **textbook hedge**. In a market where the futures contract is correctly priced, a perfect hedge is risk free and, therefore, should provide a return equal to the risk-free rate.

Risks Associated with Hedging

In practice, hedging is not simple. The amount of the loss or profit on a hedge will depend on the relationship between the cash price and the futures price at two points in time, when a hedge is placed and when it is lifted. The difference between the cash price and the futures price is called the **basis**. That is,

$$\text{Basis} = \text{Cash price} - \text{Futures price}$$

As we explained in the previous chapter, if a futures contract is priced according to its theoretical value, the difference between the cash price and the futures price should be equal to the cost of carry. The risk that the hedger takes on is that the basis will change for some reason. This possibility of change is called **basis risk**. Therefore, hedging involves the substitution of basis risk for price risk; that is, the substitution of the risk that the basis will change for the risk that the cash price will change.

When a futures contract is used to hedge a position where either the portfolio or the individual financial instrument is not identical to the instrument underlying the futures, it is called **cross hedging**. Cross hedging is common in asset/liability and portfolio management and in hedging a corporate bond issuance. The reason it is so common is that there are no futures contracts on specific common stock shares and bonds. Cross hedging introduces another risk—the risk that the price movement of the underlying instrument of the futures contract may not accurately track the price movement of the portfolio or financial instrument to be hedged. This is called **cross-hedging risk**. Therefore, the effectiveness of a cross hedge will be determined by two factors:

1. The relationship between the cash price of the underlying instrument and its futures price at the time when a hedge is placed and the time when it is lifted.
2. The relationship between the market (cash) value of the portfolio and the cash price of the instrument underlying the futures contract when the hedge is placed and when it is lifted.

Short and Long Hedges

A **short hedge** is used to protect against a decline in the cash price of a financial instrument or portfolio. To execute a short hedge, the hedger sells a futures contract (enters into the short side of a futures contract or agrees to make delivery). Consequently, a short hedge is also known as a **sell hedge**. By establishing a short hedge, the hedger has fixed the future cash price and transferred the price risk of ownership to the buyer of the futures contract.

A **long hedge** is undertaken to protect against an increase in the price of a financial instrument or portfolio to be purchased in the cash market at some future time. In a long hedge, the hedger buys a futures contract (enters into the long side of a futures contract or agrees to accept delivery). A long hedge is also known as a **buy hedge**.

Hedging Illustrations

We illustrate the principles of hedging and cross hedging using an agricultural commodity, corn, rather than a financial instrument or portfolio, because a corn futures contract is not as complicated as a stock index futures contract or an interest rate futures contract. The principles we illustrate are equally applicable to these futures contracts but easier to grasp with a farm product example not involving financial contract nuances.

Suppose that a corn farmer expects to sell 30,000 bushels of corn three months from now. Assume further that the management of a food processing company plans to purchase 30,000 bushels of corn three months from now. Both the corn farmer and the management of the food processing company want to lock in a price today. That is, each wants to eliminate the price risk associated with corn three months from now. The cash or spot price for corn is currently $2.75 per bushel.

A corn futures contract is available with the following terms: (1) The settlement date for the contract is five months from now and (2) 5,000 bushels of corn must be delivered per contract. Notice that the settlement date is two months after the parties expect to lift their hedge. The futures price for this futures contract is currently $3.20 per bushel.

As the corn farmer seeks to lock in the price of corn to eliminate the risk of a decline in the price three months from now, he will place a short or sell hedge. That is, he will promise to make delivery of corn at the current futures price. The corn farmer will sell six futures contracts because each contract calls for the delivery of 5,000 bushels of corn. Three months from now, the corn farmer will do two things: deliver his corn at the prevailing price in the cash market and lift his short futures hedge by buying the corn futures contract, which will then have two months to settlement. The price at which the corn farmer will buy the corn futures contract depends on the futures contract price three months from now.

The management of the food processing company seeks to lock in the cost of corn to eliminate the risk of an increase in the price of corn three months from now. Consequently, management will place a buy or long hedge. That is, it will agree to accept delivery of corn at the futures price. Protection is sought against a price increase for 30,000 bushels of corn, so six contracts are bought. Three months from now, the food processing company will have to purchase corn in the cash market, paying the prevailing market price. To offset the long corn futures position, which has two months remaining until settlement, the food processing company will sell the contract at the then-prevailing futures price.

Let's look at what happens under various scenarios for the cash price and the futures price of corn three months from now when both parties lift their hedges by reversing their futures contract positions.

Suppose that, when the hedges are lifted, the cash price declines to $2.00 and the futures contract price declines to $2.45. Notice what happens to the basis under this scenario. At the time the hedge is placed, the basis is −$.45 ($2.75 − $3.20). When the hedge is lifted, the basis is still $.45 ($2.00 − $2.45).

The corn farmer, when he placed the hedge, wanted to lock in a price of $2.75 per bushel of corn, or $82,500 for 30,000 bushels. He sold six futures contracts at a price of $3.20 per bushel, or $96,000 for 30,000 bushels. When he lifts his short hedge, the value of the farmer's corn is $60,000 ($2.00 × 30,000). The corn farmer realizes a decline in the cash market value of his corn of $22,500, but the futures price has declined to $2.45, so the cost to the corn farmer to liquidate his futures position is only $73,500 ($2.45 × 30,000). The corn farmer realizes a gain in the futures market of $22,500, or $96,000 − $73,500. The net result is that the gain in the futures market matches the loss in the cash market. Consequently, the corn farmer, by hedging, succeeds in ensuring a price per unit of $2.75, precisely equal to the initial price he had intended to realize for himself. This is an example of a perfect or textbook hedge.

Because there was a decline in the cash price, the food processing company would realize a gain in the cash market of $22,500 but would realize a loss in the futures market of the same amount. Therefore, this buy or long hedge is also a perfect or textbook hedge from the perspective of the food processing company, ensuring a cost per unit equal to the initial price of $2.75.

This scenario illustrates two important points. First, for both participants there was no overall gain or loss. The reason for this result is our assumption that the basis did not change while the hedges were in place. Thus, if the basis does not change, a perfect hedge will be achieved. Second, note that the management of the food processing company would have been better off if it had not hedged. The cost of corn would have fallen $22,500 in the cash market over the three months. This failure to gain from the decline in the cash price should not be interpreted as a sign of poor planning by management. Management is not in the business of speculating on the future price of corn. Hedging is a standard practice to ensure the price to be paid at the delivery date, thus eliminating future price uncertainty.

Suppose that the cash price of corn, when the hedge is lifted, increases to $3.55, and that the futures price increases to $4.00. Notice that the basis is unchanged at −$.45. As long as the basis is unchanged, the cash and futures price we have assumed in this scenario will produce a perfect hedge.

The corn farmer will gain in the cash market because the value of 30,000 bushels of corn is $106,500 ($3.55 × 30,000). This represents a $24,000 gain, compared to the cash value at the time the hedge was placed. However, the corn farmer must liquidate his position in the futures market by buying six futures contracts at a total cost of $120,000, which is $24,000 more than when the contracts were sold. The loss in the futures market offsets the gain in the cash market, which is the meaning of a perfect hedge. The food processing company would realize a gain in the futures market of $24,000 but would have to pay $24,000 more in the cash market to acquire 30,000 bushels of corn.

Note that the management of the food processing company under this scenario saved $24,000 in the cost of corn by employing a hedge. The corn farmer, though, would have been better off if he had not used a hedging strategy but rather simply sold his product on the market three months later. Again, it must be emphasized that the corn farmer, just like the management of the food processing company, employed a hedge to protect against unforeseen and adverse price changes in the cash market.

These scenarios assume that the basis does not change when the hedge is lifted. In the real world, the basis does, in fact, change between the time a hedge is placed and when it is lifted. Here is what happens when the basis changes.

Assume that the cash price of corn decreases to $2.00, just as in the first scenario; assume also that the futures price decreases to $2.70 rather than $2.45. The basis has now widened from −$.45 to −$.70 ($2.00 − $2.70). For the short (sell) hedge, the loss in the cash market of $22,500 is offset only partially by a $15,000 gain realized in the futures market (equal to 6 contracts × 5,000 bushels per contract × the per bushel price decline of $.50). Consequently, the hedge results in an overall loss of $7,500.

There are two points to note here. First, if the corn farmer had not employed the hedge, the loss would have been $22,500, because the value of 30,000 bushels of corn is $60,000, compared to $82,500 three months earlier. Although the hedge is not a perfect hedge because the basis widened, the loss of $7,500 on the hedged position is less than the loss of $22,500 which would have occurred in the absence of the hedge. So, the hedge did not eliminate all risk: As we said earlier, the hedge substitutes basis risk for price risk. Second, the management of the food processing company faces the same problem from the opposite perspective. An unexpected gain for either participant results in an unexpected loss of equal dollar value for the other. That is, the participants face a zero-sum game. Consequently, the food processing company would realize an overall gain of $7,500 from its long (buy) hedge. This gain represents a gain of $22,500 in the cash market and a realized loss of $15,000 in the futures market.

Illustrations of Cross Hedging

Suppose that a zucchini farmer plans to sell 37,500 bushels of zucchini three months from now and that a food processing company plans to purchase the same amount of zucchini three months from now. Each party wants to hedge against price risk, but zucchini futures contracts are not traded. Both parties believe there is a close price relationship between zucchini and corn. Specifically, both parties believe that the cash price of zucchini will be 80% of the cash price of corn. The cash price of zucchini is currently $2.20 per bushel, and the cash price of corn is currently $2.75 per bushel. The futures price of corn is currently $3.20 per bushel.

Let's examine various scenarios to see how effective the cross hedge will be. In each scenario, the difference between the cash price of corn and the futures price of corn will be assumed to remain unchanged at −$.45 over the interval between the time the cross hedge is placed and the time it is lifted. This assumption allows us to highlight the importance of the relationship between the two cash prices at the two times.

We must first determine how many corn futures contracts must be used in the cross hedge. The cash value of 37,500 bushels of zucchini at the cash price of $2.20 per bushel is $82,500. To protect a value of $82,500 using corn futures with a current cash price of $2.75, the price of 30,000 bushels of corn ($82,500/$2.75) must be hedged. Each corn futures contract involves 5,000 bushels, so six corn futures contracts are necessary.

Suppose that the cash prices of zucchini and corn decrease to $1.60 and $2.00 per bushel, respectively, and the futures price of corn decreases to $2.45 per bushel. The relationship between the cash price for zucchini and corn assumed when the cross hedge was placed holds at the time the cross hedge is lifted. That is, the cash price of zucchini is 80% of the cash price of corn. The basis for the cash price of corn and the futures price of corn is still −$.45 at the time the cross hedge is lifted.

The short cross hedge produces a gain in the futures market of $22,500 and an exactly offset loss in the cash market. The opposite occurs for the long cross hedge. There is neither overall gain nor loss from the cross hedge in this case. That is, we have a perfect cross hedge. The same would occur if we assume that the cash price of both commodities increases by the same percentage and the basis does not change.

Suppose that the cash prices of both commodities decrease, but the cash price of zucchini falls by a greater percentage than the cash price of corn. For example, suppose that the cash price of zucchini falls to $1.30 per bushel while the cash price of corn falls to $2.00 per bushel. The futures price of corn falls to $2.45 so that the basis is not changed. The cash price of zucchini at the time the cross hedge is lifted is 65% of the cash price of corn, rather than 80% as assumed when the cross hedge was constructed.

For the short cross hedge, the loss in the cash market exceeds the realized loss in the futures market by $11,200. For the long cross hedge, the opposite is true. There is an overall gain from the cross hedge of $11,200. Had the cash price of zucchini fallen by less than the decline in the cash price of corn, the short cross hedge would have produced an overall gain, while the long cross hedge would have generated an overall loss.

C h a p t e r   3 0

Other Derivative Markets: Swaps, Caps, Floor, and Credit Derivatives

Learning Objectives

After reading this chapter, you will understand

- what an interest rate swap is.
- how an interest rate swap can be used by institutional investors and corporate borrowers.
- why the interest rate swap market has grown so rapidly.
- the risk/return characteristics of an interest rate swap.
- two ways to interpret an interest rate swap.
- reasons for the development of an interest rate swap market.
- determinants of the swap spread.
- what a swaption is.
- what a forward start swap is.
- what an interest rate/equity swap is.
- what an interest rate cap and floor is.
- how interest rate caps and floors can be used by institutional investors and corporate borrowers.
- the relationship between an interest rate cap and floor and an option.
- how an interest rate collar can be created.
- the role of credit derivatives
- the different types of credit risk: default risk, credit spread risk, and downgrade risk.
- the basic feature of credit derivatives: credit options, credit forward contracts, and credit swaps.

Interest rate futures and options can be used to control interest rate risk. Commercial banks and investment banks also customize other contracts useful for controlling interest rate risk for their clients. These include interest rate swaps and interest rate caps and floors. In this chapter, we will review each contract and explain the way borrowers and institutional investors use them. Although interest rate derivatives can be used to control for changes in the level of interest rates, they do not protect against changes in credit spreads. At the end of this chapter we will describe derivative instruments that can be used to control for credit risk. These instruments are called credit derivatives.

INTEREST RATE SWAPS

An **interest rate swap** is an agreement whereby two parties (called *counterparties*) agree to exchange periodic interest payments. The dollar amount of the interest payments exchanged is based on some predetermined dollar principal, which is called the **notional principal amount**. The dollar amount each counterparty pays to the other is the agreed-upon periodic interest rate times the notional principal amount. The only dollars exchanged between the parties are the net interest payments, not the notional principal amount. In the most common type of swap, one party agrees to pay the other party fixed interest payments at designated dates for the life of the contract. This party is referred to as the **fixed-rate payer**. The other party, referred to as the **floating-rate payer**, agrees to make interest rate payments that float with some reference interest rate (or, simply, reference rate).

For example, suppose that for the next five years party X agrees to pay party Y 10% per year, while party Y agrees to pay party X six-month LIBOR (London Interbank Offered Rate). Party X is a fixed-rate payer/floating-rate receiver, while party Y is a floating-rate payer/fixed-rate receiver. Assume that the notional principal amount is $50 million, and that payments are exchanged every six months for the next five years. This means that every six months, party X (the fixed-rate payer/floating-rate receiver) will pay party Y $2.5 million (10% times $50 million divided by 2). The amount that party Y (the floating-rate payer/fixed-rate receiver) will pay party X will be six-month LIBOR times $50 million divided by 2. For example, if six-month LIBOR is 7%, party Y will pay party X $1.75 million (7% times $50 million divided by 2). Note that we divide by two because one-half year's interest is being paid.

The reference rates that are commonly used for the floating rate in an interest rate swap are those on various money market instruments: Treasury bills, the London Interbank Offered Rate (LIBOR), commercial paper, bankers acceptances, certificates of deposit, federal funds rate, and prime rate.

As we illustrate later, market participants can use an interest rate swap to alter the cash flow character of assets or liabilities from a fixed-rate basis to a floating-rate basis or vice versa.

Risk/Return Characteristics of a Swap

The value of an interest rate swap will fluctuate with market interest rates. To see how, let's analyze our hypothetical swap. Suppose that interest rates change immediately after parties X and Y enter into the swap. First, consider what would happen if the market demanded that the fixed-rate payer must pay 11% in order to receive six-month LIBOR in any five-year swap. If party X (the fixed-rate payer) wants to sell its position, say, to party A, then party A will benefit by only having to pay 10% (the original swap rate agreed upon) rather than 11% (the current swap rate) to receive six-month LIBOR. Party X will want compensation for this benefit. Consequently, the value of party X's position has increased. Thus, if interest rates increase, the fixed-rate payer will realize a profit and the floating-rate payer will realize a loss.

Next, consider what would happen if interest rates decline to, say, 6%. Now a five-year swap would require the fixed-rate payer to pay 6% rather than 10% to receive six-month LIBOR. If party X wants to sell its position to party B, the latter would demand compensation to take over the position. In other words, if interest rates decline, the fixed-rate payer will realize a loss, while the floating-rate payer will realize a profit.

The risk/return profile of the two positions when interest rates change is summarized in Table 30-1.

Table 30-1   Risk/Return Profile of Counterparties to an Interest Rate Swap

	INTEREST RATES DECREASE	INTEREST RATES INCREASE
Floating-rate payer	Gain	Loss
Fixed-rate payer	Loss	Gain

Interpreting a Swap Position

There are two ways that a swap position can be interpreted: (1) as a package of forward/futures contracts, or (2) as a package of cash flows from buying and selling cash market instruments. We will evaluate both interpretations. Contrast the position of the counterparties in an interest rate swap in Table 30-1 to the position of the long and short futures or a forward contract shown in Table 26-2 of Chapter 26. An interest rate futures contract has an underlying fixed-income instrument. A forward rate agreement (FRA) is one in which the underlying is a rate.

Consider first the FRA. As explained in Chapter 26, the buyer of an FRA gains if the reference rate rises above the contract rate at the settlement date (i.e., the settlement rate is greater than the contract rate) and loses if the reference rate falls below the contract rate at the settlement date (i.e., the settlement rate is less than the contract rate). The opposite is true for the seller of an FRA. Table 30-2 compares the position of the swap parties and the parties to an FRA if rates increase and decrease. Consequently, the buyer of an FRA realizes the same effect as a fixed-rate payer and the seller of an FRA the same effect as a floating-rate payer.

A swap can be viewed as a package of FRAs. In fact, an FRA can be viewed as a special case of a swap in which there is only one settlement date.

Now let's compare a swap to a futures or forward contract where the underlying is an interest rate instrument such as a Eurodollar CD. The long futures position gains if interest rates decline and loses if interest rates rise—this is similar to the risk/return profile for a floating-rate payer. The risk/return profile for a fixed-rate payer is similar to that of the short futures position: a gain if interest rates increase and a loss if interest rates decrease. Table 30-3 compares the counterparty positions for a swap, an FRA, and a forward/futures on a fixed-income instrument when rates change.

Consequently, interest rate swaps can be viewed as a package of more basic interest rate control tools, such as forwards. The pricing of an interest rate swap will then depend on the price of a package of forward contracts with the same settlement dates and in which the underlying for the forward contract is the same reference rate.

While an interest rate swap may be nothing more than a package of forward contracts, several important reasons suggest that it is not a redundant contract. First, the

Table 30-2   Effect of Rate Changes on Interest Rate Swap Counterparties and FRA Counterparties

COUNTERPARTIES TO		INTEREST RATES	
SWAP	FRA	DECREASE	INCREASE
Floating-rate payer	Seller	Gains	Losses
Fixed-rate payer	Buyer	Losses	Gains

Table 30-3   Effect of Rate Changes on Interest Rate Swap Counterparties, FRA Counterparties, and Futures and Forwards on Fixed-Income Instrument Counterparties

		Counterparties to		
		FUTURES/FORWARD ON FIXED-INCOME	INTEREST RATES	
SWAP	FRA	INSTRUMENT	DECREASE	INCREASE
Floating-rate payer	Seller	Buyer	Gains	Losses
Fixed-rate payer	Buyer	Seller	Losses	Gains

longest maturity of forward or futures contracts does not extend out as far as that of an interest rate swap. In fact, an interest rate swap with a term of 15 years or longer can be obtained. Second, an interest rate swap is a more transactionally efficient instrument. By this we mean that in one transaction two parties can effectively establish a payoff equivalent to a package of forward contracts. The forward contracts would each have to be negotiated separately. Third, the liquidity of the interest rate swap market has grown since its beginning in 1981; it is now more liquid than forward contracts, particularly long-dated (that is, long-term) forward contracts.

Package of Cash Market Instruments.

To understand why a swap can also be interpreted as package of cash market instruments, consider the following. Suppose that an investor enters into a transaction to:

➤ buy $50 million par of a five-year, floating-rate bond that pays six-month LIBOR every six months

➤ finance the purchase of the five-year, floating-rate bond by borrowing $50 million for five years with a 10% annual interest rate and payments every six months.

The cash flow of this transaction is presented in Table 30-4. The second column of the exhibit sets out the cash flow from purchasing the five-year, floating-rate bond. There is a $50 million cash outlay and then cash inflows. The amount of the cash inflows is uncertain because they depend on future LIBOR. The third column shows the cash flow from borrowing $50 million on a fixed-rate basis. The last column shows the net cash flow from the entire transaction. As can be seen in the last column, there is no initial cash flow (no cash inflow or cash outlay). In all 10 six-month periods the net position results in a cash inflow of LIBOR and a cash outlay of $2.5 million. This net position, however, is identical to the position of a fixed-rate payer/floating-rate receiver.

The net cash flow in Table 30-4 reveals that a fixed-rate payer has a cash market position that is equivalent to a long position in a floating-rate bond and borrowing the funds to purchase the floating-rate bond on a fixed-rate basis. But the borrowing can be viewed as issuing a fixed-rate bond, or equivalently, being short a fixed-rate bond. Consequently, the position of a fixed-rate payer can be viewed as being long a floating-rate bond and short a fixed-rate bond.

What about the position of a floating-rate payer? It can be demonstrated that the position of a floating-rate payer is equivalent to purchasing a fixed-rate bond and financing that purchase at a floating rate, with the floating rate being the reference interest rate for the swap. That is, the position of a floating-rate payer is equivalent to a long position in a fixed-rate bond and a short position in a floating-rate bond.

Table 30-4   Cash Flow for the Purchase of a Five-Year, Floating-Rate Bond
Financed by Borrowing on a Fixed-Rate Basis

Transaction: Purchase for $50 million a five-year, floating-rate bond:
Floating rate = LIBOR, semiannual pay
Borrow $50 million for five years: fixed rate = 10% semiannual payments

	Cash flow (in millions of dollars) from:		
SIX-MONTH PERIOD	FLOATING-RATE BOND	BORROWING COST	NET
0	−$50	+$50.0	$ 0
1	+(LIBOR$_1$/2) × 50	− 2.5	+(LIBOR$_1$/2) × 50 − 2.5
2	+(LIBOR$_2$/2) × 50	− 2.5	+(LIBOR$_2$/2) × 50 − 2.5
3	+(LIBOR$_3$/2) × 50	− 2.5	+(LIBOR$_3$/2) × 50 − 2.5
4	+(LIBOR$_4$/2) × 50	− 2.5	+(LIBOR$_4$/2) × 50 − 2.5
5	+(LIBOR$_5$/2) × 50	− 2.5	+(LIBOR$_5$/2) × 50 − 2.5
6	+(LIBOR$_6$/2) × 50	− 2.5	+(LIBOR$_6$/2) × 50 − 2.5
7	+(LIBOR$_7$/2) × 50	− 2.5	+(LIBOR$_7$/2) × 50 − 2.5
8	+(LIBOR$_8$/2) × 50	− 2.5	+(LIBOR$_8$/2) × 50 − 2.5
9	+(LIBOR$_9$/2) × 50	− 2.5	+(LIBOR$_9$/2) × 50 − 2.5
10	+(LIBOR$_{10}$/2) × 50 + 50	− 52.5	+(LIBOR$_{10}$/2) × 50 − 2.5

NOTE: *The subscript for LIBOR indicates the six-month LIBOR as per the terms of the floating-rate bond at a particular time.*

Applications

So far we have merely described an interest rate swap and looked at its characteristics. With the help of two illustrations, we now explain how swaps can be used. Although we focus on basic or **plain vanilla swaps**, the illustrations will help us understand why other types of interest rate swaps have been developed.

Application to Asset/Liability Management.

In the first illustration we look at how an interest rate swap can be used to alter the cash flow characteristics of an institution's assets so as to provide a better match between assets and liabilities. The two institutions are a commercial bank and a life insurance company.

Suppose a bank has a portfolio consisting of five-year term commercial loans with a fixed interest rate. The principal value of the portfolio is $50 million, and the interest rate on all the loans in the portfolio is 10%. The loans are interest only loans; interest is paid semiannually, and the entire principal is paid at the end of five years. That is, assuming no default on the loans, the cash flow from the loan portfolio is $2.5 million every six months for the next five years and $50 million at the end of five years. To fund its loan portfolio, assume that the bank is relying on the issuance of six-month certificates of deposit. The interest rate that the bank plans to pay on its six-month CDs is the six-month Treasury bill rate plus 40 basis points (b.p.).

The risk that the bank faces is that the six-month Treasury bill rate will be 9.6% or greater. To understand why, remember that the bank is earning 10% annually on its commercial loan portfolio. If the six-month Treasury bill rate is 9.6%, it will have to pay 9.6% plus 40 basis points to depositors for six-month funds, or 10%, and there will be no spread income. Worse, if the six-month Treasury bill rate rises above 9.6%, there will be a loss; that is, the cost of funds will exceed the interest rate earned on the loan portfolio. The bank's objective is to lock in a spread over the cost of its funds.

The other party in the interest rate swap illustration is a life insurance company that has committed itself to pay a 9% rate for the next five years on a guaranteed investment contract (GIC) it has issued. The amount of the GIC is $50 million. Suppose that the life insurance company has the opportunity to invest $50 million in what it considers an attractive five-year, floating-rate instrument in a private placement transaction. The interest rate on this instrument is the six-month Treasury bill rate plus 160 basis points. The coupon rate is set every six months.

The risk that the life insurance company faces is that the six-month interest rate will fall so that it will not earn enough to realize a spread over the 9% rate that it has guaranteed to the GIC holders. If the six-month Treasury bill rate falls to 7.4% or less, no spread income will be generated. To understand why, suppose that the six-month Treasury bill rate at the date the floating-rate instrument resets its coupon is 7.4%. Then the coupon rate for the next six months will be 9% (7.4% plus 160 basis points). Because the life insurance company has agreed to pay 9% on the GIC policy, there will be no spread income. Should the six-month Treasury bill rate fall below 7.4%, the life insurance company will incur a loss.

We can summarize the asset/liability problem of the bank and life insurance company as follows:

BANK:

1. Has lent long-term and borrowed short-term.
2. If the six-month Treasury bill rate rises, spread income declines.

LIFE INSURANCE COMPANY:

3. Has effectively lent short-term and borrowed long-term.
4. If the six-month Treasury bill rate falls, spread income declines.

Now let's suppose that an intermediary offers a five-year interest rate swap with a notional principal amount of $50 million to both the bank and life insurance company. The terms offered to the bank are as follows:

1. Every six months the bank will pay 10% (annual rate) to the intermediary.
2. Every six months the intermediary will pay the six-month Treasury bill rate plus 155 basis points to the bank.

The terms offered to the insurance company are as follows:

1. Every six months the life insurance company will pay the six-month Treasury bill rate plus 160 basis points per year to the intermediary.
2. Every six months the intermediary will pay the insurance company 10% (annual rate).

What has this interest rate contract done for the bank and the life insurance company? Consider first the bank. For every six-month period during the life of the swap agreement, the interest rate spread will be as follows:

Annual interest rate received:	
From commercial loan portfolio	= 10%
From interest rate swap	= 6-month T-bill rate + 155 b.p.
Total	= 11.55% + 6-month T-bill rate

Annual interest rate paid:	
To CD depositors	6-month T-bill rate + 40 b.p.
On interest rate swap	= 10%
Total	= 10.40% + 6-month T-bill rate
Outcome:	
To be received	= 11.55% + 6-month T-bill rate
To be paid	= 10.40% + 6-month T-bill rate
Spread income	= 1.15% or 115 b.p.

Thus, regardless of what happens to the six-month Treasury bill rate, the bank locks in a spread of 115 basis points.

Now let's look at the effect of the interest rate swap on the life insurance company:

Annual interest rate received:	
From floating-rate instrument	= 6-month T-bill rate + 160 b.p.
From interest rate swap	= 10%
Total	= 11.6% − 6-month T-bill rate
Annual interest rate paid:	
To GIC policyholders	= 9%
On interest rate swap	= 6-month T-bill rate + 160 b.p.
Total	= 10.6% + 6-month T-bill rate
Outcome:	
To be received	= 11.6% + 6-month T-bill rate
To be paid	= 10.6% + 6-month T-bill rate
Spread income	= 1.0% or 100 b.p.

Regardless of what happens to the six-month Treasury bill rate, the life insurance company locks in a spread of 100 basis points.

The interest rate swap has allowed each party to accomplish its asset/liability objective of locking in a spread.[1] The swap permits each financial institution to alter the cash flow characteristics of its assets: from fixed to floating in the case of the bank, and from floating to fixed in the case of the life insurance company. This type of transaction is referred to as an **asset swap**. The bank and the life insurance company could have used the swap market instead to change the cash flow nature of their liabilities. Such a swap is called a **liability swap**. While in our illustration we used a bank, an interest rate swap obviously would be appropriate for savings and loan associations that, because of regulation, borrow short term—on a floating-rate basis—and lend long term—on fixed-rate mortgages.

Of course, there are other ways that the two institutions could have chosen to match the cash flow characteristics of their assets and liabilities. The bank might refuse to make fixed-rate commercial loans and insist only on floating-rate loans. This approach has a major pitfall: If borrowers can find another source willing to lend on a fixed-rate basis, the bank would lose these customers. The life insurance company might refuse to purchase a floating-rate instrument. But suppose that the terms

---

[1] Whether or not the size of the spread is adequate is not an issue to us in this illustration.

offered on the private placement instrument were more attractive than what would have been offered on a floating-rate instrument of comparable credit risk. Thus, by using the swap market, the life insurance company can earn a yield higher than what it would earn if it invested directly in a five-year, fixed-rate security. For example, suppose the life insurance company can invest in a comparable credit risk five-year, fixed-rate security with a yield of 9.8%. Given the funding through the GIC with a 9% rate, this investment would result in spread income of 80 basis points—less than the 100 basis point spread income the life insurance company achieved by purchasing the floating-rate instrument and entering into the swap.

Consequently, an interest rate swap performs two important functions: (1) It can change the risk of a financial position by altering the cash flow characteristics of assets or liabilities, and (2) under certain circumstances, it also can be used to enhance returns. Obviously, this second function arises only if there are market imperfections.

There is a final point to be made in this illustration. Look at the floating-rate payments that the life insurance company makes to the intermediary and the floating-rate payments that the intermediary makes to the bank. The life insurance company pays the six-month Treasury bill rate plus 160 basis points, but the intermediary pays the bank the six-month Treasury bill rate plus only 155 basis points. The difference of 5 basis points represents the fee to the intermediary for the services of intermediation.

Application to Debt Issuance.

Our second illustration considers two U.S. entities, a triple-A rated commercial bank and a triple-B rated nonfinancial corporation; each wants to raise $100 million for 10 years. For various reasons, the bank wants to raise floating-rate funds, while the nonfinancial corporation wants to raise fixed-rate funds. The interest rates available to the two entities in the U.S. bond market are as follows:

Bank: Floating rate = 6-month LIBOR + 30 b.p.
Nonfinancial corporation: Fixed rate = 12%

Suppose also that both entities could issue securities in the Eurodollar bond market, if they wanted to. Let us assume that the following terms are available in the Eurodollar bond market for 10-year securities for these two entities:

Bank: Fixed rate = 10.5%
Nonfinancial corporation: Floating rate = 6 month LIBOR + 80 b.p.

Notice that we indicate the terms that the bank could obtain on fixed-rate financing and that the nonfinancial corporation could obtain on floating-rate securities. You will shortly see why we did this. First, let us summarize the situation for the two entities in the U.S. domestic and Eurodollar bond markets:

FLOATING-RATE SECURITIES		
Entity	Bond market	Rate
Bank	U.S. domestic	6-month LIBOR + 30 b.p.
Nonfinancial corporation	Eurodollar	6-month LIBOR + 80 b.p
		Quality spread = 50 b.p.
FIXED-RATE SECURITIES		
Entity	Bond market	Rate
Bank	Eurodollar	10.5%
Nonfinancial corporation	U.S. domestic	12.0%
		Quality spread = 150 b.p.

In this table, we use the term *quality spread*. This term simply means the differential borrowing costs that reflect the difference in the creditworthiness of the two entities.

Notice that the quality spread for floating-rate securities (50 basis points) is narrower than the quality spread for fixed-rate securities (150 basis points). This difference in spreads provides an opportunity for both entities to reduce the cost of raising funds. To see how, suppose each entity issued securities in the Eurodollar bond market, and then simultaneously entered into the following 10-year interest rate swap with a $100 million notional principal amount offered by an intermediary:

Bank:
Pay floating rate of 6-month LIBOR + 70 b.p.
Receive fixed rate of 11.3%
Nonfinancial corporation:
Pay fixed rate of 11.3%
Receive floating rate of 6-month LIBOR + 45 b.p.

The cost of the issue for the bank would then be:

Interest paid:	
On fixed-rate Eurodollar bonds issued	= 10.5%
On interest rate swap	= 6-month LIBOR + 70 b.p.
Total	= 11.2% + 6-month LIBOR
Interest received:	
On interest rate swap	= 11.3%
Net cost:	
Interest paid	= 11.2% + 6-month LIBOR
Interest received	= 11.3%
Total	= 6-month LIBOR − 10 b.p.

The cost of the issue for the nonfinancial corporation would then be:

Interest paid:	
On floating-rate Eurodollar bonds issued	= 6-month LIBOR + 80 b.p.
On interest rate swap	= 11.3%
Total	= 12.1% + 6-month LIBOR
Interest received:	
On interest rate swap	= 6-month LIBOR + 45 b.p.
Net cost:	
Interest paid	= 12.1% + 6-month LIBOR
Interest received	= 6-month LIBOR + 45 b.p.
Total	= 11.65%

The transactions are diagrammed in Figure 30-1. By issuing securities in the Eurodollar bond market and using the interest rate swap, both entities are able to reduce their cost of issuing securities. The bank was able to issue floating-rate securities for six-month LIBOR minus 10 basis points rather than issue floating-rate securities in the U.S. domestic bond market for six-month LIBOR plus 30 basis points,

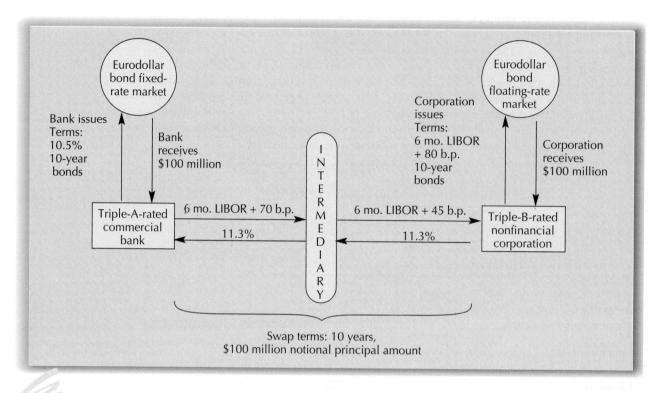

Figure 30-1   Diagram of Interest Rate Swap for Debt Issuance

thereby saving 40 basis points. The nonfinancial corporation saved 35 basis points (11.65% versus 12%) by issuing floating-rate bonds in the Eurodollar bond market and using the interest rate swap.

The point of this illustration is to show that, if differences in quality spreads exist in different sectors of the bond markets, borrowers can use the interest rate swap to arbitrage the inconsistency. Whether these differences do exist is another question, which we address below.

Finally, look once again at the intermediary in this transaction. The intermediary pays a floating rate of six-month LIBOR plus 45 basis points to the nonfinancial corporation, and receives six-month LIBOR plus 70 basis points from the bank, realizing 25 basis points for its intermediary services.

Reasons for the Development of the Interest Rate Swap Market

The interest rate swap was first developed in late 1981. By December 1990, according to a survey by the International Swap Dealers Association, the swap market (consisting of interest rate swaps and currency swaps) totaled $2.9 trillion, as measured in terms of notional principal. (Currency swaps are discussed in Chapter 31.) The interest rate swap market grew by 50% over its 1989 level.[2]

---

[2] As reported in Soma Biswas, "Derivative Pros See Growth in Customization," *Bond Week*, Special Supplement (October 14), 1991, p. 1.

What is behind this rapid growth? As our two illustrations have demonstrated, an interest rate swap is a quick way for institutional investors and corporate borrowers to change the nature of assets and liabilities or to exploit any perceived capital market imperfection.

The initial motivation for the interest rate swap market was borrower exploitation of what were perceived to be *credit arbitrage* opportunities. These opportunities were attributed to the fact that quality spreads, the difference in yields between lower- and higher-rated credits, were frequently not the same in the fixed-rate market as in the floating-rate market, and often the quality spreads were not the same in the U.S. debt markets as in the Eurodollar bond markets. Note that our second illustration assumes a spread of 50 basis points in the floating-rate markets and 150 basis points in the fixed-rate markets. Publications by dealer firms[3] and academic research have suggested this credit arbitrage motivation.[4]

Basically, this argument for swaps rested on the well-known economic principle of comparative advantage, which was developed in international economics. The argument takes this form: even though a high credit-rated issuer could borrow at a lower cost in both the fixed-rate and floating-rate markets (that is, have an absolute advantage in both), it will have a comparative advantage relative to a lower credit-rated issuer in one of the markets (and a comparative disadvantage in the other). Under these conditions, each borrower could benefit from issuing securities in the market in which it has a comparative advantage and then swapping obligations for the desired type of financing. The swap market developed as the vehicle for swapping obligations.

Several observers have challenged the notion that credit arbitrage opportunities exist. They insist that the comparative advantage argument, while based on arbitrage, does not rely on irrational mispricing, but on assumptions of equilibrium in segmented markets. That is, two completely separate markets can be perfectly competitive unto themselves, but set different prices for risk. An economic agent transacting simultaneously in both markets would see an imperfectly competitive market and an opportunity to make money.

Those who challenge the credit arbitrage notion argue that the differences in quality spreads in the fixed-rate and floating-rate markets represent differences in the risks that lenders face in these two markets. Let us consider short- and long-term markets in this regard. The interest rate for a floating-rate note effectively represents a short-term interest rate, and the quality spread on floating-rate notes, therefore, is a spread in the short-term market. In contrast, the quality spread on fixed-rate medium- and long-term notes represents the spread in that maturity sector. There is no reason why the quality spreads across those two markets have to be the same.[5]

A serious obstacle to accepting the credit arbitrage explanation of the swap market is that opportunities for credit arbitrage should be rare in reasonably efficient international credit markets. Moreover, even if such opportunities arose, market participants would quickly exploit and eliminate them. How then can we explain the fact that the number of interest rate swap transactions has grown substantially over the last decade? The May 1984 edition of *Euromoney* contained a Citicorp-sponsored contribu-

---

[3] See, for example, a January 1986 Salomon Brothers publication: T. Lipsky and S. Elhalaski, "Swap-Driven Primary Issuance in the International Bond Market."

[4] See, for example, James Bicksler and Andrew Chen, "An Economic Analysis of Interest Rate Swaps," *Journal of Finance* (July 1986), pp. 645–655.

[5] Two researchers demonstrate that differences in quality spreads between the fixed-rate and floating-rate markets are consistent with option-pricing theory. See Ian Cooper and Antonio Mello, "Default Spreads in the Fixed and in the Floating Rate Markets: A Contingent Claims Approach," *Advances in Futures and Options Research*, Vol. 3 (1988), pp. 269–290.

tion that offered this interesting explanation of the swap market and its reason for being:

> The nature of swaps is that they arbitrage market imperfections. As with any arbitrage opportunity, the more it is exploited, the smaller it becomes.
> . . .
>
> But some of the causes of market imperfections are unlikely to disappear quickly. For example, insurance companies in many countries are constrained to invest mainly in instruments that are domestic in that country. That requirement, tending to favor domestic issuers artificially, is unlikely to be changed overnight. And even in the world's most liquid markets there are arbitrage opportunities. They are small and exist only briefly, but they exist nevertheless.[6]

As this opinion demonstrates, as early as 1984, some observers attributed the difference in quality spreads among markets to differences in regulations among countries. Similarly, differences in tax treatment across countries also create differences in the price of risk and in expected returns.[7] Thus, swaps can be used for regulatory or tax arbitrage and may be explained by such differences among national markets.

Finally, another argument suggested for the growth of the interest rate swap market is the increased volatility of interest rates that has led borrowers and lenders to hedge or manage their exposure. Even though risk/return characteristics can be replicated by a package of forward contracts, interest rate forward contracts are not as liquid as interest rate swaps. And entering into or liquidating swap transactions has been facilitated by the standardization of documentation published by the International Swap Dealers Association in early 1987. Moreover, a swap to hedge or manage a position costs less than a package of interest rate forward contracts.

Consequently, we can say that the swap market originally developed around the purpose of exploiting real or perceived imperfections in the capital market, but eventually evolved into a transactionally efficient market for accomplishing asset/liability objectives.

Although there are no publicly available data on the users of swaps, a study by Leslie Lynn Rahl provides some insight into their identity.[8] She found that 25% of the end users of swaps are corporations, 60% are financial institutions that are not swap dealers, and 15% are government agencies and supranationals.

Role of the Intermediary

The role of the intermediary in an interest rate swap sheds some light on the evolution of the market. Intermediaries in these transactions have been commercial banks and investment banks, who in the early stages of the market sought out end users of swaps. That is, commercial banks and investment banking firms found in their client bases

---

[6] "Swap Financing Techniques: A Citicorp Guide," Special Sponsored Section, *Euromoney* (May 1984), pp. S1–S7. Rather than relying exclusively on an arbitrage argument, one study suggests that the swaps market grew because it allowed borrowers to raise a type of financing that was not possible prior to the introduction of interest rate swaps. See: Marcelle Arak, Arturo Estrella, Laurie Goodman, and Andrew Silver, "Interest Rate Swaps: An Alternative Explanation," *Financial Management* (Summer 1988), pp. 12–18.

[7] This applies even more so to currency swaps, which we discuss in Chapter 30. Several examples of the way swaps can be used to exploit differences in taxes are given in Clifford W. Smith, Charles W. Smithson, and Lee MacDonald Wakeman, "The Evolving Market for Swaps," *Midland Corporate Finance Journal* (Winter 1986), pp. 20–32.

[8] Leslie Lynn Rahl, "Who Is Using Swaps?" *Bond Week* (October 14, 1991), p. 4.

those entities that needed swaps to accomplish funding or investing objectives, and they matched the two entities. In essence, the intermediary in this type of transaction performed the function of a broker.

In the early years of this market, the only time that the intermediary would take the opposite side of a swap (that is, would act as a principal) was when it had to do so in order to balance out the transaction. For example, if an intermediary had two clients that were willing to do a swap but one wanted the notional principal amount to be $100 million while the other wanted it to be $85 million, the intermediary might become the counterparty to the extent of $15 million. That is, the intermediary would warehouse or take a position as a principal to the transaction in order to make up the $15 million difference between the clients' objectives. To protect itself against an adverse interest rate movement, the intermediary would hedge its position.

To explain how the intermediary's role developed over time, we need to address an important feature of the swap that we have not yet discussed. The parties to the swaps we have described had to be concerned that the other party would default on its obligation. While a default would not mean any principal was lost (because the notional principal amount had not been exchanged), a default would mean that the objective for which the swap was entered into would be impaired. As the early transactions involved a higher and a lower credit-rated entity, the former would be concerned with the potential for default of the latter. To reduce the risk of default, many early swap transactions required that the lower credit-rated entity obtain a guarantee from a highly rated commercial bank. Often, the intermediary in the swap was a bank of this type. Involvement as insurer or guarantor in this way led banks to accept the role of dealer or counterparty.

As the frequency and the size of the transactions increased, many intermediaries became comfortable with swap transactions and became principals instead of simply acting as brokers. As long as an intermediary had one entity willing to enter into a swap, the intermediary was willing to be the counterparty. Consequently, interest rate swaps became part of an intermediary's inventory of products. Advances in quantitative techniques and futures products for hedging complex positions such as swaps made the protection of large inventory positions feasible.

Yet another development encouraged intermediaries to become principals rather than brokers in swaps. As more intermediaries entered the swap market, bid–ask spreads on swaps narrowed sharply. To make money in the swaps market, intermediaries had to do a sufficient volume of business, which was possible only if they had (1) an extensive client base willing to use swaps, and (2) a large inventory of swaps. Accomplishing these objectives necessitated that the intermediaries act as principals. A survey by *Euromoney* asked 150 multinationals and supranationals to identify the characteristics that make a swap house efficient.[9] The results indicated that the speed at which a swap could be arranged for a client was the most important criterion. That speed depends on client base and inventory. The same survey also revealed clients to be less interested in brokered deals than in transactions in which the intermediary is a principal.

Market Quotes

The convention that has evolved for quoting swaps levels is for a swap dealer to set the floating rate equal to the index and then quote the fixed rate that will apply. To illus-

---

[9] Special Supplement on Swaps, *Euromoney* (July 1987), p. 14.

trate this convention, we use the swap in our second example of the application of swaps. The terms for that 10-year swap are as follows:

BANK:

> Pay floating rate of 6-month LIBOR + 70 b.p.
>
> Receive fixed rate of 11.3%

NONFINANCIAL CORPORATION:

> Pay fixed rate of 11.3%
>
> Receive floating rate of 6-month LIBOR + 45 b.p.

The offer price that the dealer would quote to the nonfinancial corporation (the fixed-rate payer) would be to pay 10.85% and receive LIBOR flat. (The term *flat* means with no spread.) The 10.85% is obtained by subtracting from the fixed rate of 11.3% the 45-basis point spread over LIBOR. The bid price that the dealer would quote to the commercial bank would be to pay LIBOR flat and receive 10.6%. The 10.6% represents the payment to be received of 11.3% minus the 70-basis point spread over LIBOR.

The dealer determines or sets the quoted fixed rate by adding some spread to the Treasury yield curve with the same term to maturity as the swap. We refer to this spread as the *swap spread*. In our illustration, suppose that the 10-year Treasury yield is 10.35%. In this case, the offer price that the dealer would quote to the fixed-rate payer is the 10-year Treasury rate plus 50 basis points versus receiving LIBOR flat. For the floating-rate payer, the bid price quoted would be LIBOR flat versus the 10-year Treasury rate plus 25 basis points. In the terminology of the market, the dealer would actually quote this particular swap as "25–50." This swap spread means that the dealer is willing to enter into a swap on either side: to receive LIBOR and pay a fixed rate equal to the 10-year Treasury rate plus 25 basis points, or to pay LIBOR and receive a fixed rate equal to the 10-year Treasury rate plus 50 basis points. The difference between the fixed rate paid and received is the bid–offer spread, which is 25 basis points. In practice, over recent years the bid–offer spread has fallen to a level of around 5 to 10 basis points.

PRIMARY DETERMINANTS OF SWAP SPREADS[10]

Earlier we provided two interpretations of a swap: (1) a package of futures/forward contracts and (2) a package of cash market instruments. The swap spread is defined as the difference between the swap's fixed rate and the rate on a Treasury whose maturity matches the swap's maturity. Although a discussion of the valuation of interest rate swaps is beyond the scope of this chapter, it can be shown that they are valued using no-arbitrage relationships relative to instruments (funding or investment vehicles) that produce the same cash flows under the same circumstances.[11]

Table 30-5 displays interest rate swap spreads (in basis points) for maturities out to 30 years on September 3, 1999. The actual swap rates can be obtained simply by adding the swap spreads to the on-the-run U.S. Treasury yield curve on that same date.

---

[10] The discussion in this section is adapted from Chapter 6 in Frank J. Fabozzi and Steven V. Mann, *Floating-Rate Securities* (New Hope, PA: Frank J. Fabozzi Associates, 2000).

[11] For an explanation of the valuation of swaps, see Jeffrey Buetow and Frank J. Fabozzi, *Valuation of Interest Rate Swaps* (New Hope, PA: Frank J. Fabozzi Associates, 2001).

Table 30-5   Swap Spreads for Various Maturities on September 3, 1999

SWAP MATURITY (IN YEARS)	SWAP SPREAD (IN BASIS POINTS)
2	65
3	78
4	86
5	92
6	97
7	100
8	103
9	105
10	107
15	121
20	124
30	114

SOURCE: Bloomberg Financial Markets.

The swap spread is determined by the same factors that drive the spread over Treasuries on instruments that replicate a swap's cash flows (i.e., produce a similar return or funding profile). As discussed below, the swap spread's key determinant for swaps with maturities of five year or less is the cost of hedging in the Eurodollar CD futures market.[12] For swaps with a longer maturity, the swap spread is largely driven by credit spreads in the corporate bond market.[13] Specifically, longer-dated swaps are priced relative to rates paid by investment-grade credits in traditional fixed- and floating-rate markets.

Given that a swap is a package of futures/forward contracts, the shorter-term swap spreads respond directly to fluctuations in Eurodollar CD futures prices. A Eurodollar CD futures contract is an instrument where a fixed dollar payment (i.e., the futures price) is exchanged for three-month LIBOR. There is a liquid market for Eurodollar CD futures contracts with maturities every three months for five years. A market participant can create a synthetic fixed-rate security or a fixed-rate funding vehicle of up to five years by taking a position in a bundle of Eurodollar CD futures contracts (i.e., a position in every three-month Eurodollar CD futures contract up to the desired maturity date).

For example, consider a financial institution that has fixed-rate assets and floating-rate liabilities. Both the assets and liabilities have a maturity of three years. The

---

[12] Naturally, this presupposes that the reference rate for the swap is LIBOR. Furthermore, part of the swap spread is attributable simply to the fact that LIBOR for a given maturity is higher than the rate of a comparable-maturity U.S. Treasury. For a discussion of non-LIBOR swaps and their valuation, see Buetow and Fabozzi, *Valuation of Interest Rate Swaps*.

[13] The default risk component of a swap spread will be smaller than for a comparable bond credit spread. There are two reasons for this. First, since only net interest payments are exchanged rather than both principal and coupon interest payments, the total cash flow at risk is lower. Second, the probability of default depends jointly on the probability of the counterparty defaulting and whether or not the swap has a positive value. See John C. Hull, *Introduction to Futures and Options Markets*, 3rd edition (Upper Saddle River, NJ: Prentice Hall, 1998).

interest rate on the liabilities resets every three months based on three-month LIBOR. This financial institution can hedge this mismatched asset/liability position by buying a three-year bundle of Eurodollar CD futures contracts. By doing so, the financial institution is receiving LIBOR over the three-year period and paying a fixed dollar amount (i.e., the futures price). The financial institution is now hedged because the assets are fixed rate and the bundle of long Eurodollar CD futures synthetically creates a fixed-rate funding arrangement. From the fixed dollar amount over the three years, an effective fixed rate that the financial institution pays can be computed. Alternatively, the financial institution can synthetically create a fixed-rate funding arrangement by entering into a three-year swap in which it pays fixed and receives three-month LIBOR. Other factors being equal, the financial institution will use the vehicle that delivers the lowest cost of hedging the mismatched position. That is, the financial institution will compare the synthetic fixed rate (expressed as a percentage over U.S. Treasuries) to the three-year swap spread. The difference between the synthetic spread and the swap spread should be within a few basis points under normal circumstances.

For swaps with maturities greater than five years, we cannot rely on the Eurodollar CD futures since liquid markets do not exist for these contracts at longer maturities. Instead, longer-dated swaps are priced using rates available to investment-grade corporate borrowers in fixed-rate and floating-rate debt markets. Since a swap can be interpreted as a package of long and short positions in a fixed-rate bond and a floating-rate bond, it is the credit spreads in those two market sectors that will be the determinant of the swap spread. Empirically, the swap rate for a given maturity is greater than the yield on U.S. Treasury securities and less than the yield for AA-rated banks.[14] Swap fixed rates are lower than AA-rated bond yields due to their lower credit due to netting and offsetting of swap positions.

In addition, a number of other technical factors influence the level of swap spreads. While the impact of some of these factors is ephemeral, their influence can be considerable in the short run. Included among these factors are (1) the level and shape of the Treasury yield curve; (2) the relative supply of fixed- and floating-rate payers in the interest rate swap market; (3) the level of asset-based swap activity; and (4) technical factors that affect swap dealers.[15]

Secondary Market for Swaps

There are three general types of transactions in the secondary market for swaps. These include (1) a swap reversal; (2) a swap sale (or assignment); and (3) a swap buy-back (or close-out or cancellation).

In a **swap reversal**, the party that wants out of the transaction will arrange for an additional swap in which (1) the maturity on the new swap is equal to the time remaining of the original swap; (2) the reference rate is the same; and (3) the notional principal amount is the same. For example, suppose party X enters into a five-year swap with a notional principal amount of $50 million in which it pays 10% and receives LIBOR, but that two years later, X wants out of the swap. In a swap reversal, X would enter into a three-year interest rate swap, with a counterparty different from the original counterparty, let's say Z, in which the notional principal amount is $50 million, and X pays LIBOR and receives a fixed rate. The fixed rate that X receives from Z will

---

[14] For a discussion of this point, see Andrew R. Young, *A Morgan Stanley Guide to Fixed Income Analysis* (New York: Morgan Stanley, 1997).

[15] For a further discussion of these technical factors, see Fabozzi and Mann, *Floating-Rate Securities*, pp. 120–123.

depend on prevailing swap terms for floating-rate receivers at the initiation of the three-year swap.

Although party X has effectively terminated the original swap in economic terms, there is a major drawback to this approach: Party X is still liable to the original counterparty Y, as well as to the new counterparty, Z. That is, party X now has two off-setting interest rate swaps on its books instead of one, and as a result it has increased its default risk exposure.

The **swap sale** or **swap assignment** overcomes this drawback. In this secondary market transaction, the party that wishes to close out the original swap finds another party that is willing to accept its obligations under the swap. In our illustration, this means that X finds another party, say, A, that will agree to pay 10% to Y and receive LIBOR from Y for the next three years. Party A might have to be compensated to accept the position of X, or A might have to be willing to compensate X. Who will receive compensation depends on the swap terms at the time. For example, if interest rates have risen so that, to receive LIBOR for three years, a fixed-rate payer would have to pay 12%, then A would have to compensate X because A has to pay only 10% to receive LIBOR. The compensation would be equal to the present value of a three-year annuity of 2% times the notional principal amount. If, instead, interest rates have fallen so that, to receive LIBOR for three years, a fixed-rate payer would have to pay 6%, then X would have to compensate A. The compensation would be equal to the present value of a three-year annuity of 4% times the notional principal amount. Once the transaction is completed, it is then A, not X, that is obligated to perform under the swap terms. (Of course an intermediary could act as principal and become party A.)

In order to accomplish a swap sale, the original counterparty, Y in our example, must agree to the sale. A key factor in whether Y will agree is whether it is willing to accept the credit of A. For example, if A's credit rating is triple-B, while X's is double-A, Y would be unlikely to accept A as a counterparty.

A **buy-back** or **close-out sale** (or **cancellation**) involves the sale of the swap to the original counterparty. As in the case of a swap sale, one party might have to compensate the other, depending on how interest rates and credit spreads have changed since the inception of the swap.

These methods for getting into or out of a swap leave much to be desired for market participants. It is this illiquidity in the secondary market that will hamper swap market growth. There have been proposals to create a swap clearing corporation, similar to the clearing corporations for futures and options, in which case swaps could be marked to market and credit exposure to a swap could be reduced. So far, these proposals have not been implemented.

Beyond the Plain Vanilla Swap

Thus far we have described the *plain vanilla* or generic interest rate swap. Nongeneric or individualized swaps have evolved as a result of the asset/liability needs of borrowers and lenders.

In a generic swap, the notional principal amount does not vary over the life of the swap. Thus, it is sometimes referred to as a **bullet swap**. In contrast, for amortizing, accreting, and roller-coaster swaps, the notional principal amount varies over the life of the swap. An **amortizing swap** is one in which the notional principal amount decreases in a predetermined way over the life of the swap. An **accreting swap** is one in which the notional principal amount increases at a predetermined way over time. In a **roller-coaster swap**, the notional principal amount can rise or fall from period to period.

The terms of a typical interest rate swap call for the exchange of fixed- and floating-rate payments. In a **basis rate swap**, both parties exchange floating-rate payments based on a different money market reference rate. As an example, assume a commercial bank has a portfolio of loans in which the lending rate is based on the prime rate, but the bank's cost of funds is based on LIBOR. The risk the bank faces is that the spread between the prime rate and LIBOR will change. This is referred to as *basis risk*. The bank can use a basis rate swap to make floating-rate payments based on the prime rate and receive floating-rate payments based on LIBOR.

Thus far we have described the plain vanilla or generic interest rate swap. Nongeneric or individualized swaps have evolved as a result of the asset/liability needs of borrowers and lenders. These include swaps where the notional principal changes in a predetermined way over the life of the swap and swaps in which both counterparties pay a floating rate. There are complex swap structures such as options on swaps (called swaptions) and swaps where the swap does not begin until some future time (called forward start swaps). We discuss all of these swaps below. It may be difficult to fully appreciate the importance of these swap structures as a tool for managing the interest rate risk of a financial institution in this book because of our limited coverage of risk management. What is important to appreciate is that these swap structures are not just "bells and whistles" added to the plain vanilla swap to make them more complicated, but features that managers have found that they need to control interest rate risk.

Varying Notional Principal Amount Swaps

In a generic or plain vanilla swap, the notional principal amount does not vary over the life of the swap. Thus, it is sometimes referred to as a *bullet swap*. In contrast, for amortizing, accreting, and roller-coaster swaps, the notional principal amount varies over the life of the swap.

An *amortizing swap* is one in which the notional principal amount decreases in a predetermined way over the life of the swap. Such a swap would be used where the principal of the asset that is being hedged with the swap amortizes over time. For example, in our illustration of the asset/liability problem faced by the bank, the commercial loans are assumed to pay only interest every six months and repay principal only at the end of the loan term. However, what if the commercial loan is a typical term loan; that is, suppose it is a loan that amortizes. Or, suppose that it is a typical mortgage loan that amortizes. In such circumstances, the outstanding principal for the loans would decline and the bank would need a swap where the notional principal amount amortizes in the same way as the loans.

Less common than the amortizing swap are the accreting swap and the roller-coaster swap. An *accreting swap* is one in which the notional principal amount increases in a predetermined way over time. In a *roller-coaster swap*, the notional principal amount can rise or fall from period to period.

Basis Swaps and Constant Maturity Swaps

The terms of a generic interest rate swap call for the exchange of fixed- and floating-rate payments. In a *basis rate swap*, both parties exchange floating-rate payments based on a different reference rate. As an example, assume a commercial bank has a portfolio of loans in which the lending rate is based on the prime rate, but the bank's cost of funds is based on LIBOR. The risk the bank faces is that the spread between the prime rate and LIBOR will change. This is referred to as *basis risk*. The bank can use a basis rate swap to make floating-rate payments based on the prime rate (because that is the reference rate that determines how much the bank is receiving on the loans) and receive floating-rate payments based on LIBOR (because that is the reference rate that determines the bank's funding cost).

Another popular swap is to have the floating leg tied to a longer-term rate such as the two-year Treasury note rather than a money market rate. So one of the parties to the swap would pay the two-year Treasury rate, for example, and the counterparty would pay LIBOR. Such a swap is called a *constant maturity swap*. The reference rate for determining the yield on the constant maturity Treasury in a constant maturity swap is typically the Constant Maturity Treasury (CMT) rate published the Federal Reserve. Consequently, a constant maturity swap tied to the CMT is called a *Constant Maturity Treasury swap*.

Swaptions

There are options on interest rate swaps. These swap structures are called **swaptions** and grant the option buyer the right to enter into an interest rate swap at a future date. The time until expiration of the swap, the term of the swap, and the swap rate are specified. The swap rate is the strike rate for the swaption. The swaption has the American-type exercise provision. That is, the option can only be exercised at the option's expiration date.

There are two types of swaptions—a payer swaption and a receiver swaption. A **payer swaption** entitles the option buyer to enter into an interest rate swap in which the buyer of the option pays a fixed rate and receives a floating rate. For example, suppose that the strike rate is 7%, the term of the swap is three years, and the swaption expires in two years. Also, assume that it is an American-type exercise provision. This means that the buyer of this swaption at the end of two years has the right to enter into a three-year interest rate swap in which the buyer pays 7% (the swap rate which is equal to the strike rate) and receives the reference rate.

In a **receiver swaption** the buyer of the swaption has the right to enter into an interest rate swap that requires paying a floating rate and receiving a fixed rate. For example, if the strike rate is 6.25%, the swap term is five years, and the option expires in one year, the buyer of this receiver swaption has the right when the option expires in one year (assuming it is an American-type exercise provision) to enter into a four-year interest rate swap in which the buyer receives a swap rate of 6.25% (i.e., the strike rate) and pays the reference rate.

How is a swaption used? We can see its usefulness in managing interest rate risk if we return to the bank-insurance company example. The bank makes the fixed-rate payments in the interest rate swap (10%) using the interest rate it is earning on the commercial loans (10%). Suppose that the commercial loan borrowers defaults on their obligations. The bank will then receive from the commercial loans the 10% to make its swap payments. This problem can be addressed at the outset of the initial swap transaction by the bank entering into a swaption that effectively gives it the right to terminate or cancel the swap. That is, the bank will enter into a receiver swaption, receiving fixed of 10% so as to offset the fixed rate it is obligated to pay under the initial swap. In fact, the borrowers do not have to fail for the swap to have an adverse impact on the bank. Suppose the commercial loans can be prepaid. Then, the bank has a similar problem. For example, suppose rates on commercial loans decline to 7% and the borrowers prepay. Then the bank would be obligated to make the 10% payments under the terms of the swap. With the proceeds received from the prepayment of the commercial loans, the bank may only be able to invest in similar loans at 7%, for example, a rate that is less than the bank's obligations.

Forward Start Swap

A **forward start swap** is a swap wherein the swap does not begin until some future date that is specified in the swap agreement. Thus, there is a beginning date for the swap at some time in the future and a maturity date for the swap. A forward start swap will also specify the swap rate at which the counterparties agree to exchange payments commencing at the start date.

Key Points That You Should Understand Before Proceeding

1. An interest rate swap is an agreement whereby two counterparties agree to exchange periodic interest payments based on a notional principal amount.

2. A position in an interest rate swap can be interpreted as a position in a package of forward contracts or a package of cash flows from buying and selling cash market instruments.

3. While the initial motivation for the swap market was borrower exploitation of what were perceived to be credit arbitrage opportunities, such opportunities are limited and depend on the presence of market imperfections.

4. The swap market has evolved into a transactionally efficient market for accomplishing asset/liability objectives to alter the cash flow characteristics of assets (an asset swap) or liabilities (a liability swap).

5. Commercial banks and investment banking firms take positions in swaps rather than act as simply intermediaries.

6. For swaps with maturities of less than five years, the swap spread is driven by rates in the Eurodollar CD futures market, but for swaps with maturities greater than five years, the spread is determined primarily by the credit spreads in the corporate bond market.

7. In addition to the generic swap structure where one party pays fixed and the other floating, there are swaps with varying notional principal amounts, basis swaps (floating payments made by both parties), constant maturity swaps, swaptions, and forward start swaps.

Interest Rate/Equity Swaps

In addition to interest rate swaps, there are currency swaps and **interest rate/equity swaps**. We will discuss the former in the next chapter. Here we will explain interest rate/equity swaps.

Illustration of an Interest Rate/Equity Swap.
To illustrate this swap, consider the following swap agreement:

➤ The counterparties to this swap agreement are the Brotherhood of Basket Weavers (a pension sponsor) and the Reliable Investment Management Corporation (a money management firm).

➤ The notional principal amount is $50 million.

➤ Every year for the next five years, the Brotherhood agrees to pay Reliable Investment Management Corporation the return realized on the Standard & Poor's 500 stock index for the year minus 200 basis points.

➤ Every year for the next five years, Reliable Investment Management Corporation agrees to pay the pension sponsor 10%.

For example, if over the past year the return on the S&P 500 stock index is 14%, then the pension sponsor pays Reliable Investment Management Corporation 12% (14% minus 2%) of $50 million, or $6 million, and the money management firm agrees to pay the pension sponsor $5 million (10% times $50 million).

Application to Creation of a Security.
Swaps can be used by investment bankers to create a security. To see how this is done, suppose the following. The Universal Information Technology Company (UIT) seeks

to raise $100 million for the next five years on a fixed-rate basis. UIT's investment banker, First Boston Corporation, indicates that if bonds with a maturity of five years are issued, the interest rate on the issue would have to be 8%. At the same time, there are institutional investors seeking to purchase bonds but that are interested in making a play on the stock market. These investors are willing to purchase a bond whose annual interest rate is based on the actual performance of the Standard & Poor's 500 stock market index.

First Boston Corporation recommends to UIT's management that it consider issuing a five-year bond whose annual interest rate is based on the actual performance of the S&P 500. The risk with issuing such a bond is that UIT's annual interest cost is uncertain, since it depends on the performance of the S&P 500. However, suppose that the following two transactions are entered into:

1. On January 1, UIT agrees to issue, using First Boston Corporation as the underwriter, a $100 million, five-year bond issue whose annual interest rate is the actual performance of the S&P 500 that year minus 300 basis points. The minimum interest rate, however, is set at zero. The annual interest payments are made on December 31.

2. UIT enters into a five-year, $100 million notional principal amount interest rate/equity swap with First Boston Corporation in which each year for the next five years UIT agrees to pay 7.9% to First Boston Corporation and First Boston Corporation agrees to pay the actual performance of the S&P 500 that year minus 300 basis points. The terms of the swap call for the payments to be made on December 31 of each year. Thus, the swap payments coincide with the payments that must be made on the bond issue. Also, as part of the swap agreement, if the S&P 500 minus 300 basis points results in a negative value. First Boston Corporation pays nothing to UIT.

Let's look at what has been accomplished with these two transactions from the perspective of UIT. Specifically, focus on the payments that must be made by UIT on the bond issue and the swap, and the payments that it will receive from the swap. These are summarized here:

Interest payments on bond issue:	S&P 500 return – 300 b.p.
Swap payment from First Boston:	S&P 500 return – 300 b.p.
Swap payment to First Boston:	7.9%
Net interest cost:	7.9%

Thus, the net interest cost is a fixed rate despite the bond issue paying an interest rate tied to the S&P 500. This was accomplished with the interest rate/equity swap.

There are several questions that should be addressed. First, what was the advantage to UIT to entering into this transaction? Recall that if UIT issued a bond, First Boston Corporation estimated that UIT would have to pay 8% annually. Thus, UIT has saved 10 basis points (8% minus 7.9%) per year. Second, why would investors purchase this bond issue? As explained in previous chapters, there are restrictions imposed on institutional investors as to types of investments. For example, a depository institution may not be entitled to purchase common stock; however, it may be permitted to purchase a bond of an issuer such as UIT despite the fact that the interest rate is tied to the performance of common stocks. Third, isn't First Boston Corporation exposed to the risk of the performance of the S&P 500? While it is difficult to demonstrate at this point, there are ways that First Boston Corporation can protect itself.

Although this may seem like a far-fetched application, it is not. In fact, it is quite common. Debt instruments created by using swaps are commonly referred to as structured notes, which we discussed in Chapter 20.

INTEREST RATE CAPS AND FLOORS

An interest rate cap and floor is an agreement between two parties in which one party, for an upfront premium, agrees to compensate the other if a designated interest rate, called the **reference rate**, is different from a predetermined level. When one party agrees to pay the other if the reference rate exceeds a predetermined level, the agreement is referred to as an **interest rate cap** or **ceiling**. The agreement is referred to as an **interest rate floor** when one party agrees to pay the other if the reference rate falls below a predetermined level. The predetermined level of the reference interest rate is called the **strike rate**. The terms of an interest rate agreement include:

1. The reference rate.
2. The strike rate that sets the ceiling or floor.
3. The length of the agreement.
4. The frequency of settlement.
5. The notional principal amount.

For example, suppose that C buys an interest rate cap from D with terms as follows:

1. The reference rate is six-month LIBOR.
2. The strike rate is 8%.
3. The agreement is for seven years.
4. Settlement is every six months.
5. The notional principal amount is $20 million.

Under this agreement, every six months for the next seven years, D will pay C whenever six-month LIBOR exceeds 8%. The payment will equal the dollar value of the difference between six-month LIBOR and 8% times the notional principal amount divided by two. For example, if six months from now six-month LIBOR is 11%, then D will pay C 3% (11% minus 8%) times $20 million divided by 2, or $300,000. If six-month LIBOR is 8% or less, D does not have to pay anything to C.

As an example of an interest rate floor, assume the same terms as the interest rate cap we just illustrated. In this case, if six-month LIBOR is 11%, C receives nothing from D, but if six-month LIBOR is less than 8%, D compensates C for the difference. For example, if six-month LIBOR is 7%, D will pay C $100,000 (8% minus 7%, times $20 million divided by 2).

Interest rate caps and floors can be combined to create an **interest rate collar**. This is done by buying an interest rate cap and selling an interest rate floor. Some commercial banks and investment banking firms now write options on interest rate agreements for customers. Options on caps are called **captions**, and options on floors are called **flotions**.

Risk/Return Characteristics

In an interest rate cap and floor, the buyer pays an upfront fee, which represents the maximum amount the buyer can lose and the maximum amount the writer of the agreement can gain. The only party that is required to perform is the writer of the interest rate agreement. The buyer of an interest rate cap benefits if the underlying interest rate rises above the strike rate because the seller (writer) must compensate the buyer. The buyer of an interest rate floor benefits if the interest rate falls below the strike rate because the seller (writer) must compensate the buyer.

How can we better understand interest rate caps and interest rate floors? In essence, these contracts are equivalent to a package of interest rate options. The question is what type of package of options is a cap and what type is a floor. Recall from our earlier discussion of the relationship between futures, forward rate agreements, and swaps that the relationship depends on whether the underlying is a rate or a fixed-income instrument. The same applies to call options, put options, caps, and floors.

If the underlying is considered a fixed-income instrument, its value changes inversely with interest rates. Therefore:

FOR A CALL OPTION ON A FIXED-INCOME INSTRUMENT:

1. interest rates increase → fixed-income instrument's price decreases → call option's value decreases and
2. interest rates decrease → fixed-income instrument's price increases → call option's value increases

FOR A PUT OPTION ON A FIXED-INCOME INSTRUMENT:

3. interest rates increase → fixed-income instrument's price decreases → put option's value increases and
4. interest rates decrease → fixed-income instrument's price increases → put option's value decreases

To summarize:

	WHEN INTEREST RATES	
Value of:	increase	decrease
Long call	Decrease	Increase
Short call	Increase	Decrease
Long put	Increase	Decrease
Short put	Decrease	Increase

For a cap and floor, the situation is as follows:

	WHEN INTEREST RATES	
Value of:	increase	decrease
Short cap	Decrease	Increase
Long cap	Increase	Decrease
Short floor	Increase	Decrease
Long floor	Decrease	Increase

Therefore, buying a cap (long cap) is equivalent to buying a package of puts on a fixed-income instrument and buying a floor (long floor) is equivalent to buying a package of calls on a fixed-income instrument.

On the other hand, if an option is viewed as an option on an interest rate (underlying), then buying a cap (long cap) is equivalent to buying a package of calls on interest rates. Buying a floor (long floor) is equivalent to buying a package of puts on interest rates.

It is important to note that, once again, a complex contract can be seen to be a package of basic contracts, or options in the case of interest rate agreements.

Applications

To see how interest rate agreements can be used for asset/liability management, consider the problems faced by the commercial bank and the life insurance company in the first illustration in the chapter of the application of interest rate swaps.

Recall that the bank's objective is to lock in an interest rate spread over its cost of funds. Yet because it raises funds through a variable-rate instrument and is basically borrowing short term, the bank's cost of funds is uncertain. The bank may be able to purchase a cap so that the cap rate plus the cost of purchasing the cap is less than the rate it is earning on its fixed-rate commercial loans. If short-term rates decline, the bank does not benefit from the cap, but its cost of funds declines. The cap therefore allows the bank to impose a ceiling on its cost of funds while retaining the opportunity to benefit from a decline in rates. This use of a cap is consistent with the view of an interest rate cap as simply a package of call options.

The bank can reduce the cost of purchasing the cap by selling a floor. In this case, the bank agrees to pay the buyer of the floor if the underlying rate falls below the strike rate. The bank receives a fee for selling the floor, but it has sold off its opportunity to benefit from a decline in rates below the strike rate. By buying a cap and selling a floor, the bank has created a range for its cost of funds (or a collar).

Consider again from that same first example of the application of interest rate swaps the problem of the life insurance company that has guaranteed a 9% rate on a GIC for the next five years and is considering the purchase of an attractive floating-rate instrument in a private placement transaction. The risk that the company faces is that interest rates will fall so that it will not earn enough to realize the 9% guaranteed rate plus a spread. The life insurance company may be able to purchase a floor to set a lower bound on its investment return, yet retain the opportunity to benefit should rates increase. To reduce the cost of purchasing the floor, the life insurance company can sell an interest rate cap. By doing so, however, it gives up the opportunity of benefiting from an increase in the six-month Treasury bill rate above the strike rate of the interest rate cap.

Key Points That You Should Understand Before Proceeding

1. An interest rate agreement is an agreement between two parties in which one party, for an upfront premium, agrees to compensate the other if the reference rate is different from the strike rate.
2. A cap is an interest rate agreement in which one party agrees to pay the other if the reference rate exceeds the strike rate; an interest rate floor is an interest rate agreement in which one party agrees to pay the other if the reference rate falls below the strike rate.
3. A collar is created by buying an interest rate cap and selling an interest rate floor.
4. An interest rate floor can be used by a depository institution to lock in an interest rate spread over its cost of funds but maintain the opportunity to benefit if rates decline.
5. The buyer of a floating-rate asset can use an interest rate floor to establish a lower bound on its investment return, yet retain the opportunity to benefit should rates increase.

CREDIT DERIVATIVES[16]

Interest rate derivatives such as Treasury futures contracts, Treasury options, interest rate swaps, caps, and floors can be used to control interest rate risk with respect to changes in the level of interest rates. However, there are also changes in the credit spread that must be controlled for by investors when investing in non-Treasury securities or by corporations when issuing bonds. The agency note futures contracts dis-

---

[16] This section draws from Chapter 5 in Frank J. Fabozzi, *Bond Portfolio Management*, 2nd edition (New Hope, PA: Frank J. Fabozzi Associates, 2001).

cussed in Chapter 26 can be used to partially control the changes in credit spread for corporate bonds. However, the correlation between the credit spread on agency debentures and corporate bonds (both investment grade and noninvestment grade) is not perfect. Moreover, the agency note futures contract is relatively new. (Initial trading began in 2000.) What has developed in the over-the-counter or dealer market are derivative instruments that provide protection against credit risk. These products are referred to as **credit derivatives**.

We will describe three main types of credit derivatives: credit options, credit forwards, and credit swaps. Before we describe these products, let's take a closer look at the meaning of credit risk.

Credit Risk

An investor who lends funds by purchasing a bond issue is exposed to three types of credit risk: (1) default risk, (2) credit spread risk, and (3) downgrade risk.

Default Risk.

Traditionally, credit risk is defined as the risk that the issuer will fail to satisfy the terms of the obligation with respect to the timely payment of interest and repayment of the amount borrowed. This form of credit risk is called *default risk*. If a default does occur, this does not mean the investor loses the entire amount invested. There is a certain percentage of the investment that can be expected to be recovered. This is called the *recovery rate*.

Credit Spread Risk.

Even in the absence of default, an investor is concerned that the market value of a bond will decline and/or the price performance of that bond will be worse than that of other bonds against which the investor is compared. To understand this, recall that the price of a bond changes in the opposite direction to the change in the yield required by the market. Thus, if yields in the economy increase, the price of a bond declines, and vice versa.

As explained in Chapter 11, the yield on a bond is made up of two components: (1) the yield on a similar default-free bond issue and (2) a premium above the yield on a default-free bond issue necessary to compensate for the risks associated with the bond. The risk premium is referred to as a *spread*. In the United States, Treasury issues are the benchmark yields because they are believed to be default free, they are highly liquid, and Treasury issues are not callable (with the exception of some old issues). The part of the risk premium or spread attributable to default risk is called the *credit spread*.

The price performance of a non-Treasury bond issue and its return that the investor will realize by holding that issue over some time period will depend on how the credit spread changes. If the credit spread increases—investors say that the spread has "widened"—the market price of the bond issue will decline (assuming Treasury rates have not changed). The risk that an issuer's debt obligation will decline due to an increase in the credit spread is called **credit spread risk**.

This risk exists for an individual issue, for issues in a particular industry or economic sector, and for all non-Treasury issues in the economy. For example, in general during economic recessions investors are concerned that issuers will face a decline in cash flows that would be used to service its bond obligations. As a result, the credit spread tends to widen for non-Treasury issuers and the prices of all such issues throughout the economy will decline.

Downgrade Risk.

While there are investors who seek to allocate funds among different sectors of the bond market to capitalize on anticipated changes in credit spreads, an investor investigating the credit quality of an individual issue is concerned with the prospects of the credit spread increasing for that particular issue. Market participants gauge the default risk of an issue by looking at the credit ratings assigned to issues by the rating agencies—Moody's Investors Service, Inc., Standard & Poor's Corporation, and Fitch. Once a credit rating is assigned to a debt obligation, a rating agency monitors the credit quality of the issuer and can reassign a different credit rating. An improvement in the credit quality of an issue or issuer is rewarded with a better credit rating, referred to as an *upgrade*; a deterioration in the credit rating of an issue or issuer is penalized by the assignment of an inferior credit rating, referred to as a downgrade. An unanticipated downgrading of an issue or issuer increases the credit spread and results in a decline in the price of the issue or the issuer's bonds. This risk is referred to as **downgrade risk** and is closely related to credit spread risk.

Credit Options

Credit options come in two types. The first type is a **credit option written on an underlying issue**. For this type of credit option the payout is determined based on whether a default occurs for the underlying issue. The amount of the payout is a fixed amount determined at the time the option is purchased. If a default does not occur by the option's expiration date, there is no payout.

The same type of credit option—which is basically a "binary option" because it has only two possible payoffs, zero if there is no default and the predetermined fixed sum if there is a default—can also be written where the payoff is based upon whether or not the issue is downgraded. Then the payoff is specified by the amount of the loss expected if there is a downgrade. A credit option can also be written in which a default is defined in broader terms than simply failure to meet an interest or principal payment. As an example, the event that triggers a payoff can be defined in terms of whether some financial measure is above or below a certain value, such as, a minimum net worth. For example, this form of a credit option can specify that if the issuer's book value falls below $150 million or less, then there is a payoff.

For the second type of credit option, the payoff is determined by the level of the credit spread over a referenced security, typically a Treasury security. The strike is specified in terms of the level of the credit spread. The payoff can specify that if the credit spread for the issue is greater than the strike spread, there is a payoff. For example, suppose that the referenced issue is a bond of company XYZ. Suppose the current spread is 200 basis points. The strike spread can be specified as 250 basis points, and that if the credit spread by the expiration date exceeds that strike spread there is a payoff. Alternatively, the payoff can specify that if the credit spread is less than the strike, then there is a payoff.

The tricky part of the payoff for an option written on a credit spread is the determination of the payoff. Remember that if interest rates increase in general, the price of the issue underlying the option will decline, and vice versa. What the payoff must do is separate the change in the price of the underlying issue due to a change in the general level of rates and the change in the credit spread. This is done by having the payoff based on the difference in the actual credit spread and the strike spread multiplied by a specified notional principal amount and by a **risk factor**. For purposes of our discussion, it is not necessary to understand how the risk factor is computed.[17] Instead,

---

[17] The risk factor is a quantitative measure that is related to the duration of the underlying asset.

let's see how the payoff is determined. The payoff function is determined as follows if the credit option is based on the credit spread being greater than the strike spread.

$$(\text{Credit spread} - \text{Strike spread}) \times \text{Notional principal amount} \times \text{Risk factor}$$

where the credit spread and the strike spread are expressed in decimal form.

For example, suppose that for the issue of company XYZ the strike spread is 250 basis points and that the notional principal amount of the credit option is $10 million. Suppose also that the risk factor for this issue is 5. If at the expiration date of this option the credit spread for this issue is 300 basis points, then the payoff is

$$(0.030 - 0.025) \times \$10,000,000 \times 5 = \$250,000$$

If the credit spread at the expiration date is 250 basis points or less, then there is no payoff.

If the credit spread option had a payoff based on the credit spread narrowing, then the payoff function would be

$$(\text{Strike spread} - \text{Credit spread}) \times \text{Notional principal amount} \times \text{Risk factor}$$

Credit Forward Contracts

The underlying for a **credit forward contract** is the credit spread. The payoff depends on the credit spread at the settlement date of the contract. The payoff is positive (i.e., the party receives cash) if the credit spread moves in favor of the party at the settlement date. The party makes a payment if the credit spread moves against the party at the settlement date.

For example, suppose that a manager has a view that the credit spread will increase (i.e., widen) to more than the current 250 basis points in one year for an issue of company XYZ. Then the payoff function for this credit forward contract would be

$$(\text{Credit spread at settlement date} - 0.025) \times \text{Notional principal amount} \times \text{Risk factor}$$

Assuming that the notional principal amount is $10 million and the risk factor is 5, then if the credit spread at the settlement date is 325 basis points, then the amount that will be received by the manager is

$$(0.035 - 0.025) \times \$10,000,000 \times 5 = \$500,000$$

Instead, suppose that the credit spread at the settlement date decreased to 190 basis points, then the manager would have to pay out $300,000 as shown below.

$$(0.019 - 0.025) \times \$10,000,000 \times 5 = \$300,000$$

In general, if an investor takes a position in a credit forward contract to benefit from an increase in the credit spread, then the payoff would be as follows:

$$(\text{Credit spread at settlement date} - \text{Credit spread in contract})$$
$$\times \text{Notional principal amount} \times \text{Risk factor}$$

For an investor taking a position that the credit spread will decrease, the payoff is

$$(\text{Credit spread in contract} - \text{Credit spread at settlement date})$$
$$\times \text{Notional principal amount} \times \text{Risk factor}$$

Credit Swaps

There are two different types of credit swaps: **credit default swaps** and **total return swaps**. Credit default swaps are used by an investor to shift credit exposure to a credit protection seller. A total return swap is used by an investor to increase credit exposure.

Credit default swaps come in two forms: credit insurance and swapping risky credit payments for certain fixed payments. With **credit insurance**, the buyer pays a fee to enter into a credit default swap. The buyer receives a payment every period for the life of the contract if a referenced credit defaults on a payment. While this contract is called a swap, it is basically a package of credit options. Rather than a payment being contingent on an individual referenced credit, the referenced credit can be a portfolio of bonds. The second form of credit default swap is one in which an investor agrees to exchange the total return on a credit risky asset for known periodic payments from the counterparty. The payments are exchanged based on what happens to the value of the credit risky asset. If it declines in value, the investor will receive a payment to compensate for the decline in value plus a periodic payment from the counterparty.

With a total return credit swap the investor agrees to pay all cash flows from the referenced asset or assets including the change in the value of the referenced asset or assets. The investor receives in exchange a floating rate plus any depreciation of the referenced asset to the credit swap seller.

Key Points That You Should Understand Before Proceeding

1. Credit derivatives can be used to control for changes in the credit spread.
2. Credit risk includes three types of risk: (1) the risk that the issuer will default (default risk), (2) the risk that the credit spread will increase (credit spread risk), and (3) the risk that an issue will be downgraded (downgrade risk).
3. Credit options include credit options written on an underlying issue and credit spread options.
4. For a credit forward contract the underlying is a credit spread, with the payoff depending on the credit spread at the settlement date of the contract;
5. There are two different types of credit swaps: credit default swaps and total return swaps.
6. Credit default swaps are used by an investor to shift credit exposure to a credit protection seller while a total return swap is used by an investor to increase credit exposure.
7. Credit default swaps come in two forms: credit insurance and swapping risky credit payments for certain fixed payments.

SUMMARY

An interest rate swap is an agreement specifying that the parties exchange interest payments at designated times. In a typical swap, one party will make fixed-rate payments and the other will make floating-rate payments, with payments based on the notional principal amount. There are more complex swap structures such as swaps with a varying notional principal amount, basis swaps, constant maturity swaps, swaptions, and forward start swaps. Participants in financial markets use interest rate swaps to alter the cash flow characteristics of their assets or liabilities, or to capitalize on perceived capital market inefficiencies. A swap has the

risk/return profile of a package of forward contracts or a combination of positions in the cash bond market.

An interest rate cap and floor allows one party the right to receive compensation from the writer of the agreement for an upfront premium if a designated interest rate is different from a predetermined level. An interest rate cap calls for one party to receive a payment if a designated interest rate is above the predetermined level. An interest rate floor lets one party receive a payment if a designated interest rate is below the predetermined level. An interest rate cap can be used to establish a ceiling on the cost of funding; an interest rate floor can be used to establish a floor return.

Interest rate derivatives can be used to control interest rate risk with respect to changes in the level of interest rates. Credit derivatives can be used to control the credit risk of a security or a portfolio of securities. Credit risk includes three types of risk: (1) the risk that the issuer will default (default risk), (2) the risk that the credit spread will increase (credit spread risk), and (3) the risk that an issue will be downgraded (downgrade risk). The three main types of credit derivatives are credit options, credit forwards, and credit swaps. Credit options include credit options written on an underlying issue and credit spread options. There are two different types of credit swaps: credit default swaps and total return swaps. Credit default swaps are used by an investor to shift credit exposure to a credit protection seller while a total return default swap is used by an investor to increase credit exposure.

KEY TERMS

- **Accreting swap, 593**
- **Amortizing swap, 593**
- **Asset swap, 583**
- **Basis rate swap, 593**
- **Bullet swap, 593**
- **Buy-back (or close-out swap or cancellation swap), 593**
- **Caption, 598**
- **Credit default swap, 604**
- **Credit derivative, 601**
- **Credit forward contract, 603**
- **Credit insurance, 604**
- **Credit option, 602**
- **Credit option written on an underlying issue, 602**
- **Credit spread risk, 601**
- **Downgrade risk, 602**
- **Fixed-rate payer, 578**
- **Floating-rate payer, 578**
- **Flotion, 598**

- **Forward start swap, 595**
- **Interest rate cap (or ceiling), 598**
- **Interest rate collar, 598**
- **Interest rate/equity swap, 596**
- **Interest rate floor, 598**
- **Interest rate swap, 578**
- **Liability swap, 583**
- **Notional principal amount, 578**
- **Payer swaption, 595**
- **Plain vanilla swap, 581**
- **Receiver swaption, 595**
- **Reference rate, 598**
- **Risk factor, 602**
- **Roller coaster swap, 593**
- **Strike rate, 598**
- **Swap reversal, 592**
- **Swap sale (or swap assignment), 593**
- **Swaption, 595**
- **Total return credit swap, 604**

QUESTIONS

1. At any time in the life of the interest rate swap, does the notional principal become a cash flow to either party or to the intermediary?
2. Consider a swap with these features: maturity is five years, notional principal is $100 million, payments occur every six months, the fixed-rate payer pays a rate of 9.05% and receives LIBOR, while the floating-rate payer pays LIBOR and receives 9%. Now, suppose that at a payment date, LIBOR is at 6.5%. What is each party's payment and receipt at that date?
3. A bank borrows funds by issuing CDs that carry a variable rate equal to the yield of the six-month Treasury bill plus 50 basis points. The bank gets the chance to invest in a seven-year loan that will pay a fixed rate of 7%. So, the bank wants to engage in an interest rate swap designed to lock in an interest spread of 75 basis points. Give the outlines of two possible swaps: one designed to change the asset's cash flow into a variable rate, and the other designed to change the liability's cash flow into a fixed rate.
4. Identify two factors that have contributed to the growth of the interest rate swap market.

5. a. Describe the role of the intermediary in a swap.
    b. What are the two factors that led swap brokers/intermediaries to act as principals or dealers?

6. Suppose a dealer quotes these terms on a five-year swap: fixed-rate payer to pay 9.5% for LIBOR flat and floating-rate payer to pay LIBOR flat for 9.2%.
    a. What is the dealer's bid–ask spread?
    b. How would the dealer quote the terms by reference to the yield on five-year Treasury notes, assuming this yield is 9%?

7. Explain the three major ways in which a party to a swap can reverse that position in the secondary market for swaps.

8. Why can a fixed-rate payer in an interest rate swap be viewed as being short the bond market, and the floating-rate payer be viewed as being long the bond market?

9. a. Why would a depository institution use an interest rate swap?
    b. Why would a corporation that plans to raise funds in the debt market use an interest rate swap?

10. Suppose that a life insurance company has issued a three-year GIC with a fixed rate of 10%. Under what circumstances might it be feasible for the life insurance company to invest the funds in a floating-rate security and enter into a three-year interest rate swap in which it pays a floating rate and receives a fixed rate?

11. The following excerpt is taken from an article entitled "IRS Rule to Open Swaps to Pension Funds" that appeared in the November 18, 1991 issue of *BondWeek*, pp. 1 and 2:

    A proposed Internal Revenue Service rule that gives tax-free status to income earned on swaps by pension funds and other tax-exempt institutions is expected to spur pension fund use of these products, say swap and pension fund professionals. . . . [Note: the proposal has subsequently been passed]

    . . . UBS Asset Management has received permission from most of its pension fund clients to use interest rate and currency swaps in its fixed-income portfolios and is awaiting the IRS regulation before stepping into the market, says Kenneth Choie, v.p. and head of research and product development . . . "The IRS' proposed rule is great news for pension fund managers," as the use of swaps can enhance returns and lower transaction costs, Choie says. . . .

    While some pension funds are exploring the swap market, pension fund consultants underscore that the funds' entrance into the market is likely to be slow. Counterparty risk has been a more formidable obstacle than the ambiguity of the tax status of income from interest rate and currency swaps, says Paul Burik, director of research at Ennis, Knupp & Associates, a pension fund consulting firm.

    a. What is meant by counterparty risk?
    b. Why would counterparty risk slow the growth of use of the swap market by pension funds?

12. A portfolio manager buys a swaption with a strike rate of 6.5% that entitles the portfolio manager to enter into an interest rate swap to pay a fixed rate and receive a floating rate. The term of the swaption is five years.
    a. Is this swaption a payer swaption or a receiver swaption? Explain why.
    b. What does the strike rate of 6.5% mean?

13. The manager of a savings and loan association is considering the use of a swap as part of its asset/liability strategy. The swap would be used to convert the payments of its portfolio of fixed-rate residential mortgage loans into a floating payment.
    a. What is the risk with using a plain vanilla or generic interest rate swap?

b. Why might a manager consider using an interest rate swap in which the notional principal amount declines over time?

c. Why might a manager consider buying a swaption?

14. Suppose that a corporation is considering using an interest rate swap in conjunction with the offering of a floating-rate bond issue. That is, the corporation wants to use the swap to change the funding arrangement from a floating rate to a fixed rate.

a. Would the corporation enter into a swap in which it pays or receives a fixed rate?

b. Suppose that the corporation does not plan to issue the bond for one year. What type of swap can the firm's management enter into in order to set the terms of the swap today?

15. The Window Wipers Union (a pension sponsor) and the All-Purpose Asset Management Corporation (a money management firm) entered into a four-year swap with a notional principal amount of $150 million with the following terms: Every year for the next four years the Window Wipers Union agrees to pay All-Purpose Asset Management the return realized on the Standard & Poor's 500 stock index for the year minus 400 basis points and receive from All-Purpose Asset Management 9%.

a. What type of swap is this?

b. If in the first year when payments are to be exchanged, suppose that the return on the S&P 500 is 7%. What is the amount of the payment that the two parties must make to each other?

16. There are several depository institutions that offer certificates of deposit where the interest rate paid is based on the performance of the Standard & Poor's 500 stock index.

a. What is the risk that a depository institution encounters by offering such certificates of deposit?

b. How do you think that a depository institution can protect itself against the risk you identified in part (a)?

17. Suppose a savings and loan association buys an interest rate cap that has these terms: the reference rate is the six-month Treasury bill rate; the cap will last for five years; payment is semiannual; the strike rate is 5.5%; and the notional principal amount is $10 million. Suppose further that at the end of some six-month period, the six-month Treasury bill rate is 6.1%.

a. What is the amount of the payment that the savings and loan association will receive?

b. What would the writer of this cap pay if the six-month Treasury rate were 5.45% instead of 6.1%?

18. What is the relationship between an interest rate agreement and an interest rate option?

19. How can an interest rate collar be created?

20. Acme Insurance Company has purchased a five-year bond whose interest rate floats with LIBOR. Specifically, the interest rate in a given year is equal to LIBOR plus 200 basis points. At the same time the insurance company purchases this bond, it enters into a floor agreement with Goldman Sachs in which the notional principal amount is $35 million with a strike rate of 6%. The premium Acme Insurance Company agrees to pay Goldman Sachs each year is $300,000.

a. Suppose at the time that it is necessary to determine if a payment must be made by Goldman Sachs, LIBOR is 9%. How much must Goldman Sachs pay Acme Insurance Company?

b. Suppose at the time that it is necessary to determine if a payment must be made by Goldman Sachs, LIBOR is 3%. How much must Goldman Sachs pay Acme Insurance Company?

    c. What is the minimum interest rate that Acme Insurance Company has locked in each year for the next five years by entering into this floor agreement and buying the five-year bond, ignoring the premium that Acme Insurance Company must make each year?

21. Why is risk factor used in determining the payoff for an option on a credit spread?

22. The manager of a bond portfolio enters into an option on a credit spread for company W based on the credit spread of an issuer widening from its current level of 320 basis points. Suppose that the strike spread for the option is 320 basis points and notional principal amount is $20 million. Suppose also that the risk factor for this issue is 4.

    a. If at the expiration date of this option the credit spread for this issue of company W is 400 basis points, what is the dollar amount of the payoff?

    b. If at the expiration date of this option the credit spread for this issue of company W is 200 basis points, what is the dollar amount of the payoff?

23. A portfolio manager has a view that the credit spread for the bonds of Zen.com will increase (i.e., widen) to more than the current 450 basis points in one year. How can the manager use a credit forward contract to capitalize on this view?

The Market for Foreign Exchange Rate Risk Control Instruments

Learning Objectives

After reading this chapter, you will understand

- what is meant by a foreign exchange rate.
- the different ways that a foreign exchange rate can be quoted (direct versus indirect).
- the conventions for quoting foreign exchange rates.
- what foreign exchange risk is.
- a cross rate and how to calculate a theoretical cross rate.
- what triangular arbitrage is.
- the foreign exchange market structure.
- what the euro is.
- the fundamental determinants of exchange rates: purchasing power parity and interest rate parity.
- the different instruments for hedging foreign exchange risk: forwards, futures, options, and swaps.
- the limitations of forward and futures contracts for hedging long-dated foreign exchange risk.
- how a forward exchange rate is determined and covered interest arbitrage.
- the basic currency swap structure and the motivation for using currency swaps.

The fundamental fact of international finance is that different countries issue different currencies, and the relative values of those currencies may change quickly, substantially, and without warning. The change, moreover, may either reflect economic developments or be a response to political events that make no economic sense. As a result, the risk that a currency's value may change adversely, which is called *foreign exchange risk* or *currency risk*, is an important consideration for all participants in the international financial markets. Investors who purchase securities denominated in a currency different from their own must worry about the return from those securities after adjusting for changes in the exchange rate. Firms that issue obligations denominated in a foreign currency face the risk that the effective value of the cash payments they owe to investors is very uncertain.

In this chapter, we provide a review of the instruments that can be used to control the risk of an adverse movement in a foreign currency. These instruments include forward contracts, futures contracts, options, and currency swaps. We begin our discussion with a review of the foreign exchange rate market.

FOREIGN EXCHANGE RATES

An **exchange rate** is defined as the amount of one currency that can be exchanged for a unit of another currency. In fact, the exchange rate is the price of one currency in terms of another currency. And, depending on circumstances, one could define either currency as the price for the other. So, exchange rates can be quoted "in either direction." For example, the exchange rate between the U.S. dollar and the Swiss franc could be quoted in one of two ways:

1. The amount of U.S. dollars necessary to acquire one Swiss franc, and this is the dollar price of one Swiss franc; or
2. The number of Swiss francs necessary to acquire one U.S. dollar, or the Swiss franc price of one dollar.

Exchange Rate Quotation Conventions

Exchange rate quotations may be either *direct* or *indirect*. The difference depends on identifying one currency as a local currency and the other as a foreign currency. For example, from the perspective of a U.S. participant, the local currency would be U.S. dollars, and any other currency, such as Swiss francs, would be the foreign currency. From the perspective of a Swiss participant, the local currency would be Swiss francs, and other currencies, such as U.S. dollars, the foreign currency. A **direct quote** is the number of units of a local currency exchangeable for one unit of a foreign currency.

An **indirect quote** is the number of units of a foreign currency that can be exchanged for one unit of a local currency. Looking at this from a U.S. participant's perspective, a quote indicating the number of dollars exchangeable for one unit of a foreign currency is a direct quote. An indirect quote from the same participant's perspective would be the number of units of the foreign currency that can be exchanged for one U.S. dollar. Obviously, from the point of view of a non-U.S. participant, the number of U.S. dollars exchangeable for one unit of a non-U.S. currency is an indirect quote; the number of units of a non-U.S. currency exchangeable for a U.S. dollar is a direct quote.

Given a direct quote, we can obtain an indirect quote (which is simply the reciprocal of the direct quote), and vice versa. For example, suppose that on December 22, 2000, a U.S. participant is given a direct quote of 0.6071 U.S. dollars for one Swiss franc. That is, the price of a Swiss franc is $0.6071. The reciprocal of the direct quote is 1.6472, which would be the indirect quote for the U.S. participant; that is, one U.S. dollar can be exchanged for 1.6472 Swiss francs, which is the Swiss franc price of a dollar.

If the number of units of a foreign currency that can be obtained for one dollar—the price of a dollar in that currency or indirect quotation—rises, the dollar is said to appreciate relative to the currency, and the currency is said to depreciate. Thus, appreciation means a decline in the direct quotation.

Foreign Exchange Risk

From the perspective of a U.S. investor, the cash flows of assets denominated in a foreign currency expose the investor to uncertainty as to the actual level of the cash flow measured in U.S. dollars. The actual number of U.S. dollars that the investor eventually gets depends on the exchange rate between the U.S. dollar and the foreign currency at the time the nondollar cash flow is received and exchanged for U.S. dollars. If the foreign currency depreciates (declines in value) relative to the U.S. dollar (that is, the U.S. dollar appreciates), the dollar value of the cash flows will be proportionately less. This risk is referred to as *foreign exchange risk*.

Any investor who purchases an asset denominated in a currency that is not the medium of exchange in the investor's country faces foreign exchange risk. For example, a Greek investor who acquires a yen-denominated Japanese bond is exposed to the risk that the Japanese yen will decline in value relative to the Greek drachma.

Foreign exchange risk is a consideration for the issuer, too. Suppose that IBM issues bonds denominated in Japanese yen. IBM's foreign exchange risk is that, at the time the coupon interest payments must be made and the principal repaid, the U.S. dollar will have depreciated relative to the Japanese yen, requiring that IBM pay more dollars to satisfy its obligation.

Key Points That You Should Understand Before Proceeding

1. An exchange rate is defined as the amount of one currency that can be exchanged for a unit of another currency and can be expressed as either a direct or indirect quote.
2. Any investor who purchases an asset denominated in a currency that is not the medium of exchange of the investor's country faces foreign exchange risk.
3. A borrower who has liabilities denominated in a currency that is not the medium of exchange of the borrower's country faces foreign exchange risk.

SPOT MARKET

The **spot exchange rate market** is the market for settlement of a foreign exchange transaction within two business days. (The spot exchange rate is also known as the *cash exchange rate*.) Since the early 1970s, exchange rates among major currencies have been free to float, with market forces determining the relative value of a currency.[1] Thus, each day a currency's price relative to that of another freely floating currency may stay the same, increase, or decrease.

A key factor affecting the expectation of changes in a country's exchange rate with another currency is the relative expected inflation rate of the two countries. Spot exchange rates adjust to compensate for the relative inflation rate. This adjustment reflects the so-called **purchasing power parity** relationship, which posits that the exchange rate—the domestic price of the foreign currency—is proportional to the domestic inflation rate, and inversely proportional to foreign inflation.

Let's look at what happens when the spot exchange rate changes between two currencies. Suppose that on day 1 the spot exchange rate between the U.S. dollar and country X is $0.7966 and on the next day, day 2, it changes to $0.8011. Consequently, on day 1, one currency unit of country X costs $0.7966. On day 2, it costs more U.S. dollars, $0.8011 to buy one currency unit of country X. Thus, the currency unit of country X *appreciated* relative to the U.S. dollar from day 1 to day 2, or, what amounts to the same thing, the U.S. dollar *depreciated* relative to the currency of country X from

---

[1] In practice, national monetary authorities can intervene in the foreign exchange market for their currency for a variety of economic reasons, so the current foreign exchange system is sometimes referred to as a "managed" floating-rate system.

day 1 to day 2. Suppose further that on day 3 the spot exchange rate for one currency of country X is $0.8000. Relative to day 2, the U.S. dollar *appreciated* relative to the currency of country X or, equivalently, the currency of country X depreciated relative to the U.S. dollar.

Although quotes can be either direct or indirect, the problem is defining from whose perspective the quote is given. Foreign exchange conventions in fact standardize the ways quotes are given. Because of the importance of the U.S. dollar in the international financial system, currency quotations are all relative to the U.S. dollar. When dealers quote, they either give U.S. dollars per unit of foreign currency (a direct quote from the U.S. perspective) or the number of units of the foreign currency per U.S. dollar (an indirect quote from the U.S. perspective). Quoting in terms of U.S. dollars per unit of foreign currency is called *American terms*, while quoting in terms of the number of units of the foreign currency per U.S. dollar is called *European terms*. The dealer convention is to use European terms in quoting foreign exchange with a few exceptions. The British pound, the Irish pound, the Australian dollar, the New Zealand dollar, and the European Currency Unit (discussed later) are exceptions that are quoted in American terms.

Cross Rates

Barring any government restrictions, riskless arbitrage will assure that the exchange rate between two countries will be the same in both countries. The theoretical exchange rate between two countries other than the United States can be inferred from their exchange rates with the U.S. dollar. Rates computed in this way are referred to as *theoretical* **cross rates**. They would be computed as follows for two countries, X and Y:

$$\frac{\text{Quote in American terms of currency X}}{\text{Quote in American terms of currency Y}}$$

To illustrate how this is done, let's calculate the theoretical cross rate between Swiss francs and Japanese yen using the following exchange rates obtained from Yahoo finance on December 22, 2000.[2] The spot exchange rate for the two currencies in American terms is $0.6071 per Swiss franc and $ 0.008864 per Japanese yen. Then, the number of units of yen (currency Y) per unit of Swiss franc (currency X) is:

$$\frac{\$0.6071}{\$0.008864} = 68.49 \text{ yen per Swiss franc}$$

Taking the reciprocal gives the number of Swiss francs exchangeable for one Japanese yen. In our example, it is 0.0146.

In the real world, it is rare that the theoretical cross rate, as computed from actual dealer dollar exchange rate quotes, will differ from the actual cross rate quoted by dealers. When the discrepancy is large by comparison with the transactions costs of buying and selling the currencies, a riskless arbitrage opportunity arises. Arbitraging to take advantage of cross-rate mispricing is called **triangular arbitrage**, so named because it involves positions in three currencies—the U.S. dollar and the two foreign currencies. The arbitrage keeps actual cross rates in line with theoretical cross rates.

---

[2] http://finance.yahoo.com. The original source for the quote is Reuters.

Dealers

Exchange rates reported in daily periodicals (such as the *Wall Street Journal* and the *New York Times*) and services such as Bloomberg Financial Markets and Reuters are indications of the rate at which a foreign currency can be purchased in the spot market. They are the rates for which the dealer is willing to sell foreign exchange. Foreign exchange dealers, however, do not quote one price. Instead, they quote an exchange rate at which they are willing to buy a foreign currency and one at which they are willing to sell a foreign currency. That is, they quote a bid–ask spread. Here are the bid and ask (in terms of the number of the currency to acquire a U.S. dollar) for selected currencies as reported by Reuters on December 24:

Currency	Bid	Ask	Updated
Japanese yen	112.88	112.93	07:48 GMT / 24 DEC 2000
British pound	1.4725	1.4735	07:51 GMT / 24 DEC 2000
Swiss franc	1.6440	1.6450	07:48 GMT / 24 DEC 2000
Canadian dollar	1.5162	1.5172	07:48 GMT / 24 DEC 2000
Hong Kong dollar	7.7985	7.7995	03:01 GMT / 23 DEC 2000

Dealers in the foreign exchange market are large international banks and other financial institutions that specialize in making markets in foreign exchange. Commercial banks dominate the market. There is no organized exchange where foreign currency is traded, but dealers are linked by telephone and cable, and by various information transfer services. Consequently, the foreign exchange market can best be described as an interbank over-the-counter market. Most transactions between banks are done through foreign exchange brokers. Brokers are agents that do not take a position in the foreign currencies involved in the transaction. The normal size of a transaction is $1 million or more.

Dealers in the foreign exchange market realize revenue from one or more sources: (1) the bid–ask spread; (2) commissions charged on foreign exchange transactions; and (3) trading profits (appreciation of the currencies that dealers hold a long position in, or depreciation of the currencies that they have a short position in), or trading losses (depreciation of the currencies that they hold a long position in, or appreciation of the currencies that they have a short position in).

The Euro

The *European Union* consists of 15 European member countries that engage in European economic and political activities. In February 1992, the *Treaty on European Union of 1992* established that monetary union would take place by January 1999. The treaty, also called the *Maastricht Treaty* because its terms were agreed to at the European Council meeting in Maastricht (Netherlands) in December 1991, called for a single currency and monetary policy for member countries in Europe. Monetary policy was to be administered by the *European Central Bank*, which we discussed in Chapter 5. The *Economic and Monetary Union* (EMU) represents the member countries that are part of the European Union that have adopted the single currency and monetary policy.

At the time of the treaty, the single currency was to be the *economic currency unit* (ECU). This was the most widely used composite currency unit for capital market transactions. It was created in 1979 by the European Economic Community (EEC). The currencies included in the ECU were those that are members of the European Monetary System (EMS). The weight of each country's currency is figured according to the relative importance of a country's economic trade and financial sector within the European Economic Community (EEC). Exchange rates between the ECU and those countries not part of the EEC float freely. The exchange rate between countries in the EEC, however, may fluctuate only within a narrow range.

However, at a meeting of the heads of government in Madrid in December 1995, it was agreed that the name of the single currency would be called the **euro**. The reason that the ECU was not selected as the single currency was due to the opinion of Germans that the ECU was perceived to be a weak currency. For the countries of the European Union electing to be members of the EMU, there is a fixed conversion rate against their national currencies and relative to the euro. However, the value of the euro against all other currencies, including member states of the European Union that did not elect to join the EMU, will fluctuate according to market conditions.

Members of the EMU are said to be part of "euroland" or the "euro zone" because the euro became the only legal currency. Initially, the member countries maintained their own physical currencies, although they were fixed in value relative to the euro, and the euro had no physical existence. The actual euro currency will physically replace the individual currencies of the participating countries on January 1, 2002. At that time, the relevant authorities of each member country will begin to withdraw their old national currency from circulation and when this process is completed, their old national currency will no longer be legal tender.

To qualify as a participating country in the EMU requires that a country satisfy certain economic standards. These standards set for fiscal policy were that the annual fiscal deficit could be no more than 3% of gross disposable product (GDP); and total outstanding government indebtedness could be no more than 60% of GDP. There were many other economic, political, and even social requirements for entry. Moreover, a provision of the treaty mandated that the voters of a country seeking membership had to approve the joining of the EMU by popular referendum.

These objectives were also, more or less, achieved, and on January 4, 1999 (a Monday, the first business day of the year), the 11 countries shown in Table 31-1 adopted the single currency, the euro. (Greece was selected as a member on June 19, 2000, and joined the common currency on January 1, 2001.) The previous currency for each country and the fixed conversion rate relative to the euro are also shown in the table. At this time, the central banks of the 11 participating countries were discontinued and replaced by the European Central Bank.

The birth of the euro on January 4, 1999, was smooth and uneventful in terms of both market volatility and operations. There have been several notable outcomes of this event. First, despite many skeptics, it has worked; it has been viable and fairly stable. Second, it has given birth to a very large public and corporate capital market denominated in the euro. With respect to the capital market, the governments of all the participating countries issue their government debt denominated in euros. Thus, the differences in the rate on the government debt is based only on differences in credit risk—since there is no difference in currency risk—and is quite small. Table 31-1 provides an estimate of the credit spread, using Germany as a base.

On the corporate side, the primary issuance of corporate debt denominated in the euro has become large and liquid. Both European and U.S. investment banks play significant roles in these fundings. The secondary markets in these issues have also become quite liquid.

There has been one disappointment in the initiation of the euro and that has been its weakness against the U.S. dollar. From its inception at $1.17 per euro, the euro weakened considerably, reaching a low of $0.8229 on October 27, 2000. Among the reasons considered for this weakness of the euro were a lack of confidence in the ECB; the need for structural reforms in the key members; and the very strong economic growth in the U.S. relative to Europe.

Table 31-1   Members of the Economic Monetary Union

COUNTRY	PREVIOUS CURRENCY*	CONVERSION 1 EURO =	SPREAD TO GERMAN 10-YEAR YIELDS**
Initial Members:			
Germany	Mark	1.95583	—
Finland	Markka	5.94573	22 b.p.
Netherlands	Guilder	2.20371	17
France	Franc	6.55957	16
Spain	Peseta	166.386	31
Italy	Lire	1936.27	37
Belgium	Franc	40.3399	36
Luxembourg	Franc	40.3399	—
Austria	Schilling	13.7603	31
Ireland	Punt	0.787564	26
Portugal	Escudo	200.48239	
Subsequent Entrant:			
Greece	Drachma	340.750	79

* *Number of previous currency units of country.*
** *Source for the spreads is Bloomberg Financial Markets.*

On September 27, 2000, the group of seven central banks (G-7), composed of U.S., European, and Japanese central banks, conducted a unified currency support intervention to support the euro, the first unified intervention in support of a currency in two years. On October 5, 2000, the ECB raised interest rates to support this intervention.

Among the most analyzed aspect of the euro, in addition to its weakness, is who the next participants will be. On September 28, 2000, Denmark voted decisively against joining the EMU. Among the other potential candidates to join are the United Kingdom and Sweden.

Key Points That You Should Understand Before Proceeding

1. The spot exchange rate market is the market for settlement of a foreign exchange transaction within two business days.

2. Foreign exchange rates between major currencies are free to float, with market forces determining the relative value of a currency.

3. Spot exchange rates adjust to compensate for the relative inflation rate between two countries.

4. Dealers in the foreign exchange market are large international banks and other financial institutions that specialize in making markets in foreign exchange.

5. Member countries of the European Union that are part of the Economic and Monetary Union have adopted a single currency, the euro, and monetary policy is administered by the European Central Bank.

6. The euro was adopted in January 1, 1999, with a fixed conversion rate against member countries national currencies and relative to the euro, but the euro against all other currencies are free to fluctuate according to market conditions.

INSTRUMENTS FOR HEDGING FOREIGN EXCHANGE RISK

There are four instruments that borrowers and investors can use to protect against adverse foreign exchange rate movements: (1) currency forward contracts; (2) currency futures contracts; (3) currency options; and (4) currency swaps.

Currency Forward Contracts

Recall that a forward contract is one in which one party agrees to buy the underlying, and another party agrees to sell that same underlying, for a specific price at a designated date in the future. There are forward contracts in which the underlying is foreign exchange.

Most forward contracts have a maturity of less than two years. Longer-dated forward contracts have relatively large bid–ask spreads; that is, the size of the bid–ask spread for a given currency increases with the maturity of the contract. Consequently, forward contracts are not attractive for hedging long-dated foreign currency exposure.

As Chapter 26 emphasized, both forward and futures contracts can be used to lock in a certain price, which in this case would be the foreign exchange rate. By locking in a rate and eliminating downside risk, the user foregoes the opportunity to benefit from any advantageous foreign exchange rate movement. Futures contracts, which are creations of an exchange, have certain advantages over forward contracts in many cases, such as stock indexes and Treasury securities. For foreign exchange, by contrast, the forward market is the market of choice, and trading there is much larger than trading on exchanges. However, as the foreign exchange forward market is an interbank market, reliable information on the amount of contracts outstanding at any time, or open interest, is not publicly available.

Pricing Currency Forward Contracts.

In Chapter 26, we showed the relationship between spot prices and forward prices, and explained how arbitrage ensures that the relationship holds. We now apply similar considerations to the pricing of foreign exchange futures contracts on the basis of the spot exchange rate, using an extended example.

Consider a U.S. investor with a one-year investment horizon who has two choices:

Alternative 1: Deposit $100,000 in a U.S. bank that pays 7% compounded annually for one year.

Alternative 2: Deposit in a bank in country X, the U.S. dollar equivalent of $100,000 in country X's currency that pays 9% compounded annually for one year.

The two alternatives and their outcomes one year from now are depicted in Figure 31-1. Which is the better alternative? It will be the alternative that produces the most U.S. dollars one year from now. Ignoring U.S. and country X taxes on interest income or any other taxes, we need to know two things in order to determine the better alternative: (1) the spot exchange rate between U.S. dollars and country X's currency, and (2) the spot exchange rate one year from now between U.S. dollars and country X's currency. The former is known; the latter is not.

We can determine, however, the spot rate one year from now between U.S. dollars and country X's currency that will make the investor indifferent between the two alternatives.

Alternative 1: The amount of U.S. dollars available one year from now would be $107,000 ($100,000 times 1.07).

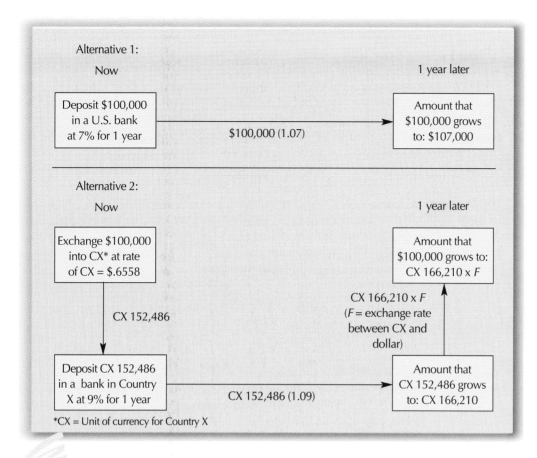

Figure 31-1   Outcome of Two Alternatives: Determination of Theoretical Forward Rate

Alternative 2:   Assume that the spot rate is $0.6558 for one unit of country X's currency at this time. We will denote country X's currency as CX. Then, ignoring commissions, $100,000 can be exchanged for CX152,486 ($100,000 divided by 0.6558). The amount of country X's currency available at the end of one year would be CX166,210 (CX152,486 times 1.09).

The number of U.S. dollars for which the CX166,210 can be exchanged will depend on the exchange rate one year from now. Let F denote the exchange rate between these two currencies one year from now. Specifically, F will denote the number of U.S. dollars that can be exchanged for one unit of country X's currency. Thus, the number of U.S. dollars at the end of one year from the second alternative is:

$$\text{Amount of U.S. dollars one year from now} = CX166{,}210 \times F$$

The investor will be indifferent between the two alternatives if the number of U.S. dollars is $107,000; that is,

$$\$107{,}000 = CX166{,}210 \times F$$

Solving, we find that F is equal to $0.6438. Thus, if one year from now the spot exchange rate is $0.6438 for one unit of country X's currency, then the two alternatives will produce the same number of U.S. dollars. If more than $0.6438 can be exchanged for one unit of country X's currency, then there will be more than $107,000 at the end of one year. An exchange rate of $0.6500 for one unit of country X's currency, for example, would produce $108,037 (CX166,210 times $0.6500). The opposite is true if less than $0.6438 can be exchanged for one unit of country X's currency. For example, if the future exchange rate is $0.6400, there will be $106,374 (CX166,210 times $0.6400).

Let us now look at this situation from the perspective of an investor in country X. Suppose that an investor in country X with a one-year investment horizon has two alternatives:

Alternative 1:   Deposit CX152,486 in a bank in country X that pays 9% compounded annually for one year.

Alternative 2:   Deposit the equivalent of CX152,486 in U.S. dollars in a U.S. bank that pays 7% compounded annually for one year.

Once again, assume that the spot exchange rate is $0.6558 for one unit of country X's currency. The investor in country X will select the alternative that generates the most CX at the end of one year. The first alternative would generate CX166,210 (CX152,486 times 1.09). The second alternative requires that CX be exchanged for U.S. dollars at the spot exchange rate at this time. Given the spot exchange rate assumed, CX152,486 can be exchanged for $100,000 (CX152,486 multiplied by $0.6558). At the end of one year, the second alternative would generate $107,000 ($100,000 times 1.07). Letting F continue to denote the number of U.S. dollars needed to purchase one unit of country X's currency one year from now, the investor in country X following alternative 2 will realize the following amount of country X's currency one year from now:

$$\text{Amount of country X's currency one year from now} = \$107{,}000/F$$

The investor will be indifferent between the two alternatives if

$$\$107{,}000/F = \text{CX166,210}$$

The equation yields a value for F of $0.6438, the same exchange rate that we found when we sought the exchange rate one year from now that would make the U.S. investor indifferent between the two alternatives facing that investor.

Now suppose that a dealer quotes a one-year forward exchange rate between the two currencies. The one-year forward exchange rate fixes today the exchange rate one year from now. Thus, if the one-year forward exchange rate quoted is $0.6438 for one unit of country X's currency, investing in the bank in country X will provide no arbitrage opportunity for the U.S. investor. If the one-year forward rate quoted is more than $0.6438 for one unit of country X's currency, the U.S. investor can arbitrage the situation by selling country X's currency forward (and buying U.S. dollars forward for CX).

To see how this arbitrage opportunity can be exploited, suppose that the one-year forward exchange rate is $0.6500 for one unit of country X's currency. Also, assume that the borrowing and the lending rates within each currency's country are the same. Suppose that the U.S. investor borrows $100,000 for one year at 7% compounded annually and enters into a forward contract agreeing to deliver CX166,210 one year from now at $0.6500 per CX. That is, one year from now the investor is agreeing to deliver CX166,210 in exchange for $108,037 (CX166,210 multiplied by $0.6500).

The $100,000 that was borrowed can be exchanged for CX152,486 at the spot rate of $0.6558 to one unit of country X's currency, which can be invested in country X at 9%. One year from now, the U.S. investor will have CX166,210 from the investment in country X, which can be delivered against the forward contract. The U.S. investor will receive $108,037 and repay $107,000 to satisfy the bank loan, netting $1,037. Assuming that the counterparty to the forward contract does not default, this is a riskless arbitrage situation, because a $1,037 profit is generated with no initial investment.[3] This riskless profit will prompt many arbitrageurs to follow this strategy and will, obviously, result in the U.S. dollar rising relative to country X's currency in the forward exchange rate market, or possibly some other adjustment.[4]

On the other hand, if the one-year forward exchange rate quoted is less than $0.6438, an investor in country X can arbitrage the situation by buying CX forward (and by selling U.S. dollars forward). This riskless arbitrage will again lead arbitrageurs to act, with the result that the forward exchange rate of U.S. dollars relative to CX will fall.[5] The conclusion of this argument is that the one-year forward exchange rate must be $0.6438, because any other forward exchange rate would result in an arbitrage opportunity for either the U.S. or the investor in country X.

Thus, the spot exchange rate and the interest rates in two countries will determine the forward exchange rate of their currencies. The relationship among the spot exchange rate, the interest rates in two countries, and the forward rate is called **interest rate parity**. The parity relationship implies that an investor, by hedging in the forward exchange rate market, will realize the same sure domestic return whether investing domestically or in a foreign country. The arbitrage process that forces interest rate parity is called **covered interest arbitrage**.

Mathematically, interest rate parity between the currencies of two countries, A and B, can be expressed in this way:

Let

I = amount of A's currency to be invested for a time period of length t
S = spot exchange rate: price of foreign currency in terms of domesic currency (units of domestic currency per unit of foreign currency)
F = t-period forward rate: price of foreign currency t periods from now
i_A = interest rate on an investment maturing at time t in country A
i_B = interest rate on an investment maturing at time t in country B

Then:

$$I(1 + i_A) = (I/S)(1 + i_B)F$$

---

[3] An investor in country X could also arbitrage this situation.
[4] Actually, a combination of things may occur when U.S. investors attempt to exploit this situation: (1) The spot exchange rate of U.S. dollars relative to country X's currency will fall as U.S. investors sell dollars and buy CX; (2) U.S. interest rates will rise in the United States as investors borrow in the United States and invest in country X; (3) Country X interest rates will fall as more is invested in country X; and (4) the one-year forward rate of U.S. dollars relative to CX will fall. In practice, the last will dominate.
[5] A combination of things may occur when country X investors attempt to exploit this situation: (1) The spot exchange rate of U.S. dollars relative to CX will rise as country X investors buy dollars and sell CX; (2) Country X interest rates will rise as investors borrow in country X and invest in the United States; (3) U.S. interest rates will fall as more is invested in the United States; and (4) the one-year forward rate of U.S. dollars relative to CX will rise. In practice, the last will dominate.

To illustrate, let country A be the United States and country B represent country X. In our example we have:

$$I = \$100,000 \text{ for one year}$$
$$S = \$0.6558$$
$$F = \$0.6438$$
$$i_A = 0.07$$
$$i_B = 0.09$$

Then, according to interest rate parity, this relationship holds:

$$\$100,000(1.07) = (\$100,000/\$0.6558)(1.09)(\$0.6438)$$
$$\$107,000 = \$107,005$$

The slight difference is due to rounding. Interest rate parity can also be expressed as:

$$(1 + i_A) = (F/S)(1 + i_B)$$

Rewriting the equation, we obtain the theoretical forward exchange rate that is implied by the interest rates and spot exchange rate:

$$F = S\left(\frac{(1 + i_A)}{(1 + i_B)}\right)$$

Although we have referred so far to investors, we could use borrowers as well to illustrate interest rate parity. That is, a borrower has the choice of obtaining funds in a domestic or foreign market. Interest rate parity provides that a borrower who hedges in the forward exchange rate market will realize the same domestic borrowing rate whether borrowing domestically or in a foreign country.

To derive the theoretical forward exchange rate using the arbitrage argument, we made several assumptions. When the assumptions are violated, the actual forward exchange rate may deviate from the theoretical forward exchange rate. First, in deriving the theoretical forward exchange rate, we assumed the investor faced no commissions or bid–ask spread when exchanging in the spot market today and at the end of the investment horizon. In practice, investors incur such costs, which cause the actual forward exchange rate to lie within a plus or minus small amount of the theoretical rate.

Second, we assumed that the borrowing and lending rates in each currency are the same. Dropping this unrealistic assumption means that there is not a single theoretical forward exchange rate, but a band around a level reflecting borrowing and lending rates. The actual rate should be within this band.

Third, we ignored taxes. In fact, the divergence between actual and theoretical forward exchange rates can be the result of the different tax structures of the two countries. Finally, we assumed that arbitrageurs could borrow, and invest in another country, as much as they wanted in order to exploit mispricing in the exchange market. It should be noted, however, that any restrictions on foreign investing or borrowing in each country impede arbitrage and may cause a divergence between actual and theoretical forward exchange rates.

Link between Eurocurrency Market and Forward Prices.

In deriving interest rate parity, we looked at the interest rates in both countries. In fact, market participants in most countries look to one interest rate in order to perform covered interest arbitrage, and that is the interest rate in the Eurocurrency market. The **Eurocurrency market** is the name of the unregulated and informal market for bank deposits and bank loans denominated in a currency other than that of the country where the bank initiating the transaction is located. Examples of transactions in the Eurocurrency market are a British bank in London that lends U.S. dollars to a French corporation, and a Japanese corporation that deposits Swiss francs in a German bank. An investor seeking covered interest arbitrage will accomplish it with short-term borrowing and lending in the Eurocurrency market.

The largest sector of the Eurocurrency market involves bank deposits and bank loans in U.S. dollars and is called the Eurodollar market. (We discussed the Eurodollar CD market in Chapter 22.) The seed for the Eurocurrency market was, in fact, the Eurodollar market. As international capital market transactions increased, the market for bank deposits and bank loans in other currencies developed.

Currency Futures Contracts

Foreign exchange futures contracts for the major currencies are traded on the International Monetary Market (IMM), a division of the Chicago Mercantile Exchange. The futures contracts traded on the IMM are for the Japanese yen, the German mark, the Canadian dollar, the British pound, the Swiss franc, and the Australian dollar. The amount of each foreign currency that must be delivered for a contract varies by currency. For example, the British pound futures contract calls for delivery of 62,500 pounds, while the Japanese yen futures contract is for delivery of 12.5 million yen. The maturity cycle for currency futures is March, June, September, and December. The longest maturity is one year. Consequently, as in the case of a currency forward contract, currency futures do not provide a good vehicle for hedging long-dated foreign exchange risk exposure.

Other exchanges trading currency futures in the United States are the Midamerica Commodity Exchange (a subsidiary of the Chicago Board of Trade) and the Financial Instrument Exchange (a subsidiary of the New York Cotton Exchange). The latter trades a futures contract in which the underlying is a U.S. dollar index. Outside the United States, currency futures are traded on the London International Financial Futures Exchange, the Singapore International Monetary Exchange, the Toronto Futures Exchange, the Sydney Futures Exchange, and the New Zealand Futures Exchange.

Currency Option Contracts

In contrast to a forward or futures contract, an option gives the option buyer the opportunity to benefit from favorable exchange rate movements but establishes a maximum loss. The option price is the cost of arranging such a risk/return profile.

There are two types of foreign currency options: options on the foreign currency and futures options. The latter are options to enter into foreign exchange futures contracts. (We described the features of futures options in Chapter 27.) Futures options are traded on the IMM, the trading location of the currency futures contracts.

Options on foreign currencies have been traded on the Philadelphia Exchange since 1982. The foreign currencies underlying the options are the same as for the futures. There are two sorts of options traded on the Philadelphia Exchange for each currency: an American-type option and a European-type option. Recall from Chapter 27 that the former permits exercise at any time up to and including the expiration date, while the latter permits exercise only at the expiration date. The number of units of foreign currency underlying each option contract traded on the Philadelphia Exchange is one-half the amount of the futures contract. For example, the Japanese yen option is for 6.25 million yen and the British pound option is for 31,250 pounds.

Options on currencies are also traded on the London Stock Exchange and the London International Financial Futures Exchange.

In addition to the organized exchanges, there is also an over-the-counter market for options on currencies. Trading in these products is dominated by commercial banks and investment banking firms. As we explained in Chapter 27, over-the-counter options are tailor-made products that accommodate the specific needs of clients. Only options on the major currencies are traded on the organized exchanges. An option on any other currency must be purchased in the over-the-counter market.

The factors that affect the price of any option were discussed in Chapter 27. One key factor is the expected volatility of the underlying over the life of the option. In the case of currency options, the underlying is the foreign currency specified by the option contract. So, the volatility that affects the option's value is the expected volatility of the exchange rate between the two currencies from the present time to the expiration of the option. The strike price also is an exchange rate, and it affects the option's value: the higher the strike price, the lower the value of a call, and the higher the value of a put. Another factor that influences the option price is the relative risk-free interest rate in the two countries.[6]

Currency Swaps

In Chapter 30, we discussed interest rate swaps—a transaction where two counterparties agree to exchange interest payments with no exchange of principal. In a **currency swap**, there is an exchange of both interest and principal. The best way to explain a currency swap is with an illustration.

Assume there are two companies, a U.S. company and a Swiss company. Each company seeks to borrow for ten years in its domestic currency; that is, the U.S. company seeks $100 million U.S. dollar-denominated debt, and the Swiss company seeks debt in the amount of 127 million Swiss francs (SF). For reasons that we will explore later, let's suppose that each wants to issue 10-year bonds in the bond market of the other country, and those bonds are denominated in the other country's currency. That is, the U.S. company wants to issue the Swiss franc equivalent of $100 million in Switzerland, and the Swiss company wants to issue the U.S. dollar equivalent of SF 127 million in the United States.

Let's also assume the following:

1. At the time when both companies want to issue their 10-year bonds, the spot exchange rate between U.S. dollars and Swiss francs is one U.S. dollar for 1.27 Swiss francs.
2. The coupon rate that the U.S. company would have to pay on the 10-year, Swiss franc-denominated bonds issued in Switzerland is 6%.
3. The coupon rate that the Swiss company would have to pay on the 10-year, U.S. dollar-denominated bonds issued in the United States is 11%.

By the first assumption, if the U.S. company issues the bonds in Switzerland, it can exchange the SF 127 million for $100 million. By issuing $100 million of bonds in

---

[6] To understand why, recall the portfolio we created in Chapter 27 to replicate the payoff of a call option on an asset. A portion of the asset is purchased with borrowed funds. In the case of a currency option, this involves purchasing a portion of the foreign currency underlying the option. However, the foreign currency acquired can be invested at a risk-free interest rate in the foreign country. Consequently, the pricing of a currency option is similar to the pricing of an option on an income-earning asset such as a dividend-paying stock or an interest-paying bond. At the same time, the amount that must be set aside to meet the strike price depends on the domestic rate. Thus, the option price, just like interest rate parity, reflects both rates.

the United States, the Swiss company can exchange the proceeds for SF 127 million. Therefore, both get the amount of financing they seek. Assuming the coupon rates given by the last two assumptions, and assuming for purposes of this illustration that coupon payments will be made annually, the cash outlays that the companies must make for the next 10 years are summarized as:

Year	U.S. Company	Swiss Company
1–10	SF 7,620,000	$ 11,000,000
10	127,000,000	100,000,000

Each issuer faces the risk that, at the time a payment on its liability must be made, its domestic currency will have depreciated relative to the other currency. Such a depreciation would require a greater outlay of the domestic currency to satisfy the liability. That is, both firms are exposed to foreign exchange risk.

In a currency swap, the two companies will issue bonds in the other's bond market and enter into an agreement requiring that:

1. The two parties exchange the proceeds received from the sale of the bonds.
2. The two parties make the coupon payments to service the debt of the other party.
3. At the termination date of the currency swap (which coincides with the maturity of the bonds), both parties agree to exchange the par value of the bonds.

In our illustration this means:

1. The U.S. company issues 10-year, 6% coupon bonds with a par value of SF 127 million in Switzerland and gives the proceeds to the Swiss company. At the same time, the Swiss company issues 10-year, 11% bonds with a par value of $100 million in the United States and gives the proceeds to the U.S. company.
2. The U.S. company agrees to service the coupon payments of the Swiss company by paying $11,000,000 per year for the next 10 years to the Swiss company; the Swiss company agrees to service the coupon payments of the U.S. company by paying SF 7,620,000 for the next 10 years to the U.S. company.
3. At the end of 10 years (this would be the termination date of this currency swap and the maturity of the two bond issues), the U.S. company would pay $100 million to the Swiss company, and the Swiss company would pay SF 127 million to the U.S. company.

This complex agreement is diagrammed in Figure 31-2 on next page.

Now let's assess what this transaction has done. Each party received the amount of financing it sought. The U.S. company's coupon payments are in dollars, not Swiss francs; the Swiss company's coupon payments are in Swiss francs, not U.S. dollars. At the termination date, both parties will receive an amount sufficient in their local currency to pay off the holders of their bonds. With the coupon payments and the principal repayment in their local currency, neither party faces foreign exchange risk.

In practice, the two companies would not deal directly with each other. Instead, either a commercial bank or investment banking firm would function as an intermediary (as either broker or dealer) in the transaction. As a broker, the intermediary simply brings the two parties together, receiving a fee for the service. If instead the intermediary serves as a dealer, it would not only bring the two parties together, but would also guarantee payment to both parties. Thus, if one party were to default, the counterparty would continue to receive its payments from the dealer. Of course, in this arrangement, both parties are concerned with the credit risk of the dealer. When the currency swap market started, transactions were typically brokered. The more prevalent arrangement today is that the intermediary acts as a dealer.

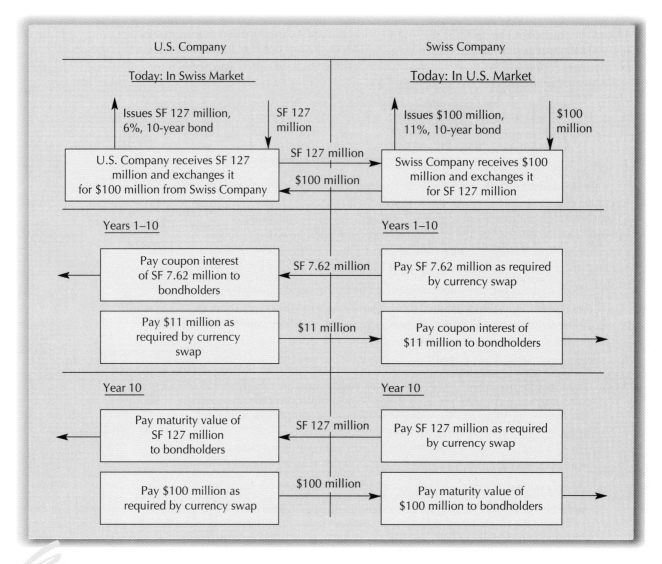

Figure 31-2   Illustration of a Currency Swap

As we explained in Chapter 30, an interest rate swap is nothing more than a package of forward contracts. The same is true for a currency swap; it is simply a package of currency forward contracts.

Currency Coupon Swap.
In our illustration, we assumed that both parties made fixed cash flow payments. Suppose instead that one of the parties sought floating-rate rather than fixed-rate financing. Returning to the same illustration, assume that instead of fixed-rate financing, the Swiss company wanted LIBOR-based financing. In this case, the U.S. company would issue floating-rate bonds in Switzerland. Suppose that it could do so at a rate of LIBOR plus 50 basis points. Because the currency swap would call for the Swiss company to service the coupon payments of the U.S. company, the Swiss company would make annual payments of LIBOR plus 50 basis points. The U.S. company would still make fixed-rate payments in U.S. dollars to service the debt obligation of the Swiss

company in the United States. Now, however, the Swiss company would make floating-rate payments (LIBOR plus 50 basis points) in Swiss francs to service the debt obligation of the U.S. company in Switzerland.

Currency swaps in which one of the parties pays a fixed rate and the counterparty a floating rate are called **currency coupon swaps**.

Reasons for Development of the Currency Swap Market.

Now we turn to the question of why the companies in this illustration may find a currency swap beneficial. In a global financial market where there are no market imperfections because of regulations, taxes, and transactions costs, the cost of borrowing should be the same whether the issuer raises funds domestically or in any foreign capital market. In a world with market imperfections, it may be possible for an issuer to reduce its borrowing cost by borrowing funds denominated in a foreign currency and hedging the associated exchange rate risk. This is what is meant by an arbitrage opportunity. The currency swap allows borrowers to capitalize on any such arbitrage opportunities.

Prior to the establishment of the currency swap market, capitalizing on such arbitrage opportunities required use of the currency forward market. The market for long-dated forward exchange rate contracts is thin, however, which increases the cost of eliminating foreign exchange risk. Eliminating foreign exchange risk in our U.S.-Switzerland illustration would have required each issuer to enter 10 currency forward contracts (one for each yearly cash payment that the issuer was committed to make in the foreign currency). The currency swap provides a more transactionally efficient means for protecting against foreign exchange risk when an issuer (or its investment banker) has identified an arbitrage opportunity and seeks to benefit from it.

As the currency swap market has developed, the arbitrage opportunities for reduced funding costs that were available in the early days of the swap market have become less common. In fact, it was the development of the swap market that reduced arbitrage opportunities. When these opportunities do arise, they last for only a short period of time, usually less than a day.

There is another motivation for currency swaps. Some companies seek to raise funds in foreign countries as a means of increasing their recognition by foreign investors, despite the fact that the cost of funding is the same as in the United States. The U.S. company in our illustration might have been seeking to expand its potential sources of future funding by issuing bonds today in Switzerland.

Key Points That You Should Understand Before Proceeding

1. The four instruments that market participants have available to control foreign exchange risk are currency forward contracts, currency futures contracts, currency options, and currency swaps.

2. Because longer-dated forward contracts have relatively large bid–ask spreads, these contracts are not attractive for hedging long-dated foreign currency exposure.

3. The forward exchange rate between two countries is determined from the spot exchange rate and the interest rates in the two countries.

4. Interest rate parity implies that, by hedging in the forward exchange rate market, an investor will realize the same sure domestic return whether investing domestically or in a foreign country, and a borrower will realize the same domestic borrowing rate whether borrowing domestically or in a foreign country.

5. There are exchange-traded options on foreign exchange and exchange-traded futures options in which the underlying is foreign exchange.

6. A currency swap is an agreement in which two counterparties agree to the exchange of both interest and principal payments.

SUMMARY

We have reviewed the spot foreign exchange market and markets for hedging foreign exchange risk. An exchange rate is defined as the amount of one currency that can be exchanged for another currency. A direct exchange rate quote is the domestic price of a foreign currency; an indirect quote is the foreign price of the domestic currency. An investor or issuer whose cash flows are denominated in a foreign currency is exposed to foreign exchange risk.

The spot exchange rate market is the market for settlement of a currency within two business days. In the developed countries, and some of the developing ones, exchange rates are free to float. According to the purchasing power parity relationship, the exchange rate between two countries—the price of the foreign currency in terms of the domestic currency—is proportional to the domestic price level and inversely proportional to the price level in the foreign country. Exchange rates are typically quoted in terms of the U.S. dollar.

The foreign exchange market is an over-the-counter market dominated by large international banks that act as dealers. Foreign exchange dealers quote one price at which they are willing to buy a foreign currency and one at which they are willing to sell a foreign currency. The difference between those prices is one cost a user of the market must pay; another cost is the explicit fee or commission to brokers arranging the purchase or sale of currency.

The Economic and Monetary Union represents the member countries that are part of the European Union that have adopted the single currency and monetary policy. The single currency adopted is the euro. Members of the EMU are said to be part of "euroland" or the "euro zone." There is a fixed conversion rate against the national currencies of EMU members and relative to the euro.

However, the value of the euro against all other currencies will fluctuate according to market conditions.

Currency forward contracts, currency futures contracts, currency options, and currency swaps are four instruments that borrowers and investors can use to protect against adverse foreign exchange rate movements.

Interest rate parity gives the relationship among the spot exchange rate, the interest rates in two countries, and the forward rate. The relationship is assured by a covered interest arbitrage. Interest rate parity implies that investors and borrowers who hedge in the forward exchange rate market will realize the same domestic return or face the same domestic borrowing rate whether investing or borrowing domestically or in a foreign country.

In implementing covered interest arbitrage, the relevant interest rates are those in the Eurocurrency market, the market for bank deposits and bank loans denominated in a currency other than that of the country where the bank initiating the transaction is located. The Eurodollar market is the largest sector of this market.

There are exchange-traded options on major foreign currencies and futures options on the same currencies traded in the United States. An option on any other currency must be purchased in the over-the-counter market.

A currency swap is effectively a package of currency forward contracts, with the advantage that it allows hedging of long-dated foreign exchange risk and it is more transactionally efficient than futures or forward contracts. Currency swaps are used to arbitrage the increasingly rare opportunities in the global financial market for raising funds at less cost than in the domestic market.

KEY TERMS

- Covered interest arbitrage, 619
- Cross rate, 612
- Currency coupon swap, 625
- Currency swap, 622
- Direct quote, 610
- Euro, 614
- Eurocurrency market, 621

- Exchange rate, 610
- Indirect quote, 610
- Interest rate parity, 619
- Purchasing power parity, 611
- Spot (or cash) exchange rate market, 611
- Triangular arbitrage, 612

QUESTIONS

1. A U.S. life insurance company that buys British government bonds faces foreign exchange risk. Specify the nature of that risk in terms of the company's expected return in U.S. dollars.

2. Explain the difference between a spot exchange rate and a forward exchange rate.

3. These spot foreign exchange rates were reported on December 24, 2000:

	Japanese yen	British pound	Canadian dollar
U.S. $	0.008864	1.477	0.6596

    The exchange rates indicate the number of U.S. dollars necessary to purchase one unit of the foreign currency.
    a. From the perspective of a U.S. investor, are the preceding foreign exchange rates direct or indirect quotes?
    b. How much of each of the foreign currencies is needed to buy one U.S. dollar?
    c. Calculate the theoretical cross rates between: (i) the Canadian dollar and the Japanese yen; (ii) the Canadian dollar and the British pound; and (iii) the Japanese yen and the British pound.

4. a. What is the euro?
    b. Comment on the following statement: "The exchange rate between the euro and the currencies of all major economic countries is fixed."

5. Explain the meaning of triangular arbitrage, and show how it is related to cross rates.

6. On February 8, 1991, the U.S. dollar/British pound spot rate was U.S. $1.9905 per pound and the U.S. dollar/Japanese yen spot rate was U.S. $0.00779 per yen. The following forward rates were also quoted:

	British pound	Japanese yen
30 days	1.9908	0.007774
60	1.9597	0.007754
90	1.9337	0.007736

    a. Explain what someone who enters into a 30-day forward contract to deliver British pounds is agreeing to do.
    b. Explain what someone who enters into a 90-day forward contract to buy Japanese yen is agreeing to do.
    c. What can you infer about the relationship between U.S. and British short-term interest rates and U.S. and Japanese short-term interest rates?

7. What is the drawback of using currency forward contracts for hedging long-dated positions?

8. How does covered interest arbitrage relate to interest rate parity?

9. Why are the interest rates in the Eurocurrency market important in covered interest arbitrage?

10. Suppose you know the following items: You can borrow and lend $500,000 at the one-year interest rate in the United States of 7.5%; in country W both the borrowing and lending rates are 9.2%; the spot exchange rate between the U.S. dollar and country W's currency is now $0.1725 per unit of currency of country W; and the one-year forward exchange rate is $0.2 per unit of currency of country W.

a. Explain how you could make a profit without risk and without investing any of your own money. (Assume commissions, fees, etc., to be equal to zero.)

b. Aside from assuming commissions, fees, and so on, to be zero, several unrealistic assumptions must be made in answering part (a). What are they?

c. Even if we incorporated realistic considerations regarding commissions and so on, the interest rate and exchange rate numbers in this question would probably produce a profit of some size. Why do you think opportunities like the one in this question are unlikely to come along very often in the real world?

11. If the one-year borrowing and lending rates in Japan were 5% and they were 7% in the United States, and if the forward exchange rate between dollars and yen were $0.007576 per yen (i.e., one dollar could buy 131.99 yen), then what should the spot exchange rate of dollars for yen be?

12. For which currencies are options and futures traded on organized U.S. exchanges?

13. What is the major difference between a currency swap and an interest rate swap?

14. The following excerpt appeared in the January 14, 1991, issue of *Wall Street Letter*:

The Philadelphia Stock Exchange plans to list the first non-dollar denominated options to trade in the United States, according to sources at the exchange. The Phlx will list cross-currency options based on the relationships between the Deutsche mark and the Japanese yen, as well as British pound/yen and pound/mark options, a spokesman confirmed. . . .

The exchange currently lists currency options that are based on the relationship between that currency and the dollar, one Phlx member explained. "If you're not American," he added, "then the dollar doesn't do it for you." The three new cross-currency options should be attractive to the same banks and broker-dealers that currently trade dollar-based currency options, as well as non-U.S. entities that have interests in other currencies.

Cross-currency options are "a very big part of international trade and international capital markets," and are big over-the-counter products, but none currently trades on an exchange. The advantage of exchange-traded options, the Phlx member said, is that "99% of the customers don't have the credit" to trade such a product over-the-counter with a big bank.

a. Explain what the representative of the Phlx means by saying: "If you're not American then the dollar doesn't do it for you."

b. Why is the credit of customers critical in the over-the-counter market but not for an exchange-traded contract?

c. When the Philadelphia Stock Exchange filed with the SEC to list cross-currency options, the exchange indicated that the demand for this product has been "spawned by recent large fluctuations and dramatic increases in volatility levels for cross-rate options." Why would this increase the demand for cross-currency options?

GLOSSARY

12b-1 fee: Fee that uses the 1980 SEC Rule 12b-1 to assess investors for selling and marketing costs.

401(k) plan: An employer-sponsored, defined contribution type of retirement plan, which allows an employee to deposit pretax dollars, often matched by the employer, into an account over which the employee can exercise a significant amount of control.

Abnormal returns: That portion of a security's returns that is above (positive) or below (negative) what one would expect from market movements and the risk class of the security.

Absolute prepayment speed: A measure of prepayments for auto loan–backed securities.

Absolute priority rule: In a bankruptcy, the principle that senior creditors are paid in full before junior creditors are paid anything.

Acceptance financing: The use of a bankers acceptance to finance a commercial transaction.

Accepting bank: A bank that creates a bankers acceptance.

Accreting swap: An interest rate swap in which the notional principal amount increases in a predetermined way over time.

Accrual tranche: A CMO bond class in which interest is accrued and eventually paid when principal is repaid.

Active investment strategy: A strategy of regular buying and selling assets that is based on the belief that they are mispriced by and in the market where they are traded.

Adjustable-rate mortgage: A mortgage design calling for the mortgage rate to reset periodically in accordance with some appropriately chosen index that reflects short-term market rates.

Adjustable-rate preferred stock (ARPS): Preferred stock for which the dividend rate is adjusted quarterly on the basis of a predetermined spread from the highest of three points on the Treasury yield curve.

Advances: Funds that savings and loan associations borrow from the Federal Home Loan Banks.

Agency pass-through security: A mortgage pass-through issued or guaranteed by either Ginnie Mae, Fannie Mae, or Freddie Mac.

Agency problems: Difficulties that can arise when a firm's managers, who are acting as agents for the firm's owners who are principals, follow their own interests at the owners' expense and to their disadvantage.

Alpha: A statistical measure of the typical unsystematic change in the price of a stock.

Alt-A loan: A loan made to borrowers whose qualifying mortgage characteristics do not meet the conforming underwriting criteria established by the government sponsored enterprises.

Alternative option (also called an either-or option): An exotic option that has a payoff that is the best independent payoff of two distinct assets.

Alternative trading system (ATS): Mechanism whereby the direct trading of stocks between customers can occur without the use of a broker or other intermediaries. The ATS market is also called the Fourth Market. There are two types of ATS, electronic communication networks (ECNs) and crossing networks.

American Depositary Receipt (ADR): A tradable right, which U.S. citizens can buy, to ownership of a specific number of a foreign company's shares, which are held in trust by a U.S. financial institution that issues the ADR.

American option: An option that the buyer may exercise at any time up to and including the expiration date.

Amortizing assets: Loans in which the borrower's periodic payment consists of scheduled principal and interest payments over the life of the loan.

Amortizing swap: An interest rate swap in which the notional principal amount decreases in a predetermined way over the life of the swap.

Annuity: A mutual fund in an insurance wrapper (often a principal guarantee), that usually cannot be withdrawn for a specified minimum period and as a result receives preferential tax treatment.

Anomalies in the market: Examples of inefficient pricing of securities.

Anticipation note: Debt with a maturity between three months and three years, which municipalities sell in anticipation of some future inflow, from taxes or revenues among other sources.

Appropriation-backed bond: Obligation of an agency or authority of a state that carries a potential state liability for making up shortfalls in the issuing entity's obligation

Arbitrage: The act of taking advantage of a difference in price and/or return of an asset that is traded in more than one market.

Arbitrage pricing theory (APT) model: The theory that a security's expected return is influenced by a variety of factors, rather than just by the movement in the value of the overall market for securities.

Asset: Broadly speaking, any possession that has value in an exchange.

Asset allocation decision: The investment decision concerning how to divide funds across major asset classes.

Asset securitization: The process by which a financial institution pools loans and sells securities backed by those loans.

Asset swap: The use of an interest rate swap to change the cash flow characteristics of assets.

Asset-backed bond (or structured bond or dedicated revenue bond): Municipal bond structured as asset-backed securities that are backed by "dedicated" revenues such as sales taxes, tobacco settlement payments, fees, and penalty payments.

Asset/liability management: Term for a financial institutions's efforts to manage its assets relative to the nature of its liabilities.

Asymmetric information: Occurs when the investors in a firm do not have the same access as managers to information relevant to a financial evaluation of the firm.

At-the-money option: An option for which the strike price is equal to the current asset price.

Auction preferred stock (APS): Preferred stock where the dividend rate is set periodically through an auction process.

Auctioneer: A market participant who facilitates trades by seeking bids from buyers and sellers that establish the market-clearing amount to be traded and the price that makes amount demanded equal amount offered.

Auto loan–backed security: An asset-backed security backed by automobile loans.

Average life: For a mortgage-backed security, the average time to receipt of principal payments (scheduled principal payments and projected prepayments), weighted by the amount of principal expected.

Back-end load: Fund that charges investors a fee to sell (redeem) shares. The formal name for the back-end load is the contingent deferred sales charge or CDSC.

Balloon/reset mortgage: A mortgage design in which the borrower is given long-term financing by the lender but at a specified date, which is considerably shorter than the maturity date, the loan is paid off and the lender agrees to provide financing for the remainder of the term of the mortgage at a new mortgage rate.

Bankassurance: The effort of banks and insurance companies to transform themselves into integrated financial conglomerates that offer both banking and insurance products.

Bank discount basis: Convention used in the Treasury market to quote the yield on Treasury bills.

Bank for International Settlements (BIS): An international organization of central banks from industrialized countries that has played a large role in the internationalization of banking and the regulation of international banking.

Bank holding company: A firm that owns one or more banks, usually by holding all or most of the equity shares of those banks.

Bank Insurance Fund (BIF): Created in 1989 and administered by the Federal Deposit Insurance Corporation, this fund insures deposits of banks.

Bank of England: The central bank in the United Kingdom, which plays many key roles in the regulation of banks.

Bank of Japan (BOJ): Japan's central bank and a major regulator of commercial banking.

Bankers acceptance (BA): A vehicle created to facilitate commercial trade transactions.

Banking Act of 1933: This law created the Federal Deposit Insurance Corporation and establishes rules on commercial banks' activities in the investment banking area, popularly referred to as the Glass-Steagall Act.

Bankruptcy Reform Act of 1978: The law governing bankruptcy in the United States.

Base interest rate (also called benchmark interest rate): The minimum yield sought on an investment as measured by the yield on an on-the-run Treasury issue of the same maturity.

Basis: The difference between the cash price and the futures price.

Basis point: A term in the financial markets for one one-hundredth (or 1%) of one percentage point.

Basis rate swap: An interest rate swap in which both parties exchange floating-rate payments based on a different money market reference rate.

Basis risk: In a hedge, the risk that the basis will change adversely.

Basle Committee on Banking Regulations and Supervisory Practices: An international committee consisting of the central banks and supervisory authorities of the large industrial and financial economies of the world.

Bermuda option (also called an Atlantic option or a limited exercise option): An option that may be exercised at several specified dates as well as the expiration date of the option.

Best efforts underwriting: An underwriting arrangement in which an investment banking firm agrees only to use its expertise to sell the securities and does not buy the entire issue from the issuer.

Beta: A statistical index of the sensitivity of an asset's price changes to changes in the value of the overall market or of assets in general.

Big Bang: In the context of equity markets, it refers to the financial reforms that were introduced in England in 1986 and in Japan in 1996 to liberalize stock trading practices.

Big Board: Common term for the New York Stock Exchange.

Block trades: Trades of 10,000 shares or more of a given stock, or trades of shares with a market value of $200,000 or more.

Board of directors: Also called fund trustees. There are "interested" or "inside" directors (i.e., directors affiliated with the investment company) and "independent" or "outside" directors (i.e., directors who have no affiliation with the investment company).

Board of Governors of the Federal Reserve: A group of seven members who are appointed by the president and approved by the Congress for 14-year terms and who are responsible for monetary policy in the United States.

Bond indenture: In a corporate bond agreement, the contract that specifies the obligations of the issuer and the rights of bondholders.

Bond-equivalent yield: The convention adopted in the bond market to annualize a semiannual yield by doubling its value.

Bootstrapping: A methodology used to construct the theoretical spot rate curve from the yield curve.

Borrowed reserves: The value (for a bank or for the banking system) of loans obtained from the Federal Reserve System through its discount window.

Bought deal: An underwriting arrangement whereby an investment banking firm or group of firms offers to buy an entire issue from the issuer.

Bourse: The stock exchange in Paris.

Broker: An agent of an investor who executes, for a commission or fee, the investor's order to buy or sell assets.

Broker's commission: The fee charged by an intermediary in a transaction of buying or selling a security.

Bullet bond (or bullet-maturity bond): A bond where no principal payments are made until the maturity date.

Bullet loan: A loan structured such that no repayment

of the principal is made until the maturity date.

Bullet swap: An interest rate swap in which the notional principal amount does not vary over the life of the swap.

Bundes bond (or Bund): A debt security issued by the central German government.

Bundesbank (or Deutsche Bundesbank): The central bank of Germany and a regulatory authority in the banking industry.

Buy-back (or close-out swap or cancellation swap): A secondary market transaction in the swap market in which a party that wishes to close out the original swap sells the swap to the original counterparty.

CAC: The acronym for *Cotation Assistée en Continu,* which is the computerized trading system on the Paris Bourse.

CAC 40 Index: A stock price index based on 40 large stocks traded on the Paris Bourse.

Call market: A secondary market where orders to buy and sell securities are batched or grouped together for simultaneous execution at the same price and at certain times in the day.

Call money rate: Also known as the broker loan rate, this is the interest rate banks charge brokers for the funding of loans to investors who buy on margin.

Call option: An option that grants the owner of the option the right to buy a financial asset from the other party (the writer) at a specified price (the strike price).

Call provision: Entitles the debtor to repay in advance, usually at some penalty and only after a number of years from the time of issuance.

Call risk (or timing risk): The disadvantages associated with the early retirement of a bond issue.

Capital adequacy standards: Rules regarding the capital requirements of depository institutions.

Capital asset pricing model (CAPM): Theory that hypothesizes that the expected return on a well-diversified portfolio should (in a linear relationship) equal the riskless rate of return plus an amount that is proportional to the portfolio beta.

Capital market: The financial market for equity instruments, and for debt instruments with a maturity greater than one year.

Capital requirements: Governmental rules about the percentage of a depository institution's funding that must be in the form of equity, or owner-supplied capital.

Capitalization (or market capitalization): The total market value of a firm's common stock, which equals the number of outstanding shares times the price per share of the stock on the market.

Caption: This is an option on an interest rate cap.

Captive finance companies: Finance companies that are subsidiaries of equipment manufacturing companies.

Cash and carry trade: Strategy in which a futures contract is sold, funds are borrowed for a period of time equal to the settlement date of the futures contract, and the underlying for the futures contract is purchased with the borrowed funds.

Cash settlement futures contract: A futures contract in which settlement is made in cash only.

Cash value life insurance (also called whole life insurance): A form of insurance that pays a stated amount upon the death of the insured, and that has a guaranteed buildup of cash value based on the general account portfolio of the insurance company.

Central Liquidity Facility (or CLF): Managed by the National Credit Union Administration, the CLF provides short-term loans to member credit unions with liquidity needs.

Certificate of deposit (CD): A financial asset issued by a bank or thrift that indicates a specified sum of money has been deposited at the issuing depository institution for a specified period of time.

Chapter 7: Chapter of the Bankruptcy Reform Act of 1978 dealing with the liquidation of a company.

Chapter 11: Chapter of the Bankruptcy Reform Act of 1978 dealing with the reorganization of a company.

Charter: The authorization, by either a federal regulatory agency for national banks or a state agency for state banks, for a financial institution to engage in banking activities.

Chartist: See technical analyst.

Cheapest-to-deliver issue: The Treasury issue that is the cheapest to deliver to satisfy the delivery requirements of a Treasury bond or Treasury note futures contract.

Clearinghouse: The corporation that is associated with an exchange and that guarantees that the two parties to the transaction will perform.

Closed-end fund: Fund that manages a pool of investments and that sells shares like any other corporation and usually does not redeem its shares, which trade on either an organized exchange or over the counter.

Closed-end home equity loan: A home equity loan that is structured the same way as a fixed-rate, fully amortizing, residential mortgage loan.

Collateral trust bond: A bond secured by stocks, notes, bonds, or other kinds of financial instruments.

Collateralized bond obligation: An asset-backed security backed by a diversified pool of one or more of the following types of debt obligations: noninvestment grade corporate bonds, emerging market bonds, and bank loans to corporate entities.

Collateralized mortgage obligation (CMO): A mortgage-backed security with multiple bond classes that is backed by one or more pools of pass-through securities or mortgages.

Commercial bank: A financial institution that accepts deposits and may use the proceeds of those deposits to make loans.

Commercial mortgage-backed securities: A mortgage-backed security backed by a pool of commercial mortgage loans.

Commercial paper: A short-term unsecured promissory note issued in the open market that represents the obligation of the issuing corporation.

Commitment letter: An agreement that the lender sends to a mortgage loan applicant that commits the lender to provide funds to the applicant.

Commodity Futures Trading Commission (CFTC): The U.S. government agency that licenses futures exchanges and monitors trading in them.

Competitive bidding underwriting: An underwriting arrangement in which the issuer announces the terms of the issue, and interested parties submit bids for the entire issue.

Competitive market: A market that brings about the efficient production of a good or service at the lowest possible cost.

Complexity: The property of an asset that represents a combination of two or more simpler assets.

Comptroller of the Currency: A U.S. government

agency with responsibility for chartering national banks and monitoring some of their key activities.

Computer Assisted Trading System (CATS): Computerized stock trading system, developed on the Toronto Stock Exchange, and now used in several countries.

Computer-Assisted Order-Routing and Execution System (CORES): The Tokyo Stock Exchange's computerized trading system.

Conditional prepayment rate: A prepayment convention that assumes that some fraction of the remaining principal in the mortgage pool is prepaid each year for the remaining term of the mortgage.

Conduit-originated deal: A commercial mortgage-backed securities deal where the pool of commercial mortgage loans backing the deal consists of multiproperties with multiple borrowers.

Conduits: Entities that pool mortgages and sell interests in these pools to investors.

Conforming mortgage: A mortgage loan that meets the underwriting standards allowing an agency to include it in a pool of mortgages that is collateral for a mortgage pass-through security.

Consolidated Quotation System (CQS): An electronic display system providing data on trades of listed stocks in different market centers.

Continuous market: A secondary market where prices are determined continuously throughout the trading day as buyers and sellers submit orders.

Contracting costs: The costs of analyzing and arranging a contract for the performance of certain tasks.

Contraction risk: A form of prepayment risk resulting from a decline in mortgage rates that will shorten the life of a mortgage or mortgage-backed security.

Conventional mortgage: A mortgage loan based solely on the credit of the borrower and on the collateral for the mortgage.

Conversion factor for a Treasury bond or note futures contracts: The factor that must be multiplied by the price of the futures contract to arrive at the invoice price for a particular deliverable Treasury bond or note.

Convertibility: Provision of a security's contract that allows the owner to convert it into another security or another type of security.

Convertible bond: A bond issue in which the bondholder has the right to exchange the bond for a specified number of shares of common stock.

Core capital: Tier 1 capital requirements for a commercial bank consisting basically of common stockholders' equity, certain types of preferred stock, and minority interest in consolidated subsidiaries.

Corporate credit union: An entity that provides a variety of investment services only to natural person credit unions.

Correlation: A statistical measure of the extent to which two variables move around their respective means.

Cost of carry (or simply carry): The net cost of financing a position in an asset; that is, the difference between the cost of financing a position in an asset and the asset's cash yield.

Coupon rate: The percentage of the principal that is a bond's contractual yearly payment, which is the yearly coupon.

Covered interest arbitrage: The arbitrage process that forces interest rate parity to hold.

Credit card asset-backed security: An asset-backed security backed by a pool of credit card receivables.

Credit default swap: A type of credit derivative that can be either credit insurance or a total return credit swap.

Credit derivative: Derivatives instruments whose payoff depends on some type of credit event and can be used to control credit risk.

Credit enhancement: Mechanism built into an asset-backed security structure to reduce the credit risk of the underlying pool of assets.

Credit forward contract: A forward contract in which the underlying is a credit spread and the payoff depends on the credit spread at the settlement date of the contract.

Credit insurance: A type of credit default swap wherein the buyer pays a fee to enter into a credit default swap. While called a swap, it is basically a package of credit options.

Credit option: A type of credit derivative.

Credit option written on an underlying issue: A type of credit option whereby the payout is determined based on whether a default occurs for the underlying issue.

Credit rating (or quality rating): Rating of an issued bond based on the perceived likelihood of default as assigned by commercial rating companies.

Credit risk-based capital requirements: Capital requirements for a depository institution that are based on the credit risk of its assets.

Credit spread risk: The risk that an issuer's debt obligation will decline due to an increase in the credit spread demanded by the market.

Credit union: An organization for people with some common bond, which accepts their savings as deposits and lends them money for purchases, mostly of consumer goods.

Crediting rate: The interest rate offered on an investment-type insurance policy.

Cross hedging: A hedging strategy in which a futures contract is used to hedge a position where either the portfolio or the individual financial instrument to be hedged is not identical to the instrument underlying the futures contract.

Cross rate: The exchange rate between two countries other than the United States.

Cross trading systems: Trading systems that allow institutional investors to match buyers and sellers directly, typically via computer.

Cross-hedging risk: The risk associated with employing a strategy of cross hedging.

Cumulative preferred stock: Preferred stock in which the dividend payment accrues until it is fully paid.

Currency: The type of nominal monetary unit in which an asset is denominated and its payments are made.

Currency coupon swap: A currency swap in which one of the parties pays a fixed rate and the counterparty a floating rate.

Currency swap: An agreement whereby two counterparties agree to swap interest and principal in two different currencies.

Daily price limit: A limit set by the exchange on the minimum and maximum price at which a futures contract may trade that day.

DAX: The acronym for the *Deutscher Aktieninex,* a stock index for the Frankfurt Stock Exchange.

Dealer: Participant in a market who takes a position in an asset, keeps an inventory of it, and is ready to buy or sell to other participants.

Dealer's position: The amount of an asset a dealer is holding in inventory.

Dealer-placed paper: Commercial paper in which the issuer uses the services of an agent to sell its paper.

Debenture bond: A bond not secured by a specific pledge of property, but giving the bondholders the claim of general creditors on all assets of the issuer not pledged specifically to secure other debt.

Debit card: A payment mechanism that allows for payment of a purchase by an immediate charge against the purchaser's account at the financial institution that sponsors the card.

Debt instrument: The claim that the holder of a financial asset has that is a fixed dollar amount. Loans and bonds are examples.

Debt-to-service coverage (DSC) ratio: Ratio used to evaluate the credit risk of a commercial property and is equal to the net operating income divided by the debt service.

Debtor-in-possession: A company that files for protection under the bankruptcy act and continues to operate its business under the supervision of the court.

Default risk (also called credit risk): The risk that the issuer or borrower will default on its obligation.

Default risk premium: The portion of the required rate of return that compensates the investor for the prospect that the issuer of a security may not make all promised payments.

Deferred coupon structure: A high-yield bond structure that permits the issuer to avoid using cash to make interest payments for a period of typically three to seven years.

Deferred-interest bond: A form of deferred coupon structure in which the issue sells at a deep discount and the issuer does not pay interest for an initial period.

Defined benefit plan: Plan whose sponsor agrees to make specified dollar payments to qualifying employees at retirement, according to factors such as the length of service and the earnings of the employee.

Defined contribution plan: Plan whose sponsor is responsible only for making specified contributions into the plan on behalf of qualifying participants.

Demand deposit: A checking account that pays no interest and funds can be withdrawn upon demand.

Demand for money: An individual's or the public's total demand, at any time, for holding wealth in the form of liquid balances, such as currency and deposits at financial intermediaries.

Denomination: The size, in units of money, of a loan or debt security.

Department of Trade and Industry (DTI): The U.K.'s government agency responsible for regulation of many markets including financial ones.

Deposit computation period: The period over which a bank must calculate its actual reserves in order to determine if it has met the required reserve ratio.

Depository institutions: Financial institutions that acquire the bulk of their funds by offering their liabilities to the public in the form of deposits.

Derivative instrument: A contract that gives the contract holder either the obligation or the choice to buy or sell a financial asset at some future time. Options and futures are examples.

Deutsche Terminbörse: Futures market in Germany.

Depository Institutions Deregulation and Monetary Control Act of 1980 (DIDMCA): Passed by Congress in 1980, the Depository Institutions Deregulation and Monetary Control Act phased out the ceilings on interest rates on time deposits and certificates of deposit.

Direct investments: The investments made by financial intermediaries; these assets can be loans or securities.

Direct quote: The convention in quoting an exchange rate expressed in terms of the number of units of a local currency exchangeable for one unit of a foreign currency.

Directly placed paper: Commercial paper sold by the issuing firm directly to investors without the help of an agent or an intermediary.

Disclosure regulation: The regulation that requires issuers of securities to make public a large amount of financial information to actual and potential investors.

Discount brokers: Brokers that charge commissions at rates much less than those charged by other brokers, but offer little or no advice or any other service apart from execution of the transaction.

Discount rate: (1) The interest rate that the Fed charges banks to borrow funds for brief periods of time; (2) the interest rate used to calculate the present value of cash flows.

Discount window: The facility by which banks can borrow short term from the Federal Reserve.

Discretionary monetary policy: The view of policy that allows the Fed to change the rate of growth in reserves or aggregates in order to achieve short-run adjustments in interest rates or levels of economic activity.

Disintermediation: The flow of funds, caused by the discrepancy between regulated and market interest rates, out of the regulated commercial banks and thrift institutions into other, unregulated financial institutions, such as money market mutual funds.

Diversifiable risk: That variability in an asset's returns that, when it is grouped with other assets in a portfolio, will be reduced or offset by variation in the returns of other members of the portfolio. This term is another name for *unsystematic risk.*

Diversification: Allocating wealth across a significant number of different assets.

Divisibility: The property of an asset that allows it to be divided into small units.

Domestic market: A classification of the global financial market. It is the financial market of a country where issuers domiciled in the country issue securities and where those securities are subsequently traded. It is part of the internal or national market.

Downgrade risk: The risk of an unanticipated downgrading of an issue or issuer resulting in a decline in the price of the issue or the issuer's bonds.

Dual-currency issue: A Eurobond in which the issuer pays coupon interest in one currency but retires the principal in a different currency.

Dual-rate mortgage (also called inflation-proof mortgage): A mortgage design in which the mortgage payments are lower than for a traditional mortgage but then rise smoothly at the rate of inflation, if any, achieving mortgage payments approximately level in terms of purchasing power.

Due diligence: Duty of an underwriter to assure that there are no misstatements or omissions of fact in the registration statement or prospectus.

Duration: A measure of the price sensitivity of an asset or liability to a change in interest rates. Duration can be interpreted as the approximate change in the price of an asset for a 100 basis point change in interest rates.

Dutch auction: An auction process for a new offering of securities in which bidders indicate the amount they are willing to buy and winning bidders agree to pay the lowest accepted bid price (or equivalently, the highest accepted bid yield).

EAFE Index: The term for the Morgan Stanley Capital International Europe, Australia, Far East Index, which covers over 20 countries.

Early amortization: In a credit card asset-backed security, this refers to the repayment of the principal prior to the end of the lockout period.

Effective duration: A duration measure that allows for the fact that the cash flow might change when interest rates change.

Effective fed funds rate: The rate most often cited for the fed funds market.

Efficient market hypothesis: The theory that the public availability of relevant information about the issuers of securities will lead to a correct pricing of those securities if they are freely traded in properly functioning markets.

Efficient (or optimal) portfolio: A portfolio that offers the highest expected return for any given level of risk.

Electronic communications networks (ECNs): Privately owned broker-dealers that operate as market participants within the Nasdaq system.

Embedded option: An option in a bond issue granted to either the bondholder or the issuer.

Employee Retirement Income Security Act of 1974 (ERISA): Comprehensive legislation regulating several key features of corporate pension plans and including the "prudent man" statutes and rules.

Equipment trust certificate: A form of borrowing secured by property such that title to the property is held in trust until the debt obligation is paid off.

Equity in a futures account: The sum, in a futures account, of all margins posted and all daily gains less all daily losses to the account.

Equity instrument (also called residual claim): A financial asset in which the issuer agrees to pay the holder an amount based on earnings, if any, after holders of debt instruments have been paid. Common stock is an example of an equity claim.

Equivalent taxable yield: The yield that must be offered on a taxable bond in order to realize a certain tax-exempt yield.

Eurex: The joint German-Swiss derivatives exchange formed in 1998 from the merger of the German Deutsche Terminborse (DTB) and Switzerland's SOFFEX. The DTB and the Swiss Exchange each own 50% of Eurex.

Euro: Currency adopted by members of the Economic and Monetary Union.

Euro medium-term notes: Medium-term notes issued in the Euromarket.

Euro straight bond: A bond that is a "plain vanilla," fixed-rate coupon Eurobond.

Eurobond: In general, a bond that is underwritten by an international syndicate, is offered simultaneously to investors in a number of countries, and is issued outside the jurisdiction of any single country.

Eurocommercial paper: Commercial paper issued and placed outside the jurisdiction of the currency of denomination.

Eurocurrency loans: Loans made by offshore banks.

Eurocurrency market: The unregulated and informal market for bank deposits and bank loans denominated in a currency other than that of the country where the bank initiating the transaction is located.

Eurodollar certificate of deposit: A CD that is denominated in U.S. dollars but is issued outside the United States.

Euroequity tranche: An issue of stock offered to investors in different countries at the same time.

Euronext: An integrated, cross border European stock exchange that was created in September 2000 by the merger of the exchanges in Amsterdam, Brussels, and Paris. It also trades some derivatives and commodities.

European option: An option that the buyer may exercise only at the expiration date.

Excess reserves: The amount of a bank's reserves that is in excess of its required reserves.

Exchange: Physical location where market participants who are members of the exchange (i.e., own a "seat") assemble to trade stocks or other securities, which are listed for trading on the exchange.

Exchange rate: The amount of one currency that can be exchanged for a unit of another currency.

Exchange-rate risk premium: The portion of the required rate of return that compensates an investor for the perceived volatility of the rate of exchange between the home currency and the currency in which an asset's cash flows are denominated.

Exchange-traded funds (ETFs): Essentially hybrid closed-end vehicles that trade on exchanges, which typically trade very close to NAV.

Exchange-traded option: An option traded on an organized exchange.

Exchangeable bond: A bond that grants the bondholder the right to exchange the bonds for the common stock of a firm other than the issuer of the bond.

Exercise (or strike) price: The price at which the underlying of an option may be bought or sold.

Exotic option: A complex over-the-counter option.

Expected return: The central tendency or mean of a probability distribution of returns.

Expiration (or maturity) date: The date after which an option expires.

Extension risk: A form of prepayment risk resulting from a rise in mortgage rates that will lengthen the life of a mortgage or mortgage-backed security.

External market (also called the international market, the offshore market, or the Euromarket): Classification of the global financial market. This financial market includes securities with the following distinguishing features: (1) at issuance they are offered simultaneously to investors in a number of countries, and (2) they are issued outside the jurisdiction of any single country.

Extra-market source of risk: A cause of the variability in the returns of securities that is independent of both movements in the general market value of securities and developments particular to the situations of the firms that issued the securities.

Fallen angel: A bond rated investment grade at the time or issuance but subsequently downgraded to noninvestment grade.

Fallout risk: In mortgage lending, the risk that applicants or those issued commitment letters by a mortgage originator will not close (complete the transaction by purchasing the property with funds borrowed from the mortgage originator).

FAZ Index: A stock market index based on the share prices for the 100 largest firms listed on the Frankfurt Stock Exchange, which is compiled by the newspaper *Frankfurter Allgemeine Zeitung.*

Federal Deposit Insurance Corporation (FDIC): Government agency that acts as an insurance company for deposits in U.S. banks.

Federal funds market: The short-term loans (also called "fed funds") that banks lend to one another, at the fed funds rate, for the purpose of meeting reserve requirements of the Federal Reserve Board.

Federal Home Loan Bank Board (FHLBB): A U.S. agency that once regulated much of the activity of savings and loan associations.

Federal Open Market Committee (FOMC): The unit of the Fed that decides on the general issues of changing the rate of growth in the money supply by open market sales or purchase of securities.

Federal Reserve Board chairman: The person appointed to be the chairman of the Fed's board of governors.

Federal Reserve District Bank: The Federal Reserve Bank in one of the 12 geographical districts.

Federal Reserve System (or Fed): An independent U.S. government agency responsible for the nation's money and banking system.

Federally related institutions: Entities that are arms of the federal government.

Fill or kill order: An order to buy or sell shares that must be executed immediately or be canceled.

Financial asset (or intangible asset): An asset that represents a legal claim to some future benefit. The terms financial asset, financial instrument, and security *are used interchangeably.*

Financial institution: A financial enterprise that may perform one of several financial services such as accepting deposits, brokering securities, managing funds, or underwriting securities.

Financial intermediary: A financial enterprise that transforms financial assets, acquired through the market, into a different and more widely preferable type of asset, which becomes the liability of the intermediary.

Financial market: A market where financial assets are exchanged (traded).

Financial Times Industrial Ordinary Index (or FT 30): An index based on the prices of shares of 30 leading companies, which is compiled by the newspaper *Financial Times.*

Financial Times World Index: An international stock market index.

Financial Times–Stock Exchange 100 (FTSE 100): An index based on the shares of the largest 100 U.K. firms.

Financing cost: In the pricing of a futures contract, the interest rate for borrowing until the settlement date.

Firm commitment underwriting: An underwriting arrangement whereby an investment banking firm agrees to buy the securities from the issuer at a set price.

Financial Institutions Reform, Recovery, and Enforcement Act of 1989 (FIRREA): Passed by Congress in 1989, the Financial Institutions Reform, Recovery, and Enforcement Act that, among other things, created the Office of Thrift Supervision.

First market: Refers to trading on exchanges of stocks listed on an exchange.

First section: The term for the stocks of the largest companies compared on the Tokyo Stock Exchange.

Fisher's Law: The theory that the observed nominal rate of interest is composed of the real rate and a premium for expected inflation.

Fisher's theory of interest: The classical analysis of the supply and demand for investment funds.

Fix: A colloquial term, used in certain U.K. markets, for the determination of the market-clearing price in a call market system.

Fixed Income Pricing System (FIPS): Nasdaq's electronic trading system for disseminating price quote and reporting trades for high-yield corporate bonds.

Fixed-income instrument: Debt instruments and preferred stock that pay a fixed dollar amount.

Fixed-rate payer: The party in an interest rate swap that agrees to pay a fixed rate and receive a floating rate.

FLEX option: Exhange-traded option where certain features of the option can be customized.

Floating rate: An interest rate whose value is based on some reference rate and is periodically reset.

Floating-rate certificate of deposit (FRCD): A CD whose interest rate changes periodically in accordance with a predetermined formula that indicates the spread above some index at which the rate will reset periodically.

Floating-rate payer: The party in an interest rate swap that agrees to pay a floating rate and receive a fixed rate.

Floating-rate security: A debt obligation in which the coupon interest is adjusted periodically on the basis of some predetermined benchmark.

Floor brokers (also called pit brokers): Floor traders who not only buy and sell for their own account but also execute customer orders.

Flotion: An option on an interest rate floor.

Foreign exchange risk: The risk of an adverse foreign exchange rate movement.

Foreign market: A classification of the global financial market. It is the financial market of a country where the securities of issuers not domiciled in the country are sold and traded. It is part of the internal or national market.

Forms of pricing efficiency: Known as the weak form, the semistrong form, and strong form, these relate to the various types of information believed to be impounded or embedded in the prices of publicly traded securities.

Forward contract: A nonstandardized contract (nonexchange-traded contract) calling for the future delivery of something at a specified price at the end of a designated period of time.

Forward rate (also called implied forward rate): The rate on an investment beginning at some future date and for some specific length of time. Since it is derived from the yield curve, it is called an implicit forward rate.

Forward rate agreement (FRA): The over-the-counter

equivalent of the exchange-traded futures contract on short-term rates, typically LIBOR, and is a cash settlement contract. The elements of an FRA are the contract rate, reference rate, settlement rate, notional amount, and settlement date.

Forward start swap: A swap wherein the swap does not begin until some future date that is specified in the swap agreement.

Fourth market: Refers to private transactions between institutional investors who deal directly with each other without utilizing the services of a broker-dealer intermediary.

Fractional reserve banking system: One in which a bank must hold or reserve some portion of its deposits in a form approved by the central bank, such as the Fed in the United States.

Frankfurter Wertpapierbörse (FWB): The Frankfurt Stock Exchange.

Free float: The portion of the outstanding total stock of a corporation that is available for trading on public stock markets.

Frictional unemployment: The unavoidable level of unemployment in the civilian workforce that arises because of the temporary unemployment of people changing jobs or those seeking new or better ones.

Frictions: Economic term for features of a market, or its environment, that keep the price it sets from being the fair market price.

Frontrun: The action of a brokerage firm, which knows of an institutional investor's plans to execute a program trade, to take positions that will benefit from the price movement that might result from the program trade.

Fundamental security analysis: Analysis of key financial and economic variables that is designed to reveal mispriced securities.

Futures commissions merchant: An authorized futures broker.

Futures contract: A standardized exchange-traded, legal agreement between a buyer and a seller in which the buyer agrees to take delivery of something at a specified price at the end of a designated period of time and the seller agrees to make delivery.

Futures option: An option on a futures contract, which gives the buyer the right to buy from or sell to the writer a designated futures contract at a designated price.

Futures price: The price at which the parties to a futures contract agree to transact at the settlement date.

G-5 countries: The five most developed economies and financial systems in the world—the United States, Japan, Great Britain, France, and Germany.

GAAP surplus (or reserves): Surplus as calculated by accountants using the Generally Accepted Accounting Principles. It is measured in a slightly different way than the statutory surplus.

Garn-St. Germain Act: This 1982 legislation permitted banks to offer money market accounts, which are similar to those offered by money market mutual funds, and it increased the types of financial activities that savings and loan associations could engage in.

General account product: A product whose guaranteed performance is supported by the insurance company to the extent of its solvency.

General obligation bond: The broadest type of tax-backed debt and includes two types of general obligation pledges: (1) an unlimited tax general obligation debt, the stronger form of general obligation pledge because it is secured by the issuer's unlimited taxing power and (2) limited tax general obligation debt which is a limited tax pledge because there is a statutory limit on tax rates that the issuer may levy to service the debt.

Global Depositary Receipt (GDR): A tradable right to ownership of a specific number of a foreign company's shares, which is issued by a financial institution holding the shares in trust.

Global Index: An international stock market index that is a joint product of First Boston Corporation and London-based *Euromoney*.

Goal of monetary policy: A condition such as high employment or price level stability that monetary policymakers seek to bring about in the economy.

Government brokers (or dealers): Brokers used by primary dealers trading Treasury securities with each other.

Government-sponsored enterprises (GSEs): Privately owned, publicly chartered entities that are created by Congress to reduce the cost of capital for certain borrowing sectors of the economy deemed to be important enough to warrant assistance.

Graduated-payment mortgage: A mortgage design in which the mortgage rate is fixed over the life of the mortgage, and the monthly mortgage payment grows at a constant rate during a portion of the life of the contract, thereafter leveling off.

Gramm-Leach-Bliley Act (GLB): Also called the Financial Modernization Act of 1999, this Act removed restrictions on commercial banks, investment banks, and insurance companies from affiliating with each other. It removed the obstacles imposed by the Glass-Steagall Act.

Gross spread (or underwriter discount): The difference between the price at which a security is reoffered to the public and the price paid by the underwriter to the issuer.

Growing-equity mortgage (GEM): Fixed-rate mortgage whose monthly mortgage payments increase over time such that the higher monthly mortgage payments serve to pay down the principal faster and shorten the term of the mortgage.

Guaranteed bond: A bond whose obligation is guaranteed by another entity.

Guaranteed investment contract or guaranteed income contract (GIC): A pure investment life insurance product in which, for a single premium, the insurance company agrees to pay the policyholder the principal amount and a predetermined annual crediting rate over the life of the contract.

Hang Seng Index: The stock index of the Hong Kong Stock Exchange.

Health insurance company: A financial intermediary that insures against medical treatment expenses.

High-grade bond: A bond with a quality rating that indicates low credit risk.

High-LTV Loans: Mortgage design for a high credit quality borrower that permits a lesser down or no down payment, resulting in loans with higher LTVs.

High-yield bond (also called junk bond): A bond whose quality rating is designated as noninvestment grade.

Hoekman: A specialist on the Amsterdam Stock Exchange.

Home equity loan-backed security: An asset-backed security backed by a pool of home equity loans.

Home Owners Loan Act: The 1933 law that allows the federal government to charter S&Ls.

Hot issue (also called special issue):   Refers to a security (collateral) that is in short supply for a repurchase agreement.

Hybrid pension plan: Plan that combines some features of the defined benefit approach and some aspects of the defined contribution method.

Immediacy: Term for a market's ability to provide an investor with a quick execution of a trade order, whether it is to buy or to sell, at a fair market price.

Impact cost: A form of execution cost resulting from the bid–ask spread and a price concession demanded by dealers in the stock to mitigate their risk that an investor's demand for the stock is motivated by information that the investor may have that is not embodied in the stock's price.

In-the-money option: An option that has intrinsic value.

Income effect: The rise in the interest rate that occurs because an increase in the money supply causes the economy's income to expand and the demand for money to increase.

Index arbitrage: A strategy that seeks to enhance returns as a result of the mispricing of the futures contract relative to the cash index.

Indexing: A passive investment strategy that involves buying stocks according to the composition of an index in order to generate the level of returns that the index achieves.

Indirect investment: An investment an investor has by holding a claim on a financial intermediary that has made direct investments.

Indirect quote: The convention in quoting an exchange rate expressed in terms of the number of units of a foreign currency that can be exchanged for one unit of a local currency.

Inflation premium: The portion of the required rate of return that compensates the investor for expected change in the purchasing power of the monetary units in which the cash flows of an asset are denominated.

Information costs: Costs associated with assessing the value of a financial asset.

Initial margin requirement: The percentage of the total market value of a security that an investor must put up in cash when buying a security on margin.

Initial margin: When a position is first taken in a futures contract, the amount per contract specified by the exchange that must be put up as margin.

Initial public offering (IPO):   The common stock offerings issued by firms that have not previously sold common shares to the public.

Insider trading: The purchase or sale of a firm's securities by its officers (among others) who are seeking to benefit from their knowledge of nonpublic information about the firm's financial prospects.

Insured benefit plan: Plan whose defined benefits the sponsor insures through an annuity policy with a life insurance company.

Insured bonds: Municipal bonds backed by insurance policies written by commercial insurance companies, as well as by the credit of the municipal issuer.

Interbank market: A market for funds in which only banks participate.

Interest rate cap (or ceiling):   An interest rate agreement in which one party agrees to pay the other if the reference rate exceeds a predetermined level.

Interest rate collar: A position created by combining an interest rate cap and an interest rate floor that confines the reference rate to a particular range of possible values.

Interest rate floor: An interest rate agreement in which one party agrees to pay the other if the reference rate falls below a predetermined level.

Interest rate parity: The relationship among the spot exchange rate, the interest rates in two countries, and the forward rate.

Interest rate risk: The risk that a depository institution will misjudge future interest rates and take positions with regard to borrowing and lending that may create a negative spread when rates change.

Interest rate risk-based capital requirements: Capital requirements for a depository institution that are based on the interest rate risk of its assets.

Interest rate swap: An agreement in which two parties (called counterparties) agree to exchange periodic interest payments.

Interest rate/equity swap: A swap in which one party pays a fixed or floating interest rate, while the other party pays a rate based on the return on some equity index.

Interest-only (IO) class: A stripped mortgage-backed security that receives all the interest payments.

Intermarket sector spread: The spread between the interest rate offered in two sectors of the bond market on issues with the same maturity.

Intermediate target: A financial or economic variable that responds in a reliable way to changes in an operating target, and that has a somewhat predictable impact on the variables constituting the central bank's economic goals.

Internal market (also called national market):   A classification of a global financial market composed of two parts: the domestic market and the foreign market.

International Bank Act of 1978 (IBA):   U.S. legislation that imposed some regulations, long familiar to domestic banks, on foreign-owned banks operating offices and branches in the United States.

International reserves: The amount of currency from large industrial countries that is held by a country's central bank and government.

Intramarket sector spread: The spread between the yield offered on two bonds in the same sector of the bond market.

Intrinsic value: The component of an option price that reflects its economic value if it is exercised immediately.

Investment advisor: The manager of a fund's portfolios.

Investment advisory fee (or management fee):   Fee charged by an investment advisory firm for managing the portfolio of an investment company.

Investment bankers: Market participants who work with issuers to distribute newly issued securities.

Investment company: A financial institution that pools funds and purchases assets on behalf of the investors.

Investment Company Act of 1940:   A major piece of legislation regarding the operations and regulations of mutual funds and closed-end funds.

Investment Company Institute: The national association for open-end or mutual funds.

Investment grade: The term for bonds rated in the

highest four quality categories of Moody's or Standard & Poor's systems.

Investment income: Revenue generated on an insurance company's portfolio of invested assets.

Investment objective: A fund's stated goal, which determines the kinds of assets in which it invests.

IRA (Individual Retirement Account):   A tax-deferred retirement plan that may be individual sponsored or employer sponsored.

Itayosa and Zaraba: Two auction methods used on the Tokyo Stock Exchange.

Japan Securities and Exchange Surveillance Commission: Created in 1992 as part of the MOF, the commission will try to prevent insider trading and favored treatment for big investors that came to light in the 1991 stock market scandal in Japan.

Japanese banks: These banks include Japanese city banks, local banks, long-term credit banks, trust banks, and mutual banks.

Jumbo loan: A mortgage loan that is nonconforming because the amount of the loan is greater than the maximum permissible loan size specified by an agency.

Junk bonds: Corporate debt securities that carry a rather high amount of credit risk or default risk and that offer a high yield commensurate with that risk.

Keynesians: Economists whose view of monetary policy largely focuses on the stimulation of demand by the targeting of short-term interest rates.

L: An inclusive measure of money and certain liquid assets.

Lessee: The party to a lease agreement that uses but does not own the equipment being leased.

Lessor: The party to a lease agreement that owns but does not use the equipment being leased.

Leveraged buyout (or LBO):   The acquisition of a company by another that uses a substantial amount of debt to finance the acquisition.

Leveraged lease: A type of leasing arrangement whereby the lessor provides only a portion of the funds to finance the cost of the leased asset, and the balance is borrowed from a third party.

Liability: An obligatory payment to a supplier of a good, a service, or funds.

Liability swap: The use of an interest rate swap to change the cash flow characteristics of liabilities.

Life insurance company: A financial intermediary that primarily insures against death but also sells investment-oriented products.

Lifetime cap: A limit placed on the maximum and minimum mortgage rate that can be set on an adjustable-rate mortgage over the life of the loan.

Limit order: An order to buy or sell a security that may be executed only when the market price of the security changes in a specific way.

Limit order book: The place where limit orders or stop orders that member firm's floor broker cannot transact immediately are recorded for later execution.

Liquidating trust: A commercial mortgage-backed securities deal where the pool of commercial mortgage loans backing the deal are nonperforming mortgage loans (i.e., loans where the borrowers are in default). A liquidating trust is also called a nonperforming trust.

Liquidity effect: The initial decline in the rate of interest that occurs because of an increase in the money supply.

Liquidity preference theory of interest: The theory, propounded by Keynes, that the interest rate is set in the market for money where the demand for money balances interacts with the central bank's supply of liquidity.

Liquidity premium: The portion of the required rate of return that compensates the investor for the perceived difficulty and cost of selling the asset in the future.

Listed stock: A stock eligible for trading on an organized exchange.

Load: Sales commission that a mutual fund may charge.

Load funds: Mutual funds that charge sales commissions.

Loan-to-value (LTV) ratio: The ratio of the amount of the loan to the market (or appraised) value of the property.

Loanable funds theory of interest: The theory that the level of the interest rate depends on the supply and demand for funds across the sectors of the economy.

LOC paper: Commercial paper supported by a letter of credit from a bank.

Locals: Floor traders who buy and sell futures contracts for their own account.

Lockout period: A time period over which no principal is paid to the investor in an asset-backed security.

London interbank offered rate (LIBOR):   The rate paid on Eurodollar CDs.

Long futures position: When an investor takes an initial position in the market by buying a futures contract.

Long hedge (also called a buy hedge):   A hedge in which futures are purchased to protect against a rise in the cash price of a financial instrument or portfolio.

Long option position: The position of one owning the option and, hence, the right to exercise it.

Long-term equity anticipation securities (LEAPs^{TM}): Options on individual stocks that have an expiration date up to three years in the future.

M$_1$:   The monetary aggregate that measures the amount of medium of exchange, defined as the sum of dollars held in the form of currency and demand deposits.

M$_2$:   The monetary aggregate that measures all forms of money that have the capacity of storing value, defined as M$_1$ plus all dollars held in time and savings accounts at banks and thrift institutions, plus all dollars invested in retail money market mutual funds, plus some additional accounts such as overnight repurchase agreements.

M$_3$:   The monetary aggregate that equals M$_2$ plus certain other financial assets, including long-term time deposits, commercial paper, bankers acceptances, and some Treasury securities.

Macaulay duration: A measure of the weighted average time to maturity of a bond.

Maintenance margin: The minimum margin level to which an investor's equity position may fall as a result of an unfavorable price movement before the investor is required to deposit additional margin.

Maintenance margin requirement: The minimum percentage of the equity in the investor's margin account to the total market value. If the investor's margin account falls below the minimum maintenance margin, the investor is required to put up additional cash.

Manufactured housing–backed security: An asset-backed security backed by a pool of manufactured housing loans.

Margin buying: Purchasing stock with money borrowed

(at some rate of interest) from the brokerage firm handling the order, with the stock serving as collateral for the loan.

Marginal productivity of capital: The additional gain from additional amounts of investment, in Fisher's theory.

Marginal rate of time preference: The willingness of someone to trade current consumption for future consumption, in Fisher's theory.

Market failure: The term used by some economists for the inability of a competitive market to remain so without the help of government, or the inability of an uncompetitive market, if not aided by government, to become competitive.

Market if touched order: An order to buy or sell shares that becomes a market order if the stock's price reaches a specified level.

Market index (or indicator):   A measure based on the prices and often number of outstanding shares of a selected number of stocks that is supposed to convey in formation about the relative value of shares traded on a market.

Market maker: Also called a dealer, this institution or individual facilitates trading in an asset by standing ready to buy or sell an asset, holding the asset in inventory, and making a profit on the difference between the two prices.

Market model: The mathematical expression of the hypothesis that the returns on a stock reflect only two forces, the overall market for securities and developments particular to the firm that issued the stock.

Market order: An order to buy or sell shares immediately at the best available price.

Market segmentation theory: A theory that recognizes that investors have preferred habitats dictated by savings and investment flows.

Market-related risk: The variability in an asset's returns that reflects changes in the average or typical value of assets. Also, another term for systematic risk.

Marking to market: The requirement that the market value of a futures position be determined at the end of each trading day so as to realize losses and gains.

Maturity: The day a debt obligation will cease to exist and the day the issuer will redeem the bond by paying the amount owed. The practice in the bond market is to refer to the *term to maturity* of a bond as simply its *maturity* or *term*.

Maturity intermediation: The function of a financial intermediary by which it transforms a longer-term asset into a shorter-term one when it gives the borrower a loan for a particular length of time and the investor/depositor a financial asset for a possibly different desired investment horizon.

Maturity premium: The portion of the required rate of return that compensates the investor for the price volatility of debt securities of long lives.

Maturity spread (or yield curve spread):   The spread between any two maturity sectors of the market.

McFadden Act of 1927:   This legislation had the goal of preventing large banks from expanding geographically and thereby forcing out or taking over smaller banking entities.

Medium of exchange: The monetary or financial item that is generally accepted in payment for goods, services, and capital transactions, and that serves as a store of value.

Medium-term note (MTN):   Debt obligations that are continuously offered to investors over a period of time by an agent of the issuer.

Ministry of Finance (MOF):   Japan's powerful regulator of many aspects of the financial system.

Mismatch problem: The mismatching of the maturity of assets and liabilities of an institution.

Modified duration: A duration measure that assumes that when interest rates change the cash flow of an asset will not change.

Monetarists: Economists whose view of monetary policy largely focuses on the need for and benefits of a steady rate of growth in the monetary aggregates.

Monetary aggregate: A sum of monetary items that helps to measure the amount of money available to the economy at any time.

Monetary base: The most basic monetary aggregate, also termed *high-powered money*, defined as currency in circulation (or coins and Federal Reserve notes held by the public) plus the total reserves in the banking system.

Money center bank: A bank that raises most of its funds from the domestic and international money markets and that relies very little on deposits or depositors.

Money market: The financial market for short-term debt instruments.

Money market mutual fund: An investment company that invests only in money market instuments.

Money multiplier: The linkage between the banking system's reserves and the amount of money, measured by one of the aggregates, in circulation.

Money supply: The amount of money in circulation within an economy at any time.

Moneyness: The property that allows an asset to function as money, which means that it is a medium of exchange and a store of value.

Moral obligation bond: A form of appropriate-backed obligation for which there is a nonbinding pledge of tax revenue but instead requires legislative approval to appropriate the funds.

Mortgage: Loan secured by real estate.

Mortgage banking (or mortgage lending):   The activity of originating mortgages.

Mortgage bond: A bond in which the issuer has granted the bondholders a lien against pledged assets.

Mortgage loan (or simply mortgage):   A loan in which there is a pledge of property to secure payment of a debt.

Mortgage market: A collection of markets, which includes a primary market, or origination market, and a secondary market where mortgages trade.

Mortgage originator: In a mortgage loan transaction, this is the original lender.

Mortgage pass-through security: Security created when one or more holders of mortgages form a collection (pool) of mortgages and sell shares or participation certificates in the pool.

Mortgage servicing: Activities including collecting monthly payments from mortgagors and forwarding proceeds to owners of the loan, sending payment notices to mortgagors, reminding mortgagors when payments are overdue, maintaining records of mortgage balances, furnishing tax information to mortgagors, administering an escrow account for real estate taxes and insurance purposes, and, if necessary, initiating foreclosure proceedings.

Mortgagee: The lender/investor in a mortgage loan.

Mortgagor: The borrower in a mortgage loan.

Most distant (or deferred) futures contract: The

futures contract for a given underlying farthest away in time from settlement.

Multiline insurance company: A financial intermediary that provides life and health as well as property and casualty insurance.

Multiple listing: The listing of a stock on an exchange in its home country and on an exchange in at least one other country.

Multiple of an index futures contract: The dollar value, for the futures contract, of a point in the index.

Multi-property single borrower deal: A commercial mortgage-backed securities deal where the pool of commercial mortgage loans backing the deal consists of multiple properties for which there is only one borrower.

Municipal bonds: Securities issued by state and local governments and by their creations, such as authorities and special districts.

Mutual holding company (MHC): A hybrid between a pure mutual insurer and a pure stock insurer. Policyholders own a mutual holding company, which in turn owns a majority stake in a stock subsidiary.

Mutual insurance company: An insurance company that has no stock and no external owners, and is essentially owned by its policyholders.

National Association of Insurance Commissioners (NAIC): A voluntary association of state insurance commissioners that develops model laws and regulations for the insurance industry.

National Association of Securities Dealers (NASD): A self-regulatory organization (or SRO), which monitors the relationships among brokers, firms issuing securities, and the investing public.

National Association of Securities Dealers Automated Quotation System (Nasdaq): Major OTC market in the U.S. that is owned and operated by the NASD (the National Association of Securities Dealers). It is an electronic quotation system that provides price quotations to market participants on Nasdaq listed stocks.

National Credit Union Administration (NCUA): The agency of the federal government that regulates credit unions.

National Credit Union Share Insurance Fund (NCUSIF): A government-sponsored insurance fund for deposits in federally chartered credit unions and state-chartered credit unions that elect to participate.

National Futures Association (NFA): The SRO in the United States that has, since the early 1980s, carried out key responsibilities in the futures markets.

Natural person credit union: Another name for a credit union that has individuals as members (as opposed to a corporate credit union).

Nearby futures contract: The futures contract for a given underlying with the closest settlement date.

Negative carry: A net financing position in which the financing cost is greater than the cash yield earned on the asset.

Negotiable certificate of deposit: A CD that allows the initial depositor (or any subsequent owner of the CD) to sell the CD in the open market prior to the maturity date.

Net asset value per share (NAV): The ratio of the market value of the portfolio less the mutual fund's liabilities to the number of mutual fund shares outstanding.

Net financing cost: The difference between the cost of financing a position in an asset and the asset's cash yield. It is also called the cost of carry or simply carry.

Neuer Markt: A German stock exchange that lists small, new companies, typically fast-growing, hi-tech companies.

Nikkei 225 Stock Average: A market index based on 225 of the largest companies on the Tokyo Stock Exchange.

No-load mutual fund: A mutual fund that charges no sales commission.

Nominal expected return: The return computed on the basis of nominal monetary units whose possible different purchasing power is not considered.

Nominal rate of interest: The rate of interest measured in terms of the units in the principal and the units paid in interest, without regard to their changes in purchasing power over the loan's life.

Nonagency pass-through security: A mortgage pass-through security not issued or guaranteed by an agency.

Nonborrowed reserves: The value (computed for a bank or the entire banking system) of total reserves less those reserves created by borrowing from the Fed through its discount window.

Nonconforming mortgage: A mortgage that does not meet the underwriting standards for inclusion in a pool that is collateral for a mortgage pass-through security issued or guaranteed by an agency.

Noncumulative preferred stock: Preferred stock in which the dividend payment, if missed, is forgone by the stockholder.

Nonprime CD: A CD issued by lower-rated domestic banks.

Notional principal amount: The dollar principal amount upon which the interest payments in an interest rate swap or interest rate agreement are based.

NOW (or Negotiable Order of Withdrawal) Account: A form of a negotiable deposit that is entirely equivalent to a checking account and that savings and loan associations or thrifts have been allowed to offer since the early 1980s.

Numeraire: The item that serves as a unit of account, which is the unit used to measure wealth.

Odd lot: Anything less than a round lot of a stock.

Off-balance sheet financing: Borrowings obtained in which debt does not appear on the balance sheet.

Off-the-run Treasury issue: A Treasury issue auctioned prior to the current coupon issues.

Office of Thrift Supervision (OTS): U.S. government agency that regulates savings and loan associations.

Official discount rate: A major element in BOJ monetary policy, this is the BOJ-set rate at which Japanese commercial banks can borrow from the BOJ's discount window.

On-the-run Treasury issue (also called current coupon issue): The most recently auctioned Treasury issue for a given maturity.

Open economy: An economy in which foreign firms and investors account for a large share of economic activity, including participation in the financial markets.

Open interest: The number of contracts that have been entered into but not yet liquidated.

Open market operations: The Fed's purchase or sale in open debt markets of government securities for its own account.

Open order: Also known as good til canceled, this type of order to buy or sell shares remains in effect until the broker is notified otherwise.

Open-end (or mutual) funds: Funds that stand ready to sell new shares to the public and to redeem outstanding shares on demand at a price equal to an appropriate share of their portfolio's value.

Operating target: A financial or monetary variable that the central bank can effectively control through the application of its tools of monetary policy.

Operational or internal efficiency: The characteristic of a market that allows investors to obtain buying and selling services at the lowest possible prices.

Option: A contract in which the writer of the option grants the buyer the right, but not the obligation, to purchase from or sell to the writer something at a specified price within a specified period of time (or at a specified date).

Option on a physical: An interest rate option whose underlying is a fixed-income instrument.

Option price (or option premium): The price of an option.

Options Clearing Corporation (OCC): Established in 1974, the OCC is the SEC-approved corporation that issues, guarantees, registers, clears, and settles all transactions involving listed options on all exchanges.

Organized exchanges: Structured markets that provide for the trading of selected corporate and governmental securities.

Origination fee: A fee, expressed in points, that a mortgage originator charges the borrower for originating a loan.

OTC Bulletin Board (OTCBB): A non-Nasdaq OTC market, sometimes called simply the Bulletin Board that displays real-time quotes, last-sale prices, and volume information for stocks not traded on NYSE, Amex, or Nasdaq.

Out-of-the-money option: A call option in which the current asset price is less than the strike price, or a put option in which the current asset price is greater than the strike price.

Outperformance option: An exotic option whose payoff is based on the relative performance of two assets at the expiration date.

Over-the-counter (OTC) market: A largely unregulated market whereby geographically dispersed traders, who are linked to one another via telecommunication systems and computers, trade in securities.

Over-the-counter (OTC) trading: Trading that results from geographically dispersed traders or market-makers linked to one another via telecommunication systems.

Overcollateralization: A form of credit enhancement in which a pool of assets is used with a greater principal amount than the principal amount of the asset-backed securities.

Overnight repo: A repurchase agreement with a maturity of one day.

Participation certificate (PC): Pass-through security issued by Freddie Mac.

Pass-through structure: An asset-backed security structure in which the principal cash flows are paid to the securityholders on a pro rata basis.

Payer swaption: A swaption that entitles the option buyer to enter into an interest rate swap in which the buyer of the option pays a fixed rate and receives a floating rate.

Payment mechanism: The financial arrangement by which the buyer of a commodity pays the seller with some form of money.

Payment-in-kind (PIK) bond: A form of deferred coupon structure that gives the issuer an option to pay cash at a coupon payment date or to give the bondholder a similar bond.

Payment-to-income (PTI) ratio: The ratio of monthly payments to monthly income, which is a measure of the ability of a mortgage applicant to make monthly payments (both mortgage and real estate tax payments).

Pension Benefit Guaranty Corporation (PBGC): The federal agency established in 1974 by the ERISA legislation to insure the vested benefits of pension plan participants.

Pension plan: A fund that is established for the payment of retirement benefits.

Perfect hedge (or textbook hedge): A hedge in which the profit and loss on the cash and futures positions are equal.

Perfect market: Term from economic theory for the kind of market that has specific characteristics of trading and price setting and that is free of the frictions that keep a fair market price from being set in trading.

Performing loan: A loan whose borrower has fulfilled all obligations to date.

Periodic cap: A restriction in an adjustable-rate mortgage as to the amount that the mortgage rate may increase or decrease at the reset date.

Perpetual (or consul): An asset that promises to pay a fixed amount per year indefinitely and not to repay the principal at any time.

Perpetual preferred stock: Preferred stock that does not have a maturity date.

Philadelphia Stock Exchange (PHLX): An organized U.S. securities market where options and other securities are traded.

Pink sheets: A non-Nasdaq OTC market.

Pipeline risk: In mortgage lending, the risk associated with originating mortgages.

Plain vanilla swap: This is a generic interest rate swap in which the counterparties exchange a fixed rate for a floating rate, and the notional principal amount is the same over the life of the swap.

Planned amortization class (PAC) tranche: A type of CMO bond class providing a specified schedule to retire the original principal of the bondholders.

Plan sponsor: The entity that establishes a pension plan for its employees, which may be a private business or a unit of a state/local government. A sponsor can also be a union acting on behalf of its members, or individuals acting for themselves.

Policy lapse: The termination of an insurance policy.

Portfolio strategy (also called dynamic hedging): A strategy that seeks to synthetically create a put option.

Portfolio: A group of financial assets or securities.

Positive carry: A net financing position in which the cash yield earned on the asset is greater than the financing cost.

Post on an exchange: The location for the trading of a particular stock or number of stocks.

Predictability: The risk that an asset's value will change over the life of an investment or the uncertainty about the return the asset will generate over that time.

Preemptive rights offering: The offering of common stock by a corporation to existing shareholders at a price below market value.

Preferred habitat theory: Theory that the term structure reflects expected future rates and a risk premium that depends on the supply-demand situation in maturity sectors and that must be offered to induce market participants to move from their preferred maturity sectors.

Preferred stock: A class of stock in which the stockholder is entitled to dividends but, unlike dividends on common stock, dividends are a specified percentage of par or face value. It also has priority over common stock in dividends and distributions in the event of liquidation.

Prerefunded bonds (or refunded bonds): Municipal bonds that originally may have been issued as general obligation or revenue bonds but that are now secured by an escrow fund consisting entirely of direct U.S. government obligations that are sufficient for paying the bondholders.

Premium on an insurance policy: The price the policyholder pays for the insurance policy.

Prepayment: A payment made in excess of the monthly mortgage payment.

Prepayment penalty mortgage (PPM): A mortgage design wherein the borrower can be assessed a penalty if there is a prepayment.

Prepayment risk: The risk associated with the ownership of a mortgage or mortgage-backed security due to the uncertainty of the cash flow arising from prepayments.

Present value: The amount of money that, if invested at a given interest rate, will generate a particular set of future cash flows.

Price discovery process: An economic function of financial markets that signals how the funds in the economy should be allocated among financial assets.

Price expectations effect: The rise in the interest rate that occurs because a rise in the money supply creates expectations of future inflation.

Price risk: A risk associated with investing in a bond that arises when a bond must be sold before its maturity date at a price that is unknown because the future yield is unknown.

Price-level-adjusted mortgage: Similar to the traditional mortgage except that monthly payments are designed to be level in purchasing power rather than in nominal terms, and that the fixed rate is the real rate rather than the nominal rate.

Pricing or external efficiency: The characteristic of a market in which the trading price reflects all relevant information about the value of the asset being traded.

Primary (or recognized) dealers: Securities firms and commercial banks that the Federal Reserve will deal with in implementing its open market operations.

Primary market: The financial market where financial claims that are newly issued are sold.

Prime CD: A CD issued by high-rated domestic banks.

Principal amortization period: The period over which the principal is repaid to investors following the lockout period.

Principal value (also called principal, par value, maturity value, redemption value, and face value): The amount that the issuer agrees to repay the bondholder at the maturity date.

Principal-only (PO) class: A stripped mortgage-backed security that receives all the principal payments.

Private placement: The sale of new securities directly to one or a few investors rather than through public offering.

Probability distribution: A listing, through a table or a mathematical formula, of the possible values of a random variable and the likelihood that each value will occur.

Program (or basket) trade: The computer-assisted and simultaneous sale (or purchase) of shares in a large number of different stocks.

Property and casualty (P&C) insurance company: Financial intermediary that insures against a wide variety of losses to personal or commercial property.

Prospectus: A part of the registration statement that is filed with the SEC by an issuer of a security and distributed to the public.

Protective put buying strategy: A strategy of buying put options on securities held in a portfolio to ensure a minimum price for the securities.

PSA prepayment benchmark: A prepayment convention that is expressed as a monthly series of annual prepayment rates assuming that prepayment rates are low for newly originated mortgages and then will speed up as the mortgages become seasoned.

Public order: An order to buy or sell shares of an exchange-listed stock that a member firm is executing for one of its customers

Purchasing power parity: The relationship that posits that the exchange rate of a foreign currency is proportional to the domestic inflation rate, and inversely proportional to foreign inflation.

Purchasing power risk (also called inflation risk): The risk attached to potential purchasing power of the expected cash flow.

Pure expectations theory: Theory that the term structure reflects only expectations of future short-term rates.

Put option: Provision in a loan or debt security that allows the buyer to demand early repayment of the security's principal. The buyer has the right to sell the underlying to the option writer.

Put provision: A provision in a bond issue that grants the bondholder the right to sell the issue back to the issuer at par value on designated dates.

Put–call parity relationship: The relationship between the price of a call option and the price of a put option on the same underlying instrument, with the same strike price and the same expiration date.

Putable bond: A bond that grants the bondholder the right to sell the issue back to the issuer at par value on designated dates.

Quality option (also called swap option): The option granted to the short of a Treasury bond (or note) futures contract to select the Treasury issue to deliver.

Quality spread (or credit spread): The spread between Treasury securities and non-Treasuries that are identical in all respects except for creditworthiness or risk of default, as represented by a quality rating.

Real expected return: The return computed on the basis of nominal monetary units adjusted for differences in purchasing power that may have developed over the life of the investment.

Real rate of interest: The expected or required annual rate of return that rewards the investor for waiting or for time.

Receiver swaption: A swaption that grants the option buyer the right to enter into an interest rate swap that requires paying a floating rate and receiving a fixed rate.

Reconstitution: The process of purchasing stripped Treasury securities to create synthetic Treasury coupon securities.

Red herring: The preliminary prospectus filed with the SEC by the issuer of a security.

Reference rate: The benchmark interest rate used in an interest rate swap and interest rate agreement.

Refunding provision: A provision that denies the issuer the right to redeem bonds during some period of time after issuance with proceeds received from issuing lower-cost debt obligations ranking equal to or superior to the debt to be redeemed.

Regional bank: A bank that relies primarily on deposits for its funding and makes less use of the money markets to obtain funds.

Registration statement: Statement filed with the SEC for the purpose of disclosing pertinent information about a security and the issuer.

Regulation Q: Rule that, at one time, allowed the Fed to impose a ceiling on the maximum interest rate that depository institutions could pay on deposits other than demand accounts.

Regulatory risk: The risk that regulators will change the rules so as to impact the earnings of financial institutions unfavorably.

Reinsurer: A financial intermediary that accepts insurance risks from a variety of primary insurers.

Reinvestment risk: A risk associated with investing in a bond that arises when proceeds received prior to the planned horizon date must be reinvested at an unknown rate.

Remarketed preferred stock: Preferred stock whose dividend rate is determined periodically by a remarketing agent who resets the dividend rate so that any preferred stock can be tendered at par and be resold (remarketed) at the original offering price.

Reopened issue: An outstanding issue that is increased at an auction instead of a new issue auctioned.

Repurchase agreement: Transaction calling for the sale of a security and its repurchase at a future date. Both the sale price and the purchase price are specified in the agreement, the difference between the two prices being the dollar interest cost of the loan.

Required reserve ratio: The Fed's ratio of mandatory reserves to deposits.

Reserve funds: A form of credit enhancement in which a fund is established by the issuer of the asset-backed security that may be used to make principal and interest payments when there are losses.

Reserve requirements: The percentage of deposits that, by Federal Reserve Board rules, depository institutions must keep in the form of cash or deposits in a Federal Reserve bank.

Reserves: The sum of the cash and deposits in the Federal Reserve Bank System that a depository institution holds for the purpose of meeting reserve requirements.

Revenue bonds: Municipal bonds issued for either project or enterprise financings where the bond issuers pledge the revenues generated by the project to the bondholders.

Reverse cash and carry trade: Strategy in which a futures contract is purchased, the underlying for the futures contract is sold short, and the proceeds from the short sale are invested in an instrument that matures at the same time as the settlement date of the futures contract.

Reverse mortgage: Mortgage design that is created for senior homeowners who want to convert their home equity into cash

Reversibility: The property of the costs of buying and selling an asset that determines how quickly an investor can buy it and turn it back into cash.

Revolving period: A time period over which no principal is paid to the investor in an asset-backed security.

Riegle-Neal Interstate Banking and Branching Efficiency Act: This act permits adequately capitalized and managed bank holding companies to acquire banks in any state subject to certain limitations and approval by the Federal Reserve and, beginning in June 1997, permitted interstate mergers between adequately capitalized and managed banks, subject to concentration limits and state laws.

Risk factor: A value used in determining the payoff of a credit option.

Risk transfer: The act of hedging a financial position so as to move some risk to another party.

Roller coaster swap: An interest rate swap in which the notional principal amount can rise or fall from period to period.

Round lot: Typically, 100 shares of a stock.

Rule 144A: An SEC rule that permits corporations—including non-U.S. firms—to issue securities without the complete and extensive registration process that SEC normally requires. That is, Rule 144A provides a "safe harbor" from the Securities Act of 1993. This rule is applicable only for the issue and sale of securities to Qualified Institutional Buyers (QIBs) and for the exchange of such securities among QIBs. A QIB is a finanicial institution that has at least $100 million invested in securities of issuers that are not affiliated with the QIB.

Saitori: Special members of the Tokyo Stock Exchange who match buy and sell orders but do not take positions for their own account.

Samurai commercial paper: Yen-denominated commercial paper sold in Japan by non-Japanese entities.

Savings and loan association (S&L): A type of depository institution that typically provides mortgage loans.

Savings bank: An early form of the savings and loan association, which appears only in certain geographical areas and that specializes in home mortgages.

Search costs: Costs in locating a counterparty to a transaction.

Seat on an exchange: Term for membership in an organized exchange.

Second market: Refers to trading in the OTC market of stocks not listed on an exchange.

Secondary market: A market in which outstanding or existing securities are traded among investors.

Secondary Mortgage Market Enhancement Act of 1984 (SMMEA): Legislation qualifying mortgage-backed securities earning a high-quality rating from one of the main commercial rating agencies as legal investments for federally chartered banks and thrifts.

Secondary reserves: Short-term or money market securities that a depository institution holds for the purpose of satisfying net withdrawals and customer loan demands.

Securities Act of 1933: Federal legislation that deals primarily with disclosure requirements for the distribution of new securities.

Securities and Exchange Commission (SEC): A federal regulatory body responsible for administering securities laws in the United States.

Securities and Investment Board (SIB): Great Britain's main governmental monitor of the securities industry.

Securities Exchange Act of 1934: Federal legislation that created the Securities and Exchange Commission, and deals with requirements for the periodic disclosure of publicly traded, seasoned securities and the regulation of activities in securities markets.

Securitized mortgage: A mortgage included in a pool of mortgages that is used as collateral for a mortgage-backed security.

Self-regulatory organization (SRO): A group that, with the sponsorship or authority of a government, monitors the behavior of its members to ensure that they meet certain well-established standards in the conduct of business.

Selling group: Syndicate formed to distribute (sell) a new issue.

Senior bank loan: A bank loan that has a priority position over subordinated lenders (bondholders) with respect to repayment of interest and principal.

Senior/subordinated structure: A form of credit enhancement in which there is a senior class and one or more subordinated classes with the subordinated classes providing credit support for the other class (i.e., the senior class).

Separate account product: A product whose performance depends solely on an account chosen by the policyholder.

Sequential-pay tranche: CMO tranches that are scheduled to be paid off in sequence.

Serial bond: A bond issue in which specified principal amounts become due on specified dates.

Serial maturity structure: A bond issue's requirement that a portion of the debt obligation be retired each year.

Settlement date (or delivery date): The designated date at which the parties to a futures contract must transact.

Settlement price: At the end of each trading day, the closing price determined by the exchange for the futures contract.

Shelf registration (or SEC Rule 415): The rule allowing firms to sell securities on a continuous basis by filing a single registration document.

Short futures position: When an investor takes an initial position in the market by selling a futures contract.

Short hedge (also called a sell hedge): A hedge in which futures are sold to protect against a decline in the cash price of a financial instrument or portfolio.

Short option position: The obligation to perform according to the specifications of an option if the long position chooses to exercise the option.

Short sale: The sale of an asset that the seller has borrowed and must repay to the lender.

Single-investor (or direct) lease: A lease in which all of the financing of the leased asset is provided by the lessor from its own funds.

Sinking fund provision: A provision that requires the issuer to retire a specified portion of an issue each year.

Skewness: The characteristic of a probability distribution that creates a greater likelihood of values on one side of the mean than on the other.

Sociedades de Valores: Term for Spanish brokerage firms.

Société de Bourse: A brokerage firm in France or Belgium.

Societá di Intermediazione Mobilaire: A brokerage firm in Italy.

Special purpose vehicle or special purpose corporation: A legal entity created in a securitization transaction to issue asset-backed securities.

Specialist: The person designated and approved by an organized exchange to function as a market-maker in a stock.

Spot market (also called cash market): The market in which a financial asset trades for immediate delivery.

Spot (or cash) exchange rate market: The market for settlement of a foreign exchange transaction within two business days.

Spot rate: The yield on a zero-coupon instrument. The term is used interchangeably with zero-coupon rate.

Spot rate curve: The graphical depiction of the relationship between the spot rate and its maturity. This curve graphically represents the term structure of interest rates.

Spread income (or margin): A depository institution's margin of profit, which is the difference between the rate earned on assets (loans and securities) and the cost of funds (deposits and other sources).

Stagflation: The condition of both inflation and recession with high unemployment.

Standard deviation: The square root of a distribution's variance.

Standby fee: Fee paid to an underwriter in a standby underwriting arrangement.

Standby underwriting arrangement: An underwriting arrangement calling for the underwriter to buy a firm's unsubscribed shares, which are those that cannot be distributed by the issuer.

Statutory surplus (or reserves): Surplus as determined by computing assets and liabilities as specified by state statutes.

Step-up bond: A form of deferred coupon structure in which the coupon rate is low for an initial period and then increases to a higher coupon rate thereafter.

Stock exchange: An organized and somewhat regulated secondary market, where trading in stock occurs in a specific geographical location.

Stock Exchange Automatic Quotation System (SEAQ): The London International Stock Exchange's computerized trading system.

Stock insurance company: An insurance company that is similar in structure to a public company, and whose stock is traded publicly.

Stop order: An order to buy or sell a set number of shares of stock that is conditional on the level of the stock's price and becomes a market order when and if the price reaches a specific level.

Stop yield: In a Treasury securities auction, the highest yield accepted by the Treasury.

Strike rate: In an interest rate cap or floor, the predetermined level of the reference rate that is used to determine when and how much the seller must compensate the buyer.

Strike spread: The spread in basis points that is used in a credit option to determine the payoff of the option.

Stripped mortgage-backed securities: A mortgage-backed security created by distributing the principal and interest from a pool of underlying mortgages on an unequal basis to two classes of securityholders.

Stripped Treasury security: A zero-coupon instrument created by stripping a Treasury security.

STRIPS: A zero-coupon instrument created from stripping a Treasury security and created as part of the Treasury's Stripped Trading of Registered Interest and Principal Securities program.

Structured note: A medium-term note created using a derivative instrument so as to create a non-traditional coupon payment.

Subordinated debenture bond: A bond in which the bondholders rank after secured debt, after debenture bonds, and often after some general creditors in their claim on assets and earnings.

Subprime loan: Mortgage loan to a borrower who has credit problems due to difficulties in repayment of debt.

Supplementary capital: Tier 2 capital requirements for a commercial bank consisting of loan-loss reserves, certain types of preferred stock, perpetual debt, hybrid capital instruments and equity contract notes, and subordinated debt.

Support bond: A type of CMO bond class that provides support for the PAC bonds in the structure.

Surplus: The difference between an insurance company's assets and liabilities.

Swap reversal: A secondary market transaction in the swap market in which a party that wants to close out a swap position arranges for an additional swap in which the maturity on the new swap is equal to the time remaining of the original swap.

Swap sale (or swap assignment): A secondary market transaction in the swap market in which a party that wishes to close out the original swap finds another party that is willing to accept its obligations under the swap.

Swaption: An option on an interest rate swap.

Swiss Performance Index (SPI): The stock market index based on almost 400 firms drawn from the Swiss stock exchanges.

Symmetric distribution: A probability distribution in which the probability for values above the mean is the same as for those below the mean.

Syndicated bank loan: A bank loan provided by a group of banks.

Systematic risk: The variability in an asset's return that derives from its relationship to the general market for securities and that cannot be eliminated by inclusion of the asset in a portfolio.

Tail: The difference between the average yield of all the bids accepted by the Treasury at an auction and the stop yield.

Tangible asset: An asset whose value depends on particular physical properties—examples are buildings, land, or machinery.

Tax status: The exposure of gains or payments from an asset to taxation by various governmental units.

Tax-backed debt: Debt obligations backed by tax revenues and that include general obligation debt, appropriation-backed obligations, and debt obligations supported by public credit enhancement programs.

Tax-oriented leases: A lease in which in exchange for tax benefits, a lessor provides lower-cost financing to the lessee than the lessee could get by purchasing the equipment with borrowed funds.

Technical analyst: Also called a chartist, this investor follows a strategy of selecting stocks solely on the basis of price patterns or trading volume.

Term certificate of deposit: A CD issued with a maturity greater than one year.

Term life insurance: A form of insurance that has no value if the insured party does not die before the end of the set policy period.

Term maturity structure: A bond issue's provision that requires the debt to be fully repaid at the end of the bond's planned life.

Term repo: A repurchase agreement with a maturity of more than one day.

Term structure of interest rates: The relationship between the yields on comparable securities with different maturities.

Term to maturity: Also called maturity, this is the time remaining in the planned life of a security.

Thickness of the market: A term referring to the frequency of transactions in a particular asset.

Thin market: Describes a market where an asset is the subject of few trades on a regular or continuing basis.

Third market: Mechanism for the trading of stocks that are listed on one or more exchanges in the OTC markets.

Third-party guarantee: A form of credit enhancement that can be either a letter of credit from a bank or a policy from an insurance company.

Thrift certificate of deposit: A CD issued by savings and loan associations and savings banks.

Tick-test rules: Rules about stock price movements that determine whether short sale orders can be executed.

Tilt problem: The fact that, in real or inflation-adjusted terms, the early payments on a mortgage can be, and often are, larger and more burdensome to a borrower than the later payments.

Time deposit (or CD): An interest-paying account that has a fixed maturity date, often called a certificate of deposit.

Time premium: The component of an option price that represents the amount by which the option's market price exceeds its intrinsic value.

Timing cost: A form of execution cost that arises when an adverse price movement of the stock during the time of the transaction can be attributed in part to other activity in the stock and is not the result of a particular transaction.

Timing option: The option granted to the short of a Treasury bond (or note) futures contract to decide when in the delivery month to deliver.

TOPIX: The Tokyo Stock Price Index, which is based on prices for the stocks of the established, large, and widely held companies.

Total reserves: The sum of a bank's required reserves and excess reserves.

Total return credit swap: A type of credit default swap wherein one party agrees to pay all cash flows from the referenced asset or assets including the change in the value of the referenced asset or assets and in exchange receive a floating rate plus any depreciation of the referenced asset to the credit swap seller.

Total risk: The standard deviation (or variance) of returns to an asset or portfolio of assets.

Tracking error risk: In an indexing strategy, the risk that the movement of a portfolio created to mimic an index does not match the targeted index.

Trademark zero-coupon Treasury securities: A zero-coupon instrument created by a particular government dealer firm by stripping a Treasury security. The resulting instrument is associated with that firm (e.g., TIGRs and CATs).

Trading Desk of the Federal Reserve Bank of New York: The unit of the Fed that implements monetary policy by its conduct of open market operations.

Trading priority rules: Rules about the sequence in which exchange specialists must execute stock orders.

Tranche: A financial term meaning a specific portion of the issue of a financial security. Often, a bond class within a CMO structure.

Treasury bills: Treasury securities with maturities of one year or less. Current Treasury practice is to issue these securities as discount securities.

Treasury bonds: Treasury coupon securities issued with original maturities greater than 10 years.

Treasury coupon securities: Treasuries that make periodic coupon interest payments. Current Treasury practice is to issue all securities with maturities of two years or longer as coupon securities.

Treasury discount securities: Treasury securities that pay only a contractually fixed amount at maturity and no periodic coupon payments. Current Treasury practice is to issue Treasury bills as discount securities.

Treasury inflation protection security (TIPS): A Treasury coupon security whose coupon rate is tied to the rate of inflation.

Treasury notes: Treasury coupon securities issued with original maturities between 2 and 10 years.

Treasury receipt (TR): A zero-coupon instrument created by a group of primary government dealers by stripping a Treasury security. The resulting instrument is not directly associated with any of the participating dealers.

Treasury security (also called Treasuries): Securities issued by the United States Department of the Treasury. There are two categories of U.S. Treasury securities—discount and coupon securities.

Triangular arbitrage: An arbitrage strategy employed to take advantage of cross rate mispricing between the U.S. dollar and the two foreign currencies.

TSE 300 Composite: The stock market index for the Toronto Stock Exchange.

Turnaround cost: Also called the round-trip cost, this is the total cost of buying and later selling an asset.

Underlying: The asset or instrument that the parties agree to exchange in a futures contract.

Underwriting: An investment banking function in which securities are purchased from the issuer for resale to the public.

Underwriting income: The difference between a property and casualty firm's annual premiums and the sum of claim expenses, claim adjustment expenses, and administrative and marketing expenses.

Underwriting syndicate: Group of investment banking firms formed to underwrite an issue.

Unit trust: In the United States, a pool of money invested in a specific and unchanging group of assets over the planned life of the trust.

Universal life insurance: An insurance policy that pays a dividend tied to market interest rates.

Unsystematic risk: The portion of the variability in a security's returns that reflects only the situations unique or specific to the firm that issued the security. This concept is the same as *diversifiable risk*.

Upstairs market: The informal but extensive arrangements, employing electronic communications systems, that institutional investors and securities firms have developed to accommodate their typically large trades.

Variable life insurance: Provides a death benefit that depends on the market value of invested premiums at the time of the insured's death or, if the value of the investments is low, pays a guaranteed minimum amount.

Variance of a probability distribution: The mean of the squared deviation of the differences between possible values and the distribution's mean.

Variation margin: The additional margin that must be deposited to bring the equity in the account back to its initial margin level.

Velocity of money: The ratio of the money supply to the economy's income (as reflected by the gross national product or some similar measure), which indicates the average amount of transactions carried by a unit of money.

Waiting period: The time interval between the initial filing of the registration statement and the time the registration statement becomes effective.

Warrant: A contract that grants the holder the right to purchase a designated security at a specified price.

Weighted average maturity (WAM): Weighted average number of months remaining for a mortgage pool.

When-issued (or wi) market: The market where Treasury securities are traded prior to the time they are issued by the Treasury.

Whole life insurance: A form of insurance that pays a stated amount upon the death of the insured, and that accumulates, over time, a cash value on which the policyholder can call.

Wild card option: The right of the short position, under CBT rules, to give notice of intent to deliver after the closing of the exchange, on the date when the futures settlement price has been fixed.

Writer of option: The entity that sells the option contract.

Xetra: Short for "Exchange Electronic Trading," this is a modern, cost efficient, order-driven trading system introduced by the Frankfurt Stock Exchange.

Yankee bank: A foreign bank that has a U.S. branch.

Yankee certificate of deposit: A CD denominated in U.S. dollars and issued by a foreign bank with a branch in the United States.

Yankee commercial paper: Commercial paper issued in the United States by foreign entities.

Yield: The annual percentage return on a debt security.

Yield curve: The graphical depiction of the relationship between the yield on bonds of the same credit quality but different maturities.

Yield curve spread: Same as *maturity spread*.

Yield spread (or spread): The difference between the yields on any two bond issues. The spread is typically measured in basis points.

Yield to maturity: The interest rate that makes the present value of the cash flow of a bond (including its principal) equal to its market price.

Zero-coupon bond: A bond that makes only one cash payment, and that is the face or par value, which is paid at maturity.

Zero-coupon instrument: Financial debt instrument that is purchased at an amount less than its maturity value and pays no interest periodically.

INDEX

647